# Praise for
## *The Moorad Choudhry Anthology*

A worthy book for professionals and students alike. Whether you want to refer to a product or a technical formula or learn afresh, the easy-to-read style of this book from an author who is very deep rooted in everyday banking business promotes great understanding, as well enjoyment from the activities of both generating profit and minimising risks.

—Dr Martin Czurda
*CEO, Austrian Anadi Bank, Klagenfurt*

"I wish this book had been around when I did my MBA. It is essential reading for anyone who wants to be both comprehensively and thoughtfully briefed about the banking sector. I particularly appreciated the section on governance, as this is rarely included in such discussions, but is always the dog that doesn't bark when things go wrong. As such, *The Moorad Choudhry Anthology* should grace the table of every bank boardroom in the world."

—Dr Eve Poole
*Ashridge Business School*

"Moorad manages to describe a comprehensive and complex area of banking in a lively and readable language. As a Group Chief Financial & Risk Officer I have had great professional benefit of the description of the role of the Asset & Liability Committee, the risk policy, reporting and stress testing as well as the description of the day-to-day management in the risk and treasury departments. It was also rewarding for me to read the final chapters about best practice in capital and funding management and corporate governance, which we should not forget, when we enter into the next period of bull markets. I can highly recommend this book as a handy reference work for anyone who is involved in banking strategy, ALM and liquidity risk management."

—Steen Blaafalk
*Group Chief Financial & Risk Officer,*
*Saxo Bank A/S, Copenhagen*

"Not very often does a monograph come along that consolidates a field's existing body of research and practitioners' insights into a comprehensive, accessible best-practice framework. *The Moorad Choudhry Anthology* achieves this feat; it builds on his earlier *Principles of Banking*, widely recognised as the bible in the ALM and bank risk management field. More than that though, *Anthology* is a fun, fascinating read, benefiting from Professor Choudhry's signature witty and straight-to-the-point writing style as well as from his substantial previous academic research and professional experience as banking executive.

*Anthology* is educational without being prescriptive, encouraging practitioners to pick and mix those elements from a rich analytical toolbox that suit their institutional and market contexts. Given the depth and breadth of its coverage and its clear, methodical organisation, the book is suitable for anyone interested in this fascinating field at the core of modern banking, from the graduate preparing for a job interview to the seasoned professional looking for a comprehensive and detailed exposition of current best practice."

—Thomas Kuehn
*Director Structured Finance Model Development Team,*
*Fitch Ratings, London*

"Moorad, you are a great team player and you have the heart that a South American footballer requires!"

—Juan Carlos Sihuincha
*Quantitative Analyst, Banco de Crédito BCP, Lima*

*Moorad Choudhry Anthology* is quite simply, the bible of banking. Anyone who is serious about a career in this industry needs a copy. We eagerly await the next book in the series from the author, who is without doubt a guru in his field.

—Julie Ashmore
*Speaker and Leadership Coach, Former Head of SME Lending, HSBC, London*

"The best book I've ever read on banking."

—David Riddell
*Director, Banking Solutions, Earnix, London*

"*The Moorad Choudhry Anthology* is that very rare thing, a textbook that shows the practitioner exactly how to go about achieving business best-practice in the real world, with templates and policy guidelines that can be applied to virtually any commercial bank. The in-depth coverage of capital, liquidity, and governance principles is particularly welcome. A heavyweight benchmark guide that all senior bankers should be thoroughly familiar with."

—David Wileman
*CEO, King & Shaxson Limited, London*

"Don't mistake the complexity and detail for a hard read. This book is a thorough anthology, complete in its coverage and with a valuable connection to the real world. It is a timely source of reference, lessons, and understanding and should help ensure that 'principles' regain their position at the forefront of banking culture."

—Steven Fine
*Managing Partner, Peel Hunt, London*

"I read it fully and can say it is one of a kind. A super useful tool for bankers and staff in the capital markets."

—Issa Soormally
*Deputy Governor, Bank of Mauritius, Port Louis*

"While working on my MBA master thesis in Finance (corporate banking), I was always reading Professor Choudhry's books as they are more valuable and better structured than most of the books in Finance."

—Piotr Lagodzinski
*VTB, Frankfurt*

"This book is an essential guide to banking in practice. *The Moorad Choudhry Anthology* is a prerequisite to understanding how banking should operate in order to be safe and sound, an imperative in today's post-crisis environment. A truly insightful and really rather fabulous book."

—Ruth Wandhöfer
*Global Banking Regulatory and Industry Expert, and author of*
Transaction Banking and the Impact of Regulatory Change *(2014)*

"This author never ceases to impress. As with all his books, Professor Choudhry has done an amazing job of concisely and clearly explaining, in a greatly appropriate and complete level of detail, all of the important aspects of banks as institutions, their products, their asset and liability management techniques, liquidity and risk management to name just a few. It is an excellent book and as always with Professor Choudhry's writing style it is very easy to read and understand. I would recommend this for anyone who wants a good, detailed insightful read about the business of banks, their products, and the regulatory and risk management aspects of the business of banking."

—Shabnam Mohammad
*Managing Director, Khalij Islamic Limited, Dubai*

"Finance text books generally don't cover bank asset–liability management, capital and liquidity in detail. I'm very impressed by this book because the author covers all important aspects of these essential disciplines in banking in a way that even a fresher can understand. Highly recommended."

—Balamurali Radhakrishnan
*FX Strategist, FXWire Pro, Bangalore*

"If you want to see how much banking has progressed in a generation, look no further than *Anthology*. And all for the better!"

—Peter Eisenhardt
*Secretary General, International Council of Securities Associations, London*

"Moorad's ability to capture the fundamentals of Banking with a particular focus on capital and liquidity risk management is laid bare in black and white for all to understand. Whether new to Banking or with multiple years of exposure, *The Moorad Choudhry Anthology* is a book that needs to be handled regularly to ascertain best practice."

—Stephen Grainger
*Chairman of the Small Banks Association, and Group Treasurer,*
*Aldermore Bank Plc, London*

"*The Moorad Choudhry Anthology* is an extremely thorough and readable book on asset–liability management and bank risk management. It covers such a wide spectrum of topics affecting a treasury and risk function that this is always the first resource I look into if I have to brush up my knowledge or look up something properly in any particular area. I find this book very authentic and relevant as it covers the latest issues in the market and is written by a practitioner who is very well regarded in the industry."

—Nehal Saghir
*Head of Asset and Liability Management,*
*Mizuho Capital Markets (UK) Ltd, London*

"Moorad's book sets a high standard that balances both academic and real world application. With the knowledge of ALM, capital and liquidity management being more relevant today in the post-crisis era, it is a must read for any serious banker."

—James Chua Pheng Kyan
*Treasurer, Bank Islam Brunei Berhad, Bandar Seri Begawan*

"This book will actually make one understand how a bank works, about their products, their asset–liability management techniques, their liquidity and risk management, and how to manage the balance sheet in aggregate, strategic terms. Any reader will see that the author covers a wide but sensibly chosen range of topics. This is a book I highly recommend to both practitioners and students.

Prof. Choudhry's writing style is very easy to read and understand. He has done a really great job in providing concise and clear explanations with a greatly useful and complete level of detail, which makes this the best reference tool for bankers everywhere. But the true beauty of this book is that it is also very readable and easily understood for non-bankers as well."

—Shahriar Azad Shashi
*Research Associate, EBL Securities Limited, wholly-owned*
*Subsidiary of Eastern Bank Limited, Dhaka*

"*The Moorad Choudhry Anthology* combines all of the strategy, capital, liquidity and asset–liability frameworks with analysis on banking practices that makes a bank thrive or fail during a financial crisis. This book serves as an invaluable guide in my work as auditor and enables me to communicate effectively with my front office and risk management colleagues."

—Chan Chee Cheong Gerard
*Vice President, Non-Credit Audit,*
*United Overseas Bank Bhd, Kuala Lumpur*

"This book contains so much about crucial things that you need to know, it gives a practical and conceptual approach to understanding the principles of modern banking. It is an indispensable guide, template and policy manual for all bankers everywhere. A well written book about important topics, I recommend this book highly."

—Budi Gunawan
*Division Head, Market & Liquidity Risk Management,*
*Bank OCBC NISP, Jakarta*

"An invaluable text that should be read by all bankers, whatever their specialism. A very high quality real-world benchmark of business best-practice."

—John Simon
*Director, Treasury & Capital Markets, CIMB Bank, Jakarta*

"A first-class guidebook that deserves to be on the bookshelf of every banker. This book will become a timeless masterpiece."

—Ekkapong Rungrojpanichkul
*Vice President, Kasikorn Bank, Bangkok*

"Nestling proudly among the Treasury team's bookshelves are: one copy of *Bank Asset & Liability Management* and two copies of *The Principles of Banking*. All copies have been suitably underlined, bookmarked, and cross-referenced. Nice testimonials!"

—Graham Laird
*Treasury Risk Manager, Aldermore Bank plc, London*

"This book gives an excellent practical overview on markets, derivatives, and risk management. Everybody preparing to take the CISI diploma should take this book as necessary reading. I would strongly recommend this book to people who are starting their career in the banking industry as an appropriate literature. This book is written in a comprehensive manner, and was very easy to understand."

—Kosta Shorko
*Head of Portfolio Management, National Bank of the Republic of Macedonia, Skopje*

"Professor Moorad Choudhry's *Anthology* is an all-encompassing practitioner's guide that comprehensively outlines best practice governance, balance sheet management, credit underwriting and risk management structures that all banks should embrace. The book is essential reading for all senior managers, board directors, and regulators, especially in frontier markets, where the importance of adopting international best practice is critical to facilitate the seamless integration into the global financial system, a key requisite for any financial institution in an increasingly globalized world."

—Njilan Senghore Njie
*General Manager, Finance & Administration, Trust Bank Ltd, Banjul*

"I've adopted elements from the *Principles of Banking* text book here in Myanmar for capacity building initiatives in the Banking sector. Great book! Thank you for sharing your knowledge Professor Choudhry."

—Tony Deary
*Head of Component – GIZ Financial Sector Reform, Yangon*

"*The Moorad Choudhry Anthology* drives home one key point – the need for the industry to return to fundamentals: manage the balance sheet. How this has been reduced by many to a residual activity should be shocking. This book provides clarity on issues of importance – a key resource and a must for bankers, board members, risk professionals, and regulators to be properly rooted in the principles of banking."

—Steven Lee
*Chair, The Financial Risk Institute (FinRisk) and Managing Director, Global Client Consulting, Washington DC*

"Prof. Choudhry's latest instalment gives a well balanced approach to finance. It demonstrates a brilliant culmination of his theoretical background and his extensive experience in the Square Mile. An essential read for anyone working in finance and those with a keen interest."

—Wei Goh
*Group Financial Controller, SRG Limited, Perth*

"To Professor Moorad Choudhry – with friendship from the author."

—Gyorgy Matolcsy
*Governor, The Central Bank of Hungary, and author
of* Economic Balance and Growth, *Budapest*

"The book helped me a lot to broaden my knowledge and I think both *The Principles of Banking* and Professor Choudhry's book *Bank Asset and Liability Management* are quite complementary. It is easy to follow, and it is better to have a handbook for people to get the main ideas because these two books cover so many things, so to understand them you need a lot of time. But they are very good."

—Vu Trong Hieu
*International Business Administration,
Foreign Trade University, Ha Noi*

"Your writing was so clear and to the point. Your books actually helped me get a job in structured finance. I'm very grateful."

—Gulshat Ibliaminova CFA
*Principal, Independent Consultancy Services, Moscow*

"This book articulates the principles of banking in a way that is easy for the beginner in banking to understand. But it is a must read for all senior executives who wish to challenge their thinking and assumptions about their business model, and provides valuable insights in how to win in the market place."

—Emmanuel O. Lamptey
*Group Head Finance & Chief Operating Officer (Group Finance Department),
Ecobank Transnational Incorporated, Lome*

"Unfortunately, I never had the chance to attend one of your classes. However, your books, articles, and views have helped me a lot during my career in banking. Thank you."

—Alexander Bell
*Managing Consultant, Horváth & Partners, Munich*

"When we received Professor Choudhry's book, we were so impressed we immediately ordered more because we wanted all our senior people in every department to have a copy."

—Dr. Nsingui Andre
*Director, Academia Banco Nacional de Angola, Luanda*

"I have always been a fan of your lucid writing and simplifying complex topics to manageable, bite-size pieces."

—Vincent Cabanero
*Director, RBS Greenwich Capital, Greenwich, CT*

"A most valuable and solid practical handbook that addresses all the key issues of bank strategy, capital, liquidity and the balance sheet. The provision of policy templates and explicit recommendations for best-practice mark this work as a standout benchmark reference text for all bankers, central bank policymakers, and finance academics."

—Martin Barber
*VP Delivery and Productivity, GTS Europe, IBM, London*

"I think everyone should have a copy of this book!"

—Carla Bester
*Senior Manager, Financial Risk Management,
KPMG, Johannesburg*

"I truly believe this book is a must for all people in banking."

—Nikolai Ivashkovsky
*Head of Treasury, International Bank for Economic
Cooperation – IBEC, Moscow*

"Professor Choudhry has written a comprehensive guide to the underlying principles in banking and finance whilst at the same time presenting the reader with practical commentary. In the process he has given us both an overall understanding of the topic and an opportunity of incorporating practical solutions into the workplace. Is it possible to learn from the mistakes of others? Yes, if you take the time to read and ponder upon the contents of this book."

—Patricia Robertson
*Chartered FCSI, Westport Global Limited, London*

"I just started to read your new book, and if it continues the way it promises this is the book I was looking for. Before banking I studied physics and always appreciated when the lecturer first explained carefully the principles of the phenomenon rather than simply jumping wildly into hours of formulas. Like legendary Feynman lectures of old, but still grasping the student's attention. I'm wishing you become the Feynman of banking!"

—Jakub Wojtasik
*Head of Capital Management, Bank Pekao, Warsaw*

"I have followed your publications and books and I found it is very useful for practitioners who want an academic base foundation like me. Thank you a lot for your inspiration."

—Pachaneeya Chongsatja
*Central Treasury Unit, United Overseas Bank Limited (UOB),*
*Singapore*

"*Moorad Choudhry Anthology* collects the most interesting parts of Professor Choudhry's extensive and well known published collection of books on financial products. As always he blends a quantitative and practical approach for readers of all levels of experience. Moorad thoroughly understands the changes in the financial industry and is always worth reading."

—Andrew Kasapis
*Director, Duff & Phelps Ltd, London, and author of*
Mastering Credit Derivatives

# The Moorad Choudhry Anthology

*"The first principle of banking is to have principles."*

— Professor Moorad Choudhry

# The Moorad Choudhry Anthology

*Past, Present and Future Principles of Banking and Finance*

+ Website

MOORAD CHOUDHRY

WILEY

**Other Wiley Editorial Offices**

*Library of Congress Cataloging-in-Publication Data is Available:*
ISBN 978-1-118-77973-6 (Hardcover)
ISBN 978-1-118-77974-3 (ePDF)
ISBN 978-1-118-77976-7 (ePub)

Cover Design: Wiley
Cover Image: © eugenesergeev / iStockphoto

Typeset in 10/12pt Sabon by SPi Global, Chennai, India

SKY086CB1D6-F5A0-40CF-B6A2-542AA87C51A4_010524

**For Lindsay**
*Ultimate Yummy Mummy*

# Contents

# Foreword

## Paul Fisher

**W**hat is a bank? Few people seem to know. As explained in this book, banks can provide many financial services, but they are defined by regulators in relation to an official authorisation to take deposits: you cannot call yourself a bank unless you are a licensed deposit taker. The meaning of banking is equally vague in the popular consciousness. Among the most notable popular *canards* are the following: you put your money in a bank and they look after it for you; they take savings and lend them to borrowers; they invest in the real economy. None of these statements is true. In fact, retail bank deposits are effectively loans by customers to the bank, so it becomes the bank's money. Banks actually create most of their deposits in the process of lending, enabling them to generate much higher leverage (assets relative to capital) than any other type of financial firm. And banks provide credit services to borrowers for a fixed or floating rate of interest rather than sharing in the risk and actual returns on an investment.[1]

Why do we regulate banks? In short, regulation could be said to reflect concerns matching those three observations. The first concern is that retail depositors are at risk of not being repaid, yet not in a position to judge that risk or get paid for it. Hence deposit insurance schemes. The second is banks' very high leverage, which increases the risk of insolvency when any sizeable loan goes bad. Hence capital requirements. And banks traditionally make long-term loans but raise funding from deposits or other short-term debt instruments – creating the maturity mismatch that generates liquidity risk. Hence liquidity regulations and central banks acting as Lender of Last Resort. Even after the Great Financial Crisis of 2007–2010 these basic facts about banking are understood by few and forgotten by many.

Why did we have a financial crisis? Well, the full answer would require another book, or several, but in my view it reflected human nature to a large extent. The 5–10 years before the crisis was one of the most stable periods in the financial history of the developed world – growth was strong,

---

[1] Except in Shariah banking, where banks must be co-investors.

unemployment and inflation were low, few risks crystallised. So, humans being human, as risks became less evident, the price of risky assets fell, controls on risk-taking were relaxed and more risk was taken. Banks held less capital and liquidity, in both quantity and quality, and the authorities allowed them to do so given the apparent contribution to economic prosperity. Meanwhile, mistakes were made globally in monetary policy (low interest rates in the US, copied across other countries to prevent exchange rate appreciation) coupled with overly lax fiscal policy. Combined, these policies led to huge short-term capital inflows into the US and UK, helping to swell financial balance sheets. And in the US there was well-intentioned but ultimately disastrous state intervention in the housing market. That probably deserves more attention as being a root cause of the explosion in sub-prime lending and thence structured products, in which the risks to the end-investor were obscured to the point of being invisible. Overall, it was a perfect storm of private and public sector failures generated through a period in which risk seemed to have receded.

After the crisis, the need to have a proper understanding of banking, and for bankers to be appropriately qualified has been recognised but not really acted upon. Moorad Choudhry's text – like his previous volumes – does something to fill the gap. Here is the knowledge that practical bankers, regulators, and financial policy makers need. I wish I had read this book in 2006, rather than learnt the hard way in the years that followed. If formal qualifications for bankers are still somewhat rare, at least we can't complain that the process of banking and the risks that it entails are not well documented, when we have such clear expositions, in detail.

The regulatory reforms of the past 10 years should have made banking much safer and the financial system much more stable. The unfortunate cost of that is a system for calculating regulatory capital and liquidity which is almost impenetrable including, in my experience, to many of those who helped design it. Again, Moorad does a great job in laying out the regulatory regime, starting from the basics. This book will benefit many, but especially those moving into the subject from other quantitative disciplines such as economics, or those practitioners who wish to have a detailed, comprehensive reference on their shelves to dip into for a reminder from time-to-time.

But what of the future? Even if the dragons of the past have been slain – or at least put to sleep for a while – new threats have emerged. One source of threat is from new technology. Without attempting to be comprehensive, we might pick out three aspects. First, the risk of cyber-hacking is one of the most dangerous. It is well-known that there are daily, routine attacks, by known actors, some of them state-sponsored, on many public institutions and private companies in the West, including banks. If the public came to believe that "their" money was not safe, and trust in banks diminished, then the financial system could be put under huge pressure once again. Second, aspects of new technology – more computing power, the approach to big data, the distributed ledger approach – means that the business models of traditional financial intermediaries are all under threat. In response, many companies, including banks, now look like IT companies with a particular customer service bolted on top! Finally, one might mention crypto-currencies such as Bitcoin. Personally I believe these to be a passing fad, with the multiplicity of such currencies being akin to a price inflation that will eventually cause a failure of trust in all such endeavours. But I have no crystal ball, and if this view is wrong, then it may lead to a significant leeching of deposits out of traditional banks.

A second existential source of threat is climate change and the wider sustainability agenda. Taking climate first, the risks to the financial sector have now been well documented – and by the Bank of England[2] no less. The economy needs to transition to much lower – actually net negative - carbon emissions. That will be driven and encouraged by public policy changes, many of which are as yet uncertain, but are beginning to emerge in China, in the EU,[3] and in the UK. Successful banks will be those who correctly spot the emerging trends and shift financing towards it – as they have done for previous economic paradigm shifts. And those firms that choose to ignore it will lose out, as they have done before. And as with climate change, so with wider social issues. The rise in political populism is likely to be met – one way or another – with radical political and social changes that banks need to follow carefully if they are not to be left behind.

In the face of these high-level threats to the future of banking, the basic principles, as recorded so well in this volume, should not be forgotten.

Paul Fisher
*Former Executive Director, Bank of England*
5 February 2018

---

[2] Matthew Scott, Julia van Huizen and Carsten Jung, "The Bank's Response to Climate Change", *Quarterly Bulletin*, Q2, 2017.
[3] High-Level Expert Group on Sustainable Finance, "Financing a Sustainable European Economy", Brussels, January 2018.

# Foreword

## Professor Alexander Lipton

It is widely assumed by the general public, and often stated in the press, that the main culprits of the global financial crisis are banks, particularly, global systemically important financial institutions. The reasons for this unflattering conclusion are manifold, but one of the more important ones is the fact that in some cases banks senior and mid-level managers are surprisingly ill equipped with the requisite technical knowledge. This is the main conclusion which Professor Moorad Choudhry arrives at in his book; he also proposes several efficient remedies to rectify this unfortunate situation.

Prof. Choudhry is uniquely equipped to accomplish this challenging task successfully. He has decades of experience in various senior roles at several leading banking institutions in the City of London. In addition, he has been teaching banking and quantitative finance for many years. He has shared his unique practical insights and theoretical findings in several best-selling books and numerous conference presentations.

This book is an anthology of the best and most relevant excerpts from the previous books of Prof. Choudhry published by Wiley. It covers several topics, which are important to anybody who wants to make a career in banking or, if they are bankers already, to stay au courant with the current trends in their chosen field. The book strikes a fine balance of being technical enough to be fit for purpose and yet not overload the reader with unnecessary details.

Specific subjects covered in the book include general principles of banking and finance; discussion of the ever-changing landscape of banking regulations, with an emphasis on regulatory capital and risk management; asset and liability management (ALM) for banks; and finally, a set of predictions on the future of banking and finance.

Personally, I find the part dealing with ALM especially important. Whilst frequently underemphasized, the fact is that banks are dividend-producing machines, which have to perform a fine balancing act by choosing sufficient levels of capital and liquidity to guarantee their survival in perpetuity, while, at the same time, maximizing their profitability to ensure the dividend flow to shareholders and steady rate of credit money creation for the economy as a whole. The fact that, in many instances, banks' senior management is ill equipped to properly appreciate this highly technical matter, unquestionably contributes to problems of the banking industry at large. Prof. Choudhry's book, which is based on his personal experience and original research, is useful in this regard and proposes several recipes for successfully solving the ALM problem.

In summary, I can wholeheartedly recommend this book to anyone who feels the need to understand how banking operates not only in theory, but in reality, and wants to apply this newly acquired understanding in practice. The accompanying website contains a treasure trove of additional technical information helpful for this purpose.

Professor Alexander Lipton
*Founder and CEO, Stronghold Labs*
*Co-Founder, Distilled Analytics*
*Fellow, Massachusetts Institute of Technology Connection*
*Science and Engineering*
*Visiting Professor of Financial Engineering,*
*École Polytechnique Fédérale de Lausanne*
22 May 2017

# Foreword

## Rundheersing Bheenick

**P**rofessor Moorad Choudhry presented me a copy of his book, *The Principles of Banking* when he visited Mauritius to attend a banking conference which the Bank of Mauritius was hosting.

I was struck by his sound down-to-earth grasp of the banking scene and impressed by his academic and publishing track record. I made it a point to plough my way through his masterly tome and emerged thoroughly convinced that this book deserves a wide readership. It is, therefore, most welcome.

Banking has gone through exceptionally turbulent times over the last few years. The bankers who brought us the spectacular global financial crisis, their regulators who failed equally spectacularly, and the reformers of the banking and finance system tasked with ensuring that we minimise risks of such bust-ups in future, have all been constantly in the news. The arcana of banking are no longer the exclusive preserve of specialists. There is keen and widespread interest to understand better what goes on in the mysterious world of banking.

This book sheds light on the subject. It returns us to basics. It is indeed a delight to have in one packed volume a text that sets out all that you wanted to know about doing the honest job of banking but perhaps did not have the nerve to ask.

As we still struggle to emerge from the 2007–2010 financial crisis in good shape, it is a boon to have such a clearly-written guide on the fundamental principles of good banking practice. *The Principles of Banking* is eminently suited to the needs of banking students, but can also enlighten experienced practitioners and bank Board members. Professor Choudhry brings to this sizeable endeavour a wealth of experience in this field as a seasoned banking practitioner and well-respected teacher.

This volume is the latest in a series he has delivered over the past decade or more covering many separate areas of banking, such as bonds, derivatives, the money market and factors underlying banking crises. With admirable skill in setting out the implications of complex numerical issues, he bridges that yawning gap between theoretical precepts of banking systems and the everyday life problems that bankers face. It is a text for everyone involved in banking from the professionals in the high-street branches interacting with the public, the decision-makers in the executive suite or the board room, to the supervisors and regulators in central banks and oversight agencies in their role as arbiters of current practice and designers of safer systems for the future.

Banking has a long history of crises, from the US banking collapse of 1792, to the latest debacle, rooted in the mismanagement of cheap mortgages and the confection of evidently misleading derivatives. This latest text book is both a survival guide for wayward practitioners and a treatise for students and their academic masters, which hopefully will help to steer this sector out of its shaky immediate past.

Professor Choudhry is a master of his subject but envelopes the mathematical devices he presents so clearly with a sound sense of priorities. He closes this most valuable contribution to the literature on banking with this wise adage, which we forget at our peril:

"The first principle of banking is to have principles. Or as the motto of the London Stock Exchange puts it: *my word is my bond.*"

I wish this book all the success it deserves in these troubled times for the banking profession.

Rundheersing Bheenick
*Governor, Bank of Mauritius*
5 May 2014

# Preface

**W**hen starting this book, I was reminded of a passage in *A Fire on the Moon*, Norman Mailer's superb work describing the Apollo 11 mission:

> *"In the study of literature, much usually depends on direct confrontation with a work. Who would dare to approach* A Farewell to Arms *by a synopsis? It is only natural to distrust a literary experience if we have been guided too carefully through it, for the act of reading must provide by itself that literary experience upon which our senses will later work. But the study of science is different. Much like the study of history, it begins with legends and oversimplifications."*
>
> — Mailer, N., *A Fire on the Moon*,
> London: Penguin Classics 1970.

If Mr. Mailer had substituted "Finance" for "Science", his point would still be well made. And this is the unfortunate thing about finance and banking. More often than not it is learnt by practitioners using legends and oversimplifications, and the primary source of many of the biggest failures in banking history lie there. It would be better if practitioners approached the practice of finance as Mr. Mailer recommends anyone should approach the study of literature.

A former boss of mine, reviewing my performance at an annual appraisal, used the following words:

"You're good on the technical stuff, but. . ."

I found that an odd remark. We worked in a bank Treasury department, after all. Treasury and ALM are by their very nature technical subjects; surely technical strength in this discipline is a pre-requisite? In other words, it isn't a strength to have technical skills in finance, they are actually essential. To me, that is like telling an airline pilot, "You're good at flying, but. . ." Would one wish to board an aeroplane whose pilot possessed poor flying skills? Equally, those without technical skills shouldn't really occupy senior positions in a bank.

Yet another boss at a different institution, the bank's Chairman no less, once remarked to me, "Why do I need to know how other banks do things? I've been in the business for 30 years, I don't care how other banks do things." I found that an astonishing comment. If ever there was a person who should read Matthew Syed's superb *Black Box Thinking* it was him, a man so suffering from cognitive dissonance that he was unable to detect the fear of failure entrenched throughout the bank, from the Board downwards. The concepts of benchmarking, of open communications and of learning from mistakes, were unknown to him.

Sadly, these gentlemen's departments contained a fair smattering of individuals who were not technically proficient in the matters of finance (and sadly outnumbering greatly those individuals who were very proficient and whose understanding of banking and risk was as good as anyone I have come across. Unfortunately, very few of these latter individuals were to be found in senior executive positions at the banks in question. This is a not uncommon occurrence). As for not benchmarking with the market and not looking to determine what is best-practice, well one doesn't need to be a genius to see that such an approach is a guarantee of absolute mediocrity and ultimate decline.

Financial markets, like the world we live in, are characterised by extreme complexity. It is an arrogant conceit to suggest that one could know everything there is to know about them, that one could fashion a model that would cover every eventuality. Mr Syed's book encapsulates with elegance and accessibility the importance of learning from one's mistakes, of accepting that failure, in any context and however large or small, is something to build on. But to do that requires intellectual honesty, an acceptance of genuine positive feedback, a willingness to test one's theories and ideas, and to be ready to adapt them if they are found to be sub-optimal. These traits are rare in banking culture. But they are important and should be adopted.

The templates and recommendations in this book are applicable to every bank in the world, but they are not set in stone. In bank operating models there is frequently more than one right answer. The key is having the right operating model *for your firm*. Banks have to be able to respond to changing conditions, whilst always pursuing the primary objectives of long-term sustainability and good customer service. That means modifying procedures and governance models where necessary. In finance, templates and policy guides must be adaptable. Certainly, principles are principles, and in banking some of them have remained good for over 600 years. But that doesn't mean one should operate in a "closed loop". For example, bankers, and especially senior bankers, should check the efficacy of their views and ideas by presenting at industry conferences, so they can gauge responses and see where they stand relative to their peers and to the market. There is no stigma, in finance anyway, in being confronted with views different to one's own: on the contrary, this is a learning opportunity. If a working environment is open and honest about mistakes, and operates without a blame culture, then the entire organisation will learn. Sadly, actively seeking feedback is not a commonly observed trait amongst senior executives in the finance industry.

Finance, and banking, is art, not science. Finance is not physics; would that it was. If the art of banking required precision and continuously consistent relationships of the kind required to, say, place a robot lander travelling at 34,000 miles per hour on a comet that was over 317 million miles away, and to calculate with unerring accuracy the precise time that the landing will take place, then we could expect to model it reasonably well. But managing a bank does not involve such relationships. The laws of physics do not apply in banking, despite what the "quants" who practise their skills on the trading floors of large banks would like us to believe. Effectiveness in bank risk management comes about first by recognising this, and then by applying oneself first-hand to the literature and practice of banking, and then acquiring over time, through practice, observation, implementation and indeed an element of trial and error, the judgement and experience needed to ensure one becomes reasonably proficient. There is no other way.

By definition then, one should not expect to reach a position of leadership and responsibility at a bank or financial institution until and unless one has acquired the correct and relevant body of knowledge in the same field. Heads of retail banks should have long experience in retail banking. Chairmen of bank boards should have long experience in banking as well as knowledge of the world of finance around them. Heads of Treasury should be good at the technical stuff. Anyone with a pretension to manage a bank should be prepared to benchmark with one's peers in the outside world and see if they are best in class, rather than just stagnating in their own bubble as the market outside moves on.

Unfortunately, the real world is not like that, thanks to what they call "office politics", and wider stakeholders have suffered after the banks they were involved with were run into the ground by CEOs, Directors, and Chairmen that at best lacked the requisite experience and knowledge of finance, and at worst were no more than empire-building charlatans. And this despite such people having been signed off by the regulatory authority as "fit and proper" persons to run a bank. We all recognise these persons: those skilled in the art of talking a lot without actually saying anything, and as good at answering questions as any professional politician.

This state of affairs is a pity, because banks play such an important role in society that they need to be managed by those skilled in the art of finance, not politics. But there is hope: not every senior bank senior executive sees things in the short-term P&L and empire-building manner that some of them have done. Here is a heartening extract from an email I received from Mark Thompson, Chairman of Holmesdale Building Society, when I informed him I was quoting from the firm's annual report:

> *"While we're currently going through our annual business planning cycle, it also takes place in the context of how our next 160 years should shape up – something that's much harder to do when you have quarterly market expectations to hit!"*

I think this thinking encapsulates perfectly the essence of banking principles, which is the need to focus on sustainability and the genuine long term. *The Moorad Choudhry Anthology* is two things: first, a collection of extracts from my previous books published by John Wiley & Sons Ltd which have remained pertinent to the banking industry and thus of continued relevance to today's market practitioners; and second, a series of brand new and previously unpublished pieces that I consider to be a best-practice guide to both current practice and the shape of things to come. In other words, this book is part "compilation album" and part "the future of bank strategy and risk management". And as such I hope the book is of value to anyone who wishes to pursue a career in banking at the senior executive level. It is not aimed at juniors, although they may well benefit from reading it. It's really for senior directors in banks, because they're the ones in a position of influence and they're the ones who can help to ensure that banks regain their position as a trusted part of society that delivers consistent excellent customer service and value. Banks need to remain viable in perpetuity, so all bank executives are really just temporary stewards of the balance sheet. And that's all that senior bank executives should be concentrating on. Because, to quote Baron Manfred Von Richthofen from another context, "Anything else is just rubbish."

## ORGANISATION OF THE BOOK

As one might expect of a work entitled "Anthology", this book is partly a collection of extracts from my earlier works. The criteria for selection for this book is that the material, no matter its age, must still be relevant and useful to practitioners today. However, the book isn't just a compilation album, it also features new material that I feel is pertinent not just to today but should remain so in the future.

The book is comprised of five parts, as follows:

Part I: Principles of Banking, Finance and Financial Products
Part II: Bank Regulatory Capital and Risk Management
Part III: Bank Treasury and Strategic Asset–Liability Management
Part IV: The Future of Banking: Strategy, Governance and Culture
Part V: Case Studies: Analysis, Coherent Advice and Problem Solving

As always, the aim is to remain accessible and practical throughout, and I hope this has been achieved. Comments on the text are welcome and should be sent to the author care of John Wiley & Sons (Asia) Pte Ltd.

## BOOK EXTRACT PAGES

Material that is extracted from the author's previous works is contained within a box. Note that Figures, Tables and Examples numbering within such extract material may not be in the same order as new material within the same chapter, reflecting the numbering that is used in the original book.

## ACCOMPANYING WEBSITE

This book features a companion website, featuring a range of models, policy templates, teaching slides, and model answers. Each item is referenced to a specific chapter in the book. Full details of all the files on the website and login information are given in Chapter 20.

## ADDITIONAL CONTRIBUTORS

During my career in the City I've been privileged to work with some great people, people who are technically expert as well as fantastic team players and all-round good eggs to boot. These people are named elsewhere in this Preface. Some of these very same people I have strong-armed into collaborating with me on writing projects, with results that you the reader are now benefitting from – as I have done – as their banking acumen and skills in written articulation are presented in this book. Various parts of the material you see here and on the associated website have been contributed by the top writers in banking, and for that my everlasting thanks to Chris Westcott, Ed Bace, Polina Bardaeva, Enrique Benito, Doo Bo Chung, Peter Eisenhardt, Adam Ginty, Rita Gnutti, Kevin Liddy, Zhuoshi Liu, Jamie Paris, Juan Ramirez, Soumya Sarkar, Christian Schmaltz, Cormac O'Connor and Graeme Wolvaardt. It is a privilege and a pleasure to know and have worked with such fantastic, genuine people.

# Acknowledgments

L ove, thanks, and respect to *The Pink Tie Brigade* (Clax, KMan Butt, Abu Abdi, Mohamoud Dualeh, Farooq Jaffrey, Kevin Zhuoshi Liu, Abukar Ali, Rod Pienaar, Richard Pereira, and Didier Joannas), Dave Beech, Phil Broadhurst, the *JPMorgan ITS Footy Boys* (Rich Lynn, Michael Nicoll, Jonathan Rossington, Stuart Medlen, Neil Lewis, Tony Fulling, Michael Beddow, and the legendary Alan Fulling), Anuk, Millie, and Leela Teasdale, Nik Slater, Professor Carol Alexander, Brian Eales, Professor Christine Oughton, Andrew Benson, Stuart Turner, Jim Harrison, Balamurali Radhakrishnan, Harry Cross, Jas Singh Ghag, Jim Croke, Sharad Samy, Wei Goh, Sean Baguley, Martin Barber, Maira Chatziperou, Mark Burgess, Suraj Gohil, and the legendary Derek Taylor. Respect. *A Solid Bond In Your Heart.*

Thanks to Frankie Routleff for reminding me of the inspiration and energy of youth.

It was great while it lasted, special thanks to the best team ever assembled in the City of London: my RBS "Project Bluebird" Treasury team, that's Patricia Geraghty, Emre Degirmenci, Bruce Walker, Steve Harris, Dorothea Sanger, Tim Hobbs, Pete Gunning, Ivo Krastev, and David Walker, plus honorary members Alan Genzel, Yusuf Surroop, Mark Smit, Mark Roberts, Tom Whalen, Angel Knott, and Damian Turner. Also at RBS thanks to David Gillespie, Ian Cowie, Kathryn Winup, Janet Adams, David Bradley, Gavin Tilling, Omar El-Tahlawi, Terry Turner, Patricia Yap, Alexander Gorokhvodatskiy, Ratica Setia, Amelia Casey, David Lammas, Cormac O'Connor, Omar Ahmed, David Connolly, Trudy Nash, Tim Evans, Raju Mandavia, Graham Corr, Gareth Walters, Mario Riet-Muller, Bill Rickard, Ross Aucutt, Bill Powell, and Graham Skeats.

Big thanks to Sherif Choudhry, Julie Ashmore, Professor Steven Mann, Professor Darrell Duffie, Professor Joel Bessis, David Wileman, Mario Cerrato, Juan Blasco Fernandez, Christine Qian Guo, Richard Pottle, Max Wong, Alex Voicu, Andy Condurache, Michael Widowitz, Liz McCormick, Jori-Pekka Rautalahti, Angela Ransley, Carla Ferreira, Phillip Jesson, James Nicholls, Andreas Simou, Valerie Maysey, Frank Spiteri, Michael Tichareva, Kim McCarthy, Ali Andani, Henry A Davis, Robert McWilliam, Frank Bock, Mia Mohamed, Samir Pandiri, Mark Arthur, Stephen Laughton, Sharon Mandeville, Eugene Banja, Lisa Bamford, David Lemmon, Pablo Fernández, Steen Blaafalk, Nathanael Yishak, Jacqui Peters, Suborna Barua, Sk. Matiur

Rahman, Amanda Jones, Nick Carpenter, Mehdi, Mark Cleere, Arif Lakhani, Shahrukh Ahmed, Vijay Makwana, Barry Howard, Evgueni Ivantsov, Kenneth Kortanek, Mike Cash, Jaafar Husain, Quintin Rayer, Paulina Krzyzanowska, Louisa Pieters, Ray Saunders, Amos Chan, Paul Newson, Gary Van Vuuren, Christian Schmaltz, Christian Buschmann, Alexander Lipton, Patrick Shim, Jan De Spiegeleer, Bonnie Buchanan, Abhijit Patharkar, Mark Mobius, Roger Drayton, Jeremy Carter, David Moskovic, Samarjeet Das Ray, Tim Sillitoe, Arno Kratky, Julie Fussell, Michael Lafferty, Libon Fung, Magdalena Ziolo, Antonio Mota Pizarro, Maurizio Pompella, Nabiha Akhter, David Marsh, Bob Bischoff, Pete McIntyre, Gary Manning, Ruth Wandhofer, Sami Sulieman, Laurie Cutting, Tamsin Harris, Hayley White, Christopher Bond, Brandon Davies, Małgorzata Tynecka, Kazi Hussain, Wolfgang Marty, Philippe Mangold, Issa Soormally, Debashis Dutta, Matthew Weilert, Irving Henry, Paul Rudd, Vincent Beard, Roddy Millar, Zia Ishaq, Tricia Lim, Jeannette Lichner, Adrianna Wozniak, Professor Jean Helwege, Asif Abdul-Razzaq, Thomas Kuehn, Raphael Chaves, Robert Reitano, Dhilnawaaz Khan, Susan Hindle Barone, Jorge Carbon, Hussain Kureshi, John D. Evans, Alastair Tyler, Enrico Castagnetti, Mark Adelson, Elenora Elroy, Vanessa Palmer, Alan Santos, Lincoln Hannah, David Fance, Panagiotis Ballis-Papanastasiou, Ruth Sunderland, Steven Lee, Murad Baig, Jean Stevenson, Caroline Andrew, Martin Day, Elizabeth Sheedy, Robert Merrifield, Will Banks, David Koenig, Randeep Gug, Tanveer Bhatti, Zumi Farooq, Jakub Wojtasik, Anthony Pereira, Sophie Linton-Sterling, Etienne Hofstetter, Jane Norris, Lina Worthing, Paul Hale, Imran Akhtar, Roland Jordan, Khalid Hottak, Mohammed Dualeh, Alistair Osborne, Mark Williams, Kristina Frykstad, Bill Forsyth, Andrea Hodgson, Andrew Kasapis, Gulser Tartan, Poonam Kaur, Kev and Jen Norman, Leila Alameddine, Tazeeb Rajwani, Paul Wilde, Simon Culhane, and Shakil Butt.

Only one publisher of Finance textbooks could put out something like *Anthology*, and that's John Wiley & Sons. Big, big thanks to Stephen Mullaly, Jeremy Chia, Thomas Hyrkiel, Cynthia Mak, Sharifah Sharomsah, Jesse Yeo, Cindy Chu, Wong Pak Yau, Lori Laker, Louise Holden, Ben Hall, Gladys Ganaden, Jennie Kitchin, Sandra Glue, Julie Attrill, Laura Cooksley, Jarene Ang, Georgie James, Laura Cooksley, Banurekha Venkatesan, Aida Ferguson, and since moved on to other things but never forgotten as it was him who got me into Wiley to start with, Mr Nick Wallwork. Thanks to you guys my Wiley Asia books look handsome – I really appreciate it.

At BTRM big thanks to Werner Coetzee, Neil Fowler, Chris Uduezue, Bobby Adjare, and the esteemed Faculty that is Chris Westcott, Ed Bace, Stefano Alberigo, Suleman Baig, Polina Bardaeva, Enrique Benito, Nicolas Bischoff, Peter Eisenhardt, Rita Gnutti, Kevin Liddy, Jamie Paris, Massimo Pedroni, Engelbert Plassmann, Juan Ramirez, Patricia Robertson, Soumya Sarkar, Graham Hillier, Doo Bo Chung, Amitabh Singhania, Andrea Cremonino, Eve Poole, and (again!) Bruce Walker.

I never thought I'd write a book about finance. Then I started teaching for the Securities Institute, and the lady running the training programme there suggested I turn my course companion into a textbook.

"Er . . . how does one do that?" I asked.

"Easy", she replied, "the Institute has a publishing arm, we'll publish it for you!"

That was in 1998, the book was *An Introduction to Value at Risk* (now in its 5$^{th}$ edition), and here we are 20 years later with the culmination of my writing career that is *Anthology*. Thank you Zena Deane, I can safely say that if it wasn't for you none of my books would have seen the light of day. The impact of the best working relationships goes on for much, much longer after the people involved have stopped working together.

## THE "UB40" VERY SPECIAL THANKS

As Derek and the Dominoes may have put it, you know who your friends are when you're unemployed! A special mention and a very, very special thanks to the following individuals for their help and support, I won't forget it:

Dan Cunningham, Professor Gautam Mitra, the legendary Colin Johnson, Chris Westcott (again!), Ed Bace (again!), Suleman Baig (again!), Polina Bardaeva (again!), Peter Eisenhardt (again!), Jamie Paris (again!), Engelbert Plassmann (again!), Balamurali Radhakrishnan (again!), Nayan Sthanakiya, Eric Scotto di Rinaldi, Bart Tkaczyk, Iain McNay, Roman Matousek, Radu Tunaru, Michael Georger, Danny Corrigan, Tony Gandy, Karen Taylor, Lawrence Ho, Adam Lawson, Cosimo Montagu, Carina Holmes, Kevin Zhuoshi Liu (legend – again!), Martin Barber (legend – again!), Stafford Bent, Russ Ives, Ionut Cristian Voicu, Richard Mitchell, George Littlejohn, Christine Whittaker, Hemraz Jankee, Lois Camberg, Cormac Lucas, Debbie Banyard, Nalin Soni, Kay Lawrence, Aleksandar Doric, Martin Ward, Chris Edwards, Tope Fasua, Michele Lizzio, Vijay Krishnaswamy, Darren Carter, John Wilson, Michael Eichhorn, Cris Kinrade, Andy Mason, David Riddell, Eric Khoo, Sachvir Cheema, Anthony Ginn, Filip Fidanoski, Martyn Hoccom, Joe Jennings, Anne Carter, Rich Lynn (again!), Philip Allen, Adam Ginty, Tony Holloway, Graeme Wolvaardt, James Philcox, Milivoje Davidovic, Konstantin Nikolaev, Soumya Sarkar (again!), David Castle, Manjula Mathew, Barney Collins, Malcolm Wood, Shakil Ashraf, and Jessica James.

## THANKS FOR GREAT LEADERSHIP

Whether in the office or on the football pitch, I have been privileged to learn from working alongside some exceptional team leaders: individuals who are naturals in the art of building and leading diverse teams, and of motivating their teams to give it that extra special effort. These people are genuinely inspiring, and it's been a pleasure to know them. I have tried my best to apply their open, honest, and straightforward approach to everything I do.

So my thanks, for setting a personal example as great leaders, to Sean Baguley, Martin Barber, Darren Carter, Martyn Hoccom, Alan Fulling, Leo Hill, and Matt Dilger. And also to Richard Smith, the first person I observed demonstrating genuine team leadership skills in the City of London, at the London Stock Exchange during in 1991.

## A GENUINE TEAM: NEWDIGATE FOOTBALL CLUB

A very big thanks to Simon Haigh and the lads at Newdigate Football Club, which plays in the West Sussex League. Mr Haigh for being a great manager and for inviting me to join the club, and the lads for being fabulous, energetic, and genuine chaps who lead by example and continually inspire me to give it my very best! Newdigate FC is a team in the true sense of the word.

So thanks, respect, and affection to Ryan Haigh, Alex Haigh, Joshua Watkins, Bobby Taylor, Jimmy Taylor, Ricki Lunn, George Corfield, Nathan Fuller, Leo Hill, Dan Townsend, Andy Longhurst, Connor Mitchell, Ben Crook, Jason Harcombe, Harry Osbourne Taylor, George Crate, Paul Bettesworth, James Humpfries, George Harrison, Matt Alderman, Ben Pankhurst, Pete Dell, Jordan Morris, Max Ridler, Jack Hazlewood, Aaron Jenkins, Jack Styles, Alexis Persaud, John Fuller, Lewis McLean, Alex Hinds, Aaron Clark, and everyone at the club.

Gentlemen, it's a pleasure and a privilege to play alongside you.

## NEAL ARDLEY FAN CLUB

I played alongside them on just two occasions (both charity football matches at AFC Wimbledon), but I must thank two ex-Premiership football players, Neal Ardley and Neil Cox, for teaching me more about teambuilding and leadership in 40 minutes of football than I'd ever learned during countless hours attending company management "offsites", business seminars, industry conferences, workshops, and MBA classes. Just observing the way they interacted with their teammates taught me a lot. Thank you gentlemen, it's a privilege to know you.[1]

---

[1] See Appendix 1.B in Chapter 1 for what I wrote in a matchday programme after playing alongside Neal Ardley, Neil Cox, Ashley Bayes, and Chris Perry in a charity match at AFC Wimbledon. They are genuinely exceptional men.

## SPECIAL BANKS THANK YOU

I'd like to thank Rafael Hurtado and all his colleagues at BCP in Lima. . . . it was a privilege and pleasure to not only conduct a workshop there on ALM in December 2014 but also to turn out with their football players! They honour me if only because they always ask my opinion on all matters balance sheet management – chaps it's a pleasure, anytime!

The Boys from South America

Big thanks to Jamel Banda, Joe Mensah, and Beatrice Nunoo at Ghana International Bank in London, a great team to work with.

Thanks to Ahmed Arbee, Conor Murphy, and Zakaria Salah at the Islamic Development Bank in Jeddah, an institution with a risk management culture that reflects the traditional bank standards of conservatism and prudence – always great to see.

## GOODBYE

As befits a "compilation album" of my previous works, this one really is my last book. Whilst there may be the odd updated edition of existing books in future, no further new titles will be forthcoming from me – at least, not on the subject of banking and finance!

So for one last time . . .

Goodbye! Stay handsome.

Goodbye.

Moorad Choudhry
Surrey, England
*31 December 2017*

## FINALLY, A SPECIAL SOMETHING . . .

. . . because "thanks" doesn't really cover it. Thank you for everything Mum and Dad. Legends.

# About the Author

Moorad Choudhry lectures on the MSc Finance programme at University of Kent Business School. He was previously with Group Treasury at The Royal Bank of Scotland, and prior to that at Europe Arab Bank, KBC Bank, JPMorgan Chase, ABN Amro Hoare Govett Ltd, and the London Stock Exchange.

Moorad is Fellow of the Chartered Institute for Securities & Investment, Fellow of the London Institute of Banking and Finance, Fellow of the Global Association of Risk Professionals, Fellow of the Institute of Sales Management, and Fellow of the Institute of Directors. He is Managing Editor of the *International Journal of Monetary Economics and Finance*, and a member of the Editorial Boards of *Journal of Structured Finance*, *International Journal of Economics and Finance*, *Qualitative Research in Financial Markets*, and *American Securitization*.

And he plays for Newdigate Football Club.

# List of Extract Book Titles

This book contains extracts from the following books authored by Professor Moorad Choudhry, published by John Wiley & Sons Limited. All titles remain in print or are available as an e-book.

*Fixed Income Markets, 2ⁿᵈ Edition* (2014)

*An Introduction to Value-at-Risk, 5ᵗʰ Edition* (2013)

*The Mechanics of Securitization* (2013)

*The Principles of Banking* (2012)

*An Introduction to Banking* (2011)

*An Introduction to Bond Markets, 4ᵗʰ Edition* (2010)

*Fixed Income Securities and Derivatives Handbook, 2ⁿᵈ Edition* (2010)

*Structured Credit Products, 2ⁿᵈ Edition* (2010)

*The Future of Finance* (2010)

*Bank Asset and Liability Management* (2007)

*The Futures Bond Basis, 2$^{nd}$ Edition* (2006)

*An Introduction to Repo Markets, 3$^{rd}$ Edition* (2006)

*The Credit Default Swap Basis* (2006)

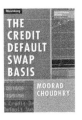

*The Money Markets Handbook* (2004)

*The Global Repo Markets* (2004)

*Analysing and Interpreting the Yield Curve* (2004)

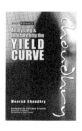

*"I have a problem with psychometric testing: it is to my mind a spurious device used by large corporations to ensure that anyone with a semblance of wit or independent thought doesn't get anywhere near securing a job. If the entire country were subjected to psychometric testing and all those who failed it humanely put down, we'd be left with a rump of deathly, grey-faced middle managers."*
——Rod Liddle, *The Sunday Times*, 18 August 2013

# PART

# I

# Principles of Banking, Finance and Financial Products

**P**art I is a primer on banking and the financial markets, as well as the products used in banking and how to analyse them. It also covers absolute essentials of finance such as the yield curve, plus various techniques in common use by many banks like securitisation, and hedging products such as interest-rate swaps. Part I is aimed at everyone and anyone who is involved in banking markets worldwide. In other words, its contents must be viewed as essential learning – the very basics of finance. Anyone with a genuine interest in finance and banking would want to be familiar with the content of Part I.

As with the book throughout, we present a mixture of extracts from the author's previous works and new material. Part I comprises material on a "primer" on banking, Eurobonds, derivative instruments and their use in hedging risk, securitisation and structured finance, and analysing and interpreting the yield curve.

"People still crave explanations even when there is no underlying under-standing about what's going on. . . .erratic stock market movements always find a ready explanation in the next day's financial columns: a price rise is attributed to sentiment that 'pessimism about interest rate increases was exaggerated,' or to the view that 'company X had been oversold.' Of course these explanations are always *a posteriori*: commentators could offer an equally ready explanation if a stock price had moved the other way."

—Professor Martin Rees, *Our Cosmic Habitat*,
Phoenix 2003, page 101

# CHAPTER 1

# A Primer on Banking, Finance and Financial Instruments

This chapter is reference material for newcomers to the market, junior bankers and finance students, or for those that require a refresher course on the core subject matter. The purpose of this primer is to introduce all the essential basics of banking, which is necessary if one is to gain a strategic overview of what banks do, what risk exposures they face and how to manage them properly. We begin with the concept of banking, and follow this with a description of bank cash flows, calculation of return, the risks faced in banking, and organisation and strategy.

Banking is a subset of "finance". The principles of finance underlay the principles of banking. It would be difficult to become conversant with the principles of banking, and thus be in a position to manage a bank efficiently and effectively to the benefit of all stakeholders, unless one was also familiar with the principles of finance. That said, it is not uncommon to encounter senior executives and non-executive directors on bank Boards who are perhaps not as *au fait* with basic principles as they should be. Hence, these basic principles are introduced here and remain the theme of Part I of this book.

## AN INTRODUCTION TO BANKING

This extract from *Bank Asset and Liability Management* (2007)

### Introduction

As Sir Arthur Conan Doyle would have put it, so elementary a form of literature as the textbook on financial economics hardly deserves the dignity of a preface. It is possible, though, to bring some instant clarity to the purpose of such a book if we open with a few words here.

The traditional view of a bank is that of a financial institution that is in the business of taking deposits and advancing loans, and which makes its money from the difference in interest rate paid and received on these two products. While this quaint image would have been true a few hundred years ago, it is decidedly incomplete today. The modern banking institution is a complex beast, which in many cases operates in a wide range of products and services and across international markets. Banks are the cornerstone of the global economy, and at the highest level the banking sector influences, and is influenced by, macroeconomic trends such as GDP growth, central bank base interest rates, equity and debt capital markets activity, and the supply and demand for investments and credit.

However, notwithstanding our first statement that banks now engage in many complex activities outside traditional borrowing and lending, we must remember that at the core of *all* capital markets activity lies the need to bring together the suppliers of capital with the borrowers of capital. This was the original business logic behind the very first banks, so in that respect very little has changed! There is much other activity surrounding this basic function in the markets, but this need is paramount. Hence a key ingredient in bank strategy is the management of its assets and liabilities. It is this that is the subject of this book: Asset and Liability Management (ALM). These days there are a large number of instruments, in cash and derivative form, that make up a bank's assets and liabilities. No matter. For the ALM desk in a bank, the cash assets and liabilities are king and must be managed prudently. That there is more to this than may meet the eye is apparent immediately from the thickness of this book!

Let us set the scene further with some discussion on banks.

## Introduction

Banking operations encompass a wide range of activities, all of which contribute to the asset and liability profile of a bank. Table P.1 shows selected banking activities, and the type of risk exposure they represent. The terms used in the table, such as "market risk", are explained elsewhere in this book. In Chapter 2 we discuss elementary aspects of financial analysis, using key financial ratios, that are used to examine the profitability and asset quality of a bank. We also discuss bank regulation and the concept of bank capital.

Before considering the concept of ALM, all readers should be familiar with the way a bank's earnings and performance are reported in its financial statements. A bank's income statement will break down the earnings by type, as we have defined in Table P.1. So we need to be familiar with interest income, trading income and so on. The other side of an income statement is the costs, such as operating expenses and bad loan provisions.

| Service or function | Revenue generated | Risk |
|---|---|---|
| Lending | | |
| – Retail | Interest income, fees | Credit, Market |
| – Commercial | Interest income, fees | Credit, Market |
| – Mortgage | Interest income, fees | Credit, Market |
| – Syndicated | Interest income, fees | Credit, Market |
| Credit cards | Interest income, fees | Credit, Operational |
| Project finance | Interest income, fees | Credit |
| Trade finance | Interest income, fees | Credit, Operational |
| Cash management | | |
| – Processing | Fees | Operational |
| – Payments | Fees | Credit, Operational |
| Custodian | Fees | Credit, Operational |
| Private banking | Commission income, interest income, fees | Operational |
| Asset management | Fees, performance payments | Credit, Market, Operational |
| Capital markets | | |
| – Investment banking | Fees | Credit, Market |
| – Corporate finance | Fees | Credit, Market |
| – Equities | Trading income, fees | Credit, Market |
| – Bonds | Trading income, interest income, fees | Credit, Market |
| – Foreign exchange | Trading income, fees | Credit, Market |
| – Derivatives | Trading income, interest income, fees | Credit, Market |

**Table P.1**　Selected banking activities and services

That the universe of banks encompasses many different varieties of beast is evident from the way they earn their money. Traditional banking institutions, perhaps typified by a regional bank in the United States or a building society in the United Kingdom, will generate a much greater share of their revenues through net interest income than trading income, and vice versa for an investment bank such as Lehman International or Merrill Lynch. The latter firms will earn a greater share of their revenues through fees and trading income.

During 2004 a regional European bank reported the following earnings breakdown, as shown in Table P.2.

| Core operating income | % share |
| --- | --- |
| Net interest income | 62 |
| Fees and commissions | 27 |
| Trading income | 11 |

**Table P.2**   European regional bank, earnings structure 2004
*Source*: Author's notes.

However, this breakdown varies widely across regions and banks, and in fact would be reversed at an investment bank whose core operating activity was market-making and proprietary trading.

Let us consider now the different types of income stream and costs.

## Interest income

Interest income, or net interest income (NII), is the main source of revenue for the majority of banks worldwide. As we saw from Table P.2, it can form upwards of 60% of operating income, and for smaller banks and building societies it reaches 80% or more.

NII is generated from lending activity and interest-bearing assets, the "net" return is this interest income minus the cost of funding the loans. Funding, which is a cost to the bank, is obtained from a wide variety of sources. For many banks, deposits are a key source of funding, as well as one of the cheapest. They are generally short-term, though, or available on demand, so they must be supplemented with longer term funding. Other sources of funds include senior debt, in the form of bonds, securitised bonds and money market paper.

NII is sensitive to both credit risk and market risk. Market risk, which we will look at later, is essentially interest-rate risk for loans and deposits. Interest-rate risk will be driven by the maturity structure of the loan book, as well as the match (or mismatch) between the maturity of the loans against the maturity of the funding. This is known as the interest-rate gap.

## Fees and commissions

Banks generate fee income as a result of the provision of services to customers. Fee income is very popular with bank senior management because it is less volatile and not susceptible to market risk like trading income or even NII. There is also no credit risk because the fees are often paid up front. There are other benefits as well, such as the opportunity to build up a diversified customer base for this additional range of services, but these are of less concern to a bank ALM desk.

Fee income uses less capital and also carries no market risk, but does carry other risks such as operational risk.

## Trading income

Banks generate trading income through trading activity in financial products such as equities (shares), bonds and derivative instruments. This includes acting as a dealer or market-maker in these products, as well as taking proprietary positions for speculative purposes. Running positions in securities (as opposed to derivatives) in some cases generates interest income, some banks strip this out of the capital gain made when the security is traded to profit, while others include it as part of overall trading income.

Trading income is the most volatile income source for a bank. It also carries relatively high market risk, as well as not inconsiderable credit risk. Many banks, although by no means all, use the Value-at-Risk (VaR) methodology to measure the risk arising from trading activity, which gives a statistical measure of expected losses to the trading portfolio under certain selected market scenarios.

## Costs

Bank operating costs comprise staff costs, as well as other costs such as premises, information technology and equipment costs. Further significant elements of cost are provisions for loan losses, which are a charge against the loan revenues of the bank. The provision is based on a subjective measure by management of how much of the loan portfolio can be expected to be repaid by the borrower.

## Bank Business and Bank Capital

### Bank Business and Bank Capital

Banking has a long and honourable history. Today it encompasses a wide range of activities, of varying degrees of complexity. Whatever the precise business, the common denominators of all banking activities are those of risk, return and the bringing together of the providers of capital. Return on capital is the focus of banking activity. The coordination of all banking activity could be said to be the focus of asset and liability management (ALM), although some practitioners will give ALM a narrower focus. Either way, we need to be familiar with the wide-ranging nature of banking business, and the importance of bank capital. This then acts as a guide for what follows.

In this introductory chapter of the first part of the book, we place ALM in context by describing the financial markets and the concept of bank capital. Subsequent chapters look at money market instruments and the basics of bank financial statements. We begin with a look at the business of banking.

We then consider the different types of revenue generated by a bank, the concept of the banking book and the trading book, and financial statements. The chapter concludes with an introduction to the money market, the key area of involvement for an ALM desk.

## Banking business

We introduced the different aspects of banking business in the Preface. For the largest banks these aspects are widely varying in nature. For our purposes we may group them together in the form shown in Figure 1.1. Put very simply, "retail" or "commercial" banking covers the more traditional lending and trust activities, while "investment" banking covers trading

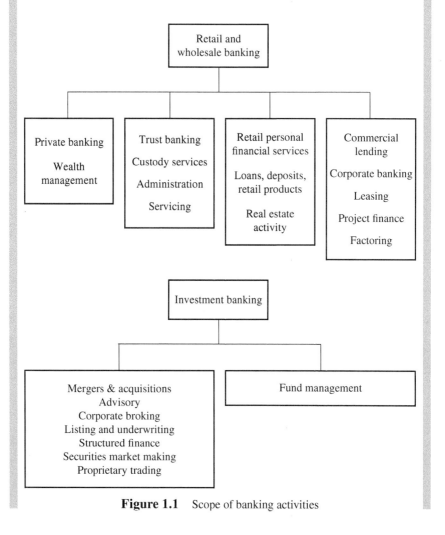

**Figure 1.1**    Scope of banking activities

activity and fee-based income such as stock exchange listing and mergers and acquisition (M&A). The one common objective of all banking activity is return on capital. Depending on the degree of risk it represents, a particular activity will be required to achieve a specified return on the capital it uses. The issue of banking capital is vital to an appreciation of the banking business; entire new business lines (such as securitisation) have been originated in response to a need to generate more efficient use of capital.

As we can see from Figure 1.1, the scope of banking business is vast. The activities range from essentially plain vanilla activity, such as corporate lending, to complex transactions such as securitisation and hybrid products trading. There is a vast literature on all these activities, so we do not need to cover them here. However, it is important to have a basic general knowledge of the basic products, so subsequent chapters will introduce these.

ALM is concerned with, among other things, the efficient management of banking capital. It therefore concerns itself with all banking operations, even if the day-to-day contact between the ALM desk (or Treasury desk) with other parts of the bank is remote. The ALM desk will be responsible for the treasury and money markets activities of the entire bank. So if we wish, we could draw a box with ALM in it around the whole of Figure 1.1. This is not to say that the ALM function does all these activities; rather, it is just to make clear that all the various activities represent assets and liabilities for the bank, and one central function is responsible for this side of these activities.

For capital management purposes a bank's business is organised into a "banking book" and a "trading book". We consider them next; first though, a word on bank capital.

## Capital

Bank capital is the equity of the bank. It is important as it is the cushion that absorbs any unreserved losses that the bank incurs. By acting as this cushion, it enables the bank to continue operating and thus avoid insolvency or bankruptcy during periods of market correction or economic downturn. When the bank suffers a loss or writes off a loss-making or otherwise economically untenable activity, the capital is used to absorb the loss. This can be done by eating into reserves, freezing dividend payments or (in more extreme scenarios) a write-down of equity capital. In the capital structure, the rights of capital creditors, including equity holders, are subordinated to senior creditors and deposit holders.

Banks occupy a vital and pivotal position in any economy, as suppliers of credit and financial liquidity, so bank capital is important. As such, banks are heavily regulated by central monetary authorities, and their capital is subject to regulatory rules governed by the Bank for International Settlements (BIS), based in Basel, Switzerland. For this reason its regulatory capital rules are often called the Basel rules. Under the original Basel rules ("Basel I") a banking institution was required to hold a minimum capital level of 8% against the assets on its book.[1] Total capital is comprised of:

- equity capital;
- reserves;
- retained earnings;
- preference share issue proceeds;
- hybrid capital instruments;
- subordinated debt.

Capital is split into Tier 1 capital and Tier 2 capital. The first three items above comprise Tier 1 capital while the remaining items are Tier 2 capital.

The quality of the capital in a bank reflects its mix of Tier 1 and 2 capital. Tier 1 or "core capital" is the highest quality capital, as it is not obliged to be repaid, and moreover there is no impact on the bank's reputation if it is not repaid. Tier 2 is considered lower quality as it is not "loss absorbing"; it is repayable and also of shorter-term than equity capital. Assessing the financial strength and quality of a particular banking institution often requires calculating key capital ratios for the bank and comparing these to market averages and other benchmarks.

Analysts use a number of ratios to assess bank capital strength. Some of the more common ones are shown in Table 1.1.

## Banking and trading books

Banks and financial institutions make a distinction between their activities for capital management, including regulatory capital, purposes. Activities are split into the "banking book" and the "trading book". Put simply, the banking book holds the more traditional banking activities such as commercial banking; for example, loans and deposits. This would cover lending to individuals as well as corporates and other banks, and so will interact with investment banking business.[2] The trading book records wholesale market transactions, such as market making and proprietary trading in bonds and derivatives. Again speaking simply, the primary difference between the two books is that the over-riding principle of the banking book is one of "buy and hold"; that is, a long-term acquisition. Assets may be held on the book for up to 30 years or longer.

---

[1] There is more to this than just this simple statement, and we consider this in chapters 26 and 27.

[2] For a start, there will be a commonality of clients. A corporate client will borrow from a bank, and may also retain the bank's underwriting or structured finance departments to arrange a share issue or securitisation for it.

| Ratio | Calculation | Notes |
|---|---|---|
| Core capital ratio | Tier 1 capital/Risk-weighted assets | A key ratio monitored in particular by rating agencies as a measure of high-quality non-repayable capital, available to absorb losses incurred by the bank |
| Tier 1 capital ratio | Eligible Tier 1 capital/ Risk-weighted assets | Another important ratio monitored by investors and rating agencies. Represents the amount of high-quality, non-repayable capital available to the bank |
| Total capital ratio | Total capital/Risk-weighted assets | Represents total capital available to the bank |
| Off-balance sheet risk to total capital | Off-balance sheet and contingent risk/Total capital | Measure of adequacy of capital against off-balance sheet risk including derivatives exposure and committed, undrawn credit lines |

**Table 1.1** Bank analysis ratios for capital strength
*Source*: Higson (1995)

The trading book is just that, it employs a trading philosophy so that assets may be held for very short terms, less than one day in some cases. The regulatory capital and accounting treatment of each book differs. The primary difference here is that the trading book employs the "mark-to-market" approach to record profit and loss (p&l), which is the daily "marking" of an asset to its market value. An increase or decrease in the mark on the previous day's mark is recorded as an unrealised profit or loss on the book: on disposal of the asset, the realised profit or loss is the change in the mark at disposal compared to its mark at purchase.

### The banking book

Traditional banking activity such as deposits and loans is recorded in the banking book. Accounting treatment for the banking book follows the accrual concept, which is accruing interest cash flows as they occur. There is no mark-to-market. The banking book holds assets for which both corporate and retail counterparties as well as banking counterparties are represented. So it is the type of business activity that dictates whether it is placed in the banking book, not the type of counterparty or which department of the bank is conducting it. Assets and liabilities in the banking book generate interest-rate and credit risk exposure for the bank. They also create liquidity and term mismatch ("gap") risks. Liquidity refers to the ease with which an asset can be transformed into cash, as well as to the ease with which funds can be raised in the market. So we see that "liquidity risk" actually refers to two related but separate issues.

All these risks form part of ALM. Interest-rate risk management is a critical part of Treasury policy and ALM, while credit risk policy will be set and dictated by the credit policy of the bank. Gap risk creates an excess or shortage of cash, which must be managed. This is the cash management part of ALM. There is also a mismatch risk associated with fixed-rate and floating-rate interest liabilities. The central role of the financial markets is to enable cash management and interest-rate management to be undertaken efficiently. ALM of the banking book will centre on interest-rate risk management and hedging, and liquidity management. Note how there is no "market risk" for the banking book in principle, because there is no marking-to-market. However, the interest rate exposure of the book creates an exposure that is subject to market movements in interest rates, so in reality the banking book is indeed exposed to market risk.

## Trading book

Wholesale market activity, including market making and proprietary trading, is recorded in the trading book. Assets on the trading book can be expected to have a high turnover, although not necessarily so, and are marked-to-market daily. The counterparties to this trading activity can include other banks and financial institutions such as hedge funds, corporates and central banks. Trading book activity generates the same risk exposure as that on the banking book, including market risk, credit risk and liquidity risk. It also creates a need for cash management. Much trading book activity involves derivative instruments, as opposed to "cash" products. Derivatives include futures, swaps and options. These can be equity, interest-rate, credit, commodity, foreign exchange (FX), weather and other derivatives. Derivatives are known as "off-balance sheet" instruments because they are recorded off the (cash) balance sheet. Their widespread use and acceptance has greatly improved the efficiency of the risk exposure hedging process, for banks and other institutions alike.

Off-balance sheet transactions refer to "contingent liabilities", which are so-called because they refer to a future exposure contracted now. These are not only derivatives contracts such as interest-rate swaps or writing an option, but include guarantees such as a credit line to a third-party customer or a group subsidiary company. These represent a liability for the bank that may be required to be honoured at some future date. In most cases they do not generate cash inflow or outflow at inception, unlike a cash transaction, but represent future exposure. If a credit line is drawn on, it represents a cash outflow and that transaction is then recorded on the balance sheet.

### EXAMPLE 1.1   The first banks[3]

Banks have a long and interesting history, and for many centuries have been the leader for economies to follow. The first records of banks come from Ancient Greece. Many private and civic entities conducted various financial transactions in the temple banks. These included loans, deposits, currency exchanges and coin validation. There is also evidence of credit, which was when a Greek port would write a credit note in exchange for the payment of a client. The port would hold the money in the temple for the customer who paid him the money, and he could collect the money in another city when he cashed in the credit note. This would save him having to carry around the gold all the time, because he could collect the money in a different city. This gave rise to a risk of being unbalanced in money at certain times. In Ancient Rome the art of banking was developed to include charging interest on loans, and paying interest on deposits.

The first bank to offer most of the basic banking functions known today was the *Bank of Barcelona* in Spain. Founded by merchants in 1401, this bank held deposits, exchanged currency, and carried out lending operations. It also introduced the bank cheque. Modern banking was introduced in what is now Italy. In the 15th century the Lombards, a group of bankers from the north of Italy began to apply accounting to work around a religious moral repugnance of usury. Accounting principles were used to keep a record of loans, and the loan was paid back "voluntarily". The oldest surviving bank today is *Monte dei Paschi di Siena*, which opened in 1472.

Modern British economic and financial history is usually traced back to the coffee houses of London. The London Royal Exchange was established in 1565 as a centre of commerce for the City of London, and trading of all sorts of commodities took place on its floors. Banking offices at that time were usually located near centers of trade, like the Royal Exchange. In London, individuals could now participate in the lucrative East India trade by purchasing bills of credit from these banks, but the price they received for commodities was dependent on the ships returning and on the cargo they carried. The commodities market was very volatile for this reason.

---

[3] This section was co-written with Darrell Hellmuth, Year 10, Wilmington Grammar School, Dartford, Kent, and Dan Slater, 2nd year mathematics, University College, Oxford.

Aside from the central Bank of England, which was founded in 1694, early English banks were privately owned goldsmiths rather than stock-issuing firms. Bank failures were common; so in the early 19th century, stock-issuing banks, with a larger capital base, were encouraged as a means of stabilising the industry. By 1833 these corporate banks were permitted to accept and transfer deposits in London, although they were prohibited from issuing money, a prerogative monopolised by the Bank of England. Corporate banking flourished after legislation in 1858 approved limited liability for stock-issuing banks.

| | |
|---|---|
| **c. 3000 – c. 2000 BC** | Development of Banking in Mesopotamia |
| **c. 350 BC** | Many banking services offered in Ancient Greece |
| **476 AD** | Roman Empire falls. Coins cease to be used as medium of exchange in Britain |
| **1232 – 1253** | Gold coins are issued by several Italian states |
| **1401** | Bank of Barcelona founded |
| **1403** | Charging interest on loans is ruled legal in Florence |
| **1407** | Bank of St George, Genoa, founded |
| **1585** | Bank of Genoa founded |
| **1587** | Banco di Rialto, Venice, founded |
| **1600** | The London East India Company is founded |
| **c. 1660** | Goldsmiths' receipts become banknotes in England |
| **1694** | Bank of England is founded |

**Table 1.2**   Timeline
*Source*: YieldCurve.com (www.yieldcurve.com)

## Financial statements and ratios

A key information tool for bank analysis is the financial statement, which is comprised of the balance sheet and the profit & loss (p&l) account. Assets on the balance sheet should equal the assets on a bank's ALM report, while receipt of revenue (such as interest and fees income) and payout of costs during a specified period is recorded in the p&l report or income statement.

### The balance sheet

The balance sheet is a statement of a company's assets and liabilities as determined by accounting rules. It is a snapshot of a particular point in time, and so by the time it is produced it is already out of date. However, it is an important information statement. A number of management information ratios are used when analysing the balance sheet and these are considered in the next chapter.

In Chapter 2 we use an hypothetical example to illustrate balance sheets. For a bank, there are usually five parts to a balance sheet, as it is split to show separately:

- lending and deposits, or traditional bank business;
- trading assets;
- treasury and interbank assets;
- off-balance sheet assets;
- long-term assets, including fixed assets, shares in subsidiary companies, together with equity and Tier 2 capital.

This is illustrated in Table 1.3. The actual balance sheet of a retail or commercial bank will differ significantly from that of an investment bank, due to the relative importance of their various business lines, but the basic layout will be similar.

## Profit & loss report

The income statement for a bank is the p&l report and it records all the income, and losses, during a specified period of time. A bank income statement will show revenues that can be accounted for as either net interest income, fees and commissions, and trading income. The precise mix of these sources will reflect the type of banking institution and the business lines it operates in. Revenue is offset by operating (non-interest) expenses, loan loss provisions, trading losses and tax expense.

A more "traditional" commercial bank such as a United Kingdom (UK) building society will have a much higher dependence on interest revenues than an investment bank that engages in large-scale wholesale capital market business. Investment banks have a higher share of revenue comprised of trading and fee income. Table 1.4 shows the components of a UK retails bank's income statement.

The composition of earnings varies widely among different institutions, Figure 1.2 shows the breakdown for a UK building society and the

| Assets | Liabilities |
|---|---|
| Cash | Short-term liabilities |
| Loans | Deposits |
| Financial instruments (long) | Financial instruments (short) |
| Fixed assets | Long-dated debt |
| Off-balance sheet (receivables) | Equity |
| | Off-balance sheet (liabilities) |

**Table 1.3**   Components of a bank balance sheet

| | % | Expressed as percentage of |
|---|---|---|
| Core operating income | 100 | |
| Net interest income | 64 | / core operating income |
| Commissions and fee income | 31 | / core operating income |
| Trading income | 8 | / core operating income |
| + Net other operating income | 8 | / core operating income |
| – Operating expenses | 61 | / revenues |
| Personnel | 38 | / revenues |
| Other, depreciation | | |
| – Loan loss provisions | 23 | / pre-provision net income |
| = Net operating income | | |
| + Other non-operating income | | |
| = Profit before tax | | |
| – Tax | | |
| = Net income | | |
| – Minority interest | | |
| = Attributable income | | |

**Table 1.4**  Components of a bank income statement, typical structure for a retail bank
*Source*: Bank financial statements.

UK branch of a US investment bank in 2005, as reported in their financial accounts for that year.

## Characteristics of the money market

The money market, worldwide, acts as a channel through which market participants exchange financial assets for cash, or raise cash on a secured and unsecured basis. Its key defining point is that it serves short-term needs. This is the short-term financing needs of participants who are short cash, and the short-term investment needs of participants who are temporarily long cash. Figure 1.5 shows a stylised structure of the money market as it would exist in most countries.

Interest rates set in the money market (well, one key interest rate) act as benchmarks and guidelines for all other rates used. The importance of the money markets to this activity is often over-looked, but cannot be denied.

The size of the market means that it, in most countries and certainly in all developed economies, carries considerable breadth and depth. It is possible to transact very large volumes of business and for this not to impact the money market in an observable way. Like most financial markets these

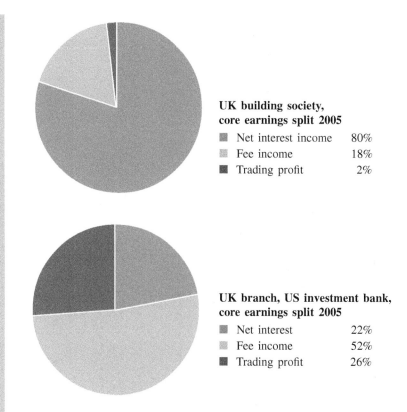

**Figure 1.2**   Composition of earnings
*Source*: Bank financial statements.

days, money market dealing is "over-the-counter", meaning it is not conducted on an exchange but over the telephone or computer terminal.

Interest rates in the money market – the rates at which participants borrow and lend funds – are set by the market and reflect a number of factors, from macroeconomic issues such as global supply and demand, to more market-specific issues such as liquidity and transparency. There are a large number of interest rates, for different products and different counterparties. The cornerstone of the market's various rates is the T-bill rate. T-bills are issued by the government to raise short-term cash (the typical maturity is 90 days). Because the bills are backed by the government, they carry no (or little) default risk. Hence the rates payable on these bills are the lowest in any market. All other rates in the market (and the bond market) will be at a positive spread over the T-bill rate.

In the following chapters we look in detail at the various instruments that go to make up the money markets. For beginners, we include a primer

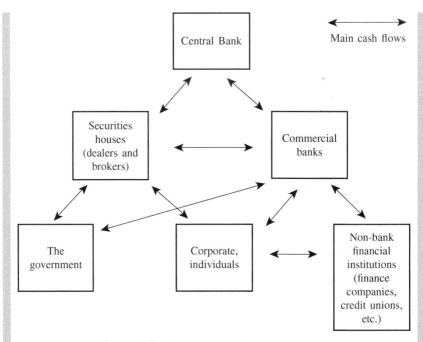

**Figure 1.5**   The structure of the money market

on financial markets arithmetic in the Appendix at the back of the book. This is required background for an understanding of interest rate mechanics.

## Money market conventions

We will see from the following pages that many money market instruments trade under similar market conventions. For example, for most currencies the basis used to calculate interest on a loan assumes a 360-day year, although sterling is an important exception to this. Again, while it is the norm for many currencies to float freely, their exchange rates to other currencies set by market supply and demand, some other important currencies are pegged to the US dollar and move with that currency. A very small number of currencies are not convertible and cannot be traded in the market.

Table 1.7 shows the characteristics of a sample of world currencies. It serves to highlight the individual detail differences that exist in the market. Terms such as "day-count" and "value date" will be fully explained in the following chapters.

Practitioners with access to Bloomberg can look up individual currency details by selecting:

[Ticker] [Currency yellow key] DES <Go>.

| Country | Currency | FX rate | Day-count | Spot FX value date |
|---|---|---|---|---|
| Argentina | Peso | Free-floating | ACT/360 | T+2 |
| Australia | Dollar | Free-floating | ACT/365 | T+2 |
| Brazil | Real | Free-floating | ACT/360 | T+3 |
| Canada | Dollar | Free-floating | ACT/365 (domestic) | T+1 |
| | | | ACT/360 (int'l) | T+2 |
| Czech Republic | Koruna | Free-floating | ACT/360 | T+2 |
| Denmark | Krone | Free-floating | ACT/360 | T+2 |
| Egypt | Pound | Free-floating | ACT/360 | T+2 |
| Euro Area[1] | Euro | Free-floating | ACT/360 | T+2 |
| Hong Kong | Dollar | Pegged to USD, HKD 7.70 per USD 1 | ACT/365 | T+2 |
| Hungary | Forint | Managed floating | ACT/360 | T+2 |
| Japan | Yen | Free-floating | ACT/360 | T+2 |
| Estonia | Kroon | Pegged to euro | ACT/360 | T+2 |
| Latvia | Lats | Pegged to Special Drawing Right (SDR)[2] | ACT/360 | T+2 |
| Lithuania | Litas | Pegged to euro, LTL 3.4528 to EUR 1 | ACT/360 | T+2 |
| Malaysia | Ringgit | Pegged to US dollar | ACT/365 | T+2 |
| New Zealand | Dollar | Free-floating | ACT/365 | T+2 |
| Norway | Krone | Free-floating | ACT/360 | T+2 |
| Poland | Zloty | Free-floating | ACT/365 | T+2 |
| Singapore | Dollar | Managed floating | ACT/365 | T+2 |
| South Africa | Rand | Free-floating | ACT/365 | T+2 |
| South Korea | Won | Free-floating | ACT/365 | T+2 |
| Switzerland | Franc | Free-floating | ACT/360 | T+2 |
| Taiwan | Dollar | Free-floating | ACT/365 | T+2 |
| Thailand | Baht | Free-floating | ACT/365 | T+2 |
| United Kingdom | Pound | Free-floating | ACT/365 | T+2 |
| United States | Dollar | Free-floating | ACT/360 | T+2 |

[1] Austria, Belgium, Finland, France, Germany, Greece, Ireland, Italy, Luxembourg, Netherlands, Portugal, Slovenia and Spain.

[2] The "currency" of the International Monetary Fund.

**Table 1.7**   Selected global currency conventions
*Sources*: Bloomberg L.P. and Reuters

```
AUD ↓  .7495  +.0056   TTOL .7493/.7497 TTOL    Curncy DES
At  9:35 Op .7448   Hi .7498   Lo .7441   Prev .7439       Value 4/21/04
                         Description                          Page 1/1
 AUD-USD       AUSTRALIAN DOLLAR SPOT              1 Dollar = 100 Cents
The Australian dollar is the official currency of the Commonwealth of Australia.
The conventional market quotation is the number of US dollars per Australian
dollar.  It is an independent, free-floating currency.

 1 )Economic Statistics           AUSTRALIA
 9) GDP               190200 12/31/03   Region:    Pacific Rim
10) Unemploymnt Rate     5.6 03/31/04   Capital:   Canberra
11) CPI                142.80 12/31/03   Population          19.55 12/31/02
12) Total Foreign De   360688 09/30/03   Area:      2966155
13) Exports (MLN)     11639.00 02/29/04   4)MAPS    Map
14) Imports (MLN)     13355.00 02/29/04   5)CDR     Calendar

 2 )News,Research & Market Information   Quick Statistics
15) Current News                    6)GPO 52Wk High        0.80 02/18/04
16) Bond Market News                    52Wk Low           0.61 04/21/03
17) Equity Market News              History Since    12/13/83
18) Economic News                   Day count        ACT/365
19) Economist Intelligence Unit     Value Date       04/21/04
20) Economic Releases
                                    7)PCS  Composite(NY)
 3 )Related Instruments             8)VOTE
Australia 61 2 9777 8600     Brazil 5511 3048 4500   Europe 44 20 7330 7500      Germany 49 69 920410
Hong Kong 852 2977 6000 Japan 81 3 3201 8900 Singapore 65 6212 1000 U.S. 1 212 318 2000 Copyright 2004 Bloomberg L.P.
                                                                   G926-802-0 19-Apr-04  9:35:26
```

**Figure 1.6**    Bloomberg page DES for Australian dollars

```
BRL   2.9130Y as of close  4/16                    Curncy DES

                         Description                          Page 1/3
 USD-BRL       BRAZILIAN REAL SPOT               1 Real = 100 Centavos
The Brazilian real is the official currency of the Federative Republic of
Brazil.  The conventional market quotation is the number of reals per US dollar.
It is an independent free-floating currency.

 1 )Economic Statistics           BRAZIL
 9) GDP% Qtr/Qtr        1.50 12/31/03   Region:    South America
10) Unemploymnt Rate    7.08 11/30/02   Capital:   Brasilia
11) CPI                 .12 03/31/04   Population         179.91 12/31/02
12) Government Debt   926680.65 02/29/04   Area:    3286500
13) Total revenue    13053.0 11/30/99   4)MAPS    Map
14) Total Expenditur 12742.0 11/30/99   5)CDR     Calendar

 2 )News,Research & Market Information   Quick Statistics
15) Current News                    6)GPO 52Wk High        3.11 08/04/03
16) Equity Market News                  52Wk Low           2.77 01/13/04
17) Economist Intelligence Unit     History Since    1/15/92
18) Economic Statistics             Day count        ACT/360
19) IMF Data                        Value Date       04/22/04
20) Related Instruments
                                    7)PCS  Composite(NY)
 3 )Related Instruments             8)VOTE
Australia 61 2 9777 8600     Brazil 5511 3048 4500   Europe 44 20 7330 7500      Germany 49 69 920410
Hong Kong 852 2977 6000 Japan 81 3 3201 8900 Singapore 65 6212 1000 U.S. 1 212 318 2000 Copyright 2004 Bloomberg L.P.
                                                                   G926-802-0 19-Apr-04  9:35:52
```

**Figure 1.7**    Bloomberg page DES for Brazilian real

**Figure 1.8**    Bloomberg page DES for Egyptian pound
© 2006 Bloomberg L.P. All rights reserved. Reprinted with permission.

We show this page for Australian dollars, Brazilian reals and Egyptian pounds in Figures 1.6, 1.7 and 1.8 respectively.

Reproduced from *Bank Asset and Liability Management* (2007)

## Interest Rate Benchmarks

A transparent and readily accessible interest rate benchmark is a key ingredient in maintaining market efficiency. Countries that do not benefit from such a benchmark are markedly less liquid as a result.

Possibly the most well-known interest rate benchmark is the London Interbank Offered Rate or Libor. It is calculated and published daily by ICE. Wikipedia describes the Libor process as follows:

*"The London Interbank Offered Rate is the average of interest rates estimated by a panel of leading banks in London on their expectation of what they would be charged were they to borrow from other banks. It is usually abbreviated to Libor or LIBOR, or more officially to ICE LIBOR (for Intercontinental Exchange Libor). It was formerly known as BBA Libor (for British Bankers' Association Libor or the trademark bba libor) before the responsibility for the administration was transferred to ICE. It is the primary benchmark, along with the Euribor, for short-term interest rates around the world. Libor rates are calculated for five currencies and seven borrowing*

*periods ranging from overnight to one year and are published each business day by Thomson Reuters. Many financial institutions, mortgage lenders and credit card agencies set their own rates relative to it. At least $350 trillion in derivatives and other financial products are tied to Libor."*

Figure 1.1 shows the Libor rates for 13 September 2016, as seen on the Bloomberg service, for USD, GBP and EUR. We note, for example, that GBP 3-month Libor was 0.38%. Figure 1.2 shows the history for GBP 3-month Libor from September 2011 to September 2016.

In developed markets, of course, there are usually a range of interest rate indicators. For example, depending on what instrument and market one is concerned with, the sovereign bond interest rates may be worth monitoring, or the overnight index swap (OIS) rate, and so on. It is important to be aware of rates relevant to the balance sheet risk management of your bank, and to understand as well as possible how they interact. Also important is some knowledge of the predictive power of yield curves and how to analyse and interpret them. For illustration, we show the GBP sovereign, interest rate swap, and overnight index swap (SONIA) yield curves for 13 September 2016 at Figure 1.3.

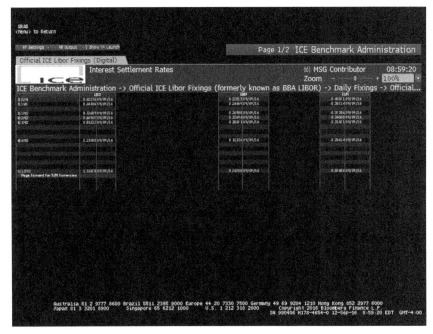

**FIGURE 1.1**    Libor screen on Bloomberg, 13 September 2016.
*Source*: © Bloomberg LP. Used with permission.

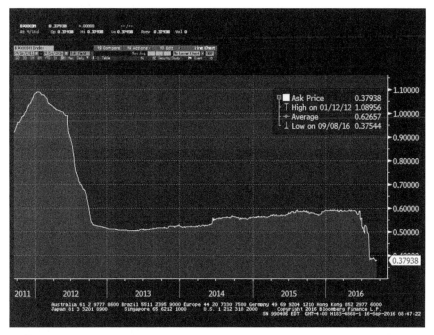

**FIGURE 1.2**    Libor history 2011–2016.
*Source*: © Bloomberg LP. Used with permission.

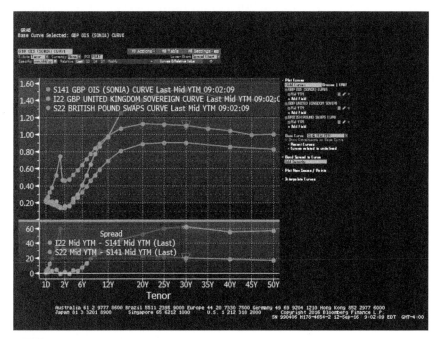

**FIGURE 1.3**    Sterling curves, 13 September 2016.
*Source*: © Bloomberg LP. Used with permission.

## AN INTRODUCTION TO DEBT FINANCIAL MARKETS

In essence, banks deal in the business of debt, either deposits from customers (banks borrowing from customers), or loans to customers (banks lending to customers). They all "clear" at the end of the day with each other or directly with the central bank.[1] Therefore we introduce the debt money markets and debt capital markets in this first chapter.

---

[1] "Clearing" or "squaring off" which refers to the process by which after all loans and deposits have been netted the bank will square the cash position to a zero balance, either through lending or borrowing from the market or the central bank direct. In the UK banks that undertake the latter process are known as "clearing" banks (although not all banks that have a settlement account with the Bank of England are also clearing banks). A bank that is not a clearing bank will settle with a bank that is, which in turn will clear with the central bank. In some jurisdictions all banks clear direct with the central bank.

**This extract from *The Money Markets Handbook* (2004)**

The Money Markets

## The Money Markets

Part of the global debt capital markets, the money markets are a separate market in their own right. Money market securities are defined as debt instruments with an original maturity of less than one year, although it is common to find that the maturity profile of banks' money market desks runs out to two years.

Money markets exist in every market economy, which is practically every country in the world. They are often the first element of a developing capital market. In every case they are comprised of securities with maturities of up to twelve months. Money market debt is an important part of the global capital markets, and facilitates the smooth running of the banking industry as well as providing working capital for industrial and commercial corporate institutions. The market provides users with a wide range of opportunities and funding possibilities, and the market is characterised by the diverse range of products that can be traded within it. Money market instruments allow issuers, including financial organisations and corporates, to raise funds for short term periods at relatively low interest rates. These issuers include sovereign governments, who issuer Treasury bills, corporates issuing commercial paper and banks issuing bills and certificates of deposit. At the same time investors are attracted to the market because the instruments are highly liquid and carry relatively low credit risk. The Treasury bill market in any country is that country's lowest-risk instrument, and consequently carries the lowest yield of any debt instrument. Indeed the first market that develops in any country is usually the Treasury bill market. Investors in the money market include banks, local authorities, corporations, money market investment funds and mutual funds and individuals.

In addition to cash instruments, the money markets also consist of a wide range of exchange-traded and over-the-counter off-balance sheet derivative instruments. These instruments are used mainly to establish future borrowing and lending rates, and to hedge or change existing interest rate exposure. This activity is carried out by both banks, central banks and corporates. The main derivatives are short-term interest rate futures, forward rate agreements, and short-dated interest rate swaps such as overnight-index seaps.

In this chapter we review the cash instruments traded in the money market. In further chapters we review banking asset and liability management, and the market in repurchase agreements. Finally we consider the market in money market derivative instruments including interest-rate futures and forward-rate agreements.

## Introduction

The cash instruments traded in money markets include the following:

- Time deposits;
- Treasury Bills;
- Certificates of Deposit;
- Commercial Paper;
- Bankers Acceptances;
- Bills of exchange.

In addition money market desks may also trade repo and take part in stock borrowing and lending activities. These products are covered in a separate chapter.

Treasury bills are used by sovereign governments to raise short-term funds, while certificates of deposit (CDs) are used by banks to raise finance. The other instruments are used by corporates and occasionally banks. Each instrument represents an obligation on the borrower to repay the amount borrowed on the maturity date together with interest if this applies. The instruments above fall into one of two main classes of money market securities: those quoted on a *yield* basis and those quoted on a *discount* basis. These two terms are discussed below. A *repurchase agreement* or "repo" is also a money market instrument and is considered in a separate chapter.

The calculation of interest in the money markets often differs from the calculation of accrued interest in the corresponding bond market. Generally the day-count convention in the money market is the exact number of days that the instrument is held over the number of days in the year. In the UK sterling market the year base is 365 days, so the interest calculation for sterling money market instruments is given by (1.1):

$$i = \frac{n}{365} \tag{1.1}$$

However the majority of currencies including the US dollar and the euro calculate interest on a 360-day base so the denominator in (1.1) would be changed accordingly. The process by which an interest rate quoted on one basis is converted to one quoted on the other basis is shown in Appendix 1.1. Those markets that calculate interest based on a 365-day year are also listed at Appendix 1.1.

Dealers will want to know the interest day-base for a currency before dealing in it as FX or money markets. Bloomberg users can use screen DCX to look up the number of days of an interest period. For instance, Figure 1.1 shows screen DCX for the US dollar market, for a loan taken out value 7 May 2004 for a straight three-month period. Ordinarily this would mature on 7 August 2004, however from Figure 1.1 we see that this is not a good day so the loan will actually mature on 9 August 2004. Also from Figure 1.1 we see that this period is actually 94 days, and 92 days under the 30/360 day convention (a bond market accrued interest convention). The number of business days is 64, we also see that there is a public holiday on the 31 May.

For the same loan taken out in Singapore dollars, look at Figure 1.2. This shows that the same loan taken out for value on 7 May will actually mature on 10 August, because 9 August 2004 is a public holiday in that market.

Settlement of money market instruments can be for value today (generally only when traded in before mid-day), tomorrow or two days forward, known as *spot*.

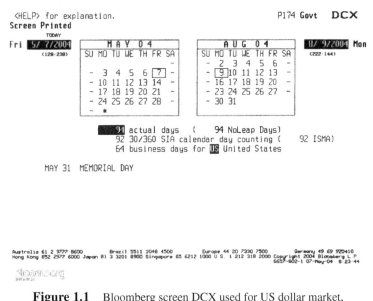

**Figure 1.1**    Bloomberg screen DCX used for US dollar market,
three-month loan taken out 7 May 2004
© Bloomberg L.P. Used with permission

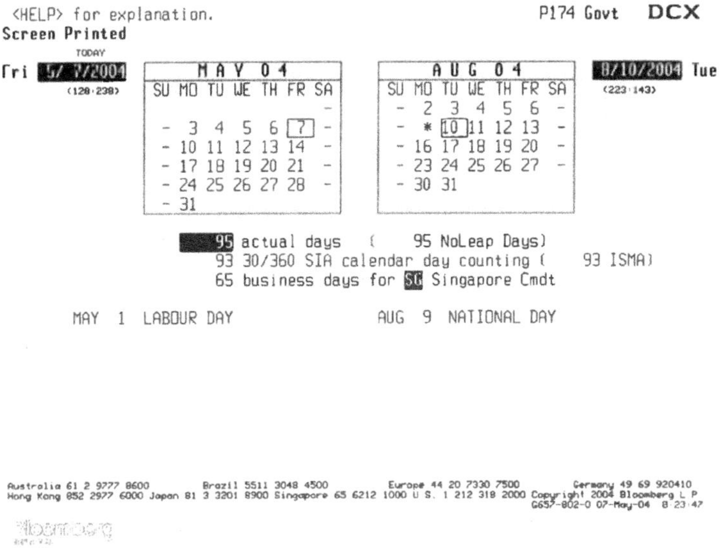

<HELP> for explanation.                              P174 Govt   **DCX**
Screen Printed

**Figure 1.2**   Bloomberg screen DCX for Singapore dollar market,
three-month loan taken out 7 May 2004
© Bloomberg L.P. Used with permission

# UK INTEREST RATES

| Mar 10 | Over-night | 7 days notice | One month | Three months | Six months | One year |
|---|---|---|---|---|---|---|
| Interbank Sterling | $3\frac{13}{16} - 3\frac{9}{16}$ | $3\frac{7}{8} - 3\frac{3}{4}$ | $4\frac{1}{8} - 4$ | $4\frac{9}{32} - 4\frac{5}{32}$ | $4\frac{7}{16} - 4\frac{5}{16}$ | $4\frac{5}{8} - 4\frac{1}{2}$ |
| BBA Sterling | $3\frac{3}{4}$ | $3\frac{7}{8}$ | $4\frac{1}{8}$ | $4\frac{9}{32}$ | $4\frac{13}{32}$ | $4\frac{19}{32}$ |
| Sterling CDs | | | $4\frac{1}{8} - 4\frac{1}{16}$ | $4\frac{1}{4} - 4\frac{7}{32}$ | $4\frac{3}{8} - 4\frac{11}{32}$ | $4\frac{17}{32} - 4\frac{1}{2}$ |
| Treasury Bills | | | $4 - 3\frac{15}{16}$ | $4\frac{1}{16} - 4$ | | |
| Bank Bills | | | $4\frac{3}{32} - 4\frac{1}{32}$ | $4\frac{7}{32} - 4\frac{5}{32}$ | | |
| †Local authority deps. | | $4\frac{1}{16} - 3\frac{15}{16}$ | $4\frac{1}{8} - 4$ | $4\frac{1}{4} - 4\frac{1}{8}$ | $4\frac{3}{8} - 4\frac{1}{4}$ | $4\frac{5}{8} - 4\frac{1}{2}$ |
| Discount Market deps | $3\frac{7}{8} - 3\frac{11}{16}$ | $4 - 3\frac{13}{16}$ | | | | |

Av. tndr rate of discount Mar 4, 4.0651pc. ECGD fixed rate Stlg. Export Finance. make up day Feb 27,2003.
Agreed rate for period Feb 25 2004 to Mar 25, 2004, Scheme III 5.30pc. Reference rate for period Jan 31, 2004
to Feb 27, 2004, Scheme IV & V 4.164%. Finance House Base Rate 4.5pv for Feb 2004
UK clearing bank base lending rate 4 per cent from Feb 5, 2004      Source: Reuters, RBS, †Tradition (UK) Ltd.

| | Up to 1 month | 1-3 month | 3-6 months | 6-9 months | 9-12 months |
|---|---|---|---|---|---|
| Certs of Tax dep. (£100,000) | ¼ | 3 | 3 | 3 | 3 |

Certs of Tax dep under £100,000.is ¼pc. Deposits withdrawn for cash 0pc.

**Figure 1.3**   London sterling money market rates.
Extract from *Financial Times*, 11 March 2004.
© *Financial Times* 2004. Reproduced with permission.

## Securities quoted on a yield basis

Two of the instruments in the list above are yield-based instruments.

### Money market deposits

These are fixed-interest term deposits of up to one year with banks and securities houses. They are also known as *time deposits* or *clean deposits*. They are not negotiable so cannot be liquidated before maturity. The interest rate on the deposit is fixed for the term and related to the London Interbank Offer Rate (LIBOR) of the same term. Interest and capital are paid on maturity.

$$
\text{Effective rate of return} = \left( \frac{\text{Total proceeds}}{\text{Initial investment}} \right)^{\frac{M}{n}} - 1
$$

$$
= \left( \frac{261,000}{250,000} \right)^{\frac{365}{270}} - 1
$$

$$
= 5.9938\%
$$

## Certificates of Deposit

Certificates of Deposit (CDs) are receipts from banks for deposits that have been placed with them. They were first introduced in the US dollar market in 1964, and in the sterling market in 1958. The deposits themselves carry a fixed rate of interest related to LIBOR and have a fixed term to maturity, so cannot be withdrawn before maturity. However the certificates themselves can be traded in a secondary market, that is, they are negotiable.[1] CDs are therefore very similar to negotiable money market deposits, although the yields are about 0.15% below the equivalent deposit rates because of the added benefit of liquidity. Most CDs issued are of between one and three months' maturity, although they do trade in maturities of one to five years. Interest is paid on maturity except for CDs lasting longer than one year, where interest is paid annually or occasionally, semi-annually.

Banks, merchant banks and building societies issue CDs to raise funds to finance their business activities. A CD will have a stated interest rate and fixed maturity date and can be issued in any denomination. On issue a CD is sold for face value, so the settlement proceeds of a CD on issue are always equal to its nominal value. The interest is paid, together with the face amount, on maturity. The interest rate is sometimes called the *coupon,*

---

[1] A small number of CDs are non-negotiable.

but unless the CD is held to maturity this will not equal the yield, which is of course the current rate available in the market and varies over time. The largest group of CD investors are banks, money market funds, corporates and local authority treasurers.

Unlike coupons on bonds, which are paid in rounded amounts, CD coupon is calculated to the exact day.

## CD yields

The coupon quoted on a CD is a function of the credit quality of the issuing bank, and its expected liquidity level in the market, and of course the maturity of the CD, as this will be considered relative to the money market yield curve. As CDs are issued by banks as part of their short-term funding and liquidity requirement, issue volumes are driven by the demand for bank loans and the availability of alternative sources of funds for bank customers. The credit quality of the issuing bank is the primary consideration however; in the sterling market the lowest yield is paid by "clearer" CDs, which are CDs issued by the clearing banks such as Royal Bank of Scotland, HSBC and Barclays Bank plc. In the US market "prime" CDs, issued by highly-rated domestic banks, trade at a lower yield than non-prime CDs. In both markets CDs issued by foreign banks such as French or Japanese banks will trade at higher yields.

Euro-CDs, which are CDs issued in a different currency to that of the home currency, also trade at higher yields, in the US because of reserve and deposit insurance restrictions.

If the current market price of the CD including accrued interest is $P$ and the current quoted yield is $r$, the yield can be calculated given the price, using (1.2):

$$r = \left( \frac{M}{P} \times \left( 1 + C\left( \frac{N_{im}}{B} \right) \right) - 1 \right) \times \left( \frac{B}{N_{sm}} \right). \tag{1.2}$$

The price can be calculated given the yield using (1.3):

$$P = M \times \left( 1 + C\left( \frac{N_{im}}{B} \right) \right) / 1 + r\left( \frac{N_{sm}}{B} \right) \tag{1.3}$$

$$= F / \left( 1 + r\left( \frac{N_{sm}}{B} \right) \right)$$

Where $C$    is the quoted coupon on the CD
$M$    is the face value of the CD
$B$    is the year day-basis (365 or 360)
$F$    is the maturity value of the CD
$N_{im}$    is the number of days between issue and maturity
$N_{sm}$    is the number of days between settlement and maturity
$N_{is}$    is the number of days between issue and settlement.

After issue a CD can be traded in the secondary market. The secondary market in CDs in developed economies is very liquid, and CDs will trade at the rate prevalent at the time, which will invariably be different from the coupon rate on the CD at issue. When a CD is traded in the secondary market, the settlement proceeds will need to take into account interest that has accrued on the paper and the different rate at which the CD has now been dealt. The formula for calculating the settlement figure is given at (1.4) which applies to the sterling market and its 365-day count basis.

$$\text{Proceeds} = \frac{M \times \text{Tenor} \times C \times 100 + 36500}{\text{Days remaining} \times r \times 100 + 36500} \tag{1.4}$$

The settlement figure for a new issue CD is of course, its face value. . .![2]

The *tenor* of a CD is the life of the CD in days, while *days remaining* is the number of days left to maturity from the time of trade.

The return on holding a CD is given by (1.5):

$$R = \left( \frac{\left(1 + \text{purchase yield} \times \left(\text{days from purchase to maturity} / B\right)\right)}{1 + \text{sale yield} \times \left(\text{days from sale to maturity} / B\right)} - 1 \right) \tag{1.5}$$

$$\times \left( \frac{B}{days\ held} \right).$$

---

**EXAMPLE 1.2**

A three-month CD is issued on 6 September 1999 and matures on 6 December 1999 (maturity of 91 days). It has a face value of £20,000,000 and a coupon of 5.45%. What are the total maturity proceeds?

$$\text{Proceeds} = 20\text{million} \times \left(1 + 0.0545 \times 91 / 365\right) = £20,271,753.42.$$

What is the secondary market proceeds on 11 October if the yield for short 60-day paper is 5.60%?

$$P = \frac{20.271\text{m}}{\left(1 + 0.056 \times 56 / 365\right)} = £20,099,066.64$$

---

[2] With thanks to Del Boy during the time he was at Tradition for pointing out this very obvious fact after I'd just bought a sizeable chunk of Japanese bank CDs. . .

On 18 November the yield on short three-week paper is 5.215%. What rate of return is earned from holding the CD for the 38 days from 11 October to 18 November?

$$R = \left( \frac{1 + 0.0560 \times 56 / 365}{1 + 0.05215 \times 38 / 365} - 1 \right) \times \frac{365}{38} = 9.6355\%$$

## US Dollar market rates

### Treasury Bills

The Treasury bill market in the United States is the most liquid and transparent debt market in the world. Consequently the bid-offer spread on them is very narrow. The Treasury issues bills at a weekly auction each Monday, made up of 91-day and 182-day bills. Every fourth week the Treasury also issues 52-week bills as well. As a result there are large numbers of Treasury bills outstanding at any one time. The interest earned on Treasury bills is not liable to state and local income taxes. T-bill rates are the lowest in the dollar market (as indeed any bill market is in respective domestic environment) and as such represents the corporate financier's *risk-free* interest rate.

### Federal Funds

Commercial banks in the US are required to keep reserves on deposit at the Federal Reserve. Banks with reserves in excess of required reserves can lend these funds to other banks, and these interbank loans are called *federal funds* or *fed funds* and are usually overnight loans. Through the fed funds market, commercial banks with excess funds are able to lend to banks that are short of reserves, thus facilitating liquidity. The transactions are very large denominations, and are lent at the *fed funds rate*, which is a very volatile interest rate because it fluctuates with market shortages.

### Prime Rate

The *prime interest rate* in the US is often said to represent the rate at which commercial banks lend to their most creditworthy customers. In practice many loans are made at rates below the prime rate, so the prime rate is not the best rate at which highly rated firms may borrow. Nevertheless the prima rate is a benchmark indicator of the level of US money market rates, and is often used as a reference rate for floating-rate instruments. As the market for bank loans is highly competitive, all commercial banks quote a single prime rate, and the rate for all banks changes simultaneously.

# Securities quoted on a discount basis

The remaining money market instruments are all quoted on a *discount* basis, and so are known as "discount" instruments. This means that they are issued on a discount to face value, and are redeemed on maturity at face value. Treasury bills, bills of exchange, bankers acceptances and commercial paper are examples of money market securities that are quoted on a discount basis, that is, they are sold on the basis of a discount to par. The difference between the price paid at the time of purchase and the redemption value (par) is the interest earned by the holder of the paper. Explicit interest is not paid on discount instruments, rather interest is reflected implicitly in the difference between the discounted issue price and the par value received at maturity.

## Treasury bills

Treasury bills or T-bills are short-term government "IOUs" of short duration, often three-month maturity. For example if a bill is issued on 10 January it will mature on 10 April. Bills of one-month and six-month maturity are issued in certain markets, but only rarely by the UK Treasury. On maturity the holder of a T-Bill receives the par value of the bill by presenting it to the Central Bank. In the UK most such bills are denominated in sterling but issues are also made in euros. In a capital market, T-Bill yields are regarded as the *risk-free* yield, as they represent the yield from short-term government debt. In emerging markets they are often the most liquid instruments available for investors.

A sterling T-bill with £10 million face value issued for 91 days will be redeemed on maturity at £10 million. If the three-month yield at the time of issue is 5.25%, the price of the bill at issue is:

$$P = \frac{10m}{\left(1 + 0.0525 \times \dfrac{91}{365}\right)} = £9,870,800.69.$$

In the UK market the interest rate on discount instruments is quoted as a *discount rate* rather than a yield. This is the amount of discount expressed as an annualised percentage of the face value, and not as a percentage of the original amount paid. By definition the discount rate is always lower than the corresponding yield. If the discount rate on a bill is $d$, then the amount of discount is given by (1.12):

$$d_{value} = M \times d \times n / B. \tag{1.12}$$

where $B$ is the day-count basis.

The price $P$ paid for the bill is the face value minus the discount amount, given by (1.13):

$$P = 100 \left( 1 - \frac{d \times \left( N_{sm} / 365 \right)}{100} \right) \tag{1.13}$$

If we know the yield on the bill then we can calculate its price at issue by using the simple present value formula, as shown at (1.14):

$$P = M / \left( 1 + r \left( N_{sm} / 365 \right) \right). \tag{1.14}$$

The discount rate $d$ for T-Bills is calculated using (1.15):

$$d = \left( 1 - P \right) \times B / n \tag{1.15}$$

where $n$ is the T-bill number of days.

The relationship between discount rate and true yield is given by (1.16):

$$d = \frac{r}{\left( 1 + r \times \dfrac{n}{B} \right)}$$

$$r = \frac{d}{1 + d \times \dfrac{n}{B}} \tag{1.16}$$

**EXAMPLE 1.4**

A 91-day £100 Treasury bill is issued with a yield of 4.75%. What is its issue price?

$$P = \frac{£100}{\left( 1 + 0.0475 \left( \dfrac{91}{365} \right) \right)}$$

$$= £98.80$$

A UK T-bill with a remaining maturity of 39 days is quoted at a discount of 4.95% What is the equivalent yield?

$$r = \frac{0.0495}{1 - 0.0495\left(\dfrac{39}{365}\right)}$$

$$= 4.976\%$$

If a T-Bill is traded in the secondary market, the settlement proceeds from the trade are calculated using (1.17):

$$\text{Proceeds} = M - \left(\frac{M \times \text{days remaining} \times d}{B \times 100}\right) \qquad (1.17)$$

Reproduced from *The Money Markets Handbook* (2004)

This extract from *The Money Markets Handbook* (2004)

## Foreign Exchange Markets

## Foreign Exchange Markets

The market in foreign exchange is an excellent example of a liquid, transparent and immediate global financial market. Rates in the foreign exchange (FX) markets move at an extremely rapid pace and in fact, trading in FX is a different discipline to bond trading or money markets trading. There is a considerable literature on the FX markets, as it is a separate subject in its own right. However some banks organise their forward FX desk as part of the money market desk and not the foreign exchange desk, necessitating its inclusion in this book. For this reason we present an overview summary of FX in this chapter, both spot and forward.

The quotation for currencies generally follows the ISO convention, which is also used by the SWIFT and Reuters dealing systems, and is the three-letter code used to identify a currency, such as USD for US dollar and GBP for sterling. The rate convention is to quote everything in terms of one unit of the US dollar, so that the dollar and Swiss franc rate is quoted as USD/CHF, and is the number of Swiss francs to one US dollar. The exception is for sterling, which is quoted as GBP/USD and is the number of US dollars to the pound. This rate is also known as "cable". The rate for euros has been quoted both ways round, for example EUR/USD although some banks, for example Royal Bank of Scotland in the UK, quote euros to the pound, that is GBP/EUR.

The complete list of currency codes was given at Appendix 1.2.

## Spot exchange rates

A *spot* FX trade is an outright purchase or sale of one currency against another currency, with delivery two working days after the trade date. Non-working days so not count, so a trade on a Friday is settled on the following Tuesday. There are some exceptions to this, for example trades of US dollar against Canadian dollar are settled the next working day; note that in some currencies, generally in the Middle-East, markets are closed on Friday but open on Saturday. A settlement date that falls on a public holiday in the country of one of the two currencies is delayed for settlement by that day. An FX transaction is possible between any two currencies, however to reduce the number of quotes that need to be made the market generally quotes only against the US dollar or occasionally against sterling or euro, so that the exchange rate between two non-dollar currencies is calculated from the rate for each currency against the dollar. The resulting exchange rate is known as the *cross-rate*. Cross-rates themselves are also traded between banks in addition to dollar-based rates. This is usually because the relationship between two rates is closer than that of either against the dollar, for example the Swiss franc moves more closely in line with the euro than against the dollar, so in practice one observes that the dollar / Swiss franc rate is more a function of the euro / franc rate.

The spot FX quote is a two-way bid-offer price, just as in the bond and money markets, and indicates the rate at which a bank is prepared to buy the base currency against the variable currency; this is the "bid" for the variable currency, so is the lower rate. The other side of the quote is the rate at which the bank is prepared to sell the base currency against the variable currency. For example a quote of 1.6245 - 1.6255 for GBP/USD means that the bank is prepared to buy sterling for $1.6245, and to sell sterling for $1.6255. The convention in the FX market is uniform across countries, unlike the money markets. Although the money market convention for bid-offer quotes is for example, 5½% - 5¼%, meaning that the "bid" for paper - the rate at which the bank will lend funds, say in the CD market - is the higher rate and always on the left, this convention is reversed in certain countries. In the FX markets the convention is always the same one just described.

The difference between the two side in a quote is the bank's dealing spread. Rates are quoted to 1/100th of a cent, known as a *pip*. In the quote above, the spread is 10 pips, however this amount is a function of the size of the quote number, so that the rate for USD/JPY at say, 110.10 - 110.20, indicates a spread of 0.10 yen. Generally only the pips in the two rates are quoted, so that for example the quote above would be simply "45-55". The "big figure" is not quoted.

**EXAMPLE 2.1**   Exchange cross-rates

Consider the following two spot rates:

$$EUR / USD \quad 1.0566 - 1.0571$$
$$AUD / USD \quad 0.7034 - 0.7039$$

The EUR/USD dealer buys euros and sells dollars at 1.0566 (the left side), while the AUD/USD dealer sells Australian dollars and buys US dollars at 0.7039 (the right side). To calculate the rate at which the bank buys euros and sells Australian dollars, we need to do

$$1.0566 / 0.7039 = 1.4997$$

which is the rate at which the bank buys euros and sells Australian dollars. In the same way the rate at which the bank sells euros and buys Australian dollars is given by

1.0571 / 0.7034 or 1.5028.
Therefore the spot EUR / AUD rate is 1.4997 − 1.5028.

The derivation of cross-rates can be depicted in the following way. If we assume two exchange rates XXX/YYY and XXX/ZZZ, the cross-rates are:

$$YYY / ZZZ = XXX / ZZZ \div XXX / YYY$$
$$ZZZ / YYY = XXX / YYY \div XXX / ZZZ$$

Given two exchange rates YYY/XXX and XXX/ZZZ, the cross-rates are:

$$YYY / ZZZ = YYY / XXX \times XXX / ZZZ$$
$$ZZZ / YYY = 1 \div \left( YYY / XXX \times XXX / ZZZ \right)$$

Figure 2.1 shows the Bloomberg major currency FX monitor, page FXC, as at 10 May 2004.

# Forward exchange rates

## Forward outright

The spot exchange rate is the rate for immediate delivery (notwithstanding that actual delivery is two days forward). A *forward contract* or simply *forward* is an outright purchase or sale of one currency in exchange for another

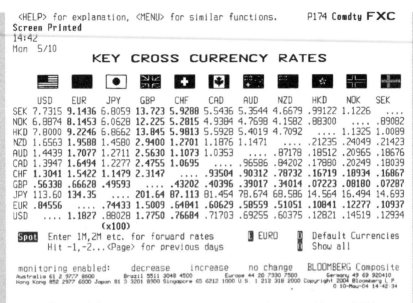

<HELP> for explanation, <MENU> for similar functions.    P174 Comdty **FXC**
Screen Printed
14:42
Mon  5/10

### KEY CROSS CURRENCY RATES

|     | USD | EUR | JPY | GBP | CHF | CAD | AUD | NZD | HKD | NOK | SEK |
|-----|-----|-----|-----|-----|-----|-----|-----|-----|-----|-----|-----|
| SEK | 7.7315 | 9.1436 | 6.8059 | 13.723 | 5.9288 | 5.5436 | 5.3544 | 4.6679 | .99122 | 1.1226 | .... |
| NOK | 6.8874 | 8.1453 | 6.0628 | 12.225 | 5.2815 | 4.9384 | 4.7698 | 4.1582 | .88300 | .... | .89082 |
| HKD | 7.8000 | 9.2246 | 6.8662 | 13.845 | 5.9813 | 5.5928 | 5.4019 | 4.7092 | .... | 1.1325 | 1.0089 |
| NZD | 1.6563 | 1.9588 | 1.4580 | 2.9400 | 1.2701 | 1.1876 | 1.1471 | .... | .21235 | .24049 | .21423 |
| AUD | 1.4439 | 1.7077 | 1.2711 | 2.5630 | 1.1073 | 1.0353 | .... | .87178 | .18512 | .20965 | .18676 |
| CAD | 1.3947 | 1.6494 | 1.2277 | 2.4755 | 1.0695 | .... | .96586 | .84202 | .17880 | .20249 | .18039 |
| CHF | 1.3041 | 1.5422 | 1.1479 | 2.3147 | .... | .93504 | .90312 | .78732 | .16719 | .18934 | .16867 |
| GBP | .56338 | .66628 | .49593 | .... | .43202 | .40396 | .39017 | .34014 | .07223 | .08180 | .07287 |
| JPY | 113.60 | 134.35 | .... | 201.64 | 87.113 | 81.454 | 78.674 | 68.586 | 14.564 | 16.494 | 14.693 |
| EUR | .84556 | .... | .74433 | 1.5009 | .64041 | .60629 | .58559 | .51051 | .10841 | .12277 | .10937 |
| USD | .... | 1.1827 | .88028 | 1.7750 | .76684 | .71703 | .69255 | .60375 | .12821 | .14519 | .12934 |

(x100)

**Spot** Enter 1M,2M etc. for forward rates     **E** EURO   **D** Default Currencies
Hit -1,-2...<Page> for previous days             **A** Show all

monitoring enabled:    decrease    increase    no change    BLOOMBERG Composite
Australia 61 2 9777 8600        Brazil 5511 3048 4500         Europe 44 20 7330 7500        Germany 49 69 920410
Hong Kong 852 2977 6000 Japan 81 3 3201 8900 Singapore 65 6212 1000 U.S. 1 212 318 2000 Copyright 2004 Bloomberg L.P.
                                                                                         O 10-May-04 14:42:34

**Figure 2.1**   Bloomberg major currency monitor page, 10 May 2004
© Bloomberg L.P. Used with permission

currency for settlement on a specified date at some point in the future. The exchange rate is quoted in the same way as the spot rate, with the bank buying the base currency on the bid side and selling it on the offered side. In some emerging markets no liquid forward market exists so forwards are settled in cash against the spot rate on the maturity date. These *non-deliverable forwards* are considered at the end of this section.

Although some commentators have stated that the forward rate may be seen as the market's view of where the spot rate will be on the maturity date of the forward transaction, this is incorrect. A forward rate is calculated on the current interest rates of the two currencies involved, and the principle of no-arbitrage pricing ensures that there is no profit to be gained from simultaneous (and opposite) dealing in spot and forward. Consider the following strategy:

- borrow US dollars for six months starting from the spot value date;
- sell dollars and buy sterling for value spot;
- deposit the long sterling position for six months from the spot value date;
- sell forward today the sterling principal and interest which mature in six months time into dollars.

The market will adjust the forward price so that the two initial transactions if carried out simultaneously will generate a zero profit/loss.

The forward rates quoted in the trade will be calculated on the six months deposit rates for dollars and sterling; in general the calculation of a forward rate is given as (2.1)

$$Fwd = Spot \times \frac{\left(1 + \text{variable currency deposit rate} \times \dfrac{days}{B}\right)}{\left(1 + \text{base currency deposit rate} \times \dfrac{days}{B}\right)} \tag{2.1}$$

The year day-count base $B$ will be either 365 or 360 depending on the convention for the currency in question.

So in other words, a forward is more a deposit instrument than an FX instrument.

---

**EXAMPLE 2.2**    **Forward rate**

90 - day GBP deposit rate :   5.75%

90 - day USD deposit rate :   6.15%

Spot GBP / USD rate :     1.6315 $\left(\text{mid - rate}\right)$

The forward rate is given by:

$$1.6315 \times \frac{\left(1 + 0.0575 \times \dfrac{90}{365}\right)}{\left(1 + 0.0615 \times \dfrac{90}{360}\right)} = 1.6296$$

Therefore to deal forward the GBP/USD mid-rate is 1.6296, so in effect £1 buys \$1.6296 in three months time as opposed to \$1.6315 today. Under different circumstances sterling may be worth more in the future than at the spot date.

---

**EXAMPLE 2.2**    **Forward rate arbitrage**

The following rates are quoted to a bank:

| | | |
|---|---|---|
| USD / CHF | spot : | 1.4810 - 1.4815 |
| | 3 - month swap : | 116 - 111 |
| USD | 3 - month deposit rates : | 7.56 - 7.43 |
| CHF | 3 - month deposit rates : | 4.62 - 4.50 |

The bank requires funding of CHF10 million for three months (91 days). It deals on the above rates and actions the following:

- it borrows USD 6,749,915,63 for 91 days from spot at 7.56%
- at the end of the 91 days the bank repays the principal plus the interest, which is a total of USD 6,880,324.00
- the bank "buys and sells" USD against CHF at a swap price of 11, based on the spot rate of 1.4815, that is:
  - the bank sells USD 6,749,915.63/buys CHF10 million spot at 1.4815;
  - the bank buys USD 6,880,324/sells CHF 10,116,828.42 for three months forward at 1.4704;

The net USD cash flows result in a zero balance.

The effective cost of borrowing is therefore interest of CHF 116,828.41 on a principal sum of CHF10 million for 91 days, which is:

$$\frac{116,828}{10,000,000} \times \frac{360}{91} = 4.57\%$$

The net effect is therefore a CHF10 million borrowing at 4.57%, which is 5 basis points lower than the 4.62% quote at which the bank could borrow directly in the market. If the bank has not actually required funding but was able to deposit the Swiss francs at a higher rate than 4.57%, it would have been able to lock in a profit.

## Forward swaps

The calculation given above illustrates how a forward rate is calculated and quoted in theory. In practice as spot rates change rapidly, often many times even in one minute, it would be tedious to keep re-calculating the forward rate so often. Therefore banks quote a forward spread over the spot rate, which can then be added or subtracted to the spot rate as it changes. This spread is known as the *swap points*. An approximate value for the number of swap points is given by (2.2) below.

$$\text{Forward swap} \approx \text{Spot} \times \text{deposit rate differential} \times \frac{days}{B} \qquad (2.2)$$

The approximation is not accurate enough for forwards maturing more than 30 days from now, in which case another equation must be used. This is given as (2.3). It is also possible to calculate an approximate deposit rate differential from the swap points by re-arranging 2.2.

$$Fwd\ swap = Spot \times \frac{\left( \text{variable currency depo rate} \times \frac{days}{B} - \text{base currency depo rate} \times \frac{days}{B} \right)}{\left( 1 + \text{base currency depo rate} \times \frac{days}{B} \right)} \quad (2.3)$$

---

**EXAMPLE 2.3**   **Forward swap points**

Spot EUR / USD :   1.0566 - 1.0571

Forward swap :   0.0125 - 0.0130

Forward outright :   1.0691 - 1.0701

The forward outright is the spot price + the swap points, so in this case,

$$1.0691 = 1.0566 + 0.0125$$
$$1.0701 = 1.0571 + 0.0130.$$

Spot EUR / USD rate : 0.9501

31 - day EUR rate :     3.15%

31 - day USD rate :     5.95%

$$Fwd\ swap = 0.9501 \times \frac{\left( 0.0595 \times \frac{31}{360} - 0.0315 \times \frac{31}{360} \right)}{\left( 1 + 0.0315 \times \frac{31}{360} \right)} = 0.0024$$

or $+24$ points.

---

The swap points are quoted as two-way prices in the same way as spot rates. In practice a middle spot price is used and then the forward swap spread around the spot quote. The difference between the interest rates of the two currencies will determine the magnitude of the swap points and whether they are added or subtracted from the spot rate. When the swap points are positive and the forwards trader applies a bid-offer spread to quote a two-way price, the left-hand side of the quote is smaller than the right-hand side as usual. When the swap points are negative, the trader must quote a "more negative" number on the left and a "more positive" number on the right-hand side. The "minus" sign is not shown however, so that the left-hand side may appear to be the larger number. Basically when the swap price appears larger on the right, it means that it is negative and must be subtracted from the spot rate and not added.

Forwards traders are in fact interest rate traders rather than foreign exchange traders; although they will be left with positions that arise from customer orders, in general they will manage their book based on their view of short-term deposit rates in the currencies they are trading. In general a forward trader expecting the interest rate differential to move in favour of the base currency, for example, a rise in base currency rates or a fall in the variable currency rate, will "buy and sell" the base currency. This is equivalent to borrowing the base currency and depositing in the variable currency. The relationship between interest rates and forward swaps means that banks can take advantage of different opportunities in different markets. Assume that a bank requires funding in one currency but is able to borrow in another currency at a relatively cheaper rate. It may wish to borrow in the second currency and use a forward contract to convert the borrowing to the first currency. It will do this if the all-in cost of borrowing is less than the cost of borrowing directly in the first currency.

### Forward cross-rates

A forward cross-rate is calculated in the same way as spot cross-rates. The formulas given for spot cross-rates can be adapted to forward rates.

### Forward-forwards

A forward-forward swap is a deal between two forward dates rather than from the spot date to a forward date; this is the same terminology and meaning as in the bond markets, where a forward or a forward-forward interest rate is the zero-coupon interest rate between two points both beginning in the future. In the foreign exchange market, an example would be a contract to sell sterling three months forward and buy it back in six months time. Here, the swap is for the three-month period between the three-month date and the six-month date. The reason a bank or corporate might do this is to hedge a forward exposure or because of a particular view it has on forward rates, in effect deposit rates.

---

**EXAMPLE 2.4**   Forward–forward contract

GBP / USD spot rate :   $1.6315 - 20$

3 - month swap :   $45 - 41$

6 - month swap :   $135 - 125$

If a bank wished to sell GBP three month forward and buy it back six months forward, this is identical to undertaking one swap to buy GBP spot and sell GBP three months forward, and another to sell GBP spot and buy it six months forward. Swaps are always quoted as the quoting bank buying the base currency forward on the bid side, and selling the base currency forward on the offered side; the counterparty bank can "buy and sell" GBP "spot against three months" at a swap price of −45, with settlement rates of spot and (spot − 0.0045). It can "sell and buy" GBP "spot against six months" at the swap price of −125 with settlement rates of spot and (spot − 0.0125). It can therefore do both simultaneously, which implies a difference between the two forward prices of (−125) − (−45) = −90 points. Conversely the bank can "buy and sell" GBP "three months against six months" at a swap price of (−135) − (−41) or −94 points. The two-way price is therefore 94–90 (we ignore the negative signs).

## Long-dated forward contracts

The formula for calculating a forward rate was given earlier (see 2.2). This formula applies to any period that is under one year, hence the adjustment of the deposit rate by the fraction of the day-count. However if a forward contract is traded for a period greater than one year, the formula must be adjusted to account for the fact that deposit rates are compounded if they are in effect for more than one year. To calculate a long-dated forward rate, in theory (2.4) should be used. In practice the formula may not give an answer to the required accuracy, because it does not consider reinvestment risk. To get around this it is necessary to use spot (zero-coupon) rates in the formula. However the market in long-dated forward contracts is not as liquid as the sub-1-year market, so banks may not be as keen to quote a price.

$$Long\text{-}dated\ forward = Spot \times \frac{\left(1 + \text{variable currency deposit rate}\right)^N}{\left(1 + \text{base currency deposit rate}\right)^N} \quad (2.4)$$

where $N$ is the contract's maturity in years.

Reproduced from *The Money Markets Handbook* (2004)

This extract from *Fixed Income Markets, Second Edition* (2014)

### The Bond Instrument

## The Bond Instrument

Bonds are debt-capital market instruments that represent a cash flow payable during a specified time period heading into the future. This cash flow represents the interest payable on the loan and the loan redemption. So, essentially, a bond is a loan, albeit one that is tradable in a secondary market. This differentiates bond-market securities from commercial bank loans.

In the analysis that follows, bonds are assumed to be default-free, which means that there is no possibility that the interest payments and principal repayment will not be made. Such an assumption is reasonable when one is referring to government bonds such as U.S. Treasuries, UK gilts, Japanese JGBs, and so on. However, it is unreasonable when applied to bonds issued by corporates or lower-rated sovereign borrowers. Nevertheless, it is still relevant to understand the valuation and analysis of bonds that are default-free, as the pricing of bonds that carry default risk is based on the price of risk-free securities. Essentially, the price investors charge borrowers that are not of risk-free credit standing is the price of government securities plus some credit risk premium.

## BOND MARKET BASICS

All bonds are described in terms of their issuer, maturity date, and coupon. For a default-free conventional, or plain-vanilla, bond, this will be the essential information required. Nonvanilla bonds are defined by further characteristics such as their interest basis, flexibilities in their maturity date, credit risk, and so on.

Figure 1.1 shows screen DES from the Bloomberg system. This page describes the key characteristics of a bond. From Figure 1.1, we see a description of a bond issued by the Singapore government, the 4.625% of 2010. This tells us the following bond characteristics:

| | |
|---|---|
| Issue date | July 2000 |
| Coupon | 4.625% |
| Maturity date | 1 July 2010 |
| Issue currency | Singapore dollars |
| Issue size | SGD 3.4 million |
| Credit rating | AAA/Aaa |

Calling up screen DES for any bond, provided it is supported by Bloomberg, will provide us with its key details. Later on, we will see how nonvanilla bonds include special features that investors take into consideration in their analysis.

We will consider the essential characteristics of bonds later in this chapter. First, we review the capital market, and an essential principle of finance, the time value of money.

## CAPITAL MARKET PARTICIPANTS

The debt capital markets exist because of the financing requirements of governments and corporates. The source of capital is varied, but the

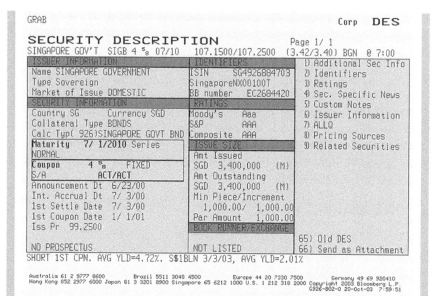

**Figure 1.1**　Bloomberg Screen DES Showing Details of 4⅝ % 2010 Issued by
Republic of Singapore as of 20 October 2003
Used with permission of Bloomberg L.P. Copyright© 2014. All rights reserved.

total supply of funds in a market is made up of personal or household
savings, business savings, and increases in the overall money supply.
Growth in the money supply is a function of the overall state of the
economy, and interested readers may wish to consult the references at
the end of this chapter, which include several standard economic texts.
Individuals save out of their current income for future consumption,
while business savings represent retained earnings. The entire savings
stock represents the capital available in a market. The requirements of
savers and borrowers differ significantly, in that savers have a short-
term investment horizon while borrowers prefer to take a longer-term
view. The constitutional weakness of what would otherwise be *uninter-
mediated* financial markets led, from an early stage, to the development
of financial intermediaries.

## Financial Intermediaries

In its simplest form a financial intermediary is a *broker* or *agent*. Today we
would classify the broker as someone who acts on behalf of the borrower
or lender, buying or selling a bond as instructed. However, intermediaries
originally acted between borrowers and lenders in placing funds as required.

A broker would not simply on-lend funds that have been placed with it, but would accept deposits and make loans as required by its customers. This resulted in the first banks. A *retail bank* deals mainly with the personal financial sector and small businesses, and in addition to loans and deposits also provides cash transmission services. A retail bank is required to maintain a minimum cash reserve, to meet potential withdrawals, but the remainder of its deposit base can be used to make loans. This does not mean that the total size of its loan book is restricted to what it has taken in deposits: loans can also be funded in the wholesale market. An *investment bank* will deal with governments, corporates, and institutional investors. Investment banks perform an agency role for their customers, and are the primary vehicle through which a corporate will borrow funds in the bond markets. This is part of the bank's corporate finance function; it will also act as wholesaler in the bond markets, a function known as *market making*. The bond-issuing function of an investment bank, by which the bank will issue bonds on behalf of a customer and pass the funds raised to this customer, is known as *origination*. Investment banks will also carry out a range of other functions for institutional customers, including export finance, corporate advisory, and fund management.

Other financial intermediaries will trade not on behalf of clients but for their own *book*. These include *arbitrageurs* and speculators. Usually such market participants form part of investment banks.

## Investors

There is a large variety of players in the bond markets, each trading some or all of the different instruments available to suit their own purposes. We can group the main types of investors according to the time horizon of their investment activity.

*Short-term institutional investors*. These include banks and building societies, money-market fund managers, central banks, and the treasury desks of some types of corporates. Such bodies are driven by short-term investment views, often subject to close guidelines, and will be driven by the total return available on their investments. Banks will have an additional requirement to maintain *liquidity*, often in fulfilment of regulatory authority rules, by holding a proportion of their assets in the form of easily tradable short-term instruments.

*Long-term institutional investors*. Typically these types of investors include pension funds and life assurance companies. Their investment horizon is long term, reflecting the nature of their liabilities; often they will seek to match these liabilities by holding long-dated bonds.

*Mixed horizon institutional investors*. This is possibly the largest category of investors and will include general insurance companies, most corporate bodies, and sovereign wealth funds. Like banks and financial-sector companies, they are also very active in the primary market, issuing bonds to finance their operations.

*Market professionals*. This category includes the banks and specialist financial intermediaries mentioned earlier, firms that one would not automatically classify as "investors" although they will also have an investment objective. Their time horizon will range from one day to the very long term. Proprietary traders will actively position themselves in the market in order to gain trading profit, for example in response to their view on where they think interest rate levels are headed. These participants will trade directly with other market professionals and investors, or via brokers. Market makers or *traders* (called *dealers* in the United States) are wholesalers in the bond markets; they make two-way prices in selected bonds. Firms will not necessarily be active market makers in all types of bonds; smaller firms often specialise in certain sectors. In a two-way quote the *bid price* is the price at which the market maker will buy stock, so it is the price the investor will receive when selling stock. The *offer price* or *ask price* is the price at which investors can buy stock from the market maker. As one might expect, the bid price is always higher than the offer price, and it is this *spread* that represents the theoretical profit to the market maker. The bid-offer spread set by the marketmaker is determined by several factors, including supply and demand, and liquidity considerations for that particular stock, the trader's view on market direction and *volatility* as well as that of the stock itself and the presence of any market intelligence. A large bid-offer spread reflects low liquidity in the stock, as well as low demand.

## Markets

Markets are that part of the financial system where capital market transactions, including the buying and selling of securities, takes place. A market can describe a traditional stock exchange; that is, a physical trading floor where securities trading occurs. Many financial instruments are traded over the telephone or electronically; these markets are known as *over-the-counter* (OTC) markets. A distinction is made between financial instruments of up to one year's maturity and instruments of over one year's maturity. Short-term instruments make up the *money market* while all other instruments are deemed to be part of the *capital market*. There is also a distinction made between the *primary market* and the *secondary market*. A new issue of bonds made by an investment bank on behalf of its client is made in the primary market. Such an issue can be a *public* offer, in which anyone can apply to buy the bonds, or a *private* offer where the customers of the investment bank are offered the stock. The secondary market is the market in which existing bonds and shares are subsequently traded.

| | Credit Rating | Maturity Range | Dealing Mechanism | Benchmark Bonds | Issuance | Coupon and Day-Count Basis |
|---|---|---|---|---|---|---|
| Australia | AAA | 2–15 years | OTC Dealer network | 5, 10 years | Auction | Semiannual, act/act |
| Canada | AAA | 2–30 years | OTC Dealer network | 3, 5, 10 years | Auction, subscription | Semiannual, act/act |
| France | AAA | BTAN: 1–7 years OAT: 10–30 years | OTC Dealer network Bonds listed on Paris Stock Exchange | BTAN: 2, 5 years OAT: 10, 30 years | Dutch auction | BTAN: Semiannual, act/act OAT: Annual, act/act |
| Germany | AAA | OBL: 2, 5 years BUND: 10, 30 years | OTC Dealer network Listed on Stock Exchange | The most recent issue | Combination of Dutch auction and proportion of each issue allocated on fixed basis to institutions | Annual, act/act |
| South Africa | A | 2–30 years | OTC Dealer network Listed on Johannesburg SE | 2, 7, 10, 20 years | Auction | Semiannual, act/365 |
| Singapore | AAA | 2–15 years | OTC Dealer network | 1, 5, 10, 15 years | Auction | Semiannual, act/act |
| Taiwan | AA– | 2–30 years | OTC Dealer network | 2, 5, 10, 20, 30 years | Auction | Annual, act/act |
| United Kingdom | AAA | 2–50 years | OTC Dealer network | 5, 10, 30 years | Auction, subsequent issue by "tap" subscription | Semiannual, act/act |
| United States | AAA | 2–20 years | OTC Dealer network | 2, 5, 10 years | Auction | Semiannual, act/act |

**Table 1.1**   Selected Government Bond Market Characteristics

| Term (years) | Australia | Germany | Japan | United Kingdom | United States |
|---|---|---|---|---|---|
| 1 | | | | 0.43 | 0.110 |
| 2 | 2.74 | 0.12 | 0.08 | 0.48 | 0.250 |
| 3 | | | | | |
| 4 | | | | | |
| 5 | 3.49 | 0.66 | 0.18 | 1.58 | 1.251 |
| 7 | | | | | |
| 10 | 4.32 | 1.7 | 0.61 | 2.83 | 2.753 |
| 15 | 4.63 | | | 3.17 | |
| 20 | | | | 3.36 | |
| 30 | | 2.62 | 1.65 | 3.64 | 3.756 |

**Table 1.2**   Selected Government Bond Markets, Yield Curves as at
2 December 2013
*Source*: Bloomberg LP.

# BOND PRICING AND YIELD: THE TRADITIONAL APPROACH

## Bond Pricing

The interest rate that is used to discount a bond's cash flows (and therefore called the discount rate) is the rate required by the bondholder. This is therefore known as the bond's yield. The yield on the bond will be determined by the market and is the price demanded by investors for buying it, which is why it is sometimes called the bond's return. The required yield for any bond will depend on a number of political and economic factors, including what yield is being earned by other bonds of the same class. Yield is always quoted as an annualised interest rate, so that for a bond paying semiannually exactly half of the annual rate is used to discount the cash flows.

The fair price of a bond is the present value of all its cash flows. Therefore, when pricing a bond, we need to calculate the present value of all the coupon interest payments and the present value of the redemption payment, and sum these. The price of a conventional bond that pays annual coupons can therefore be given by (1.11).

$$P = \frac{C}{(1+r)} + \frac{C}{(1+r)^2} + \frac{C}{(1+r)^3} + \ldots\ldots \frac{C}{(1+r)^N} + \frac{M}{(1+r)^N} \quad (1.11)$$

$$= \sum_{n=1}^{N} \frac{C}{(1+r)^n} + \frac{M}{(1+r)^N}$$

Where    $P$    is the price

           $C$    is the annual coupon payment

           $r$    is the discount rate (therefore, the required yield)

           $N$    is the number of years to maturity (therefore, the number of interest periods in an annually paying bond)

           $M$    is the maturity payment or par value (usually 100% of currency)

Note that (1.11) applies only for fixed coupon bonds where the "recovery rate" (RR) on default of the issuer is zero. In other words, we can only assume it for default-risk free bonds. The RR term will be explained and considered in later chapters.

For long-hand calculation purposes, the first half of (1.11) is usually simplified and is sometimes encountered in one of the two ways shown in (1.12).

$$\sum_{n=1}^{N} \frac{C}{(1+r)^n} = C\left[\frac{1-\left[\frac{1}{(1+r)^N}\right]}{r}\right]$$

or                                          (1.12)

$$\sum_{n=1}^{N} \frac{C}{(1+r)^n} = \frac{C}{r}\left[1-\frac{1}{(1+r)^N}\right]$$

The price of a bond that pays semiannual coupons is given by the expression in (1.13), which is our earlier expression modified to allow for the twice-yearly discounting:

$$
\begin{aligned}
P &= \frac{C/2}{\left(1+\frac{1}{2}r\right)} + \frac{C/2}{\left(1+\frac{1}{2}r\right)^2} + \frac{C/2}{\left(1+\frac{1}{2}r\right)^3} + \ldots\ldots \frac{C/2}{\left(1+\frac{1}{2}r\right)^{2N}} + \frac{M}{\left(1+\frac{1}{2}r\right)^{2N}} \\
&= \sum_{n=1}^{2N} \frac{C/2}{\left(1+\frac{1}{2}r\right)^n} + \frac{M}{\left(1+\frac{1}{2}r\right)^{2N}} \\
&= \frac{C}{r}\left[1-\frac{1}{\left(1+\frac{1}{2}r\right)^{2N}}\right] + \frac{M}{\left(1+\frac{1}{2}r\right)^{2N}}
\end{aligned}
$$

(1.13)

Note how we set $2N$ as the power to which to raise the discount factor, as there are two interest payments every year for a bond that pays semiannually. Therefore, a more convenient function to use might be the number of interest periods in the life of the bond, as opposed to the number of years to maturity, which we could set as $n$, allowing us to alter the equation for a semiannually paying bond as:

$$P = \frac{C}{r}\left[1 - \frac{1}{\left(1 + \frac{1}{2}r\right)^{2n}}\right] + \frac{M}{\left(1 + \frac{1}{2}r\right)^{2n}} \tag{1.14}$$

The formula in (1.14) calculates the fair price on a coupon-payment date, so that there is no accrued interest incorporated into the price. It also assumes that there is an even number of coupon-payment dates remaining before maturity. The concept of accrued interest is an accounting convention, and treats coupon interest as accruing every day that the bond is held; this amount is added to the discounted present value of the bond (the *clean* price) to obtain the market value of the bond, known as the *dirty* price.

The date used as the point for calculation is the settlement date for the bond, the date on which a bond will change hands after it is traded. For a new issue of bonds, the settlement date is the day when the stock is delivered to investors and payment is received by the bond issuer. The settlement date for a bond traded in the secondary market is the day when the buyer transfers payment to the seller of the bond and when the seller transfers the bond to the buyer. Different markets will have different settlement conventions. For example, Australian government bonds normally settle two business days after the trade date (the notation used in bond markets is "T + 2"), whereas Eurobonds settle on T + 3. The term *value date* is sometimes used in place of settlement date. However, the two terms are not strictly synonymous. A settlement date can only fall on a business date, so that an Australian government bond traded on a Friday will settle on a Tuesday. However, a value date can sometimes fall on a non-business day; for example, when accrued interest is being calculated.

The standard formula also assumes that the bond is traded for a settlement on a day that is precisely one interest period before the next coupon payment. The price formula is adjusted if dealing takes place in between coupon dates. If we take the value date for any transaction, we then need to calculate the number of calendar days from this day to the next coupon date. We then use the following ratio $i$ when adjusting the exponent for the discount factor:

$$i = \frac{\text{Days from value date to next coupon date}}{\text{Days in the interest period}}$$

The number of days in the interest period is the number of calendar days between the last coupon date and the next one, and it will depend on the day-count basis used for that specific bond. The price formula is then modified as shown in (1.15).

$$P = \frac{C}{(1+r)^i} + \frac{C}{(1+r)^{1+i}} + \frac{C}{(1+r)^{2+i}} + \ldots \ldots \frac{C}{(1+r)^{n-1+i}} + \frac{M}{(1+r)^{n-1+i}} \quad (1.15)$$

where the variables $C$, $M$, $n$ and $r$ are as before. Note that (1.15) assumes $r$ for an annually paying bond and is adjusted to $r/2$ for a semiannually paying bond.

**EXAMPLE 1.1**

In these examples we illustrate the long-hand price calculation, using both expressions for the calculation of the present value of the annuity stream of a bond's cash flows.

## 1.1 (A)

Calculate the fair pricing of a U.S. Treasury, the 4% of February 2014, which pays semiannual coupons, with the following terms:

$C$ = $4.00 per $100 nominal

$M$ = $100

$N$ = 10 year (that is, the calculation is for value the 17th February 2004)

$r$ = 4.048%

$$P = \frac{\$4.00}{0.04048} \left\{ 1 - \frac{1}{1 + \frac{1}{2}(0.04048)]^{20}} \right\} + \frac{\$100}{\left[1 + \frac{1}{2}(0.04048)\right]^{20}}$$

$$= \$32.628 + \$66.981$$

$$= \$99.609 \text{ or } 99 - 19 +$$

The fair price of the Treasury is $99 – 19+, which is composed of the present value of the stream of coupon payments ($32.628) and the present value of the return of the principal ($66.981).

This yield calculation is shown at Figure 1.3, the Bloomberg YA page for this security. We show the price shown as 99 – 19+ for settlement on 17 Feb 2004, the date it was issued.

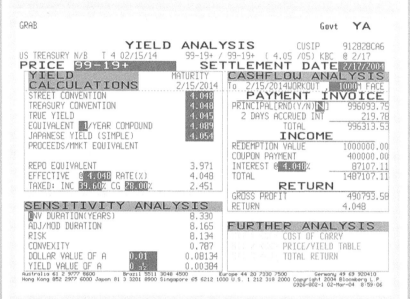

**Figure 1.3** Bloomberg YA Page for Yield Analysis
Used with permission of Bloomberg L.P. Copyright© 2014. All rights reserved.

## 1.1(B)

What is the price of a 5% coupon sterling bond with precisely five years to maturity, with semiannual coupon payments, if the yield required is 5.40%?

As the cash flows for this bond are 10 semiannual coupons of £2.50 and a redemption payment of £100 in 10 six-month periods from now, the price of the bond can be obtained by solving the following expression, where we substitute $C = 2.5$, $n = 10$, and $r = 0.027$ into the price equation (the values for $C$ and $r$ reflect the adjustments necessary for a semiannual paying bond).

$$P = 2.5 \left[ \frac{1 - \left[ \frac{1}{(1.027)^{10}} \right]}{0.027} \right] + \frac{100}{(1.027)^{10}}$$

$$= 21.65574 + 76.61178$$

$$= \$98.26752$$

The price of the bond is $98.2675 per $100 nominal.

## 1.1(C)

What is the price of a 5% coupon euro bond with five years to maturity paying annual coupons, again with a required yield of 5.4%?

In this case there are five periods of interest, so we may set $C = 5$, $n = 5$, with $r = 0.05$.

$$P = 5 \left[ \frac{1 - \left[ \frac{1}{(1.054)^5} \right]}{0.054} \right] + \frac{100}{(1.054)^5}$$

$$= 21.410121 + 76.877092$$

$$= £98.287213$$

Note how the annual-paying bond has a slightly higher price for the same required annualised yield. This is because the semiannual paying sterling bond has a higher effective yield than the euro bond, resulting in a lower price.

## 1.1(D)

Consider our 5% sterling bond again, but this time the required yield has risen and is now 6%. This makes $C = 2.5$, $n = 10$, and $r = 0.03$.

$$P = 2.5 \left[ \frac{1 - \left[ \frac{1}{(1.03)^{10}} \right]}{0.03} \right] + \frac{100}{(1.03)^{10}}$$

$$= 21.325507 + 74.409391$$

$$= £95.7349$$

As the required yield has risen, the discount rate used in the price calculation is now higher, and the result of the higher discount is a lower present value (price).

## 1.1(E)

Calculate the price of our sterling bond, still with five years to maturity but offering a yield of 5.1%.

$$P = 2.5 \left[ \frac{1 - \left[ \frac{1}{(1.0255)^5} \right]}{0.0255} \right] + \frac{100}{(1.0255)^5}$$

$$= 21.823737 + 77.739788$$

$$= £99.563523$$

To satisfy the lower required yield of 5.1%, the price of the bond has fallen to £99.56 per £100.

## 1.1(F)

Calculate the price of the 5% sterling bond one year later, with precisely four years left to maturity and with the required yield still at the original 5.40%. This sets the terms in 1.1(b) unchanged, except now $n = 8$.

$$P = 2.5 \left[ \frac{1 - \left[ \frac{1}{(1.027)^8} \right]}{0.027} \right] + \frac{100}{(1.027)^8}$$

$$= 17.773458 + 80.804668$$

$$= £98.578126$$

The price of the bond is £98.58. Compared to 1.1(B) this illustrates how, other things being equal, the price of a bond will approach par (£100 percent) as it approaches maturity.

There also exist *perpetual* or *irredeemable* bonds which have no redemption date, so that interest on them is paid indefinitely. They are also known as undated bonds. An example of an undated bond is the 3½% War Loan, a UK gilt originally issued in 1916 to help pay for the 1914–1918 war effort. Most undated bonds date from a long time in the past, and it is unusual to see them issued today. In structure, the cash flow from an undated bond can be viewed as a continuous annuity. The fair price of such a bond is given from (1.11) by setting $N = \infty$, such that:

$$P = \frac{C}{r} \tag{1.16}$$

In most markets, bond prices are quoted in decimals, in minimum increments of 1/100ths. This is the case with Eurobonds, euro-denominated bonds, and gilts, for example. Certain markets—including the U.S. Treasury market and South African and Indian government bonds, for example—quote prices in ticks, where the minimum increment is 1/32nd. One tick is therefore equal to 0.03125. A U.S. Treasury might be priced at "98-05" which means "98 and five ticks". This is equal to 98 and 5/32nds which is 98.15625.

Bonds that do not pay a coupon during their life are known as zero-coupon bonds or strips, and the price for these bonds is determined by modifying (1.11) to allow for the fact that $C = 0$. We know that the only cash flow is the maturity payment, so we may set the price as:

$$P = \frac{M}{\left(1 + r\right)^{N}} \tag{1.17}$$

where $M$ and $r$ are as before and $N$ is the number of years to maturity. The important factor is to allow for the same number of interest periods as coupon bonds of the same currency. That is, even though there are no actual coupons, we calculate prices and yields on the basis of a quasi-coupon period. For a U.S. dollar or a sterling zero-coupon bond, a five-year zero coupon bond would be assumed to cover 10 quasi-coupon periods, which would set the price equation as:

$$P = \frac{M}{\left(1 + \frac{1}{2}r\right)^{n}} \tag{1.18}$$

EXAMPLE 1.2

What is the total consideration for £5 million nominal of a gilt, where the price is 114.50?

The price of the gilt is £114.50 per £100, so the consideration is:

$$1.145 \times 5,000,000 = £5,725,000$$

What consideration is payable for $5 million nominal of a U.S. Treasury, quoted at an all-in price of 99-16?

The U.S. Treasury price is 99-16, which is equal to 99 and 16/32, or 99.50 per $100. The consideration is therefore:

$$0.9950 \times 5,000,000 = £4,975,000$$

If the price of a bond is below par, the total consideration is below the nominal amount; whereas if it is priced above par, the consideration will be above the nominal amount.

**EXAMPLE 1.3**

## 1.3(A)

Calculate the price of a gilt strip with a maturity of precisely five years, where the required yield is 5.40%.

These terms allow us to set $N = 5$ so that $n = 10$, $r = 0.054$ (so that $r/2 = 0.027$), with $M = 100$ as usual.

$$P = \frac{100}{(1.027)^{10}}$$
$$= £76.611782$$

## 1.3(B)

Calculate the price of a French government zero-coupon bond with precisely five years to maturity, with the same required yield of 5.40%.

$$P = \frac{100}{(1.054)^{5}}$$
$$= £76.877092$$

We have to note carefully the quasi-coupon periods in order to maintain consistency with conventional bond pricing.

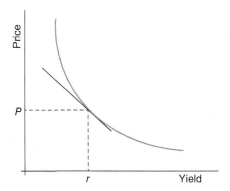

**Figure 1.4**    The Price/Yield Relationship

An examination of the bond price formula tells us that the yield and price for a bond are related. A key aspect of this relationship is that the price changes in the opposite direction to the yield. This is because the price of the bond is the net present value of its cash flows; if the discount rate used in the present value calculation increases, the present values of the cash flows will decrease. This occurs whenever the yield level required by bondholders increases. In the same way, if the required yield decreases, the price of the bond will rise. This property was observed in Example 1.2. As the required yield decreased, the price of the bond increased, and we observed the same relationship when the required yield was raised.

The relationship between any bond's price and yield at any required yield level is illustrated in a stylised manner in Figure 1.4, which is obtained if we plot the yield against the corresponding price; this shows a convex curve. In practice the curve is not quite as perfectly convex as illustrated in Figure 1.4, but the diagram is representative.

## SUMMARY OF THE PRICE/YIELD RELATIONSHIP

At issue, if a bond is priced at par, its coupon will equal the yield that the market requires from the bond.

If the required yield rises above the coupon rate, the bond price will decrease.

If the required yield goes below the coupon rate, the bond price will increase.

## BOND YIELD

We have observed how to calculate the price of a bond using an appropriate discount rate known as the bond's yield. We can reverse this procedure to find the yield of a bond where the price is known, which would be equivalent to calculating the bond's internal rate of return (IRR). The IRR calculation is taken to be a bond's yield to maturity or redemption yield and is one of various yield measures used in the markets to estimate the return generated from holding a bond. In most markets, bonds are generally traded on the basis of their prices, but because of the complicated patterns of cash flows that different bonds can have they are generally compared in terms of their yields. This means that a marketmaker will usually quote a two-way price at which she will buy or sell a particular bond, but it is the yield at which the bond is trading that is important to the marketmaker's customer. This is because a bond's price does not actually tell us anything useful about what we are getting. Remember, that in any market there will be a number of bonds with different issuers, coupons, and terms to maturity. Even in a homogenous market such as the Treasury market, different bonds and notes will trade according to their own specific characteristics. To compare bonds in the market, therefore, we need the yield on any bond, and it is yields that we compare, not prices.

The yield on any investment is the interest rate that will make the present value of the cash flows from the investment equal to the initial cost (price) of the investment. Mathematically, the yield on any investment, represented by $r$, is the interest rate that satisfies (1.19), which is simply the bond price equation we've already reviewed.

$$P = \sum_{n=1}^{N} \frac{C_n}{\left(1+r\right)^n} \qquad (1.19)$$

But as we have noted there are other types of yield measure used in the market for different purposes. The simplest measure of the yield on a bond is the current yield, also known as the flat yield, interest yield or running yield. The running yield is given by (1.20).

$$rc = \frac{C}{P} \times 100 \qquad (1.20)$$

where $rc$ is the current yield.

In (1.20) $C$ is not expressed as a decimal. Current yield ignores any capital gain or loss that might arise from holding and trading a bond and does not consider the time value of money. It essentially calculates the bond coupon income as a proportion of the price paid for the bond, and to be accurate would have to assume that the bond was more like an annuity rather than a fixed-term instrument.

The current yield is useful as a rough-and-ready interest-rate calculation; it is often used to estimate the cost of or profit from a short-term holding of a bond. For example, if other short-term interest rates such as the one-week or three-month rates are higher than the current yield, holding the bond is said to involve a running cost. This is also known as *negative carry* or *negative funding*. The term is used by bond traders and market makers and leveraged investors. The carry on a bond is a useful measure for all market practitioners as it illustrates the cost of holding or funding a bond. The funding rate is the bondholder's short-term cost of funds. A private investor could also apply this to a short-term holding of bonds.

The yield to maturity or gross redemption yield is the most frequently used measure of return from holding a bond.[5] Yield to maturity (YTM) takes into account the pattern of coupon payments, the bond's term to maturity, and the capital gain (or loss) arising over the remaining life of the bond. We saw from our bond price formula in the previous section that these elements were all related and were important components determining a bond's price. If we set the IRR for a set of cash flows to be the rate that applies from a start-date to an end-date we can assume the IRR to be the YTM for those cash flows. The YTM therefore is equivalent to the internal rate of return on the bond, the rate that equates the value of the discounted cash flows on the bond to its current price. The calculation assumes that the bond is held until maturity, and therefore it is the cash flows to maturity that are discounted in the calculation. It also employs the concept of the time value of money.

As we would expect, the formula for YTM is essentially that for calculating the price of a bond. For a bond paying annual coupons, the YTM is calculated by solving (1.11). Note that the expression in (1.11) has two variable parameters, the price $P$ and yield $r$. It cannot be rearranged to solve for yield $r$ explicitly, and, in fact, the only way to solve for the yield is to use the process of numerical iteration. The process involves estimating a value for $r$ and calculating the price associated with the estimated yield. If the calculated price is higher than the price of the bond at the time, the yield estimate is lower than the actual yield, and so it must be adjusted until it converges to the level that corresponds with the bond price.[6] For the YTM of a semiannual coupon bond, we have to adjust the formula to allow for the semiannual payments, shown in (1.13).

---

[5] In this book the terms yield to maturity and gross redemption yield are used synonymously. The latter term is encountered in sterling markets.

[6] Bloomberg also uses the term yield-to-workout, where workout refers to the maturity date for the bond.

**EXAMPLE 1.4**   Yield to maturity for semiannual coupon bond

A semiannual paying bond has a dirty price of $98.50, an annual coupon of 6%, and there is exactly one year before maturity. The bond therefore has three remaining cash flows, comprising two coupon payments of $3 each and a redemption payment of $100. Equation 1.12 can be used with the following inputs:

$$98.50 = \frac{3.00}{\left(1 + \frac{1}{2}rm\right)} + \frac{103.00}{\left(1 + \frac{1}{2}rm\right)^2}$$

Note that we use half of the YTM value $rm$ because this is a semiannual paying bond. The preceding expression is a quadratic equation, which is solved using the standard solution for quadratic equations, which is noted in the following equations.

$$ax^2 + bx + c = 0$$

$$x = \frac{-b \pm \sqrt{b^2 - 4ac}}{2a}$$

In our expression, if we let $x = (1 + rm/2)$, we can rearrange the expression as follows:

$$98.50x^2 - 3.0x - 103.00 = 0$$

We then solve for a standard quadratic equation, and there will be two solutions, only one of which gives a positive redemption yield. The positive solution is $rm/2 = 0.037929$ so that $rm = 7.5859\%$.

As an example of the iterative solution method, suppose that we start with a trial value for $rm$ of $r_1 = 7\%$ and plug this into the right-hand side of (1.12). This gives a value for the right-hand side of:

$$RHS_1 = 99.050$$

which is higher than the left-hand side (LHS = 98.50); the trial value for $rm$ was therefore too low. Suppose then that we try next $r_2 = 8\%$ and use this as the right-hand side of the equation. This gives:

$$RHS_2 = 98.114$$

$$rm = r_1 + \left(r_2 - r_1\right)\frac{RHS_1 - LHS}{RHS_1 - RHS_2}$$

our linear approximation for the redemption yield is $rm = 7.587\%$, which is near the exact solution.

To differentiate redemption yield from other yield and interest-rate measures described in this book, we henceforth refer to it as *rm*.

Note that the redemption yield, as discussed earlier in this section, is the gross redemption yield, the yield that results from payment of coupons without deduction of any withholding tax. The net redemption yield is obtained by multiplying the coupon rate *C* by (1 − marginal tax rate). The net yield is what will be received if the bond is traded in a market where bonds pay coupon net, which means net of a withholding tax. The net redemption yield is always lower than the gross redemption yield.

We have already alluded to the key assumption behind the YTM calculation, namely that the rate *rm* remains stable for the entire period of the life of the bond. By assuming the same yield, we can say that all coupons are reinvested at the same yield *rm*. For the bond in Example 1.4, this means that if all the cash flows are discounted at 7.59% they will have a total net present value of 98.50. This is patently unrealistic since we can predict with virtual certainty that interest rates for instruments of similar maturity to the bond at each coupon date will not remain at this rate for the life of the bond. In practice, however, investors require a rate of return that is equivalent to the price that they are paying for a bond, and the redemption yield is, to put it simply, as good a measurement as any. A more accurate measurement might be to calculate present values of future cash flows using the discount rate that is equal to the forward interest rates at that point, known as the forward interest rate. However, forward rates are simply interest rates today for execution at a future date, and so a YTM measurement calculated using forward rates can be as speculative as one calculated using the conventional formula. So a YTM calculation made using forward rates would not be realised in practice either. We shall see later how the zero-coupon interest rate is the true interest rate for any term to maturity. However, despite the limitations presented by its assumptions, the YTM is the main measure of return used in the markets.

We have noted the difference between calculating redemption yield on the basis of both annual and semiannual coupon bonds. Analysis of bonds that pay semiannual coupons incorporates semiannual discounting of semiannual coupon payments. This is appropriate for most UK and U.S. bonds. However, government bonds in most of continental Europe and most Eurobonds pay annual coupon payments, and the appropriate method of calculating the redemption yield is to use annual discounting. The two yields measures are not therefore directly comparable. We could make a Eurobond directly comparable with a UK gilt by using semiannual discounting of the Eurobond's annual coupon payments. Alternatively we could make the gilt comparable with the Eurobond by using annual discounting of its semiannual coupon payments. The price/yield formulae for different discounting possibilities we encounter in the markets are listed in the following equations (as usual we assume that the calculation takes place on a coupon payment date so that accrued interest is zero).

Semiannual discounting of annual payments:

$$P_d = \frac{C}{\left(1 + \frac{1}{2}rm\right)^2} + \frac{C}{\left(1 + \frac{1}{2}rm\right)^4} + \frac{C}{\left(1 + \frac{1}{2}rm\right)^6} + \ldots \frac{C}{\left(1 + \frac{1}{2}rm\right)^{2N}} + \frac{M}{\left(1 + rm\right)^{2N}}$$

(1.21)

Annual discounting of semiannual payments:

$$P_d = \frac{C/2}{\left(1 + rm\right)^{\frac{1}{2}}} + \frac{C/2}{\left(1 + rm\right)} + \frac{C/2}{\left(1 + rm\right)^{\frac{3}{2}}} + \ldots \frac{C/2}{\left(1 + rm\right)^N} + \frac{M}{\left(1 + rm\right)^N}$$

(1.22)

Consider a bond with a dirty price of 97.89, a coupon of 6%, and five years to maturity. This bond would have the following gross redemption yields under the different yield-calculation conventions:

| Discounting | Payments | Yield to Maturity (%) |
| --- | --- | --- |
| Semiannual | Semiannual | 6.500 |
| Annual | Annual | 6.508 |
| Semiannual | Annual | 6.428 |
| Annual | Semiannual | 6.605 |

This proves what we have already observed: namely, that the coupon and discounting frequency will affect the redemption yield calculation for a bond. We can see that increasing the frequency of discounting will lower the yield, while increasing the frequency of payments will raise the yield. When comparing yields for bonds that trade in markets with different conventions, it is important to convert all the yields to the same calculation basis. Intuitively we might think that doubling a semiannual yield figure will give us the annualised equivalent; in fact, this will result in an inaccurate figure due to the multiplicative effects of discounting and one that is an underestimate of the true annualised yield. The correct procedure for producing an annualised yields from semiannual and quarterly yields is given by the following expressions. The general conversion expression is given by (1.23):

$$rm_a = \left(1 + \text{interest rate}\right)^m - 1$$

(1.23)

where $m$ is the number of coupon payments per year.

Specifically we can convert between yields using the expressions given in (1.24) and (1.25).

$$rm_a = \left[ \left( 1 + \tfrac{1}{2} rm_s \right)^2 - 1 \right]$$

$$rm_s = \left[ \left( 1 + rm_a \right)^{\frac{1}{2}} - 1 \right] \times 2 \qquad (1.24)$$

$$rm_a = \left[ \left( 1 + \tfrac{1}{4} rm_q \right)^4 - 1 \right]$$

$$rm_q = \left[ \left( 1 + rm_a \right)^{\frac{1}{4}} - 1 \right] \times 4 \qquad (1.25)$$

where $rm_q$, $rm_s$, and $rm_a$ are, respectively, the quarterly, semiannually, and annually compounded yields to maturity.

The market convention is sometimes simply to double the semi-annual yield to obtain the annualised yields, despite the fact that this produces an inaccurate result. It is only acceptable to do this for rough calculations. An annualised yield obtained by multiplying the semiannual yield by two is known as a bond equivalent yield.

While YTM is the most commonly used measure of yield, it has one major disadvantage. The disadvantage is that implicit in the calculation of the YTM is the assumption that each coupon payment as it becomes due is reinvested at the rate $rm$.

---

**EXAMPLE 1.5**

A UK gilt paying semiannual coupons and a maturity of 10 years has a quoted yield of 4.89%. A European government bond of similar maturity is quoted at a yield of 4.96%. Which bond has the higher effective yield?

The effective annual yield of the gilt is:

$$rm = \left( 1 + \tfrac{1}{2} \times 0.0489 \right)^2 - 1 = 4.9498\%$$

Therefore, the gilt does indeed have the lower yield.

---

This is clearly unlikely, due to the fluctuations in interest rates over time and as the bond approaches maturity. In practice, the measure itself will not equal the actual return from holding the bond, even if it is held to maturity. That said, the market standard is to quote bond returns as yields to maturity, bearing the key assumptions behind the calculation in mind.

Another disadvantage of this measure of return arises where investors do not hold bonds to maturity. The redemption yield measure will not be of great value where the bond is not being held to redemption. Investors might then be interested in other measures of return, which we can look at later.

To reiterate then, the redemption yield measure assumes that:

1. The bond is held to maturity;
2. All coupons during the bond's life are reinvested at the same (redemption yield) rate.

Therefore the YTM can be viewed as a prospective yield if the bond is purchased on issue and held to maturity. Even then the actual realised yield on maturity would be different from expected or anticipated yield and is closest to reality only where an investor buys a bond on first issue and holds the YTM figure because of the inapplicability of the second condition in the preceding list.

In addition, as coupons are discounted at the yield specific for each bond, it actually becomes inaccurate to compare bonds using this yield measure. For instance, the coupon cash flows that occur in two years time from both a two-year and five-year bond will be discounted at different rates (assuming we do not have a flat yield curve). This would occur because the YTM for a five-year bond is invariably different from the YTM for a two-year bond. However, it would clearly not be correct to discount a two-year cash flow at different rates, because we can see that the present value calculated today of a cash flow in two years' time should be the same whether it is sourced from a short- or long-dated bond. Even if the first condition noted earlier for the YTM calculation is satisfied, it is clearly unlikely for any but the shortest maturity bond that all coupons will be reinvested at the same rate. Market interest rates are in a state of constant flux and would thus affect money reinvestment rates. Therefore, although yield to maturity is the main market measure of bond levels, it is not a true interest rate. This is an important result, and we shall explore the concept of a true interest rate in Chapter 2.

## Accrued Interest, Clean and Dirty Bond Prices

Our discussion of bond pricing up to now has ignored coupon interest. All bonds accrue interest on a daily basis, and this is then paid out on the coupon date. The calculation of bond prices using present-value analysis does not account for coupon interest or *accrued interest*. In all major bond markets, the convention is to quote price as a *clean price*. This is the price of the bond as given by the net present value of its cash flows, but excluding coupon interest that has accrued on the bond since the last dividend payment. As all bonds accrue interest on a daily basis, even if a bond is held for only one day, interest will have been earned by the bondholder. However, we have referred already to a bond's *all-in* price, which is the price that is actually paid for the bond in the market. This is also known as the *dirty price* (or *gross price)*, which is the clean price of a bond plus accrued interest. In other words, the accrued interest must be added to the quoted price to get the total consideration for the bond.

Accruing interest compensates the seller of the bond for giving up all of the next coupon payment even though she will have held the bond for part of the period since the last coupon payment. The clean price for a bond will move with changes in market interest rates; assuming that this is constant in a coupon period, the clean price will be constant for this period. However, the dirty price for the same bond will increase steadily from one interest payment date until the next. On the coupon date, the clean and dirty prices are the same and the accrued interest is zero. Between the coupon payment date and the next ex-dividend date the bond is traded cum dividend, so that the buyer gets the next coupon payment. The seller is compensated for not receiving the next coupon payment by receiving accrued interest instead. This is positive and increases up to the next ex-dividend date, at which point the dirty price falls by the present value of the amount of the coupon payment. The dirty price at this point is below the clean price, reflecting the fact that accrued interest is now negative. This is because after the ex-dividend date the bond is traded "ex-dividend"; the seller not the buyer receives the next coupon, and the buyer has to be compensated for not receiving the next coupon by means of a lower price for holding the bond.

The net interest accrued since the last ex-dividend date is determined as follows:

$$AI = C \times \left[ \frac{N_{xt} - N_{xc}}{Day\ Base} \right] \tag{1.26}$$

Where    $AI$      is the next accrued interest
          $C$      is the bond coupon
          $N_{xc}$     is the number of days between the ex-dividend date and the coupon payment date (seven business days for UK gilts)
          $N_{xt}$     is the number of days between the ex-dividend date and the date for the calculation
          *Day Base*    is the day-count base (365 or 360)

Certain bonds do not have an ex-dividend period (for example, Eurobonds) and accrue interest right up to the coupon date.

Interest accrues on a bond from and including the last coupon date up to and excluding what is called the value date. The value date is almost always the settlement date for the bond, or the date when a bond is passed to the buyer and the seller receives payment. Interest does not accrue on bonds whose issuer has subsequently gone into default. Bonds that trade without accrued interest are said to be trading flat or clean. By definition therefore,

Clean price of a bond = Dirty price − Accrued interest

For bonds that are trading ex-dividend, the accrued coupon is negative and would be subtracted from the clean price. The calculation is given by (1.27).

$$AI = -C \times \left[ \frac{\text{Days to next coupon}}{\text{Day Base}} \right] \tag{1.27}$$

As we noted, certain classes of bonds—for example, U.S. Treasuries and Eurobonds—do not have an ex-dividend period and therefore trade cum dividend right up to the coupon date.

The accrued-interest calculation for a bond is dependent on the day-count basis specified for the bond in question. When bonds are traded in the market, the actual consideration that changes hands is made up of the clean price of the bond together with the accrued that has accumulated on the bond since the last coupon payment; these two components make up the dirty price of the bond. When calculating the accrued interest, the market will use the appropriate day-count convention for that bond. A particular market will apply one of five different methods to calculate accrued interest:

| | |
|---|---|
| Actual/365 | Accrued = Coupon × Days/365 |
| Actual/360 | Accrued = Coupon × Days/360 |
| Actual/actual | Accrued = Coupon × Days/actual number of days in the interest period |
| 30/360 | See following text |
| 30E/360 | See following text |

When determining the number of days in between two dates, include the first date but not the second; thus, under the actual/365 convention, there are 37 days between 4th August and 10th September. The last two conventions assume 30 days in each month; so, for example, there are "30 days" between 10th February and 10th March. Under the 30/360 convention, if the first date falls on the 31st, it is changed to the 30th of the month, and if the second date falls on the 31st *and* the first date is on the 30th or 31st, the second date is changed to the 30th. The difference under the 30E/360 method is that if the second date falls on the 31st of the month, it is automatically changed to the 30th.

| Market | Coupon Frequency | Day-Count Basis | Ex-Dividend Period |
|---|---|---|---|
| Australia | Semiannual | Actual/actual | Yes |
| Austria | Annual | Actual/actual | No |
| Belgium | Annual | Actual/actual | No |
| Canada | Semiannual | Actual/actual | No |
| Denmark | Annual | 30E/360 | Yes |
| Eurobonds | Annual | 30/360 | No |
| France | Annual | Actual/actual | No |
| Germany | Annual | Actual/actual | No |
| Eire | Annual | Actual/actual | No |
| Italy | Annual | Actual/actual | No |
| New Zealand | Semiannual | Actual/actual | Yes |
| Norway | Annual | Actual/365 | Yes |
| Spain | Annual | Actual/actual | No |
| Sweden | Annual | 30E/360 | Yes |
| Switzerland | Annual | 30E/360 | No |
| United Kingdom | Semiannual | Actual/actual | Yes |
| United States | Semiannual | Actual/actual | No |

**Table 1.5**   Selected Country Market Accrued Interest Day-Count Basis

The accrued interest day-count basis for selected country bond markets is given in Table 1.5.

Van Deventer (1997) presents an effective critique of the accrued interest concept, believing essentially that it is an arbitrary construct that has little basis in economic reality. He states:

> The amount of accrued interest bears no relationship to the current level of interest rates.
>
> *Van Deventer, 1997, p. 11*

This is quite true; the accrued interest on a bond that is traded in the secondary market at any time is not related to the current level of interest rates, and is the same irrespective of where current rates are. As Example 1.6 makes clear, the accrued interest on a bond is a function of its coupon, which reflects the level of interest rates at the time the bond was issued. Accrued interest is therefore an accounting concept only, but at least it serves to recompense the holder for interest earned during the period the bond was held. It is conceivable that the calculation could be adjusted for present value, but, at the moment, accrued interest is the convention that is followed in the market.

---

EXAMPLE 1.6

## 1.6(A): ACCRUAL CALCULATION FOR 7% TREASURY 2002

This gilt has coupon dates of 7th June and 7th December each year. £100 nominal of the bond is traded for value 27th August 1998. What is accrued interest on the value date?

On the value date, 81 days have passed since the last coupon date. Under the old system for gilts, act/365, the calculation was:

$$7 \times 81 / 365 = 1.55342$$

Under the current system of act/act, which came into effect for gilts in November 1998, the accrued calculation uses the actual number of days between the two coupon dates, giving us:

$$7 \times 81 / 183 \times 0.5 = 1.54918$$

## 1.6(B)

Mansur buys £25,000 nominal of the 7% 2002 gilt for value on 27th August 1998, at a price of 102.4375. How much does he actually pay for the bond?

The clean price of the bond is 102.4375. The dirty price of the bond is 102.4375 + 1.55342 = 103.99092.

The total consideration is therefore

$$1.0399092 \times 25,000 = £25,997.73$$

## EXAMPLE 1.6(C)

A Norwegian government bond with a coupon of 8% is purchased for settlement on 30th July 1999 at a price of 99.50. Assume that this is seven days before the coupon date and therefore the bond trades ex-dividend. What is the all-in price?

The accrued interest $= -8 \times 7 / 365 = -0.153424$

The all-in price is therefore $99.50 - 0.1534 = 99.3466$

## EXAMPLE 1.6(D)

A bond has coupon payments on 1st June and 1st December each year. What is the day-base count if the bond is traded for value date on 30th October, 31st October and 1st November 1999, respectively? There are 183 days in the interest period.

|         | 30th October | 31st October | 1st November |
|---------|--------------|--------------|--------------|
| Act/365 | 151          | 152          | 153          |
| Act/360 | 151          | 152          | 153          |
| Act/Act | 151          | 152          | 153          |
| 30/360  | 149          | 150          | 151          |
| 30E/360 | 149          | 150          | 150          |

Reproduced from *Fixed Income Markets, Second Edition* (2014)

**This extract from *The Global Repo Markets* (2004)**

## The Repo Instrument

## The Repo Instrument

In this chapter we define repo and illustrate its use. We will see that the term *repo* is used to cover one of two different transactions—the *classic repo* and the *sell/buy-back*, and sometimes is spoken of in the same context as another instrument, the *stock loan*. A fourth instrument, known as the *total return swap* which is now commonly encountered as part of the market in credit derivatives, is economically similar in some respects to a repo so we will also look at this product. However, although these transactions differ in terms of their mechanics, legal documentation and accounting treatment, the economic effect of each of them is often very similar. The structure of any particular market and the motivations of particular counterparties will determine which transaction is entered into and there is also some crossover between markets and participants.

Market participants enter into classic repo transactions either because they wish to invest cash, for which the transaction is deemed to be *cash-driven*, or because they wish to borrow a certain stock, for which purpose the trade is *stock-driven*. A sell/buy-back, which is sometimes referred to as a *buy-sell*, is entered into for similar reasons but the trade itself operates under different mechanics and documentation.[1] A stock loan is just that, a borrowing of stock against a fee. Long-term holders of stock will therefore enter into stock loans simply to enhance their portfolio returns. Similar motivations lie behind the use of total return swaps as a funding instrument.

In this chapter we look in detail at the main repo structures, their mechanics and the different reasons for entering into them. It's a long chapter, but well worth studying closely.

# Repo Instruments

## Definition

A repo agreement is a transaction in which one party sells securities to another, and at the same time and as part of the same transaction commits to repurchase identical securities on a specified date at a specified price. The seller delivers securities and receives cash from the buyer. The cash is supplied at a predetermined rate of interest–*the repo rate*–that remains constant during the term of the trade. On maturity the original seller receives collateral of equivalent type and quality, and returns the cash plus repo interest. One party to the repo requires either the cash or the securities and provides *collateral* to the other party, as well as some form of compensation for the temporary use of the desired asset. Although legal title to the securities is transferred, the seller retains both the economic benefits and the market risk of owning them. This means that the "seller" will suffer loss if the market value of the collateral drops during the term of the repo, as they still retain beneficial ownership of the collateral. The "buyer" in a repo is not affected in profit/loss account terms if the value of the collateral drops, although as we shall see later, there are other concerns for the buyer if this happens.

We have given here the legal definition of repo. However, the purpose of the transaction as we have described above is to borrow or lend cash, which is why we have used inverted commas when referring to sellers and buyers. The "seller" of stock is really interested in borrowing cash, on which they will pay interest at a specified interest rate. The "buyer" requires security or *collateral* against the loan they have advanced, and/or the specific security to borrow for a period of time. The first and most important thing to emphasize is that repo is a secured loan of cash, and is categorized as a money market yield instrument.[2]

---

[1] We shall use the term "sell/buy-back" throughout this book. A repo is still a repo whether it is cash-driven or stock-driven, and one person's stock-driven trade may well be another's cash-driven one.

[2] That is, a money market product quoted as a yield instrument, similar to a bank deposit or a certificate of deposit. The other class of money market products are discount instruments such as a Treasury bill or commercial paper.

# The Classic Repo

The *classic repo* is the instrument generally used in the US, UK and other markets. In a classic repo one party enters into a contract to sell securities, simultaneously agreeing to purchase them back at a specified future date and price. The securities can be bonds or equities but also money market instruments such as T-bills. The buyer of the securities is effectively handing over cash, which on the termination of the trade will be returned to them, and on which they will receive interest.

The seller in a classic repo is selling or *offering* stock, and therefore receiving cash, whereas the buyer is buying or *bidding* for stock, and consequently paying cash. So if the one-week repo interest rate is quoted by a market-making bank as "5.50–5.25", this means that the market maker will bid for stock, that is, lend the cash, at 5.50% and offers stock or pays interest on borrowed cash at 5.25%. In some markets the quote is reversed.

## Illustration of Classic Repo

There are two parties to a repo trade, let us say Bank A (the seller of securities) and Bank B (the buyer of securities). On the trade date the two banks enter into an agreement whereby on a set date, the *value* or *settlement* date, Bank A will sell to Bank B a nominal amount of securities in exchange for cash.[3] The price received for the securities is the market price of the stock on the value date. The agreement also demands that on the termination date Bank B will sell identical stock back to Bank A at the previously agreed price, consequently, Bank B will have its cash returned with interest at the agreed repo rate.

In essence, a repo agreement is a secured loan (or *collaterized* loan) in which the repo rate reflects the interest charged on the cash being lent.

On the value date, stock and cash change hands. This is known as the start date, *on-side* date, *first leg* or *opening leg*, while the termination date is known as the *second leg, off-side leg* or *closing leg*. When the cash is returned to Bank B, it is accompanied by the interest charged on the cash during the term of the trade. This interest is calculated at a specified rate known as the *repo rate*. It is important to remember that although in legal terms the stock is initially "sold" to Bank B, the economic effects of ownership are retained with Bank A. This means that if the stock falls in price it is Bank A that will suffer a capital loss. Similarly, if the stock involved is a bond and there is a coupon payment during the term of the trade, this coupon is to the benefit of Bank A, and although Bank B will have received it on the coupon date, it must be handed over on the same day or immediately

---

[3] The two terms are not necessarily synonymous. The value date in a trade is the date on which the transaction acquires value, for example, the date from which accrued interest is calculated. As such, it may fall on a non-business day such as a weekend or public holiday. The settlement date is the day on which the transaction settles or clears, and so can only fall on a business day.

after to Bank A. This reflects the fact that although legal title to the collateral passes to the repo buyer, economic costs and benefits of the collateral remain with the seller.

A classic repo transaction is subject to a legal contract signed in advance by both parties. A standard document will suffice; it is not necessary to sign a legal agreement prior to each transaction.

Note that although we have called the two parties in this case "Bank A" and "Bank B", it is not only banks that get involved in repo transactions, and we have used these terms for the purposes of illustration only.

The basic mechanism is illustrated in Figure 4.1.

A seller in a repo transaction is entering into a repo, whereas a buyer is entering into a *reverse repo*. In Figure 4.1 the repo counterparty is Bank A, while Bank B is entering into a reverse repo. That is, a reverse repo is a purchase of securities that are sold back on termination. As is evident from Figure 4.1, every repo is a reverse repo, and the name given to a deal is dependent on whose viewpoint one is looking at the transaction.

## Examples of Classic Repo

The basic principle is illustrated with the following example. This considers a *specific* repo, that is, one in which the collateral supplied is specified as a particular stock, as opposed to a *general collateral* (GC) trade in which a basket of collateral can be supplied, of any particular issue, as long as it is of the required type and credit quality.

We consider first a classic repo in the UK gilt market between two market counterparties, in the 5.75% Treasury 2009 gilt stock. The terms of the trade are given in Table 4.1 and illustrated in Figure 4.2. Note that the terms of a classic repo trade are identical, irrespective of which market the deal is taking place in. So the basic trade, illustrated in Table 4.1, would be recognizable as a bond repo in European and Asian markets.

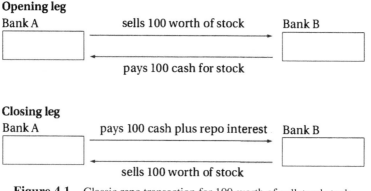

**Figure 4.1**    Classic repo transaction for 100-worth of collateral stock.

| Trade date | 5 July 2000 |
| --- | --- |
| Value date | 6 July 2000 |
| Repo term | 1 week |
| Termination date | 13 July 2000 |
| Collateral (stock) | UKT 5.75% 2009 |
| Nominal amount | £10,000,000 |
| Price | 104.60 |
| Accrued interest (29 days) | 0.4556011 |
| Dirty price | 105.055601 |
| Settlement proceeds (*wired amount*) | £10,505,560.11 |
| Repo rate | 5.75% |
| Repo interest | £11,584.90 |
| Termination proceeds | £10,517,145.01 |

**Table 4.1**   Terms of classic repo trade.

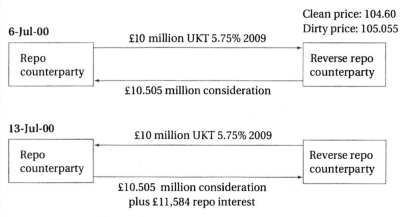

**Figure 4.2**   Diagram of classic repo trade.

The repo counterparty delivers to the reverse repo counterparty £10 million nominal of the stock, and in return receives the purchase proceeds. The clean market price of the stock is £104.60. In this example no *margin* has been taken so the start proceeds are equal to the market value of the stock that is £0,505,560.11. It is common for a rounded sum to be transferred on the opening leg. The repo interest is 5.75%, so the repo interest charged for the trade is:

$$10,505,560 \times 5.75\% \times \frac{7}{365}$$

or £11,584.01. The sterling market day-count basis is actual/365, and the repo interest is based on a seven-day repo rate of 5.75%. Repo rates are agreed at the time of the trade and are quoted, like all interest rates, on an annualised basis. The settlement price (dirty price) is used because it is the market value of the bonds on the particular trade date and therefore indicates the cash value of the gilts. By doing this the cash investor minimises credit exposure by equating the value of the cash and the collateral.

On termination the repo counterparty receives back its stock, for which it hands over the original proceeds plus the repo interest calculated above.

Market participants who are familiar with the Bloomberg trading system will use screen RRRA for a classic repo transaction. For this example the relevant screen entries are shown in Figure 4.3. This screen is used in conjunction with a specific stock, so in this case it would be called up by entering:

UKT 5.75 09 〈GOVT〉 RRRA 〈GO〉

where "UKT" is the ticker for UK gilts. Note that the date format for Bloomberg screens is the US style, which is mm/dd/yy. The screen inputs are relatively self-explanatory, with the user entering the terms of the trade that are detailed in Table 4.1. There is also a field for calculating margin, labelled "collateral" on the screen. As no margin is involved in this example, it is left at its default value of 100.00%. The bottom of the screen shows the opening leg cash proceeds or "wired amount", the repo interest and the termination proceeds.

What if a counterparty is interested in investing £10 million against gilt collateral? Let us assume that a corporate treasury with surplus cash wishes to invest this amount in repo for a one-week term. It invests this cash with a bank that deals in gilt repo. We can use Bloomberg screen RRRA to calculate the nominal amount of collateral required. Figure 4.4 shows the screen for this trade, again against the 5.75% Treasury 2009 stock as collateral. We see from Figure 4.4 that the terms of the trade are identical to that in Table 4.1, including the bond price and the repo rate, however, the opening leg wired amount is entered as £10 million, which is the cash being invested. Therefore the nominal value of the gilt collateral required will be different, as we now require a market value of this stock of £10 million. From the screen we see that this is £9,518,769. The cash amount is different from the example in Figure 4.3 so the repo interest charged is different, and is £11,027 for the seven-day term. The diagram at Figure 4.5 illustrates the transaction details.

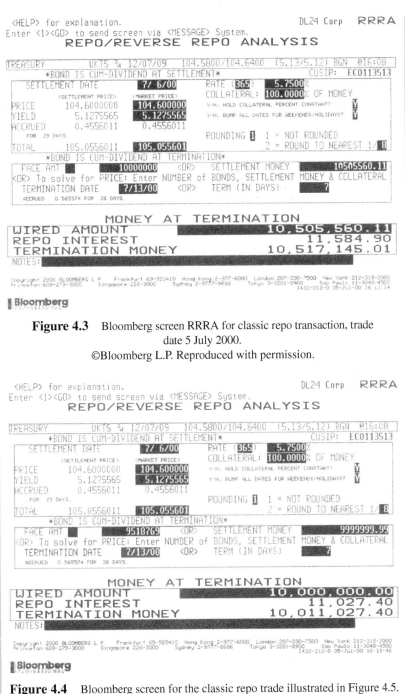

**Figure 4.3**   Bloomberg screen RRRA for classic repo transaction, trade
date 5 July 2000.
©Bloomberg L.P. Reproduced with permission.

**Figure 4.4**   Bloomberg screen for the classic repo trade illustrated in Figure 4.5.
©Bloomberg L.P. Reproduced with permission.

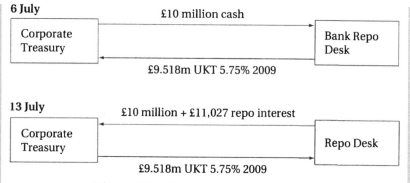

**Figure 4.5**    Corporate treasury classic repo.

## Stock-lending

### Definition

Stock-lending or *securities lending* is defined as a temporary transfer of securities in exchange for collateral. It is not a repo in the normal sense, because there is no sale or repurchase of the securities. The temporary use of the desired asset (the stock that is being borrowed), is reflected in a fixed fee payable by the party temporarily taking the desired asset. In a stock loan, the lender does not monitor interest rates during the term of the trade, but instead realizes value by receiving this fixed fee during the term of the loan. This makes administration of stock-lending transactions less onerous compared to repo transactions. The formal definition of a stock loan is a contract between two parties in which one party lends securities to another for a fixed, or *open*, term. The party that borrows must supply collateral to the stock lender, which can be other high-quality securities, cash or a letter of credit. This protects against credit risk. Fabozzi (2001) states that in the US, the most common type of collateral is cash, however, in the UK market it is quite common for other securities to be given as collateral, typically gilts. In addition, the lender charges a fixed fee, usually quoted as a basis point charge on the market value of the stock being lent, payable by the borrower on termination. The origins and history of the stock-lending market are different from that of the repo market. The range of counterparties is also different, although a large number of counterparties are involved in both markets. Most stock loans are on an "open" basis, meaning that they are confirmed (or terminated) each morning, although term loans also occur.

Institutional investors such as pension funds and insurance companies often prefer to enhance the income from their fixed interest portfolios by lending their bonds, for a fee, rather than entering into repo transactions.

| Classic Repo | Sell/Buy-back |
|---|---|
| "Sale" and repurchase | Outright sale; forward buy-back |
| Bid at repo rate: bid for stock, lend the cash (Offer at repo rate: offer the stock, take the cash) | Repo rate implicit in forward buy-back price |
| Sale and repurchase prices identical | Forward buy-back price different |
| Return to cash lender is repo interest on cash | Return to cash lender is the difference between sale price and forward buy-back price (the "repo" interest) |
| Bond coupon received during trade is returned to seller | Coupon need not be returned to bond seller until termination (albeit with compensation) |
| Standard legal agreement (BMA/ ISMA GMRA) | No standard legal agreement (but may be traded under the GMRA) |
| Initial margin may be taken | Initial margin may be taken |
| Variation margin may be called | No variation margin unless transacted under a legal agreement |
| Specific repo dealing systems required | May be transacted using existing bond and equity dealing systems |

**Table 4.2**   Summary of highlights of classic repo and sell/buy-back.

This obviates the need to set up complex settlement and administration systems, as well as the need to monitor what is, in effect, an interest rate position. An initial *margin* is given to institutional lenders of stock, usually in the form of a greater value of collateral stock than the market value of the stock being lent.

## Basic Concepts

Stock-lending transactions are the transfer of a security or basket of securities from a lending counterparty, for a temporary period, in return for a fee payable by the borrowing counterparty. During the term of the loan the stock is lent out in exchange for collateral, which may be in the form of other securities or cash. If other securities are handed over as collateral, they must be high-quality assets such as Treasuries, gilts or other highly-rated paper. Lenders are institutional investors such as pension funds, life assurance companies, local authority treasury offices and other fund managers, and loans of their portfolio holdings are often facilitated via the use of a broking agent, known as a *prime broker* or a clearing agent custodian such as Euroclear or Clearstream. In addition, banks and securities houses that require stock to cover short positions sometimes have access to their own source of stock lenders, for example, clients of their custody services.

Stock-lending is not a sale and repurchase in the conventional sense but is used by banks and securities houses to cover short positions in securities put on as part of market-making or proprietary trading activity. In some markets (for example, the Japanese equity market), regulations require a counterparty to have arranged stock-lending before putting on the short trade.

Other reasons why banks may wish to enter into stock loan (or stock-borrowing, from their viewpoint) transactions include:

- where they have effected a purchase, and then on-sold this security, and their original purchase has not settled, putting them at risk of defaulting on their sale;
- as part of *disintermediation* between the stock loan market and the repo and unsecured money market.

An institution that wishes to borrow stock must pay a fee for the term of the loan. This is usually a basis point charge on the market value of the loan, and is payable in arrears on a monthly basis. In the Eurobond market, the fee is calculated at the start of the loan, and unless there is a significant change in the market value of the stock, it will be paid at the end of the loan period. In the UK gilt market the basis point fee is calculated on a daily basis on the market value of the stock that has been lent, and so the total charge payable is not known until the loan maturity. This arrangement requires that the stock be *marked-to-market* at the end of each business day. The fee itself is agreed between the stock borrower and the stock lender at the time of each loan, but this may be a general fee payable for all loans. There may be a different fee payable for specific stocks, so in this case the fee is agreed on a trade-by-trade basis, depending on the stock being lent. Any fee is usually for the term of the loan, although it is possible in most markets to adjust the rate through negotiation at any time during the loan. The fee charged by the stock lender is a function of supply and demand for the stock in the market. A specific security that is in high demand in the market will be lent at a higher fee than one that is in lower demand. For this reason it is important for the bank's Treasury desk[7] to be aware of which stocks are in demand, and more importantly to have a reasonable idea of which stocks will be in demand in the near future. Some banks will be in possession of better *market intelligence* than others. If excessive demand is anticipated, a prospective short seller may borrow stock in advance of entering into the short sale.

The term of a stock loan can be fixed, in which case it is known as a *term loan*, or it can be open. A term loan is economically similar to a classic repo transaction. An open loan is just that—there is no fixed maturity term, and the borrower will confirm on the telephone at the start of each day whether it wishes to continue with the loan or will be returning the security.

---

[7] Or whichever desk is responsible for covering short positions by borrowing or reverse repoing stock.

As in a classic repo transaction, coupon or dividend payments that become payable on a security or bond during the term of the loan will be to the benefit of the stock lender. In the standard stock loan legal agreement, known as the OSLA agreement,[8] there is no change of beneficial ownership when a security is on loan. The usual arrangement when a coupon is payable is that the payment is automatically returned to the stock lender via its settlement system. Such a coupon payment is known as a *manufactured dividend*.

Clients of prime brokers and custodians will inform their agent if they wish their asset holdings to be used for stock-lending purposes. At this point a stock-lending agreement is set up between the holder of the securities and the prime broker or custodian. Borrowers of stock are also required to set up an agreement with brokers and custodians. The return to the broker or custodian is the difference between the fee paid by the stock borrower and that paid to the stock lender. Banks that have their own internal lending lines can access this stock at a lower borrowing rate. If they wish to pursue this source they will set up a stock-lending agreement with institutional investors directly.

## Example of Stock Loan

Let us now illustrate a stock loan where the transaction is "stock-driven". Assume that a securities house has a requirement to borrow a UK gilt, the 5.75% 2009, for a one-week period. This is the stock from our earlier classic repo and sell/buy-back examples. We presume the requirement is to cover a short position in the stock, although there are other reasons why the securities house may wish to borrow the stock. The bond that it is offering as collateral is another gilt, the 6.50% Treasury 2003. The stock lender, who we assume is an institutional investor, such as a pension fund, another securities house or a bank, requires a margin of 5% as well as a fee of 20 basis points. The transaction is summarised in Table 4.3.

Note that in reality, in the gilt market the stock loan fee (here quoted as 20 bps) is calculated on the daily mark-to-market stock price, automatically within the gilt settlement mechanism known as CREST–CGO, so the final charge is not known until termination. Within the Eurobond market, for example in Clearstream, the fee on the initial loan value is taken, and adjustments are made only in the case of large movements in stock price.

There is no specialist screen for stock loan transactions on Bloomberg, but it is sometimes useful to use the RRRA screen for calculations and analysis, for example Figure 4.12 shows this screen being used to calculate the nominal amount of collateral required for the loan of £10 million nominal of the 5.75% 2009 gilt shown in Table 4.3. The margin-adjusted market value of the collateral is £11,030,838, and if this is entered into the

---

[8] After the trade association overseeing the stock loan market.

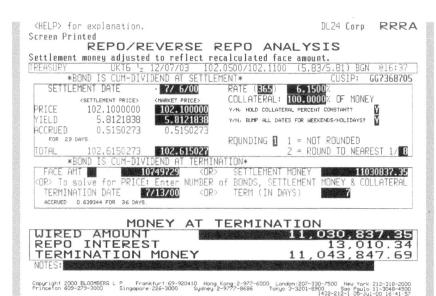

**Figure 4.12**    Bloomberg screen used to calculate nominal value of collateral
required in a stock loan transaction.
©Bloomberg L.P. Used with permission.

| | |
|---|---|
| Value date | 6 July 2000 |
| Termination date | 13 July 2000 |
| Stock borrowed | 5.75% 2009 |
| Nominal borrowed | £10 million |
| Term | 1 week |
| Loan value | £10,505,560.11 |
| Collateral | 6.50% 2003 |
| Clean price | 102.1 |
| Accrued interest (29 days) | 0.5150273 |
| Dirty price | 102.615027 |
| Margin required | 5% |
| Market value of collateral required = 10, 505, 560 × 1.05 | £11,030,837.35 |
| Nominal value of collateral | £10,749,729 |
| Stock loan fee (20 bps) | £402.95 |

**Table 4.3**    Stock loan transaction.

"wired amount" field on the screen, with the current price of the stock, we see that it shows a required nominal of £10,749,729 of the 6.50% 2003 gilt.

# Margin

To reduce the level of exposure in a repo transaction, it is common for the lender of cash to demand a margin, which is where the market value of collateral is higher than the cash value of cash lent in the repo. This is a form of protection should the cash-borrowing counterparty default on the loan. Another term for margin is *over-collateralisation* or *haircut*. There are two types of margin—an *initial margin* taken at the start of the trade, and *variation margin*, which is called if required during the term of the trade.

## Initial Margin

The cash proceeds in a repo are typically no more than the market value of the collateral. This minimises credit exposure by equating the value of the cash to that of the collateral. The market value of the collateral is calculated at its *dirty* price, not clean price—that is, including accrued interest. This is referred to as *accrual pricing*. To calculate the accrued interest on the (bond) collateral, we require the day-count basis for the particular bond.

The start proceeds of a repo can be less than the market value of the collateral by an agreed amount or percentage. This is known as the *initial margin* or *haircut*. The initial margin protects the buyer against:

- a sudden fall in the market value of the collateral;
- illiquidity of collateral;
- other sources of volatility of value (for example, approaching maturity);
- counterparty risk.

The margin level of repo varies from 0–2% for collateral such as UK gilts or German Bunds, to 5% for cross-currency and equity repo, to 10–35% for emerging market debt repo.

In both classic repo and sell/buy-back, any initial margin is given to the supplier of cash in the transaction. This remains true in the case of specific repo. For the initial margin, the market value of the bond collateral is reduced (or given a "*haircut*") by the percentage of the initial margin and the nominal value determined from this reduced amount. In a stock loan transaction the lender of stock will ask for the margin.

There are two methods for calculating the margin; for a 2% margin this could be one of the following:

- (dirty price of the bonds) × 0.98
- ((dirty price of the bonds)/1.02)

The two methods do not give the same value. The RRRA repo page on Bloomberg uses the second method for its calculations and this method is increasingly the market convention.

For a 2% margin level the BMA/ISMA GMRA defines a "margin ratio" as:

$$\frac{\text{collateral value}}{\text{cash}} = 102\%$$

The size of the margin required in any particular transaction is a function of the following:

- the credit quality of the counterparty supplying the collateral; for example, a central bank, interbank and corporate counterparty will all suggest different margin levels;
- the term of the repo; an overnight repo is inherently lower risk than a one-year repo;
- the duration (price volatility) of the collateral; for example, a T-bill compared to the long bond;
- the existence or absence of a legal agreement; repo traded under a standard agreement is considered lower risk.

Certain market practitioners, particularly those that work on bond research desks, believe that the level of margin is a function of the volatility of the collateral stock. This may be either, say, one-year historical volatility or the implied volatility given by option prices. For example, given a volatility level of 10%, suggesting a maximum expected price movement of −10% to +10%, the margin level may be set at, say, 5% to cover expected movements in the market value of the collateral. This approach to setting the initial margin is regarded as onerous by most repo traders, given the differing volatility levels of stocks within GC bands. The counterparty credit risk and terms of trade remain the most influential elements in setting the margin, followed by the quality of collateral.

In the final analysis, the margin is required to guard against market risk — the risk that the value of collateral will decrease during the course of the repo. Therefore the margin call must reflect the risks prevalent in the market at the time, therefore extremely volatile market conditions may call for large increases in the initial margin.

## Variation Margin

The market value of the collateral is maintained through the use of the *variation margin*. So if the market value of the collateral falls, the buyer calls for extra cash or collateral. If the market value of the collateral rises, the seller calls for extra cash or collateral. In order to reduce the administrative burden, margin calls can be limited to changes in the market value of the collateral in excess of an agreed amount or percentage, which is called a *margin maintenance limit.*

The standard market documentation that exists for the three structures covered so far includes clauses that allow parties to a transaction to call for a variation margin during the term of a repo. This can be in the form of extra collateral (if the value of the collateral has decreased in relation to the asset exchanged) or a return of collateral, if the value has increased. If the cash-borrowing counterparty is unable to supply more collateral where required, they will have to return a portion of the cash loan. Both parties have an interest in making and meeting margin calls, although there is no obligation. The level at which the variation margin is triggered is often agreed before-hand in the legal agreement put in place between individual counterparties. Although primarily viewed as an instrument used by the supplier of cash against a fall in the value of the collateral, a variation margin can also be called by the repo seller if the value of the collateral has risen in value.

An illustration of a variation margin being applied during the term of a trade is given in Example 4.4.

---

**EXAMPLE 4.4**    **Variation margin**

- Figure 4.20 shows a 60-day repo in the 5% Treasury 2004, a UK gilt where a margin of 2% is taken. The repo rate is 5.5%. The start of the trade is 5 January 2000. The clean price of the gilt is 95.25.

| | |
|---|---|
| Nominal amount | 1,000,000 |
| Principal | £952,500.00 |
| Accrued interest (29 days) | £3961.75 |
| **Total consideration  £956,461.75** | |

The consideration is divided by 1.02, the amount of the margin, to give £937,707.60. Assume that this is rounded up to the nearest pound.

| | |
|---|---|
| Loan amount | £937,708.00 |
| Repo interest at 5½% | £8477.91 |
| **Termination proceeds** | **£946,185.91** |

Assume that one month later there has been a severe downturn in the bond market and the 5% 2004 gilt is trading down at 92.75. Following this downturn, the market value of the collateral is now:

| | |
|---|---|
| Principal | £927,500 |
| Accrued interest (59 days) | £8082.19 |
| **Market value £935,582.19** | |

However, the repo desk has lent £937,708 against this security, which exceeds its market value. Under a variation margin arrangement, it can call a margin from the counterparty in the form of general collateral securities or cash.

The formula used to calculate the amount required to restore the original margin of 2% is given by:

$$\text{Margin adjustment} = \big((\text{original consideration} + \text{repo interest charged to date})$$
$$\times (1 + \text{initial margin})\big)$$
$$- (\text{new all - in price} \times \text{nominal amount})$$

This therefore becomes:

$$\big((937,708 + 4238.96) \times (1 + 0.02)\big) - (0.93558219 \times 1,000,000) = £25,203.71.$$

The margin requirement can be taken as additional stock or cash. In practice, margin calls are made on what is known as a portfolio basis, based on the net position resulting from all repo and reverse repo transactions in place between the two counterparties, so that a margin delivery may be made in a general collateral stock rather than more of the original repo stock. The diagrams below show the relevant cash flows at the various dates.

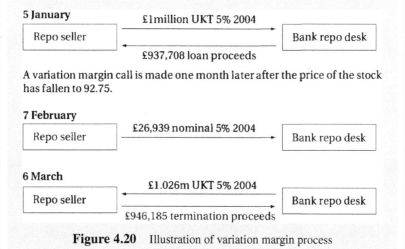

**5 January**    £1million UKT 5% 2004

| Repo seller | | Bank repo desk |

£937,708 loan proceeds

A variation margin call is made one month later after the price of the stock has fallen to 92.75.

**7 February**    £26,939 nominal 5% 2004

| Repo seller | | Bank repo desk |

**6 March**    £1.026m UKT 5% 2004

| Repo seller | | Bank repo desk |

£946,185 termination proceeds

**Figure 4.20**    Illustration of variation margin process

Reproduced from *The Global Repo Markets* (2004)

## AN INTRODUCTION TO FINANCIAL MARKET PRODUCTS

There is almost, but not quite, infinite variety in financial market products. But more than the 80–20 rule, in finance it is more like the 95–5 rule, whereby 95% of the customer needs of the global financial marketplace can be met with 5% of its product types. We summarise the main "cash" products in Table 1.1. We'll cover derivative instruments and structured finance products in subsequent chapters.

**TABLE 1.1**  "Cash" Products

| Retail products | Corporate banking products | Wholesale banking products |
| --- | --- | --- |
| **Assets** | | |
| Personal loan (unsecured, fixed- or floating-rate) | Corporate loan, unsecured, secured | Money market (CD / CP) |
| Personal loan (secured, fixed- or floating-rate) | Corporate loan, fixed- or floating-rate | Fixed income securities |
| Personal loan, bullet or amortising | Corporate loan, bullet or amortising | Equity market-making |
| Residential mortgage | Commercial mortgage | |
| Credit card | Credit card | |
| Overdraft | Overdraft | |
| Foreign exchange (spot) | Liquidity line, revolving credit, etc. | |
| | Trade Finance (Letter of Credit, Trade Bill, Guarantee, etc.) | |
| | Invoice Discounting, Factoring | |
| | Foreign exchange (spot and forward) | |
| **Liabilities** | | |
| Current account | Current account | Structured products (MTNs, etc.) |
| Deposit account | Deposit account | Structured deposit |
| Notice and Fixed-Term, Fixed-Rate Deposit accounts | Call account | |
| Call account | Structured deposit | |

## Commercial Bank Products

Banking is a commoditised product (or service). Most financial products are essentially of long standing and all of them nothing more (or less) than a series of cash flows. Thus to a great extent most of the main products can be obtained (provided the specific customer is acceptable to the bank in question) from most banks. They are summarised in Table 1.1.

Note that "products" does not mean "customer interface". Hence a mobile banking app for use on Apple or Android is not a "product". "Contactless" is not a product, although we would suggest that Credit Cards *are* a product because they are a specific form of bank loan.

From an accounting perspective, the essential distinction to make is whether the product is "on" or "off" balance sheet (or "cash" or "derivative"). However off-balance sheet products, a term still in common use to describe derivative instruments, are still a package of cash flows. From an asset–liability management (ALM) perspective the distinction between cash and derivative is something of a red herring, because both products give rise to balance sheet risk issues. The ALM practitioner is concerned with cash impact on both sides of the balance sheet, so making a distinction between on- and off-balance-sheet is to miss the point.

In the ALM discipline, cash and its impact on the balance sheet are everything. So it is important to have an intimate understanding of the cash flow behaviour of every product that the bank deals in. This may seem like a statement of the obvious, but there is no shortage of senior (and not so senior) bankers who are unfamiliar with the product characteristics of some of the instruments on their balance sheet. When we say "understanding" we mean:

- The product's contractual cash flows, their pattern and timing;
- The cash flows' sensitivity (if any) to changes in external and/or relevant market parameters such as interest rates, FX rates, inflation, credit rating, and so on;
- The cash flows' sensitivity to customer behaviour;
- The cash flows' sensitivity to factors impacting the bank itself.

Without this understanding it is not possible to undertake effective NIM management, let alone effective ALM.

**This extract from *The Principles of Banking* (2012)**

**Loan Valuation**

# Loan Valuation

This section may seem obvious to many readers, as well as very basic, but one would be surprised how often its main tenets are not followed in corporate and commercial bank loan origination desks. So think of this as a refresher course.

The concept of shareholder value-added arises the instant one sets a target RoE at the strategy level. Holding all else equal, the bank shareholder will not continue to hold shares in the bank unless its target return is met. This target therefore drives strategy. All business undertaken by the bank must meet this target, otherwise it is not creating value. Thus the target RoE, together with the other variables introduced in the previous section, drives loan pricing. This is shown in the simple illustration at Example 1.1. Economic value-added, with respect to the capital employed, must be the guiding principle of all bank business.[11] In other words, the business must generate a return that exceeds the target RoE. If it does not, then it is creating zero value, which means the shareholder would not rationally embark upon it.

---

**EXAMPLE 1.1**    **LOAN PRICING ILLUSTRATION**

| Asset | | Liability | |
|---|---|---|---|
| Loan | 100 | Deposit | 90 |
| | | Equity | 10 |

The equity base of the bank is exclusively Tier 1 (equity and retained profits)

*Assumptions*

| | |
|---|---|
| Loan maturity = | 1 year |
| The customer deposit pay rate = | 5% |
| The target RoE = | 10% |
| The corporate tax rate = | 20% |
| Loan interest rate = | X% |

---

[11] Beware of arguments advanced along the lines of "in the real world, it is not as simple as that". Thus we observe "loss leader" products, we observe loss-making overseas subsidiaries being maintained because the bank's competitors are based there, we observe loss-making businesses retained for a tax write-off advantage. We observe a myriad of businesses being maintained in existence that, far from creating value, actively destroy it. Ultimately, this is all complete nonsense. Any business line that destroys value must be discontinued. It really is as simple as that.

The main principle is that the business, in this case the loan, must create value that exceeds the RoE target of equity invested.

We set the following relationship, which equates the capital employed with the after-tax discounted cash flow of the business:

$$10 = [(1 - 20\%) * ((X*100) - (5\% *90))] + 100 - 90/1.10$$

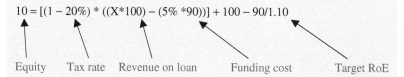

Equity    Tax rate    Revenue on loan    Funding cost    Target RoE

Rearranging for X we obtain an interest rate of 5.75%. The interpretation of this is as follows: by setting an interest rate of 5.75%, the present value of the revenue earned on the loan, after tax, is equal to 10, which is the capital set aside for the loan.

Therefore the loan interest rate must be set above 5.75%. At this rate or below, there is zero value creation.

Note that the break-even loan rate of 5.75% is 75 bps (basis points) above the funding rate of 5%. This is the break-even margin.

Following naturally from this illustration in Example 1.1, we see that a bank should calculate the break-even interest rate charge on business as a function of its funding rate, the break-even margin, as well as its RoE and the corporate tax rate. This is of course a very simple example that ignores all other operating costs, but these additional expenses can be incorporated in the analysis easily enough.

Note that the break-even margin is what is required to create shareholder value. For business lines that do not require any capital, for example AAA-rated government bonds, the margin can be lower. In our simple example, the loan is backed with the full capital base. In reality, the amount of capital required will depend on the "risk weighting" of the asset (loan). But the essential principle remains the same.

Let us now make the illustration more like the real world (see Example 1.2).

**EXAMPLE 1.2**    **LOAN PRICING INCORPORATING DEFAULT RISK**

| Asset | | Liability | |
|---|---|---|---|
| Loan | 100 | Deposit | 90 |
| | | Equity | 10 |

The equity base of the bank is exclusively Tier 1 (equity and retained profits)

### Assumptions

| | |
|---|---|
| Loan maturity = | 2 years (annual interest) |
| Customer deposit pay rate = | 5% (fixed for two years) |
| Target RoE = | 10% |
| Corporate tax rate = | 20% |
| Loan default probability (Year 1) = | 0% |
| Loan default probability (Year 2) = | 5% |
| Recovery rate = | 40% |
| Loan interest rate = | X% |

The same principle is applied again, whereby the break-even loan rate of X% must be set such that the present value of the expected cash flow of the loan, after tax, equates the value of the equity used to back the loan. Thus we have:

$$10 = [(X*100) - (90 *5\%)] * (1 - 0.2) / 1.10 \longleftarrow \text{Year 1 cash flow present value (zero default probability)}$$

plus $\qquad$ Year 2 cash flow present value (incorporates default probability)

$$95\% * [(1 - 0.2) * X*100 + 100] + 5\% * [40 + (0.2 * 60)] / 1.10^2$$

Allowing for no default (95% probability)  Allowing for default (5% probability)

minus

$$90 * 5\% * (1 - 0.2) + 90 / 1.10^2 \longleftarrow \text{Year 2 funding cost}$$

Rearranging for X we obtain an interest rate of 7.72%. This is the break-even loan rate that must be applied to the loan.

In this example, we allow for the possibility of default by the borrower in Year 2 of the two-year loan. There are now two parameters to allow for in addition to the equity backing the loan, and these are the default probability of the loan and the amount of recovery in the event of default (called the "recovery rate", in the manner of the credit derivative market). Should default occur, the bank will recover 40 cents on the dollar. We also allow for a tax recovery on the amount that is lost in the event of default, which is the tax rate of 20% multiplied by the loss amount of 60 cents on the dollar.

We see then that in setting the loan rate at a level that creates value, we need to adjust the expected cash flows for the possibility of customer default, and the amount we expect to recover should there be a default. From this point on, we have introduced an element of subjectivity in the calculation: the recovery rate is an *assumed* value (we have no firm idea what we will recover in the event of a customer going into bankruptcy) and the default probability of any customer can never be known with certainty, although one can infer it from observing the prices of loans and bonds in the market.[12] But one can see how once one enters the real world, pricing loans to create shareholder value and allow for credit risk becomes as much an art as a science.

This example also highlights the issue of setting aside part of each year's profit to cover for future loan defaults. This is known as loan provisioning; it is the method by which a proportion of bank capital is earmarked as a buffer to enable the bank to withstand losses arising from customer default in the future. In this process, part of the profit generated by the loan at the end of Year 1, which is essentially the interest income minus the funding cost and expenses, after tax, is not recorded as profit but is instead set aside as a loan loss provision for the following year. In other words, loan provisions reduce the after-tax profit of the business.

What should the amount of loss provision be? The calculation of this amount again uses the default probability and recovery rate parameters (which may have changed from the time the loan was originated). We illustrate this in Example 1.3.

---

**EXAMPLE 1.3** **LOAN LOSS PROVISION**

**Net loan value:**

$$0.95*\left[100+\left(11.1\right)*\left(1-0.2\right)\right]+0.05*\left[40+\left(0.2*60\right)\right]/1.10$$

minus

$$\left[90*0.05*\left(1-0.2\right)\right)+90\right]/1.10$$

=

9.305

---

[12] See pages 815–18 of the author's book *Bank Asset and Liability Management* (John Wiley & Sons, 2007) for a detailed look from first principles on how to extract default probabilities from bond market prices.

**Interest margin after tax:**

$$(1-0.2)*\left[\left(11.1\%*100\right)-\left(5\%*90\right)\right]$$
$$= 5.28$$

**Attributable profit**

$$= 5.28 - 0.695$$
$$= 4.585$$

We see that the net loan value is now 9.305. At loan origination the loan value was 10, so the loan has fallen in value by [10 − 9.305] or 0.695.

The fall in the net value of the loan at the end of the year is used to calculate the amount of interest income from it that can be attributed as profit, and what should be set aside as a loan provision. This is given as:

Attributable profit = Post − tax interest margin − fall in loan value.

This is shown in the second half of Example 1.3. The balance of the interest income not assigned to attributable profit is set aside as a credit provision.

We see then that to arrive at a sensible lending rate for any type of business that it undertakes, a bank must have a good idea of its cost base as well as a good idea of what the expected frequency of bad loans will be in the following 12 months. It also needs to have a target RoE to aim for. The interest rate on a loan is then set as a spread over the bank's funding cost, being calculated as a function of the target RoE, a credit spread to cover anticipated loan losses, and any additional spread to cover its operating expenses.

The above may be obvious, but one would be surprised just how many banks do not observe this very basic principle.

Reproduced from *The Principles of Banking* (2012)

## BANK STRUCTURES AND BUSINESS MODELS

### The Role of Banking Institutions in the Global Economy

Although different countries will exhibit different levels of development and sophistication in their individual banking sectors, ultimately all jurisdictions will desire a well-developed banking system, such that their banks are well-managed with fit-for-purpose risk management systems and good corporate governance. This is because banks play an important role in every economy.

**As Agents of Liquidity**    Banks play a vital role in providing liquidity to the financial system. Their deposit-taking activities allow them to on-lend these funds to institutions and individuals, in order to provide liquidity to market operations. Financial intermediaries offer the ability to transform assets into money at relatively low cost. By collecting funds from a large number of small investors, a bank can reduce the cost of their combined investment, offering the individual investor both liquidity and rates of return. Financial intermediaries enable us to diversify our investments and reduce risk. As a last resort in exceptional circumstances, banks also may have access to funding from the country's central bank or "reserve bank".

**To Facilitate Investment by Firms and to Enable Growth and Job Creation**    Banking institutions play the role of financial intermediaries. These are business entities that bring together providers and users of capital. Banks can act as either agents acting on behalf of clients or they can act as principals conducting financial transactions for their own account. Financial intermediaries develop the facilities and financial instruments which make lending and borrowing possible. They provide the means by which funds can be transferred from surplus units (for example, someone with savings to invest in the economy) to deficit units (for example, someone who wants to borrow money to buy a house).

If lending and borrowing or other financial transactions between unrelated parties takes place without financial intermediation, they are said to be dealing directly.

Banks also provide capital, technical assistance and other facilities which promote trade. They finance agricultural and industrial development and help increase the rate of capital formation. They increase a country's production capabilities by strengthening capital investment.

**To Facilitate Local and International Trade**    Banks make possible the reliable transfer of funds and the transmission of business practices between different countries and different customs all over the world. The global nature of banking also makes possible the distribution of valuable economic and business information among customers and capital markets of all countries. Banking also serves as a worldwide barometer of economic health and business trends. Banks help traders from different countries undertake business opportunities by arranging cross-border facilities and foreign exchange.

## Types of Banks

Banks come in different shapes, sizes, and types. At one end of the spectrum are small specialist or "niche" banks, while at the other end are the global cross-border banks. Generally, a vanilla bank that offers deposit and loan products to firms and individuals would be a "commercial bank". We summarise here the different types of institutions.

**Traditional Deposit Taking Banks** Traditional deposit taking banks are also known as commercial banks or retail banks. Commercial banks provide services such as accepting deposits, providing loans, mortgage lending, and basic investment products like savings accounts and certificates of deposit. Commercial banks are usually public limited companies that are regulated, listed on major stock exchanges, and owned by their shareholders. They may work alongside an associated investment bank in the banking group that can, and will, use the assets (depositors' savings) from the commercial (retail) bank.

**Wholesale Funding Operations** Wholesale banking involves providing banking services to other banks, medium and large corporate clients, fund managers, and other non-bank financial institutions. Individual loans and deposits are generally much larger in wholesale than in retail banking. Often banks will fund their wholesale or retail lending by borrowing in financial markets themselves. For a traditional bank, most of its assets will consist of loans and financial securities, such as shares and bonds. These are funded by liabilities, which are mainly customer deposits in most cases, but can also be wholesale funding.

Banks that provide money market services to other banks are known as "clearing" banks or "money centre" banks.

**Investment Banking** "Investment banking" is the term used to refer to financial market activities such as debt raising and equity financing for corporations, other banks, or governments. This includes originating the securities, underwriting them, and then placing them with investors. In a normal arrangement, a company seeks out an investment bank provider, proposing that it wants to raise a given amount of financing in the form of debt, equity, or hybrid instruments, such as convertible bonds. The bank acts as underwriter for the securities, which are originated to investors along with legal documentation describing the rights of the security holders.

Besides helping companies with new issues of securities, investment banking also involves offering advice to companies on mergers, acquisitions, divestitures, corporate restructurings, and so on. The service also may include assistance in finding merger partners and takeover targets, and also aiding companies in finding buyers for units or subsidiaries which they wish to divest. They also advise a corporation's management which is itself a target for merger or takeover.

Note that what we describe above is not "banking" as such, as it does not involve the bank itself lending money or taking deposits.

**Community Banks**    The broad definition of community banks encompasses membership-based, decentralised, and self-help financial institutions. Under this definition fall several variants, such as credit unions and building societies.

**Development Banks**    Development banks are, generically speaking, alternative financial institutions including microfinance institutions, community development institutions, and revolving loan funds. These entities fill a critical role in providing credit through higher risk loans, equity stakes and risk guarantee instruments to private sector initiatives in developing countries. Typically they are supported by states with developed economies. They provide finance to the private sector for investment to promote development and to aid companies in investing, particularly in nations with various market restrictions.

Examples of development banks include the Asian Development Bank and the Islamic Development Bank. The African Development Bank (AfDB) is a regional multilateral development bank that finances development projects in Africa. Financing mainly takes the form of loans to or guaranteed by sovereign institutions, the rest being loans to the private sector and equity participations.

**Reserve Bank**    The role of the central or reserve bank, which is the government bank of the country, is to achieve and maintain price stability in the interests of balanced and sustainable economic growth. Along with other institutions (the public and private sectors) it plays a critical part in helping to ensure financial stability in the country. For example, the Bank of England (BoE) and the South African Reserve Bank (SARB) carry out these missions in their respective countries through the formulation and implementation of inflation targeting and monetary policy. They issue banknotes and coinage, supervise the domestic banking system, and ensure the effective functioning of the national payments system. Their remit extends to managing the official gold and foreign exchange reserves, and they act as banker to the government.

A critical role of the central bank in many countries is as the country's banking supervisory authority, responsible for bank regulation and supervision. The purpose is to achieve a sound, efficient banking system in the interest of the depositors of banks and the economy as a whole. In order to achieve this purpose, a central bank monitors different functions within the banks themselves to help ensure they are run in a sustainable manner. Some of these checks extend to the regular monitoring of the capital requirements of the bank (based on the "Basel" requirements as well as the Internal Capital Adequacy Assessment Process (ICAAP) models), scrutinising of the models used in formulating the risk parameters used within the capital calculations, periodically performing end-to-end product level reviews (or reviewing processes within the banks), and performing periodic regulatory checks within the banks to ensure regulatory and prudential compliance.

## Activities Carried Out by Banks

**Retail Banking Activities** Retail banks offer investment and loan products to customers. On the investment side, there are a number of deposit account varieties provided, which could be long-term savings accounts (for example, fixed deposits) or current accounts with checking facilities. Money market accounts are another type of short-term investment account. Portfolio cash accounts earn a return from a portfolio of cash and money market investments.

**Corporate Banking Activities** Today's large banks operate on a global basis and transact business in many different sectors. They are still occupied with the traditional commercial banking activities of taking deposits, making loans, and clearing cheques (both domestically and internationally). They also offer retail customers credit cards, telephone banking, internet banking, and automatic teller machines (ATMs), and provide payroll services to businesses.

Large banks also offer lines of credit to businesses and individual customers. They provide a variety of services to companies exporting goods and services. Companies can enter into a range of contracts with banks which are designed to hedge the risks, relating to foreign exchange, commodity prices, interest rates, and other market variables, they may confront.

Larger banks may conduct research on securities and offer recommendations on individual stocks. They offer brokerage services, as well as trust services where they are willing to manage portfolios of assets for clients. They possess economics departments that consider macroeconomic trends and actions likely to be taken by central banks. These departments deliver forecasts on interest rates, exchange rates, commodity prices, inflation rates, and other variables. Large banks also offer a slate of mutual funds and in some cases have their own hedge funds. Increasingly they also offer insurance products (for example, life insurance).

**Investment Banking Activities**   Valuation, strategy, and tactics pursued represent fundamental aspects of the advisory services offered by investment banks. Banks, and particularly investment banks, often are involved in securities trading, providing brokerage services, and making markets in individual securities. In so doing, they enter into competition with smaller securities firms that are not in a position to offer other banking services.

Brokers intermediate in the trading of securities by taking orders from clients and arranging for them to be fulfilled on an exchange. Some brokers have a national presence, while others may serve only a particular region. So-called full-service brokers typically offer investment research and advice. Discount brokers, on the other hand, charge lower commissions, and provide no advice. Frequently, online services are offered. Some, like E-trade, make available a platform for customers to trade without a broker.

Market-making involves the quotation of a bid price (the price at which you are prepared to buy) and an offer price (the price at which you are willing to sell). When consulted for a price, a market-maker also quotes both bid and offer without knowing whether the person asking for the price wishes to buy or sell. Market-makers make a profit from the spread between bid and offer, but bear the risk that they will be left with an exposure that is unacceptably high.

Trading is very closely related to market-making. Many large investment and even commercial banks undertake extensive trading activities. Their counterparties are typically other banks, corporations, and fund managers. Banks trade for three primary reasons:

- To meet the needs of counterparties. A bank may sell a currency option to a corporate client to aid in reducing foreign exchange risk, or purchase a credit derivative from a hedge fund to help in following a trading strategy;
- To lower its own risks;
- To take a speculative position in the hope of making a profit. This activity is referred to as trading for its own account or proprietary ("prop") trading.

Trading activity undertaken by banks is regulated under a different set of regulatory and accounting rules to banking activity.

## Financial Statements

**Bank Income Statement and Components**   The majority of a commercial bank's revenues will come from net interest income, representing the positive spread between the gross interest earned on loans and securities, less the cost of funding those loans. Other revenue line items in a bank's income statement will include net fees and commissions, and trading profits. There may also be income from insurance activities and other operating income. This results in a level of pre-impairment operating income. Each year a certain amount of loan impairment charges will be subtracted from this level, depending on credit loss experience, to result in an operating profit or loss, which is then adjusted for non-recurring and non-operating income and expenses. The resultant pre-tax income has income tax deducted from it, as well as any income from discontinued operations. The bottom line is thus the overall net income of the bank. An example of a typical income statement for a bank (a simplified version) is shown at Figure 1.4.

**Bank Balance Sheet and Components**   By far the majority of a typical bank's assets will be its loan book, which can be subdivided into residential mortgage loans, vehicle asset finance, other consumer loans (unsecured loans, credit cards, overdrafts), and corporate and commercial loans. This gross loan book, or bank book, has a loan loss reserve set against it to cover expected loan losses based on the experience of nonperforming loans (NPLs) historically. Other earning assets will include loans and advances to other

| | | Rm | Rm |
|---|---|---|---|
| Net Interest Income | | | 14495 |
| | Gross Interest Income | 21050 | |
| | Less Cost of Funding | −6205 | |
| | Less ISP (Interest Suspended on NPL's) | −350 | |
| Impairments | | | −2256 |
| (Bad Debt Charge) | | | |
| | Write-offs | −2105 | |
| | Net Provision Adjustments | −451 | |
| | Post Write-off Recoveries | 300 | |
| Income from Lending | | | 12239 |
| Activities | | | |
| Non-Interest Revenue | | | 6540 |
| | Credit Life Insurance Income | 2010 | |
| | Fee Income (Initiation, Admin Fees) | 4530 | |
| Total Operating Expenses | | | −11712 |
| VAT | | | −300 |
| Profit Before Tax (PBT) | | | 6767 |
| Direct Taxation | | | −1628 |
| Profit After Tax | | | 5139 |

**FIGURE 1.4**   Typical income statement for a simple bank.

banks, trading securities, and derivatives (the trading book), as well as securities, debt, equity, or related, intended to be held to maturity.

Besides these earning assets, banks will possess non-earning assets such as cash and amounts due from banks, fixed assets and goodwill, or other intangibles.

These assets are balanced by liabilities and equity. For commercial banks, the major liability is customer deposits, and there will also be deposits and cash-collateralised instruments from other banks. Many banks also have short- and long-term debt issued in the wholesale markets for funding purposes. Also reflected will be liabilities associated with derivatives and the trading book. While the above are interest-bearing liabilities, there may also be non-interest bearing liabilities such as tax or insurance liabilities.

On the equity side, in addition to common equity, banks may also have hybrid capital, which possesses features of both debt and equity, and typically qualifies for some regulatory recognition as core capital.

**Accounting for Impairments**　The major impairment a lending bank would typically encounter is that of loan losses, as discussed above. This requires loan loss reserves to be set aside to absorb the expected losses (exactly how this "expectation" is defined will depend on the accounting principles in place in the country in question). In addition, impairments on the value of securities held can also occur in the daily marking-to-market process. Fair value accounting is discussed in the following section.

**Fair Value Accounting**　Accountants refer to marking-to-market as "fair value accounting". As explained above, a financial institution is required to mark-to-market its trading book on a daily basis. This means it has to estimate a value for each financial instrument in its trading portfolio and then calculate the total value of the portfolio. The valuations are used in value-at-risk calculations to determine capital requirements, and by accountants to calculate financial statements.

A number of different approaches are used to calculate the mark-to-market price of an asset:

- When there are market-makers for an asset, or an asset is traded on an exchange, the price of the asset can be based on the most recent quotes.
- When the financial institution itself has traded the asset in the last day, the price of the asset can be based on the price it paid or received.
- When interdealer brokers provide information on the prices at which the asset has been traded by other financial institutions in the over-the-counter market, the financial institution can base the price of the asset on this information.

- When interdealer brokers provide price indications (not the prices of actual trades), the financial institution will (in the absence of anything better) base its prices on this information.
- For exotic deals and structured products, the price is usually based on a model developed by the financial institution. Using a model instead of a market price for daily marking-to-market is sometimes called marking-to-model.

The fair value accounting rules of the International Accounting Standards Board (IASB) require banks to classify instruments as "held for sale" or "held to maturity". Those "held to maturity" are in the banking book and their values are not changed unless they become impaired. Those "held for sale" are in the trading book and must be marked-to-market. Three types of valuation are reported for instruments "held for sale". Level 1 instruments are those for which there are quoted prices in active markets. Level 2 instruments are those for which there are quoted prices for similar assets in active markets, or quoted prices for the same assets in markets that are not active. Level 3 instruments require some valuation assumptions by the bank.

## Types of Capital Held by Banks

Central bank regulators require banks to hold enough capital for the risks that they are bearing. In 1987, international standards were developed to determine this capital, which have evolved since then. The Basel rules assign capital for three types of risk: credit risk, market risk, and operational risk. The total required capital is the capital for credit risk along with the capital for market risk and the capital for operational risk.

We discuss bank regulatory capital in Chapter 8.

## Sources of Funds Used to Fund Operations

**Deposit Taking**   The major funding source for most lending banks is deposits made by retail and corporate customers. For banks, this is seen as a low-cost and relatively reliable source. The arrangement also tends to be low risk for the depositors, given the existence of deposit insurance in most major bank markets. To maintain public confidence in banks, government regulators in many nations have introduced guarantee programmes, which typically insure depositors against losses up to a certain level. After the 1929 US stock market crash, the US government created the Federal Deposit Insurance Company to protect depositors. Banks pay a premium that is a percentage of their domestic deposits and upon failure of a bank, the insurance pays out claims to the depositors that lost funds as a result of the bank failure. In the UK, deposit insurance covers up to £85,000 per depositor.

In countries where deposit insurance has not been implemented by the regulators, it is up to the banks themselves to ensure that they are capitalised to sufficiently reduce the risk of failure.

**Wholesale Markets Funding**   Wholesale funding is a method that banks use in addition to core demand deposits to finance operations and manage risk. Wholesale funding sources include, but are not limited to, reserve bank funds, public funds (such as state and local governments), foreign deposits, and borrowing from institutional investors. While core deposits remain a key liability funding source, some depository institutions experience difficulty attracting core deposits and increasingly look to wholesale funding to meet loan funding and liquidity management needs.

Wholesale funding providers are generally sensitive to changes in the credit risk profile of the banks to which these funds are provided and to the interest rate environment. For example, such providers closely track the institution's financial condition and are likely to cut back such funding if other investment opportunities offer more attractive interest rates. As a consequence, an institution may experience liquidity problems due to lack of wholesale funding availability when needed. The wide use of short-term wholesale funding was one of the contributors to many banks' vulnerability during the 2007–2010 financial crisis.

**Central Bank Funding**   Many central banks use a classical cash reserve system as the framework for their monetary policy implementation. An appropriate liquidity requirement is created by levying a cash reserve requirement on banks in the country. The primary refinancing operation is a weekly 7-day repurchase (repo) auction, which is conducted with commercial banks at the repo rate set by the central bank's Monetary Policy Committee. The reserve bank lends funds to the banks against eligible collateral, comprising assets that also qualify as liquid assets. Besides the main repo facility, many central banks offer a range of end-of-day facilities to help commercial banks square off their daily positions, i.e., to access to their cash reserve balances.

Beyond that, open market operations are conducted to manage market liquidity in realisation of monetary policy. These include issuance of debentures, reverse repos, movement of public sector funds, and foreign exchange money market swaps.

### Main Types of Financial and Non-Financial Risk Faced by Banks

**Credit Risk**   The reason for the original 1988 Basel Accord, focusing on credit risk, was a recognition of its primary importance in the risk profile of many financial institutions. At the most basic level, credit risk is simply the risk that, having extended a loan to another party, it is not repaid as agreed. Therefore, techniques can be examined that can be used to assess the probability that third parties default (i.e., fail to repay). These techniques can be applied to individual third parties (known as counterparties) or the industry within which they operate, or even the country within which they are based. This is because the likelihood of a counterparty defaulting is strongly correlated with the success of their industry as well as the economic state of their home country.

Larger counterparties are credit-rated by firms known as ratings agencies: the higher the rating, the better the credit risk – or to put it another way, the lower the likelihood of default. Smaller firms are not rated by an agency, and so lending institutions have to perform their own assessment of the likelihood of default. This is also true for retail customers.

Another important consideration when assessing credit risk is the quality of any assets which have been used as collateral in the event of default. The higher the quality, the less concerned the lending institution is about default because the underlying security (perhaps the house of one of the borrowing company's directors) can be sold to recoup the loss.

Credit risk is the risk of loss caused by the failure of a counterparty or issuer to meet its obligations. The party that has the financial obligation is called the obligor. The goal of credit risk management is to maximise a firm's risk-adjusted rates of return by maintaining credit risk exposure within acceptable parameters.

Credit risk exists in two broad forms: counterparty risk and issuer risk. Counterparty risk is the risk that a counterparty fails to fulfil its contractual obligations. A counterparty is one of the parties to a transaction – either the buyer or the seller. Examples of counterparty credit risk from a bank's perspective would include:

- The risk that a customer fails to pay back a loan;
- The risk that a company with whom the bank does business declares bankruptcy before having paid for goods or services supplied by the bank;
- The risk that a broker from whom the bank has purchased a bond fails to deliver – or delivers late;
- In the third of the above examples, the bond itself also carries issuer risk. This is the risk that the issuer of the bond could default on its obligations to pay coupons or repay the principal on the bond.

Concentration risk in credit portfolios arises through an uneven distribution of bank loans to individual issuers or counterparties (single-name concentration), or within industry sectors and geographical regions (sectorial concentration).

If a bank is overly dependent on a small number of counterparties – single-name concentration risk – then, if any of those counterparties default, the bank's revenues could drop by a significant amount. Over-concentration at the country, sector, or industry levels also holds risk for a bank – if, for example, the country in which it is overly concentrated suffers an economic downturn, then its revenues will again be adversely affected compared to competitors who are better diversified.

For most banks, loans are the largest and most obvious source of credit risk. However, other sources of credit risk exist throughout the activities of a bank, including in the banking book and in the trading book, and both on and off the balance sheet. These sources include:

- The extension of commitments and guarantees;
- Inter-bank transactions;
- Financial instruments such as futures, options, swaps, and bonds;
- The settlement of these and other transactions.

Transaction settlement is a key source of counterparty risk. This is the point at which the buyer and seller exchange the instrument and the cash to pay for it. Here is a risk that one party delivers, but the other fails to do so.

Ideally, the transfer of the purchased item and the transfer of cash would occur at exactly the same time, and there are electronic settlement systems to ensure that this happens. However, this is not always possible – and even when it is, there is always the chance that the mechanism may fail and one party to the agreement is still owed what they are due.

Certain financial instruments also carry "pre-settlement risk". This is the risk that an institution defaults before the settlement of the transaction, where the traded instrument has a positive economic value to the other party.

**Market Risk**    Market risk can be subdivided into the following types:

- Volatility risk: the risk of price movements that are more uncertain than usual affecting the pricing of products. All priced instruments suffer from this form of volatility. This especially affects options pricing because if the market is more volatile, then the pricing of an option is more difficult and options will become more expensive.
- Trading liquidity risk: in the context of market risk, this is the risk of loss through not being able to trade in a market or obtain a price on a desired product when required. This can occur in a market due to either a lack of supply or demand or a shortage of market-makers.
- Currency risk: this exists due to adverse movements in exchange rates. It affects any portfolio or instrument with cash flows denominated in a currency other than the base currency of the business underpinning

the financial instrument and/or where an investment portfolio contains holdings in investments priced in non-base currencies.

- Basis risk: this occurs when one risk exposure is hedged with an offsetting exposure in another instrument that behaves in a similar, but not identical, manner. If the two positions were truly "equal and opposite", then there would be no risk in the combined position. Basis risk exists to the extent that the two positions do not exactly mirror each other.
- Interest rate risk: this exists due to adverse movements in interest rates and will directly affect fixed-income securities, loans, futures, options, and forwards. It may also indirectly affect other instruments.
- Equity price risk: the returns from investing in equities comes from capital growth (if the company does well the price of its shares goes up) and income (through the distribution by the company of its profits as dividends). Therefore, investing in equities carries risks that can affect the capital (the share price may fall, or fail to rise in line with inflation, or with the performance of other, less risky investments) and the income (if the company is not as profitable as hoped, the dividends it pays may not keep pace with inflation; indeed they may fall or even not be paid at all. Unlike bond coupons, dividend payments are not compulsory).

As discussed above, there is a link between market risk and a firm's capital adequacy. The ability of a firm to bear market risk is linked to the amount of capital it possesses and the losses it can absorb.

**Currency Risk**   This exists due to adverse movements in exchange rates. It affects any portfolio or instrument with cash flows denominated in a currency other than the base currency of the business. One way that banks attempt to address this risk is through matching of assets, liabilities, and cash inflows, and inflows in the same currency. Where this is not possible, then the usual course of action is to use the wholesale inter-bank market to hedge the FX mismatch, using forwards and other products. Of course funding mismatch – lending in a currency funded by another currency – cannot be hedged with any real effectiveness, to any practical purpose, and is a significant risk if ever wholesale markets dry up as they did in 2008–2009.

**Interest Rate Risk**   This exists due to adverse movements in interest rates and will directly affect loans, deposits, fixed-income securities, futures, options, and forwards. It may also indirectly affect other instruments. Interest-rate risk can be mitigated through hedging using market instruments and through careful matching.

**Liquidity Risk**   The term liquidity is used in various ways, all relating to availability of, or access to, or convertibility into cash. Liquidity risk is discussed in detail in Chapters 11–12.

**Operational Risk**   Operational risks arise from the people, processes, and systems in use within a firm, or from external events. There is very little commonality between people, or processes, or IT systems, or external events (such as bomb threats or power cuts). The techniques used to understand and manage operational risk are therefore very diverse.

In addition to managing expected operational risks, firms also need to hold capital against unexpected losses. Firms can choose between one of three regulatory methods for calculating their operational risk capital requirement. The methods are associated with increasing levels of risk management sophistication, and moving up the levels results in firms having to hold less capital. The three method levels are called:

- The basic indicator approach (BIA);
- The standardised approach (TSA); and
- The advanced measurement approach (AMA).

As well as working out the known risks and holding capital for the unknowns, firms also need to remain vigilant to changes in their risk profile. The two common methods of achieving this are the creation of key risk indicators, and the capture and analysis of loss data.

Firms also have choices to make on how to keep their operational risk exposure within their operational risk appetite. This can be achieved firstly by avoiding the risk altogether, for example, by choosing to withdraw a product which has proved too complex to administer at an acceptable cost without repeated processing errors. A second method for reducing the risk profile to within appetite is to transfer the risk to a third party. This can take several forms including:

- Outsourcing an area of the company, such as back office administration, to another company which specialises in this type of business;
- Taking out insurance against certain events such as fraud or loss of premises through flooding.

As observed above, the simplest approach is to use the basic indicator approach. This sets the operational risk capital equal to the bank's average annual gross income, over the last 3 years, multiplied by 0.15.

**Re-Investment Risk**   This is the risk that future payments from a bond or a loan will not be reinvested at the prevailing interest rate when the bond was initially bought or the loan extended. Reinvestment risk is more likely when interest rates are declining. It affects the yield-to-maturity of a bond or loan, which is calculated on the assumption that all future payments will be reinvested at the interest rate in effect when the bond was first bought or the loan was made. Zero coupon instruments are the only ones to have no reinvestment risk, since they have no interim payments. Two factors that have an effect on the extent of reinvestment risk are:

1. The maturity of the instrument: the longer the maturity, the higher the likelihood that interest rates will be lower than they were at the time of investment.
2. The interest rate on the bond: the higher the interest rate, the bigger the payments which have to be reinvested, and thus the reinvestment risk.

**Pre-Payment Risk**   Pre-payment risk is the risk associated with the early, unscheduled return of principal on an instrument. Some fixed-income securities, such as mortgage-backed securities, have embedded call options which may be exercised by the issuer or the borrower.

The yield-to-maturity of such instruments cannot be known for certain at the time of investment since the cash flows are not known. When principal is returned early, future interest payments will not be paid on that part of the principal. If a bond were purchased at a premium, the bond's yield will be less than what was estimated at the time of purchase.

This risk also extends to typical retail lending products (for instance, unsecured loans, mortgages, and vehicle finance). This risk is twofold:

1. A loan product that is repaid quicker than anticipated within the pricing models will cause the loan to make a smaller profit than anticipated. If the loan is settled particularly quickly, the acquisition costs of writing the loan may not be recovered before it is settled and the loan may actually be loss-making.
2. Where the loan product is a fixed-rate product, banks will often look to hedge out some of the interest rate risk by purchasing interest rates swaps available to them within the market. The duration of these swaps will be based on the anticipated repayment period of the product. Should the loan product be repaid quicker (or slower) than anticipated, the bank will incur breakage charges on the swaps purchased.

**Model Risk**   Models are approximations of reality. They are needed for determining the price at which an instrument should be traded. They are also needed for marking-to-market a financial institution's position in an instrument once it has been traded, as well as for estimating the reserves required on a portfolio of assets (loans).

There are two primary types of model risk. One is the risk that the model will give the wrong price at the time a product is bought or sold. This can result in a company buying a product for too high a price or selling it at too low a price. The other risk involves hedging. If a company does not use the right model, the risk measures it calculates and the hedges it arranges based on those measures, are liable to be wrong (this would include raising reserves to cover loss expectations on the portfolio).

The skill in building a model for a financial product lies in capturing the key features of the product without permitting the model to become so complicated that it is difficult to use.

**Country Risk**    This refers to the risk of investing in a country, which is mainly dependent on changes in the business environment that may adversely affect operating profits or the value of assets in a specific country. For instance, financial factors such as currency controls, devaluation, or regulatory changes, or stability factors such as mass riots, civil war, and other potential events contribute to bank operational risks. This phenomenon is also sometimes referred to as political risk. However, country risk is a more general term that refers only to risks affecting all companies operating within a particular country.

**Business Risk**    As described above, operational risk includes model risk and legal risk, but does not include risk arising from strategic decisions (for example, related to a bank's decision to enter new markets and develop new products), or reputational risk. This type of risk is collectively referred to as business risk. Regulatory capital is not required under Basel II for business risk, but some banks do assess economic capital for business risk.

**Counterparty Credit Risk**    Counterparty risk, also known as a default risk, is a risk that a counterparty will not pay as obliged on a bond, credit derivative, trade credit insurance or payment protection insurance contract, or other trade or transaction. Financial institutions may hedge or take out credit insurance. Offsetting counterparty risk is not always possible, for example, because of temporary liquidity issues or longer-term systemic reasons. Counterparty risk increases due to positively correlated risk factors. Accounting for correlation among portfolio risk factors and counterparty default in risk management can be challenging.

# APPENDIX 1.A: Financial Markets Arithmetic

This extract from *An Introduction to Banking* (2011)

## Simple interest

A loan that has one interest payment on maturity is accruing simple interest. On short-term instruments there is usually only the one interest payment on maturity, hence simple interest is received when the instrument expires. The terminal value of an investment with simple interest is given by:

$$FV = PV(1+r) \tag{B.1}$$

here

FV =   Terminal value or future value;
PV =   Initial investment or present value;
$R$ =   Interest rate.

So, for example, if PV is £100, $r$ is 5% and the investment is 1 year. Then

$$FV = £100(1+r) = £105$$

The market convention is to quote interest rates as *annualized* interest rates, which is the interest that is earned if the investment term is 1 year. Consider a 3-month deposit of £100 in a bank, placed at a rate of interest of 6%. In such an example the bank deposit will earn 6% interest for a period of 90 days. As the annual interest gain would be £6, the investor will expect to receive a proportion of this:

$$£6.00 \times \frac{90}{365}$$

So, the investor will receive £1.479 interest at the end of the term. The total proceeds after the 3 months is therefore £100 plus £1.479. If we wish to calculate the terminal value of a short-term investment that is accruing simple interest we use the following expression:

$$FV = PV\left(1 + r \times \frac{Days}{Year}\right) \tag{B.2}$$

The fraction $\dfrac{Days}{Year}$ refers to the numerator, which is the number of days the investment runs, divided by the denominator, which is the number of days in the year. In sterling markets the number of days in a year is taken to be 365; however, certain other markets (including euro currency markets) have a 360-day year convention. For this reason we simply quote the expression as 'days' divided by 'year' to allow for either convention.

## Compound interest

Let us now consider an investment of £100 made for 3 years, again at a rate of 6%, but this time fixed for 3 years. At the end of the first year the investor will be credited with interest of £6. Therefore, for the second year the interest rate of 6% will be accruing on a principal sum of £106, which means that at the end of Year 2 the interest credited will be £6.36. This illustrates how *compounding* works, which is the principle of earning interest on interest. What will the terminal value of our £100 3-year investment be?

In compounding we are seeking to find a *future value* given a *present value*, a *time period* and an *interest rate*. If £100 is invested today (at time $t_0$) at 6%, then 1 year later ($t_1$) the investor will have £100 × (1 + 0.06) = £106. In our example the capital is left in for another 2 years, so at the end of Year 2 ($t_2$) we will have:

$$\pounds100\times\left(1+0.06\right)\times\left(1+0.06\right) = \pounds100\times\left(1+0.06\right)^2$$
$$= \pounds100\times\left(1.06\right)^2$$
$$= \pounds112.36$$

The outcome of the process of compounding is the *future value* of the initial amount. We don't have to calculate the terminal value long hand as we can use:

$$FV = PV\left(1+r\right)^n \qquad (B.3)$$

Where
$r =$ Periodic rate of interest (expressed as a decimal);
$n =$ Number of periods for which the sum is invested.

In our example, the initial £100 investment after 3 years becomes £100 × (1 + 0.06)³ which is equal to £119.10.

When we compound interest we have to assume that the reinvestment of interest payments during the investment term is at the same rate as the first year's interest. That is why we stated that the 6% rate in our example was *fixed* for 3 years. However, we can see that compounding increases our returns compared with investments that accrue only on a simple interest basis. If we had invested £100 for 3 years fixed at a rate of 6% but paying on a simple interest basis our terminal value would be £118, which is £1.10 less than our terminal value using a compound interest basis.

## Compounding more than once a year

Now let us consider a deposit of £100 for 1 year, again at our rate of 6% but with quarterly interest payments. Such a deposit would accrue interest of £6 in the normal way, but £1.50 would be credited to the account every quarter, and this would then benefit from compounding. Again assuming that we can reinvest at the same rate of 6%, the total return at the end of the year will be:

$$100 \times \left( (1+0.015) \times (1+0.015) \times (1+0.015) \times (1+0.015) \right)$$
$$= 100 \times (1+0.015)^4$$

which gives us $100 \times 1.06136$, a terminal value of £106.136. This is some 13 pence more than the terminal value using annual compounded interest.

In general, if compounding takes place $m$ times per year, then at the end of $n$ years $mn$ interest payments will have been made and the future value of the principal is given by:

$$FV = PV\left(1+\frac{r}{m}\right)^{mn} \qquad (B.4)$$

As we showed in our example, the effect of more frequent compounding is to increase the value of total return when compared with annual compounding. The effect of more frequent compounding is shown below, where we consider annualized interest rate factors, for an annualized rate of 5%.

| Compounding frequency | Interest rate factor |
|---|---|
| Annual | $(1 + r) = 1.050000$ |
| Semi-annual | $\left(1+\dfrac{r}{2}\right)^2 = 1.050625$ |
| Quarterly | $\left(1+\dfrac{r}{4}\right)^2 = 1.050945$ |
| Monthly | $\left(1+\dfrac{r}{4}\right)^{12} = 1.051162$ |
| Daily | $\left(1+\dfrac{r}{365}\right)^{365} = 1.051267$ |

This shows us that the more frequent the compounding the higher the interest rate factor. The last case also illustrates how a limit occurs when interest is compounded continuously. Equation (B.4) can be rewritten as:

$$FV = PV\left(\left(1+\frac{r}{m}\right)^{m/r}\right)^{rn} = PV\left(\left(1+\frac{1}{m/r}\right)^{m/r}\right)^{rn}$$

$$= PV\left(\left(1+\frac{1}{n}\right)^{n}\right)^{rn} \qquad (B.5)$$

where $n = m/r$. As compounding becomes continuous and $m$ and hence $n$ approach infinity, equation (B.5) approaches a value known as $e$, which is shown by:

$$e = \lim_{n\to\infty}\left(1+\frac{1}{n}\right)^{n} = 2.718281...$$

If we substitute this into (B.5) we get:

$$FV = PVe^{rn} \qquad (B.6)$$

where we have continuous compounding. In equation (B.6) $e^{rn}$ is known as the *exponential function* of $rn$; it tells us the continuously compounded interest rate factor. If $r = 5\%$ and $n = 1$ year then:

$$e^{r} = (2.718281)^{0.05} = 1.051271$$

This is the limit reached with continuous compounding. To illustrate continuous compounding from our initial example, the future value of £100 at the end of 3 years – when the interest rate is 6% – can be given by:

$$FV = 100e^{(0.06)\times3} = £119.72$$

## Effective interest rates

The interest rate quoted on a deposit or loan is usually the *flat* rate. However, we are often required to compare two interest rates which apply for a similar investment period but have different interest payment frequencies – for example, a 2-year interest rate with interest paid quarterly compared with a 2-year rate with semi-annual interest payments. This is normally done by comparing equivalent *annualized* rates. The annualized rate is the interest rate with annual compounding that results in the same return at the end of the period as the rate we are comparing.

The concept of the effective interest rate allows us to state that:

$$PV \times \left(1 + \frac{r}{n}\right)^n = PV \times \left(1 + AER\right) \qquad (B.7)$$

where AER is the equivalent annual rate. Therefore, if $r$ is the interest rate quoted that pays $n$ interest payments per year, AER is given by:

$$AER = \left(\left(1 + \frac{r}{n}\right)^n - 1\right) \qquad (B.8)$$

The equivalent annual interest rate AER is known as the *effective* interest rate. We have already referred to the quoted interest rate as the 'nominal' interest rate. We can rearrange equation (B.8) to give us equation (B.9) which allows us to calculate nominal rates:

$$r = \left(\left(1 + AER\right)^{1/n} - 1\right) \times n \qquad (B.9)$$

We can see then that the effective rate will be greater than the flat rate if compounding takes place more than once a year. The effective rate is sometimes referred to as the *annualized percentage rate* or APR.

## Interest rate conventions

The convention in both wholesale or personal (retail) markets is to quote an annual interest rate. A lender who wishes to earn interest at the rate quoted has to place her funds on deposit for 1 year. Annual rates are quoted irrespective of the maturity of a deposit, from overnight to 10 years or longer. For example, if one opens a bank account that pays interest at a rate of 3.5% but then closes it after 6 months, the actual interest earned will be equal to 1.75% of the sum deposited. The actual return on a 3-year building society bond (fixed deposit) that pays 6.75% fixed for 3 years is 21.65% after 3 years. The quoted rate is the annual 1-year equivalent. An overnight deposit in the wholesale or *inter-bank* market is still quoted as an annual rate, even though interest is earned for only one day.

The convention of quoting annualized rates is to allow deposits and loans of different maturities and different instruments to be compared on the basis of the interest rate applicable. We must also be careful when comparing interest rates for products that have different payment frequencies. As we have seen from the foregoing paragraphs the actual interest earned will be greater for a deposit earning 6% on a semi-annual basis compared with 6% on an annual basis. The convention in the money markets is to quote the equivalent interest rate applicable when taking into account an instrument's payment frequency.

## Discount factors

The calculation of present values from future values is also known as *discounting*. The principles of present and future values demonstrate the concept of the *time value* of money which is that in an environment of positive interest rates a sum of money has greater value today than it does at some point in the future because we are able to invest the sum today and earn interest. We will only consider a sum in the future compared with a sum today if we are compensated by being paid interest at a sufficient rate. Discounting future values allows us to compare the value of a future sum with a present sum.

The rate of interest $r$, known as the *discount rate*, is the rate we use to *discount* a known future value in order to calculate a present value. We can rearrange equation (B.1) to give:

$$PV = FV(1+r)^{-n}$$

The term $(1 + r)^{-n}$ is known as the *n*-year discount factor:

$$df_n = (1+r)^{-n} \tag{B.10}$$

where $df_n$ is the *n*-year discount factor.
The 3-year discount factor when the discount rate is 9% is:

$$df_3 = (1+0.09)^{-3} = 0.77218$$

We can calculate discount factors for all possible interest rates and time periods to give us a *discount function*. Fortunately, we don't need to calculate discount factors ourselves as this has been done for us (discount tables for a range of rates are provided in Table B.1).

---

### Formula summary

Discount factor with simple interest $df = \dfrac{1}{\left(1 + r\dfrac{\text{Days}}{\text{Year}}\right)^n}$

Discount factor with compound interest $df_n = \left(\dfrac{1}{1+r}\right)^n$

---

Earlier we established the continuously compounded interest rate factor as $e^{rn}$. Therefore, using a continuously compounded interest rate we can establish the discount factor to be:

$$\left. \begin{aligned} df &= \frac{1}{1+(e^{r \times \text{Days/Year}}-1)} = e^{-r \times \text{Days/Year}} \\ \therefore df_n &= e^{-rn} \end{aligned} \right\} \tag{B.11}$$

**Table B.1** Discount Factor Table

Discount rate (%)

| Years | 1 | 2 | 3 | 4 | 5 | 6 | 7 | 8 | 9 | 10 | 12 | 15 | 20 |
|---|---|---|---|---|---|---|---|---|---|---|---|---|---|
| | 0.01 | 0.02 | 0.03 | 0.04 | 0.05 | 0.06 | 0.07 | 0.08 | 0.09 | 0.1 | 0.12 | 0.15 | 0.2 |
| 1 | 0.990099 | 0.980392 | 0.970874 | 0.961538 | 0.952381 | 0.943396 | 0.934579 | 0.925926 | 0.917431 | 0.909091 | 0.892857 | 0.869565 | 0.833333 |
| 2 | 0.980296 | 0.961169 | 0.942596 | 0.924556 | 0.907029 | 0.889996 | 0.873439 | 0.857339 | 0.841680 | 0.826446 | 0.797194 | 0.756144 | 0.694444 |
| 3 | 0.970590 | 0.942322 | 0.915142 | 0.888996 | 0.863838 | 0.839619 | 0.816298 | 0.793832 | 0.772183 | 0.751315 | 0.711780 | 0.657516 | 0.578704 |
| 4 | 0.960980 | 0.923845 | 0.888487 | 0.854804 | 0.822702 | 0.792094 | 0.762895 | 0.733030 | 0.708425 | 0.683013 | 0.635518 | 0.571753 | 0.482253 |
| 5 | 0.951466 | 0.905731 | 0.862609 | 0.821927 | 0.783526 | 0.747258 | 0.712986 | 0.680583 | 0.649931 | 0.620921 | 0.567427 | 0.497177 | 0.401878 |
| 6 | 0.942045 | 0.887971 | 0.837484 | 0.790315 | 0.746215 | 0.704961 | 0.666342 | 0.630170 | 0.596267 | 0.564474 | 0.506631 | 0.432328 | 0.334898 |
| 7 | 0.932718 | 0.870560 | 0.813092 | 0.759918 | 0.710681 | 0.665057 | 0.622750 | 0.583490 | 0.547034 | 0.513158 | 0.452349 | 0.375937 | 0.279082 |
| 8 | 0.923483 | 0.853490 | 0.789409 | 0.730690 | 0.676839 | 0.627412 | 0.582000 | 0.540269 | 0.501866 | 0.466507 | 0.403883 | 0.326902 | 0.232568 |
| 9 | 0.914340 | 0.836755 | 0.766417 | 0.702587 | 0.644609 | 0.591898 | 0.543934 | 0.500249 | 0.460428 | 0.424098 | 0.360610 | 0.284262 | 0.193807 |
| 10 | 0.905287 | 0.820348 | 0.744094 | 0.675564 | 0.613913 | 0.558395 | 0.508349 | 0.463193 | 0.422411 | 0.385543 | 0.321973 | 0.247185 | 0.161506 |
| 11 | 0.896324 | 0.804263 | 0.722421 | 0.649581 | 0.584679 | 0.526788 | 0.475093 | 0.428883 | 0.387533 | 0.350494 | 0.287476 | 0.214943 | 0.134588 |
| 12 | 0.887449 | 0.788493 | 0.701380 | 0.624597 | 0.556837 | 0.496969 | 0.444012 | 0.397114 | 0.355535 | 0.318631 | 0.256675 | 0.186907 | 0.112157 |
| 13 | 0.878663 | 0.773033 | 0.680951 | 0.600574 | 0.530321 | 0.468839 | 0.414964 | 0.367698 | 0.326179 | 0.289664 | 0.229174 | 0.162528 | 0.093464 |
| 14 | 0.869963 | 0.757875 | 0.661118 | 0.577475 | 0.505068 | 0.442301 | 0.387817 | 0.340461 | 0.299246 | 0.263331 | 0.204620 | 0.141329 | 0.077887 |
| 15 | 0.861349 | 0.743015 | 0.641862 | 0.555265 | 0.481017 | 0.417265 | 0.362446 | 0.315242 | 0.274538 | 0.239392 | 0.182696 | 0.122894 | 0.064905 |
| 16 | 0.852821 | 0.728446 | 0.623167 | 0.533908 | 0.458112 | 0.393646 | 0.338735 | 0.291890 | 0.251870 | 0.217629 | 0.163122 | 0.106865 | 0.054088 |
| 17 | 0.844377 | 0.714163 | 0.605016 | 0.513373 | 0.436297 | 0.371364 | 0.316574 | 0.270269 | 0.231073 | 0.197845 | 0.145644 | 0.092926 | 0.045073 |
| 18 | 0.836017 | 0.700159 | 0.587395 | 0.493628 | 0.415521 | 0.350344 | 0.295864 | 0.250249 | 0.211994 | 0.179859 | 0.130040 | 0.080805 | 0.037561 |
| 19 | 0.827740 | 0.686431 | 0.570286 | 0.474642 | 0.395734 | 0.330513 | 0.276508 | 0.231712 | 0.194490 | 0.163508 | 0.116107 | 0.070265 | 0.031301 |
| 20 | 0.819544 | 0.672971 | 0.553676 | 0.456387 | 0.376889 | 0.311805 | 0.258419 | 0.214548 | 0.178431 | 0.148644 | 0.103667 | 0.061100 | 0.026084 |
| 21 | 0.811430 | 0.659776 | 0.537549 | 0.438834 | 0.358942 | 0.294155 | 0.241513 | 0.198656 | 0.163698 | 0.135131 | 0.092560 | 0.053131 | 0.021737 |
| 22 | 0.803396 | 0.646839 | 0.521893 | 0.421955 | 0.341850 | 0.277505 | 0.225713 | 0.183941 | 0.150182 | 0.122846 | 0.082643 | 0.046201 | 0.018114 |
| 23 | 0.795442 | 0.634156 | 0.506692 | 0.405726 | 0.325571 | 0.261797 | 0.210947 | 0.170315 | 0.137781 | 0.111678 | 0.073788 | 0.040174 | 0.015095 |
| 24 | 0.787566 | 0.621721 | 0.491934 | 0.390121 | 0.310068 | 0.246979 | 0.197147 | 0.157699 | 0.126405 | 0.101526 | 0.065882 | 0.034934 | 0.012579 |
| 25 | 0.779768 | 0.609531 | 0.477606 | 0.375117 | 0.295303 | 0.232999 | 0.184249 | 0.146018 | 0.115968 | 0.092296 | 0.058823 | 0.030378 | 0.010483 |
| 26 | 0.772048 | 0.597579 | 0.463695 | 0.360689 | 0.281241 | 0.219810 | 0.172195 | 0.135202 | 0.106393 | 0.083905 | 0.052521 | 0.026415 | 0.008735 |
| 27 | 0.764404 | 0.585862 | 0.450189 | 0.346817 | 0.267848 | 0.207368 | 0.160930 | 0.125187 | 0.097608 | 0.076278 | 0.046894 | 0.022970 | 0.007280 |
| 28 | 0.756836 | 0.574375 | 0.437077 | 0.333477 | 0.255094 | 0.195630 | 0.150402 | 0.115914 | 0.089548 | 0.069343 | 0.041869 | 0.019974 | 0.006066 |
| 29 | 0.749342 | 0.563112 | 0.424346 | 0.320651 | 0.242946 | 0.184557 | 0.140563 | 0.107328 | 0.082155 | 0.063039 | 0.037383 | 0.017369 | 0.005055 |
| 30 | 0.741923 | 0.552071 | 0.411987 | 0.308319 | 0.231377 | 0.174110 | 0.131367 | 0.099377 | 0.075371 | 0.057309 | 0.033378 | 0.015103 | 0.004213 |

The continuously compounded discount factor is part of the formula used in option-pricing models. It is possible to calculate discount factors from the prices of government bonds. The traditional approach described in most textbooks requires that we first use the price of a bond that has only one remaining coupon, its last one, and calculate a discount factor from this bond's price. We then use this discount factor to calculate the discount factors of bonds with ever-increasing maturities, until we obtain the complete discount function.

## Present values with multiple discounting

Present values for short-term investments of under 1-year maturity often involve a single interest payment. If there is more than one interest payment then any discounting needs to take this into account. If discounting takes place $m$ times per year then we can use equation (B.4) to derive the present value formula:

$$PV = FV\left(1 + \frac{r}{m}\right)^{-mn} \qquad (B.12)$$

For example, what is the present value of the sum of £1,000 which is to be received in 5 years where the discount rate is 5% and there is semi-annual discounting?

Using equation (B.12) we see that

$$PV = 1,000\left(1 + \frac{0.05}{2}\right)^{-2 \times 5} = £781.20$$

The effect of more frequent discounting is to lower the present value. As with continuous compounding, the limiting factor is reached by means of continuous discounting. We can use equation (B.6) to derive the present value formula for continuous discounting

$$PV = FVe^{-rn} \qquad (B.13)$$

If we consider the same example as before but now with continuous discounting, we can use this expression to calculate the present value of £1,000 to be received in 5 years' time as:

$$PV = 1,000e^{-(0.05) \times 5} = £778.80$$

Reproduced from *An Introduction to Banking* (2011)

## APPENDIX 1.B: Leadership Lessons From The World of Sport

The following is reproduced from the matchday programme for AFC Wimbledon, published 13 September 2013.

---

### FEATURE

# LESSONS IN LEADERSHIP

IN HIS ROLES AS A PROFESSOR OF FINANCE AT BRUNEL UNIVERSITY AND A CITY OF LONDON BANKER, PROGRAMME SPONSOR **MOORAD CHOUDHRY** OFTEN ADDRESSES ASPIRING ENTREPRENEURS ON WHAT IT TAKES TO BE A TEAM LEADER. BUT, HE SAYS, HE MAY HAVE TO REWRITE HIS LECTURE NOTES AFTER SEEING AT FIRST HAND HOW NEAL ARDLEY AND NEIL COX LEAD A TEAM OF PLAYERS.

 ecently I had the privilege to play in the annual shirt sponsors' match alongside the Dons management team. An XI made up of staff from the shirt sponsors, Sports Interactive, faced an XI led by the Dons management and supplemented by other club commercial sponsors. The game was played in an appropriate spirit, exemplified by Ivor Heller kicking off the match for the management team.

It was all great fun, but for me it was also something of a revelation. My time on the pitch was limited to around 20 minutes in the first half and 25 minutes in the second. But I learnt more about team leadership in those 45 minutes playing alongside Messrs Ardley and Cox than I have during thousands of hours spent in seminars and MBA programmes over the past 24 years in the City.

So here is my eight-point guide to leadership, based on seeing Neal and Neil in action. It can be applied in virtually any walk of life, but it should be required reading for anyone in an office environment aspiring to lead teams – and it's a lot cheaper than an MBA!

**1. Treat everyone as equals in the way you speak to them and communicate instructions.** Neil Cox didn't vary the way he spoke to individuals in the team, whatever their ability, familiarity or position. He delivered instructions in exactly the same way to everyone. This builds tremendous loyalty and confidence.

**2. Lead by example.** This is nothing new. The difference was that these two guys *really did* it. They put in the effort and, what's more, it was obvious that they were putting in the effort. This has a tremendous inspirational effect on team members.

**3. Provide continuous encouragement.** Everyone likes to feel appreciated, both when things are going well and when they are going badly. Ardley and Cox delivered encouragement at every possible opportunity. This makes a big difference.

**4. Don't dwell on mistakes, and don't apportion blame.** When a player made a mistake, it wasn't dwelt on because the player was aware he had made it. We've done it – let's move on and try again. This is tremendously inspiring and makes everyone try harder.

**5. Make everyone feel part of the same team: no cliques, no favourites, no inner circles.** Whatever the situation, it is enough that everyone feels part of the same team and that no one person is favoured more than any other. This is a platitude espoused by every office manager in every company; sadly, in nine out of ten offices it just isn't true.

**6. Involve everyone, and keep involving them.** This follows on from the previous point. One way to inspire people to want to follow you is to involve them: it makes them feel that you believe they'll do a good job. The modern office equivalent of this is "don't micromanage, and learn to delegate". The difference between most corporate managers and the Wimbledon management team was that the latter *really did this*.

**7. Trust your subordinates' judgement.** It will make them want to do well and inspire them even more. They are there to do a job, and to build a truly effective team one has to accept their answers. A leader who does this will inspire loyalty. A leader who can't do this needs to rebuild the team. You won't inspire dedication if you always question your team members' judgement.

**8. Act so that everyone is aware they have the same objective.** This is the easy bit with a football team. There are no individual winners if the team loses. But by applying points 1 to 7 above, Neal Ardley and Neil Cox cover the essentials of team management first. After that, it's up to the players.

People define "leadership" in various ways, but really it boils down to inspiring people to want to follow you. This sponsors' game was just a bit of fun, and a million miles away from the serious business of a professional football match. But character comes across in any situation, and a transparent approach to leadership is tremendously inspiring. Unlike in an office, on a football pitch there is little if any room for artifice and platitudes. It was fantastic for me to see that Neal Ardley and his entire management team possess leadership and motivational skills that would make them not only a success in football, but would also make them ideal team leaders in any business environment. Not that I want them to change profession just yet!

*Adapted with permission from "Leadership Lessons from the World of Sport", first published by CNBC at www.cnbc.com/id/100973768 on 20 August 2013.*

Reproduced from CNBC, AFC Wimbledon

## APPENDIX 1.C: The Global Master Repurchase Agreement

To view the GMRA, please go to this website and download the document from the link on this page: http://www.icmagroup.org/Regulatory-Policy-and-Market-Practice/repo-and-collateral-markets/global-master-repurchase-agreement-gmra/.

### SELECTED BIBLIOGRAPHY AND REFERENCES

Basel III proposals: www.bis.org/bcbs/basel3.htm.
Country risk: www.businessmonitor.com/bmo/country-risk.
Development banks: www.ft.com/reports/development-banks-2012.
Hull, J. (2010). *Risk Management and Financial Institutions*, Boston: Pearson, Chapters 2, 11, 14, 18–20.

*"The spread of secondary and tertiary education has created a large population of people, often with well-developed literary and scholarly tastes, who have been educated far beyond their capacity to undertake analytical thought."*

—Peter Medawar, quoted in Richard Dawkins,
*The Greatest Show on Earth: The Evidence for Evolution*,
Bantam Press, 2009.

# CHAPTER 2

# Derivative Instruments and Hedging

**R**eiterating our "95–5" rule from Chapter 1, most customer finance requirements – whether long or short of cash – can be met with essentially plain vanilla products. That said, some financial market derivatives have made a positive contribution to society; a good example of this would be the humble interest-rate swap, without which banks in many countries would not be able to offer fixed-rate residential mortgages or corporate loans to their customers.

This illustrates the principal reason why derivative instruments are "popular" – they enable an institution to hedge risk exposure. An inability to hedge exposure is the main impediment to a bank offering a customer a desired product such as a fixed-rate loan. So in this chapter we present previous book extracts that are pertinent to an understanding of the main derivative instruments and the main hedging applications that such products are used for.

The new material in the chapter includes an up-to-date discussion on using the asset swap measure to ascertain bond relative value. We also consider the impact of the 2008 crash on the hitherto "standard" pricing principles used for valuing interest-rate swaps. Swaps have been a collateralised market for some years now, and the previous approach of using solely Libor as the driver of the swap discount factor has had to be modified. The approach described here is important general knowledge for all banks using derivatives in any capacity. Finally, we provide a brief introduction to hedge accounting, again a topic of importance to banks using derivatives.

This extract from *Bank Asset and Liability Management* (2007)

## Money Market Derivatives

## Money Market Derivatives

ALM practitioners use a variety of derivative instruments for the purposes of trading and hedging. These are primarily interest-rate derivatives. In this chapter we review the two main contracts used in money markets trading, the short-term *interest-rate future* and the *forward rate agreement* (FRA). Money market derivatives are priced on the basis of the *forward rate*, and are flexible instruments for hedging against or speculating on forward interest rates. The FRA and the exchange-traded interest-rate future both date from around the same time, and although initially developed to hedge forward interest-rate exposure, they now have a variety of uses. In this chapter we review the instruments and their main uses.

## Forward rate agreements

An FRA is an OTC derivative instrument that trades as part of the money markets. It is essentially a forward-starting loan, but with no exchange of principal, so that only the difference in interest rates is exchanged. Trading in FRAs began in the early 1980s and the market now is large and liquid; turnover in London exceeds $5 billion each day.[1] In effect, an FRA is a forward-dated loan, dealt at a fixed rate, but with no exchange of principal – only the interest applicable on the notional amount between the rate dealt at and the actual rate prevailing at the time of settlement changing hands. That is, FRAs are *off-balance sheet* (OBS) instruments. By trading today at an interest rate that is effective at some point in the future, FRAs enable banks and corporates to hedge forward interest-rate exposure. They are also used to speculate on the level of future interest rates.

## Definition of an FRA

An FRA is an agreement to borrow or lend a *notional* cash sum for a period of time lasting up to 12 months, starting at any point over the next 12 months, at an agreed rate of interest (the FRA rate). The "buyer" of an FRA is borrowing a notional sum of money while the "seller" is lending this cash

---

[1] *Source*: British Bankers Association (BBA).

sum. Note how this differs from all other money market instruments. In the cash market, the party buying a CD or Bill, or bidding for stock in the repo market, is the lender of funds. In the FRA market, to "buy" is to "borrow". Of course, we use the term "notional" because with an FRA no borrowing or lending of cash actually takes place, as it is an OBS product. The notional sum is simply the amount on which interest payment is calculated.

So when an FRA is traded, the buyer is borrowing (and the seller is lending) a specified notional sum at a fixed rate of interest for a specified period, the "loan" to commence at an agreed date in the future. The *buyer* is the notional borrower, and so if there is a rise in interest rates between the date that the FRA is traded and the date that the FRA comes into effect, he or she will be protected. If there is a fall in interest rates, the buyer must pay the difference between the rate at which the FRA was traded and the actual rate, as a percentage of the notional sum. The buyer may be using the FRA to hedge an actual exposure, that is an actual borrowing of money, or simply speculating on a rise in interest rates. The counterparty to the transaction, the *seller* of the FRA, is the notional lender of funds, and has fixed the rate for lending funds. If there is a fall in interest rates the seller will gain, and if there is a rise in rates the seller will pay. Again, the seller may have an actual loan of cash to hedge or be a speculator.

In FRA trading only the payment that arises as a result of the difference in interest rates changes hands. There is no exchange of cash at the time of the trade. The cash payment that does arise is the difference in interest rates between that at which the FRA was traded and the actual rate prevailing when the FRA matures, as a percentage of the notional amount. FRAs are traded by both banks and corporates, and between banks. The FRA market is very liquid in all major currencies, and rates are readily quoted on screens by both banks and brokers. Dealing is over the telephone or over a dealing system such as Reuters.

The terminology quoting FRAs refers to the borrowing time period and the time at which the FRA comes into effect (or matures). Hence, if a buyer of an FRA wished to hedge against a rise in rates to cover a three-month loan starting in three months' time, he or she would transact a "three-against-six-month" FRA, or more usually denoted as a 3x6 or 3-v-6 FRA. This is referred to in the market as a "threes-sixes" FRA, and means a three-month loan beginning in three months' time. So correspondingly a "ones-fours" FRA (1v4) is a three-month loan beginning in one month's time, and a "three-nines" FRA (3v9) is six-month money beginning in three month's time.

Note that when one buys an FRA one is "borrowing" funds. This differs from cash products such as CD or repo, as well as interest-rate futures, where to "buy" is to lend funds.

---

**EXAMPLE 13.1** A forward-date interest-rate exposure

A company knows that it will need to borrow £1 million in three months' time for a 12-month period. It can borrow funds today at Libor + 50 basis points. Libor rates today are at 5%, but the company's treasurer expects rates to go up to about 6% over the next few weeks. So the company will be forced to borrow at higher rates unless some sort of hedge is transacted to protect the borrowing requirement. The treasurer decides to buy a 3v15 ("threes-fifteens") FRA to cover the 12-month period beginning three months from now. A bank quotes 5½% for the FRA, which the company buys for a notional £1 million. Three months from now rates have indeed gone up to 6%, so the treasurer must borrow funds at 6½% (the Libor rate plus spread). However, she will receive a settlement amount that will be the difference between the rate at which the FRA was bought and today's 12-month Libor rate (6%) as a percentage of £1 million, which will compensate for some of the increased borrowing costs.

---

## FRA mechanics

In virtually every market FRAs trade under a set of terms and conventions that are identical. The British Bankers Association (BBA) has compiled standard legal documentation to cover FRA trading. The following standard terms are used in the market.

- *Notional sum*: the amount for which the FRA is traded.
- *Trade date*: the date on which the FRA is dealt.
- *Settlement date*: the date on which the notional loan or deposit of funds becomes effective; that is, is said to begin. This date is used, in conjunction with the notional sum, for calculation purposes only as no actual loan or deposit takes place.
- *Fixing date*: the date on which the *reference rate* is determined; that is, the rate to which the FRA dealing rate is compared.
- *Maturity date*: the date on which the notional loan or deposit expires.
- *Contract period*: the time between the settlement date and maturity date.
- *FRA rate*: the interest rate at which the FRA is traded.
- *Reference rate*: the rate used as part of the calculation of the settlement amount, usually the Libor rate on the fixing date for the contract period in question.

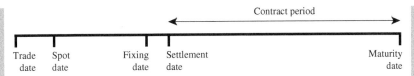

**Figure 13.1**   Key dates in an FRA trade

- *Settlement sum*: the amount calculated as the difference between the FRA rate and the reference rate as a percentage of the notional sum, paid by one party to the other on the settlement date.

These terms are illustrated in Figure 13.1.

The spot date is usually two business days after the trade date; however, it can by agreement be sooner or later than this. The settlement date will be the time period after the spot date referred to by the FRA terms; for example, a 1x4 FRA will have a settlement date one calendar month after the spot date. The fixing date is usually two business days before the settlement date. The settlement sum is paid on the settlement date, and as it refers to an amount over a period of time that is paid up front, at the start of the contract period, the calculated sum is discounted present value. This is because a normal payment of interest on a loan/deposit is paid at the end of the time period to which it relates; because an FRA makes this payment at the *start* of the relevant period, the settlement amount is a discounted present value sum.

With most FRA trades the reference rate is the Libor setting on the fixing date.

The settlement sum is calculated after the fixing date, for payment on the settlement date. We may illustrate this with an hypothetical example. Consider a case where a corporate has bought £1 million notional of a 1v4 FRA, and dealt at 5.75%, and that the market rate is 6.50% on the fixing date. The contract period is 90 days. In the cash market the extra interest charge that the corporate would pay is a simple interest calculation, and is:

$$\frac{\left(6.50 - 5.75\right)}{100} \times 1,000,000 \times \frac{91}{365} = £1,869.86.$$

This extra interest that the corporate is facing would be payable with the interest payment for the loan, which (as it is a money market loan) is when the loan matures. Under an FRA then, the settlement sum payable should, if it were paid on the same day as the cash market interest charge, be exactly equal to this, which would make it a perfect hedge. As we noted above though, FRA settlement value is paid at the start of the contract period; that is, the beginning of the underlying loan and not the end. Therefore the settlement sum has to be adjusted to account for this, and the amount of the adjustment is the value of the interest that would be earned if the unadjusted cash value was invested for the contract period in the money market. The settlement value is given by (13.1):

$$\text{Settlement} = \frac{\left(r_{ref} - r_{FRA}\right) \times M \times {}^{n}\!\!\big/\!{}_{B}}{1 + \left(r_{ref} \times {}^{n}\!\!\big/\!{}_{B}\right)} \qquad (13.1)$$

where   $r_{ref}$        is the reference interest-fixing rate
        $r_{FRA}$       is the FRA rate or *contract rate*
        $M$             is the notional value
        $n$             is the number of days in the contract period
        $B$             is the day-count base (360 or 365).

The expression in (13.1) simply calculates the extra interest payable in the cash market, resulting from the difference between the two interest rates, and then discounts the amount because it is payable at the start of the period and not, as would happen in the cash market, at the end of the period.

In our illustration, as the fixing rate is higher than the dealt rate, the corporate buyer of the FRA receives the settlement sum from the seller. This then compensates the corporate for the higher borrowing costs that he or she would have to pay in the cash market. If the fixing rate had been lower than 5.75%, the buyer would pay the difference to the seller, because the cash market rates will mean that he or she is subject to a lower interest rate in the cash market. What the FRA has done is hedge the interest rate, so that whatever happens in the market, it will pay 5.75% on its borrowing.

A market-maker in FRAs is trading short-term interest rates. The settlement sum is the value of the FRA. The concept is exactly as with trading short-term interest-rate futures; a trader who buys an FRA is running a long position, so that if on the fixing date $r_{ref} > r_{FRA}$, the settlement sum is positive and the trader realises a profit. What has happened is that the trader, by buying the FRA, "borrowed" money at an interest rate, which subsequently rose. This is a gain, exactly like a *short* position in an interest-rate future, where if the price goes down (that is, interest rates go up), the trader realises a gain. Equally, a "short" position in an FRA, put on by selling an FRA, realises a gain if on the fixing date $r_{ref} < r_{FRA}$.

## FRA pricing

As their name informs us, FRAs are forward rate instruments and are priced using standard forward rate principles.[2] An introduction to the concept of spot and forward rates can be found. Consider an investor who has two alternatives, either a six-month investment at 5% or a one-year investment at 6%. If the investor wishes to invest for six months and then roll-over the investment for a further six months, what rate is required for the roll-over period such that the final return equals the 6% available from the one-year investment? If we view an FRA rate as the breakeven forward rate between the two periods, we simply solve for this forward rate and that is our approximate FRA rate. This rate is sometimes referred to as the interest-rate "gap" in the money markets (not to be confused with an interbank desk's *gap risk*, the interest-rate exposure arising from the net maturity position of its assets and liabilities, and which was considered in Chapter 5).

We can use the standard forward-rate breakeven formula to solve for the required FRA rate; we established this relationship in Chapter 9 when discussing the calculation of forward rates that are arbitrage-free. The relationship given in (13.2) below connects simple (bullet) interest rates for periods of time up to one year, where no compounding of interest is required. As FRAs are money market instruments we are not required to calculate rates for periods in excess of one year,[3] where compounding would need to be built into the equation. The expression is given by (13.2):

$$(1 + r_2 t_2) = (1 + r_1 t_1)(1 + r_f t_f) \qquad (13.2)$$

where    $r_2$    is the cash market interest rate for the long period
          $r_1$    is the cash market interest rate for the short period
          $r_f$    is the forward rate for the gap period
          $t_2$    is the time period from today to the end of the long period
          $t_1$    is the time period from today to the end of the short period
          $t_f$    is the forward gap time period, or the contract period for the FRA.

---

[2] An introduction to the basics of spot and forward rates can be found in any number of finance textbooks; the author particularly likes Windas (1993) and Rubinstein (1999) for their accessibility for beginners. His own treatment of the subject is in Chapter 9.

[3] Although it is of course possible to trade FRAs with contract periods greater than one year, for which a different pricing formula must be used.

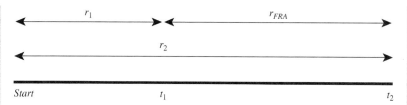

**Figure 13.2** Rates used in FRA pricing

This is illustrated diagrammatically in Figure 13.2.

The time period $t_1$ is the time from the dealing date to the FRA settlement date, while $t_2$ is the time from the dealing date to the FRA maturity date. The time period for the FRA (contract period) is $t_2$ minus $t_1$. We can replace the symbol "$t$" for time period with "$n$" for the actual number of days in the time periods themselves. If we do this and then rearrange the equation to solve for $r_{fra}$ the FRA rate, we obtain (13.3):

$$r_{FRA} = \frac{r_2 n_2 - r_1 n_1}{n_{fra}\left(1 + r_1 \dfrac{n_1}{365}\right)} \qquad (13.3)$$

where    $n_1$    is the number of days from the dealing date or spot date to the settlement date

        $n_2$    is the number of days from dealing date or spot date to the maturity date

        $r_1$    is the spot rate to the settlement date

        $r_2$    is the spot rate from the spot date to the maturity date

        $n_{fra}$    is the number of days in the FRA contract period

        $r_{FRA}$    is the FRA rate.

If the formula is applied to, say, the US dollar money markets, the 365 in the equation is replaced by 360, the day-count base for that market.

In practice FRAs are priced off the exchange-traded short-term interest-rate future for that currency, so that sterling FRAs are priced off LIFFE short-sterling futures. Traders normally use a spreadsheet pricing model that has futures prices directly fed into it. FRA positions are also usually hedged with other FRAs or short-term interest-rate futures.

**EXAMPLE 13.2**   Pricing FRAs from futures

The following are interest-rate futures prices for short-sterling contracts:

| | |
|---|---|
| Jun 00 | 94.70 (implied three-month interest rate: 5.30%) |
| Sep 00 | 94.65 (implied three-month interest rate: 5.35%) |
| Dec 99 | 94.60 (implied three-month interest rate: 5.40%). |

A trader is asked for the offer side of a 3v6 FRA in £5 million and also to advise on the hedge by futures. If we assume there are no bid–offer spreads, what should the rate on the FRA be?

The FRA dates are given below:

Contract period: 20 June to 20 September (92 days)
Settlement date: 18 June.

As the expiry date for the June futures contract is 18 June, the FRA rate will be the implied June futures rate of 5.30%. The settlement amount is:

$$\frac{5,000,000 \times (0.0530 - \text{Libor}) \times \frac{92}{365}}{1 + \text{Libor} \times \frac{92}{365}}.$$

The profit or loss on the futures contract, which is not discounted is calculated as:

No. of contracts $\times 500,000 \times (0.0530 - \text{Libor}) \times 90 / 365.$

In a hedge the FRA buyer requires these two values to be equal, so we have:

$$\text{No. of contracts} = 10 \times \frac{\frac{92}{90}}{\left(1 + \text{Libor} \times \frac{92}{365}\right)}.$$

The future Libor rate is of course not known at this point, but if we estimate it as 5.30%, we obtain:

$$\text{No. of contracts} = 10 \times \frac{\frac{92}{90}}{\left(1 + 0.0530 \times \frac{92}{365}\right)} = 10.08746.$$

The hedge here is 10 contracts.

---

**EXAMPLE 13.3**    FRA hedging (1)

Using the same prices as in Example 13.2, what is the hedge and price for a sale of a 3v6 FRA against a 6v12 FRA?
The 3v6 FRA is priced at 5.30% as before. A 6v9 FRA, which is the 91 days from 20 September to 20 December, is also priced at the September futures price of 5.35%, and hedged with 10 futures contracts. This is only completely accurate if the futures contract delivery date is the same as the settlement date of the FRA, but it is close enough for our purposes. The 3v9 FRA is equivalent to a *strip* combining the 3v6 FRA and a 6v9 FRA, due to the principle of arbitrage-free pricing, so the 3v9 FRA price is calculated as:

$$\left(\left(1+0.0530\times\frac{92}{365}\right)\times\left(1+0.0535\times\frac{91}{365}\right)-1\right)\times\frac{365}{182}$$

$$= 5.38987\%.$$

The price of the 6v12 FRA may be obtained from the price of a 6v9 FRA and a 9v12 FRA (90 days from 20 December to 20 March), because a strip of these two FRAs is the same as the 6v12 FRA. The price is calculated below.

$$\left(\left(1+0.0535\times\frac{91}{365}\right)\times\left(1+0.0540\times\frac{90}{365}\right)-1\right)\times\frac{365}{183}$$

$$= 5.39815\%.$$

---

**EXAMPLE 13.4**    FRA hedging (2)

Again using the prices in Example 13.2, our trader now wishes to sell a 3v8 FRA (153 days from 20 June to 20 November) and a 6v11 FRA (153 days from 20 Septmeber to 20 February). How are these priced?
The 3v8 FRA is the implied rate for five-month money in three months' time. We do not have the spot or futures rates that allow us to calculate this rate exactly, so we must interpolate using the rates we do have. This then becomes:

$$3v6+\left(3v9-3v6\right)\times\frac{\text{Days in } 3v8-\text{Days in } 3v6}{\text{Days in } 3v8-\text{Days in } 3v6}$$

$$= 5.35\%+\left(\left(5.39-5.35\right)\times\left(153-92/182-92\right)\right)$$

$$= 5.3771\%.$$

**EXAMPLE 13.5** Valuation of an existing FRA

In order to value an FRA, it must be decomposed into its constituent parts, which are equivalent to a loan and deposit. Both these parts are then present valued, and the value of the FRA is simply the net present value of both legs. For example, a 6v9 FRA is equivalent to a six-month asset and a nine-month liability. If we assume that the six-month rate is 5% and the nine-month rate is 6%, on a notional principal of £1 million, the value of the FRA is given by:

| Value | Term (yr) | Rate (%) | PV |
|---|---|---|---|
| £1 million | 0.4932 | 5.00 | +£976,223 |
| £1 million | 0.7397 | 6.00 | −£957,814 |

The value of the FRA is therefore £18,409.

## Short-term interest-rate futures

### Description

A *futures* contract is a transaction that fixes the price today for a commodity that will be delivered at some point in the future. Financial futures fix the price for interest rates, bonds, equities and so on, and trade in the same manner as commodity futures. Contracts for futures are standardised and traded on recognised exchanges. In London the main futures exchange is LIFFE, although other futures are also traded on, for example, the International Petroleum Exchange and the London Metal Exchange. The money markets trade short-term interest-rate futures, which fix the rate of interest on a notional fixed-term deposit of money (usually for 90 days or three months) for a specified period in the future. The sum is notional because no actual sum of money is deposited when buying or selling futures; the instrument is off-balance sheet. Buying such a contract is equivalent to making a notional deposit, while selling a contract is equivalent to borrowing a notional sum.

The three-month interest-rate future is the most widely used instrument used for hedging interest-rate risk.

The LIFFE exchange in London trades short-term interest-rate futures for major currencies, including sterling, euros, yen and Swiss francs. Table 13.1 summarises the terms for the short sterling contract as traded on LIFFE.

| Name: | 90-day sterling Libor interest-rate future |
|---|---|
| Contract size: | £500,000 |
| Delivery months: | March, June, September, December |
| Delivery date: | First business day after the last trading day |
| Last trading day: | Third Wednesday of delivery month |
| Price: | 100 minus interest rate |
| Tick size: | 0.005 |
| Tick value: | £6.25 |
| Trading hours: | LIFFE CONNECT™ 0805 – 1800 hours |

**Table 13.1**  Description of LIFFE short sterling future contract
*Source*: LIFFE.

The original futures contracts related to physical commodities, which is why we speak of *delivery* when referring to the expiry of financial futures contracts. Exchange-traded futures such as those on LIFFE are set to expire every quarter during the year. The short sterling contract is a deposit of cash, so as its price refers to the rate of interest on this deposit, the price of the contract is set as $P = 100 - r$ where $P$ is the price of the contract and $r$ is the rate of interest at the time of expiry implied by the futures contract. This means that if the price of the contract rises, the rate of interest implied goes down, and vice versa. For example, the price of the June 1999 short sterling future (written as Jun99 or M99, from the futures identity letters of H, M, U and Z for contracts expiring in March, June, September and December respectively) at the start of trading on 13 March 1999 was 94.880, which implied a three-month Libor rate of 5.12% on expiry of the contract in June. If a trader bought 20 contracts at this price and then sold them just before the close of trading that day, when the price had risen to 94.96, an implied rate of 5.04%, she would have made 16 ticks profit or £2000. That is, a 16 tick upward price movement in a long position of 20 contracts is equal to £2000. This is calculated as follows:

$$\text{Profit} = \text{Ticks gained} \times \text{Tick value} \times \text{Number of contracts}$$
$$\text{Loss} = \text{Ticks lost} \times \text{Tick value} \times \text{Number of contracts}.$$

The tick value for the short sterling contract is straightforward to calculate, since we know that the contract size is £500,000. There is a minimum price movement (tick movement) of 0.005% and the contract has a three-month "maturity". So we have:

$$\text{Tick value} = 0.005\% \times £500,000 \times 3/12 = £6.25.$$

The profit made by the trader in our example is logical because if we buy short sterling futures we are depositing (notional) funds; if the price of the futures rises, it means the interest rate has fallen. We profit because we have "deposited" funds at a higher rate beforehand. If we expected sterling interest rates to rise, we would sell short sterling futures, which is equivalent to borrowing funds and locking in the loan rate at a lower level.

Note how the concept of buying and selling interest rate futures differs from FRAs: if we buy an FRA we are borrowing notional funds, whereas if we buy a futures contract we are depositing notional funds. If a position in an interest-rate futures contract is held to expiry, cash settlement will take place on the delivery day for that contract.

Short-term interest-rate contracts in other currencies are similar to the short sterling contract and trade on exchanges such as Eurex in Frankfurt and MATIF in Paris.

## Pricing interest-rate futures

The price of a three-month interest-rate futures contract is the implied interest rate for that currency's three-month rate at the time of expiry of the contract. Therefore there is always a close relationship and correlation between futures prices, FRA rates (which are derived from futures prices) and cash market rates. On the day of expiry the price of the future will be equal to the Libor rate as fixed that day. This is known as the Exchange Delivery Settlement Price (EDSP) and is used in the calculation of the delivery amount. During the life of the contract its price will be less closely related to the actual three-month Libor rate *today*, but closely related to the *forward rate* for the time of expiry.

Equations (13.2) and (13.3) were our basic forward rate formulas for money market maturity forward rates, which we adapted to use as our FRA price equation. If we incorporate some extra terminology to cover the dealing dates involved it can also be used as our futures price formula. Let us say that:

$T_0$ is the trade date
$T_M$ is the contract expiry date
$T_{CASH}$ is the value date for cash market deposits traded on $T_0$
$T_1$ is the value date for cash market deposits traded on $T_M$
$T_2$ is the maturity date for a three-month cash market deposit traded on $T_M$.

We can then use Equation (13.3) as our futures price formula to obtain $P_{fut}$, the futures price for a contract up to the expiry date.

$$P_{fut} = 100 - \frac{r_2 n_2 - r_1 n_1}{n_f \left(1 + r_1 \dfrac{n_1}{365}\right)} \tag{13.6}$$

where $P_{fut}$ is the futures price

$r_1$ is the cash market interest rate to $T_1$

$r_2$ is the cash market interest rate to $T_2$

$n_1$ is the number of days from $T_{CASH}$ to $T_1$

$n_2$ is the number of days from $T_{CASH}$ to $T_2$

$n_f$ is the number of days from $T_1$ to $T_2$.

The formula uses a 365-day count convention that applies in the sterling money markets; where the market convention is a 360-day base this is used in the equation instead.

In practice, the price of a contract at any one time will be close to the theoretical price that would be established by (13.6) above. Discrepancies will arise for supply and demand reasons in the market, as well as because Libor rates are often quoted only to the nearest sixteenth or 0.0625. The price between FRAs and futures are correlated very closely; in fact, banks will often price FRAs using futures, and use futures to hedge their FRA books. When hedging an FRA book with futures, the hedge is quite close to being exact, because the two prices track each other almost tick for tick.[4] However, the tick value of a futures contract is fixed, and uses (as we saw above) a 3/12 basis, while FRA settlement values use a 360- or 365-day base. FRA traders will be aware of this when putting on their hedge.

In any good discussion of forward rates it would be emphasised that they are the market's view on future rates using all information available today. As the available information is constantly updated, the forward rate will change. However, forward rates should not be taken to be the market's *prediction* of interest rates in the future; rather, they are the rate that a bank would write on a trade ticket for dealing today at value in the future, using all available information up to the minute the ticket is written. Of course, a futures price today is very unlikely to be in line with the actual three-month interest rate that is prevailing at the time of the contract's expiry. This explains why prices for futures and actual cash rates will differ on any particular day. Up until expiry the futures price is the implied forward rate; of course, there is always a discrepancy between this forward rate and the cash market rate *today*. The gap between the cash price and the futures price is known as the *basis*. This is defined as:

$$\text{Basis} = \text{Cash price} - \text{Futures price.}$$

At any point during the life of a futures contract prior to final settlement – at which point futures and cash rates converge – there is usually a difference

---

[4] That is, the basis risk is minimised.

between current cash market rates and the rates implied by the futures price. This is the difference we've just explained; in fact, the difference between the price implied by the current three-month interbank deposit and the futures price is known as *simple basis*, but it is what most market participants refer to as the basis. Simple basis consists of two separate components, *theoretical basis* and *value basis*. Theoretical basis is the difference between the price implied by the current three-month interbank deposit rate and that implied by the theoretical fair futures price based on cash market forward rates, given by (13.6) above. This basis may be either positive or negative, depending on the shape of the yield curve; this is illustrated in Example 13.7.

---

**EXAMPLE 13.7** **Theoretical basis**

Let us examine the relationship between the shape of the yield curve and the basis. Assume that today is 14 March.
(1) Negative yield curve; negative theoretical basis:

| | |
|---|---|
| 3-month Libor: | 6.50% |
| 6-month Libor: | 6.375% |
| 9-month Libor: | 6.25% |
| One-year Libor: | 6.1875%. |

| Cash price (100 – Libor) | Contract | Fair futures price | Theoretical basis |
|---|---|---|---|
| 93.5 | Jun. | 93.85 | −0.35 |
| | Sep. | 94.19 | −0.69 |
| | Dec. | 94.27 | −0.77 |

(2) Flat yield curve; negative theoretical basis:

| | |
|---|---|
| 3-month Libor: | 6.50% |
| 6-month Libor: | 6.50% |
| 9-month Libor: | 6.50% |
| One-year Libor: | 6.50%. |

| Cash price (100 – Libor) | Contract | Fair futures price | Theoretical basis |
|---|---|---|---|
| 93.50 | Jun. | 93.60 | −0.10 |
| | Sep. | 93.70 | −0.20 |
| | Dec. | 93.80 | −0.30 |

(3) Positive yield curve; positive theoretical basis:

| 3-month Libor: | 6.50% |
|---|---|
| 6-month Libor: | 6.75% |
| 9-month Libor: | 6.9375% |
| One-year Libor: | 7.125%. |

| Cash price (100 – Libor) | Contract | Fair futures price | Theoretical basis |
|---|---|---|---|
| 93.50 | Jun. | 93.11 | 0.39 |
| | Sep. | 92.93 | 0.57 |
| | Dec. | 92.69 | 0.81 |

The above is a very simple example and the steepness and shape of the yield curve will have an impact on the assumptions shown.

The value basis is the difference between the theoretical fair futures price and the actual futures price. It is a measure of how under- or over-valued the futures contract is relative to its fair value. Value basis reflects the fact that a futures contract does not always trade at its mathematically calculated theoretical price, due to the impact of market sentiment and demand and supply. The theoretical price and value can and do move independently of one another and in response to different influences. Both however converge to zero on the last trading day when final cash settlement of the futures contract is made.

Futures contracts do not in practice provide a precise tool for locking into cash market rates today for a transaction that takes place in the future, although this is what they are in theory designed to do. Futures do allow a bank to lock in a rate for a transaction to take place in the future, and this rate is the *forward rate*. The basis is the difference between today's cash market rate and the forward rate on a particular date in the future. As a futures contract approaches expiry, its price and the rate in the cash market will converge (the process is given the name *convergence*). As we noted earlier this is given by the EDSP and the two prices (rates) will be exactly in line at the exact moment of expiry.

## Futures trading

Trading with derivatives is often preferred, for both speculative or hedging purposes, to trading in the cash markets mainly because of the liquidity of the market and the ease and low cost of undertaking transactions. The essential features of futures trading are volatility and leverage. To establish a futures position on an exchange, the level of margin required is very low proportional to the notional value of the contracts traded. For speculative purposes, traders often carry out open – that is, uncovered trading – which is a directional bet on the market. So, therefore, if traders believed that short-term sterling interest rates were going to fall, they could buy a short sterling contract on LIFFE. This may be held for under a day (in which case, if the price rises the traders will gain), or for a longer period, depending on their view. The 1 basis point tick value of a short sterling contract is £12.50; so, if they bought one lot at 92.75 (that is, 100 – 92.75 or 7.25%) and sold it at the end of the day for 98.85, they made a profit of £125 on their one lot, from which brokerage will be subtracted. The trade can be carried out with any futures contract. The same idea could be carried out with a cash-market product or an FRA, but the liquidity, narrow price spread and the low cost of dealing make such a trade easier on a futures exchange. It is much more interesting, however, to carry out a spread trade on the difference between the rates of two different contracts. Consider Figures 13.6 and 13.7, which relate to the prices for the LIFFE short-sterling futures contract on 25 March 2004.

Futures exchanges use the letters H, M, U and Z to refer to the contract months for March, June, September and December. So the June 2004

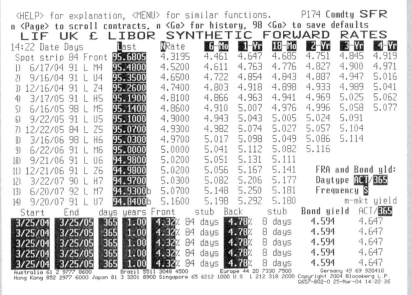

**Figure 13.6** LIFFE short-sterling contract analysis, 25 March 2004

contract would be denoted by "M4". From Chapter 9 we know that forward rates can be calculated for any term, starting on any date. In Figure 13.6, we see the future prices on that day, and the interest rate that the prices imply. The "stub" is the term for the interest rate from today to the expiry of the first futures contract, which is called the front month contract (in this case the front month contract is the June 2004 contract) and is 84 days. Figure 13.7 lists the forward rates from the spot date to six months, one year and so on. It is possible to trade a strip of contracts to replicate any term, out to the maximum maturity of the contract. This can be done for hedging or speculative purposes. Note from Figure 13.7 that there is a spread between the cash curve and the futures curve. A trader can take positions on cash against futures, but it is easier to transact only on the futures exchange.

Short-term money market interest rates often behave independently of the yield curve as a whole. A money markets trader may be aware of cash-market trends – for example, an increased frequency of borrowing at a certain point of the curve – as well as other market intelligence that suggests that one point of the curve will rise or fall relative to others. One way to exploit this view is to run a position in a cash instrument such as a CD against a futures contract, which is a *basis spread* trade.

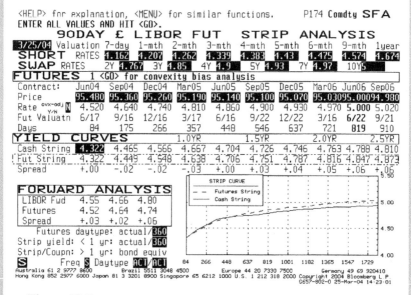

**Figure 13.7** LIFFE short-sterling forward rates analysis, 25 March 2004

However, the best way to trade on this view is to carry out a spread trade, shorting one contract against a long position in another trade. Consider Figure 13.6; if we feel that three-month interest rates in June 2004 will be lower than where they are implied by the futures price today, but that September 2004 rates will be higher, we will buy the M4 contract and short the U4 contract. This is not a market-directional trade; rather, it's a view on the relative spread between two contracts. The trade must be carried out in equal weights; for example, 100 lots of the June against 100 lots of the September. If the rates do move in the direction that the trader expects, the trade will generate a profit. There are similar possibilities available from an analysis of Figure 13.7, depending on our view of forward interest rates.

Spread trading carries a lower margin requirement than open position trading, because there is no directional risk in the trade. It is also possible to arbitrage between contracts on different exchanges. If the trade is short the near contract and long the far contract (that is, the opposite of our example) this is known as buying the spread and the trader believes the spread will widen. The opposite is shorting the spread and is undertaken when the trader believes the spread will narrow. Note that the difference between the two price levels is not limitless, because the theoretical price of a futures contract provides an upper limit to the size of the spread or the basis. The spread or the basis cannot exceed the cost of carry; that is, the net cost of buying the cash security today and then delivering it into the futures market on the contract expiry. The same principle applies to short-dated interest-rate contracts; the net cost is the difference between the interest cost of borrowing funds to buy the "security" and the income accruing on the security while it is held before delivery. The two associated costs for a short-sterling spread trade are the notional borrowing and lending rates from having bought one and sold another contract. If traders believe that the cost of carry will decrease, they could sell the spread to exercise this view.

Traders may have a longer time horizon and trade the spread between the short-term interest-rate contract and the long bond future. This is usually carried out only by the proprietary trading desk, because it is unlikely that one person would be trading both three-month and 10-year (or 20-year, depending on the contract specification) interest rates. A common example of such a spread trade is a yield-curve trade. If traders believe that the sterling yield curve will steepen or flatten between the three-month and the 10-year terms, they can buy or sell the spread by using the LIFFE short-sterling contract and the long gilt contract. To be first-order risk-neutral, however, the trade must be duration-weighted, as one short-sterling contract is not equivalent to one gilt contract. The tick value of the gilt contract is £10, however, although the gilt contract represents £100,000 of a notional gilt and the short-sterling contract represents a £500,000 time deposit. We use (13.7) to calculate the hedge ratio, with £1,000 being the value of a 1% change in the value of the gilt contract against £1,250 for the short sterling contract.

$$h = \frac{(100 \times Tick) \times P_b \times D}{(100 \times Tick) \times P_f} \tag{13.7}$$

Where    *Tick*    is the tick value of the contract
         *D*     is the duration of the bond represented by the long bond contract
         $P_b$    is the price of the bond futures contract
         $P_f$    is the price of the short-term deposit contract.

The notional maturity of a long bond contract is always given in terms of a spread; for example, for the long gilt it is 8¾–13 years. Therefore, in practice, one would use the duration of the cheapest-to-deliver bond.

A butterfly spread is a spread trade that involves three contracts, with the two spreads between all three contracts being traded. This is carried out when the middle contract appears to be mispriced relative to the two contracts either side of it. The trader may believe that one or both of the outer contracts will move in relation to the middle contract. If the belief is that only one of these two will shift relative to the middle contract, then a butterfly will be put on if the trader is not sure which of these will adjust. For example, consider Figure 13.6 again. The prices of the front three contracts are 95.48, 95.35 and 95.26. A trader may feel that the September contract is too low, having a spread of +13 basis points to the June contract, and +9 basis points to the December contract. The trader feels that the September contract will rise, but will that be because June and December prices fall or because the September price will rise? Instead of having to answer this question, all the trader need believe is that the June–September spread will widen and the September–December spread will narrow. To put this view into effect, the trader puts on a butterfly spread, which is equal to the September–December spread minus the June–September spread, which she expects to narrow. Therefore, she buys the June–September spread and sells the September–December spread, which is also known as *selling the butterfly spread*.

---

**EXAMPLE 13.8**    **The Eurodollar futures contract**

The Eurodollar futures contract is traded on the Chicago Mercantile Exchange, although it can be traded globally on a 24-hour basis on SIMEX and GLOBEX. The underlying asset is a deposit of US dollars in a bank outside the United States, and the contract is on the rate on dollar 90-day Libor. The Eurodollar future is cash settled on the second business day before the third Wednesday of the delivery month (London business day). The final settlement price is used to set the price of the contract, given by:

$$10,000(100 - 0.25r)$$

where $r$ is the quoted Eurodollar rate at the time. This rate is the actual 90-day Eurodollar deposit rate.

The longest-dated Eurodollar contract has an expiry date of 10 years. The market assumes that futures prices and forward prices are equal; Appendix 13.1 shows that this is indeed the case under conditions where the risk-free interest rate is constant and the same for all maturities. In practice it is also holds for short-dated futures contracts, but is inaccurate for longer-dated futures contracts. Therefore using futures contracts with a maturity greater than five years to calculate zero-coupon rates or implied forward rates will produce errors in results, which need to be taken into account if the derived rates are used to price other instruments such as swaps.

Figure 13.8 shows the Bloomberg description page for the Eurodollar contract.

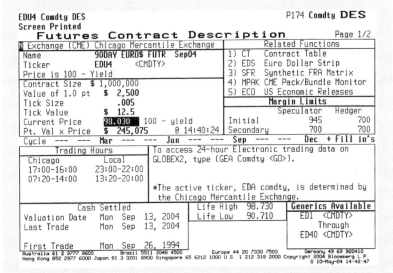

**Figure 13.8**   Bloomberg page DES for Eurodollar contract

## Hedging using interest-rate futures

ALM desks use interest-rate futures to hedge interest rate risk exposure in cash and off-balance sheet instruments. Bond trading desks also often use futures to hedge positions in bonds of up to two or three years' maturity, as contracts are traded up to three years' maturity. The liquidity of such "far-month" contracts is considerably lower than for near-month contracts and the "front month" contract (the current contract, for the next maturity month). When hedging a bond with a maturity of say two years' maturity, the trader will put on a *strip* of futures contracts that matches as near as possible the expiry date of the bond.

The purpose of a hedge is to protect the value of a current or anticipated cash market or OBS position from adverse changes in interest rates. The hedgers will try to offset the effect of the change in interest rates on the value of their cash position with the change in value of their hedging instruments. If the hedge is an exact one the loss on the main position should be compensated by a profit on the hedge position. If traders are expecting a fall in interest rates and wish to protect against such a fall they will buy futures, known as a long hedge, and they will sell futures (a short hedge) if wishing to protect against a rise in rates.

Bond traders also use three-month interest-rate contracts to hedge positions in short-dated bonds; for instance, market-makers running a short-dated bond book would find it more appropriate to hedge their books using short-dated futures rather than the longer-dated bond futures contract. When this happens it is important to accurately calculate the correct number of contracts to use for the hedge. To construct a bond hedge it will be necessary to use a strip of contracts, thus ensuring that the maturity date of the bond is covered by the longest-dated futures contract. The hedge is calculated by finding the sensitivity of each cash flow to changes in each of the relevant forward rates. Each cash flow is considered individually and the hedge values are then aggregated and rounded to the nearest whole number of contracts.

Figure 13.9 is a reproduction of page TED on Bloomberg, which calculates the strip hedge for short-dated bonds. The example shown is for a short-sterling contract hedge for a position in the UK 8½% 2005 gilt, for settlement on 11 November 2003. The screen shows the number of each contract that must be bought (or sold) to hedge the position, which in the example is a holding of £10 million of the bond. The "stub" requirement is met using the near-month contract. A total of 165 contracts are required.

## Options

The interest-rate risk management needs of a large number of banks can be met by the use of plain vanilla derivatives such as interest-rate swaps and

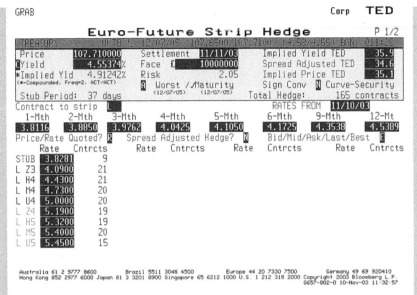

**Figure 13.9** Bloomberg screen TED page, used to calculate hedge
requirements for UK 8½% 2005 gilt, 11 November 2003
© 2006 Bloomberg L.P. All rights reserved. Reprinted with permission.

exchange-traded futures. In some circumstances though, it may be more
efficient and cost effective to use option products to effect the risk hedging.
As such, ALM managers need to be familiar with the use and application of
options, particularly interest-rate options such as caps and floors. For this
reason we discuss options in this chapter.

As a risk management tool, option contracts allow banks to hedge market risk exposure but also to gain from upside moves in the market; thus they
are unique among hedging instruments. Options have special characteristics
that make them stand apart from other classes of derivatives. As they confer
a right to conduct a certain transaction, but not an obligation, their payoff
profile is different from other financial assets, both cash and off-balance
sheet. This makes an option more of an insurance policy rather than a pure
hedging instrument, as the person who has purchased the option for hedging
purposes need only exercise it if required. The price of the option is in effect
the insurance premium that has been paid for peace of mind. Options are
also used for purposes other than hedging, as part of speculative and arbitrage trading. Many banks also act as option market-makers and generate
returns from profitably managing the risk on their option books.

The subject of options is a large one, and there are a number of specialist texts devoted to them. In this chapter we introduce the basics of options,

including a primer on option pricing. We also provide an example of the risk hedging application of an interest-rate option.

## Introduction

An option is a contract in which the buyer has the right, but not the obligation, to buy or sell an underlying asset at a predetermined price during a specified period of time. The seller of the option, known as the writer, grants this right to the buyer in return for receiving the price of the option, known as the premium. An option that grants the right to buy an asset is a call option, while the corresponding right to sell an asset is a put option. The option buyer has a long position in the option and the option seller has a short position in the option.

Because options confer on a buyer the right to effect a transaction, but not the obligation (and correspondingly on a seller the obligation, if requested by the buyer, to effect a transaction), their risk/reward characteristics are different from other financial products. The payoff profile from holding an option is unlike that of any other instrument. Let us consider the payoff profiles for a vanilla call option and a gilt futures contract. Suppose that a trader buys one lot of the gilt futures contract at 114.00 and holds it for one month before selling it. On closing the position, the profit made will depend on the contract sale price. If it is above 114.00, the trader will have made a profit, and if below 114.00 a loss. On one lot, this represents a £1,000 gain for each point above 114.00. The same applies to someone who had a short position in the contract and closed it out – if the contract is bought back at any price below 114.00 the trader will realise a profit. The profile is shown in Figure 13.13.

This profile is the same for other derivative instruments such as FRAs and swaps, and, of course, for cash instruments such as bonds or equity.

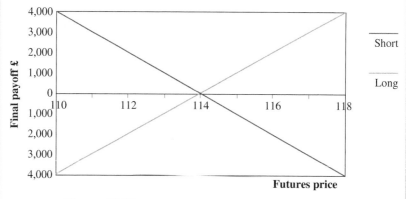

**Figure 13.13**    Payoff profile for a bond futures contract

The payoff profile therefore has a linear characteristic, and it is linear whether one has bought or sold the contract.

The profile for an option contract differs from the conventional one. Because options confer a right, but not an obligation to one party (the buyer), and an obligation but not a right to the seller, the profile will differ according to whether one is the buyer or seller. Consider a trader who buys a call option that grants the right to buy a gilt futures contract at a price of 114.00 at some point during the life of the option, the resulting payoff profile will be like that shown in Figure 13.14 on page 584. If during the life of the option the price of the futures contract rises above 114.00, the trader will exercise the right to buy the future, under the terms of the option contract. This is known as exercising the option. If, on the other hand, the price of the future falls below 114.00, the trader will not exercise the option and, unless there is a reversal in price of the future, it will eventually expire worthless on its maturity date. In this respect, it is exactly like an equity or bond warrant. The seller of this particular option has a very different payout profile. If the price of the future rises above 114.00 and the option is exercised, the seller will bear the loss equal to the profit that the buyer has made. The seller's payoff profile is also shown in Figure 13.14, as the dashed line. If the option is not exercised and expires, the trade will have generated premium income for the seller, which is revenue income that contributes to the p&l account.

So the holders of long and short positions in options do not have the same symmetrical payoff profile. The buyer of the call option will benefit if the price of the underlying asset rises, but will not lose if the price falls

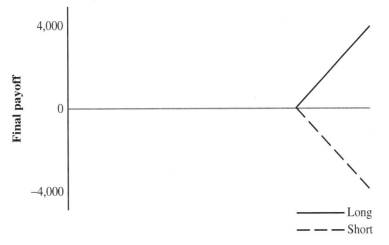

**Figure 13.14** Payoff profile for call-option contract

(except the funds paid for purchasing the rights under the option). The seller of the call option will suffer loss if the price of the underlying asset rises, but will not benefit if it falls (except realising the funds received for writing the option). The buyer has a right but not an obligation, while the seller has an obligation if the option is exercised. The premium charged for the option is the seller's compensation for granting such a right to the buyer.

## Option terminology

Let us now consider some basic terminology used in the options markets.

A call option grants the buyer the right to buy the underlying asset, while a put option grants the buyer the right to sell the underlying asset. There are, therefore, four possible positions that an option trader may put on: long a call or put; and short a call or put. The payoff profiles for each type are shown at Figure 13.15.

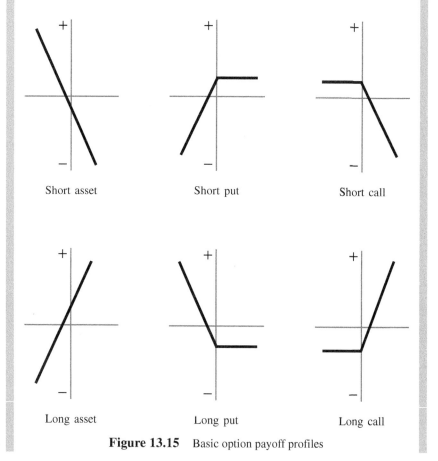

**Figure 13.15** Basic option payoff profiles

The strike price describes the price at which an option is exercised. For example, a call option to buy ordinary shares of a listed company might have a strike price of £10.00. This means that if the option is exercised, the buyer will pay £10 per share. Options are generally either American- or European-style, which defines the times during the option's life when it can be exercised. There is no geographic relevance to these terms, as both styles trade can be traded in any market. It is very rare for an American option to be exercised ahead of its expiry date, so this distinction has little impact in practice, although of course the pricing model being used to value European options must be modified to handle American options. The holders of European options cannot exercise them prior to expiry. However, if they wish to realise their value, they will sell them in the market.

The premium of an option is the price at which the option is sold. Option premium is made up of two constituents: intrinsic value and time value.

The intrinsic value of an option is the value of the option if it is exercised immediately, and it represents the difference between the strike price and the current underlying asset price. If a call option on a bond futures contract has a strike price of 100.00 and the future is currently trading at 105.00, the intrinsic value of the option is 5.00, as this would be the immediate profit gain to the option holder if it were exercised. Since an option will only be exercised if there is benefit to the holder from so doing, its intrinsic value will never be less than zero. So, in our example, if the bond future was trading at 95.00, the intrinsic value of the call option would be zero, not −5.00. For a put option, the intrinsic value is the amount by which the current underlying price is below the strike price. When an option has intrinsic value, it is described as being *in-the-money*. When the strike price for a call option is higher than the underlying price (or for a put option is lower than the underlying price) and has no intrinsic value it is said to be *out-of-the-money*. An option for which the strike price is equal to the current underlying price is said to be *at-the-money*. This term is normally used at the time the option is first traded, in cases where the strike price is set to the current price of the underlying asset.

The time value of an option is the amount by which the option value exceeds the intrinsic value. An option writer will almost always demand a premium that is higher than the option's intrinsic value, because of the risk that the writer is taking on. This reflects the fact that over time the price of the underlying asset may change sufficiently to produce a much higher intrinsic value. During the life of an option, the option writer has nothing more to gain over the initial premium at which the option was sold. However, until expiry there is a chance that the writer will lose if the markets move against him or her, hence the inclusion of a time-value element. The value of an option that is out-of-the-money is composed entirely of time value.

| | |
|---|---|
| **Call** | The right to buy the underlying asset |
| **Put** | The right to sell the underlying asset |
| **Buyer** | The person who has purchased the option and has the right to exercise it if he or she wishes |
| **Writer** | The person who has sold the option and has the obligation to perform if the option is exercised |
| **Strike price** | The price at which the option may be exercised, also known as the *exercise price* |
| **Expiry date** | The last date on which the option can be exercised, also known as the maturity date |
| **American** | The style of option; an American option can be exercised at any time up to the expiry date |
| **European** | An option which may be exercised on the maturity date only, and not before |
| **Premium** | The price of the option, paid by the buyer to the seller |
| **Intrinsic value** | The value of the option if it were exercised today, which is the difference between the strike price and the underlying asset price |
| **Time value** | The difference between the current price of the option and its intrinsic value |
| **In-the-money** | The term for an option that has intrinsic value |
| **At-the-money** | An option for which the strike price is identical to the underlying asset price |
| **Out-of-the-money** | An option that has no intrinsic value |

**Table 13.4**   Basic option terminology

Table 13.4 summarises the main option terminology that we have just been discussing.

## Option pricing

The price of an option is a function of six different factors, which are:

- the strike price of the option;
- the current price of the underlying;
- the time to expiry;
- the risk-free rate of interest that applies to the life of the option;
- the volatility of the underlying asset's price returns;
- the value of any dividends or cash flows paid by the underlying asset during the life of the option.

We review the basic parameters next.

## Pricing inputs

Let us consider the parameters of option pricing. Possibly the two most important are the current price of the underlying and the strike price of the option. The intrinsic value of a call option is the amount by which the strike price is below the price of the underlying, as this is the payoff if the option is exercised. Therefore, the value of the call option will increase as the price of the underlying increases, and will fall as the underlying price falls. The value of a call will also decrease as the strike price increases. All this is reversed for a put option.

Generally, for bond options a higher time to maturity results in higher option value. All other parameters being equal, a longer-dated option will always be worth at least as much as one that had a shorter life. Intuitively we would expect this because the holder of a longer-dated option has the same benefits as someone holding a shorter-dated option, in addition to a longer time period in which the intrinsic value may increase. This rule is always true for American options, and usually true for European options. However, certain factors, such as the payment of a coupon during the option life, may cause a longer-dated option to have only a slightly higher value than a shorter-dated option.

The risk-free interest-rate is the rate applicable to the period of the option's life. So for our table of gilt options in the previous section, the option value reflected the three-month rate. The most common rate used is the T-bill rate, although for bond options it is more common to see the government-bond repo rate being used. A rise in interest rates will increase the value of a call option, although not always for bond options. A rise in rates lowers the price of a bond, because it decreases the present value of future cash flows. However, in the equity markets it is viewed as a sign that share price growth rates will increase. Generally, however, the relationship is the same for bond options as equity options. The effect of a rise in interest rates for put options is the reverse: they cause the value to drop.

A coupon payment made by the underlying asset during the life of the option will reduce the price of the underlying asset on the ex-dividend date. This will result in a fall in the price of a call option and a rise in the price of a put option.

## Pricing methodology

The interest-rate products described in this book so far, both cash and derivatives, can be priced using rigid mathematical principles, because on maturity of the instrument there is a defined procedure that takes place such that one is able to calculate a fair value. This does not apply to options because there is uncertainty as to what the outcome will be on expiry; an option seller does not know whether the option will be exercised or not. This factor makes options more difficult to price than other financial-market instruments. In this section we review the parameters used in the pricing of an option, and introduce the Black–Scholes pricing model.

Pricing an option is a function of the probability that it will be exercised. Essentially, the premium paid for an option represents the buyer's expected profit on the option. Therefore, as with an insurance premium, the writer of an option will base his or her price on the assessment that the payout on the option will be equal to the premium, and this is a function on the probability that the option will be exercised. Option pricing, therefore, bases its calculation on the assessment of the probability of exercise and derives from this an expected outcome and, hence, a fair value for the option premium. The expected payout, as with an insurance company premium, should equal the premium received.

The following factors influence the price of an option.

- *the behaviour of financial prices*: one of the key assumptions made by the Black–Scholes model (B–S) is that asset prices follow a lognormal distribution. Although this is not strictly accurate, it is close enough of an approximation to allow its use in option pricing. In fact, observation shows that while prices themselves are not normally distributed, asset returns are, and we define returns as $\ln\left(\dfrac{P_{t+1}}{P_t}\right)$ where $P_t$ is the market price at time $t$ and $P_{t+1}$ is the price one period later. The distribution of prices is called a lognormal distribution because the logarithm of the prices is normally distributed. The asset returns are defined as the logarithm of the price relatives and are assumed to follow the normal distribution. The expected return as a result of assuming this distribution is given by $E\left[\ln\left(\dfrac{P_t}{P_0}\right)\right] = rt$ where $E[\ ]$ is the expectation operator and $r$ is the annual rate of return. The derivation of this expression is given in Appendix 13.2;
- *the strike price*: the difference between the strike price and the underlying price of the asset at the time the option is struck will influence the size of the premium, as this will have an impact on the probability that the option will be exercised. An option that is deeply in-the-money has a greater probability of being exercised;
- *volatility*: the volatility of the underlying asset will influence the probability that an option is exercised, as a higher volatility indicates a higher probability of exercise. This is considered in detail below;
- *the term to maturity*: a longer-dated option has greater time value and a greater probability of eventually being exercised;

- *the level of interest rates*: the premium paid for an option in theory represents the expected gain to the buyer at the time the option is exercised. It is paid up-front so it is discounted to obtain a present value. The discount rate used, therefore, has an effect on the premium, although it is less influential than the other factors presented here.

The volatility of an asset measures the variability of its price returns. It is defined as the annualised standard deviation of returns, where variability refers to the variability of the returns that generate the asset's prices, rather than the prices directly. The standard deviation of returns is given by (13.10):

$$\sigma = \sqrt{\sum_{i=1}^{N} \frac{\left(x - \mu\right)^2}{N-1}} \tag{13.10}$$

where $x_i$ is the $i$'th price relative, $\mu$ the arithmetic mean of the observations and $N$ is the total number of observations. The value is converted to an annualised figure by multiplying it by the square root of the number of days in a year, usually taken to be 250 working days. Using this formula from market observations it is possible to calculate the *historic volatility* of an asset. The volatility of an asset is one of the inputs to the B–S model. Of the inputs to the B–S model, the variability of the underlying asset, or its volatility is the most problematic. The distribution of asset prices is assumed to follow a lognormal distribution, because the logarithm of the prices is normally distributed (we assume lognormal rather than normal distribution to allow for the fact that prices cannot – as could be the case in a normal distribution – have negative values). The range of possible prices starts at zero and cannot assume a negative value.

Note that it is the asset price *returns* on which the standard deviation is calculated, and the not the actual prices themselves. This is because using prices would produce inconsistent results, as the actual standard deviation itself would change as price levels increased.

However, calculating volatility using the standard statistical method gives us a figure for historic volatility. What is required is a figure for *future* volatility, since this is relevant for pricing an option expiring in the future. Future volatility cannot be measured directly, by definition. Market-makers get around this by using an option-pricing model "backwards". An option-pricing model calculates the option price from volatility and other parameters. Used in reverse, the model can calculate the volatility implied by the option price. Volatility measured in this way is called implied volatility. Evaluating implied volatility is straightforward using this method and generally more appropriate than using historic volatility, as it provides a clearer measure of an option's fair value. Implied volatilities of deeply in-the-money or out-of-the-money options tend to be relatively high.

## The Black–Scholes (B–S) option model

Most option-pricing models are based on one of two methodologies, although both types employ essentially identical assumptions. The first method is based on the resolution of the partial differentiation equation of the asset–price model, corresponding to the expected payoff of the option security. This is the foundation of the B–S model. The second type of model uses the martingale method, and was first introduced by Harrison and Kreps (1979) and Harrison and Pliska (1981), where the price of an asset at time 0 is given by its discounted expected future payoffs, under the appropriate probability measure, known as the risk-neutral probability. There is a third type that assumes lognormal distribution of asset returns but follows the two-step binomial process.

In order to employ the pricing models, we accept a state of the market that is known as a *complete market*,[7] one where there is a viable financial market. This is where the rule of no-arbitrage pricing exists, so that there is no opportunity to generate risk-free arbitrage due to the presence of, say, incorrect forward interest rates. The fact that there is no opportunity to generate risk-free arbitrage gains means that a zero-cost investment strategy that is initiated at time $t$ will have a zero maturity value. The martingale property of the behavior of asset prices states that an accurate estimate of the future price of an asset may be obtained from current price information. Therefore, the relevant information used to calculate forward asset prices is the latest price information. This was also a property of the semi-strong and strong-form market-efficiency scenarios described by Fama (1970).

In this section, we describe the B–S option model in accessible fashion. More technical treatments are given in the relevant references listed in the bibliography.

### Assumptions

The B–S model describes a process to calculate the fair value of a European call option under certain assumptions, and apart from the price of the underlying asset $S$ and the time $t$, all the variables in the model are assumed

---

[7] First proposed by Arrow and Debreu (1953, 1954), for reference details, see Choudhry (2001).

to be constant, including – most crucially – the volatility. The following assumptions are made:

- there are no transaction costs, and the market allows short selling;
- trading is continuous;
- underlying asset prices follow geometric Brownian motion, with the variance rate proportional to the square root of the asset price;
- the asset is a non-dividend-paying security;
- the interest rate during the life of the option is known and constant;
- the option can only be exercised on expiry.

The B–S model is neat and intuitively straightforward to explain, and one of its many attractions is that it can be readily modified to handle other types of options such as foreign-exchange or interest-rate options. The assumption of the behavior of the underlying asset price over time is described by (13.11), which is a generalised Weiner process, and where $a$ is the expected return on the underlying asset and $b$ is the standard deviation of its price returns.

$$\frac{\mathrm{d}S}{S} = a\mathrm{d}t + b\mathrm{d}W \tag{13.11}$$

## The Black–Scholes model and pricing derivative instruments

We assume a financial asset is specified by its terminal payoff value. Therefore, when pricing an option we require the fair value of the option at the initial time when the option is struck, and this value is a function of the expected terminal payoff of the option, discounted to the day when the option is struck. In this section, we present an intuitive explanation of the B–S model, in terms of the normal distribution of asset–price returns. Background on the log-normal distribution of price returns is given in Appendix 13.2.

From the definition of a call option, we can set the expected value of the option at maturity $T$ as:

$$E\left(C_T\right) = E\left[\max\left(S_T - X, 0\right)\right] \tag{13.12}$$

where $S_T$ is the price of the underlying asset at maturity $T$
$X$ is the strike price of the option.

From (13.12) we know that there are only two possible outcomes that can arise on maturity; either the option will expire in-the-money and the outcome is $S_T - X$, or the option will be out-of-the-money and the outcome will be 0. If we set the term $p$ as the probability that on expiry $S_T > X$, equation (13.12) can be re-written as (13.13).

$$E(C_T) = p \times \left( E\left[ S_T \mid S_T > X \right] - X \right) \tag{13.13}$$

where $E[S_T \mid S_T > X]$ is the expected value of $S_T$ given that $S_T > X$. Equation (13.12) gives us an expression for the expected value of a call option on maturity. Therefore, to obtain the fair price of the option at the time it is struck, the value given by (13.13) must be discounted back to its present value, and this is shown as (13.14).

$$C = p \times e^{-rt} \times \left( E\left[ S_T \mid S_T > X \right] - X \right) \tag{13.14}$$

where $r$ is the continuously compounded risk-free rate of interest, and $t$ is the time from today until maturity. Therefore, to price an option we require the probability $p$ that the option expires in-the-money, and we require the expected value of the option given that it does expire in-the-money, which is the last term of (13.14). To calculate $p$ we assume that asset prices follow a stochastic process, which enables us to model the probability function.

The B–S model is based on the resolution of the following partial differential equation,

$$\tfrac{1}{2}\sigma^2 S^2 \left( \frac{\partial^2 C}{\partial S^2} \right) + rS \left( \frac{\partial C}{\partial S} \right) + \left( \frac{\partial C}{\partial t} \right) - rC = 0, \tag{13.15}$$

under the appropriate parameters. We do not demonstrate the process by which this equation is arrived at. The parameters refer to the payoff conditions corresponding to a European call option, which we considered above. We do not present a solution to the differential equation at (13.15), which is beyond the scope of the book, but we can consider now how the probability and expected-value functions can be solved. For a fuller treatment, readers may wish to refer to the original account by Black and Scholes. Other good accounts are given in Ingersoll (1987), Neftci (1996) and Nielsen (1999), among others.

We wish to find the probability $p$ that the underlying asset price at maturity exceeds $X$ is equal to the probability that the return over the time period the option is held exceeds a certain critical value. Remember that we assume normal distribution of asset–price returns. As asset returns are defined as the logarithm of price relatives, we require $p$ such that:

$$p = prob[S_T > X] = prob\left[ return > \ln\left( \frac{X}{S_0} \right) \right] \tag{13.16}$$

where $S_0$ is the price of the underlying asset at the time the option is struck. Generally, the probability that a normally distributed variable $x$ will exceed a critical value $x_c$ is given by (13.17):

$$p[x > x_c] = 1 - N\left(\frac{x_c - \mu}{\sigma}\right) \qquad (13.17)$$

where $\mu$ and $\sigma$ are the mean and standard deviation of $x$ respectively and $N(\ )$ is the cumulative normal distribution.

We know from our earlier discussion of the behaviour of asset prices that an expression for $\mu$ is the natural logarithm of the asset–price returns. We already know that the standard deviation of returns is $\sigma\sqrt{t}$. Therefore, with these assumptions, we may combine (13.16) and (13.17) to give us (13.18); that is,

$$p = prob.[S_T > X] = prob.\left[return > \ln\left(\frac{X}{S_0}\right)\right] = 1 - N\left[\frac{\ln\left(\dfrac{X}{S_0}\right) - \left(\dfrac{r - \sigma^2}{2}\right)t}{\sigma\sqrt{t}}\right].$$

$$(13.18)$$

Under the conditions of the normal distribution, the symmetrical shape means that we can obtain the probability of an occurrence based on $1 - N(d)$ being equal to $N(-d)$. Therefore, we are able to set the following relationship, as (13.19):

$$p = prob.[S_T > X] = N\left[\frac{\ln\left(\dfrac{S_0}{X}\right) + \left(r - \dfrac{\sigma^2}{2}\right)t}{\sigma\sqrt{t}}\right]. \qquad (13.19)$$

Now we require a formula to calculate the expected value of the option on expiry, the second part of the expression in (13.14). This involves the integration of the normal distribution curve over the range from $X$ to infinity. This is not shown here, but the result is given in (13.20):

$$E[S_T | S_T > X] = S_0 e^{rt} \frac{N(d_1)}{N(d_2)} \qquad (13.20)$$

where

$$d_1 = \frac{\ln\left(\dfrac{S_0}{X}\right) + \left(r + \dfrac{\sigma^2}{2}\right)t}{\sigma\sqrt{t}}$$

and

$$d_2 = \frac{\ln\left(\dfrac{S_0}{X}\right) + \left(r - \dfrac{\sigma^2}{2}\right)t}{\sigma\sqrt{t}} = d_1 - \sigma\sqrt{t}.$$

We now have expressions for the probability that an option expires in-the-money as well as the expected value of the option on expiry, and we incorporate these into the expression at (13.14), which gives us (13.21):

$$C = N\left(d_2\right) \times e^{-rt} \times \left[ S_0 e^{-rt}\, \frac{N\left(d_1\right)}{N\left(d_2\right)} - X \right]. \qquad (13.21)$$

Equation (13.21) can be rearranged to give (13.22), which is the famous and well-known B–S option-pricing model for a European call option:

$$C = S_0 N\left(d_1\right) - X e^{-rt} N\left(d_2\right) \qquad (13.22)$$

where  $S_0$   is the price of the underlying asset at the time the option is struck

$X$   is the strike price

$r$   is the continuously compounded risk-free interest rate

$t$   is the maturity of the option.

and $d_1$ and $d_2$ are as before.

What the expression in (13.22) states is that the fair value of a call option is the expected present value of the option on its expiry date, assuming that prices follow a lognormal distribution.

$N(d_1)$ and $N(d_2)$ are the cumulative probabilities from the normal distribution of obtaining the values $d_1$ and $d_2$, given above. $N(d_1)$ is the delta of the option. The term $N(d_2)$ represents the probability that the option will be exercised. The term $e^{-rt}$ is the present value of one unit of cash received $t$ periods from the time the option is struck. Where $N(d_1)$ and $N(d_2)$ are equal to 1, which is the equivalent of assuming complete certainty, the model is reduced to:

$$C = S - X e^{-rt}$$

which is the expression for Merton's lower bound for continuously compounded interest rates, and which we introduced in intuitive fashion in the previous chapter. Therefore, under complete certainty, the B–S model reduces to Merton's bound.

## The put-call parity relationship

Up to now we have concentrated on calculating the price of a call option. However, the previous section introduced the boundary condition for a put option, so it should be apparent that this can be solved as well. In fact, the price of a call option and a put option are related via what is known as the put-call parity theorem. This is an important relationship and obviates the need to develop a separate model for put options.

Consider a portfolio $Y$ that consists of a call option with a maturity date $T$ and a zero-coupon bond that pays $X$ on the expiry date of the option. Consider also a second portfolio $Z$ that consists of a put option also with maturity date $T$ and one share. The value of portfolio $A$ on the expiry date is given by (13.23):

$$MV_{Y,T} = \max.\left[S_T - X, 0\right] + X = \max\left[X, S_T\right]. \tag{13.23}$$

The value of the second portfolio $Z$ on the expiry date is:

$$MV_{Z,T} = \max.\left[X - S_T, 0\right] + S_T = \max\left[X, S_T\right]. \tag{13.24}$$

Both portfolios have the same value at maturity. Therefore, they must also have the same initial value at start time $t$, otherwise there would be an arbitrage opportunity. Prices must be arbitrage-free; therefore, the following put-call relationship must hold:

$$C_t - P_t = S_t - Xe^{-r(T-t)}. \tag{13.25}$$

If the relationship in (13.24) did not hold, then arbitrage would be possible. So, using this relationship, the value of a European put option is given by the B–S model as shown below, in (13.26):

$$P(S,T) = -SN\left(-d_1\right) + Xe^{-rT}N\left(-d2\right). \tag{13.26}$$

> EXAMPLE 13.11    The Black–Scholes model: Example

Here we illustrate a simple application of the B–S model. Consider an underlying asset, assumed to be a non-dividend-paying equity, with a current price of 25, and volatility of 23%. The short-term risk-free interest rate is 5%. An option is written with strike price 21 and a maturity of three months. Therefore, we have:

$S = 25$
$X = 21$
$r = 5\%$
$T = 0.25$
$\sigma = 23\%.$

To calculate the price of the option, we first calculate the discounted value of the strike price, as follows:

$$Xe^{-rT} = 21e^{-0.05(0.25)} = 20.73913.$$

We then calculate the values of $d_1$ and $d_2$:

$$d_1 = \frac{\ln(25/21) + \left[0.05 + (0.5)(0.23)^2\right]0.25}{0.23\sqrt{0.25}} = \frac{0.193466}{0.115}$$

$$= 1.682313$$

$$d_2 = d_1 - 0.23\sqrt{0.25} = 1.567313.$$

We now insert these values into the main price equation:

$$C = 25N(1.682313) - 21e^{-0.05(0.25)}N(1.567313).$$

Using the approximation of the cumulative normal distribution at the points 1.68 and 1.56, the price of the call option is:

$$C = 25(0.9535) - 20.73913(0.9406) = 4.3303$$

or 4.3303.

What would be the price of a put option on the same stock?
The values of $N(d_1)$ and $N(d_2)$ are 0.9535 and 0.9406; therefore, the put price is calculated as:

$$P = 20.7391(1 - 0.9406) - 25(1 - 0.9535) = 0.06943.$$

If we use the call price and apply the put-call parity theorem, the price of the put option is given by:

$$P = C - S + Xe^{-rT}$$
$$= 4.3303 - 25 + 21e^{-0.05(0.25)}$$
$$= 0.069434.$$

This is exactly the same price that was obtained by the application of the put-option formula in the B–S model above.

As we noted early in this chapter, the premium payable for an option will increase if the time to expiry, the volatility or the interest rate is increased (or any combination is increased). Thus, if we keep all the parameters constant, but price a call option that has a maturity of six months or $T = 0.5$, we obtain the following values:

$$d_1 = 1.3071, \text{ giving } N(d_1) = 0.9049$$
$$d_2 = 1.1445, \text{ giving } N(d_2) = 0.8740.$$

The call price for the longer-dated option is 4.7217.

## The B–S model as an Excel spreadsheet

In Appendix 13.3, we show the spreadsheet formulas required to build the B–S model into Microsoft® Excel. The user must ensure that the Analysis Tool-Pak add-in is available, otherwise some of the function references may not work. By setting up the cells in the way shown, the fair value of a vanilla call or put option may be calculated. The put-call parity is used to enable calculation of the put price.

## B–S and the valuation of bond options

In this section, we illustrate the application of the B–S model to the pricing of an option on a zero-coupon bond and a plain vanilla fixed-coupon bond.

For a zero-coupon bond, the theoretical price of a call option written on the bond is given by 13.27:

$$C = PN(d_1) - Xe^{-rT}N(d_2) \qquad (13.27)$$

where $P$ is the price of the underlying bond and all other parameters remain the same. If the option is written on a coupon-paying bond, it is necessary to subtract the present value of all coupons paid during the life of the option from the bond's price. Coupons sometimes lower the price of a call option because a coupon makes it more attractive to hold a bond rather than an option on the bond. Call options on bonds are often priced at a lower level than similar options on zero-coupon bonds.

---

**EXAMPLE 13.12** B–S model and bond option pricing

Consider a European call option written on a bond that has the following characteristics:

| | |
|---|---|
| Price: | £98 |
| Coupon: | 8.00% (semiannual) |
| Time to maturity: | Five years |
| Bond price volatility: | 6.02% |
| Coupon payments: | £4 in three months and nine months |
| Three-month interest rate: | 5.60% |
| Nine-month interest rate: | 5.75% |
| One-year interest rate: | 6.25% |

The option is written with a strike price of £100 and has a maturity of one year. The present value of the coupon payments made during the life of the option is £7.78, as shown below:

$$4e^{-0..056\times0.25} + 4e^{-0.057\times0.25} = 3.9444 + 3.83117 = 7.77557.$$

This gives us $P = 98 - 7.78 = £90.22$.
Applying the B–S model we obtain:

$$d_1 = \left[ \ln\left(90.22/100\right) + 0.0625 + 0.001812 \right] / 0.0602 = -0.6413$$

$$d_2 = d_1 - \left(0.0602\times1\right) = -0.7015$$

$$C = 90.22N\left(-0.6413\right) - 100e^{-0.0625}N\left(-0.7015\right)$$

$$= 1.1514.$$

Therefore, the call option has a value of £1.15, which will be composed entirely of time value. Note also that a key assumption of the model is constant interest rates, yet it is being applied to a bond price – which is essentially an interest rate – that is considered to follow a stochastic price process.

| EXAMPLE 13.13 | Using options to hedge interest-rate risk exposure |

Let us consider a hypothetical small-sized retail bank with a USD200 million balance sheet. Its simplified gap report is shown at Table 13.5 on page 614. This shows that the majority of the bank's assets are fixed rate, while a majority of its funding (liabilities) are floating-rate. This liability sensitivity is indicated by the "instant" gap of −80.00, as shown in the Table.[10] In other words, the bank exhibits an earnings stream that is at risk from a rise in interest rates. We illustrate this in Table 13.6 on page 615, which shows the impact of a 100 basis point parallel shift in market interest rates (we assume that all the floating-rate assets and liabilities would reprice immediately following the change in market rates). We observe that if there is a 1% upward parallel shift in rates, NII is reduced by USD800,000.00. Thus the bank is carrying currently approximately 7.8% of earnings-at-risk exposure (EAR). Put another way, the risk represents a 40 basis point reduction in the net interest margin (NIM).[11] It may be that this is acceptable to ALCO, although typically ALCO will set a ±5% or ±10% limit on EAR. For our hypothetical bank under the current scenario the latter would not present a problem, however the former would. The ALM desk would want to reduce the EAR to within the formal limit, and this can be undertaken in a number of ways. If derivatives are not available, the ALM desk could reduce the amount of floating-rate funding and increase fixed-rate funding; equally it could increase the amount of floating-rate assets.[12] The problem with using cash assets to reduce EAR exposure is that they cannot be effected right away.

By using derivatives the risk exposure can be adjusted immediately. An FRA can be used to cover the funding risk; or, the ALM desk can use an interest-rate cap. If it believes rates are going up, it can buy a cap. In this case, the bank can buy a cap of notional

---

[10] This gap report is simplified because we do not take into account the tenor of the assets and liabilities. Rather, we view this as a snapshot gap report of interest-rate sensitivity to a change in rates today.

[11] We define NIM as the dollar difference between interest income and interest expenses, expressed as a percentage of average earning assets. In our example, all USD200 million of assets are earning a return – there are no non-earning assets on the balance sheet.

[12] The ALM desk might consider this if it firmly believed that the next move in interest rates was upward.

USD80 million (the amount of the funding gap at risk), which would remove the EAR completely. A lower notional would leave some exposure, and a higher notional would change the interest-rate sensitivity of the bank to one that benefited from a rise in rates. The tenor of the option would be set to match the risk horizon of the bank; if for example the ALM desk believes rates will change in the next six to 12 months, it would buy a one-year cap. Generally, the strike price of the option would be set at the prevailing interest rate (at-the-market), so if the current three-month Libor rate is 3% then the cap strike would be set at 3%. This removes any downside risk. For a lower option premium, the ALM desk may want to set a higher strike rate, say 4%, which is "out-of-the-money" and leaves some residual EAR. This would be done to reduce the cost of the hedge, and also if the bank feels that it can live with a small increase in rates.

By buying a 3% strike USD80 million one-year cap, the bank is hedged if rates rise above the strike rate. If on option maturity rates are indeed higher, the seller of the cap (usually a bank that is a market-maker in options) will pay to the buyer the difference between the current rate and the strike rate, multiplied by the notional. If rates have not risen or if they have fallen, the option expires worthless (the buyer would have paid the option premium on purchase and this remains income for the market-maker). Table 13.7 on page 616 shows the effect on EAR if the bank buys the cap to hedge its interest-rate risk. The cap is an off-balance sheet instrument, but its cash flows on execution and expiry impact the bank's balance sheet position, in this case altering its risk profile. The risk exposure has been reduced such that if rates do increase, there is no negative impact for the bank.[13] The NII and NIM are unchanged even when rates have moved upward, and the EAR has been eliminated completely, so on paper this hedge looks very effective. The option premium is key to the analysis; of course, in our example it is sufficiently low to be not material, but this may not necessarily be the case in practice.

The illustration in Table 13.7 shows one advantage of using options to hedge rather than other derivatives: the ability to gain from an upside move and yet not pay – option premium excepted – on a downside move. In a falling interest-rate environment the NIM

---

[13] We have set a premium price of 0.1 to make the illustration clear. The payout on the option is shown in Table 13.7.

increases, but the option hedge is unused. If the hedge was constructed with an interest-rate swap or FRA, the bank would have to pay out on either of these instruments if rates moved lower. This is not the case with the option, and when the hedge is in place the only cost is the one-off premium. In other words, a swap removes earnings volatility in both a rising and a falling interest-rate environment, so while the risk protection is complete there is no chance of upside gain. With an option the bank has a chance to benefit from an upward move in rates. The cost of the hedge is the premium, which is of course paid irrespective of whether the option expires in-the-money or not. In our example, this hedge cost amounted to 5 basis points in NIM terms.

Note that a bank that was "asset sensitive" would do the opposite to what is described here, it would purchase a floor option that would pay out if the Libor rate on expiry was below the strike rate.

**Asset–liability gap**

| *Assets* | (million) | Fixed rate or current floating-rate |
|---|---|---|
| Loans: fixed rate | 140 | 8% |
| Bonds: fixed rate | 40 | 7% |
| Bonds: floating-rate | 20 | 5% |
| Total assets | 200 | |
| Risk-sensitive assets (RSA) | 20 | |
| *Liabilities* | | |
| Deposits: floating-rate | 100 | 3% |
| Deposits: fixed rate | 60 | 3% |
| NIBLs | 20 | 0% |
| Capital | 20 | 0% |
| | 200 | |
| Risk-sensitive liabilities (RSL) | 100 | |
| Gap | −80.0 | |
| RSA/RSL | 20% | |

**Table 13.5**   Bank simplified gap report

| | No rate change | | −1% parallel shift | | +1% parallel shift | |
|---|---|---|---|---|---|---|
| *Interest income* | | | | | | |
| Loans: fixed rate | 11.2 | [140 * 0.08] | 11.2 | [140 * 0.08] | 11.2 | [140 * 0.08] |
| Bonds: fixed rate | 2.8 | [40 * 0.07] | 2.8 | [40 * 0.07] | 2.8 | [40 * 0.07] |
| Bonds: floating-rate | 1.0 | [20 * 0.05] | 0.8 | [20 * 0.04] | 1.2 | [20 * 0.06] |
| Total | 15.0 | | 14.8 | | 15.2 | |
| *Interest cost* | | | | | | |
| Deposits: floating-rate | 3.0 | [100 * 0.03] | 2.0 | [100 * 0.02] | 4.0 | [100 * 0.04] |
| Deposits: fixed rate | 1.8 | [60 * 0.03] | 1.8 | [60 * 0.03] | 1.8 | [60 * 0.03] |
| Total | 4.8 | | 3.8 | | 5.8 | |
| Net interest income (NII) | **10.2** | | **11** | | **9.4** | |
| Net interest margin (NIM) | 5.10% | | 5.50% | | 4.70% | |
| Earnings at risk | | | | | 7.84% | |

**Table 13.6**   Net interest income scenarios

| | No rate change | | −1% parallel shift | | +1% parallel shift | |
|---|---|---|---|---|---|---|
| ***Interest income*** | | | | | | |
| Loans: fixed rate | 11.2 | [140 * 0.08] | 11.2 | [140 * 0.08] | 11.2 | [140 * 0.08] |
| Bonds: fixed rate | 2.8 | [40 * 0.07] | 2.8 | [40 * 0.07] | 2.8 | [40 * 0.07] |
| Bonds: floating-rate | 1 | [20 * 0.05] | 0.8 | [20 * 0.04] | 1.2 | [20 * 0.06] |
| Payments from Cap | 0 | 0 | 0.8 | [80mm * (5% − 4%)] | | |
| Total | 15 | | 14.8 | | 16 | |
| ***Interest cost*** | | | | | | |
| Deposits: floating-rate | 3 | [100 * 0.03] | 2 | [100 * 0.02] | 4 | [100 * 0.04] |
| Deposits: fixed rate | 1.8 | [60 * 0.03] | 1.8 | [60 * 0.03] | 1.8 | [60 * 0.03] |
| Cap premium | 0.1 | | 0.1 | | 0.1 | |
| Total | 4.9 | | 3.9 | | 5.9 | |
| Net interest income (NII) | **10.1** | | **10.9** | | **10.1** | |
| Net interest margin (NIM) | 5.05% | | 5.45% | | 5.05% | |
| Earnings at risk | | | | | 0.00% | |

**Table 13.7** Net interest income and option hedge

## Hedging considerations when using options

The simple example above serves to illustrate how an ALM desk can reduce or eliminate interest-rate risk through the use of options. The desk should also be aware of other issues when using options to construct the hedge.

### Basis risk

Basis risk exists for all hedging instruments, not just options. If all the cash assets on the bank's balance sheet were referenced to Libor, then basis risk would be zero because the option fix on expiry is also with reference to Libor. However, some assets will be linked to other reference rates such as the Prime rate or the T-bill rate. Risk hedging needs to be aware of any divergence between the hedge index and the reference index, and rebalance the hedge accordingly.

### Counterparty risk

When buying options for hedging purposes, a bank will need to monitor the credit quality of the option seller, as it will have an exposure to it should the option expire in-the-money. This can be carried out as part of the standard credit analysis carried out by the bank for its own customers. Generally, option market-makers are of interbank quality and this is considered more than acceptable credit risk.

### Option pricing

Interest-rate options are generally priced using the Black model or a binomial or trinomial pricing model. However, different banks may use slightly different parameter values for implied volatility, when pricing the same option. A bank looking to use options can ensure that it is paying fair value for the hedge by asking more than one market-maker for a price quote. A more efficient method would be for the bank to implement its own option pricing model, which it can then use to compare prices and also to mark-to-market.

Reproduced from *Bank Asset and Liability Management* (2007)

This extract from *Fixed Income Markets, Second Edition* (2014)

## Swaps

### Swaps

Swaps are one of the most important and useful instruments in the debt-capital markets, indeed the global economy. The main types of swap are interest-rate swaps, asset swaps, basis swaps, cross-currency swaps, and currency-coupon swaps. The market for swaps is organised by the International Swaps and Derivatives Association (ISDA). They are used by a wide range of institutions, including banks, mortgage banks and building societies, corporates, and local authorities. As the market has matured, the instrument has gained wider acceptance, and it is regarded as a plain-vanilla product in the debt-capital markets. Virtually all commercial and investment banks will quote swap prices for their customers, and as they are over-the counter (OTC) instruments, dealt over the telephone, it is possible for banks to tailor swaps to match the precise requirements of individual customers. There is also a close relationship between the bond market and the swap market, and corporate finance teams and underwriting banks keep a close eye on the government yield curve and the swap yield curve, looking out for possibilities regarding new issue of debt.

In this chapter, we review the use of interest-rate swaps from the point of view of the bond-market participant; this includes pricing and valuation and its use as a hedging tool. The bibliography lists further reading on important topics such as pricing, valuation, and credit risk.

## INTEREST–RATE SWAPS

### Background

Interest-rate swaps are the most important type of swap in terms of volume of transactions. They are used to manage and hedge interest-rate risk and exposure, while market makers will also take positions in swaps that reflect their view on the direction of interest rates. An interest-rate swap is an agreement between two counterparties to make periodic interest payments to one another during the life of the swap, on a predetermined set of dates, based on a notional principal amount. One party is the fixed-rate payer, and this rate is agreed at the time of trade of the swap; the other party is the floating-rate payer, the floating rate being determined during the life of the swap by reference to a specific market index. The principal or notional amount is not physically exchanged; hence, the term "off-balance-sheet", but is used merely to calculate the interest payments.[1] The fixed-rate payer receives floating-rate interest and is said to be "long" or to have "bought" the swap. The long side has conceptually purchased a floating-rate note (because it receives floating-rate interest) and issued a fixed-coupon bond (because it

---

[1] The author himself eschews the term "off-balance-sheet" because it is misleading; all derivatives have a very definite on-balance-sheet impact on any person transacting them, whether it is the contractual cash flows and/or the collateral cash flows. From an understanding of the balance sheet perspective, forget the accounting terminology; derivatives are on your balance sheet because their associated cash flows are on your balance sheet.

pays out fixed interest at intervals); that is, it has in principle borrowed funds. The floating-rate payer is said to be "short" or to have "sold" the swap. The short side has conceptually purchased a coupon bond (because it receives fixed-rate interest) and issued a floating-rate note (because it pays floating-rate interest). So an interest-rate swap is:

- An agreement between two parties
- To exchange a stream of cash flows
- Calculated as a percentage of a *notional* sum
- Calculated on different interest bases

For example, in a trade between Bank A and Bank B, Bank A may agree to pay fixed semiannual coupons of 10% on a notional principal sum of £1 million, in return for receiving from Bank B the prevailing six-month sterling Libor rate on the same amount. The known cash flow is the fixed payment of £50,000 every six months by Bank A to Bank B.

Interest-rate swaps trade in a secondary market, so their value moves in line with market interest rates, in exactly the same way as bonds. If a five-year interest-rate swap is transacted today at a rate of 5%, and five-year interest rates subsequently fall to 4.75%, the swap will have decreased in value to the fixed-rate payer, and correspondingly increased in value to the floating-rate payer, who has now seen the level of interest payments fall. The opposite would be true if five-year rates moved to 5.25%. Why is this? Consider the fixed-rate payer in an IR swap to be a borrower of funds; if she fixes the interest rate payable on a loan for five years, and then this interest rate decreases shortly afterwards, is she better off? No, because she is now paying above the market rate for the funds borrowed. For this reason, a swap contract decreases in value to the fixed-rate payer if there is a fall in rates. Equally a floating-rate payer gains if there is a fall in rates, as he can take advantage of the new rates and pay a lower level of interest; hence, the value of a swap increases to the floating-rate payer if there is a fall in rates.

A bank swaps desk will have an overall net interest-rate position arising from all the swaps it has traded that are currently on the book. This position is an interest-rate exposure at all points along the term structure, out to the maturity of the longest-dated swap. At the close of business each day, all the swaps on the book will be *marked-to-market* at the relevant tenor interest rate quoted for that day.

A swap can be viewed in two ways; either as a bundle of forward or futures contracts, or as a bundle of cash flows arising from the "sale" and "purchase" of cash-market instruments. If we imagine a strip of futures contracts, maturing every three or six months out to three years, we can see how this is conceptually similar to a three-year interest-rate swap. However, in the author's view it is better to visualise a swap as being a bundle of cash flows arising from cash instruments.

Let us imagine we have only two positions on our book:

1. A long position in £100 million of a three-year floating-rate note (FRN) that pays six-month Libor semiannually, and is trading at par
2. A short position in £100 million of a three-year gilt with coupon of 6% that is also trading at par

Being short a bond is the equivalent to being a borrower of funds. Assuming this position is kept to maturity, the resulting cash flows are shown in Table 13.1.

There is no net outflow or inflow at the start of these trades, as the £100 million purchase of the FRN is netted with receipt of £100 million from the sale of the gilt. The resulting cash flows over the three-year period are shown in the last column of Table 13.1. This net position is exactly the same as that of a fixed-rate payer in an (interest-rate) IR swap. As we had at the start of the trade, there is no cash inflow or outflow on maturity. For a floating-rate payer, the cash flow would mirror exactly a long position in a fixed-rate bond and a short position in an FRN. Therefore, the fixed-rate payer in a swap is said to be short in the bond market; that is, a borrower of funds. The floating-rate payer in a swap is said to be long the bond market.

## Market Terminology

Virtually all swaps are traded under the legal terms and conditions stipulated in the ISDA standard documentation. The trade date for a swap is, not

---

**Cash Flows Resulting from Long Position in FRN and Short Position in Gilt**

| Period (6 mo) | FRN | Gilt | Net Cash Flow |
|---|---|---|---|
| 0 | −£100m | +£100m | £0 |
| 1 | +(Libor × 100)/2 | −3 | +(Libor × 100)/2 − 3.0 |
| 2 | +(Libor × 100)/2 | −3 | +(Libor × 100)/2 − 3.0 |
| 3 | +(Libor × 100)/2 | −3 | +(Libor × 100)/2 − 3.0 |
| 4 | +(Libor × 100)/2 | −3 | +(Libor × 100)/2 − 3.0 |
| 5 | +(Libor × 100)/2 | −3 | +(Libor × 100)/2 − 3.0 |
| 6 | +[(Libor × 100)/2] + 100 | −103 | +(Libor × 100)/2 − 3.0 |

The Libor rate is the six-month rate prevailing at the time of the setting; for instance, the Libor rate at period 4 will be the rate actually prevailing at period 4.

**Table 13.1**   Three-Year Cash Flows

surprisingly, the date on which the swap is transacted. The terms of the trade include the fixed interest rate, the maturity and notional amount of the swap, and the payment bases of both legs of the swap. The date from which floating interest payments are determined is the setting date, which may also be the trade date. Most swaps fix the floating-rate payments to Libor, although other reference rates that are used include the U.S. Prime rate, the Fed Funds rate, euribor, the Treasury-bill rate, and the commercial-paper rate. In the same way as for a forward-rate agreement (FRA) and for eurocurrency deposits, the rate is fixed two business days before the interest period begins. The second (and subsequent) setting date will be two business days before the beginning of the second (and subsequent) swap periods. The effective date is the date from which interest on the swap is calculated, and this is typically two business days after the trade date. In a forward-start swap, the effective date will be at some point in the future, specified in the swap terms. The floating interest rate for each period is fixed at the start of the period, so that the interest payment amount is known in advance by both parties (the fixed rate is known, of course, throughout the swap by both parties).

Although for the purposes of explaining swap structures, both parties are said to pay interest payments (and receive them), in practice only the net difference between both payments changes hands at the end of each interest period. This eases the administration associated with swaps and reduces the number of cash flows for each swap. The counterparty that is the net payer at the end of each period will make a payment to the other counterparty. The first payment date will occur at the end of the first interest period, and subsequent payment dates will fall at the end of successive interest periods. The final payment date falls on the maturity date of the swap. The calculation of interest is given by equation (13.1).

$$I = M \times r \times \frac{n}{B} \qquad (13.1)$$

where $I$ is the interest amount, $M$ is the nominal amount of the swap, and $B$ is the interest day-base for the swap. Dollar- and euro-denominated swaps use an actual/360 day-count, similar to other money-market instruments in those currencies, while sterling swaps use an actual/365 day-count basis.

The cash flows in a vanilla interest-rate swap are illustrated in Figure 13.1. The counterparties in a swap transaction only pay across net cash flows, however, so at each interest payment date only one actual cash transfer will be made, by the net payer. This is shown as Figure 13.1(iii).

## Swap Spreads and the Swap Yield Curve

In the market, banks will quote two-way swap rates on screens or via a dealing system such as Reuters. Brokers will also be active in relaying prices in

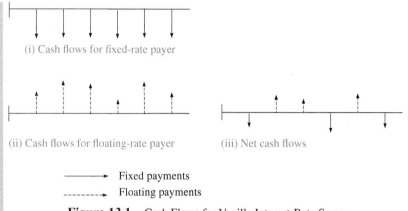

(i) Cash flows for fixed-rate payer

(ii) Cash flows for floating-rate payer        (iii) Net cash flows

→ Fixed payments

----→ Floating payments

**Figure 13.1**   Cash Flows for Vanilla Interest-Rate Swap

the market. The convention in the market is for the swap market maker to set the floating leg at Libor and then quote the fixed rate that is payable for that maturity. So for a five-year swap, a bank's swap desk might be willing to quote the following:

Floating-rate payer:   Pay 6-month-Libor
                       Receive fixed rate of 5.19%
Fixed-rate payer:      Pay fixed rate of 5.25%
                       Receive 6-month Libor

In this case, the bank is quoting an offer rate of 5.25%, which the fixed-rate payer will pay, in return for receiving Libor flat. The bid price quote is 5.19%, which is what a floating-rate payer will receive fixed. The bid-offer spread in this case is therefore 6 basis points. The fixed-rate quotes are always at a spread above the government bond yield curve. Let us assume that the five-year gilt is yielding 4.88%. In this case, then, the five-year swap bid rate is 31 basis points above this yield. So the bank's swap trader could quote the swap rates as a spread above the benchmark-bond yield curve, say 37-31, which is her swap spread quote. This means that the bank is happy to enter into a swap paying fixed 31 basis points above the bench-mark yield and receiving Libor, and receiving fixed 37 basis points above the yield curve and paying Libor. The bank's screen on, say, Bloomberg or Reuters might look something like Table 13.2, which quotes the swap rates as well as the current spread over the government-bond benchmark.

The swap spread is a function of the same factors that influence the spread over government bonds for other instruments. For shorter-duration swaps of, say, up to three years, there are other yield curves that can be used in comparison, such as the cash-market curve or a curve derived from

| 1-yr | 4.50 | 4.45 | +17 |
| 2-yr | 4.69 | 4.62 | +25 |
| 3-yr | 4.88 | 4.80 | +23 |
| 4-yr | 5.15 | 5.05 | +29 |
| 5-yr | 5.25 | 5.19 | +31 |
| 10-yr | 5.50 | 5.40 | +35 |

**Table 13.2**   Swap Quotes

futures prices. For longer-dated swaps, the spread is determined mainly by the credit spreads that prevail in the corporate-bond market. Because a swap is viewed as a package of long and short positions in fixed- and floating-rate bonds, it is the credit spreads in these two markets that will determine the swap spread. This is logical; essentially, it is the premium for greater credit risk involved in lending to corporates that dictates that a swap rate will be higher than the same maturity government-bond yield. Technical factors will be responsible for day-to-day fluctuations in swap rates, such as the supply of corporate bonds and the level of demand for swaps, plus the cost to swap traders of hedging their swap positions.

We can summarise by saying that swap spreads over government bonds reflect the supply and demand conditions of both swaps and government bonds, as well as the market's view on the credit quality of swap counter-parties. There is considerable information content in the swap yield curve, much like that in the government-bond yield curve. During times of credit concerns in the market, such as the corrections in Asian and Latin American markets in the summer of 1998, and the 2008 bank crash, the swap spread will increase, more so at higher maturities. After the Lehman default in September 2008, the overnight index swap (OIS) spread over Libor widened considerably. The change in swap spreads is shown in Figure 13.2.

**Figure 13.2**   Libor-OIS Spread, 2002–2008

# GENERIC SWAP VALUATION

Banks generally use par-swap (zero-coupon) swap pricing. We will look at this method in the next section. First, however, we will introduce an intuitive swap valuation method.

## Par Swap Pricing

Assume we have a vanilla interest-rate swap with a notional principal of $N$ that pays $n$ payments during its life, to a maturity date of $T$. The date of each payment is on $t_i$ with $i = 1, \ldots n$. The present value today of a future payment is denoted by $PV(0, t)$. If the swap rate is $r$, the value of the fixed-leg payments is given by (13.2).

$$PV_{fixed} = N \sum_{i=1}^{n} PV\left(0, t_i\right) \times \left[ r \times \left( \frac{t_i - t_{i-1}}{B} \right) \right] \qquad (13.2)$$

where $B$ is the money-market day base. The term $(t_i - t_{i-1})$ is simply the number of days between the $i$th and the $i-1$th payments.

The value of the floating-leg payments at the date $t_1$ for an existing swap is given by,

$$PV_{float} = N \times \left[ rl \times \frac{t_1}{B} \right] + N - \left[ N \times PV\left(t_1, t_n\right) \right] \qquad (13.3)$$

where $rl$ is the Libor rate that has been set for the next interest payment. We set the present value of the floating-rate payment at time 0 as follows:

$$PV\left(0, t_1\right) = \frac{1}{1 + rl\left(t_1\right)\left(\dfrac{t_1}{B}\right)} \qquad (13.4)$$

For a new swap, the value of the floating payments is given by

$$PV_{float} = N \left\{ \left[ rl \times \frac{t_1}{B} + 1 \right] \times PV\left(0, t_1\right) - PV\left(0, t_n\right) \right\} \qquad (13.5)$$

The swap valuation is then given by $PV_{fixed} - PV_{float}$. The swap rate quoted by a market-making bank is that which sets $PV_{fixed} = PV_{float}$ and is known as the par or zero-coupon swap rate. We consider this next.

## Zero-Coupon Swap Pricing

So far, we have discussed how vanilla swap prices are often quoted as a spread over the benchmark government-bond yield in that currency, and how this swap spread is mainly a function of the credit spread required by the market over the government (risk-free) rate. This method is convenient and also logical because banks use government bonds as the main instrument when hedging their swap books. However, because much bank swap trading is now conducted in nonstandard, tailor-made swaps, this method can sometimes be unwieldy, as each swap needs to have its spread calculated to suit its particular characteristics. Therefore, banks use a standard pricing method for all swaps known as zero-coupon swap pricing.

In Chapter 3, we referred to zero-coupon bonds and zero-coupon interest rates. Zero-coupon or spot rates, are true interest rates for their particular term to maturity. In zero-coupon swap pricing, a bank will view all swaps, even the most complex, as a series of cash flows. The zero-coupon rates that apply now for each of the cash flows in a swap can be used to value these cash flows. Therefore, to value and price a swap, each of the swap's cash flows are present-valued using known spot rates; the sum of these present values is the value of the swap.

In a swap, the fixed-rate payments are known in advance, and so it is straightforward to present-value them. The present value of the floating rate payments is usually estimated in two stages. First, the implied forward rates can be calculated using (13.6). We are quite familiar with this relationship from our reading of Chapter 3

$$rf_i = \left( \frac{df_i}{df_{i+1}} - 1 \right) N \qquad (13.6)$$

where   $rf_i$   is the one-period forward rate starting at time $i$
        $df_i$   is the discount factor for the maturity period $i$
        $df_{i+1}$ is the discount factor for the period $i + 1$
        $N$     is the number of times per year that coupons are paid

By definition, the floating-payment interest rates are not known in advance, so the swap bank will predict what these will be, using the forward rates applicable to each payment date. The forward rates are those that currently implied from spot rates. Once the size of the floating-rate payments has been estimated, these can also be valued by using the spot rates. The total value of the fixed and floating legs is the sum of all the present values, so the value of the total swap is the net of the present values of the fixed and floating legs.

While the term "zero-coupon" refers to an interest rate that applies to a discount instrument that pays no coupon and has one cash flow (at maturity), it is not necessary to have a functioning zero-coupon bond market in order to construct a zerocoupon yield curve. In practice, most financial pricing models use a combination of the following instruments to construct zero-coupon yield curves:

- Money-market deposits
- Interest-rate futures
- FRAs
- Government bonds.

Frequently an overlap in the maturity period of all instruments is used. FRA rates are usually calculated from interest-rate futures so it is only necessary to use one of either FRA or futures rates.

Once a zero-coupon yield curve (term structure) is derived, this may be used to value a future cash flow maturing at any time along the term structure. This includes swaps: to price an interest-rate swap, we calculate the present value of each of the cash flows using the zero-coupon rates and then sum all the cash flows. As we noted above, while the fixed-rate payments are known in advance, the floating-rate payments must be estimated, using the forward rates implied by the zero-coupon yield curve. The net present value of the swap is the net difference between the present values of the fixed- and floating-rate legs.

## Calculating the Forward Rate from Spot-Rate Discount Factors

Remember that one way to view a swap is as a long position in a fixed-coupon bond that was funded at Libor, or against a short position in a floating-rate bond. The cash flows from such an arrangement would be paying floating-rate and receiving fixed-rate. In the former arrangement, where a long position in a fixed-rate bond is funded with a floating-rate loan, the cash flows from the principals will cancel out, as they are equal and opposite (assuming the price of the bond on purchase was par), leaving a collection of cash flows that mirror an interest-rate swap that pays floating and receives fixed. Therefore, as the fixed-rate on an interest-rate swap is the same as the coupon (and yield) on a bond priced at par, calculating the fixed-rate on an interest-rate swap is the same as calculating the coupon for a bond that we wish to issue at par.

The price of a bond paying semiannual coupons is given by (13.7), which may be rearranged for the coupon rate $r$ to provide an equation that enables us to determine the par yield, and hence the swap rate $r$, given by (13.8).

$$P = \frac{r_n}{2} df_1 + \frac{r_n}{2} df_2 + \ldots\ldots + \frac{r_n}{2} df_n + M df_n \qquad (13.7)$$

where $r_n$ is the coupon on an $n$-period bond with $n$ coupons and $M$ is the maturity payment. Assuming $P = 1$ and $M = 1$, it can be shown then that

$$
\begin{aligned}
r_n &= \frac{1 - df_n}{\dfrac{df_1}{2} + \dfrac{df_2}{2} + \ldots\ldots + \dfrac{df_n}{2}} \\[2ex]
&= \frac{1 - df_n}{\displaystyle\sum_{i=1}^{n} \frac{df_i}{2}}
\end{aligned}
\qquad (13.8)
$$

For annual coupon bonds, there is no denominator for the discount factor, while for bonds paying coupons on a frequency of $N$ we replace the denominator 2 with $N$.[2] The expression in (13.8) may be rearranged again, using $F$ for the coupon frequency, to obtain an equation that may be used to calculate the $n$th discount factor for an $n$-period swap rate, given in (13.9).

$$df_n = \frac{1 - r_n \displaystyle\sum_{i=1}^{n-1} \frac{df_i}{N}}{1 + \dfrac{r_n}{N}} \qquad (13.9)$$

The expression in (13.9) is the general expression for the *bootstrapping* process that we first encountered in Chapter 1. Essentially, to calculate the $n$-year discount factor we use the discount factors for the years 1 to $n - 1$, and the $n$-year swap rate or zero-coupon rate. If we have the discount factor for any period, we may use (13.9) to determine the same period zero-coupon rate, after rearranging it, shown in (13.10).

$$rs_n = \sqrt[t_n]{\frac{1}{df_n}} - 1 \qquad (13.10)$$

---

[2] The expression also assumes an actual/365 day-count basis. If any other day-count convention is used, the 1/N factor must be replaced by a fraction made up of the actual number of days as the numerator and the appropriate year base as the denominator.

Discount factors for spot rates may also be used to calculate forward rates. We know that

$$df_1 = \frac{1}{\left(1 + \dfrac{rs_1}{N}\right)} \tag{13.11}$$

where $rs$ is the zero-coupon rate. If we know the forward rate we may use this to calculate a second discount rate, shown by (13.12).

$$df_2 = \frac{df_1}{\left(1 + \dfrac{rf_1}{N}\right)} \tag{13.12}$$

where $rf_1$ is the forward rate. This is of no use in itself; however, we may derive from it an expression to enable us to calculate the discount factor at any point in time between the previous discount rate and the given forward rate for the period $n$ to $n + 1$, shown in (13.13), which may then be rearranged to give us the general expression to calculate a forward rate, given in (13.14).

$$df_{n+1} = \frac{df_n}{\left(1 + \dfrac{rf_n}{N}\right)} \tag{13.13}$$

$$rf_n = \left(\frac{df_n}{df_{n+1}} - 1\right) N \tag{13.14}$$

The general expression for an $n$-period discount rate at time $n$ from the previous period forward rates is given by (13.15).

$$df_n = \frac{1}{\left(1 + \dfrac{rf_{n-1}}{N}\right)} \times \frac{1}{\left(1 + \dfrac{rf_{n-2}}{N}\right)} \times \dots \dots \times \frac{1}{\left(1 + \dfrac{rf_n}{N}\right)} \tag{13.15}$$

$$df_n = \prod_{i-0}^{n-1} \left[\frac{1}{\left(1 + \dfrac{rf_i}{N}\right)}\right]$$

From the above (13.7 to 13.15), we may combine equations (13.8) and (13.14) to obtain the general expression for an $n$-period swap rate and zero-coupon rate, given by (13.16) and (13.17), respectively.

$$r_n = \frac{\displaystyle\sum_{i=1}^{n} \frac{rf_{i-1} df_i}{N}}{\displaystyle\sum_{i=1}^{n} \frac{df_i}{F}} \tag{13.16}$$

$$1 + rs_n = \sqrt[t_n]{\prod_{i=0}^{n-1}\left(1 + \frac{rf_i}{N}\right)} \tag{13.17}$$

The two expressions do not tell us anything new, as we have already encountered their results in Chapter 3. The swap rate, which we have denoted as $r_n$ is shown by (13.16) to be the weighted average of the forward rates. If we consider that a strip of FRAs constitutes an interest-rate swap, then a swap rate for a continuous period could be covered by a strip of FRAs. Therefore, an average of the FRA rates would be the correct swap rate. As FRA rates are forward rates, we may be comfortable with (13.16), which states that the $n$-period swap rate is the average of the forward rates from $rf_0$ to $rf_n$. To be accurate, we must weight the forward rates, and these are weighted by the discount factors for each period. Note that although swap rates are derived from forward rates, interest payments under a swap are paid in the normal way at the end of an interest period, while payments for an FRA are made at the beginning of the period and must be discounted.

Equation (13.17) states that the zero-coupon rate is calculated from the geometric average of (one plus) the forward rates. The $n$-period forward rate is obtained using the discount factors for periods $n$ and $n - 1$. The discount factor for the complete period is obtained by multiplying the individual discount factors together, and exactly the same result would be obtained by using the zero-coupon interest-rate for the whole period to obtain the discount factor.

## Illustrating Interest–Rate Swap Pricing

The rate charged on a newly transacted interest-rate swap is the one that gives its net present value as zero. The term *valuation* of a swap is used to denote the process of calculating the net present value of an existing swap, when marking-to-market the swap against current market interest rates. Therefore, when we price a swap, we set its net present value to zero; while, when we value a swap, we set its fixed rate at the market rate and calculate the net present value.

To illustrate the basic principle, we price a plain-vanilla interest-rate swap with the terms set out below; for simplicity we assume that the annual fixed-rate payments are the same amount each year, although in practice there would be slight differences. Also assume that we already have our zero-coupon yields as shown in Table 13.3.

We use the zero-coupon rates to calculate the discount factors, and then use the discount factors to calculate the forward rates. This is done using

| Period | Zero-Coupon Rate % | Discount Factor | Forward Rate % | Fixed Payment | Floating Payment | PV Fixed Payment | PV Floating Payment |
|--------|--------------------|-----------------|----------------|---------------|------------------|------------------|---------------------|
| 1 | 5.50 | 0.94 | 5.50 | 689,625 | 550,000.00 | 653,672.98 | 521,327.01 |
| 2 | 6.00 | 0.88 | 6.50 | 689,625 | 650,236.96 | 613,763.79 | 578,708.58 |
| 3 | 6.25 | 0.83 | 6.75 | 689,625 | 675,177.02 | 574,944.84 | 562,899.47 |
| 4 | 6.50 | 0.77 | 7.25 | 689,625 | 725,353.49 | 536,061.43 | 563,834.02 |
| 5 | 7.00 | 0.71 | 9.02 | 689,625 | 902,358.47 | 491,693.09 | 643,369.11 |
| | | 4.16 | | | | 2,870,137.00 | 2,870,137.00 |

**Table 13.3** Generic Interest-Rate Swap

equation (13.14). These forward rates are then used to predict what the floating-rate payments will be at each interest period. Both fixed-rate and floating-rate payments are then present-valued at the appropriate zero-coupon rate, which enables us to calculate the net present value.

The fixed-rate for the swap is calculated using equation (13.8) to give us:

$$\frac{1 - 0.71298618}{4.16187950}$$

or 6.8963%.

The swap terms are:

| | |
|---|---|
| Nominal principal | £10 million |
| Fixed rate | 6.8963% |
| Day count fixed | Actual/365 |
| Day count floating | Actual/365 |
| Payment frequency fixed | Annual |
| Payment frequency floating | Annual |
| Trade date | 31st January 2000 |
| Effective date | 2nd February 2000 |
| Maturity date | 2nd February 2005 |
| Term | Five years |

For reference, the Microsoft Excel formulae are shown in Table 13.4. It is not surprising that the net present value is zero, because the zero-coupon curve is used to derive the discount factors, which are then used to derive the forward rates, which are used to value the swap. As with any financial instrument, the fair value is its break-even price or hedge cost, and in this case the bank that is pricing the five-year swap shown in Table 13.3 could hedge the swap with a series of FRAs transacted at the forward rates shown. If the bank is paying fixed and receiving floating, value of the swap to it will rise if there is a rise in market rates, and fall if there is a fall in market rates.

| CELL C | D | E | F | G | H | I | J |
|---|---|---|---|---|---|---|---|
| 21 | | 10000000 | | | | | |
| 22 | | | | | | | |
| 23 | Zero-Coupon Rate % | Discount Factor | Forward Rate % | Fixed Payment | Floating Payment | PV Fixed Payment | PV Floating Payment |
| Period | | | | | | | |
| 24 1 | 5.50 | 0.94 | 5.50 | 689,625 | "=(F24*10000000)/100 | "=G24/1.055 | "=H24/(1.055) |
| 25 2 | 6.00 | 0.88 | "=((E24/E25)-1)*100 | 689,625 | "=(F25*10000000)/100 | "=G24/(1.06)^2 | "=H25/(1.06)^2 |
| 26 3 | 6.25 | 0.83 | "=((E25/E26)-1)*100 | 689,625 | "=(F26*10000000)/100 | "=G24/(1.0625)^3 | "=H26/((1.0625)^3) |
| 27 4 | 6.50 | 0.77 | "=((E26/E27)-1)*100 | 689,625 | "=(F27*10000000)/100 | "=G24/(1.065)^4 | "=H27/((1.065)^4) |
| 28 5 | 7.00 | 0.71 | "=((E27/E28)-1)*100 | 689,625 | "=(F28*10000000)/100 | "=G24/(1.07)^5 | "=H28/((1.07)^5) |
| | | "=SUM(E24:E28) | | | | 2,870,137.00 | 2,870,137.00 |

**Table 13.4**  Generic Interest-Rate Swap (Excel formulae)

Conversely, if the bank was receiving fixed and paying floating, the swap value to it would fall if there was a rise in rates, and vice versa.

This method is used to price any interest-rate swap, even an exotic one.

## Valuation Using Final-Maturity Discount Factor

A shortcut to valuing the floating-leg payments of an interest-rate swap involves using the discount factor for the final maturity period. This is possible because, for the purposes of valuation, an exchange of principal at the beginning and end of the swap is conceptually the same as the floating-leg interest payments. This holds because, in an exchange of principal, the interest payments earned on investing the initial principal would be uncertain, as they are floating rate, while on maturity the original principal would be returned. The net result is a floating-rate level of receipts, exactly similar to the floating-leg payments in a swap. To value the principals, then, we need only the final maturity discount rate.

To illustrate, consider Table 13.3, where the present value of both legs was found to be £2,870,137. The same result is obtained if we use the five-year discount factor, as shown below.

$$PV_{\text{floating}} = \left(10,000,000 \times 1\right) - \left(10,000,000 \times 0.71298618\right) = 2,870,137$$

The first term is the principal multiplied by the discount factor 1; this is because the present value of an amount valued immediately is unchanged (or rather, it is multiplied by the immediate-payment discount factor, which is 1.0000).

Therefore, we may use the principal amount of a swap if we wish to value the swap. This is, of course, for valuation only, as there is no actual exchange of principal in a swap.

## Summary of IR Swap

Let us summarise the chief characteristics of swaps. A plain-vanilla swap has the following characteristics:

- One leg of the swap is fixed-rate interest, while the other will be floating-rate, usually linked to a standard index such as Libor.
- The fixed rate is fixed through the entire life of the swap.
- The floating rate is set in advance of each period (quarterly, semi-annually, or annually) and paid in arrears.
- Both legs have the same payment frequency.
- The maturity can be standard whole years up to 30 years, or set to match the customer's requirements.
- The notional principal remains constant during the life of the swap.

Of course, to meet customer demand banks can set up swaps that have variations on any or all of the above standard points. Some of the more common variations are discussed in a following section.

## SONIA Swaps

SONIA is the average interest rate of interbank (unsecured) overnight sterling deposit trades undertaken before 1530 hours each day between members of the London Wholesale Money Brokers' Association. Recorded interest rates are weighted by volume. A SONIA swap is a swap contract that exchanges a fixed interest rate (the swap rate) against the geometric average of the overnight interest rates that have been recorded during the life of the contracted. Exchange of interest takes place on maturity of the swap. SONIA swaps are used to speculate on or to hedge against interest rates at the very short end of the sterling yield curve; in other words, they can be used to hedge an exposure to overnight interest rates.[7] The swaps themselves are traded in maturities of one week to one year, although two-year SONIA swaps have also been traded.

Conventional swap rates are calculated off the government bond yield curve and represent the credit premium over government yields of interbank default risk. Essentially they represent an average of the forward rates derived from the government spot (zero-coupon) yield curve. The fixed rate quoted on a SONIA swap represents the average level of the overnight interest rates expected by market participants over the life of the swap. In practice, the rate is calculated as a function of the Bank of England's repo rate. This is the two-week rate at which the Bank conducts reverse repo trades with banking counterparties as part of its open market operations. In other words, this is the Bank's base rate. In theory one would expect the SONIA rate to follow the repo rate fairly closely, since the credit risk on an overnight deposit is low. In practice, however, the spread between the SONIA rate and the Bank repo rate is very volatile, and for this reason the swaps are used to hedge overnight exposures.

The daily turnover in SONIA swaps is considerably lower than cash instruments such as gilt repo (£20 billion) or more established derivative instruments such as short sterling (£45 billion); however, it is now a key part of the sterling market. Most trades are between one-week and three-month maturity, and the bid-offer spread has been reported by the BoE as around 2 basis points, which compares favourably with the 1-basis-point spread of short sterling.

---

[7] Traditionally overnight rates fluctuate in a very wide range during the day, depending on the day's funds shortage, and although volatility has reduced since the introduction of gilt repo, it is still unpredictable on occasion.

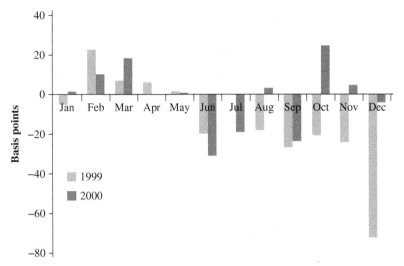

**Figure 13.5**   SONIA Average Rate Minus BoE Repo Rate, 1999–2000
*Source*: Bank of England.

Figure 13.5 illustrates the monthly average of the SONIA index minus Bank's repo rate during 1999 and 2000, with the exaggerated spread in December 1999 reflecting millenium bug concerns.

An illustration of the use of OIS to hedge a funding position is given in Example 13.3.

---

**EXAMPLE 13.3**   **Using an OIS swap to hedge a funding requirement**

A structured hedge fund derivatives desk at an investment bank offers a leveraged investment product to a client in the form of a participating interest share in a fund of hedge funds. The client's investment is leveraged up by funds lent to it by the investment bank, for which the interest rate charged is overnight Libor plus a spread. (In other words, for instance for each $25 invested by the client, the investment bank puts up $75 to make a total investment of $100. This gives the investor a leveraged investment in the hedge fund of funds. In most cases, the client would also bear the first $15 of loss of the $100 share of the investment.)

GRAB                                                                M-Mkt  **TTDE**

**11:37 TULLETT & TOKYO**                                           PAGE  1 / 1

| | USD Cash Deposits | Non-Japanese Bid | Ask | Time | | USD Cash Deposits | Japanese Bid | Ask | Time |
|---|---|---|---|---|---|---|---|---|---|
| 1) | Spot | 1.0000 | 1.0200 | 9:33 | 18) | T/N | 1.0000 | 1.0300 | 11/07 |
| 2) | T/N | 1.0100 | 1.0300 | 11/07 | 19) | 1 Week | 1.0400 | 1.0600 | 9:33 |
| 3) | 1 Week | 1.0300 | 1.0500 | 9:33 | 20) | 2 Week | 1.0500 | 1.0700 | 9:33 |
| 4) | 2 Week | 1.0300 | 1.0500 | 9:33 | 21) | 3 Week | 1.0600 | 1.0800 | 9:33 |
| 5) | 3 Week | 1.0300 | 1.0500 | 9:33 | 22) | 1 Month | 1.0800 | 1.1000 | 9:33 |
| 6) | 1 Month | 1.0400 | 1.0500 | 9:33 | 23) | 2 Month | 1.1800 | 1.2100 | 9:33 |
| 7) | 2 Month | 1.1200 | 1.1400 | 9:33 | 24) | 3 Month | 1.1900 | 1.2200 | 9:33 |
| 8) | 3 Month | 1.1300 | 1.1500 | 9:33 | 25) | 4 Month | 1.2000 | 1.2300 | 9:33 |
| 9) | 4 Month | 1.1400 | 1.1700 | 9:33 | 26) | 5 Month | 1.2100 | 1.2400 | 9:33 |
| 10) | 5 Month | 1.1600 | 1.1900 | 9:33 | 27) | 6 Month | 1.2300 | 1.2600 | 9:33 |
| 11) | 6 Month | 1.2000 | 1.2200 | 9:33 | 28) | 7 Month | 1.2700 | 1.3000 | 9:33 |
| 12) | 7 Month | 1.2300 | 1.2500 | 9:33 | 29) | 8 Month | 1.3100 | 1.3400 | 9:33 |
| 13) | 8 Month | 1.2700 | 1.2900 | 9:33 | 30) | 9 Month | 1.3800 | 1.4100 | 9:33 |
| 14) | 9 Month | 1.3300 | 1.3600 | 9:33 | 31) | 10 Month | 1.4600 | 1.4900 | 9:33 |
| 15) | 10 Month | 1.3800 | 1.4100 | 9:33 | 32) | 11 Month | 1.5300 | 1.5600 | 9:33 |
| 16) | 11 Month | 1.4500 | 1.4800 | 9:33 | 33) | 12 Month | 1.5500 | 1.5800 | 9:33 |
| 17) | 12 Month | 1.5000 | 1.5300 | 9:33 | | | | | |

Australia 61 2 9777 8600    Brazil 5511 3048 4500    Europe 44 20 7330 7500    Germany 49 69 920410
Hong Kong 852 2977 6000 Japan 81 3 3201 8900 Singapore 65 6212 1000 U.S. 1 212 318 2000 Copyright 2003 Bloomberg L.P.
G657-802-0 10-Nov-03 11:37 50

**Figure 13.6**   Tullet US Dollar Deposit Rates, 10 November 2003
Used with permission of Bloomberg L.P. Copyright© 2014.
All rights reserved. © Tullet & Tokyo. Used with permission.

Assume that this investment product has an expected life of at least two years, and possibly longer. As part of its routine asset-liability management operations, the bank's Treasury desk has been funding this requirement by borrowing overnight each day. It now wishes to match the funding requirement raised by this product by matching asset term structure to the liability term structure. Let us assume that this product creates a USD 1 billion funding requirement for the bank.

The current market deposit rates are shown in Figure 13.6. The Treasury desk therefore funds this requirement in the following way:

| | |
|---|---|
| Assets | $1 billion, > 1-year term |
| | Receiving overnight Libor + 130 bps |
| Liability | $350 million, six-month loan |
| | Pay 1.22% |
| | $350 million, 12-month loan |
| | Pay 1.50% |
| | $300 million, 15-month loan |
| | Pay 1.70% (not shown in figure 13.6) |

This matches the asset structure more closely to the term structure of the assets; however, it opens up an interest-rate basis mismatch in that the bank is now receiving an overnight-Libor-based income but paying a term-based liability. To remove this basis mismatch, the Treasury desk transacts an OIS swap to match the amount and term of each of the loan deals, paying overnight floating-rate interest and receiving fixed-rate interest. The rates for OIS swaps of varying terms are shown in Figure 13.7, which shows two-way prices for OIS swaps up to two years in maturity. So for the six-month OIS the hedger is receiving fixed-interest at a rate of 1.085% and for the 12-month OIS he is receiving 1.40%. The difference between what it is receiving in the swap and what it is paying in the term loans is the cost of removing the basis mismatch, but more fundamentally reflects a key feature of OIS swaps versus deposit rates: deposit rates are Libor-related, whereas U.S. dollar OIS rates are driven by the Fed Funds rate. On average, the Fed Funds rate lies approximately 8–10 bps below the dollar deposit rate, and sometimes as much as 15 bps below cash levels. Note that at the time of this trade, the Fed Funds rate was 1% and the market was not expecting a rise in this rate until at least the second half of 2004. This sentiment would have influenced the shape of the USD OIS curve.

GRAB                                                           Corp  **ICAU**

11:34 **USD  OIS  -  ICAU**                                    PAGE  1  /  1

| USD OIS | | Ask | Bid | Time |
|---|---|---|---|---|
| 1) | 1 Month | 1.0190 | 0.9990 | 9:30 |
| 2) | 2 Month | 1.0240 | 1.0040 | 9:30 |
| 3) | 3 Month | 1.0310 | 1.0110 | 9:30 |
| 4) | 4 Month | 1.0440 | 1.0240 | 10:59 |
| 5) | 5 Month | 1.0710 | 1.0510 | 10:59 |
| 6) | 6 Month | 1.1050 | 1.0850 | 11:04 |
| 7) | 7 Month | 1.1420 | 1.1220 | 10:59 |
| 8) | 8 Month | 1.1920 | 1.1720 | 11:00 |
| 9) | 9 Month | 1.2420 | 1.2220 | 11:05 |
| 10) | 10 Month | 1.2930 | 1.2730 | 11:00 |
| 11) | 11 Month | 1.3580 | 1.3380 | 11:00 |
| 12) | 12 Month | 1.4210 | 1.4000 | 11:06 |
| 13) | 15 Month | 1.6250 | 1.6040 | 11:00 |
| 14) | 18 Month | 1.8090 | 1.7890 | 11:00 |
| 15) | 21 Month | 2.0080 | 1.9880 | 11:00 |
| 16) | 24 Month | 2.2030 | 2.1820 | 11:00 |

Australia 61 2 9777 8600      Brazil 5511 3048 4500      Europe 44 20 7330 7500      Germany 49 69 920410
Hong Kong 852 2977 6000 Japan 81 3 3201 8900 Singapore 65 6212 1000 U.S. 1 212 318 2000 Copyright 2003 Bloomberg L.P.
G657-802-0 10-Nov-03 11:34:17

**Figure 13.7**   Garban ICAP U.S. Dollar OIS Rates, 10 November 2003 Used with permission of Bloomberg L.P.
Copyright© 2014. All rights reserved.

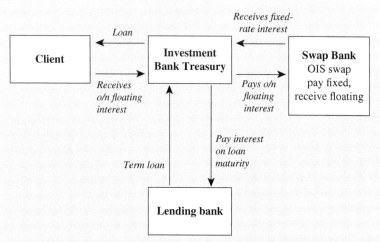

**Figure 13.8**    Illustration of Interest Basis Mismatch Hedging
Using OIS Instrument

The action taken above hedges out the basis mismatch and also
enables the Treasury desk to match its asset profile with its liability
profile. The net cost to the Treasury desk represents its hedging costs.
Figure 13.8 illustrates the transaction.

## OIS Swap Terms

To illustrate OISs further, we give here the terms of one of the OIS executed
in Example 13.3, the six-month swap. The counterparties to the trade are as
labelled in Figure 13.8.

| | |
|---|---|
| Notional | $350 million |
| Trade date | 10 November 2003 |
| Effective date | 12 November 2003 |
| Termination date | 12 May 2004 |
| Payment terms | The net interest payment is paid |
| | as a bullet amount on maturity |

---

***Fixed Amounts***

| | |
|---|---|
| Fixed rate payer | OIS swap bank |
| Fixed rate period end date | 12 May 2004 |
| Fixed rate | 1.085% |
| Fixed rate day-count fraction | Act/360 |

***Floating Amounts***

| | |
|---|---|
| Floating rate payer | Treasury desk |
| Floating rate period end date | 12 May 2004 |
| Floating rate option | USD-Fed Funds |

---

The floating rate is calculated as follows:

$$F_{OIS} = \left[ \prod \left( 1 + \frac{FedFunds_i \times n_i}{360} \right) - 1 \right] \times \frac{360}{d} \qquad (13.24)$$

where $d_0$      is the number of New York banking days in the calculation period

$i$      is a series of whole numbers from 1 to $d_0$, each representing a New York banking day

$FedFunds_i$      is a reference rate equal to the overnight USD Federal Funds interest rate, as displayed on Telerate page 118 and Bloomberg page BTMM

$n_i$      is the number of calendar days in the calculation period on which the rate is $FedFunds_i$

$d$      is the number of days in the calculation period

---

| | |
|---|---|
| Floating rate day-count | Act/360 |
| Reset dates | The last day of each calculation period |
| Compounding | Inapplicable |
| Business day convention | Modified following business day |
| Calculation agent | OIS swap bank |

---

Reproduced from *Fixed Income Markets, Second Edition* (2014)

This extract from *Fixed Income Markets, Second Edition* (2014)

## Bond Futures Contracts

## Bond Futures Contracts

The most widely used risk management instrument in the bond markets is the government-bond futures contract. This is usually an exchange-traded standardised contract that fixes the price today at which a specified quantity and quality of a bond will be delivered at a date during the expiry month of the futures contract. Unlike short-term interest-rate futures, which only require cash settlement, and which we encountered in the section on money markets, bond futures require the actual physical delivery of a bond when they are settled. In this chapter we review bond futures contracts and their use for trading and hedging purposes.

## BACKGROUND

The concept of a bond futures contract is probably easier to grasp intuitively than a short-dated interest-rate future. This reflects the fact that a bond futures contract represents an underlying physical asset, the bond itself, and a bond must be delivered on expiry of the contract. In this way, bond futures are similar to commodity futures, which also require physical delivery of the underlying commodity.

A futures contract is an agreement between two counterparties that fixes the terms of an exchange that will take place between them at some future date. They are standardised agreements, as opposed to over-the-counter (OTC) ones, when traded on an exchange, so they are also referred to as exchange-traded futures. In the United Kingdom, financial futures are traded on London International Financial Futures Exchange (LIFFE), which opened in 1982. There are four classes of contract traded on LIFFE: short-term interest-rate contracts; long-term interest-rate contracts (bond futures); currency contracts; and stock-index contracts. We discussed interest-rate futures contracts, which generally trade as part of the money markets, in an earlier chapter. In this section we will look at bond futures contracts, which are an important part of the bond markets; they are used for hedging and speculative purposes. Most futures contracts on exchanges around the world trade at three month maturity intervals, with maturity dates fixed at March, June, September, and December each year. This includes the contracts traded on LIFFE. Therefore, at preset times during the year a contract for each of these months will expire, and a final settlement price is determined for it. The further out one goes, the less liquid the trading is in that

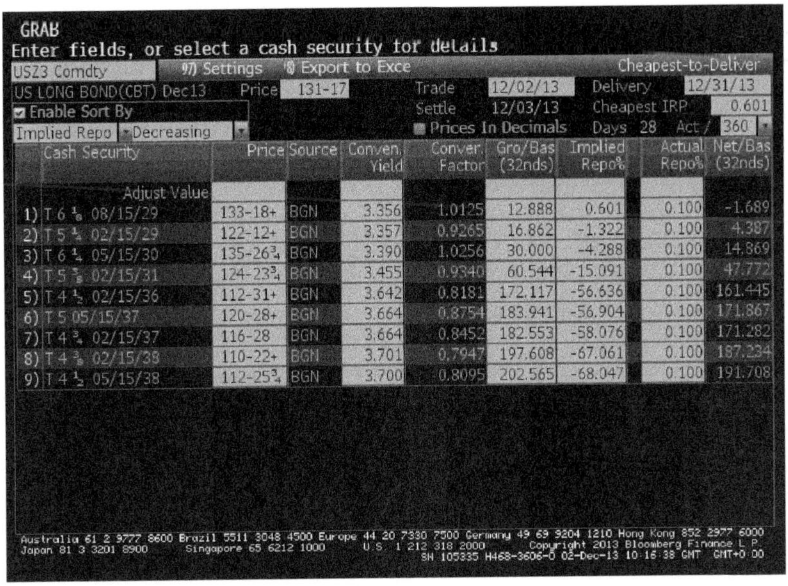

**Figure 12.1** Bond Futures Delivery Quotes, Bloomberg Page DLV, 2 December 2013

Used with permission of Bloomberg L.P. Copyright© 2014. All rights reserved.

contract. It is normal to see liquid trading only in the "front month" contract (the current contract, so that if we are trading in April 2013 the front month is the June 2013 future), and possibly one or two of the next contracts, for most bond futures contracts. The liquidity of contracts diminishes the further one trades out in the maturity range.

When a party establishes a position in a futures contract, it can either run this position to maturity or close out the position between the trade date and maturity. If a position is closed out, the party will have either a profit or loss to book. If a position is held until maturity, the party who is long the future will take delivery of the underlying asset (bond) at the settlement price; the party who is short futures will deliver the underlying asset. This is referred to as physical settlement or sometimes, confusingly, as cash settlement. Figure 12.1 shows the deliverable bonds into the US Treasury futures contract, and the prices of each cash bond at the time.

There is no counterparty risk associated with trading exchange-traded futures, because of the role of the clearing house, such as the London Clearing House (LCH). This is the body through which contracts are settled. A clearing house acts as the buyer to all contracts sold on the exchange, and the seller to all contracts that are bought. So in the London market, the LCH acts as the counterparty to all transactions, so that settlement is effectively guaranteed. The LCH requires all exchange participants to deposit margin with it, a cash sum that is the cost of conducting business (plus broker's commissions). The size of the margin depends on the size of a party's net open position in contracts (an open position is a position in a contract that is held overnight and not closed out). There are two types of margin, maintenance margin and variation margin. Maintenance margin is the minimum level required to be held at the clearing house; the level is set by the exchange. Variation margin is the additional amount that must be deposited to cover any trading losses and as the size of the net open positions increases. Note that this is not like margin in, say, a repo transaction. Margin in repo is a safeguard against a drop in value of collateral that has been supplied against a loan of cash. The margin deposited at a futures exchange clearing house acts essentially as "good faith" funds, required to provide comfort to the exchange that the futures trader is able to satisfy the obligations of the futures contract that are being traded.

| | |
|---|---|
| Unit of Trading | U.S. Treasury bond with notional value of $100,000 and a coupon of 8% |
| Deliverable grades | U.S. T-bonds with a minimum maturity of 15 years from first day of delivery month |
| Delivery months | March, June, September, December |
| Delivery date | Any business day during the delivery month |
| Last trading day | 12:00 noon, seventh business day before last business day of delivery month |
| Quotation | Percent of par expressed as points and thirty-seconds of a point, e.g., 108–16 is 108 16/32 or 108.50 |
| Minimum price movement | 1/32 |
| Tick value | $31.25 |
| Trading hours | 07.20–14.00 (trading pit) |
| | 17.20–20.05 |
| | 22.3006.00 hours (screen trading) |

**Table 12.1**    CBOT U.S. T-Bond Futures Contract Specifications

# BOND FUTURES CONTRACTS

We have noted that futures contracts traded on an exchange are standardised. This means that each contract represents exactly the same commodity, and it cannot be tailored to meet individual customer requirements. In this section, we describe two very liquid and commonly traded contracts, starting with the U.S. T-Bond contract traded on the Chicago Board of Trade (CBOT). The details of this contract are given in Table 12.1.

The terms of this contract relate to a U.S. Treasury bond with a minimum maturity of 15 years and a notional coupon of 8%. We introduced the concept of the notional bond in the chapter on repo markets. A futures contract specifies a notional coupon to prevent delivery and liquidity problems that would arise if there was shortage of bonds with exactly the coupon required, or if one market participant purchased a large proportion of all the bonds in issue with the required coupon. For exchange-traded futures, a short future can deliver any bond that fits the maturity criteria specified in the contract terms. Of course, a long future would like to be delivered a high-coupon bond with significant accrued interest, while the short future would want to deliver a low-coupon bond with low interest accrued. In fact, this issue does not arise because of the way the invoice amount (the amount paid by the long future to purchase the bond) is calculated. The invoice amount on the expiry date is given in equation (12.1).

$$Inv_{amt} = P_{fut} \times CF + AI \qquad (12.1)$$

where  $Inv_{amt}$   is the invoice amount
  $P_{fut}$   is the price of the futures contract
  $CF$   is the conversion factor
  $AI$   is the bond accrued interest

## CONVERSION FACTOR

The conversion factor (or price factor) gives the price of an individual cash bond such that its yield to maturity on the delivery day of the futures contract is equal to the notional coupon of the contract. The product of the conversion factor and the futures price is the forward price available in the futures market for that cash bond (plus the cost of funding, referred to as the gross basis).

Any bond that meets the maturity specifications of the futures contract is said to be in the delivery basket, the group of bonds that are eligible to be delivered into the futures contract. Every bond in the delivery basket will have its own *conversion factor*, which is used to equalise coupon and accrued interest differences of all the delivery bonds. The exchange will announce the conversion factor for each bond before trading in a contract begins; the conversion factor for a bond will change over time, but remains fixed for one individual contract. That is, if a bond has a conversion factor of 1.091252, this will remain fixed for the life of the contract. If a contract specifies a bond with a notional coupon of 7%, like the long gilt future on LIFFE, then the conversion factor will be less than 1.0 for bonds with a coupon lower than 7% and higher than 1.0 for bonds with a coupon higher than 7%. A formal definition of conversion factor is given below.

Although conversion factors equalise the yield on bonds, bonds in the delivery basket will trade at different yields, and, for this reason, they are not "equal" at the time of delivery. Certain bonds will be cheaper than others, and one bond will be the cheapest-to-deliver bond. The cheapest-to-deliver bond is the one that gives the greatest return from a strategy of buying a bond and simultaneously selling the futures contract, and then closing out positions on the expiry of the contract. This so-called cash-and-carry trading is actively pursued by proprietary trading desks in banks. If a contract is purchased and then held to maturity, the buyer will receive, via the exchange's clearing house, the cheapest-to-deliver gilt. Traders sometimes try to exploit arbitrage price differentials between the future and the cheapest-to-deliver gilt, known as basis trading. This is discussed in Choudhry (2003), where the mathematical calculation of the conversion factor for the gilt future is given in Appendix 12.1.

We summarise the contract specification of the long gilt futures contract traded on LIFFE in Table 12.2. There is also a medium gilt contract on LIFFE, which was introduced in 1998 (having been discontinued in the early 1990s). This trades a notional five-year gilt, with eligible gilts being those of four to seven years maturity.

# HEDGING USING FUTURES

## The Theoretical Position

Bond futures are used for a variety of purposes. Much of one day's trading in futures will be speculative; that is, a punt on the direction of the market. Another main use of futures is to hedge bond positions. In theory, when hedging a cash-bond position with a bond futures contract, if cash and futures prices move together, then any loss from one position will be offset by a gain from the other. When prices move exactly in lock-step with each other, the hedge is considered perfect. In practice, the price of even the cheapest-to-deliver bond (which one can view as being the bond being traded—implicitly—when one is trading the bond future) and the bond future will not move exactly in line with each other over a period of time. The difference between the cash price and the futures price is called the basis. The risk that the basis will change in an unpredictable way is known as *basis risk*.

Futures are a liquid and straightforward way of hedging a bond position. By hedging a bond position, the trader or fund manager is hoping to balance the loss on the cash position by the profit gained from the hedge. However, the hedge will not be exact for all bonds except the cheapest-to-deliver (CTD) bond, which we can assume is the futures contract underlying bond. The basis risk in a hedge position arises because the bond being hedged is not identical to the CTD bond. The basic principle is that if the trader is long (or net long, where the desk is running long and short positions in different bonds) in the cash market, an equivalent number of futures contracts will be sold to set up the hedge. If the cash position is short, the trader will buy futures. The hedging requirement can arise for different reasons. A market-maker will wish to hedge positions arising out of client business, when she is unsure when the resulting bond positions will be unwound. A fund manager may, for example, know that she needs to realise a cash sum at a specific time in the future to meet fund liabilities, and sell bonds at that time. The market maker will want to hedge against a drop in value of positions during the time the bonds are held. The fund manager will want to hedge against a rise in interest rates between now and the bond sale date, to protect the value of the portfolio.

When putting on the hedge position, the key is to trade the correct number of futures contracts. This is determined by using the hedge ratio of the bond and the future, which is a function of the volatilities of the two instruments. The number of contracts to trade is calculated using the hedge ratio, which is given by

$$\text{Hedge ratio} = \frac{\text{Volatility of bond to be hedged}}{\text{Volatility of hedging instrument}}$$

Therefore one needs to use the volatility values of each instrument. We can see from the calculation that if the bond is more volatile than the hedging instrument, then a greater amount of the hedging instrument will be required. Let us now look in greater detail at the hedge ratio.

## THE FUTURES BASIS

The term "basis" is also used to describe the difference in price between the future and the deliverable cash bond. The basis is of considerable significance. It is often used to establish the fair value of a futures contract, as it is a function of the cost of carry. The gross basis is defined (for deliverable bonds only) as follows:

Gross basis = Clean bond price − (futures price × conversion factor).

There are different methods available to calculate hedge ratios. The most common ones are the conversion-factor method, which can be used for deliverable bonds (also known as the price-factor method) and the modified-duration method (also known as the basis-point value method).

Where a hedge is put on against a bond that is in the futures delivery basket, it is common for the conversion factor to be used to calculate the hedge ratio. A conversion factor hedge ratio is more useful, as it is transparent and remains constant, irrespective of any changes in the price of the cash bond or the futures contract. The number of futures contracts required to hedge a deliverable bond using the conversion-factor hedge ratio is determined using the following equation:

$$Number\ of\ contracts = \frac{M_{bond} \times CF}{M_{fut}} \tag{12.4}$$

where $M$ is the nominal value of the bond or futures contract.

The conversion-factor method may only be used for bonds in the delivery basket. It is important to ensure that this method is only used for one bond. It is an erroneous procedure to use the ratio of conversion factors of two different bonds when calculating a hedge ratio. This will be considered again later.

Unlike the conversion-factor method, the modified-duration hedge ratio may be used for all bonds, both deliverable and nondeliverable. In calculating this hedge ratio the modified duration is multiplied by the dirty price of the cash bond to obtain the basis-point value (BPV). As we discovered in Chapter 2, the BPV represents the actual impact of a change in the yield on the price of a specific bond. The BPV allows the trader to calculate the hedge ratio to reflect the different price sensitivity of the chosen bond (compared to the CTD bond) to interest-rate movements. The hedge ratio calculated using BPVs must be constantly updated, because it will change if the price of the bond and/or the futures contract changes. This may necessitate periodic adjustments to the number of lots used in the hedge. The number of futures contracts required to hedge a bond using the BPV method is calculated using the following

$$Number\ of\ contracts = \frac{M_{bond}}{M_{fut}} \times \frac{BPV_{bond}}{BPV_{fut}} \qquad (12.5)$$

where the BPV of a futures contract is defined with respect to the BPV of its CTD bond, as given by equation (12.6).

$$BPV_{fut} = \frac{BPV_{CTD\ bond}}{CF_{CTD\ bond}} \qquad (12.6)$$

The simplest hedge procedure to undertake is one for a position consisting of only one bond, the cheapest-to-deliver bond. The relationship between the futures price and the price of the CTD given by equation (12.3) indicates that the price of the future will move for moves in the price of the CTD bond; so, therefore, we may set:

$$\Delta P_{fut} \cong \frac{\Delta P_{bond}}{CF} \qquad (12.7)$$

where $CF$ is the CTD conversion factor.

The price of the futures contract, over time, does not move tick for tick (although it may on an intraday basis) but rather by the amount of the change divided by the conversion factor. It is apparent, therefore, that to hedge a position in the CTD bond we must hold the number of futures contracts equivalent to the value of bonds held multiplied by the conversion factor. Obviously, if a conversion factor is less than one, the number of futures contracts will be less than the equivalent nominal value of the cash position; the opposite is true for bonds that have a conversion factor greater than one. However, the hedge is not as simple as dividing the nominal value of the bond position by the nominal value represented by one futures contract (!); this error is frequently made by graduate trainees and those new to the desk.

To measure the effectiveness of the hedge position, it is necessary to compare the performance of the futures position with that of the cash-bond position, and to see how much the hedge instrument mirrored the performance of the cash instrument. A simple calculation is made to measure the effectiveness of the hedge, given by equation (12.8), which is the percentage value of the hedge effectiveness.

$$Hedge\ effectiveness = -\left[\frac{Fut\ P/L}{Bond\ P/L}\right] \times 100 \qquad (12.8)$$

## Hedging a Bond Portfolio

The principles established above may be applied when hedging a portfolio containing a number of bonds. It is more realistic to consider a portfolio as holding not just bonds that are outside the delivery basket, but are also nongovernment bonds. In this case, we need to calculate the number of futures contracts to put on as a hedge based on the volatility of each bond in the portfolio compared to the volatility of the CTD bond. Note that, in practice, there is usually more than one futures contract that may be used as the hedge instrument. For example, in the sterling market it would be more sensible to use LIFFE's medium gilt contract, whose underlying bond has a notional maturity of four to seven years, if hedging a portfolio of short- to medium-dated bonds. However, for the purposes of illustration we will assume that only one contract, the long gilt, is available.

To calculate the number of futures contracts required to hold as a hedge against any specific bond, we use the expression in equation (12.9).

$$Hedge = \frac{M_{bond}}{M_{fut}} \times Vol_{bond/CTD} \times Vol_{CTD/fut} \qquad (12.9)$$

where $M$ is the nominal value of the bond or future

$Vol_{bond/CTD}$    is the relative volatility of the bond being hedged compared to that of the CTD bond

$Vol_{CTD/fut}$    is the relative volatility of the CTD bond compared to that of the future

It is not necessarily straightforward to determine the relative volatility of a bond vis-à-vis the CTD bond. If the bond being hedged is a government bond, we can calculate the relative volatility using the two bonds' modified duration. This is because the yields of both may be safely assumed to be strongly positively correlated. If, however, the bond being hedged is a corporate bond and/or a nonvanilla bond, we must obtain the relative volatility using regression analysis, as the yields between the two bonds may not be strongly positively correlated. This is apparent when one remembers that the yield spread of corporate bonds over government bonds is not constant and will fluctuate with changes in government-bond yields. To use regression analysis to determine relative volatilities, historical price data on the bond is required. The daily price moves in the target bond and the CTD bond are then analysed to assess the slope of the regression line. In this section, we will restrict the discussion to a portfolio of government bonds.

If we are hedging a portfolio of government bonds, we can use (12.10) to determine relative volatility values, which are based on the modified duration of each of the bonds in the portfolio.

$$Vol_{bond/CTD} = \frac{\Delta P_{bond}}{\Delta P_{CTD}} = \frac{MD_{bond} \times P_{bond}}{MD_{CTD} \times P_{CTD}} \qquad (12.10)$$

where $MD$ is the modified duration of the bond being hedged or the CTD bond, as appropriate. This preserves the terminology we introduced in Chapter 2.[1]

Once we have calculated the relative volatility of the bond being hedged, equation (12.11) (obtained by rearranging (12.7)) tells us that the relative volatility of the CTD bond to that of the futures contract is approximately the same as its conversion factor. We are then in a position to calculate the futures hedge for each bond in a portfolio.

$$Vol_{CTD/fut} = \frac{\Delta P_{CTD}}{\Delta P_{fut}} \approx CF_{CTD} \qquad (12.11)$$

Table 12.3 shows a portfolio of five UK gilts on 20th October 1999. The nominal value of the bonds in the portfolio is £200 million, and the bonds have a market value, excluding accrued interest, of £206.84 million. Only one of the bonds is a deliverable bond, the 5¾% 2009 gilt, which is in fact the CTD bond. For the Dec99 futures contract, the bond had a conversion factor of 0.9124950. The fact that this bond is the CTD explains why it has a relative volatility of 1. We calculate the number of futures contracts required to hedge each position, using the equations listed above. For example, the hedge requirement for the position in the 7% 2002 gilt was calculated as follows:

$$\frac{5,000,000}{100,000} \times \frac{2.245 \times 101.50}{7.235 \times 99.84} \times 0.9124950 = 14.39$$

The volatility of all the bonds is calculated relative to the CTD bond, and the number of futures contracts determined using the conversion factor for the CTD bond. The bond with the highest volatility is, not surprisingly, the 6% 2028, which has the longest maturity of all the bonds and hence the highest modified duration. We note from Table 12.3 that the portfolio

---

[1]  In certain textbooks and research documents, it is suggested that the ratio of the conversion factors of the bond being hedged (if it is in the delivery basket) and the CTD bond can be used to determine the relative volatility of the target bond. This is a fallacious argument. The conversion factor of a deliverable bond is the price factor that will set the yield of the bond equal to the notional coupon of the futures contract on the delivery date, and it is a function mainly of the coupon of the deliverable bond. The price volatility of a bond, on the other hand, is a measure of its modified duration, which is a function of the bond's duration (that is, the term to maturity). Therefore, using conversion factors to measure volatility levels will produce erroneous results. It is important not to misuse conversion factors when arranging hedge ratios.

|  | | CTD | | | 5.75% 2009 | | |
|  | | Modified duration | | | 7.2345656 | | |
|  | | Conversion factor | | | 0.9124950 | | |
|  | | Price | | | 99.84 | | |
| Bond | Nominal Amount (£m) | Price | Yield % | Duration | Modified Duration | Relative Volatility | Number of Contracts |
|---|---|---|---|---|---|---|---|
| UKT 8% 2000 | 12 | 102.17 | 5.972 | 1.072 | 1.01158797 | 0.143090242 | 15.67 |
| UKT 7% 2002 | 5 | 101.50 | 6.367 | 2.388 | 2.24505721 | 0.315483336 | 14.39 |
| UKT 5% 2004 | 38 | 94.74 | 6.327 | 4.104 | 3.85979102 | 0.50626761 | 175.55 |
| UKT 5.75% 2009 | 100 | 99.84 | 5.770 | 7.652 | 7.23456557 | 1 | 912.50 |
| UKT 6% 2028 | 45 | 119.25 | 4.770 | 15.031 | 14.3466641 | 2.368603078 | 972.60 |
| Total | 200 | | | | | | 2,090.71 |

**Table 12.3**   Bond Futures Hedge for Hypothetical Gilt Portfolio, 20 October 1999

requires a hedge position of 2,091 futures contracts. This illustrates how a rough-and-ready estimate of the hedging requirement, based on nominal values, would be insufficient, as that would suggest a hedge position of only 2,000 contracts.

The effectiveness of the hedge must be monitored over time. No hedge will be completely perfect, however, and the calculation illustrated above, as it uses modified-duration value, does not take into account the convexity effect of the bonds. The reason why a futures hedge will not be perfect is because, in practice, the price of the futures contract will not move tick for tick with the CTD bond, at least not over a period of time. This is the basis risk that is inherent in hedging cash bonds with futures. In addition, the calculation of the hedge is only completely accurate for a parallel shift in yields, as it is based on modified duration, so as the yield curve changes around pivots, the hedge will move out of line. Finally, the long gilt future is not the appropriate contract to use to hedge three of the bonds in the portfolio, or over 25% of the portfolio by nominal value. This is because these bonds are short- or medium-dated, and so their price movements will not track the futures price as closely as longer-dated bonds. In this case, the more appropriate futures contract to use would have been the medium gilt contract, or (for the first bond, the 8% 2000) a strip of short sterling contracts. Using shorter-dated instruments would reduce some of the basis risk contained in the portfolio hedge.

## THE MARGIN PROCESS

Institutions buying and selling futures on an exchange deal with only one counterparty at all times, the exchange clearing house. The clearing house is responsible for the settlement of all contracts, including managing the delivery process. A central clearing mechanism eliminates counterparty risk for anyone dealing on the exchange, because the clearing house guarantees the settlement of all transactions. The clearing house may be owned by the exchange itself, such as the one associated with the Chicago Mercantile Exchange (the CME Clearinghouse) or it may be a separate entity, such as the London Clearing House, which settles transactions on LIFFE. The LCH is also involved in running clearing systems for swaps and repo products in certain currencies.

One of the key benefits to the market of the clearing-house mechanism is that counterparty risk, as it is transferred to the clearing house, is virtually eliminated. The mechanism that enables the clearing house to accept the counterparty risk is the margining process that is employed at all futures exchanges. A bank or local trader must deposit margin before commencing dealing on the exchange; each day a further amount must be deposited or returned, depending on the results of the day's trading activity.

The exchange will specify the level of margin that must be deposited for each type of futures contract that a bank wishes to deal in. The initial margin will be a fixed sum per lot. So, for example, if the margin was £1,000 per lot, an opening position of 100 lots would require margin of £100,000. Once initial margin has been deposited, there is a mark-to-market of all positions at the close of business; exchange-traded instruments are the most transparent products in the market, and the closing price is not only known to everyone, it is also indisputable. The closing price is also known as the settlement price. Any losses suffered by a trading counterparty, whether closed out or run overnight, are entered as a debit on the party's account and must be paid the next day. Trading profits are credited and may be withdrawn from the margin account the next day. This daily process is known as variation margining. Thus, the margin account is updated on a daily basis, and the maximum loss that must be made up on any morning is the maximum price movement that occurred the previous day. It is a serious issue if a trading party is unable to meet a margin call. In such a case, the exchange will order it to cease trading, and will also liquidate all its open positions; any losses will be met out of the firm's margin account. If the level of funds in the margin account is insufficient, the losses will be made good from funds paid out of a general fund run by the clearing house, which is maintained by all members of the exchange.

Payment of margin is made by electronic funds transfer between the trading party's bank account and the clearing house. Initial margin is usually paid in cash, although clearing houses will also accept high-quality securities, such as T-bills or certain government bonds, to the value of the margin required. Variation margin is always cash. The advantage of depositing securities rather than cash is that the depositing firm earns interest on its margin. This is not available on a cash margin, and the interest forgone on a cash margin is effectively the cost of trading futures on the exchange. However, if securities are used, there is effectively no cost associated with trading on the exchange (we ignore, of course, infrastructure costs and staff salaries).

The daily settlement of exchange-traded futures contracts, as opposed to when the contract expires or the position is closed out, is the main reason why futures prices are not equal to forward prices for long-dated instruments.

Reproduced from *Fixed Income Markets, Second Edition* (2014)

This extract from *The Futures Bond Basis, Second Edition* (2006)

## The Bond Basis: Basic Concepts

# 2.3 THE BOND BASIS: BASIC CONCEPTS

## 2.3.1 Introduction

The previous section introduced the no-arbitrage forward pricing principle and the concept of the basis. We will look at this again later. So, we know that the price of an asset, including a bond, that is agreed today for immediate delivery is known as its *spot* price.[9] In essence, the forward price of an asset, agreed today for delivery at some specified future date, is based on the spot price and the cost or income of foregoing delivery until the future date. If an asset carries an income stream, with-holding delivery until, say, 3 months in the future, it would present an opportunity cost to an investor in the asset, so the prospective investor would require a discount on the spot price as the price of dealing in a forward. However, if an asset comes with a holding cost – for example, storage costs – then an investor might expect to pay a premium on the spot price, as he would not be incurring the holding costs that are otherwise associated with the asset.

Commodities such as wheat or petroleum are good examples of assets whose forward delivery is associated with a holding cost. For a commodity whose price is agreed today but for which delivery is taken at a forward date, economic logic dictates that the futures price must exceed the spot price. That is, a commodity basis is usually negative. Financial assets such as bonds have zero storage costs, as they are held in electronic form in a clearing system such as CREST, the settlement system for UK gilts;[10] moreover, they provide an income stream that would offset the cost of financing a bond-holding until a future date. Under most circumstances when the yield curve is positively sloping, the holding of a bond position until delivery at a future date will generate a net income to the holder. For these and other reasons it is common for the bond basis to be positive, as the futures price is usually below the spot price.

As we have noted, bond futures contracts do not specify a particular bond, rather a generic or *notional* bond. The actual bond that is delivered against an expired futures contract is the one that makes the cost of

---

[9] We use the term 'immediate' delivery, although for operational, administrative and settlement reasons, actual delivery may be a short period in the future: say, anything up to several days or even longer.

[10] CREST itself was formed by a merger of the equity settlement system of the same name and the Bank of England's gilt settlement system known as the Central Gilts Office (*CGO*). CREST merged with Euroclear, the international settlement system owned by a consortium of banks, in 2002.

delivering it as low as possible. The bond that is selected is known as the cheapest-to-deliver. Considerable research has been undertaken into the concept of the *cheapest-to-deliver* (*CTD*) bond. In fact, certain commodity contracts also trade with an underlying CTD. Burghardt *et al.* (1994) point out that wheat is not an homogenous product, as wheat from one part of the country exhibits different characteristics from wheat from another part of the country, and may have to be transported a longer distance (hence at greater cost) to delivery. Therefore, a wheat contract is also priced based on the designated cheapest-to-deliver. There is no physical location factor with government bonds, but futures contracts specify that any bond may be delivered that falls into the required maturity period.

In this section we look at the basic concepts necessary for an understanding of the bond basis, and introduce all the key topics. Basis trading itself is the simultaneous trading of the cash bond and the bond futures contract, an arbitrage trade that seeks to exploit any mis-pricing of the future against the cash or *vice versa*.[11] In liquid and transparent markets such mis-pricing is rare, of small magnitude and very short-lived. The arbitrageur will therefore also try to make a gain from the difference between the costs of holding (or shorting) a bond against that of delivering (or taking delivery of) it at the futures expiry date: essentially, then, the difference between the bond's running yield and its repo financing cost. We'll save the trading principles for Chapter 3. First, let us introduce some basic terminology.

### 2.3.3 The conversion factor

So, we know that a bond futures contract represents any bond whose maturity date falls in the period described in the contract specifications. During the delivery month, and up to the expiry date, the party that is short the future has the option on which bond to deliver and on what day in the month to deliver it. Let us consider the long gilt contract on LIFFE. If we assume the person that is short the future delivers on the expiry date, for each contract they must deliver to the exchange's clearing house £100,000 nominal of a notional 6% gilt of between $8\frac{3}{4}$ and 13 years' maturity.[12] Of course, no such specific bond exists, so the seller delivers a bond from within the delivery basket. However, if the seller delivers a bond of, say, 5% coupon and 9 years' maturity, intuitively we see that the value of this bond is lower than a 6% bond of 13 years' maturity. While the short future

---

[11] Another term for basis trading is *cash-and-carry* trading. The terms are used interchangeably.

[12] In our example, to the London Clearing House. The *LCH* then on-delivers to the party that is long the contract. The long pays the settlement invoice price.

| Gilt | Futures contract | | | | | |
| --- | --- | --- | --- | --- | --- | --- |
| | Dec00 | Mar01 | Jun01 | Sep01 | Dec01 | Mar02 |
| 5.75% Treasury 2009 | 0.917 472 8 | 0.918 980 2 | | | | |
| 6.25% Treasury 2010 | 0.946 747 8 | 0.947 561 1 | 0.948 641 5 | 0.949 495 6 | 0.950 587 4 | |
| 9% Conversion 2011 | 1.147 928 1 | 1.145 557 8 | 1.143 102 6 | 1.140 593 6 | 1.138124 0 | 1.135 585 9 |
| 5% Treasury 2012 | | | | 0.852 8791 | 0.855172 7 | 0.857 727 0 |
| 9% Treasury 2012 | 1.157 636 8 | 1.155 551 2 | 1.153 162 6 | | | |
| 8% Treasury 2013 | 1.083 567 6 | 1.082 620 6 | 1.081 499 0 | 1.080 511 4 | 1.079 356 0 | 1.078 336 3 |

**TABLE 2.3**  Conversion factors for deliverable gilts, Dec00 to Mar02 long gilt contracts.
*Source:* LIFFE.

may well think, 'fine by me', the long future will most certainly think not. There would be the same aggrieved feelings, just reversed, if the seller was required to deliver a bond of 7% coupon. To equalise all bonds, irrespective of which actual bond is delivered, the futures exchange assigns a *conversion factor* to each bond in the delivery basket. This serves to make the delivery acceptable to both parties. Conversion factors are used in the invoice process to calculate the value of the delivered bond that is equal to that specified by the contract. In some texts the conversion factor is known as the *price factor*. The concept of the conversion factor was developed by CBOT in the 1970s.

Table 2.3 shows the conversion factors for all gilts that were eligible for delivery for the December 2000 to March 2002 contracts. Notice how the conversion factors exhibit the 'pull to par', decreasing towards 1.00 for those with a coupon above the notional 7% and increasing towards 1.00 for bonds with a coupon below 7%. The passage of time also shows bonds falling out of the delivery basket, and the introduction of a new issue into the basket, the 5% gilt maturing 7 March 2012.

The yield obtainable on bonds that have different coupons but identical maturities can be equalised by adjusting the price for each bond. This principle is used to calculate the conversion factors for different bonds. The conversion factor for a bond is the price per £1 (or per $1, €1 and so on) at which the bond would give a yield equal to the yield of the notional coupon specified in the futures contract. This is 7% in the case of the long gilt contract, 6% for the Treasury long bond and so on. In other words, the conversion factor for each bond is the price such that every bond would provide an investor with the same yield if purchased; or, the price at which a deliverable bond would trade if its gross redemption yield was 7% (or 6% and so on). The yield calculation is rounded to whole quarters, given the delivery month cycle of futures. Futures exchanges calculate conversion factors effective either on the exact delivery date, where a single date is defined, or (as at LIFFE) on the 1st day of the delivery month if delivery can take place at any time during the delivery month.

The conversion factor is assigned by the exchange to each bond in the delivery basket at the start of trading of each contract. It remains constant throughout the life of the contract. A particular bond that remains in the delivery basket over a length of time will have different conversion factors for successive contracts. For example, the 9% UK Treasury maturing on 13 October 2008 had conversion factors of 1.145 431 7, 1.142 995 5 and 1.140 715 5 for the LIFFE long gilt contracts that matured in June, September and December 1998, respectively.

Other things being equal, bonds with a higher coupon will have larger conversion factors than those with lower coupons. For bonds with the same coupon, maturity has an influence, though this is slightly less obvious. For bonds with coupons below the notional rate defined in the contract description, the conversion factor is smaller for bonds with a longer maturity. The opposite is true for bonds carrying coupons in excess of the notional coupon rate, for which the conversion factor will be larger the longer the maturity. This effect arises from the mathematics of fixed-interest securities. Bonds with coupon below current market yields will trade at a discount. This discount is larger the longer the maturity, because it is a disadvantage to hold a bond paying a coupon lower than current market rates, and this disadvantage is greater the longer the period to the bond maturing. Conversely, bonds with coupons above current market yields trade at a premium which will be greater the longer the maturity.

To help calculate the *invoice price* of a bond on delivery, we multiply the price of the final settlement price of the futures contract with its conversion factor. This gives us the *converted price*. The price payable by the long future on delivery of the bond is the invoice price, and this is the futures settlement price plus accrued interest. This was shown in simple fashion as (2.1). The actual invoice price, calculated once the actual bond being delivered is known, is given by:

$$P_{inv} = \left( M_{fut} \times P_{futsett} \times CF \right) + AI \qquad (2.8)$$

where $P_{inv}$ = Invoice price;
$M_{fut}$ = Nominal value of the delivered bonds as specified in the contract;
$P_{futsett}$ = Futures settlement price.

**Invoice amount**

When the bond is delivered, the long pays the short an invoice amount:

$$Invoiced = \left( \frac{EDSP}{100 \times CF \times Nominal} \right) + AI \qquad (2.9)$$

The settlement price (or *exchange delivery settlement price, EDSP*) is the trading price per £100 nominal for the futures contract on the last day of trading, and is confirmed by the exchange. The invoice amount includes accrued interest because the futures contract is traded at a *clean* price and does not include accrued interest.

**Box 2.1** Calculating the invoice price.

A futures contract settles at 102.50. The contract specifies £100,000 nominal of the underlying bond. The delivered bond has a conversion factor of 1.14579 and accrued interest of 0.73973. The settlement price is equal to 1.025% of the nominal value (par value). The invoice price is calculated as:

$$P_{inv} = \left(100,000 \times 1.025 \times 1.145\ 79\right) + 0.739\ 73$$
$$= £117,443 + 0.739\ 73$$

For the Treasury long bond the conversion factor is calculated using (2.10):

$$CF = \frac{1}{1.03^{t/6}}\left[\frac{C}{2} + \frac{C}{0.06}\left(1 - \frac{1}{1.03^{2N}}\right) + \frac{1}{1.03^{2N}}\right] \qquad (2.10)$$

where $N$ = Complete years to maturity as at the delivery month;
$t$ = Number of months in excess of the whole $N$ (rounded *down* to whole quarters).

The LIFFE conversion factor for the long gilt was given in Appendix 1.A. The formula is actually the same, beginners are invited to explain that this is indeed so. To illustrate (2.10), if a deliverable Treasury bond has a maturity of 19 years and 5 months, $t$ is 3 because the 5 months is rounded down to one quarter or 3 months. Hence, if the maturity is 19 years and 9 months, $t$ is 6.

It is worth summarising what we know so far about conversion factors:

- conversion factors remain constant for a bond from the moment they are assigned to the expiry of the contract;
- conversion factors are different for each bond and for each contract;[13] from Table 2.3, which relates to the long gilt contract and its then notional coupon of 7%, we see that conversion factors for bonds with coupons higher than 7% diminish in value for each successive contract month, while those for bonds with coupons lower than 7% rise in value for successive contract months.[14] This reflects the 'pull to par' effect which for bonds with the higher coupon is falling from a premium and for bonds with the lower coupon is rising from a discount;

---

[13] If two bonds had identical coupons and maturity dates, then they would have the same conversion factor for a specific contract. However, under these terms the two bonds would be identical as well . . .

[14] The notional coupon for the long gilt was changed from 7% to 6% in March 2004.

- the conversion factor is used to calculate the invoice price of a bond that is delivered into a futures contract;
- bonds with coupons greater than the notional coupon of the futures contract have a conversion factor higher than 1, while bonds with coupons lower than the notional coupon have a conversion factor lower than 1.

The conversion factor is not a hedge ratio, as has been strongly emphasised by both Burghardt and Kolb,[15] and should not be used as such. Certain textbooks and market practitioners have suggested that using the ratio of two bonds' conversion factors can be an effective hedge ratio for hedging a bond position, rather than the traditional approach of using the ratio of basis point values. This is fallacious and will lead to serious errors. The conversion factor of a bond is influenced primarily by its coupon, whereas the modified duration of a bond – from which is derived the Basis Point Value (*BPV*) – is a function mainly of its term to maturity. Hence, it is not correct to substitute them. If an investor was hedging a position in a long-dated bond of low coupon, and the current CTD bond was a short-dated bond of high coupon, the volatility ratio calculated using the respective conversion factors would be lower than unity. However, using respective BPVs would result in a volatility ratio higher than 1. This example illustrates how using a ratio of conversion factors can result in serious hedging errors, and this approach must not be adopted.

Using conversion factors provides an effective system for making all deliverable bonds perfect substitutes for one another. The system is not perfect, of course. Conversion factors are calculated to equalise returns at a single uniform yield, the notional coupon rate specified in the contract specification. In practice though, bonds trade at different yields, resulting in the yield curve. Hence, despite the use of conversion factors, bonds will not be precisely 'equal at the time of delivery. Some bonds will be relatively more expensive, some cheaper; one particular bond will be the CTD bond. The CTD bond is an important concept in the pricing of bond futures contracts.

## 2.3.4 The bond basis

Basis trading arises from the difference between the current clean price of a bond and the (implied) forward clean price at which the bond is bought through the purchase of a futures contract. The difference between these two prices is known as the *gross basis*. This is the bond basis to which the

---

[15] Burghardt *et al.* (1994, p. 9 and ch. 5); Kolb (2000, p. 217).

```
<HELP> for explanation, <MENU> for similar functions.     P139 Comdty DLV
Hit (NUMBER) <GO> to view Historical Basis/Repo
Cheapest  to  Deliver              Trade 3/15/00 Dlv 6/30/00
LONG GILT FUTURE  Jun00    G  MO 112.98     Set 3/16/00 Cheapest IRP= 7.38
                                        DECIMAL  106 Days Act/365  DECIMAL
PRICES AS DECIMALS? Y   (Mid)       Conv.      Gross  Implied  Actual  Net
Order DR re-sort? Y  Price Source  Yield C.Factor  Basis  Repo%   Repo%  Basis
       MASTER:                                                6.24
1) UKT 5 ¾ 12/07/09  102.7328 BFV  5.384  .9142255 -.556  7.38    6.24 -.344
2) UKT 9 07/12/11    131.4610 BFV  5.273 1.1525705 1.244  3.56    6.24 1.032
3) UKT 6 ¼ 11/25/10  107.8777 BFV  5.275  .9449312 1.119  2.20    6.24 1.275
4) UKT 9 08/06/12    134.4551 BFV  5.194 1.1619558 3.177 -1.41    6.24 3.009
```

**FIGURE 2.6**    Delivery basket for Jun00 long gilt, Bloomberg page DLV,
15 March 2000.
© Bloomberg L.P. Used with permission. Visit *www.bloomberg.com*

market refers, the difference between the bond's spot cash price and the price implied by the current price of the futures contract. The latter is given by multiplying the futures price by the relevant bond's conversion factor. The formula for calculating the gross basis is therefore:

$$Basis = P_{bond} - \left( P_{fut} \times CF \right) \qquad (2.11)$$

From (2.11) we might think that if we sell a futures contract short, in effect this guarantees an ability to deliver the bond at the futures delivery date and receive a known price for the bond. However, the price payable for the bond at delivery is based on the future's final settlement price, and not the trading price of the future at any time beforehand, and so this thinking is erroneous.

In the Treasury market both cash and futures prices are quoted as points and ticks (32nds) per $100 nominal value, and if necessary as half-ticks or 64ths. A 64th price is indicated by a +.

The gross basis can be explained essentially as the difference between the running yield on the bond and the current repo (money market) rate. However, a residual factor exists due to the delivery option implicit in the design of the futures contract and to the daily marking-to-market of the contract, both of which are more difficult to quantify. This residual amount is known as the *net basis*. Net basis is the gross basis adjusted for net carry. Net carry is the actual coupon income and re-investment less borrowing expense, which is at the security's actual repo or money market financing rate.

Figure 2.6 is the Bloomberg page DLV of the deliverable bonds for the June 2000 long gilt contract, and shows the conversion factors and gross basis value for each bond in the basket.

---

**Box 2.2**  **The gross basis**

Consider the following market details, all relating to one instantaneous point in time:

| | |
|---|---:|
| Settlement date | 16 March 2000 |
| Futures delivery date | 30 June 2000 |
| Days to delivery | 106 |
| Bond price (UKT 9% 2011) | 131.461 0 |
| Accrued interest | 1.578 082 2 |
| Accrued to delivery | 4.191 780 8 |
| Futures price (M0 LIFFE long gilt) | 112.98 |
| Conversion factor | 1.152 570 5 |
| Cash market repo rate | 6.24% |

We can calculate the gross basis that would apply in a hypothetical cash-and-carry trade, where there is a simultaneous purchase of the bond and sale of the futures contract as shown below.

Bond purchase – outflow of funds:

$$131.461 + 1.578\ 1 = 133.039\ 082\ 2$$

Futures sale – inflow of funds:

$$(112.98 \times 1.152\ 570\ 5) + 4.192 = 134.409\ 19\ 6$$

The gross basis is:

$$131.461\ 0 - (112.98 \times 1.152\ 570\ 5)$$

or 1.243 584 91.

## 2.3.5 The net basis

We've seen from the previous section that gross basis measures the carry on a bond that applies during the life of the futures contract. Because of other factors associated with the delivery into a futures contract, principally that delivery is at the option of the short future, the gross basis is not the actual carry that would be incurred if a trader put on a cash versus futures trade. This is measured by the *net basis*. The net basis causes much confusion amongst market participants, but it is a straightforward concept. Burghardt *et al.* (1994) state that the net basis is the difference between a bond's basis and its total carry to delivery.[16] Plona describes net basis as the difference between the *implied repo rate* (*IRR*) and the general collateral repo rate. We consider the IRR in Section 2.3.6.[17]

Both descriptions are good ways in which to consider net basis. Essentially, the net basis is the gross basis adjusted for net carry. Net carry is the actual coupon income (and any re-investment income) minus borrowing expense, which is at the security's actual repo (money market) rate. The net basis is therefore the true 'economic basis and measures the net gain from a simultaneous position in the cash bond and the futures contract. A positive value represents a *loss* or net cost to the long cash/short futures position, and the net basis is the expected *profit* for the short cash/long futures position (where the actual repo rate used is the reverse repo rate). The opposite is true for negative net basis values.

The net basis is calculated on the assumption that a basis trade is conducted by the arbitrageur borrowing funds to purchase the CTD bond, financing it in the repo market, and shorting the futures contract. It measures the maximum *loss* that would be suffered by holding this position until the contract expiry date. The net basis should be negative as a loss measure; a positive net basis indicates the potential profit from such a trade.[18] On the other hand, a negative net basis theoretically indicates the potential profit from a short bond/long futures position.

To calculate the net basis, we need to make an assumption about the financing rates that would apply to a basis trade.[19] This centres on the repo rate that is applicable to the cash bond element of the trade. Analysts use one of two methods:

- the specific repo rate for the cash bond, fixed to the maturity date. This is a logical approach, as it provides an accurate measure of the financing cost associated with running a long position in the bond, and then

---

[16] Burghardt *et al.* (1994, p. 33). It is also known as the *basis net of carry*.

[17] Plona (1997, p. 32).

[18] Note that in some cases and vendor systems the net basis appears to be positive because the negative sign is left off, under the assumption that users are aware that the net basis represents the loss from a long cash/short futures trade.

[19] As we shall see in Section 2.3.6, no assumptions need to be made when determining the IRR, which is calculated from actual market-observed prices.

delivering it into the futures exchange. Calculating net basis under this method provides a measure of the value of the delivery option;
* the overnight *general collateral* (*GC*) repo rate, assuming therefore that the bond position is financed on a daily basis. Assuming that the overnight rate will be maintained more or less over the term of the trade is risky.

Box 2.3 illustrates the calculation of the net basis.

**Box 2.3**    **The net basis.**

Consider this calculation for the June 1998 long gilt future contract. At this time the 'special ex' rule applies to delivery of bonds into the contract, something that no longer applied with the removal of special ex-trading in August 1998.

| | |
|---|---|
| Trade date | 24 April 1998 |
| Settlement date | 25 April 1998 |
| M8 long gilt future price | 109.656 25 |
| CTD bond ($8\frac{1}{2}$% Treasury 2007) | 106.343 75 |
| Accrued interest | 2.305 48 |
| Accrued to delivery | 3.423 288 2 |
| Dirty price | 108.649 32 |
| Conversion factor ($8\frac{1}{2}$% 2007) | 0.967 406 4 |
| Repo rate | 6.36% |

The converted price of the bond (that is, through the futures contract) is:

$$109.656\ 25 \times 0.967\ 406\ 4 = 106.082\ 16$$

The market clean price is 106.343 75, therefore the gross basis is:

$$106.343\ 75 - 106.082\ 16 = 0.261\ 59$$

Due to the special-ex rule in this case, the last day for delivery of $8\frac{1}{2}$% Treasury 2007 into the futures contract is 12 June. This makes the term 48 days. The total price paid including accrued interest will be 108.649 23. To finance that using repo for 48 days until 12 June will cost £0.908 724 3. The holder of the gilt will however earn 48 days' accrued interest of £1.117 808 2. Therefore, buying the bond direct gives the owner an income advantage of £0.209 083 9.

The difference between the gross basis and this income advantage is £0.216 159 – £0.209 083 9, that is £0.0525. It therefore represents the gain by buying the gilt using the futures contract rather than buying directly in the market.

Of course, the long gilt contract gives the futures seller the right to deliver any of the gilts in the delivery basket and on any day of the delivery month. If the CTD is bought through a futures contract the buyer may find that, because of market movements, a different gilt is delivered. The short future in effect holds an option which decreases the value of the futures contract to the long.

For this reason the *net* basis is usually positive. The futures contract is also marked-to-market which means that the gain or loss on the contract is spread over the life of the contract, in contrast to a forward contract. This effect is small but will again lead to the net basis differing from 0.

The net basis is given by:

$$
\begin{aligned}
Net\ Basis &= \left[108.649\ 23 \times \left(1{+}6.36 \times \frac{48}{36\ 500}\right)\right] \\
&\quad - \left(\left(109.656\ 25 \times 0.967\ 406\ 4\right) + 3.423\ 882\right) \\
&= 109.557\ 954\ 3 - 109.505\ 446\ 25 \\
&= 0.052\ 508\ 05
\end{aligned}
$$

### 2.3.6 The implied repo rate

In a basis trade the rate implied by the strategy is known as a repo rate because it is equivalent to a *repurchase* agreement with the futures market. In effect, the short future lends money to the futures market: the short future agrees to buy a bond with a simultaneous provision to sell it back to the market at a predetermined price and to receive a rate of interest on his money, the repo rate. It is the *implied repo rate* because it is an expected repo rate gain if the trade was carried out. In some literature it is suggested as a complex and obscure calculation; in fact, the Implied Repo Rate (IRR) is very straightforward to calculate. It is the theoretical return from a basis trade of long cash bond against short future, with the bond delivered into the future on expiry.

The IRR is a measure of return from a basis trade. Consider the cash flows involved when one is long bond/short future. We have:

- a cash outflow from purchasing the bond;
- a cash inflow on delivery into the future, including the accrued interest to the delivery date;
- the cash borrowed to finance the trade.

We simply therefore wish to have the percentage return of the investment over the borrowing cost. That is:

$$IRR = \frac{\left(\left(P_{futs} \times CF\right) + AI_{del}\right) - \left(P_{bond} + AI\right)}{P_{bond} + AI} \times \frac{M}{Days} \qquad (2.12)$$

where   $M$ = Day-base, either 360 or 365;
        $Days$ = Term of the trade.

There is no need to remember this version though, Burghardt *et al.* (1994, p. 14) simplify it to:

$$IRR = \left[\frac{P_{invoice} - P_{bond}}{P_{bond}}\right] \times \left(\frac{360}{n}\right) \qquad (2.13)$$

which is identical to (2.12), with $n$ for the number of days to delivery, and all prices still include accrued interest, at the time of the trade (bond) or to delivery (future). The formula written as (2.13) is easy to explain. The invoice price is the futures invoice price, the amount from the delivery on expiry. Of course, the actual invoice price is a function of the final futures settlement price, but we adjust the current futures price with the conversion factor to allow for this.

Note that Bloomberg quotes the formula in still more simplified fashion, as:

$$IRR = \left[\frac{P_{FutsInvoice}}{P_{bond}} - 1\right] \times \left(\frac{360}{n}\right) \qquad (2.14)$$

with the 360-day base associated with the US Treasury market.

Both (2.12) and (2.13) assume that no coupon is paid during the trade. If a coupon is paid during the trade, it is considered as being reinvested, and the cash flow total must therefore include both the coupon and the reinvestment income generated. The re-investment rate used in the market is one of the following:

- the implied repo rate;
- the bond's yield-to-maturity. This is described as being consistent with the bond yield calculation itself, which assumes reinvestment of coupon at the bond yield;
- the overnight repo rate, and rolled over. This is justified on the basis that traders in fact do not reinvest the coupon but use the cash to reduce funding costs.

The first two are assumed to apply to maturity, while the second must be calculated at the prevailing rate each day. If the reinvestment rate is assumed to be the IRR, it is the rate that results in:

$$P_{bond} \times \left(1 + IRR\left(\frac{n}{M}\right)\right) = P_{invoice} + \left(\frac{C}{2}\right) \times \left[1 + IRR\left(\frac{n_2}{M}\right)\right] \qquad (2.15)$$

where $n_2$ is the number of days between the coupon payment and the futures expiry (delivery) date. Expression (2.15) is then rearranged for the IRR, to give us:

$$IRR = \frac{\left(P_{invoice} + \frac{C}{2} - P_{bond}\right) \times M}{\left(P_{bond} \times n\right) - \left(\frac{C}{2} \times n_2\right)} \qquad (2.16)$$

The deliverable bond that has the highest IRR is the *cheapest-to-deliver* bond or *CTD*. We see from (2.16) that the IRR is a function of the bond price, the value of which is compared to the forward price for the bond implied by futures price. As such the status of the CTD bond reflects the bond's price (in other words, its yield). If the yield of a bond within the delivery basket moves sufficiently *vis-à-vis* the other deliverable bonds, it may become the CTD bond. A change in the cheapest bond is an important development and any such change should be anticipated in advance by good traders.

The bond with the highest IRR will, almost invariably, have the lowest net basis. On rare occasions this will not be observed. When two bonds each have IRRs that are very similar, it is sometimes the case that the bond with the (slightly) lower IRR has a (slightly) lower net basis.

The CTD bond is just that: it is the cheapest bond to deliver into the futures contract in terms of running costs. The short future has the delivery option, and will elect to deliver the CTD bond unless there is a reason it cannot, in which case it will deliver the next cheapest at greater cost to itself. Assuming that a basis trade is put on with the CTD bond against the future, if the CTD changes then the position becomes useless and will be unwound at great loss. The CTD bond is what the market will treat as the actual underlying bond of the futures contract, and it is closely observed. Pricing theory informs us that the futures price will track the CTD bond price; in fact, it is the other way around, with the liquidity and transparency of the futures contract and its price meaning that the CTD bond price tracks that of the future. Under the terms of the long gilt contract, the CTD gilt can be delivered on any business day of the delivery month, but in practice only one of two days are ever used to make delivery: the first (business) day of the delivery month or the last (delivery) day of the month. If the current yield on the CTD gilt exceeds the money market repo rate, the bond will be delivered on the last business day of the month, because the short future earns more by holding on to the bond than by delivering it and investing the proceeds in the money market; otherwise, the bond will be delivered on the first business day of the delivery month. Until very recently a gilt that was eligible for trading *special exdividend* on any day of the delivery month was not eligible for delivery into that gilt contract. However, from August 1998 the provision for special ex-dividend trading was removed from gilts, so this consideration no longer applies. Other gilts that are not eligible for delivery are index-linked, partly paid or convertible gilts.[20] For gilts the IRR for all deliverable bonds can be calculated using (2.12) in the normal way. However, if a bond goes ex-dividend between trade date and delivery date, a modification is required in which the interest accrued is negative during the ex-dividend period.

---

**Box 2.4**    **The implied repo rate.**

Another way of looking at the concept of the CTD bond is in terms of the IRR. The CTD bond is the bond that gives the highest IRR to the short from a cash-and-carry trade; that is, a strategy of buying the bond (with borrowed funds) in the cash market and selling it forward into the futures market. The bond is funded in the repo market, and by selling it forward the trade is in effect a repo with the futures market, hence *implied* repo rate.

To illustrate we calculate the IRR for the 9% Treasury 2008, a UK gilt, at the time that the 'front month' contract was the December 1998 contract. The price of the gilt is 129.083 4. The December 1998 long gilt futures contract is trading at 114.50. The date is 1 October.

---

[20] Gilts go ex-dividend 7 business days before the coupon date, this being the record date to determine the investors that will receive the coupon. Prior to its withdrawal, counterparties could agree between themselves to trade ex-dividend up to 2 weeks before the ex-dividend date, this being known as *special ex-dividend*. During trading for the September 1997 long gilt contract, some market participants forgot (or were unaware) that gilts that were special ex-dividend at any time during the delivery month became ineligible for delivery, and had traded in the current CTD bond – the 9% 2008 – under the assumption that they could deliver, or would be delivered into, this bond. When the CTD bond changed it resulted in losses for parties that had not been aware of this. This despite the fact that LIFFE sent out a notice informing the market that the CTD for September 1997 would not be the 9% 2008 for this reason . . .

The money market rate on this date is 7.25%. As the current (or *running*) yield on the 9% 2008, at 6.972%, is lower than the money market rate, it will be delivered at the beginning of December (that is, in 61 days from now). To identify the CTD bond we would need to calculate the IRR for all eligible bonds. We use the conversion factor for the bond which is 1.140 715, calculated and given out by LIFFE before the futures contract began trading.

The cash outflow in a cash-and-carry trade is:

| | |
|---|---|
| Bond dirty price | 129.083 4 |
| Interest cost (1 October–1 December) | 129.083 4 × (0.072 5 × (61/365)) |
| Total outflow | 130.647 4 |

The bond (whose price includes 171 days' accrued interest on 1 October) has to be financed at the money market rate of 7.25% for the 61 days between 1 October and 1 December, when the bond (if it is still the CTD) is delivered into the futures market.

The cash inflow per £100 nominal as a result of this trade is:

| | |
|---|---|
| Implied clean price of bond on 1 December (futures price on 1 October multiplied by conversion factor) | 114.50 × 1.140 715 5 |
| Accrued interest 1 October–1 December | £9 × (61/365) |
| Total inflow | 132.11603 |

The implied price of the bond on 1 December equals the futures price on 1 October multiplied by the conversion factor for the bond. Because the futures price is quoted clean, accrued interest has to be added to obtain the implied dirty price on 1 December.

This cash-and-carry trade which operates for 61 days from 1 October to 1 December generates a rate of return or IRR of:

$$IRR = \left( \frac{132.116\ 03 - 130.647\ 4}{130.647\ 4} \right) \times \frac{365}{61} \times 100$$
$$= 6.726\%$$

**Box 2.5**   Calculating gross basis, net basis and implied repo rate.

The gross basis is the difference between the actual price of the bond and the forward price of the bond as implied by the price of the futures contract, and represents the carrying cost of the bond. This is the actual difference between the coupon gain and re-investment minus the carry costs (which is at the actual money market repo rate). A positive net basis represents the loss that would result from a long cash/short futures position, and therefore the theoretical gain from a short cash/long futures trade, where the actual repo rate is the reverse repo rate transacted when covering the short cash position. The IRR is the theoretical return from a long cash/short futures trade, assuming that the trader is short the number of futures equal to the bond's conversion factor for each £100,000 nominal of bonds held. Any coupon payments are assumed to be reinvested at the IRR.

Earlier in this book we presented the formulae for gross basis and IRR. The net basis is given by:

$$\text{Net basis} = \left( P_{bond} \times \left(1 + r \times \frac{Del}{36\ 500}\right)\right) - \left(\left(P_{fut} \times CF\right) + AI_{del}\right)$$

where   $P_{bond}$ = Bond dirty price;
   $r$   = Actual repo rate (expressed as per cent × 100);
   $Del$ = Days to delivery;
   $P_{fut}$ = Futures price;
   $CF$ = Bond's conversion factor;
   $AI_{del}$ = Bond's accrued interest to delivery.

For net basis calculations in Treasury or euro markets the appropriate 360-day basis is used.

The calculations are for the CTD bond for the long gilt contract, which was the $6\frac{1}{4}\%$ 2010 gilt. We use mid prices for the bond. The trade is buying the cash and simultaneously selling the future. Note that gilts accrue on actual/actual basis and there were 184 days in the interest period 25 May–25 November 2001. The accrued interest calculation is therefore (80/184 × (6.25 × 0.5)) for the first date and (126/184 × (6.25 × 0.5)) for the delivery date.

| | |
|---|---|
| Settlement date | 13 August 2001 |
| Futures price | 115.94 |
| $6\frac{1}{4}\%$ Treasury 25/11/2010 price | 110.20 |
| Conversion factor | 0.949 495 6 |
| Repo rate | 4.90% |

*Calculations*

Cash out on 13/8/2001:

$$110.20 \text{ plus accrued } (80 \text{ days}) = 111.558 \ 696$$

Cash in on 28/9/2021:

$$(115.94 \times 0.949 \ 495 \ 6) \text{ plus accrued} = 110.084 \ 52 + 2.139 \ 946$$
$$(46 \text{ days later})$$
$$= 112.224 \ 465 \ 9$$

*Gross basis*

$$110.20 - 110.084 \ 519 \ 9 = \mathbf{0.115 \ 480 \ 1}$$

*Net basis*

$$\left( 111.558 \ 696 \times \left( 1 + 4.90 \times \frac{46}{36 \ 500} \right) \right) - 112.224 \ 465 \ 9$$
$$= \mathbf{0.023 \ 143 \ 2}$$

*Implied repo rate*

$$\left( \frac{112.224 \ 465 \ 9}{111.558696} - 1 \right) \times \frac{365}{46} \times 100 = \mathbf{4.735 \ 390\%}$$

These calculations are confirmed by looking at the Bloomberg screens YA and DLV for value on 13 August 2001, as shown in Figures 2.7 and 2.8, respectively. Figure 2.7 is selected for the $6\frac{1}{4}\%$ 2010 gilt and Figure 2.8 is selected for the front month contract at the time, the Sep01 gilt future. Figure 2.9 shows the change in CTD bond status between the $6\frac{1}{4}\%$ 2010 gilt and the 9% 2011 gilt, the second cheapest bond at the time of the analysis, with changes in the futures price. The change of CTD status with changes in the IRR is shown in Figure 2.10. Both are Bloomberg page HCG.

Page DLV on Bloomberg lists deliverable bonds for any selected futures contract. Bonds are listed in order of declining *implied repo rate*; the user can select in increasing or decreasing order of implied repo rate, basis, yield, maturity, coupon or duration. The user can also select the price source for the bonds (in our example set at 'Bloomberg Generic' rather than any specific bank or market maker) and the current cash repo rate.

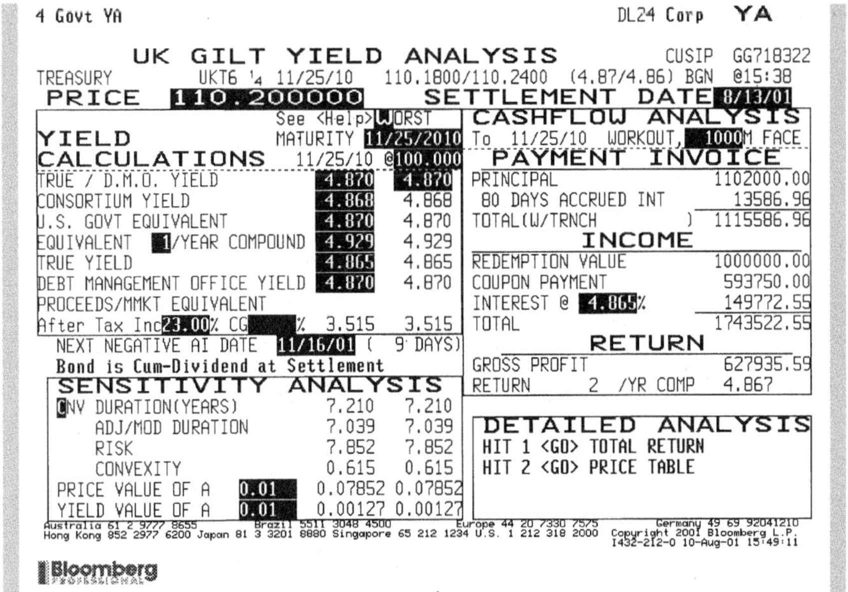

**Figure 2.7** Bloomberg YA page for $6\frac{1}{4}$% 2010 gilt, showing accrued interest for value 13 August 2001.
© Bloomberg L.P. Used with permission. Visit *www.bloomberg.com*

**Figure 2.8** Bloomberg DLV page for Sep01 (U1) gilt contract, showing gross basis, net basis and IRR for trade date 12 August 2001.
© Bloomberg L.P. Used with permission. Visit *www.bloomberg.com*

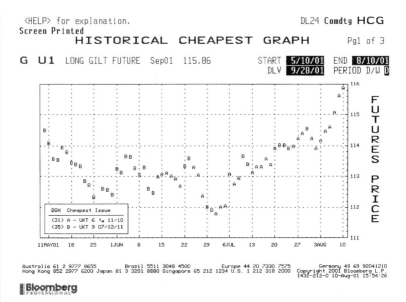

**Figure 2.9**   Bloomberg HCG page for Sep01 (U1) gilt contract, showing CTD
bond history up to 12 August 2001 with changes in futures price.
© Bloomberg L.P. Used with permission. Visit *www.bloomberg.com*

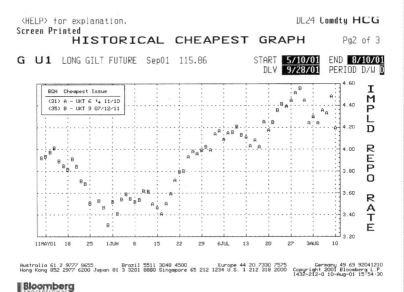

**Figure 2.10**   Bloomberg HCG page for Sep01 (U1) gilt contract, showing CTD
bond history up to 12 August 2001, with changes in IRR.
© Bloomberg L.P. Used with permission. Visit *www.bloomberg.com*

Reproduced from *The Futures Bond Basis, Second Edition* (2006)

**This extract from *Structured Credit Products, Second Edition* (2010)**

## Credit Risk and Credit Derivatives

# CREDIT RISK AND CREDIT DERIVATIVES

Credit derivatives are financial contracts designed to reduce or eliminate credit risk exposure by providing insurance against losses suffered due to *credit events*. A payout under a credit derivative is triggered by a credit event associated with the credit derivative's *reference asset* or *reference entity*. As banks define default in different ways, the terms under which a credit derivative is executed usually include a specification of what constitutes a credit event. The principle behind credit derivatives is straightforward. Investors desire exposure to debt that is not risk-free because of the higher returns this debt offers. However, such exposure brings with it concomitant credit risk. This can be managed with credit derivatives. At the same time, the exposure itself can be taken on synthetically if, for instance, there are compelling reasons why a cash market position cannot be established. The flexibility of credit derivatives provides users with a number of advantages and as they are over-the-counter (OTC) products they can be designed to meet specific user requirements. Some of the most common reasons for which they are used include:

- hedging credit risk: this includes credit default risk, dynamic credit risks and changes in credit quality;
- reducing credit risk with a specific client (*obligor*) so that lending lines to this client are freed up for other business;
- diversifying investment options; in other words, acquiring credit exposure without having to buy the cash product.

The intense competition among commercial banks, combined with rapid disintermediation, has meant that banks have been forced to evaluate their lending policies, with a view to improving profitability and return on capital. The use of credit derivatives assists banks with restructuring their businesses, because they allow banks to repackage and transfer credit risk, while retaining assets on balance sheet (when required) and thus maintain client relationships. As the instruments isolate certain aspects of credit risk from the underlying loan or bond and transfer them to another entity, it becomes possible to separate the ownership and management of credit risk from the other features of ownership associated with the assets in question. This means that illiquid assets such as bank loans, and illiquid bonds, can have their credit risk exposures transferred—the bank owning the assets can protect against credit loss even if it cannot transfer the assets themselves.[5]

---

[5] The bank may not wish to transfer the physical assets, in order to maintain client relationships. It can always transfer the assets in a securitisation transaction, which can also bring in funding (cash securitisation).

The same principles apply to the credit risk exposures of portfolio managers. For fixed-income portfolio managers, some of the advantages of using credit derivatives include the following:

- they can be tailor-made to meet the specific requirements of the entity buying the risk protection, as opposed to the liquidity or term of the underlying reference asset;
- they can be 'sold short' without risk of a liquidity or delivery squeeze, as it is a specific credit risk that is being traded. In the cash market, it is not possible to 'sell short' a bank loan for example, but a credit derivative can be used to establish synthetically the economic effect of such a position;
- as they isolate credit risk from other factors such as client relationships and interest rate risk, credit derivatives introduce a formal pricing mechanism to price credit issues only. This means a market is available in credit only, allowing more efficient pricing, and it becomes possible to model a term structure of credit rates;
- they are off-balance sheet instruments[6] and as such incorporate flexibility and leverage, exactly like other financial derivatives. For instance, bank loans are not particularly attractive investments for certain investors because of the administration required in managing and servicing a loan portfolio. However, an exposure to bank loans and their associated return can be achieved using credit derivatives while simultaneously avoiding the administrative costs of actually owning the assets. Hence credit derivatives allow investors access to specific credits while allowing banks access to further distribution for bank loan credit risk.

Thus credit derivatives can be an important instrument for bond portfolio managers as well as commercial banks, who wish to increase the liquidity of their portfolios, gain from the relative value arising from credit pricing anomalies and enhance portfolio returns.

## CREDIT DERIVATIVE INSTRUMENTS

Before analysing the main types of credit derivatives, we now consider some generic features of all credit derivatives.

---

[6] When credit derivatives are embedded in certain fixed-income products, such as structured notes and credit-linked notes, they are then off-balance sheet but part of a structure that will have on-balance sheet elements. Funded credit derivatives are on-balance sheet.

# Background

Credit derivative instruments enable participants in the financial market to trade in credit as an asset, as they effectively isolate and transfer credit risk. They also enable the market to separate funding considerations from credit risk. A number of instruments come under the category of credit derivative. In this and the next chapter we consider the most commonly encountered credit derivative instruments. Irrespective of the particular instrument under consideration, all credit derivatives can be described as having the following characteristics:

- the *reference entity*: which is the asset or name on which credit protection is being bought and sold;[7]
- the credit event, or events: which indicate that the reference entity is experiencing or about to experience financial difficulty and which act as trigger events for termination of and payments under the credit derivative contract;
- the settlement mechanism for the contract: whether cash settled or physically settled;
- (under physical settlement), the deliverable obligation: that the protection buyer delivers to the protection seller on the occurrence of a trigger event.

Within this broad framework, it is common to see wide variations in detail among specific types of credit derivative instruments.

## Funded and Unfunded Contracts

Credit derivatives are grouped into *funded* and *unfunded* instruments. In a funded credit derivative, typified by a credit-linked note (CLN), the investor in the note is the credit-protection seller and is making an upfront payment to the protection buyer when it buys the note. This upfront payment is the price of the CLN. Thus, the protection buyer is the issuer of the note. If no credit event occurs during the life of the note, the redemption value (par) of the note is paid to the investor on maturity. If a credit event does occur, then on termination (in effect, maturity of the bond), a value less than par will be paid to the investor. This value will be reduced by the nominal value of the reference asset that the CLN is linked to. The exact process will differ

---

[7] Note that a contract may be written in relation to a *reference entity*, which is the corporate or sovereign name, or a *reference obligation*, which is a specific debt obligation of a specific reference entity. Another term for reference obligation is *reference asset* or *reference credit*. We will use these latter terms interchangeably in the book.

according to whether *cash settlement* or *physical settlement* has been specified for the note. We will consider this later.

In an unfunded credit derivative, typified by a CDS, the protection seller does not make an upfront payment to the protection buyer. Thus the main difference between funded and unfunded is that in a funded contract, the insurance protection payment is made to the protection buyer at the start of the transaction: if there is no credit event, the payment is returned to the protection seller. In an unfunded contract, the protection payment is made on termination of the contract on occurrence of a triggering credit event. Otherwise it is not made at all. Therefore, when entering into a funded contract transaction, the protection seller (that is, the investor) must find the funds at the start of the trade.

Credit derivatives such as CDS have a number of applications and are used extensively for flow trading of single reference name credit risks or, in *portfolio swap* form, for trading a basket of reference obligations. CDSs and CLNs are used in structured products, in various combinations, and their flexibility has been behind the growth and wide application of the synthetic collateralised debt obligation (CDO) and other credit hybrid products. We look at these later.

Compared to cash market bonds and loans, an unfunded credit derivative isolates and transfers credit risk only. In other words, its value reflects only the credit quality of the reference entity. Compare this to a fixed-coupon corporate bond, the value of which is a function of both interest rate risk and credit quality, where the return to the investor depends on the investor's funding costs.[8] The interest rate risk element of the bond can be removed by combining the bond with an interest rate swap, to create an *asset swap*. An asset swap removes the interest rate risk of the bond, leaving only the credit quality and the funding aspects of the bond. With an unfunded credit derivative, the funding aspect is removed as well, leaving only the credit element. This is because no upfront payment is required, resulting in no funding risk to the protection seller. The protection seller, who is the investor, receives a return that is linked only to the credit quality of the reference entity.

This separation of credit risk from other elements of the cash market is shown in Figure 2.5.

---

[8] Funding refers to the cost of funds of the investor. For a bank, funding is based on LIBID. For a traditional investor, such as a pension fund manager, funding is more problematic, as the funds are in theory invested directly with the pension fund and so acquired 'free'. However, for economic purposes, such funds are valued at the rate that they can be invested in the money markets. For other investors, funding is based on LIBOR plus a spread, except for very highly rated market participants such as the World Bank, who can fund at sub-LIBOR rates.

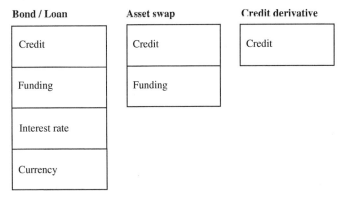

**Figure 2.5**    Credit derivatives isolate credit as an asset class and risk element.

---

**EXAMPLE 2.1**    Reference entity and reference obligation

A reference obligation or reference asset is an obligation issued by a reference entity for which credit protection is required. The reference obligation usually has a pre-specified seniority, to facilitate ease of determination of the settlement payment. A higher seniority usually leads to a better recovery rate and hence a lower loss rate following a credit event. It is also reflected in a lower price for the credit derivative contract.

---

## Credit Events

The occurrence of a specified credit event will trigger the termination of the credit derivative contract, and result in the transfer of the default protection payment from the protection seller to the protection buyer.

The following may be specified as 'credit events' in the legal documentation between counterparties:

- downgrade in S&P and/or Moody's credit rating below a specified minimum level;
- financial or debt restructuring; for example, occasioned under administration or as required under US bankruptcy protection;
- bankruptcy or insolvency of the reference asset obligor;
- default on payment obligations such as bond coupon and continued non-payment after a specified time period;
- technical default; for example, the non-payment of interest or coupon when it falls due;
- a change in credit spread payable by the obligor above a specified maximum level.

The International Swap and Derivatives Association (ISDA) compiled standard documentation governing the legal treatment of credit derivative contracts. The standardisation of legal documentation promoted ease of execution and was a factor in the rapid growth of the market. The 1999 ISDA CDS documentation specified bankruptcy, failure to pay, obligation default, debt moratorium and restructuring to be credit events. Note that it does not specify a rating downgrade to be a credit event.[9]

A summary of the credit events as set forth in the ISDA definitions is given in Appendix 2.1. Note that for North American contracts rate these were affected in 2009, as discussed later in the chapter.

The precise definition of 'restructuring' is open to debate and has resulted in legal disputes between protection buyers and sellers. Prior to issuing its 1999 definitions, ISDA had specified restructuring as an event or events that resulted in making the terms of the reference obligation 'materially less favourable' to the creditor (or protection seller) from an economic perspective. This definition was open to more than one interpretation and it caused controversy when determining if a credit event had occurred. The 2001 definitions specified more precise conditions, including any action that resulted in a reduction in the amount of principal. In the European market, restructuring is generally retained as a credit event in contract documentation, but in the US market it is less common to see it included. Instead, US contract documentation tends to include as a credit event a form of *modified restructuring*, the impact of which is to limit the options available to the protection buyer as to the type of assets it could deliver in a physically settled contract. Further clarification was provided in the 2003 ISDA definitions,[10] and again as part of the 2009 ISDA 'Big Bang'.

---

[9] The ISDA definitions from 1999, the restructuring supplement from 2001, the 2003 definitions and the 2009 protocols are available at www.ISDA.org.

[10] The debate on restructuring as a credit event arose out of a number of events, notably the case involving a corporate entity, Conseco, in the US in 2000. It concerned the delivery option benefit afforded to the protection buyer in a physically settled credit derivative, and the *cheapest-to-deliver* asset. Under physical settlement, the protection buyer may deliver any senior debt obligation of the reference entity. When the triggering credit event is default, all senior obligations of the reference entity generally trade at approximately equal levels, mainly because of the expected recovery rate in a bankruptcy proceeding. However, where the triggering event is restructuring short-dated bank debt, which has been restructured to give lending banks better pricing and collateral, the short-dated bonds will trade at a significant premium to longer dated bonds. The pricing differential between the short-dated, restructured obligations and the longer dated bonds results in the delivery option held by the protection buyer carrying significant value, as the protection buyer will deliver the cheapest-to-deliver obligation. Under the modified restructuring definition, where the triggering event is restructuring, the delivered obligation cannot have a maturity that is longer than the original maturity date of the credit derivative contract, or more than 30 months after the original maturity date.

## Comparing Credit Derivatives to Cash Instruments

Both funded and unfunded credit derivatives act as alternatives to cash market products for investors. Funded credit derivatives are similar to cash bonds, but investors will need to assess their requirements more fully when assessing the relative merits of cash versus synthetic products.

---

### RESTRUCTURING, MODIFIED RESTRUCTURING AND MODIFIED-MODIFIED RESTRUCTURING

The original 1999 ISDA credit definitions defined restructuring among the standard credit events. The five specified definitions included events such as a reduction in the rate of interest payable, a reduction in the amount of principal outstanding and a postponement or deferral of payment. Following a number of high-profile cases where there was disagreement or dispute between protection buyers and sellers on what constituted precisely a restructuring, the Supplement to the 1999 ISDA limited the term to maturity of deliverable obligations. This was modified restructuring or Mod-R, which was intended to reduce the difference between the loss suffered by a holder of the actual restructured obligation and the writer of a CDS on that reference name. In practice this has placed a maturity limit on deliverable obligations of 30 months.

The 2003 Definitions presented further clarification and stated that the restructuring event had to be binding on all holders of the restructured debt. The modified-modified restructuring definition or Mod-Mod-R described in the 2003 ISDA defines the modified restructuring term to maturity date as the later of:

- the scheduled termination date;
- 60 months following the restructuring date

in the event that a restructured bond or loan is delivered to the protection seller. If another obligation is delivered, the limitation on maturity is the scheduled maturity date and 30 months following the restructuring date.

Restructuring does not now apply as a credit event in North American contracts.

---

In certain respects both products offer the same thing. The coupon cash flows of a corporate bond can be replicated using a CDS contract, and an investor can get synthetic access to a particular sovereign or corporate name in this way. In some cases the return can be higher for essentially the same commensurate risk. We can illustrate this with a hypothetical example. Assume

| Buy Jackfruit 5-year bonds | Sell 5-year protection on Jackfruit |
| --- | --- |
| Funded position | Unfunded position |
| Earn 195 bps over LIBOR | Earn 225 bps |
| Fund at LIBOR + 10.0 | No funding cost |
| Net return 185 bps | Return 225 bps |

**Table 2.1**   Jackfruit Music Ltd, buying bonds versus selling protection.

a pension fund investor wishes to invest in the bonds of a hypothetical corporate credit, call it Jackfruit Music Limited, which is rated BBB–/Baa3. The investor can buy Jackfruit Music bonds or sell protection on Jackfruit Music instead. Either way, the investor is acquiring risk in Jackfruit Music. Market makers quote the following for Jackfruit Music:

- 5-year bonds offered at 250 bps over benchmark government bonds;
- the CDS bid–offer price is 225–230 bps;
- the bond asset swap price is LIBOR + 195 bps (the 5-year inter-bank swap spread is 55 bps).

Assume further that the investor is part of a Group entity and funds at LIBOR plus 10 bps.

The alternatives are illustrated in Table 2.1.

By investing via the synthetic product, the investor earns a yield pick up of 40 bps over the cash position. This sounds too good to be true and in some cases will be; also, in some cases the CDS will be trading below the cash. However it illustrates the key issues. As we will see in Chapter 9, the CDS position in many cases exposes the investor to a greater risk exposure than the

| Buy cash bonds | Sell credit protection |
| --- | --- |
| Funded position | Unfunded position |
| Investor holds a specific bond and its risk exposure is to that specific bond | Unless written into the contract specifically, investor is selling protection on all obligations of the reference issuer |
| Risk to specific bond that is marked-to-market and may be sold in market if buyer is available | In event of credit event, which may not be complete default or full administration, protection seller will settle at par, minus market price of cheapest eligible reference bond (or receive this bond, for which it pays par) |
| Return on bond is net amount of funding cost | Return is CDS bid price |

**Table 2.2**   Cash versus synthetic market considerations.

cash bond position, which is why the CDS price is in many cases higher. This difference between the CDS price and the cash bond price is known as the *basis*. The size of the basis is used as an indicator of deteriorating credit quality (or, as significant, potentially deteriorating credit quality) in a reference name.

Table 2.2 shows the key investor considerations for both markets.

We now consider the individual credit derivative instruments.

# CREDIT DEFAULT SWAPS

We describe first the credit default swap (CDS), the most commonly traded credit derivative instrument.

## Structure

The most common credit derivative is the *credit default swap*, sometimes called the *credit swap* or *default swap*.[11] This is a bilateral contract that provides protection on the par value of a specified reference asset, with a protection buyer that pays a periodic fixed fee or a one-off premium to a *protection seller*, in return for which the seller will make a payment on the occurrence of a specified credit event. The fee is usually quoted as a basis point multiplier of the nominal value. It is usually paid quarterly in arrears. The swap can refer to a specific single asset, known as the reference asset or underlying asset, a basket of assets, or a reference entity. The default payment can be paid in whatever way suits the protection buyer or both counterparties. For example, it may be linked to the change in price of the reference asset or another specified asset, it may be fixed at a pre-determined recovery rate, or it may be in the form of actual delivery of the reference asset at a specified price. The basic structure is shown in Figure 2.6.

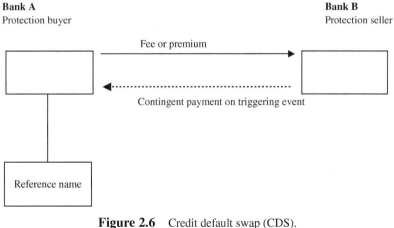

**Figure 2.6**   Credit default swap (CDS).

---

[11] The author prefers the first term, but the other two terms are also observed.

The CDS enables one party to transfer its credit risk exposure to another party. Banks may use default swaps to trade sovereign and corporate credit spreads without trading the actual assets themselves; for example, someone who has gone long a default swap (the protection buyer) will gain if the reference asset obligor suffers a rating downgrade or defaults, and can sell the default swap at a profit if they can find a buyer counterparty.[12] This is because the cost of protection on the reference asset will have increased as a result of the credit event. The original buyer of the credit default swap need never have shorted the bond issued by the reference asset obligor.

The maturity of the CDS does not have to match the maturity of the reference asset and often does not. On occurrence of a credit event, the swap contract is terminated and a settlement payment is made by the protection seller, or *guarantor,* to the protection buyer. This termination value is calculated at the time of the credit event, and the exact procedure that is followed to calculate the termination value depends on the settlement terms specified in the contract. This will be either cash settlement or physical settlement. We look at these options later.

For illustrative purposes, Figure 2.7 shows investmentgrade credit default swap levels during 2001 and 2002 for US dollar and euro reference entities (average levels taken), while Table 2.3 shows sample CDS prices during September 2003. We update the latter for December 2008 at Table 2.4.

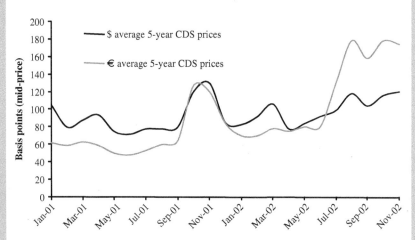

**Figure 2.7**    Investment-grade CDS levels, 2001–2002.
*Source*: Bloomberg L.P.

---

[12] Be careful with terminology here. To 'go long' of an instrument generally is to purchase it. In the cash market, 'going long the bond' means one is buying the bond and so receiving coupon—the buyer has therefore taken on credit risk exposure to the issuer. In a CDS, 'going long' is to buy the swap, but the buyer is purchasing protection and therefore paying premium. The buyer has in effect 'gone short' on the reference name (the equivalent of 'shorting a bond' in the cash market and paying coupon). So buying a CDS is frequently referred to in the market as 'shorting' the reference entity.

| Reference name | Mid-price bps | Moody's/S&P |
|---|---|---|
| *Automobiles* | | |
| Ford Motor Co. | 318 | Baa1/BBB2 |
| General Motors | 269 | Baa1/BBB |
| GMAC | 229 | A3/BBB |
| *Banks* | | |
| Bank of America | 23 | Aa2/A1 |
| Wells Fargo | 33 | Aa2/A1 |
| **Asia-Pacific region** | **Bid–ask** | **Moody's/S&P** |
| Hutchison Whampoa | 96/106 | A3/A2 |
| PR China | 22/26 | A3/BBB |
| Republic of Korea | 67/74 | A3/A2 |
| NEC | 46/53 | Baa2/BBB2 |
| Qantas | 74/84 | Baa1/BBB1 |

**Table 2.3**   Sample 5-year CDS premiums, September 2003.
*Sources*: Morgan Stanley, Bloomberg, Risk.

| Reference name | Mid-price bps | Rating: S&P/Moody's/Fitch |
|---|---|---|
| *Automobiles* | | |
| Ford Motor Co. | 2508 | CCC+/Caa2/CCC |
| General Motors | 11064 | CCC+/NR/CCC |
| GMAC | 3443 | CC/C/CCC |
| *Banks* | | |
| Bank of America | 193 | AA–/Aa2/A+ |
| Wells Fargo | 155 | AA–/Aa2/A+ |
| **Asia-Pacific region** | **Bid-Ask** | **S&P/Moody's/Fitch** |
| Hutchison Whampoa | 423 | A–/A3/A |
| PR China | 239 | NR/A1/NR |
| Republic of Korea | 419 | A/A2/AA |
| NEC | 195 | BBB/Baa1/BBB |
| Qantas | 348 | BBB+/Baa1/NR |

**Table 2.4**   Sample 5-year CDS premiums, 8 December 2008.
*Source*: Bloomberg L.P.

---

| EXAMPLE 2.2 | Credit default swap example |

XYZ plc credit spreads are currently trading at 120 bps over 5-year government bond maturities and 195 bps over 10-year government bond maturities. A portfolio manager hedges a $10 million holding of 10-year paper by purchasing the following CDS, written on the 5-year bond. This hedge protects for the first five years of the holding, and in the event of XYZ's credit spread widening, will increase in value and may be sold before expiry at profit. The 10-year bond holding also earns 75 bps over the shorter term paper for the portfolio manager.

| | |
|---|---|
| Term: | 5 years |
| Reference credit: | XYZ plc 5-year bond |
| Credit event: | The business day following occurrence of specified credit event |
| Default payment: | Nominal value of bond × 3 × [100 × 2 × price of bond after credit event] |
| Swap premium: | 3.35% |

Assume that midway into the life of the swap there is a technical default on the XYZ plc 5-year bond, such that its price now stands at $28. Under the terms of the swap the protection buyer delivers the bond to the seller, who pays $7.2 million to the buyer.

# TOTAL RETURN SWAPS

A *total return swap* (TRS), sometimes known as a *total rate of return swap* or *TR swap*, is an agreement between two parties that exchanges the total return from a financial asset between them. This is designed to transfer the credit risk from one party to the other. It is one of the principal instruments used by banks and other financial instruments to manage their credit risk exposure, and as such is a credit derivative. One definition of a TRS is given in Francis *et al* (1999), which states that a TRS is a swap agreement in which the *total return* of a bank loan or credit-sensitive security is exchanged for some other cash flow, usually linked to LIBOR or some other loan or credit-sensitive security.

The TRS trade itself can be to any maturity term; that is, it need not match the maturity of the underlying security. In a TRS, the total return from the underlying asset is paid to the counterparty in return for a fixed or floating cash flow. This makes it slightly different to other credit derivatives, as the payments between counterparties to a TRS are connected to changes in the market value of the underlying asset, as well as changes resulting from the occurrence of a credit event. So, in other words, TRS cash flows are not solely linked to the occurrence of a credit event—in a TRS the interest rate risk is also transferred. The transaction enables the complete cash flows of a bond to be received without the recipient actually buying the bond, which makes it a synthetic bond product and therefore a credit derivative. An investor may wish to receive such cash flows synthetically for tax, accounting, regulatory capital, external audit or legal reasons. On the other hand, it may be easier to source the reference asset synthetically—via the TRS—than in the cash market. This happens sometimes with illiquid bonds.

In some versions of a TRS, the underlying asset is actually sold to the counterparty, with a corresponding swap transaction agreed simultaneously. In other versions, there is no physical change of ownership of the underlying asset. This makes TRS akin to a synthetic repo transaction. This is discussed in Appendix 2.3.

Figure 2.25 illustrates a generic TRS. The two counterparties are labelled as banks, but the party termed 'Bank A' can be another financial institution, including cash-rich fixed-income portfolio managers such as insurance companies and hedge funds. In Figure 2.25, Bank A has contracted to pay the 'total return' on a specified reference asset, while simultaneously receiving a LIBOR-based return from Bank B. The reference or underlying asset can be a bank loan such as a corporate loan or a sovereign or corporate bond. The total return payments from Bank A include the interest payments on the underlying loan as well as any appreciation in the market value of the asset.

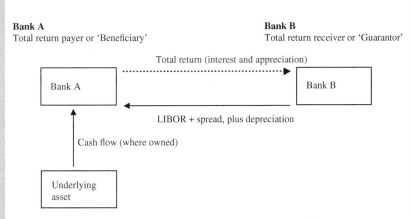

Bank A
Total return payer or 'Beneficiary'

Bank B
Total return receiver or 'Guarantor'

Total return (interest and appreciation)

Bank A

Bank B

LIBOR + spread, plus depreciation

Cash flow (where owned)

Underlying asset

**Figure 2.25**   Total return swap.

Bank B will pay the LIBOR-based return and it will also pay any difference if there is a depreciation in the price of the asset. The economic effect is as if Bank B owned the underlying asset, so as such TR swaps are synthetic loans or securities. A significant feature is that Bank A will usually hold the underlying asset on its balance sheet, so that if this asset were originally on Bank B's balance sheet, this is a means by which the latter can have the asset removed from its balance sheet for the term of the TR swap.[21] If we assume Bank A has access to LIBOR funding, it will receive a spread on this from Bank B. Under the terms of the swap, Bank B will pay the difference between the initial market value and any depreciation, so it is sometimes termed the 'guarantor' while Bank A is the 'beneficiary'.

The total return on the underlying asset is the interest payments and any change in the market value if there is capital appreciation. The value of an appreciation may be cash settled, alternatively there may be physical delivery of the reference asset on maturity of the swap, in return for a payment of the initial asset value by the total return 'receiver'. The maturity of the TR swap need not be identical to that of the reference asset, and in fact it is rare for it to be so.

The swap element of the trade will usually pay on a monthly, quarterly or semi-annual basis, with the underlying asset being revalued or *marked-to-market* on the re-fixing dates. The asset price is usually obtained from an independent third party source such as Bloomberg or Reuters, or as the average of a range of market quotes. If the *obligor* of the reference asset defaults, the swap may be terminated immediately, with a net present value payment changing hands according to what this value is, or it may be continued with each party making appreciation or depreciation payments as appropriate. This second option is only available if there is a market for the asset, which is less likely in the case of a bank loan. If the swap is terminated, each counterparty is liable to the other for accrued interest plus any appreciation or depreciation of the asset. Commonly under the terms of the trade, the guarantor bank has the option to purchase the underlying asset from the beneficiary bank, and then deal directly with loan defaulter.

The TRS can also be traded as a funded credit derivative, and we look at this in the next chapter.

Banks employ a number of methods to price credit derivatives and TR swaps. Essentially the pricing of credit derivatives is linked to that of other instruments; however, the main difference between credit derivatives and

---

[21] Although it is common for the receiver of the LIBOR-based payments to have the reference asset on its balance sheet, this is not always the case.

other off-balance sheet products such as equity, currency or bond derivatives is that the latter can be priced and hedged with reference to the underlying asset, which can be problematic when applied to credit derivatives. Credit products pricing uses statistical data on likelihood of default, probability of payout, level of risk tolerance and a pricing model. With a TRS the basic concept is that one party 'funds' an underlying asset and transfers the total return of the asset to another party, in return for a (usually) floating return that is a spread to LIBOR. This spread is a function of:

- the credit rating of the swap counterparty;
- the amount and value of the reference asset;
- the credit quality of the reference asset;
- the funding costs of the beneficiary bank;
- any required profit margin;
- the capital charge associated with the TRS.

The TR swap counterparties must consider a number of risk factors associated with the transaction, which include:

- the probability that the TR guarantor or receiver may default while the reference asset has declined in value;
- the reference asset obligor defaults, followed by default of the TR swap receiver before payment of the depreciation has been made to the payer or 'provider'.

The first risk measure is a function of the probability of default by the TR swap receiver and the market volatility of the reference asset, while the second risk is related to the joint probability of default of both factors as well as the recovery probability of the asset.

Reproduced from *Structured Credit Products, Second Edition* (2010)

**This extract from *The Credit Default Swap Basis* (2006)**

# CDS Valuation

We consider now two approaches to pricing a CDS contract, both of which are used in the market. The first we describe is termed the "reduced form" model, developed by Hull and White (2000). The second is a market approach first described by JPMorgan, which extracts a default term structure from bond market prices and is straightforward to apply in practice.

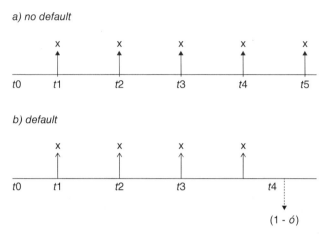

**Figure 1.10**   Illustration of cash flows in a default swap

## Pricing Methodology Based on Reduced-Form Model Approach[12]

A credit default swap, like an interest-rate swap, consists of two legs—one corresponding to the premium payments, and the other to the contingent default payment. This is illustrated in **FIGURE 1.10.** The present value (PV) of a default swap can be viewed as the algebraic sum of the present values of its two legs. The market premium is similar to an interest rate swap in that the premium makes the current aggregate PV equal to zero.

The CDS is priced on the assumption that there is a recovery amount that is a fraction of the recovery rate $R$ of par value, plus any accrued interest.

Because these cash flows may terminate at an unknown time during the life of the deal, their values are computed in a probabilistic sense, using the discounted expected value as calculated under the risk-neutral method and assumptions.

The theoretical pricing of credit derivatives has attracted attention in the academic literature. Longstaff and Schwartz (1995) present the pricing of credit spread options based on an exogenous mean-reverting process for credit spreads. Duffie (1999) presents a simple reduced-form pricing model. Here, we introduce another reduced-form pricing model developed by Hull and White (2000). Their approach was to calibrate their model based on the traded bonds of the underlying reference name, on a time series of credit default swap prices.

Like most other approaches, their model assumes that there is no counterparty default risk. Default probabilities, interest rates, and recovery rates are independent.

Finally, Hull and White also assume that the claim in the event of default is the face value plus accrued interest. To illustrate, we consider the valuation of a plain vanilla credit default swap with $1 notional principal.

---

[12]   This section was coauthored with Abukar Ali.

We use the following notation:

| | |
|---|---|
| $T$ | is life of credit default swap in years |
| $q(t)$ | is risk-neutral probability density at time $t$ |
| $R$ | is expected recovery rate on the reference obligation in a risk-neutral world (independent of the time of default) |
| $u(t)$ | is present value of payments at the rate of \$1 per year on payment dates between time zero and time $t$ |
| $e(t)$ | is present value of an accrual payment at time $t$ equal to $t - t^*$ where $t^*$ is the payment date immediately preceding time $t$ |
| $v(t)$ | is present value of \$1 received at time $t$ |
| $w$ | is total payment per year made by credit default swap buyer |
| $s$ | is value of $w$ that causes the value of the credit default swap to have a value of zero |
| $\pi$ | is the risk-neutral probability of no credit event during the life of the swap |
| $A(t)$ | is accrued interest on the reference obligation at time $t$ as a percentage of face value |

The value $\pi$ is one minus the probability that a credit event will occur by time $T$. This is also referred to as the survival probability, and can be calculated from $q(t)$ as follows:

$$\pi = 1 - \int_0^T q(t)\,dt. \tag{1.1}$$

The payments last until a credit event or until time $T$, whichever is sooner. If default occurs at $t(t<T)$, the present value of the payment is $w[u(t)]$. If there is no default prior to time $T$, the present value of the payment is $wu(T)$. The expected present value of the payment is therefore

$$w\int_0^T q(t)\big[u(t)+e(t)\big]dt + w\pi u(T). \tag{1.2}$$

Given the assumption about the claim amount, the risk-neutral expected payoff from the CDS contract is derived as follows:

$$1 - R\big[1+A(t)\big] \text{multiplying} - R \text{ by } \big[1+A(t)\big]$$
$$1 - R\big[1+A(t)\big] = 1 - R - A(t)R.$$

The present value of the expected payoff from the CDS is given as

$$\int_0^T \big[1-R-A(t)R\big]q(t)v(t)dt. \tag{1.3}$$

The value of the CDS to the buyer is the present value of the expected payoff minus the present value of the payments made by the buyer, or

$$\int_0^T \big[1-R-A(t)R\big]q(t)v(t)dt - w\int_0^T q(t)\big[u(t)+e(t)\big]dt + w\pi u(T). \tag{1.4}$$

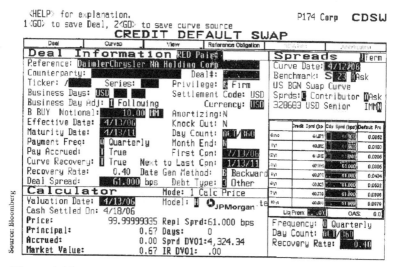

**Figure 1.11**   Bloomberg page CDSW using modified Hull-White pricing for selected credit default swap, April 12, 2006

In equilibrium, the present value of each leg of the above equation should be equal. We can now calculate the credit default swap spread $s$, which is the value of $w$ that makes the equation equal to zero, by simply rearranging the equation, as shown below.

$$s = \frac{\int_0^T \left[1 - R - A(t)R\right]q(t)v(t)dt}{\int_0^T q(t)\left[u(t) + e(t)\right]dt + \pi u(T)} \tag{1.5}$$

The variable $S$ is referred to as the CDS spread.

The formula at equation (1.5) is simple and intuitive for developing an analytical approach for pricing credit default swaps because of the assumptions used. For example, the model assumes that interest rates and default events are independent; also, the possibility of counterparty default is ignored. The spread $s$ is the payment per year, as a percentage of notional principal, for a newly issued credit default swap.

**FIGURE 1.11** shows the CDSW page on the Bloomberg using the modified Hull and White model.[13] Certain default parameter inputs (for the DaimlerChrysler five5-year CDS) are selected. This implementation links the rates observed in the credit-protection market and the corporate bond market, via probabilities of default of the issuer. The input used to price the CDS contract is selected from a range of market-observed yield curves, and can include:

- A curve of CDS spreads
- An issuer (credit-risky) par yield curve

---

[13] A description of this page is given in Appendix I.

- A default probability curve (derived from the default probabilities of the underlying reference for each maturity implied by the par credit default swap spreads)

The assumptions based on the independence of recovery rates, default probabilities, and interest rates may not hold completely in practice, since high interest rates may cause companies to experience default or administration. As a result, default probabilities would increase. Hence, a positive relation between interest rates and default probabilities may be associated with high discount rates for the CDS payoffs. This would have the effect of reducing the credit default swap spread. Nevertheless, the modified Hull-White approach presents a neat and intuitive approach that allows for a closed-form pricing approach for credit default swaps, using parameter inputs from the market.

## Market Pricing Approach[14]

We now present a discrete form pricing approach that is used in the market, using market-observed parameter inputs.

We stated earlier that a CDS has two cash-flow legs; the fee premium leg and the contingent cash-flow leg. We wish to determine the par spread, or premium, of the CDS, remembering that for a par spread valuation, in accordance with no-arbitrage principles, the net present value of both legs must be equal to zero (that is, they have the same valuation).

The valuation of the fee leg is given by the following relationship:

$$PV \text{ of No-default fee payments} = S_N \times \text{Annuity}_N,$$

which is given by

$$PV = S_N \sum_{i=1}^{N} DF_i.PND_i.A_i, \qquad (1.6)$$

where
$\quad S_N \quad$ is the par spread (CDS premium) for maturity $N$
$\quad DF_i \quad$ is the risk-free discount factor from time $T_0$ to time $T_i$
$\quad PND_i \quad$ is the no-default probability from $T_0$ to $T_i$
$\quad A_i \quad$ is the accrual period from $T_i-1$ to $T_i$.

Note that the value for *PND* is for the specific reference entity for which a CDS is being priced.

If the accrual fee for the CDS is paid upon default and termination,[15] then the valuation of the fee leg is given by the following relationship:

$$PV \text{ of no-default fee payments} + PV \text{ of default accruals}$$

$$= S_N \times \text{Annuity}_N + S_N \times \text{DefaultAccrual}_N$$

---

[14] A more descriptive explanation of this approach, including Excel spreadsheet formulas, is given in Appendix II.

[15] This is the amount of premium payable from the last payment date up to termination date, and similar to accrued coupon on a cash bond. Upon occurrence of a credit event and termination, the accrued premium to date is payable immediately. No protection payment is due from the protection seller until and after the accrual payment is made.

which is given by

$$PV_{NoDefault+DefaultAccrual} = S_N \sum_{i=1}^{N} DF_i.PND_i.A_i$$

$$+S_N \sum_{i=1}^{N} DF_i.\left(PND_{i-1} - PND_i\right).\frac{A_i}{2}, \quad (1.7)$$

where

$(PND_{i-1} - PND_i)$ is the probability of a credit event occurring during the period $T_{i-1}$ to $T_i$

$\frac{A_i}{2}$ is the average accrual amount from $T_{i-1}$ to $T_i$.

The valuation of the contingent leg is approximated by

$$PV \text{ of Contingent} = \text{Contingent}_N,$$

which is given by

$$PV_{Contingent} = \left(1 - R\right) \sum_{i=1}^{N} DF_i.\left(PND_{i-1} - PND_i\right), \quad (1.8)$$

where $R$ is the recovery rate of the reference obligation.
For a par credit default swap, we know that

$$\text{Valuation of leg fee} = \text{Valuation of contingent leg,}$$

and therefore we can set

$$S_N \sum_{i=1}^{N} DF_i.PND_i.A_i + S_N \sum_{i=1}^{N} DF_i.\left(PND_{i-1} - PND_i\right).\frac{A_i}{2} \quad (1.9)$$

$$= \left(1 - R\right) \sum_{i=1}^{N} DF_i.\left(PND_{i-1} - PND_i\right)$$

which may be rearranged to give us the formula for the CDS premium $s$ as follows:

$$S_N = \left(1 - R\right) \sum_{i=1}^{N} \frac{DF_i.\left(PND_{i-1} - PND_i\right)}{\sum_{i=1}^{N} DF_i.PND_i.A_i + DF_i.\left(PND_{i-1} - PND_i\right).\frac{A_i}{2}} \quad (1.10)$$

In **TABLE 1.1,** we illustrate an application of the expression in equation (1.10) for a CDS of varying maturities, assuming a recovery rate of the defaulted reference asset of 30% and a given term structure of interest rates. It uses actual/360-day count convention.

| MATURITY $t$ | SPOT RATES | DISCOUNT FACTORS $DF_j$ | SURVIVAL PROBABILITY $PS_j$ | DEFAULT PROBABILITY $PD_j$ |
|---|---|---|---|---|
| 0.5 | 3.57% | 0.9826 | 0.9993 | 0.0007 |
| 1.0 | 3.70% | 0.9643 | 0.9983 | 0.0017 |
| 1.5 | 3.81% | 0.9455 | 0.9972 | 0.0028 |
| 2.0 | 3.95% | 0.9254 | 0.9957 | 0.0043 |
| 2.5 | 4.06% | 0.9053 | 0.9943 | 0.0057 |
| 3.0 | 4.16% | 0.8849 | 0.9932 | 0.0068 |
| 3.5 | 4.24% | 0.8647 | 0.9900 | 0.0100 |
| 4.0 | 4.33% | 0.8440 | 0.9886 | 0.0114 |
| 4.5 | 4.42% | 0.8231 | 0.9859 | 0.0141 |
| 5.0 | 4.45% | 0.8044 | 0.9844 | 0.0156 |
| RECOVERY RATE | | | | |
| 0.3 | | | | |

**Table 1.1**  Example of CDS spread pricing

| PROBABILITY-WEIGHTED PVs | | | |
|---|---|---|---|
| PV OF RECEIPTS IF NO DEFAULT | PV OF RECEIPTS IF DEFAULT | DEFAULT PAYMENT IF DEFAULT | CDS PREMIUM $s$ |
| 0.4910 | 0.0002 | 0.0005 | 0.10% |
| 0.9723 | 0.0006 | 0.0016 | 0.17% |
| 1.4437 | 0.0012 | 0.0035 | 0.24% |
| 1.9044 | 0.0022 | 0.0063 | 0.33% |
| 2.3545 | 0.0035 | 0.0099 | 0.42% |
| 2.7939 | 0.0050 | 0.0141 | 0.50% |
| 3.2220 | 0.0072 | 0.0201 | 0.62% |
| 3.6392 | 0.0096 | 0.0269 | 0.74% |
| 4.0450 | 0.0125 | 0.0350 | 0.86% |
| 4.4409 | 0.0156 | 0.0438 | 0.98% |

For readers' reference, we present a fuller explanation of this valuation approach in Appendix II.

We can use CDS prices to extract a market-implied timing of default. Given that the CDS has a specified fixed term to maturity, it is possible by applying break-even analysis to extract a market-implied timing of default for the reference credit in question. This is done by calculating the amount of time that has to elapse before the premium income on the CDS equals the recovery value. By definition therefore, we require an assumed recovery rate to perform this calculation. An illustration of this process is given in Appendix III.

Reproduced from *The Credit Default Swap Basis* (2006)

## ASSET SWAPS AND RELATIVE VALUE

This section can be found in the companion website, in the folder for Chapter 2. Please see Chapter 20 for more details.

**This extract from *Fixed Income Securities and Derivatives Handbook, Second Edition* (2010)**

Bond Spreads and Relative Value

## Bond Spreads and Relative Value

Return from a holding of fixed-income securities may be measured in more than one way. The most common approach is to consider the asset-swap spread. More sophisticated investors also consider the basis spread between the cash bond and the same-name credit default swap price, which is known as the basis.[2] In this chapter we consider the most accessible way to measure bond return.

## Bond Spreads

Investors measure the perceived market value, or relative value, of a corporate bond by measuring its yield spread relative to a designated benchmark. This is the spread over the benchmark that gives the yield of the corporate bond. A key measure of relative value of a corporate bond is its swap spread. This is the basis point spread over the interest-rate swap curve and is a measure of the credit risk of the bond. In its simplest form, the swap spread can be measured as the difference between the yield-to-maturity of the bond and the interest rate given by a straight-line interpolation of the swap curve. In practice, traders use the asset-swap spread and the Z-spread as the main measures of relative value. The government bond spread is also used. In addition, now that the market in synthetic corporate credit is well established, using credit derivatives and CDS, investors consider the Cash-CDS spread as well, which is the *basis* and which we consider in greater detail later.

The spread that is selected is an indication of the relative value of the bond and a measure of its credit risk. The greater the perceived risk, the greater the spread should be. This is best illustrated by the credit structure of interest rates, which will (generally) show AAA- and AA-rated bonds trading at the lowest spreads and BBB- , BB- and lower-bonds trading at the highest spreads. Bond spreads are the most commonly used indication of the risk-return profile of a bond.

In this section we consider the Treasury spread, asset swap spread, Z-spread, and basis.

### Swap Spread and Treasury Spread

A bond's swap spread is a measure of the credit risk of that bond, relative to the interest-rate swaps market. Because the swaps market is traded by banks, this risk is effectively the interbank market, so the credit risk of the bond over and above bank risk is given by its spread over swaps. This is a simple calculation to make and is simply the yield of the bond minus the swap rate for the appropriate maturity swap. **FIGURE 19.2** shows Bloomberg page IRSB for Pounds sterling as of August 10, 2005. This shows the GBP swap curve on the left-hand side. The right-hand side of the screen shows the swap rates' spread over U.K. gilts. It is the spread over these swap rates that would provide the simplest relative value measure for corporate bonds denominated in GBP. If the bond has an odd maturity, say 5.5 years, we would interpolate between the five-year and six-year swap rates.

British Pound

GBP Swap Rates

| Ticker | TiME | Bid | Ask | Change | Open | High | Low | Prev Cls |
|---|---|---|---|---|---|---|---|---|
| 2) 1 YR | 11:22 | 4.4940 | 4.5020 | -- | 4.4980 | 4.5005 | 4.4870 | 4.4980 |
| 3) 18 MO | 11:22 | 4.3925 | 4.4225 | -.0087 | 4.4150 | 4.4175 | 4.3960 | 4.4163 |
| 4) 2 YR | 11:18 | 4.4070 | 4.4150 | -.0055 | 4.4150 | 4.4225 | 4.3975 | 4.4175 |
| 5) 3 YR | 11:23 | 4.4110 | 4.4350 | -.0008 | 4.4225 | 4.4275 | 4.4000 | 4.4238 |
| 6) 4 YR | 11:23 | 4.4150 | 4.4150 | -.0118 | 4.4250 | 4.4515 | 4.4085 | 4.4263 |
| 7) 5 YR | 11:23 | 4.4230 | 4.4240 | -.0127 | 4.4350 | 4.4370 | 4.4125 | 4.4363 |
| 8) 6 YR | 11:23 | 4.4340 | 4.4625 | -.0030 | 4.4600 | 4.4650 | 4.4233 | 4.4513 |
| 9) 7 YR | 11:23 | 4.4440 | 4.4620 | -.0157 | 4.4600 | 4.4690 | 4.4355 | 4.4638 |
| 10) 8 YR | 11:23 | 4.4520 | 4.4690 | -.0158 | 4.4675 | 4.4750 | 4.4422 | 4.4713 |
| 11) 9 YR | 11:23 | 4.4580 | 4.4630 | -.0157 | 4.4725 | 4.4800 | 4.4478 | 4.4763 |
| 12) 10 YR | 11:23 | 4.4610 | 4.4640 | -.0138 | 4.4750 | 4.4840 | 4.4550 | 4.4763 |
| 13) 12 YR | 11:23 | 4.4610 | 4.4640 | -.0138 | 4.4750 | 4.4750 | 4.4585 | 4.4763 |
| 14) 15 YR | 11:23 | 4.4520 | 4.4650 | -.0128 | 4.4650 | 4.4735 | 4.4335 | 4.4663 |
| 15) 20 YR | 11:23 | 4.4210 | 4.4230 | -.0118 | 4.4325 | 4.5250 | 4.3912 | 4.4338 |
| 16) 25 YR | 11:21 | 4.3175 | 4.4475 | -.0125 | 4.3975 | 4.4367 | 4.3763 | 4.3963 |
| 17) 30 YR | 11:21 | 4.3430 | 4.3550 | -.0078 | 4.3550 | 4.4500 | 4.3225 | 4.3588 |

Page 1

GBP Swap Spread

| Ticker | TiME | Bid | Ask | Change | Open | High | Low | Prev Cls |
|---|---|---|---|---|---|---|---|---|
| 19) 1 YR | 11:22 | 33.80 | 39.80 | +2.10 | 31.40 | 33.80 | 29.90 | 31.7000 |
| 20) 2 YR | 11:21 | 29.50 | 33.50 | +1.00 | 29.00 | 32.25 | 28.50 | 30.5000 |
| 21) 3 YR | 11:21 | 31.00 | 35.00 | +.75 | 30.75 | 33.25 | 30.00 | 32.2500 |
| 22) 4 YR | 11:23 | 30.50 | 35.50 | +.50 | 30.50 | 33.25 | 30.00 | 32.5000 |
| 23) 5 YR | 11:14 | 26.50 | 36.00 | -4.50 | 30.50 | 30.50 | 28.50 | 33.0000 |
| 24) 6 YR | 11:23 | 32.75 | 37.75 | +.50 | 32.50 | 35.50 | 32.50 | 34.7500 |
| 25) 7 YR | 11:23 | 32.00 | 37.00 | +.50 | 32.00 | 34.75 | 32.00 | 34.0000 |
| 26) 8 YR | 11:21 | 31.00 | 36.00 | +.50 | 30.75 | 33.75 | 30.75 | 33.0000 |
| 27) 9 YR | 11:21 | 29.75 | 34.75 | +.50 | 29.75 | 32.50 | 29.75 | 31.7500 |
| 28) 10 YR | 8:05 | 29.75 | 34.75 | +.25 | 32.25 | 32.50 | 32.25 | 32.0000 |
| 29) 15 YR | 11:21 | 22.75 | 31.75 | +.25 | 27.25 | 28.00 | 27.00 | 27.0000 |
| 30) 20 YR | 11:21 | 19.00 | 32.00 | +.13 | 25.50 | 26.00 | 25.25 | 26.3750 |
| 31) 30 YR | 11:23 | 14.75 | 27.50 | +.25 | 21.00 | 21.50 | 20.63 | 20.8750 |

For UK Govt Yield Curve, Click on any Tickers above & Select: IYC1 122
For GBP Swap Curve, Click on any Tickers above & Select: IYC1 155

Page 2

**Figure 19.2** *Bloomberg Page IRSB for Pounds Sterling, Showing GBP Swap Rates and Swap Spread over U.K. Gilts*

The spread over swaps is sometimes called the *I-spread*. It has a simple relationship to swaps and Treasury yields, shown here in the equation for corporate bond yield,

$$Y = I + S + T \qquad 19.1$$

where   $Y$    is the yield on the corporate bond
       $I$      is the I-spread or spread over swap
       $S$      is the swap spread
       $T$     is the yield on the Treasury security (or an interpolated yield).

In other words, the swap rate itself is given by $T + S$.

The I-spread is sometimes used to compare a cash bond with its equivalent CDS price, but for straightforward relative value analysis is usually dropped in favor of the asset-swap spread, which we look at later in this section.

Of course, the basic relative value measure is the Treasury spread or government bond spread. This is simply the spread of the bond yield over the yield of the appropriate government bond. Again, an interpolated yield may need to be used to obtain the right Treasury rate to use. The bond spread is given by:

$$BS = Y - T$$

Using an interpolated yield is not strictly accurate because yield curves are smooth in shape and so straight-line interpolation will produce slight errors. The method is still commonly used, though.

## Asset-Swap Spread

An asset swap is a package that combines an interest-rate swap with a cash bond, the effect of the combined package being able to transform the interest-rate basis of the bond. Typically, a fixed-rate bond will be combined with an interest-rate swap in which the bond holder pays fixed coupon and received floating coupon. The floating coupon will be a spread over LIBOR (see Choudhry et al. 2001). This spread is the asset-swap spread and is a function of the credit risk of the bond over and above interbank credit risk.[3] Asset swaps may be transacted at par or at the bond's market price, usually par. This means that the asset swap value is made up of the difference between the bond's market price and par, as well as the difference between the bond coupon and the swap fixed rate.

The zero-coupon curve is used in the asset swap valuation. This curve is derived from the swap curve, so it is the implied zero-coupon curve. The asset swap spread is the spread that equates the difference between the present value of the bond's cash flows, calculated using the swap zero rates, and the market price of the bond. This spread is a function of the bond's market price and yield, its cash flows, and the implied zero-coupon interest rates.[4]

**FIGURE 19.3** shows the Bloomberg screen ASW for a GBP-denominated bond, GKN Holdings 7 percent 2012, as of August 10, 2005. We see that the asset-swap spread is 121.5 basis points. This is the spread over LIBOR that will be received if the bond is purchased in an asset-swap package. In essence, the asset swap spread measures a difference between the market price of the bond and the value of the bond when cash flows have been valued using zero-coupon rates. The asset-swap spread can therefore be regarded as the coupon of an annuity in the swap market that equals this difference.

## Z-Spread

The conventional approach for analyzing an asset swap uses the bond's yield-to-maturity (YTM) in calculating the spread. The assumptions implicit in the YTM calculation (see Chapter 2) make this spread problematic for relative analysis, so market practitioners use what is termed the Z-spread instead. The Z-spread uses the zero-coupon yield curve to calculate spread, so is a more realistic, and effective, spread to use. The zero-coupon curve used in the calculation is derived from the interest-rate swap curve.

Put simply, the Z-spread is the basis point spread that would need to be added to the implied spot yield curve such that the discounted cash flows

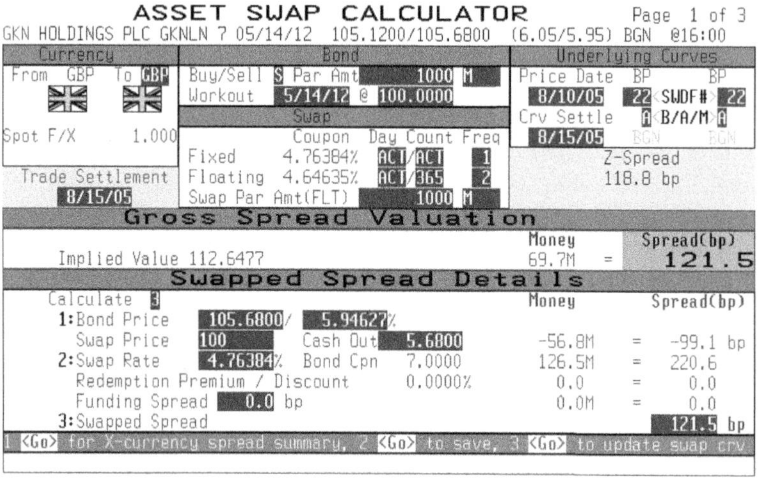

**Figure 19.3**  Bloomberg Page ASW for GKN Bond, August 10, 2005

*Source*: © Bloomberg. All rights reserved. Reprinted with permission.

of the bond are equal to its present value (its current market price). Each bond cash flow is discounted by the relevant spot rate for its maturity term. How does this differ from the conventional asset-swap spread? Essentially, in its use of zero-coupon rates when assigning a value to a bond. Each cash flow is discounted using its own particular zero-coupon rate. The bond's price at any time can be taken to be the market's value of the bond's cash flows. Using the Z-spread we can quantify what the swap market thinks of this value, that is, by how much the conventional spread differs from the Z-spread. Both spreads can be viewed as the coupon of a swap market annuity of equivalent credit risk of the bond being valued.

In practice, the Z-spread, especially for shorter-dated bonds and for better credit-quality bonds, does not differ greatly from the conventional asset-swap spread. The Z-spread is usually the higher spread of the two, following the logic of spot rates, but not always. If it differs greatly, then the bond can be considered to be mispriced.

**FIGURE 19.4** is the Bloomberg screen YAS for the same bond shown in Figure 19.3, as of the same date. It shows a number of spreads for the bond. The main spread of 151.00 bps is the spread over the government yield curve. This is an interpolated spread, as can be seen lower down the screen, with the appropriate benchmark bind identified. We see that the asset-swap spread is 121.6 bps, while the Z-spread is 118.8 bps. When undertaking relative value analysis, for instance, if making comparisons against cash funding rates or the same company name credit default swap (CDS), it is this lower spread that should be used.[5]

```
YIELD & SPREAD ANALYSIS              CUSIPEC563412 PCS BGN
GKN HOLDINGS PLC GKNLN 7 05/14/12  105.1200/105.6800  (6.05/5.95) BGN  @16:00
   SETTLE  8/15/05      FACE AMT     1000 M  or PROCEEDS        1,074,635.62
1) YA          YIELDS        2) YASD RISK &  GKNLN 7 05/14/12
PRICE 105.680000 No Rounding     N  HEDGE     workout      HEDGE BOND
YIELD     5.860 st              RATIOS    5/14/12  OAS      OAS
SPRD     151.00 bp  yld-decimals3/3  Mod Dur  5.39   5.40    5.47
      versus                          Risk    5.795  5.801   5.784
       UKT 5 03/07/12          BENCHMARK Convexity 0.35  0.35  0.36
  PRICE 103.680000   Save  Delete  Workout HEDGE Amount:1,001 M
  YIELD     4.350 %    sd:  8/11/05  OAS HEDGE Amount:1,003 M
  Yields are: Semi-Annual
3) OAS        SPREADS       4) ASW  5) FPA      FINANCING
OAS:   151.1 CRV# 110   VOL     Opt  Repo% 4.540  (360/365)365   Days 1
OAS:   118.7 CRV# I55   TED:        Int Income   191.78     Carry P&L
ASW (A/A)  121.6 ZSPR  118.8 11) History Fin Cost   -133.67      58.11
CRV# I55   U.K. POUND SWAP          Amortiz    -21.70<->     36.41
ISPRD   115.9 DSPRD   116.6         Forwrd Prc 105.674189
 Yield Curve:122   U.K. GOVT BNCHMARK  Prc Drop   0.005811
+ 151  v  6.8yr ( 4.353 %)  INTERPOLATED Drop (bp)    0.06
+ 160  v  3yr ( 4.26) UKT 5 03/07/08  Accrued Interest /100  1.783562
+ 157  v  4yr ( 4.29) UKT 4 03/07/09  Number Of Days Accrued   93
+ 154  v  5yr ( 4.32) UKT 4 ¾ 06/07/10
```

**Figure 19.4**   Bloomberg Page YAS for GKN Bond, August 10, 2005
*Source*: © Bloomberg. All rights reserved. Reprinted with permission.

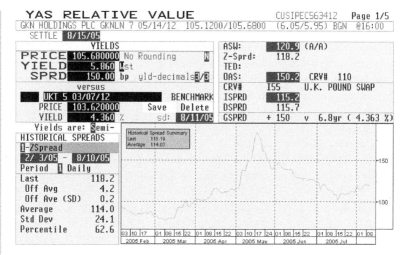

**Figure 19.5** Bloomberg Page YAS for GKN Bond, August 10, 2005 Showing Z-Spread History
*Source*: © Bloomberg. All rights reserved. Reprinted with permission.

The same screen can be used to check spread history. This is shown at **FIGURE 19.5**, the Z-spread graph for the GKN bond for the six months prior to our calculation date.

The Z-spread is closely related to the bond price, as shown by:

$$P = \sum_{i=1}^{n}\left[\frac{C_i + M_i}{\left(1 + \left(\left(Z + S_i + T_i\right)/m\right)\right)^i}\right] \quad (19.2)$$

where
- $n$    is the number of interest periods until maturity
- $P$    is the bond price
- $C$    is the coupon
- $M$    is the redemption payment (so bond cash flow is all $C$ plus $M$)
- $Z$    is the Z-spread
- $m$    is the frequency of coupon payments

In effect, this is the standard bond price equation with the discount rate adjusted by whatever the Z-spread is; it is an iterative calculation. The appropriate maturity swap rate is used, which is the essential difference between the I-spread and the Z-spread. This is deemed to be more accurate, because the entire swap curve is taken into account rather than just one point on it. In practice, though, as we have seen in the previous example, there is often little difference between the two spreads.

To reiterate, then, using the correct Z-spread, the sum of the bond's discounted cash flows will be equal to the current price of the bond.

We illustrate the Z-spread calculation at **FIGURE 19.6**. This is done using a hypothetical bond, the XYZ PLC 5 percent of June 2008, a three-year bond at the time of the calculation. Market rates for swaps, Treasury, and CDS are also shown. We require the spread over the swaps curve that equates the present values of the cash flows to the current market price. The cash flows are discounted using the appropriate swap rate for each cash flow maturity. With a bond yield of 5.635 percent, we see that the I-spread is 43.5 basis points, while the Z-spread is 19.4 basis points. In practice, the difference between these two spreads is rarely this large.

For readers' benefit we also show the Excel formula in Figure 19.6. This shows how the Z-spread is calculated; for ease of illustration, we have assumed that the calculation takes place for value on a coupon date, so that we have precisely an even period to maturity.

## Cash-CDS Basis

The difference between the premium on a CDS contract and the same name (and same tenor) cash bond yield is known as the basis. That is, the basis is the CDS spread minus the ASW spread. Alternatively, it can be the CDS spread minus and the Z-spread. So the basis is given by

$$B = D - CashSpread \qquad (19.3)$$

where $D$ is the CDS price. Where $D - CashSpread > 0$ it is a positive basis; the opposite is a negative basis.

**FIGURE 19.7** shows page G <go> on Bloomberg, set up to show the Z-spread and CDS price history for the GKN 2012 bond, for the period March–September 2005. We can select the "Table" option to obtain the actual values, which can then be used to plot the basis. This is shown at **FIGURE 19.8**, for the period August 22 to September 22, 2005. Notice how the basis was always negative during August–September; we see from Figure 19.8 that earlier in the year the basis had briefly been positive. Changes in the basis give rise to arbitrage opportunities between the cash and synthetic markets. This is discussed in greater detail in Choudhry (2009).

A wide range of factors drive the basis, which are described in detail in Choudhry (2010). The existence of a non-zero basis has implications for investment strategy. For instance, when the basis is negative, investors may prefer to hold the cash bond, whereas if, for liquidity, supply, or other reasons, the basis is positive, the investor may wish to hold the asset synthetically by selling protection using a credit default swap. Another approach is to arbitrage between the cash and synthetic markets, in the case of a negative basis by buying the cash bond and shorting it synthetically by buying protection in the CDS market. Investors have a range of spreads to use when performing their relative value analysis.

**Issuer** XYZ PLC
Settlement date 6/1/2005
Maturity date 6/1/2008
Coupon 5%
Price 98.95

Par 100
Semiannual coupon 2
act/act 1

| | |
|---|---|
| **YIELD** | 0.05635 |
| [Cell formula = YIELD(C4,C5,C6, C7,C8,C9,C10)] | |
| **PRICE** | 98.95000 |
| [Cell formula = PRICE(C4,C5,C6, C6,C8,C9,C10)] | |

Bond yield 5.635%
Sovereign bond yield 4.880%
Swap rate 5.200%
3-year CDS price 28 bps
**Treasury spread**
5.635 – 4.88   55 bps
**I-spread**
5.635–5.20   43.5 bps
**Z-spread (Z)**   19.4 bps
The Z-spread is found using iteration   0.00194

| Cash flow date | 12/1/2005 | 6/1/2006 | 12/1/2006 | 6/1/2007 | 12/1/2007 | 6/1/2008 | SUM OF PVS |
|---|---|---|---|---|---|---|---|
| Cash flow maturity (years) | 0.50 | 1.00 | 1.50 | 2.00 | 2.50 | 3.00 | |
| 0.5-year swap rate (S) | 4.31% | 4.84% | 4.99% | 5.09% | 5.18% | 5.20% | |
| Cash flow (CF) | 2.50 | 2.50 | 2.50 | 2.50 | 2.50 | 102.50 | |
| Discount factor (DF Calculation) | 0.97797598 | 0.951498751 | 0.926103469 | 0.900947692 | 0.875835752 | 0.852419659 | |
| | $1/(1+(S+Z)/2)^1$ | $1/(1+(S+Z)/2)^2$ | $1/(1+(S+Z)/2)^3$ | $1/(1+(S+Z)/2)^4$ | $1/(1+(S+Z)/2)^5$ | $1/(1+(S+Z)/2)^6$ | |
| CF present value (PV) | 2.445 | 2.379 | 2.315 | 2.252 | 2.190 | 87.373 | 98.95 |

A Z-spread of 19.4 basis points gives us the current bond price, so is the correct one.
Using this value, the sum of all the discounted cash flows is equal to the market price.

**CDS Basis**
28 – 19.4
8.6 bps
**The basis is positive in this example.**

**Figure 19.6** Calculating the Z-Spread. Hypothetical 5% 2008 Bond Issued by XYZ PLC

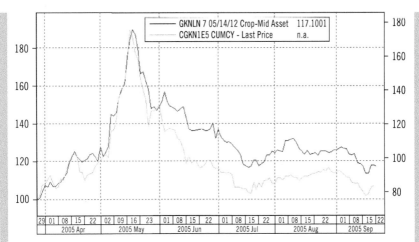

**Figure 19.7**   Bloomberg Graph Using Screen G <GO>, Plot of Asset-Swap
Spread and CDS Price for GKN Bond, April–September 2005
*Source*: © Bloomberg. All rights reserved. Reprinted with permission.

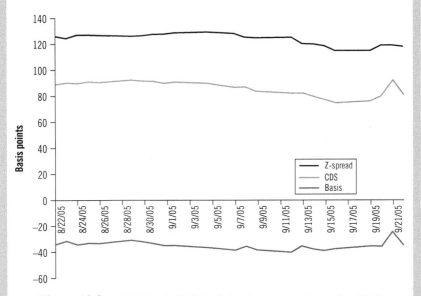

**Figure 19.8**   GKN Bond, CDS Basis During August–September 2005
*Data source*: Bloomberg L.P.

## Summary of Fund Managers' Approach to Value Creation

The management of a portfolio of bonds may be undertaken either passively or actively. Passive fund management does not involve any actual analysis or portfolio selection, because the manager merely constructs the bond portfolio to mirror the benchmark or index whose performance he wishes to replicate. As such, passive fund management is more of an administrative function than an analytical or strategic one.

Active fund management involves just that: the manager makes the decision on which bonds to buy and the time at which to buy (and subsequently sell) them. The performance of an actively managed fixed-income portfolio is still measured against the relevant benchmark or index, because this serves to illustrate how well the manager is doing. If the portfolio does not outperform the index, then the manager has not added value.

What approach is adopted by the active fund manager? Portfolio managers employ four basic strategies to add value over and above the benchmark. We summarize these here:

*Extend duration before a market rally, shorten duration before a market correction:* This is the most basic approach, and in its crudest form amounts to "punting" the market. The fund manager basically decides when he or she expects the market to rally and buys longer-dated bonds ahead of the anticipated move upward, which benefit from such a move more than shorter-dated bonds. Unfortunately, very few fund managers consistently get such a call right, and this approach is not often adopted, at least not explicitly anyway.

*Yield curve trades:* In this approach, the fund manager puts on steepening trades before the yield curve steepens, and flattening trades before the curve flattens. A common approach is to put on barbell and bullet trades; generally the former is adopted for curve flattening trades, while a steepening yield curve tends to favor bullet trades. This strategy has a bit more intellectual cachet than the straight directional "punt" trade, and generally fund managers are given more latitude to put on relative value-style curve shaping trades compared to directional trades. However, this approach ultimately calls for the manager to call the directional move in the market right.

*Convexity and volatility trades:* This strategy also has a directional element to it and involves employing convexity and volatility trades to outperform benchmarks. When there is a mismatch between a manager's view on volatility and the implied volatility of bonds with embedded options, buying or selling convexity before realized volatility increases or decreases can enhance return. An alternative approach is, rather than realized volatility differing from implied volatility, the market as a whole may change its opinion about future volatility and thereby produce a change in implied volatility, which may enhance returns. Convexity and volatility trades can also be effected using barbell and bullet positions, or via derivatives.

*Security selection:* Portfolio managers can attempt to outperform benchmarks through security selection. This entails being overweight in "cheap" bonds and underweight in "rich" bonds, which will produce higher total return relative to the benchmark. Security selection requires effective relative value analysis to determine which bonds are cheap compared to their peer group and to the risk-free benchmark. Such analysis makes use of measures such as the asset-swap spread. A basic analysis would use this metric and compare it across an (otherwise equivalent) set of bonds. The approach is as follows: after selecting portfolio average duration, and the level of credit risk that is acceptable, purchase the bonds that have the highest asset-swap spread. The resulting portfolio then represents the best relative value for a given duration target and credit risk exposure. In practice, the asset-swap spread is nowadays compared also to the same-name credit default swap premium. The difference between the two measures (the CDS basis) gives another measure of the relative value of the bond, by implying the level of mispricing in either or both of the cash and synthetic markets.

Active fund management, whichever method or combination of methods is adopted, ultimately still requires the manager to have an idea of market direction. If the fund manager gets this right, this makes it more likely that the portfolio will outperform the benchmark.

## NOTES

[2] For more details on the cash-CDS basis, see Choudhry (2010).

[3] This is because in the interbank market, two banks transacting an interest-rate swap will be paying/receiving the fixed rate and receiving/paying LIBOR-flat. See also the "Learning Curve" article on asset swaps available on www.yieldcurve.com.

[4] Bloomberg refers to this spread as the Gross Spread.

[5] On the date in question, the 10-year CDS for this reference entity was quoted as 96.8 bps, which is an example of a negative basis, in this case of −22 bps.

Reproduced from *Fixed Income Securities and Derivatives Handbook, Second Edition* (2010)

## POST-2008 CRASH SWAP DISCOUNTING AND VALUATION PRINCIPLES[1]

Interest-rate swaps (IRS) were introduced in the earlier extracts. This section looks at the impact on the swap market of the 2008 bank crash, specifically with respect to pricing and valuation. A large proportion of swaps are now settled via a centralised clearing counterparty (CCP); before that the swap market had become essentially a fully secured market in any case, at least between bank counterparties. The operation of this entailed the mark-to-market (MTM) of the swap being passed between the two bilateral counterparties as collateral under the auspices of the credit support annexe (CSA) of the standard ISDA derivatives agreement. Under a CSA, the party that is offside on the swap value (negative MTM) will post collateral to the counterparty equivalent to this MTM value. There is considerable optionality availability in a CSA, which is a legal agreement negotiated between the two parties but if we assume a "gold standard" CSA, which describes (among other things):

- Daily margin, equal to end-of-day MTM;
- Margin in the form of cash, in the currency of the IRS;
- No "threshold" amount, so whatever the MTM value the posting takes place at end of day

then this makes the following discussion simpler.

### Basic Terms

Herewith some swap basics to ensure everyone is familiar with the key features:

### Example definition of an IRS
Notional: 10m EUR
Start Date: 30th August 2016
End Date (Tenor): 30th August 2021 (5 years)
Frequency of payments: Annual fixed, Semi-annual floating
Fixed Leg accruals: Unadjusted
Floating leg date rolling convention: Modified following (MF)
Floating leg business day calendar for accruals: "Target"
Business day calendar for payments: "Target" for both legs
Business day calendar for resets (floating leg): "Target"

---

[1] Thanks to David Moskovic for his BTRM lecture slides which form the basis of parts of this section.

Day count conventions: A/360 floating, 30U/360 fixed
Fixed rate: 1%
Reference for floating rate: 6 month Euribor, reset two days in advance

A "par" swap is defined as a swap with zero mark-to-market (MTM). The fixed rate on a par swap can be interpreted as the (discounted) average forward rate over the life of the swap (Figure 2.1).

**Fixed Leg**

| Period | Unadjusted Period Start Date | Accrual Start Date | Payment Date | DCF numerator | DCF | Comments on accrual start dates |
|---|---|---|---|---|---|---|
| 1 | Tue 30-Aug-16 | Tue 30-Aug-16 | Tue 30-Aug-16 | 360 | 1.0000 | |
| 2 | Wed 30-Aug-17 | Wed 30-Aug-17 | Wed 30-Aug-17 | 360 | 1.0000 | |
| 3 | Thu 30-Aug-18 | Thu 30-Aug-18 | Thu 30-Aug-18 | 360 | 1.0000 | |
| 4 | Fri 30-Aug-19 | Fri 30-Aug-19 | Fri 30-Aug-19 | 360 | 1.0000 | |
| 5 | Sun 30-Aug-20 | Mon 31-Aug-20 | Mon 31-Aug-20 | 360 | 1.0000 | We roll forward to Monday. DCF unaffected as 31 replaced with 30 |
| 6 | Mon 30-Aug-21 | Mon 30-Aug-21 | Mon 30-Aug-21 | 360 | 1.0000 | |
| 7 | Tue 30-Aug-22 | Tue 30-Aug-22 | Tue 30-Aug-22 | 360 | 1.0000 | |
| 8 | Wed 30-Aug-23 | Wed 30-Aug-23 | Wed 30-Aug-23 | 360 | 1.0000 | The roll-back of the end-date reduced the DCF |
| 9 | Fri 30-Aug-24 | Fri 30-Aug-24 | Fri 30-Aug-24 | 360 | 1.0000 | Rolling forwards would take us into Sept, so we roll back |
| End Date | Sat 30-Aug-25 | Sat 30-Aug-25 | | | | |

**Floating Leg**

| Period | Unadjusted Period Start Date | Accrual Start Date | Payment Date | DCF numerator | DCF | Comments on accrual start dates | Reset Date |
|---|---|---|---|---|---|---|---|
| 1 | Tue 30-Aug-16 | Tue 30-Aug-16 | Tue 28-Feb-17 | 178 | 0.4944 | | Fri 26-Aug-16 |
| 2 | Tue 28-Feb-17 | Tue 28-Feb-17 | Wed 30-Aug-17 | 182 | 0.5056 | | Fri 24-Feb-17 |
| 3 | Wed 30-Aug-17 | Wed 30-Aug-17 | Wed 28-Feb-18 | 178 | 0.4944 | If the swap had started on 28Feb17, we would have rolled to Monday | Mon 28-Aug-17 |
| 4 | Wed 28-Feb-18 | Wed 28-Feb-18 | Thu 30-Aug-18 | 182 | 0.5056 | | Mon 26-Feb-18 |
| 5 | Thu 30-Aug-18 | Thu 30-Aug-18 | Thu 28-Feb-19 | 178 | 0.4944 | | Tue 28-Aug-18 |
| 6 | Thu 28-Feb-19 | Thu 28-Feb-19 | Fri 30-Aug-19 | 182 | 0.5056 | | Tue 26-Feb-19 |
| 7 | Fri 30-Aug-19 | Fri 30-Aug-19 | Fri 28-Feb-20 | 178 | 0.4944 | | Wed 28-Aug-19 |
| 8 | Fri 28-Feb-20 | Sat 29-Feb-20 | Mon 31-Aug-20 | 183 | 0.5083 | Leap year, but rolled back to Friday | Wed 26-Feb-20 |
| 9 | Sun 30-Aug-20 | Mon 31-Aug-20 | Mon 01-Mar-21 | 176 | 0.4889 | Rolled forward from Sunday | Wed 27-Aug-20 |
| 10 | Sun 28-Feb-21 | Mon 01-Mar-21 | Mon 30-Aug-21 | 178 | 0.4944 | Rolled back from Sunday | Wed 24-Feb-21 |
| 11 | Mon 30-Aug-21 | Mon 30-Aug-21 | Mon 28-Feb-22 | 182 | 0.5056 | | Thu 26-Aug-21 |
| 12 | Mon 28-Feb-22 | Mon 28-Feb-22 | Tue 30-Aug-22 | 178 | 0.4944 | | Thu 24-Feb-22 |
| 13 | Tue 30-Aug-22 | Tue 30-Aug-22 | Tue 28-Feb-23 | 182 | 0.5056 | | Fri 26-Aug-22 |
| 14 | Tue 28-Feb-23 | Tue 28-Feb-23 | Thu 29-Feb-24 | 179 | 0.4972 | | Fri 24-Feb-23 |
| 15 | Wed 30-Aug-23 | Wed 30-Aug-23 | Fri 30-Aug-24 | 181 | 0.5028 | Leap year | Mon 28-Aug-23 |
| 16 | Thu 29-Feb-24 | Thu 29-Feb-24 | Fri 30-Aug-24 | 178 | 0.4944 | | Wed 26-Feb-24 |
| 17 | Fri 30-Aug-24 | Fri 30-Aug-24 | Fri 28-Feb-25 | 181 | 0.5028 | | Wed 28-Aug-24 |
| 18 | Fri 28-Feb-25 | Fri 28-Feb-25 | Sat 29-Aug-25 | | | Rolled back from Saturday | Wed 26-Feb-25 |
| End Date | Sat 29-Aug-25 | Fri 29-Aug-25 | | | | | |

**FIGURE 2.1** Worked example of a Euribor swap

## CSA

The CSA is a bilateral agreement governing the collateral posting process. Its most important features describe:

- What instruments can be posted as collateral, or if this can be only cash;
- The interest rate to be paid on collateral;
- Minimum thresholds;
- Minimum transfer amounts (MTA).

In theory, a CSA in place removes all credit risk between the two counterparties. (Except an operational risk, known as margin period of risk, arising out of the fact that the MTM value at close of business yesterday may be different the next day when the bank that has posted collateral defaults and the collateral process is finalised so that the non-defaulting party now has legal ownership of the collateral. This period is accepted to be about 10 days.) A CSA may require, depending on the credit quality of the counterparty, an initial amount (IA) of margin, a standing value, to be posted by one party to the other. Note that CCPs require IA amounts from all their members.

The CSA sets the risk-free rate for all transactions between the two counterparties; the "CSA rate" is typically the OIS overnight rate in that currency (OIS USD, SONIA for GBP, and EONIA for EUR)

CSAs introduced additional complexity to the swap market because of the optionality that is inherent in them, although the market generally speaks of a "gold standard" CSA with standard terms. For market-makers in swaps (dealers), issues arise because some swaps on their book will be under a gold standard CSA, others under non-standard CSAs and some will be uncollateralised.

## CCP

The CCP is the central clearing counterparty. They include for example the London Clearing House (LCH) and the Chicago Mercantile Exchange (CME). Virtually all inter-bank swaps trade through CCPs. The CCP sets the collateral rate, usually the OIS rate in the swap's payment currency. They also charge risk-based IAs to all members, as we noted above.

### Day Count Conventions (Accrual/Payment basis)

Applied to the accrual dates to calculate the weighting of each payment, also known as the Day Count Fraction (DCF) or Accrual Factor. The principal ones are:

- Actual/x (Act/x, A/x), where x=360 or 365 most commonly;
- $(d_2 - d_1)/x$, where $d_i$ are the accrual start and end dates;
- Number of calendar days in the accrual period, divided by the number of days assumed to be in a year, either 360 or 365;

- 30/360, where [360(Y2 – Y1) ⊦ 30(M2  M1) ⊦ (D2 – D1)] / 360.

The ISDA method specifies two further rules:

- If $D_1$ is 31, then change $D_1$ to 30.
- If $D_2$ is 31 and $D_1$ is 30 or 31, then change $D_2$ to 30.

In some cases a convention is denoted as "U": unadjusted. This is often used with 30/360 to give almost all periods equal weighting.

## Determination of the Main (L)ibor Rates

**Euribor (Euro Interbank Offered Rate)**  This is set by a panel of 24 banks, determined by the European Banking Federation, that have the highest volume of business in the euro zone money markets. Each bank submits its rate: the top and bottom 15% are eliminated, and the remaining quotes are averaged. Results are published at 11am CET. In theory, Euribor represents the rate at which these banks lend money to each other on unsecured loans. The tenors that are quoted are overnight, 1-week, 2-week, 1-, 2-, 3-, 6-, 9- and 12-month rates.

### LIBOR (London Interbank Offer Rate)

This was discussed in Chapter 1.

Note that the reference swaps are very liquid but that not every bank is able to borrow unsecured in the inter-bank market at Libor-flat. Some banks, with lower credit ratings, will pay a spread over the relevant term Libor rate for borrowing unsecured, where they have borrowing lines with other banks (again, not every bank has such access).

### Alternative Fixing Source: Overnight Indexed Swaps (OIS)

The OIS rate is the average of unsecured overnight lending rates between banks. It is closer to the risk-free, but of course still contains some credit and liquidity risk. (We assume the risk-free rate to be the US T-bill rate.)

The USD OIS swap references the Federal Funds Effective Rate, whereas other currencies references overnight Libor or Euribor. The common currencies are:

- GBP Over-Night Indexed Average (SONIA);
- EUR Over-Night Indexed Average (EONIA);
- JPY Over-Night Indexed Average (TONAR).

The mechanics of OIS swaps are covered elsewhere in this chapter, in the extract from the book *Bank Asset Liability Management*.

### Example Structure Diagrams

Figures 2.2 and 2.3 show a cross-currency basis swap example and a swap transacted under a CSA agreement.

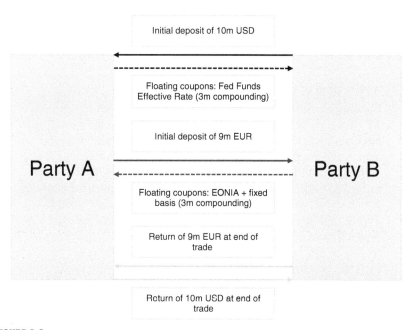

**FIGURE 2.2**　Cross-currency basis swap example

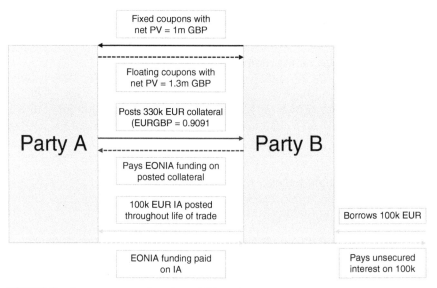

**FIGURE 2.3**　Swap transacted under a CSA agreement

## Discounting

The discount factor represents the present value of a £1 (or $1) unit cash flow paid at a specified future date. The rate is the expected cost of funding the cash flow continuously overnight until maturity.

At the inception of the bilateral OTC swaps market, due to the definition of a swap, banks were already using Libor (or Euribor) in forecasting future cash flows. At that time, swaps were uncollateralised, and the valuation process assumed that all banks could fund at Libor-flat; hence Libor-flat would be the rate used to fund swap cash flows. Hence, future cash flows associated with a swap were discounted at the same rate where banks were assumed to fund themselves (Libor-flat). Of course, in the lead-up to the 2008 crash and subsequently, many banks were not able to fund themselves at Libor-flat and instead funded at Libor+spread, hence the origination of the funding value adjustment (FVA), to reflect the actual funding cost of banks. This is very material in a collateralised swap market, as we have now, as banks have to fund the collateral requirement.

Discounting affects the par swap rate. This is not necessarily relevant if every swap transacted by a bank is collateralised under a CSA (although

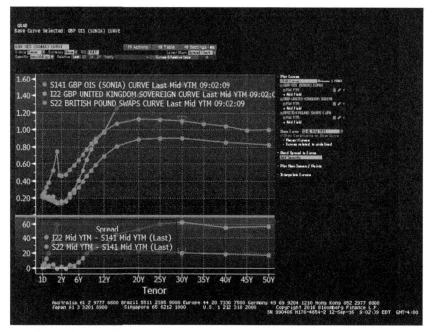

**FIGURE 2.4**   GBP Swaps and OIS curves, September 2016
*Source*: © Bloomberg LLP. Reproduced with permission.

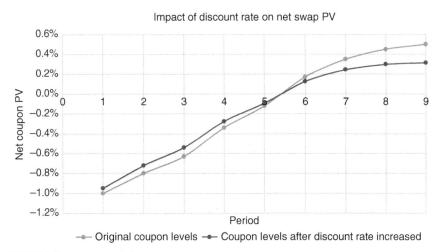

**FIGURE 2.5** Impact of discount rate on swap NPV

it may be), but given that a swap is funded (in terms of collateral) at the OIS rate, but the floating-rate re-fix references the Libor rate showing the UK sovereign curve, GBP vanilla swaps curve, and the SONIA curve) there may be valuation issues especially for longer-dated swaps. (The Libor and OIS yield curves are different, see Figure 2.4 which is a Bloomberg screen as at 13 September 2016.) To agree the MTM for collateral posting, bilateral swaps would have to agree the discounting curve in order to agree the collateral margin. CCP-cleared swaps will all value to the CCP convention.

Note, typically yield curves are upward-sloping. A high discount rate reduces the value of longer-dated cash flows more, and this reduces their weighting in the total PV, causing the par swap rate to fall. If one discounts "wrongly" (such as with Libor), one will misprice steep yield curves and out-of-money swaps. A stylised illustration of this effect is shown at Figure 2.5.

Uncollateralised swaps are discounted at a rate that depends on the credit-risk of the two counterparties. Bilaterally collateralised swaps are discounted at the CSA rate, and swaps cleared through the CCP are collateralised at a standard OIS rate.

Independent Amounts (IAs) can be charged by banks facing customers. CCPs charge banks IAs which the bank will fund at its specific funding rate.

The relationship between Libor and discount factors is illustrated using Figure 2.6 and expressions below. This shows in effect a dual-purpose Libor; first a forecasting rate for future cash flows and second a measure for how to discount cash flows.

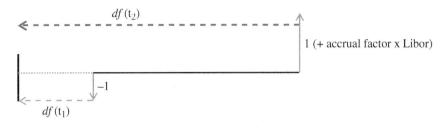

**FIGURE 2.6** Relationship between Libor and discount factors

When pricing a swap on Day 1, we assume that par swap rates have zero net present value (NPV), hence a single swap curve is sufficient both to forecast Libors and determine discount factors. The basic description for this is given in Appendix 2.1.

### How Does Collateral Impact the Discount Rate?

Consider the collateralised deal shown at Figure 2.7.

At $t_0$ we lend EUR X, to receive EUR 1 at $t_1$. As collateral we immediately receive the mutually agreed NPV which is $df(t_1)$ hence it is analogous to a secured loan. Since both parties agree this is the contract NPV, the following must hold:

$$X = df(t_1).$$

This implies our net cash position is equal to zero: our portfolio is in balance and there is no need to fund via the money market.

On the collateral cash we have specified an interest rate payable of $R$, which gives an amount of:

$$\alpha * df(t_1) * R$$

where $\alpha$ is the day-count accrual factor and the earlier expression is for the notional amount X.

At $t_1$ two cash flows take place.

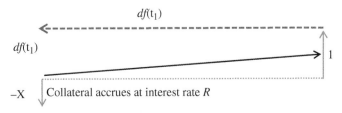

**FIGURE 2.7** How collateral impacts the discount rate

We receive EUR 1 and we pay the collateral amount back plus interest. Assuming a no-arbitrage environment these cash flows must be identical and so the following will hold:

$$df(t_1) + \alpha * df(t_1 * R = 1) \Leftrightarrow df(t_1) = 1 + \alpha * R$$

It is the interest R on the collateral that determines the discount factor. Moving to swap valuation, the collateral cash is the swap MTM, so since the collateral rate (generally OIS, SONIA, or EONIA for USD, GBP, and EUR respectively) determines the discounting curve, we need to use two curves to value the swap book. This is shown at Figure 2.8.

So when valuing a collateralised swap, we consider both curves. Interbank swap quotes are based on the CSA (or CCP as appropriate) collateral funding rate, generally OIS. The swap curve and the overnight curve forecast Libors, so the forecasting curve is known. The same Libor forecast is used for all secured swaps, irrespective of the actual form of the collateral. Hence, the NPV of a swap is calculated with a discounting curve that is based on the actual posted collateral. As the posted collateral is designed to reflect the swap MTM, the logic is clear.

Figure 2.9 summarises this principle, where the expressions used are again:

| | |
|---|---|
| α | the day-count accrual factor; |
| R | the swap fixed rate; |
| L | Libor. |

In practice, banks will use an FVA adjustment to account for their own funding rate (where they are borrowing to post cash collateral) in the swap valuation.

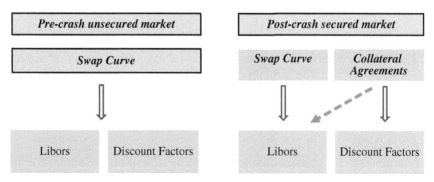

**FIGURE 2.8** Separating the forecasting and discounting curve

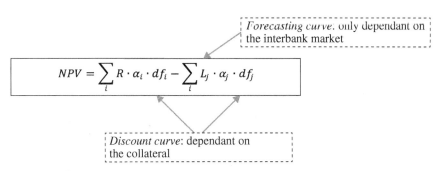

**FIGURE 2.9** Valuing a collateralised swap

**Cross-Currency Swaps** With respect to cross-currency swaps, in the lead-up to the Lehman default and subsequently, a cross-currency basis swap appeared, due to supply/demand, credit, and liquidity. The market had assumed that it could always discount using 3m USD Libor, cross-currency swapped. For example, euro cash flows would be discounted at 3m Euribor + XCCY basis spread. Post-Lehman's, the Libor-OIS spreads blew up, and this assumption failed. (Even pre-Lehman it was a poor assumption.) At the present time, we know the single currency OIS rates from OIS swaps. The discount factor depends on the trade currency and the collateral type (or lack thereof). Cross-currency swaps also trade against OIS. The basis spread allows us to calculate our CSA discount factors.

We can use the ratio of two discount rates to calculate the forward FX rate:

$$USD_t = USD_o \times df_{USD}$$

$$JPY_t = JPY_o \times df_{JPY}$$

$$\frac{USD}{JPY_t} = \frac{USD}{JPY_o} \times \frac{df_{USD}}{df_{JPY}}$$

$$FX_t = FX_o \times \frac{df_{foreign}}{df_{domestic}}$$

## ALM and Hedge Accounting[2]

A large number of banks around the world employ financial derivative instruments when hedging interest-rate and FX risk exposure on the balance sheet. Derivatives are treated as "trading book" products requiring daily

---

[2] This section was co-written with Juan Ramirez.

marking-to-market revaluation. This generates a P&L impact, which can be addressed by the application of the "hedge accounting" concept.

In this section, we consider the ALM implications of hedge accounting, as well as the capital reporting issues associated with the trading book.

A banking book exposes a bank to interest rate and credit risks. A banking book may also comprise financial instruments denominated in foreign currency, equities and commodities, exposing the bank to foreign exchange (FX), equity, and commodity risks.

These risks are commonly hedged with derivatives. The international accounting standard that sets out the guidelines to recognise derivatives is IFRS 9. In July 2014, the International Accounting Standards Board (IASB) issued IFRS 9 *Financial Instruments*, which replaced IAS 39 *Financial Instruments: Recognition and Measurement*, and included requirements for classification and measurement of financial assets and liabilities, impairment of financial assets, and hedge accounting. IFRS 9 came into force on 2 January 2018.

Derivatives are recognised initially, and are subsequently measured, at fair value, regardless of whether they are held for trading or hedging purposes. Fair values of derivatives are obtained either from quoted market prices or by using valuation techniques. Derivatives are classified as assets when their fair value is positive or as liabilities when their fair value is negative.

Gains and losses from changes in the fair value of derivatives that do not qualify for hedge accounting are reported in "net trading income" (i.e., not reported in "net interest income").

## Accounting Approach

In a hedge accounting relationship there are two elements: the hedged item and the hedging instrument.

- The **hedged item** is the item that exposes the entity to a market risk(s). It is the element that is designated as being hedged;
- The **hedging instrument** is the element that hedges the risk(s) to which the hedged item is exposed. Most of the time, the hedging instrument is a derivative.

For example, a bank hedging an issued variable rate bond with a pay-fixed receive-floating interest-rate swap and applying hedge accounting would designate the bond as the hedged item and the swap as the hedging instrument.

Hedge accounting is a technique that modifies the normal basis for recognising gains and losses (or revenues and expenses) associated with a hedged item or a hedging instrument to enable gains and losses on the hedging instrument to be recognised in profit or loss in the same period as offsetting losses and gains on the hedged item.

The application of hedge accounting is voluntary. In other words, were a bank to hedge a specific market risk with a derivative, it is not obliged to apply hedge accounting. However, were a bank willing to apply hedge accounting, it may not be able to do so. To qualify for hedge accounting, these are the three requirements that a hedging relationship must meet:

- The hedging relationship consists only of eligible hedging instruments and eligible hedged items;
- At the inception of the hedging relationship there is formal designation and documentation of the hedging relationship and the entity's risk management objective and strategy for undertaking the hedge. That documentation shall include identification of the hedging instrument, the hedged item, the nature of the risk being hedged and how the entity will assess whether the hedging relationship meets the hedge effectiveness requirements (including its analysis of the sources of hedge ineffectiveness and how it determines the hedge ratio); and
- The hedging relationship meets all the three hedge effectiveness requirements.

The three hedge effectiveness requirements are the following:

- There is an economic relationship between the hedged item and the hedging instrument;
- The effect of credit risk does not dominate the value changes that result from that economic relationship; and
- The weightings of the hedged item and the hedging instrument (i.e., the hedge ratio of the hedging relationship) is the same as that resulting from the quantity of the hedged item that the entity actually hedges and the quantity of the hedging instrument that the entity actually uses to hedge that quantity of hedged item. However, that designation shall not reflect an imbalance between the weightings of the hedged item and the hedging instrument that would create hedge ineffectiveness (irrespective of whether recognised or not) that could result in an accounting outcome that would be inconsistent with the purpose of hedge accounting.

Hedge accounting takes three forms under IFRS 9: fair value hedge, cash flow hedge, and net investment hedge.

## Fair Value Hedge

A fair value hedge hedges the change in fair value of a recognised asset or liability or firm commitment.

In the case of interest rate risk hedges, a bank enters into fair value hedges, using primarily interest rate swaps and options, in order to protect itself against movements in the fair value of fixed-rate financial instruments due to movements in market interest rates.

In a fair value hedge, the changes in the fair value of the hedged asset, liability or unrecognised firm commitment, or a portion thereof, attributable to the risk being hedged, are recognised in the profit or loss statement along with changes in the entire fair value of the derivative. When hedging interest rate risk, any interest accrued or paid on both the derivative and the hedged item is reported in "net interest income", and the unrealised gains and losses from the hedge accounting fair value adjustments are reported in "net trading income" (i.e., not reported in "net interest income") in profit or loss.

Let us assume that Megabank provided a fixed-rate loan to a corporate. Because the fair value of the loan was exposed to changes in interest rates (and the corporate credit spread), Megabank decided to enter into a pay-fixed receive-floating interest rate swap. The combination of the loan and the swap resembled an origination of a variable-rate loan, as shown at Figure 2.10.

Let us assume that Megabank decided not to apply hedge accounting. In such a case, the interest income stemming from the loan and the swap settlement amounts were recognised in profit or loss. The loan was recognised at amortised cost. In contrast, the swap was recognised at fair value through profit or loss, meaning that the changes in fair value of the swap were recognised in profit or loss. Ignoring the loan interest income and the swap settlement amounts, the hedging strategy added volatility to Megabank's profit or loss statement, as shown at Figure 2.11, although the strategy mitigated Megabank's exposure to interest rates stemming from the loan fair value.

Let us assume instead that the hedging relationship met the requirements for the application of hedge accounting and that Megabank decided to apply hedge accounting. As in the case of no application of hedge accounting, the

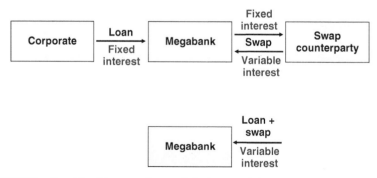

**FIGURE 2.10**    Combined interest flows of the loan and the interest rate swap

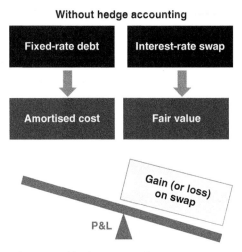

**FIGURE 2.11**    No application of hedge accounting

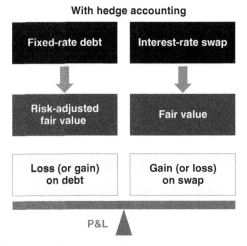

**FIGURE 2.12**    Application of fair value hedge accounting

interest income stemming from the loan and the swap settlement amounts were recognised in profit or loss. As in the case of no application of hedge accounting, the changes in fair value of the swap were recognised in profit or loss. Through the application of fair value hedge, the loan was fair valued and changes in its fair value due to changes in interest rates were recognised in profit or loss. If the hedge was well constructed, the changes in fair value of the swap would be offset by the changes in fair value of the loan (for changes in interest rates) and, therefore, the hedge would not add volatility in profit or loss, as shown at Figure 2.12 (ignoring the loan interest income and the swap settlement amounts). Therefore, the application of hedge accounting changed the recognition of the loan to align it with the recognition of the swap.

## Cash Flow Hedge

These are hedges set up to address variability in expected future cash flows that are attributable to a recognised specific asset or liability, or to a future expected transaction.

In the case of interest-rate risk hedges, a bank enters into cash flow hedges, using primarily interest rate swaps and options, futures, and cross-currency swaps, in order to protect itself against exposures to variability, due to movements in market interest rates, in future interest cash flows on banking book assets, and liabilities which bear interest at variable rates or which are expected to be re-funded or reinvested in the future.

In a cash flow hedge, there is no change to the accounting for the hedged item and the derivative is carried at fair value, with changes in value reported initially in other comprehensive income to the extent the hedge is effective. These amounts initially recorded in other comprehensive income are subsequently reclassified into the profit or loss statement in the same periods during which the forecast transaction affects the profit or loss statement. (There is an exception for hedges of equities recognised at fair value though other comprehensive income.) For hedges of interest rate risk, the amounts are amortised into "net interest income" at the same time as the interest is accrued on the hedged transaction.

Hedge ineffectiveness is recorded in "net trading income" in profit or loss and is measured as changes in the excess (if any) in the absolute cumulative change in fair value of the actual hedging derivative over the absolute cumulative change in the fair value of the hypothetically perfect hedge.

## Net Investment Hedge

A net investment hedge is a hedge of the net investment in a foreign operation. In other words, it is the hedge of the translation adjustments resulting from translating the functional currency financial statements of the foreign operation into the presentation currency of the parent entity. Imagine that Megabank was a British bank with the GBP as its presentation currency and that it controlled a French bank which reported in EUR. The financial statements of the French subsidiary will be disclosed in EUR and translated into GBP when the group prepares its consolidated financial statements. As a result, Megabank would be exposed to a potential depreciation of the EUR against the GBP. Megabank may hedge such an exposure by entering into, for example, a GBP/EUR FX forward in which the bank receives a fixed amount of GBP in exchange for a fixed amount of EUR.

In a net investment hedge, the portion of the change in fair value of the derivative due to changes in the spot (or forward) foreign exchange rate is recorded as a foreign currency translation adjustment in other comprehensive income to the extent the hedge is effective; the remainder is recorded in "net trading income" in profit or loss.

Changes in fair value of the hedging instrument relating to the effective portion of the hedge are subsequently recognised in profit or loss on disposal of the foreign operations.

## APPENDIX 2.A: The Par Asset Swap Spread

We assume we have constructed a market curve of Libor discount factors where $Df(t)$ is the price today of \$1 to be paid at time $t$. From the perspective of the asset swap seller, it sells the bond for par plus accrued interest. The net up-front payment has a value $100 - P$ where $P$ is the market price of the bond. If we assume both parties to the swap are inter-bank credit quality, we can price the cash flows off the Libor curve.

For the calculation we cancel out the principal payments of par at maturity. We assume that cash flows are annual and take place on the same coupon dates. The breakeven asset swap spread $A$ is calculated by setting the present value of all cash flows equal to zero. From the perspective of the asset swap seller, the present value is

$$100 - P + C\sum_{i=1} Df\left(t_i\right) - \sum_{i=1} D_i\left(L_i + A\right) Df\left(t_i\right) = 0 \qquad (2A.1)$$

There is a $100 - P$ upfront payment to purchase the asset in return for par. For the interest rate swap we have

$$C\sum_{i=1} Df\left(t_i\right) \qquad (2A.2)$$

for the fixed payments and

$$\sum_{i=1} D_i\left(L_i + A\right) Df\left(t_i\right) \qquad (2A.3)$$

for the floating payments, where $C$ equals the bond annual coupon, $L_i$ is the Libor rate set at time $t_i - 1$ and paid at time $t_i$, and $D_i$ is the accrual factor in the corresponding basis (day-count adjustment). We then solve for the asset swap spread $A$.

## SELECTED BIBLIOGRAPHY AND REFERENCES

Choudhry, M., "An alternative bond relative value measure: determining a fair value of the swap spread using Libor and GC repo rates", *Journal of Asset Management* 7 (1), June 2005, pp. 17–21.

Gale, G., "Using and trading asset-swaps: interest rate strategy", *Morgan Stanley Fixed Income Research*, May 2006.

O'Kane, D., Sen, S., "Credit spreads explained", *Journal of Credit Risk* 1 (2), Spring 2005, pp. 61–78.

*"Raisuli, what shall we do? We have lost everything . . ."*

*"Sherif, was there never anything in your life for which it was worth losing everything for?"*

—From *The Wind and The Lion*,
MGM Films, Columbia Pictures, 1975.

# CHAPTER 3

# The Yield Curve

This is probably the most important chapter in the book. Interest rates and the term structure of rates are the very foundation of modern principles of finance, yet this topic is not one that most senior bank executives are most *au fait* with. No doubt many of them would suggest that it is not an area they need to be technically expert in, but the fact remains that an understanding of the yield curve is fundamental to an understanding of the principles of finance.

The extracts in this chapter cover every aspect of interest rates, their term structure, spot and forward rates, dynamics of asset prices, fitting the curve, the secured curve, the multicurrency curve – everything but the kitchen sink, as they might say in 1940s Britain.

The new material in this book follows the book extracts, and ties in curve interpolation methodology with issues of relevance for the bank's internal funding or "funds transfer pricing" curve.

**This extract from *The Principles of Banking* (2012)**

## The Yield Curve

### The Yield Curve

The art of banking, indeed all of finance, revolves around the yield curve. Understanding and appreciating the curve is important to all financial market participants. It is important to debt capital market participants, and especially important to bank ALM practitioners. So if one is reading this book it is safe to assume that the yield curve is a very important subject.

This is a long chapter but well worth the close attention of all bankers, irrespective of their function or seniority. In it, we discuss the main concepts behind the yield curve, as well as its uses and information content. An ability to interpret the yield curve is vital for all market practitioners.

We discuss the zero-coupon (or spot) and forward yield curves, and present the main theories that seek to explain their shape and behaviour. We will see that the spread of different curves to another, such as the swap yield curve compared to the government yield curve, is also noteworthy and so we seek to explain the determinants of these spreads in this chapter.

We begin with an introduction to the curve and interest rates in general.

# IMPORTANCE OF THE YIELD CURVE

As we noted in Chapter 1, banks deal in interest rate and credit risk, as well as liquidity risk. These are the fundamental tenets of banking, as important today as they were when banking first began. The first of these, interest rates, is in effect an explicit measure of the cost of borrowing money, and is encapsulated in the yield curve. For bankers, understanding the behaviour and properties of the yield curve is an essential part of the risk management process. The following are some, but not all, of the reasons that this is so:

- changes in interest rates have a direct impact on bank revenue; the yield curve captures the current state of term interest rates, and also presents the current market expectation of the future state of the economy;
- the interest-rate gap reflects the state of bank borrowing and lending; gaps along the term structure are sensitive to changes in the shape and slope of the yield curve;
- current and future trading strategy, including the asset allocation and credit policy decision, will impact interest-rate risk exposure and therefore will take into account the shape and behaviour of the yield curve;
- the balance sheet itself, from both an asset and a liability viewpoint, is sensitive to changes in the shape, level and slope of the yield curve;
- balance sheet management and valuation requires an accurate yield curve, reflecting liquid market.

We see then that understanding and appreciating the yield curve is a vital part of banks' ALM operations, at both a strategic and tactical level. This chapter provides a detailed look at the curve from the banker's viewpoint. It is divided into three parts – Parts I and II focus on interest rates and interpreting the yield curve, and other curves; and Part III looks at fitting the curve.

## Part I: THE MONEY MARKET YIELD CURVE

The main measure of return associated with holding debt market assets is the yield-to-maturity (YTM) or *gross redemption yield*. In developed markets, as well as certain emerging economies, there is usually a large number of bonds trading at one time, at different yields and with varying terms to maturity. Investors and traders frequently examine the relationship between the yields on bonds that are in the same class; plotting yields of bonds that differ only in their term to maturity produces what is known as a *yield curve*. This curve is an important indicator and knowledge source of the state of a debt capital market. It is sometimes referred to as the *term structure of interest rates*, but strictly speaking this is not correct, as this expression should be reserved for the zero-coupon yield curve only. We shall examine this in detail later.

Much of the analysis and pricing activity that takes place in the capital markets revolves around the yield curve. This curve describes the relationship between a particular redemption yield and that yield's maturity. Plotting the yields along the term structure will give us our yield curve. It is very important that only rates from the same class of issuer or with the same degree of liquidity are used when plotting the yield curve; for example, a curve may be constructed for UK gilts or for AA-rated sterling Eurobonds, but not a mixture of both, because gilts and Eurobonds are bonds from different class issuers. The primary yield curve in any domestic capital market is the government bond yield curve, so for example in the US market it is the US Treasury yield curve. In the eurozone, in theory any euro-currency government bond can be used to plot a euro yield curve. In practice, only bonds from the same government are used, as for various reasons different country bonds within euro-land trade at different yields (the *de facto* euro benchmark is the German bund).

Outside the government bond markets yield curves are plotted for money-market instruments, off-balance sheet instruments; in fact, virtually all debt market instruments. Money market instruments trade on a simple yield basis, as the cash market is comprised essentially of bullet interest payment securities. So the money market yield curve is simple to construct. The "Libor curve" for money markets is the main measure of money market return, and in theory goes out to 12 months only. In fact, money market derivatives frequently trade out to 18 months and two years, and for tenors beyond that the interest-rate swap fixed rate is also referred to as "Libor". We show in Figures 5.1 and 5.2 the Bloomberg screen for Libor fixing and a broker's screen (Garban ICAP) for US dollar overnight-index swaps (OIS) swaps. These show that the maximum accepted maturity for the money market yield curve is 24 months. Another money market yield curve, in fact the most widely used by participants, is the exchange-traded futures curve for short-dated deposits; for instance, the Eurodollar curve or the short-sterling curve. This is taken as the most reliable and liquid indicator of expected money market rates. Figure 5.3 shows the Eurodollar curve as at 10 May 2004.

1
Screen Printed

P3007a Govt **BBAM**

BRITISH BANKERS'
ASSOCIATION

Page 1 of 4

| 05/10 13:34 GMT [BRITISH BANKERS ASSOCIATION LIBOR RATES] | | | | | 3750 |
|---|---|---|---|---|---|
| [10/05/04] RATES AT 11:00 LONDON TIME 10/05/2004 | | | | 10/05 11:18 GMT | |
| CCY | USD | GBP | CAD | EUR | JPY | EUR 365 |
| O/N | 1.05250 | 4.27875 | 2.07000 | 2.00125 | SN0.03250 | 2.02905 |
| 1WK | 1.08000 | 4.32813 | 2.06833 | 2.04613 | 0.03375 | 2.07455 |
| 2WK | 1.08125 | 4.37500 | 2.07000 | 2.05063 | 0.03500 | 2.07911 |
| 1MO | 1.10000 | 4.40500 | 2.07500 | 2.06263 | 0.03750 | 2.09128 |
| 2MO | 1.16000 | 4.43875 | 2.08500 | 2.08038 | 0.04313 | 2.10927 |
| 3MO | 1.24000 | 4.47188 | 2.10833 | 2.08950 | 0.04750 | 2.11852 |
| 4MO | 1.34000 | 4.52750 | 2.13167 | 2.10613 | 0.05075 | 2.13538 |
| 5MO | 1.43750 | 4.59500 | 2.15833 | 2.12275 | 0.05525 | 2.15223 |
| 6MO | 1.53000 | 4.65625 | 2.20000 | 2.14038 | 0.05975 | 2.17011 |
| 7MO | 1.62000 | 4.70750 | 2.23833 | 2.16150 | 0.06250 | 2.19152 |
| 8MO | 1.71250 | 4.76375 | 2.27500 | 2.19150 | 0.06750 | 2.22194 |
| 9MO | 1.81000 | 4.82125 | 2.32667 | 2.22363 | 0.07188 | 2.25451 |
| 10MO | 1.89375 | 4.86875 | 2.37000 | 2.25275 | 0.07750 | 2.28404 |
| 11MO | 1.98125 | 4.91625 | 2.41000 | 2.27788 | 0.08438 | 2.30952 |
| 12MO | 2.07000 | 4.95875 | 2.46333 | 2.31538 | 0.08875 | 2.34754 |

Australia 61 2 9777 8600    Brazil 5511 3048 4500    Europe 44 20 7330 7500    Germany 49 69 920410
Hong Kong 852 2977 6000 Japan 81 3 3201 8900 Singapore 65 6212 1000 U.S. 1 212 318 2000 Copyright 2004 Bloomberg L.P.
O 10-May-04 14:24:11

**Figure 5.1** Bloomberg screen BBAM, daily Libor fixing page, as at 10 May 2004.
© 2006 Bloomberg L.P. All rights reserved. Reproduced with permission.

ICAU2
Screen Printed
14:34 **USD OIS - ICAU**

P1P300 Govt **ICAU**

PAGE 1 / 1

| USD OIS | | Ask | Bid | Time |
|---|---|---|---|---|
| 1) | 1 Month | 1.0230 | 1.0030 | 14:12 |
| 2) | 2 Month | 1.0670 | 1.0470 | 14:12 |
| 3) | 3 Month | 1.1350 | 1.1150 | 14:26 |
| 4) | 4 Month | 1.2430 | 1.2230 | 14:31 |
| 5) | 5 Month | 1.3220 | 1.3020 | 14:31 |
| 6) | 6 Month | 1.4030 | 1.3830 | 14:31 |
| 7) | 7 Month | 1.4920 | 1.4720 | 14:31 |
| 8) | 8 Month | 1.5810 | 1.5600 | 14:34 |
| 9) | 9 Month | 1.6680 | 1.6470 | 14:34 |
| 10) | 10 Month | 1.7490 | 1.7290 | 14:34 |
| 11) | 11 Month | 1.8280 | 1.8070 | 14:34 |
| 12) | 12 Month | 1.9120 | 1.8920 | 14:34 |
| 13) | 15 Month | 2.1590 | 2.1390 | 14:34 |
| 14) | 18 Month | 2.3900 | 2.3690 | 14:34 |
| 15) | 21 Month | 2.6120 | 2.5920 | 14:34 |
| 16) | 24 Month | 2.8010 | 2.7810 | 14:34 |

Australia 61 2 9777 8600    Brazil 5511 3048 4500    Europe 44 20 7330 7500    Germany 49 69 920410
Hong Kong 852 2977 6000 Japan 81 3 3201 8900 Singapore 65 6212 1000 U.S. 1 212 318 2000 Copyright 2004 Bloomberg L.P.
O 10-May-04 14:34:21

**Figure 5.2** Bloomberg screen ICAU2, Garban ICAP broker's price screen for
US dollar OIS swaps, 10 May 2004.
© Garban ICAP © 2006 Bloomberg L.P. All rights reserved.
Reproduced with permission.

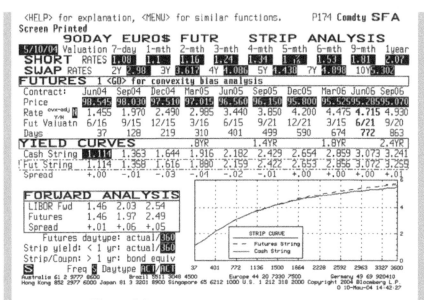

**Figure 5.3** Eurodollar yield curve, 10 May 2004.
© 2006 Bloomberg L.P. All rights reserved. Reproduced with permission.

Figure 5.4 shows the inter-bank fixings for HKD and SGD, and the AUD deposit rates as at 6 September 2004, as money market yield curves on Bloomberg screen MMCV.

The principles behind the money market yield curve are exactly the same as those behind the longer dated bond market yield curve. So in this chapter we will consider the YTM yield curve and how to derive spot and forward yields from a current redemption yield curve.

## USING THE YIELD CURVE

All participants in the capital markets have an interest in the current shape and level of the yield curve, as well as what this information implies for the future. Its main uses are summarised below.

### Setting the Yield for all Debt Market Instruments

The yield curve essentially fixes the cost of money over the maturity term structure. The yields of government bonds from the shortest maturity instrument to the longest set the benchmark for yields for all other debt instruments in the market, around which all debt instruments are analysed. Issuers of debt (and their underwriting banks) therefore use the yield curve to price bonds and all other debt instruments. Generally, the zero-coupon yield curve is used to price new issue securities, rather than the redemption yield curve.

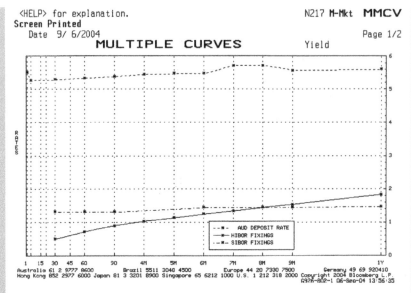

**Figure 5.4**    Bloomberg screen MMCV, inter-bank fixings for HKD and SGD, and AUD deposit rates as at 6 September 2004.
© 2006 Bloomberg L.P. All rights reserved. Reproduced with permission.

## Acting as an Indicator of Future Yield Levels

As we discuss later in this chapter, the yield curve assumes certain shapes in response to market expectations of future interest rates. Bond market participants analyse the present shape of the yield curve in an effort to determine the implications regarding the future direction of market interest rates. This is perhaps one of the most important functions of the yield curve. The yield curve is scrutinised for its information content, not just by bond traders and fund managers, but also by corporate financiers as part of the project appraisal process. Central banks and government treasury departments also analyse the yield curve for its information content, with regard to expected inflation levels.

## Measuring and Comparing Returns Across the Maturity Spectrum

Portfolio managers use the yield curve to assess the relative value of investments across the maturity spectrum. The yield curve indicates the returns that are available at different maturity points and is therefore very important to fixed-income fund managers, who can use it to assess which point of the curve offers the best return relative to other points.

## Indicating Relative Value Between Different Bonds of Similar Maturity

The yield curve can be analysed to indicate which bonds are cheap or dear to the curve. Placing bonds relative to the zero-coupon yield curve helps to highlight which bonds should be bought or sold either outright or as part of a bond spread trade.

## Pricing Interest-rate Derivatives

The price of derivatives revolves around the yield curve. At the short-end, products such as forward rate agreements (FRAs) are priced off the futures curve, but futures rates reflect the market's view on forward 3-month cash deposit rates. At the longer end, interest-rate swaps are priced off the yield curve, while hybrid instruments that incorporate an option feature such as convertibles and callable bonds also reflect current yield curve levels. The "risk-free" interest rate, which is one of the parameters used in option pricing, is the T-bill rate or short-term government repo rate, both constituents of the money market yield curve.

# TYPES OF YIELD CURVE

## Yield-to-maturity Yield Curve

The most commonly occurring yield curve is the YTM yield curve. The equation used to calculate the YTM is available in countless fixed income textbooks. The curve itself is constructed by plotting the YTM against the term to maturity for a group of bonds of the same class. Three different types are shown in Figure 5.5. Bonds used in constructing the curve will only rarely have an exact number of whole years to redemption; however, it is often common to see yields plotted against whole years on the *x*-axis. This is because once a bond is designated the *benchmark* for that term, its yield is taken to be the representative yield. For example, the then 10-year benchmark bond in the UK gilt market, the 4¾% of 2020, maintained its benchmark status throughout 2010 and into 2011, even as its term to maturity fell below 10 years. The YTM yield curve is the most commonly observed curve simply because YTM is the most frequent measure of return used. The business sections of daily newspapers, where they quote bond yields at all, usually quote bond yields to maturity. As we might expect, given the source data from which it is constructed, the YTM yield curve contains some inaccuracies. The main weakness of the YTM measure is the assumption of a constant rate for coupon reinvestment during the bond's life at the redemption yield level. Since market rates will fluctuate over time, it

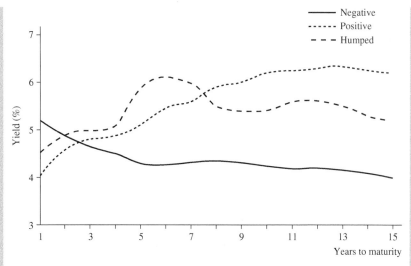

**Figure 5.5**　YTM yield curves.

will not be possible to achieve this (a feature known as *reinvestment risk*). Only zero-coupon bondholders avoid reinvestment risk as no coupon is paid during the life of a zero-coupon bond.

The YTM yield curve does not distinguish between different payment patterns that may result from bonds with different coupons; that is, the fact that low-coupon bonds pay a higher portion of their cash flows at a later date than high-coupon bonds of the same maturity. The curve also assumes an even cash flow pattern for all bonds. Therefore in this case cash flows are not discounted at the appropriate rate for the bonds in the group being used to construct the curve. To get around this, bond analysts may sometimes construct a *coupon yield curve*, which plots YTM against term to maturity for a group of bonds with the same coupon. This may be useful when a group of bonds contains some with very high coupons; high coupon bonds often trade "cheap to the curve"; that is, they have higher yields than corresponding bonds of the same maturity but lower coupon. This is usually because of reinvestment risk and, in some markets, for tax reasons.

The market often uses other types of yield curve for analysis when the YTM yield curve is deemed unsuitable. That there are a number of yield curves that can be plotted, each relevant to its own market, can be seen from Figure 5.6, which shows the curves that can be selected for the US dollar market, from screen IYC on Bloomberg. We see that curves can be selected for US Treasuries, US dollar swaps, strips, agency securities and so on. Figure 5.7 shows the curves for Treasuries, interest-rate swaps and strips as at August 2006.

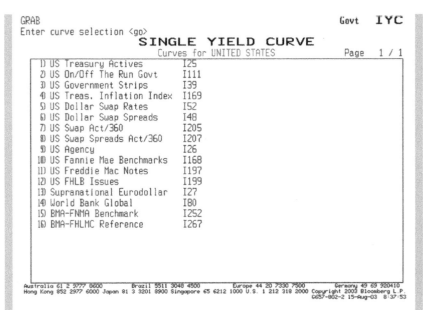

**Figure 5.6**   US menu page from screen IYC on Bloomberg.

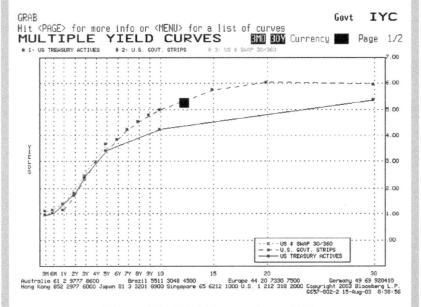

**Figure 5.7**   US yield curves, August 2006.

## The Coupon Yield Curve

The coupon yield curve is a plot of the YTM against term to maturity for a group of bonds with the same coupon. If we were to construct such a curve we would see that in general high-coupon bonds trade at a discount (have higher yields) relative to low-coupon bonds, because of reinvestment risk and for tax reasons (in the UK, for example, on gilts the coupon is taxed as income tax, while any capital gain is exempt from capital gains tax; even in jurisdictions where capital gain on bonds is taxable, this can often be deferred, whereas income tax cannot). It is frequently the case that yields vary considerably with coupons for the same term to maturity, and with term to maturity for different coupons. Put another way, usually we observe different coupon curves not only at different levels but also with different shapes. Distortions arise in the YTM curve if no allowance is made for coupon differences. For this reason bond analysts frequently draw a line of "best fit" through a plot of redemption yields, because the coupon effect in a group of bonds will produce a curve with humps and troughs. Figure 5.8 shows a hypothetical set of coupon yield curves. However, since in any group of bonds it is unusual to observe bonds with the same coupon along the entire term structure this type of curve is observed rarely.

## The Par Yield Curve

The *par yield curve* is not usually encountered in secondary market trading; however, it is often constructed for use by corporate financiers and others in the new issues or *primary* market. The par yield curve plots YTM against

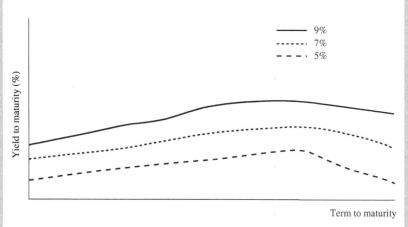

**Figure 5.8**    Coupon yield curves.

term to maturity for current bonds trading at par.[1] The par yield is therefore equal to the coupon rate for bonds priced at par or near to par, as the YTM for bonds priced exactly at par is equal to the coupon rate. Those involved in the primary market will use a par yield curve to determine the required coupon for a new bond that is to be issued at par. This is because investors prefer not to pay over par for a new-issue bond, so the bond requires a coupon that will result in a price at or slightly below par.

The par yield curve can be derived directly from bond yields when bonds are trading at or near par. If bonds in the market are trading substantially away from par then the resulting curve will be distorted. It is then necessary to derive it by iteration from the spot yield curve. As we would observe at almost any time, it is rare to encounter secondary market bonds trading at par for any particular maturity. The market therefore uses actual non-par vanilla bond yield curves to derive *zero-coupon yield curves* and then constructs hypothetical par yields that would be observed were there any par bonds being traded.

## The Zero-coupon (or Spot) Yield Curve

The *zero-coupon* (or *spot*) yield curve plots zero-coupon yields (or spot yields) against term to maturity. A zero-coupon yield is the yield prevailing on a bond that has no coupons. In the first instance if there is a liquid zero-coupon bond market we can plot the yields from these bonds if we wish to construct this curve. However, it is not necessary to have a set of zero-coupon bonds in order to construct the curve, as we can derive it from a coupon or par yield curve; in fact, in many markets where no zero-coupon bonds are traded, a spot yield curve is derived from the conventional YTM yield curve. This is of course *a theoretical* zero-coupon (spot) yield curve, as opposed to the *market* or *observed* spot curve that can be constructed using the yields of actual zero-coupon bonds trading in the market.[2]

### Basic Concepts
Spot yields must comply with equation (5.1). This equation assumes a bond with annual coupon payments and that the calculation is carried out on a coupon date so that accrued interest is zero.

---

[1] Par price for a bond is almost invariably 100%. Certain bonds have par defined as 1,000 per 1,000 nominal of paper.

[2] It is common to see the terms "spot rate" and "zero-coupon rate" used synonymously. However, the spot rate is a theoretical construct and cannot be observed in the market. The definition of the spot rate, which is the rate of return on a single cash flow that has been dealt today and is received back almost instantaneously, comes very close to that of the yield on a very short-dated zero-coupon bond, which can be observed directly in the market. Zero-coupon rates can therefore be taken to be spot rates in practice, which is why the terms are frequently used interchangeably.

$$P_d = \sum_{n=1}^{N} \frac{C}{\left(1+rs_n\right)^n} + \frac{M}{\left(1+rs_N\right)^N} \tag{5.1}$$

$$= \sum_{n=1}^{N} C \times df_n + M \times df_N$$

where   $rs_n$ = is the spot or zero-coupon yield on a bond of dirty price
$P_d$ with $n$ years to maturity
$df$ = is the corresponding *discount factor.*

In (5.1) $rs_1$ would be the current 1-year spot yield, $rs_2$ the current 2-year spot yield and so on. Theoretically the spot yield for a particular term to maturity is the same as the yield on a zero-coupon bond of the same maturity, which is why spot yields are also known as zero-coupon yields.

This last is an important result, as spot yields can be derived from redemption yields that have been observed in the market. As with the yield-to-redemption yield curve, the spot yield curve is commonly used in the market. It is viewed as the true term structure of interest rates because there is no reinvestment risk involved; the stated yield is equal to the actual annual return. That is, the yield on a zero-coupon bond of $n$ years maturity is regarded as the true $n$-year interest rate. Because the observed government bond redemption yield curve is not considered to be the true interest rate, analysts often construct a theoretical spot yield curve. Essentially, this is done by breaking down each coupon bond that is being observed into its constituent cash flows, which become a series of individual zero-coupon bonds. For example, £100 nominal of a 5% 2-year bond (paying annual coupons) is considered equivalent to £5 nominal of a 1-year zero-coupon bond and £105 nominal of a 2-year zero-coupon bond.

Let us assume that in the market there are 30 bonds all paying annual coupons. The first bond has a maturity of one year, the second bond of two years and so on, out to 30 years. We know the price of each of these bonds, and we wish to determine what the prices imply about the market's estimate of future interest rates. We naturally expect interest rates to vary over time, but assume that all payments being made on the same date are valued using the same rate. For the 1-year bond we know its current price and the amount of the payment (comprised of one coupon payment and the redemption proceeds) we will receive at the end of the year; therefore, we can calculate the interest rate for the first year: assume the 1-year bond has a coupon of 5%. If the bond is priced at par and we invest £100 today we will receive £105 in one year's time; hence, the rate of interest is apparent and is 5%. For the 2-year bond we use this interest rate to calculate the future value of its current price in one year's time: *this is how much we would receive if we had invested the same amount in the 1-year bond*. However, the 2-year bond pays a coupon at the end of the first year; if we subtract this amount from the future value of the current price, the net amount is what we should be giving up in one year in return for the one remaining payment. From these numbers we can calculate the interest rate in year 2.

Assume that the 2-year bond pays a coupon of 6% and is priced at 99.00. If the 99.00 were invested at the rate we calculated for the 1-year bond (5%), it would accumulate £103.95 in one year, made up of the £99 investment and interest of £4.95. On the payment date in one year's time, the 1-year bond matures and the 2-year bond pays a coupon of 6%. If everyone expected that at this time the 2-year bond would be priced at more than 97.95 (which is 103.95 minus 6.00), then no investor would buy the 1-year bond, since it would be more advantageous to buy the 2-year bond and sell it after one year for a greater return. Similarly, if the price was less than 97.95 no investor would buy the 2-year bond, as it would be cheaper to buy the shorter bond and then buy the longer dated bond with the proceeds received when the 1-year bond matures. Therefore the 2-year bond must be priced at exactly 97.95 in 12 months' time. For this £97.95 to grow to £106.00 (the maturity proceeds from the 2-year bond, comprising the redemption payment and coupon interest), the interest rate in year 2 must be 8.20%. We can check this by using the standard present value formula. At these two interest rates, the two bonds are said to be in equilibrium.

This is an important result and shows that (in theory) there can be no arbitrage opportunity along the yield curve; using interest rates available today the return from buying the 2-year bond must equal the return from buying the 1-year bond and rolling over the proceeds (or *reinvesting*) for another year. This is the known as the *break-even principle*, the law of no-arbitrage.

Using the price and coupon of the 3-year bond we can calculate the interest rate in year 3 in precisely the same way. Using each of the bonds in turn, we can link together the *implied 1-year rates* for each year up to the maturity of the longest dated bond. This process is known as *bootstrapping*. The "average" of the rates over a given period is the spot yield for that term: in the example given above, the rate in year 1 is 5% and in year 2 it is 8.20%. An investment of £100 at these rates would grow to £113.61. This gives a total percentage increase of 13.61% over two years, or 6.588% per annum (the average rate is not obtained by simply dividing 13.61 by 2, but – using our present value relationship again – by calculating the square root of "1 plus the interest rate" and then subtracting 1 from this number). Thus, the 1-year yield is 5% and the 2-year yield is 8.20%.

In real-world markets it is not necessarily as straightforward as this; for instance, on some dates there may be several bonds maturing, with different coupons, and on some dates there may be no bonds maturing. It is most unlikely that there will be a regular spacing of bond redemptions exactly one year apart. For this reason it is common for analysts to use a software model to calculate the set of implied spot rates which best fits the market prices of the bonds that do exist in the market. For instance, if there are several 1-year bonds, each of their prices may imply a slightly different rate of interest. We choose the rate that gives the smallest average price error. In practice all bonds are used to find the rate in year 1, all bonds with a term longer than one year are used to calculate the rate in year 2 and so on. The zero-coupon curve can also be calculated directly from the coupon yield curve using a method similar to that described above; in this case the bonds would be priced at par and their coupons set to the par yield values.

The zero-coupon yield curve is ideal to use when deriving implied forward rates, which we consider next, and defining the term structure of interest rates. It is also the best curve to use when determining the *relative value*, whether cheap or dear, of bonds trading in the market, and when pricing new issues, irrespective of their coupons. However, it is not an absolutely accurate indicator of average market yields because most bonds are not zero-coupon bonds.

## Zero-coupon Discount Factors

Having introduced the concept of the zero-coupon curve in the previous paragraph, we can illustrate more formally the mathematics involved. When deriving spot yields from redemption yields, we view conventional bonds as being made up of an *annuity*, which is the stream of fixed coupon payments, and a zero-coupon bond, which is the redemption payment on maturity. To derive the rates we can use (5.1), setting $Pd = M = 100$ and $C = rm_N$ as shown in (5.2) below. This has the coupon bonds trading at par, so that the coupon is equal to the yield. So we have:

$$100 = rm_N \times \sum_{n=1}^{N} df_n + 100 \times df_n \qquad (5.2)$$

$$= rm_n \times A_N + 100 \times df_n$$

where $rm_N$ is the par yield for a term to maturity of $N$ years, where $df_n$, the discount factor, is the fair price of a zero-coupon bond with a par value of £1 and a term to maturity of $N$ years, and where

$$A_N = \sum_{n=1}^{N} df_n = A_{N-1} + df_N \qquad (5.3)$$

is the fair price of an annuity of £1 per year for $N$ years (with $A_0$ by convention). Substituting (5.3) into (5.2) and rearranging them will give us the expression below for the $N$-year discount factor, shown in (5.4):

$$df_N = \frac{1 - rm_N \times A_{N-1}}{1 + rm_N}. \tag{5.4}$$

If we assume 1-year, 2-year and 3-year redemption yields for bonds priced at par to be 5%, 5.25% and 5.75% respectively, we will obtain the following solutions for the discount factors:

$$df_1 = \frac{1}{1 + 0.05} = 0.95238$$

$$df_2 = \frac{1 - (0.0525)(0.95238)}{1 + 0.0525} = 0.90261$$

$$df_3 = \frac{1 - (0.0575)(0.95238 + 0.90261)}{1 + 0.0575} = 0.84476.$$

We can confirm that these are the correct discount factors by substituting them back into equation (5.2); this gives us the following results for the 1-year, 2-year and 3-year par value bonds (with coupons of 5%, 5.25% and 5.75% respectively):

$$100 = 105 \times 0.95238$$
$$100 = 5.25 \times 0.95238 + 105.25 \times 0.90261$$
$$100 = 5.75 \times 0.95238 + 5.75 \times 0.90261 + 105.75 \times 0.84476.$$

Now that we have found the correct discount factors it is relatively straightforward to calculate the spot yields using equation (5.1), and this is shown below:

$$df_1 = \frac{1}{(1 + rs_1)} = 0.95238, \text{ which gives } rs_1 = 5.0\%$$

$$df_2 = \frac{1}{(1 + rs_2)} = 0.90261, \text{ which gives } rs_2 = 5.256\%$$

$$df_3 = \frac{1}{(1 + rs_3)} = 0.84476, \text{ which gives } rs_3 = 5.784\%.$$

Equation (5.1) discounts the $n$-year cash flow (comprising the coupon payment and/or principal repayment) by the corresponding $n$-year spot yield. In other words, $rs_n$ is the *time-weighted rate of return* on an $n$-year bond. Thus, as we said in the previous section the spot yield curve is the correct method for pricing or valuing any cash flow, including an irregular cash flow, because it uses the appropriate discount factors. That is, it matches each cash flow to the discount rate that applies to the time period in which the cash flow is paid. Compare this to the approach for the YTM procedure, which discounts all cash flows by the same yield to maturity. This illustrates neatly why the $N$-period zero-coupon interest rate is the true interest rate for an $N$-year bond.

The expressions above are solved algebraically in the conventional manner, although those wishing to use a spreadsheet application such as Microsoft Excel® can input the constituents of each equation into individual cells and solve using the "Tools" and "Goal Seek" functions.[3]

---

**EXAMPLE 5.1**    **Zero-coupon yields**

Consider the following zero-coupon market rates:

1-year (1y): 5.000%
2y: 5.271%
3y: 5.598%
4y: 6.675%
5y: 7.213%.

---

[3] To calculate these values the steps are summarised below:

$$Df = \frac{1}{(1 + rs_1)}$$

$$(1 + rs_1) = \frac{1}{Df}$$

$$rs = \left[\frac{1}{Df}\right] - 1$$

$$Df = \frac{1}{(1 + rs_2)^2}$$

$$rs_2 = \left[\sqrt{\frac{1}{Df}}\right] - 1$$

In the example in the text the working is:

| Par yeields | 0.05 | Df | 0.952381 | | |
|---|---|---|---|---|---|
| | 0.0525 | | 0.9026128 | | |
| | 0.0575 | | 0.8447639 | Working | 0.1066621 |
| | | | | | 0.8933379 |
| | | | | | 1.0575 |

With special thanks to Praveen Murthy, iflexsolutions, for assistance with the calculations.

Calculate the zero-coupon discount factors and the prices and yields of:

a. a 6% 2-year bond;
b. a 7% 5-year bond.

Assume both are annual coupon bonds.
The zero-coupon discount factors are:

1y: $1/1.05$ $= 0.95238095$
2y: $1/(1.05271)^2 = 0.90236554$
3y: $1/(1.05598)^3 = 0.84924485$
4y: $1/(1.06675)^4 = 0.77223484$
5y: $1/(1.07213)^5 = 0.70593182.$

The price of the 6% 2-year bond is then calculated in the normal fashion using present values of the cash flows:

$$(6 \times 0.95238095) \times (106 \times 0.90236554) = 101.365.$$

The YTM is 5.263%, obtained using the iterative method, with a spreadsheet function such as Microsoft Excel® "Goal Seek" or a Hewlett Packard (HP) calculator. The price of the 7% 5-year bond is:

$$(7 \times 0.95238095) + (7 \times 0.90236554) + (7 \times 0.84924485) +$$
$$(7 \times 0.77223484) + (107 \times 0.70593182)$$
$$= 99.869.$$

The yield to maturity is 7.05%.

## Formula Summary

Example 5.1 illustrates that if the zero-coupon discount factor for $n$ years is $df_n$ and the par yield for $N$ years is $rp$, then the expression in (5.5) is always true.

$$(rp \times df_1) + (rp \times df_2) + \ldots + (rp \times df_N) + (1 \times df_N) = 1$$
$$rp \times (df_1 + df_2 + \ldots + df_N) = 1 - df_N$$
$$rp = \frac{1 - df_N}{\sum_{n=1}^{N} df_N} \tag{5.5}$$

## The Forward Yield Curve

### Forward Yields

Most transactions in the market are for immediate delivery, which is known as the *cash* market, although some markets also use the expression *spot* market, which is more common in foreign exchange. Cash market transactions are settled straight away, with the purchaser of a bond being entitled to interest from the settlement date onwards.[5] There is a large market in *forward* transactions, which are trades carried out today for a forward settlement date. For financial transactions that are forward transactions, the parties to the trade agree today to exchange a security for cash at a future date, but at a price agreed today. So the forward rate applicable to a bond is the spot bond yield as at the forward date. That is, it is the yield of a zero-coupon bond that is purchased for settlement at the forward date. It is derived today, using data from a present-day yield curve, so it is not correct to consider forward rates to be a prediction of the spot rates as at the forward date. Rather, the correct way to view forward rates is simply the forward-starting equivalent of spot rates; that they are saying one-and-the-same thing is immediately apparent when one considers the mathematical relationships below.

Forward rates can be derived from spot interest rates. Such rates are then known as implied forward rates, since they are implied by the current range of spot interest rates. The *forward* (or *forward–forward*) *yield curve* is a plot of forward rates against term to maturity. Forward rates satisfy expression (5.6):

$$
P_d = \frac{C}{\left(1+_0 rf_1\right)} + \frac{C}{\left(1+_0 rf_1\right)\left(1+_0 rf_2\right)} + \ldots + \frac{M}{\left(1+_0 rf_1\right)\ldots\left(1+_{N-1} rf_N\right)} \tag{5.6}
$$

$$
= \sum_{n=1}^{N} \frac{C}{\prod_{n=1}^{n}\left(1+_{i-1} rf_i\right)} + \frac{M}{\prod_{n=1}^{N}\left(1+_{i-1} rf_i\right)}
$$

where $_{n-1}rf_n$ is the implicit forward rate (or forward–forward rate) on a 1-year bond maturing in year $N$, with coupons $C$ and redemption payment $M$.

As a forward or forward–forward yield is implied from spot rates, the forward rate is a forward zero-coupon rate. Comparing (5.1) and (5.6) we see that the spot yield is the geometric mean of the forward rates, as shown below:

$$
\left(1+rs_n\right)^n = \left(1+_0 rf_1\right)\left(1+_1 rf_2\right)\cdots\left(1+_{n-1} rf_n\right). \tag{5.7}
$$

---

[5] We refer to "immediate" settlement, although of course there is a delay between trade date and settlement date, which can be anything from one day to seven days, or even longer in some markets. The most common settlement period is known as "spot" and is two business days.

This implies the following relationship between spot and forward rates:

$$\left(1+_{n-1}rf_n\right) = \frac{\left(1+rs_n\right)^n}{\left(1+rs_{n-1}\right)^{n-1}} \tag{5.8}$$

$$= \frac{df_{n-1}}{df_n}.$$

Using the spot yields we calculated in the earlier paragraph we can derive the implied forward rates from (5.8). For example, the 2-year and 3-year forward rates are given by:

$$\left(1+_1rf_2\right) = \frac{\left(1+0.05256\right)^2}{\left(1+0.05\right)} = 5.5138\%$$

$$\left(1+_2rf_3\right) = \frac{\left(1+0.05778\right)^3}{\left(1+0.05256\right)^2} = 6.8479\%.$$

Using our expression gives us $_0rf_1$ equal to 5%, $_1rf_2$ equal to 5.514% and $_2rf_3$ as 6.848%. This means, for example, that given current spot yields, which we calculated from the 1-year, 2-year and 3-year bond redemption yields (which were priced at par), the market would set the yield on a bond with one year to mature in three years' time at 6.848% (that is, the 3-year 1-period forward–forward rate is 6.848%).

The relationship between the par yields, spot yields and forward rates is shown in Table 5.1.

Figure 5.10 highlights our results for all three yield curves graphically. This illustrates another important property of the relationship between the three curves, in that as the original coupon yield curve was positively sloping, so the spot and forward yield curves lie above it. The reasons behind this will be considered later in the chapter.

Let us now consider the following example. Suppose that a 2-year bond with cash flows of £5.25 at the end of year 1 and £105.25 at the end of

| Year | Coupon yield (%) | Zero-coupon yield (%) | Forward rate (%) |
|------|------------------|-----------------------|------------------|
| 1    | 5.000            | 5.000                 | 5.000            |
| 2    | 5.250            | 5.2566                | 5.5138           |
| 3    | 5.750            | 5.7844                | 6.8479           |

**Table 5.1**  Coupon, spot and forward yields.

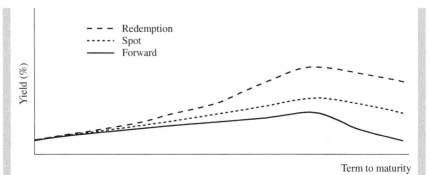

**Figure 5.10**    Redemption, spot and forward yield curves: traditional analysis.

year 2 is trading at par, hence it has a redemption yield (indeed, a par yield) of 5.25% (this is the bond in Table 5.1 above). To be regarded as equivalent to this a pure zero-coupon bond or discount bond making a lump-sum payment at the end of year 2 only (so with no cash flow at the end of year 1) would require a rate of return of 5.257%, which is the spot yield. That is, for the same investment of £100 the maturity value would have to be £110.79 (this figure is obtained by multiplying 100 by $(1 + 0.05257)^2$).

This illustrates why the zero-coupon curve is important to corporate financiers involved in new bond issues. If we know the spot yields, then we can calculate the coupon required on a new 3-year bond that is going to be issued at par in this interest-rate environment by making the following calculation:

$$100 = \frac{C}{(1.05)} + \frac{C}{(1.05257)^2} + \frac{C+100}{(1.05784)^3}.$$

This is solved in the conventional algebraic manner to give $C$ equal to 5.75%.

The relationship between spot rates and forward rates was shown in (5.8). We can illustrate it as follows. If the spot yield is the average return, then the forward rate can be interpreted as the marginal return. If the marginal return between years 2 and 3 increases from 5.514% to 6.848%, then the average return increases from 5.257% up to the 3-year spot yield of 5.784% as shown below:

$$\{[(1.05257)^2 \, (1.06848)]^{1/3} - 1\} = 0.05784$$

or 5.784%, as shown in Table 5.1.

## Formula Summary

The forward zero-coupon rate from interest period $a$ to period $b$ is given by (5.9):

$$_a rf_b = \left[ \frac{\left(1+rs_b\right)^b}{\left(1+rs_a\right)^a} \right]^{1/(b-a)} - 1 \qquad (5.9)$$

where $rs_a$ and $rs_b$ are the $a$ and $b$ period spot rates respectively, and $_a rf_b$ is an annualised forward rate.

The forward rate from interest period $a$ to period $(a + 1)$ is given by (5.10):

$$_a rf_{a+1} = \frac{\left(1+rs_{a+1}\right)^{a+1}}{\left(1+rs_a\right)^a} - 1. \qquad (5.10)$$

## Calculating Spot Rates from Forward Rates

The previous section showed the relationship between spot and forward rates. Just as we have derived forward rates from spot rates based on this mathematical relationship, it is possible to reverse this and calculate spot rates from forward rates. If we are presented with a forward yield curve, plotted from a set of one-period forward rates, we can use this to construct a spot yield curve. Equation (5.7) states the relationship between spot and forward rates, rearranged as (5.11) to solve for the spot rate:

$$rs_n = \left[ \left(1 + _1 rf_1\right) \times \left(1 + _2 rf_1\right) \times \left(1 + _3 rf_1\right) \times \ldots \times \left(1 + _n rf_1\right) \right]^{1/n} - 1 \qquad (5.11)$$

where $_1 rf_1, _2 rf_1, _3 rf_1$ are the 1-period versus 2-period, 2-period versus 3-period forward rates up to the $(n - 1)$ period versus $n$-period forward rates.

Remember to adjust (5.11) as necessary if dealing with forward rates relating to a deposit of a different interest period. If we are dealing with the current 6-month spot rate and implied 6-month forward rates, the relationship between these and the $n$-period spot rate is given by (5.11) in the same way as if we were dealing with the current 1-year spot rate and implied 1-year forward rates.

**EXAMPLE 5.2A**     Spot rates

The 1-year cash market yield is 5.00%. Spot prices imply 1-year rates in one year's time at 5.95% and in two years' time at 7.25%. What is the current 3-year spot rate that would produce these forward rate views?

To calculate this we assume an investment strategy dealing today at forward rates, and calculate the return generated from this strategy. The return after a 3-year period is given by the future value relationship, which in this case is $1.05 \times 1.0595 \times 1.0725 = 1.1931$.

The 3-year spot rate is then obtained by:

$$\left(\frac{1.1931}{1}\right)^{1/3} - 1 = 6.062\%.$$

**EXAMPLE 5.2B**     Forward rates

Consider the following 6-month implied forward rates, when the 6-month spot rate is 4.0000%.

$_1rf_1$    4.0000%
$_2rf_1$    4.4516%
$_3rf_1$    5.1532%
$_4rf_1$    5.6586%
$_5rf_1$    6.0947%
$_6rf_1$    7.1129%

An investor is debating between purchasing a 3-year zero-coupon bond at a price of £72.91028 per £100 nominal, or buying a 6-month zero-coupon bond and then rolling over her investment every six months for the 3-year term. If the investor was able to reinvest her proceeds every six months at the actual forward rates in place today, what would her proceeds be at the end of the 3-year term? An investment of £72.91028 at the spot rate of 4% and then reinvested at the forward rates in our table over the next three years would yield a terminal value of:

72.91028
$$\times (1.04)(1.044516)(1.051532)(1.056586)(1.060947)(1.071129)$$
$$= 100.$$

This merely reflects our spot and forward rates relationship, in that if all the forward rates are indeed realised, our investor's £72.91 will produce a terminal value that matches the investment in a 3-year zero-coupon bond priced at the 3-year spot rate. This illustrates the relationship between the 3-year spot rate, the 6-month spot rate and the implied 6-month forward rates. So what is the 3-year zero-coupon bond trading at? Using (5.11) the solution to this is given by:

$$rs_6$$
$$= \left[ (1.04)(1.044516)(1.051532)(1.056586)(1.060947)(1.071129) \right]^{1/6} - 1$$
$$= 5.4068\%$$

which solves our 3-year spot rate $rs_6$ as 5.4068%. Of course, we could have also solved for $rs_6$ using the conventional price/yield formula for zero-coupon bonds; however, the calculation above illustrates the relationship between spot and forward rates.

## An Important Note on Spot and Forward Rates

Forward rates that exist at any one time reflect everything that is known in the market *up to that point*. Certain market participants believe that the forward rate curve is a forecast of the future spot rate curve. This is implied by the *unbiased expectations hypothesis* that we consider below. In fact, this interpretation of implied forward rates is incorrect; for an excellent analysis of this see Jarrow (1996). It is possible, for example, for the forward rate curve to be upward sloping at the same time that short-dated spot rates are expected to decline, but this is simply explained by the mathematical properties of forward rates (the best explanation for this is given in Campbell, Lo and MacKinlay (1997), see also Example 5.9 on page 284). To view the forward rate curve as a predictor of rates is a misuse of it. The derivation of forward rates reflects all currently known market information. Assuming that all developed country markets are at least in a semi-strong form,[6] to preserve market equilibrium there can only be one set of forward rates from a given spot rate curve. However, this does not mean that such rates are a prediction because the instant after they have been calculated new market knowledge may become available that alters the market's view of current interest rates. This will cause the forward rate curve to change.

---

[6] See Fama (1970).

Forward rates are important because they are needed if we are to make prices today for dealing at a future date. For example, a bank's corporate customer may wish to fix today the interest rate payable on a loan that begins in one year from now; what rate does the bank quote? The forward rate is used by market-makers to quote prices for dealing today, and is the best *implied expectation* of future interest rates given everything that is known in the market up to now, but it is not a prediction of future spot rates. What would happen if a bank were privy to insider information; for example, it knew that central bank base rates would be changed very shortly? A bank in possession of such information (if we ignore the ethical implications) would not quote forward rates based on the spot rate curve, but would quote rates that reflected its insider knowledge.

## The Bootstrapping Approach Using Discount Factors

In this section we describe how to obtain zero-coupon and forward rates from the yields available from coupon bonds, using the *bootstrapping* technique. In a government bond market such as US Treasuries, the bonds are considered to be default-free. The rates from a government bond yield curve describe the risk-free rates of return available in the market today; however, they also *imply* (risk-free) rates of return for future time periods. These implied future rates, known as *implied forward rates*, or simply *forward rates*, can be derived from a given discount function or spot yield curve using bootstrapping. This term reflects the fact that each calculated spot rate is used to determine the next period spot rate, in successive steps. We illustrate the technique using discount factors. Once we have obtained the discount curve, it is a straightforward process to obtain the spot rate curve, as we saw earlier when we described the relationship that exists between discount factors, spot rates and forward rates.

A $t$-period discount factor is the present value of $1 that is payable at the end of period $t$. Essentially it is the present value relationship expressed in terms of $1. If $d(t)$ is the $t$-year discount factor, then the 5-year discount factor at a discount rate of 6% is given by:

$$d(5) = \frac{1}{\left(1 + 0.06\right)^5} = 0.747258.$$

The set of discount factors for the time period from one day to 30 years (or longer) is termed the *discount function*. Discount factors are used to price any financial instrument that is comprised of a future cash flow. For example, if the 6-month discount factor is 0.98756, the current value of the maturity payment of a 7% semi-annual coupon bond due for receipt in six months' time is given by $0.98756 \times 103.50$ or 102.212.

Discount factors may be used to calculate the future value of any current investment. From the example above, $0.98756 would be worth $1 in six months' time, so by the same principle a present sum of $1 would be worth at the end of six months:

$$1/d(5) = 1/0.98756 = 1.0126.$$

As we saw earlier in the chapter, the interrelationship between discount factors and spot and forward rates means we may obtain discount factors from current bond prices. Assume a hypothetical set of semi-annual coupon bonds and bond prices as given in Table 5.2, and assume further that the first bond matures in precisely six months' time. All other bonds then mature at 6-month intervals.

Taking the first bond, this matures in precisely six months' time, and its final cash flow will be 103.50, comprised of the $3.50 final coupon payment and the $100 redemption payment. The market-observed price of this bond is $101.65, which allows us to calculate the 6-month discount factor as:

$$d(0.5) \times 103.50 = 101.65$$

which gives us $d(0.5)$ equal to 0.98213.

From this step we can calculate the discount factors for the following 6-month periods. The second bond in Table 5.2, the 8% 2001, has the following cash flows:

- $4 in six months' time
- $104 in one year's time.

The price of this bond is 101.89, the bond's present value, and this is comprised of the sum of the present values of the bond's total cash flows. So we are able to set the following:

$$101.89 = 4 \times d(0.5) + 101 \times d(1).$$

| Coupon | Maturity date | Price |
|--------|---------------|-------|
| 7% | 7/6/2001 | 101.65 |
| 8% | 7/12/2001 | 101.89 |
| 6% | 7/6/2002 | 100.75 |
| 6.50% | 7/12/2002 | 100.37 |

**Table 5.2**  Hypothetical set of bonds and bond prices.

| Coupon | Maturity date | Term (years) | Price | *dn* |
|--------|---------------|--------------|-------|------|
| 7% | 7/6/2001 | 0.5 | 101.65 | 0.98213 |
| 8% | 7/12/2001 | 1 | 101.89 | 0.94194 |
| 6% | 7/6/2002 | 1.5 | 100.75 | 0.92211 |
| 6.50% | 7/12/2002 | 2 | 100.37 | 0.88252 |

**Table 5.3**  Discount factors calculated using the bootstrapping technique.

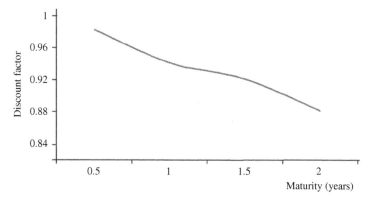

**Figure 5.11**  Discount function.

However, we already know $d(0.5)$ to be 0.98213, which leaves only one unknown in the above expression. Therefore we may solve for $d(1)$ and this is shown to be 0.94194.

If we carry on with this procedure for the remaining two bonds, using successive discount factors, we obtain the complete set of discount factors as shown in Table 5.3. The continuous function for the 2-year period is shown as the discount function in Figure 5.11.

Once we have the discount function we are able to compute the zero-coupon rates and hence also the forward rates. As a result, we can fit the yield curve from the discount function.

The theoretical approach described above is neat and appealing, but in practice there are a number of issues that will complicate the attempt to extract zero-coupon rates from bond yields. The main problem is that it is highly unlikely that we will have a set of bonds that are both precisely six months (or one interest) apart in maturity and priced precisely at par. We also require our procedure to fit as smooth a curve as possible. Setting our coupon bonds at a price of par simplified the analysis in our illustration of bootstrapping, so in reality we need to apply more advanced techniques. A standard approach for extracting zero-coupon bond prices is described in Choudhry (2004b).

# THE DETERMINANTS OF THE SWAP SPREAD

Up to now we have been looking in detail at the risk-free yield curve. An important hedging tool in bank ALM is the interest-rate swap, and so the swap curve is also analysed by market practitioners. Therefore an important issue for interest-rate analysis is the swap spread, which is the spread of the swap curve over the government bond yield curve, and the relationship between the two yield curves. The swap spread is an indicator of value in the market, as well as an indicator of the overall health of the economy. Understanding the determinants of the swap spread is important for ALM practitioners for this reason. We also consider the impact of macro-level geo-political factors on the swap spread.

## Interest-rate Swaps in Banking

Interest-rate swaps, which are described in Chapter 15 of the author's book *Fixed Income Markets*, are an important ALM and risk management tool in banking. The rate payable on a swap represents bank risk, if we assume that a swap is paying (receiving) the fixed swap rate on one leg and receiving (paying) Libor-flat on the other leg. If one of the counterparties is not a bank, then either leg is adjusted to account for the different counterparty risk; usually the floating leg will have a spread added to Libor. We can see that this produces a swap curve that lies above the government bond yield curve, if we compare Figure 5.24 with Figure 5.25. Figure 5.24 is the USD swap rates page from Tullett & Tokyo brokers, and Figure 5.25 is the US Treasury yield curve, both as at 3 July 2006. The higher rates payable on swaps represents the additional risk premium associated with bank risk compared to government risk. The spread itself is the number of basis points the swap rate lies above the equivalent maturity government bond yield, quoted on the same interest basis.

In theory, the swap spread represents only the additional credit risk of the inter-bank market above the government market. However, as the spread is variable, it is apparent that other factors influence it. An ALM desk will want to be aware of these factors, because they influence swap rates. Swaps are an important risk hedging tool, if not the most important, for banks so it becomes necessary for practitioners to have an appreciation of what drives swap spreads.

2                                                     P1P122 Govt   **TTIS**
200<Go> to view in Launchpad
10:10 **TULLETT & TOKYO**                                    PAGE  1 / 2

| USD | | | | USD | | | |
|---|---|---|---|---|---|---|---|
| Swaps | Bid | Ask | Time | Swaps | Bid | Ask | Time |
| IMM SWAPS | | | | 19) 15 Year | 5.7380 | 5.7780 | 1:46 |
| 1) 1st | 5.6900 | 5.7100 | 10:08 | 20) 20 Year | 5.8060 | 5.8460 | 1:46 |
| 2) 2nd | 5.6580 | 5.6790 | 10:08 | 21) 25 Year | 5.8080 | 5.8490 | 3:02 |
| 3) 3rd | 5.6150 | 5.6350 | 10:10 | 22) 30 Year | 5.7740 | 5.8150 | 1:46 |
| 4) 4th | 5.5800 | 5.6000 | 10:01 | SEMI-ANNUAL SWAPS | | | |
| ANNUAL SWAPS | | | | 23) 2 Year | 5.6310 | 5.6710 | 7/03 |
| 5) 1 Year | 5.6770 | 5.6970 | 9:36 | 24) 3 Year | 5.6120 | 5.6520 | 7/03 |
| 6) 2 Year | 5.6240 | 5.6650 | 7/03 | 25) 4 Year | 5.6210 | 5.6610 | 7:16 |
| 7) 3 Year | 5.6070 | 5.6480 | 7/03 | 26) 5 Year | 5.6410 | 5.6810 | 0:01 |
| 8) 4 Year | 5.6180 | 5.6590 | 7:16 | 27) 6 Year | 5.6600 | 5.7000 | 0:01 |
| 9) 5 Year | 5.6390 | 5.6790 | 0:01 | 28) 7 Year | 5.6770 | 5.7170 | 0:01 |
| 10) 6 Year | 5.6560 | 5.6970 | 0:01 | 29) 8 Year | 5.6910 | 5.7310 | 0:01 |
| 11) 7 Year | 5.6740 | 5.7150 | 0:01 | 30) 9 Year | 5.7080 | 5.7480 | 0:01 |
| 12) 8 Year | 5.6890 | 5.7300 | 0:01 | 31) 10 Year | 5.7270 | 5.7670 | 7:40 |
| 13) 9 Year | 5.7070 | 5.7470 | 0:01 | 32) 11 Year | 5.7370 | 5.7770 | 0:01 |
| 14) 10 Year | 5.7250 | 5.7650 | 7:40 | 33) 12 Year | 5.4570 | 5.4970 | 1:46 |
| 15) 11 Year | 5.7350 | 5.7760 | 0:01 | 34) 13 Year | 5.7620 | 5.8020 | 0:01 |
| 16) 12 Year | 5.4520 | 5.4920 | 1:46 | 35) 14 Year | 5.7720 | 5.8120 | 0:01 |
| 17) 13 Year | 5.7610 | 5.8020 | 0:01 | LIVE | Treasury Mid-Yields & | | |
| 18) 14 Year | 5.7700 | 5.8110 | 0:01 | | Treasury Swap Spreads -> SMKR<GO> |

Australia 61 2 9777 8600       Brazil 5511 3048 4500       Europe 44 20 7330 7500       Germany 49 69 920410
Hong Kong 852 2977 6000 Japan 81 3 3201 8900 Singapore 65 6212 1000 U.S. 1 212 318 2000 Copyright 2006 Bloomberg L.P.
                                                                              Z 04-Jul-06 10:10:46

**Figure 5.24**    Tullet & Tokyo brokers USD interest-rate swaps page on
Bloomberg, as at 3 July 2006.

<HELP> for explanation.                               P122 Govt   **IYC**
Cancel: Screen not saved
**YIELD CURVE – US TREASURY ACTIVES**               Page  2/2
                                                      DATE    7/ 4/06

| | DESCRIPTION | PRICE | SRC | UPDATE | YIELD | HEDGED YIELD |
|---|---|---|---|---|---|---|
| 3MO | 1) B 0 09/28/06 | B  4.8900 | BGN | 4:00 | 5.0158 | 5.0158 |
| 6MO | 2) B 0 12/28/06 | B  5.0700 | BGN | 4:00 | 5.2711 | 5.2711 |
| 1YR | 3) | | | | | |
| 2YR | 4) T 5 ⅛ 06/30/08 | B 99.9063 | BGN | 4:00 | 5.1748 | 5.1748 |
| 3YR | 5) T 4 ⅞ 05/15/09 | B 99.2969 | BGN | 4:00 | 5.1400 | 5.1400 |
| 4YR | 6) | | | | | |
| 5YR | 7) T 5 ⅛ 06/30/11 | B100.0625 | BGN | 4:00 | 5.1104 | 5.1104 |
| 6YR | 8) | | | | | |
| 7YR | 9) | | | | | |
| 8YR | 10) | | | | | |
| 9YR | 11) | | | | | |
| 10YR | 12) T 5 ⅛ 05/15/16 | B 99.7813 | BGN | 4:00 | 5.1527 | 5.1527 |
| 15YR | 13) | | | | | |
| 20YR | 14) | | | | | |
| 30YR | 15) T 4 ½ 02/15/36 | B 89.4531 | BGN | 4:00 | 5.2017 | 5.2017 |
| 1MO | 16) B 0 07/27/06 | B  4.5500 | BGN | 4:00 | 4.6261 | 4.6261 |

To change price source for securities, use <FMPS>.
To change price source for swaps, use <XDF>.
Yields are based on STANDARD settlement and are Conventional
Australia 61 2 9777 8600       Brazil 5511 3048 4500       Europe 44 20 7330 7500       Germany 49 69 920410
Hong Kong 852 2977 6000 Japan 81 3 3201 8900 Singapore 65 6212 1000 U.S. 1 212 318 2000 Copyright 2006 Bloomberg L.P.
                                                                              3 04-Jul-06 10:30:31

**Figure 5.25**    US Treasury yield curve as at 3 July 2006.

## Historical Pattern

If we plot swap spreads over the period 1997–2006, we note that they tightened in the second half of this period. Figure 5.26 shows the spread for USD and GBP for the period 1997 to the first quarter of 2006. This reflects the bull market period of 2002–2006 when credit spreads fell in all markets.

During this period the widest spread for both currencies was reached during 2000, when the 10-year sterling swap spread peaked at around 140 bps above the gilt yield. The tightest spreads were reached during 2003, when the 10-year sterling spread reached around 15 bps towards the end of that year. At the beginning of 2006 sterling spreads were still lower than the 10-year average of 55 bps. This implies that the perceived risk premium for the sterling capital markets had fallen.

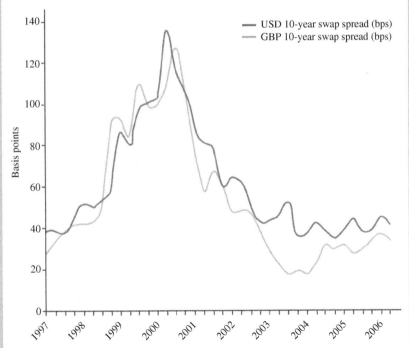

**Figure 5.26**   USD and GBP interest-rate swap spreads over government curve, 1997–2006.
Yield source: Bloomberg L.P.

The change in spread levels coincides with macro-level factors and occurrences. For instance, spreads moved in line with:

- the Asian currency crisis of 1997;
- the Russian government bond default and collapse of the Long Term Capital Management (LTCM) hedge fund in 1998;
- the "dot.com" crash in 2000;
- the subsequent loosening of monetary policy after the dot.com crash and the events of 9/11.

This indicates to us, if just superficially, that swap spreads react to macro-level factors that are perceived by the market to affect their business risk, credit risk and liquidity risk. Spreads also reflect supply and demand, as well as the absolute level of base interest rates.

## Determinants of the Spread

We have already noted that in theory the swap spread, representing inter-bank counterparty risk, should reflect only the market's perception of bank risk over and above government risk. Bank risk is captured in the Libor rate – the rate paid by banks on unsecured deposits to other banks. So in other words, the swap spread is meant to adequately compensate against the risk of bank default. (In fact, post-crash many banks fund at a rate above Libor, so Libor itself is less accurate a gauge of bank credit risk). The Libor rate is the floating-rate paid against the fixed rate in the swap transaction, and moves with the perception of bank risk. As we implied in the previous section though, it would appear that other factors influence the swap spread. We can illustrate this better by comparing the swap spread for 10-year quarterly paying swaps with the spread between 3-month Libor and the 3-month general collateral (GC) repo rate. The GC rate is the risk-free borrowing rate, whereas the Libor rate represents bank risk again. In theory, the spread between 3-month Libor and the GC rate should therefore move closely with the swap spread for quarterly resetting swaps, as both represent bank risk. A look at Figure 5.27 shows that this is not the case. Figure 5.27 compares the two spreads in the US dollar market, but we do not need to calculate the correlation or the $R_2$ for the two sets of numbers. Even on cursory visual observation we can see that the correlation is not high. Therefore we conclude that other factors, in addition to perceived bank default risk, drive one or both spreads. These other factors influence swap rates and government bond yields, and hence the swap spread, and we consider them below.

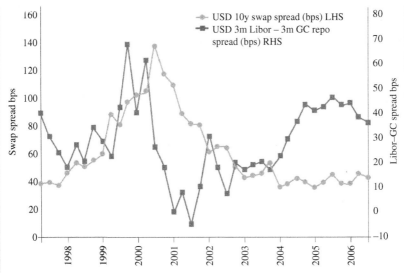

**Figure 5.27**  Comparison of USD 10-year swap spread and 3-month
Libor–GC repo spread.
Yield source: Bloomberg L.P.

## Level and Slope of the Swap Curve

The magnitude of the swap spread is influenced by the absolute level of
base interest rates. If the base rate is 10%, so that the government short-term
rate is around 10%, with longer term rates being recorded higher, the spread
tends to be greater than that seen if the base rate is 5%. The shape of the
yield curve has even greater influence. When the curve is positively sloping,
under the expectations hypothesis (see earlier in this chapter) investors will
expect future rates to be higher; hence, floating-rates are expected to rise.
This would suggest the swap spread will narrow. The opposite happens if
the yield curve inverts.

Figure 5.28 shows the GBP 10-year swap spread compared to the GBP
gilt yield curve spread (10-year gilt yield minus 2-year yield). We see that
the slope of the curve has influenced the swap spread; as the slope is narrowing, swap spreads are increasing and vice-versa.

## Supply and Demand

The swap spread is influenced greatly by supply and demand for swaps.
For example, greater trading volume in cash market instruments increases
the need for hedging instruments, which will widen swap spreads. The best
example of this is corporate bond issuance; as volumes increase, the need
for underwriters to hedge issues increases. However, greater bond issuance

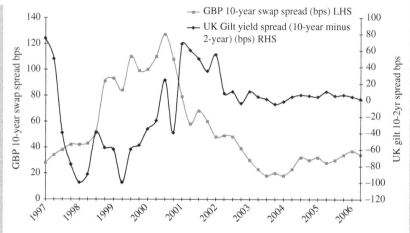

**Figure 5.28**    GBP swap spreads and gilt spreads compared 1997–2006.
Yield source: Bloomberg L.P.

also has another impact, as issuers seek to swap their fixed-rate liabilities to floating-rate. This also increases demand for swaps.

## Market Volatility
As suggested by Figure 5.26, swap spreads widen during times of market volatility. This may be in times of market uncertainty (for example, the future direction of base rates or possible inversion of the yield curve) or in times of market shock such as 9/11. In some respects spread widening during periods of volatility reflects the perception of increased bank default risk. It also reflects the "flight to quality" that occurs during times of volatility or market correction: this is the increased demand for risk-free assets such as government bonds that drives their yields lower and hence swap spreads wider.

## Government Borrowing
The level of government borrowing influences government bond yields, so perforce it will also impact swap spreads. If borrowing is viewed as being in danger of getting out of control, or the government runs persistently large budget deficits, government bond yields will rise. All else being equal, this will lead to narrowing swap spreads. We can see then that a number of factors influence swap spreads. An ALM or Treasury desk should be aware of these and assess them because the swap rate represents a key funding and hedging rate for a bank.

## Impact of Macro-level Economic and Political Factors on Swap Spreads

The Treasury or ALM desk of a bank must always have a keen understanding of macro-level economic factors, and the overall geo-political situation, because these factors also influence swap spreads. It is worth considering the impact of these factors, in general terms, on spreads and the overall level of interest rates because the ALM desk will need to take them into account as part of its strategy. Also, geo-political events often arrive unannounced – for example, the Iraqi invasion of Kuwait in 1990, the attack on the World Trade Centre in New York ("9/11"), and the conflict between Israel and Lebanese Hezbollah guerrillas in July 2006. An ability to work effectively under the circumstances prevailing in such occurrences is crucial to efficient ALM.

Events that impact the financial markets at a macro level are often termed market "shocks" or external geo-political events. Such events invariably result in higher market volatility. The immediate impact of this is a market sell-off and a "flight to quality", which is when investors move out of higher risk assets such as equities and emerging market sovereign bonds and into risk-free assets such as US Treasuries and UK gilts. This is an almost knee-jerk reaction as investors become more risk-averse.

Swap spreads reflect the market perception about the general health of the economy and its future prospects, as well as the overall macro-level geo-political situation. Because the swap curve is an indicator of inter-bank credit quality, the swap spread can be taken to be the market perception of the health and prospects of the inter-bank market specifically and the bank sector generally.

Speaking generally, swap spreads widen during periods of increased market volatility. By implication a flight-to-quality should be reflected in a widening of the spread. This is expected because investors' new risk aversion manifests itself in lower government bond yields, arising from higher demand for government bonds. However, on occasion this analysis might be overly simplistic, because other micro-level factors will still be in play and can be expected to influence market rates. How can we consider the interaction between government yields, swap rates and possible influences on the swap spread?

The research team at Lloyds Banking Group produced a report[31] that suggests a novel way for us to analyse this, and we summarise their findings here with permission. We require an indicator of market volatility; one measure of this for the US dollar market is the VIX index. The VIX index is produced by the Chicago Board Options Exchange (CBOE) and is a proxy measure of market volatility. It uses a weighted average of implied volatilities to calculate an estimate of future volatility. An increase in the level of the index indicates increased market volatility.

---

[31] "Geo-politics Returns to the Limelight", in *Economics Perspectives*, 8 August 2006 (Lloyds Banking Group). With thanks to Mark Miller for his generous assistance.

We illustrate the relationship between geo-political events and the magnitude of the swap spread by looking at the correlation between the US dollar 10-year swap spread and the VIX index. Table 5.9 shows – as expected – a positive correlation between the VIX index and the swap spread during a period of both economic events, as well as macro-level geopolitical events. For instance, the period covers the 9/11 events as well as the Ford and GM credit-rating downgrades of 2005. There is a notable exception for the period September 2001 to March 2002, when there is a negative correlation. This is our first indication that the relationship is not as simplistic as we might think. Although the geopolitical situation was negative, with the events of 9/11 leading to the US war in Afghanistan, suggesting that swap spreads should widen, this was also a period of successive cuts in the US base interest rate (the "Fed rate"). During this time the swap rate fell by more than 100 bps as the Fed rate was cut by 175 bps. So here we observe that the impact of specific financial market factors was greater than macro-level geo-political issues. Generally though, we observe the strong positive correlation between the swap spread the volatility index.

Figure 5.29 is a chart of the spread to the level of the VIX index.

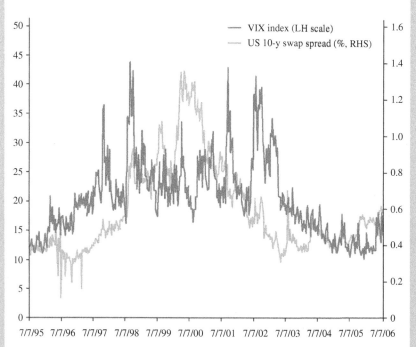

**Figure 5.29**    VIX index versus US 10-year swap spread.
*Source*: Lloyds Banking Group. Reproduced with permission.

| Event | Correlation between VIX and 10-year swap spread | Correlation between VIX and 10-year US Treasury yield |
|---|---|---|
| Asian currency crisis (1997–1998) | 0.71 | −0.52 |
| LTCM and Russian debt default (Jun.–Sept. 1998) | 0.90 | −0.78 |
| 9/11 to Afghan war (Sept. 2001–Mar. 2002) | −0.17 | −0.67 |
| Iraq War (Mar.–May 2003) | 0.54 | −0.08 |
| Ford and GM credit rating downgrade (Mar.–May 2005) | 0.38 | −0.53 |

**Table 5.9** Correlation between the USD 10-year swap spread, the CBOE VIX index, the 10-year US Treasury yield and the CBOE VIX index. *Source*: Lloyds Banking Group. Reproduced with permission.

By the same analysis, we can expect a negative correlation between the US Treasury yield and the VIX index level. This is generally borne out in Table 5.9. However, as with the case of the swap spread correlation, we see an occasion when other factors impact the correlation value. The low negative value for the period in 2003 leading up to, and after, the second Iraq war shows other factors influencing the Treasury yield. The flight-to-quality had taken place before the war actually began and was fully priced-in to Treasury yields.

Figure 5.30 illustrates the lower government bond yields that are observed at times of higher market volatility.

The purpose of the foregoing has been to illustrate how the swap spread interacts with macro-level geo-political factors. However, even during periods of high market tension, characterised by high levels of market volatility, the swap spread will respond also to more micro-level financial factors. ALM practitioners need to be aware of the nature of this interaction, and allow for this in their strategy and planning.

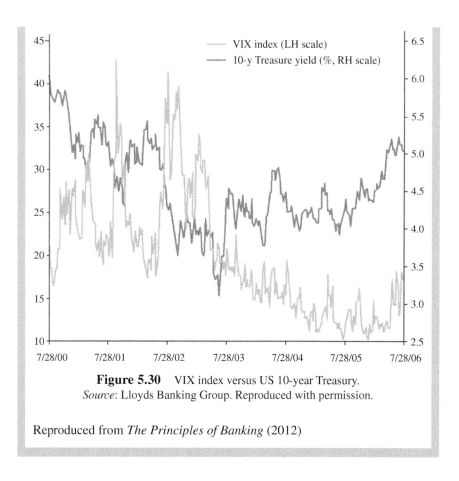

**Figure 5.30** VIX index versus US 10-year Treasury.
*Source*: Lloyds Banking Group. Reproduced with permission.

Reproduced from *The Principles of Banking* (2012)

This extract from *Analysing and Interpreting the Yield Curve* (2004)

## Interest Rate Modeling: The Dynamic of Asset Prices

## Interest Rate Modeling Part II: The Dynamic of Asset Prices

The pricing of derivative instruments such as options is a function of the movement in the price of the underlying asset over the lifetime of the option, and valuation models describe an environment where the price of an option is related to the behavior process of the variables that drive asset prices. This process is described as a *stochastic* process, and pricing models describe the stochastic dynamics of asset price changes, whether this is a change in share prices, interest rates, foreign exchange rates or bond prices. To understand the mechanics of interest rate modeling therefore, we must familiarize ourselves with the behavior of functions of *stochastic variables*. The concept of a stochastic process is a vital concept in finance theory. It describes random phenomena that evolve over time, and these include asset prices. For this reason an alternative title for this chapter could be *An Introduction to Stochastic Processes*.

This is a text on bonds after all, not mathematics, and it is outside the scope of this book comprehensively to derive and prove the main components of dynamic asset pricing theory. There are a number of excellent textbooks that the reader is encouraged to read which provide the necessary detail, in particular Ingersoll (1987), Baxter and Rennie (1996), Neftci (1996) and James and Webber (2000). Another recommended text that deals with probability models in general, as well as their application in derivatives pricing, is Ross (2000). In this chapter, we review the basic principles of the dynamics of asset prices, which are then put into context in the following chapters, which look at term structure models.

## The Behavior of Asset Prices

The first property that asset prices, which can be taken to include interest rates, are assumed to follow is that they are part of a *continuous* process. This means that the value of any asset can and does change at any time and from one point in time to another, and can assume any fraction of a unit of measurement. It is also assumed to pass through every value as it changes, so for example if the price of a bond moves from 92.00 to 94.00, it must also have passed through every point in between. This feature means that the asset price does not exhibit *jumps*, which is not the case in many markets, where price processes do exhibit jump behavior. For now however, we may assume that the price process is continuous.

## Stochastic Processes

Models that seek to value options or describe a yield curve also describe the dynamics of asset price changes. The same process is said to apply to changes in share prices, bond prices, interest rates and exchange rates. The process by which prices and interest rates evolve over time is known as a *stochastic process*, and this is a fundamental concept in finance theory.[1] Essentially a stochastic process is a time series of random variables. Generally the random variables in a stochastic process are related in a non-random manner, and so therefore we can capture in a *probability density function*. A good introduction is given in Neftci (1996), and following his approach, we very briefly summarize the main features here.

Consider the function $y = f(x)$. Given the value of $x$, we can obtain the value of $y$. If we denote the set $W$ as the state of the world, where $w \in W$,

---

[1] A formal definition of a stochastic process is given in Appendix 5.1.

the function $f(x, w)$ has the property that given a value $w \in W$, it becomes a function of $x$ only. If we say that $x$ represents the passage of time, two functions $f(x, w_1)$ and $f(x, w_2)$ will be different because the second element $w$ in each case is different. With $x$ representing time, these two functions describe two different processes that are dependent on different states of the world $W$. The element $w$ represents an underlying random process, and so therefore the function $f(x, w)$ is a *random function*. A random function is also called a *stochastic process*, one in which $x$ represents time and $x \geq 0$. The random characteristic of the process refers to the entire process, and not any particular value in that process at any particular point in time.

Examples of functions include the *exponential* function denoted by $y = e^x$ and the *logarithmic* function $\log_e(y) = x$.

The price processes of shares and bonds, as well as interest rate processes, are stochastic processes. That is, they exhibit a random change over time. For the purposes of modeling, the change in asset prices is divided into two components. These are the *drift* of the process, which is a *deterministic* element,[2] also called the mean, and the random component known as the *noise*, also called the volatility of the process.

We introduce the drift component briefly as follows. For an asset such as an ordinary share, which is expected to rise over time (at least in line with assumed growth in inflation), the drift can be modeled as a geometric growth progression. If the price process has no "noise", the change in price of the stock from over the time period d$t$ can be given by:

$$\frac{dS_t}{dt} = \mu S_t \qquad (5.1)$$

where the term $\mu$ describes the growth rate. Expression (5.1) can be rewritten in the form:

$$dS_t = \mu S_t dt \qquad (5.2)$$

which can also be written in integral form. For interest rates, the movement process can be described in similar fashion, although as we shall see interest rate modeling often takes into account the tendency for rates to return to a mean level or range of levels, a process known as *mean reversion*. Without providing the derivation here, the equivalent expression for interest rates takes the form

$$dr_t = \alpha \left( \mu - r_t \right) dt \qquad (5.3)$$

---

[2] There are two types of model: *deterministic*, which involves no randomness so the variables are determined exactly, and *stochastic*, which incorporates the random nature of the variables into the model.

where $\alpha$ is the mean reversion rate that determines the pace at which the interest rate reverts to its mean level. If the initial interest rate is less than the drift rate, the rate $r$ will increase, while if the level is above the drift rate it will tend to decrease.

For the purposes of employing option pricing models, the dynamic behavior of asset prices are usually described as a function of what is known as a *Weiner process*, which is also known as *Brownian motion*. The noise or volatility component is described by an *adapted* Brownian or Weiner process, and involves introducing a random increment to the standard random process. This is described next.

## Weiner process or Brownian motion

The stochastic process we have briefly discussed above is known as Brownian motion or a Weiner process. In fact, a Weiner process is only a process that has a mean of 0 and a variance of 1, but it is common to see these terms used synonymously. Weiner processes are a very important part of continuous-time finance theory, and interested readers can obtain more detailed and technical data on the subject in Neftci (1996) and Duffie (1996)[3] among others. It is a well-researched subject.

One of the properties of a Weiner process is that the sample pathway is continuous, that is, there are no *discontinuous* changes. An example of a discontinuous process is the Poisson process. Both are illustrated in Figures 5.1 and 5.2 below.

In the examples illustrated, both processes have an expected change of 0 and a variance of 1 per unit of time. There are no discontinuities in the Weiner process, which is a plot of many tiny random changes. This is reflected in the "fuzzy" nature of the sample path. However the Poisson process has no fuzzy quality and appears to have a much smaller number of random changes. We can conclude that asset prices, and the dynamics of interest rates, are more akin to a Weiner process. This, therefore, is how asset prices are modeled. From observation we know that, in reality asset prices and interest rates do exhibit discontinuities or *jumps*, however, there are other advantages in assuming a Weiner process, and in practice because continuous-time stochastic processes can be captured as a combination of Brownian motion and a Poisson process, analysts and researchers use the former as the basis of financial valuation models.

The first step in asset pricing theory builds on the assumption that prices follow a Brownian motion. The properties of Brownian motion $W$ state that it is continuous, and the value of $W_t(t > 0)$ is normally distributed

---

[3] Duffie's text requires a very good grounding in continuous-time mathematics.

**Figure 5.1**   An example of a Weiner process.

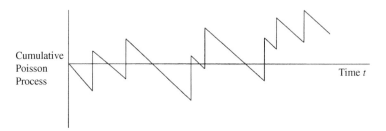

**Figure 5.2**   An example of a Poisson process.

under a probability measure $P$ as a *random* variable with parameters $N(0, t)$. An incremental change in the asset value over time $dt$, which is a very small or *infinitesimal* change in the time, given by $W_{s+t} - W_s$, is also normally distributed with the parameters $N(0, t)$ under $P$. Perhaps the most significant feature is that the change in value is independent of whatever the history of the price process has been up to time $s$. If a process follows these conditions, it is Brownian motion. In fact, asset prices do not generally have a mean of 0, because over time we expect them to rise. Therefore modeling asset prices incorporates a *drift* measure that better reflects asset price movement, so that an asset movement described by:

$$S_t = W_t + \mu t \tag{5.4}$$

would be a Brownian motion with a drift given by the constant $\mu$. A second parameter is then added, a *noise* factor, which scales the Brownian motion by another constant measure, the standard deviation $\sigma$. The process is then described by:

$$S_t = \sigma W_t + \mu t \tag{5.5}$$

which can be used to *simulate* the price path taken by an asset, as long as we specify the two parameters. An excellent and readable account of this is given in Baxter and Rennie (1996, Chapter 3), who also state that under (5.5) there is a possibility of achieving negative values, which is not realistic for asset prices. However, using the exponential of the process given by (5.5) is more accurate, and is given by (5.6):

$$S_t = \exp(\sigma W_t + \mu t). \tag{5.6}$$

Brownian motion or the *Weiner process* is employed by virtually all option pricing models, and we introduce it here with respect to a change in the variable $W$ over an interval of time $t$. If $W$ represents a variable following a Weiner process and $\Delta W$ is a change in value over a period of time $t$, the relationship between $\Delta W$ and $\Delta t$ is given by (5.7):

$$\Delta W = \varepsilon \sqrt{\Delta t} \tag{5.7}$$

where $\varepsilon$ is a random sample from a normal distribution with a mean 0 and a standard deviation of 1. Over a short period of time the values of $\Delta W$ are independent and therefore also follow a normal distribution with a mean 0 and a standard deviation of $\sqrt{\Delta t}$. Over a longer time period $T$ made up of $N$ periods of length $\Delta t$ the change in $W$ over the period from time 0 to time $T$ is give by (5.8):

$$W(T) - W(0) = \sum_{i=1}^{N} \varepsilon_i \sqrt{\Delta t} \tag{5.8}$$

The successive values assumed by $W$ are serially independent, therefore from (5.8) we conclude that changes in the variable $W$ from time 0 to time $T$ follow a normal distribution with mean 0 and a standard deviation of $\sqrt{T}$. This describes the Weiner process, with a mean of zero or a zero drift rate and a variance of $T$. This is an important result because a zero drift rate implies that the change in the variable (in this case, the asset price) in the future is equal to the current change. This means that there is an equal chance of an asset return ending up 10% or down 10% over a long period of time.

The next step in the analysis involves using stochastic calculus. Without going into this field here, we summarize from Baxter and Rennie (1996) and state that a stochastic process $X$ incorporates a *Newtonian* term that is based on d$t$ and a Brownian term based on the infinitesimal increment of $W$ that is denoted by $dW_t$. The Brownian term has a "noise" factor of $\alpha_t$. The infinitesimal change of $X$ at $X_t$ is given by the differential equation:

$$dX_t = \sigma_t dW_t + \mu_t dt \tag{5.9}$$

where $\sigma_t$ is the *volatility* of the process $X$ at time $t$ and $\mu_t$ is the drift of $X$ at time $t$. For interest rates that are modeled on the basis of mean reversion, the process is given by:

$$dr_t = \sigma_t dW_t + \alpha \left( u_t + r_t \right) dt \tag{5.10}$$

where the mean reverting element is as before. Without providing the supporting mathematics, which we have not covered here, the process described by (5.10) is called an Ornstein–Uhlenbeck process, and has been assumed by a number of interest rate models.

One other important point to introduce here is that a random process described by (5.10) operates in a continuous environment. In continuous-time mathematics the *integral* is the tool that is used to denote the sum of an infinite number of objects, that is where the number of objects is *uncountable*. A formal definition of the integral is outside the scope of this book, but accessible accounts can be found in the texts referred to previously. A basic introduction is given at Appendix 5.4. However the continuous stochastic process $X$ described by (5.9) can be written as an integral equation in the form:

$$X_t = X_0 + \int_0^t \sigma_s dW_s + \int_0^t \mu_s ds \tag{5.11}$$

where $\sigma$ and $\mu$ are processes as before. The volatility and drift terms can be dependent on the time $t$ but can also be dependent on $X$ or $W$ up to the point $t$. This is a complex technical subject and readers are encouraged to review the main elements in the referred texts.

## The distribution of the risk-free interest rate

The continuously compounded rate of return is an important component of option pricing theory. If $r$ is the continuously compounded rate of return, we can use the lognormal property to determine the distribution that this follows. At a future date $T$, the asset price $S$ may be written as (5.2):

$$S_T = S_t e^{r(T-t)} \tag{5.21}$$

and
$$r = \frac{1}{T-t} \ln \left( \frac{S_T}{S_t} \right)$$

Using the lognormal property we can describe the distribution of the risk-free rate as:

$$r \sim N\left( (\mu - \tfrac{1}{2}\sigma^2), \frac{\sigma}{\sqrt{T-t}} \right). \tag{5.22}$$

# Stochastic Calculus Models: Brownian Motion and Itô Calculus

We noted at the start of the chapter that the price of an option is a function of the price of the underlying stock and its behavior over the life of the option. Therefore, this option price is determined by the variables that describe the process followed by the asset price over a continuous period of time. The behavior that asset prices follow is a stochastic process, and so option pricing models—and term structure models—must capture the behavior of stochastic variables behind the movement of asset prices. To accurately describe financial market processes, a financial model depends on more than one variable. Generally, a model is constructed where a function is itself a function of more than one variable. Itô's lemma, the principal instrument in continuous time finance theory, is used to differentiate such functions. This was developed by a mathematician, K. Itô, in 1951. Here we simply state the theorem, as a proof and derivation are outside the scope of the book. Interested readers may wish to consult Brys *et al.* (1998), and Hull (1997) for a background on Itô's lemma. We also recommend Neftci (1996). Basic background on Itô's lemma is given in Appendices 5.2 and 5.3.

## Brownian motion

Brownian motion is very similar to a Weiner process, which is why it is common to see the terms used interchangeably. Note that the properties of a Weiner process requires that it be a martingale, while no such constraint is required for a Brownian process. A mathematical property known as the *Lévy theorem* allows us to consider any Weiner process $W_t$ with respect to an information set $F_t$ as a Brownian motion $Z_t$ with respect to the same information set.

We can view Brownian motion as a continuous time *random walk*, visualized as a walk along a line, beginning at $X_0 = 0$ and moving at each incremental time interval $dt$ either up or down by an amount $\sqrt{dt}$. If we denote the position of the walk as $X_n$ after the $n$th move, the position would be:

$$X_n = X_{n-1} \pm \sqrt{dt} \qquad n = 1,2,3\ldots \qquad (5.23)$$

where the + and − signs occur with an equal probability of 0.5. This is a simple random walk. We can transform this into a continuous path by applying linear interpolation between each move point, so that:

$$\bar{X}_t = X_n + (t - ndt)\cdot(X_{n+1} - X_n), \qquad ndt \le t \le (n+1)dt \qquad (5.24)$$

It can be shown (but not here) that the path described at (5.24) has a number of properties, including that the incremental change in value each time it moves is independent of the behavior leading up to the move, and that the mean value is 0 and variance is finite. The mean and variance of the set of moves is independent of $dt$.

What is the importance of this? Essentially this—the probability distribution of the motion can be shown, as $dt$ approaches 0, to be normal or *Gaussian*.

## Stochastic calculus

Ito's theorem provides an analytical formula that simplifies the treatment of stochastic differential equations, which is why it is so valuable. It is an important rule in the application of stochastic calculus to the pricing of financial instruments. Here we briefly describe the power of the theorem.

The standard stochastic differential equation for the process of an asset price $S_t$ is given in the form:

$$dS_t = a\left(S_t, t\right)dt + b\left(S_t, t\right)dW_t \qquad (5.25)$$

where $a(S_t, t)$ is the drift coefficient and $b(S_t, t)$ is the volatility or *diffusion* coefficient. The Weiner process is denoted $dW_t$ and is the unpredictable events that occur at time intervals $dt$. This is sometimes denoted $dZ$ or $dz$.

Consider a function $f(S_t, t)$ dependent on two variables $S$ and $t$, where $S$ follows a random process and varies with $t$. If $S_t$ is a continuous-time process that follows a Weiner process $W_t$, then it directly influences the function $f(\ )$ through the variable $t$ in $f(S_t, t)$. Over time, we observe new information about $W_t$ as well the movement in $S$ over each time increment, given by $dS_t$. The sum of both these effects represents the *stochastic differential* and is given by the stochastic equivalent of the chain rule known as *Itô's lemma*. So for example, if the price of a stock is 30 and an incremental time period later is 30.5, the differential is 0.5.

If we apply a Taylor expansion in two variables to the function $f(S_t, t)$ we obtain:

$$df_t = \frac{\partial f}{\partial S_t}dS_t + \frac{\partial f}{\partial t}dt + \frac{1}{2}\frac{\partial^2 f}{\partial S_t^2}b_t^2 dt \qquad (5.26)$$

Remember that $\partial t$ is the partial derivative while $dt$ is the derivative.

If we substitute the stochastic differential equation (5.25) for $S_t$, we obtain *Itô's lemma* of the form:

$$df_t = \left(\frac{\partial f}{\partial S_t}a_t + \frac{\partial f}{\partial t} + \frac{1}{2}\frac{\partial^2 f}{\partial S_t^2}b_t^2\right)dt + \frac{\partial^2 f}{\partial S_t}b_t dW_t. \qquad (5.27)$$

What we have done is taken the stochastic differential equation ("SDE") for $S_t$ and transformed it so that we can determine the SDE for $f_t$. This is a valuable mechanism by which we can obtain an expression for pricing derivatives that are written on an underlying asset whose price can be determined using conventional analysis. In other words, using Ito's formula enables us to determine the SDE for the derivative, once we have set up the SDE for the underlying asset. This is the value of Itô's lemma.

The SDE for the underlying asset $S_t$ is written in most textbooks in the following form:

$$dS_t = \mu S_t dt + \sigma S_t dW_t \qquad (5.28)$$

which has denoted the drift term $a(S_t, t)$ as $\mu S_t$ and the diffusion term $(S_t, t)$ as $\sigma S_t$. In the same way, Itô's lemma is usually seen in the form:

$$dF_t = \left[ \frac{\partial F}{\partial S_t} \mu S_t + \frac{\partial F}{\partial t} + \frac{1}{2} \frac{\partial^2 F}{\partial S_t^2} \sigma^2 S_t^2 \right] dt + \frac{\partial F}{\partial S_t} \sigma S_t dW_t \qquad (5.29)$$

although the noise term is sometime denoted $dZ$. Further applications are illustrated in Example 5.2(i).

---

**EXAMPLE 5.2(i)**　**Lognormal distribution**

A variable (such as an asset price) may be assumed to have a *lognormal distribution* if the natural logarithm of the variable is normally distributed. Therefore, if an asset price $S$ follows a stochastic process described by:

$$dS_t = \mu(Sdt) + \sigma SdW \qquad (5.30)$$

how would we determine the expression for $\ln S$? This can be achieved using Itô's lemma.

If we say that $F = \ln S$, then the first derivative:

$\dfrac{dF}{dS} = \dfrac{1}{S}$ and as there is no $t$ we have $\dfrac{dF}{dt} = 0$.

The second derivative is $\dfrac{d^2 F}{dS^2} = \dfrac{-1}{S^2}$.

We substitute these values into Itô's lemma given at (5.29) and this gives us:

$$d \ln S = \left( \mu - \frac{\sigma^2}{2} \right) dt + \sigma \, dW. \tag{5.31}$$

So we have moved from $dF$ to $dS$ using Itô's lemma, and (5.31) is a good representation of the asset price over time.

**EXAMPLE 5.2(ii)**    **The bond price equation**

The continuously compounded gross redemption yield at time $t$ on a default-free zero-coupon bond that pays £1 at maturity date $T$ is $x$. We assume that the movement in $x$ is described by:

$$dx = a(\alpha - x) dt + sxdZ$$

where $a$, $\alpha$ and $s$ are positive constants. What is the expression for the process followed by the price $P$ of the bond? Let us say that the price of the bond is given by:

$$P = e^{-x(T-t)}.$$

We have $dx$, and we require $dP$. This is done by applying Itô's lemma. We require:

$$\frac{\partial P}{\partial x} = -(T-t)e^{-x(T-t)} = -(T-t)P$$

$$\frac{\partial^2 P}{\partial x^2} = -(T-t)e^{-x(T-t)} = -(T-t)^2 P$$

$$\frac{\partial P}{\partial t} = xe^{-x(T-t)} = xP$$

From Itô's lemma:

$$dP = \left[ \frac{\partial P}{\partial x} a(\alpha - x) + \frac{\partial P}{\partial t} + \frac{1}{2} \frac{\partial^2 P}{\partial x^2} s^2 x^2 \right] dt + \frac{\partial P}{\partial x} sxdZ$$

which gives:

$$dP = \left[ -(T-t)Pa(\alpha - x) + xP + \tfrac{1}{2}(T-t)^2 Ps^2 x^2 \right] dt$$
$$-(T-t)PsxdZ$$

which simplifies to:

$$dP = [-a(\alpha - x)(T-t) + x + \tfrac{1}{2}s^2 x^2 (T-t)^2] Pdt - sx(T-t) PdZ$$

Therefore, using Itô's lemma we have transformed the SDE for the bond yield into an expression for the bond price.

## Stochastic integrals

Whilst in no way wishing to trivialize the mathematical level, we will not consider the derivations here, but simply state that the observed values of the Brownian motion up to the point at time $t$ determine the process immediately after, and that this process is Gaussian. Stochastic integrals are continuous path martingales. As described in Neftci (1996), the integral is used to calculate sums where we have an infinite or uncountable number of items, in contrast with the $\Sigma$ sum operator, which is used for a finite number of objects. In defining integrals, we begin with an approximation, where there is a countable number of items, and then set a limit and move to an uncountable number. A basic definition is given in Appendix 5.4. Stochastic integration is an operation that is closely associated with Brownian paths—a path is partitioned into consecutive intervals or increments, and each increment is multiplied by a random variable. These values are then summed to create the stochastic integral. Therefore, the stochastic integral can be viewed as a random walk Brownian motion with increments that have varying values, a random walk with non-homogeneous movement.

## Generalized Itô formula

It is possible to generalize Itô's formula in order to produce a multidimensional formula, which can then be used to construct a model to price interest rate derivatives or other asset class options where there is more than one variable. To do this, we generalize the formula to apply to situations where the dynamic function $f(.)$ is dependent on more than one Itô process, each expressed as standard Brownian motions.

Consider $W_T = \left( W_t^1, \ldots, W_T^n \right)$ where $\left( W_T^t \right)_{t \geq 0}$ are independent standard Brownian motions and $W_T$ is an $n$-dimensional Brownian motion. We can express Itô's formula mathematically with respect to $p$ Itô processes $\left( X_t^1, \ldots, X_T^p \right)$ as:

$$X_T^i = X_0^i + \int_0^t K_s^i ds + \sum_{i=1}^N \int_0^t H_s^{ij} dX_s^i.$$

(5.32)

Where the function $f(.)$ contains second-order partial derivatives with respect to $x$ and first-order partial derivatives with respect to $t$, which are a continuous function in $(x, t)$, the generalized Itô formula is given by:

$$
\begin{aligned}
f\left(t, X_t^1, \ldots, X_T^p\right) &= f\left(0, X_0^1, \ldots, X_0^p\right) + \int_0^t \left( \frac{\partial f}{\partial s} \right)\left(s, X_s^1, \ldots, X_s^p\right) ds \\
&+ \sum_{i=1}^p \int_0^t \left( \frac{\partial f}{\partial x_i} \right)\left(s, X_s^1, \ldots, X_s^p\right) dX_s^i \\
&+ \frac{1}{2} \sum_{i,j=1}^p \int_0^t \left( \frac{\partial^2 f}{\partial x_i \partial x_j} \right)\left(s, X_s^1, \ldots, X_s^p\right) d\left(X^i, X^j\right)_s
\end{aligned}
$$

(5.33)

with:

$$
\begin{aligned}
dX_s^i &= K_s^i ds + \sum_{j=1}^n H_s^{im} dW_s^j \\
d\left(X^i, X^j\right)s &= \sum_{m=1}^n H_s^{im} H_s^{jm} ds.
\end{aligned}
$$

(5.34)

Reproduced from *Analysing and Interpreting the Yield Curve* (2004)

**This extract from *Analysing and Interpreting the Yield Curve* (2004)**

## Yield Curves and Relative Value

### Yield Curves and Relative Value

Bond market participants take a keen interest in both cash and zero-coupon (spot) yield curves. In markets where an active zero-coupon bond market exists, much analysis is undertaken into the relative spreads between derived and actual zero-coupon yields. In this chapter we review some of the yield curve analysis used in the market, with respect to bonds that are default-free, such as US and UK government bonds. We then look at specific case study examples in the next (and final) chapter.

## The Determinants of Government Bond Yields

Market-makers in government bond markets analyze various factors in the market in deciding how to run their book. Customer business apart, decisions to purchase or sell securities is a function of their views on:

- market direction itself, that is the direction in which short-term and long-term interest rates are headed;
- which maturity point along the entire term structure offers the best value;
- which specific issue within a particular maturity point offers the best value.

All three areas are related but react differently to certain pieces of information. A report on the projected size of the government's budget deficit for example, will not have much effect on two-year bond yields, whereas if the expectations come as a surprise to the market it may have an adverse effect on long-bond yields. The starting point for analysis is the yield curve, both the traditional coupon curve plotted against duration and the zero-coupon curve. Figure 12.1 illustrates the traditional yield curve for gilts in October 1999.

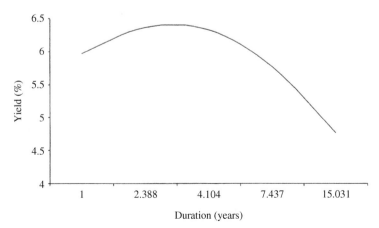

**Figure 12.1**  Yield and duration of gilts, 21 October 1999.
*Source*: Bloomberg.

For a first-level analysis, many market practitioners go no further than Figure 12.1. An investor who has no particular view on the future shape of the yield curve or the level of interest rates may well adopt a neutral outlook and hold bonds that have a duration that matches their investment horizon. If they believe interest rates are likely to remain stable for a time, they might hold bonds with a longer duration in a positively-sloping yield curve environment, and pick up additional yield but with higher interest rate risk. Once the decision has been made on which part of the yield curve to invest in or switch in to, the investor must decide on the specific securities to hold, which then brings us on to relative value analysis. For this, the investor analyzes specific sectors of the curve, looking at individual stocks. This is sometimes called looking at the "local" part of the curve.

An assessment of a local part of the yield curve includes looking at other features of individual stocks in addition to their duration. This recognizes that the yield of a specific bond is not only a function of its duration, and that two bonds with near-identical duration can have different yields. The other determinants of yield are liquidity of the bond and its coupon. To illustrate the effect of coupon on yield, let us consider Table 12.1. This shows that, where the duration of a bond is held roughly constant, a change in coupon of a bond can have a significant effect on the bond's yield.

In the case of the long bond, an investor could, under this scenario, both shorten duration and pick up yield, which is not the first thing that an investor might expect. However, an anomaly of the markets is that, liquidity issues aside, the market does not generally like high coupon bonds, so they usually trade cheap to the curve.

The other factors affecting yield are supply and demand, and liquidity. A shortage of supply of stock at a particular point in the curve has the affect of depressing yields at that point. A reducing public sector deficit is the main reason why such a supply shortage might exist. In addition, as interest rates decline, for example, ahead of or during a recession, the stock of high coupon bonds increases, as the newer bonds are issued at lower levels,

| Coupon | Maturity | Duration | Yield |
|--------|----------|----------|-------|
| 8% | 20-Feb-02 | 1.927 | 5.75% |
| 12% | 5-Feb-02 | 1.911 | 5.80% |
| 10% | 20-Jun-10 | 7.134 | 4.95% |
| 6% | 1-Jul-10 | 7.867 | 4.77% |

**Table 12.1**    Duration and yield comparisons for bonds in a hypothetical inverted curve environment, October 1999.

and these "outdated" issues can end up trading at a higher yield. Demand factors are driven primarily by the investor's views of the country's economic prospects, but also by government legislation, for example the Minimum Funding Requirement in the UK compelled pension funds to hold a set minimum amount of their funds in long-dated gilts, which had the effect of permanently keeping demand high.[1]

Liquidity often results in one bond having a higher yield than other, despite both having similar durations. Institutional investors prefer to hold the benchmark bond, which is the current two-year, five-year, ten-year or thirty-year bond and this depresses the yield on the benchmark bond. A bond that is liquid also has a higher demand, thus a lower yield, because it is easier to convert into cash if required. This can be demonstrated by valuing the cash flows on a six-month bond with the rates obtainable in the Treasury bill market. We could value the six-month cash flows at the six-month bill rate. The lowest obtainable yield in virtually every market[2] is the T-bill yield, therefore valuing a six-month bond at the T-bill rate will produce a discrepancy between the observed price of the bond and its theoretical price implied by the T-bill rate, because the observed price will be lower. The reason for this is simple, because the T-bill is more readily realizable into cash at any time, it trades at a lower yield than the bond, even though the cash flows fall on the same day.

We have therefore determined that a bond's coupon and liquidity level, as well as its duration, will affect the yield at which it trades. These factors can be used in conjunction with other areas of analysis, which we look at next, when deciding which bonds carry relative value over others.

## Characterizing the complete term structure

As many readers would have concluded, the yield versus duration curve illustrated in Figure 12.1 is an ineffective technique with which to analyze the market.

This is because it does not highlight any characteristics of the yield curve other than its general shape and this does not assist in the making of trading decisions. To facilitate a more complete picture, we may wish to employ the technique described here. Figure 12.2 shows the bond par yield curve[3] and T-bill yield curve for gilts in October 1999. Figure 12.3 shows the difference between the yield on a bond with a coupon that is 100 basis points below the par yield level, and the yield on a par bond. The other curve

---

[1] The requirements of the MFR were removed in 2002.
[2] The author is not aware of any market where there is a yield lower than its shortest-maturity T-bill yield, but that does not mean such a market doesn't exist!
[3] See Chapter 2 for a discussion of the par yield curve.

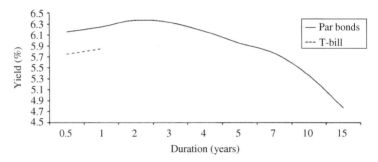

**Figure 12.2**   T-bill and par yield curve, October 1999.

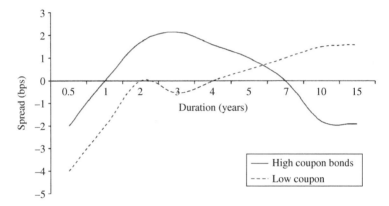

**Figure 12.3**   Structure of bond yields, October 1999.

in Figure 12.3 shows the level for a bond with a coupon that is 100 basis points above the par yield. These two curves show the "low coupon" and "high coupon" yield spreads. Using the two figures together, an investor can see the impact of coupons, the shape of the curve and the effect of yield on different maturity points of the curve.

## Identifying relative value in government bonds

Constructing a zero-coupon yield curve provides the framework within which a market participant can analyze individual securities. In a government bond market, there is no credit risk consideration (unless it is an emerging market government market), and therefore no credit spreads to consider. There are a number of factors that can be assessed in an attempt to identify relative value.

The objective of much of the analysis that occurs in bond markets is to identify value, and identify which individual securities should be purchased and which should be sold. At the overview level, this identification is a function of whether one thinks interest rates are going to rise or fall. At the local level though, the analysis is more concerned with a specific sector of the yield curve, whether this will flatten or steepen, whether bonds of similar duration are trading at enough of a spread to warrant switching from one into another. The difference in these approaches is one of identifying which stocks have absolute value, and which have relative value. A trade decision based on the expected direction of interest rates is based on assessing absolute value, whether interest rates themselves are too low or too high. Yield curve analysis is more a matter of assessing relative value. On (very!) rare occasions, this process is fairly straightforward, for example if the three-year bond is trading at 5.75% when two-year yields are 5.70% and four-year yields are at 6.15%, the three-year appears to be overpriced. However, this is not really a real-life situation. Instead, a trader might assess the relative value of the three-year bond compared to much shorter- or longer-dated instruments. That said, there is considerable difference between comparing a short-dated bond to other short-term securities and comparing say, the two-year bond to the thirty-year bond. Although it looks like it on paper, the space along the x-axis should not be taken to imply that the smooth link between one-year and five-year bonds is repeated from the five-year out to the thirty-year bonds. It is also common for the very short-dated sector of the yield curve to behave independently of the long end.

One method used to identify relative value is to quantify the coupon effect on the yields of bonds. The relationship between yield and coupon is given by (12.1):

$$rm = rm_P + c \cdot \max\left(C_{PD} - rm_P, 0\right) + d \cdot \min\left(C_{PD} - rm_P, 0\right) \quad (12.1)$$

where;    $rm$    is the yield on the bond being analyzed;
              $rm_P$    is the yield on a par bond of specified duration;
              $C_{PD}$    is the coupon on an arbitrary bond of similar duration to the part bond.

and $c$ and $d$ are coefficients. The coefficient $c$ reflects the effect of a high coupon on the yield of a bond. If we consider a case where the coupon rate exceeds the yield on the similar-duration par bond ($C_{PD} > rm_P$), (12.1) reduces to (12.2):

$$rm = rm_P + c \ \left(C_{PD} - rm_P\right) \quad (12.2)$$

Equation (12.2) specifies the spread between the yield on a high coupon bond and the yield on a par bond as a linear function of the spread between the first bond's coupon and the yield and coupon of the par bond. In reality this relationship may not be purely linear, for instance the yield spread may widen at a decreasing rate for higher coupon differences. Therefore (12.2) is an approximation of the effect of a high coupon on yield where the approximation is more appropriate for bonds trading close to par. The same analysis can be applied to bonds with coupons lower than the same-duration par bond.

The value of a bond may be measured against comparable securities or against the par or zero-coupon yield curve. In certain instances the first measure may be more appropriate when for instance, a low coupon bond is priced expensive to the curve itself but fair compared to other low coupon bonds. In that case, the overpricing indicated by the par yield curve may not represent unusual value, rather a valuation phenomenon that is shared by all low coupon bonds. Having examined the local structure of a yield curve, the analysis can be extended to the comparative valuation of a group of similar bonds. This is an important part of the analysis, because it is particularly informative to know the cheapness or dearness of a single stock compared to the whole yield curve, which might be somewhat abstract. Instead we may seek to identify two or more bonds, one of which is cheap and the other dear, so that we might carry out an outright switch between the two, or put on a spread trade between them. Using the technique we can identify excess positive or negative yield spread for all the bonds in the term structure. This has been carried out for our five gilts, together with other less liquid issues as at October 1999 and the results are summarized in Table 12.2.

| Coupon | Maturity | Duration | Yield % | Excess yield spread (bp) |
|--------|----------|----------|---------|--------------------------|
| 8% | 07/12/2000 | 1.072 | 5.972 | −1.55 |
| 10% | 26/02/2001 | 1.2601 | 6.051 | 4.5 |
| 7% | 07/06/2002 | 2.388 | 6.367 | −1.8 |
| 5% | 07/06/2004 | 4.104 | 6.327 | −3.8 |
| 6.75% | 26/11/2004 | 4.233 | 6.351 | 2.7 |
| 5.75% | 07/12/2009 | 7.437 | 5.77 | −4.7 |
| 6.25% | 25/11/2010 | 7.957 | 5.72 | 1.08 |
| 6% | 07/12/2028 | 15.031 | 4.77 | −8.7 |

**Table 12.2**   Yields and excess yield spreads for selected gilts, 22 October 1999.

| Coupon | Maturity | Duration | Yield % | Price | BPV |
|--------|----------|----------|---------|-------|-----|
| 8% | 07/12/2000 | 1.072 | 5.972 | 102.17 | 0.01095 |
| 10% | 26/02/2001 | 1.2601 | 6.051 | 105.01 | 0.01880 |
| 7% | 07/06/2002 | 2.388 | 6.367 | 101.5 | 0.02410 |
| 5% | 07/06/2004 | 4.104 | 6.327 | 94.74 | 0.03835 |
| 6.75% | 26/11/2004 | 4.233 | 6.351 | 101.71 | 0.03980 |
| 5.75% | 07/12/2009 | 7.437 | 5.77 | 99.84 | 0.07584 |
| 6.25% | 25/11/2010 | 7.957 | 5.72 | 104.3 | 0.07526 |
| 6% | 07/12/2028 | 15.031 | 4.77 | 119.25 | 0.17834 |

**Table 12.2**   Bond basis point value, 22 October 1999.

From Table 12.2 as we might expect the benchmark securities are all expensive to the par curve, and the less liquid bonds are cheap. Note that the 6.25% 2010 appears cheap to the curve, but the 5.75% 2009 offers a yield pick-up for what is a shorter-duration stock—this is a curious anomaly and one that disappeared a few days later.[4]

## Yield Spread Trades

In the earlier section on futures trading, we introduced the concept of spread trading, which is not market-directional trading, but rather the expression of a view point on the shape of a yield curve, or more specifically the spread between two particular points on the yield curve. Generally, there is no analytical relationship between changes in a specific yield spread and changes in the general level of interest rates. That is to say, the yield curve may flatten when rates are both falling or rising, and equally may steepen under either scenario as well. The key element of any spread trade is that it is structured so that a profit (or any loss) is made only as a result of a change in the spread, and not due to any change in overall yield levels. That is, spread trading eliminates market-directional or first-order market risk.

### Bond spread weighting

Table 12.3 shows data for our selection of gilts but with additional information on the basis point value (BPV) for each point. This is also known as the "dollar value of a basis point" or DV01.

If a trader believed that the yield curve was going to flatten, but had no particular strong feeling about whether this flattening would occur in

---

[4]In other words, we've missed the opportunity! This analysis used mid-prices, which are not available in practice.

an environment of falling or rising interest rates, and thought that the flattening would be most pronounced in the two-year versus ten-year spread, they could put on a spread consisting of a short position in the two-year and a long position in the ten-year. This spread must be duration-weighted to eliminate first-order risk. At this stage we must point out, and it is important to be aware of, the fact that basis point values, which are used to weight the trade, are based on modified duration measures. From an elementary understanding of bond maths we know that this measure is an approximation, and will be inaccurate for large changes in yield. Therefore the trader must monitor the spread to ensure that the weights are not going out of line, especially in a volatile market environment.

To weight the spread, the trader should use the ratios of the BPVs of each bond to decide on how much to trade. Assume that the trader wants to purchase £10 million of the ten-year. In this case, he must sell $((0.07584/0.02410) \times 10,000,000)$ or £31,468,880 of the two-year bond. It is also possible to weight a trade using the bonds' duration values, but this is rare. It is common practice to use the BPV.

The payoff from the trade depends on what happens to the two-year versus ten-year spread. If the yields on both bonds move by the same amount, there will be no profit generated, although there will be a funding consideration. If the spread does indeed narrow, the trade will generate profit. Note that disciplined trading calls for both an expected target spread as well as a fixed time horizon. So for example, if the current spread is 59.7 basis points, the trader may decide to take the profit if the spread narrows to 50 basis points, with a three-week horizon. If, at the end of three weeks, the spread has not reached the target, the trader should unwind the position anyway, because that was their original target. On the other hand, what if the spread has narrowed to 48 basis points after one week and looks like narrowing further—what should the trader do? Again, disciplined trading suggests the profit should be taken. If contrary to expectations, the spread starts to widen, if it reaches 64.5 basis points the trade should be unwound, this "stop-loss" being at the half-way point of the original profit target.

The financing of the trade in the repo markets is an important aspect of the trade, and will set the trade's break-even level. If the bond being shorted (in our example, the two-year bond) is *special*, this will have an adverse impact on the financing of the trade. The repo considerations are reviewed in Choudhry (2002).

## Types of bond spreads

A bond spread has two fundamental characteristics; in theory there should be no profit or loss effect due to a general change in interest rates, and any profit or loss should only occur as a result of a change in the specific spread being traded. Most bond spread trades are yield curve trades where a view is taken on whether a particular spread will widen or narrow. Therefore it is important to be able to identify which sectors of the curve to sell. Assuming that a trader is able to transact business along any part of the yield curve, there are a number of factors to consider. In the first instance, the historic spread between the two sectors of the curve. To illustrate in simplistic fashion, if the 2–10 year spread has been between 40 and 50 basis points over the last six months, but very recently has narrowed to less than 35 basis points, this may indicate imminent spread widening. Other factors to consider are demand and liquidity for individual stocks relative to others, and any market intelligence that the trader gleans. If there has been considerable customer interest in certain stocks relative to others, because investors themselves are switching out of certain stocks and into others, this may indicate a possible yield curve play. It is a matter of individual judgement.

An historical analysis requires that the trader identifies some part of the yield curve within which he expects to observe a flattening or steepening. It is, of course, entirely possible that one segment of the curve will flatten while another segment is steepening, in fact this scenario is quite common. This reflects the fact that different segments respond to news and other occurrences in different ways.

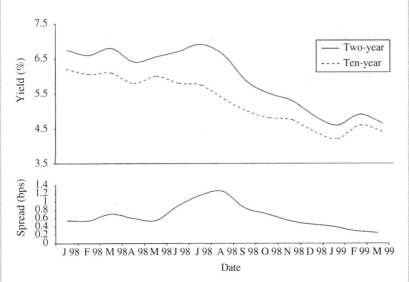

**Figure 12.4**  2-year and 10-year spread, UK gilt market March 1999.
*Source*: Bloomberg.

A more exotic type of yield curve spread is a *curvature* trade. Let us consider for example, a trader who believes that three-year bonds will out-perform on a relative basis, both two-year and five-year bonds. That is, he believes that the two-year/three-year spread will narrow relative to the three-year/five-year spread, in other words that the curvature of the yield curve will decrease. This is also known as a *butterfly/barbell* trade. In our example, the trader will buy the three-year bond, against short sales of both the two-year and the five-year bonds. All positions are duration-weighted.

Reproduced from *Analysing and Interpreting the Yield Curve* (2004)

## CONSTRUCTING THE BANK'S INTERNAL YIELD CURVE[1]

The construction of an internal yield curve is one of the major steps in the implementation of the internal funds pricing or "funds transfer pricing" (FTP) system in a bank. It should be done after the Trading book and the Banking book are split, but before internal funding methodologies for all balance sheet items and the internal bank result calculation methodology are approved and implemented in the balance sheet management information.

As is pointed out in regulatory recommendations, "the transfer prices should reflect current market conditions as well as the actual institution-specific circumstances"[2]. Putting it simply, that means the curve should contain a market component responsible for interest rate risk and a bank-specific spread over the market which will reflect the term liquidity cost for the bank.

There are several approaches for construction of an FTP curve. The choice of the approach depends on the scale of your bank, as well on the market where the bank operates. These main approaches are:

- *Market approach* (based on market interest rates): FTP rates reflect the rate of alternative placement of funds or borrowing in the market and change according to market dynamics;
- *Cost approach* (based on the borrowing rates): FTP rates motivate placement of funds at a higher rate than the rate at which the funds were raised;
- *Mixed approach* (based on the sum of the interest rate curves): FTP rates take into consideration diversified contents of liabilities at different tenors;

---

[1] This section was co-authored with Polina Bardaeva.
[2] Guidelines on Liquidity Cost Benefit Allocation. CEBS, October 2010.

- *Marginal approach* (based on the price of the following additional asset or liability): FTP rates represent the most relevant pricing levels. This approach can be based on:

  - Marginal rates of lending; or
  - Marginal rates of borrowing.

We consider each of these approaches in turn. We also show in the Appendix the ALCO submission prepared by one of the authors on implementing an internal curve methodology, when he was working in the investment banking division of a global multinational bank.

## MARKET APPROACH FOR FTP CURVE CONSTRUCTION

As implied by the name and definition of the approach, both components of an FTP curve should be derived from market quotes and indicators. The following is a list of requirements defining the characteristics of these market indicators:

- They should reflect accurately market conditions;
- The quotes should be published in well-known sources and should be available for all market participants (or calculated according to a widely accepted formula);
- Instruments referenced should enable the user to define the spread to the market indicator, in order to obtain the funding cost for the bank.

Usually, as market indicators for FTP curve construction we understand Libor (Euribor, etc.), interest rate swap (IRS), cross-currency swap (CCS), and credit default swap (CDS). Although as CDS is not available for each bank and sometimes is not representative when it is available, bond yields as market quotes can also be used. An FTP curve based on bond yields can be constructed using several methods which are deeply analysed in the special section. (See Application of Ordinary Least Squares method and Nelson-Siegel family approaches.)

The market approach can be applied by large banks which have a lot of operations in financial markets. The deep and developed market of financial instruments (including derivatives) is required.

The advantages of this approach are:

- Objectivity and transparency (as a consequence, high level of trust);
- Instant reflection of the level of the market rates;
- Possibility to define FTP rates even for those tenors at which no balance sheet items exist;
- Construction of a smoothed curve without distortions.

Although this method also has limitations:

- Too high volatility of the money market indicators;
- Sometimes lack of market indicators for middle-term and long-term;
- Sometimes low volume of deals with government bonds and as a result loss of marketability of quotes;
- Insufficient volume of deals and instruments for representativeness of the results for mathematical modelling.

## APPLICATION OF ORDINARY LEAST SQUARES METHOD AND NELSON-SIEGEL FAMILY APPROACHES

The topic of constructing a yield curve was widely investigated in scientific literature and by practitioners of central banks. The reason for such a deep investigation for these researches was that each country which has government bonds needs to construct a realistic, trustworthy, and flexible zero-coupon yield curve to reflect the level of the country's debt cost. Such reasons and the grade of responsibility for fair curve construction do not stop debates around the best methods and approaches. However not all approaches are feasible for use in ALM applications.

What are the main criteria for choosing the optimal approach? This approach should be *simple enough* to be executed without complicated technical packages, but at the same time reflect the market of a particular country, even when *bond quotes* are *not available for all tenors*.

According to a Bank for International Settlements survey about zero-coupon yield curve estimation procedures at central banks (2005), the most commonly used approaches are spline-based (for example, McCulloch, 1971, 1975) and parametric methods (Nelson, Siegel, 1987 and Svensson, 1994). Although the spline methods gain more positive assessments due to their provision of smoothness and accuracy, they are more complex. At the same time, Nelson and Siegel state in their work that their objective is simplicity rather than accuracy. The following part of this section is devoted to comparison and contrasting of parametric approaches and their practical implementation.

All the parametric methods are based on minimisation of the price / yield errors. Among parametric methods the most basic approach is the **Ordinary Least Squares (OLS) method**. This is the simplest parametric method which applies calculation of squares of deviations of actual quotes from the calculated approximated values and minimisation of their sum. Formula used to construct the curve is $f(x) = a * x^2 + b * x + c$, where $x$ – duration, $f(x)$ – yield, parameters $a$, $b$, and $c$ should satisfy the following: sum of the squares of deviations from the mean should be minimal.

The implementation in practice consists of three steps:

1. Collecting data from the information sources and placing in Excel spreadsheet (on the graph the bond quotes with different durations would represent a so-called "starry sky");
2. Calculation of approximations according to the formula with some initial values of parameters a, b, and c, deviations from the actual values, squares of deviations and sum of squares; next through the "Goal Seek" in Excel determination of the most appropriate parameters a, b, and c;
3. Solving the equation for some tenor in order to get the yield for this tenor.

The advantages of applying this method for ALM purposes are its simplicity and transparency. However, there are disadvantages which can significantly impact the result. The first and the main one is that the function which is used for approximation is parabolic – and, thus, is increasing in its first half, but after the extremum it starts to decline (see Figure 3.1). It's evident that this is not the best function to describe the market structure of interest rates – at least due to the reason that according to the expectations hypothesis theory, in the long run the rates tend to increase.

This method can, though, be used by an ALM unit of a bank in the following cases: a) the market does not have long tenors (so the declining part of the curve won't be used); b) the market yield curve is increasing (that means that it is not inverted and does not have troughs); c) the ALM unit doesn't have resources to try to implement any more complicated method (usually in small banks).

Figure 3.1 shows an example of the difference in output of the N-S and OLS methodologies when using the same inputs.

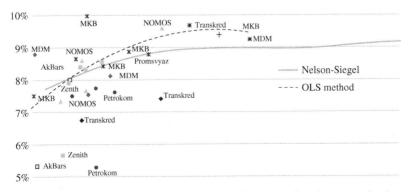

**FIGURE 3.1** Curve results when employing Nelson-Siegel and OLS methods
*Source*: www.micex.ru, Author's calculations.

In order to make the curve more flexible **Nelson-Siegel family curves** are used.

The first approach was suggested by **Nelson** and **Siegel** (basic N-S). They use four parameters in the equation to describe the yield curve:

$$f(x) = \beta_0 + (\beta_1 + \beta_2) * \frac{\left(1 - e^{-\frac{x}{\tau}}\right)}{\frac{x}{\tau}} - \beta_2 * e^{-\frac{x}{\tau}}$$

where $\beta_0$  is a long-term interest rate;

$\beta_1$  represents the spread between short-term and long-term rates (this parameter defines the slope of the curve: if parameter is positive, then the slope is negative). $\beta_0 + \beta_1$ – is the starting point of the curve at the short end;

$\beta_2$  is the difference between the middle-term and the long-term rates, defining the hump of the curve (if $\beta_2 > 0$ then the hump is observed in period ô, if $\beta_2 < 0$ then the curve will have an "U"-shape);

$\tau$  is a constant parameter, representing the tenor at which the maximum of the hump is achieved.

The main difference between the basic N-S approach and the OLS method is the addition of dependence between short-term and long-term rates, which tend to make the curve more flexible. This model assumes that long-term rates directly impact the short-term rates and, thus, some segments of the curve can't change while other segments are stable. Moreover, this basic approach provides a curve with only one hump or trough. And that is not always true in practice.

**Svensson** suggested an extension to basic N-S approach and implemented an additional component to provide a better description of the first part of the curve:

$$f(x) = \beta_0 + (\beta_1 + \beta_2) * \frac{\left(1 - e^{-\frac{x}{\tau_1}}\right)}{\frac{x}{\tau_1}} - \beta_2 * e^{-\frac{x}{\tau_1}} + \beta_3 * \frac{\left(1 - e^{-\frac{x}{\tau_2}}\right)}{\frac{x}{\tau_2}} - \beta_3 * e^{-\frac{x}{\tau_2}}$$

Thus the curve can have two extremums, $\beta_3$ determines the size and the form of the second hump, $\tau_2$ specifies the tenor for the second hump.

The advantages of the Svensson method in comparison to OLS and basic N-S approaches are even better flexibility and better accuracy. However even two humps do not perfectly reflect the market curve. That is why in practice further adjustments were made.

One of them is the **adjusted Nelson-Siegel (adjusted N-S) approach** with a set of seven parameters. The vector of curve's parameters is recalculated after each new bond / new quote is added. The first four parameters $(\beta_s)$ are responsible for the level of yields on short-term, middle-term, and long-term segments of the yield curve (the shifts up and down), and the remaining three parameters $(\tau_s)$ are responsible for convexity / concavity of the appropriate segments.

Such adjustment provides even more advantages: such flexibility that the yield curve by adjusted N-S approach can have all types of forms: monotonous increasing, or decreasing, convex, U-form, or S-form; memory, because the calculation is based on the previous parameters, so additional data doesn't change the form suddenly. This may be especially useful for markets with low liquidity of some bond issues – when on one day bonds are traded, there's a quote and the bond is included in the calculation, but on another day they are not traded, there's no quote and, thus, there's no input for calculation.

The disadvantage of all types of Nelson-Siegel approaches is their complexity in comparison with the OLS method. As far as one needs to assign initial values to parameters and then apply the "goal seek" function – there's risk that at this moment a mistake is made and further calculations are incorrect.

Nevertheless, one of the Nelson-Siegel family approaches would be recommended to be used for ALM purposes in the following cases: a) for larger banks with bigger ALM units, equipped with automatic systems; b) on the markets where the curve is supposed to demonstrate several humps on different tenors; c) on bond markets with low liquidity.

To summarise, not all of the existing methods to construct a yield curve can be successfully applied by ALM units. Parametric approaches are most simple in their implementation. The choice between the most "plain vanilla" OLS method and more complicated Nelson-Siegel family approaches should be done according to the size of the bank and market conditions and peculiarities.

# SONIA YIELD CURVE[3]

An important reference yield curve today is the overnight index swap (OIS) curve. This is similar to the conventional swap curve except it refers to the overnight rate on the floating leg of the swap, compared to the 3-month or 6-month rate on the floating leg of a conventional swap.

---

[3] This section was co-written with Kevin Liddy.

Prior to the 2008 crash derivative pricing and valuations were based on the simple principle of the time value of money. A breakeven price was calculated such that when all the future implied cash flows were discounted back to today the Net Present Value of all the cash flows was zero. The breakeven price was used for valuations or spread by a bid–offer price to create a trading price. Bid–offers would generally incorporate a counterparty-dependent mark-up to cover various costs and a return on capital in a fairly ill-defined way.

A breakeven price required the construction of a projection curve for the index being referenced, which could be a tenor of Libor, such as 3-month, for 3-month Libor swaps or an overnight rate in the case of overnight index swaps. The projection curve would use market observable inputs and various interpolation methodologies to derive market implied future rates used to project the future floating-rate fixings. In other words:

- A conventional swap curve is a projection curve based on the 3-month (or 6-month) Libor fix; whereas
- An OIS curve is a projection curve based on the overnight rate.

Once the market implied future fixings are known, a discount curve was then used to discount cash flow mismatches in such a way that the breakeven fixed rate gives a result where all the cash flow mismatches have a present value of zero. Historically market practice was to discount cash flows using a Libor discount curve, the assumption being that all cash flow mismatches could be borrowed or reinvested at Libor. It was implicitly assumed that Libor was the risk-free rate at which these cash flow mismatches could be funded.

Figure 3.2 shows the GBP OIS (known as SONIA) and GBP swap curves as at 13 October 2016. The OIS curve lies below the conventional swap curve because of the term liquidity premium (TLP) difference between the two tenors (the TLP is higher the longer the tenor).

In the case of a collateralised trade transacted under the terms of a CSA, the posting of collateral ensures that the NPV of a trade is always zero net of collateral held or posted. All future funding mismatches are therefore explicitly funded directly by the exchange of collateral and as a result do not require any external funding. The collateral remuneration rate is defined by the CSA and is normally the relevant OIS rate. As it is the relevant OIS rate that becomes the applicable rate for funding cash flow mismatches, market practice has evolved to discount future cash flows using OIS rates when pricing or valuing a collateralised trade, so-called OIS discounting. It is impossible to determine when this market practice changed but it is generally accepted that when the London Clearing House (which clears derivative

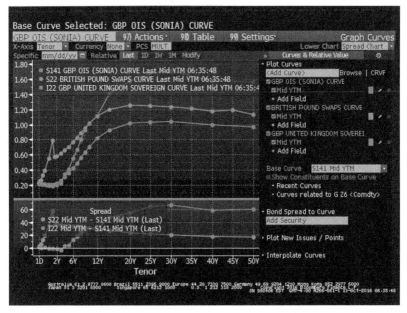

**FIGURE 3.2**    GBP SONIA and GBP Swap curves, 13 October 2016
*Source*: © Bloomberg LP. Reproduced with permission.

transactions) changed to OIS discounting in 2010 it was doing so to reflect best market practice.

Where multiple forms of collateral were permissible under a CSA, market practice evolved to take into account the embedded option for the collateral poster. Pricing assumed that a counterparty would always act rationally and post the cheapest to deliver collateral with the discount curve reflecting the relevant collateral OIS rate, so-called CTD or CSA discounting. A further enhancement is often used where the collateral is non-cash such as a government bond, in these instances the discount curve reflects the price at which the bonds can be traded in the repo market. For complex CSAs where collateral was multicurrency, the discount curve is often a multicurrency hybrid curve which reflects that the CTD may change at a future date.

For uncollateralised trades, not only was the use of a Libor rate to discount cash flow mismatches clearly inappropriate given the increase in funding spreads during the 2008 crisis but also, in the absence of collateral, the NPV of an uncollateralised trade represented a potential funding requirement. Pricing for uncollateralised trades now generally contains an upfront adjustment to the price to take into account the expected funding costs of non-collateralisation referred to as the Funding Valuation Adjustment or FVA. FVA along with a Credit Valuation Adjustment CVA now represent a more rigorously defined part of the bid–offer price adjustment.

Collateral posted at the LCH has no optionality allowed – it must be in cash and in the currency of the transaction. Hence the swap screen price now reflects the price for a cleared swap at LCH. Because the collateral is unambiguous (cash in the currency of the trade) remunerated at the relevant OIS, so the discount / funding rate is always known and is not counterparty dependent. Anything other than a LCH cleared trade means the swap price is different to take into account the impact of the type of collateral. This is an important point: observable swap rates are for LCH cleared trades only.

## CONCLUSION

The yield curve is the best snapshot of the state of the financial markets. It is not the sole driver of customer prices in banking, but it is the most influential. Hence it is important that all practitioners understand the behaviour of the curve and how to analyse and interpret it. Being aware of the relationship between spot rates, forward rates, and yield to maturity is also important. Ultimately, there should be no short-cuts when it comes to understanding the yield curve.

# APPENDIX 3.A: ALCO Submission Paper

## ALCO submission paper

The Royal Bank of Scotland

Author: Moorad Choudhry
GBM Treasury

**Global Banking & Markets**
135 Bishopsgate
London EC2M 3UR

Date: 29 March 2011

Subject: **Formalising the procedure for constructing the GBM internal yield curve**

A significant risk management decision at every bank is selecting the internal yield curve construction methodology. The internal curve is an important tool in the pricing and risk management process, driving resource allocation, business line transaction pricing, hedge construction and RAROC analysis. It is given therefore that curve construction methodology should follow business best-practice. In this paper we describe a recommended procedure on curve formulation to adopt at GBM, as well as a secondary procedure to liaise with Group Treasury (GT) aimed at maintaining a realistic and market-accurate public issuance curve.

### Background

Orthodox valuation methodology in financial markets follows the logic of risk-neutral no-arbitrage pricing [1]. The same logic should apply when setting a bank's internal pricing term structure. The risk-free curve is given by sovereign bond prices, while the banking sector risky curve was traditionally the Libor or swap curve. Banks now fund at "cost of funds" as opposed to Libor-flat; therefore, the logic of the no-arbitrage approach dictates that a bank's risky pricing yield curve should be extracted from market prices, because the latter dictate the rate at which the bank can raise liabilities. Such an approach preserves consistency because the same no-arbitrage principles drive market prices in the first place. In other words, the logic behind setting a bank's yield curve would be identical to the logic used when pricing derivatives.

Best-practice at peer group banks is to adopt an interpolation method that uses prices (yields) of the issuer's existing debt as model inputs, and extracts a discount function from these prices. The output is then used to derive a term structure that represents the issuer's current risky yield curve. To adopt such an approach requires a liquid secondary market in the issuer's bonds. This is a not unreasonable assumption in the case of RBS.

The two most common interpolation methods in use are the cubic spline approach and the parametric approach. The former produces markedly oscillating forward rates and is also less accurate at the short-end [2], [3]. Therefore we propose adopting the parametric method. The original parametric model is Nelson-Siegel [4], which is a forward rate model; however we recommend an extension of Nelson-Siegel for use at GBM, the Svensson (94) model, which produces a smoother forward curve, partly as a result of incorporating one extra parameter [5].

### Recommended procedure

In line with business best-practice we recommend immediate adoption of the following procedure:

1) Fit Svensson 94 to market data

2) Extract the RBS risky yield curve. This is the baseline EUR yield curve that determines the fixed coupon for a vanilla coupon fixed-maturity bond issued at par

3) Use the continuous discount function obtained from (2) above to create a par-par asset swap curve

4) This is the market-implied EUR Term Liquidity Premium (TLP) curve, which sets the spread for a vanilla FRN issued at par.

The curve at (4) is therefore the GBM TLP as dictated by market rates. By definition, under the no-arbitrage principles we refer to above, this curve is the baseline GBM pricing curve, and therefore will be used as such in GBM going forward.

The curve construction procedure logic is shown in the Appendix. It has been reviewed by the GBM Head of Front Office Risk Management and Quantitative Analytics.

Following approval at ALCO, we will implement the procedure via the Quantitative Analytics function, to create an application that can produce the RBS risky curve at the touch of a button.

The baseline EUR curve will be the source for creating all cross-currency funding curves. This procedure will be articulated formally in a later submission to GBM ALCO.

### Maintenance in line with market: liaison with Group Treasury

One of the issues raised by the FSA during the recent ILAA review, and also as part of the KPMG s166 review, referred to the risks created by a bank's public funding curve falling out of line with market prices.

To manage this risk, we recommend that GBM liaise with Group Treasury on a regular basis to ensure that the public issuance curve set by GT remains within a 10-15 basis point range of the 2-week moving average of the GBM market-implied TLP curve.

The tolerance level will be reviewed on a quarterly basis (or as required by market events) by GBM ALCO and in liaison with GT.

**REFERENCES**

[1] The most appropriate references in this field are Feynman-Kac (1949), Ito (1951), Markowitz (1959), Fama (1970), Black-Scholes (1973) and Merton (1973).

[2] James, J., and N. Webber (2000), *Interest Rate Modelling*, Chichester: John Wiley & Co Ltd

[3] Choudhry, M. (2003), *Analysing and Interpreting the Yield Curve*, Singapore: John Wiley & Sons Pte Ltd

[4] Nelson, C., and A.F. Siegel, (1987), "Parsimonious Modeling of Yield Curves", *Journal of Business*, 60, pp.473-489

[5] Svensson, Lars E. O. (1994), "Estimating and Interpreting Forward Rates: Sweden 1992-4," *National Bureau of Economic Research Working Paper* #4871

## APPENDIX

We desire to extract the RBS credit-risky curve from market prices. To do this we require a liquid secondary market of RBS-issued bonds, and an interpolation model. Practitioners generally use either the cubic spline approach or a parametric model approach.

For the reasons cited above, we recommend using the parametric methodology. The original parametric model is Nelson-Siegel (1987), which suffers to an extent from oscillating forward curves, so we recommend Svensson (1994) which has one extra parameter, and reduced oscillation, and also produces smoother short-date forwards.

A working Svensson model with Excel front-end is available on request.

The procedure we implement involves the following:

1 – Extract the RBS risky yield curve using RBS money-market funding rates and prices of secondary market bonds. We set the model's Beta and Tau parameters ourselves, or otherwise allow for the model to extract the ordinary least-squares best fit. The parameters include the long-run expected interest rate, which in general would be user-specified. This will be set as part of regular discussion within GBM, co-ordinated by GBM Treasury, and in liaison with GT.

2 – Running the model produces a discount function in near-continuous time. (See Exhibit 1, which shows the function in annual time steps. This can be adjusted for monthly or daily time steps if desired). This is the Svensson discount function (DF). We convert this DF to match to EUR swap dates, and to spot settlement (this is because the EUR curve in the bank's common analytics function (CAF) is defined with spot settlement).

3 – We extract the par yield curve. We now have a set of discrete rates corresponding to the RBS fair value yield curve, which tells us the coupon to set on a vanilla fixed coupon bond we issue at par for the relevant tenor.

4 – We use these rates to construct a full yield curve in CAF. Note that until the CAF methodology is set up to incorporate the Svensson model, this part of the process will use cubic spline methodology. However the procedure will ensure that the CAF output matches the input precisely (that is, a 0.000% error) so we have preserved our market-determined Svensson curve.

From the curve at (4) we extract the implied TLP. (Exhibit 2) This shows the fair-value spread we should pay on an FRN we issue of relevant tenor with a floating re-set of 3 months Euribor. It is also the GBM internal private placement curve.

(Note: this also sets the rate we would pay on a fixed coupon bond issue that was asset-swapped, but for an unsecured swap [as this is the unsecured pricing curve]. Hence it would not be the correct fair-value spread to pay on an asset swap, because that would involve a secured derivative. If we assume an unsecured derivative, we now have the par-par asset swap curve.).

We should note that the above is the market-implied curve process. The model output extrapolates beyond the latest tenor of our issued bonds to as long a maturity as the user wishes, and as a function of the long-run expected forward rate. Exhibit 2 shows yields up to 10-year because that is within the life of existing RBS debt issuance. The user can set the model to extrapolate fair-value output to a tenor of its choice. Note that extrapolated rates represent the current secondary market-implied value, and hence the fair-value rate to pay for that tenor.

The implied TLP is the same curve that GBM would be feeding back to GT on a regular basis. The suggested procedure to GT is that they will set the RBS public curve to within a specified tolerance (such as plus/minus 15 bps) of the 2-week moving average of the GBM curve.

**EXHIBITS**

| Maturity (year) | discount factor | forward rates | spot rates |
|---|---|---|---|
| 0 | 1 | 0.48% | 0.48% |
| 1 | 0.981433988 | 3.10% | 1.87% |
| 2 | 0.942635953 | 4.85% | 2.95% |
| 3 | 0.892551064 | 5.98% | 3.79% |
| 4 | 0.837510049 | 6.68% | 4.43% |
| 5 | 0.781645775 | 7.08% | 4.93% |
| 6 | 0.727458537 | 7.26% | 5.30% |
| 7 | 0.676326573 | 7.30% | 5.59% |
| 8 | 0.628899097 | 7.23% | 5.80% |
| 9 | 0.585375249 | 7.10% | 5.95% |
| 10 | 0.545690715 | 6.93% | 6.06% |

Exhibit 1 Svensson discount function, annual time steps

| Point | Basis Swap | Implied 3m spreads |
|---|---|---|
| 3m | ##66.Unity.Swap | -17 |
| 6m | ##67.Unity.Swap | -1 |
| 1y | ##35.Unity.Swap | 33 |
| 18m | ##41.Unity.Swap | 66 |
| 2y | ##40.Unity.Swap | 95 |
| 3y | ##39.Unity.Swap | 147 |
| 4y | ##38.Unity.Swap | 184 |
| 5y | ##37.Unity.Swap | 210 |
| 6y | ##36.Unity.Swap | 228 |
| 7y | ##42.Unity.Swap | 240 |
| 8y | ##43.Unity.Swap | 248 |
| 9y | ##44.Unity.Swap | 253 |
| 10y | ##45.Unity.Swap | 255 |

Exhibit 2 Extracted implied TLP

## SELECTED BIBLIOGRAPHY AND REFERENCES

Choudhry, M. (2012), *The Principles of Banking*, Wiley.

Ferstl, R., Hayden, J., Zero-Coupon Yield Curve Estimation with the Package termstrc. https://r-forge.r-project.org/scm/viewvc.php/*checkout*/pkg/doc/termstrc. pdf?revision=253&root=termstrc&pathrev=253.

Guidelines on Liquidity Cost Benefit Allocation, CEBS, October 2010.

Klein, S. and van Deventer, D. (2009), Yield Curve Smoothing: Nelson-Siegel versus Spline Technologies, Part 1, Kamakura Corporation Honolulu, 21 July 2009.

Nelson, Ch. and Siegel, A. "Parsimonious Modeling of Yield Curves", *The Journal of Business*, Vol. 60, No. 4, October 1987, pp. 473–489.

Principles for Sound Liquidity Risk Management and Supervision. BIS, September 2008.

Zero-coupon yield curves: technical documentation, BIS Papers, No. 25, Bank for International Settlements, October 2005.

*"It does not seem to me as though anything I've ever done was quite well enough done. That is an aching, unsatisfied feeling and ends up by making me wish I hadn't done anything."*
—T. E. Lawrence, quoted in Orlans, H., editor, *Lawrence of Arabia, Strange Man of Letters – the Literary Criticism and Correspondence of T. E. Lawrence*, London 1993, p.32.

# CHAPTER 4

# Eurobonds, Securitisation and Structured Finance

A s we noted previously, there is almost infinite variety in debt capital market products. This chapter highlights just some of the variety, starting with the more or less plain vanilla Eurobond onto other instruments such as convertible bonds and "CoCos", and then finally the structured products that arise out of the securitisation process. Along the way we introduce ratings agencies and the credit rating process. There is further material on the book's website, which contains a number of PowerPoint decks on securitisation and the credit ratings process.

**This extract from *An Introduction to Bond Markets, Fourth Edition* (2010)**

## The Eurobond Market

The Eurobond market is an important source of funds for many banks and corporates, as well as central governments. The Eurobond market has benefited from many of the advances in financial engineering, and has undergone some innovative changes in the debt capital markets. It continues to develop new structures, in response to the varying demands and requirements of specific groups of investors. The range of innovations have customised the market to a certain extent, and often the market is the only opening for certain types of government and corporate finance. Investors also often look to the Eurobond market due to constraints in their domestic market, and Euro securities have been designed to reproduce the features of instruments that certain investors may be prohibited from investing in in their domestic arena. Other instruments are designed for investors in order to provide tax advantages. The traditional image of the Eurobond investor – the so-called

'Belgian dentist' – has changed and the investor base is both varied and geographically dispersed worldwide.

The key feature of Eurobonds, which are also known as *international securities*, is the way they are issued, internationally across borders and by an international underwriting syndicate. The method of issuing Eurobonds reflects the cross-border nature of the transaction, and unlike government markets where the auction is the primary issue method, Eurobonds are typically issued under a 'fixed price re-offer' method or a 'bought deal'. There is also a regulatory distinction as no one central authority is responsible for regulating the market and overseeing its structure.

This chapter reviews the Eurobond market in terms of the structure of the market, the nature of the instruments themselves, the market players, the issuing process and technical aspects – such as taxation and swap arrangements.

## EUROBONDS

A Eurobond is a debt capital market instrument issued in a 'Eurocurrency' through a syndicate of issuing banks and securities houses, and distributed internationally when issued – that is, sold in more than one country of issue and subsequently traded by market participants in several international financial centres. The Eurobond market is divided into sectors depending on the currency in which the issue is denominated. For example, US dollar Eurobonds are often referred to as *Eurodollar* bonds, similar sterling issues are called *Eurosterling* bonds. The prefix 'Euro' was first used to refer to deposits of US dollars in continental Europe in the 1960s. The Euro-deposit now refers to any deposit of a currency outside the country of issue of that currency, and is not limited to Europe. For historical reasons and also due to the importance of the US economy and investor base, the major currency in which Eurobonds are denominated has always been US dollars. The volume of all non-sovereign Eurobond and domestic bond issues during 2004–2008 is shown at Figure 6.1.

The first ever Eurobond is generally considered to be the issue of $15 million nominal of 10-year $5\frac{1}{2}\%$ bonds by Autostrada, the Italian state highway authority, in July 1963.[1] The bonds were denominated in US dollars and paid an annual coupon in July each year. This coincides with the imposition in the US of the Interest Equalisation Tax, a withholding tax on domestic corporate bonds, which is often quoted as being a prime

---

[1] Decovny (1998) states that the first Eurobond issue was in 1957, but its identity is not apparent.

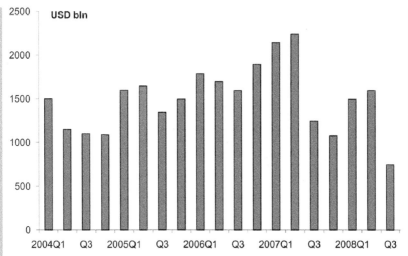

**Figure 6.1**  Non-government international bond issuance, 2004–2008.
*Source*: Thomson Reuters.

reason behind the establishment of overseas deposits of US dollars. Table 6.1 shows the diversity of the market with a selection of Eurobond issues in June 2005.

## FOREIGN BONDS

At this stage it is important to identify 'foreign bonds' and distinguish them from Eurobonds. Foreign bonds are debt capital market instruments that are issued by foreign borrowers in the domestic bond market of another country. As such, they trade in a similar fashion to the bond instruments of the domestic market in which they are issued. They are usually underwritten by a single bank or a syndicate of domestic banks, and are denominated in the currency of the market in which they are issued. For those familiar with the sterling markets, the best example of a foreign bond is a *Bulldog* bond, which is a sterling bond issued in the UK by a non-UK domiciled borrower. Other examples are *Yankee* bonds in the US, *Samurai* bonds in Japan, *Rembrandt* bonds in the Netherlands, *Matador* bonds in Spain, and so on. Hence, a US company issuing a bond in the UK, denominated in sterling and underwritten by a domestic bank would be issuing a Bulldog bond, which would trade as a gilt, except with an element of credit risk attached. In today's integrated global markets, however, the distinction is becoming more and more fine. Many foreign bonds pay gross coupons and are issued

| Issuer | Moody's/ S&P rating | Coupon | Maturity | Issue size | Launch speed to benchmark (bps) |
|---|---|---|---|---|---|
| Daimler Chrysler NA | A3/BBB | 4.875% | 15 June 2010 | USD 1,000 million | 130 |
| Development Bank of Japan | Aaa/AAA | 4.25% | 9 June 2015 | USD 700 million | 38.8 |
| Federal Home Loan Bank | AAA | 3.625% | 20 June 2007 | USD 4,000 million | 17 |
| GE Capital | Aaa/AAA | 4.75% | 15 June 2011 | GBP 250 million | 52 |
| General Electric Capital Corp. | Aaa/AAA | 4.00% | 15 June 2009 | USD 500 million | 48 |
| If Skadeforsakring AB | Baa2/BBB | 4.943% | Perpetual/Callable | EUR 150 million | 179.8; fixed coupon to June 2015, thereafter, 3-month Euribor + 265 |
| ING Group N.V. | A2/A– | 4.176% | Perpetual/Callable | EUR 500 million | 95.3; fixed coupon to June 2015, thereafter, 3-month Euribor + 180 |
| Kingdom of Belgium | Aa1/AA+ | 3.000% | 28 March 2010 | EUR 6,145 million | 9 |
| Korea Exchange Bank | Baa3/BB+ | 5.00% | 10 June 2015 | USD 300 million | 151 |
| Lambay Capital Securities | Baa1 | FRN | Perpetual | GBP 300 million | 3-month Libor + 166. Coupon step-up after 2015 |
| LB Baden-Wuerttemberg | Aaa/AAA | 6.50% | 26 November 2007 | NZD 50 million | 23 |
| Legal & General Group | A2/A | 4.00% | 8 June 2025 | EUR 600 million | 85.1 |
| Portugal Telecom | A3/A– | 4.50% | 16 June 2025 | EUR 500 million | 137 |
| Republic of El Salvador | Baa2/BB+ | 7.65% | 15 June 2035 | USD 375 million | 345 |
| Republic of Turkey | B1/BB– | 7.00% | 5 June 2020 | USD 1,250 million | 332.4 |
| Zurich Finance (USA) Inc. | Baa2/BBB+ | 4.50% | 15 June 2025 | EUR 500 million | 135.00 to June 2015; thereafter, 3-month Euribor + 220 |

**Table 6.1**   Selected Eurobond issues in first half of June 2005.

by a syndicate of international banks, so the difference between them and Eurobonds may be completely eroded in the near future.

The most important domestic market for foreign bond issues has been the US dollar market, followed by euros, Swiss francs and Japanese yen. There are also important markets in Canadian and Australian dollars, and minor markets in currencies such as Hong Kong dollars, Kuwaiti dinars and Saudi Arabian riyals.

# EUROBOND INSTRUMENTS

There is a wide range of instruments issued in the Eurobond market, designed to meet the needs of borrowers and investors. We review the main types in this section.

## Conventional bonds

The most common type of instrument issued in the Euromarkets is the conventional vanilla bond, with fixed coupon and maturity date. Coupon frequency is on an annual basis. The typical face value of such Eurobonds is $1,000, €1,000, £1,000 and so on. The bond is unsecured, and therefore depends on the credit quality of its issuer in order to attract investors. Eurobonds have a typical maturity of 5–10 years, although many high-quality corporates have issued bonds with maturities of 30 years or even longer. The largest Eurobond market is in US dollars, followed by issues in euros, Japanese yen, sterling and a range of other currencies such as Australian, New Zealand and Canadian dollars, South African rand and so on. Issuers will denominate bonds in a currency that is attractive to particular investors at the time, and it is common for bonds to be issued in more 'exotic' currencies, such as East European, Latin American and Asian currencies.

Eurobonds are not regulated by the country in whose currency the bonds are issued. They are typically registered on a national stock exchange, usually London or Luxembourg. Listing of the bonds enables certain institutional investors, who are prohibited from holding assets that are not listed on an exchange, to purchase them. The volume of trading on a registered stock exchange is negligible, however; virtually all trading is on an over-the-counter (*OTC*) basis directly between market participants.

Interest payments on Eurobonds are paid gross and are free of any withholding or other taxes. This is one of the main features of Eurobonds, as is the fact that they are 'bearer' bonds – that is, there is no central register. Historically, this meant that the bond certificates were bearer certificates with coupons attached; these days bonds are still designated 'bearer' instruments but are held in a central depository to facilitate electronic settlement.

## Floating rate notes

An early innovation in the Eurobond market was the floating rate note (*FRN*). They are usually short- to medium-dated issues, with interest quoted as a spread to a reference rate. The reference rate is usually the London interbank offered rate (*Libor*), or the Singapore interbank offered rate for issues in Asia (*Sibor*). The euro interbank rate (*Euribor*) is also now commonly quoted. The spread over the reference rate is a function of the credit quality of the issuer, and can range from 10 to 150 basis points over the reference rate or even higher. Bonds typically pay a semiannual coupon, although quarterly coupon bonds are also issued. The first FRN issue was by ENEL, an Italian utility company, in 1970. The majority of issuers are financial institutions – such as banks and securities houses.

There are also perpetual, or undated, FRNs, the first issue of which was by National Westminster Bank plc in 1984. They are essentially similar to regular FRNs except that they have no maturity date and are therefore 'perpetual'. Most perpetual FRNs are issued by banks, for whom they are attractive because they are a means of raising capital, similar to equity but with the tax advantages associated with debt. They also match the payment characteristics of the bank's assets. Traditionally, the yield on perpetuals is higher than both conventional bonds and fixed-term FRNs.

## Zero-coupon bonds

An innovation in the market from the late 1980s was the zero-coupon bond, or *pure discount* bond, which makes no interest payments. Like zero-coupon bonds initially in government markets, the main attraction of these bonds for investors was that, as no interest was payable, the return could be declared entirely as capital gain, thus allowing the bondholder to avoid income tax. Most jurisdictions including the US and UK have adjusted their tax legislation so that the return on zero-coupon bonds now counts as income and not capital gain.

## Convertible bonds[2]

Another instrument that is common in the Eurobond market is the convertible bond. A Eurobond is convertible if it may be exchanged at some point for another instrument, usually the ordinary shares (equity) of the issuing company. The decision to elect to convert is at the discretion of the bondholder. Convertibles are analysed as a structure comprised of a conventional bond and an embedded option.

---

[2] Convertible bonds are reviewed in Chapter 7.

The most common conversion feature is an *equity convertible*, which is a conventional bond that is convertible into the equity of the issuer. The conversion feature allows the bondholder to convert the Eurobond, on maturity or at specified times during the bond's life, into a specified number of shares of the issuing company at a set price. In some cases the bond is convertible into the shares of the company that is guaranteeing the bond. The issuing company must release new shares in the event of conversion. The price at which the bond is convertible into shares, known as the 'exercise price', is usually set at a premium above the market price of the ordinary shares in the market on the day the bond is issued. Investors will exercise their conversion rights only if the market price has risen sufficiently that a gain will be realised by converting. The incorporation of a conversion feature in a bond is designed to make the bond more attractive to investors, as it allows them to gain from a rise in the issuing company's share price. The conversion feature also acts as a floor for the bond price.

The advantages of convertibles for borrowers include the following:

- as the bond incorporates an added attraction in the form of the conversion feature, the coupon payable on the bond is lower than it otherwise would be – this enables the borrower to save on interest costs;
- issuing convertibles is one method by which companies can broaden the geographical base of their equity holders;
- companies are usually able to raise a higher amount at one issue if the bond is convertible, compared with a conventional bond.

Against these factors must be weighed certain disadvantages associated with convertibles, which include the following:

- the investor's insurance against the volatility of share price movements – an attraction of the convertible – is gained at the cost of a lower coupon than would be obtained from a conventional bond;
- convertibles are often issued by companies that would have greater difficulty placing conventional paper. Convertibles are usually subordinated and are often viewed more as equity rather than debt. The credit and interest-rate risk associated with them is consequently higher than for conventional bonds.

*Currency convertibles* are bonds that are issued in one currency and are redeemed in another currency or currencies. Often this is at the discretion of the bondholder; other currency convertibles pay their coupon in a different currency from the one they are denominated in. In certain respects, currency convertibles possess similar characteristics to a conventional bond issued in conjunction with a forward contract. The conversion rate is specified at the time of issue, and may be either a fixed-rate option or a floating-rate option.

With a fixed-rate option the exchange rate between the currencies is fixed for the entire maturity of the bond at the time it is issued; with a floating-rate option the exchange rate is not fixed and is the rate prevailing in the market at the time the conversion is exercised. Initially, most currency convertibles offered a fixed-rate option, so that the foreign exchange risk resided entirely with the issuer. Floating-rate options were introduced in the 1970s when exchange rates began to experience greater volatility.

## THE ISSUE PROCESS: MARKET PARTICIPANTS

When a company raises a bond issue its main concerns will be the success of the issue, and the interest rate that must be paid for the funds borrowed. An issue is handled by an international syndicate of banks. A company wishing to make a bond issue will invite a number of investment banks and securities houses to bid for the role of lead manager. The bidding banks will indicate the price at which they believe they can get the issue away to investors, and the size of their fees. The company's choice of lead manager will be based not only on the bids, but also the reputation and standing of the bank in the market. The lead manager when appointed will assemble a syndicate of other banks to help with the issue. This syndicate will often be made up of banks from several different countries. The lead manager has essentially agreed to underwrite the issue, which means that he guarantees to take the paper off the issuer's hands (in return for a fee). If there is an insufficient level of investor demand for the bonds the lead manager will be left holding ('wearing') the issue, which in addition to being costly will not help its name in the market. When we referred to an issuer assessing the reputation of potential lead managers, this included the company's view on the 'placing power' of the bank, its perceived ability to get the entire issue away. The borrowing company would prefer the issue to be over-subscribed, which is when demand outstrips supply.

In many cases the primary issue involves a *fixed price re-offer* scheme. The lead manager will form the syndicate which will agree on a fixed issue price, a fixed commission and the distribution amongst themselves of the quantity of bonds they agreed to take as part of the syndicate. The banks then re-offer the bonds that they have been allotted to the market, at the agreed price. This technique gives the lead manager greater control over a Eurobond issue. It sets the price at which other underwriters in the syndicate can initially sell the bonds to investors. The fixed price re-offer mechanism is designed to prevent underwriters from selling the bonds back to the lead manager at a discount to the original issue price – that is, 'dumping' the bonds.

Before the bond issue is made, but after its basic details have been announced, it is traded for a time in the *grey market*. This is a term used to describe trading in the bonds before they officially come to the market – that is, mainly market makers selling the bond short to other market players or investors. Activity in the grey market serves as useful market intelligence to the lead manager, who can gauge the level of demand that exists in the market for the issue. A final decision on the offer price is often delayed until dealing in the grey market indicates the best price at which the issue can be got away.

Let us now consider the primary market participants in greater detail.

## The borrowing parties

The range of borrowers in the Euromarket is very diverse. From virtually the inception of the market, borrowers representing corporates, sovereign and local governments, nationalised corporations, supranational institutions and financial institutions have raised finance in the international markets. The majority of borrowing has been by governments, regional governments and public agencies of developed countries, although the Eurobond market is increasingly a source of finance for developing country governments and corporates.

Governments and institutions access the Euromarket for a number of reasons. Under certain circumstances it is more advantageous for a borrower to raise funds outside its domestic market, due to the effects of tax or regulatory rules. The international markets are very competitive in terms of using intermediaries, and a borrower may well be able to raise cheaper funds in them. Other reasons why borrowers access Eurobond markets include:

- a desire to diversify sources of long-term funding. A bond issue is often placed with a wide range of institutional and private investors, rather than the more restricted investor base that may prevail in a domestic market. This gives the borrower access to a wider range of lenders, and for corporate borrowers this also enhances the international profile of the company;
- for both corporates and emerging country governments, the prestige associated with an issue of bonds in the international market;
- the flexibility of a Eurobond issue compared with a domestic bond issue or bank loan, illustrated by the different types of Eurobond instruments available.

Against this are balanced the potential downsides of a Eurobond issue, which include the following:

- for all but the largest and most creditworthy of borrowers, the rigid nature of the issue procedure becomes significant during times of interest and exchange-rate volatility, reducing the funds available for borrowers;

- issuing debt in currencies other than those in which a company holds matching assets, or in which there are no prospects of earnings, exposes the issuer to foreign exchange risk.

Generally though, the Euromarket remains an efficient and attractive market in which a company can raise finance for a wide range of maturities.

The nature of the Eurobond market is such that the ability of governments and corporates to access it varies greatly. Access to the market for a first-time borrower has historically been difficult, and has been a function of global debt market conditions. There is a general set of criteria, first presented by van Agtmael (1983), that must be fulfilled initially, which for corporates includes the following:

- the company should ideally be domiciled in a country that is familiar to Eurobond issuers, usually as a result of previous offerings by the country's government or a government agency. This suggests that it is difficult for a corporate to access the market ahead of a first issue by the country's government;
- the borrowing company must benefit from a level of name recognition or, failing this, a sufficient quality credit rating;
- the company ideally must have a track record of success, and needs to have published financial statements over a sufficient period of time, audited by a recognised and respected firm, and the company's management must make sufficient financial data available at the time of the issue;
- the company's requirement for medium-term or long-term finance, represented by the bond issue, must be seen to fit into a formal strategic plan.

Generally, Eurobond issuers are investment-grade rated, and only a small number, less than 5%,[3] are not rated at all.

## The underwriting lead manager

Issuers of debt in the Eurobond market select an investment bank to manage the bond issue for them. This bank is known as the underwriter because in return for a fee it takes on the risk of placing the bond amongst investors. If the bond cannot be placed in total, the underwriting bank will take on the paper itself. The issuer will pick an investment bank with whom it already has an existing relationship, or it may invite a number of banks to bid for the mandate. In the event of a competitive bid, the bank will be selected on the basis of the prospective coupon that can be offered, the fees and other

---

[3] *Source*: IMF.

expenses that it will charge, the willingness of the bank to support the issue in the secondary market, the track record of the bank in placing similar issues and the reach of the bank's client base. Often it is a combination of a bank's existing relationship with the issuer and its reputation in the market for placing paper that will determine whether or not it wins the mandate for the issue.

After the mandate has been granted, and the investment bank is satisfied that the issuer meets its own requirements on counterparty and reputational risk, both parties will prepare a detailed financing proposal for the bond issue. This will cover topics such as the specific type of financing, the size and timing of the issue, approximate pricing, fees and so on. The responsibilities of the lead manager include the following:

- analysing the prospects of the bond issue being accepted by the market – this is a function of both the credit quality of the issuer and the market's capacity to absorb the issue;
- forming the *syndicate* of banks to share responsibility for placing the issue – these banks are co-lead managers and syndicate banks;
- assisting the borrower with the prospectus, which details the bond issue and also holds financial and other information on the issuing company;
- assuming responsibility for the legal issues involved in the transaction, for which the bank's in-house legal team and/or external legal counsel will be employed;
- preparing the documentation associated with the issue;
- taking responsibility for the handling of the fiduciary services associated with the issue, which is usually handled by a specialised agent bank;
- if deemed necessary, establishing a pool of funds that can be used to stabilise the price of the issue in the *grey market*, used to buy (or sell) bonds if required.

These duties are usually undertaken jointly with other members of the syndicate. For first-time borrowers the prospectus is a very important document, as it is the main communication media used to advertise the borrower to investors. In a corporate issue, the prospectus may include the analysis of the company by the underwriters, financial indicators and balance sheet data, a detailed description of the issue specifications, the members of the underwriting syndicate and details of placement strategies. In a sovereign issue, the prospectus may cover a general description of the country's economy, including key economic indicators such as balance of payments figures and export and import levels, the state of the national accounts and budget, a description of the political situation (with an eye on the stability of the country), current economic activity, and a statement of the current external and public debt position of the country.

## The co-lead manager

The function of the co-lead manager in Eurobond issues developed as a consequence of the distribution of placing ability across geographic markets. For example, as the Eurobond market developed, underwriters who were mainly US or UK banks did not have significant client bases in, say, the continental European market, and so banking houses that had a customer base there would be invited to take on some of the issue. For a long time the ability to place $500,000 nominal of a new Eurobond issue was taken as the benchmark against a potential co-lead manager.

The decision by a lead manager to invite other banks to participate will depend on the type and size of the issue. Global issues such as those by the World Bank, which have nominal sizes of $1 billion or more, have a fairly large syndicate. The lead manager will assess whether it can place all the paper or, in order to achieve geographic spread (which may have been stipulated by the issuer), it needs to form a syndicate. It is common for small issues to be placed entirely by a single lead manager.

## Investors

The structure of the Eurobond market, compared with domestic markets, lends a certain degree of anonymity, if such is desired, to end-investors. This is relevant essentially in the case of private investors. The institutional holders of investors are identical to those in the domestic bond markets, and include institutional investors such as insurance companies, pension funds, investment trusts, commercial banks and corporations. Other investors include central banks and government agencies; for example, the Kuwait Investment Office and the Saudi Arabian Monetary Agency both have large Eurobond holdings. In the UK, banks and securities houses are keen holders of FRN Eurobonds, usually issued by other financial institutions.

# FEES, EXPENSES AND PRICING

## Fees

The fee structure for placing and underwriting a Eurobond issue is relatively identical for most issues. The general rule is that fees increase with maturity and decreasing credit quality of the issuer, and decrease with nominal size. Fees are not paid directly but are obtained by adjusting the final price paid to the issuer – that is, taken out of the sale proceeds of the issue. The allocation of fees within a syndicate can be slightly more complex, and in the form of an *underwriting allowance*. This is usually paid out by the lead manager.

Typical fees will vary according to the type of issue and issuer, and also whether the bond itself is plain vanilla or more exotic. Fees range from 0.25% to 0.75% of the nominal of an issue. Higher fees may be charged for small issues.

## Expenses

The expenses associated with the launch of a Eurobond issue vary greatly. Table 4.2 illustrates the costs associated with a typical Eurobond transaction. Not every bond issue will incur every expense; however, these elements are common.

The expense items in Table 6.2 do not include the issuer's own expenses with regard to financial accounting and marketing. The reimbursement for underwriters is intended to cover such items as legal expenses, travel, delivery of bonds and other business expenses.

In general, Eurobonds are listed on either the London, Dublin or Luxembourg Stock Exchanges. Certain issues in the Asian markets are listed on the Singapore Exchange. To enable listing to take place an issuer will need to employ a listing agent, although this is usually arranged by the lead manager. The function of the listing agent is to (i) provide a professional opinion on the prospectus, (ii) prepare the documentation for submission to the stock exchange and (iii) make a formal application and conduct negotiations on behalf of the issuer.

## Pricing

One of the primary tasks of the lead manager is the pricing of the new issue. The lead manager faces an inherent conflict of interest between its need to maximise its returns from the syndication process and its obligation to secure the best possible deal for the issuer, its client. An inflated issue price invariably causes the yield spread on the bond to rise as soon as the bond trades in the secondary market. This would result in a negative impression being associated with the issuer, which would affect its next offering. On

| | |
|---|---|
| Printing (prospectus, certificates, etc.) | Clearing and bond issuance |
| Legal counsel (issuer and investment bank) | Paying agent |
| Stock exchange listing fee | Trustee |
| Promotion | Custodian |
| Underwriter's expenses | Common depositary |

**Table 6.2** Expense elements, Eurobond issue.

the other hand, too low a price can permanently damage a lead manager's relationship with the client.

For Eurobonds that are conventional vanilla fixed-income instruments, pricing does not present too many problems in theory. The determinants of the price of a new issue are the same as those for a domestic bond offering, and include the credit quality of the borrower, the maturity of the issue, the total nominal value, the presence of any option feature, and the prevailing level and volatility of market interest rates. Eurobonds are perhaps more heavily influenced by the target market's ability to absorb the issue, and this is gauged by the lead manager in its preliminary offering discussions with investors. The credit rating of a borrower is often similar to that granted to it for borrowings in its domestic market, although in many cases a corporate will have a different rating for its foreign currency debt compared with its domestic currency debt.

In the grey market the lead manager will attempt to gauge the yield spread over the reference pricing bond at which investors will be happy to bid for the paper. The reference bond is the benchmark for the maturity that is equivalent to the maturity of the Eurobond. It is commonly observed that Eurobonds have the same maturity date as the benchmark bond that is used to price the issue. As lead managers often hedge their issue using the benchmark bond, an identical maturity date helps to reduce basis risk.

# ISSUING THE BOND

The three key dates in a new issue of Eurobonds are the announcement date, the offering day and the closing day. Prior to the announcement date the borrower and the lead manager (and co-lead managers if applicable) will have had preliminary discussions to confirm the issue specifications, such as its total nominal size, the target coupon and the offer price. These details are provisional and may well be different at the time of the closing date. At these preliminary meetings the lead manager will appoint a fiscal agent or trustee, and a principal paying agent. The lead manager will appoint other members of the syndicate group, and the legal documentation and prospectus will be prepared.

On the announcement date the new issue is formally announced, usually via a press release. The announcement includes the maturity of the issuer and a coupon rate or range in which the coupon is expected to fall. A telex is also sent by the lead manager to each prospective underwriter, which is a formal invitation to participate in the syndicate. These banks will also receive the preliminary offering circular, a timetable of relevant dates for the issue and documentation that discloses the legal obligations that they are expected to follow should they decide to participate in the issue. The decision to join is mainly, but not wholly, a function of the bank's clients' interest in the issue, which the bank needs to sound out.

The *pricing day* signals the end of the subscription period, the point at which the final terms and conditions of the issue are agreed between the borrower and the syndicate group. If there has been a significant change in market conditions, the specifications of the bond issue will change. Otherwise, any required final adjustment of the price is usually undertaken by a change in the price of the bond relative to par. The ability of the lead manager to assess market conditions accurately at this time is vital to the successful pricing of the issue.

Once the final specifications have been determined, members of the syndicate have roughly 24 hours to accept or reject the negotiated terms; the bonds are then formally offered on the *offering day*, the day after the pricing day, when the issuer and the managing group sign the subscription or underwriting agreement containing the final specifications of the issue. The underwriting syndicate then enters into a legal commitment to purchase the bonds from the issuer at the price announced on the pricing day. A final offering circular is then produced, and the lead manager informs the syndicate of the amount of their allotments. The lead manager may wish to either over-allocate or under-allocate the number of available bonds, depending on its view on future levels and direction of interest rates. There then begins the *stabilisation period*, when the bonds begin to trade in the secondary period, where Eurobonds trade in an over-the-counter market. About 14 days after the offering day, the *closing day* occurs. This is when syndicate members pay for bonds they have purchased, usually by depositing funds into a bank account opened and run by the lead manager on behalf of the issuer. The bond itself is usually represented by a *global note*, held in Euroclear or Clear-stream, initially issued in temporary form. The temporary note is later changed to a *permanent* global note. Tranches of an issue targeted at US investors may be held in the Depositary Trust Corporation as a registered note.

## The grey market

The subscription period of a new Eurobond issue is characterised by uncertainty about potential changes in market conditions. After the announcement of the issue, but before the bonds have been formally issued, the bonds trade in the *grey market*. The grey market is where bonds are bought and sold pre-issue for settlement on the first settlement date after the offering day. Grey market trading enables the lead manager to gauge the extent of investor appetite for the issue, and make any adjustment to coupon if required. A grey market that functions efficiently will at any time reflect the market's view on where the bond should trade, and at what yield the bond should be offered. It enables investors to trade in the primary market possessing information as to the likely price of the issue in the secondary market.

Another principal task of the lead manager is to stabilise the price of the bond issue for a short period after the bond has started trading in the secondary market. This is known as the stabilisation period, and the process is undertaken by the lead manager in concert with some or all of the syndicate members. A previously established pool of funds may be used for this purpose. The price at which stabilisation occurs is known as the *syndicate bid*.

## Alternative issue procedures

In addition to the traditional issue procedure where a lead manager and syndicate offer bonds to investors based on a price set on pricing day, based on a yield over the benchmark bond, there are a number of other issue procedures that are used. One of these methods includes the *bought deal*, where a lead manager or a managing group approaches the issuer with a firm bid, specifying issue price, amount, coupon and yield. Only a few hours are allowed for the borrower to accept or reject the terms. If the bid is accepted, the lead manager purchases the entire bond issue from the borrower. The lead manager then has the option of selling part of the issue to other banks for distribution to investors, or doing so itself. In a volatile market the lead manager will probably parcel some of the issue to other banks for placement. However, it is at this time that the risk of banks dumping bonds on the secondary market is highest; in this respect lead managers will usually pre-place the bonds with institutional investors before the bid is made. The bought deal is focused primarily on institutional rather than private investors. As the syndicate process is not used, the bought deal requires a lead manager with sufficient capital and placement power to enable the entire issue to be placed.

In a *pre-priced offering* the lead manager's bid is contingent on its ability to form a selling group for the issue. Any alterations in the bid required for the formation of the group must be approved by the borrower. The period allocated for the formation of the group is usually 2–4 days, and after the group has been formed the process is identical to that for the bought deal.

Yet another approach is the *auction issue*, under which the issuer will announce the maturity and coupon of a prospective issue and invite interested investors to submit bids. The bids are submitted by banks, securities houses and brokers, and include both price and amount. The advantages of the auction process are that it avoids the management fees and costs associated with a syndicate issue. However, the issuer does not have the use of a lead manager's marketing and placement expertise, which means it is a method that can only be employed by very high quality, well-known borrowers.

# COVENANTS

Eurobonds are unsecured and, as such, the yield demanded by the market for any particular bond will depend on the credit rating of the issuer. Until the early 1980s Eurobonds were generally issued without covenants, due to the high quality of most issuers. Nowadays it is common for covenants to be given with Eurobond issues. Three covenants in particular are frequently demanded by investors:

- a negative pledge;
- an 'event risk' clause;
- a gearing ratio covenant.

## Negative pledge

A negative pledge is one that restricts the borrowings of the group which ranks in priority ahead of the debt represented by the Eurobond. In the case of an unsecured Eurobond issue this covenant restricts new secured borrowings by the issuer, as well as new unsecured borrowings by any of the issuer's subsidiaries, since these would rank ahead of the unsecured borrowings by the parent company in the event of the whole group going into receivership.

## Disposal of assets covenant

This sets a limit on the number of assets that can be disposed of by the borrower during the tenor (term to maturity) of the debt. The limit on disposals could be, typically, a cumulative total of 30% of the gross assets of the company. This covenant is intended to prevent a break-up of the company without reference to the Eurobond investors.

## Gearing ratio covenant

This places a restriction on the total borrowings of the company during the tenor of the bond. The restriction is set as a maximum percentage – say, 150–175% of the company's or group's net worth (share capital and reserves).

# TRUST SERVICES

A Eurobond issue requires an agent bank to service it during its life. The range of activities required are detailed below.

## Depositary

The depositary for a Eurobond issue is responsible for the safekeeping of securities. In the Euromarket well over 90% of investors are institutions, and so as a result issues are made in dematerialised form and are represented by a global note. Trading and settlement is in computerised book-entry form via the two main international clearing systems, Euroclear and Clearstream. Both these institutions have appointed a group of banks to act on their behalf as depositaries for book-entry securities; this is known as *common depositaries*, because the appointment is common to both Euroclear and Clear-stream. Both clearing firms have appointed separately a network of banks to act as specialised depositaries, which handle securities that have been issued in printed note or *definitive* form.

As at February 2009 there were 20 banks that acted as common depositaries on behalf of Euroclear and Clearstream, although the majority of the volume was handled by just three banks, Citibank NA, Bank of New York Mellon and Deutsche Bank. The common depositary is responsible for:

- representing Euroclear and Clearstream and facilitating delivery-versus-payment of the primary market issue by collecting funds from the investors, taking possession of the temporary global note (which allows securities to be released to investors) and making a single payment of funds to the issuer;
- holding the temporary global note in safe custody, until it is exchanged for definitive notes or a permanent global note;
- making adjustments to the nominal value of the global note that occur after the exercise of any options or after conversions, in line with instructions from Euroclear or Clearstream and the fiscal agent;
- surrendering the cancelled temporary global note to the fiscal agent after the exchange into definitive certificates or a permanent global note, or on maturity of the permanent global note.

A specialised depositary will hold definitive notes representing aggregate investor positions held in a particular issue; on coupon and maturity dates it presents the coupons or bond to the paying agent and passes the proceeds on to the clearing system.

## Paying agent

Debt issuance in the Euromarkets requires a fiscal or principal paying agent, or in the case of a programme of issuance (e.g., a Euro-MTN programme) an issuing and paying agent. The responsibility of the paying agent is to provide administrative support to the issuer throughout the lifetime of the issue. The duties of a paying agent include:

- issuing securities upon demand in the case of a debt programme;
- authenticating definitive notes;
- collecting funds from the issuer and paying these out to investors as coupon and redemption payments;

- in the case of global notes, acting on behalf of the issuer to supervise payments of interest and principal to investors via the clearing systems, and in the case of definitive notes, paying out interest and coupon on presentation by the investor of the relevant coupon or bond to the paying agent;
- transferring funds to sub-paying agents, where these have been appointed – a security that has been listed in Luxembourg must have a local sub-paying agent appointed for it;
- maintaining an account of the cash flows paid out on the bond;
- arranging the cancellation and subsequent payment of coupons, matured bonds and global notes, and sending destroyed certificates to the issuer.

A paying agent will act solely on behalf of the issuer, unlike a trustee who has an obligation to look after the interests of investors. For larger bond issues there may be a number of paying agents appointed, of which the *principal paying agent* is the coordinator. A number of *sub-paying agents* may be appointed to ensure that bondholders in different country locations may receive their coupon and redemption payments without delay. The term *fiscal agent* is used to describe a paying agent for a bond issue for which no trustee has been appointed.

## Registrar

The role of the registrar is essentially administrative; it is responsible for keeping accurate records of bond ownership for registered securities. As most Eurobonds are issued in bearer form, there is not a great deal of work for registrars in the Euromarket, and the number of holders of registered notes is normally quite low.

The responsibilities of the registrar include:

- maintaining a register of all bondholders and records of all transfers of ownership;
- coordinating the registration, transfer or exchange of bonds;
- issuing and authenticating new bonds should any transfer or exchange take place;
- maintaining a record of the outstanding principal value of the bond;
- undertaking administrative functions relating to any special transfers.

## Trustee

An issuer may appoint a trustee to represent the interests of investors. In the event of default, the trustee is required to discharge its duties on behalf of bondholders. In certain markets a trustee is required by law – for instance, in the US a trustee has been a legal requirement since 1939. In other markets an issuer may appoint a trustee in order to make the bond issue more attractive to investors, as it means that there is an independent body to help look after their interests. This is particularly important for a secured issue, where the trustee sometimes holds collateral for the benefit of investors. Assets that are held by the trustee can be protected from the creditors of the issuer in the event of bankruptcy. A trustee has a variety of powers and discretion, which are stated formally in the issue trust deed, and these include its duties in relation to the monitoring of covenants and duties to bondholders.

## Custodian

A custodian provides safekeeping services for securities belonging to a client. The client may be an institutional investor, such as a pension fund, that requires a portfolio of securities in many locations to be kept in secure custody on their behalf. As well as holding securities, the custodian usually manages corporate actions such as dividend payments.

Reproduced from *An Introduction to Bond Markets, Fourth Edition* (2010)

**This extract from *Fixed Income Markets, Second Edition* (2014)**

### Convertible Bonds

## CONVERTIBLE BONDS

Convertible bonds have a long history in the capital markets, having been issued by utility companies in the United States in the nineteenth century. Today they are common in all global debt markets.

A convertible bond is a corporate debt security that gives the bondholder the right, without imposing an obligation, to convert the bond into another security under specified conditions, usually the ordinary shares of the issuing company. Thus a convertible bond provides an investor with an exposure to the underlying equity, but allied with a regular coupon payment and promise of capital repayment on maturity if no conversion takes place. From the investor's viewpoint a convertible usually presents higher value compared to the dividend stream of the equity, as well as an opportunity to share in any upside performance of the equity. The option represented by the convertibility feature carries value, for which investors are willing to pay a premium. This premium is in the form of a lower bond yield compared to a vanilla bond of equivalent liquidity and credit quality. Because of their structure, convertibles display the characteristics of both debt and equity instruments, and are often referred to as *hybrid* instruments.

In this section we provide a description of convertible bonds and an overview of issues in their valuation. We also describe a bond type that was introduced in the wake of the crash of 2008–09, the contingent convertible (CoCo) bond.

## Basic Features

Convertible bonds are typically fixed-coupon securities that are issued with an option to be converted into the equity of the issuing company under specified terms and conditions. They have been issued as both senior and subordinated securities. The investors' view on the performance of the issuing company's shares is a major factor, because investors are buying into the right to subscribe for the shares at a later date and, if exercised, at a premium on the open market price prevailing at first issue. For this reason the price of a convertible bond at any time will reflect changes in the price of the underlying equity; it also reflects changes in interest rates. Convertibles are typically medium- to long-dated instruments with maturities of 5 to 10 years. The coupon on a convertible is below the level payable on the same issuer's nonconvertible bond of the same maturity, reflecting the additional value of the equity option element. This is a key reason why issuer companies favour convertibles, because through them they can raise funds at a below-market (to them) interest rate. The bonds are usually convertible into shares under a set ratio and at a specified price.

The option element in a convertible cannot be stripped out of the bond element, and so is termed an "embedded option". The valuation of the bond takes into account this embedded optionality. Note also that unlike a straight equity option, there is no additional payment to make on conversion: the holder simply exchanges the bond for the specified number of shares. One could view the price paid for exercising the option as being the loss of the "bond" element, which is the regular coupon and redemption proceeds on maturity, but this should be viewed as more of an "opportunity cost" rather than a payment. This bond element is often referred to as the "bond floor", which is the straight debt element of the convertible. The bond floor can be viewed as the level at which a vanilla bond issued by the same company would trade; that is, its yield and price. It generally accounts for between 50 and 80% of the total value.

Some convertibles are callable by the issuer, under prespecified conditions. These are known as *convertible calls* and remove one of the advantages of the straight convertible—that conversion is at the discretion of the bondholder—because by calling a bond the issuer is able to force conversion, on terms potentially unfavourable to the investor. There are two types of call option. *Hardcall* is nonconditional while *softcall* is conditional. If a bond is hardcall protected for any time after issue, then the issuer may not early redeem the bond. During softcall protection, early redemption is possible under certain conditions, normally that the underlying share price must trade above a certain level for a specific period. This level is usually around 130% of the conversion price.

Investors rarely convert voluntarily. They may do so during an event such as a call or a tender offer, or if the share price has risen by a considerable amount. The main reason why early redemption is not generally in the investor's interest is because it will erode the "time value" of the option element, as well as remove the yield advantage of holding the convertible. It also removes the downside protection afforded by the bond. That is why softcall options build in a significant equity upside element before the issuer can redeem early. Issuers will call a bond to effect conversion into shares, at which point the bondholder will convert or simply receive cash for par value. Generally, there will be value in conversion at this point so converting is not problematic. Issuers also call convertibles if there is an opportunity to reissue debt at a lower interest rate.

## Investor Analysis

When evaluating convertible securities, the investor will consider the expected performance of the underlying shares, the future prospects of the company itself, and the relative attraction of the bond as a pure fixed income instrument in the event that the conversion feature proves to be worthless. He will also take into account the credit quality of the issuer, the yield give-up suffered as a result of purchasing the convertible over a conventional bond, the conversion premium ratio, and the fixed-income advantage gained over a purchase of the underlying shares in the first place.

Consider a convertible bond issued by hypothetical borrower ABC plc, which confers a right, but not the obligation, to the bondholder to convert into the underlying shares of ABC plc at a specified price during the next 10 years (see Table 7.4).

The terms and conditions under which a convertible is issued, and the terms under which it may be converted into the issuer's ordinary shares, are listed in the offer particulars or *prospectus*. The legal obligations of issuers and the rights of bondholders are stated in the *indenture* of the bond.

The ratio of exchange between the convertible bond and the ordinary shares can be stated either in terms of a *conversion price* or a *conversion ratio*. The conversion ratio is given by (7.4).

Conversion ratio = Bond denomination / Conversion price     (7.4)

| | |
|---|---|
| Issuer | ABC plc |
| Coupon | 10% |
| Maturity | December 2019 |
| Issue size | £50,000,000 |
| Face value | £1,000 |
| Number of bonds | 50,000 |
| Issue price | £100 |
| Current price | £103.50 |
| Conversion price | £8.50 |
| Dividend yield | 3.50% |

**Table 7.4** ABC plc 10% 2019 Convertible Hypothetical Bond Terms.

so that for the ABC plc bond it is

$$£1,000 / £8.50 = 117.64 \text{ shares}$$

Conversion terms for a convertible do not necessarily remain constant over time. In certain cases convertible issues will provide for increases or *step ups* in the conversion price at periodic intervals. A £1,000 denomination face value bond may be issued with a conversion price of, say, £8.50 a share for the first three years, £10 a share for the next three years, and £12 for the next five years, and so on. Under this arrangement, the bond will convert to fewer ordinary shares over time, which is a logical arrangement, given that the share price is expected to rise during this period. The conversion price is also adjusted for any corporate actions that occur after the convertibles have been issued, such as rights issues or stock dividends. For example, if there was a 2-for-1 rights issue, the conversion price would be halved. This provision protects the convertible bondholders and is known as an *antidilution* clause.

The *parity* or *intrinsic value* of a convertible refers to the value of the underlying equity, expressed as a percentage of the nominal value of the bond. Parity is given by (7.5).

$$\text{Parity} = \text{Share price} / \text{Conversion price} \qquad (7.5)$$

or

$$(\text{Share price} \times \text{Conversion ratio}) / \text{Face value}$$

The bond itself may be analysed—in the first instance—as a conventional fixed-income security, so using its coupon and maturity date we may calculate a current yield (running yield) and yield-to-maturity. The *yield advantage* is the difference between the current yield and the *dividend yield* of the underlying share, given by (7.6).

$$\text{Yield advantage} = \text{Current yield} - \text{Dividend yield} \qquad (7.6)$$

For the ABC plc bond the current yield of the bond is 9.66%, which results in a yield advantage of 6.16%. Equity investors also use another measure, the *break-even* value, which is given by (7.7).

$$\text{Break-even} = \left(\text{Bond price} - \text{Parity}\right) / \text{Yield advantage} \qquad (7.7)$$

The conversion price is the price paid for the shares when conversion takes place.

$$\text{Conversion price} = \frac{\text{Par value of bond}}{\text{Conversion ratio}} \qquad (7.8)$$

The *conversion premium* is the percentage by which the conversion price exceeds the current share price. The ABC plc bond has a conversion ratio of 117.64 (that is, 117.64 shares are received in return for the bond with a par value of £1,000) and therefore a conversion price of £8.50. If the current price of the share is £6.70, then we have:

$$
\begin{aligned}
\text{Percentage conversion permium} &= \frac{\text{Conversion price} - \text{Share price}}{\text{Share price}} \\
&= \frac{£8.50 - £6.70}{£6.70} \qquad (7.9) \\
&= 26.87\%
\end{aligned}
$$

The *conversion value* of the bond is given by:

$$\text{Conversion value} = \text{Share price} \times \text{Conversion ratio} \qquad (7.10)$$

This shows the current value of the shares received in exchange for the bond. As the current share price is £6.70, then the current conversion value is given by:

$$\text{Conversion value} = £6.70 \times 117.64 = £788.19$$

If the bond is trading at 103.50 (per 100), then the *percentage conversion price premium*, or the percentage by which the current bond price exceeds the current conversion value is given by (7.11).

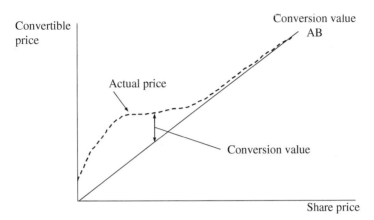

**Figure 7.2**   Convertible Bond and Conversion Premium

$$\text{Percentage conversion price premium} = \frac{\text{Price of bond} - \text{Conversion value}}{\text{Conversion value}}$$

$$(7.11)$$

In our example the premium value is:

$$= \frac{1,035 - 788.19}{788.19} = 31.32\%$$

The premium value in a convertible is illustrated in Figure 7.2, which shows the value of the convertible bond minus the conversion feature (represented by the line AB). It is sometimes referred to as the *straight line* value and is the conventional redemption yield measure. The minimum value of a convertible bond is the higher of its straight line value and conversion value.

Investors are concerned with the point at which the ratio of the parity of the bond to the investment value moves far above the bond floor. At this point, the security trades more like equity than debt, the "equity exposure investment" we described earlier. The opposite to this is when the equity price falls to low levels, to the point at which it will need to appreciate by a very large amount before the conversion option has any value; at this point the convertible trades as a yield investment.

Reproduced from *Fixed Income Markets, Second Edition* (2014)

This extract from *An Introduction to Bond Markets, Fourth Edition* (2010)

## Credit Ratings

The risks associated with holding a fixed-interest debt instrument are closely connected with the ability of the issuer to maintain regular coupon payments as well as redeem the debt on maturity. Essentially, *credit risk* is the main risk of holding a bond. Only the highest quality government debt, and a small number of supranational issues, may be considered to be entirely free of credit risk. Therefore, at any time the yield on a bond reflects investors' views on the ability of the issuer to meet its liabilities as set out in the bond's terms and conditions. A delay in paying a cash liability as it becomes due is known as technical default and is a cause for extreme concern for investors; failure to pay will result in the matter being placed in the hands of the legal court as investors seek to recover their funds. To judge the ability of an issue to meet its obligations for a particular debt issue, for the entire life of the issue, requires judgemental analysis of the issuer's financial strength and business prospects. There are a number of factors that must be considered, and larger banks, fund managers and corporates carry out their own *credit analysis* of individual borrowers' bond issues. The market also makes a considerable use of formal *credit ratings* that are assigned to individual bond issues by a formal credit-rating agency. In the international markets arguably the two influential rating agencies are Standard & Poor's Corporation (*S&P*) and Moody's Investors Service, Inc. (*Moody's*), based in the US. Fitch Investors Service, Inc. (*Fitch*) also has a high profile.

The specific factors that are considered by a ratings agency, and the methodology used in conducting the analysis, differ slightly amongst the individual ratings agencies. Although in many cases the ratings assigned to a particular issue by different agencies are the same, they occasionally differ, and in these instances investors usually seek to determine what aspect of an issuer is given more weight in an analysis by which individual agency. Note that a credit rating is not a recommendation to buy (or, equally, sell) a particular bond, nor is it a comment on market expectations. Credit analysis does take into account general market and economic conditions; the overall purpose of credit analysis is to consider the financial health of the issuer and its ability to meet the obligations of the specific issue being rated. Credit ratings play a large part in the decision-making of investors, and also have a significant impact on the interest rates payable by borrowers.

## CREDIT RATINGS

A credit rating is a formal opinion given by a rating agency, of the *credit risk* for investors in a particular issue of debt securities. Ratings are given to public issues of debt securities by any type of entity, including governments, banks and corporates. They are also given to short-term debt such as commercial paper as well as bonds and medium-term notes.

## Purpose of credit ratings

Investors in securities accept the risk that the issuer will default on coupon payments or fail to repay the principal in full on the maturity date. Generally, credit risk is greater for securities with a long maturity, as there is a longer period for the issuer potentially to default. For example, if a company issues 10-year bonds, investors cannot be certain that the company will still exist in 10 years' time. It may have failed and gone into liquidation some time before that. That said, there is also risk attached to short-dated debt securities; indeed, there have been instances of default by issuers of commercial paper, which is a very short-term instrument.

The prospectus or offer document for an issue provides investors with some information about the issuer so that some credit analysis can be performed on the issuer before the bonds are placed. The information in the offer documents enables investors themselves to perform their own credit analysis by studying this information before deciding whether or not to invest. Credit assessments take up time, however, and also require the specialist skills of credit analysts. Large institutional investors do in fact employ such specialists to carry out credit analysis; however, often it is too costly and time-consuming to assess every issuer in every debt market. Therefore, investors commonly employ two other methods when making a decision on the credit risk of debt securities:

- name recognition;
- formal credit ratings.

*Name recognition* is when the investor relies on the good name and reputation of the issuer and accepts that the issuer is of such good financial standing, or sufficient financial standing, that a default on interest and principal payments is highly unlikely. An investor may feel this way about, say, Microsoft or Coca Cola. However, the experience of Barings in 1995 suggested to many investors that it may not be wise to rely on name recognition alone in today's market place. The tradition and reputation behind the Barings name allowed the bank to borrow at the London Interbank Offer Rate (*Libor*) and occasionally at sub-Libor interest rates in the money markets, which put it on a par with the highest quality clearing banks in terms of credit rating. However, name recognition needs to be augmented by other methods to reduce the risk against unforeseen events, as happened with Barings. Credit ratings are a formal assessment, for a given issue of debt securities, of the likelihood that the interest and principal will be paid in full and on schedule. They are increasingly used to make investment decisions about corporate or lesser developed government debt.

## Formal credit ratings

Credit ratings are provided by the specialist agencies, including S&P's, Fitch's and Moody's.[1] There are other agencies both in the US and other countries. On receipt of a formal request the credit-rating agencies will carry out a rating exercise on a specific issue of debt capital. The request for a rating comes from the organisation planning the issue of bonds. Although ratings are provided for the benefit of investors, the issuer must bear the cost. However, it is in the issuer's interest to request a rating as it raises the profile of the bonds, and investors may refuse to buy paper that is not accompanied with a recognised rating. Although the rating exercise involves a credit analysis of the issuer, the rating is applied to a specific debt issue. This means that, in theory, the credit rating is applied not to an organisation itself, but to specific debt securities that the organisation has issued or is planning to issue. In practice, it is common for the market to refer to the creditworthiness of organisations themselves in terms of the rating of their debt. A highly rated company such as Rabobank is therefore referred to as a 'triple-A rated' company, although it is the bank's debt issues that are rated as triple-A.

The rating for an issue is kept constantly under review, and if the credit quality of the issuer declines or improves the rating will be changed accordingly. An agency may announce in advance that it is reviewing a particular credit rating, and may go further and state that the review is a precursor to a possible downgrade or upgrade. This announcement is referred to as putting the issue under *credit watch*. The outcome of a credit watch is in most cases likely to be a rating downgrade; however, the review may re-affirm the current rating or possibly upgrade it. During the credit watch phase the agency will advise investors to use the current rating with caution. When an agency announces that an issue is under credit watch, the price of the bonds will fall in the market as investors look to sell out of their holdings. This upward movement in yield will be more pronounced if an actual downgrade results. For example, in October 2008 the entity of Ireland was placed under credit watch and subsequently lost its AAA credit rating; as a result, there was an immediate and sharp sell-off in Irish government Eurobonds, before the rating agencies had announced the actual results of their credit review.

Credit ratings vary between agencies. Separate categories are used by each agency for short-term debt (with original maturity of 12 months or less) and long-term debt of over 1 year original maturity. It is also usual to distinguish between higher 'investment grade' ratings where the credit risk is low and lower quality 'speculative grade' ratings, where the credit risk is greater. High-yield bonds are speculative-grade bonds and are generally rated no

---

[1] The first ever credit rating was published by John Moody in the US in 1909, in a document that rated US Railway bonds.

higher than double B, although some issuers have been upgraded to triple-B in recent years and a triple-B rating is still occasionally awarded to a high-yield bond. A summary of long-term ratings is shown at Table 8.1 (overleaf).

Ratings can be accessed on the Bloomberg system. Composite pages are shown at Figures 8.1 and 8.2 (see p. 203) – Bloomberg screen RATD.

| Fitch | Moody's | S&P | Summary description |
|-------|---------|-----|---------------------|
| **Investment grade – high credit quality** | | | |
| AAA | Aaa | AAA | Gilt edged, prime, lowest risk, risk-free |
| AA+ | Aa1 | AA+ | High-grade, high credit quality |
| AA | Aa2 | AA | |
| AA– | Aa3 | AA– | |
| A+ | A1 | A+ | Upper-medium grade |
| A | A2 | A | |
| A– | A3 | A– | |
| BBB+ | Baa1 | BBB+ | Lower-medium grade |
| BBB | Baa2 | BBB | |
| BBB– | Baa3 | BBB– | |
| **Speculative – lower credit quality** | | | |
| BB+ | Ba1 | BB+ | Low grade; speculative |
| BB | Ba2 | BB | |
| BB– | Ba3 | BB– | |
| B+ | B1 | B+ | Highly speculative |
| B | B2 | B | |
| B– | B3 | B– | |
| **Highly speculative, substantial risk or in default** | | | |
| | | CCC+ | Considerable risk, in poor standing |
| CCC | Caa | CCC | |
| | | CCC– | |
| CC | Ca | CC | May already be in default, very speculative |
| C | C | C | Extremely speculative |
| | | CI | Income bonds – no interest being paid |
| DDD | | | Default |
| DD | | | |
| D | | D | |

**Table 8.1** Summary of credit rating agency bond ratings.
*Source*: Rating agencies.

| GRAB | | | | | | | | | Govt | RATD | |
|---|---|---|---|---|---|---|---|---|---|---|---|

**LONG-TERM RATING SCALES COMPARISON** Page 1/2

| MOODY'S | Aaa | Aa1 | Aa2 | Aa3 | A1 | A2 | A3 | Baa1 | Baa2 | Baa3 |
|---|---|---|---|---|---|---|---|---|---|---|
| S&P | AAA | AA+ | AA | AA- | A+ | A | A- | BBB+ | BBB | BBB- |
| COMP | AAA | AA+ | AA | AA- | A+ | A | A- | BBB+ | BBB | BBB- |
| TBW | AAA | AA+ | AA | AA- | A+ | A | A- | BBB+ | BBB | BBB- |
| FITCH | AAA | AA+ | AA | AA- | A+ | A | A- | BBB+ | BBB | BBB- |
| CBRS | AAA | AA+ | AA | AA- | A+ | A | A- | BBB+ | BBB | BBB- |
| DOMINION | AAA | AAH | AA | AAL | AH | A | AL | BBBH | BBB | BBBL |
| R&I | AAA | AA+ | AA | AA- | A+ | A | A- | BBB+ | BBB | BBB- |
| JCR | AAA | AA+ | AA | AA- | A+ | A | A- | BBB+ | BBB | BBB- |
| MI | AAA | | AA | | | A | | | BBB | |

Note: white = investment grade, yellow = non-investment grade

Australia 61 2 9777 8600     Brazil 5511 3048 4500     Europe 44 20 7330 7500     Germany 49 69 920410
Hong Kong 852 2977 6000 Japan 81 3 3201 8900 Singapore 65 6212 1000 U.S. 1 212 318 2000 Copyright 2005 Bloomberg L.P.
G479-793-0 29-Mar-05 7:50:48

**Figure 8.1**   Bloomberg screen RATD showing rating agency
investment-grade ratings scale.
© Bloomberg Finance L.P. All rights reserved. Used with permission.

| GRAB | | | | | | | | | Govt | RATD | |
|---|---|---|---|---|---|---|---|---|---|---|---|

**LONG-TERM RATING SCALES COMPARISON** Page 2/2

| MOODY'S | Ba1 | Ba2 | Ba3 | B1 | B2 | B3 | Caa1 | Caa2 | Caa3 | Ca | C |
|---|---|---|---|---|---|---|---|---|---|---|---|
| S&P | BB+ | BB | BB- | B+ | B | B- | CCC+ | CCC | CCC- | CC | C | D |
| COMP | BB+ | BB | BB- | B+ | B | B- | CCC+ | CCC | CCC- | CC | C | DDD |
| TBW | BB+ | BB | BB- | CCC+ | CCC | CCC- | CC+ | CC | CC- | | | D |
| FITCH | BB+ | BB | BB- | B+ | B | B- | CCC+ | CCC | CCC- | CC | C | D |
| CBRS | BB+ | BB | BB- | B+ | B | B- | | | | | C | D |
| DOMINION | BBH | BB | BBL | BH | B | BL | CCCH | CCC | CCCL | CC | C | D |
| R&I | BB+ | BB | BB- | B+ | B | B- | CCC+ | CCC | CCC- | CC+ | CC | CC- |
| JCR | BB+ | BB | BB- | B+ | B | B- | | CCC | | CC | C | D |
| MI | | BB | | | B | | | CCC | | CC | | DDD |

Note: white = investment grade, yellow = non-investment grade

Australia 61 2 9777 8600     Brazil 5511 3048 4500     Europe 44 20 7330 7500     Germany 49 69 920410
Hong Kong 852 2977 6000 Japan 81 3 3201 8900 Singapore 65 6212 1000 U.S. 1 212 318 2000 Copyright 2005 Bloomberg L.P.
G479-793-0 29-Mar-05 7:51:33

**Figure 8.2**   Bloomberg screen RATD showing rating agency sub-investment
grade ratings scale.
© Bloomberg Finance L.P. All rights reserved. Used with permission.

| CDO vintage | Collateral loss % | % current subordination | | | | Coverage ratio | | | | Estimated write-down % | | | | |
|---|---|---|---|---|---|---|---|---|---|---|---|---|---|---|
| | | AAA | AA | A | BBB | AAA | AA | A | BBB | AAA | AA | A | BBB | Equity |
| *Mezz SF* | | | | | | | | | | | | | | |
| 2003 | 16.4 | 25.9 | 16.3 | 12.0 | 6.8 | 1.6 | 1.0 | 0.7 | 0.4 | 0.0 | 1.4 | 100.0 | 100.0 | 100.0 |
| 2004 | 14.1 | 24.4 | 15.0 | 10.7 | 5.6 | 1.7 | 1.1 | 0.8 | 0.4 | 0.0 | 0.0 | 79.5 | 100.0 | 100.0 |
| 2005 | 18.8 | 23.6 | 14.4 | 10.3 | 5.2 | 1.3 | 0.8 | 0.5 | 0.3 | 0.0 | 48.5 | 100.0 | 100.0 | 100.0 |
| 2006 | 40.9 | 23.1 | 14.1 | 10.1 | 5.1 | 0.6 | 0.3 | 0.2 | 0.1 | 23.0 | 100.0 | 100.0 | 100.0 | 100.0 |
| 2007 | 47.1 | 23.1 | 14.1 | 10.1 | 5.0 | 0.5 | 0.3 | 0.2 | 0.1 | 31.2 | 100.0 | 100.0 | 100.0 | 100.0 |
| *HG SF* | | | | | | | | | | | | | | |
| 2003 | 2.9 | 7.4 | 4.1 | 2.5 | 1.4 | 2.6 | 1.4 | 0.9 | 0.5 | 0.0 | 0.0 | 25.0 | 100.0 | 100.0 |
| 2004 | 2.9 | 7.0 | 3.8 | 2.2 | 1.1 | 2.4 | 1.3 | 0.7 | 0.4 | 0.0 | 0.0 | 46.2 | 100.0 | 100.0 |
| 2005 | 5.7 | 6.7 | 3.6 | 2.1 | 1.0 | 1.2 | 0.6 | 0.4 | 0.2 | 0.0 | 68.1 | 100.0 | 100.0 | 100.0 |
| 2006 | 12.2 | 6.5 | 3.5 | 2.0 | 1.0 | 0.5 | 0.3 | 0.2 | 0.1 | 6.0 | 100.0 | 100.0 | 100.0 | 100.0 |
| 2007 | 20.4 | 6.5 | 3.5 | 2.0 | 1.0 | 0.3 | 0.2 | 0.1 | 0.0 | 14.9 | 100.0 | 100.0 | 100.0 | 100.0 |

**Table 8.2**  Average CDO portfolio losses and tranche write-down. Source: JPMorgan

The rating agencies did make changes to their structured finance rating methodologies after the crisis, although in the main these were not conceptual changes.[3] In the long run, short of the rating agencies introducing, say, a new AAA* rating exclusively for sovereign securities such as Treasuries and Gilts, investors should remember that it is possible for AAA structured finance securities to be downgraded in a way that should conceivably never happen for a AAA G7 sovereign security.

We should remember that a difference of opinion is what drives markets. Without a difference of opinion there is no liquidity. If investors were sceptical about the rating methodology, they were always in a position not to agree the valuation, or demand a higher premium for holding the securities – or to simply not buy the securities! It does appear that investors looked at AAA-rated CDO and other structured finance securities paying anything from 20 to 50 basis points above AAA sovereign securities and perceived an economist's free lunch. But of course this difference in credit spread existed for a reason, namely that higher paying securities reflect greater relative risk. Little thought was paid by many investors as to what the CDO or ABS bond's underlying assets were, or as to how the mark-to-market valuation of the CDO tranches changed with changes in exogenous factors and could fall even without a large number of underlying defaults. As the first defaults started to feed through from the sub-prime market to ABS and then CDO bonds, the overlying securities were downgraded, which resulted in mark-to-market losses and consequent write-downs.

A clear lesson learned from the crash is not necessarily to avoid securitisation, structured finance securities or credit derivatives, but rather to "know your risk".

Reproduced from *An Introduction to Bond Markets, Fourth Edition* (2010)

**This extract from *The Mechanics of Securitization* (2013)**

## Introduction to Securitization and Asset-Backed Securities

## Introduction to Securitization and Asset-Backed Securities

Perhaps the best illustration of the flexibility, innovation, and user-friendliness of the debt capital markets is the rise in the use and importance of securitization. As defined in Sundaresan (1997, page 359), securitization

---

[3] For example, Fitch no longer rated what were known as 'market value CDOs', and also no longer assigned AAA ratings to certain types of CDO securities.

is "a framework in which some illiquid assets of a corporation or a financial institution are transformed into a package of securities backed by these assets, through careful packaging, credit enhancements, liquidity enhancements, and structuring."

The flexibility of securitization is a key advantage for both issuers and investors. Financial engineering techniques employed by investment banks today enable bonds to be created from any type of cash flow. The most typical such flows are those generated by high-volume loans such as residential mortgages and car and credit card loans, which are recorded as assets on bank or financial house balance sheets. In a securitization, the loan assets are packaged together, and their interest payments are used to service the new bond issue.

In addition to the more traditional cash flows from mortgages and loan assets, investment banks underwrite bonds secured with flows received by leisure and recreational facilities, such as health clubs, and other entities, such as nursing homes. Bonds securitizing mortgages are usually treated as a separate class, termed *mortgage-backed securities*, or MBSs. Those with other underlying assets are known as *asset-backed securities*, or ABSs. The type of asset class backing a securitized bond issue determines the method used to analyze and value it.

The asset-backed market represents a large and diverse group of securities suited to a varied group of investors. Often these instruments are the only way for institutional investors to pick up yield while retaining assets with high credit ratings. They are considered by issuers because they represent a cost-effective means of removing assets from their balance sheets, thus freeing up lines of credit and enabling them to access lower-cost funding.

Instruments are available backed by a variety of assets covering the entire yield curve, with either fixed or floating coupons. In the United Kingdom, for example, it is common for mortgage-backed bonds to have floating coupons, mirroring the interest basis of the country's mortgages. To suit investor requirements, however, some of these structures have been modified, through swap arrangements, to pay fixed coupons.

The market in structured finance securities was hit hard in the wake of the 2007–2008 financial crisis. Investors shunned asset-backed securities in a mass flight to quality. As the global economy recovered from recession, interest in securitization resumed. We examine the fallout in the market later in this chapter. First we discuss the principal concepts that drive the desire to undertake securitization.

## THE CONCEPT OF SECURITIZATION

Securitization is a well-established practice in the global debt capital markets. It refers to the sale of assets, which generate cash flows, from the institution that owns them, to another company that has been specifically set up for the purpose, and the issuing of notes by this second company. These notes are backed by the cash flows from the original assets. The technique was introduced first as a means of funding for mortgage banks in the United States, with the first such transaction generally recognized as having been undertaken by Salomon Brothers in 1979. Subsequently, the technique was applied to other assets such as credit card payments and leasing receivables, and has been employed worldwide. It has also been employed as part of asset-liability management, as a means of managing balance sheet risk.

## Reasons for Undertaking Securitization

The driving force behind securitization has been the need for banks to realize value from the assets on their balance sheet. Typically these assets are residential mortgages, corporate loans, and retail loans such as credit card debt. The following are factors that might lead a financial institution to securitize a part of its balance sheet:

- If revenues received from assets remain roughly unchanged but the size of assets has decreased, this will lead to an increase in the return on equity ratio.
- The level of capital required to support the balance sheet will be reduced, which again can lead to cost savings or allow the institution to allocate the capital to other, perhaps more profitable, business.
- The financial institution can obtain cheaper funding: Frequently the interest payable on ABS securities is considerably below the level payable on the underlying loans. This creates a cash surplus for the originating entity.

In other words, a bank will securitize part of its balance sheet for one or all of the following reasons:

- Funding the assets it owns
- Balance sheet capital management
- Risk management and credit risk transfer.

We consider each of these in turn.

**Funding** Banks can use securitization to (1) support rapid asset growth, (2) diversify their funding mix and reduce cost of funding, and (3) reduce maturity mismatches. All banks will not wish to be reliant on only a single or a few sources of funding, as this can be risky in times of market liquidity difficulty. Banks aim to optimize their funding between a mix of retail, interbank, and wholesale sources. Securitization has a key role to play in this mix. It also enables a bank to reduce its funding costs. This is because the securitization process separates the credit rating of the originating institution from the credit rating of the issued notes. Typically most of the notes issued by special purpose vehicles (SPVs) will be more highly rated than the bonds issued directly by the originating bank itself. Although the liquidity of the secondary market in ABSs is frequently lower than that of the corporate bond market, and this adds to the yield payable by an ABS, it is frequently the case that the cost to the originating institution of issuing debt is still lower in the ABS market because of the latter's higher rating. Finally, there is the issue of maturity mismatches. The business of bank asset-liability management (ALM) is inherently one of maturity mismatch, because a bank often funds long-term assets, such as residential mortgages, with short-asset liabilities, such as bank account deposits or interbank funding. This funding "gap" can be mitigated via securitization, as the originating bank receives funding from the sale of the assets, and the economic maturity of the issued notes frequently matches that of the assets.

**Balance Sheet Capital Management** Banks use securitization to improve balance sheet capital management. This provides (1) regulatory capital relief, in some cases (depending on the form of the transaction), (2) "economic" capital relief, and (3) diversified sources of funding. As stipulated in the Bank for International Settlements (BIS) capital rules,[1] also known as the Basel rules, banks must maintain a minimum capital level for their assets, in relation to the risk of these assets. Under Basel I, for every $100 of risk-weighted assets a bank must hold at least $8 of capital; however, the designation of each asset's risk-weighting is restrictive. For example, with the exception of mortgages, customer loans are 100 percent risk weighted regardless of the underlying rating of the borrower or the quality of the security held. The anomalies that this raises, which need not concern us here, were partly addressed by the Basel II rules, which became effective from 2007. However, the Basel rules that have been in place since 1988 (and effective from 1992) were a key driver of securitization. Because an SPV is not a bank, it is not subject to Basel rules, and needs only such capital as is economically required by the nature of the assets it contains. This is not a set amount, but is significantly below the 8 percent level required by banks in all cases. Although an originating bank does not obtain 100 percent regulatory capital relief when it sells assets off its balance sheet to an SPV where it will have retained a first-loss piece out of the issued notes, its regulatory capital charge may be significantly reduced after the securitization.[2]

To the extent that securitization provides regulatory capital relief, it can be thought of as an alternative to capital raising, compared with the traditional sources of Tier 1 (equity), preferred shares, and perpetual loan notes

---

[1] For further information on this, see Choudhry (2007).
[2] The "first loss" piece refers to the most junior tranche on the liabilities sides of the securitization (the issued notes), and is the tranche that is exposed to the first of any default losses suffered by the underlying asset pool. In other words, it carries the most performance risk for the investor.

with step-up coupon features. By reducing the amount of capital that has to be used to support the asset pool, a bank can also improve its returnon-equity (ROE) value. This will be received favorably by shareholders.

**Risk Management**  Once assets have been securitized, the credit risk exposure on these assets for the originating bank is reduced considerably and, if the bank does not retain a first-loss capital piece (the most junior of the issued notes), it is removed entirely. This is because assets have been sold to the SPV. Securitization can also be used to remove non-performing assets from banks' balance sheets. This has the dual advantage of removing credit risk and removing a potentially negative sentiment from the balance sheet, as well as freeing up regulatory capital as before. Further, there is a potential upside from securitizing such assets: If any of them start performing again, or there is a recovery value obtained from defaulted assets, the originator will receive any surplus profit made by the SPV.

## Potential Benefits of Securitization to Investors

In theory there are a number of benefits available to investors from investing in ABS notes, centered mainly on the alternative sectors that they allow investors to diversify into. The potential attractions include:

- Ability to diversify into sectors of exposure that might not be available in the regular bond markets (for example, residential mortgages or project finance loans).
- Access to different (and sometimes superior) risk-reward profiles.
- Access to sectors that are otherwise not open to them.

A key benefit of ABS notes is the ability to tailor risk-return profiles. For example, if there is a lack of assets of any specific credit rating, these can be created via securitization. Securitized notes sometimes produce a better risk-reward performance than corporate bonds of the same rating and maturity. Although this might seem peculiar (why should one AA-rated bond perform better in terms of credit performance than another just because it is asset backed?), this occurs because the originator holds the first-loss piece in the structure.

A holding in an ABS also diversifies investor risk exposure. For example, rather than invest $100 million in an AA-rated corporate bond and be exposed to event risk associated with the issuer, investors can gain exposure to, for instance, 100 pooled assets. These pooled assets will, in theory, have lower concentration risk, although the experience of 2007–2008 showed that this theoretical diversification of concentration did not always occur in practice.

# THE PROCESS OF SECURITIZATION

We look now at the process of securitization, the nature of the SPV structure, and issues such as credit enhancements and the cash flow waterfall.

## Securitization Process

The securitization process involves a number of participants. First there is the *originator*, the firm whose assets are being securitized. The most common process involves an *issuer* acquiring the assets from the originator. The issuer is usually a company that has been specially set up for the purpose of the securitization, which is the SPV and is usually domiciled offshore. The creation of an SPV ensures that the underlying asset pool is held separate from the other assets of the originator. This is done so that in the event that the originator is declared bankrupt or insolvent, the assets that have been transferred to the SPV will not be affected. This is known as being "bankruptcy remote." Conversely, if the underlying assets begin to deteriorate in quality and are subject to a ratings downgrade, investors have no recourse to the originator.

By holding the assets within an SPV framework, defined in formal legal terms, the financial status and credit rating of the originator becomes almost irrelevant to the bondholders. The process of securitization often involves *credit enhancements*, in which a third-party guarantee of credit quality is obtained, so that notes issued under the securitization are often rated at investment grade and up to AAA-grade.

The process of structuring a securitization deal ensures that the liability side of the SPV—the issued notes—carries lower cost than the asset side of the SPV. This enables the originator to secure lower-cost funding that it would not otherwise be able to obtain in the unsecured market. This is a tremendous benefit for institutions with lower credit ratings

Exhibit 1.1 illustrates the process of securitization in simple fashion.

**Mechanics of Securitization**   Securitization involves a true sale of the underlying assets from the balance sheet of the originator. This is why a separate legal entity, the SPV, is created to act as the issuer of the notes. The assets being securitized are sold onto the balance sheet of the SPV. The process involves:

- Undertaking due diligence on the quality and future prospects of the assets.
- Setting up the SPV and then effecting the transfer of assets to it.
- Underwriting of loans for credit quality and servicing.
- Determining the structure of the notes, including how many tranches are to be issued, in accordance to originator and investor requirements.
- The notes being rated by one or more credit rating agencies.
- The placing of notes in the capital markets.

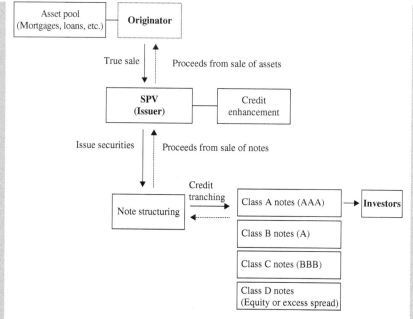

**Exhibit 1.1**   The securitization process

The sale of assets to the SPV needs to be undertaken so that it is recognized as a true legal transfer. The originator will usually hire external legal counsel to advise it in such matters. The credit rating process will consider the character and quality of the assets, and also whether any enhancements have been made to the assets that will raise their credit quality. This can include *overcollateralization*, which is when the principal value of notes issued is lower than the principal value of assets, and a liquidity facility is provided by a bank.

A key consideration for the originator is the choice of the underwriting bank that structures the deal and places the notes. The originator will award the mandate for its deal to an investment bank on the basis of fee levels, marketing ability, and track record with assets being securitized.

**Securitization Note Tranching**   As illustrated in Exhibit 1.1, in a securitization the issued notes are structured to reflect specified risk areas of the asset pool, and thus are rated differently. The senior tranche is usually rated AAA. The lower-rated notes usually have an element of *overcollateralization* and are thus capable of absorbing losses. The most junior note is the lowest rated or nonrated. It is often referred to as the *first-loss piece*, because it is impacted by losses in the underlying asset pool first. The first-loss piece is sometimes called the *equity piece* or equity note (even though it is a bond) and is usually held by the originator.

**Financial Modeling**   The originator will construct a cash flow model to estimate the size of the issued notes. The model will consider historical sales values, any seasonal factors in sales, credit card cash flows, and so on. Certain assumptions will be made when constructing the model, for example growth projections, inflation levels, tax levels, and so on. The model will consider a number of different scenarios, and also calculate the minimum asset coverage levels required to service the issued debt. A key indicator in the model will be the debt service coverage ratio (DSCR). The more conservative the DSCR, the more comfort there will be for investors in the notes. For a residential mortgage deal, this ratio might be approximately 2.5 to 3.0; however, for an exotic asset class like an airline ticket receivables deal, the DSCR would be unlikely to be lower than 4.0. The model will therefore calculate the amount of notes that can be issued against the assets while maintaining the minimum DSCR.

**Credit Rating**   It is common for securitization deals to be rated by one or more of the formal credit ratings agencies such as Moody's, Fitch, or Standard & Poor's. A formal credit rating will make it easier for the originator to place the notes with investors. The methodology employed by the ratings agencies takes into account both qualitative and quantitative factors, and will differ according to the asset class being securitized. The main issues in a typical ABS deal include:

- Corporate credit quality: These are risks associated with the originator, and are factors that affect its ability to continue operations, meet its financial obligations, and provide a stable foundation for generating future receivables. This might be analyzed according to (1) the issuer's historical financial performance, including its liquidity and debt structure; (2) its status within its domicile country, for example whether it is state-owned; (3) the general economic conditions for industry and for airlines; and (4) the historical record and current state of the airline—for instance its safety record and age of its airplanes.
- The competition and industry trends: the issuer's market share, the competition on its network.
- Regulatory issues, such as need for the issuer to comply with forthcoming legislation that would impact its cash flows.
- Legal structure of the SPV and transfer of assets.
- Cash flow analysis.

Based on the findings of the ratings agency, the arranger may redesign some aspect of the deal structure so that the issued notes are rated at the required level.

Above is a summary of the key issues involved in the process of securitization. Depending on investor sentiment, market conditions, and legal issues, the process from inception to closure of the deal may take anything from three to 12 months or more. After the notes have been issued, the arranging bank will no longer have anything to do with the issue; however, the bonds themselves require a number of agency services for their remaining life until they mature or are paid off. These agency services include paying agent, cash manager, and custodian.

## SPV Structures

There are essentially two main securitization structures: amortizing (pass-through) and revolving. A third type, the master trust, is used by frequent issuers.

**Amortizing Structures** Amortizing structures pay principal and interest to investors on a coupon-by-coupon basis throughout the life of the security, as illustrated in Exhibit 1.1. They are priced and traded based on expected maturity and weighted-average life (WAL), which is the time-weighted period during which principal is outstanding. A WAL approach incorporates various prepayment assumptions, and any change in this prepayment speed will increase or decrease the rate at which principal is repaid to investors. Pass-through structures are commonly used in residential and commercial mortgage-backed deals (RMBS and CMBS) and consumer loan ABS.

**Revolving Structures** Revolving structures revolve the principal of the assets; that is, during the revolving period, principal collections are used to purchase new receivables that fulfill the necessary criteria. The structure is used for short-dated assets with a relatively high prepayment speed, such as credit card debt and auto loans. During the amortization period, principal payments are paid to investors in a series of equal installments (*controlled amortization*) or principal is "trapped" in a separate account until the expected maturity date and then paid in a single lump sum to investors (*soft bullet*).

**Master Trust** Frequent issuers under U.S. and UK law use *master trust* structures, which allow multiple securitizations to be issued from the same SPV. Under such schemes, the originator transfers assets to the master trust SPV. Notes are then issued out of the asset pool based on investor demand. Master trusts have been used by MBS and credit card ABS originators.

## Credit Enhancement

Credit enhancement refers to the group of measures that can be instituted as part of the securitization process for ABS and MBS issues so that the credit rating of the issued notes meets investor requirements. The lower the quality of the assets being securitized, the greater the need for credit enhancement. This is often by one of the following methods:

*Overcollateralization*: Where the nominal value of the assets in the pool is in excess of the nominal value of issued securities.

*Pool insurance*: An insurance policy provided by an insurance company to cover the risk of principal loss in the collateral pool. The claims-paying rating of the insurance company is important in determining the overall rating of the issue.

*Senior/junior note classes*: Credit enhancement is provided by subordinating a class of notes (class B notes) to the senior class notes (class A notes). The class B notes' right to their proportional share of cash flows is subordinated to the rights of the senior noteholders. Class B notes do not receive payments of principal until certain rating agency requirements have been met; specifically, satisfactory performance of the collateral pool over a predetermined period, or in many cases until all of the senior note classes have been redeemed in full.

*Margin step-up*: A number of ABS issues incorporate a step-up feature in the coupon structure, which typically coincides with a call date. Although the issuer is usually under no obligation to redeem the notes at this point, the step-up feature was introduced as an added incentive for investors and serves to imply from the outset that the economic cost of paying a higher coupon is unacceptable, and so the issuer will seek to refinance by exercising its call option.

*Excess spread*: This is the difference between the return on the underlying assets and the interest rate payable on the issued notes (liabilities). The monthly excess spread is used to cover expenses and any losses. If any surplus is left over, it is held in a reserve account to cover against future losses or (if not required for that) as a benefit to the originator. In the meantime, the reserve account is a credit enhancement for investors.

All securitization structures incorporate a *cash waterfall* process, whereby the cash that is generated by the asset pool is paid in order of payment priority. Only when senior obligations have been met can more junior obligations be paid. An independent third-party agent is usually employed to run tests on the vehicle to confirm that there is sufficient cash available to pay all obligations. If a test is failed, then the vehicle will start to pay off the notes, starting from the senior notes. The waterfall process is illustrated in Exhibit 1.2.

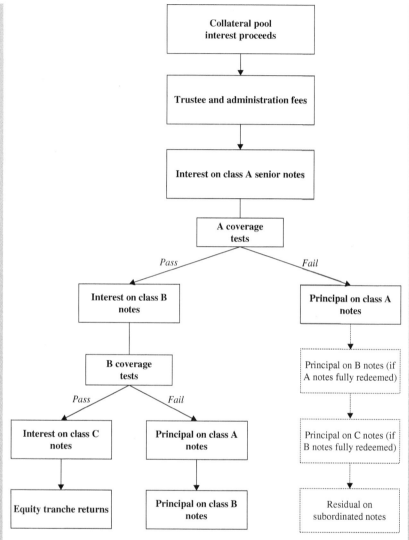

**Exhibit 1.2** Cash flow waterfall (priority of payments)

---

**EXAMPLE 1.1** Impact on balance sheet

The exhibit in this example illustrates by a hypothetical example the effect on the liability side of an originating bank's balance sheet from a securitization transaction. Following the process, selected assets have been removed from the balance sheet, although the originating bank may have retained the first-loss piece. With regard to the regulatory capital impact, this first-loss amount is deducted from the bank's total capital position. For example, assume a bank has $100 million of risk-weighted assets and a target Basel ratio of 12 percent,[3] and securitizes all $100 million of these assets. It retains the first-loss tranche, which forms 1.5 percent of the total issue. The remaining 98.5 percent will be sold on to the market. The bank will still have to set aside 1.5 percent of capital as a buffer against future losses, but it has been able to free itself of the remaining 10.5 percent of capital.

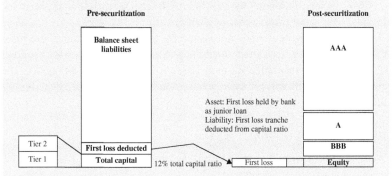

Regulatory capital impact of securitization

## SECURITIZING MORTGAGES

A mortgage is a long-term loan taken out to purchase residential or commercial property, which itself serves as security for the loan. The term of the loan is usually 20 to 25 years, but a shorter period is possible if the borrower, or *mortgagor*, wishes one. In exchange for the right to use the property during the term of the mortgage, the borrower provides the lender, or *mortgagee*, with a *lien*, or claim, against the property and agrees to make regular payments of both principal and interest. If the borrower defaults on the interest payments, the lender has the right to take over and sell the property, recovering the loan from the proceeds of the sale. The lien is removed when the debt is paid off.

---

[3] The minimum is 8 percent, but many banks set aside an amount well in excess of this minimum required level.

A lending institution may have many hundreds of thousands of individual residential and commercial mortgages on its books. When these are pooled together and used as collateral for a bond issue, the result is an MBS. In the U.S. market, certain mortgage-backed securities were backed, either implicitly or explicitly, by the government. A government agency, the Government National Mortgage Association (GNMA, known as Ginnie Mae), and two government-sponsored agencies, the Federal Home Loan Mortgage Corporation and the Federal National Mortgage Association (Freddie Mac and Fannie Mae, respectively), purchased mortgages to pool and hold in their portfolios and, possibly, securitize. The MBSs created by these agencies traded essentially as risk-free instruments and were not rated by the credit agencies. Following the 2007–2008 financial crash, Fannie Mae and Freddie Mac were taken under explicit government control.

Mortgage-backed bonds not issued by government agencies are rated in the same way as other corporates. Some nongovernment agencies obtain mortgage insurance for their issues to boost their credit quality. The credit rating of the insurer then becomes an important factor in the bond's credit rating.

## Growth of the Market

We list the following features of mortgage-backed bonds:

- Their yields were traditionally higher than those of corporate bonds with the same credit rating. In the mid-1990s, mortgage-backed bonds traded around 100 to 200 basis points above Treasury bonds; by comparison, corporates traded at a spread of around 80 to 150 for bonds of similar credit quality. This yield gap stems from the mortgage bonds' complexity and the uncertainty of mortgage cash flows. At the height of the structured finance market in 2007, MBS securities rated AAA paid a comfortable 20 to 30 bps over government security. That this was underpriced is reflected in spreads post-2008, which remain higher by some margin over equivalent rated conventional securities.
- They offer investors a wider range of maturities, cash flows, and security collateral to choose from.
- The market is large and until the 2007 crash was very liquid; agency mortgage-backed bonds had the same liquidity as Treasury bonds. Post-2008 the liquidity reduced considerably.
- Unlike most other bonds, mortgage-backed securities pay monthly coupons, an advantage for investors who require frequent income payments.

### EXAMPLE 1.2  Securitization transaction

We illustrate the impact of securitizing the balance sheet under original Basel I regulatory rules using a hypothetical example from ABC Bank PLC.

The bank has a mortgage book of £100 million, and the regulatory weight for this asset is 50 percent. The capital requirement is therefore £4 million (that is, 8 percent × 0.5 percent × £100 million). The capital is composed of equity, estimated to cost 25 percent, and subordinated debt, which has a cost of 10.2 percent. The cost of straight debt is 10 percent. The ALM desk reviews a securitization of 10 percent of the asset book, or £10 million. The loan book has a fixed duration of 20 years, but its effective duration is estimated at seven years, due to refinancings and early repayment. The net return from the loan book is 10.2 percent.

The ALM desk decides on a securitized structure that is made up of two classes of security, subordinated notes and senior notes. The subordinated notes will be granted a single-A rating due to their higher risk, whereas the senior notes are rated triple-A. Given such ratings the required rate of return for the subordinated notes is 10.61 percent, and that of the senior notes is 9.80 percent. The senior notes have a lower cost than the current balance sheet debt, which has a cost of 10 percent. To obtain a single-A rating, the subordinated notes need to represent at least 10 percent of the securitized amount. The costs associated with the transaction are the initial cost of issue and the yearly servicing cost, estimated at 0.20 percent of the securitized amount (see the accompanying summary information).

ABC Bank PLC mortgage loan book and securitization proposal

| | |
|---|---|
| **Current funding** | |
| Cost of equity | 25% |
| Cost of subordinated debt | 10.20% |
| Cost of debt | 10% |
| **Mortgage book** | |
| Net yield | 10.20% |
| Duration | 7 years |
| Balance outstanding | £100 million |
| **Proposed structure** | |
| Securitized amount | £10 million |
| Senior securities: | |
| Cost | 9.80% |
| Weighting | 90% |

| Maturity | 10 years |
|---|---|
| Subordinated notes: | |
| Cost | 10.61% |
| Weighting | 10% |
| Maturity | 10 years |
| Servicing costs | 0.20% |

A bank's cost of funding is the average cost of all the funds it employed. The funding structure in our example is capital 4 percent, divided into 2 percent equity at 25 percent, 2 percent subordinated debt at 10.20 percent, and 96 percent debt at 10 percent. The weighted funding cost $F$ therefore is:

$$F_{\text{balance sheet}} = \left(96\% \times 10\%\right) + \left[\left(8\% \times 50\%\right) \times \left(25\% \times 50\%\right)\right.$$
$$\left. + \left(10.20\% \times 50\%\right)\right]$$
$$= 10.30\%$$

This average rate is consistent with the 25 percent before-tax return on equity given at the start. If the assets do not generate this return, the received return will change accordingly, because it is the end result of the bank's profitability. As currently the assets generate only 10.20 percent, they are performing below shareholder expectations. The return actually obtained by shareholders is such that the average cost of funds is identical to the 10.20 percent return on assets. We may calculate this return to be:

$$\text{Asset return} = 10.20\% = \left(96\% \times 10\%\right) + \left(8\% \times 50\%\right)$$
$$\times \left(\text{ROE} \times 50\% + 10.20\% \times 50\%\right)$$

Solving this relationship we obtain a return on equity of 19.80 percent, which is lower than shareholder expectations. In theory, the bank would find it impossible to raise new equity in the market because its performance would not compensate shareholders for the risk they are incurring by holding the bank's paper. Therefore, any asset that is originated by the bank would have to be securitized, which would also be expected to raise the shareholder return.

The ALM desk proceeds with the securitization, issuing £9 million of the senior securities and £1 million of the subordinated notes. The bonds are placed by an investment bank with institutional investors. The outstanding balance of the loan book decreases from £100 million to £90 million. The weighted assets are therefore £45 million. Therefore, the capital requirement for the loan book is now

£3.6 million, a reduction from the original capital requirement by £400,000, which can be used for expansion in another area, a possible route for which is given here.

Impact of securitization on balance sheet

| Outstanding balances | Value (£m) | Capital required (£m) |
|---|---|---|
| Initial loan book | 100 | 4 |
| Securitized amount | 10 | 0.4 |
| Senior securities | 9 | Sold |
| Subordinated notes | 1 | Sold |
| New loan book | 90 | 3.6 |
| Total assets | 90 | |
| Total weighted assets | 45 | 3.6 |

The benefit of the securitization is the reduction in the cost of funding. The funding cost as a result of securitization is the weighted cost of the senior notes and the subordinated notes, together with the annual servicing cost. The cost of the senior securities is 9.80 percent, whereas the subordinated notes have a cost of 10.61 percent (for simplicity here we ignore any differences in the duration and amortization profiles of the two bonds). This is calculated as:

$$(90\% \times 9.80\%) + (10\% \times 10.61\%) + 0.20\% = 10.08\%$$

This overall cost is lower than the target funding cost obtained from the balance sheet, which was 10.30 percent. This is the quantified benefit of the securitization process. Note that the funding cost obtained through securitization is lower than the yield on the loan book. Therefore, the original loan can be sold to the structure issuing the securities for a gain.

# ABS STRUCTURES: A PRIMER ON PERFORMANCE METRICS AND TEST MEASURES

This section is an introduction to the performance measures on the underlying collateral of the ABS and MBS product. These would be of most interest to potential investors in ABS notes, but would also be noted by (amongst others) ratings agencies.

## Collateral Types

ABS performance is largely dependent on consumer credit performance, so typical ABS structures include trigger mechanisms (to accelerate amortization) and reserve accounts (to cover interest shortfalls) to safeguard against poor portfolio performance. Though there is no basic difference in terms of the essential structure between CDO and ABS/MBS, some differences arise by the very nature of the collateral and the motives of the issuer. Interestingly, whereas a CDO portfolio may have 100–200 loans, ABS portfolios will often have thousands of obligors, in theory providing the necessary diversity in the pool of consumers.

We discuss briefly some prominent asset classes.

**Auto Loans**  Auto loan pools were some of the earliest to be securitized in the ABS market and still remain a major segment of the U.S. market. Investors traditionally have been attracted to the high asset quality involved and the fact that the vehicle offers an easily sellable, tangible asset in the case of obligor default. In addition, because a car is seen as an essential purchase and a short loan exposure (three to five years) provides a disincentive to refinance, no real prepayment culture exists. Prepayment speed is extremely stable and losses are relatively low, particularly in the prime sector.

Performance analysis:

- **Loss Curves** show expected cumulative loss through the life of a pool and so, when compared to actual losses, give a good measure of performance. In addition, the resulting loss forecasts can be useful to investors buying subordinate classes. Generally, prime obligors will have losses more evenly distributed, while nonprime and subprime lenders will have losses recognized earlier and so show a steeper curve. In both instances, losses typically decline in the latter years of the loan.
- **The Absolute Prepayment Speed** (also abbreviated as APS)[4] is a standard measure for prepayments, comparing actual period prepayments as a proportion to the whole pool balance. As with all prepayment metrics, this measure provides an indication of the expected maturity of the issued ABS and, essentially, the value of the call option on the issued ABS at any time.

**Credit Cards**  For specialized credit card banks, particularly in the United States, the ABS market has become the primary vehicle to fund increases in the volume of unsecured credit loans to consumers. Credit card pools

---

[4] First developed by Credit Suisse First Boston.

arc different from other types of ABSs in that loans have no predetermined term. A single obligor's credit card debt is often no more than six months, so the structure has to differ from other ABSs in that repayment speed needs to be controlled either through scheduled amortization or the inclusion of a revolving period (where principal collections are used to purchase additional receivables).

Since 1991, the stand-alone trust has been replaced with a master trust as the preferred structuring vehicle for credit card ABS. The master trust structure allows an issuer to sell multiple issues from a single trust and from a single, albeit changing, pool of receivables. Each series can draw on the cash flows from the entire pool of securitized assets with income allocated to each pro rata based on the invested amount in the master trust.

Consider the example structure represented by Exhibit 1.3. An important feature is excess spread, reflecting the high yield on credit card debt. In addition, a financial guarantee is included as a form of credit enhancement, given the low rate of recoveries and the absence of security on the collateral. Excess spread released from the trust can be shared with other series suffering interest shortfalls.

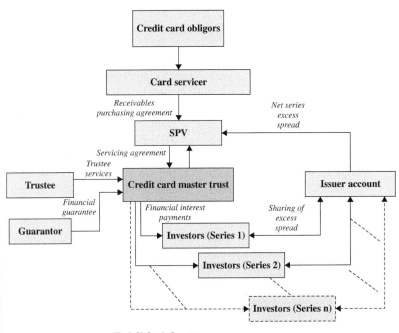

**Exhibit 1.3**  Master trust structure

Performance analysis:

- The **Delinquency Ratio** is measured as the value of credit card receivables overdue for more than 90 days as a percentage of total credit card receivables. The ratio provides an early indication of the quality of the credit card portfolio.
- The **Default Ratio** refers to the total amount of credit card receivables written off during a period as a percentage of the total credit card receivables at the end of that period. Together, these two ratios provide an assessment of the credit loss on the pool and are normally tied to triggers for early amortization and so require reporting through the life of the transaction.
- The **Monthly Payment Rate (MPR)**[5] reflects the proportion of the principal and interest on the pool that is repaid in a particular period. The ratings agencies require every non-amortizing ABS to establish a minimum as an early-amortization trigger.

**Mortgages**   The MBS sector is notable for the diversity of mortgage pools that are offered to investors. Portfolios can offer varying duration as well as both fixed and floating debt. The most common structure for agency MBS is pass-through, where investors are simply purchasing a share in the cash flow of the underlying loans. Conversely, nonagency MBS (including CMBS), have a senior and a tranched subordinated class with principal losses absorbed in reverse order.

The other notable difference between RMBS and CMBS is that the CMBS is a nonrecourse loan to the issuer as it is fully secured by the underlying property asset. Consequently, the debt service coverage ratio (DSCR) becomes crucial to evaluating credit risk.

Performance analysis:

- **Debt Service Coverage Ratio (DSCR)** is given by net operating income/debt payments, and so indicates a borrower's ability to repay a loan. A DSCR of less than 1.0 means that there is insufficient cash flow generated by the property to cover required debt payments.
- The **Weighted Average Coupon (WAC)** is the weighted coupon of the pool, which is obtained by multiplying the mortgage rate on each loan by its balance. The WAC will therefore change as loans are repaid, but at any point in time, when compared to the net coupon payable to investors, it gives us an indication of the pool's ability to pay.
- The **Weighted Average Maturity (WAM)** is the average weighted (weighted by loan balance) of the remaining terms to maturity

---

[5] This is not a prepayment measure because credit cards are non-amortizing assets.

(expressed in months) of the underlying pool of mortgage loans in the MBS. Longer securities are by nature more volatile, so a WAM calculated on the stated maturity date avoids the subjective call of whether the MBS will mature and recognizes the potential liquidity risk for each security in the portfolio. Conversely, a WAM calculated using the reset date will show the shortening effect of prepayments on the term of the loan.

The **Weighted Average Life (WAL)** of the notes at any point in time is

$$s = \sum t \cdot \text{PF}(s)$$

where

$$\text{PF}(s) = \text{Pool factor at } s$$
$$t = \text{Actual} / 365$$

We illustrate this measure using the example shown in Exhibit 1.4.

It is the time-weighted maturity of the cash flows that allows potential investors to compare the MBS with other investments with similar maturity. These tests apply uniquely to MBS because principal is returned through the life of the investment on such transactions.

Forecasting prepayments is crucial to computing the cash flows of MBS. Though the underlying payment remains unchanged, prepayments, for a given price, reduce the yield on the MBS. There are a number of methods used to estimate prepayment; two commonly used ones are the constant prepayment rate (CPR) and the PSA method.

The CPR approach is:

$$\text{CPR} = 1 - (1 - \text{SMM})^{12}$$

where **Single Monthly Mortality (SMM)** is the single-month proportional prepayment.

An SMM of 0.65 percent means that approximately 0.65 percent of the remaining mortgage balance at the beginning of the month, less the scheduled principal payment, will prepay that month.

The CPR is based on the characteristics of the pool and the current expected economic environment, as it measures prepayment during a given month in relation to the outstanding pool balance.

The **Public Securities Association (PSA)** has a metric for projecting prepayment that incorporates the rise in prepayments as a pool seasons. A pool of mortgages is said to have 100 percent PSA if its CPR starts at 0 and increases by 0.2 percent each month until it reaches 6 percent in month 30. It is a constant 6 after that. Other prepayment scenarios can be specified as multiples of 100 percent PSA. This calculation helps derive an implied prepayment speed assuming mortgages prepay slower during their first 30 months of seasoning.

| IPD | Dates | Actual Days (a) | PF(t) | Principal Paid | O/S | a/365 | PF(t)*(a/365) |
|---|---|---|---|---|---|---|---|
| 0 | 21/11/2003 | 66 | 1.00 | | 89,529,500.00 | 0.18082192 | 0.18082192 |
| 1 | 26/01/2004 | 91 | 0.94 | 5,058,824.00 | 84,470,588.00 | 0.24931507 | 0.23522739 |
| 2 | 26/04/2004 | 91 | 0.89 | 4,941,176.00 | 79,529,412.00 | 0.24931507 | 0.22146757 |
| 3 | 26/07/2004 | 91 | 0.83 | 4,823,529.00 | 74,705,882.00 | 0.24931507 | 0.20803536 |
| 4 | 25/10/2004 | 91 | 0.78 | 4,705,882.00 | 70,000,000.00 | 0.24931507 | 0.19493077 |
| 5 | 24/01/2005 | 91 | 0.73 | 4,588,235.00 | 65,411,765.00 | 0.24931507 | 0.18215380 |
| 6 | 25/04/2005 | 91 | 0.68 | 4,470,588.00 | 60,941,176.00 | 0.24931507 | 0.16970444 |
| 7 | 25/07/2005 | 91 | 0.63 | 4,352,941.00 | 56,588,235.00 | 0.24931507 | 0.15758269 |
| 8 | 24/10/2005 | 92 | 0.58 | 4,235,294.00 | 52,352,941.00 | 0.25205479 | 0.14739063 |
| 9 | 24/01/2006 | 90 | 0.54 | 4,117,647.00 | 48,235,294.00 | 0.24657534 | 0.13284598 |
| 10 | 24/04/2006 | 91 | 0.49 | 4,000,000.00 | 44,235,294.00 | 0.24931507 | 0.12318314 |
| 11 | 24/07/2006 | 92 | 0.45 | 3,882,353.00 | 40,352,941.00 | 0.25205479 | 0.11360671 |
| 12 | 24/10/2006 | 92 | 0.41 | 3,764,706.00 | 36,588,235.00 | 0.25205479 | 0.10300784 |
| 13 | 24/01/2007 | 90 | 0.37 | 3,647,059.00 | 32,941,176.00 | 0.24657534 | 0.09072408 |
| 14 | 24/04/2007 | 91 | 0.33 | 3,529,412.00 | 29,411,765.00 | 0.24931507 | 0.08190369 |
| 15 | 24/07/2007 | 92 | 0.29 | 3,411,765.00 | 26,000,000.00 | 0.25205479 | 0.07319849 |
| 16 | 24/10/2007 | 92 | 0.25 | 3,294,118.00 | 22,705,882.00 | 0.25205479 | 0.06392448 |
| 17 | 24/01/2008 | 91 | 0.22 | 3,176,471.00 | 19,529,412.00 | 0.24931507 | 0.05438405 |
| 18 | 24/04/2008 | 91 | 0.18 | 3,058,824.00 | 16,470,588.00 | 0.24931507 | 0.04586606 |
| 19 | 24/07/2008 | 91 | - | 16,470,588.00 | - | | - |
| | | | | | WAL | | 2.57995911 |

**Exhibit 1.4**   Sample weighted average life (WAL) calculation

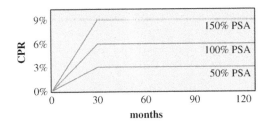

$$PSA = \left[ CPR / (.2)(m) \right] * 100$$

where $m$ = number of months since origination

## Summary of Performance Metrics

Exhibit 1.5 lists the various performance measures we have introduced in this chapter, and the asset classes to which they apply.

## In-House Securitization Transactions

Following the July–August 2007 implosion of the asset-backed commercial paper market, investor interest in ABS product dried up virtually completely. The growing illiquidity in the interbank market, which resulted in even large AA-rated banks finding it difficult to raise funds for tenures longer than one month, became acute following the collapse of Lehman Brothers in September 2008. To assist banks in raising funds, central banks starting with the U.S. Federal Reserve and European Central Bank (ECB), and subsequently the Bank of England (BoE), relaxed the criteria under which they accepted collateral from banks to whom they were advancing liquidity. In summary, the central banks announced that asset-backed securities, including mortgage-backed securities and other ABS, would now be eligible as collateral at the daily liquidity window.

As originally conceived, the purpose of these moves was to enable banks to raise funds from their respective central bank, using existing ABS on their balance sheet as collateral. Very quickly, however, the banks began to originate new securitization transactions, using illiquid assets held on their own balance sheet (such as residential mortgages or corporate loans) as collateral in the deal. The issued notes would be purchased by the bank itself, making the deal completely in-house. These new purchased ABS tranches would then be used as collateral at the central bank repo window.

This activity continued well beyond the period immediately after the 2008 crash and it is still common. In an effort to create assets that are eligible for use as collateral at central bank funding facilities, banks may elect to undertake an in-house securitization.

| Performance Measure | Calculation | Typical Asset Class |
|---|---|---|
| Public Securities Association (PSA) | PSA = [CPR/(.2) (months)]*100 | Mortgages, home equity, student loans |
| Constant prepayment rate (CPR) | $1 - (1 - SMM)^{12}$ | Mortgages, home equity, student loans |
| Single monthly mortality (SMM) | Prepayment / Outstanding pool balance | Mortgages, home equity, student loans |
| Weighted average life (WAL) | $\sum(a/365) \cdot PF(s)$ where $PF(s) =$ | Mortgages |
| Weighted average maturity (WAM) | Weighted maturity of the pool | Mortgages |
| Weighted average coupon (WAC) | Weighted coupon of the pool | Mortgages |
| Debt service coverage ratio (DSCR) | Net operating income / Debt payments | Commercial mortgages |
| Monthly payment rate (MPR) | Collections / Outstanding pool balance | All non-amortizing asset classes |
| Default ratio | Defaults / Outstanding pool balance | Credit card |
| Delinquency ratio | Delinquents / Outstanding pool balance | Credit card |
| Absolute prepayment speed (APS) | Prepayments / Outstanding pool balance | Auto loans, truck loans |
| Loss curves | Show expected cumulative loss | Auto loans, truck loans |

**Exhibit 1.5**    Summary of ABS analysis and performance metrics.

**Structuring Considerations** Essentially, a central bank deal is like any other deal, except that there is no buyer for the notes. Of course the issued notes must be structured such that they are eligible as collateral at the central bank where they are intended to be placed as collateral. There are also haircut considerations and the opportunity to structure it without consideration for investors. To be eligible for repo at the ECB, for example, deals have to fulfill certain criteria. These include:

Minimum requirements

- Public rating of triple-A or higher at first issue.
- Only the senior tranche can be repoed.
- No exposure to synthetic securities. The ECB rules state that the cash flow in generating assets backing the asset-backed securities must not consist in whole or in part, actually or potentially, of credit-linked notes or similar claims resulting from the transfer of credit risk by means of credit derivatives. Therefore, the transaction should expressly exclude any types of synthetic assets or securities;
- Public presale or new issue report issued by the agency rating the facility, either listed in Europe (e.g., the Irish Stock Exchange) or with book entry capability in Europe (e.g., Euroclear, Clearstream).

Haircut considerations

- Collateralized loan obligation (CLO) securities denominated in euro will (taking effect from March 2009) incur a haircut of 12 percent regardless of maturity or coupon structure.
- For the purposes of valuation, in the absence of a trading price within the past five days, or if the price is unchanged over that period, a 5 percent valuation markdown is applied. This equates to an additional haircut of 4.4 percent.
- CLO securities denominated in USD will incur the usual haircuts but with an additional initial margin of between 10 percent and 20 percent to account for foreign exchange (FX) risk.

Other considerations

- Can incorporate a revolving period (external investors normally would not prefer this).
- Can be a simple two-tranche setup. The junior tranche can be unrated and subordinated to topping off the cash reserve.
- Off-market swap.
- One rating agency (the BoE requires two).
- There can be no in-house currency swap (this must be with an external counterparty).

The originator also must decide whether the transaction is to be structured to accommodate replenishment of the portfolio or whether the portfolio should be static. ECB transactions are clearly financing transactions for the bank and as such the bank will wish to retain flexibility to sell or refinance some or all of the portfolio at any time should more favorable financing terms become available to it. For this reason there is often no restriction on the ability to sell assets out of the portfolio, provided that the price received by the issuer is not less than the price paid by it for the asset (par), subject to adjustment for accrued interest. This feature maintains maximum refinancing flexibility and has been agreed to by the rating agencies in previous transactions.

Whether or not replenishment is incorporated into the transaction depends on a number of factors. If it is considered likely that assets will be transferred out of the portfolio (in order to be sold or refinanced), then replenishment enables the efficiency of the CDO structure to be maintained by adding new assets rather than running the existing transaction down and having to establish a new structure to finance additional or future assets. However, if replenishment is incorporated into the transaction, the rating agencies will have to carry out diligence on the bank to satisfy themselves on the capabilities of the bank to manage the portfolio. Also, the recovery rates assigned to a static portfolio will be higher than those assigned to a manager portfolio. The decision on whether to have a managed or static transaction will have an impact on the documentation for the transaction and the scope of the bank's obligations and representations.

**Example of In-House Deal**    During 2007–2009 over 100 banks in the European Union undertook in-house securitizations in order to access the ECB discount window, as funding sources in the interbank market dried up.[8] A United Kingdom banking institution, the Nationwide Building Society, acquired an Irish banking entity during 2008 it was rumored solely in order to access the ECB's discount window (a requirement for which was to have an office in the eurozone area).

---

[8] The entire business model of a large number of banks as well as shadow banks such as structured investment vehicles (SIVs) had depended on available liquidity from the interbank market, which was rolled over on a short-term basis such as weekly or monthly and used to fund long-dated assets such as RMBS securities that had much longer maturities and that themselves could not be realized in a liquid secondary market once the 2007 credit crunch took hold. This business model unraveled after the credit crunch, with its most notable casualties being Northern Rock PLC and the SIVs themselves, which collapsed virtually overnight. Regulatory authorities responded by requiring banks to take liquidity risk more seriously, with emphasis on longer-term average tenor of liabilities and greater diversity on funding sources (for example, see the UK FSA's CP 08/22 document at www.fsa.org). We discuss liquidity management in *Bank Asset and Liability Management* (John Wiley & Sons Limited, 2007) and *The Principles of Banking* (John Wiley & Sons Limited, 2012).

**EXAMPLE 1.3**    **Fastnet securities 3 limited**

| | | Fastnet securities 3 limited | | | | |
| --- | --- | --- | --- | --- | --- | --- |
| Class | Balance | % of total | Rating (S&P) | WAL (years) | Legal final basis | Margin (bp) |
| A1 | 1,920,000,000 | 24% | AAA | 2.91 | Nov-2049 1-mo Euribor | 40 |
| A2 | 5,040,000,000 | 63% | AAA | 3.15 | Nov-2049 1-mo Euribor | 45 |
| B | 1,040,000,000 | 13% | n/r | 3.08 | Nov-2049 1-mo Euribor | 200 |
| | 8,000,000,000 | | | | | |
| Cash reserve | 400,000,000 | 5% | | | | |
| Swap spread | | | | | | 150 |

**Timing**

| | |
| --- | --- |
| Cut-off date | 12/5/2007 |
| Final OC | 12/17/2007 |
| Settlement | 12/17/2007 |
| First payment date | 2/11/2008 |

**Key terms**

| | |
| --- | --- |
| Issuer | Fastnet Securities 3 Ltd |
| Originator | Irish Life and Permanent |
| Sole arranger | Deutsche Bank AG |
| Trustee | Deutsche Trustee Company Ltd |
| First payment date | Monday, February 11, 2008 |
| Day count | Actual/360 |

*(Continued)*

**EXAMPLE 1.3**   Fastnet securities 3 limited *(Continued)*

**Fastnet securities 3 limited**

| Class | Balance | % of total | Rating (S&P) | WAL (years) | Legal final basis | Margin (bp) |
|---|---|---|---|---|---|---|
| Listing | Irish Stock Exchange | | | | | |
| Settlement | Euroclear/Clearstream | | | | | |
| Legal maturity date | Thursday, November 11, 2049 | | | | | |
| **Asset pool** | | | | | | |
| Mortgage pool | Residential mortgages originated by Irish Life in the Republic of Ireland | | | | | |
| Number of obligors | 35,672 | | | | | |
| Aggregate balance | EUR 8,319,049,200.22 | | | | | |
| Average balance | EUR 226,190 | | | | | |
| Largest mortgage | EUR 8,502,202 | | | | | |
| Weighted average Loan-to-Value Ratio (LTV) | 83% | | | | | |
| Weighted average seasoning | 21 months | | | | | |
| Weighted average remaining term | 27.3 years | | | | | |
| Longest maturity date | 2-Nov-47 | | | | | |

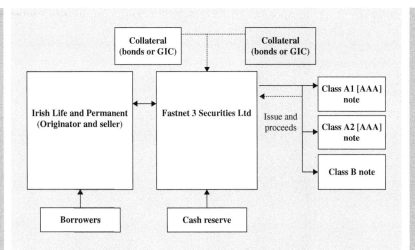

Note that this transaction was closed in December 2007, a time when the securitization market was essentially moribund in the wake of the credit crunch. An ABS note rated AAA could be expected to be marked to market at over 200 bps over LIBOR. Because the issued notes were purchased in entirety by the originator, who intended to use the senior tranche as collateral to raise funds at the ECB, the terms of the deal could be set at a purely nominal level; this explains the "40 bps over Euribor" coupon of the senior tranche.

One such public deal was Fastnet Securities 3 Limited, originated by Irish Life and Permanent PLC. Example 1.3 shows the deal highlights.

## Market Yields and Prices Post Credit Crunch

During July and August 2009 a secondary market began to reemerge in European markets as investors began to pull back from the flight to quality exhibited during 2007–2008.

As an example of the yields that were trading during this time, see Exhibit 1.6. This shows the Bloomberg page DES for Columbus Nova, a CLO transaction closed in August 2006. At issue: The senior tranche of this deal, which was rated AAA, paid 26 bps over three-month LIBOR, and was priced at par. At the start of September 2009, the tranche was being offered at 87, over 400 bps over LIBOR. It was still rated AAA.

We consider postcrash developments in the market in Chapter 2.

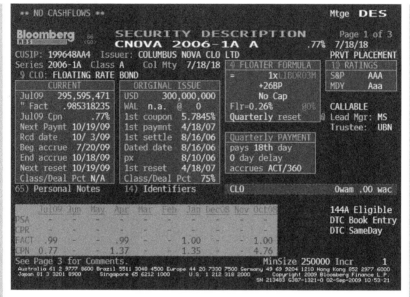

**Exhibit 1.6**   Columbus Nova CLO DES page
*Source*: Bloomberg LP. Reproduced with permission.

## SUMMARY AND CONCLUSIONS

Securitization is a long-established technique that enables banks to manage their balance sheets with greater flexibility and precision. By employing it, a bank can work toward ensuring optimum treatment of its assets for funding, regulatory capital, and credit risk management purposes. In addition, in the postcrash era the securitization tool continues to be used to create tradable notes that can then be used as collateral at the central bank.

The primary driver behind the decision to securitize part of the asset side of the balance sheet is one or more of the following:

- Funding: Assets that are unrepo-able may be securitized, which enables the bank to fund them via the capital market, or by creating notes that can be used as collateral at the central bank.
- Regulatory capital: This is a rarer reason driving securitization in the postcrash, Basel III era, however it is still possible to structure a deal that reduces regulatory capital requirement, principally if "significant risk transfer" has taken place.
- Risk management: Assets on the balance sheet expose the originator to credit risk, and this can be managed (either reduced, removed, or hedged) via securitization.

A secondary driver is client demand: The process of securitization creates bonds that can be sold, and investor demand for a note of specified credit risk, liquidity, maturity, and underlying asset class may well cause a bond to be created, via securitization, to meet this specific investor requirement. Whether a transaction is demand driven or issuer driven, it will always be created to meet at least one of the preceding requirements.

The mechanics of closing a securitization deal, which we cover in detail in subsequent chapters, can take anything from a few months to up to a year or more. The most important parts of the process are the legal review and drafting of transaction documents, and the rating agency review. The involvement of third parties, such as lawyers, trustees, agency services providers, and the rating agencies, is the key driver behind the cost of closing a securitization deal, and these costs are covered either by the deal itself or directly by the originating institution.

A wide range of asset classes can be securitized, with the most common being residential mortgages and corporate loans. Other asset classes include auto loans and credit card receivables. When assessing the risk exposure and performance of different types of ABS, investors will consider the behaviors and characteristics of the specific type of underlying asset. Some performance metrics are of course common to all types of assets, such as delinquency rate or the percentage of nonperforming loans.

A type of securitization unknown before the 2008 crash but now common is the in-house transaction. In this process, the originating bank will undertake all the usual steps to structure the deal, but will buy the ABS notes itself. These notes, which would be rated by a rating agency in the normal way, are then available to the bank to use as collateral, either in a repo transaction or to place with the central bank. The deal has thereby transformed illiquid assets on the bank's balance sheet into liquid notes that can then be used to raise funding.

Reproduced from *The Mechanics of Securitization* (2013)

## SELECTED BIBLIOGRAPHY AND REFERENCES

Buchanan, B. (2017), *Securitization and the Global Economy: History and Prospects for the Future*, Palgrave Macmillan.

Sundaresan, S. (1997). *Fixed Income Markets and their Derivatives*, Cincinnati, OH: South-Western Press.

*"He is a passionate, emotional player, and those characters will always argue with people. He is a winner and that is what I love about him. He confronts people, he demands more. He is a better player than anyone else at Arsenal and he works harder than the lot of them . . . Very few players have Sanchez's natural ability, but there is no reason why they shouldn't have his work ethic too."*
—Danny Murphy describing Arsenal FC player Alexis Sanchez,
*London Evening Standard,* 6 January 2017

# PART

# II

# Bank Regulatory Capital and Risk Management

art II of the book comprises essential breadth and depth on bank risk management for practitioners. In other words, now we are beyond the theory. In banking, to be effective from all stakeholder viewpoints one has to have an ability to take decisions, to understand both risk and return. Often the most difficult process in banks is the one that requires an actual decision to be taken; inaction (actually a decision in itself) can be as risky, if not more so, than deciding on a proactive course of action. Board members are prone to suffer considerable angst when a decision needs to be taken, except when there is consensus or the boss has spoken.

The best preparation and grounding for decision-making ability in a bank is to understand the balance sheet, what its current shape and structure are, what its sensitivities are to changes in market factors, and what shape one would like it to be in the medium-term. To be at this stage requires experience and some measure of technical expertise. Part II hopes to supply some of the latter, and possibly a proxy form of the former. It comprises chapters on:

- Risk "taxonomy", in other words, coverage of the different types of balance sheet risks (credit, market, and liquidity) as well as operational risk;
- Regulatory capital basics and requirements.

There is also a chapter on financial statements and accounting. As we describe later in Part III, managing the balance sheet of a bank effectively requires good interaction and process between Treasury, Risk, and Finance, as well as the business lines. Not everyone in these various departments will be familiar with elements of finance and financial reporting, yet it is important for bankers to know the basics, which is why we include material on the topic in this book.

*"People aren't friends till they have said all they can say, and are able to sit together, at work or rest, hour-long without speaking. . ."*
—T. E. Lawrence, quoted in J. Wilson, *Lawrence of Arabia: The Authorised Biography of T. E. Lawrence,* London 1989, p. 704

# CHAPTER 5

# Banks and Risk Management

The practice of finance brings with it risk exposures that have to be understood and managed, for all participants. Banks are (or should be) at the forefront of this discipline. In fact the art of banking is the art of managing risk on both sides of the balance sheet. In this chapter, we introduce the "universe" of risk for banks, and develop the individual segments in subsequent chapters. In addition, there is a primer on the value-at-risk (VaR) risk measurement tool. Many regulators request the banks they supervise to employ the VaR technique when calculating risk exposure and thereby their minimum capital requirement, and as such it is worthwhile being aware of the methodology, the assumptions behind it, and its weaknesses.

## THE RISK MANAGEMENT UNIVERSE FOR BANKS[1]

It is sensible to group balance sheet related risks in banking separate from other risks. The former includes the main one for banks, credit risk, as well as market risk, non-traded market risk, and liquidity risk. The latter would include technology risk, operational risk, and conduct risk.

### Introduction

Banks are by their nature risk-taking institutions and as far as possible seek to meet the precise needs of their customers. This "business as usual" gives rise to balance sheet risk exposure which must be managed. Essentially banks offer the lending terms, maturities, rate options, currency, optionality, and contingencies demanded by their clients, and take on the range of risks associated with providing these services. Because banks have a wide range of clients with varying borrowing and deposit requirements, exposures may to some degree offset each other, but will not match completely in terms of timing, amount, and currency.

---

[1] This section was co-written with Ed Bace and Peter Eisenhardt.

Banks must have the scale, systems, expertise and staff to concentrate on financial risk. Throughout history, banks have generally charged their clients sufficiently for taking on the range of risks and consequently earned profits. Banks can match fund loans to maturity immediately to offset interest-rate risks, which sometimes negates profitability. Banks can also choose to hedge through a range of mechanisms. Finally, balance sheet positions can be left open with risk retained if the view is taken that markets will move in a direction favourable to the exposure, and be reduced or offset in the course of new business.

In this chapter, we take a high-level view of risk management before detailing the risks in subsequent chapters. Specifically, we will focus on the aggregation of risk, concentration and correlation, determination of risk tolerance and its translation into limits, and means of risk mitigation.

### Risk Management: High Level

A bank is defined by its risk management approach and framework. It is integral to strategy, and must be determined at the Board and senior management level. The regulatory framework merely sets out minimum standards. Management must use all its experience and knowledge to establish risk policies that fit the bank's markets and capabilities, by means of:

- Defining a business model based on competitive strengths in markets and products;
- Identifying and understanding the risks and returns of the model, and reviewing and adjusting constantly as conditions change and markets evolve;
- Quantifying the risks and developing and maintaining risk management monitoring capabilities supported by robust IT systems;
- Constructing a broad array of possible techniques for mitigating risks;
- Instilling a strong culture of risk management and ensuring objectives and the risk strategy are understood at all levels of the bank.

Risk oversight is the responsibility of the Board and stands apart from risk management, which is the responsibility of management. Internal audit teams are important in risk management, focusing on protecting against fraud and the preparation of sound financial reports. However, the Board is accountable ultimately for all aspects of risk management at every level. Good practice dictates that the Board defines risk management issues that will always require direct elevation for its attention. In other words, the Board must own every aspect of risk tolerance and risk appetite for the bank, from credit risk on origination through to market risk and operational risk as a business-as-usual (BAU) function. This culminates in a formal risk appetite and guidance statement that every member of the Board must sign up to and must maintain responsibility for.

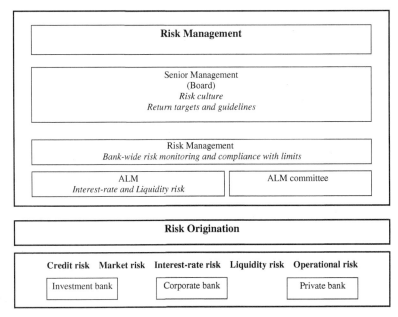

**FIGURE 5.1**   Overview of a risk management framework
*Source*: The Principles of Banking (2012).

The reward system of the bank must encourage employees to seek out business and realise returns without taking excessive or disproportionate risks. It is crucial that banks have a strong independent risk function to ensure "producers" (lending officers, sales teams, and traders) keep revenues and new business in balance with risk. This risk function must be backed up and fully supported by senior management. A key challenge is to ensure consistency across all areas, so that perceived banking "stars" or over-hyped "businesses of the future" are held to the same risk–reward standards. Figure 5.1 is a stylised view of the central risk management function in a bank.

## Aggregation of Risk

Banks must place sufficient emphasis on their processes to identify, monitor, and aggregate risk. Action cannot be taken to dispose of or mitigate risk and limit losses without a complete picture. It is inefficient to take aggressive steps to deal with risk in individual parts of the bank when these risks may actually have some offset in others, so that the need for selling or hedging is limited. This includes lending, trading, funding, interest-rate risk exposure, and off-balance sheet businesses.

In order to understand both the diversification and correlation of the portfolio, and likely outcomes in various environments, the bank requires aggregate data. In times of economic stress, regulators and other banks cannot help, and potential merger partners with fresh capital cannot be found, without comprehensive management information systems to assess the situation in a timely manner.

The Financial Stability Board issued a report in 2011 noting that aggregate data reporting at global systemically important banks was inadequate, and set a deadline of 2016 to meet supervisory expectations. Complex group structures and businesses ranging across legal entities and regions must not hinder risk data aggregation.

Risk aggregation models include:

- *Summation*: add together individual capital components;
- *Constant diversification*: subtract fixed risk percentage from summation to reflect diversification;
- *Variance-Covariance*: components weighted based on bilateral correlation;
- *Copulas*: use of multi-variate probability theory to evaluate marginal risks;
- *Full modelling*: simulate impact of multiple risk factors on all components.

Banks must consider clarity and simplicity, IT cost, non-linearity of risks, and over-reliance on assumptions in assessing the most appropriate of these models.

The simplest and most traditional approach in a credit risk setting is to consider just two scenarios, default and no default. A binomial tree is built over a number of time periods until maturity. A more advanced approach was, however, developed, where the observable market prices, data for bonds, indices for credit rating and sector categories were used to compute a volatility value for the credit portfolio.

Variance-Covariance value-at-risk (VaR) was introduced in the mid-1990s and quickly became popular, revolutionising credit portfolio risk management. The model joined previous market risk methodologies to estimate portfolio VaR to include upgrades and downgrades, as well as defaults. Credit risk monitoring shifted to a more mark-to-market approach.

Risk management models must be effective not only in normal conditions, but also in extreme situations. However, in the past a VaR confidence level was generally calibrated to only two standard deviations (95%). This was not effective in the extreme markets of the late 1990s with financial crises in Asia and Russia. Tail risk (three standard deviations beyond the mean) must also be captured and monitored. Risks with disproportionately high probabilities of extreme outcomes are referred to as having "fat tails".

Nasim Taleb's book, *The Black Swan: The Impact of the Highly Improbable*, is a widely discussed and popular study of the extreme impact of unpredictable outlier events. That said, the book offers very little if anything in the way of practical guidance as to how the impact of such tail events can be mitigated in practice. For this reason, the most important aspect of the risk management culture at a bank must be that every bank must know its risk and understand the nature of its exposure to economic fluctuations to a sufficient degree of familiarity that it can mitigate the exposures in a satisfactory manner.

Any model is dependent on assumptions, which are generally based on historical experience. The key assumption in using historical experience is that this is representative of future experience. Numbers generated by a model therefore cannot be taken as the final assessment of risk. One of the worst assumptions in banking history was that, because there had never been a nation-wide housing slump, a portfolio of US retail mortgages could be made safe by diversifying across regions. This helped lead to the creation of high volumes of mortgage-backed securities that suffered large financial losses.

Banks may choose to compare and benchmark their risk management against peers and competitors to validate models. While helpful, adherence to the same methodologies and assumptions can lead to systemic (as opposed to idiosyncratic) risk. Homogeneity in credit risk assumptions is in part addressed by the BIS by allowing banks to assign their own internal ratings to individual credits.

Management judgement is also an important element of risk management, as not all risks can be quantified using mathematical and statistical techniques. Some risks, such as reputational risk, are largely unquantifiable.

Regulatory capital requirements address diversification, concentration, and correlation risk to some extent; however, sound judgements by experienced management can be used to provide greater insights into these risks.

## Diversification

The concept of diversification is intuitive and well known to all, as evidenced by the popular saying "don't put all your eggs in one basket". Diversification helps protect against losses arising from idiosyncratic risk. It does not help with systemic risk, which is what would lead to catastrophic losses or total failure of the financial system. A well-diversified portfolio will perform in line with overall markets and the economy, and have more predictable volatility and manageability.

Diversification can be a problem for specialised and regional banks. Examples in the US include specialised mortgage banks and regional Savings and Loans Associations. Prior to a relaxation of interstate banking laws, many US banks were forced to lend within their states, some of which were dominated by just a few industries.

Diversification is not a solution to all the risks faced by banks. Banks that diversify by lending to sectors and regions where they have limited expertise, insufficient ability to monitor transactions, and competitive disadvantages may find that there are other risks which arise as a result. This issue would be greater for smaller banks with limited resources. In short, banks must focus on both individual risks and the overall portfolio.

Diversification is not a substitute for quality lending. Although banks have put in place mechanisms, such as credit provisions and risk capital, which allow them to absorb losses up to a certain point, and only those within their estimation of their risk exposure, badly considered diversification can lead to diminished returns or even large losses. Diversification of a portfolio for the purpose of investment returns must be viewed very differently from diversification for credit risk management. Managing the portfolio in terms of investment returns will be more focused on the "upside", while credit risk management is concerned with the "downside" risk. Default correlation increases significantly in deteriorating market conditions, while asset return correlation is less sensitive.

Diversification analysis will review industry sectors, size, products, and regions. In doing so, methodologies to quantify expected losses given varying degrees of diversification can be a useful tool in decision-making.

## Concentration

Excessive concentration of credit risk has been identified by global regulators as one of the key causes of bank crises and failures. Traditionally, concentration risk was viewed as the risk of over-exposure to single borrowers, but the emphasis is now on excessive correlation across the entire portfolio. BIS studies have concluded that sector concentrations have had a bigger impact on bank credit portfolios than single name exposures. While name concentration is straightforward, correlation risk management is challenging in terms of both setting appropriate assumptions and performing analytics.

Basel II is based on the Asymptotic Single Risk Factor model, where each asset class (for example, corporate, bank, sovereign, retail) is assigned a single correlation to the overall performance of the economy. No form of concentration risk was considered in the previous calculation of capital requirements, and thus did not fully incentivise diversification. As banks realised the need to more fully analyse correlations in the portfolio, more sophisticated methodologies have been developed.

Historically, many regulatory regimes across the world set a large exposure limit to a single entity or related entities of 25% of a bank's regulatory capital.

In April 2014, the BIS issued a new standard addressing concentration risk, considering exposure to both instrument-based asset classes (for example, asset backed securities and collateralised debt obligations) and systemically important financial institutions (SIFIs) and individual companies. The revised framework will help ensure a common minimum standard for measuring, aggregating, and controlling concentration risk across jurisdictions.

## Correlation

Even if single name exposures are limited, and transactions are evaluated and structured on a sound basis, management must make correlation assessments on the aggregate portfolio. If different borrowers are sensitive to the same changes in economic, business, regulatory, financial market, and political conditions, a much larger exposure akin to a single large borrower is created, which can result in heavy losses.

The US Comptroller of the Currency has identified as highly correlated credit exposures to borrowers, those:

- Related through group structure;
- Dependent on the same guarantor;
- Dependent on the selling of the same manufacturer's product;
- In the same industry or economic sector;
- In the financial sector;
- Within a geographic area dominated by few business enterprises;
- Owned by a foreign government;
- Secured by a common debt or equity instrument.

Product areas where correlation risk has been identified by global regulators as having created large concentration risk include retail products (for example, credit cards, home equity), leveraged loans, CDOs, and commercial real estate.

Once pools of correlated risks are identified, it is necessary to examine whether there is further correlation across those pools. As one example, there could be a correlation between transportation and hotel sector exposures.

For maximum diversification, banks would construct a loan portfolio with the lowest possible correlations. The lower the correlation, the fewer the number of loans needed for a diverse portfolio. New loans might increase diversification. But again, this must be balanced against expertise and competitive position in markets and clients.

It should also be noted that correlation is difficult to measure as a result of data constraints. For example, in order to determine correlation between asset classes and default rates for an asset class and the economy as accurately as possible, one would need data points for all possible scenarios. This would include periods of low, medium, and high economic stress, as well as corresponding default rate data. In reality, this data is difficult to obtain and validate, and often does not contain sufficient information around extreme scenarios to allow for accurate calibration of correlation.

## Risk Management Tolerance and Parameters

The risk appetite of a bank is driven to a large extent by the size of its free or available capital, and to a material extent by its funding model and its ability to raise sufficient levels of long-term (or stable) liquidity. Banks must maintain minimum regulatory capital ratios. Any strategy must be based on having enough capital to meet these requirements in even the most challenging environments. However, banks must not stop at main-taining minimum regulatory capital, but should also perform a thorough analysis of their business model and capital needs under various scenarios. The amount of capital required as assessed by a bank is known as risk cap-ital or economic capital.

A risk appetite statement must be coordinated by the risk management team and include senior management before being approved by the Board. Shareholders, regulators, and rating agencies will be part of the process. Parameters are likely to include:

- Desired External Risk Rating;
- Risk-adjusted Return on Capital (RAROC) hurdle rate for new business;
- Weighted Average Portfolio Rating;
- Relative internal capital allocation to Credit, Interest Rate, Market and Operational Risk;
- Concentration Thresholds (Obligor, Sector, Country);
- Asset–Liability Management mismatch;
- Liquidity Thresholds and metrics;
- Connection to Business Strategy;
- Acceptable earnings volatility;
- Controlled or undesirable exposures;
- Targeted levels of Risk Asset Ratios or leverage.

The statement will anticipate scenarios of market stress and plan pos-sible responses. Mechanisms for early identification and escalation of limits breaches also need to be constructed.

**Allocation of Risk Based Capital**    Allocation of risk based capital is not only about risk, but must be linked also to potential rewards. In order to increase returns, the bank will need to take on additional risk, and it is necessary to optimise risk capital allocation to the portfolio in seeking higher profitability. Banker and trader pay must be linked not only to returns, but also to the amount of risk based capital used in its generation, as higher risk positions attract higher regulatory and economic capital. In assessing returns, banks must consider potential "ancillary" business (for example, investment banking and custody fees) which might be realised as the client relationship is strengthened through the extension of credit.

Capital must be allocated with a view towards sustainability. Business plans must anticipate ongoing capital needs, costs, and availability, without which growth and continued competitiveness will not be attainable. Consideration must be given to the time value of money, in that businesses generate cash flows and returns in differing time frames. Management must consider tax consequences and varying rates when assessing returns.

In allocating capital, banks can perform a comparison between the economic capital and regulatory capital charges applicable to different areas of their business. In doing so, they can identify those areas of their business which attract high amounts of regulatory capital, but low amounts of economic capital. Management would then need to understand why the regulator believes this area of business to be significantly more risky than the bank does. Similarly, the bank can identify those areas of their business which attract low amounts of regulatory capital, but high amounts of economic capital. Performing this type of analysis will help the bank with strategic business planning and in setting growth and performance targets for the future.

**Setting Loan Sanctioning Criteria** New loans must be sanctioned only within the context of the risk appetite statement and risk weighted capital criteria. For corporate and wholesale banking, a request to provide credit should involve the completion of a form to be submitted to a separate entity from the relationship bankers, whether it be a credit committee, or (in the case of smaller banks) executive management and ALCO. The request will contain all the information needed for the committee to discuss the risk and return of the loan, terms, and the client, so a determination can be made as to whether it fits into the broader strategy. For retail banking, new loans can be granted via automated applications, which will be approved or referred by loan origination officers.

"Know Your Customer" (KYC) is a key element of the loan origination process. For corporate and wholesale banking, relationship bankers should have an extensive dialogue with clients to have a thorough understanding of their business, strategy, and risks. The extension of credit will be only part of an ongoing process. Any entity is likely to undergo some difficulties over the term of a loan, and good communication will enable the bank to work with the borrower. For retail banking, the bank will maintain behavioural scorecards and delinquency information, which will enable them to monitor loan performance and take action should the loan be at risk of defaulting.

Beyond the credit risk of the borrower and the rate charged, the committee must also evaluate the specifics of the loan, these specifics being:

- Legal framework and jurisdiction risks;
- Collateral: acceptable forms and enforceability;
- Disclosure requirements;
- Ability to terminate: material adverse change clauses and covenants;
- Transferability: can the loan be sold?;
- Currencies;
- Fixed or floating rate;
- Pre-payment options.

The Loan Market Association (LMA) strives to improve liquidity, efficiency, and transparency in the primary and secondary syndicated loan markets in Europe, the Middle East, and Africa by issuing recommended standard market practices and documentation.

### Survival Models for Credit Risk Management

Just as survival analysis is used in insurance to predict mortality rates, at the same time, duration analysis can be used to predict frequencies of default throughout the economic cycle. An example of survival analysis being used to calculate the Loss Given Default (LGD) parameter is presented below:

1. The probability of an account being written off, given that it has "survived" to a certain duration in default (P(W|D)), is calculated for each duration in default. This is calculated as the exposure which is written off at the end of the period divided by the exposure at risk at the start of the period;
2. The next step is to calculate the loss given write-off at that duration in default (LGW). This is calculated as the loss at write-off (which is the difference between the outstanding balance and any recoveries made) divided by the outstanding balance at write-off.

In this way the two parameters, probability of write-off and loss, can be combined to provide an estimate of loss given default that is dependent on the duration spent in default. This curve is usually upward sloping, with loans suffering a higher loss the longer they have remained in default.

Unlike with mortality rates, recurring or repeated event models are required in banking, i.e. "default" is a non-absorbing state from which cure is possible.

**Asset–Liability Modelling for Balance Sheet Management**    Actuaries have traditionally been involved in performing asset–liability modelling for life insurers and pension funds. Actuaries determine funding status, cash requirements, and balance sheet positions, and make projections under varying future economic and capital market environments. Projections are deterministic (scenario based) or stochastic (using Monte Carlo techniques). These same skills and techniques are applicable to banks in their Asset–Liability Management process.

**Cash Flow Models for Budgeting and Balance Sheet Management**    Cash flow is an important measure of sustainability of a bank or business. Banks must be able to estimate cash flows (timing and severity) in the most extreme scenarios so as to be able to devise a strategy to ensure adequate funding. Understanding cash flows under stressed economic conditions also forms part of a bank's regulatory reporting requirements.

## Risk Management and Mitigation

Before focusing on technical and complicated risk management matters, management should always know and be thinking about a few basic questions: what are the bank's largest individual, sector, product, and regional exposures? In what circumstances should these exposures be reduced or grown? And, very importantly, what are the means and options for reducing these exposures under a range of circumstances? The bank would also want to understand how to grow certain exposures to meet their strategic and business objectives, without taking on excessive risk.

**Positions**    The risk portfolio of a bank can be adjusted by monitoring maturing business and adjusting policies for new assets accordingly. New business for sectors can be frozen, reduced, or subjected to stricter standards (for example, increased spread and fees, more collateral, tighter covenants). Emphasis can be placed on booking business in sectors that can be expected to perform in a manner counter to the concentration risk. These sectors may outperform in different phases of the economic cycle (for example, consumer staples are usually relatively strong in a downturn).

A more direct approach is the outright sale of loan and bond positions. Selling has the advantage of immediacy and avoids the risk that a hedging instrument does not perform as expected (basis risk). Liquidity varies based on factors including market size and standardisation, complexity and terms of the debt instrument, and borrower credit rating. In stressed markets, liquidity can be expected to diminish when it is needed most.

**Credit Hedging**   Historically, best-practice credit risk management discipline dictated that banks apply a sound credit policy at origination. In other words, prevention is better than cure. This reflects the fact that credit risk is, for practical purposes, difficult to hedge. This remains true in the era of credit derivatives, which (despite being in use since 1994) are used by only a small minority of the world's banks to mitigate credit risk. It remains the case that the optimum approach to credit risk for most banks involves diversification of the loan book, avoiding concentration with one borrower or sector and the operation of conservative origination principles.

For a more proactive approach, one means of hedging credit risk was to short the bonds of the borrower or similar borrowers. However, it is not always possible to borrow the bonds in sufficient size (if at all), and the repo rate can be prohibitively expensive. Basis risk can again be a challenge. This is not a feasible hedge approach for the vast majority of the world's banks.

Since the early 1990s, the management and transfer of credit risk has been transformed by the emergence of credit derivatives, which are contracts and instruments that separate and transfer credit or default risk from the lender/noteholder to another party. Credit Default Swaps (CDS) spreads are watched closely by issuers, investors, and banks, and are key to issuance, investment and pricing decisions.

Credit derivatives have been a source of discussion and debate. In the early years, growing pains were experienced in coping with processing of increasing volumes and there were controversies in agreeing exactly when credit events were triggered. Many buyers of protection were dismayed when there was no payout on Greece because default was accepted "voluntarily". As with all derivatives, greater scrutiny has been brought to bear since the crisis given the size and complexity of the market.

In essence then, managing credit risk is all about sound origination policies, sticking to one's knitting, and avoiding concentration. Prevention, to reiterate, is better than cure.

This extract from *An Introduction to Value-at-Risk, Fifth Edition* (2013)

## Introduction to Risk

### Chapter 1: INTRODUCTION TO RISK

The risk management department was one of the fastest growing areas in investment and commercial banks during the 1990s, and again after the crash of 2008. A string of high-profile banking losses and failures, typified by the fall of Barings Bank in 1995, highlighted the importance of risk management to bank managers and shareholders alike. In response to the volatile and complex nature of risks that they were exposed to, banks set up specialist risk management departments, whose functions included both measuring and managing risk. As a value-added function, risk management can assist banks not only in managing risk, but also in understanding the nature of their profit and loss, and so help increase return on capital. It is now accepted that senior directors of banks need to be thoroughly familiar with the concept of risk management. One of the primary tools of the risk manager is *value-at-risk* (*VaR*), which is a quantitative measure of the risk exposure of an institution. For a while VaR was regarded as somewhat inaccessible, and only the preserve of mathematicians and quantitative analysts. Although VaR is indeed based on statistical techniques that may be difficult to grasp for the layman, its basic premise can, and should, be explained in straightforward fashion, in a way that enables non-academics to become comfortable with the concept. The problem with VaR is that while it was only ever a measure, based on some strong assumptions, of approximate market risk exposure (it is unsuited to measuring risk exposure in the banking book), it suffers in the eyes of its critics in having the cachet of science. This makes it arcane and inaccessible, while paradoxically being expected to be much more accurate than it was ever claimed to be. Losses suffered by banks during the crash of 2007–08 were much larger than any of their VaR values, which is where the measure comes in for criticism. But we can leave that aside for now, and concentrate just on introducing the technicalities.

Later in the book we describe and explain the calculation and application of VaR. We begin here with a discussion of risk.

## DEFINING RISK

Any transaction or undertaking with an element of uncertainty as to its future outcome carries an element of risk: risk can be thought of as uncertainty. To associate particular assets such as equities, bonds or corporate cash flows with types of risk, we need to define 'risk' itself. It is useful to define risk in terms of a risk *horizon*, the point at which an asset will be realised, or turned into cash. All market participants, including speculators, have an horizon, which may be as short as a half-day. Essentially then, the horizon is the time period relating to the risk being considered.

Once we have established a notion of horizon, a working definition of risk is *the uncertainty of the future total cash value of an investment on the investor's horizon date*. This uncertainty arises from many sources. For participants in the financial markets risk is essentially a measure of the volatility of asset returns, although it has a broader definition as being any type of uncertainty as to future outcomes. The types of risk that a bank or securities house is exposed to as part of its operations in the bond and capital markets are characterised below.

# THE ELEMENTS OF RISK: CHARACTERISING RISK

Banks and other financial institutions are exposed to a number of risks during the course of normal operations. The different types of risk are broadly characterised as follows:

- *Market risk* – risk arising from movements in prices in financial markets. Examples include foreign exchange (*FX*) risk, interest rate risk and basis risk. In essence market risk applies to 'tradeable instruments, ones that are *marked-to-market* in a trading book, as opposed to assets that are held to maturity, and never formally repriced, in a banking book.
- *Credit risk* – something called *issuer risk* refers to risk that a customer will default. Examples include sovereign risk, marginal risk and *force majeure* risk.
- *Liquidity risk* – this refers to two different but related issues: for a Treasury or money markets' person, it is the risk that a bank has insufficient funding to meet commitments as they arise. That is, the risk that funds cannot be raised in the market as and when required. For a securities or derivatives trader, it is the risk that the market for assets becomes too thin to enable fair and efficient trading to take place. This is the risk that assets cannot be sold or bought as and when required. We should differentiate therefore between funding liquidity and trading liquidity whenever using the expression *liquidity*.

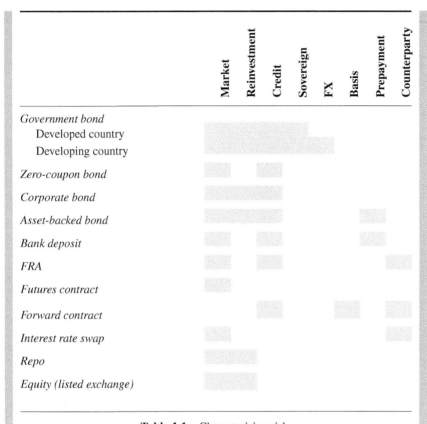

**Table 1.1**   Characterising risk.

- *Operational risk* – risk of loss associated with non-financial matters such as fraud, system failure, accidents and ethics. Table 1.1 assigns sources of risk for a range of fixed interest, FX, interest rate derivative and equity products. The classification has assumed a 1-year horizon, but the concepts apply to any time horizon.

## Forms of market risk

Market risk reflects the uncertainty as to an asset's price when it is sold. Market risk is the risk arising from movements in financial market prices. Specific market risks will differ according to the type of asset under consideration:

- *Currency risk* – this arises from exposure to movements in FX rates. A version of currency risk is *transaction* risk, where currency fluctuations affect the proceeds from day-to-day transactions.
- *Interest rate risk* – this arises from the impact of fluctuating interest rates and will directly affect any entity borrowing or investing funds. The most common exposure is simply to the level of interest rates but some institutions run positions that are exposed to changes in the shape of the yield curve. The basic risk arises from revaluation of the asset after a change in rates.
- *Equity risk* – this affects anyone holding a portfolio of shares, which will rise and fall with the level of individual share prices and the level of the stock market.
- *Other market risk* – there are residual market risks which fall in this category. Among these are *volatility* risk, which affects option traders, and *basis* risk, which has a wider impact. Basis risk arises whenever one kind of risk exposure is hedged with an instrument that behaves in a similar, but not necessarily identical manner. One example would be a company using 3-month interest rate futures to hedge its commercial paper (*CP*) programme. Although eurocurrency rates, to which futures prices respond, are well correlated with CP rates, they do not invariably move in lock step. If CP rates moved up by 50 basis points but futures prices dropped by only 35 basis points, the 15-bps gap would be the basis risk in this case.

## Other risks

- *Liquidity risk* – in banking, this refers to the risk that a bank cannot raise funds to refinance loans as the original borrowing becomes past due. It is sometimes also referred to as *rollover* risk. In other words, it refers to the risk of an inability to continue to raise funds to replace maturing liabilities. There is also another (related) liquidity risk, which refers to *trading liquidity*. This is the risk that an asset on the balance sheet cannot be sold at a previously perceived fair value, or cannot be sold at all, and hence experiences *illiquidity*.
- *Credit risk* – the risk that an *obligor* (the entity that has borrowed funds from you) defaults on the loan repayments.
- *Counterparty risk* – all transactions involve one or both parties in counterparty risk, the potential loss that can arise if one party were to default on its obligations. Counterparty risk is

most relevant in the derivatives market, where every contract is marked-to-market daily and so a positive MTM is taken to the profit & loss (P&L) account. If the counterparty defaults before the contract has expired, there is risk that the actual P&L will not be realized. In the credit derivatives market, a counterparty that has sold protection on the third-party reference name on the credit derivative contract and which subsequently defaults will mean the other side to the trade is no longer protected against the default of that third party.

- *Reinvestment risk* – if an asset makes any payments before the investor's horizon, whether it matures or not, the cash flows will have to be reinvested until the horizon date. Since the reinvestment rate is unknown when the asset is purchased, the final cash flow is uncertain.
- *Sovereign risk* – this is a type of credit risk specific to a government bond. Post 2008, there is material risk of default by an industrialised country. A developing country may default on its obligation (or declare a debt 'moratorium') if debt payments relative to domestic product reach unsustainable levels.
- *Prepayment risk* – this is specific to mortgage-backed and asset-backed bonds. For example, mortgage lenders allow the homeowner to repay outstanding debt before the stated maturity. If interest rates fall prepayment will occur, which forces reinvestment at rates lower than the initial yield.
- *Model risk* – some financial instruments are heavily dependent on complex mathematical models for pricing and hedging. If the model is incorrectly specified, is based on questionable assumptions or does not accurately reflect the true behaviour of the market, banks trading these instruments could suffer extensive losses.

## RISK MANAGEMENT

The risk management function grew steadily in size and importance within commercial and investment banks during the 1990s. Risk management departments exist not to eliminate the possibility of all risk, should such action indeed be feasible or desirable; rather, to control the frequency, extent and size of such losses in such a way as to provide the minimum surprise to senior management and shareholders.

Risk exists in all competitive business although the balance between financial risks of the type described above and general and management risk varies with the type of business engaged in. The key objective of the risk management function within a financial institution is to allow for a clear understanding of the risks and exposures the firm is engaged in, such that monetary loss is deemed acceptable by the firm. The acceptability of any loss should be on the basis that such (occasional) loss is to be expected as a result of the firm being engaged in a particular business activity. If the bank's risk management function is effective, there will be no over-reaction to any unexpected losses, which may increase eventual costs to many times the original loss amount.

## The risk management function

While there is no one agreed organisation structure for the risk management function, the following may be taken as being reflective of the typical bank set-up:

- an independent, 'middle office' department responsible for drawing up and explicitly stating the bank's approach to risk, and defining trading limits and the areas of the market that the firm can have exposure to;
- the head of the risk function reporting to an independent senior manager, who is a member of the executive board;
- monitoring the separation of duties between front, middle and back office, often in conjunction with an internal audit function;
- reporting to senior management, including firm's overall exposure and adherence of the front office to the firm's overall risk strategy;
- communication of risks and risk strategy to shareholders;
- where leading edge systems are in use, employment of the risk management function to generate competitive advantage in the market as well as control.

The risk management function is more likely to deliver effective results when there are clear lines of responsibility and accountability. It is also imperative that the department interacts closely with other areas of the front and back office.

In addition to the above the following are often accepted as ingredients of a risk management framework in an institution engaged in investment banking and trading activity:

- proactive management involvement in risk issues;
- daily overview of risk exposure profile and profit & loss (*P&L*) reports;
- VaR as a common measure of risk exposure, in addition to other measures including 'jump risk' to allow for market corrections;

- defined escalation procedures to deal with rising levels of trading loss, as well as internal 'stop-loss' limits;
- independent daily monitoring of risk utilisation by middle-office risk management function;
- independent production of daily P&L, and independent review of front-office closing prices on a daily basis;
- independent validation of market pricing, and pricing and VaR models.

These guidelines, adopted universally in the investment banking community, should assist in the development of an influential and effective risk management function for all financial institutions. We say 'should', but of course the experience of JPMorgan, Soc Gen and UBS in the 21st century, shows that the existence of large and seemingly sophisticated risk management infrastructures does not preclude multi-billion dollar trading losses.

## Managing risk

The different stakeholders in a bank or financial institution will have slightly different perspectives on risk and its management. If we were to generalise, shareholders will wish for stable earnings as well as the highest possible return on capital. From the point of view of business managers though, the perspective may be slightly different and possibly shorter term. For them, risk management often takes the following route:

- create as diversified a set of business lines as possible, and within each business line diversify portfolios to maximum extent;
- establish procedures to enable some measure of forecasting of market prices;
- hedge the portfolio to minimise losses when market forecasts suggest that losses are to be expected.

The VaR measurement tool falls into the second and third areas of this strategy. It is used to give an idea of risk exposure (generally, to market and credit risk only) so that banks can stay within trading limits, and to feed into the hedge calculation.

## Chapter 2: VOLATILITY AND CORRELATION

Value-at-Risk (*VaR*) is essentially a measure of volatility, specifically how volatile a bank's assets are. Assets that exhibit high volatility present higher risk. VaR also takes into account the correlation between different sets of assets in the overall portfolio. If the market price performance of assets is closely positively correlated, this also presents higher risk. So, before we begin the discussion of VaR we need to be familiar with these two concepts. Readers who have an investor's understanding of elementary statistics may skip this chapter and move straight to Chapter 3.

# STATISTICAL CONCEPTS

The statistics used in VaR calculations are based on well-established concepts. There are standard formulae for calculating the mean and standard deviation of a set of values. If we assume that $X$ is a random variable with particular values $x$, we can apply the basic formula to calculate the mean and standard deviation. Remember that the mean is the average of the set of values or observations, while the standard deviation is a measure of the dispersion away from the mean of the range of values. In fact, the standard deviation is the square root of the variance, but the variance, being the sum of squared deviations of each value from the mean divided by the number of observations, has less practical value for us.

## Arithmetic mean

We say that the random variable is $X$, so the mean is $E(X)$. In a time series of observations of historical data, the probability values are the frequencies of the observed values. The mean is:

$$E(X) = \frac{\sum_i x_i}{n} \tag{2.1}$$

where   $1/n$ = Assigned probability to a single value among $n$; and

        $n$ = Number of observations.

The standard deviation of the set of values is:

$$\sigma(X) = \frac{1}{n}\sqrt{\sum_i \left[x_i - E(X)\right]^2} \tag{2.2}$$

The probability assigned to a set of values is given by the type of distribution and, in fact, from a distribution we can determine the mean and standard deviation depending on the probabilities $p_i$ assigned to each value $x_i$ of the random variable $X$. The sum of all probabilities must be 100%. From probability values then, the mean is given by:

$$E(X)\frac{\sum_i p_i x_i}{n} \tag{2.3}$$

The variance is the average weighted by the probabilities of the squared deviations from the mean; so, of course, the standard deviation – which we now call the volatility – is the square root of this value. The volatility is given by:

$$\sigma(X) = \sqrt{\sum_i p_i \left[ x_i - E(X) \right]^2} \tag{2.4}$$

In the example in Table 2.1 we show the calculation of the mean, the variance and the standard deviation as calculated from an Excel spreadsheet. The expectation is the mean of all the observations, while the variance is, as we noted earlier, the sum of squared deviations from the mean. The standard deviation is the square root of the variance.

| Dates | Observations | Deviations from mean | Squared deviation |
|---|---|---|---|
| 1 | 22 | 4.83 | 23.36 |
| 2 | 15 | −2.17 | 4.69 |
| 3 | 13 | −4.17 | 17.36 |
| 4 | 14 | −3.17 | 10.03 |
| 5 | 16 | −1.17 | 1.36 |
| 6 | 17 | −0.17 | 0.03 |
| 7 | 16 | −1.17 | 1.36 |
| 8 | 19 | 1.83 | 3.36 |
| 9 | 21 | 3.83 | 14.69 |
| 10 | 20 | 2.83 | 8.03 |
| 11 | 17 | −0.17 | 0.03 |
| 12 | 16 | −1.17 | 1.36 |
| Sum | 206 | Sum | 85.66 |
| Mean | 17.17 | Variance | 7.788 |
| | | Standard deviation | 2.791 |

**Table 2.1**  Calculation of standard deviation.

What happens when we have observations that can assume any value within a range, rather than the discrete values we have seen in our example? When there is a probability that a variable can have a value of any measure between a range of specified values, we have a continuous distribution.

## Probability distributions

A probability distribution is a model for an actual or empirical distribution. If we are engaged in an experiment in which a coin is tossed a number of times, the number of heads recorded will be a discrete value of 0, 1, 2, 3, 4, or so on, depending on the number of times we toss the coin. The result is called a 'discrete' random variable. Of course, we know that the probability of throwing a head is 50%, because there are only two outcomes in a coin-toss experiment, heads or tails. We may throw the coin three times and get three heads (it is unlikely but by no means exceptional); however, performing the experiment a great number of times should produce something approaching our 50% result. So, an experiment with a large number of trials would produce an empirical distribution which would be close to the theoretical distribution as the number of tosses increases.

This example illustrates a discrete set of outcomes (0, 1, 2, 3); in other words, a discrete probability distribution. It is equally possible to have a continuous probability distribution: for example, the probability that the return on a portfolio lies between 3% and 7% is associated with a continuous probability distribution because the final return value can assume any value between those two parameters.

### The normal distribution

A very commonly used theoretical distribution is the normal distribution, which is plotted as a bell-shaped curve and is familiar to most practitioners in business. The theoretical distribution actually looks like many observed distributions such as the height of people, shoe sizes, and so on. The distribution is completely described by the mean and the standard deviation. The normal distribution $N(\mu, \sigma)$ has mean $\mu$ and standard deviation $\sigma$. The probability function is given by:

$$P(X = x) = \frac{1}{\sigma\sqrt{2\pi}} \exp\left[ -\frac{(x - \mu)^2}{2\sigma^2} \right] \tag{2.5}$$

The distribution is standardised as $N(0, 1)$ with a mean of 0 and a standard deviation of 1. It is possible to obtain probability values for any part of the distribution by using the standardised curve and converting variables to this standardised distribution; thus, the variable $Z = (X - \mu)/\sigma$ follows the standardised normal distribution $N(0, 1)$ with probability:

$$P\left(Z = Z\right) = \frac{1}{\sigma\sqrt{2\pi}} \exp\left[-\frac{Z^2}{2\sigma^2}\right] \qquad (2.6)$$

The *Central Limit Theorem* (known also as the law of large numbers) is the basis for the importance of the normal distribution in statistical theory, and in real life a large number of distributions tend towards the normal, provided that there are a sufficient number of observations. This explains the importance of the normal distribution in statistics. If we have large numbers of observations – for example, the change in stock prices, or closing prices in government bonds – it makes calculations straightforward if we assume that they are normally distributed.

For both option pricing theory and VaR, it is assumed that the returns from holding an asset are normally distributed. It is often convenient to define the return in logarithmic form as:

$$\ln\left(\frac{P_t}{P_{t-1}}\right)$$

where     $P_t$ = Price today;

          $P_{t-1}$ = Previous price.

If this is assumed to be normally distributed, then the underlying price will have a log-normal distribution. The log-normal distribution never goes to a negative value, unlike the normal distribution, and hence is intuitively more suitable for asset prices. The distribution is illustrated as Figure 2.1.

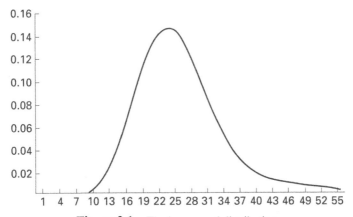

**Figure 2.1**    The log-normal distribution.

The normal distribution is assumed to apply to the returns associated with stock prices, and indeed all financial time series observations. However, it is not strictly accurate, as it implies extreme negative values that are not observed in practice. For this reason the log-normal distribution is used instead, in which case the logarithm of the returns is used instead of the return values themselves; this also removes the probability of negative stock prices. In the log-normal distribution, the logarithm of the random variable follows a normal distribution. The log-normal distribution is asymmetric, unlike the normal curve, because it does not have negatives at the extreme values.

## Confidence intervals

Assume an estimate $x$ of the average of a given statistical population where the true mean of the population is $\mu$. Suppose that we believe that on average $\bar{x}$ is an unbiased estimator of $\mu$. Although this means that on average $\bar{x}$ is accurate, the specific sample that we observe will almost certainly be above or below the true level. Accordingly, if we want to be reasonably confident that our inference is correct, we cannot claim that $\mu$ is precisely equal to the observed $\bar{x}$.

Instead, we must construct an interval estimate or confidence interval of the following form:

$$\mu = \bar{x} \pm \text{Sampling error}$$

The crucial question is: How wide must this confidence interval level be? The answer, of course, will depend on how much $\bar{x}$ fluctuates. We first set our requirements for level of confidence; that is, how certain we wish to be statistically. If we wish to be incorrect only 1 day in 20 – that is, we wish to be right 19 days each month (a month is assumed to have 20 working days) – that would equate to a 95% confidence interval that our estimate is accurate. We also assume that our observations are normally distributed. In that case we would expect that the population would be distributed along the lines portrayed in Figure 2.2.

In the normal distribution, 2.5% of the outcomes are expected to fall more than 1.96 standard deviations from the mean. So, that means 95% of the outcomes would be expected to fall within ±1.96 standard deviations. That is, there is a 95% chance that the random variable will fall between −1.96 standard deviations and +1.96 standard deviations. This would be referred to as a 'two-sided' (or 'two-tailed') confidence interval. It gives the probability of a move upwards or downwards by the random variable outside the limits we are expecting.

In the financial markets, we do not however expect negative prices, so that values below 0 are not really our concern. In this scenario, it makes sense to consider a one-sided test if we are concerned with the risk of loss: a move upward into profit is of less concern (certainly to a risk manager

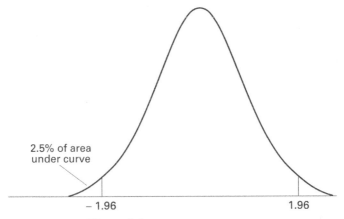

**Figure 2.2**   Confidence intervals.

anyway!). From the statistical tables associated with the normal distribution we know that 5% of the outcomes are expected to fall more than 1.645 (rounded to 1.65) standard deviations from the mean. This would be referred to as a one-sided confidence interval.

## VOLATILITY

In financial market terms, volatility is a measure of how much the price of an asset moves each day (or week or month, and so on). Speaking generally, higher volatility equates to higher profit or loss risk. Bankers must be familiar with volatility, as assets that exhibit higher volatility must be priced such that their returns incorporate a 'risk premium' to compensate the holder for the added risk exposure.

**EXAMPLE 2.1**

We demonstrate volatility from first principles here. Table 2.2 shows two portfolios, outwardly quite similar. They have virtually identical means from an observation of portfolio returns over ten observation periods. However, the standard deviation shows a different picture, and we see that Portfolio B exhibits much greater volatility than Portfolio A. Its future performance is much harder to predict with any reasonable confidence. Portfolio B carries higher risk and so would carry higher VaR. We see also from Table 2.2 that the standard deviation is a measure of the dispersion away from the mean of all the observations. To be comfortable that the statistical measures are as accurate as possible, we need the greatest number of observations.

The volatility demonstrated in Table 2.2 is historical volatility; it is based on past performance. Options traders deal in implied volatility, which is the volatility value given by backing out the Black–Scholes options pricing formula from market prices to obtain an implied volatility value for an asset.

Volatility is important for both VaR measurement and in the valuation of options. It is a method of measuring current asset price against the distribution of the asset's future price. Statistically, volatility is defined as the fluctuation in the underlying asset price over a certain period of time. Fluctuation is derived from the change in price between one day's closing price and the next day's closing price. Where the asset price is stable it will exhibit low volatility, and the opposite when price movements are large and/or unstable.

We saw from Table 2.2 that the average values for low- and high-volatility portfolios were similar; however, the distribution of the recordings differ. The low-volatility portfolio showed low variability in the distribution. High-volatility assets show a wider variability around the mean.

Market practitioners wish to obtain a volatility value that approximates around the normal distribution. This is done by recording a sufficiently large volume of data and reducing the price change intervals to as small an amount as possible; this means that the price changes can be described statistically by the normal distribution curve. We saw earlier in the chapter that the normal distribution curve has two numerical properties known as the mean and the standard deviation. The mean is the average reading taken at the centre of the curve, and the standard deviation is a value which represents the dispersion around the mean. We demonstrate some examples at Figures 2.3 and 2.4.

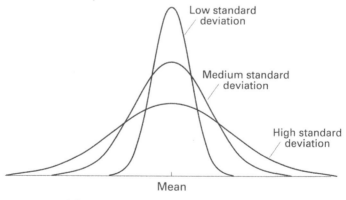

**Figure 2.3**   Differing standard deviations.

|  | Excel column B | C | D |
|---|---|---|---|
| Excel row | *Observations* | *Portfolio A* | *Portfolio B* |
| 6 |  |  |  |
| 7 | 1 | 5.08% | 3.50% |
| 8 | 2 | 5.00% | 5.00% |
| 9 | 3 | 5.05% | 6.25% |
| 10 | 4 | 5.00% | 7.10% |
| 11 | 5 | 5.05% | 3.75% |
| 12 | 6 | 5.00% | 5.75% |
| 13 | 7 | 5.01% | 2.50% |
| 14 | 8 | 5.20% | 4.75% |
| 15 | 9 | 5.06% | 5.25% |
| 16 | 10 | 5.00% | 6.75% |
| 17 |  |  |  |
| 18 |  |  |  |
| 19 |  |  |  |
| 20 | Mean | 5.05% | 5.06% |
| 21 | Standard deviation | 0.000 622272 | 0.014813282 |
| 22 |  |  |  |
| 23 | Excel formula | = AVERAGE(C7:C16) | = AVERAGE(D7:D16) |
| 24 |  | = STDEV(C7:C16) | = STDEV(D7:D16) |

**Table 2.2**   Standard deviation.

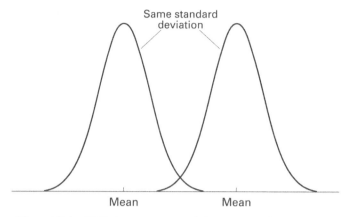

**Figure 2.4**   Differing means around the same standard deviation.

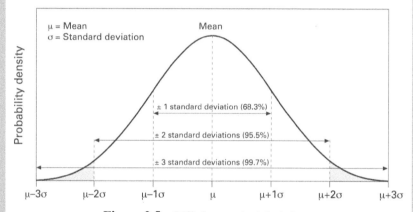

**Figure 2.5**   Differing standard deviations.

In Figure 2.5, the standard deviation is shown correlated with dispersion. The curve can be divided into segments which represent specific percentages within each band.

We see from Figure 2.5 that 68.3% of data fall within ±1 standard deviation, 95.5% of data fall within ±2 standard deviations and 99.7% fall within ±3 standard deviations.

The normal distribution curve can also be used to predict future daily share fluctuation over a measured period of time. Future price distribution uses volatility expressed as a 1 standard deviation price change at the end of 1 year. This can be expressed as a percentage:

1 standard deviation price change $(p)$ = Volatility $(\%)$

$\times$ Current asset price $(p)$

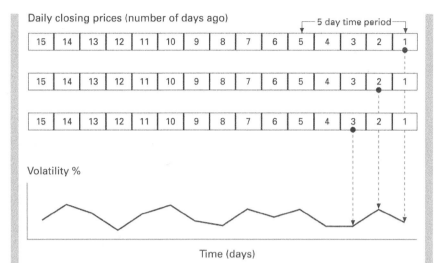

**Figure 2.6**   Historical volatility chart.

Although the value of an option relies upon estimated future volatility, volatility is shown also as historical volatility and implied volatility. *Historical volatility* is the actual price fluctuation in a given time period. The value will depend on the length of the observation period and when the value was observed. This naturally smoothes out day-to-day fluctuations – a moving average of historical volatility can be shown graphically in a similar way as conventional share prices. Figure 2.6 shows a 5-day historical volatility chart reversing through a specified time period.

Although historical volatility can show trends over a greater period of time – for example, 4 years – it can also make distinctly significant and highly variable changes. Therefore, there can be no certainty that a past trend is in any way indicative of a share's future performance.

Implied volatility is a necessary tool to obtain the predicted value of an option which has been obtained from the present value of that option by entering different levels of volatility into an option pricing model, until the current market price is reached. This iterative process effectively reduces the margin of error. In a working situation, most option pricing models allow the calculation of implied volatility by entering the present market price for an option.

Future volatility is the predicted or expected price fluctuation of a period of time until the option has expired. Evidently, this will be affected not only by the calculated implied volatility but also by the expectation of the share's price trend.

## THE NORMAL DISTRIBUTION AND VaR

As we will see from Chapter 3 there is more than one way to calculate VaR for an asset portfolio. Many VaR models use the normal curve to calculate the

| | E | F | G | H | I | J |
|---|---|---|---|---|---|---|
| 8 | No. of standard deviations | −1.645 | −1.000 | 0.000 | 1.000 | 1.650 | 2.450 |
| 9 | Probability | 5.00% | 15.87% | 50.00% | 84.13% | 95.05% | 99.29% |
| 10 | Excel formula | = NORMSDIST(E8) | | | | | |

**Table 2.3**  Probabilities extracted from the normal distribution table.

| | C | D | E | F | G | H | I |
|---|---|---|---|---|---|---|---|
| 6 | | | | | | | |
| 7 | Observation | 1 | 2 | 3 | 4 | 5 | 6 |
| 8 | Mean return | 5% | 5% | 5% | 5% | 5% | 5% |
| 9 | Target return | 4% | 5% | 6% | 7% | 8% | 8% |
| 10 | Standard deviation of return | 1.63% | 1.63% | 1.63% | 1.63% | 1.63% | 1.63% |
| 11 | Number of standard deviations | −0.612369 871 | 0 | 0.612369 871 | 1.224 739 743 | 1.837 109 614 | 1.837 109 614 |
| 12 | Probability | 27.01% | 50.00% | 72.99% | 88.97% | 96.69% | 96.69% |

Excel formula

Number of standard deviations = (D9-D8)/D10

Probability = NORMSDIST(D11)

**Table 2.4**  Normal distribution illustrated for portfolio return.

estimation of losses over a specified time period. Normal distribution curve tables, which can be looked up in any number of statistics textbooks or on the Internet, show the probability of an observation moving a specific distance away from the recorded mean. Some specific probabilities are given in Table 2.3.

Table 2.3 shows that 95% of all observations in a normal distribution lie within ±1.65 standard deviations of the mean. A 95% percentile is often used in VaR calculations. Let us take this further. Consider a gilt portfolio of £20 million with a mean return of 5% per annum. If the standard deviation of the returns is 1.63 what probability is there that returns will fall to 4% within the holding period of 1 year? We require the area of the normal curve at which the 4% value is marked – that is, 27% of the area to the left of the mean. The results are shown at Table 2.4, which also shows the Excel formula.

We should note that, although the markets assume a normal distribution of asset (equity and bond) prices, from observation we know that prices follow a more skewed distribution. In practice, asset prices exhibit what is termed 'leptokurtosis', also known as 'fat tails', which is a normal distribution with fatter tails than the theoretical. In other words, extreme price movements such as stock market corrections occur more frequently than the normal distribution would suggest.

Options traders need to correct for this more than others. The standard option pricing model, the Black–Scholes formula, which we look at in Chapter 5, uses the normal distribution to calculate the delta of the option – the $N(d1)$ part of the formula – and the probability that the option will be exercised, the $N(d2)$ part. In practice, the implied volatility of an option is higher if it is deeply in-the-money or out-of-the-money. This is known as the option 'smile', and reflects market understanding that the normal distribution is not a completely accurate description of market price behaviour.

## CORRELATION

The correlation between different assets and classes of assets is an important measure for risk managers because of the role diversification plays in risk reduction. Correlation is a measure of how much the price of one asset moves in relation to the price of another asset. In a portfolio comprised of only two assets, the VaR of this portfolio is reduced if the correlation between the two assets is weak or negative.

The simplest measure of correlation is the correlation coefficient. This is a value between −1 and +1, with a perfect positive correlation indicated by 1, while a perfect negative correlation is given by −1. Note that this assumes a linear (straight line) relationship between the two assets. A correlation of 0 suggests that there is no linear relationship.

We illustrate these values at Table 2.5, which is a hypothetical set of observations showing the volatilities of four different government benchmark bonds. Note also the Excel formula so that readers can reproduce their own analyses. We assume these bonds are different sovereign names. Bonds 1, 3 and 4 have very similar average returns, but the relationship between Bond 3 and Bond 1 is negatively closely correlated, whereas Bond 4 is positively closely correlated with Bond 1. Bond 2 has a very low positive correlation with Bond 1, and we conclude that there is very little relationship in the price movement of these two bonds.

What are we to make of these four different sovereign names with regard to portfolio diversification? On first glance, Bonds 1 and 3 would appear to offer perfect diversification because they are strongly negatively correlated. However, calculating a diversified VaR for such a portfolio would underestimate risk exposure in times of market correction – which is, after all, when managers most want to know what their risk is. This is because, even though the bonds are negatively related, they can both be expected to fall in value when the market overall is dropping. Bond 2 is no good for risk mitigation, it is strongly positively correlated. Bond 2 has essentially no relationship with Bond 1; however, it is also the most risky security in the portfolio.

We will apply what we have learned here in Chapter 3.

## Value-At-Risk

### Chapter 3: VALUE-AT-RISK

The advent of value-at-risk (*VaR*) as an accepted methodology for quantifying market risk and its adoption by bank regulators are part of the development of risk management. The application of VaR has been extended from its initial use in securities houses to commercial banks and corporates, following its introduction in October 1994 when JPMorgan launched Risk-Metrics free over the Internet.

In this chapter we look at the different methodologies employed to calculate VaR, and also illustrate its application to simple portfolios. We look first at the variance–covariance method, which is arguably the most popular estimation technique.

# WHAT IS VaR?

VaR is an estimate of an amount of exposure cash value. It is based on probabilities, so cannot be relied on with certainty, but reflects rather a level of confidence which is selected by the user in advance. VaR measures the

| Cell | C | D | E | F | G |
|---|---|---|---|---|---|
| | | Government bond 1 | Government bond 2 | Government bond 3 | Government bond 4 |
| 5 | Observation | | | | |
| 6 | 1 | 5.35% | 11.00% | 7.15% | 5.20% |
| 7 | 2 | 6.00% | 9.00% | 7.30% | 6.00% |
| 8 | 3 | 5.50% | 9.60% | 6.90% | 5.80% |
| 9 | 4 | 6.00% | 13.70% | 7.20% | 6.30% |
| 10 | 5 | 5.90% | 12.00% | 5.90% | 5.90% |
| 11 | 6 | 6.50% | 10.80% | 6.00% | 6.05% |
| 12 | 7 | 7.15% | 10.10% | 6.10% | 7.00% |
| 13 | 8 | 6.80% | 12.40% | 5.60% | 6.80% |
| 14 | 9 | 6.75% | 14.70% | 5.40% | 6.70% |
| 15 | 10 | 7.00% | 13.50% | 5.45% | 7.20% |
| 16 | | | | | |
| 17 | | | | | |
| 18 | Mean return | 6.30% | 11.68% | 6.30% | 6.30% |
| 19 | Volatility | 0.006 31 | 0.018 97 | 0.007 60 | 0.006 22 |
| 20 | Correlation with bond 1 | | 0.357 617 936 | −0.758 492 885 | 0.933 620 205 |
| 21 | | | | | |
| 22 | Excel formula | | | | |
| 23 | Mean return | | = AVERAGE(E6:E15) | | |
| 24 | Volatility | | = STDEV(E6:E15) | | |
| 25 | Correlation with bond 1 | | = CORREL(E6:E15,D6:D15) | | |

**Table 2.5** Correlation.

volatility of a company's asset prices, and so the greater the volatility, the higher the probability of loss.

## Definition

Essentially VaR is a measure of the volatility of a bank trading book. It is the characteristics of volatility that traders, risk managers and others wish to become acquainted with when assessing a bank's risk exposure. The mathematics behind measuring and estimating volatility is slightly involved, and we do not go into it here. However, by making use of a volatility estimate, a trader or senior manager can gain some idea of the risk exposure of the trading book, using the VaR measure.

VaR is defined as follows:

**VaR is a measure of market risk. It is the maximum loss which can occur with X% confidence over a holding period of t days.**

VaR is the expected loss of a portfolio over a specified time period for a set level of probability. So, for example, if a daily VaR is stated as £100,000 to a 95% level of confidence, this means that during the day there is a only a 5% chance that the loss will be *greater* than £100,000. VaR measures the potential loss in market value of a portfolio using estimated volatility and correlations. It is measured within a given confidence interval, typically 95% or 99%. The technique seeks to measure possible losses from a position or portfolio under 'normal' circumstances. The definition of normality is critical to the estimation of VaR and is a statistical concept; its importance varies according to the VaR calculation methodology that is being used.

Broadly speaking, the calculation of a VaR estimate follows four steps:

1. *Determine the time horizon over which one wishes to estimate a potential loss* – this horizon is set by the user. In practice, time horizons of 1 day to 1 year have been used. For instance, bank front-office traders are often interested in calculating the amount they might lose in a 1-day period. Regulators and participants in illiquid markets may want to estimate exposures to market risk over a longer period. In any case a time horizon must be specified by the decision-maker.
2. *Select the degree of certainty required, which is the confidence level that applies to the VaR estimate* – knowing the largest likely loss a bank will suffer 95 times out of 100, or in fact on 1 day out of 20 (i.e., a 95% degree of confidence in this estimate, or confidence interval) may be sufficient. For regulatory requirements a 99% confidence interval may be more appropriate. Senior management and shareholders are often interested in the potential loss arising from catastrophe situations, such as a stock market crash, so for them a 99% confidence level is more appropriate.

3. *Create a probability distribution of likely returns for the instrument or portfolio under consideration* – several methods may be used. The easiest to understand is the distribution of recent historical returns for the asset or portfolio which often looks like the curve associated with the normal distribution. After determining a time horizon and confidence interval for the estimate, and then collating the history of market price changes in a probability distribution, we can apply the laws of statistics to estimate VaR.

4. *Calculate the VaR estimate* – this is done by observing the loss amount associated with that area beneath the normal curve at the critical confidence interval value that is statistically associated with the probability chosen for the VaR estimate in Step 2.

These four steps will in theory allow us to calculate a VaR estimate 'longhand', although in practice mathematical models exist that will do this for us. Bearing these steps in mind, we can arrive at a practical definition of VaR not much removed from our first one:

**VaR is the largest likely loss from market risk (expressed in currency units) that an asset or portfolio will suffer over a time interval and with a degree of certainty selected by the user.**

We stress, of course, that this would be under 'normal', that is, unstressed conditions. There are a number of methods for calculating VaR, all logically sustainable but nevertheless reliant on some strong assumptions, and estimates prepared using the different methodologies can vary dramatically. At this point it is worthwhile reminding ourselves what VaR is *not*. It is not a unified method for measuring risk, as the different calculation methodologies each produce different VaR values. In addition, as it is a quantitative statistical technique, VaR only captures risks that can be quantified. Therefore, it does not measure (nor does it seek to measure) other risks that a bank or securities house will be exposed to, such as liquidity risk or operational risk. Most importantly, VaR is not 'risk management'. This term refers to the complete range of duties and disciplines that are involved in minimising and managing bank risk exposure. VaR is but one ingredient of risk management, a measurement tool for market risk exposure. So the mean and standard deviation parameters of the statistical distribution are key to the VaR estimate.

# METHODOLOGY

## Centralised database

To implement VaR, all of a firm's positions data must be gathered into one centralised database. Once this is complete the overall risk has to be calculated by aggregating the risks from individual instruments across the entire portfolio. The potential move in each instrument (i.e., each risk factor) has to be inferred from past daily price movements over a given observation period. For regulatory purposes this period is at least 1 year. Hence, the data on which VaR estimates are based should capture all relevant daily market moves over the previous year. The main assumption underpinning VaR – and which in turn may be seen as its major weakness – is that the distribution of future price and rate changes will follow past variations. Therefore, the potential portfolio loss calculations for VaR are worked out using distributions from historic price data in the observation period.

## Correlation assumptions

VaR requires that the user decide which exposures are allowed to offset each other and by how much. For example, is the Japanese yen correlated to movements in the euro or the Mexican peso? Consider also the price of crude oil to movements in the price of natural gas: if there is a correlation, to what extent is the degree of correlation? VaR requires that the user determine correlations *within* markets as well as *across* markets. The mapping procedures used as part of the VaR process also have embedded correlation assumptions. For example, mapping individual stocks into the S&P 500 or fixed interest securities into the swap curve translate into the assumption that individual financial instruments move as the market overall. This is reasonable for diversified portfolios but may fall down for undiversified or illiquid portfolios.

To calculate the VaR for a single security, we would calculate the standard deviation of its price returns. This can be done using historical data, but also using the *implied volatility* contained in exchange-traded option prices. We would then select a confidence interval and apply this to the standard deviation, which would be our VaR measure. This is considered in more detail later.

There are three main methods for calculating VaR. As with all statistical models, they depend on certain assumptions. They are:

- the correlation method (or variance/covariance method);
- historical simulation;
- Monte Carlo simulation.

## Correlation method

This is also known as the variance–covariance, *parametric* or analytic method. This method assumes the returns on risk factors are normally distributed, the correlations between risk factors are constant and the delta (or price sensitivity to changes in a risk factor) of each portfolio constituent is constant. Using the correlation method, the volatility of each risk factor is extracted from the historical observation period. Historical data on investment returns are therefore required. The potential effect of each component of the portfolio on the overall portfolio value is then worked out from the component's delta (with respect to a particular risk factor) and that risk factor's volatility.

There are different methods of calculating relevant risk factor volatilities and correlations. We consider two alternatives:

(i) Simple *historic volatility* (correlation) – this is the most straightforward method but the effects of a large one-off market move can significantly distort volatilities (correlations) over the required forecasting period. For example, if using 30-day historic volatility, a market shock will stay in the volatility figure for 30 days until it drops out of the sample range and, correspondingly, causes a sharp drop in (historic) volatility 30 days *after* the event. This is because each past observation is equally weighted in the volatility calculation.

(ii) A more sophisticated approach is to weight past observations unequally. This is done to give more weight to recent observations so that large jumps in volatility are not caused by events that occurred some time ago. Two methods for unequal weighting are the generalised autoregressive conditional heteroscedasticity (*GARCH*) models and exponentially weighted moving averages. GARCH models are fine-tuned to each risk factor time series, while exponentially weighted averages can be computed with little more complication than simple historic volatility. Both methods rely on the assumption that future volatilities can be predicted from historic price movements.

## Historical simulation method

The historical simulation method for calculating VaR is the simplest and avoids some of the pitfalls of the correlation method. Specifically, the three main assumptions behind correlation (normally distributed returns, constant correlations, constant deltas) are not needed in this case. For historical simulation the model calculates potential losses using actual historical returns in the risk factors and so captures the non-normal distribution of risk factor returns. This means rare events and crashes can be included in the results. As the risk factor returns used for revaluing the portfolio are actual past movements, the correlations in the calculation are also actual past correlations. They capture the dynamic nature of correlations as well as scenarios when the usual correlation relationships break down.

## Monte Carlo simulation method

The third method, Monte Carlo simulation, is more flexible than the previous two. As with historical simulation, Monte Carlo simulation allows the risk manager to use actual historical distributions for risk factor returns rather than having to assume normal returns. A large number of randomly generated simulations are run forward in time using volatility and correlation estimates chosen by the risk manager. Each simulation will be different, but in total the simulations will aggregate to the chosen statistical parameters (i.e., historical distributions and volatility and correlation estimates). This method is more realistic than the previous two models and, therefore, is more likely to estimate VaR more accurately. However, its implementation requires powerful computers and there is also a trade-off in that the time to perform calculations is longer.

## Validity of the volatility–correlation VaR estimate

The level of confidence in the VaR estimation process is selected by the number of standard deviations of variance applied to the probability distribution. A standard deviation selection of 1.645 provides a 95% confidence level (in a one-tailed test) that the potential estimated price movement will not be more than a given amount based on the correlation of market factors to the position's price sensitivity. This confidence level is advocated by the RiskMetrics version of volatility–correlation VaR.

## HOW TO CALCULATE VaR

A conceptual illustration of the normal distribution being applied for VaR is given at Figure 3.1.

A market risk estimate can be calculated by following these steps:

1. Value the current portfolio using today's prices, the components of which are 'market factors'. For example, the market factors that affect the value of a bond denominated in a foreign currency are the term structure of that currency's interest rate (either the zero-coupon curve or the par yield curve) and the exchange rate.
2. Revalue the portfolio using alternative prices based on changed market factors and calculate the change in the portfolio value that would result.
3. Revaluing the portfolio using a number of alternative prices gives a distribution of changes in value. Given this, a portfolio VaR can be specified in terms of confidence levels.
4. The risk manager can calculate the maximum the firm can lose over a specified time horizon at a specified probability level.

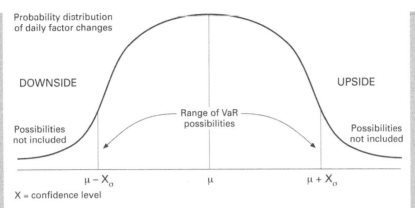

**Figure 3.1**   VaR and the normal distribution.

In implementing VaR the main problem is finding a way to obtain a series of vectors of different market factors. We will see how the various methodologies try to resolve this issue for each of the three methods that can be used to calculate VaR.

## Historical method

Values of the market factors for a particular historical period are collected and changes in these values over the time horizon are observed for use in the calculation. For instance, if a 1-day VaR is required using the past 100 trading days, each of the market factors will have a vector of observed changes that will be made up of the 99 changes in value of the market factor. A vector of alternative values is created for each of the market factors by adding the current value of the market factor to each of the values in the vector of observed changes.

The portfolio value is found using the current and alternative values for the market factors. The changes in portfolio value between the current value and the alternative values are then calculated. The final step is to sort the changes in portfolio value from the lowest value to highest value and determine the VaR based on the desired confidence interval. For a 1-day, 95% confidence level VaR using the past 100 trading days, the VaR would be the 95th most adverse change in portfolio value.

## Simulation method

The first step is to define the parameters of the distributions for the changes in market factors, including correlations among these factors. Normal and log-normal distributions are usually used to estimate changes in market factors, while historical data are most often used to define correlations among market factors. The distributions are then used in a Monte Carlo simulation to obtain simulated changes in the market factors over the time horizon to be used in the VaR calculation.

A vector of alternative values is created for each of the market factors by adding the current value of the market factor to each of the values in the vector of simulated changes. Once this vector of alternative values of the market factors is obtained, the current and alternative values for the portfolio, the changes in portfolio value and the VaR are calculated exactly as in the historical method.

## Variance–covariance, analytic or parametric method

This is similar to the historical method in that historical values of market factors are collected in a database. The next steps are then to:

(i) decompose the instruments in the portfolio into the cash-equivalent positions in more basic instruments;
(ii) specify the exact distributions for the market factors (or 'returns'); and
(iii) calculate the portfolio variance and VaR using standard statistical methods.

We now look at these steps in greater detail.

### Decompose financial instruments

The analytic method assumes that financial instruments can be decomposed or 'mapped' into a set of simpler instruments that are exposed to only one market factor. For example, a 2-year UK gilt can be mapped into a set of zero-coupon bonds representing each cash flow. Each of these zero-coupon bonds is exposed to only one market factor – a specific UK zero-coupon interest rate. Similarly, a foreign currency bond can be mapped into a set of zero-coupon bonds and a cash foreign exchange amount subject to movement in the spot foreign exchange ($FX$) rate.

### Specify distributions

The analytic method makes assumptions about the distributions of market factors. For example, the most widely used analytic method, JPMorgan's RiskMetrics, assumes that the underlying distributions are normal. With normal distributions all the historical information is summarised in the mean and standard deviation of the returns (market factors), so users do not need to keep all the historical data.

## Calculate portfolio variance and VaR

If all the market factors are assumed to be normally distributed, the portfolio, which is the sum of the individual instruments, can also be assumed to be normally distributed. This means that portfolio variance can be calculated using standard statistical methods (similar to modern portfolio theory), given by:

$$\sigma_p = \sqrt{\alpha_j^2 \sigma_j^2 + \alpha_k^2 \sigma_k^2 + 2\alpha_j \alpha_k \rho_{jk} \sigma_j \sigma_k} \qquad (3.1)$$

where  $\alpha_j$ = Home currency present value of the position in market factor $j$;
$\sigma_j^2$ = Variance of market factor $j$;
$\rho_{jk}$ = Correlation coefficient between market factors $j$ and $k$.

The portfolio VaR is then a selected number of portfolio standard deviations; for example, 1.645 standard deviations will isolate 5% of the area of the distribution in the lower tail of the normal curve, providing 95% confidence in the estimate. Consider an example where, using historical data, the portfolio variance for a package of UK gilts is £348.57. The standard deviation of the portfolio would be $\sqrt{348.57}$, which is £18.67. A 95% 1-day VaR would be $1.645 \times £18.67$, which is £30.71.

Of course, a bank's trading book will contain many hundreds of different assets, and the method employed above, useful for a two-asset portfolio, will become unwieldy. Therefore, matrices are used to calculate the VaR of a portfolio where many correlation coefficients are used. This is considered below.

## Matrix calculation of variance–covariance VaR

Consider the following hypothetical portfolio of £10,000,000.00 invested in two assets, as shown in Table 3.1(i). The standard deviation of each asset has been calculated on historical observation of asset returns. Note that *returns* are returns of asset prices, rather than the prices themselves; they are calculated from the actual prices by taking the ratio of closing prices. The returns are then calculated as the logarithm of price relatives. The mean and standard deviation of the returns are then calculated using standard statistical formulae. This would then give the standard deviation of daily price relatives, which is converted to an annual figure by multiplying it by the square root of the number of days in a year, usually taken to be 250.

We wish to calculate the portfolio VaR at the 95% level. The Excel formulae are shown at Table 3.1(ii).

The standard equation is used to calculate the variance of the portfolio, using the individual asset standard deviations and the asset weightings; the VaR of the book is the square root of the variance. Multiplying this figure

| D | E | F | G | H |
|---|---|---|---|---|
| | | Asset | | |
| 8 | | Bond 1 | Bond 2 | |
| 9 | Standard deviation | 11.83% | 17.65% | |
| 10 | Portfolio weighting | 60% | 40% | |
| 11 | Correlation coefficient | | | 0.647 |
| 12 | Portfolio value | | | £10,000,000.00 |
| 13 | Confidence level | | | 95% |
| 14 | | | | |
| 15 | Portfolio variance | | | 0.016506998 |
| 16 | Standard deviation | | | 12.848% |
| 17 | | | | |
| 18 | 95% c.i. standard deviations | | | 1.644853627 |
| 19 | | | | |
| 20 | Value-at-Risk | | | 0.211330072 |
| 21 | Value-at-Risk £ | | | £2,113,300.72 |
| 22 | | | | |
| 23 | | | | |
| 24 | | | | |
| 25 | | | | |
| 26 | | | | |

**Table 3.1(i)**    Two-asset portfolio VaR.

by the current value of the portfolio gives us the portfolio VaR, which is £2,113,300.72.

Using historical volatility means that we must define the horizon of the time period of observations, as well as the frequency of observations. Typically, a daily measure is used due to the ease of collating information, with the result that we need to use the 'square root of time' rule when moving to another time period. This applies when there are no bounds to returns data. This was illustrated above when we referred to the square root for the number of working days in a year. As an example, if we assume a 2% daily volatility, the 1-year volatility then becomes:

$$\sigma_{1\ year} = \sigma_{1\ day}\ \sqrt{250}$$
$$= 2\% \times 15.811$$
$$= 31.622\%$$

| D | E | F | G | H |
|---|---|---|---|---|
| | | Asset | | |
| 8 | | Bond 1 | Bond 2 | |
| 9 | Standard deviation | 11.83% | 17.65% | |
| 10 | Portfolio weighting | 60% | 40% | |
| 11 | Correlation coefficient | | | 0.647 |
| 12 | Portfolio value | | | £10,000,000.00 |
| 13 | Confidence level | | | 95% |
| 14 | | | | |
| 15 | Portfolio variance | | | =F9^2*F10^2+G9^2*G10^2+2*F9*F10*G9*G10 |
| 16 | Standard deviation | | | =H15^0.5 |
| 17 | | | | |
| 18 | 95% c.i. standard deviations | | | =NORMSINV(H13) |
| 19 | | | | |
| 20 | Value-at-Risk | | | =H18*H16 |
| 21 | Value-at-Risk £ | | | =H20*H12 |
| 22 | | | | |
| 23 | | | | |

**Table 3.1(ii)**   Spreadsheet formulae for Table 3.1(i).

Using this rule we can convert values for market volatility over any period of time.

The RiskMetrics VaR methodology uses matrices to obtain the same results that we have shown here. This is because, once a portfolio starts to contain many assets, the method we described above becomes unwieldy. Matrices allow us to calculate VaR for a portfolio containing many hundreds of assets, which would require assessment of the volatility of each asset and correlations of each asset to all the others in the portfolio. We can demonstrate how the parametric methodology uses variance and correlation matrices to calculate the variance, and hence the standard deviation, of a portfolio. The matrices are shown at Figure 3.2. Note that multiplication of matrices carries with it some unique rules; readers who are unfamiliar with matrices should refer to a standard mathematics text.

As shown at Figure 3.2, using the same two-asset portfolio described, we can set a 2 × 2 matrix with the individual standard deviations inside; this is labelled the 'variance' matrix. The standard deviations are placed on the horizontal axis of the matrix, and a '0' entered in the other cells. The second matrix is the correlation matrix, and the correlation of the two assets is placed in cells corresponding to the other asset; that is why a '1' is placed in the other cells, as an asset is said to have a correlation of 1 with itself. The two matrices are then multiplied to produce another matrix, labelled 'VC' in Figure 3.2.[1]

|  | Variance matrix | | Correlation matrix | | VC matrix | |
|---|---|---|---|---|---|---|
|  |  |  | Bond 1 | Bond 2 |  |  |
| Bond 1 | 11.83% | 0 | 1 | 0.647 | 0.1183 | 0.076 54 |
| Bond 2 | 0 | 17.65% | 0.647 | 1 | 0.114 196 | 0.1765 |

| VC matrix | | Variance matrix | | VCV matrix | |
|---|---|---|---|---|---|
| 0.1183 | 0.076 54 | 11.83% | 0 | 0.013 995 | 0.013 509 |
| 0.114 196 | 0.1765 | 0 | 17.65% | 0.013 509 | 0.031 152 |

| Weighting matrix | | VCV matrix | | WVCV | |
|---|---|---|---|---|---|
| 60% | 40% | 0.013 995 | 0.013 509 | 0.013 801 | 0.020 566 |
|  |  | 0.013 509 | 0.031 152 |  |  |

| WVCV | | W | WVCVW |
|---|---|---|---|
| 0.013 801 | 0.020 566 | 60% | 0.016 507 |
|  |  | 40% |  |

| | Standard deviation | 0.128 48 |
|---|---|---|

**Figure 3.2**  Matrix variance–covariance calculation for the two-asset portfolio shown in Table 3.1.

[1] A spreadsheet calculator such as Microsoft Excel has a function for multiplying matrices which may be used for any type of matrix. The function is '=MMULT()' typed in all the cells of the product matrix.

The VC matrix is then multiplied by the V matrix to obtain the variance–covariance matrix or VCV matrix. This shows the variance of each asset; for Bond 1 this is 0.013 99, which is expected as that is the square of its standard deviation, which we were given at the start. The matrix also tells us that Bond 1 has a covariance of 0.0135 with Bond 2. We then set up a matrix of the portfolio weighting of the two assets, and this is multiplied by the VCV matrix. This produces a 1 × 2 matrix, which we need to change to a single number; so, this is multiplied by the W matrix, reset as a 2 × 1 matrix, which produces the portfolio variance. This is 0.016 507. The standard deviation is the square root of the variance, and is 0.128 4795 or 12.848%, which is what we obtained before. In our illustration it is important to note the order in which the matrices were multiplied, as this will obviously affect the result. The volatility matrix contains the standard deviations along the diagonal, and '0's are entered in all the other cells. So, if the portfolio we were calculating has 50 assets in it, we would require a 50 × 50 matrix and enter the standard deviations for each asset along the diagonal line. All the other cells would have a '0' in them. Similarly, for the weighting matrix this is always one row, and all the weights are entered along the row. To take the example just given the result would be a 1 × 50 weighting matrix.

The correlation matrix in the simple example above is set up as shown in Table 3.2.

The correlation matrix at Table 3.2 shows that Asset 1 has a correlation of 0.647 with Asset 2. All correlation tables always have unity along the diagonal because an asset will have a correlation of 1 with itself. So, a three-asset portfolio of the following correlations

| | |
|---|---|
| Correlation 1, 2 | 0.647 |
| Correlation 1, 3 | 0.455 |
| Correlation 2, 3 | 0.723 |

would look like Table 3.3.

The matrix method for calculating the standard deviation is more effective than the first method we described, because it can be used for a portfolio containing a large number of assets. In fact, this is exactly the methodology used by RiskMetrics, and the computer model used for the calculation will

| | Asset 1 | Asset 2 |
|---|---|---|
| Asset 1 | 1 | 0.647 |
| Asset 2 | 0.647 | 1 |

**Table 3.2**    Asset correlation.

|          | **Asset 1** | **Asset 2** | **Asset 3** |
|----------|---------|---------|---------|
| Asset 1  | 1       | 0.647   | 0.455   |
| Asset 2  | 0.647   | 1       | 0.723   |
| Asset 3  | 0.455   | 0.723   | 1       |

**Table 3.3**   Correlation matrix: three-asset portfolio.

be set up with matrices containing the data for hundreds, if not thousands, of different assets.

The variance–covariance method captures the diversification benefits of a multi-product portfolio because the correlation coefficient matrix is used in the calculation. For instance, if the two bonds in our hypothetical portfolio had a negative correlation the VaR number produced would be lower. It was also the first methodology introduced by JPMorgan in 1994. To apply it, a bank would require data on volatility and correlation for the assets in its portfolio. These data are actually available from the RiskMetrics website (and other sources), so a bank does not necessarily need its own data. It may wish to use its own datasets, however, should it have them, to tailor the application to its own use. The advantages of the variance–covariance methodology are that:

- it is simple to apply and fairly straightforward to explain;
- datasets for its use are immediately available.

The drawbacks of the variance–covariance method are that it assumes stable correlations and measures only linear risk; it also places excessive reliance on the normal distribution, and returns in the market are widely believed to have 'fatter tails' than a true to normal distribution. This phenomenon is known as *leptokurtosis*; that is, the non-normal distribution of outcomes. Another disadvantage is that the process requires mapping. To construct a weighting portfolio for the RiskMetrics tool, cash flows from financial instruments are mapped into precise maturity points, known as *grid points*. We will review this later in the chapter; however, in most cases assets do not fit into neat grid points, and complex instruments cannot be broken down accurately into cash flows. The mapping process makes assumptions that frequently do not hold in practice.

Nevertheless, the variance–covariance method is still popular in the market, and is frequently the first VaR method installed at a bank.

## Confidence intervals

Many models estimate VaR at a given confidence interval, under normal market conditions. This assumes that market returns generally follow a random pattern but one that approximates over time to a normal distribu tion. The level of confidence at which the VaR is calculated will depend on the nature of the trading book's activity and what the VaR number is being used for. The original amendment to the Basel Capital Accord stipulated a 99% confidence interval and a 10-day holding period if the VaR measure is to be used to calculate the regulatory capital requirement. However, certain banks prefer to use other confidence levels and holding periods; the decision on which level to use is a function of asset types in the portfolio, quality of market data available and the accuracy of the model itself, which will have been tested over time by the bank.

For example, a bank may view a 99% confidence interval as providing no useful information, as it implies that there should only be two or three breaches of the VaR measure over the course of 1 year; that would leave no opportunity to test the accuracy of the model until a relatively long period of time had elapsed, in the meantime the bank would be unaware if the model was generating inaccurate numbers. A 95% confidence level implies the VaR level being exceeded around 1 day each month, if a year is assumed to contain 250 days. If a VaR calculation is made using 95% confidence, and a 99% confidence level is required for, say, regulatory purposes, we need to adjust the measure to take account of the change in standard deviations required. For example, a 99% confidence interval corresponds to 2.32 standard deviations, while a 95% level is equivalent to 1.645 standard deviations. Thus, to convert from 95% confidence to 99% confidence, the VaR figure is divided by 1.645 and multiplied by 2.32.

In the same way there may be occasions when a firm will wish to calculate VaR over a different holding period from that recommended by the Basel Committee. The holding period of a portfolio's VaR calculation should represent the period of time required to unwind the portfolio; that is, sell off the assets on the book. A 10-day holding period is recommended but would be unnecessary for a highly liquid portfolio; for example, a market-making book holding government bonds.

To adjust the VaR number to fit it to a new holding period we simply scale it upwards or downwards by the square root of the time period required. For example, a VaR calculation measured for a 10-day holding period will be $\sqrt{10}$ times larger than the corresponding 1-day measure.

## COMPARISON BETWEEN METHODS

The three methods produce different VaR estimates and these are more marked with portfolios that contain options. The analytic method usually estimates the market risk of option positions based on delta (or delta and gamma). This results in inaccurate risk estimates for large changes in the

|                                              | Historical | Simulation | Analytic |
|----------------------------------------------|------------|------------|----------|
| **Ease of implemenation**                    |            |            |          |
| *Easy to aggregate risk across markets*      | Yes        | Yes        | Yes      |
| *Data available at no charge*                | No         | No         | Yes      |
| *Ease of programming (spreadsheet)*          | Easiest    | Hardest    | Medium   |
| **Distributions for market factors**         |            |            |          |
| *Must specific distributions be assumed?*    | No         | Yes        | Yes      |
| *Are actual volatilities and correlations used?* | Yes    | Possible   | Yes      |
| **Handling of individual instruments**       |            |            |          |
| *Are pricing models required?*               | Yes        | Yes        | No       |
| *Is it necessary to map instruments?*        | No         | No         | Yes      |
| *Accurate handling of options*               | Yes        | Yes        | No       |
| **Communication with senior management**     |            |            |          |
| *Ease of explanation*                        | Easiest    | Medium     | Hardest  |
| *Can sensitivity analyses be done?*          | No         | Yes        | Some     |

**Table 3.7**    Comparison of VaR methods.
*Source*: Smitson/Minton, *Risk*.

price of the underlying; it also ignores the potential effect of changes in the volatility of the underlying. The historic and simulation methods can account for changes in all the market factors that affect an option price, and the revaluation process allows the market risk of options to be more accurately measured for larger changes in market factors.

A comparison of the three methodologies is presented at Table 3.7, summarised from *Risk* in November 1997.

## Choosing between methods

The composition of a bank's portfolio is a prime factor in deciding which method to implement. For portfolios with no options the analytic method may be most suitable because it does not require pricing models. Publicly available software and data (e.g., RiskMetrics) makes installation simpler.

Historical or simulation methods are more appropriate for portfolios with option positions. The historical method is conceptually simple and the required pricing models are often available as add-ins for spreadsheet packages. The main obstacle to using the simulation method is the complex task of doing Monte Carlo simulations; although the software is available the process is time-consuming.

To calculate a single position VaR example in simple fashion, consider Example 3.2.

**EXAMPLE 3.2** **VaR calculation**

| | |
|---|---|
| VaR | Amount of position * Volatility of instrument; |
| Volatility | % of value which may be lost with a certain possibility (e.g., 95%); |
| Position | A bond trader is long of $40 million US 10-year Treasury benchmark; |
| Market risk | US 10-year volatility is 0.932%; |
| VaR = | $40 million * 0.932% = $372,800. |

For a two-position VaR example the portfolio now needs to consider correlations and the following expression is applied:

$$VaR = \sqrt{VaR_1^2 + VaR_2^2 + 2\rho VaR_1\ VaR_2}$$

where  $VaR_1$ = Value-at-risk for Instrument 1;
$VaR_2$ = Value-at-risk for Instrument 2;
$\rho$ = Correlation between the price movements of Instrument 1 and 2.

The individual VaRs are calculated as before.

Essentially, RiskMetrics follows the procedure detailed in the previous section for analytic method VaR estimates.

The core of RiskMetrics is:

- a method mapping position, forecasting volatilities and correlations, and risk estimation;
- a daily updated set of estimated volatilities and correlations of rates and prices.

The DEaR and VaR are the maximum estimated loss in market value of a given position that can be expected to be incurred with 95% certainty until the position can be neutralised or reassessed.

**Assessment**

The key technical assumptions made by RiskMetrics are:

- conditional multivariate normality of returns and assets;
- exponentially weighted moving average forecasts of volatility (as against GARCH or stochastic models);
- variance–covariance method of calculation (as against historical simulation).

The key limitations are:

- limited applicability to options and non-linear positions generally;
- simplicity of its mapping process, assuming cash flows on standardised grid points on the time line;
- like any VaR model, no coverage of liquidity risk, funding risk, credit risk, or operational risk.

## Comparison with the historical approach

The historical approach is preferred in some firms because of its simplicity. It differs from RiskMetrics in three respects:

- it makes no explicit assumption about the variances of portfolio assets and the correlations between them;
- it makes no assumptions about the shape of the distribution of asset returns, including no assumption of normality;
- it requires no simplification or mapping of cash flows.

To calculate VaR using this approach all that is required is a historical record of the daily profit and loss (*P&L*) of the portfolio under consideration. Hence, a major strength of the historical approach is the minimal analytical capability required. An additional benefit is the lack of cash flow mapping. The simplification process can create substantial risk distortion, particularly if there are options in the portfolio. Under RiskMetrics, options are converted into their delta equivalents.

The main drawback of the historical approach is that since it is based strictly on the past it is not useful for scenario analysis. With RiskMetrics we can alter the assumed variances and correlations to see how the VaR would be affected. This is not possible under the historical approach.

## COMPARING VaR CALCULATION FOR DIFFERENT METHODOLOGIES

The different approaches to calculating VaR produce a wide range of results. As we illustrate here, this difference occurs even with the simplest portfolio (in this case, a holding of just one vanilla fixed income instrument). If this variation is so marked for just one asset holding, how much more dispersion must there be for complex portfolios that include exotic instruments? The point here is that one must be aware that care needs to be taken when interpreting and using VaR numbers. The actual loss that might occur in practice can bear no relation to the previous day's VaR calculation. This being the case, it suggests that banks should be ultra conservative when setting VaR limits for credit and market risk, on the grounds that the true risk exposure might be many times what the bank's model is suggesting. Relying excessively on VaR model output is not recommended.

Figure 3.3 shows Bloomberg screen PORT, which needs to be set up by the user to hold the desired securities (in other words, the portfolio is bespoke to the user's needs). We see that the portfolio consists of one bond, the Aston Martin Capital Ltd $9\frac{1}{4}\%$ 2018, a £304 million issue from 2011 and quoted at £100.30 as at 18 December 2012. At that price the holding of £1 million had a market value of £1,030,563.

This Bloomberg screen has a VaR functionality built in, which allows you to compare VaR numbers by methodology. We see this at Figure 3.4. From this screen we observe the following values, for the 95% confidence interval:

| | |
|---|---|
| Monte Carlo VaR | 9,579 |
| 1-year historical VaR | 1,778 |
| 2-year historical VaR | 4,101 |
| 3-year historical VaR | 3,050 |
| Parametric VaR | 11,570 |

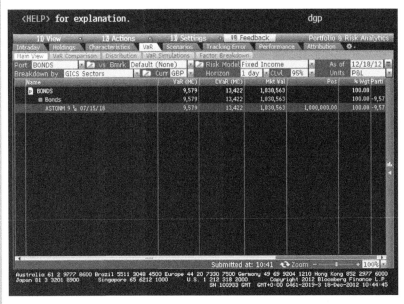

**Figure 3.3** PORT screen showing holding of GBP1 million Aston Martin Capital Ltd $9\frac{1}{4}\%$ 2018 sterling corporate bond.

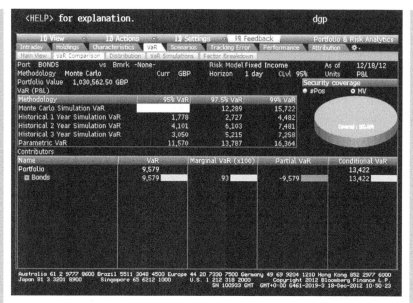

**Figure 3.4** PORT screen showing VaR results by methodology, for bond holding at Figure 3.3
© Bloomberg L.P. Used with permission. Visit *www.bloomberg.com*

This variation is so great as to render the results almost unusable. The investor can take the entire range or simply select an average or the worst-case scenario. It is at this point that using VaR itself becomes slightly subjective. The other interesting observation is the 2-year historical VaR exceeding the 3-year historical VaR. This forces the question, what time horizon is most appropriate if selecting historical VaR as the preferred methodology? The answer is not clear-cut, and of course there is no one right answer. Banks generally tend to obtain a feel for their preferred approach based on a number of market and operational factors.

Finally, Figure 3.5 is the distribution of VaR results by confidence interval selected. As expected we observe reducing estimates the closer we decrease towards 95% c.i., and this trend continuing the further below 95% c.i. the user falls. It also shows the resulting P&L distribution.

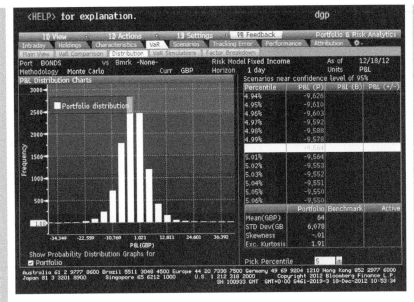

**Figure 3.5** PORT screen showing the VaR distribution of values by selected confidence interval.

© Bloomberg L.P. Used with permission. Visit *www.bloomberg.com*.

Reproduced from *An Introduction to Value-at-Risk, Fifth Edition* (2013)

## POLICY TEMPLATES

For practitioners we have placed the following policy document templates on the book's website, contained in the folder for Chapter 5:

- Trading Book policy;
- FX hedging policy.

## SELECTED BIBLIOGRAPHY AND REFERENCES

*Principles for effective risk data aggregation and risk reporting*, BIS, June 2012, http://www.bis.org/publ/bcbs222.pdf.

*Developments in Modelling Risk Aggregation*, BIS, October 2010, http://www.bis.org/publ/joint25.pdf.

*Supervisory framework for measuring and controlling large exposures*, BIS, March 2013, http://www.bis.org/publ/bcbs246.pdf.

*Should banks be diversified? Evidence from individual bank loan portfolios,* Iftekhar Hasan, Anthony Saunders, and Viral Acharya, http://www.bis.org/publ/work118.htm.

*Diversification and the Banks' risk-return-characteristics – evidence from loan portfolios of German Banks,* Behr, Kamp, Memmel, Pfingsten / Bundesbank, 2007, https://www.bundesbank.de/Redaktion/EN/Downloads/Publications/Discussion_Paper_2/2007/2007_04_02_dkp_05.pdf?__blob=publicationFile.

*Studies on credit risk concentration,* BIS, November 2006, http://www.bis.org/publ/bcbs_wp15.pdf.

*An Explanatory Note on the Basel II IRB Risk Weight Functions,* BIS, July 2005, http://www.bis.org/bcbs/irbriskweight.pdf.

*Concentrations of Credit,* U.S. Comptroller of the Currency, December 2011, http://www.occ.gov/publications/publications-by-type/comptrollers-handbook/Concentration-HB-Final.pdf.

*Measuring portfolio credit risk correctly: why parameter uncertainty matters,* BIS, April 2009, http://www.bis.org/publ/work280.htm.

Supervisory framework for measuring and controlling large exposures – final standard, BIS, April 2014, http://www.bis.org/publ/bcbs283.htm.

*Principles for an Effective Risk Appetite Framework,* Financial Stability Board, November 2013, https://www.financialstabilityboard.org/publications/r_131118.pdf.

*Documents and Guidelines,* Loan Market Association, http://www.lma.eu.com/landing_documents.aspx.

*"Unfortunately Vic came off rather badly [in the squadron], as he suffered from two career-limiting character faults: firstly he was outspokenly honest and always said what he really thought, and secondly he was invariably right."*
—Michael Napier, *Tornado Over the Tigris: Recollections of a Fast Jet Pilot*, Pen & Sword Books, 2015

# CHAPTER 6

# Banks and Credit Risk

For a very large majority of the world's banks, by far the biggest driver of their regulatory capital requirement is credit risk. Specifically this is the exposure arising from lending money to borrowers who are not risk-free and present default risk to the lender. The author once undertook a short consulting engagement at a regional bank in southern Austria for which credit risk represented 91% of the bank's total regulatory capital requirement! The remainder was made up of miniscule amounts for non-traded market risk, liquidity risk, and operational risk. This is possibly somewhat extreme an example but serves to illustrate the point.

Given the significance of credit risk on the balance sheet, it is clear that it is a subject that needs to be understood. It is as important to a bank's good health as liquidity risk is. Therefore this chapter deals with the topic in some depth, and we consider the concept of the credit risk management framework in a banking operation.

## UNDERSTANDING AND MANAGING CREDIT RISK: PART 1

Credit is the core business of a bank and is also its key to profitability and primary risk. As credit risk cannot be avoided, it must be well-managed. Strategy, decision-making, risk–reward optimisation, diversification, and minimisation of loss are not possible without extensive and thorough credit risk measurement. Management must use all of its qualitative and quantitative judgement capabilities to best assess credit risk.

### Credit Risk Measurement Process

The Basel Committee on Banking Supervision (BCBS) was established by central bank governors in 1974. Headquartered at the Bank for International Settlements in Basel, Switzerland, it serves as a forum for cooperation on banking supervision and formulates broad standards and recommendations to be used by national regulators. The Basel Committee has developed extensive guidance on credit risk management measures, parameters, and models. These remain guidance however, and do not carry the force of law. It is the responsibility of national regulatory authorities to ensure that guidelines and recommendations are enshrined in their country's legislative framework.

### Qualitative Factors: Retail and Non-Retail Exposures

Financial information, metrics, and analysis are central to the extension of credit. However, decision makers must balance what numbers and models indicate with their own judgements. Qualitative factors are less tangible and harder to quantify, but crucial. Ultimately, there is no substitute for "Know-Your-Customer".

**Non-Retail**   Traditional banking was very much an "expert system", where bankers allocated credit in their sectors using subjective judgements. A popular framework was the "five C's" – character, capital, capacity, collateral, and cycle – weighted as deemed appropriate. Without rigorous analytics, credit was sometimes extended to clients sponsored by the relationship banker who shouted loudest. But, again, soft factors are important and two broad areas for consideration are management and business.

**Management**   Management needs technical and organisational skills to succeed. The team must understand their business, demonstrate adaptability to changing environments, and have the capacity to control risk and act decisively. Do they have the ability to execute their plan? Experience and background checks should be completed to assess past track records of key leaders.

Consistency of message is important and progress in implementing plans can be checked against past annual reports and press releases. The quality and thoroughness of financial reporting are paramount. Face-to-face meetings are highly desirable and an opportunity to ask probing questions. The openness of responses is a good indicator as to whether a good working relationship is possible, through both good and difficult times. Will problems be disclosed promptly, so they can be worked out with action taken?

Corporate governance must be examined so that the relationships and responsibilities between management and directors are understood. Good corporate governance ensures that proper checks and balances and protections are in place in the interests of investors, lenders, and other stakeholders, and also against unethical and illegal activities. Policies are defined and determined in the company charter and its bylaws, along with corporate rules and regulations. Strong internal controls, authorisation and approval procedures, and the independence of the internal audit department are vital.

Ownership structure is another important factor. Is the ownership structure stable? What are the objectives of the owners? Do the owners (private or government?) have the capacity and willingness to assist in the event of difficulties? How much control do they have and exert over management? A Board can hire and fire management on behalf of the shareholders, but if too many members are insiders it may not serve its role as objective critic.

**Business**   As a first step, a lender must understand the basics of its client's business. Beyond knowing the company's business sector, exactly what does it provide, and in so doing how does it make money? In other words, what is the business model? If a bank cannot meet the company and attain a clear understanding of its business and external operating environment, it does not make sense to extend credit.

Success and long-term viability often depend on competitive advantage, or franchise value. Is the company innovative, unique, or efficient? Does it benefit from a strong brand? Does it have sufficient market share? How high are the barriers for new entrants to challenge its position?

A bank needs to develop informed views on industry sectors and regions. A company can have a strong financial profile and top market share, but a weak or volatile business environment will reduce its credit quality. The state of the economy in its markets, diversification of buyer base, regulation, labour markets, and the pace and depth of structural change are all key factors.

**Retail**   For many years, retail credit decisions were made by local bank relationship managers based on qualitative factors. Models used to analyse wholesale loans could not be applied to small, unrated borrowers. Data has been expensive to collect and verify, with the cost amplified given small potential profit. Often, sound retail credit decision frameworks have been developed by smaller banks with dedicated resources, local knowledge, and relationships. Part of the decision should be based on not just a borrower's ability to pay, but also their sense of obligation to pay. Borrowers may have a local business and range of other debts (credit cards, mortgages, loans) to consider.

## Internal Ratings

Ratings act as the basis for bank credit approval, pricing, monitoring, and loan loss provisioning. Whereas external ratings agencies were founded in the 19th century, bank internal ratings only took off in the 1990s with Basel I.

**Pricing, Provisioning, and Capital Management**   The Basel Committee defines a rating as a "summary indicator of the risk inherent in an individual credit". Ratings "typically embody an assessment of the risk of loss due to failure by a given borrower to pay as promised". A rating system is defined as "the conceptual methodology, management processes, and systems that play a role in the assignment of a rating". Ratings have two dimensions: 1) borrower propensity to default; and 2) transaction characteristics (for example, product, terms, seniority, and collateral).

Under the Basel "Standardised Approach", banks use ratings developed by external rating agencies. The starting point for capital required against assets is 8% of the nominal, against which a risk weighting is applied according to a matrix of ratings and types (sovereign, bank, or corporate).

A bank loan pricing model is based on the capital required and the target return on that capital. The model considers funding, default probability, recovery rate, and taxes as costs against the interest rate charged in calculating a net gain to weigh against the capital required. If loan rates in the marketplace are below the rate needed to meet the target return, the bank needs to decide whether it will accept a lower return to maintain market share or the client relationship.

Since Basel II, banks meeting strict criteria are permitted to use internal ratings to calculate regulatory capital for credit risk. The rationale is that "internal ratings can prove to be more sensitive to the level of risk in a bank's portfolio. Internal ratings may incorporate supplementary customer information, which is usually out of the reach of external credit assessment institutions. Banks will (have incentives to) further refine internal credit risk management and measurement techniques.

To use the "IRB" approach, a bank must:

- Define a risk grading methodology based on an assessment horizon reflected in the bank's rating philosophy (shorter or longer term);
- Maintain at least seven borrower grades for non-defaulted exposures, and one for those in default;
- Assign ratings to all borrowers;
- Review ratings annually;
- Review the model annually;
- Stress test the rating system under adverse economic and market conditions;
- Document the rating system with clear definitions and criteria so as to enable replication of ratings by auditors;
- Provide adequate disclosure and data and demonstrate its use over three years;
- Obtain approval from national supervisors.

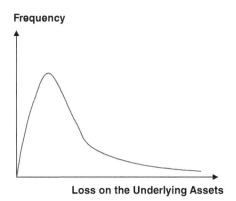

**Frequency**

**Loss on the Underlying Assets**

**FIGURE 6.1**   Credit loss distribution

Internal ratings must satisfy the "use test" and serve as the basis of risk, limits, pricing, provisioning, and capital management decisions, and not be simply for regulatory risk capital calculations.

Both Basel I and Basel II were designed to ensure that banks maintain an adequate capital buffer based on an expected loss methodology. The standard credit loss profile, illustrated at Figure 6.1 below, lies behind the capital calculation.

Figure 6.2 shows how this general credit losses distribution drives the minimum capital level. Expected losses are covered in the loan asset pricing, typically via the target rate of return (given by the cost of capital). Unexpected losses (UL) are covered by the capital reserves, shown at Figure 6.2 as Economic Capital. Of course, regulatory capital rules assign risk weightings

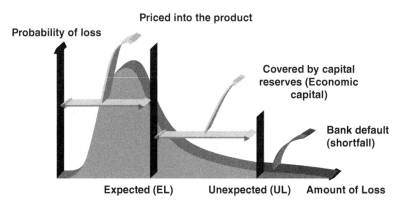

**Priced into the product**

**Probability of loss**

**Covered by capital reserves (Economic capital)**

**Bank default (shortfall)**

**Expected (EL)**      **Unexpected (UL)**      **Amount of Loss**

**FIGURE 6.2**   Applying credit loss distributions into capital calculation

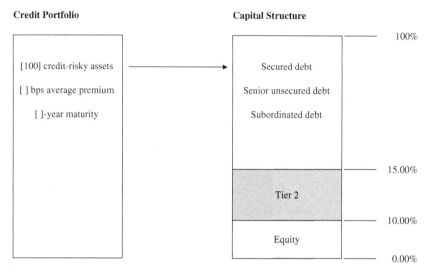

**FIGURE 6.3**    Risky asset portfolio and capital structure

based on the type of loan asset counterparty, and these risk weightings drive the regulatory capital minimum. In the Basel II regime, credit ratings are used to determine risk weightings for banks that use the standardised approach.

Where losses exceed the unexpected losses used to derive the capital calculation, the shortfall results in cessation of the bank as a going concern.

In theory, (and in practice if one was putting together a bank's capital structure from scratch today) the expected loss profile effectively drives the capital structure. As Figure 6.3 shows, if the UL is 10% then this is the minimum equity base requirement.

**Retail, Non-Retail, and Specialised Lending Exposures**    The dominant practice of banks is to use ratings to manage corporate credit risk as described. Ratings remain relatively constant, and are often linked to a schedule of average default probabilities. Rating mobility is a function of a bank's philosophy, which can be either Through-the-Cycle (TtC – more active migration) or Point-in-Time (PiT – less migration).

The quality of the portfolio shifts as the distribution of ratings evolves.

Retail exposures are not generally managed using ratings on an individual borrower basis. Exposures are grouped into segments with similar risk characteristics. Often, the distinction between borrower and product is limited or eliminated. Borrower characteristics (for example, population segment, income, credit history) and those of the facility (for example, product type, credit limit, collateral) are blended in formulating segments.

To demonstrate homogencity of risk, genuine segmentation requires all borrowers within a segment to be treated the same.

Retail exposures include loans (for example, personal finance, education loans, auto loans, or leasing), revolving credits (for example, overdrafts, revolving credit plans, or home equity lines), credit cards, residential mortgages, and small business facilities. Typically (and from a BIS regulatory stand point), retail exposures are managed on a product (facility) basis as opposed to an obligor basis.

There are four tests for characterisation as retail exposure:

- Product;
- Credit to individuals;
- Manageable as a pool of exposures;
- Low value.

For retail exposures, delinquent exposures are managed separately.

In specialised lending, both the source of repayment of a loan and prospects for recovery in an event of default are based on the cash flow from a project or property rather than on the ongoing, open-ended operations of the borrower. Assets pledged as collateral serve to mitigate risk and as a secondary source of repayment. Types of specialised lending include project finance, income producing real estate, high volatility commercial real estate, object finance, and commodities finance.

Specialised lending possesses unique loss distribution and risk characteristics. Given the source of repayment, the exposures exhibit greater risk volatility, with both high default rates and high loss rates in times of distress. Banks use different internal risk rating criteria. Historical data is often not as readily available or comparable and relevant to the current special financing exposures being assessed.

A special risk management focus for specialised lending includes financial strength and flexibility, collateral control, project phase, and marketability.

### Counterparty Risk Parameters

Assigning risk parameters to each loan counterparty is a vital step in the internal ratings (and hence loan approval) process.

**Counterparty Risk Parameters for Non-Defaulted Assets**  After assigning ratings, banks estimate risk parameters for key exposures including probability of default (PD), loss given default (LGD), and exposure at default (EAD). Exposures are risk-weighted by Basel-mandated asset class (corporate, sovereign, bank, retail, and equity) to arrive at total risk weighted assets (RWA) to determine capital requirements.

**Probability of Default (PD)** describes the likelihood of default over a particular time horizon. PD estimates are derived from internal default experience, mapping to external data, and statistical default models. Except for pooled retail exposures, PD for a particular grade must be a long-run average of 1-year default rates. Retail PD estimates must be derived primarily from internal data.

**Expected Loss Given Default (ELGD or LGD)** is defined as the "economic" loss for non-defaulted assets, accounting for inflows (via sale of supporting collateral, unsecured recoveries and guarantor payments) and outflows (via additional post-default draw downs on the credit facility, internal administrative costs, and external legal and valuation fees) measured relative to the exposure at default.

An "economic" loss (unlike an accounting loss) takes into account all relevant factors including material discount effect, and material direct and indirect costs associated with holding and collecting the defaulted facilities.

Methods used to estimate ELGD for credit facilities fall into one of two categories. Subjective methods are primarily driven by expert judgement and used mainly on portfolios with few defaults and/or by banks in the early stage of internal model development. Objective methods largely rely on formal mathematical procedures, and can be further divided into explicit methods (i.e., market LGD approach and workout LGD approach) and implicit methods (i.e., implied market LGD approach). The decision to select one of these objective methods is largely driven by the nature of the portfolio in question, the exposure type (loan vs bond), and the availability of data.

Estimates are based on historical recoveries (including collateral) in economic downturn conditions and used in calculating regulatory capital. LGD is economic rather than accounting loss, which includes direct and indirect costs discounted back to the point of default. Interpretations of key parameters differ by bank and are not always comparable. Definitions of downturn vary, with some banks using two consecutive quarters of negative GDP growth, while others emphasise product downturn rather than overall economic conditions. The relative financial condition and capabilities by bank are important, as funding levels affect discount rates, stronger banks negotiate better collateral terms, and more capable and well-staffed teams work through defaults more quickly and efficiently. While PD is largely the same across all types of exposures to a borrower, LGD is likely to vary significantly by product. Banks are expected to be conservative, and auditors, and external supervisors must be able to validate the model. Repurchase Value Estimators are used when banks need to take possession of and sell property and goods.

**Expected Exposure at Default (EAD)** is the gross exposure upon default. For fixed-credit facilities (such as term loans), EAD is simply the amount outstanding (although EADs slightly above 100% are not uncommon given interest accrual). For revolving facilities (such as lines of credit, liquidity facilities, and overdrafts), EAD is the drawn amount plus an estimate of the amount of the remainder of the commitment likely to be drawn at the time of default. These estimates are often referred to as either the Credit Conversion Factor or Loan Equivalent.

LGD and EAD for corporate, sovereign, and bank exposures are based on a BIS required period of no shorter than seven years. Estimates for retail exposures are based on at least five years of data unless the bank demonstrates that recent data is a better predictor.

If a supervisor agrees that a bank's total expected loss is less than its provisions, the difference can be included in Tier II capital. This can occur in practice as the assumptions used in modelling the provisions required do not necessarily align with those for the capital calculations (for example, a point in time LGD is often used for provisioning, while a downturn LGD is used as a basis for capital calculations).

**Counterparty Risk Parameters for Defaulted Assets**   When exposures default, actual losses can exceed LGD estimates. At this stage, banks need to make a Best Estimate of Expected Losses (BEEL) for each defaulted asset considering the current economic climate, so as to cover the possibility of additional losses. Again, historical data from a full economic cycle should be used as a basis, with losses consistent with any provisions or charge-offs taken.

**Impaired Assets**   Treatment of assets with a reduced likelihood of performing in full was a source of controversy in the financial crisis, as with hindsight it is clear that often problems should have been identified and loss provisions taken earlier. Under the IAS 39 "incurred loss" model, recognition of credit losses was delayed until there was evidence of a trigger event. While designed to limit the ability to build hidden reserves that could be used to boost earnings in future difficult periods, the model enabled earnings management that postponed losses.

Under the global accounting standard IFRS 9, banks are required to recognise expected credit losses at all times and to update the amount of expected credit losses recognised at each reporting date. IFRS 9 broadens the information that banks are required to consider when determining expected credit losses (for example, reasonable and supportable historical, current, and forecast information). To reduce complexity, the same impairment accounting will now be applied to all financial assets.

This forward-looking approach is much more transparent for central banks, regulators, creditors, and shareholders. The model eliminates thresholds and triggers for loss reporting, which should reduce "cliff effects". Disclosure is enhanced, with banks required to explain the basis for their expected credit loss calculations, to explain how they measure expected credit losses, and to explain how they assess changes in credit risk.

## Default Events and Measures

Even default has no simple definition. While some advocate a quantitative standard for clarity and easy understanding, most regulators believe interpreting default as only non-payment fails to capture clear indicators of loss and recognition of increased expected losses.

The most common objective definition of default is when the borrower is:

- 90 days past due on payment (with allowance made for failure to pay given technical / administrative issues); and/or
- Placed in bankruptcy protection.

Rating agencies use this above narrow definition.
Wider definitions include when the borrower is:

- In default on another obligation; and/or
- In breach of any contractual condition (technical default, for example, breach of covenants, failure to submit audit statements on time).

In practice, banks can only use broader definitions if information is available to them. Sometimes the definition of default is addressed in product documentation, which includes covenant breach and cross-default. Products specifying a broad range of technical defaults mean that default may likely occur well before non-payment. Laws vary by jurisdiction as to the lender's ability to place the borrower in default, so banks may have difficulties in being consistent.

**Default Events and Measures: Specialised Lending**  The cash waterfall is the priority of payments by which classes of lenders receive interest and principal. Senior lenders are paid first, followed by junior (also called subordinated or mezzanine) lenders. On loan initiation or bond purchase, senior lenders receive lower returns in exchange for lower credit risk. In a default, equity holders receive what (if anything) remains after assets are distributed to debt holders.

Lenders analyse the size of the company or project assets and collateral relative to debt to assess the value of seniority. If the loan is a general obligation of a large company to finance a small project, seniority may be less important. If repayment is secured only on the asset financed and the cash flow it can generate, a higher priority of payment may be more important.

Loan covenants require borrowers to meet certain conditions over the period of a loan. Breaches of covenants may trigger default, higher pricing, penalties, or termination ("call", or "acceleration") of the loan. Covenants can relate to reporting standards, financial performance, ownership, or business activities.

Common financial covenants include:

- **Debt Service Coverage Ratio** is the ratio of income less expenses to interest and principal payments. DSCR is the main measure to determine whether cash flow is sufficient to service debt. It can be applied to all types of transactions and used as a covenant set at the minimum level acceptable to the lender.
- **Loan Life Coverage Ratio** is the net present value of cash flow available for debt servicing to total debt. LLCR is like DSCR but is a useful standard in project finance as the analysis covers the term of the transaction. LLCR is more difficult to monitor if project cash flows are likely to be inconsistent.
- **Loan to Value Ratio** is central to residential mortgage lending. LTV allows banks to gauge how far prices can fall before loss is incurred should they need to foreclose on the loan and liquidate the property.

Covenants may be waived, and only serve to ensure early alerts and constructive dialogue when conditions become more difficult. However, covenants do cede some control to banks, and management can be forced to take actions not believed by them to be in the best interests of the company.

**Default Events and Measures: Cross-Border Lending**   Currency convertibility and transfer risk is the loss that can occur if local currency cannot be converted to another currency and/or transferred abroad. The situation can arise when a country is experiencing capital outflows in a time of political and economic crisis. Governments may impose currency controls, or there may be simply no market for the currency. The risk is different from devaluation, or appropriation of assets.

Risk assessment must include analysis of economic conditions, political situation, and legal framework. To the extent the country is integrated into the global economy through trade and capital markets activity, currency restrictions would be more likely to be avoided given the severe repercussions.

Risk can be mitigated by the use of cash collateral and letters of credit with banks in other jurisdictions, or increases in interest rates linked to currency disruption.

**Impairment vs. Default**   As discussed earlier, definitions of default vary. Impairment can be described generally as when an exposure is judged by management to have deteriorated so there is no longer a reasonable expectation as to the collection of the full amount as scheduled.

Banks can analyse a number of triggers for borrower deterioration to determine whether an asset is impaired:

- Macroeconomic deterioration:
  - National or local economic conditions relevant to the asset class;
  - Unemployment rate;
  - Property prices for mortgages;
  - Industry (or sector).

- Company:
  - Borrower requests for forbearance;
  - Breach of contract or covenants;
  - Credit rating;
  - Debt service capacity;
  - Financial performance;
  - Cash flow;
  - Net worth;
  - Decrease in turnover;
  - Loss of customers or market share;
  - Diversion of cash flows from earning assets to support non-earning assets;
  - Prospects of the guarantors;
  - Collateral;
  - Country risks.

- Mortgage portfolio:
  - Decrease in rents received;
  - Absence of refinancing options.

- Retail portfolio:
  - Early delinquency (for example, one payment in arrears);
  - Continual high utilisation of facilities;
  - Steady increase in total debt for the client;
  - Income less than total debt repayments.

Banks should disclose impairment triggers to regulatory supervisors.

Loans generally appear on bank balance sheets as assets using nominal principal values. Once a loan is identified as impaired, the current probability of default and loss given default is applied and discounted to establish the new value. Both the loan and capital (shareholders' equity) are marked down on the balance sheet. Impairment provisions appear on the income statement as an expense. Debate as to the optimal balance accounting for loans is ongoing, with some arguing that constant marking-to-market is needed.

## Product Credit Risk Measurement

Credit risk measurement for standard loans involves basic credit risk measures. Some products are undrawn, so exposure is dependent on usage. These contingent liabilities are off-balance sheet, and Credit Conversion Factors (CCF) are applied as estimates of risk. The exposure is multiplied by the CCF to assess capital required.

Banks provide liquidity facilities for clients to draw down as needed. Facilities can be committed or uncommitted. Clients issuing Commercial Paper (marketable notes maturing in one year or less) need backstop liquidity facilities to repay maturing issuance should rollover not be possible. Backstops are a rating agency requirement for the high credit ratings demanded by CP investors.

Under Basel I, the CCF for liquidity facilities under one year was 0%. Under Basel II, the CCFs for standard banks providing facilities under one year and over one year were 20% and 50%, respectively. In reassessing risk and increasing capital requirements under Basel III, the distinction based on term is eliminated and the CCF for all facilities is 50%. Lower CCFs for facilities that could be drawn only in the event of market disruption (not client credit deterioration) have been eliminated.

Any facility which is uncommitted and can be cancelled unconditionally and without notice, and requires the bank to proactively approve new drawdowns has a CCF of 0%.

Guarantees of financial indebtedness are integral to world trade. These include loan guarantees, letters of credit, and banker's acceptances. Banks must categorise guarantee facilities in three ways: unutilised, utilised, and utilised with payment / obligations owing to the beneficiary. CCFs are generally 0–50%, 50–100%, and 100%, respectively.

BIS rules stated previously that bank exposure to another bank's letter of credit was subject to a "sovereign floor", for example, the risk weighting could not be lower than that of the sovereign. This was prohibitive for importers using local banks to issue letters of credit in countries where the sovereign was unrated and external ratings were used by the other bank. The BIS has now waived the sovereign floor to allow the risk weighting to go below 100%. The BIS also eased proposals for stricter capital measures for trade finance in certain short-term, self-liquidating, trade-related contingent liability products collateralised by the underlying shipments, allowing the CCF of 20% to apply to the actual remaining maturity rather than a 1-year floor.

## Credit Risk Terminology

The following terms are important in understanding credit risk measurement:

**Lending Exposure (Legal Entity)**    As a first step, lenders must know exactly to whom they are lending. The legal entity and type (individual, partnership, trust, or corporation) and its powers to conduct business and engage in borrowing must be fully understood. The structure can be simple or highly complex, involving organisational charts and legal shells.

**Facilities / Accounts (Transactions): Draw Down Profile**    Credit agreements include the terms of drawing down the amounts of a facility and types of accounts (for example, revolving credit account, term loan account). A schedule of drawdown amounts and dates can be specified, particularly in project finance. Drawdowns are subject to meeting the conditions precedent, which can involve providing these documents:

- Articles of incorporation demonstrating that the company can enter into the transaction;
- Financial statements;
- Project agreements, licenses, consents;
- Rating agency confirmations;
- Legal opinions;
- Corporate authorisations or Board approvals for the transaction which confirm execution by specified individuals.

Often the provision of collateral is the precedent for another condition.

The timing and likelihood of drawdown are necessary to estimate exposure and risk.

**Collateral**    Collateral is (an) asset(s) pledged by the borrower to the lender to secure a loan. In the event of default, and where the bank decides not to restructure the transaction (and the counterparty cannot refinance externally), the bank will take possession of the collateral in order to offset their loss exposure. It is essential that the lender "perfect a security interest" in the collateral, so that it can easily take control and sell without dispute should the borrower fail to meet the terms of the loan.

Collateral ranges from cash, securities as well as property, to the asset being financed. The lender is best protected if the collateral is marketable in all economic conditions, characterised by low price volatility, and denominated in the same currency. Banks can choose to lend up to a percentage of the value of the asset to protect against a decline in value. This is called taking a "haircut", and the concept behind fixing loan-to-value percentages in the residential mortgage market. Some loans are "over collateralised", meaning the bank receives collateral worth more than the loan. Collateral value must be monitored regularly, with additional collateral ("margin") required if the value declines.

Taking collateral must not be seen as risk-free lending. Banks must only lend to clients they believe have the ability to repay from their operations. Reputation risk, collateral value volatility, and the process of taking and liquidating collateral must be considered.

**Guarantees** Guarantees take many forms and are issued by all types of entities including banks, corporations, and sovereigns, as well as individuals. Banks issue direct guarantees and indirect or counter-guarantees (where non-performance of a second party's guarantee is guaranteed).

Guarantees include:

- A payment guarantee, which ensures the seller that the purchase price will be paid on the agreed date if all contractual obligations are met;
- An advance payment guarantee, which ensures the buyer that the advanced payment will be reimbursed if the seller does not meet contractual delivery obligations in full;
- A performance bond, which serves as collateral for costs incurred by the buyer due to failure of the seller to provide goods and services promptly and as contractually agreed;
- A Bid bond (tender bond), which secures the organiser's expenses in tenders by requiring participants to pay if their bid is accepted but withdrawn;
- A warranty obligations guarantee, which secures any claims by the buyer for defects appearing after delivery;
- A letter of indemnity, which secures the shipping company against any claims if goods are delivered prior to receipt of the original bill of lading;
- A credit security bond, which serves as collateral for loan repayment.

Sovereign guarantees back projects deemed in the public interest, and support development and promotion of infrastructure, new industries, regions, and exports. Many sovereigns have state-owned development and export-import banks.

**On-Balance-Sheet Netting** Banks offset client loans against deposits to reduce risk and capital requirements through netting. This is possible when:

- A bank has a well-founded legal basis for concluding that netting is enforceable in each relevant jurisdiction in all conditions, supported by documents such as legal opinions and netting agreements;
- The maturity of the deposit is at least as long as the loan;
- A bank has adequate reporting and monitoring systems in place, so it can always identify the relevant assets and liabilities as well as rollovers.

Netting allows a bank to do more business with its clients.

Netting is key to non-balance-sheet activities and businesses including securities clearing, payment systems, and derivatives.

## Model Development

Credit risk management models serve many purposes. While generating outputs mandated by regulation, models must be built to meet the needs of the bank and its business for optimal decision-making. Different measures provide a variety of insights in both normal and stressed conditions, and aid in balancing profitability and business objectives with risk. It is imperative that models are built on sound and reliable data.

Risk estimates (PDs, EADs and LGDs) for capital purposes may not be the same for pricing or impairment purposes. Point-in-time or through-the-cycle views may differ. For example, one will not necessarily price a 12-month loan on a through-the-cycle credit expectation.

**Probability of Default** Probability of Default is estimated from a range of sources. The simplest and most widely used throughout the world is rating agency ratings. Banks also use their own historical default databases or purchase those compiled by third parties. For some sectors, decades of default data is available. PD can also be estimated by monitoring bond and credit default prices; that is, by implying the default probability of a particular issuer from market prices.

Statistical methods to estimate PDs include:

- Linear regression;
- Discriminant analysis;
- Logit and Probit models;
- Panel models;
- Cox proportional hazards model;
- Neural Networks.

Banks must make careful judgements as to how data is used. While default is rare (roughly 2% on average globally), consequences for debt portfolios are severe given small earnings margins and no upside as there is with equities. While modelling monthly or quarterly data from portfolio segments is common, defaults observed may not be a good indicator for forward-looking analysis if a portfolio is growing or the market is new. The risk of PD being understated is significant.

An important concept in PD is "distance to default". PD increases as the market value of the assets of a company decreases towards the book value of the liabilities. Issues considered are:

- The current asset value;
- The distribution of asset values at time horizon;
- The volatility of the future assets value at time horizon;
- The level of the default point, the book value of the liabilities;
- The expected rate of growth in the asset value over the horizon;
- The length of time horizon.

The default point is sometimes when the two values converge, although companies may continue to trade if the liabilities are longer term and creditors believe in the business.

Models must provide PD in both unstressed and stressed economic scenarios. Higher interest rates, which make debt more costly, can be integral to stress scenarios. "Point-in-Time" PDs are estimated for unstressed conditions while "Through-the-Cycle" PDs estimate the trough. Both are fixed for one year, but PiT PDs will be volatile as the economy evolves while TtC PDs will be more stable. Obligors must be classified as to how they are likely to respond to the economic cycle at both peaks and troughs.

**Loss Given Default** The most common LGD measure is "Gross" (total losses are divided by EAD) because it is simple to calculate and requires the least data. Another LGD measure is "Blanco" (losses divided by the unsecured portion of a credit line), which is important when a bank has significant collateralisation. As a conservative measure, collateral is "haircut" in the calculation to allow for a fall in value, thereby decreasing LGD. Banks calculate "Downturn" LGD.

LGD can be difficult to calculate as bank recovery rates vary and workouts take different lengths of time, so peer data is not always useful. Formulas have been developed to best achieve comparability. Models "time weight" LGD, meaning historical data is not analysed simply by averaging loss severity of each default but also considers the time periods in the economic cycle when they are likely to occur.

There are three objective LGD estimation methods:

- Market LGD, which is observed from market prices of defaulted bonds and marketable loans soon after default events. The main benefit is that actual prices can be used. This is the methodology used most by the rating agencies.
- Workout LGD, which is estimated cash flows from the workout process, based on estimated exposure and a discount rate. Users must monitor the timing of payments received and consider the riskiness of any restructured debt.
- Implied Market LGD, which is derived from prices of bonds deemed to be high risk. This is the least developed of the methods, but has the benefit of a large pool of market data

Given the challenges involved in calibrating LGD models, banks reference external data sources, such as Pan European Credit Data Consortia (PECDC), S&P LossStat, and Paris Club restructure data.

**Exposure at Default** Exposure at Default (EAD) is the gross total of extended credit plus estimated additional drawings for one year or until maturity.

The greatest analytical challenge in setting Credit Conversion Factors (or Loan Equivalents) is estimating additional drawings. Globally, unused commitments are huge and it is logical that a corporation would seek to drawn down in stress scenarios. Examples of products where modelling is needed include committed loan and liquidity facilities, and credit cards.

Strong information management systems are vital in assessing EAD, as the bank must ensure that troubled entities draw only under the terms permitted by the facility and up to the limit. Collateral must be monitored, priced, and margined. The bank must deal efficiently and quickly in default situations.

## Risk Monitoring and Model Validation

Banks must have a standard and regular process for validation and review of credit risk models. Validation must assess the accuracy and consistency of ratings and risk components in an independent manner, with input from relevant departments. A fundamental role of supervisory authorities is to ensure this process is conducted in a meaningful and thorough manner, with banks making available the inputs and calculations.

Back-testing is an important part of model validation, and includes comparison of model results against actual ratings migration and loss experience by category. Benchmarking of internal estimates against external sources is another useful quantitative review, and can add objectivity. The entire process should make apparent changes in drivers, trends, and correlations. Outcomes can include revision of risk categories and adjustments to data timeframes. Strong risk aggregation capabilities are vital and deficiencies (a problem in the crisis) should be exposed to ensure business grows only as quickly as control infrastructure. Business line leaders must have a basic understanding of the models and ensure their risks are fully incorporated into the bank-wide risk process.

**Risk Appetite Statement**   Risk appetite is the quantum of risk a bank is prepared to assume in pursuit of its strategy, and is established, integrated into business plans, and monitored by the Board. The risk appetite statement sets out the risk profile by identifying risks and boundaries. The statement should be actionable and include quantitative measures. High level limit and target measures can be set against earnings at risk, probability of insolvency, and the chance of experiencing an annual loss. Best-practice discipline dictates that the bank's Board sign off on the risk appetite statement. By being a Board-issued document, it ensures that adherence to risk tolerance is taken seriously as a requirement of senior management.

Implementation requires proper policies, procedures, and controls. Regulators will monitor the level of Board involvement, adherence to policies, breach of limits, and policy changes. Crucially, the risk appetite statement must be used to identify excessive risk taking which can threaten a bank.

## Trading Book Credit Exposures

Trading book exposures must be managed actively and held for "trading intent", or short-term gain. Positions may be proprietary or arise from market-making to serve clients. Capital should be allocated to cover losses from a very short period (10–20 days). Standardised method banks must use set parameters, but advanced banks with approved internal models banks can use their own EAD and Value-at-Risk. In addition to the risk of default of the issuer of the securities, there is a small credit risk in trading, as the counterparty could default before settlement with the position needing to be replaced at a worse price. Most securities trade on a delivery-vs-payment basis (DVP), so there is little or no settlement risk in exchanging securities and cash.

## Potential Future Exposures and Regulatory Add-ons

Swaps, foreign exchange and interest rate forwards, options, other derivatives, and securities finance transactions (repo) are subject to fluctuations in value over the life of the contract. Besides replacement value, credit risk measurement must include Potential Future Exposure (PFE), defined as the maximum expected credit exposure. PFE is important because some transactions have longer maturities where losses may emerge over time. Also, positions with large downsides in extreme markets (for example, options sold) are more fully captured.

CCR "add-ons" are determined by multiplying the notional principal amount by Credit Conversion Factors set by type (interest rate, commodities, credit, currency, and equities), features, position, and term.

## Netting

Netting agreements allow parties to net the mark-to-market values of their trades so that in the event of default the credit exposure is limited to the net positive value of the total. Netting is generally effected under an International Swap Dealer Association (ISDA) Master Agreement signed between the parties, which specifies methods for calculating a single settlement amount in the termination currency. ISDA has obtained legal opinions from major jurisdictions confirming the enforceability of netting. "The ISDA" also specifies margining arrangements and collateral terms so that CCR in the normal course of business is further reduced with less capital required.

Securities finance transactions have similar netting and are generally executed under the ICMA Global Master Repo Agreement.

## Basel III

While Basel III retains the concepts of replacement cost and potential future exposure, it strengthens CCR capital requirements with new charges and measures:

- **Effective Expected Positive Exposure:** a stress calibrated measure of the total portfolio of CCR used for capital requirements, if greater than the sum of market values of the portfolio. EEPE focuses on out-of-the-money positions that could become credit exposures and also addresses "wrong way risk", meaning the positions of counterparties can be correlated to their probability of default.
- **Credit Valuation Adjustment:** a charge to cover mark-to-market losses, which were twice as large as CCR losses from defaults in the crisis.
- **Asset Value Correlation:** the correlation coefficient to large regulated and all unregulated financial entities is increased, thus increasing risk weights.
- **Central Clearing Parties:** risk weights are substantially lower and the CVA does not apply if the CCP meets certain requirements as well as collateral and margining standards, which allows for strong incentives to clear OTC trades centrally.

Basel III includes enhanced management requirements for policies, processes, reporting, and testing.

## Market Implied Probability of Default and Survival Curves

Bond and CDS prices can be used to extract the market view on probability of default and guide the pricing of loans and securities.

**Default and Survival Curves**   Default curves can be constructed by extracting credit spreads over risk-free (for example, treasury) rates using as many securities and maturity pricing observations as possible. Assumptions, requiring carefully thought-out best estimates, must be then made as to:

- Linearity (given infrequent data points);
- Discount rates;
- Recovery rates;

- Role of investor premium in credit spread for:
  - Volatility; and
  - Liquidity.

The process of curve construction is also known as "bootstrapping". Given the investor premiums described above, it must be noted that actual historical default rates are less than those implied by bond and CDS prices.

The default intensity or hazard rate is the default probability for each time period. This is used to construct cumulative probability of default rates and cumulative probability survival rates (the two are inverses) for each time period. Investors generally demand relatively higher increases in credit spreads earlier along the curve for lower rated credits, implying increasing default intensity with time.

**Closed Form Analytical Approximations vs. Monte Carlo Simulation**   With the rapid growth and complexity of derivatives markets since the 1980s, credit risk models have advanced in sophistication. Early systems of managing risk were closed form approximations, with limited and static credit categories, default probabilities, recovery rates, term structure, potential future exposure, and netting measures. Little focus was directed to correlation, diversification, and credit migration. With limited historical data and less computing power, more elaborate models were not possible.

Given the complexity, number of dimensions, and uncertainty of the CCR of a bank's derivatives portfolio, Monte Carlo simulations are now the norm. While it is data and IT system intensive, Monte Carlo can incorporate the multiple sources of risk, correlations, and mitigants (including netting). Modelling therefore shifts from the deterministic setting to the probabilistic setting.

Large numbers of joint scenarios are generated based on numerous risk-based factors pertaining to market conditions, defaults, credit migration, correlations, and recovery over the term of the portfolio. This is especially necessary as credit events and in particular defaults are rare, yet have huge impacts. Besides estimating risk, the simulations provide many insights into profit maximisation and hedging. Figure 6.4 shows an example of an RWA calculation, highlighting the various parameter inputs.

The exposure at default value (EAD) is based on the specific asset drawn amount plus the expectation that the facility usage will increase, up to and beyond limit, as the obligor approaches default. Historical data and observation of sector in default is used to drive this. The EAD is, therefore, invariably above the drawn amount and up to the Facility limit and beyond (includes some "costs" in certain cases.)

# Example: RWA calculation

**CRE = Commercial Real Estate**

|  |  |  | CRE | | | | |
|---|---|---|---|---|---|---|---|
|  |  |  | Drawn | EAD | RWA | EL | RW % |
| **Curr Acc** | Performing |  |  |  |  |  |  |
|  | Non-performing |  |  |  |  |  |  |
| **Loans** | Performing |  |  |  |  |  |  |
|  | Non-performing |  |  |  |  |  |  |
| **Mortgages** | Performing |  |  |  |  |  |  |
|  | Non-performing |  |  |  |  |  |  |
| **Cards** | Performing |  |  |  |  |  |  |
|  | Non-performing |  |  |  |  |  |  |
| **RETAIL TOTAL** |  |  |  |  |  |  |  |
| Retail | Performing | BIB (business segment) | 24 | 50 | 27 | 0 | 55% |
|  |  | BBB | 18 | 25 | 14 | 0 | 55% |
|  |  | BB Dev | 352 | 388 | 213 | 5 | 55% |
|  | Non-performing | BIB | 0 | 0 | 0 | 0 | 46% |
|  |  | BBB | 52 | 64 | 8 | 29 | 13% |
|  |  | BB Dev | 33 | 37 | 12 | 16 | 31% |
| *BB Retail Total* |  |  | 478 | 563 | 274 | 52 | 49% |
| Corporate CRE | Performing | BIB | 3 | 3 | 2 | 0 | 81% |
|  |  | BBB | 30 | 30 | 24 | 0 | 81% |
|  |  | BB Dev | 265 | 268 | 286 | 4 | 107% |
|  | Non-performing | BIB | - | - | - | - | - |
|  |  | BBB | - | - | - | - | - |
|  |  | BB Dev | - | - | - | - | 150% |
| *BB Corp CRE Total* |  |  | 297 | 301 | 312 | 4 | 104% |
| Corporate Non CRE | Performing | BIB | - | - | - | - | - |
|  |  | BBB | - | - | - | - | - |
|  |  | BB Dev | - | - | - | - | - |
|  | Non-performing | BIB | - | - | - | - | - |
|  |  | BBB | - | - | - | - | - |
|  |  | BB Dev | - | - | - | - | - |
| *BB Corp Non CRE Total* |  |  | - | - | - | - | - |
| **Business Banking Total** |  |  | 775 | 864 | 587 | 56 | 68% |

Based on drawn amount plus expectation that the facility usage will increase, up to and beyond limit, as the obligor approaches default. [Historical data and observation of sector in default is used to drive this]

The EAD therefore invariably above the Drawn amount and up to Facility limit and beyond (includes some "costs")

RW% driven by the credit model

RW% for Retail based on IRB (uses firm-specific PD and LGD)

RW% for CRE uses "Slotting" (PRA)

RW% for non-CRE is Standardised (no model needed uses internal rating, which will be model derived)

**FIGURE 6.4** Summary of a risk-weighted assets calculation for a retail and corporate customer commercial bank

The risk weighting percentage (RW%) is driven by the credit model. In Figure 6.4, the RW% for Retail based on IRB (uses firm-specific PD and LGD), while the RW% for commercial real-estate (CRE) has been calculated via the regulatory authority's "Slotting" technique (whereby the regulator applies its own risk-weight value because it does not deem the bank's internal model and/or data analytics to be robust enough for this asset class). The RW% for non-CRE is the standardised approach (no model is needed, and it uses internal rating, which will be model derived).

Note the 150% RW level is used if there are any non-performing assets on the balance sheet.

## DE(RE)CONSTRUCTING THE B2 CREDIT RISK AIRB FORMULA[1]

At first the "Basel 2 Credit Risk Advanced Internal Ratings Based Risk Weighted Asset", B2 Credit RWA formula for short, is not only a mouthful to say but seemingly also made up of a set of arbitrary constants and numbers (see Equation 6.1).

$$RWA = 1.06 \times 12.5 \times EAD \times LGD \times RW \qquad (6.1)$$

Here we present a deconstruction of the B2 Credit RWA formula with the aim of presenting a logical derivation of the formula.

As a graduate trainee in a financial institution at the same time as being presented with the above B2 formula, one is informed that bank capital is meant to absorb unexpected losses, while expected losses should be recognised as a cost of doing business, as shown at Figure 6.5.

To link the concept of unexpected losses and required capital to absorb losses (Regulatory Capital or "Reg Cap") to RWA, it might be helpful to introduce a segue and consider RWA as an artificial artefact that is simply Reg Cap scaled by the inverse of the Minimum Capital Ratio set by regulators, that is:

$$(1) \qquad RWA = \left(\text{Minimum Capital Ratio}\right)^{-1} \times \text{Reg Cap} \qquad (6.2)$$

In Equation (2) Reg Cap is the capital needed to cover Unexpected Losses at a given confidence interval of $\alpha$ minus Expected Losses

$$(2) \qquad \text{Reg Capital} = UL(\alpha) - EL \qquad (6.3)$$

---

[1] This section was co-authored with Doo Bo Chung.

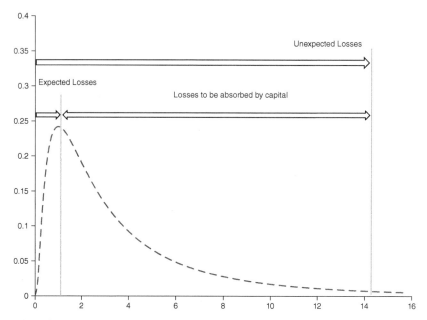

**FIGURE 6.5**   Losses to be absorbed by capital

The confidence interval for the Basel II RWA formula is set at 99.9%, while the implied minimum capital ratio used in the Basel II formula is

$$(3) \qquad \text{Minimum Capital Ratio} = \frac{8\%}{1.06} \qquad (6.4)$$

Formally, the B2 Minimum Capital Ratio is 8%. A 1.06 scaling factor is applied to "broadly maintain the aggregate level of minimum capital requirements"; as a consequence the effective Minimum Capital Ratio as shown in Equation (3) is 7.55%. In Equation (4), the Expected Loss is the result of a series of conditional expectations

$$(4) \qquad \text{EL} = \text{EAD} \cdot \text{LGD} \cdot \text{PD} \qquad (6.5)$$

where EAD is the Exposure at Default, LGD is the Loss Given Default and PD is the Probability of Default. Unexpected Loss can be interpreted as the Credit Value-At-Risk measure and in a similar vein as shown in Equation (5) can be expressed as

$$(5) \qquad \text{UL}(\alpha) = \text{CVAR}(\alpha) = \text{EAD} \cdot \text{LGD} \cdot P_{UL}(\alpha) \qquad (6.6)$$

where $P_{UL}(\alpha)$ is the Probability of Unexpected Losses.

To derive the Probability of Unexpected Losses, a portfolio model is needed and we consider a model where default is deemed to have occured where total asset value $A_i$, which follows a standard normal distribution, falls below the value of liabilities $L_i$ (known as the Merton Model named after Nobel Laureate Robert Merton)

(6)
$$PD = p\left(A_i \leq L_i\right) = \Phi_N\left(L_i\right)$$
(6.7)

where $\Phi_N$ is the standard normal cumulative distribution function. Total asset value $A_i$ is described using Vasicek's one factor model where asset value is a function of both a systemic factor $\eta$ and an idiosyncratic factor $\epsilon_i$, which both follow a standard normal distribution

(7)
$$A_i = \sqrt{\rho}\eta + \sqrt{1-\rho}\ \epsilon_i$$
(6.8)

where $\rho$ is the correlation coefficient to the systemic factor. For a given state of $\eta$ the conditional probability can be rearranged as

(8)
$$P\left(A_i \leq L_i \mid \eta\right) = P\left(\sqrt{\rho}\eta + \sqrt{1-\rho}\ \epsilon_i \leq L_i \mid \eta\right)$$
(6.9)

Rearranging Equation (8) yields

(9)
$$P\left(A_i \leq L_i \mid \eta\right) = P\left(\epsilon_i \leq \frac{L_i - \sqrt{\rho}\eta}{\sqrt{1-\rho}_i} \mid \eta\right)$$
(6.10)

Given $\epsilon_i$ follows a standard normal distribution, Equation (9) can be written as

(10)
$$P\left(A_i \leq L_i \mid \eta\right) = \Phi_N\left(\frac{L_i - \sqrt{\rho}\eta}{\sqrt{1-\rho}}\right)$$
(6.11)

As Equation (6) implies $L_i = \Phi_N^{-1}\left(PD\right)$, equation (10) can be further simplified to

(11)
$$P\left(A_i \leq L_i \mid \eta\right) = \Phi_N\left(\frac{\Phi_N^{-1}\left(PD\right) - \sqrt{\rho}\eta}{\sqrt{1-\rho}}\right)$$
(6.12)

For a given confidence interval $\alpha$, Equation (11) can be written as

(12)

$$P_{UL}(\alpha) = \Phi_N\left(\frac{\Phi_N^{-1}(PD) - \sqrt{\rho}\Phi_N^{-1}(1-\alpha)}{\sqrt{1-\rho}}\right) = \Phi_N\left(\frac{\Phi_N^{-1}(PD) + \sqrt{\rho}\Phi_N^{-1}(\alpha)}{\sqrt{1-\rho}}\right)$$

(6.13)

As a final step the B2 Credit RWA formula can be reconstructed as

(13)

$$RWA = 1.06 \times \frac{1}{8\%} \times EAD \times LGD \times \left[\Phi_N\left(\frac{\Phi_N^{-1}(PD) + \sqrt{\rho}\Phi_N^{-1}(\alpha)}{\sqrt{1-\rho}}\right) - PD\right]$$

(6.14)

or the more familiar version [2]

(14)

$$RWA = 1.06 \times 12.5 \times EAD \times LGD \times \left[\Phi_N\left(\frac{\Phi_N^{-1}(PD) + \sqrt{\rho}\Phi_N^{-1}(\alpha)}{\sqrt{1-\rho}}\right) - PD\right]$$

(6.15)

Note above formula is assuming maturity of 1Y. The Basel formula introduces a Maturity adjustment factor to account for different maturities.

# UNDERSTANDING AND MANAGING CREDIT RISK: PART 2

In Part 2 we examine the credit process of a bank, including how it organises the credit function, and approves, analyses, structures, prices, monitors, and works out credit assets.

## Credit Risk Organisational Structures

As made clear in previous chapters, the Board of Directors has overall responsibility for all risks of the bank and sets strategy, policy, and limits. The Board must have a Risk Management sub-committee, which includes the

CEO and the heads of the management level Credit, Market, Asset Liability, and Liquidity as well as the Operational Risk Management Committees. The Board sub-committee must take a coordinated and integrated approach to the range of risks. It is vital that its integrity and independence is maintained, with a system in place to report to internal and external auditors for when and reasons why the full Board does not accept recommendations.

Given the critical importance of credit risk, the Credit Policy Committee (also called the Credit Risk Management Committee) should be chaired by the CEO and include the Chief Risk Officer, Heads of Credit, Credit Risk Management, Treasury, and the Chief Economist. Our recommended operating model is to place the credit committee under the oversight of the bank's ALCO (see Chapter 10).

The credit committee is responsible for implementing Board-level credit strategy and policy as well as the following:

**Credit Approval:**
- Formulating standards for credit proposals:
  - Credit analysis;
  - Ratings;
  - Loan structures, covenants, and collateral;

- Setting credit pricing policy;
- Delegating credit approval authority;
- Monitoring, Risk Management, and Reporting;
- Measuring and monitoring credit risk with precision and consistency across the bank;
- Maintaining credit risk within approved limits;
- Managing the credit portfolio;
- Establishing a review mechanism for loans;
- Setting policy for provisioning;
- Devising a process for loan workout;
- Ensuring compliance with all regulatory requirements.

The Board and Credit Committee policies and strategies must be communicated effectively throughout the bank and permeate to each level and function. Delegation of authority and responsibility with clear reporting lines and accountability are paramount. Credit risk functions must be staffed and resourced sufficiently.

On an operating level, banks need to have separate Banking and Credit Risk Management Departments. The Banking Department (often organised by industry specialisation) manages customer relationships and takes a commercial approach in identifying business opportunities, pitching for deals, and negotiating and closing transactions. The Credit Risk Management Department measures risk and enforces limits and standards, with constant overseeing of the entire portfolio. Sub-departments of the CRMD include Credit Portfolio, Credit Modelling, Monitoring and Collection, Collateral Management, and Restructuring.

While separate, all departments and functions must rely on each other for credit risk management to be effective. Credit Modelling must receive timely and accurate data to provide useful risk measures to the Credit Department and Credit Portfolio for action.

### Credit Scores and Credit Bureaus

A credit score is a numerical expression of creditworthiness generated by a statistical model using pertinent data. In contrast to commercial lending where extensive analysis is performed on the borrower with judgements being made, high volume / small size transactions generally dictate that retail lending is based on automated scoring without any human intervention. This applies to approval, pricing, terms, monitoring, control, and collections. Credit scores are sometimes also used for Small to Medium Enterprise (SME) lending. Banks must satisfy supervisors that the data is relevant to exposures, the model has a sound track record in predicting default and is regularly tested and updated, and a system is in place for governing the use of the credit scores.

Credit bureaus (also referred to as consumer reporting or credit reference agencies) collect and aggregate personal and financial information from sources including creditors, lenders, utilities, debt collection agencies, and public records. A particular focus is past borrowing and bill paying habits. Bureaus provide their clients with credit reports for credit risk assessment and scoring, or for other purposes such as offering employment or renting of property.

While formats vary, all credit reports contain the same basic information:

- Identity of the counterparty;
- Trade lines: accounts with date of opening, classification (for example, credit card, auto loan), activity, balances, minimum payments, and payment history;
- Credit enquiries: list of parties accessing reports to evaluate requests for credit;
- Public records: bankruptcy, foreclosure, wage attachment (garnishes / admin orders), lien, lawsuit, and judgements information;
- Collection items: information on overdue payments.

In the past, credit reporting involved only negative information, but now scheduled repayment of debt is used as a positive. Negative items closed out are removed from credit reports over time (there are regulations that govern these time periods that are often country specific).

The minimum for a report is generally one undisputed account opened for six months or more with no indication that one of the holders is deceased.

Credit reports do not contain information on race, religion, national origin, sex and marital status; location of residence; age; income and employment history; interest rates charged on accounts; child support obligations; customer initiated report checks; history of credit counselling; or any information not proven to be predictive of future credit performance. Much of this information is stored at the credit bureaus themselves, and can be used for validating client information required by the local regulations, if required.

Data quality is fundamental to the generation of useful credit scores. Potential sources of mistakes include:

- Lender error in recording payments;
- Incorrect / incomplete data submissions to the bureaus;
- Incorrect recording of identity, transposition of digits;
- Ex-spouse's credit issues linked;
- Identity theft.

Consumers can check their credit reports and notify credit bureaus of any errors. Credit bureaus have a legal duty to respond promptly, however, there is criticism about their efficiency in that a greater burden is placed on the consumer.

Credit scores are modelled by both credit bureaus and banks. The most widely used credit scoring system is FICO, pioneered in the United States in the 1950s by what was then Fair, Isaac and Company. Consumers need to know the basics and means to improve their credit scores to meet their financial goals. Steps for consumers to take with the greatest effect are:

- Paying bills on time (setting up payment reminders and automatic payments or debit orders can help);
- Catching up on missed payments;
- Reducing debt (achieved most quickly by paying off highest interest rate debt first);
- Avoiding opening new accounts simply to increase available credit (but not closing accounts likely to be needed);
- Avoiding searching extensively for a single loan, as it may appear as an effort to increase borrowing rapidly (by increasing the number of recent bureau enquiries);

- Avoiding moving debt around to put off repayment;
- Having some active accounts that reflect on the credit bureaus (this allows an "active credit" score to be generated with positive payment information).

While credit scoring methodologies vary and are not disclosed in detail, overall weighting of factors has been estimated as follows: payment history 35%, debt to credit ratio 30%, average age of accounts 15%, types of credit 10%, and enquiries 10%.

Credit scores constantly change, therefore consumers must be reminded, educated, and be provided with incentives for good personal financial management.

### Limits and Risk Appetite

As discussed in previous chapters, the Board uses the risk appetite statement to set the quantity and type of risk the bank will tolerate within its total capacity to pursue its business objectives. Highest level limits for broad exposure groupings are set after considering the impact of the potential transaction on the regulatory and/or economic capital required to support the credit position. This includes using probabilities of default to estimate expected losses under different scenarios (from normal to recession or to major disruption and with consideration of frequency). These may be expressed in absolute amounts for the riskiest exposures or as a percentage of total exposure. An internal economic capital framework considering correlation, concentration, and large single exposures are all integral to setting limits. Risk is then allocated on an operating level across business lines, products, industries, and regions, as well as individual borrowers in the form of further limits.

Limits are incorporated in Pillar II of Basel II as part of the supervisory review process. Limits must not be merely a "rubber stamp" of business requests leading to the approval of further increases when requested only. Forward thinking credit management involves consideration of reasonable exposure levels in anticipation of new business opportunities and the potential medium-term movements of the credit cycle. For instance, when there is an expectation of a downturn in the credit cycle, risk limits may be tightened to alleviate future volatility in the credit outcome (bad debt charge or default rates).

Limits serve varying purposes. In some instances, limits are a firm form of policing against taking on risks not deemed tolerable. In other instances, limits are essentially a form of an early warning system, where credit officers and management are alerted to an increase in risk that merits further discussion and analysis. Sometimes a client is involved in multiple products (including trading) and the bank may not be able to ensure that the total intra-day exposure limits are not breached, in which case limits should be set conservatively low. As credit risk is constantly changing due to portfolio effects and new data, limits need regular adjustments irrespective of whether nominal exposures change or remain the same.

## Credit Risk Assessment

In extending credit to a corporation, banks will consider attributes such as market share, quality of products and services, innovation, brand, and operating efficiency. However, a company's performance and ability to meet debt obligations is strongly linked to macroeconomic and industry factors.

Key factors include the phase of the economic cycle, interest, inflation, and exchange rates. Sensitivity to these factors varies by industry. While the durable goods, auto, transportation, and information technology industries tend to perform in line with the economy (cyclical), the household goods, food, and utilities industries are more constant (non-cyclical). Historically, the performance of the financial and homebuilding industries have been highly interest rate sensitive.

Industry characteristics to consider include:

- Size and growth prospects;
- Competition;
- Profit margins;
- Supplier power;
- Buyer power;
- Labour supply and relations;
- Barriers to entry for new entrants;
- Innovation;
- New markets;
- Threat of substitute products;
- Research and development costs;
- Regulatory environment;
- Political risks.

With a broader understanding of the industry, it is then possible to analyse a company's competitive advantages, positioning, and its prospects in the future.

## Financial Analysis

Corporate financial statements include volumes of data which can be used to perform extensive credit analysis. The most widely used technique is financial ratios, with four main categories:

- Leverage ratios:
  - Indicate the extent of reliance on debt financing;
  - Measure the relative contribution of stockholders and creditors or the extent to which debt is used in the capital structure;
  - Measure the degree of protection of suppliers of long-term funds;
  - Aid in assessing the ability to pay liabilities and raise new additional debt.

- Liquidity ratios:
  - Measure the ability to meet current obligations as they come due;
  - Indicate the ease of turning current assets into cash.

- Profitability ratios:
  - Measure the ability to generate revenues in excess of costs;
  - Measure the ability to earn a return on resources.

- Efficiency ratios:
  - Indicate how well assets are used to generate sales and profits;
  - Measure the ability to control expenses.

It is possible to generate dozens of financial ratios from a company's balance sheet and income statement. However, credit analysts do not rely on ratios as much as in the past or they do not have the same expectation, as in the past, that benchmark ratio levels must be met. Often one ratio appearing weak is offset by a stronger one, and more sophisticated statistical modelling techniques are available now.

Ratio by industry sector and company size (for example, large corporate, middle market, SME) is used to assess norms and relative strength. Historical ratios are useful in identifying trends, we list some common ones in Table 6.1.

## Loan Facilities

Once the credit strength of a potential borrower is analysed, a bank can consider the structure and risks of the proposed facility. The bank must understand the purpose, amount, and duration of the borrowing. The loan must be for an activity within a company's business remit or an individual's financial goals. It is acceptable to finance the repayment of existing debts,

**TABLE 6.1** Formulae and description for the key ratios

| Ratio | Formula | Measures |
|---|---|---|
| **Leverage** | | |
| Debt to Equity | Debt / equity | Owed compared to owned |
| Interest Coverage | EBIT* / interest expense | Ability to pay interest using cash-flow |
| **Liquidity** | | |
| Current or Working Capital Ratio | Current assets / current liabilities | Liquidity reserves |
| Quick Ratio or Acid Test | (Cash+marketable securities+receivables) / current liabilities | Ready liquidity (excludes inventory) |
| **Profitability** | | |
| Gross Profit Margin | (Revenue-cost of goods sold) / revenue | Ability to generate profit |
| Return on Equity | Net income / shareholder equity | Return on shareholder's investment |
| Return on Assets | Net income / average assets | Return on assets used |
| **Efficiency** | | |
| Asset Turnover | Net sales / average assets | Use of assets to generate sales |
| Payables Turnover | Cost of sales / trade payables | Speed of paying bills |
| Operating Cycle | average inventory / cost of sales per day | Time between acquisition of inventory and realisation of cash |

*$EBIT$: earnings before interest and taxes

providing the new loan terms can accommodate the client's needs better and can be serviced.

By understanding a borrower's requirements, the bank can offer the most suitable facilities, which may include the following:

- Line of Credit:
  - Credit availability is established but approval is needed for each draw down;
  - Drawings to be repaid in fixed, short periods of time;
- Revolving Line of Credit:
  - Allows for continuous borrowing up to a limit;
  - Repayments allow for automatic borrowing back up to the limit;

- Asset Based:
  - Attractive to companies with less free cash flow due to rapid growth or difficult markets which are less able to obtain unsecured credit;
  - Funds advanced against collateral:
    - Working capital (accounts receivable, inventories);
    - The assets financed;
  - Factoring is when accounts receivable are sold outright to the bank at a discount which reflects the cost of credit.
- Term Loan:
  - Finances longer term assets:
    - Factory and equipment for companies;
    - For individuals, this could include Home Loans and Vehicle Finance; as funds are advanced against assets, the bank's assessment of potential losses would be more favourable, resulting in more favourable lending parameters (for example, interest rates) to the customer, compared to say unsecured Personal Loans;
  - Ensures funding;
  - Fixed and regular repayment schedule;
    - Bullet: single repayment of principal at maturity;
    - Amortising: principal paid in multiple payments on a schedule (for example, mortgage);
  - Fixed or floating rate interest;
  - Larger company loans may be syndicated across a number of banks.

In analysing the risk of a facility, bankers must always ask the question "Just how am I going to be repaid?" The bank must identify the primary source of repayment and consider whether there are secondary sources of repayment. For example, in a revolving line of credit to a company, the bank is looking to the successful conversion of the working capital into cash. Should that fail (decline in sales, receivables not collected), secondary sources could be other cash flow from operations, new business, fees, the sale of other assets, and divestitures.

Figure 6.6 illustrates the nature of outstanding loan balances of different facilities. As the revolver is on demand, usage is unknown and will vary. The bullet payment means principal risk remains for the life of the loan. Amortising loans generally require regular payments combining principal and interest, with the proportion for interest declining as principal is reduced.

## Loan Balances

For many loans, the bank's exit strategy is important. When a loan to help a company make an acquisition results in high debt levels, the bank needs to believe the merger will be cash generative to reduce leverage in a reasonable

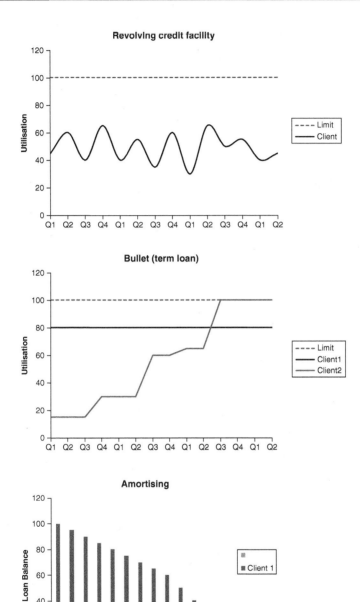

**FIGURE 6.6** Loan principal cash flow profile

timeframe. The bank might also take the view that the company would have access to the bond markets as an alternative funding in the future.

To the extent that a bank's internal rating / scoring, industry, facility, source of repayment, and exit strategy analysis raises questions about the extension of credit, it may still wish to proceed by requiring credit "mitigants". These include covenants and guarantees.

Borrowers are assigned a single internal rating / credit score, but risk varies depending on facility type and credit mitigants. Internal ratings assess probability of default, but guarantees and collateral mean some facilities can have much lower expected losses. Basel II includes a methodology for "notching" internal ratings upward to generate higher "facility ratings" for secured borrowing.

### Risk-Adjusted Loan Pricing

RAROC (Risk-adjusted return on capital) is the profitability of capital after considering all costs. This profitability measure expresses expected profit (net of all costs including expected losses) as a percentage of economic capital, or worse case loss. RAROC is preferred to risk-adjusted return on equity (RAROE) as it includes all capital rather than purely core Tier 1 equity. The relationship to Economic Capital needs to be understood although it is regulatory capital that ultimately should drive the overall target and strategy, given that the regulatory capital level is required by legislative fiat.

The RAROC (or RAROE) model expresses facility and connection level income net of expected losses (i.e., it is risk-adjusted) as a return on regulatory capital. It should be a key component of principal front book asset pricing calculators. By applying a RAROC target the bank is able to:

- Facilitate comparative analysis of investments of differing risk profiles;
- Understand the cost of risk undertaken and reward received for the process;
- Improve MI and decision-making.

The formula is given by:

$$\text{RAROC} = \frac{\begin{bmatrix} \text{Income} + \text{Capital Benefit} - \text{Operating Costs} \\ - \text{Funding} - \text{Expected Loss} \end{bmatrix}}{\text{Total Tier 1 Capital}} \quad (6.16)$$

The element "capital benefit" is contentious and is not an input that is applied at every bank. It is not something the author agrees with. Capital benefit is included by some banks who argue that because the business line is charged the cost of capital held against it, it should also benefit from income received when the capital liabilities are "hedged". That this leads to inconsistencies should be evident when one realises that a business line can start the year with "profit" on the books simply because of this capital benefit, before having undertaken any genuine shareholder value-added work of any kind. Nevertheless it is not uncommon to see this element on the numerator line. The better-managed banks will dispense with this element, and it is a true test of a bank CFO's genuine understanding of the principles of corporate finance to witness whether this element is included in the bank's RAROC analysis.

RAROC enables a bank to compare opportunities more consistently by ensuring that relative risks are considered. Capital can be better allocated to business areas and products, right down to individual loans. RAROC is useful in evaluating ongoing performance as well as deal flow.

Banks set target or "hurdle" RAROCs for the use of capital. Opportunities that do not meet the required RAROC should be rejected or escalated to senior management for additional consideration. Business decisions to proceed can be made because a product is a "loss leader" valued by clients or a new line of business where profitability takes time to develop.

EVA (Economic Value Added) is net profit less the cost of use of economic capital (also known as NIACC – net income after capital charge). The cost is usually calculated as a weighted average cost of the bank's sources of capital. Unlike RAROC, EVA is an absolute measure. EVA is sometimes described as "excess return". This "economic profit" is different from simple accounting profit because it considers implicit costs as well as tangible costs.

A comparison of RAROC and EVA is summarised at Figure 6.7.

**The Basics of Loan Pricing**   A conventional vanilla pricing approach for a corporate bank relationship manager would use these inputs:

1. Set the target margin for the asset (a function of the cost of capital of the bank, including the cost of equity, the rate on which is realistically difficult to ascertain with any real accuracy unless one has issued a contingent convertible bond. Debt capital cost is explicit and another guide. Nevertheless this cost drives the target rate of return;)

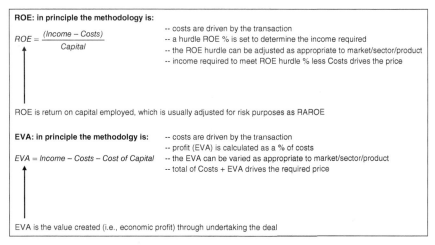

**ROE: in principle the methodology is:**

$$ROE = \frac{(Income - Costs)}{Capital}$$

-- costs are driven by the transaction
-- a hurdle ROE % is set to determine the income required
-- the ROE hurdle can be adjusted as appropriate to market/sector/product
-- income required to meet ROE hurdle % less Costs drives the price

ROE is return on capital employed, which is usually adjusted for risk purposes as RAROE

**EVA: in principle the methodolgy is:**

$$EVA = Income - Costs - Cost \; of \; Capital$$

-- costs are driven by the transaction
-- profit (EVA) is calculated as a % of costs
-- the EVA can be varied as appropriate to market/sector/product
-- total of Costs + EVA drives the required price

EVA is the value created (i.e., economic profit) through undertaking the deal

**FIGURE 6.7**   Comparison of RAROC versus EVA

2. Factor in margin (spread) for default probability and loss-given-default of the specific obligor, so in effect its risk weighting, together with any adjustment for size of loan;
3. Factor in margin reduction arising from extent of collateral (so unsecured highest margin, lowest to zero margin for fully collateralised or over-collateralised lending);
4. Factor in term liquidity premium.

Input [4] is the Treasury-applied "term liquidity premium" which is mainly, though not wholly, a function of the tenor of the lending and the liquidity of the asset once originated.

Figure 6.8 shows what the pricing screen might look like.

## Credit Authorisation Process

Beyond risk appetite and measurement, the Credit Policy Committee establishes and monitors the credit authorisation process. This includes:

- Minimum requirements for information and analysis:
  - Client identity verification (may be a regulatory requirement);
  - Financial data (for example, payslip for individual, audited financials for SME / corporate);
- Minimum underwriting standards:
  - Terms;
  - Documentation (for instance, sufficient detail on the contract);
  - Collateral, covenants, and guarantees.

**Asset Pricing Calculator**

| Product type | Loan |
|---|---|
| Utilisation | 100% |
| Interest rate basis | LIBOR |
| Amount | £1,000,000 |
| Term (months) | 60 |
| PD | 0.064% |
| LGD | 5% |

*Customer*    *ANO & Sons*

**Asset costs illustration**

| Tier 1 capital | £12,640 | Cost of capital | £2,100 |
|---|---|---|---|
| TLP bps | 236 | TLP | £8,325 |
| Expected loss rate | 0.06% | Expected loss | £480 |
| Undrawn liquidity buffer | 0.00% | Liquidity buffer | £0 |
| | | Total costs | |

| Recommended pricing | | RM proposed pricing | |
|---|---|---|---|
| Margin bps | 431 | Proposed margin bps | 325 |
| Target margin bps | 331 | Proposed fee | £0 |
| Minimum margin bps | 306 | Proposed non-util fee | £0 |

**FIGURE 6.8** Corporate lending pricing screen

Larger and more complicated loans are generally approved by credit committees. The client officer sponsors the loan proposal memorandum and is responsible for completeness. The committee scrutinises the proposal to ensure underwriting standards are met and uses their experience and knowledge of similar customers as well as their own facilities to evaluate risk and reward in making a decision. Smaller and less complicated loans are approved through delegation of authority.

Monitoring the credit authorisation process is an important control function and can yield business insights. This includes tracking:

- Processing time and cost per approval;
- Approval rates (rising or falling);
- Acceptance rates (and NTU – not taken up – rates);
- Volume of policy exceptions.

Breaking data down by client, product, and facility can demonstrate where underwriting standards are falling in line with the market.

The credit policy committee should ensure that minutes of credit committee meetings are complete and include the justification for their decisions.

## Collateral Management

Banking and collateral are synonymous with each other. Collateral is an excellent risk mitigant and is recognised in the Basel Accord's loss given default methodology. However, – and while banks would almost always prefer to receive collateral – credit should only be extended when it is deemed that the borrower is likely to be able to repay without it. The liquidation of collateral can involve legal, market, and reputational risk, as well as time and resources.

The lending bank must have clear legal rights over the collateral, and must be able to liquidate or take possession in a timely manner in the event of default, insolvency, bankruptcy, or defined credit event. This is called "perfecting" an interest in the collateral. Collateral rights vary by jurisdiction therefore business collateral transactions with multi-national corporations will require focused legal advice.

The amounts and types of collateral are negotiated and depends on:

- Client risk;
- Facility risk and maturity;
- Available collateral;
- Volatility of collateral value;
- Liquidity of collateral;
- Legal terms.

Collateral for loans is most commonly real estate (mortgages), equipment, inventory, cash, or securities. The borrower must prove it holds the deed to the collateral, and certify that it is not already pledged to another creditor (unless the bank is willing to take a second charge).

Where possible, banks should use historical data to project liquidation value. Banks consider potential links between borrower default and declines in collateral value. For example, if a company fails because of lack of sales, buyers for equipment for the manufacture of its products may be limited.

Collateral management is often the responsibility of a dedicated department whose responsibilities include:

- Monitoring collateral amounts and value;
- Collecting additional collateral when collateral value declines, as per facility terms (margining);
- Monitoring and limiting collateral concentrations.

In most jurisdictions, a lien refers to a transaction where the bank does not hold the collateral. Banks will ideally hold securities collateral in their own custody department. However, only clear terms in lending documentation ensure the ability to sell the collateral and keep the proceeds in the event of default.

Demand for securities collateral is growing because banks are required increasingly to post collateral for their own financing, derivatives, and clearing businesses. Central bank trades with banks designed to provide liquidity and effect monetary policy are collateralised. Banks seek to re-hypothecate (use collateral received for its own collateral pledges) whenever possible.

## Credit Portfolio Monitoring and Control

When new loans are booked and the economy, industries, and companies change, the risk and profitability of the overall credit portfolio also change. Credit policy adapts to rebalance the portfolio by adjusting limits, pricing, maturities, and requirements (for example, collateral, guarantees, and covenants) for new business. However, the credit portfolio management team have the tools to control risk and optimise the profitability of the portfolio, which can then complement lending policy and be quicker and more efficient. This is particularly important should concentrations build and credit concerns develop rapidly. Furthermore, portfolio management techniques can reduce risk and maximise the lending capacity for banks to offer competitive market pricing for important clients and products as often as possible.

The effectiveness of credit portfolio management depends on accurate, uniform, aggregated, and timely data.

Strategies may include:

- Selling loans;
- Securitise assets (for example, mortgages, loans, trade receivables, credit cards) for sale:
- Hedge using Credit Default Swaps (CDS):
  - Single-name;
  - Index;
  - Options on CDS (Swaptions).

Selling and securitising loans frees capacity and can improve profitability if returns are low. While basis risk and liquidity are factors, the global credit default swap (CDS) market has grown significantly with gross notional CDS amount reported by the Depository Trust Clearing Corporation to have exceeded $25.5 trillion at year end 2010 alone. However, it must be noted that for most banks, CDS is not a viable option to hedge credit risk because the reference names are just not there.

Traditionally, loan profit and loss was attributed to the responsible lending officer from start date through to maturity. Now, many banks credit the lending officer with the EVA or excess return of the loan (spread between expected return and economic capital) at inception, and then transfer the loan and P&L to the credit portfolio team to manage. Regardless, the relationship banker must remain engaged with the loan throughout its duration in working through any issues with the client and keeping credit portfolio informed.

Banks need to have a periodic, objective, and comprehensive loan review function, which includes audit and is ultimately responsible to the Board. Smaller banks may outsource loan review. Key functions include:

- Identify loans with potential weaknesses;
- Re-grade loans and create a watch list;
- Develop a watch list strategy for monitoring and potential action;
- Assess risk trends and underwriting standards in segments of the portfolio;
- Review loan documentation;
- Confirm adherence to credit policy;
- Evaluate data and reporting.

Behavioural scoring is an additional means of assessing credit risk made possible once a credit facility is extended. Banks can observe the patterns of activity and gain insights into how a customer manages her financial affairs. Exceeding credit limits, missed payments, and returned cheques are negative behaviours. Excessive utilisation of overdrafts or numerous credit card advances can be indicators of financial difficulties. Behavioural scores are generated by weighting recent trends, and are used in evaluating renewals or requests for new or larger borrowings.

Vintage analysis is another means of using existing business to better understand risk. Loan underwriting characteristics and standards vary over different periods of time. Similar loans from time periods are grouped together to create vintage pools, which are further segmented by borrower rating. Pools are tracked to assess how performance is linked to changes in the economy, interest rates, and other variables. Vintage analysis is particularly useful for longer-term mortgages in forecasting repayment rates, delinquencies, and charge-offs. Newer loans can be compared to earlier vintages at similar points in their lifecycle to test the impact of risk credit policy changes, for instance, a decision to cut back on risk.

## Workout Process

The definition of default is when a borrower fails to meet the conditions of a loan. Default can be a failure to make a payment as scheduled or technical, involving a breach of covenants. Default must be distinguished from the legal terms insolvency (borrower without means to pay) and bankruptcy (borrower under court supervision due to default or insolvency).

Corporations, individuals, banks, and even countries default. Difficult economic conditions, financial mismanagement, poor strategy and investment, excess leverage, and fraud all contribute to default. In almost all instances, it is preferable to work with the borrower to try to maximise value going forward than to become enmeshed in lengthy legal proceedings where lawyers and administrators rank first in order of payments.

**Corporate Debt Restructuring**   Banks attempt first to refinance debt, which involves extending the maturity and thus reducing and rescheduling payments. If a realistic assessment of the company's finances and business outlook shows the debt burden is still too great, a debt restructuring is necessary. This will include a distressed situation, if the company has defaulted on payments or moved into bankruptcy. Banks have restructuring departments to review businesses and work with the company and other creditors to create a workout plan.

Beyond refinancing, a workout can involve exchanging debt for equity and reduction of debt. Before agreeing to concessions, creditors need to agree that the new business plan will rehabilitate the company and make debt levels serviceable. Parties involved will have different incentives and interests, consequently agreement is not straightforward.

- Creditors: senior, collateralised creditors have less incentive to keep the company going and continue their exposure relative to junior, unsecured creditors;
- Shareholders: do not want the company wound down with their investment lost;
- Management: do not want the company wound down with their jobs lost.

If parties cannot agree that the company continuing as an ongoing concern is worth more than the assets, the parties should then work towards an orderly liquidation.

**This extract from *The Principles of Banking* (2012)**

## Understanding Credit Risk

## UNDERSTANDING CREDIT RISK

Credit risk management is a judgement call. The one single factor that most assists effective credit risk management is knowing one's market. An unfamiliarity with a particular market or customer set, or an over-reliance on "black box" models to assess loan origination quality, hampers the application of credit risk, because it renders it too susceptible to the business cycle. So beyond understanding the drivers of credit risk, and their dynamics, the over-riding principle remains to understand the market one is operating in. Never originate loans or invest in assets that one does not understand. This principle does not change, irrespective of the level of sophistication of the product or customer. In other words, the complexity of a product or transaction does not alter the requirement to understand the borrower and its business risks. That is what credit risk is. Even with sophisticated transactions or complex products, while the evaluation of the risk exposure may be more difficult, the need to understand the nature of the risk does not alter. Ultimately, the question of credit risk management remains the same: what is the chance that the investment will incur losses, and how much will the lender lose if the borrower is unable to repay? And is the lender able to survive this potential loss? The answer to these questions, which are dynamic, guides the approach to bank credit risk management.

In this section we define credit risk and exposure, and consider recovery rate in the event of default.

## Definition of Credit Risk

Credit risk is the risk of loss due to a "credit event". This was the case before the advent of the credit derivative market placed this term into regular usage. A credit event can be a number of things, from outright default due to bankruptcy, liquidation or administration, or it can be something short of full default. It can also mean loss due to credit migration, such as a downgrade in credit rating. In the credit derivatives market, the range of credit events is defined in the legal documentation governing the market. In a full default, the extent of loss can be observed immediately to be the full notional amount of the loan; however, typically over time the lender will receive an amount of the loan back from the administrators, known as the "recovery value". In a credit loss event short of default, the amount of loss is determined by applying mark-to-market valuation.

Default itself is defined in more than one way. Generally it is one or more of the following:

- non-payment of interest 90 days after the interest-due date;
- non-payment of loan 90 days after the loan maturity date;
- a restructuring of the borrower's loans;
- filing for bankruptcy, appointment of administrators, liquidation and so on.

Late payment is often termed an NPL or a delinquent loan rather than a defaulted loan if the borrower itself is still undertaking business. However, at some point, irrespective of the state of the borrower, an NPL will be written off as a default loss. The write-down, which must be funded out of the bank's capital, is often at 100% of outstanding notional value, even though the bank will probably recover a percentage, however small, at some later date. Another definition of default is that presented by Merton in his 1974 paper. This states that default occurs when the value of a company falls below the value of its debts. The definition of default is relevant because for some models it is a driver of the calculation of default probability; it is also relevant to credit rating agencies when they compile the historical frequency of default. Rating agencies generally apply the delay in payment definition.

## The Asset Exposure

The notional, or absolute level of risk exposure is the first port of call. It is also the easiest to calculate. It is given by the amount of the loan or investment with the customer or "counterparty".[3] This amount may be fixed, sometimes called a "bullet" loan, or it may reduce steadily, which is an amortising loan. If the exposure is a vanilla loan that is recorded in the bank's balance sheet, the amount will not change from the origination date to the maturity date. If it is a loan that is tradeable, such as a bond, or otherwise subject to mark-to-market valuation, then the exposure amount will vary according to its valuation, but should always be 100% of notional by the maturity date.

---

[3] We have to be careful with the use of the word "investment". Here we mean it from the viewpoint of the bank. In general conversation, investment is often used to mean an equity investment, by a shareholder in the business. A bank is advancing debt funds to the customer, but this is of course also an investment in the future well-being of the company.

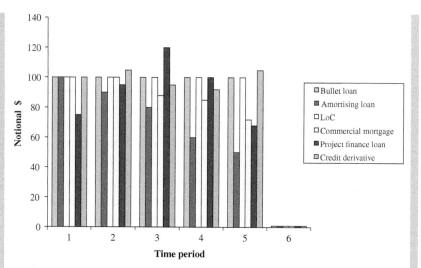

**Figure 3.5**    Notional value risk exposure profiles of different product types.

Figure 3.5 is a stylised representation of the behaviour of asset risk exposure by type of asset, each of which has the same maturity date.[4]

Trading book assets apply mark-to-market. The value of a loan that is under mark-to-market will change because of changes to the general level of interest rates, and/or changes to the credit standing of the borrower (or the borrower's industrial sector, or to credit conditions generally in the market). As such, trading book assets capture changes in value, at least theoretically, that arise due to, for instance, changes in credit rating. This is known as credit migration risk. The banking book, which does not apply mark-to-market, cannot by definition capture migration risk of its assets. It only captures the risk of loss due to default. This might be seen to be some sort of disadvantage, because the changes in credit standing of a borrower also change its probability of default. However, use of mark-to-market in a trading book is less of an advantage than one might think, and in stressed market conditions it can be self-defeating (lower mark-to-market values can generate a vicious circle of falling prices that impacts confidence and can itself lead to default).

The asset exposure on a balance sheet is not comprised solely of live loans. It also includes potential future liabilities, such as letters of credit (LoC), third-party liquidity lines and other guarantees. The notional

---

[4] This is for illustration. It is highly uncommon to observe this different range of asset types with identical maturity dates. Mortgage and project finance loans have the longest legal final maturity dates.

amount of such off-balance sheet exposures is also part of the bank's credit risk exposure.

The main risk management mechanism for asset exposure risk is by means of credit limits. This is the maximum amount that can be outstanding at any time to the individual customer, the industrial sector, the country and so on. Limits can also be set by currency.

## Recovery Value

It is quite common for banks to write down the entire notional value of an NPL. In practice, virtually all defaulted assets return an element of recovery value, although the time taken to realise this value can be very long indeed. In general therefore a prudent approach is to assign a 0% recovery value for risk management purposes.

The concept of recovery value is relevant in the credit derivative markets as well, as it is a parameter that feeds into pricing.

### Recovery Rates

The concept of RR is a key parameter in credit derivative valuation. This is somewhat unfortunate, because the nature of markets is such that an assumed rate must be used. In the real world, actual recovery value from a defaulted obligation may not be known for years.

The procedure for determining RR in the cash market is a long drawn-out affair. Debt investors take their place in the queue with all other creditors and receive their due after the administrators have completed their work. This process can take a matter of months or over 10 years. The rating agencies make an assumption of what the final recovery amount will be from the market price of the debt asset at the time bankruptcy or default is announced. This approach is carried over to an extent into the credit derivative market.

The definition of recovery rate in the CDS market differs slightly from that in the cash bond market, for reasons of practicality. This is because the contract must settle fairly soon after the notice of a credit event has been announced, and the real "RR" is not at that point. At the same time, the model approach under which the CDS would have been priced and valued up to now would have used a "RR" as one of its parameters. So in the CDS market, recovery is defined as the market value of the "delivered obligation". This market value is determined by a poll of CDS dealers bidding for the defaulted assets of the reference entity.

Note that recovery rates for the two markets will therefore differ from those in the cash market in practice. This arises for a number of reasons, one of which is that in the CDS market a credit event will encompass circumstances that fall short of full default in the cash market. For example,

Moody's notes three categories of default for the purposes of its ratings and historical default statistics:

- delayed or failed coupon or principal payments;
- bankruptcy or receivership;
- distressed exchange that results in investors having a lower obligation value, undertaken by the obligor in order to avoid default.

Recovery rates in practice vary widely, as we note below. In essence, what the 2007–08 credit crunch has taught us is that if one is using CDS to hedge credit risk, the safest approach is to assume a 0% recovery rate. This is because in the event of default it will be some time before the investor receives the recovery value, while in the meantime the payment from the CDS that was used to hedge the asset will be (100 − RR) so the investor will actually have lost out on some of the investment until recovery is received. In the meantime, the investor's accountants would most probably have written down the entire par value of the investment. Therefore for complete hedging it is best to assume a zero recovery value when calculating the notional amount of the CDS used to hedge the investment.

Despite the RR being a key parameter in CDS pricing models, it is not apparent that it is influencing CDS premiums heavily, or that actual historical RRs are used when selecting the input level. A look at CDS spreads during the period 2000–2004 shows that while "RR" varies widely, the CDS premium across all industries is fairly similar (see Figure 3.6).

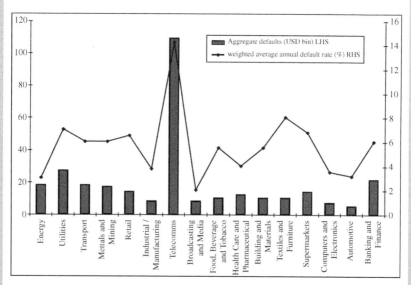

**Figure 3.6**   BBB CDS level versus historic recovery rate
(rates are average for industry in April 2005).
*Source:* Fitch.

We observe that most industries were trading at levels fairly close: within 10 or 20 bps of each other. Industries traditionally regarded as higher risk (for example, computers and electronics), or in more difficult circumstances such as automotive, are marked up. But otherwise the closeness is significant.

These observations are noteworthy because RR assumption is a required, and important, parameter in CDS pricing. However, it is usually set at 40% for all reference names (for example, the Bloomberg page CDSW defaults to this value. Post the credit crunch and global recession, however, it is more usually set at 50% for most names). The chart is interesting because it implies there is little variation in RR assumption – if we adjusted for it we should have observed greater variation in CDS prices.

Note the approximation of market implied default probability in a flat term structure environment, which uses the RR assumption, showing the relationship between them which is as follows:

$$P(\text{default}) = CDS \text{ spread} / [1 - RR].$$

Generally, the market gives little weight to the RR assumption when the probability of default is low. But during a recession or in a bear market environment when default probability is higher, this approach is risky and can lead to less accuracy in hedging. A report from Fitch[5] (that pre-dated the credit crunch) suggests the following reasons behind the small differences between industry spread, given that the variation in recovery rate is so much larger:

- at the time, the low-default environment may have made this a non-issue;
- when actual recovery values are received, the ultimate result will probably be very similar;
- given the real difficulty in estimating actual recovery values, which may be many years into the future, the market may prefer a standardised assumption;
- historical rates may not be any more realistic a guide to future rates;
- historical data on recovery values varies widely year-to-year across industries, rendering them less meaningful.

The recovery value of an investment-grade reference name can be more difficult to estimate than a high-yield name given that for the former, any default is likely to occur further in the future.

---

[5] Fitch special report, 8 June 2005.

In practice, as we might expect, there is considerable variation in default rates over time. Average default and recovery rate by industry and loan seniority for the US market (see Table 3.5 and Figure 3.7) shows the variation over time historically, although if we standardised by credit rating some of this variation would reduce.

Recovery rates also exhibit great variation. In practice, recovery rates and default rates tend to be inversely related: high default rates are associated with lower average recovery rates (see Figure 3.8). Note that most market practitioners, and the Fitch report we quote from, measure **RR** as recovery value, and the market price of the defaulted loan 30 days after default. As we noted above this will be different from the actual recovery value. The

**Recovery rates according to loan seniority**

| Seniority | Mean (%) | Standard deviation (%) |
|---|---|---|
| Senior secured bank loans | 60.70 | 26.31 |
| Senior secured | 55.83 | 25.41 |
| Senior unsecured | 52.13 | 25.12 |
| Senior subordinated | 39.45 | 24.79 |
| Subordinated | 33.81 | 21.25 |
| Junior subordinated | 18.51 | 11.26 |
| Preference shares | 8.26 | 10.45 |

**Table 3.5** Moody's recovery rates for varying levels of loan seniority, 2006.

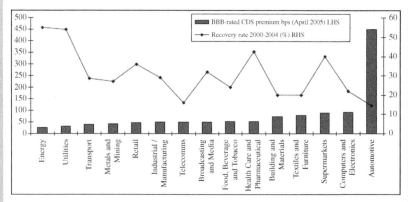

**Figure 3.7** Default rate versus recovery rate.
*Source:* Fitch.

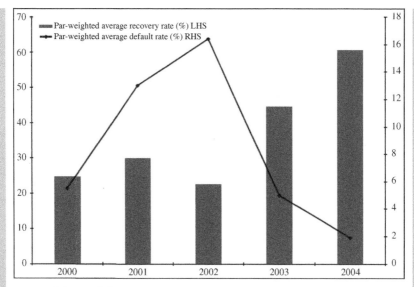

**Figure 3.8** High yield sector default rate versus recovery rate. *Source:* Fitch.

actual loss experienced by investors will be increased by poor recovery rates during times of high default rate. A rough calculation is given by:

$$Loos = Notional \times \left[ Default\ rate\ \times (1 - RR) \right].$$

Low recoveries are more likely during a period of high defaults and this reflects economic reality, as supply and demand depresses secondary market price for defaulted loans. This was observed during the 2008–2009 recession and is in effect a "double whammy" for investors. It also means it is difficult to estimate a "normal" recovery rate (one more reason for the standard level used in CDS pricing).

## Collateral and Third-Party Guarantees

Much bank lending involves the use of collateral and/or guarantees from third parties to back the loan. The existence of these features complicates the credit risk management process. From a prudent, perhaps conservative viewpoint, the assessment of risk exposure should take no account of these features. It is always the credit quality of the borrower, and that only, that should drive the loan origination process and the credit risk management approach. The existence of guarantees or collateral also does not influence the performance of the borrower and hence the loan. In practice banks do factor such security features into their risk calculations, especially when to do so enables them to reduce their regulatory capital requirement. While this might not be business best-practice, the fact that Basel II allows for it encourages such behaviour.

Security or backing for a loan can be arranged in the following forms:

- Loan collateral: company assets such as plant or machinery, or other assets of value such as government bonds. The collateral is written into the loan documentation as security transferable to the lender in the event of default.
- Guarantee: this may be in the form of third-party that assumes the liability of the borrower in the event of default, in which case the lender is exposed to the credit quality of the guarantor, or in the form of credit insurance or credit protection such as a credit derivative contract.
- Liquidity line: a line of credit arranged by the borrower, from a third-party bank or financial institution, which can be drawn on in the event of financial difficulty of the borrower. This type of facility is common in structured finance transactions that involve the use of an SPV legal entity. It exposes the cash lender to the credit quality of the third-party institution, as well as the soundness and strength of the legal documentation governing the obligations of the third party.

These arrangements do not impact the fortunes of the borrower or the performance of the loan. An arrangement that does so to an extent, but does not provide any additional security for the lender, is a loan covenant. A covenant is a provision written in the legal documents describing the loan that requires the borrower to adhere to certain specific requirements, such as the absolute level of borrowing or the leverage ratio. Some covenants also describe certain business activities that the borrower is prohibited from entering into. Whatever their form, they serve to restrict the borrower in certain ways and thus are a risk management mechanism for the lender.

In practice, collateral and guarantees often serve to reduce a lender's risk aversion, under the impression that the risk exposure is less than it might otherwise be. However, whatever their form, they do not eliminate credit risk (unless the third-party guarantor is a AAA-rated government), and so should not be viewed ultimately as risk mitigating tools. In the event of default, the lender will still suffer some form of loss. Equally, an "implicit" guarantee is often worthless, because unless the guarantor is legally obliged to back the loan, it may walk away from it in the event of default (even at risk to its reputation). A bank should always ensure that third-party backing is written into the loan documentation, otherwise it has no value.

The impact of a guarantee on credit risk calculations is assessed using the recovery rate assumption for the loan. We discussed recovery rate earlier. The LGD of a loan is given by:

$$LGD = \text{Notional value} \times \left(100\% - RR\right)$$

where RR is the recovery rate as before.

As we saw earlier, recovery rates vary widely across industry and even within industries, and also by the seniority of the loan in the corporate capital structure. Historically, recovery rates have been higher for senior loans and secured loans than for subordinated loans and unsecured loans. The bank must therefore make a distinction between recovery rate assumptions according to the type of guarantee and the type of loan in question.

For risk management practice that is adequate throughout the business cycle, the impact of the credit risk reducing measures described above should be set at negligible or zero. This is because in the event of default, there is a legal process to be followed, affecting all creditors, which may take many months or years. Recovery of any kind – including collateral – may be some distance away. Even a third-party guarantee may not be enforceable, while a covenant clause is of no value if the borrower is in breach of them. As a going concern, a bank cannot rely on a legal process as part of its support to ensure that it can carry on business as usual. Also, in a stress situation such as a recession or financial market crisis, the legal process may take even longer than usual.

The bottom line for senior management is this: credit enhancements in themselves should not be viewed as alternatives to sound loan origination and credit risk management.

Reproduced from *The Principles of Banking* (2012)

**This extract from *An Introduction to Value-at-Risk, Fifth Edition* (2013)**

## Modelling Credit Risk

# MODELLING CREDIT RISK

The main credit risk VaR methodologies take a *portfolio* approach to credit risk analysis. This means that:

- the credit risks to each obligor across the portfolio are restated on an equivalent basis and aggregated in order to be treated consistently, regardless of the underlying asset class;
- correlations of credit quality moves across obligors are taken into account.

This allows portfolio effects – the benefits of diversification and risks of concentration – to be quantified.

The portfolio risk of an exposure is determined by four factors:

- size of the exposure;
- maturity of the exposure;
- probability of default of the obligor;
- systematic or concentration risk of the obligor.

Credit VaR – like market risk VaR – considers (credit) risk in a mark-to-market framework. It arises from changes in value due to credit events; that is, changes in obligor credit quality including defaults, upgrades and downgrades.

Nevertheless, credit risk is different in nature from market risk. Typically, market return distributions are assumed to be relatively symmetrical and approximated by normal distributions. In credit portfolios, value changes will be relatively small upon minor upgrades/downgrades, but can be substantial upon default. This remote probability of large losses produces skewed distributions with heavy downside tails that differ from the more normally distributed returns assumed for market VaR models. This is shown in Figure 8.4.

This difference in risk profiles does not stop City quantitative analysts from assessing risk on a comparable basis. Analytical method market

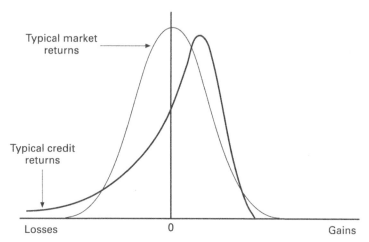

**Figure 8.4** Comparison of distribution of market returns and credit returns.

VaR models consider a time horizon and estimate VaR across a distribution of estimated market outcomes. Credit VaR models similarly look to a horizon and construct a distribution of value given different estimated credit outcomes.

When modelling credit risk the two main measures of risk are:

- *distribution of loss* – obtaining distributions of loss that may arise from the current portfolio. This considers the question of what the expected loss is for a given confidence level;
- *identifying extreme or catastrophic outcomes* – this is addressed through the use of scenario analysis and concentration limits.

To simplify modelling, no assumptions are made about the causes of default. Mathematical techniques used in the insurance industry are used to model the event of an obligor default.

## Time horizon

The choice of time horizon will not be shorter than the time frame over which risk-mitigating actions can be taken. Most analysts suggest two alternatives:

- a constant time horizon such as 1 year;
- a hold-to-maturity time horizon.

## Data inputs

Modelling credit risk requires certain data inputs; generally these are the following:

- credit exposures;
- obligor default rates;
- obligor default rate volatilities;
- recovery rates.

These data requirements present some difficulties. There is a lack of comprehensive default and correlation data, and assumptions need to be made at certain times.

Reproduced from *An Introduction to Value-at-Risk, Fifth Edition* (2013).

## SELECTED BIBLIOGRAPHY AND REFERENCES

*Asset encumbrance, financial reform and the demand for collateral assets*, BIS, May 2013. www.bis.org/publ/cgfs49.pdf.

*Collateral asset terms, BIS Quarterly Review,* September 2013. http://www.bis.org/ publ/qtrpdf/r_qt1309z.htm.

*Credit risk: internal ratings based approaches*, Bank of England, March 2013. http://www.bankofengland.co.uk/pra/Documents/publications/policy/2013/creditriskirbapproachcp4-13.pdf.

*Definition of Default*, IFRS, September 2013. http://www.ifrs.org/Meetings/MeetingDocs/WSS%202013/Agenda%20Paper%2005D%20Impairment-Definition%20of%20default.pdf.

*Euroclear collateral management.* www.euroclear.com/en/services/processing-your-transactions/collateral-management0.html.

*Guiding principles for the replacement of IAS 39*, BIS, August 2009. www.bis.org/publ/bcbs161.pdf.

*ICMA Global Master Repo Agreement.* http://www.icmagroup.org/Regulatory-Policy-and-Market-Practice/short-term-markets/Repo-Markets/global-master-repurchase-agreement-gmra/.

*Impairment Provisioning and Disclosure Guidelines*, Central Bank of Ireland, May 2013. https://www.centralbank.ie/regulation/industry-sectors/credit-institutions/Documents/Impairment%20Provisioning%20Guidelines%20May%202013.pdf.

*Internal Ratings-Based Approach to Specialised Lending Exposures*, BIS, October 2001. http://www.bis.org/publ/bcbs_wp9.htm.

*International Convergence of Capital Measurement and Capital Standards – A Revised Framework – Comprehensive Version*, Basel Committee on Banking Supervision, June 2006, pages 12, 64.

*ISDA Master Agreement.* http://www.isda.org/publications/pubguide.aspx.

*Principles for effective risk data aggregation and risk reporting*, BIS, June 2012. http://www.bis.org/publ/bcbs222.pdf.

*Principles for an effective risk appetite framework*, Financial Stability Board, July 2013. www.financialstabilityboard.org/publications/r_130717.pdf.

*Project Summary: IFRS 9 Financial Instruments*, IFRS, July 2014. http://www.ifrs.org/current-projects/iasb-projects/financial-instruments-a-replacement-of-ias-39-financial-instruments-recognitio/Pages/Financial-Instruments-Replacement-of-IAS-39.aspx.

*Sound practices for back testing counterparty credit risk models*, BIS, April 2010. http://www.bis.org/publ/bcbs171.pdf.

*Studies on the Validation of Internal Rating Systems (revised)*, BIS, May 2005. http://www.bis.org/publ/bcbs_wp14.htm.

*The Internal Ratings-Based Approach*, BIS, May 2001. http://www.bis.org/publ/bcbsca05.pdf.

*The IRB Use Test: Background and Implementation*, BIS, September 2006. http://www.bis.org/publ/bcbs_nl9.htm.

*Treatment of trade finance under the Basel capital framework*, BIS, October 2011. http://www.bis.org/publ/bcbs205.pdf.

*Validating Risk Rating Systems under the IRB Approaches*, HKMA 2006. www.hkma.gov.hk/media/eng/doc/key-functions/.../CA-G-4.pdf.

*"I think that people should be recognized for their achievements and the value that adds to society's progress. But it can be easily overdone. I think highly of many people and their accomplishments, but I don't believe that that should be paramount over the actual achievements themselves. Celebrity shouldn't supersede the things they've accomplished."*
—Neil Armstrong, quoted in James Hansen, *First Man: The Life of Neil Armstrong*, Simon & Schuster 2005

# CHAPTER 7

# Understanding and Managing Operational Risk[1]

In this chapter, we introduce the concept of operational risk management in banking. Operational risk is as old as banking, but its management has only recently been given some of the focus afforded to credit, interest rate, market, and liquidity risk. For instance, in some banks operational risk was often simply placed in the same category as credit risk, despite it being markedly different. Measurement, modelling, and capital allocation associated with operational risk are challenging and are the topic of much debate. However, operational risk management requires focus because it is a driver of part of a bank's regulatory capital requirement.

As with other risks, the Board of Directors should approve appropriate limits for specific and overall operational risk in the risk appetite statement.

## OPERATIONAL RISK OVERVIEW

Whether huge and headline-making or relatively small, banks suffer losses regularly from risks outside of credit, interest rates, and markets. In the 1990s, once the Basel Committee had determined that operational risk should be formalised as a concept in Basel II – with capital allocated against it – market participants made attempts to create a working definition. For many, operational risk was simply "other" risk, or a residual category for difficult to measure risk. Presently, most accept the Basel II definition of "the risk of direct or indirect loss resulting from inadequate or failed internal processes, people and systems or from external events". For regulatory capital purposes, this includes legal risk but not reputational and strategic risks.

---

[1] This chapter was co-written with Ed Bace and Peter Eisenhardt.

**TABLE 7.1** Operational risk failure: types and examples

| Type | Category | Description | Bank | Year |
|------|----------|-------------|------|------|
| Internal Fraud | fraud / unauthorised trading | derivatives | Barings | 1995 |
| | fraud / unauthorised trading | US treasury bonds | Daiwa | 1995 |
| | fraud / unauthorised trading | commodities | Sumitomo | 1996 |
| | fraud / unauthorised trading | foreign exchange | Allied Irish | 2002 |
| | fraud / unauthorised trading | foreign exchange | National Australia Bank | 2004 |
| | fraud / unauthorised trading | proprietary trading | Société Générale | 2008 |
| | fraud / unauthorised trading | exchange traded funds | UBS | 2011 |
| External Fraud | accounting fraud / Parmalat | overstated earnings | numerous | 2003 |
| | accounting fraud / World Com | overstated earnings | numerous | 2004 |
| | accounting fraud / Enron | overstated earnings | numerous | 2004 |
| Employment | discrimination | racial bias | Merrill Lynch | 2013 |
| Business Practices | mutual funds trading abuse | late trading | Bank of America | 2003 |
| | market manipulation | European treasury bonds | Citi | 2006 |
| | ABS mis-selling | CDOs | Goldman Sachs | 2007 |
| | LIBOR rigging | collusion | numerous | 2008 |

*(Continued)*

| | | | |
|---|---|---|---|
| discriminatory lending | racial bias | Wells Fargo | 2012 |
| aid tax evasion | inadequate reporting | Swiss banks | 2013 |
| swaps mis-selling | over-selling | UK banks | 2013 |
| **Physical** | | | |
| terrorist attack – 9/11 | disruption, destruction | numerous | 2011 |
| **Systems / Execution** | | | |
| faulty mortgage underwriting | incomplete data, records | numerous | 2008 |
| payment processing failure | no client access to funds | RBS | 2012 |
| trading risk controls failure | proprietary trading | J.P. Morgan | 2012 |
| money laundering risk controls failure | inadequate checks | numerous | 2013 |
| accounting failure | capital position | Bank of America | 2014 |

Operational risk is a test of management and corporate governance and can stem from:

- Internal processes: must have clear, orderly, and complete processes to meet responsibilities to clients, manage risk, control payments, protect against fraud and comply with regulation;
- People: must communicate and enforce rules, minimise conflicts of interest, and set proper incentives to maintain an ethical culture;
- Systems: must have adequate technology resources that are backed up and protected from security breaches;
- External events: must know and monitor clients to guard against fraud and protect people and facilities.

Operational risk management encompasses quality, change, and business continuity management disciplines, and also crisis management in adverse situations. While not included in the regulatory definition of operational risk or capital allocation, operational risk failings affect reputation, client satisfaction, business and earnings volatility, as well as shareholder value.

Basel II specified seven Level 1 categories of operational risk: Internal Fraud; External Fraud; Employment Practices and Workplace Safety; Clients, Products and Business Practices; Damage to Physical Assets, Business Disruption and System Failures; and Execution, Delivery, and Process Management. These are further broken down into Level 2 and Level 3 categories. Examples of actual operational risk failures are shown in Table 7.1.

Banks extend the grouping loss events along eight business lines to create a matrix. Business lines include commercial banking, retail banking, payment and settlement, agency services, trading and sales, corporate finance, asset management, and retail brokerage. Regulators have worked with banks to map business activities to business lines to avoid distortions and arbitrage.

Unlike lending or trading, new operational risks are not acquired to build revenue and profits. Operational risks can be more difficult to foresee and cannot be diversified, sold off, or hedged in the banking market. The only potential mitigation and pricing tool is insurance which depends on availability. While operational risk cannot be eliminated, the goal must be to keep it within acceptable limits and prevent it from surpassing potential gains. Improvement to processes is necessary and protection increased when benefits are likely to exceed costs.

When the concept of Operational Risk was first formulated, some banks drew on inspiration from other institutions which had extensive experience monitoring operational risk, such as the military, in building their own methodologies.

## CONDUCT RISK

While not an explicit part of the Basel framework, the concept of conduct risk has gained intensive focus following the 2008–2009 financial crisis. The OECD has published multi-laterally agreed, government-backed guidelines for corporate behaviour, as well as guidelines for consumer financial protection. When the UK's Financial Conduct Authority was formed in 2013, it placed conduct risk at the centre of its agenda. While not formally defined, conduct risk is the risk that a bank's performance will result in poor outcomes for customers. From the perspective of shareholders, this could be an issue as serious as market risk because such a negative outcome could have an impact as extreme as any other risk exposure and ultimately result in the bank's collapse.

Simply stated, banks must demonstrate fair regard for the interests of their customers in order to maintain the integrity of markets.

The FCA defines drivers of conduct risk as:

- Inherent: information asymmetries, biases and heuristics, inadequate financial capability;
- Structures and Behaviours: ineffective competition, culture and incentives, conflicts of interest;
- Environmental: regulatory and policy changes, technological developments, economic and market trends.

Negative behaviours the FCA is working to eradicate include:

- Putting profits ahead of ethics and customer interests;
- Taking tick box and legalistic approaches in dealing with customers, where compliance is limited to the letter rather than the spirit of the law;
- Treating disclosure at the point of sale as the end of responsibility to ensure a good outcome for the customer.

The FCA is striving to keep "the wrong products from ending up in the wrong hands" and avoiding "people not being able to get access to the right products, to the detriment of society".

While much of the focus of conduct risk pertains to consumers, the principles apply to wholesale business as well. Products with high growth and margins have potentially high conduct risk, and warrant added management scrutiny.

The management of conduct risk falls to the Chief Risk Officer's (CRO) department.

## OPERATIONAL RISK MEASUREMENT

The key to developing operational risk management has been the building of operational risk measurement. To achieve this, historical data is gathered and organised into an internal loss database. Consequently, operational risk measurement and therefore, management, has become more robust, objective, and credible. Rather than relying simply on "expert" opinion, data is measured and audited. Risk can be replicated, referred to, and compared. This leads to a greater understanding of business area processes and can further highlight the risks to back up hard decisions on resources, limits, and capital.

The data process must consider:

- Automation: makes for ease of access and consistency;
- Frequency: some data can be collected daily (for example, transaction processing) while other data (for example, fraud or losses can only be collected in a more meaningful way on a monthly or quarterly basis);
- Detail: some types of data can be collected more easily (for example, legal fees, customer compensation, fines) than others (for example, increased funding costs for failed trades).

Once risk is identified and classified, data can be collected and modelling can begin.

## OPERATIONAL RISK MEASUREMENT CONCEPTS

Data capture should include gross loss amounts, dates, and any recoveries, as well as qualitative descriptions of events and causes.

### Loss Definition

Gross loss is the loss from an operational risk before recoveries. The loss may be recorded for risk management purposes prior to the consequences that this will have on the financial statements. Net loss is the loss after recoveries which could be amended over time. Insurance should be treated as a special recovery category otherwise it will obscure the measurement of the riskiness of the activity.

### Loss Data Thresholds

Loss collection thresholds are the minimum values above which loss amounts must be collected and recorded in the internal loss database. In setting thresholds, banks must ensure that all material exposure is captured.

Thresholds are a supervisory requirement. Levels may vary across business lines, but regulators seek consistency amongst peer banks.

Banks generally use judgement rather than statistical evidence to set thresholds. However, the level can affect modelling of expected losses. Losses must not be disregarded only because they are relatively small, and in fact recording "near losses" can be valuable. The higher the threshold, the more difficult it may be to reconcile operational risk totals within the financial statements.

A simple test of the appropriateness of the current threshold is to calculate the total sub-threshold losses as a percentage of all losses.

### Date of Loss Allocation

Losses from operational risk often build up over time and are not identified for months or years. The Daiwa unauthorised trading scandal proceeded for more than 10 years ("incurred") before it was exposed ("reported"). Legal settlements and regulatory fines are generally incurred well after events. Recognition of loss may vary for risk measurement and financial statement purposes.

Losses may best be modelled when assigned to a wider timeframe.

### Grouping of Loss Events

Banks sometimes group a number of losses into a single loss for purposes of efficiency. If the individual losses are small and unrelated, the group should be excluded in the modelling process to prevent distortion of the results.

### Model Granularity, Model Validation, and Monitoring

Limiting the number of loss groupings makes for a critical mass of data and overall simplicity. This may be unsatisfactory if risks within groups are substantially different and independent. According to the Basel text, measurement "must be sufficiently 'granular' to capture the major drivers of operational risk affecting the shape of the tail of the loss estimates". If data is limited, external data sources or different modelling techniques are required.

As with other types of risks, methods and models must be monitored and validated on a periodic basis, and if necessary reviewed by specialist external parties. This includes:

- Integrity of inputs, assumptions, processes, and outputs;
- Independence from business lines;
- Relevance and soundness of model through testing;
- Consistency with policies approved by the Board of Directors.

The monitoring and validation process should ask whether the framework is a realistic reflection of the operational risk position and highlight any issues or deficiencies.

## Distribution Assumptions

Distribution assumptions form the basis of all operational risk models, and are made for severity and frequency. Banks use a range of distributions to estimate severity, including generalised power law Pareto distributions of extreme value theory, empirical distributions, and lognormal distributions.

In estimating frequency, there is a consensus amongst most banks that a Poisson distribution should be used, but some assume a negative binomial distribution. In using a Poisson distribution, banks must consider how capital needs could be met if loss frequency exceeds what would seem the most reasonable of conservative assumptions.

It is important not to restrict the analysis to one type of distribution, but to rather test and parameterise several based on the available data. Banks can model "working" (expected losses / provisioning) and "non-working" (unexpected) losses separately.

## Correlation and Dependence

Correlation is a measure of the dependency of operational risk losses across groupings. Losses may be correlated based on factors such as deterioration in economic conditions; changes in management, processes, and systems; and external events. Complex dependencies can be estimated across high- and low-severity risk events.

Banks can use their own correlation assumptions, provided supervisors are satisfied as to the soundness of methods, integrity of implementation, allowances for uncertainty and high stress situations, and validation. In practice, this is very difficult to achieve. Correlation emphasises the need for granularity, as it is generally assumed that risks within a loss grouping are 100% correlated.

Dependence assumptions must be fully supported by empirical data and expert judgment and be biased towards conservatism. Expert judgement is particularly important in making correlation parameters forward looking, while a bias towards conservatism is achieved by overestimating correlation.

## Data Integration

Data integration involves combining internal loss, external loss, scenario, and control factor data to quantify operational risk. Bayesian inference can be used to update loss estimates as new data is acquired. Many banks began operational risk measurement relying on external loss data, given that internal loss data was limited. As internal loss data accumulated and its variation with other sources decreased, credibility models could be used to increase its weighting. This allows for a greater focus on bank-specific rather than industry-wide and less relevant risk data over time.

Regardless, it must be remembered that using data is backward looking, and is only a guide for the future.

## BASIC INDICATOR APPROACH

Under Basel II, the Basic Indicator Approach (BIA) uses a single indicator (gross income) as the proxy for overall operational risk exposure. Banks hold capital for operational risk equal to the average over the previous three years of a fixed percentage of annual gross income ("alpha" – typically 15%). Any year which shows a negative or zero annual gross income will be excluded.

Gross income is net interest and non-interest income before deduction of operational losses.

The Basic Indicator Approach is the simplest of Basel II operational risk approaches and is most often used by smaller banks with limited international operations. However, the BIA does not help measure, monitor, and respond to risks and larger banks are expected to use advanced approaches. Banks approved for more sophisticated approaches cannot revert to the BIA without supervisory approval.

## STANDARDISED APPROACH

Also based on the original Basel Accord, the Standardised Approach differs from the BIA in that the percentage of gross income varies by business line. Standard "betas" serve as a proxy for industry-wide business line operational risk loss:

- 18%: corporate finance, trading and sales, payment and settlement;
- 15%: commercial banking, agency services;
- 12%: retail banking, asset management, retail brokerage.

Total capital charge is the 3-year average of the summation of the capital charges for each business line. In any year, negative capital charges (from negative gross income) in a business line may offset positive capital charges in others without limit.

The Alternative Standardised Approach allows some large, diversified banks to use loans and advances as the exposure indicator rather than gross income for retail and commercial banking.

In using the Standardised Approach, banks are differentiated according to business mix and must collect data and focus on their operational risk by business line. When capital is based on actual risk, there is an incentive to reduce it. Before use of the Standardised Approach is approved, banks must implement a sound framework backed by adequate resources that is actively supervised by the Board and senior management.

## ADVANCED MEASUREMENT APPROACH

Under Basel II, the Advanced Measurement Approach (AMA) allowed banks to use their internal risk measurement systems to generate the regulatory capital requirement for operational risk. However its use is being discontinued under Basel III from 2022 onwards, so consequently we do not cover it in detail in this chapter. AMA requires use of four types of data.

- Internal loss: database supported by a minimum of five years of history;
- External loss: database of competitor experience, purchased from vendors, or built with available information and is most important in measuring severity;
- Scenario analysis: provides information where losses have not been adequately captured or discovered, extends loss distribution beyond experiences.
- Business environment control factors: objective Key Risk Indicators (KRIs), Key Performance Indicators (KPIs), and Key Control Indicators (KCIs) that can be expressed in counts, total values, percentages, and ratios (for example, unmatched trades, failed trades, disputed collateral calls).

Correlation and diversification may be recognised, but banks must be prepared to justify calculations.

## KEY RISK INDICATORS

As described earlier, business environment control factors are risk metrics and statistics used to monitor drivers of risk exposure.

- Key Performance Indicators (KPIs): monitor operational efficiency (for example, system downtime, staff turnover);
- Key Control Indicators (KCIs): monitor effectiveness of controls (for example, outstanding confirmations, audit exceptions);
- Key Risk Indicators (KRIs): a selection of KPIs and KCIs (typically 10–15) used to warn of escalating risk to trigger management attention and action. Composite KRIs can be rolled up to top management.

Indicators must be measurable and not complicated so as not to become a control issue in and of themselves, as well as a representative of the business line and its risk. If an indicator is broken down to the lowest level and assigned a cost centre, it can be kept in use throughout organisational changes.

The Basel Committee assumes the use of risk indicators to be subjective in nature and cautions against overweighting.

## OPERATIONAL RISK MANAGEMENT FRAMEWORK

The Basel Committee has outlined eleven principles for operational risk management. These are intended to be a high-level operating framework that should set the culture for management of operational risk at the right level. They are as follows:

1. The Board of Directors should establish a strong risk management culture that provides appropriate standards and incentives for responsible behaviour throughout the bank.
2. Banks should develop, implement, and maintain a framework that is fully integrated into the bank's overall risk management processes.
3. The Board of Directors should establish, approve, and periodically review the framework and oversee senior management to ensure effective implementation.
4. The Board of Directors should approve an operational risk appetite and tolerance statement.
5. Senior management should develop a clear and robust governance structure for Board approval with well-defined lines of responsibility.
6. Senior management should ensure identification and assessment of risk.
7. Senior management should ensure an approval process for new products and systems.
8. Senior management should implement a process for monitoring and reporting to support proactive management of operational risk.
9. Banks should have a strong control environment to utilise processes and systems, internal controls, and risk mitigation and transfer.
10. Banks should have continuity plans for severe business disruption.
11. Banks' public disclosures should allow stakeholders to assess operational risk management.

Governance structure involves the "three lines of defence" concept: business line management, risk management, and independent review (for example, Internal Audit). The latter two report to Board level committees. Risk management encompasses a number of areas including compliance, legal, IT and data protection, new account opening, health and safety, HR screening, and building security.

Further defence comes from national supervisors and shareholders.

A good test of an operational risk management system is whether it addresses causes, events, and impact:

- Causes: classifies reasons for losses, helps perform "root cause" analysis, seeks prevention;
- Events: ensures risks are captured, integral to the Advanced Measurement Approach;
- Impact: helps set priorities and mitigation strategies.

Banks will want to assess whether their approach to operational risk is more "top-down" or "bottom-up" orientated. "Top-down" allows management to drive strategy and policy, unify standards, use firm-wide experience, and mitigate risk on an aggregated basis. "Bottom-up" fully utilises the dynamic, "real world" knowledge of those closest to the business and emphasises personal responsibility and ownership. The best approach is a combination of the two with neither over-emphasised.

## OPERATIONAL RISK CAPITAL ALLOCATION

In its publication of the "final chapter" of Basel III in December 2017, which some commentators refer to erroneously as "Basel IV", the Basel Committee acknowledged that the Advanced Measurement Approach (AMA) for operational risk regulatory capital had not worked as intended. Operational risk capital held by banks had been insufficient to cover operational risk losses, and internal models had proved ineffective in assessing capital requirements for risks such as misconduct and inadequate systems and controls.

Thus, the AMA and the three standardised methods will be replaced with a single standardised approach. From 2022 onwards, operational risk capital will be a function of:

- A three year average of certain Business Indicators (BI), for example, interest, lease and dividends, services and financial;
- A Marginal Coefficient, which will increase as the BI rises (0.12 - 0.18);
- An Internal Loss Multiplier (based upon 15 × a bank's average historical losses over the preceding 10 years).

This approach means that the internal models developed and implemented up to now will no longer be required from 2022 onwards, when there will be a single standardised approach for operational risk regulatory capital for all banks.

Operational risk management is not only about allocating capital (Pillar I). Otherwise it assumes that operational risk losses are merely "accidents", with limited scope for prevention and mitigation. Operational risk management should not be a "box ticking" compliance exercise but integral to systems, processes, and culture. Hence, a Pillar II risk management approach in partnership with supervisors and Pillar III disclosure in partnership with stakeholders should be embraced.

**This extract from *The Principles of Banking* (2012)**

## Operational Risk

# OPERATIONAL RISK

The operational risk capital charge introduced in Basel II is the most significant departure in regulatory capital rules when compared to the previous regime. The primary objective of the new charge is to cover for the possibility of catastrophic loss situations *à la* Barings or Kidder Peabody.

## The Nature of Operational Risk

The BIS defines operational risk as "the risk of loss resulting from inadequate or failed internal processes, people and systems or from external events".[25] Put in this way, operational risk covers a very wide range of risk exposures; some of these include the following:

- *fraud*: the risk of loss arising from fraudulent activity, both internal to the bank undertaken by employees and external to the bank and undertaken by a third party. This would cover trading fraud of the type perpetrated by Nick Leeson at Barings, and (allegedly) by Kweku Adoboli at UBS;
- *system failures*: the risk of loss arising from a breakdown of systems and processes;
- *employment practice and workplace safety*: risk of loss due to litigation for personal or other injury, including sexual harassment claims;
- *physical plant and assets*: risk of loss arising from damage to office property and buildings, say from natural disaster or other such events.

---

[25] BIS document of 26 June 2004.

The above is only a small sample. We observe then that the operational risk category is a wide one, and in fact can be taken as a catch-all for all unforeseen risks and losses that are not market risks. Essentially, the operational risk capital charge is designed to protect against low-frequency, but large-impact, rare events.

## Calculation Methodology

Basel II specifies three methods by which the operational risk charge may be calculated. These are the:

- basic indicator approach (BIA);
- standardised approach (SA);
- advanced measurement approach (AMA).

The BIS has suggested that banks adopt the more sophisticated SA or AMA methods over the BIA approach. Banks are allowed to select more than one method if they wish to apply different approaches for different parts of their business.

### Basic Indicator Approach (BIA)
This is fairly simple calculation which states that the operational risk charge is the average over the bank's last three years of 15% of its positive annual gross income. It is given by:

$$BIA = \frac{\left(15\% \times \sum \text{Years } 1-3 \text{ Annual gross income}\right)}{3}. \qquad (2.11)$$

The definition of gross income is given as net interest income plus net non-interest income: a fairly wide coverage. However, it would exclude the insurance income of bancassurance groups.

### Standardised Approach (SA)
The SA method is slightly more sophisticated. It divides a bank's activities into eight different business lines, which are:

- corporate finance;
- trading and sales;
- retail banking
- commercial banking;
- payment and settlements;
- agency services;
- asset management;
- retail brokerage.

Gross income is taken for each business line; the capital charge is the product of the gross income and a factor termed the *beta* for that business line. Beta is prescribed by the BIS, and is meant to denote the relationship between the level of operational risk for that business line and the aggregate level of gross income for that line. The formula for the capital charge is:

$$SA = \frac{\left(\sum \text{Years } 1-3 \ \max.[\sum(\text{Annual gross income}_{1-8} \times \beta_{1-8}),0]\right)}{3}. \quad (2.12)$$

The business line beta factors are:

| | |
|---|---|
| Corporate finance: | 18% |
| Trading and sales: | 18% |
| Retail banking: | 12% |
| Commercial banking: | 15% |
| Payment and settlements: | 18% |
| Agency services: | 15% |
| Asset management: | 12% |
| Retail brokerage: | 12%. |

The beta factors are lower for more "traditional" banking factors, which suggests that the SA method would be favoured by retail and commercial banks; conversely, investment banks may prefer the BIA approach, or adopt the AMA approach.

### Advanced Measurement Approach (AMA)

The AMA might be said to be the advanced IRB approach for operational risk, as it uses a bank's internal operational risk measurements and requires the approval of the national supervisor. A 5-year database of internal operational risk measurement data is required to implement AMA. This includes five years of historical observation.

Calculating the capital charge requires that the bank maps the historical loss data for each of the eight business lines from its internal measures, for each of the risk types that are defined to be "operational risk". This requires complex and sophisticated systems, which not all banks will have in place.

## Insurance Policy Mitigation

Under Basel II a bank can make use of insurance policies to offset a maximum of 20% of its operational risk capital charge. The BIS prescribes the circumstances in which a bank can use insurance to achieve this. These include terms such as: (i) the insurance policy must have a minimum initial term of one year with a minimum 90-day cancellation notice period;

(ii) the policy must contain no exclusions for events triggered by supervisory action; and (iii) the policy must be provided by a third-party institution. The maximum relief that can be granted is 20% of a bank's operational risk capital charge. The insurance policy cannot cover any fines levied by bank regulatory authorities.

Reproduced from *The Principles of Banking* (2012)

## SELECTED BIBLIOGRAPHY AND REFERENCES

*A Tale of Tails: An Empirical Analysis of Loss Distribution Models for Estimating Operational Risk Capital*, Federal Reserve Bank of Boston, April 2007 http://www.bostonfed.org/economic/wp/wp2006/wp0613.htm.

*Basel II: International Convergence of Capital Measurement and Capital Standards: A Revised Framework – Comprehensive Version*, BIS, June 2006 http://www.bis.org/publ/bcbs128.htm.

Bühlmann *et al* (2007) "A 'Toy' Model for Operational Risk Quantification Using Credibility Theory", *The Journal of Operational Risk*, 2(1), pp. 3–19, 2007.

*FCA Risk Outlook 2013*, FCA, March 2013 www.fca.org.uk/static/fca/documents/fca-risk-outlook-2013.pdf.

*G-20 High-Level Principles on Financial Consumer Protection*, OECD, October 2011, www.oecd.org/daf/fin/financial-markets/48892010.pdf.

*Guidelines on the management of operational risks in market-related activities*, European Banking Authority, October 2010 https://www.eba.europa.eu/regulation-and-policy/operational-risk/guidelines-on-the-management-of-operational-risk-in-market-related-activities.

*Observed range of practice in key elements of Advanced Measurement Approaches (AMA)*, BIS, July 2009 http://www.bis.org/publ/bcbs160b.pdf.

*Observed range of practice in key elements of Advanced Measurement Approaches (AMA)*, BIS, July 2009 http://www.bis.org/publ/bcbs160b.pdf.

*OECD Guidelines: Responsible Business Matters*, OECD, 2010, www.mneguidelines.oecd.org/MNEguidelines_RBCmatters.pdf.

*Operational Risk Management*, BIS, September 1998 http://www.bis.org/publ/bcbs42.htm.

*Operational Risk*, BIS, January 2001 www.bis.org/publ/bcbsca07.pdf.

*Operational Risk – Supervisory Guidelines for the Advanced Measurement Approaches*, BIS, June 2011 http://www.bis.org/publ/bcbs196.htm.

*Our Risk Outlook 2014*, FCA, March 2014 www.fca.org.uk/news/about-us/risk-outlook-2014.

*Principles for the Sound Management of Operational Risk*, BIS, June 2011 http://www.bis.org/publ/bcbs195.htm.

*Results from the 2008 Loss Data Collection Exercise for Operational Risk*, BIS, July 2009 http://www.bis.org/publ/bcbs160.htm.

*The Quantitative Impact Study for Operational Risk: Overview of Individual Loss Data and Lessons Learned*, BIS, January 2002 http://www.bis.org/bcbs/qis/qisoprisk.htm.

*Working Paper on the Regulatory Treatment of Operational Risk*, BIS, September 2001 http://www.bis.org/publ/bcbs_wp8.htm.

*"But sometimes I decide that it's time to jut out, to moan about a bill, to make a stand, to damn well not blend in any more. To dare, to take a leap, do those things that the Hollywood stars tell you to do with the idealistic backing music – it worked for them. . .so yes, I was going to make up for those times. . . .look the world in the eye, set my jaw with a sense of character. And man, did I pay the price."*

—Laurie Tallack, *Not a Natural Pilot,*
CreateSpace Independent Publishing Platform, 2015

# Regulatory Capital and the Capital Adequacy Assessment Process

# CHAPTER 8

## REGULATORY CAPITAL FRAMEWORK

The ultimate responsibility for the management of regulatory capital in a bank over the cycle – in effect, in perpetuity (because we have yet to discover, anywhere in the world, a bank whose mission statement includes an objective of winding itself up at some point in the future) – lies with the Board. Therefore every aspect of this responsibility needs to be addressed with care, expertise, and sound judgement, from the Board of Directors downwards. The risk management framework in a bank, within which regulatory capital adequacy is managed, is essentially the corporate governance committee organisation structure. It's such an important topic that we have devoted an entire chapter to it (Chapter 17), and readers may want to tackle that one before proceeding here.

After that, regulatory capital management and liquidity risk management are the important topics to master. This chapter looks in detail at the former, and we reserve the latter for Part III.

### Key Elements of the Basel I Framework and Perceived Shortcomings

**Capital Adequacy**   In just about every country in the world, local legislation describing incorporated companies will cover issues related to their share capital and unimpaired reserve funds. The regulations relating to banks dictate the capital requirements. These regulations are set in line with the Basel Accord. The Basel Accord is not a law. Most governments worldwide are committed to implementing the accord. Under Basel I, the minimum capital requirement was based on the allocated qualifying capital and reserve funds approved and assigned by a bank's Board of Directors and designated to provide for risk pertaining to the particular nature of a bank's business. Minimum capital included the sum of its primary and secondary capital and primary and secondary unimpaired reserve funds.

For trading banks, additional tertiary capital was required. The regulators could increase the required capital depending on a bank's risk assets, thereby ensuring that an adequate amount of capital and reserves was maintained to safeguard the bank's solvency. Most country banking regulators imposed capital adequacy standards that are based on the 1988 Basel I Accord, which became live in 1992.

Capital was divided into Tier 1 (primary capital) and Tier 2 (secondary capital). Banks had to maintain the minimum amount of qualifying primary and secondary reserve funds relating to banking and trading activities. Tier 1 must make up at least 50% of a bank's capital base.

Tier 1 capital consists of:

- Ordinary shares;
- Non-redeemable, non-cumulative preference shares;
- Share premium;
- Accumulated profits;
- Surplus on realisation of capital assets;
- Other general or special reserves.

The following items (amongst others) must be deducted from Tier 1 capital:

- Goodwill;
- Deferred tax debits arising from assessed loss;
- Accumulated losses.

Tier 2 capital consists of:

- Cumulative preference shares and premium;
- 50% capitalisation of specified revaluation reserves;
- General provisions;
- Subordinated long-term debt.

The following items (amongst others) must be deducted from Tier 2 capital:

- Debt instruments held by the bank or its non-bank subsidiary that rank as secondary capital of another bank.

Conventionally, capital adequacy requirements (CAR) have been based on credit risk. In addition, capital requirements imposed on the trading activities of a bank relate to position risk.

While Basel I improved the way capital requirements were determined, it did have significant weaknesses. Under its provisions, all loans by a bank to a corporation had a risk weight of 100% and required the same amount of capital. A loan to a company with an AA+ credit rating was treated in the same way as one to a corporation with a B rating. In Basel I, there was no model of default correlation.[1] Also, the requirements for assessing risk in the trading book, including value-at-risk methodologies, were rudimentary and failed to recognise the risk inherent in the books.

Furthermore, Basel I did not make any allowance for the funding mismatch and consequential liquidity risk that a bank was running. (This was deliberate: neither Basel I nor Basel II addressed liquidity risk. The logic behind this appears to be the academic view of a clearing market: a bank must, almost by definition, always be liquid because customers would not deposit funds with a bank that was perceived to be weak in terms of liquidity strength and liquidity management. Of course the events of 2007 and 2008 proved this line of thinking to be unrealistic.)

Because of Basel I's demonstration of these shortcomings which affected banks globally, it was succeeded by the Basel II Accord in 2008. The goal of the new accord was to maintain an adequate amount of regulatory capital which addressed the risk inherent in asset exposure and their default correlation and incorporated operational risk. Basel II was based on three "pillars", namely: minimum capital requirements, a supervisory review process, and effective use of market discipline through minimum disclosure standards. Many developed country banks also applied the internal ratings-based approach (IRB). Shortcomings with respect to the trading book and liquidity profile assessment were addressed in Basel III, after the bank crash events of 2008.

The three pillars encompass:

- Pillar 1: minimum capital requirements were beefed up to cover operational as well as credit risk, with a formula provided to help banks refine their risk weighted assets;
- Pillar 2: the supervisory review process needed to be more thorough and uniform, emphasising early intervention where needed;
- Pillar 3: market discipline had to be reinforced to demand greater disclosure of the scope and application of Basel II, the regulatory capital requirements, and the nature of the bank's risk exposures.

In June 1999, the Basel Committee proposed the new rules that became known as Basel II. These were revised in January 2001 and April 2003.

---

[1] In the post-2008 era, this is not necessarily a weakness. Remember, "default correlation" is a statistic that cannot be observed in the market. In a discipline such as Physics, there would be no place for a model parameter with such characteristics. . .

Several quantitative impact studies (QISs) were undertaken to test the application of the new rules and the amount of capital required. A final set of new rules agreed to by all members of the Basel Committee was published in June 2004. This was updated in November 2005. Implementation of the new rules began in 2007 after a further QIS. Note that the advent of Basel III did not mean that Basel II was replaced in its entirety; rather, amendments were made to Basel II. The core text can be found at http://www.bis.org/publ/bcbs128.pdf.

What we call "regulatory capital" differs from what is known as "economic capital". In effect, there are two approaches to consider supply and demand of capital. The regulatory approach dictates the rules on which the demand is to be set, as well as the admissibility of supply, while an internal or economic approach considers the internal best estimate of demand and supply. Regulatory capital supply compared to a predetermined scalar of demand is what the regulators determine as adequate for a bank's operations. Economic capital is what the bank itself views as appropriate for its activities. Almost invariably it is lower than regulatory capital, in that it incorporates a portfolio effect reflecting diversification of activities and also uses the bank's own calculating models, which "benefit" from knowledge of portfolio behaviour based on past experience and understanding of the customer.

Through the Pillar 2 requirements of the internal capital adequacy assessment process (ICAAP) banks have had to become more sophisticated at estimating their economic capital, based on their own risk appetite and strategy and contrasting this to the regulatory capital requirements. This process is refined in line with the requirements imposed under Basel III.

Some jurisdictions in emerging markets still apply the Basel I framework. For multinational banking groups, their exposure may therefore be subject to Basel I in a specific country, Basel II in another country, and Basel III on consolidation.

### Basel II Framework and Implications for Banking Operations

**Pillar 1: Minimum Capital Requirements (Rules-based)**   The Basel II requirements applied to "internationally active" banks, which include most large banks in the world. In Pillar 1 the minimum capital requirement for credit risk in the banking book is calculated in a way that reflects the credit ratings of counterparties. The capital requirement for market risk remained unchanged from the 1996 Amendment, but there was a new capital charge for operational risk. The general requirement in Basel I that banks hold a total capital equal to 8% of risk-weighted assets (RWA) remained unchanged.

When the capital requirement for a risk is calculated in a way that does not involve RWAs, it is multiplied by 12.5 to convert it to an RWA. As a result, it is always the case that:

$$\text{Total capital} = 0.08 \times \left( \begin{array}{c} \text{Credit risk RWA} + \text{Market risk RWA} \\ + \text{Operational risk RWA} \end{array} \right) \quad (8.1)$$

This approach has been adopted given the original Basel I approach to assess risk as a percentage of the value of an asset rather than calculating the capital requirement explicitly.

For credit risk, three approaches of calculation were introduced under Basel II, namely:

1. The standardised approach (BCBS128 Part 2.II);
2. The foundation internal ratings based (IRB) approach (BCBS128 Part 2.III);
3. The advanced IRB approach (also, BCBS128 Part 2.III).

The standardised approach has been used by banks which are not sufficiently sophisticated enough (in the view of the regulators) to use the internal ratings approaches. The standardised approach is similar to Basel I except for the calculation of risk weights. The risk weight for a country (sovereign) exposure ranges from 0% to 150%, and the risk weight for an exposure to another bank or a corporation ranges from 20% to 150%. Supervisors are allowed to apply lower risk weights (20% rather than 50%, 50% rather than 100%, and 100% rather than 150%) when exposures are to the country in which the bank is incorporated or to that country's central bank.

For claims on banks, the rules are somewhat complicated. Instead of using the standard risk weights, national supervisors can choose to base capital requirements on the rating of the country in which the bank is incorporated. The risk weight assigned to the bank will be 20% if the country of incorporation has a rating between AAA and AA−, 50% if it is between A+ and A−, 100% if it is between BBB+ and B−, as in the case of South Africa (2014), 150% if it is below B−, and 100% if it is unrated.

The standard rule for retail lending is that a risk weight of 75% be applied, compared with 100% in Basel I. When claims are secured by a residential mortgage, the risk weight is 35%, compared with 50% in Basel I. Due to poor historical loss experience, the risk weight for claims secured by commercial real estate is 100%. So in other words, while a bank may take some comfort in the "security" afforded by commercial real-estate collateral, it is actually not the most efficient deployment given that the RW remains 100%, the same as unsecured lending but at much lower lending spreads than unsecured loans.

There are two ways that banks can adjust risk weights for collateral. The first is called the simple approach and is similar to the approach used in Basel I. The second is called the comprehensive approach. Banks have a choice as to which approach is used in the banking book, but they must use the comprehensive approach to calculate capital for counterparty credit risk in the trading book.

Under the simple approach, the risk weight of the counterparty is replaced by the risk weight of the collateral for the part of the exposure covered by the collateral (the exposure is calculated after netting). For any exposure not covered by the collateral, the risk weight of the counterparty is used. The minimum level for the risk weight applied to the collateral is 20%. A requirement is that the collateral must be revalued at least every six months and must be pledged for at least the life of the exposure.

Under the comprehensive approach, banks adjust the size of their exposure upwards to allow for possible decreases in the value of the collateral (the adjustments depend on the volatility of the exposure and the collateral). A new exposure equal to the excess of the adjusted exposure over the adjusted value of the collateral is calculated and the counterparty's risk weight is applied to this exposure. The adjustments applied to the exposure and the collateral can be calculated using rules specified in Basel II or, with regulatory approval, using a bank's internal models. Where netting arrangements apply, exposures and collateral are separately netted and the adjustments made are weighted averages.

## EXAMPLE 8.1    CREDIT EXPOSURE

Suppose that a $800 million exposure to a particular counterparty is secured by collateral worth $700 million. The collateral consists of bonds issued by a BBB-rated company. The counterparty has a rating of B–. The risk weight for the counterparty is 150% and the risk weight for the collateral is 100%. The risk-weighted assets applied to the exposure using the simple approach is:

$$(1.0 \times 700) + (1.5 \times 100) = 850, \text{ or } \$850 \text{ million.}$$

Consider next the comprehensive approach. Assume that the adjustment to exposure to allow for possible future increases in the exposure is +10% and the adjustment to the collateral to allow for possible future decreases in its value is –15%. The new exposure is:

$$(1.1 \times 800) - (0.85 \times 700) = 285, \text{ or } \$285 \text{ million;}$$

and a risk weight of 150% is applied to this exposure to give risk-adjusted assets equal to $427.5 million.

Under the internal ratings-based (IRB) approach, regulators base the capital requirement on the value-at-risk calculated using a 1-year time horizon and a 99.9% confidence level. They recognise that expected losses are usually covered by the way a financial institution prices its products (for example, the interest charged by a bank on a loan is designed to recover expected loan losses). The capital required is therefore the value-at-risk minus the expected loss.

The value-at-risk is calculated using a Gaussian copula model (single factor Vašíček) of time to default. Assume that a bank has a very large number of obligors, all of which have the same 1-year probability of default (PD). The correlation between each pair of obligors is p. There is a probability of 99.9% that the percentage of defaults during a 1-year period will be less than:

$$\text{WCDR} = N\left[\left(N^{-1}(\text{PD}) + \sqrt{p}N^{-1}(0.999)\right)/\sqrt{1-p}\right] \qquad (8.2)$$

WCDR denotes the "worst case default rate", which we are 99.9% certain will not be exceeded next year provided all exposures are equal and no correlation exists between loss given default (LGD) and PD. It follows that, for a large portfolio of instruments (loans, loan commitments, derivatives, etc.) that have the same PD and p, there is a 99.9% chance that the loss on the portfolio will be less than:

$$\sum_I \text{EAD}_I \times \text{LGD}_I \times \text{WCDR} \qquad (8.3)$$

where    $\text{EAD}_I$    is the exposure at default of the i-th counterparty; and
         $\text{LGD}_I$    is the loss given default for the i-th counterparty.

The variable $\text{EAD}_I$ is the currency amount that is expected to be owed by the i-th counterparty at the time of default. If there is a single loan outstanding to the i-th counterparty, this is likely to equal the principal amount outstanding on the loan. If there is a single swap or other derivative, a credit equivalent amount must be estimated. The variable $\text{LGD}_I$ is the proportion of $\text{EAD}_I$ that is expected to be lost in the event of default. For example, if a bank expects to recover 30% of the amount owed in the event of default, then $\text{LGD}_I = 0.7$.

The expected loss from defaults is $\sum_I \text{EAD}_I \times \text{LGD}_I \times \text{PD}$. The capital required is the excess of the 99.9% worst-case loss minus the expected loss:

$$\sum_I \text{EAD}_I \times \text{LGD}_I \times (\text{WCDR} - \text{PD}) \qquad (8.4)$$

When contrasting this approach to economic capital frameworks, it is apparent that a collective risk model approach has not been applied and all input parameters are independent of each other.

When counterparties have different PDs and different p's, an extension of the model can be used to show that the capital required is:

$$\sum_i EAD_I \times LGD_I \times (WCDR_I - PD_I) \qquad (8.5)$$

where $PD_I$ and $WCDR_I$ are PD and WCDR for the i-th counterparty. WCDR depends on PD and p. When the correlation p is zero, WCDR = PD because in that case there is no default correlation and the percentage of loans defaulting can be expected to be the same in all years. As p increases, WCDR increases.

In the case of corporate, sovereign, and bank exposures, Basel II assumes a relationship between the correlation parameter p and the probability of default PD in an equation based on empirical research. Using this approach, the formula for the capital required is:

$$EAD \times LGD \times (WCDR - PD) \times MA \qquad (8.6)$$

where MA is the maturity adjustment. The maturity adjustment is designed to allow for the fact that, if an instrument lasts longer than one year, there is a 1-year credit exposure arising from a possible decline in the creditworthiness of the counterparty as well as from a possible default by the counterparty. As mentioned earlier, the risk-weighted assets (RWA) are calculated as 12.5 times the capital required:

$$RWA = 12.5 \times EAD \times LGD \times (WCDR - PD) \times MA \qquad (8.7)$$

so that the capital is 8% of RWA, 4% of which must be Tier 1.

Under an economic capital framework, maturity impact and the term structure of PDs could be considered explicitly. Furthermore, the correlation parameter can be considered to be more flexible and explained by multiple factors.

Under the foundation IRB approach, banks supply PD while LGD, EAD, and maturity M are supervisory values set by the Basel Committee. PD is subject to a floor of 0.03% for bank and corporate exposures, LGD is set at 45% for senior claims and 75% for subordinated claims. When there is eligible collateral, in order to correspond to the comprehensive approach that was described earlier, LGD is reduced by the ratio of the adjusted value of the collateral to the adjusted value of the exposure, both calculated using the comprehensive approach. The EAD is calculated in a way similar to the credit equivalent amount in Basel I and includes the impact of netting. M is set at 2.5 in most cases.

Under the advanced IRB approach, banks supply their own estimates of the PD, LGD, EAD, and M for corporate, sovereign, and bank exposures, subject to regulatory approval and therefore not necessarily the same as internal estimates. The PD can be reduced by credit mitigants such as credit triggers. The two main factors influencing the LGD are the seniority of the debt and the collateral. In calculating EAD, banks can, with regulatory approval, use their own estimates of credit conversion factors.

The capital given by the above equations is intended to be enough to cover unexpected losses over a 1-year period that we are 99.9% certain will not be exceeded. The WCDR is the probability of default that (theoretically) happens once every thousand bank years. The Basel Committee reserves the right to apply a scaling factor (less than or greater than 1.0) to the result of the calculations, if it finds that the aggregate capital requirements are too high or low.

---

### EXAMPLE 8.2

Suppose the assets of a bank consist of $1 billion of loans to BBB-rated corporations. The PD for the corporations is estimated as 0.1% and the LGD is 60%. Average maturity of the corporate loans is 2.5 years. Adjusted maturity is 1.59, which according to our equation makes the WCDR 3.4%. Under the Basel II IRB approach, the risk-weighted assets for the corporate loans are:

$$12.5 \times 1000 \times 0.6 \times (0.034 - 0.0001) \times 1.59 = 393$$

or $393 million. This compares with $1 billion under Basel I and $1 billion under the standardised approach of Basel II.

---

The model underlying the calculation of capital for retail exposures is similar to that underlying the calculation of corporate, sovereign, and bank exposures. However, the foundation IRB and advanced IRB approaches are merged, and all banks using the IRB approach provide their own estimates of PD, LGD, and EAD. There is no maturity adjustment. The capital requirement is therefore:

$$EAD \times LGD \times (WCDR - PD) \tag{8.8}$$

and the risk-weighted assets are:

$$RWA = 12.5 \times EAD \times LGD \times (WCDR - PD) \qquad (8.9)$$

where WCDR is calculated as before. For residential mortgages, p is set equal to 0.15 in this equation. For qualifying revolving exposures, p is set equal to 0.04. For all other retail exposures, a relationship between p and PD is specified for the calculation of WCDR, wherein correlations are assumed to be much lower for retail exposures.

---

### EXAMPLE 8.3

Suppose the assets of a bank consist of $500 million of residential mortgages where the PD is 0.005 and the LGD is 20%. In this case, p = 0.15 and

$$WCDR = N \times \left[ \left( N^{-1}(0.005) + \sqrt{0.15}\, N^{-1}(0.999) \right) / \sqrt{1 - 0.15} \right] = 0.67$$

The risk-weighted assets are:

$$12.5 \times 500 \times 0.2 \times (0.067 - 0.005) = 78$$

or $78 million. This compares with $250 million under Basel I and $17.5 million under the standardised approach of Basel II.

---

The approach traditionally taken by the Basel Committee for handling guarantees is the credit substitution approach. Suppose that a BBB-rated company guarantees a loan to a BB-rated company. For the purposes of calculating capital, the credit rating of the guarantor is substituted for the credit rating of the borrower, so that capital is calculated as though the loan had been made to the BBB-rated company. This overstates the credit risk because, for the lender to lose money, both the guarantor and the borrower must default (with the guarantor defaulting before the borrower). This issue of double default was addressed by Basel in 2005. As an alternative to using the credit substitution approach, the capital requirement can be calculated as the capital that would be required without the guarantee multiplied by 0.15 + (160 × $PD_G$), where $PD_G$ is the 1-year probability of default of the guarantor.

In determining capital requirements for defaulted assets, the WCDR formula above sets N and PD equal to 1, and both EAD and LGD have to be estimated.

*Operational Risk* Besides changing the manner in which banks calculate credit risk capital, Basel II required banks to possess sufficient capital to cover operational risk. This is the risk of losses from occurrences where the bank's procedures fail to work as they are meant to, or where there is an adverse external event such as an explosion in a key facility. The effect of the Basel II credit risk calculation is to reduce the credit risk capital requirements for most banks and the capital charge for operational risk has the impact of restoring the total level of capital in the banking system roughly to where it was under Basel I.

Three approaches of calculating capital for operational risk were introduced in Chapter 7.

**Pillar 2: Supervisory Review Process (Non-rules Based) Including the Internal Capital Adequacy Assessment Process (ICAAP) (BCBS128 Part III)** Pillar 2, which is concerned with the supervisory review process, allows regulators in different countries some discretion in how rules are applied (so that they can take account of local conditions), but seeks to achieve overall consistency in the application of the principles. It places more emphasis on early intervention when problems arise. Supervisors are required to do far more than simply ensuring that the minimum capital required under Basel II is held. Part of their role is to encourage banks to develop and use better risk management techniques and to evaluate these techniques. They should evaluate risks that are not covered by Pillar 1 and enter into an active dialogue with banks when deficiencies are identified.

Four key principles of supervisory review are specified:

1. Banks should have a process for assessing their overall capital adequacy in relation to their risk profile and strategy for maintaining capital levels.
2. Supervisors should review and evaluate banks' internal capital adequacy assessments and strategies, as well as their ability to monitor and ensure compliance with regulatory capital ratios. Supervisors should take appropriate supervisory action if they are not satisfied with the result of the process.
3. Supervisors should expect banks to operate above the minimum regulatory capital and should be able to require banks to hold capital in excess of this minimum.
4. Supervisors should seek to intervene at an early stage to prevent capital from falling below the minimum levels required to support the risk characteristics of a particular bank and should require rapid remedial action if capital is not maintained or restored.

The first point is achieved by requiring banks to perform an internal capital adequacy assessment process (ICAAP). The key components required in an ICAAP include the following two types of capital assessment:

1. Point-in-time capital assessment as at the date chosen for the ICAAP submission:
   - Pillar 1 – 8% of RWA of Credit, Market and Operational Risks;
   - Pillar 2A – additional capital requirements for risks not captured in Pillar 1 (for example, Interest Rate Risk in the Banking Book (IRRBB), Pension Risk, and Credit Concentration Risk). A Material Integrated Risk Assessment (MIRA) is performed to ensure that all material risks are managed / capitalised adequately.
2. Forward-looking capital assessment using stress test results:
   - Maintain a capital surplus – total available less total required capital must be in surplus after taking into account management and recovery options where necessary;
   - Determine whether an additional capital buffer is required to enable a bank to remain in surplus during periods of stress: determine the Capital Planning Buffer (CPB) (under the current regime) equal to the most adverse movement in the capital surplus.

In the European Union, Capital Requirements Directive (CRD) IV introduces the Capital Conservation Buffer (CCoB), the Countercyclical Buffer (CCyB), and the Domestic Systemically Important Financial Institution (D-SIFI) buffers.

Table 8.1 provides an overview of the key ICAAP processes. Figure 8.1 illustrates the recommended governance structure of the ICAAP framework

**TABLE 8.1**  Overview of the ICAAP processes

| Process | Short Description |
|---|---|
| Risk Appetite | Risk Appetite is an integral part of ABC's Risk Management Framework, designed to deliver the strategic risk objectives of capital adequacy, market confidence, stable earnings growth, and access to funding and liquidity. |
| Material Integrated Risk Assessment | An exercise that identifies, evaluates, and assesses all material financial and non-financial risks whether quantifiable or not. |
| Stress Testing Programme | A comprehensive programme of stress testing which is designed to ensure senior management involvement, is aligned to regulatory requirements, and integrated into the budgeting and capital planning processes. |
| 9+3 Capital Planning and Budgeting | An annual budgeting and capital planning process incorporating business and financial plans for the current year and project at least an additional two years under a base case (normal conditions) and three years under stressed conditions. |

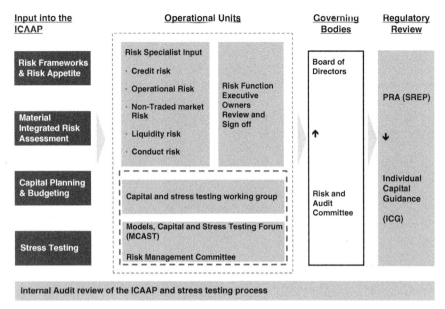

**FIGURE 8.1**   Recommended governance structure for the ICAAP

for a typical commercial bank, mapping the components of the ICAAP to the internal processes, governance, and approvals, ultimately for regulatory review, the supervisory review and evaluation process (SREP).

The Basel Committee suggests that regulators pay particular attention to credit risk, operational risk, market risk, interest rate risk in the banking book, and liquidity risk. Key issues in credit risk are stress tests used, default definitions used, credit risk concentration, and the risks associated with the use of collateral, guarantees, and credit derivatives.

In the United Kingdom and other countries the regulatory authority places significant emphasis on the "usage" of the process in practice. Banks are encouraged not to simply comply with the regulation but to use the processes in practice. This is referred to as the "use test" in the ICAAP and supervisory review process.

**Pillar 3: Market Review (Public Disclosure)**   Pillar 3 (market discipline) requires banks to disclose more information about the way they allocate capital and the risks they take. The idea is that banks will be subjected to added pressure to make sound risk management decisions if shareholders and potential shareholders have more information about those decisions.

The extent to which regulators can force banks to increase their disclosure varies from region to region. However, banks are unlikely to ignore directives on this from their supervisors, given the potential of supervisors to make their life difficult. Moreover, banks sometimes have to increase their disclosure in order to be allowed to use particular methodologies for calculating capital.

Regulatory disclosures are likely to be different in form from accounting disclosures and need not be made in annual reports. It is largely left to the bank to choose disclosures that are material and relevant. Among the items that banks should disclose are:

1. The entities in the banking group to which Basel III is applied and adjustments made for entities to which it is not applied;
2. The terms and conditions of the main features of all capital instruments;
3. A list of the instruments constituting Tier 1 capital and the amount of capital provided by each item;
4. The total amount of Additional Tier 1 and Tier 2 capital;
5. Capital requirements for credit, market, and operational risk;
6. Other general information on the risks to which a bank is exposed and the assessment methods used by the bank for different categories of risk;
7. The structure of the risk management function and how it operates.

The emphasis in Basel II was on self-regulation. Banks were allowed to use internal models to handle many aspects of assessing capital requirements. The financial crisis and subsequent bank bail-outs led to market commentators to suggest that Basel II's reliance on internal models should be reduced, with the more proactive and granular approach of regulators today in the Basel III era being the result.

**New Definition of Tier 2 and Tier 2 Capital**   Basel III increased the minimum common equity Tier 1, total Tier 1, and total capital adequacy ratios. There is a requirement to form core capital predominantly through common shares and retained earnings. The leverage ratio has been introduced as a non-risk based measure of the capital structure, requiring a minimum Tier 1 ratio of 3%, which some regulators (for example, the South Africa Reserve Bank) raise to 4%. International harmonisation of capital deductions and prudential filters is sought (for example, limited recognition of investments in financial institutions). These measures are all expected to be in place by 2019, if not sooner, in effect raising total capital up to 10.5% of RWA if not higher.

**Capital Conservation Buffer**   Basel III introduced an additional 2.5% capital conservation buffer (2.5% of RWA) to withstand future stress periods.

**Countercyclical Capital Buffer**   Basel III further introduced an additional countercyclical buffer, ranging from 0–2.5%, to withstand future stresses.

**Domestic Systemically Important Banks (D-SIB)**   Basel III further introduces an additional buffer for domestic systemically important banks, ranging from 0–2.5%, to withstand future stresses. Implementation of this measure is from 2016, but set only for those banks deemed by the local regulator to be systemically important.

**Basel III Liquidity: Liquidity Coverage Ratio (LCR) and Long-term Structural Ratio (NSFR)**   Basel III introduces two structural liquidity ratio minimums: the LCR identifies the amount of unencumbered, high quality liquid assets a bank is required to hold in order to offset the cumulative net cash outflows it would encounter under an acute short-term (30-day) stress scenario; and the Net Stable Funding Ratio (NSFR) measures the amount of longer-term, stable funding sources required by a bank given the liquidity profile of its assets and liabilities and the contingent liquidity risk arising from off-balance sheet exposures (OBEs). The standard requires a minimum amount of funding that is expected to be stable over a 6-month horizon based on liquidity risk factors assigned to assets / liabilities and OBEs. This is intended to promote longer-term structural funding of a bank's balance sheet.

These metrics are discussed in detail in Chapter 12.

**Minimum Leverage Ratio**   As mentioned above, Basel III introduces a non-risk based measure of capital structure, called the minimum leverage ratio. This requires banks to keep a minimum Tier 1 ratio of 3%, but some regulators require their banks to keep a 4% minimum.

## CAPITAL AND BALANCE SHEET MANAGEMENT AND THE ICAAP PROCESS

A bank's strategy is closely linked to its capital position. That said, a bank's capital position also drives its strategy. Like all commercial enterprises, the return shareholders receive for their investment in a bank or financial holding company, is of critical importance when considering the value generated. Furthermore, the regulators and society, in general, require banks to be well capitalised to reduce friction to the financial system. Well-regulated and strongly capitalised banks are fundamental to a robust financial system.

Bank capital is a concept that is central to the understanding, and management, of a bank's business strategy and the risk exposure associated with that strategy. In the business media, it is often suggested that capital is the most important aspect of bank risk management, but although such a view is incorrect (liquidity and funding are as important certainly, if not more so), it is indeed the case that effective capital management is essential if a bank is to continue to deliver shareholder returns through the economic cycle. Put simply, understanding capital is key to understanding what banks do, the risks they take, and how best these risks should be managed.

Often capital is spoken of as being "held" or "put aside" by a bank in order to support lending operations, as if it was an asset. This is an unfortunate turn of phrase. Far from being an asset, capital is a liability, alongside all the other forms of liability the bank has, and as such is a form of funding for the bank. However, unlike the other forms of liability it has no fixed interest cost, indeed core capital is not obliged to pay out any form of coupon at any time (as such it has no explicit interest cost). Moreover, because it has no repayment date it is able to absorb losses. Such losses could otherwise threaten a bank's solvency, so it is easy to see why a sufficient capital base to cover all eventualities is essential for every bank. Alternative sources of "non-core Tier 1" capital with contractual costs and different levels of loss absorption are also available to banks.

## The Banking Model and Capital

Having discussed the Basel II and III regulatory regime we now consider the best-practice framework within which capital should be planned and managed within a bank, including the internal processes undertaken to ensure regulatory compliance (exemplified by the ICAAP process). Before that, however, the concepts of capital and its purpose are introduced. The best-practice recommended approach to use of capital is also presented.

**The Business Model and Capital**   The importance of capital to a bank and an appropriate appreciation of its importance requires a genuine understanding of what banks actually do. In essence they:

1. Provide transaction services for customers, primarily payments, which enable them to settle commercial transactions;
2. Provide funding, in the form of credit, to customers to enable them to enter into commercial transactions; and
3. Provide risk management services to customers, ranging from the simple current account ("checking account") to more complex services that enable customers to manage and hedge their foreign exchange and interest rate risk exposures.

Services 2 and 3 require a bank to undertake two fundamentally contradictory things: lend money for as long a period as the customer requires, and accept deposits on an "instant access" basis from customers. This is the process of "maturity transformation", the very definition of the banking business model, and it is the risk exposures generated by operating this model which make capital and liquidity so important for a bank. Liquidity management is covered in Part III, while here we concentrate on capital.

A stylised bank balance sheet is shown at Figure 8.2.

**Bank Balance Sheet** The balance sheet is a snapshot in time of the bank's financial strength. Note that the capital amount must, at all times, be more than sufficient to absorb customer loan losses (or losses incurred for other reasons, such as the result of proprietary trading losses or ineffective hedging resulting in unexpected losses). However, the reality of government regulation, which every bank in the world is subject to, means that banks don't need sufficient capital to absorb only losses. They also need sufficient capital to absorb losses *and* still, after such absorption, be able to demonstrate capital levels which are above the regulatory minimum. In other words,

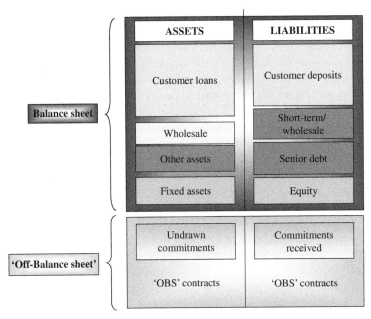

**FIGURE 8.2**  Stylised representation of a typical commercial bank balance sheet

they require sufficient capital base such that they *remain a going concern* after absorbing unexpected losses. Banking is all about confidence. If customers have confidence in the bank, they will continue to place their funds on deposit there. If they do not, they will not. A bank which dips below its regulatory minimum capital ratios, even if it has still absorbed all its losses to date, will not be able to maintain that confidence.

In other words, good capital management, is all about managing capital on a *going concern* basis. The Board of a bank takes responsibility to articulate its risk appetite such that this requirement is met. It is generally considered bad practice to manage capital on a gone-concern basis. *The available capital*, the actual amount that can be used to absorb losses, is the surplus above the minimum required by the regulator. Capital that meets the regulator's requirement is not, in truth, available to absorb losses on a going concern basis. It is essential that bank Boards and executive directors manage the institution on this basis.

Invariably banks may fail. In such circumstances the capital sources must be adequate to recover the bank or, if this is not possible, resolve the bank without undue stress to the financial system. This, however, is more feasible in theory than in practice. If a bank fails, one can assume, to a reasonable and safe extent, that its capital base will be insufficient to recover it, and for large banks to resolve it either.

**Treatment of Bank Capital**  The core Tier 1 capital base of a bank comprises its initial capital, or start-up capital, and retained earnings that have been placed in the reserves. Generally, the simplest and most transparent model is to consider that the complete capital base is used as part of a leveraged business model in which it represents equity backing for borrowed funds, which are invested in assets. The return on the assets covers for the cost of borrowing, and the surplus over this and all other costs is the shareholder value-added for the equity owner.

In its simplest form, the bank's capital should not be exposed to risk. Ideally, it must be placed in an instantly liquid risk-free asset, with zero counterparty risk, so that it itself is not in danger of erosion and can be retrieved easily if needed, either to cover unexpected losses and/or to fund further expansion and investment. The only assets that fit this category are a deposit at the central bank or an investment in the sovereign bonds of the same currency. All other investments carry an element of counterparty and/ or liquidity risk and may be considered unsuitable assets in which to invest the bank's capital.

The logic is straightforward: given that capital available must be sufficient to cover unexpected losses, as well as expected losses, if the capital itself was placed at risk then there would be no guarantee that it would be able to absorb all losses at any one time. A loss elsewhere in the portfolio may occur at the same time as losses from assets that were funded with capital. This is what is meant when managing capital on a going concern basis is referred to.

The equity and funding provide the sources of funding to invest in assets. The bank has to hold sufficient liquid assets and cash to ensure liquidity pressures can be met immediately. Given that capital is generally only returned through dividends, the capital therefore has a very long behavioural term. The Treasury of the bank acts as the "bank to the bank", that is, to provide funding to all assets and pay for all liabilities. From an accounting perspective, the cost of funding of capital is nil. An endowment benefit therefore arises as no expense is incurred for this funding. In order to ensure that businesses in a bank group do not unduly benefit from such capital structures, Treasury should charge a funding cost on all assets and pays a funding cost to all liabilities, including capital.

So the capital base itself should not be expected to generate a return. Where it does, for example, the coupon return from a holding of government bonds, this income on capital should accrue to a central book or "ALCO" book, and not to any business line. Neither should it be allocated on a pro-rata basis to the business lines, otherwise the calculation of shareholder value-added by the businesses will be skewed. The business lines are assumed to utilise matched funding instruments to fund their operations. Certain banks also charge a capital risk premium which will also accrue to the "ALCO" book. Views vary on the treatment of this endowment benefit. Some banks keep the benefit in the ALCO book and implement an economic profit type of management account framework, while others allocate some or all of the benefit to incentivise business, hence there is no cost to allocate.

The target return on equity, set by the shareholder and therefore the Board as their representatives, sets the hurdle rate for the business or the legal entities in the group. Senior management generally then translate these hurdles for each of the business lines, who benefit indirectly from the existence of the capital base. This hurdle rate can be a minimum for all the businesses (which is very unlikely as the returns per line of business vary greatly, for example, between asset and liability lines), or it can be modified to suit the differing requirements of each business. It is imperative to note how important it is for the bank's ROC target to be set at a Board level, reflecting the needs of the shareholder and thereby the "cost" of that equity.

The example below describes further the treatment of share capital.

## EXAMPLE 8.4    TREATMENT OF SHARE CAPITAL

The share capital of a legal entity represents a source of funding like any other, except it has one main defining characteristic – it need bear no real actual interest cost and is perpetual. That said, there is a cost that is imputed to it, this being the shareholder's targeted return on equity. This "cost" must be attributed to the equity base, otherwise there is a risk that it ends up representing "free capital" to the benefit of the business lines. This would result in an incorrect and inaccurate reporting of genuine shareholder valued-added (SVA).

There are different approaches as to where the share capital is booked and where the benefit of this free source of funding is assigned. That said, often in reality because the share capital is a specific type of external funding source, it is often recorded in the Treasury book of the entity in which the capital resides, with the cash forming part of the general cash funding pool of the entity that is then managed by Treasury.

The net interest benefit of the utilisation of this "free" cash should then be subject to the same internal funds pricing ("Funds Transfer Pricing") rules as any other funding in the bank (see Chapter 12). In any case, the treatment of capital should be consistent with the treatment of retained earnings: since retained earnings and share capital are both similar sources of funding in that neither have a real interest cost, it is important that the benefit of retained earnings is allocated to a central ALCO book, and not to any of the business lines.

The treatment and allocation of capital described here represents what is considered business best-practice by the author. However, it is not universal. In some cases a deviation from the above is justified where a portion of the capital base is allocated for use as "working capital", for example, in a start-up situation to cover cash requirements such as rental and salary expenses. In this case, the amount to be allocated should be identified in advance and once the business has declared a profit, then the same amount should be restored to the capital base or the bank needs to adjust its reported capital base. So we accept that there could well be other treatments of the capital base that are justified, hence some banks may adopt a different approach from the above. However, just because some banks do something doesn't make it "best-practice".

**Expected and Unexpected Losses**   Banks' normal course of business involves exposing themselves to risk of loss due to customer loan default. Losses will vary from one year to the next, unsurprisingly closely correlated to the economic cycle. The extent of exposure also varies, from "AAA"-rated exposure to lower-rated exposure, by type of customer and product. The extent of collateral provided by a loan customer also dictates the level of loss.

Obviously it is not possible to know in advance what the extent of loss in the next 12 months (or any time period) will be. Banks estimate the average level of losses they expect to incur over the next budgeting period based on their historical experience and internal modelling. This is the bank's *expected losses*. The level of expected loss dictates the nature of future business. For example, since it can be seen as part of the cost of doing business, expected loss levels will influence:

- The level of future balance sheet expansion and lending levels;
- The rate of interest charged to customers.

Banks must also, however, account for *unexpected losses*. This should be self-evident: it would not be possible to estimate accurately what future losses will be. It is common for actual loss rates to far exceed expected loss rates, especially if historical rates were used to estimate expected losses and the last five years had seen the economy booming with the central bank raising interest rates. It is these unexpected losses that banks require a buffer of capital to absorb, and as was said earlier, if the bank is to manage itself on a going concern basis this buffer must be sufficient to absorb losses and still remain above the regulatory minimum. Otherwise, of course, it would no longer be a going concern. This is because a bank that falls even 1 basis point below the regulator's minimum will suffer a loss of confidence and a run on the bank (as well as the inevitable credit rating downgrade to junk status and withdrawal of banking licence).

Unexpected losses are harder to estimate than expected losses. The way it is approximated is the basis of the orthodox credit risk management methodology process in banks. Figure 8.3 provides a stylised illustration of the distribution of credit losses.

**Understanding the Difference Between Capital and Liquidity**   It is evident then that a bank's capital base and its holding of genuinely liquid assets are of equal importance in helping to mitigate against the main bank balance sheet risks. Arguably, the liquidity risk is of greater importance because a failure of liquidity sourcing can kill a bank in an instant. But this aside, it should be noted that in the same way as banks' construction as "financial resources" differs, so does the type of risk exposure that each resource is used to manage against differ. We reiterate that capital is a liability, on the same side

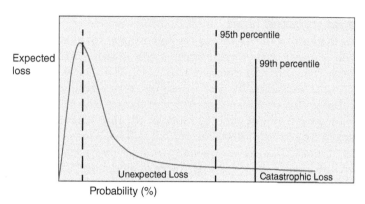

**FIGURE 8.3**   Expected and unexpected losses

of the balance sheet as all other liabilities, and is a source of funding. The balance sheet has to balance of course, and liquid assets are on the other side of the balance sheet as a use of funding (the most liquid asset is a deposit at the central bank, or failing that the domestic sovereign Treasury bill). The requirement to have both sufficient capital and sufficient liquid assets requires balance sheet managers to be aware of the details surrounding the source of funds and the use of funds. In other words, how much capital is available capital that is perpetual (it has no repayment date), has no obligation to pay dividends ever, and can absorb losses on a going concern basis, and how truly liquid are the liquid assets?

**Capital Regulation**   How much capital a bank needs is determined by legislation – so the answer to this question is straightforward. Indeed, Basel III enshrines in law a limit on how much balance sheet leverage a bank can employ. But it is a useful exercise to determine what the capital requirement would look like if there was no regulator.

Certain key ratios (including the leverage ratio) help to provide an estimate answer to this question. This is because not all assets on a bank's balance sheet are the same – some assets are (credit) riskier than others, so each asset type is assigned a risk weight to reflect how risky it is deemed to be. These weights are then applied to the bank's assets to give a risk-weighted asset value (RWA). This is then used to calculate the capital ratio, the bank's capital amount as a percentage of the RWA amount. It is seen that it is easy enough to alter the capital ratio value by adjusting either the numerator or the denominator – or both.

In such an instance, the capital requirement would be based on the internal view of risk and the level of financial resources required to ensure the bank remains a going concern within the tolerances set by its risk appetite.

**Regulatory Capital Requirements** In the first instance, capital structure consid-erations are essentially given by the CRR/CRDIV (in the EU) and in other jurisdictions by the local interpretation of Basel III. Figure 8.4 is a summary of this requirement.

For Basel III, paper BCBS 189 (June 2011) footnote 47 states:

*Common Equity Tier 1 must first be used to meet the minimum cap-ital requirements (including the 6 per cent Tier 1 and 8 per cent Total capital requirements if necessary) before the remainder can contribute to the capital conservation buffer.*

For banks in the EU, the requirement of CRDIV as stated in Article 124 (July 2011) is that:

*Institutions shall meet the requirement imposed by the Countercyclical Capital Buffer with Common Equity Tier 1 capital, which shall be addi-tional to any Common Equity Tier 1 capital maintained to meet the own funds requirement imposed by Article 87 of Regulation [total capital ratio of 8 per cent], the requirement to maintain a Capital Conservation Buffer. . .*

**Sources of Capital** Core equity Tier 1 capital consists in principle of share capital, share premium, and retained earnings attributed as regulatory capi-tal. Certain deductions apply.

The features that make a long-dated liability eligible as Additional Tier 1 (AT1) and Tier 2 (T2) are as follows:

**AT1**
- Perpetual; not callable prior to Year 5;
- Non-cumulative, discretionary distributions;
- Deeply subordinated;

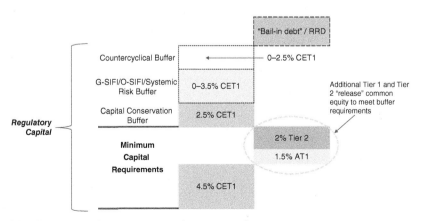

**FIGURE 8.4** Capital structure considerations under CRR / CRDIV

- Conversion to equity or principal write-down at a trigger of CET1 < 5.875% (or higher)
- Conversion or write-down at the point of non-viability, where the point of non-viability is determined at the discretion of the SARB prior to the failure of the bank.

**T2**
- Minimum maturity of five years (with capital credit amortising 20% per year five years prior to maturity);
- Subordinated;
- Conversion or write-down at the point of non-viability.

Given the requirements of Basel III, at a strategic level the main ingredients of capital planning are essentially given: that is, the attachment points for maximum distributable amounts can be set quite easily.

The Pillar 2A add-on is stipulated by the national regulator.

In other jurisdictions, as in the UK, the PRA has stated that the Pillar 2A add-on of up to 2% must comprise at least 56% CET1 and the remainder of a combination of AT1 and T2. For a new bank, the minimum capital requirement would allow the requirements under Basel III to be met as well as to allow for sufficient capital should a countercyclical buffer requirement be implemented by the regulator SARB (Figure 8.5).

**Hypothetical Example: Vanilla Commercial Bank**   To illustrate the considerations involved from a first-principles basis, an assumed example of a UK commercial bank that is being set up from scratch, with an inherited portfolio, is considered. What would be the primary factors driving the capital planning

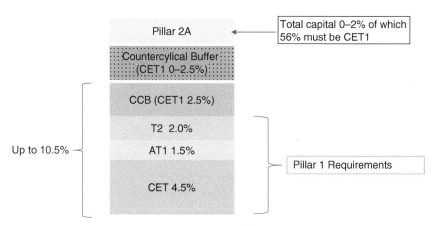

**FIGURE 8.5**   Estimating the combined buffer requirement for a bank under Basel III

process? The balance sheet risk-weighted assets (RWA) breakdown is as at Figure 8.6.

The main factors that (say) a ratings agency review would consider include: asset mix (for example, whether there is a concentration in assets such as commercial real-estate (CRE)); advanced- versus foundation-IRB being applied; Pillar 2 impacts; stress buffers required and any capital release opportunities. With a total balance sheet RWA here of just over GBP 13 billion, the bank is below 1% of UK GDP in size so the countercyclical, G-SIFI and ring-fence buffers do not apply. Hence, the capital considerations which must be accounted for are shown at Figure 8.7.

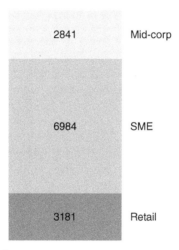

**FIGURE 8.6** RWA breakdown

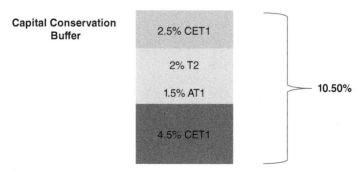

**FIGURE 8.7** Capital considerations

This argues for an indicative capital structure of 15%. However, as this is a fairly small portfolio, the individual capital guidance received from the regulator will more likely impose a higher requirement. This would be a working assumption taking into account:

- Regulator feedback (for example, the requirement for the amount of total loss-absorbing capacity (TLAC));
- Potential impact of stress tests on the capital plan. Such stresses are then accounted for to a certain level of confidence using economic capital principles;
- Peer-group analysis;
- Market expectations;
- Rating agency feedback.

Assuming the 15% capital base is accepted as minimum requirement, there are two main scenarios which present themselves. The first is Scenario 1, the all-equity scenario, while Scenario 2 describes an equity plus other capital structure. The latter is shown at Figure 8.8.

A capital base as shown at Figure 8.8 would enable the bank to meet both the standing buffer requirements and the macro-prudential one. Note that the PRA has stipulated that CET1 must be used to fill Pillar 2A requirements prior to the combined capital buffer. The residual 3.0% of CET1 would be available to meet any remaining capital or buffer requirements, including the Pillar 2A requirements.

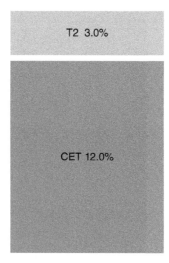

**FIGURE 8.8**  Hypothetical new bank capital structure minimum compliance with Basel III

What factors should guide the capital planning process with respect to the structure of the capital base? The all-equity scenario presents the following features:

- The most robust form from a regulatory perspective;
- It may result in an incremental (one-notch) rating benefit;
- As the most expensive structure, it is least efficient from a shareholder return perspective;
- Compared to the equity plus other capital format, there is a substantial decrease in RoC.

The equity plus other capital liability structure has the following features:

- It is a more efficient capital structure;
- Ultimately, it remains subject to national regulatory approval;
- The rating agency position towards this structure is neutral to negative;
- The T2 issuance would of course be subject to investor demand for this paper;
- The structure allows for further gearing / leverage of the capital base.

Table 8.2 is a summary of the requirements for capital instruments to be AT1 and T2 eligible. In its capital planning, a bank may consider the following rationale for issuance of one or both of these instruments:

- Free up common equity to count towards buffer requirements (capital buffers are additive to minimum total capital requirements);
- Pillar 2 / bail-in capital requirements;
- Non-dilutive (absent conversion);
- Tax-deductible;
- Able to be sold to a fixed-income investor base;
- Acts as a cushion for senior debt investors;
- Supports credit rating requirements (S&P RAC-eligible).

In undertaking its capital planning, a bank must consider the Pillar 2 requirements. When conducting its Pillar 2 review the local regulator will consider both those risks to banks that are not fully captured under Pillar 2A and those risks a firm may be exposed to in future, for example, regulatory changes (Pillar 2B). The key considerations are:

- Pillar 2A: in addition to the Pillar 1 requirements of Basel III (in the EU, CRR / CRDIV), certain regulators including the PRA regard Pillar 2A capital as the minimum level of regulatory capital a bank should maintain at all times to cover against risks, with the implication being

**TABLE 8.2** AT1 and T2 instrument requirements

|  | Additional Tier 1 | Tier 2 |
|---|---|---|
| Tenor | Perpetual | May be dated. Must have minimum 5 years maturity |
| Subordination | Subordinated to depositors, general creditors and subordidated debt of the bank | Subordinated to depositors and general creditors of the bank |
| Distribution | Bank must have full discretion to cancel payments (non-cumulative) | No requirement for deferral / cancellation of coupon |
| Call Features | May be callable by the issuer after a minimum of 5 years (subject to regulatory approval) | May be callable by the issuer after a minimum of 5 years (subject to regulatory approval) |
| Going concern loss absorption | Must have principal loss absorption through either conversion to shares or a write-down mechanism | N/a |
| Gone concern loss absorption | Write-off or conversion if required by the regulator | Write-off or conversion if required by the regulator |

that CET1 must be used to fill the Pillar 2A requirement prior to being used for the CCB.

- Pillar 2B: Pillar 2B buffers will be required for firms where the regulator (PRA included) deems that the Basel III / CRDIV buffers may not be sufficient to enable a firm to meet its capital requirements under stress. The Pillar 2B buffer will replace the existing (in the UK jurisdiction) Capital Planning Buffer, and will be set based upon a range of factors including firm-specific stress test results.

**Leverage Ratio** The leverage ratio limit is a Basel III requirement. In the European Union's CRDIV definition the leverage ratio is defined as T1 capital divided by a total exposure measure, with a limit of 3%; the simplest form is given by:

$$\text{Leverage ratio} = \frac{\text{Tier 1 capital}}{\text{Funded assets}} \qquad (8.10)$$

## Capital Management Policy

Bank capital management should be articulated formally in a policy standard in the same way that liquidity management is (described in Part III). The objective of the policy is to describe how the bank will:

- Meet its regulatory and other legal obligations;
- Maintain its capital resources and buffer as required and in line with the stated risk profile of the business;
- Manage its capital planning in an efficient and cost-effective manner;
- Recover from stress events.

A benchmark standard template for a bank's capital management policy follows.

**Capital Management**  The starting point for capital management policy is the regulatory capital ratios. The requirements of any overseas regulators, from jurisdictions that the bank also operates in, are also included. The next step is a consideration of internal capital requirements (economic capital) as the Board has a duty to meet regulatory requirements but where these requirements are inadequate, as indicated by the internal risk assessment, to demand higher capital ratios. The buffers on regulatory ratios are required to reduce the likelihood of a limit breach and form the basis of the capital risk appetite of the bank. This is followed by a description of the monitoring process and escalation process for limit breaches.

The policy template would cover the following.

**Capital Targets**  The bank will monitor and report its forecast regulatory capital base and risk-weighted assets (RWA) per business line to Finance and Treasury. The responsibility for regulatory reporting lies with a dedicated department. The bank's current operational targets are:

> Core Tier 1:   [ ] per cent
> Total Tier 1:   [ ] per cent
> Total capital:   [ ] per cent.

The Finance department will maintain a 3-year rolling forecast and report this to ALCO. Forecast or actual breaches of the internal capital ratios and ultimately the regulatory capital ratios will be reported to the Head of Treasury and to ALCO as well as the regulatory authority. A regulatory breach should be very rare and the bank's risk management processes will require escalation prior to such an event. Upon escalation, management actions will be considered to rectify the position.

The Treasury department will undertake capital stress testing to assess the potential capital impact of changes in firm-specific and market-wide business conditions. Where the test results indicate a potential breach of target rations, this must be reported to ALCO. Mitigating action should then be undertaken after approval from ALCO.

The actions considered to rectify any capital adequacy positions will also be tested during the stress testing exercises. There, actions range from the improvement of business processes, the sell-down of assets, and the change in balance sheet strategy, to a rights issue to obtain more capital. Each action will have wide ranging impact and therefore needs to be considered in detail.

**Risk-weighted Assets and Economic Capital Demand**   RWA balances (i.e., the regulatory Pillar 1 view of risk) and economic capital demand (the internal view of risk) must be reported to Finance, Treasury, and the business lines. The frequency of reporting may vary from inter-day to monthly depending on the type of risks. RWA forecasts are prepared at month-end; any inconsistency with the Finance general forecast must be reported to ALCO. The RWA forecast should be in line with the bank's capital allocation process. The impact of any business line transaction, whether asset or liability, that is likely to result in a reduction in capital must be reported immediately to ALCO. The process applied is similar in nature to the actuarial control cycle.

**Business Restructuring**   The transfer or disposal of any asset or business line, or any such reorganisation that has an impact on regulatory capital and/or RWAs, must be approved in advance by ALCO.

**Business Line Profit**   The net profit after direct and indirect costs of each business line must be transferred to the central book at year-end. This is a direct cash transfer.

**Capital Resource Management**   A subset of capital management policy is capital resource management policy. The object of this document is to articulate formally how each business line will meet its requirements with regard to adherence to the capital management policy standard, and to ensure that use of capital at the business level is at an optimum in terms of allocation, planning, and management. The efficient use of capital is also a metric in business performance evaluation. The capital resource management policy is part of the process to ensure that capital is allocated efficiently and as part of the bank's strategy.

**Capital Allocation**   Each business line prepares a business case for capital demand, based on RWA and economic capital. Each business case contains key metrics including return on capital, net generation of equity, and economic profit. The Balance Sheet Management department sets targets for RWAs and capital usage as part of the budget forecast and allocation process. Capital is allocated to produce optimum return, in line with the strategy and risk appetite of the bank. The strategy and risk appetite will drill down to each business line. Treasury Balance Sheet Management will present capital usage limits at month-end, for approval by ALCO (see elsewhere for template Treasury organisation structure). Treasury BSM will report current and forecast capital usage to ALCO on a weekly basis.

If a forecast exceeds a limit, the business line will submit a request for mitigating action to be taken or for an increase in limit.

**Performance Metrics**    The Board, having delegated authority to Executive Management Committee (ExCo), will set performance metrics targets for each business line. This will include RoC and capital usage (RWA) metrics, against which performance of each business is evaluated. Some banks also consider economic profit or profit after regulatory capital cost depending on which view of risk is more onerous.

**Portfolio Credit Risk Management**    ALCO is responsible for reviewing and approving the asset pool for credit risk management purposes. This is to ensure that provisions are signed off in a consistent manner, that all trans-actions are in line with the business strategy and risk profile, and that they follow policy on capital usage and regulatory requirements.

**Capital Management Strategy**    We conclude that bank strategy should focus on serving customers, and driving the business via this customer focus. This strategy will be articulated in terms of a financial plan containing all key metrics. It should include an RoC target set in advance, which is aligned to the bank's risk–reward preference. The capital strategy follows on from the overall strategy, and describes how and what capital is allocated to each business line. The plans are then stress tested. The outcomes indicate the potential frictions which may be experienced by each business area. At that point, the bank sets its core Tier 1 capital target level to achieve in line with the risk appetite set by the Board. The point being made here is that capital strategy is a coherent, articulated, and formal plan of action that builds on a regular review of the business, allocation of capital to those businesses, and desired return on capital. This should all be documented as part of the bank's capital strategy, which feeds into the overall strategy. This may sound obvious, but the layperson would be surprised how few banks actually do this.

A bank's management may think that the core Tier 1 ratio to have in place is the starting point of the strategy. In fact almost the contrary could be true: the desired core equity Tier 1 ratio should be arrived at after consideration of the business lines, the results of stress testing and the share of capital allocated to each to support the revenue and RoE target that is desired. The bank should compile an annual, 3-year, and 5-year capital ratio target, aligned to a strategic funding plan, and then target the optimum Tier 1 ratio through setting optimal capital structures. This will be achieved through management of dividends (regular or special), rights issues for significant opportunities, AT1 and T2 issuances, or repurchases and liability management exercises.

As a key part of strategy, the capital management framework at a bank should address the requirements of all the various stakeholders. It should be communicated in a transparent fashion to all internal and external stakeholders, articulating:

- How the risk appetite is aligned to their needs and expectations;
- How and why capital allocation and capital constraints are integrated with funding capabilities and assigned to each business line;
- The extent of tolerance for earnings volatility;
- The framework in which each of the business lines operate, with respect to risk exposure and the type of business undertaken.

Figure 8.9 is a stylised representation of this strategy formulating process. It reiterates that a bank's capital management process is part of

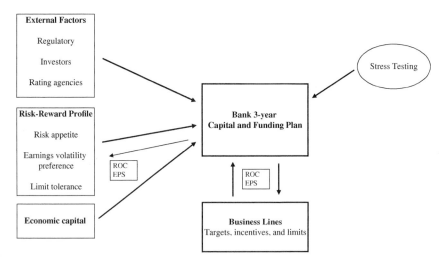

**FIGURE 8.9**    Formulating capital management strategy
*Source: The Principles of Banking* (2012).

overall strategy and is encompassed in a "capital management framework". This process must be the right way round; in other words, it should reflect the priorities for the bank of maintaining confidence, delivering on its customer-focus strategy, and in optimising risk-adjusted return on capital – and in that order.

## "Basel IV" Key Principles

The implementation of Basel II internal models in different jurisdictions has produced considerable variation in RWA outputs, which has resulted in new rules to reduce variation in Credit RWA arising from IRB models by harmonising input parameters, excluding IRB for certain categories, for example, large corporates and applying a capital floor at portfolio level. The capital floor for what is the final form of Basel III, but often referred to erroneously as "Basel IV", is 72.5%, and this standardised floor will be universal in 2022.

Other aspects of Basel III final form include the introduction of a new Standardised Approach to operational risk and abolishing the internal model approach for operational risk. The key aspect of the final form, however, is the revised Standardised Credit Risk approach, with the minimum capital floor and reduced reliance on external ratings. Table 8.3 summarises the key aspects of the rules.

**TABLE 8.3**   Basel III Final Form key features

| | |
|---|---|
| Constraints on IRB models | Remove the Internal Ratings Based (IRB) approach altogether for the following low default portfolios:<br>- banks and other financial institutions<br>- large corporates (total assets > EUR 50bn) |
| | To remove IRB for specialised lending that use banks' estimates of model parameters leaving only the Standardised Approach or the IRB Supervisory Slotting Approach |
| | For the remaining exposures, that can continue to use A-IRB, there will be new floors at exposure-level in respect of PD, LGD and the credit conversion factors used to determine EAD for off-balance sheet items, e.g., the minimum PD for any corporate exposure or mortgage will be 5bps |
| | To introduce a floor at the portfolio level for A-IRB based on a percentage of the applicable Standardised Approach (72.5%) |

(*continued*)

**TABLE 8.3**   Basel III Final Form key features (*Continued*)

| | |
|---|---|
| Revisions to Standardised Credit Risk Approach | Even when banks use an External Credit Risk Assessment Approach, separate due diligence must be performed at origination and thereafter on a regular basis |
| | Bank risk weightings remain a function of credit rating, e.g. A+ to BBB– will have weighting of 50%, but short term exposures with original maturity of less than 3 months may attract a lower weighting |
| | Corporate exposures will also follow credit rating varying from 20% for AAA to AA– up to 150% for BB– or lower. Unrated exposures will continue to attract 100% weighting. SMEs (sales less than €50m) will be given preferential weighting of 85% |
| | Object and Commodities finance will attract a weighting of 120% whereas Project Finance will be weighted at 150% pre-operational phase and reduce to 100% during operational phase |
| | Retail unsecured exposures of < €1m continue to attract 75% weighting |
| | Significant increase in weighting for buy to let mortgages (from 35%) |
| | Facilities secured by commercial real estate may attract a preferential weighting of 60% if the LTV <= 60%, but if the property is the prime source of the cash flows then the weightings will vary from 80% to 130%. Land acquisition, development and construction lending will attract a weighting of 150% |
| | Some increases in off-balance sheet exposures, e.g., undrawn credit card exposures will go from 0% to 10–20%. For some full-payer books this increase will be significant |
| | Changes to methodology for repo-style transactions do allow firms to incorporate up to 40% of the benefits arising from correlation between positions |

## CAPITAL ADEQUACY AND STRESS TESTING

To recap, Pillar 1 of the Basel regulatory capital framework describes the capital requirements for credit, market and operational risk, while Pillar 2 focuses on the economic and internal perspective of banks' capital adequacy. Banks are required to employ satisfactory procedures and systems in order to ensure their capital adequacy is sufficient over the long term, with due attention to all material risks. These procedures are referred to collectively as the internal capital adequacy assessment process (ICAAP). The standard process by which the regulator determines whether a bank is managing capital on a satisfactory basis is also referred to, almost universally, as the ICAAP, which sometimes is taken to refer to the *individual* capital adequacy assessment process. It is known by other terms in certain jurisdictions, but irrespective of the name, we refer here to the process by which a bank "stress tests" its capital level for sufficiency through a range of scenarios and presents its results to the regulator. The regulatory authority will determine if it agrees with the results and thereby determine the level of capital required.

The ICAAP enables the bank (and the regulator) to identify, measure, and aggregate all material risk types and calculate the economic, or internal, capital necessary to cover these risks. As such the ICAAP process is key to the preservation of financial stability and is subject to a high degree of supervisory scrutiny, which does make the process very bureaucratic and administrative. That said, because banks come in many different shapes and sizes, and a variety of balance sheet risk exposures, a number of different approaches may be observed when it comes to the ICAAP process. Business best-practice for a vanilla commercial banking institution is described here.

## ICAAP Primer

In essence, the Basel Accord and its amendments form the basis for the ICAAP. In the EU, the legislative framework was described in CRDII. Further guidance was provided by CEBS (2006), which published 10 principles for the implementation of a consistent and comprehensive ICAAP. In short, all banks are required to document and specify fully the ICAAP, integrate it into the regular risk management process, and review it continuously to ensure it remains fit-for-purpose.

The ICAAP needs to be a risk-based document, comprehensive and detailed, as well as forward-looking. Of course, the results of the ICAAP process need to be consistent with the bank remaining a going concern – if they are not, the bank's Board must implement management actions to redress the matter before presenting results to the regulator. While there is considerable commonality, each ICAAP is ultimately unique to the bank in question, reflecting its specific balance sheet structure and exposure.

**Risk Taxonomy and Quantification**  Before quantifying balance sheet risk exposure, it is important to categorise it, or as some banks term it, compile a taxonomy of risk. Not all banks exhibit all identified risk type exposures.

Under Pillar 2, all material risk types need to be quantified, and thereby covered with adequate capital provision. Certain types of risk (conduct risk, reputation, etc.) are not straightforward to quantify, so banks will apply a qualitative assessment. Typically banks and, crucially, certain regulators employ the value-at-risk (VaR) technique to estimate risk exposure on the balance sheet. For those familiar with VaR, the logic of its methodology is consistent with a trading book, or a pool of assets that are re-priced on a regular basis. However, this logic is less consistent in a banking book. Nevertheless, the VaR approach remains the one that is most in use and often demanded by the regulator to assess the value at risk to the firm. The actual methods vary from simply risk weights to detailed economic risk assessments. In addition, regulators use peer group comparisons as well and any outliers per business area are interrogated further.

Table 8.4 summarises the Level 1 risks within the risk taxonomy for a vanilla UK commercial bank.

It is common to see the variance–covariance ("parametric"), historical simulation, and Monte Carlo simulation approaches used in equal measure amongst banks. Typically, banks apply a 1-year holding period and 1-sided confidence levels of 95% or 99%. For market risk, banks often apply a 1-day and 10-day holding period. Note that most banks classify interest rate risk in the banking book (IRRBB) as a market risk, albeit a non-traded market risk. Again, it is common to observe VaR as the preferred measurement technique for IRRBB as well; however, the author's recommended approach is to supplement this with traditional modified duration analysis ("gap" analysis) as well.

**Stress Tests**  In the post-2008 era, all banks, except perhaps the very smallest, specify a large number and variety of stress tests. That said, there is considerable commonality in approach. Generally, the primary focus is on scenario analyses, often based on 5-year historical worst-case values or hypothetical scenarios. The latter are sometimes also required to include a "reverse stress test", which is a hypothetical scenario that would break the bank. In theory, as stress tests allow for the identification of sensitivities to specific risk factors, they should be a worthwhile exercise as they provide value-added input to the bank's risk management process and subsequent management actions. The danger, as with all exercises subject to considerable regulatory supervision, is that the stress testing process becomes an excessively bureaucratic one and more of a "box-ticking" exercise. This must be avoided and ALCO is the appropriate forum to review the process and ensure this does not happen.

**TABLE 8.4** Level 1 risk taxonomy

| Level 1 Risk | 1st LoD Risk Owners | 2nd LoD Risk Owner | Definition |
|---|---|---|---|
| CREDIT | MD's of each Business area / MD Sales & Marketing | CRO | Risk of loss from the failure of a customer to meet its obligations to settle outstanding amounts, including Concentration Risk. |
| OPERATIONAL | COO, Head of HR, Legal & CFO | | The risk of loss resulting from inadequate or failed internal processes, people, or from external events, including legal risk and supplier risk. |
| IT | Head of IT | | Loss of technology services due to loss of data, system, or data centre including, where applicable, failure of back up processes and/or a third party to restore services. |
| COMPLIANCE | ExCo members | | The risk of material financial costs (including rectification and remediation costs), legal, and regulatory sanctions, or reputational damage the bank may suffer as a result of its failure to comply with relevant laws, regulations, principles, rules, standards, and codes of conduct applicable to its activities, in letter and spirit. <br>▪ Conduct is the risk that actions undertaken by the bank and/or its staff could lead to customer detriment, employee detriment (outside of appetite), inappropriate control of financial crime, and related activity or negative impact on market stability. <br>▪ Prudential Compliance is the risk of material loss or liability, legal or regulatory sanctions, or reputational damage arising from breaching existing relevant prudential policy, laws, or regulations, in any jurisdiction in which the entity operates. |

*(continued)*

**TABLE 8.4**  Level 1 risk taxonomy (*Continued*)

| Level 1 Risk | 1st LoD Risk Owners | 2nd LoD Risk Owner | Definition |
|---|---|---|---|
| NON TRADED MARKET | Head of Treasury | | The Market Risk arising in non-trading assets and liabilities. |
| CAPITAL & STRESS TESTING | CFO | | The risk of not being able to conduct business in base or stress conditions due to insufficient qualifying capital as well as the failure to assess, monitor, plan, and manage capital adequacy requirements. |
| FUNDING & LIQUIDITY | Head of Treasury | | The risk that the company is not able to meet its liabilities as they fall due, or has insufficient resources to repay withdrawals. |
| REPUTATIONAL | ExCo members | | The risk of brand damage and/or financial cost due to the failure to meet stakeholder expectations of the company's conduct and/or performance. |
| BUSINESS | CFO / (+MD's of Biz areas / S&M) | | The risk that the company suffers losses as a result of adverse variance in its revenues and/or costs relative to its business plan and strategy. |
| STRATEGIC | CEO (Board) | | The risk that the company will make inappropriate strategic choices, is unable to successfully implement selected strategies, or changes arise which invalidate strategies. This includes all divestment programme-related risks. |
| GROUP (for subsidiary entities) | CEO | | The dependency of the company on the Group for key support areas, e.g., Funding, Liquidity, Capital, and other Back Office functions. |

## ICAAP Process Guidelines

To recap, Basel II introduced the three-pillar architecture for capital and risk management (Figure 8.10).

On the one hand, Pillar 2 (Supervisory Review and Evaluation Process – SREP) requires banks to implement a process for assessing their capital adequacy in relation to their risk profiles as well as a strategy for maintaining their capital levels. This is the ICAAP. On the other hand, Pillar 2 also requires the regulatory authority to review all banks for their capital adequacy and to impose any necessary supervisory measures following such review. So there are two parts to this process:

- The ICAAP which comprises all of a bank's procedures and measures designed to ensure that there exists:
    - The appropriate identification and measurement of all balance sheet risks;
    - An appropriate level of internal capital in relation to the bank's risk profile;
    - The application and further development of suitable risk management systems.
- The supervisory review process or SRP (sometimes SREP) which covers the processes and measures defined in the principles listed above, including the review and evaluation of the ICAAP process, an independent assessment of the bank's risk profile, and where necessary instructing the bank to undertake further prudential measures.

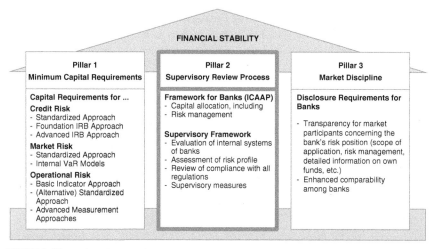

**FIGURE 8.10**   The Three Pillars of Capital and Risk Management
*Source*: BCBS.

**ICAAP Implementation**   Before a bank can begin designing its ICAAP, it should first define its relevant target state. The steps involved are illustrated at Figure 8.11.

What does Figure 8.11 mean in practice? Each step is considered in turn below.

- Definition of Bank-Specific Requirements (target state)
  In the first step, the bank compiles and sets its strategy based on its goal or vision. It will test this strategy against a list of requirements based on national regulator statements (for example, the EU CRDIV). Next, these requirements have to be specified for the individual bank. Thus in the course of a self-assessment, the bank should identify its material risks, which arise from the implementation of its strategy. The ICAAP therefore facilitates assessing the sensitivity and risks in a firm's strategy. The requirements with regard to ICAAP methods should be defined in light of the bank's risk profile, as they need to be fit for purpose but also meet regulatory rigour. Typically, the introduction of new methods begins with relatively simple, robust solutions which are then developed and refined on an ongoing basis. The full list of requirements then represents the target state for ICAAP purposes and defines requirements with regard to methods, procedures, processes, and organisation.
- Gap Analysis
  Once the target state has been defined, the bank should analyse those requirements which are currently not (or not completely) fulfilled. These gaps pertain both to the execution of strategy as well as the capital assessment process. It is the business team's responsibility to address the former and its risk management teams would survey the current state of methods, processes, and organisation in place in the internal risk management system. This might include the regulator's requirements for calculating capital amounts, or activities aimed at fulfilling the minimum standards for the credit origination business. The process is not restricted to risk managers. In terms of the three lines of defence model, the process starts with all business lines which should analyse their current state and report it centrally to Risk (and ALCO). Gaps in implementation can then be identified by comparing the requirements

**FIGURE 8.11**   Steps involved in the design of ICAAP

with the current state. This comparison of target and actual states could be carried out in the course of a workshop attended by representatives from the business lines, with the results documented and reported to all relevant stakeholders. The bank can then assess the significance and consequences of the gaps identified as well as identify the necessary management actions as a result.

■ Implementation Planning
In implementation planning, the first step is to prioritise the required measures identified in the previous process. This way a clear ranking can be defined in order to deploy implementation resources effectively. Measures identified should be combined in individual work packages and coordinated with business lines; this process requires that specific roles and responsibilities be identified and assigned. As part of the process, the bank should set binding deadlines which reflect resource and capacity available within the firm.

■ Implementation
Put simply, this stage involves undertaking and delivering on the process measures identified in the previous stage. This includes employing human resources as well as IT capacity as required by the ICAAP. The process-related aspects and responsibilities within the ICAAP can then be defined and documented. This may involve quantifying and aggregating risks and coverage capital, monitoring limits, or taking measures in the *ex-post* control process. The ICAAP is integrated into the bank's strategic and operational control mechanisms (for example, annual budgeting and planning on the basis of risk indicators and coverage capital). Once implementation is completed, the bank should have in place adequate methods, processes, and systems to ensure its risk-bearing capacity over the long term.

**What Makes a Good ICAAP?** In essence, the ICAAP process and its published output as presented to the national regulator should be a value-added exercise that reflects the interests of all stakeholders in the long-term viability of the bank as a going concern. This is not a platitude. However, because of the onerous regulation and reporting process in place in most jurisdictions, the process often boils down to producing something which the regulator signs off on. This is not the best approach to ICAAP production. To the question, "What makes a good ICAAP?" the obvious answer is a document which presents the firm's strategy with all material risk exposures, on a forward-looking basis, and demonstrates that these exposures are covered by adequate capital levels, risk management systems, and management actions to rectify stresses in order to ensure the successful implementation of the strategy.

As a checklist, we should note that the following factors are crucial in the actual implementation and successful presentation of an ICAAP:

- Early Detection of Gaps in Fulfilment
  A bank should make efforts to detect gaps in the fulfilment of requirements as early as possible so that it can take the appropriate measures in a timely and economical manner. Closing these gaps quickly will improve the bank's internal risk management and thus enhances its ability to ensure its risk-bearing capacity.
- Selection of Methods
  The bank should determine the methods and procedures which best suit its needs, as these determine the validity of the ICAAP as well as the required implementation resources. In the course of selecting methods, the bank should not only consider its current risk profile but also anticipate planned developments in individual risk types. If, for example, a decision has already been made that trading will be expanded in the medium term, then it makes sense to introduce more advanced procedures from the outset when designing the ICAAP.
- Master Plan and Project Management
  The bank should develop a master implementation plan which covers planning, budgeting, and a prioritisation of all ICAAP implementation tasks. There should be one overall, dedicated project manager (most probably someone within Risk or Treasury). This master plan forms the basis for requesting internal and external capacities and may well involve planning resources over a period of several years. For example, implementation might already be well underway for the most important risk types while measures for other risk types are still being planned. Once it reaches a certain scale, the master plan should be transformed into a detailed project plan, which serves to reduce complexity and create transparency with regard to the current implementation status. It is also important to set binding deadlines and responsibilities on the basis of this plan. A project manager should then monitor and control the performance of individual tasks. Project management should seek to prevent any conflicts of interest between the business lines involved in implementation and to maintain an aggregate and holistic view of the project.
- Communication
  The need for, and benefits of, the ICAAP have to be clearly communicated to all staff. The fundamental concept of the ICAAP is not something for senior executives only to appreciate, but for all business lines. An example is a newly designed limit allocation system or a change to the organisation chart more likely to be supported by staff if they

arc informcd about thc nccd for thcsc mcasures in a transparent and understandable manner. Insufficient communication in implementation projects often results in low levels of identification or even rejection and demotivation. By applying an appropriate communication policy and setting a good example, senior executives should generate the employee acceptance necessary for successful implementation of the ICAAP.

▪ Know-how and Resources
One major objective of the ICAAP is to foster the development of an appropriate internal risk management culture. For this reason, expertise in this area is a key success factor in the implementation of the ICAAP. It is important for the bank to have the necessary resources (employees, systems) at its disposal in the ICAAP implementation process. Resource requirements will depend on the bank's size and risk profile, as well as the difference between the current status and the defined requirements.

▪ Data Quality and IT Systems
Data quality (completeness, availability) is especially important because it determines the reliability and accuracy of calculated results (for example, risk indicators and coverage capital). The process of data quality assurance begins with accurate data capture and goes as far as ensuring data availability in the ICAAP. Especially for risk management, it is necessary and worthwhile to ensure timely automated evaluations due to the large data quantities involved and the sometimes complex calculation algorithms used. In its ICAAP, the bank can rely on existing risk management systems (risk measurement, limit monitoring) if they meet the defined requirements. Historically, maintaining and updating the IT structures of many banks requires copious resources. It is a required investment, however, because the lack of uniform data pools can create considerable difficulties in assessing the true extent of balance sheet risk.

## Principal ICAAP Requirements

Based on supervisory requirements and the benefits from a business perspective, the basic requirements to be taken into account in the production of an ICAAP are:

▪ *Securing capital adequacy*: Banks should define a risk strategy which contains descriptions of its risk policy instruments and objectives. This is a Board-level statement. The explicit formulation of such a risk strategy aids in the early detection of deviations from appetite and tolerance.
▪ *ICAAP as an internal management tool*: The ICAAP should form an integral part of the management and decision-making process.

- *Responsibility of the management*: The overall responsibility for the ICAAP is assigned to the Board and senior executive, which must ensure that the bank's risk-bearing capacity is secured and that all material risks are identified, measured, and limited.
- *Assessment of all material risks*: The ICAAP focuses on ensuring bank-specific internal capital adequacy from a business perspective. For this purpose, all material risks must be assessed. Therefore, the focus is laid on those risks which are (or could be) significant for the individual bank.
- *Processes and internal review procedures*: Merely designing risk assessment and control methods is not sufficient to secure a bank's risk-bearing capacity. It is only in the implementation of appropriate processes and reviews that the ICAAP is actually brought to bear. This ensures that every employee knows which steps to take in various situations. For the sake of improving risk management on an ongoing basis, the development of an ICAAP should be regarded not as a one-time project but as a continuous development process. In this way, input from ongoing experience can be used to develop simpler methods into a more complex system with enhanced control functions.

## Risk Indicators

The ICAAP should present all relevant material balance sheet risk through a series of risk exposure indicators. These are specific to the risk types. Indicators presenting the aggregate view are also required, i.e. the firm's capital adequacy ratios as well as risk-adjusted performance indicators.

**Credit Risk Indicators** The structure of the credit portfolio provides initial indications of a bank's risk appetite. A large share of loans in a certain asset class (for example, commercial real-estate) may point to increased risk. In addition, the presence of complex financing transactions such as specialised lending (project finance, for instance) may also indicate a larger risk appetite. A bank can use credit assessments (such as credit ratings) to measure the share of borrowers with poor creditworthiness in its portfolio; this provides an indication of default risk. The bank will also consider the portfolio in terms of delinquency and impairment. The amount of available collateral – and thus the unsecured volume – also plays a role in this context. The lower the unsecured volume is, the lower the risk generally is; this relationship is also reflected in future supervisory regulations for calculating capital requirements. In this context, however, the type and quality of collateral are decisive; this can be assessed by asking the following questions:

- To what extent is the retention or liquidation of the collateral legally enforceable?
- How will the value of the collateral develop?
- Is there any correlation between the value of the collateral and the creditworthiness of the debtor?

A close inspection of the credit portfolio will provide further insights with regard to any existing concentration risks. In order to assess the size structure or granularity of its portfolio, the bank can also assess the size and number of large exposures. The bank should also consider the distribution of exposures among industries (for example, construction business, transport, tourism, and so on) in assessing its concentration risk. If a bank conducts extensive operations overseas (share of foreign assets), it is appropriate to take a close look at the risks associated with those activities as well, such as country and transfer risks. The share of foreign currency loans in a bank's credit portfolio can also point to concentration risks. If the share of foreign currency loans is very high, exchange rate fluctuations can have adverse effects on the credit quality of the borrowers. If the foreign currency loans are serviced using a repayment vehicle which is heavily exposed to market risks, this indicates an additional source of risk which should be monitored accordingly and controlled as necessary.

**Market Risks in the Trading Book, Foreign Exchange Risks at the Overall Bank Level**   This exposure is calculated typically using a VaR approach. A bank can determine its sensitivity to foreign exchange fluctuations on the basis of its open foreign exchange positions and (in the broadest sense) open term positions. The influence of foreign exchange fluctuations on the default probability of borrowers with foreign currency loans is also considered.

**Interest Rate Risk in the Banking Book (IRRBB)**   The results reported in interest rate risk statistics (part of regulatory reporting requirements) constitute an essential indicator of the level of interest rate risk in the banking book. The traditional approach here is to apply modified duration analysis such as parallel yield curve shifts (for example, the effects of a 200 basis point interest rate shock on the present value of the balance sheet). Of course if this method demonstrates that material interest rate risks exist in the banking book, regulators usually require more "sophisticated" risk measurement methods to be applied, with output including a precise quantification of risks in terms of their effects on the income statement. Another risk indicator should cover proprietary trading both on- and off-balance sheet. In accordance with the proportionality principle in the ICAAP (larger, more sophisticated balance sheets require larger, more sophisticated ICAAPs) the corresponding requirements increase in line with the scale of derivatives trading activities. Even in cases where a bank primarily uses derivatives to hedge other transactions or portfolios, the effectiveness of hedging transactions (the hedge effectiveness) should be examined in order to avoid undesirable side effects. In the case of on-balance sheet proprietary transactions, the need for more precise risk control grows along with the scale and complexity of the positions held, for example, "alternative investments" or structured bonds.

**Operational Risk Indicators**   Two important indicators of operational risk are the size and complexity of a bank. As the number of employees, business partners, customers, branches, systems, and processes at a bank increases, its risk potential also tends to rise. Another risk indicator in this category is process intensity, for example, the number of transactions and volumes handled in payments processing, loan processing, securities operations, and proprietary trading. Failures (for example, due to overloaded systems) can bring about severe economic losses in banks with high levels of process intensity.[2] The number of lawsuits filed against a bank can also serve as an indicator of operational risks. A large number of lawsuits suggests that there are substantial sources of risk within the bank, such as inadequate system security or insufficient care in processes and control mechanisms. In cases where business operations (for example, the processing activities mentioned above) are outsourced, the bank cannot automatically assume that operational risks have been eliminated completely. This is because a bank's dependence on an outsourcing service provider means that risks incurred by the latter can have negative repercussions for the bank. Therefore, the content and quality of the service level agreement as well as the quality and creditworthiness of the outsourcing service provider can also serve as risk indicators in this context.

The risk indicators may be presented as per the following template (note that more than one bank has been amalgamated to reflect different approaches), as illustrated in Table 8.5.

In Table 8.5, for Bank A the risk types mentioned above would have little significance under the proportionality principle. The bank shows a low level of complexity and low risk levels. Besides, Bank A does not have any

---

[2] A good example of this was the failure of Royal Bank of Scotland's ATM machines over a three-day period in June 2012. In 2014, the UK Financial Conduct Authority imposed a several hundred million pound fine on the bank for this IT failure.

**TABLE 8.5**   Example risk indicator levels

| Risk Indicator   Risk Subtype | Bank A | Bank B | Bank C | Bank D |
|---|---|---|---|---|
| General risk indicators (e.g., size) | Small | Small | Medium | Large |

Specific risks
    Credit risk
    Equity risk
    Concentration risk
    - Foreign currency loans
    - Industries
    - Size classes
    - Country risks
Market risks
Interest rate risk in the banking book
Operational risks
Liquidity risks
Other risks

High significance
Medium significance
Low significance

trading positions. For the purpose of measuring its risks and calculating its internal capital needs, Bank A could calculate its capital requirements using the Standardised Approach, or the Basic Indicator Approach in the case of operational risk.

In terms of its total assets and number of employees, Bank B is comparable to Bank A, but Bank B's transactions show a markedly higher risk level. In addition, concentration risks exist with regard to size classes (for example, several relatively large loans to medium-sized businesses), borrowers in the same industry, and foreign currency loans. In this bank, methods which go beyond the Standardised Approach should be employed and/or adequate qualitative measures (monitoring / reporting) should be set. Furthermore, Bank B should pay attention to concentration risks, for example, by adhering to suitable individual borrower limits based on creditworthiness or by implementing minimum standards for foreign currency loans. In this example, using more advanced systems may be appropriate in other areas, such as interest rate risk in the banking book.

Bank C shows high credit exposures to SMEs and has also granted a number of relatively large loans. This results in a certain degree of concentration risk. In addition, the bank is exposed to relatively high interest rate risks. In fact, Bank D has large exposures to almost all risk types. The bank's size and structure can be described (such as a VaR model) for interest rate risk at Banks C and D; Bank D should also use a more sophisticated model for market risk. Due to the higher risk level and the existing complexity with regard to credit risk, the bank may use other risk-sensitive techniques based on the IRB approach or a credit portfolio model.

The individual institutions in this example have to define the scale and type of risk management system which is appropriate to their activities, with due attention to the regulator's requirements. The choice of suitable risk measurement procedures to determine risks and internal capital needs plays a key role in this context. Moreover, the proportionality concept also has effects on process and organisational design: banks which demonstrate a high level of complexity or a large risk appetite have to fulfil more comprehensive requirements.

An example of the presentation of the risk indicators is given in Table 8.6.

## Documentation Requirements

The ICAAP must remain a living document. That means the Board must use the ICAAP document to familiarise and challenge risk as well as capital management processes in the bank. The ICAAP has to be designed in a transparent and comprehensible manner. This will not only aid bank staff in understanding, accepting, and applying the defined procedures, it will also make it easier for the bank to review the adequacy of its methods and rules regularly, and to enhance them on an ongoing basis. Critically, it makes the SRP (or SREP) process by the regulator a smoother one.

For this reason, it is necessary to compile formal written documentation on all essential elements of the ICAAP. In creating the required documentation, the bank should ensure that the depth and scope of its explanations are tailored to the relevant target group. It is sensible to use various levels of detail in the actual implementation of documentation requirements. For illustration purposes, a sample scenario with three levels is shown at Figure 8.12.

At the top level, it is advisable to articulate the bank's fundamental strategic attitude toward risk management. This will reflect the institution's basic orientation and guide all ICAAP-related decisions. The basic strategic attitude can be documented in the form of the firm's strategy – that is the purpose and objectives of the bank and how it executes on this purpose. This

**TABLE 8.6**   Sample Incorporation of an Institution's Relevant Risk Types in the ICAAP

| Risk Type | Risk Subtype | Risk Level | Justification (if immaterial) | Risk Assessment Procedure Used |
|---|---|---|---|---|
| Credit risk | Counterparty / default risk | Very high | | Foundation IRB Approach |
| | Equity risk | Immaterial | Equity investments as share of total assets < 0.5% | Foundation IRB Approach |
| | Country / transfer risk | Medium | | Strict limitation (structural limit) |
| | Securitisation risk | Immaterial | No involvement in securitisation programmes (neither as originator nor as investor) | Not considered |
| | Credit risk concentrations | High | | Strict limitation (structural limit) and increased monitoring |
| | Residual risk from credit risk mitigation techniques | Medium | | Qualitative assessment, process-based reduction of risk (use of standard contracts, "four eyes" principle, regular revaluation of collateral, etc.) |
| Market risk | Market risks in the trading book | Low | | Standard supervisory methods |
| | Foreign exchange risks in the banking book | Medium | | Standard supervisory methods |
| Interest rate risks in the banking book | | High | | Value-at-risk model |
| Operational risk | | Medium | | Basic Indicator Approach |
| Liquidity risk | | Low | | Qualitative measures |
| Other risks | Strategic risk | Medium | | Cushion |
| | Reputation risk | Low | | Cushion |
| | Capital risk | Medium | | Cushion |
| | Earnings risk | Medium | | Cushion |

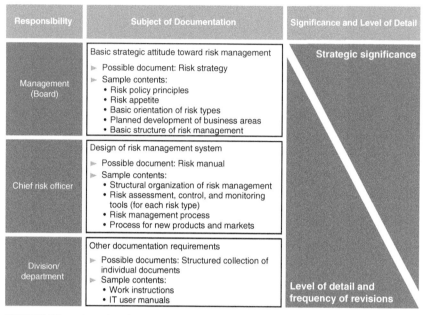

| Responsibility | Subject of Documentation | Significance and Level of Detail |
|---|---|---|
| Management (Board) | Basic strategic attitude toward risk management<br>▶ Possible document: Risk strategy<br>▶ Sample contents:<br>• Risk policy principles<br>• Risk appetite<br>• Basic orientation of risk types<br>• Planned development of business areas<br>• Basic structure of risk management | Strategic significance |
| Chief risk officer | Design of risk management system<br>▶ Possible document: Risk manual<br>▶ Sample contents:<br>• Structural organization of risk management<br>• Risk assessment, control, and monitoring tools (for each risk type)<br>• Risk management process<br>• Process for new products and markets | |
| Division/ department | Other documentation requirements<br>▶ Possible documents: Structured collection of individual documents<br>▶ Sample contents:<br>• Work instructions<br>• IT user manuals | Level of detail and frequency of revisions |

**FIGURE 8.12**    Three-level scenario

will be executed via a business plan. The business plan will be delivered subject to a risk strategy. The essential components of such a strategy include:

- Risk policy principles;
- Statements as to the bank's appetite;
- A description of the bank's fundamental orientation with regard to individual risk types;
- Comments on the current business strategy and future development of the business;
- Areas of risk and uncertainty in the business strategy, and how these risks are managed in terms of the risk policy principles and the bank's risk appetite.

The risk strategy should be approved by the entire management Board of the bank and so it should be in summary form. At the next level down, the bank should provide a more detailed explanation of the methods and instruments employed for risk control and management. In practice, such a document is frequently referred to as the bank's risk management policy manual. Essentially, the risk manual contains a description of the risk management process, definitions of all relevant risk types, explanations of evaluation, control and monitoring procedures for risk positions (separate for each risk type), and a discussion of the process of launching new products or entering new markets. In general, the depth of these explanations also implies that it will be necessary to revise at least certain parts of the document on a regular basis.

This level of detail will be contained in the executive summary of the report. Further outline will be provided in the body, while all technical detail required will be provided in appendices to the document.

## ICAAP Process: Worked Example of Presentation

In this section, we show a worked example of a typical ICAAP presentation to a regulator. The bank in question is a vanilla UK commercial bank with retail and corporate business line exposure, and with a balance sheet of approximately £22 billion.

In Table 8.1 we showed a summary of the key ICAAP processes undertaken in the bank. Figure 8.1 illustrated the governance structure of the ICAAP framework, mapping the components of the ICAAP to the internal processes, governance, and approvals, ultimately for the regulatory SREP review.

However the ICAAP also must pass the "use test", which requires that the process and planning are to be derived from the business strategy, and that the business lines take an active part in the process. Hence Figure 8.13 is an illustration of an all-embracing process for ICAAP preparation and submission, in that it shows the incorporation of the business lines. Figure 8.14 is a qualitative description of the process.

**Components of the Internal Capital Assessment**    The Basel regulatory regime prescribes three "pillars" of risk exposure capital input. In the UK, generally the capital assessment process combines two views: a point-in-time (Pillar 1

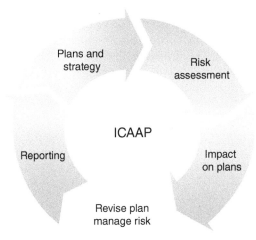

**FIGURE 8.13**    All-embracing ICAAP governance process

---

**Process summary**

A level of risk appetite will be set or revised from previous iterations. The **strategy** drivers include balance sheet and revenue growth, profitability and capital consumption, as well as wider stakeholder objectives and a strategic ALM focus

In the **plans** a projection of the income statement as well as the corresponding change in the balance sheet forms the **baseline.**

The **risks** inherent in the business (as articulated by the baseline) must be identified, measured, and monitored through the process. These risks are tested to appetite.

The impact of each risk on the plan must be assessed. In particular this assessment will drive the **capital required** both on an internal and regulatory basis as well as the **funding profile** to support the business.

Based on the risk assessment, their impact will be tested through scenario analysis and stress testing. **Plans or risk appetite may be revised** to optimise the strategy or contingent management action plans developed.

The results of the risk assessment, capital requirement assessment, and consequential value metrics will be **reported** to the business areas. Analysis of change forms part of this process.

---

**FIGURE 8.14**  Summary of the ICAAP planning and implementation process, linking strategy, and capital management

and Pillar 2A) and a forward-looking (Pillar 2B) view. These are described as follows:

- Point-in-Time Capital Assessment (1-year horizon) Pillar 1 and Pillar 2A: these form part of an Individual Capital Guidance (ICG), which is the minimum capital requirements the bank has to meet at all times. Pillar 2A assesses risks not in Pillar 1 or risks not adequately captured under the Pillar 1 framework. The process is illustrated at Figure 8.15.
- Pillar 2B refers to the individual capital guidance and is set for each bank based on the output of the bilateral SREP process where the regulatory capital requirement is compared to the internal / economic capital requirement.
- The capital planning buffer (CPB) which is part of the internal capital target is the amount of capital to be held, in addition to the ICG such that it can be used in stress to absorb losses in order to prevent the bank from breaching its ICG. It reflects the change in the capital surplus / deficit and is illustrated at Figure 8.16 below.

The governance of this process is not cast in stone: different banks will organise it in different ways. Certainly there is no one single correct

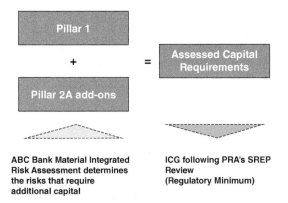

**FIGURE 8.15**  Point-in-Time Capital Assessment (1-year horizon) Pillar 1 and Pillar 2A

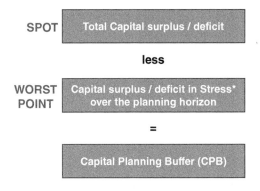

\* Impact of management actions/ recovery options is included

**FIGURE 8.16**  Capital surplus / deficit

way to approach this, but the governance structure must be fit-for-purpose in a way which provides confidence to the regulator and clearly articulates the risk appetite to the Board. The author's recommendation is to first compile a "Risk Taxonomy" associated with the capital management and ICAAP process, and then allocate roles and responsibilities based on this taxonomy.

In order to ensure a consistent approach to risk identification and measurement, it is preferable to compile a "Risk Taxonomy" associated with the risk management framework of the bank and used in the capital management and ICAAP process.

Roles and responsibilities will be defined based on the risk management framework of the bank. This is often based on the three lines of defence framework based on business as the first line, risk as the second line, and audit and the Board as the third line, affirming that the second line review process functions properly.

Table 8.7 is a summary of a template risk taxonomy for the ICAAP and capital stress testing process.

**TABLE 8.7** Capital management risk taxonomy

| Aspect | Key Facts |
|---|---|
| Definition | The Risk Taxonomy is a catalogue of the inherent risks associated with the bank's business, its customers, and the regulatory environment in which it operates. |
| Rationale | In order to establish and maintain the Risk Framework and its various components, it is important to agree a list of risks (Risk Taxonomy) and associated accountabilities around which the Framework is designed and built. The Risk Taxonomy provides a common risk language for all stakeholders whether internal or external. |
| Preparation | The Group Taxonomy has been used as a starting point and then tailored to the ABC Bank business based on discussion with Business and Risk stakeholders (Subject Matter Experts), coupled with a review of ABC Bank's strategy, including product strategy, profit and loss account, and balance sheet and other related information / documentation. This will need to change and evolve as the company's internal and external environments change. |
| Structure | There are three levels of risks as follows: <br> Level 1: These are the headline risk types common to most financial institutions, e.g., Credit, Market, and Operational. <br> Level 2: These are the identifiable sub-risks of the Level 1; for example, Core Lending risk and Concentration risk are sub-risks of Level 1 Credit Risk. <br> Level 3: These arise where Level 2 risks require to be sub-divided further into specific risks requiring risk management. |
| Status | ExCo have approved the Risk Taxonomy and this will now be used when rolling out the Risk Framework. |
| Importance for ICAAP | The Risk Taxonomy is an important starting point for the MIRA process, which in turn is used in the capital assessment process. |

## The MIRA

The material integrated risk assessment (MIRA) is a key part of the ICAAP process. It helps to place the key drivers of the ICAAP in context. It is a basic "Top Down" risk assessment tool across all risk types. It identifies material risks and assesses the risk and control framework in place to mitigate those risks. The MIRA is an important input to the capital assessment process because it identifies material risks and then assesses the capital treatment required for each of those risks. Material risks are either managed and have capital set aside, or else are managed away, not requiring capital. An example illustration of the output is given in the next section.

**Capital Treatment of Material Risks** In our example illustration, the MIRA material risks are summarised below. These are used to determine whether the risk is either "managed and capitalised" or else just "managed". In this case, the MIRA has identified that the material add-on risks are for credit risk concentration, operational risk, and non-traded market risk, and these are then discussed in more detail in Table 8.8.

**Pillar 2 Add-on** From the above, the bank in question has to calculate its Pillar 2 add-on for credit risk concentration and non-traded interest rate risk. The relevant points here are:

- Single name concentration (SNC)
- Sector Concentrations (SRC)
  It is an add-on for excess concentration in certain sectors such as CRE.
- Non-Traded Market Risk (NTMR) – Method of Assessment
  The bank does not incur traded market risk. Non-Traded Market Risk arises from:
  - Re-pricing risk: arises from timing differences in the maturity (for fixed-rate) and re-pricing (for floating-rate) of assets and liabilities. There re-pricing mismatches can expose net interest income and economic value to fluctuations in interest rates;
  - Yield Curve risk: arises when yield curve shifts differently between the short end and the long end and this can have adverse effects on a bank's economic value where re-pricing mismatches exist. The Liquid Asset Buffer of £3.5bn is expected to be held in gilts for an average duration of four to seven years, and this would be subject to fluctuating gilts prices if unhedged or to swap spread risk if hedged with swaps. For the purpose of an interim capital assessment, NTMR is

**TABLE 8.8**    MIRA material risks

| Risk Type | Pillar 1 | Pillar 2A |
|---|---|---|
| Credit Risk | Advanced Internal Ratings Based (subject to PRA approval) and Standardised approaches are utilised. | Single Name, Sector, Geographical – Methodology to calculate capital charges is work in progress. |
| Operational Risk (including IT risk) | The Standardised Approach (TSA) is utilised. The 3-year average gross income grouped by business line is multiplied by a % factor (12%, 15%) depending on business line. | The bank will be developing a comprehensive programme for scenario analysis for the next 3 years. Consequently, two interim approaches have been developed for the purpose of determining current capital assessments, based on scaling Group Group operational risk capital modelling results, using gross income as the scaling factor. |
| Compliance Risk (conduct and prudential) | Covered through the Operational Risk capital charge. | |
| Non-Traded Market Risk | Not covered in Pillar 1 | VaR approach is adopted for capital assessment. |
| Liquidity and Funding Risk | Liquidity and Funding risk is covered by the ILAA | |
| Capital and Stress Testing Risk | Capital and Stress Testing Risk is managed through the capital planning process, stress testing, and scenario analysis. | |
| Strategic Risk | Not covered in Pillar 1 | Managed through the Business and Risk strategy and not capitalised. |
| Reputational Risk | Not covered in Pillar 1 | Any financial losses related to reputational risk are covered by the capital treatment relevant to the risk type through which the loss manifests. For non-financial events the relevant capital treatment is predominantly covered by the operational risk capital charge. |
| Business Risk | Not covered in Pillar 1 | The risk is managed and taken into account under integrated stress testing where income and expenses are stressed. For capital purposes, this risk is captured through the Capital Planning Buffer (Pillar 2B). |

**Key:**

Risk is managed and capitalised

Risk is managed

Pillar 2A Risk

measured using a Value-at-Risk model based on a 99% confidence interval over a 1-year holding period. In addition a parallel shift of +/–100 and +/–200 basis point parallel shifts are also calculated and reported to ALCO. Non-Traded Market Risk (NTMR) – Estimates of Exposure: The risk exposure on the estimated LAB is a PV01 of *circa* £820k for an average 4-year duration. The VaR estimated on a hedged or unhedged basis (using a 99% confidence interval for a 1-year holding period) is between £50 and £80m. Thus, the Pillar 2 add-on will be £80mm.

**Operational Risk**　In normal circumstances, to calculate a robust Pillar 2 operational risk capital charge, a bank would use a variety of data including internal loss event data, external loss event data, key risk indicators, and the output of scenario analyses. For a new bank, there may be insufficient internal loss event data specific to its operations to be able to undertake any meaningful modelling capability. As a consequence, such a bank (as in our case study here) would develop a comprehensive programme for scenario analysis which it would use until such time as three years' worth of loss event data was accumulated.

In the meantime, while the scenario analysis approach is being developed, the example bank here adopts a scaling approach based on the Group operational risk economic capital model, which considers Group internal loss event experience, its own programme of scenario analyses outputs, and relevant external loss event data.

**ICAAP Approach**　In order to deliver a credible Pillar 2A operational risk capital charge, the bank takes its five largest risks based on its Material Integrated Risk Assessment (MIRA) and subjects them to workshopped scenario analysis. All other MIRA risks will be reviews to ensure that their exclusion from this process would not have a meaningful impact on the capital number generated by the five largest risks. These are:

- Technology / business process change / system Failure;
- Third-party Supplier Failure (RBS);
- Customer Retention;
- AML and Sanctions; and
- Change Management.

The outcomes of these scenarios will be subjected to a scenario analysis economic capital model.

## Stress Testing

Stress tests show the effects of events which cannot (or not sufficiently) be accounted for under business as usual circumstances. Banks are repeatedly confronted with these exceptional scenarios: market crashes, country crises, critical political events, or major bankruptcies, for example. For situations of this kind, the assumptions of the usual assessment methods do not appear sufficient, which can lead to substantial underestimation of risk. For this reason, it is important for a bank to define relevant stress scenarios.

For example, fluctuations on international financial markets will have a different effect on a bank with high market risks than on a regional bank which primarily focuses on customer business. Nevertheless, it is necessary to account for the fact that these shocks can also have a noticeable impact on banks operating in more remote segments. After a market crisis, interest in funds and equities diminishes, which in turn brings about a decline in fee and commission income for many banks (even those which only operate regionally). For this reason, it may be helpful to define relevant stress scenarios for all of a bank's material risk types and to analyse the effect the simultaneous occurrence of such exceptional situations would have on the bank's risk-bearing capacity. The institution-specific business focuses can be taken into account by assigning different weights, for example. Banks which assume correlations in their ICAAP calculations should not assume any diversification effects in their stress scenarios. In practice, banks will apply systemic stress tests where the correlation between risk types is implicit in the risk factors evaluated in the macroeconomic scenario. Banks also use specific stress events and reverse stress tests to obtain a broad understanding of the impact of individual risks and the interplay between them on the business plans and their inherent risk profiles.

Moreover, tests prescribed by supervisory authorities also have to be integrated into the design of relevant stress scenarios (for example, when certain methods are used to calculate capital requirements or large exposures). A bank can depict the effects of stress scenarios within the framework of risk-bearing capacity analysis. In this context, the bank should consider stress scenarios on the risk side, as well as the effects of exceptional situations on the capital side. The results of the stress tests provide indications which may be helpful in identifying any existing weaknesses. This information can be used to develop countermeasures such as restricting dividend pay-outs, raising additional forms of capital, limiting certain business lines, redeveloping business architectures, or in terms of certain specific risk criteria, limiting certain asset concentrations, or introducing security checks and access authorisations in order to reduce operational risks, or drawing up general contingency plans.

### ICAAP Stress Testing Framework: Worked Example

For the example UK commercial bank introduced earlier, we present the templates used to describe the stress testing framework.

Stress testing is a key internal risk management tool and is used as an input into a number of bank key business processes (including strategic planning, risk appetite, ICAAP, ILAA, and so on). This section summarises the different objectives of stress testing within the bank, structured across four main areas as follows:

- Strengthen risk management
  1. Assess the impact of certain macroeconomic and systemic events on a portfolio and bank as a whole;
  2. Identify a variety of hidden, un-matured risks at a Group, portfolio, and divisional level;
  3. Formulate risk appetite and better manage the business through improved understanding of the underlying risks and sensitivities;
  4. Reverse Stress Testing: test the vulnerabilities of the business model and the resulting actions would improve the resilience of the entity under stress.
- Inform capital and liquidity requirements
  1. Support the assessment of capital and liquidity requirements for the bank;
  2. Contribute to continuous improvement of the bank's capital and liquidity models.
- Maintain confidence in the bank's resilience to stress
  1. Evaluate all of the material consequences of stress events, across all risk classes;
  2. Facilitate the development of risk mitigation plans and implement a framework of early warning indicators.
- Meet regulatory requirements
  1. Respond promptly and effectively to regulator-mandated stresses;
  2. Support regulatory assessment of capital and liquidity requirements (for example, the UK, PRA, ICG, and ILG requirements).

**Stress Testing Approaches**   Table 8.9 is a slide that would be presented at the start of the ICAAP deck to the regulator during the SREP.

**TABLE 8.9**  SREP slide

| Type of stress testing | Objectives | Type of activities |
|---|---|---|
| Entity wide or Integrated Stress Testing | ▪ Assess the impact of certain macro-economic and systemic events on a portfolio and the Banks as a whole. <br> ▪ Support the assessment of capital and liquidity requirements for the Bank. <br> ▪ Facilitate the development of risk mitigation plans and implement a framework of early warning indicators. <br> ▪ Support regulatory assessment of capital and liquidity requirements (i.e., CPB, ICG, and ILG requirements). | ▪ Top down, integrated, macro-economic stress testing to support the following: <br> - ICAAP and other Supervisory mandated stress tests (e.g., CPP); <br> - Risk appetite setting; <br> - Sensitivity analysis of the business plan (covering business and strategic risk). |
| Risk specific | ▪ Better manage the business through improved understanding of the underlying risks and sensitivities. <br> ▪ Contribute to continuous improvement of the bank's capital and liquidity models. | ▪ Bottom up, risk specific stress testing to cover the risk types defined in the ABC Bank Risk Taxonomy <br> - Credit risk <br> - Non-traded market risk <br> - Funding and liquidity risk <br> - Operational risk (including compliance and reputational risk) |
| Reverse stress testing | ▪ Identify a variety of hidden, un-matured risks at a total, portfolio, and divisional level. <br> ▪ Identify the circumstance where the business model fails. <br> ▪ Remain in line with regulatory requirements related to stress testing, including completing regulator-mandated stresses. | ▪ Developing scenarios that would threaten the bank's business model. <br> ▪ Calibrating a level of stress that would lead to bank failure. <br> ▪ Complementing setting of risk appetite and Recovery and Resolution Planning. |

The stress testing framework should emphasise integrated stress testing for the aggregate balance sheet. Remember that the ICAAP is designed to be a forward-looking process, so that the anchor point for start of testing would be today and then built around scenarios over the next one, three and five years.

For the case study here on the UK commercial bank, the top-level scenario planning looked like this:

- A recession for the first two years, triggered by contagion from a re-intensification of Eurozone sovereign concerns; this scenario is relevant for the UK bank as it is a UK-based recession although the trigger is outside the UK. The scenario addresses the key vulnerabilities in the bank's portfolio, being UK focused, affecting CRE and mortgage exposures with the key economic parameters below:
  - UK real GDP falls at an annualised rate of 5.7% at the trough of the recession;
  - Unemployment peaks at the highest to 11.4% affecting household consumption and business consumption;
  - House prices fall by more 20% over the first two scenarios and remain volatile thereafter;
  - M4 lending and holdings contract but at different rates;
  - Interest rates (3m Libor) increase in the first three years and then fall for the next two years.
- The contraction is followed by a slow recovery, with growth eventually returning close to trend towards the end of the scenario.

Of course, banks would design their stress test relevant to their operating environment. A South African bank, for instance, would concentrate on the economic impact of recession in South Africa.

The scenario is then subject to drill down to see the impact on financials:

- Balance Sheet under Stress:
  - Asset balances decline under stress due to debt flow, fall in new lending, and in consumer / household spending as reflected in the relevant economic parameters;
  - Additional assumptions are being taken with regard to CRE decline as shown in scenario 3.
- Operating and Funding costs:
  - Balance sheet decline will cause a corresponding fall in income in the first two years of the stress and then picks up the following three years;
  - Net interest margin declines compared to base case and remains low in the first few years of the recovery;

- Costs will follow the base balance sheet forecast and any cost cutting will be taken as a management action;
- Funding costs would reflect the scenario interest rates but would increase if the funding gap increases.
- Impairments:
  - Impairments are equal to EL and taken into the P&L.
  - The scenario has a negative effect on unemployment, house prices, and the CRE index and this has a significant impact on impairments during the stress period as creditworthiness deteriorates. Consequently, PDs and expected losses increase causing impairments more than double during the stress period.
  - Similarly, an economic recovery would result in lower impairments.
- RWA Credit:
  - The effects of a decline in house prices and property values during stress would decrease the value of the security of the loan and hence increase LGDs. This and the increase in PDs would cause a sharp increase in RWAs and this is offset by debt flow (defaults) and contraction of the balance sheet.
- Operational Risk Losses and RWAs:
  - It is assumed that certain OR losses (for example, external fraud) crystallise under stress;
  - OR RWAs are recalculated according to the Standardised Approach and would decline in line with income.
- Capital Plans:
  - Capital deductions remain, although there will be no Excess Provisions over EL as provisions are equal or greater than EL;
  - The assets in the Liquid Asset Buffer (LAB), also termed Available For Sale (AFS), are revalued and profits / losses taken against capital and not P&L in line with accounting rules;
  - The combined effects of a deterioration in P&L and an increase in RWAs causes CT1 and Total capital ratios to decline compared to base. This will then be assessed against regulatory minima.

The above summary is presented as a template as to how a bank could set the stress testing framework for impact on financials.

### Dividend Policy

As part of its capital management and capital planning process, it is important for a bank to have in place a formal dividend policy statement. This should reflect the bank's overall risk appetite and be referred to in the risk appetite statement. Dividend policy is a critical part of the capital management process, because it is part of the process by which capital buffers are built up and retained.

For example, where one has observed a dividend payment made to the shareholder which was in excess of 50% of the reported post-tax profit, this would suggest a Board that was not placing capital preservation as a priority. Such an approach would not be a common one for, for instance, at a new bank or "challenger" bank. Typically, banks that are in some form of challenger mode, such as start-ups, niche players, or those operating under a revised business model, pay little or no dividend for the first few years. A good example of this is TSB Bank in the UK, which was divested in 2014 from Lloyds Banking Group, with a balance sheet of approximately £25 billion. It stated on listing that it expected to pay no dividend for at least the next five years. The statement went on to describe the rationale for this policy, which included the desire to build up regulatory capital buffers to above peer group levels. A policy similar to that of TSB would be more in line with what one would expect to observe at most banks under competitive or other stress.

## Case Study: Internal Capital Assessment

Here we illustrate the quantitative output from an "internal capital assessment" (ICA) exercise at an EU commercial bank ("ABC Bank"). It is a baseline input to the ICAAP process (the headings are the same as would be used in the ICAAP) as well as valuable management information in its own right, provided the output is used to inform management actions. An example of the list of possible management actions in stress is also illustrated. This output would be for senior management and the Board to approve before its content was submitted to the regulator.

**Example Quantitative Output** The summary of the ICA was presented as follows:

A Material Risk Assessment was conducted in order to identify material risks and assess whether sufficient capital is set aside for these risks. The capital adequacy assessment has been conducted using two approaches:

- Mixed approach: assumes capital requirements for ABC's Retail exposures are assessed under the AIRB approach, while wholesale exposures are assessed under either standardised (non-Commercial Real Estate) or slotting (CRE) approaches;
- Standardised approach: assumes capital requirements for all ABC exposures apart from wholesale CRE are assessed under the Standardised Approach (CRE remains under the slotting approach).

This includes an assessment of additional Pillar 2A risk capital for those risks that are not sufficiently covered under the Pillar 1 framework. Assessed Pillar 2A risk capital totals £447m as at 30 June 2015 or 42% of Pillar 1 under the mixed approach (36% of Pillar 1 under the Standardised Approach).

Note the regulator will, after the ICAAP process, issue an individual capital guidance (ICG) which states the minimum capital required, as a percentage of the RWA total.

Alongside that the ICA included a timeline for key metrics and targets to be met, as progress towards target, shown at Figure 8.17.

Table 8.10 shows the "Point-in-Time" capital assessment, using both the mixed and standardised approaches. There are also explanatory notes which are presented below.

Note that this has been assessed assuming the current credit quality of assets. Any increase in the riskiness of the ABC's portfolio would lead to an increase in the SNC buffer.

- The sector concentration add-on is the difference between the economic capital requirements for the existing ABC Bank portfolio and that of a fully diversified portfolio (without sector and regional concentration).
- A fully diversified portfolio has been defined as one where the unexpected loss contribution of each individual sector does not exceed 10% of the total portfolio unexpected loss.

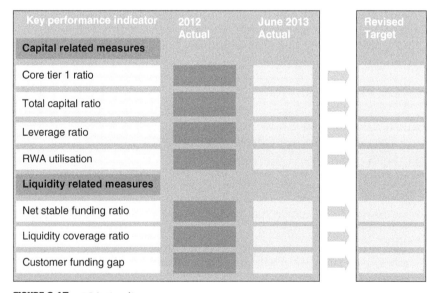

**FIGURE 8.17**  ICA timeline

**TABLE 8.10**  Point-in-time capital assessment

Assessment as at 30 June 2013, £mn

|  | RWAs Mixed | Capital @8% Mixed | RWAs Standardised | Capital @8% Standardised |
|---|---|---|---|---|
| **Pillar 1** | | | | |
| Credit | 11,279 | 902.3 | 13,380 | 1070.4 |
| Credit Counterparty Risk (Derivatives) | 295 | 23.6 | 295 | 23.6 |
| Non Credit Assets (Fixed Assets) | 106 | 8.5 | 106 | 8.5 |
| Operational Risk | 1,576 | 126.1 | 1,576 | 126.1 |
| **Total Pillar 1** | **13,256** | **1060.5** | **15,357** | **1228.6** |
| **Pillar 2A Add-ons** | | | | |
| Single Name Concentration | | 10.0 | | 10.0 |
| Sector Concentration | | 267.0 | | 267.0 |
| Non-Traded Market Risk | | 80.0 | | 80.0 |
| Operational Risk | | 90.0 | | 90.0 |
| Total Pillar 2A | | 447.0 | | 447.0 |
| Total Pillar 1 and Pillar 2A Capital | | 1507.5 | | 1675.6 |
| ICG Multiplier | | 42% | | 36% |

- The sector concentration add-on is mainly driven by ABC Bank's exposure to the Corporate Real Estate (CRE) asset class.

Note that neither product nor geographical concentration risk has been considered in this analysis.

Non-traded market risk has been assessed using a Value-at-Risk model calibrated to a 99% confidence interval over a 1-year holding period.

ABC Bank has undertaken its capital add-on assessment for operational risk by applying a scaling factor to Peer Bank's operational risk economic capital results, which takes into account published internal loss event experience, its own programme of scenario analyses outputs and relevant external loss event data.

The scaling factor has been applied based on comparing ABC's gross income as at year-end 2012 to published data.

**ICG Multiplier Explained**    The Pillar 2A add-on has been converted into a percentage of Pillar 1 capital requirements based on actual RWAs from June 2013.

This results in a Pillar 2A add-on of 42% of Pillar 1 capital requirements under the mixed approach and 36% of Pillar 1 capital requirements under the standardised approach. The lower percentage Pillar 2 add-on under the standardised approach reflects the fact that Pillar 1 capital requirements are higher compared to the mixed approach.

The presentation then considers the Base Case forward-looking capital assessment. This is shown as a projection of capital surplus, and the approach is illustrated in Table 8.11 and Figure 8.18.

The exercise has assumed that ABC's starting point capital (in 2014) will ensure that it has a CET1 ratio of 12% and a total capital ratio of 15%. Under the mixed approach, this will require starting CET1 capital to be

**TABLE 8.11**   Base Case capital projection

| Base Case | | | | | |
|---|---|---|---|---|---|
| £m | 2014 | 2015 | 2016 | 2017 | 2018 |
| Required | | | | | |
| RWAs | 12,647 | 12,870 | 13,387 | 13,877 | 14,488 |
| Pillar 1 – Capital | 1,012 | 1,030 | 1,071 | 1,110 | 1,159 |
| Pillar 2A (proposed ICG) – Capital | 426 | 434 | 451 | 468 | 489 |
| Total Required Capital | 1,438 | 1,464 | 1,522 | 1,578 | 1,648 |
| Total CT1 | 1,748 | 1,970 | 2,206 | 2,478 | 2,757 |
| Deductions | –230 | –290 | –268 | –246 | –225 |
| Total Tier 1 / CT1 | 1,518 | 1,680 | 1,938 | 2,231 | 2,532 |
| Tier 2 | 374 | 374 | 374 | 374 | 374 |
| Total Available Capital (T1 and T2) | 1,892 | 2,054 | 2,312 | 2,605 | 2,906 |
| Surplus | 453 | 591 | 790 | 1,027 | 1,258 |
| Ratios | | | | | |
| Core Tier 1 (based on Pillar 1 RWA) | 12.0% | 13.1% | 14.5% | 16.1% | 17.5% |
| Total Capital (based on Pillar 1 RWA) | 15.0% | 16.0% | 17.3% | 18.8% | 20.1% |

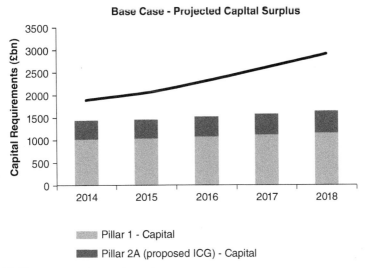

**FIGURE 8.18**   Projected capital surplus

£1,518 million post deductions and starting Tier 2 capital to be £374 million. The 2014 proposed ICG is based on the Pillar 2A calculations presented earlier. These Pillar 2A items have been projected as a fixed percentage (42%) of Pillar 1 capital requirements over the time horizon. Retained earnings grow throughout the forecast period leading to a significant increase in the capital surplus (£1,258 million in 2018).

The base case shows a sizeable surplus throughout the 5-year projection period with the lowest surplus in the first year (2014) reflecting ABC's starting point *capital* position. During the forecast period, the CT1 ratio steadily increases to attain 17.5% in 2018.

## Summary of Management Actions in Stress

Table 8.12 is a summary of the analysis on management action in stress, which is an Appendix to the ICA and also an integral part of the ICAAP submission. The table is the complete list of possible capital-related management and recovery actions that could be put in place at ABC Bank, including a summary of their impact on capital, liquidity, and P&L. Of course the exact content of the table will differ by type of banking institution and specific business model. It is important to remember that not all of the management actions in Table 8.12 are realistic with the goal of maintaining the institution as a *going concern*. Some of the actions, such as stopping new business or not renewing existing customer business, could so damage the

**TABLE 8.12** Summary of potential management actions in stress

| Management options | Description | Damage to franchise | Numbers | | |
|---|---|---|---|---|---|
| | | | Capital | Liquidity | P&L Impact |
| **A. Stop selling** | | | | | |
| A.1 Business lending | Cease all new business lending via loans and overdrafts | High | £202m | £2bn | £60m pa |
| A.2 Mortgages | Cease all new mortgages | Low | £17.2m | £1.2bn | £44.4m pa |
| A.3 Personal lending | Cease all new personal loans This is normally unsecured borrowing and carries significant RWA | Medium | £45.1m | £376m | £37m pa |
| A.4 Stop renewals | Loans, commercial bullet facilities that do not contractually require renewal | Medium | £9.6m | £80m | £2.4m pa |
| **B. Capital maximisation** | | | | | |
| B.1 Adjust limits | Cancel all undrawn limits on accounts including utilised overdrafts | High | £50.4m | Nil | £21m |
| B.2 RWA | Stop High RWA items | Medium | See A1 | See A1 | See A1 |
| **C. Capital raising** | | | | | |
| C.1 Sell a stake in the business | Seek buyers for element of the business via Private Placement | Low | £200m | £200m | £30m pa |
| C.2 Debt | Convert debt to shares. (Bail in senior debt holders) | Low | £200m | Nil | £18m |
| C.3 Rights issue | Launch rights issue | Low | £200m | £150m | Nil |

| | | | Capital | Liquidity | P&L Impact |
|---|---|---|---|---|---|
| **D. Debt buyback** | | | | | |
| D.1 | Debt | Buy back own debt if opportunity for capital gain | Low | £129m (in retained profits) | £180m | £129m |
| **E. Capital retention** | | | | | |
| E.1 | Dividends | Withhold any unpaid dividends, stop new ones | Low | £45m | £45m | Nil |
| **F. Fixed asset sales** | | | | | |
| F.1 | Property | Sale & Leaseback or sub-lease | Low | Net Negligible | £32m | Nil |
| **G. Sell assets** | | | | | |
| G.1 | Operations | Outsource with "free" period up front | Medium | £20.2m (in retained profits) | £26m | £26m |
| G.2 | Mortgage book | Sell Mortgage book | Medium | £104.4m | £5800m | £435m |
| G.3 | Credit card book | Sell receivables | Low | £36m | £300m | £6m |
| G.4 | Data | Sell marketing data | Medium | £0.78m | £1m | £1m |
| G.5 | Sale "Tall Trees" debt | Sell off debt for customers over £30m debt | Low | £187.5m | £1860m | £56m |
| **H. Repricing** | | | | | |
| H.1 | Deposits | Increase rate paid to customers to enhance liquidity | None | **Corporate:** £0.58m **Retail:** £1.55m | **Corporate:** £100m **Retail:** £100m | **Corporate:** £0.75m **Retail:** £2m |
| H.2 | Lending | Increase pricing to enhance profitability and retain liquidity by reducing demand | Medium | £211.4m | £2860.8m | –£113.1m |

*(continued)*

**TABLE 8.12** Summary of potential management actions in stress (*Continued*)

| Management options | | Description | Damage to franchise | | Numbers | |
|---|---|---|---|---|---|---|
| H.3 | MTA | Increase pricing to enhance profitability | Medium | £1.0m | £1.3m | £1.3m |
| H.4 | LOBO | Exercise review clause under "Lender Option - Borrower Option" contracts (LOBO) | Low | ? | ? | ? |
| **I. Radical cost cutting** | | | | | | |
| I.1 | Bonus / incentives | Stop all discretionary salary elements | Low | £12.4m (in retained profits) | £16m | £16m |
| I.2 | Pay cut | 10% pay cut for staff | Low | £13.2m (in retained profits) | £17m | £17m |
| I.3 | Non-staff | Stop all discretionary payments, e.g., marketing, travel | Low | £14.9m (in retained profits) | £19.2m | £19.2m |
| I.4 | Reduce footprint | Close branches | High | 0 | –0£2.5m | £0.3m |
| I.5 | Recruitment | Stop all recruitment activity including in-flight. Give notice to terminate consultants/agency, etc. Stop all recruitment | Low | £0.38m (in retained profits) | £0.5m | £0.5m |
| I.6 | Cost reduction | Impose flat 10% budget reduction across all areas | Low | £38.75m (in retained profits) | £50m | £50m |

brand and the customer franchise that the bank ceased to be a viable entity. In that case, one has to ask oneself what exactly is being "saved" in such a situation, other than a potential orderly wind-down.

## PRACTICAL ISSUES AND BEST-PRACTICE ICAAP PREPARATION[3]

We have already noted that **the main beneficiary of the ICAAP** is a bank's management as the process will reveal vital information about the level and types of risk the organisation is exposed to. As a result, it is essential that the ICAAP is not viewed as a regulatory tick-box exercise.

**The end to end ICAAP process** can take around 12 months to complete in large organisations. A key challenge is the continuing relevance of a firm's ICAAP as the business will develop during the course of ICAAP preparation and PRA review / feedback, meaning that the document produced is quickly out of date.

When assessing their **material risks**, banks should seek to ensure that the modelling approach is appropriate for the type of risk being evaluated. Also, as well as capturing material risks in risk maps, risk appetite statements, etc., it is important to document any risk classified as "non-material" with reasons.

ICAAP inputs can originate from many different parts of a bank. If the nature of the agreed **stress scenarios** is not well understood by all stakeholders at the outset, then inconsistencies will arise in ICAAP outputs. For example, Business Unit A deduces that a particular stress scenario has positive implications for lending volumes, whereas Business Unit B, engaged in related activities, concludes the opposite. Workshops should be arranged by the central project team in the early phases of the project to discuss the stress scenarios with all stakeholders and ensure that there is a common understanding. Also, a broad range of internal stakeholders should be involved in the development of plausible but severe scenarios to stress test the key vulnerabilities of the firm.

A **good data history** is of paramount importance. Weaknesses in the availability or quality of historic data is likely to adversely affect the predictive capability of models and lead to greater subjectivity in the production of stress testing results. A bank with poor data history, inaccurate entries, and missing values will have to allocate time and resources to developing alternative data sources, data cleansing, and subjective overlays, which will divert attention away from the development of models with a good predictive capability.

Banks must check that their list of **risk mitigation actions** is reviewed against the background of the stress scenario that is being tested to ensure

---

[3] This section was co-authored with Chris Westcott.

they are still valid. For example, many organisations rely upon disposal of discretionary trading portfolios to free up balance sheet resources in a stress situation, but this approach would not have worked during the 2007–2008 financial crisis as there was a flight to quality and no market whatsoever in many instruments.

If the ICAAP is viewed as a tick-box exercise to satisfy a set of regulatory rules, its preparation will most likely be under-resourced and, as a consequence, little will be learnt about the risks to which the firm is exposed. A strong **central project team** is required, made up of both project management resources and subject matter experts (SMEs). The project managers are responsible for planning the exercise, managing its completion to a tight timeline, and putting necessary governance arrangements in place. SMEs, on the other hand, assess the full range of risks to which the firm is exposed, ensure that the modelled answers are realistic, and check the hand-offs between functions. The level of effort involved should match that given to the annual planning cycle and a full resource commitment is required by all stakeholders to the process.

ICAAP preparation requires **cross-functional collaboration**, which is not always easy to achieve in large organisations. Senior management must agree where the stress testing function sits in the organisational structure and a clearly defined operating model (reviewed by Internal Audit). Figure 8.19 illustrates how the different functions within the bank must work together closely and efficiently when working on the ICAAP process.

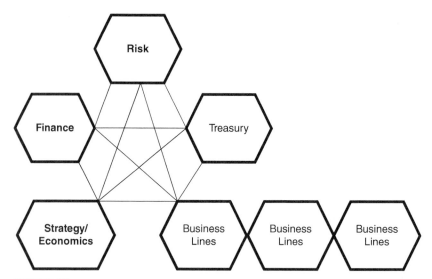

**FIGURE 8.19**    Cross-functional collaboration: Different functions of a bank must work together closely to produce the ICAAP

In terms of governance, a single owner of the ICAAP will help to drive a consistent comprehensive approach (we recommend Treasury, rather than Finance or Risk). For optimum results, key stakeholders in business units, Risk, Finance, Treasury, Strategy, Economics, etc., must be involved in its construction. Both senior management and the Board should be actively involved in the review and challenge process and there should be a formal sign-off.

According to the PRA, "the ICAAP should be an integral part of the firm's management process and decision-making culture". This "Use Test" could, for example, be achieved by capturing the outputs from the ICAAP process in the setting of risk limits, pricing, and/or capital allocation.

In an ideal world, all aspects of the business's financial plan and stress testing activity would be undertaken in one **integrated model** (base case economic scenario, base case business financial plan, capital plan, and stress modelling of each key risk faced by the firm). In reality, though, these tend to be modelled as separate components, which means that care is required to ensure that the inter-relationships between the components are explored. There will inevitably be a degree of subjectivity in the production of the final result.

If a **Pillar 2A or 2B overlay** is applied as part of Individual Capital Guidance, banks must decide how it should be **allocated to business lines**, if at all. If the level of the regulatory overlay differs from the bank's internal calculations of the level of capital required, the challenge is increased. If this process is not carefully managed, gaps can arise between the business unit view of the level of capital required, on which incentive schemes are based and the aggregate view.

It is important to recognise that ICAAP / SREP / ICG is only part of the capital story. In the US, the comparable process, CCAR (Comprehensive Capital Analysis and Review) also captures Recovery and Resolution Planning to deliver a fully integrated "end to end" capital assessment, which is updated by firms annually. In the UK, the PRA has introduced Recovery and Resolution Planning, but it is separate to the ICAAP.

## CONCLUSIONS

Capital management is a critical part of managing a bank. Indeed, to suggest it is "risk management" is to somehow underplay its importance; capital along with liquidity is the lifeblood of banking and must be managed on a conservative basis, with a going concern outlook throughout the economic cycle.

This chapter has presented the role of capital management within the business of banking. The ICAAP process has been designed to ensure that long-term thru-the-cycle capital planning is an inherent part of banking, but with any regulatory supervision process it tends to be downgraded to a bureaucratic "tick-box" exercise. This is an undesirable route for any bank to take.

Risk is a significant aspect of business activities in a market economy. As risk taking or transformation of risks constitutes a major characteristic of the banking business, it is especially important for banks to address risk management issues. The necessity from a business perspective has arisen from developments on the financial markets and the increasing complexity of the banking business. These circumstances call for functioning systems which support the limitation and control of risk exposure. The implementation of an ICAAP is not rooted exclusively in regulatory considerations; rather it is in the best interest of all stakeholders of an institution. The owners are inherently interested in the continued existence of the bank as they expect a reasonable return on their investment and wish to avoid capital losses. But certainly a bank's employees, customers, and lenders also have an interest in its survival. The individual interests of these groups are not mutually exclusive; in fact all stakeholders should be interested in ensuring that the institution does not take on risk positions which might endanger its continued existence. The main motive for the ICAAP can therefore be seen in ensuring a viable risk position by dealing with risks in the appropriate manner. In particular, it is important to detect developments which may endanger the institution as early as possible in order for the bank to take suitable management action in response. In this regard, delivering an ICAAP serves the interests of all the internal and external stakeholders of the bank.

This raises two issues: first, when calculating the bank's risk-bearing capacity, it is necessary to determine the extent to which a bank can afford to take certain risks at all. For this purpose, the bank needs to ensure that the available risk coverage capital is sufficient at all times to cover the risks taken. Second, the bank must review the extent to which risks are worth assuming; that is, it is necessary to analyse the opportunities arising from risk taking (evaluation of the risk–return ratio, typically a risk-adjusted measure such as RAROC). The main objective of the ICAAP is to secure the bank's risk-bearing capacity. Comprehensive risk–return management follows as a next step. Done properly (that is, not as a bureaucratic or tick-box exercise), the ICAAP thus constitutes a comprehensive package which delivers significant benefits and balance sheet understanding from a business perspective.

## SELECTED BIBLIOGRAPHY AND REFERENCES

BIS Enhancements to the Basel II framework, Available at http://www.bis.org/publ/bcbs157.pdf.

BIS Principles for sound stress testing practices and supervision, http://www.bis.org/publ/bcbs155.pdf.

Committee of European Banking Supervisors (2006), Guidelines on the Application of the Supervisory Review Process under Pillar 2 (CP03 revised).

Churm and Radia, "The Funding for Lending Scheme", *Bank of England Quarterly Bulletin* 2012 Q4, Available at http://www.bankofengland.co.uk/publications/Documents/quarterlybulletin/qb120401.pdf.

De La Mora, Matten, and Barfield, "Capital management in banking: The way forward", *The Journal*, PWC, December 2010, Available at http://www.pwc.com/gx/en/banking-capital-markets/pdf/capital-management.pdf.

EBA, *Guidelines on retail deposits*, 2013. Available at http://www.eba.europa.eu/regulation-and-policy/liquidity-risk/guidelines-on-retail-deposits-subject-to-higher-outflows-for-the-purposes-of-liquidity-reporting.

Freer, J., "Capital management: banking's trickiest juggling act", *Bank Director*, 3 June 2011. Available at www.bankdirector.com/magazine/archives/4th-quarter-2009/capital-management-bankings-trickiest-juggling-act.

Gropp, R. and Heider, F., *The determinants of bank capital structure*, 2009. Available at www.ecb.europa.eu/pub/pdf/scpwps/ecbwp1096.pdf.

Marshall, P., *Capital management in stressful times: taking a holistic approach*, 2012. Available at http://businessfinancemag.com/article/capital-management-stressful-times-taking-holistic-approach-0106.

*"He critically failed to delegate or appoint talented people lest they under-mine his overall authority. Instead he promoted those whose weaknesses he understood and could exploit. Competence was not an issue."*
—James Wyllie, *Goering and Goering: Hitler's Henchman and his Anti-Nazi Brother*, The History Press, 2006

# CHAPTER 9

# Financial Statements, Ratio Analysis, and Credit Analysis

I n this chapter, we present basic concepts in investment analysis for equities, beginning with the financial structure of the firm. We then consider the fair pricing of an equity, dividend policy, financial ratio analysis and basic concepts in assessing the cost of capital. The book extract section considers relative value analysis in the context of debt instruments, so that the reader can determine the differences in approach compared to equity instruments.

## Firm Financial Structure and Company Accounts

A corporate entity or *firm* is governed by the types of equity capital it can issue as stipulated in its *memorandum* and *articles of association*. In the past, in the UK market at least, firms would issue different classes of shares including "A" shares that carried restricted voting rights. However, this was not encouraged by the Stock Exchange and the most common form of share in the market is the *ordinary share*, which is known as *common stock* in the US market. The holders of ordinary shares are entitled to certain privileges, including the right to vote in the running of the company, the right to dividend payments, and the right to subscribe for further shares ahead of non-shareholders, in the event of a new issue. Dividends are only payable after liabilities to all other parties with a claim on the company, including bondholders, have been discharged. Shares are issued with a par value, but this has no relevance to their analysis and is frequently for a token amount such as £0.10 or £0.25. Firms also issue *preference shares* which are a type of hybrid between shares and bonds.

We begin by considering the financial structure of the firm, which traditionally is of vital importance to shareholders. We can consider the importance to shareholders of the financial structure of a firm by comparing the interests of shareholders with those of bondholders. Unlike shareholders, bondholders have a prior contractual claim on the firm. This means that as and when the contractual claim is covered, bondholders have no further interest in the firm. Put another way, as long as the firm is able to meet its contractual commitments, which are interest and principal payments owing to creditors, bondholders will be satisfied.[1] Shareholders, however, have what is known as a *residual* claim on the firm. As the owners of the firm, they will be concerned about the overall value of the firm and that this is being maximised. Hence they are (in theory) keenly concerned with the financial structure of their firm, as well as its long-term prospects.

We begin therefore, with a review of company accounts. Firms are required by law to produce accounts, originally under the belief that owners should be kept informed about how the directors are managing the company.

**The Balance Sheet**    The balance sheet is a snapshot in time of the asset value of a company. A company balance sheet may be put together using one of three different approaches, namely *historic cost book value*, *current cost*, or *market value*. Equity analysts' preference is for the market value basis, which records the value of assets and liabilities in the balance sheet using current market values. For liabilities this is relatively straightforward to undertake if the firm is listed on an exchange and there is a liquid market in its shares; the net value of the firm can be taken to be the difference between the market value of the firm's ordinary shares and the *book value* of the shares. The latter is the par value of the shares plus the share premium and accumulated retained earnings. It is more problematic to determine market value for firm assets, however. For instance, what is the market value of 2-year-old photocopying machines? In fact the majority of incorporated institutions do not have their shares traded on an exchange and so a market value balance sheet is rarely released.

The most common balance sheet approach uses the historic cost book value approach, in which assets and liabilities are valued at their original cost, known as historic cost. The net worth of the company is calculated as the sum of the share capital and retained profits (reserves). It is rare to observe balance sheets presented using the current cost book value approach, which values assets at current replacement cost.

A hypothetical company balance sheet is shown at Figure 9.1.

Note that the balance sheet orders assets and liabilities in terms of their maturity. Fixed assets are recorded first, followed by current assets

---

[1] This is perhaps too simplistic; bondholders will also be concerned if any developments affect the *perceived* ability of the firm to meet its future liabilities, such as a change of credit rating. Such events will affect the value of the bonds issued by the firm, which is why they will be of concern to bondholders.

| Balance sheet as at 31 December 2001 | | |
|---|---|---|
| | £m | £m |
| Fixed assets | | 675 |
| Long-term investments | | 98 |
| | | 773 |
| | | |
| Current assets | | |
| Stock | 365 | |
| Debtors | 523 | |
| Cash | 18 | |
| | 906 | |
| | | |
| Short-term liabilities | | |
| Creditors | 355 | |
| Short-dated loans | 109 | |
| Bank overdraft | 88 | |
| Corporation tax | 91 | |
| Planned dividend | 66 | |
| | 709 | |
| | | |
| Net current assets | | 197 |
| | | |
| Total assets less current liabilities | | 970 |
| Liabilities falling due after 12 months | | |
| Creditors | 28 | |
| Long-dated debt, bonds | 400 | (428) |
| | | |
| Net assets | | 542 |
| | | |
| Share capital | | |
| Ordinary shares issued | | 170 |
| Preference shares | | 30 |
| | | 200 |
| Capital and Reserves | | |
| Paid-up capital | 25 | |
| Share premium | 109 | |
| Profit and loss account (reserves) | 208 | 342 |
| | | |
| Shareholders' funds | | 542 |

Fixed assets include items such as factory buildings, property holdings, etc. Short-term liabilities are those falling due within 12 months.

**FIGURE 9.1**  Hypothetical corporate balance sheet

less current liabilities. This value, the net current assets, indicates if the company is able to cover its short-term liabilities with its current assets. The net current asset value is added to fixed assets value, resulting in the value of the firm's assets less current liabilities. The balance sheet then records long-term liabilities, and after subtracting from the previous figure, shows the total value of the company once all liabilities have been discharged. This is also known as shareholders' funds, and would be distributed to them in the event that the firm was wound up at this point. Shareholders' funds are represented by the capital and reserves entries. Share capital is the sum of the issued share par value and the share premium. These are defined as follows:

- Paid-up share capital: the nominal value of the shares, which represents the total liabilities of the shareholders in the event of winding up, and which has been paid by shareholders;
- Share premium: the difference between market value of the shares and the nominal or par value.

The entry for "profit and loss account" sometimes appears as *retained earnings*. This is the accumulated profit over the life of the company that has not been paid out as dividend to shareholders, but has been reinvested back into the company. The profit and loss account is part of the firm's reserves, and its calculation is arrived at via a separate financial statement.

**The Profit and Loss Account**   The profit and loss account, also known as the *income statement*, shows the profit generated by a firm, separating out the amount paid to shareholders and that retained in the company. Hence, the profit and loss account is also a statement of retained earnings. Unlike the balance sheet, which is a snapshot in time, the income statement is a rolling total of retained profit from the last accounting period to the current one. Generally, this period is one year.

The calculation of the profit and loss account[2] is relatively straightforward, recording income less expenses. A firm's income is that generated from its business activities, and so excludes share capital or loan funding. The expenses are daily costs of running the business, and so exclude items such as plant and machinery which are considered "capital" expenditure and recorded as fixed assets in the balance sheet. Due to the different accounting conventions and bases in use, it is possible for two identical companies to

---

[2] Strictly speaking, it is a profit *or* loss account, as the firm would have made one or the other in the accounting period.

produce very different profit and loss statements. This is a complex and vast subject, well outside of the scope of this book, and so we will not enter into it. A good overview of accounting principles in the context of corporate finance is given in Higson (1995).

A hypothetical profit and loss statement is shown at Figure 9.2.

In the context of a profit and loss statement, the *net profit* is the gross profit minus business operating expenses. This is an accurate measure of the profit that the firm's managers have generated. The more efficiently managers run the business, the lower its expenses will be, and correspondingly the higher the net profit will be. Tax expenses are outside the control of the firm's managers and so appears afterwards. *Extraordinary items* are deemed to be those generating income that are outside the ordinary business activities of the company, and expected to be one-off or rare occurrences. This might include the disposal of a subsidiary, for example.

**Consolidated Accounts**   Consolidated accounts are produced when a company has one or more subsidiaries; the accounts of the individual undertakings

|  | £m | £m | £m |
|---|---|---|---|
| Operating revenue | 737 | | |
| Operating costs | (389) | | |
| Gross operating profit | | 348 | |
| | | | |
| Expenses | | | |
| Administration | (19) | | |
| Sales | (67) | | |
| Financial | (27) | | |
| | | (113) | |
| | | | |
| Net profit | | 235 | |
| | | | |
| Taxation | | (78) | |
| Profit on ordinary activities after tax | | 157 | |
| Extraordinary items | | - | |
| | | 157 | |
| Dividends | | | 30 |
| Retained profit | | | 127 |
| Retained profit brought forward | | | 81 |
| Retained profit carried forward | | | 208 |

**FIGURE 9.2**   Hypothetical corporate profit and loss statement

are combined into a single consolidated account for shareholders. In the UK, this is required under the Companies Act 1985, based on the belief that a company's business will be closely linked to that of any subsidiary that it owns, and therefore its shareholders require financial statements on the combined entity. At the same time, the subsidiaries also produce their balance sheet and profit and loss account.

### Valuation of Shares

In this section, we present some fundamental concepts in equity valuation. The approaches described seek to determine a share's *fair value*, which would then be compared against its market value. We consider first dividend valuation methods and then the *expected earnings* method.

**Dividend Valuation Model**   We assume a corporate entity that pays an annual dividend. An investor thinking of purchasing a number of shares of this company, and holding them for one year, will expect to receive the annual dividend payment during the time he holds it, as well as the share proceeds on disposal. The fair value that the investor would be prepared to pay today for the shares is given by

$$P_t = \frac{E(DV_{t+1})}{1+r} + \frac{E(P_{t+1})}{1+r} \qquad (9.1)$$

where   $P_t$          is the price of the shares at time $t$;
        $r$           is the required rate of return;
        $E(DV_{t+1})$  is the expected annual dividend one year after $t$;
        $E(P_{t+1})$   is the expected price of the share one year after $t$.

The rate of return $r$ may be related to the company's cost of capital plus a spread, or some other market-determined discount rate. The return generated by the shareholding is split between the income element, given by the dividend amount $(DV_{t+1})$ and the capital gain element given by $(P_{t+1} - P_t)$. Following (9.1) we may say that

$$E(P_{t+1}) = \frac{E(DV_{t+2})}{1+r} + \frac{E(P_{t+2})}{1+r} \qquad (9.2)$$

and by using substitution and continuing for successive years we obtain

$$P_0 = \sum_{t=1}^{T} \frac{E(DV_t)}{(1+r)^t} + \frac{E(P_T)}{(1+r)^T} \qquad (9.3)$$

for the period beginning now (at $t = 0$) and where $DV_t$ is the dividend per share in year $t$. If we extend $T$ to the limiting factor as it becomes close to infinity, the share price element will disappear and so (9.3) transforms to

$$P_0 = \sum_{t=1}^{\infty} \frac{E(DV_t)}{(1+r)^t} \tag{9.4}$$

Expression (9.4) is the dividend discount model and one can observe its similarity to the bond price / redemption yield expression straight away. However, the comparison of share and bond values using this method is fraught with complications, and so is rarely undertaken. This reflects problems with the approach. First, the model assumes a constant discount rate or cost of capital over time, which is unrealistic. For this reason, the appropriate $t$-period zero-coupon interest rate is sometimes used as the discount rate, with a spread added to the government rate to reflect additional risk associated with holding the share. Other problems associated with the model include:

- Problems of divergence associated with the infinite time period implied by (9.4);
- An expectation of infinite dividend payments.

These issues may be resolved in practice by introducing further assumptions, considered in the next section as part of corporate dividend policy.

**Dividend Growth Model**   Following the dividend valuation model, let us assume a constant growth rate in dividend payments given by $c$. The dividend valuation model is then given by

$$P_0 = \sum_{t=0}^{\infty} \frac{DV_t}{(1+r)^t} = \sum_{t=0}^{\infty} \frac{DV_0(1+c)^t}{(1+r)^t} \tag{9.5}$$

Assuming further that $r > c$, then it can be shown[3] that the sum of this infinite series is given by

$$P_0 = \frac{DV_1}{r - c} \tag{9.6}$$

What (9.6) states is that, under a constant dividend growth rate $c$ that is less than the required rate of return $r$, the value of a company's share is

---

[3] For instance, see the appendix in Chapter 5 of Higson (1995).

the Year 1 dividend divided by the dividend yield of $r - c$, which itself is the required rate of return minus the dividend growth rate.

We can re-arrange (9.6) to give

$$r = \frac{DV_1}{P_0} + c \qquad (9.7)$$

which states that the share's fair value is the dividend yield together with the expected dividend growth rate.

**Expected Earnings Valuation Model**  In the expected earnings model, again the cash flow stream of the expected earnings are discounted at the required rate of return or market-determined discount rate $r$. To ensure consistency, the values given by the earnings model and the dividend model must be identical. This is achieved by using what are known as *economic earnings* rather than reported earnings when undertaking the valuation. Economic earnings of a share are defined as the maximum quantity of resources that may be withdrawn from the share and consumed before the share becomes unable to provide real consumption at a future date. A *cash flow statement* is used to convert reported earnings into economic earnings. Put simply for sources this is:

> reported earnings + new external funds = total sources;

while for uses this is:

> dividends + net investment = total uses.

The relationship just given describes a *net* cash flow statement. If stated per share issued, the cash flow statement is given by

$$y_t + F_t \equiv DV_t + x_t \qquad (9.8)$$

where  $y_t$    is the reported earnings per share in year $t$;
       $F_t$    are the new external funds per share in year $t$;
       $DV_t$   is the dividend per share in year $t$;
       $x_t$    is the net investment per share in year $t$.

The relationship at (9.8) illustrates that if the firm raises new external finance, so that $F_t \neq 0$, a company can make the decision to proceed with new investment independently of the funding decision. However, if all the new investment in the company is sourced from retained earnings, an increase in dividends will decrease net investment, which will then reduce the company's ability to generate further real income in the future. By reinvesting a portion of its earnings and guaranteeing financial health, a company's retained earnings do not represent genuine economic income that are available to shareholders. From this reasoning, economic earnings per share are defined as $y_t + F_t - x_t$, where $\sum_{t=1}^{\infty} F_t / (1+r)^t = 0$

We therefore reason that the present value of externally-sourced funds must be equal to zero, and as we assume this funding to be debt, all its debt is required to be repaid during the life of the company.

Therefore we say that

economic earnings = reported earnings + new external funds

– net investment

From this relationship and the expression above, we can value shares on the basis of economic earnings using the expression at (9.9).

$$P_0 = \sum_{t=1}^{\infty} \frac{E(y_t + F_t - x_t)}{(1+r)^t} = \sum_{t=1}^{\infty} \frac{E(y_t - x_t)}{(1+r)^t} \qquad (9.9)$$

Identical valuations will be produced irrespective of the method used. This would be expected from no-arbitrage principles, but also because as (9.8) shows, the value of dividends would be equal to that of economic earnings.

## FINANCIAL RATIO ANALYSIS

The second part of our look at equity analysis considers some key concepts in finance, followed by an introduction to financial ratio analysis.

### Introduction: Key Concepts in Finance

The cornerstone of financial theory is the concept of the time value of money, which we introduced early in the book. This principle underpins discounted cash flow analysis, which is long established as a key element in financial analysis. The academic foundation of the *present value rule* as a corporate finance project appraisal technique is the Fisher–Hirshleifer model, generally quoted as first being presented by Fisher (1930) and Hirshleifer (1958). The present value rule established that in order to maximise shareholder wealth, a firm would be on safe ground accepting all projects with a positive net present value. The milestones in finance that followed this landmark are generally cited as being the *efficient markets hypothesis, portfolio theory*, and the Capital Asset Pricing Model (CAPM). Without going into the mathematics and derivation, we briefly introduce these topics in this section.

The efficient market hypothesis is attributed to Fama (1965). Its primary message was that it is not possible to outperform the market. Investors who found they beat the market in the short term would not be able to sustain this over time because information reaches the market very quickly and other investors will react to this information immediately. This reaction to buy or sell assets will in turn impact share prices so that shares rapidly become fully valued; after this only unexpected events will influence these prices. These events may have either a negative or positive impact on share prices, so that it becomes impossible to discern a clear trend in the movement of prices. The key aspects of the efficient markets hypothesis are that:

- The current price of a stock reflects all that is known about the stock and the issuing company, as well as relevant market and economic information;
- If we accept market efficiency, share prices can be accepted to be fair value, and given all *publicly available* information, neither under- or over-valued;
- It is not possible for an investor to beat the market, unless he is privy to information ahead of the market;
- Only unpredictable relevant news can cause share prices to change, and all previously released news has already been incorporated into the share price;
- Since unpredictable news is, by its nature, unpredictable, changes in share prices are also unpredictable and follow what is known as a *random walk*.

The key assumptions underlying the efficient market hypothesis are that investors are rational operators, and that being rational they will undertake dealing only on the receipt of new information, and not using intuition. The assumption of rationality later gave rise to the CAPM.

Portfolio theory was first presented by Markowitz (1959), and suggests that an investor who diversifies will achieve superior returns compared to one that doesn't. It also follows naturally from the efficient market hypothesis; as it is not possible to outperform the market, the most logical investment decision would be to hold the market itself in the form of a basket of shares that represent the entire market. The two main assumptions of the theory are that:

- Investment appraisal risk is given by the amount of variation in the returns over time;
- The overall risk level may be reduced if the assets are combined into a portfolio.
- CAPM was developed from portfolio theory, and assumes that rational investors require a premium when holding risk-bearing assets. The model defines the risk premium of an individual share in relation to the

market, and can be used as a project appraisal tool. The risk premium is measured by quantifying the volatility of an individual share in relation to the market as a whole, by means of the share's *beta*. Assuming that markets absorb all relevant information efficiently, share prices will react to information rapidly, and their adjusted price will then fully reflect all information received to date, as well as all expectations of the company's future prospects. Individual shares are more or less risky than the average of the market as a whole, and this is captured by its beta. Regression techniques are commonly used to measure beta, using historical share price data. For example, the London Business School's *Risk Measurement Service* uses monthly share price movements of the previous five years to estimate beta values for liquid securities.

The CAPM is attributed to Sharpe (1964) and it states that:

- The return on a risk-bearing asset is the sum of the *risk-free* interest rate together with a risk *premium*, which is a multiple of the beta and the premium of the market itself;
- The constituents of share prices include their perceived risk bearing level, and discounts built into them explain the higher returns achieved by certain investors;
- A portfolio of shares with high volatility will have a lower price for a specified return, so in order to generate higher returns, investors must accept higher risk.

Under CAPM the market itself has a beta value of 1. An individual share exhibiting identical price movements identical to the market therefore also has a beta of 1. A share that was three times as volatile as the market[4] would have a beta of 3.

A critique of the CAPM and review of its strengths and weaknesses is outside the scope of this book. Comments about the effectiveness of beta as a measure of risk later led to the development of Arbitrage Pricing Theory (APT), first presented by Ross (1976). This states that:

- Two assets possessing identical risk exposures must offer investors identical returns, otherwise an arbitrage opportunity will arise;
- The various elements of market risk can be measured in terms of a number of economic factors, including inflation levels, interest rates, production figures, and so on, which influence all share prices;
- By using regression techniques it is possible to calculate an estimate of the impact of each of these economic factors on the overall level of risk.

---

[4] So that if the market rose by 10% the share price would rise by 30%, and a fall in the market of 10% would equally observe a fall in the share price of 30%.

There have been a number of criticisms of both the CAPM and APT[5], and the valuation of companies that had yet to make a profit illustrated how analysts could no longer apply the traditional techniques to all companies. Essentially CAPM and APT assume that the past is a good representation of the future, which may be unrealistic for companies that have undergone or which are undergoing significant changes, or which operate in rapidly changing or developing industries. As beta is measured by a regression of past returns over a relatively long period of time, any impact on the level of beta will be felt only slowly. Hence the historical beta of a company that has say, changed its view on risk exposure, will not be a reliable estimate of its future beta. Finally, it is difficult to use either method for firms that now have publicly traded shares, or for divisions within companies. However, generally both CAPM and APT and the efficient markets hypothesis are still considered because no alternative models have been presented, which explains why these approaches are still used in the markets.

## Ratio Analysis

Ratio analysis is used heavily in financial analysis. In this section, we present a review of the general application of ratio analysis and its use in peer group analysis.

**Overview of Ratio Analysis**   A number of performance measures are used as management information in the financial analysis of corporations. Generally, they may be calculated from published accounts. The following key indicators are used by most listed companies to monitor their performance:

- Return on capital employed;
- Profit on sales;
- Sales multiple on capital employed;
- Sales multiple of fixed assets;
- Sales per employee;
- Profit per employee.

These indicators are all related and it is possible to measure the impact of an improvement in one of them on the others. Return on capital employed (ROCE) is defined in a number of ways, the two most common being return on net assets (RONA) and return on equity (RoE). RONA measures the

---

[5] Most significantly, in Fama and French (1992). However, see Roll and Ross (1992) for an argument that the CAPM and APT can still be applied.

overall return on capital irrespective of the long-term source of that capital, while RoE measures return on shareholders' funds only, thereby ignoring interest payments to providers of debt capital. Focusing on RONA, which gives an indication of the return generated from net assets (that is, fixed assets and current assets minus current liabilities), analysts frequently split this into return on sales and sales multiples. Such measures are commonly calculated for quoted and unquoted companies, and are used in the comparison of performance between different companies.

We illustrate the calculation and use of these ratios in the next section.

**Using Ratio Analysis**   At Figures 9.3 and 9.4 we show the published accounts for a fictitious manufacturing company, Constructa plc. These are the balance sheet and profit and loss account. (Their notes are at Figure 9.5.) From

| | Notes | 2000 £m | 1999 £m | 1998 £m |
|---|---|---|---|---|
| Fixed assets | | 97.9 | 88.2 | 79.4 |
| | | | | |
| Current assets | | | | |
| Stock | | 80.6 | 67.3 | 65.4 |
| Debtors | (2) | 44.3 | 40.5 | 39.6 |
| Cash | | 2.4 | 2.7 | 1.4 |
| | | 127.3 | 110.5 | 106.4 |
| | | | | |
| Creditors: amounts due within one year | (3) | 104.8 | 85.8 | 70.0 |
| | | | | |
| Net current assets | | 22.5 | 24.7 | 36.4 |
| | | | | |
| Total assets less current liabilities | | 120.4 | 112.9 | 115.8 |
| | | | | |
| Creditors: amounts due after one year | (3) | 31.4 | 36.9 | 35.5 |
| | | 89.0 | 76.0 | 80.3 |
| | | | | |
| | | | | |
| Capital and reserves | | | | |
| Paid up share capital | (4) | 15.0 | 15.0 | 15.0 |
| Share premium account | | 45.5 | 37.2 | 46.1 |
| Profit and loss account | | 28.5 | 23.8 | 19.2 |
| Shareholders' funds | | 89.0 | 76.0 | 80.3 |

**FIGURE 9.3**   Constructa plc balance sheet for the year ended 31 December 2000

| | Notes | 2000 £m | 1999 £m | 1998 £m |
|---|---|---|---|---|
| Turnover | | 251.6 | 233.7 | 211.0 |
| Cost of sales | | 118.2 | 109.3 | 88.7 |
| Gross profit | | 133.4 | 124.4 | 122.3 |
| Operating expenses | | 109.0 | 102.7 | 87.9 |
| Operating profit | | 24.4 | 21.7 | 34.4 |
| Interest payable | (1) | 7.6 | 6.2 | 7.1 |
| Profit before tax | | 16.8 | 15.5 | 27.3 |
| Tax liability | | 5.04 | 4.65 | 8.19 |
| Shareholders' profit | | 11.8 | 10.9 | 19.1 |
| Dividends | | 7.1 | 6.2 | 8.5 |
| Reserves | | 4.7 | 4.6 | 10.6 |
| Earnings per share | | 7.87 | 7.27 | 12.7 |

**FIGURE 9.4** Constructa plc profit and loss account for the year ended 31 December 2000

the information in the accounts we are able to calculate the RONA, return on sales, and sales multiples ratios, shown in Table 9.1.

From Table 9.1 we see that Constructa's RONA measure was 20.3% in 2000; however, on its own this figure is meaningless. In order to gauge the relative importance of this measure we would have to compare it to previous years' figures, to see if any trend was visible. Other useful comparisons would be to the same measure for Constructa's competitor companies, as well as industry sector averages. From the information available here, it is possible only to make a historical comparison. We see that the measure has fallen considerably from the 29.7% figure in 1998, but that the most recent year has improved from the year before. The sales margin shows exactly the

| | 2000 £m | 1999 £m | 1998 £m |
|---|---|---|---|
| **(1) Interest payable** | | | |
| Bank loans and short-term loans | 5.8 | 4.1 | 5.4 |
| Hire purchase | 1.0 | 1.0 | 1.0 |
| Leases and other loans | 0.8 | 1.1 | 0.7 |
| | 7.6 | 6.2 | 7.1 |
| | | | |
| **(2) Debtors** | | | |
| Trade debtors | 34.3 | 31.8 | 32.1 |
| Other debtors | 10 | 8.7 | 7.5 |
| | 44.3 | 40.5 | 39.6 |
| | | | |
| **(3) Creditors:** amounts due within one year | | | |
| Bank loans | 31.7 | 26 | 21.1 |
| Bond | 7 | 7 | 7 |
| Trade creditors | 30.6 | 28.4 | 19.4 |
| Tax and national insurance | 10.8 | 6.8 | 3.8 |
| Leases | 3.5 | 2.6 | 11.7 |
| Other creditors | 8.9 | 4.1 | 1.4 |
| Accruals | 6.8 | 5.8 | 1.6 |
| Dividend | 5.5 | 5.1 | 4 |
| | 104.8 | 85.8 | 70.0 |
| | | | |
| **(3) Creditors:** amounts due after one year | | | |
| Bank loans | 12.1 | 11.8 | 10.2 |
| Bond | 7 | 7 | 7 |
| Leases | 8.9 | 9.4 | 9.1 |
| Other creditors | 3.4 | 8.7 | 9.2 |
| | 31.4 | 36.9 | 35.5 |
| | | | |
| **(4) Paid-up share capital** | | | |
| 10p ordinary shares, 150 million | | | |

**FIGURE 9.5**   Constructa plc: notes to the accounts

same pattern; however, the sales generation figure has not decreased. During a period of falling return such as this, which is commonly encountered during a recession, a company would analyse its asset base, with a view to increasing the sales generation ratio and countering the decrease in decreasing margin ratio.

**TABLE 9.1**  Constructa plc RONA ratio measures

| Ratio | Calculation | 2000 | 1999 | 1998 |
|---|---|---|---|---|
| RONA % | (3) / (5) × 100 | 20.3% | 19.2% | 29.7% |
| Return on sales % | (3) / (4) × 100 | 9.7% | 9.3% | 16.3% |
| Sales multiple (x) | (4) / (5) | 2.1x | 2.1x | 1.8x |
| | Source | £m | £m | £m |
| (1) Profit before tax | P&L account | 16.8 | 15.5 | 27.3 |
| (2) Interest payable | P&L account | 7.6 | 6.2 | 7.1 |
| (3) Profit before interest and tax | (1) + (2) | 24.4 | 21.7 | 34.4 |
| (4) Sales ("turnover") | P&L account | 251.6 | 233.7 | 211.0 |
| (5) Net assets | Balance sheet | 120.4 | 112.9 | 115.8 |

This illustration is a very basic one. Any management-level ratio analysis would need to look at a higher level if it is to provide any meaningful insight. We consider this in the next section.

## Management-level Ratio Analysis

**Return on Equity**  We now consider a number of performance measures that are used in corporate level analysis. Table 9.2 shows performance for a UK listed company in terms of return on equity (RoE). The terms we have considered, together with a few we have not, are shown as a historical trend. "Asset turnover" refers to the sales generation or sales multiple, while "leverage factor" is a measure of the *gearing* level, which we consider shortly.

**TABLE 9.2**  UK plc corporate performance 1995–1999

| Performance measure | 1999 | 1998 | 1997 | 1996 | 1995 |
|---|---|---|---|---|---|
| Asset Turnover (Sales generation) | 2.01 | 1.97 | 1.85 | 1.91 | 1.79 |
| Return on Net Sales | 4.26% | 4.43% | 3.99% | 4.77% | 4.12% |
| Return on Net Assets* | 8.56% | 8.73% | 7.38% | 9.11% | 7.37% |
| Leverage Factor (Gearing) | 2.43 | 2.54 | 2.83 | 2.95 | 2.71 |
| Return on Equity~ | 20.80% | 22.17% | 20.89% | 26.87% | 19.97% |

*This is Asset Turnover x Return on Net Sales
~This is Return on Net Assets x Leverage Factor

Our analysis of the anonymous UK plc shows how RoE is linked to RONA which we illustrated in the earlier analysis. How do the figures turn out for the hypothetical Constructa plc? These are listed in Table 9.3.

Unlike our actual examples from the anonymous UK plc, the ratios for Constructa plc do not work out as a product of lower level ratios. This is because different profit measures have been used to calculate the RONA and RoE; this is deliberate. With RONA we wish to measure the profit generated by the business irrespective of the source of funds used in generating this profit. RoE on the other hand measures profit attributable to shareholders, so we use the profit after tax and interest figure. The actual results illustrate a downtrend in the RoE and senior management will be concerned about this.

**Gearing** In Table 9.2 we encountered a leverage ratio, known as gearing in the UK. We also observed that gearing combined with RONA results in RoE. Put simply, gearing is the ratio of debt capital to equity capital, and measures the extent of indebtedness of a company. Gearing ratios are used by analysts and investors because they indicate the impact on ordinary shareholders' earnings of a change in operating profit. For a company with high gearing, such change in profit can have a disproportionate impact on shareholders' earnings because more of the profit has to be used to service debt. There is no one "right" level of gearing, but at some point the level will be

**TABLE 9.3**   Constructa plc corporate-level ratios

| Ratio | Calculation | 2000 | 1999 | 1998 |
|---|---|---|---|---|
| RONA % | See Table 9.1 | 20.3% | 19.2% | 29.7% |
| Return on sales % | See Table 9.1 | 9.7% | 9.3% | 16.3% |
| Sales multiple (x) | See Table 9.1 | 2.1x | 2.1x | 1.8x |
| ROE % | $(6) / (7) \times 100$ | 13.26% | 14.21% | 23.78% |
| Gearing (x) | $(5) / (7)$ | 1.35x | 1.49x | 1.44x |
| | **Source** | **£m** | **£m** | **£m** |
| (1) Profit before tax | P&L account | 16.8 | 15.5 | 27.3 |
| (2) Interest payable | P&L account | 7.6 | 6.2 | 7.1 |
| (3) Profit before interest and tax | (1) + (2) | 24.4 | 21.7 | 34.4 |
| (4) Sales ("turnover") | P&L account | 251.6 | 233.7 | 211.0 |
| (5) Net assets | Balance sheet | 120.4 | 112.9 | 115.8 |
| (6) Shareholders' profit | P&L account | 11.8 | 10.8 | 19.1 |
| (7) Shareholders' funds | Balance sheet | 89.0 | 76.0 | 80.3 |

high enough to raise both shareholders' and rating agency concerns, as doubts creep in about the company's ability to meet its debt interest obligations.[6] The acceptable level of gearing for any company is dependent on a number of issues, including the type of business it is involved in, the average gearing level across similar companies, the stage of the business cycle (companies with high gearing levels are more at risk if the economy is heading into recession), the level of and outlook for interest rates, and so on. The common view is that a firm with a historically good track record and less prone to the effects of changes in the business cycle can afford to be more highly geared than a company that does not boast these features.

As the values for debt and equity capital can be measured in more than one way, so a company's gearing level can take more than one value. We illustrate this below. Table 9.4 shows hypothetical company results.

From the data in Table 9.4 it is possible to calculate a number of different gearing ratios. These are shown in Table 9.5. So any individual measure of gearing is essentially meaningless unless it is also accompanied by a note of how it was calculated.

**Market-book and Price-earnings Ratio**    The remaining performance measures we wish to consider are the market-to-book ratio (MB) and the price-earnings or p/e ratio. It was not possible to calculate these for the hypothetical

**TABLE 9.4**    Hypothetical company results

|                                         | £m    |
| --------------------------------------- | ----- |
| Short-term debt                         | 190   |
| Long-term debt                          | 250   |
| Preference shares                       | 35    |
| Shareholders' funds                     | 500   |
| Cash at bank                            | 89    |
| Market value of long-term debt          | 276   |
| Market value of shareholders' funds     | 2,255 |

---

[6] A good illustration of this was the experience of telecommunications companies after they borrowed heavily in the debt capital market to pay for so-called "third generation" mobile phone licences, which were auctioned off by respective European governments. As a result of the multi-billion dollar sums involved in the purchase of each licence, some of the telecoms companies saw their credit ratings downgraded by Moody's and S&P (in the case of BT plc, to one level above non-investment grade) as concerns were raised about their resulting high gearing levels.

**TABLE 9.5**  Gearing ratios

| Measure | Gearing |
|---|---|
| Long-term debt / Equity [250 / (35 + 595)] | 39.7% |
| Short-term and long-term debt / Shareholders' funds [(190 + 250) / 595] | 74.0% |
| Short-term and long-term debt less cash at bank / Shareholders' funds [(190 + 250 − 89) / 595] | 59.0% |
| Market value of long-term debt / Market value of equity [276 / 1,977] | 14.0% |

Constructa plc because we don't have a publicly quoted share price for it.[7] However, these ratios are widely used and quoted by analysts and investors. For valuation purposes, they are used to obtain an estimated value of a company or subsidiary. Provided we have data for shareholders' earnings and shareholders' funds, as well as MB and p/e figures for comparable companies, it is possible to calculate an approximation of fair market value for an unquoted company.

The p/e ratio is considered to be an important performance indicator and for stock exchange listed companies is quoted in, for example, the London *Financial Times*. It is given by

$$p/e = \frac{P_{share}}{EPS} \qquad (9.10)$$

where $P_{share}$ is the market price of the company's shares and *EPS* is the earnings per share. For quoted companies, both these values may be obtained with ease.

The p/e ratio is an indication of the price that investors are prepared to pay for a company's shares in return for its current level of earnings. It relates shareholder profit to the market value of the company. Companies that are in "high growth" sectors, such as (during the late 1990s) the "dot .com" or technology sector, are observed generally to have high p/e ratios,

---

[7] Not every "public listed company" (plc) actually has its shares quoted on the stock exchange. It is possible for a company to be a plc without having quoted shares.

while companies in low growth sectors will have lower p/e ratios. This illustrates one important factor of p/e ratio analysis: an individual figure on its own is of no real use, rather, it is the sector average as well as the overall level of the stock market that are important considerations for the investor. In the *Financial Times* the company pages list the p/e ratio for each industry sector, thus enabling investors to compare specific company p/e ratios with the sector level and the market level.[8] The *p/e relative* is calculated by comparing specific and industry-level p/e ratios, given at (9.12), which is an indication of where investors rate the company in relation to the industry it is operating in, or the market as a whole.

$$p/e\,relative = \frac{p/e_{company}}{p/e_{market}} \qquad (9.11)$$

A very high p/e relative for a specific company may indicate a highly-rated company and one that is a sector leader. However, it may also indicate, and this is very topical, a "glamour" company that is significantly overvalued and so overdue for a correction and decline in its share price.

The MB ratio relates a company's market value to shareholder funds value. If we see the p/e ratio as emanating from the P&L account, then the MB ratio emanates from the balance sheet. It is given by

$$MB = ROE\% \times p/e\,ratio \qquad (9.12)$$

We consider the MB and p/e ratios in the context of business valuation in the next section.

## Corporate Valuation

We have noted how for a company listed on a stock exchange, it is straightforward to know its market value: its share price. However, for subsidiaries and divisions of quoted companies or unquoted companies, a proper market value is not so simple to obtain. In this section, we provide an introduction of how analysis from within a "peer group" of companies may be used to obtain an estimated valuation for unquoted companies.

We wish to calculate an estimated market share price for Constructa plc, our hypothetical manufacturing company. Assume that we are fortunate to observe a peer group that consists of three other manufacturing companies of comparable size and performance, operating in a similar line of business as Constructa plc. The three companies are known as "X", "Y",

---

[8] These figures are not listed in the Monday edition of the FT, which contains other relevant data.

and "Z". Table 9.6 shows financial data and key performance indicators for the year 2000 for each of these three companies.

The next step is to use this observed data in conjunction with Constructa plc data to obtain a range of possible values for the latter's market value. First, we calculate the mean p/e and MB ratios of the three peer group companies, and then from the range of ratios for these companies calculate the estimated Constructa plc values, using that company's own earnings per share value. In this way, we obtain a highest and lowest possible market valuation and a mean valuation. We have not previously calculated a book value per share for Constructa plc, so this is done now; the result is 59.3 pence, obtained by dividing the shareholders' funds figure of £89 million by the number of shares (150 million).

The mean value p/e and MB ratios are shown in Table 9.7, together with the range of possible market values for Constructa plc using each method.

With this approach we obtain a mean value for the Constructa plc share price of £1.53 or £2.79 depending on which method we use. It is a subjective issue as to which approach is the better one, and the motivation of the

**TABLE 9.6**  Comparable company financial indicators, year 2000

|  |  | X plc | Y plc | Z plc |
|---|---|---|---|---|
| Turnover £m |  | 821.4 | 369.7 | 211.3 |
| Profit before interest and tax £m |  | 97.6 | 41.9 | 18.7 |
| Net profit (profit after interest and tax) £m |  | 56.2 | 26.7 | 15.4 |
| Book value of shareholders' funds £m |  | 331.2 | 219.6 | 46.9 |
| Shares in issue |  | 167m | 55m | 48m |
| Share market price |  | 712p | 408p | 926p |
| Return on sales % | (1) | 11.88 | 11.33% | 8.85% |
| Earnings per share | (2) | 33.7p | 48.5p | 32.1p |
| p/e ratio | (3) | 21.1 | 8.4 | 28.8 |
| Book value per share | (4) | 198p | 399p | 97.7p |
| MB ratio | (5) | 3.6 | 1.02 | 9.5 |

*Notes:*
(1) Return on sales is [profit before interest and tax / turnover]
(2) EPS is [net profit / number of shares in issue]
(3) The p/e ratio is [share price / earnings per share]
(4) Book value per share is [book value of shareholders' funds / number of shares in issue]
(5) MB ratio is [share market price / book value per share]

**TABLE 9.7** Peer group company ratios, mean values, and Constructa plc market valuation

|  | Mean value | X plc | Y plc | Z plc |
|---|---|---|---|---|
| p/e ratio | 19.4 | 21.1 | 8.4 | 28.8 |
| MB ratio | 4.7 | 3.6 | 1.02 | 9.5 |

| Constructa plc |  | Mean value | High value | Low value |
|---|---|---|---|---|
| Valuation using p/e ratio |  |  |  |  |
| EPS | 7.87 |  |  |  |
| p/e ratio |  | 19.4 | 28.8 | 8.4 |
| Share market value (1) |  | 152.7p | 226.7p | 66.1p |
| Valuation using MB ratio |  |  |  |  |
| Book value per share | 59.3p |  |  |  |
| MB ratio |  | 4.7 | 9.5 | 1.02 |
| Share market value (2) |  | 278.7p | 563.4p | 60.5p |

analyst undertaking the calculation is key. In practice, analysts will consider a peer group with a greater number of companies, which usually results in a wider range of possible values. Of course the true market valuation for any good is the price at which there is both a buyer and seller for it, and similarly the true value for a company will lie somewhere in between the high and low limits that arise from using the method we have just described.

## EXAMPLE 9.1 THE "TRUE" COST OF EQUITY: CONTINGENT CONVERTIBLE BOND

As this chapter will have made clear, equity valuation is very much an inexact science. There is logic in taking the market valuation of a listed company to determine the cost of capital, but as the share price is volatile this does not make it relevant for a long-term analysis. Perhaps the "truest" cost of equity available is for any company that issues Contingent Convertible (CoCo) bonds: these are capital market securities that were issued by banks in the wake of the 2008 crash. Their special feature is that under certain circumstances they convert from debt to equity. For this reason, investors treat the bonds as equity; hence the coupon payable on CoCo securities is a good proxy for the cost of equity. Figure 9.6 shows basic features of such bonds.

Of course a company, be it a bank or otherwise, that has not issued CoCo will have to continue to use one of the assumptions-based estimation methods described in standard texts on corporate finance.

- Hybrid capital securities
- Mandatory action occurs when the capital of the bank breaches a pre-determined threshold. The bond is
  - Partially or wholly written down OR
  - Converted to equity
- Most AT1 but some AT2
- Despite being less favourable, demand has been strong for investors seeking yield
  - Some investors believe bank equity holders are treated well in a crisis
- Besides analysing bank credit, investor must also consider
  - Trigger threshold
  - Definition of capital
  - Method of applying losses – write-down or equity, shut-off of coupons/dividends

| TYPE | TRIGGER | ACTION |
|---|---|---|
| Conversion | core Tier 1 ratio falls below 5% | automatically converted into ordinary shares |
| Conversion | 1) common equity Tier 1 ratio falls below 7% OR 2) regulator determines bank requires public sector support to prevent it from becoming insolvent, bankrupt, or unable to pay material amount of debts | automatically converted into ordinary shares |
| Write-down | equity capital ratio (equity capital divided by risk-weighted assets) falls below 7% | automatic and permanent write-down of 1) principal amount to 25% of par and 2) accrued and unpaid interest |
| Write-down | equity capital ratio (equity capital divided by risk-weighted assets) falls below 8% | cancel any accrued but unpaid interest and write-down the prevailing principal amount |

**FIGURE 9.6**   Features of contingent convertible bonds
*Source*: Peter Eisenhardt, 2017.

## EXAMPLE 9.2    IFRS9

The IFRS9 accounting framework makes great demands on a bank's reporting and stress testing framework. The topic is outside the scope of this book but we introduce it here so that readers are aware of its main focus.

In essence, IFSR9 dictates the process by which banks set aside provisions for loan losses or impaired loans. The key change from previous regimes is that an element of provision is required even for loans that are not yet marked as impaired or non-performing. The approach to recognising impairment is based on a three-stage process which is intended to reflect the deterioration in credit quality of a financial instrument. This "three-stages" model for impairment based on changes in credit quality since initial recognition is shown at Figure 9.7, which describes how the "expected credit loss" (ECL) will be determined based on loan quality deterioration.

In IFRS9 impairment, a time slice approach is used within the ECL model:

$$ECL = \sum_{i=1}^{n} EAD_i \; PD_i \; LGD_i \; DF_i$$

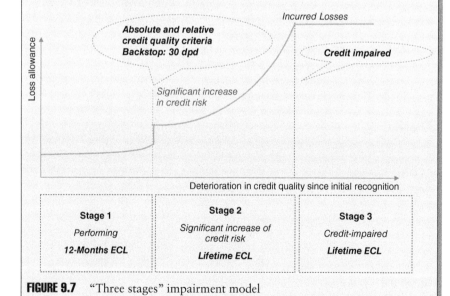

**FIGURE 9.7**    "Three stages" impairment model

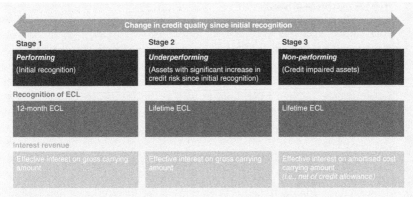

**FIGURE 9.8**   IFRS9 Framework

IFRS 9 replaces IAS 39's incurred loss impairment approach, with the forward looking ECL approach to impairment provisions for financial assets drawing on Risk data in order to report through Finance. The standard covers classification and measurement of assets and hedge accounting but the largest impact on business is the new approach for measuring impairment using an expected loss approach. Figure 9.8 describes Figure 9.7 in greater detail.

Bank stress testing regimes (see chapters 8 and 12 on ICAAP and ILAAP respectively) must incorporate IFRS9 requirements into their scenario frameworks.

This extract from *Structured Credit Products, Second Edition* (2010)

## Credit Analysis and Relative Value Measurement

### Credit Analysis and Relative Value Measurement

Credit analysis is concerned with issuer-specific considerations (as opposed to macro considerations). This will include a quantitative analysis and a qualitative analysis that results in the assignment of an internal credit rating. Investors sometimes substitute the credit rating given by a third-party company such as Moody's or S&P. The qualitative factors to consider include those both internal and exogenous to the company.

In this chapter, we consider the process of credit analysis, as this is important for investors to be familiar with. We then look at measuring credit relative value.

# CREDIT ANALYSIS

When ratings agencies were first set up the primary focus of credit analysis was on the default risk of the bond, or the probability that the investor would not receive the interest payments and the principal repayment as they fell due. Although this is still important, credit analysts now also consider overall macroeconomic conditions, as well as the chance that an issuer will have its rating changed during the life of the bond. There are differences in approach, depending on which industry or market sector the issuing company is part of.

In this section we review the main issues of concern to a credit analyst when rating bond issues. Analysts usually adopt a 'top-down' approach, or a 'big picture' approach, and concentrate on the macro issues first before looking at the issuer-specific points in detail. The process therefore involves reviewing the issuer's industry, before looking at its financial and balance sheet strength, and finally the legal provisions concerning the bond issue. There are also detail differences in analysis depending on which industry the issuer is in.

## The Issuer Industry

In the first instance the credit analysis process of a specific issue will review the issuer's industry. This is in order to place the subsequent company analysis in context. For example, a company that has recorded growth rates of 10% each year may appear to be a quality performer, but not if its industry has been experiencing average growth rates of 30%. Generally, the industry analysis will review the following issues:

- *Economic cycle*. The business cycle of the industry and its correlation with the overall business cycle are key indicators. That is, how closely does the industry follow the rate of growth of its country's GNP? Certain industries such as the electricity and food retail sectors are more resistant to recession than others. Other sectors are closely tied to changes in population and birth patterns, such as residential homes, while the financial services industry is influenced by the overall health of the economy, as well as by the level of interest rates. As well as the correlation with macro-factors, credit analysts review traditional financial indicators in context; for example, the issuing company's *earnings per share* (EPS) against the growth rate of its industry.
- *Growth prospects*. This review is of the issuer industry's general prospects. A company operating within what is considered a high-growth industry is generally deemed to have better credit quality expectations than one operating in a low-growth environment.

A scenario of anticipated growth in the industry has implications for the issuing company; for example, the extent to which the company will be able cope with capacity demands and the financing of excess capacity. A fast-growth industry also attracts new entrants, which will lead to over-supply, intensified competition and reduced margins. A slow-growth industry has implications for diversification, so that a company deemed to have plans for diversifying when operating in stagnant markets will be marked up.

* *Competition.* A review of the intensity of competitive forces within an industry, and the extent of pricing and over- or under-capacity, is an essential ingredient of credit analysis. Competition is now regarded as a global phenomenon and well-rated companies are judged able to compete successfully on a global basis while concentrating on the highest growth regions. Competition within a particular industry is related to that industry's structure and has implications for pricing flexibility. The type of market—for example, monopoly, oligopoly and so on—also influences pricing policy and relative margins. Another issue arises if there is obvious overcapacity in an industry; this has been exemplified in the past in the airline industry and financial services (of some countries) when overcapacity often leads to intense price competition and price wars. This is frequently damaging for the industry as a whole, as all companies suffer losses and financial deterioration in the attempt to maintain or grow market share.

* *Supply sources.* The availability of suppliers in an industry influences a company's financial wellbeing. Monopoly sources of supply are considered a restrictive element and have negative implications. A vertically integrated company that is able to supply its own raw materials is less susceptible to economic conditions that might affect suppliers or leave it hostage to price rises. A company that is not self-sufficient in its factors of production, but is nevertheless in strong enough a position to pass on its costs, is in a good position.

* *Research and development.* A broad assessment of the growth prospects of a company must also include a review of its research and development (R&D) position. In certain industries, such as telecommunications, media and information technology, a heavy investment in R&D is essential simply in order to maintain market share. In a hightechnology field it is common for products to obsolesce very quickly, therefore it is essential to maintain high R&D spending. In the short term, however, a company with a low level of research expenditure may actually post above-average (relative to the industry) profits because it is operating at higher margins. This is not

considered a healthy strategy for the long term, though. Evaluating the R&D input of a company is not necessarily a straightforward issue of comparing ratios, however, as it is also important to assess correctly the direction of technology. That is, a successful company needs not only to invest a sufficient amount in R&D, it must also be correct in its assessment of the direction the industry is heading, technology-wise. A heavy investment in developing Betamax videos, for example, would not have assisted a company in the early 1980s.

- *Level of regulation.* The degree of regulation in an industry, its direction and its effect on the profitability of a company are relevant in a credit analysis. A highly regulated industry such as power generation, production of medicines or (in certain countries) telecommunications can have a restrictive influence on company profits. On the other hand, if the government has announced a policy of deregulating an industry, this is considered a positive development for companies in that industry.

- *Labour relations.* An industry with a highly unionised labour force or generally tense labour relations is viewed unfavourably compared to one with stable labour relations. Credit analysts will consider historic patterns of, say, strikes and production days lost to industrial action. The status of labour relations is also more influential in a highly labour-intensive industry than one that is more automated for example.

- *Political climate.* The investment industry adopts an increasingly global outlook and the emergence of sizeable tradable debt markets in, for example, 'emerging' countries means that ratings agencies frequently must analyse the general political and economic climate in which an industry is operating. Failure to foresee certain political developments can have far-reaching effects for investors; for example in Indonesia when that country experienced a change of government foreign investors lost funds as several local banks went bankrupt.

# FINANCIAL ANALYSIS

The traditional approach to credit analysis concentrated heavily on financial analysis. The more modern approach involves a review of the industry the company is operating in first, discussed above, before considering financial considerations. Generally, the financial analysis of the issuer is conducted in three phases, namely:

- the ratio analysis for the bonds;
- analysing the company's return on capital;
- non-financial factors such as management expertise and the extent of overseas operations.

## Ratio analysis

In themselves ratios do not present very much insight, although there are various norms that can be applied. Generally, ratio analysis is compared to the levels prevalent in the industry, as well as historical values, in an effort to place the analysis in context and compare the company with those in its peer group. The ratios that can be considered are:

- pre-tax interest cover, the level of cover for interest charges in current pre-tax income;
- fixed interest charge level;
- *leverage*, which is commonly defined as the ratio of long-term debt as a percentage of the total capitalisation;
- level of leverage compared to industry average;
- nature of debt, whether fixed- or floating-rate, short- or long-term;
- cash flow, which is the ratio of cash flow as a percentage of total debt. Cash flow itself is usually defined as net income from continuing operations, plus depreciation and taxes, while debt is taken to be long-term debt;
- net assets, as a percentage of total debt. The liquidity of the assets—meaning the ease with which they can be turned into cash—is taken into account when assessing the net asset ratio.

The ratings agencies maintain benchmarks that are used to assign ratings, and these are monitored and if necessary modified to allow for changes in the economic climate. For example, Standard & Poor's guidelines for pre-tax interest cover, leverage level and cash flow in 1997 are shown in Table 4.1. A pre-tax cover of above 9.00, for example, was consistent with a double-A rating.

| Credit Rating | Pre-Tax Interest Cover | Leverage | Cash Flow |
|---|---|---|---|
| AAA | 17.99 | 13.2 | 97.5 |
| AA | 9.74 | 19.7 | 8.5 |
| A | 5.35 | 33.2 | 43.8 |
| BBB | 2.91 | 44.8 | 29.9 |

**Table 4.1**   S&P ratio benchmarks, 1997.
*Source*: S&P.

Other ratios that are considered include:

- intangibles; that is, the portion of intangibles relative to the asset side of a balance sheet;
- unfunded pension liabilities; generally a fully funded pension is not seen as necessary; however, an unfunded liability that is over 10% of net assets would be viewed as a negative point;
- age and condition of plant;
- working capital.

## Return on equity

There is a range of performance measures used in the market that are connected with return on equity (generally, the analysis concentrates on return on capital, or more recently return on risk-adjusted capital or RORAC). In analysing measures of return, analysts seek to determine trends in historical performance and comparisons with peer group companies. Different companies also emphasise different target returns in their objectives, usually an expression of their corporate philosophy, so it is common for companies in the same industry to have different return ratios. The range of ratios used by the credit ratings agencies is shown below. Note that 'EBIT' is 'earnings before interest and tax'.

$$\text{Return on net assets} = \frac{\text{Profit}}{\text{Net assets}} \times 100$$

$$\text{Return on sales} = \frac{\text{Profit}}{\text{Sales turnover}} \times 100$$

$$\text{Return on equity} = \left(\text{Return on net assets} \times \text{Gearing}\right) \times 100$$

$$\text{Pre-tax interest cover} = \frac{\text{Pre-tax income from continuing operations}}{\text{Gross interest}}$$

$$\text{EBIT interest cover} =$$

$$\frac{\text{Pre-tax income from continuing operations} + \text{Interest expense}}{\text{Gross interest}}$$

$$\text{Long-term debt as \% of capitalisation} = \frac{\text{Long-term debt}}{\text{Long-term debt} + \text{Equity}} \times 100$$

$$\text{Funds flow as \% of debt} = \frac{\text{Funds from operations}}{\text{Total debt}} \times 100$$

$$\text{Free cash flow as \% of debt} = \frac{\text{Free cash flow}}{\text{Total debt}} \times 100$$

The agencies make available data that may be consulted by the public; for example, default rates, recovery rates and so on.

## Non-financial factors

The non-financial element of a company credit analysis has assumed a more important role in recent years, especially with regard to companies in exotic or emerging markets. Credit analysts review the non-financial factors relevant to the specific company after they have completed the financial and ratio analysis. These include the strength and competence of senior management, and the degree of exposure to overseas markets. The depth of overseas exposure is not always apparent from documents such as the annual report, and analysts sometimes need to conduct further research to determine this. Companies with considerable overseas exposure, such as petroleum companies, also need to be reviewed with respect to the political situation in their operating locations. A bank such as Standard Chartered, for example, has significant exposure to more exotic currencies in Asian, Middle-Eastern and African countries, and so is more at risk from additional market movements than a bank with almost exclusively domestic operations. The global, integrated nature of the bond markets also means that the foreign exchange exposure of a company must be evaluated and assessed for risk. The quality of management is a subjective, qualitative factor that can be reviewed in a number of ways. A personal familiarity with senior directors, acquired over a period of time, may help in the assessment. A broad breadth of experience, diversity of age and strong internal competition for those aspiring to very senior roles is considered positive. A company that had been founded by one individual, and in which there were no clear plans of 'succession', might be marked down.

## INDUSTRY-SPECIFIC ANALYSIS

Specific industries will be subject to review that is more relevant to the particular nature of the operations of the companies within them. In this section we briefly consider two separate industries: power generation, water and certain other public service companies (or utilities); and financial companies.

### Utility Companies

The industry for power generation, water supply and until recently telecommunications has a tradition of being highly regulated. Until the mid- 1980s, utility companies were public-sector companies, and the first privatisation of such a company was for British Telecom in 1984. In certain European countries, utility companies are still nationalised companies, and their debt trades virtually as government debt. Credit analysis for utility companies therefore emphasises non-financial factors such as the depth of regulation and the direction in which regulation is heading; for example, towards an easing or tightening. Even in a privatised industry, for example, new government regulation maybe targeted only at the utility sector. In May 1997, the Labour government in the UK imposed a 'windfall tax' on several privatised utility companies shortly after being elected.

Another consideration concerns government direction on how the companies may operate, such as restrictions on where a power generation company may purchase coal from. In some countries, such as Germany, coal must be bought from the country's own domestic coal industry only, which imposes costs on the generating company that it would escape if it were free to purchase coal from other, lower cost producers. The financial analysis of a utility company essentially follows the pattern we described earlier.

## Financial Sector Companies

The financial sector encompasses a large and diverse group of companies. They conduct an intermediary function in that they are a conduit for funds between borrowers and lenders of capital. At its simplest, financial service companies such as banks may earn profit by taking the spread between funds lent and borrowed. In analysing a financial sector company the credit analyst will consider the type of customer base served by the company; for example, how much of a bank's lending is to the wholesale sector, how much is retail and so on. The financial strength and prospects of its customer base are important elements of a bank's credit rating.

Financial analysis of banks and securities houses is concerned (in addition to the factors discussed above) with the asset quality of the institution; for example, the extent of diversification of a bank's lending book. Diversification can be across customer base as well as geographically. A loan book that is heavily concentrated in one sector is considered to be a negative factor in the overall credit assessment of the bank. A credit analyst will be concerned with the level of loans compared with levels in peer companies and the risk involved with this type of lending. For example, the expected frequency of bad loans from direct unsecured retail customer loans is higher than for retail customer loans secured by a second mortgage on a property. The higher lending rate charged for the former is designed to compensate for this higher lending risk.

There is a range of financial ratios that can be used to assess a bank's asset quality. These include:

- loss reserves/net charge-off level;
- net losses/average level of receivables;
- non-performing loans/average level of receivables.

However, unlike the more 'concrete' financial ratios given earlier, there is a higher subjective element with these ratios as banks themselves will designate which loans are non-performing and those loans against which have been assigned charges. Nevertheless, these ratios are useful indicators and may be used to identify trends across the sector as well. The loss reserves/net charge-off ratio is perhaps the most useful as it indicates the level of 'cushion' that a bank has; a falling ratio suggests that the bank may not be adding sufficient reserves to cover for future charge-offs. This trend, if continued, may then result in a future increase in the reserves and therefore a decrease in earnings levels as the expense of the reserves increase.

The leverage ratio is particularly important for financial sector companies, as the industry and business itself are highly leveraged. Banks and securities companies are therefore permitted a significantly higher leverage level than other companies. For example, in a diversified banking group with a high level of asset quality, a leverage ratio of 20:1 or even higher is considered satisfactory by ratings agencies. Another important measure for financial companies is *liquidity*. Due to the nature of the industry and the capital structure of banks, liquidity or, more accurately, the lack of liquidity is the primary reason behind banking failures. A bank that is unable to raise funds sufficiently quickly to meet demand will most probably fail, and certainly so if external support is not provided. An inability to raise funds may arise due to internal factors, such as a deterioration in earnings or a very poorly performing loan book, connected perhaps with a downgrade in credit rating, or from external factors such as a major structural fault in the money markets. This latter was exactly what happened to Northern Rock in 2007.

For credit analysis purposes the traditional liquidity measures are:

- cash;
- cash equivalents;
- level of receivables under one year/level of short-term liabilities.

A higher ratio indicates a greater safety cushion. A further consideration is the extent of lines of credit from other banks in the market. Other measures of strength for financial companies are *asset coverage*, the bank's earnings record including *earnings per share* (profit attributable to shareholders/number of shares in issue) and finally, the size of the institution. There is an element of thought which states that a very large institution, measured by asset size, cannot go bankrupt. This type of thinking can lead to complacency however, and it did not prevent several large Japanese banks from getting into financial difficulty in the 1990s.[1] It was also plainly no defence against the problems suffered by Citigroup and Royal Bank of Scotland in 2008.

Reproduced from *Structured Credit Products, Second Edition* (2010)

## SELECTED BIBLIOGRAPHY AND REFERENCES

Fridson, M., and F. Alvarez, (2011). *Financial Statement Analysis: A Practitioner's Guide*, 4th edition, John Wiley & Sons Ltd.

Sagner, J., (2010). *Essentials of Working Capital Management*, John Wiley & Sons Ltd.

# PART III

# Bank Treasury and Strategic Asset–Liability Management

Part III contains our "big idea". Having provided the necessary background and technical detail on finance and bank risk management in Parts I and II, we are now in a position to elaborate on what is the "must have" for all banks, irrespective of size or business model, to ensure sustainability and good practice: strategic asset–liability management (ALM). We spend a bit of time discussing this concept, why it's important, and how to implement it. It is not a trivial process.

The purpose of Part III is to provide an idea of business best-practice in banking, including recommendations on strategy and structure. To this end we describe optimum Treasury and ALM committee (ALCO) operating models and governance structures. The topic breakdown is:

- Treasury operating model and ALCO best-practice framework;
- Strategic ALM concept and how to implement it;
- Liquidity risk, everything from basic principles and metrics to policy and strategy;
- Market risk, traded and non-traded.

Having presented these ingredients we attempt to wrap it up with a chapter on the future of bank balance sheet risk management. Finally in Chapter 15 we also provide a listing of the various policy templates that are available for practitioners, contained on the book's website.

*"Gene Kranz is a leader. He is a man who gives others the feeling that they are about to go through the door together into the stadium where they are each going to play the game of their life."*

—Norman Mailer, *A Fire on the Moon*,
Boston: Little, Brown & Company, 1970

CHAPTER **10**

# The Bank Treasury Operating Model and ALCO Governance Process Best-Practice

There are certain functions in a bank that are understood universally and which require very little effort in their definition. For example, it will be clear to every banker in every country in the world what the "corporate lending" department does. And while some departments in banks are relatively recent in their historical origins (think of the "correlation trading" desk), some departments will be as old as banks themselves.

The "Treasury" function is just such an ancient department. Whatever they may have been called at the time, the very first banks would have had an individual or team of individuals responsible for collecting all the deposits and for transmitting all the loans, and for dealing with the surplus or shortage of cash at the end of the day. However, mention "Treasury" to a banker (or University economics department professor) and it will not be entirely clear to them quite exactly what the Treasury department does in any one specific bank. There is considerable variety observable. This is not an uncommon thing in finance, which as a practical discipline is almost as much art as science, and while there is no one "right" or "wrong" Treasury operating model, what is important is that the Treasury function in any bank is *the right one for that bank*.

Treasury is an important part of the *balance sheet risk management triumvirate* in a bank. Figure 10.1 is a simple but effective illustration of this triumvirate.

What Figure 10.1 shows is that Treasury is a peer of the Finance and Risk functions, led respectively by the Chief Financial Officer and Chief Risk Officer. When it comes to managing the bank's balance sheet, all three departments play an equally important function, and therefore the interaction between all three teams must be efficient and effective. There is one crucial aspect of operations that is unique to Treasury, however, and that

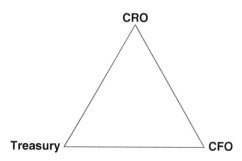

**FIGURE 10.1**   Balance sheet risk management triumvirate

is that Treasury is the only department in a bank that is both inward and outward looking, *and* has responsibility for the entire balance sheet. That makes the Treasury function the cornerstone and vital underpinning of the entire bank.[1] Given this importance, we can say without exaggeration that it is important that the Treasury function is organised and managed in a way that represents best-practice for the bank and which ensures that the bank itself is run along the best possible lines. Therefore in this chapter, we will cover the recommended operating model for the Treasury function in some detail.

The extracts from the author's previous works describe the "traditional" approach to bank asset–liability management (ALM), and the role of the bank's ALM committee (ALCO). This historically orthodox approach might be termed "reactive" ALM. As we shall see, for best-practice balance sheet management and optimisation it is important that banks move to a more "proactive" ALM discipline, and this is described in the author's new material.

We will also describe what this means for the asset-liability committee (ALCO), and present a recommended best-practice governance structure for the bank's ALCO. We do not exaggerate when we say that the ALCO is the most important risk and operating committee in the entire bank, and must function in an effective way. The book extracts consider the ALCO operating process, and we provide an ALCO Terms of Reference template at Appendix 10.A. This would be appropriate for virtually all commercial banking institutions.

The remainder of Part III in this book looks in further detail at the technical side of the Treasury function, and concludes with a preview of the future of the bank Treasury organisation structure.

---

[1] This ignores whether the Treasury function has an explicit trading and P&L target or not.

This extract from *Bank Asset and Liability Management* (2007)

## Asset-Liability Management III: The ALCO

## Asset-Liability Management III: The ALCO

The third and final strand of our look at traditional ALM considers the reporting process, often overseen by the ALM committee (ALCO). The ALCO will have a specific remit to oversee all aspects of ALM, from the front-office money market function to back-office operations and middle-office reporting and risk management. In this chapter we consider the salient features of ALCO procedures.

## ALCO POLICY

The ALCO is responsible for setting, and implementing, the ALM policy. Its composition varies in different banks but usually includes heads of business lines, as well as director-level staff such as the finance director. The ALCO also sets hedging policy.

The ALM process may be undertaken by the Treasury desk, ALM desk or another dedicated function within the bank. In traditional commercial banks it will be responsible for management reporting to the ALCO. The ALCO will consider the report in detail at regular meetings, usually weekly. Main points of interest in the ALCO report include variations in interest income, the areas that experienced fluctuations in income and what the latest short-term income projections are. The ALM report will link these three strands across the group entity and also to each individual business line. That is, it will consider macro-level factors driving variations in interest income as well as specific desk-level factors. The former includes changes in the shape and level of the yield curve, while the latter will include new business, customer behaviour and so on. Of necessity the ALM report is a detailed, large document.

Table 8.1 is a summary overview of the responsibilities of the ALCO, and is essentially a banking ALM strategic overview.

The ALCO will meet on a regular basis; the frequency depends on the type of institution but is usually once a month. The composition of the ALCO also varies by institution but may be comprised of the heads of Treasury, Trading and Risk Management, as well as the finance director. Representatives from the credit committee and loan syndication may also be present. A typical agenda would consider all the elements listed in Table 8.1. Thus the meeting will discuss and generate action points on the following:

| Mission | Components |
|---|---|
| ALCO management and reporting | Formulating ALM strategy |
| | Management reporting |
| | ALCO agenda and minutes |
| | Assessing liquidity, gap and interest-rate risk reports |
| | Scenario planning and analysis |
| | Interest income projection |
| Asset management | Managing bank liquidity book (CDs, Bills) |
| | Managing the FRN book |
| | Investing bank capital |
| ALM strategy | Yield curve analysis |
| | Money market trading |
| Funding and liquidity management | Liquidity policy |
| | Managing funding and liquidity risk |
| | Ensuring funding diversification |
| | Managing lending of funds |
| Risk management | Formulating hedging policy |
| | Interest-rate risk exposure management |
| | Implementing hedging policy using cash and derivative instruments |
| Internal treasury function | Formulating transfer pricing system and level |
| | Funding group entities |
| | Calculating the cost of capital |

**Table 8.1**   ALCO main mission

- Management reporting: this will entail analysing the various management reports and either signing off on them or agreeing to items for actioning. The issues to consider include lending margin, interest income, variance from last projection, customer business and future business. Current business policy with regard to lending and portfolio management will be reviewed and either continued or adjusted.
- Business planning: existing asset (and liability) books will be reviewed, and future business direction drawn up. This will consider the performance of existing business, most importantly with regard to return on capital. The existing asset portfolio will be analysed

from a risk-reward perspective, and a decision taken to continue or modify all lines of business. Any proposed new business will be discussed and if accepted in principle will be moved on to the next stage.[1] At this stage any new business will be assessed for projected returns, revenue and risk exposure.

- Hedging policy: overall hedging policy will consider the acceptance of risk exposure, existing risk limits and the use of hedging instruments. The latter also includes use of derivative instruments. Many bank ALM desks find that their hedging requirements can be met using plain vanilla products such as interest-rate swaps and exchange-traded short-money futures contracts. The use of options, and even vanilla instruments such as FRAs,[2] is much less common than one might think. Hedging policy takes into account the cash book revenue level, current market volatility levels and the overall cost of hedging. On occasion, certain exposures may be left unhedged because the cost associated with hedging them is deemed prohibitive (this includes the actual cost of putting on the hedge as well as the opportunity cost associated with expected reduced income from the cash book). Of course, hedging policy is formulated in coordination with overall funding and liquidity policy. Its final form must consider the bank's views of the following:
  - expectations on the future level and direction of interest rates;
  - balancing the need to manage and control risk exposure with the need to maximise revenue and income;
  - the level of risk aversion, and how much risk exposure the bank is willing to accept.

The ALCO is dependant on management reporting from the ALM or Treasury desk. The reports may be compiled by the Treasury middle office. The main report is the overall ALM report, showing the composition of the bank's ALM book. This was discussed in Chapter 5. Other reports will look at specific business lines, and will consider the return on capital generated by these businesses. These reports will need to break down aggregate levels of revenue and risk by business line. Reports will also drill down by product type, across business lines. Other reports will consider the gap, the gap risk, the VaR or DV01 (interest-rate risk)

---

[1] New business will follow a long process of approval, typically involving all the relevant front, middle- and back-office departments of the bank, and culminating in a "new products committee" meeting at which the proposed new line of business will be either approved, sent back to the sponsoring department for modification or rejected.

[2] See Chapter 13. But, as a well-known old boy from the market is fond of saying, "Hedging is for gardeners!"

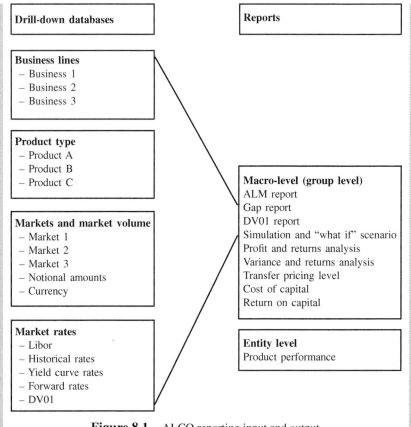

**Figure 8.1**     ALCO reporting input and output

report and credit risk exposures. Overall, the reporting system must be able to isolate revenues, return and risk by country sector, business line and product type. There is also an element of scenario planning; that is, expected performance under various specified macro- and micro-level market conditions.

Figure 8.1 illustrates the general reporting concept.

Reproduced from *Bank Asset and Liability Management* (2007)

**This extract from *The Principles of Banking* (2012)**

## The ALCO: Terms of Reference and Treasury Operating Model

### The ALCO: Terms of Reference and Treasury Operating Model

In the previous chapter we introduced the Asset–Liability Committee or ALCO, the most important operating committee in a bank. In this chapter we consider further the governance aspects of the ALCO, and a basic reporting pack that is part of ALCO MI reporting. We review a business best practice approach to ALCO governance in a group banking structure, for a bank that operates across multiple legal entities and country jurisdictions. We also describe the organisation of a business best-practice Treasury function.

A presentation summary of the ALCO role and policy is available at the Wiley website (see Chapter 19 for details). This also holds examples of ALCO reporting packs.

# THE ALCO GOVERNANCE MODEL

It is important that the ALCO function be set up and run with a governance structure and authority that befits its importance. For this reason, its terms of reference (ToR) must be articulated clearly to all bank management. Regular attendance by members of the ALCO must also be stressed. A common point of discussion is the frequency with which the ALCO should meet. At the minimum it should meet once every four weeks, ideally at the same time and on the same day each month. This establishes a pattern and ensures that the meeting is embedded in the firm's risk and management culture. If for any reason a discussion is required ahead of the next scheduled meeting, for example during periods of market stress or because of a firm-specific issue of urgency, then certainly an extraordinary meeting should be able to be called at short notice.

We review here the ALCO ToR and some sample agendas.

## ALCO Terms of Reference

Among the supplementary materials to this book appearing on the Wiley website (see Chapter 19 for details), we enclose a recommended sample template for an ALCO ToR. This is certainly appropriate for a small or medium-sized bank. We consider the ALCO ToR for a larger or multinational institution later in the chapter.

The most significant element of ALCO organisation is its membership, which reflects its status as a high-level management committee and key

**ALCO Membership**

*Members*

CEO or Deputy CEO

Chief Financial Officer (Chair)

Head of Treasury (Deputy Chair)

Head of Corporate Banking

Head of Retail Banking

Head of Private Banking

Head of Research *or* Chief Economist

Chief Risk Officer

*Guests*

Head of ALM/Money Markets

Head of Market & Liquidity Risk

Head of Valuation Control/Product Control

Head of Financial Institutions Group

*Secretariat*

Treasury Business Manager or Liquidity team member

**Table 10.1**    ALCO membership.

policymaking body. Table 10.1 is an extract from the ToR template. This is the criteria recommended for ALCO membership in a medium-sized bank. What one observes from Table 10.1 is the seniority as well as the slant of the ALCO, which is ultimately a risk management mechanism. Note the following:

- the committee is chaired by the Finance Director, or in case of absence, the Head of Treasury, and not by the CEO or any of the business line heads (where the Treasury desk is a profit centre and not a cost centre, the Head of Treasury is less likely to act as Chair, but if no alternative is possible, this person must be mindful to not allow any conflict of interest whenever required to act as chair in the CFO's absence);
- the head of each business line must be represented, as must the head of risk management (more often now termed the Chief Risk Officer);
- selected members of staff of relevant departments can also be invited to attend as guests; for example, the head of money markets or ALM (who reports to the head of Treasury). Where this occurs, the ToR must make clear that such persons have voting powers in the absence of their

department head. For effective management and decision-making, it is recommended that deputies be given such authority, so that the bank can function correctly in the absence of key senior individuals.

The author believes that the Head of Credit, or a senior person from the Credit Committee, should also attend ALCO, and certainly some banks do follow such an arrangement. However, credit decisions, including risk-related issues such as expected losses, forecasts and loss provisions, are often handled at the Executive Credit Committee level, and because the Credit department does not have a day-to-day involvement, from either an operational or policy level, with asset–liability issues it reduces the need to have it represented at the ALCO level. Ultimately, it is a decision for the CEO and ALCO chairman.

The membership of ALCO should be reasonably stable, but also flexible enough to allow for additional persons and expertise as and when necessary; for example, technical experts by invitation.

The ToR is a formal statement of the primary aims and objective of the ALCO. It should be a succinct document. We observe that its remit covers every aspect of asset, liability, liquidity and capital management of the bank's operations. We show at Figure 10.1 an extract from the ToR, which is the committee's operating agenda. The list is not exhaustive. The agenda makes clear that any aspect of the bank's operations that impact ALM issues – which is essentially anything that a bank might undertake – must be addressed, for risk management purposes, at the ALCO level.

## Agenda Setting

The ALCO agenda is varied and wide ranging, and by definition dynamic in line with market and firm-specific events. On the Wiley website we include a sample of hypothetical agendas from past ALCO meetings at different banks. Figure 10.2 is an example of one of these agendas, from a bank ALCO meeting. Specific items must be the responsibility of named individuals, who will present in accordance with the agenda. The agenda and supporting documents should be circulated at least one week before the meeting date, to enable members to have sufficient time to review the contents. Where this is not possible, for example for late items or for extraordinary meetings, the emphasis should be on making the meeting documents available to the circulation list as soon as possible.

Items for inclusion at the next meeting should be discussed, informally or formally, with the Chairperson before then being sent to the committee secretary for circulation on the agenda.

- Review gap limits, actual gaps, and their sensitivities, together with any recommendations to amend the limits;
- Review the liquidity ratio and other liquidity metrics, and adherence to regulatory and internal liquidity limits, and assess forecasted values for risk control purposes and adequacy;
- Review and discuss deposit and funding trends, including deposit concentrations, programs/products, deposit promotion campaigns, and forecasts;
- Review exceptions/excesses to internal and regulatory policies and limits as reported by the Head of Financial Planning and Control;
- Review current allocation of capital and profit contribution by business line, and present regulatory capital adequacy forecasts and requests for Board review;
- Review the market environment and potential impact on the branch's interest-rate risk and trading activities;
- Review and approve authorised instruments and permissible hedging and position-taking strategies for gap management, trading and customer sales;
- Review and discuss recommendations to change policies, objectives or limits;
- Review internal funds transfer pricing arrangements and consider whether changes are required;
- Set standards and methodology for measuring and monitoring the quantitative limits on all trading activities;
- In liaison with CRO's office, set and review stress testing scenarios;
- Review new trading activities recommended under the policy for New Products & Services; and
- Act as the centre for excellence for all ALM-related policy and governance issues.

**Figure 10.1**   ALCO operating agenda: extract from the formal ToR.

# THE GROUP ALCO

Larger banks that operate across national boundaries and/or legal entities and subsidiaries will need to organise their governance on the basis of a central Group function and outlying regional and/or legal entity functions. This applies most crucially to the ALCO function. We present here recommended best practice for a Group ALCO (GALCO) organisation structure in a multinational and/or multi-entity bank.

---

**ALCO Agenda**
Date:                       Wednesday 25 November
Time:                      15:00
Location:              Board Room

1. **Apologies**
2. **Minutes of last meeting**
3. **Matters arising**
4. **Review of ALCO monthly pack**
5. **ALCO Capital Investment Options for following year**: update on recommendations to replace current practice (Head of Treasury)
6. **Finance department interest-rate sensitivity: Scenario Analysis** present agreed daily analysis already in production, highlighting key aspects, and parallel limits (CFO)
7. **IPV Results for Q3** Following ALCO approval of the IPV policy, report results formally to ALCO on a calendar quarter basis, the first being Q3. (Head of Product Control)
8. **Private Bank client deposit results and targets** (Head of PB)
9. **Internal Funds "Transfer Pricing" Model – update on** implementation (Head of Financial Accounting)
10. **European Central Bank Amendment to Collateral Rules** (Head of Treasury)
11. **Update and review of the bank's Liquidity Policy Statement** (Head of Market and Liquidity Risk)
12. **Any other business**
13. **Date of next meeting**

**Circulation:**
| | | |
|---|---|---|
| CFO (Chairman) | CEO | Head of Treasury |
| Head of Corporate Banking | Head of Market Risk | Head of Money Markets |
| Head of Product Control | Head of FI | CRO |
| Secretariat | | |

**Attachments:**
Minutes (Item 2)
ALCO Reports Pack (Item 4)

---

**Figure 10.2**   Sample ALCO agenda.

## Group Treasury Operating Model

A large or multinational bank should put in place a formal "operating model" that states formally what the objectives, roles, responsibility and ToR of the Group Treasury and branch and subsidiary Treasuries are. This forms the basis of the Group ALCO ToR. We describe here our recommended Group Treasury operating model framework.

## Treasury Roles and Responsibilities

Group Treasury is responsible for overseeing that balance sheet capital and resources are utilised at their optimum level and on a sustainable basis across the bank. This is achieved via the following parallel tracks:

- Strategic and tactical governance
  - Ensure transparent governance and communication of policies and limits across the bank
- Balance sheet management
  - Compile board-approved Treasury policy statements for governance of the balance sheet, with regard to capital, liquidity, funding, transfer pricing and interest-rate and FX risk management). Implement and ensure compliance with these policies
  - Monitor the various balance sheet limits (including capital and asset limits) across the Group, legal entities and subsidiaries
- Liaising and working with business lines
  - Ensure seamless liaison with the business lines across the Group, to facilitate application of Treasury policy guidelines at the business line level
  - Ensure that capital, liquidity, funding, transfer pricing and interest-rate and FX risk management policies are adhered to at the business line level and part of the origination process.

The above can be drilled down into a more detailed document that includes the various policy statements, limits and approval levels. This would also include department organisation and names of individuals responsible for implementing policy. The communication process would be organised as shown at Figure 10.4.

## Group Treasury Role and Responsibility

At a vanilla commercial bank operating in one jurisdiction, Treasury will typically be a profit centre, while also being responsible for overall ALM, funding, liquidity risk management, and policy setting and implementation. In a Group Treasury structure for a multinational and/or multi-entity bank group, it is more likely to be organised for the latter activity only, although the home country money market desk (a profit-making activity) may also be included within it.

Generally, Group Treasury will define Treasury policy for the entire bank and implement this across the group. It will also manage and be responsible overall for the relationship with the national and all external regulators, and the credit rating agencies. Overseas entities will also manage the local regulatory relationship on a day-to-day basis.

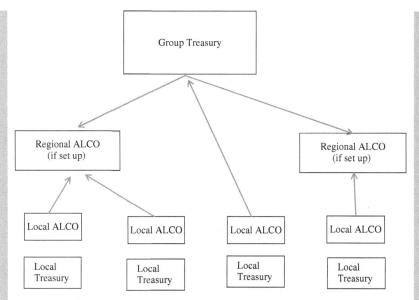

**Figure 10.4**   Group Treasury and local ALCO communication structure.

As a standard template, GALCO on an overview basis and Group Treasury on a delegated basis are responsible for all Treasury-related issues in the bank. These include the following:

- managing the capital base of the bank;
- monitoring at aggregate level the Group's balance sheet risk;
- compiling for board approval the Group's liquidity risk appetite and funding policy. This includes responsibility for all capital raising, including equity, hybrid capital instruments, and senior and subordinated debt;
- managing the Group's funding structure, in line with approved guidelines, with respect to regulatory requirements and internal funding policy;
- managing the liquidity reporting to the national regulators;
- managing the Group's non-traded interest-rate risk for the Banking book;
- setting policy for the management of the Group's FX exposure risk, which is implemented as delegated authority to the individual local Treasury desks.

Again, this high-level operating model ToR can be drilled down into detailed policy statements and outlines of roles and responsibilities for each desk.

## Local ALCO Organisation

Where the overseas business of the Group is organised as a branch, no local ALCO structure is necessary as the Head of Treasury at the branch will report direct to Group Head of Treasury (with a dotted line to the local CEO), and thus branch business is covered at the GALCO level.

A local ALCO organisation arrangement is necessary at any overseas business operation that is a subsidiary, partnership or separate legal entity to the parent. The ToR of the local ALCO will be virtually identical to that for a general ALCO of a domestic banking operation, described earlier, with the exception that the local Treasury is not responsible for any bank policy setting. The role of the local ALCO is to ensure that GALCO policy and all Treasury-related matters are adhered to in the local jurisdiction. The local ALCO ToR would include the following:

- managing the local regulatory relationship;
- ensuring that GALCO and Group Treasury policy is adhered to;
- overseeing balance sheet management for the local entity;
- in line with Group Treasury policy and principles, devising and implementing a liquidity and funding plan for the local entity;
- approving capital and funding, via the approval process at ALCO level, for local business origination, in line with overall bank strategy;
- managing the liquidity book or Liquid Asset Buffer (delegated to local Treasury).

The operating model should describe a clear delineation of roles and responsibilities, as well as a structure of transparent communication between GALCO, Group Treasury, local ALCO and the local Treasury, and thence to the business lines. For example, Table 10.4 shows how the approval levels for capital allocation may be set from GALCO downwards.

| GALCO | Any amount |
|---|---|
| Group Finance Director | Up to $100 m |
| Group Head of Treasury | Up to $50 m |
| Local ALCO | Up to $10 m |
| Local Head of Treasury | Up to $1 m |

**Table 10.4**    Hypothetical capital approval limit structure.

## Local Treasury

Both branches and subsidiaries overseas will have a local Treasury desk, managed by the local Head of Treasury. This person, in conjunction with the local ALCO, is responsible for compliance with local regulations and Group Treasury policy. This includes the following:

- ensure that the local entity adheres to the requirements of the national regulator;
- compile a local market liquidity contingency funding plan;
- chair the local ALCO and compliance with the set ALCO ToR;
- manage the day-to-day relations with the local regulator.

In addition, the local Treasury is responsible for managing the branch/subsidiary liquidity requirement and risk exposure, in line with internal limits and targets to comply with local requirements. That is, liquidity is managed at local entity level (in line with Group Treasury policy) and all liquidity modelling and stress testing (see Chapter 14) is undertaken locally. Assumptions used in stress testing would follow Group standards, modified where necessary to reflect local market conditions.

## Organisation Structure

There is of course more than one way to organise the GALCO governance structure at a multinational or multi-entity bank. We illustrate our recommendation at Figure 10.5. A Regional ALCO is not common and not

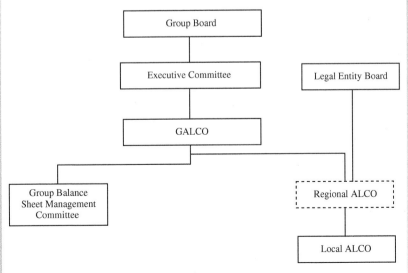

**Figure 10.5**   GALCO and Group Treasury organisation.

necessarily recommended; however, for banks with a number of overseas operations in the same defined region (such as the Gulf Cooperation Council, or in Asia-Pacific), it may be logical to organise the local entities into a Regional ALCO structure. This should only be done where value is added through a regional set-up. Otherwise, incorporating both local and regional ALCOs may create unnecessary bureaucracy and duplication.

For larger banks and multi-entity banking groups, it is frequently the case that the ALCO does not have sufficient time to review adequately all policies and relevant aspects of the balance sheet. Where this is the case, business best-practice suggests that a separate Balance Sheet Management Committee (BSMCO) be set up to review more technical items, and feed up to ALCO where necessary. The membership of BSMCO would include:

- Head of Balance Sheet Management;
- Deputy Head of Treasury;
- Regional or Subsidiary Treasury delegates;
- Interest-rate Risk Management delegates;
- Chief Economist.

The role of BSMCO is essentially to review interest rate and liquidity risk aspects of the balance sheet from a macro-level perspective, and to recommend action in advance of expected stress events. It will also bring relevant items to the attention of ALCO, and there will be some commonality of membership between the two committees. The Chair would usually be the Deputy Head of Treasury.

Figure 10.6 shows the Treasury organisation at the subsidiary and/or overseas level for a bank that operates as a Group entity. Figure 10.6A is where the Treasury function is not also a profit centre (so that all dealing and money market trading is conducted as part of the front office environment,

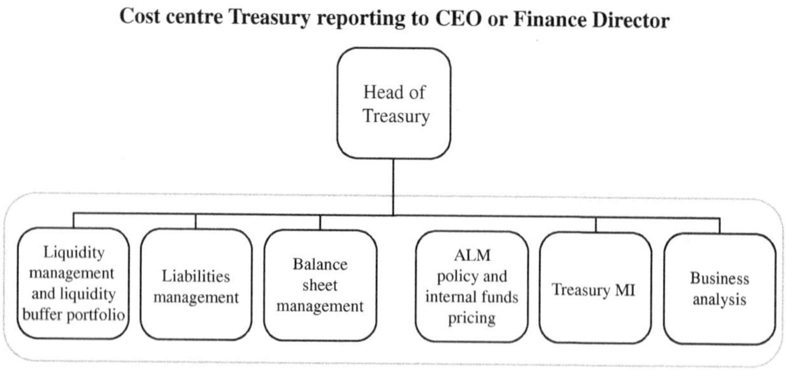

**Cost centre Treasury reporting to CEO or Finance Director**

**Figure 10.6A**    Treasury organisation, cost centre.

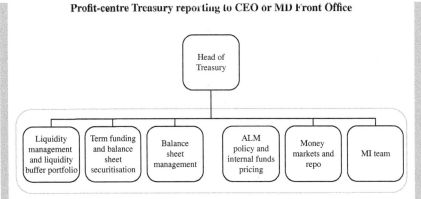

**Profit-centre Treasury reporting to CEO or MD Front Office**

**Figure 10.6B** Treasury organisation, profit centre.

and Treasury is a middle office cost centre), and Figure 10.6B is the more common arrangement with the Treasury as a front-office profit centre, incorporating the money markets dealing function.

## GALCO Agenda Setting

The agenda items for GALCO are conceptually identical to what we discussed earlier for the ALCO agenda. However, much of the operating level business will be discussed at the local ALCO level and, where they are set up, regional ALCO level. This means that much GALCO business concerns Group policy issues, or high-level strategic decision-making issues. A sample GALCO agenda is shown at Figure 10.7.

**For attention of GALCO**
CEO
Deputy CEO
Head of Corporate Banking
Head of Portfolio Management
Head of Investment Banking
Head of Money Markets
Finance Director
Group Risk Officer
Group Head of Treasury
Deputy Group Head of Treasury

**Figure 10.7** Sample GALCO agenda.

---

Subject
Group ALCO Agenda

Minutes/Actions:

1. Minutes of previous GALCO
2. MI Pack
3. Macroeconomics update

Approval items:

4. Year-end forecast and budget update
5. Year-end asset and capital limits
6. Capital stress testing
7. Revised approval process, capital allocation
8. New business: MENA capital injection request
9. Private bank business organisation review
10. Internal funds pricing for liquidity lines

Updated items:

11. Risk-weighted assets limit transfer
12. Intra-group limits: regulatory update
13. Revised Funds Transfer Pricing policy
14. Term funding strategy

---

**Figure 10.7** *(Continued)*

---

EXAMPLE 10.1 ALCO BEST-PRACTICE GUIDELINES: THE UK REGULATOR

The ALCO is the most important senior management and risk committee in a bank. It must always be run as a value-added committee, which means it needs to have the correct composition, review up-to-date management information that reflects accurately the balance sheet position and risk exposures of the bank and be the centre of robust discussion and debate. Policies and recommendations approved by ALCO will have a considerable influence on the bank's condition and future state, so it is important that all banks seek to manage their ALCO on best-practice lines.

The UK FSA opined on this in a publication in January 2011.[1] It presented good practice guidelines that all ALCOs should seek to adhere to, in the following areas:

- the role of ALCO;
- the composition and authority of ALCO;

---

[1] Financial Services Authority, *Finalised Guidance: Asset and Liability Management*, January 2011

- the forward-looking nature of the ALCO discussion and the decisions it makes;
- the degree of senior management challenge during meetings, and evidence of this in the approved ALCO minutes;
- regular attendance from all members.

We list the FSA's recommended guidelines here.

### Role of the Committee
- Proactively controls the business in line with the bank's strategy and objectives, and focuses on the entire balance sheet;
- Ensures that risks remain within the stated risk appetite;
- Considers the impact on earnings volatility of changing economic and market conditions;
- Ensures that an appropriate internal funds pricing mechanism is in place that correctly charges for the cost of liquidity, incentivises the desired behaviour and is in line with the bank's strategic objectives and risk appetite;
- Acts as the arbitrator in the debate and challenge process between business lines.

### Committee Membership
- Attended by the CEO or Deputy CEO, and chaired by the CFO;
- Includes all business group heads, the CRO, the Head of Research/Economics and the Head of Internal Audit.

### Nature of Discussion
- Is forward-looking in nature, focusing on the impact of future plans and strategy at the business line level;
- Takes proactive decisions to manage ALM risks, act to solve issues raised or otherwise escalating to the Executive Committee/Board rather than simply noting or observing the risks;
- Ensures issues are fully articulated and debated;
- Considers recommendations from a tactical sub-committee that excludes the CEO and other ExCo members. Where appropriate, delegates decision-making authority to an ALCO sub-committee;
- Ensures an active dialogue and debate among committee members, and shows evidence of a strong degree of challenge;
- Provides minutes summarising the extent of discussion and debate, and do not only record action points.

### Management Information (the ALCO "Pack")
- Is content-focused on future plans and strategy;
- Presents market and economic outlook, together with impact assessment on ALM issues pertinent to the bank;

- Shows liquidity and funding metrics by currency; also provides a forecast of metrics based on current market expectations;
- Provides results of stress tests under specified stress conditions;
- Provides analysis of interest-rate risk using modified duration and VaR methodologies, NII/NIM sensitivity and basis risk, as part of an assessment of earnings volatility;
- Reports its current funding composition, and assesses potential refinancing risk stress points, based on its funding maturities, its market funding position and the position of the market generally;
- Presents liquidity stress testing scenarios of varying severity;
- Presents the Contingency Funding Plan (CFP) for the bank, and regularly updates it;
- Provides the required level of granularity and invites challenge from members.

The author endorses these recommendations, particularly the ones on regular attendance and management challenge.

An example of an ALCO pack is provided on the Wiley website link that accompanies THIS book.

## TREASURY OPERATING MODEL

As the previous section showed, there is more than one way to organise the bank Treasury function. The principle decision to take is whether it should be a profit centre, incorporating the money market trading desk, or a cost centre "middle office" that sets policy and governance but is not a market-facing function. Both approaches have their merits, but in a well-run and well-governed institution it is more likely that effective control and discipline can be enforced if the Treasury set-up is as a market-facing profit centre.

When organising the bank's Treasury operating model, it is recommended that a review of the functions be undertaken first, before then deciding which department they best fit in. Table 10.8 shows the relevant bank activities by discipline, illustrated as a matrix function.

There is no "right" way to organise the Treasury operating model with respect to the functions shown in Table 10.8. What is important, however, is that the structure that is selected is appropriate to the strategy and culture of the specific bank. All the alternative approaches shown here would be suitable. There is a large variety of models that can be selected, but in general the ones described here are a business best-practice approach; the author would not recommend structures outside what is described in Figures 10.9 to 10.12.

A common organisation structure is for Treasury to encompass both market facing and policy functions. This is shown at Figure 10.9, and describes a Treasury function that reports to the CEO, but with a "dotted

| | Capital and balance sheet | Liquidity | NII/NIM |
|---|---|---|---|
| **Strategic management** | *Capital management* Risk limits (risk-weighted assets, or RWA) Cost of capital Budget forecasting Setting capital policy Setting return metrics Defining capital structure and ratios Capital allocation | *Liquidity risk management* Liquidity limits Liquidity stress tests Liquidity policy Contingency funding plan LAB policy Liquidity cost calculation Funding strategy Internal funds pricing policy (FTP) | *Banking book interest-rate risk* Interest-rate risk management Interest-rate risk modelling Forecasting NII/NIM |
| **Market facing functions** | *Term Liabilities Issuance* Senior unsecured debt Subordinated debt Equity instruments Securitisation Secured – ABS/MBS – Covered bonds | *Money Markets Desk* Cash management Money markets – depos – CD/CP Repo *Collateral management* *Counterparty risk management* *Investor Relations* Rating Agencies Investors | *Swaps and Derivatives desks* Banking book Trading book Market risk hedging |
| **Governance** | | *Finance and Risk Management* Financial control and reporting Regulatory reporting Risk and product control | |

**Table 10.8** Bank operating functions relevant to Treasury.

line" reporting responsibility to the CFO. The areas of responsibility given to Treasury are shaded.

In a large bank the reporting line to the CEO may be replaced with one to the head of markets or the head of an operating division. We observe from Figure 10.9 that in this arrangement the Treasury desk has a P&L responsibility, but is also the control function for capital and liquidity policy. The financial reporting for Treasury therefore must separate activities conducted with the external market from internal activities, to ensure that the P&L shown is only for external business. So, for example, internal transactions undertaken as part of the internal funding policy, otherwise known as funds transfer pricing (FTP; see Chapter 15) would be reported separately, usually as part of the ALCO book and not as Treasury P&L.

The opposite to this structure is a "middle office" Treasury that is responsible for policy setting and implementation, but has no market facing function. The governance function would not encompass financial reporting, but may include regulatory reporting. In this arrangement the reporting line is typically to the CFO, although we recommend that it be to the CEO or Deputy CEO. This is shown at Figure 10.10.

The first two methodologies represent the most common arrangements. A mixture of the two, which must be implemented with care because it risks generating control and policy implementation problems, is for Treasury to manage the term liabilities functions, but not the money markets and collateral management functions. In this arrangement it has a market facing function, but not the day-to-day cash management side of this function. This is shown at Figure 10.11. This model also includes the Investor Relations department, and may or may not include the regulatory reporting (not shown as shaded, as this responsibility may reside within Finance). The Treasury head would report to the CFO or CEO. However, for most banks, the effective operating model would be either Figure 10.9 or Figure 10.10.

A final option is shown at Figure 10.12. This is a larger Treasury that is again front office facing and so would report to the CEO. It holds the policy

| Capital management | Liquidity risk management | Banking book interest rate risk |
|---|---|---|
| Term Liabilities Issuance | Money Markets Desk | Swaps and Derivatives desks |
| | Collateral management | |
| | Counterparty risk management | |
| Investor Relations | | |
| Finance and Risk Management | | |

**Figure 10.9**   Front office treasury operating model.

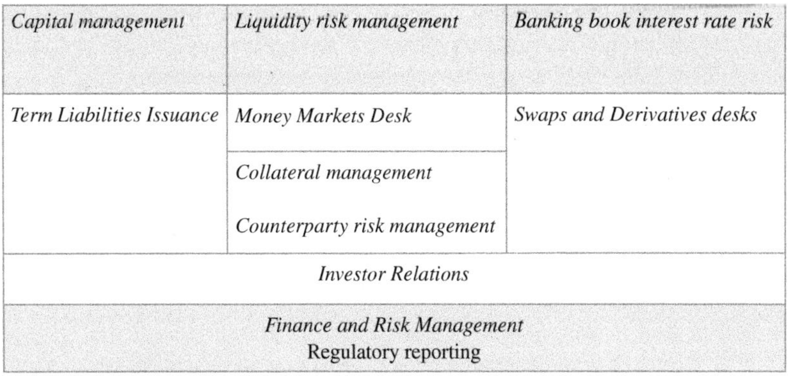

| Capital management | Liquidity risk management | Banking book interest rate risk |
|---|---|---|
| Term Liabilities Issuance | Money Markets Desk | Swaps and Derivatives desks |
| | Collateral management | |
| | Counterparty risk management | |
| | Investor Relations | |
| | Finance and Risk Management<br>Regulatory reporting | |

**Figure 10.10**    Middle office treasury operating model.

| Capital management | Liquidity risk management | Banking book interest rate risk |
|---|---|---|
| Term Liabilities Issuance | Money Markets Desk | Swaps and Derivatives desks |
| | Collateral management | |
| | Counterparty risk management | |
| | Investor Relations | |
| | Finance and Risk Management<br>Regulatory reporting | |

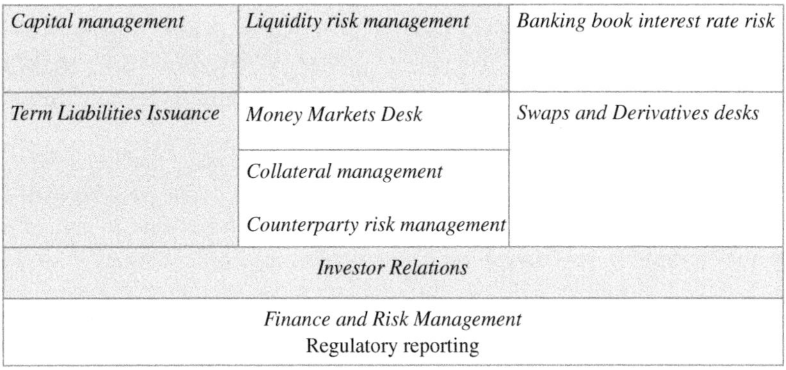

**Figure 10.11**    Treasury operating model with market facing function.

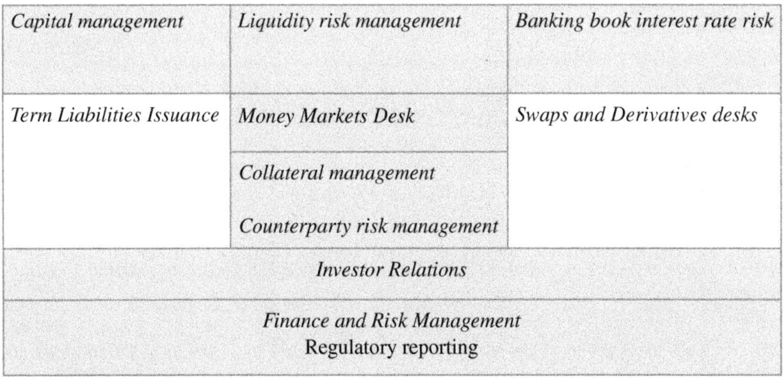

| Capital management | Liquidity risk management | Banking book interest rate risk |
|---|---|---|
| Term Liabilities Issuance | Money Markets Desk | Swaps and Derivatives desks |
| | Collateral management | |
| | Counterparty risk management | |
| | Investor Relations | |
| | Finance and Risk Management<br>Regulatory reporting | |

**Figure 10.12**    Treasury operating model with market facing
governance function.

and governance responsibility as well as the money market function, but the term liabilities and securitisation roles are placed elsewhere, perhaps within an investment bank division or a debt capital markets department.

As we noted at the start, there is more than one way to arrange the Treasury operating model. It is important that the method selected be fit for purpose. The critical areas of capital and liquidity management policy and operation, both day-to-day and long term, are best placed within a strong central Treasury function, which is why the author prefers the option shown at Figure 10.9.

Reproduced from *The Principles of Banking* (2012)

## THE TREASURY AND ALCO OPERATING MODELS: SINGLE LEGAL ENTITY STRUCTURE

Before looking at the Treasury operating model in detail, consider the following illustrations on the Treasury function, at Figures 10.2, 10.3, 10.4 and 10.5. Rather than necessarily providing the "right" solutions, these figures ask the right questions.

Figure 10.2 shows the various functions that *may* sit in a Treasury department, and how the department itself might be organised. Figures 10.3 and 10.4 show orthodox "front office" Treasury functions in banks, and are quite common in combining a market-facing P&L element with a risk management liquidity and capital management element. Figure 10.4 is not uncommon in smaller banks which seek to extract more shareholder

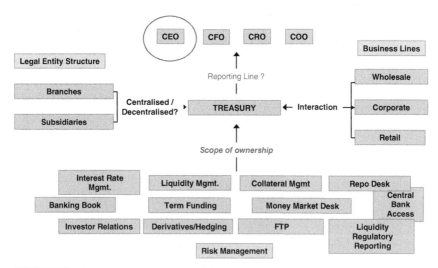

**FIGURE 10.2**   Treasury operating model overview

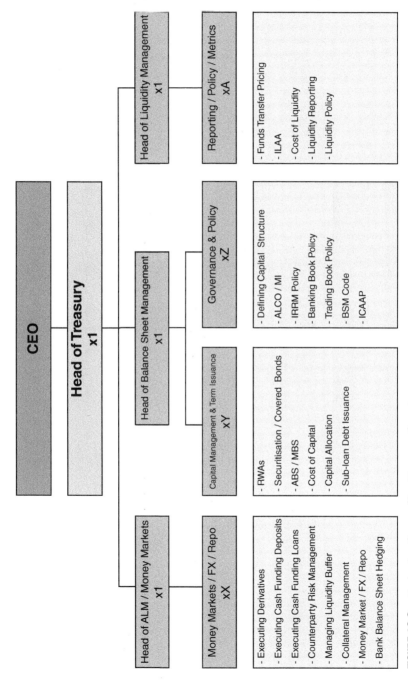

**CEO**

**Head of Treasury**
**x1**

**Head of ALM / Money Markets**
**x1**

**Head of Balance Sheet Management**
**x1**

**Head of Liquidity Management**
**x1**

Money Markets / FX / Repo
xX

- Executing Derivatives
- Executing Cash Funding Deposits
- Executing Cash Funding Loans
- Counterparty Risk Management
- Managing Liquidity Buffer
- Collateral Management
- Money Market / FX / Repo
- Bank Balance Sheet Hedging

Capital Management & Term Issuance
xY

- RWAs
- Securitisation / Covered Bonds
- ABS / MBS
- Cost of Capital
- Capital Allocation
- Sub-loan Debt Issuance

Governance & Policy
xZ

- Defining Capital Structure
- ALCO / MI
- IRRM Policy
- Banking Book Policy
- Trading Book Policy
- BSM Code
- ICAAP

Reporting / Policy / Metrics
xA

- Funds Transfer Pricing
- ILAA
- Cost of Liquidity
- Liquidity Reporting
- Liquidity Policy

**FIGURE 10.3** Orthodox front-office Treasury function

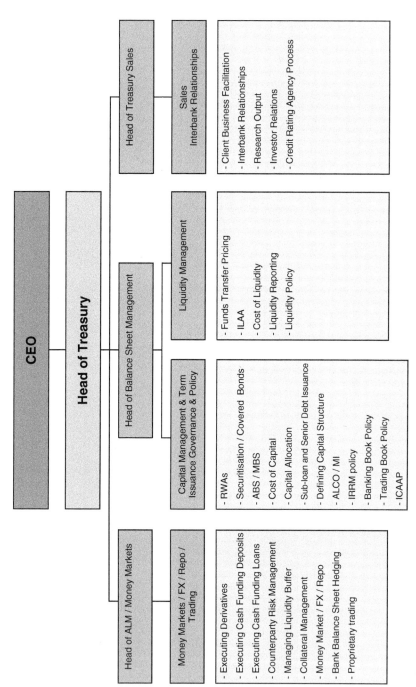

**FIGURE 10.4** Front-office Treasury function with Sales function

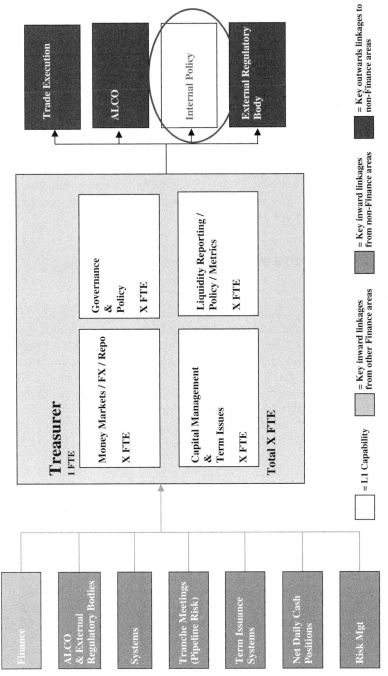

**FIGURE 10.5**  Treasury high-level operating model overview and linkages

value-added by having the Treasury function work directly with the business lines (usually a corporate banking team) to facilitate customer business. Finally Figure 10.5 is a high level overview of the Treasury operating model illustrating recommended core capabilities within the function, along with key linkages to other areas.

We note in the ALCO ToR that one of its strategic objectives is to maintain a forward-looking review of the balance sheet. To that end, just one of the key tools used to assist this process must be an "early warning indicator" (EWI) report that highlights key risk indicators (KRIs) for the bank. We provide a template ALCO EWI report at Appendix 10.B. Note that what exactly constitutes an EWI for a bank will depend on the type of bank concerned, its strategy, business model, product line, customer franchise, and geographical spread. The template we present would be appropriate for a medium-sized vanilla commercial bank.

## THE TREASURY AND ALCO OPERATING MODELS: GROUP STRUCTURE[2]

A bank that operates across national jurisdictions and/or with multiple legal entities must pay careful attention to its Treasury operating model, or more accurately to its Group Treasury operating model. This is to ensure that uniformity of policy and adherence to minimum standards are maintained throughout the institution's balance sheet management discipline. Hence, a group or multinational bank should put in place a formal operating model that states formally what the objectives, roles, responsibility, and terms of reference (ToR) of the Group Treasury and branch and subsidiary Treasuries are. This forms the basis of the Group ALCO ToR. Group Treasury is responsible for overseeing that balance sheet resources such as capital and liquidity are utilised at their optimum level and on a sustainable basis across the entire bank worldwide.

A summary of the Group function responsibilities should include the following:

- Strategic and tactical governance: transparent governance and communication of policies and limits across the bank;
- Balance sheet management: compile Board-approved Treasury policy statements for governance of the balance sheet, with regard to capital, liquidity, funding, internal funds transfer pricing, and interest-rate and FX risk management; implement and ensure compliance with these policies; monitor the various balance sheet limits (including capital and asset limits) across the Group, legal entities, and subsidiaries;

---

[2] This section was co-authored with Polina Bardaeva.

- Liaising and working with business lines: ensure seamless liaison with the business lines across the Group, to facilitate application of Treasury policy guidelines at the business line level; ensure capital, liquidity, funding, internal funds transfer pricing, and interest-rate and FX risk management policies are adhered to at the business line level and as part of the origination process.

The above tasks can be drilled down into the various policy statements, limits, and approval levels. At the same time, there are practical issues faced by the Group function that often argue towards a more decentralised operating model. These include the following:

- Different regulatory requirements:
  - Local lending limits;
  - Capital adequacy ratios;
  - Liquidity buffer requirements;
  - Regulatory constraints to transfer funds across legal entities and jurisdictions.
- Local specifics of markets (opportunities for growth, market share, types of business lines, and products):
  - Availability of different products;
  - Availability (or lack) of some funding maturities;
  - Difference in interest rates levels and costs of funding;
  - Volatility of exchange rates of local currencies.
- Double reporting lines may cause conflicts or ambiguity. This needs careful attention to ensure a proper establishment of the structure and governance within the Group in adherence with the requirements of Group Treasury. Of course exemptions from Group policy may be arranged for specific areas of local responsibility.

Ultimately, from the shareholder point of view the overarching objective is for balance sheet funding and capital consumption optimisation across the Group.

Figures 10.6 to 10.9 present the cases for and against a centralised versus a decentralised Group Treasury arrangement in a multinational banking entity. When organising the Group Treasury function, the same rules apply as when considering the single legal entity Treasury function: first, the imperative is to craft the structure that is the best fit for that specific bank's business model and culture; and second, the existing structure and what has transpired in the past are irrelevant.

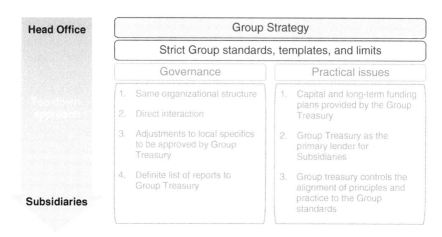

**FIGURE 10.6**  Centralised Group Treasury model

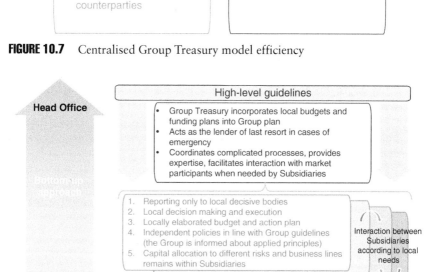

**FIGURE 10.7**  Centralised Group Treasury model efficiency

**FIGURE 10.8**  Decentralised Group Treasury model

| Virtues | Drawbacks |
|---|---|
| ✓ Accounting local specifics of different countries / environments<br><br>✓ Local teams have better knowledge about requirements and opportunities in capital and liquidity management | • Requirements for high competences at each local level<br>• More expensive to have multiple ALM & Treasury teams<br>• Lack of scale => less possible funding sources and hedging instruments<br>• Lack of transparency and control<br>• Problem of clients' arbitrage against the banking group<br>• Comparative advantages not used => influence on the Group financial result |

**FIGURE 10.9**   Decentralised Group Treasury model efficiency

## TREASURY POLICY STATEMENT: EXAMPLE TEMPLATE

We noted at the start that the Treasury department of a bank is its cornerstone, the vital risk management function that is responsible not simply for basic cash management but also for ensuring stewardship of the balance sheet such that the bank is able to remain a going concern over multiple economic cycles, whatever the external market conditions may be. Subsequent chapters in Part III consider the technical challenges facing the Treasury function and the tools it uses to carry out its function. We end this chapter by including a template Treasury Policy Statement for a hypothetical medium-sized commercial bank, with balance sheet assets and liabilities in more than its reporting currency. This can be applied at any commercial banking institution. Please go to the files relevant to Chapter 10 held on the companion website for this book to download the policy statement, which is a Word file. Full details on the companion website are in Chapter 20.

## CONCLUSION

It is difficult to exaggerate the importance to a bank of its ALM function, and its approach to balance sheet origination. To reiterate, there is more than one "right" Treasury and ALM organisation structure; the key requirement is that the Treasury operating model be appropriate to the bank in question. Changes to the external environment, the internal business model, the customer franchise, the product suite – indeed any change in internal or external factors – demands a review of the Treasury structure to ensure it is still fit-for-purpose. And the final authority on whether this is always the case should sit with the bank's ALCO.

## APPENDIX 10.A: Bank Asset and Liability Management Committee (ALCO) Template Terms of Reference

ALCO Recommended Terms of Reference

| | |
|---|---|
| Chair | ▪ Chief Financial Officer |
| | In the absence of the Chief Financial Officer, the Head of Treasury will act as the meeting Chair. If the Head of Treasury is unavailable a suitable alternative for the Chair shall be appointed by the Chief Executive Officer. |
| Members | ▪ Chief Financial Officer<br>▪ Chief Executive Officer<br>▪ Head of Treasury<br>▪ Global Head of Balance Sheet Management, Group Treasury [for GROUP entities] or alternate<br>▪ Head of Corporate Banking<br>▪ Head of Retail Banking<br>▪ Head of Private Banking<br>▪ Chief Risk Officer<br>▪ Head of Strategy |
| Attendees | ▪ MD Products & Marketing<br>▪ Head of ALM / Money Markets<br>▪ Head of Liquidity Risk<br>▪ Head of Valuation Control / Product Control<br>▪ Chief Economist<br>▪ [Head of Internal Audit]<br>▪ [Board NED] |
| Additional Invitees | As appropriate. |
| Deputies | If a Member is unable to attend a meeting, he/she shall appoint a deputy to attend on his/her behalf. Such deputy's attendance shall not count towards the quorum and the deputy shall not hold the right to vote. |
| Quorum | Three members, at least one of whom shall be the Chief Financial Officer or the Chief Risk Officer, one from the 1st line of defence and one from the 2nd line of defence. |
| Meeting Frequency | Monthly and *ad hoc* as required by any member. |
| | *Ad hoc* meetings are permitted to take place via email if necessary. Rules regarding decision making and quorum remain the same as for face to face meetings. |

| | |
|---|---|
| Voting protocol | Items presented for approval may be approved by majority vote in favour, provided at least one from the 1ˢᵗ line of defence and one from the 2ⁿᵈ line of defence are in favour. |
| Secretary | Provided by Treasury. |
| Committee Authority | ALCO operates as a sub-committee of the Board. |
| Authority Delegated by the Committee | ALCO may delegate any of its powers to a sub-committee consisting of one or more ALCO members. Any sub-committee so formed shall conform to any regulations that may be imposed on it by ALCO and the acts and proceedings of a sub-committee shall be reported to ALCO. |
| | ALCO shall review and approve the ToR of those committees to which it has delegated authority at least annually and on an ad hoc basis should material amendment be proposed. |
| | The ABC Bank Products Pricing Committee will report as a sub-committee of ALCO. |
| | The ABC Bank Balance Sheet Management Committee will operate as a technical sub-committee of ALCO |
| | Specific delegated authorities are set out within "Scope of the Board/Committee's oversight and responsibility" |
| Committee accountability | ALCO operates as a sub-committee of the Board and reports to the Board. |
| Escalation | Management decisions beyond this Committee's authority and matters which this Committee deems necessary for escalation will be escalated to the Board or appropriate other Board committees where relevant. |
| Purpose of the Committee | It is responsible for identifying, managing and controlling all of the bank's balance sheet risks and capital management in executing its chosen business strategy. Balance sheet risks are managed by setting limits, monitoring exposures and implementing controls across the dimensions of capital, credit, FX, funding and liquidity, and non-traded interest rate risk. |
| | It is responsible for the implementation of ALCO strategy and policy for the bank's balance sheet. |

*(continued)*

ALCO Recommended Terms of Reference (*Continued*)

| | |
|---|---|
| Scope of the Committee's oversight and responsibility | **Strategic overview**<br>▪ Provide a single forum where the balance sheet risks of the bank can be monitored and managed.<br>▪ Ensure a consistency of approach across a range of Treasury issues.<br>▪ Establish risk appetite for the individual business lines and monitor exposures against limits.<br>▪ Provide oversight of business line Stress Testing<br>▪ Provide a single forum to consider developments in Treasury policy and regulation.<br>▪ Approve significant transactions where appropriate.<br>▪ Ensure that the decisions and policies from the Board are fully adhered to<br>▪ Ensure compliance with regulatory requirements<br><br>**Capital**<br>▪ Monitor long-term RWA trends and oversee actions to optimise RWA levels<br>▪ Monitor and review capital usage and return on capital metrics for each business against targets<br>▪ Review capital budgets / forecasts by business to ensure compliance with Board strategy.<br>▪ Approve allocation of capital between businesses where appropriate<br>▪ Review strategic transactions as required.<br>▪ Review proposed changes in bank risk policy and drive action as required<br>▪ Exercise responsibility for the overall oversight, preparation, drafting, and approval of the internal capital adequacy assessment process (ICAAP), for upward submission to the Board.<br><br>**Non-Trading Interest Risk & Foreign Currency Exposure**<br>▪ Establish risk appetite and set appropriate business limits.<br>▪ Review principle positions and hedging strategies and approve excesses as required.<br>▪ Review proposed changes in Board policy and drive action as required<br>▪ Review the effects of stress tests and potential impact of significant external events on interest rate and FX exposure |

**Liquidity and Funding**
- Establish liquidity risk appetite and set appropriate business limits (where measurable) and targets.
- Set liquidity risk tolerances via specific metric limits, at bank, corporate banking, retail banking, and business line level
- Review liquidity and funding positions by business (where possible) against limits and approve excesses as required.
- Review liquidity and funding budgets/forecasts by business to ensure compliance with Group strategy.
- Review stress testing and underlying assumptions. Consider whether alterations to modelling scenarios are required.
- Approve and sign off on the bank's Contingency Funding Plan
- Approve the sign off Treasury Funding Policy statements
- Exercise responsibility for the overall oversight, preparation, drafting, and approval of the individual liquidity adequacy assessment process (ILAAP), for upward submission to the Board.

**Pricing**
- Support business pricing strategy through transparent identification and communication of liquidity, funding and capital costs.
- Review and monitor portfolio pricing initiatives and implications for strategic balance sheet management
- Review and challenge margin trends/movements.
- Ensure that pricing methodologies remain appropriate, including the FTP and RAROE pricing model (where appropriate), particularly the assumptions of funding costs.

**Credit risk**
- Credit risk oversight in within the scope of ALCO governance to the extent that it approval of all credit policies and direction, and approval of country and sectir limits.
- Includes high level reporting and review of key credit risk parameters which have implications for RWA reporting and trends.

**Intra Group Limits (IGLs)**
- [For GROUP entities] Oversight, approval, and monitoring of all intra-group limits and limit usage by business lines and [subsidiaries for GROUP entities]

*(continued)*

ALCO Recommended Terms of Reference (*Continued*)

> Internal funds pricing regime
> - Approve the Bank's internal funds pricing regime ("FTP") and sign off the FTP policy on semi-annual basis.
> - Delegate authority for FTP implementation to Treasury.
> - Approve and sign off FTP policy statements for Retail banking and Corporate Banking
>
> - Other
> - Approve all funding cost re-charge mechanisms.
> - Other issues relating to the management of financial risk and the balance sheet, as the Chair and members identify from time to time.
> - Ensure effective operation of the ALCO in line with best-practice and regulator requirements, including as the appropriate forum for challenge and debate of all balance sheet-related issues and concerns
> - Promote and ensure a culture of good corporate governance.
> - Escalation of issues to Board where necessary.

| | |
|---|---|
| Board Administration/ Secretariat | The Treasury team is responsible for meeting administration. The draft agenda for each meeting is agreed with the Head of Treasury and the Chief Financial Officer in advance of meetings. Papers are circulated to Members and Attendees a minimum of three business days before each meeting. Draft minutes and agreed actions are circulated for approval as soon as possible after each meeting, preferably within a period of one week. |

The minutes of the meeting shall include:
- A record of all material issues discussed and agreed by the Committee;
- All agreed actions and items approved by the Committee; and
- Any matters which require escalation.

The Chair of the meeting has responsibility for ensuring the meeting minutes are reviewed before circulation to the Members and Attendees for review and comment. The minutes from the previous Committee meeting will be submitted for formal approval at its next meeting.

Copies of the approved minutes and record sets for all meetings are retained by the secretary.

# APPENDIX 10.B:  Liquidity Risk Early Warning Indicators (EWI) Template

Liquidity risk early warning indicators (EWI) - Choudhry Bank Group

| No. | Indicator description | EWI specification | Threshold | Latest | Group 9/30-15 | Group 6/30-15 | Group 3/31-15 | Parent 9/30-15 | Parent 6/30-15 | Parent 3/31-15 |
|-----|----------------------|-------------------|-----------|--------|--------|--------|--------|--------|--------|--------|
| 1 | Liquidity Coverage Ratio («LCR») | Stock of HQLA / net cash outflows over 30 days | < 120% | 180.7% | 246.5% | 205.1% | 273.8% | 161.8% | 181.2% | 202.8% |
| 2 | Rapid asset growth funded by volatile liabilities | Monitored through Advance / Deposit (A/D) Ratio | > 75% | 37.3% | 37.0% | 38.4% | 41.3% | 40.7% | 42.5% | 43.5% |
| 3 | Deposit Coverage Ratio («DCR») | Overall liquidity reserve / Deposits due < 90 D | < 60% | 112.3% | 112.3% | 107.9% | 100.8% | 76.8% | 71.3% | 71.8% |
| 4 | Funding concentration ratio («FCR») | Largest single bank commitment or depositor < 30D / Total due to banks < 30D + total depositors < 30 D | > 8% | 9.7% | 9.7% | 2.0% | 5.8% | 1.8% | 1.9% | 1.5% |
| 5 | Withdrawal of deposits during last 30 days («WD30») | Percentage of deposit withdrawal | > 10% | no data | no data | no data | no data | no data | no data | no data |
| 6 | Correspondent banks eliminate / decrease credit and FX lines | Total amount of credit and FX line decreases | > CHF 50 million | No | No | No | No | No | No | No |
| 7 | Key FX rate development | USD / CHF rate largely deviating from budget rate | > 25% | 9.3% | 5.7% | 1.1% | 5.5% | 5.7% | 1.1% | 5.5% |
| 8 | Overall market volatility | VIX (CBOE Volatility Index) | > 25% | 27.0% | 24.5% | 17.6% | 15.0% | 24.5% | 17.6% | 15.0% |
| 9 | Negative publicity about the Bank | Immediate Notifiable Event («INE») | significant case | No | No | No | No | No | No | No |

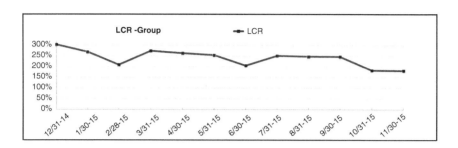

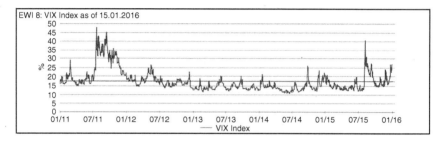

**Comments:**

- The Group's LCR decreased during 2015. However, the 180.7% LCR ratio at 11/30-15 largely exceeds both the internal requirement (110%) as well as the future regulatory requirement (100%).

- On August 24, 2015, the VIX volatility index peaked to 40.7% mainly driven by China's devaluation of the Yuan by 1.9% to boost exports earlier in August, the subsequent FX / stock market turmoil, the Chinese slowdown as well as reduced global growth outlook. Since then the volatilitx index had its low at 14.2% on November 2, 2015. In 2016 the volatility index increased rapidly to the peak of 27% on January 8, 2016. After some decrease the following week, the index reached again 27% on January 15, 2016, and exceeds the stipulated threshold of 25%.

- In Q4 the countries performed further liquidity stress tests. The Group and all countries have sufficient liquidity to absorb the market driven stress outflows (LST 1) as well as to absorb the projected deposit outflows (LST 2) at 9/30-15.

- GALCO to consider to substitute KRI 5 "Withdrawal of deposits" with "Net deposit movement" (for which data is readily available).

Liquidity risk early warning indicators (EWI) (*Continued*)

Glossary

| Indicator / Term | Description | Characteristics |
|---|---|---|
| **Loan to Deposit Ratio («LDR»)** | The L-D Ratio shows to what extent customer advances are financed with customer deposits. It is also used for the early identification of rapid asset growth, which cannot be funded by deposits and needs to be financed alternatively. Funding by volatile liabilities, e.g., wholesale financing, increases liquidity funding risk. | L-D Ratio is closely monitored by Management with regard to strategic risk and the achievement of lending targets / revenue generation. |
| **Credit & FX line cancellation** | Correspondent banks may cancel credit or FX lines granted to Group companies, which reduces the Group's flexibility for liquidity management and may indicated negative opinion or sentiment in the market. | Only limit cancellations by counterparty to be reported. |
| **Deposit Coverage Ratio («DCR»)** | The DCR is a liquidity funding risk indicator, which highlights to which extent the total deposits due within 90 days are covered by the Overall Liquidity Reserve («OLR»). | Overall liquidity reserve / Deposits due < 90 days |
| **Funding Concentration Ratio («FCR»)** | Funding concentrations are determined to identify potential dependencies. The FCR puts the largest commitment to a single bank / banking group or largest amount due to a depositor in relation to total due to banks and depositors for a 30-day timeframe. | Largest single bank commitment or depositor < 30 days / Total due to banks < 30 days + total depositors < 30 days |
| **High-Quality Liquid Assets («HQLA»)** | HQLA have to be unencumbered and the stock of HQLA has to be managed so that a Group entity is able to use the HQLA immediately during the 30-day stress period without restriction on the liquidity generated. | To be eligible as HQLA, the assets must neither be issued by, nor an obligation of a financial institution. |
| **Immediate Notifiable Event («INE»)** | INEs are triggered by the following: (i) Operational loss > CHF 100'000 or equivalent, (ii) Fraud cases / fraud attempts (regardless of size), (iii) Systems down and affecting > 25% of all clients, (iv) Robbery, kidnapping and branch attack and (v) Reputational risk identification (e.g., unfavourable mention in the press). In case of the latter, significant cases reported are to be included in the EWI table above. | INE reporting within 24 hours |
| **Key FX rate development** | As the GBPUSD rate is of utmost importance to the Group and the achievement of defined objectives (e.g., the Group's annual results and budget in USD equivalents), large fluctuations and deviations from the budget rate are monitored. | 2015: The budgeted GBPUSD rate amounts to 1.42 |
| **Liquidity Coverage Ratio («LCR»)** | To promote the short-term resilience of the liquidity risk profile of banks, the LCR ensures that banks have an adequate stock of unencumbered HQLA that can be converted easily and immediately in private markets into cash to meet their liquidity needs for a 30-calendar-day liquidity stress scenario. | Stock of high HQLA / Net cash stressed outflows over next 30 days |

Liquidity risk early warning indicators (EWI) (*Continued*)

| Negative publicity about the Bank | Negative publicity about a bank may result in significant deposit outflows and cancellation of correspondent banking relationships. Therefore, the Group monitors INE reports and in particular reputation risk situation (e.g., unfavourable mention in the press). | Overall liquidity reserve / Deposits due < 90 days |
|---|---|---|
| Net Stable Funding Ratio («NSFR») | To promote more medium- and long-term funding of the assets and activities of banking organisations, the NSFR establishes a minimum acceptable amount of stable funding based on the liquidity characteristics of an institution's assets and activities over a one-year horizon. | Available amount of stable funding / Required amount of stable funding Effective date: January 1, 2018. |
| Overall Liquidity Reserve («OLR») | The OLR complements the LCR computation and focuses on a 90-day horizon under normal markets.<br><br>The liquidity reserve comprises net liquid assets, which are unencumbered and freely disposable, as well as unused committed funding lines. While required minimum reserve balances to be held with central banks are excluded from the "freely disposable liquidity", they are added back when computing the OLR as they can be used in case of large deposit withdrawals. | The OLR comprises the following:<br>- Cash & central banks<br>- Due from / to banks < 90 days, net<br>- Marketable securities, unencumbered<br>- Valuation haircut (5%)<br>- Unused committed lines received / granted, net<br>- Regulatory minimum reserve holdings |
| Overall market volatility | Market volatility is a measure of prevailing market price fluctuations. Higher overall market volatility expresses increased uncertainty and fears. | VIX (CBOE Volatility Index) as measure of implied volatility of S&P 500 index options |
| Red-Amber-Green («RAG») | The benchmarks of the Group's Key Risk Indicators (KRI) are applied to the EWI, too. The EWI are primarily geared to the identification of situations or trends, which deviate from the desired level ("green"). Furthermore, if an excess over threshold is identified during the reporting period, it is highlihgted, as well. | An excess over threshold first results in "amber" colouring. |
| **Withdrawal of deposits during last 30 days** («WD30») | WD30 or the percentage of deposits withdrawn within the last 30 days is used as an indicator for potential additional deposit withdrawals in the immediate future. | WD30 = Deposits withdrawn during last 30 days / Total deposits at beginning of the year |

Distribution: GALCO members

Liquidity risk early warning indicators (EWI) (*Continued*)

# SELECTED BIBLIOGRAPHY AND REFERENCES

Baritsch, V., (2004). *Bank Treasury Management*, Financial World Publishing.

Bragg, S., (2010). *Treasury Management: The Practitioner's Guide*, John Wiley & Sons Ltd.

*"The inconvenient truth is that mathematical models, though often touted as risk management tools, work best for everyday situations, when they are least needed. They are often wrong in a crisis, precisely when you need them most, but their wrongness is dressed up in mathematical pseudo-precision. . .they are designed to work in perfectly calibrated, artificial conditions, not in reality."*

—Stephen Davis, Jon Lukomnik, and David Pitt-Watson,
*What They Do With Your Money*, New Haven, CT:
Yale University Press, 2016

# CHAPTER 11

# Bank Asset–Liability Management (ALM) and "Strategic ALM"

The asset–liability management (ALM) function in a bank is as old as banking itself, although it was not codified into a formal discipline in any real way until the early 1970s. The breakdown of the Bretton-Woods system, greater volatility in interest rates and FX rates, and high inflation placed more emphasis on the business of bank balance sheet management, and hence the importance of the ALM desk in a bank grew. It was the economic and geo-political circumstances prevailing in the early 1970s that acted as a catalyst towards the development of the ALM discipline. However, the function never really acquired any formal academic cachet and has never attracted the research interest that, say, derivatives or structured finance has. That is something of a paradox because unlike derivatives or structured products, the active use of which is the preserve of only a small percentage of the world's banks, ALM must be practised – and practised competently – by every bank in the world, irrespective of size, business model, jurisdiction, customer franchise, or product set.

Responsibility for ALM is generally, but not always, placed within the Treasury department of a bank, and this is the main reason we spent so much time discussing the Treasury operating model in Chapter 10. However. as with so much in the finance space, there is more than one way to arrange the function and there is actually some considerable variation observable in the world's banks when it comes to the operating model for ALM.

In this chapter, we delve deeper into the ALM discipline. This is the focus of the book extracts, which we begin with here. These extracts are describing the traditional, reactive approach to ALM. The new material in this chapter describes the ALM discipline of today and the future, the more proactive integrated methodology. We then discuss the interaction of Treasury, Finance, and Risk as part of the balance sheet risk "triumvirate".

As we make clear in the second half of this chapter, what is needed for 21ˢᵗ century banks is an integrated, more proactive ALM approach. Therefore we consider the author's concept of "Strategic ALM", which is essentially the necessary evolution of the ALM function for the post-crash Basel III era. In a nutshell, if a bank is to manage its balance sheet efficiently, it has to move from the historically reactive and silo-like approach to ALM towards a more proactive integrated balance sheet risk management approach. We present our recommendations for the Strategic ALM function later in this chapter. (Interestingly, in 2016 some of the large consulting firms began to speak about a concept they called "Strategic Treasury", a more limited version of the strategic ALM concept the author first presented in 2006 and which we recommend in this chapter.)

This extract from *Bank Asset and Liability Management* (2007)

## Bank Asset–Liability Management

## Bank Treasury Asset–Liability Management

Having introduced the market instruments, we are in a position to introduce the basics of asset–liability management (ALM). In Part II we review the main strands of the discipline, including a look at the role of the ALM Committee (ALCO) and ALCO reporting. We also consider the yield curve, relative value analysis, determinants of the swap spread and the expected magnitude of the term premium, all of which feed into ALM decision-making.

We describe the ALM function in four chapters. In Chapter 5 we introduce basic concepts, such as liquidity, gap and the cost of funds. This is illustrated with case studies that show how an hypothetical medium-sized bond and derivatives trading house, which we call XYZ Securities Limited, would structure its ALM policy. There are also case studies that illustrate how XYZ would use floating-rate notes (FRNs) and sovereign bond portfolios as part of its treasury management. Chapter 6 develops these concepts with real-world illustrations. We take an interlude with Chapter 7 which introduces the basic techniques of money market trading and hedging; these are essential elements in the daily ALM process. Finally we describe in detail the function of the bank ALM committee or ALCO, in Chapter 8.

# Asset–Liability Management I

Asset–liability management (ALM) is a generic term that is used to refer to a number of things by different market participants. We believe however that it should be used to denote specifically the high-level management of a bank's assets and liabilities; as such it is a strategy-level discipline and not a tactical one. It may be set within a bank's Treasury division or by its asset–liability committee (ALCO). The principle function of the ALM desk is to manage interest-rate risk and liquidity risk. It will also set overall policy for credit risk and credit risk management, although tactical-level credit policy is set at a lower level within credit committees. Although the basic tenets of ALM would seem to apply more to commercial banking rather than investment banking, in reality it is important that it is applied to both functions. A trading desk still deals in assets and liabilities, and these must be managed for interest-rate risk and liquidity risk. In a properly integrated banking function the ALM desk must have a remit overseeing all aspects of a bank's operations.

In this chapter we introduce the key ALM concepts of liquidity, management policy and the internal cost of funds.

## BASIC CONCEPTS

In financial markets the two main strands of risk management are interest-rate risk and liquidity risk. ALM practice is concerned with managing this risk. Interest-rate risk exists in two strands. The first strand is the more obvious one, the risk of changes in asset–liability value due to changes in interest rates. Such a change impacts the cash flows of assets and liabilities, or rather their present value, because financial instruments are valued with reference to market interest rates. The second strand is that associated with optionality, which arises with products such as early redeemable loans. The other main type of risk that ALM seeks to manage is liquidity risk, which refers both to the liquidity of markets and the ease with which assets can be translated to cash.

ALM is conducted primarily at an overview, balance sheet level. The risk that is managed is an aggregate, group-level risk. This makes sense because one could not manage a viable banking business by leaving interest-rate and liquidity risk management at individual operating levels. We illustrate this in Figure 5.1, which highlights the cornerstones of ALM. Essentially, interest-rate risk exposure is managed at the group level by the Treasury desk. The drivers are the different currency interest rates, with each exposure being made up of the net present value (NPV) of cash flow as it changes with movements in interest rates. The discount rate used to

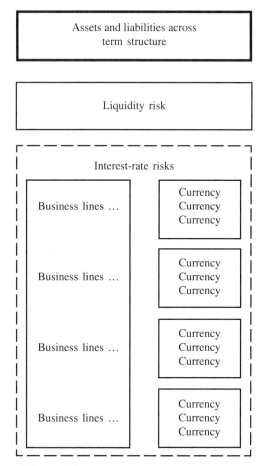

**Figure 5.1**    Cornerstone of ALM philosophy

calculate the NPV is the prevailing market rate for each time bucket in the term structure.

The interest-rate exposure arises because rates fluctuate from day to day, and continuously over time. The primary risk is that of interest-rate reset, for floating-rate assets and liabilities. The secondary risk is liquidity risk: unless assets and liabilities are matched by amount and term, assets must be funded on a continuous rolling basis. Equally, the receipt of funds must be placed on a continuous basis. Whether an asset carries a fixed or floating-rate reset will determine its exposure to interest-rate fluctuations. Where an asset is marked at a fixed rate, a rise in rates will reduce its NPV and so reduce its value to the bank. This is intuitively easy to grasp, even without recourse to financial arithmetic, because we can see that the asset is now paying a below-market rate of interest. Or we can think of it as a loss due to opportunity cost foregone, since the assets are earning below what they could earn if they were employed elsewhere in the market. The opposite applies if there is a fall in rates: this causes the NPV of the asset to rise. For assets marked at a floating-rate of interest, the risk exposure to fluctuating rates is lower, because the rate receivable on the asset will reset at periodic intervals, which will allow for changes in market rates.

We speak of risk exposure as being for the group as a whole. This exposure must therefore aggregate the net risk of all the bank's operating business. Even for the simplest banking operation, we can see that this will produce a net mismatch between assets and liabilities, because different business lines will have differing objectives for their individual books. This mismatch will manifest itself in two ways:

- the mismatch between the different terms of assets and liabilities across the term structure;
- the mismatch between the different interest rates that each asset or liability contract has been struck at.

This mismatch is known as the ALM *gap*. The first type is referred to as the *liquidity gap*, while the second is known as the *interest-rate gap*. We value assets and liabilities at their NPV; hence, we can measure the overall sensitivity of the balance sheet NPV to changes in interest rates. As such ALM is an art that encompasses aggregate balance sheet risk management at the group level.

Figure 5.2 shows the aggregate group-level ALM profile for a securities and derivatives trading house based in London. There is a slight term mismatch as no assets are deemed to have "overnight" maturity whereas a significant portion of funding (liabilities) is in the overnight term. One thing we do not know from looking at Figure 5.2 is how this particular institution is defining the maturity of its assets.[1] To place these in the relevant maturity buckets, one can adopt one of two approaches, namely:

- the actual duration of the assets;
- the "liquidity duration", which is the estimated time it would take the firm to dispose of its assets in an enforced or "fire sale" situation, such as a withdrawal from the business.

---

[1] This report is discussed in full in the Case Study later in the chapter.

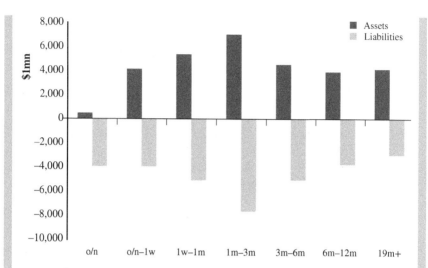

**Figure 5.2**   Securities and derivatives trading house ALM profile

Each approach has its adherents, and we believe that actually there is no "right" way. It is up to the individual institution to adopt one method and then consistently adhere to it. The second approach has the disadvantage, however, of being inherently subjective – the estimate of the time taken to dispose of an asset book is not an exact science and is little more than educated guesswork. Nevertheless, for long-dated and/or illiquid assets, it is at least a workable method that enables practitioners to work around a specified ALM framework with regard to structuring the liability profile.

# LIQUIDITY GAP

There is an obvious risk exposure arising because of liquidity mismatch of assets and liabilities. The maturity terms will not match, which creates the liquidity gap. The amount of assets and liabilities maturing at any one time will also not match (although overall, as we saw in Chapter 2, by definition assets must equal liabilities). Liquidity risk is the risk that a bank will not be able to refinance assets as liabilities become due, for any reason.[2] To manage this, the bank will hold a large portion of assets

---

[2] The reasons can be macro-level ones, affecting most or all market participants, or more firm- or sector-specific. The former might be a general market correction that causes the supply of funds to dry up, and would be a near-catastrophe situation. The latter is best illustrated with the example of Barings plc in 1995: when it went bust overnight due to large, hitherto covered-up losses on the Simex exchange, the supply of credit to similar institutions was reduced or charged at much higher rates, albeit only temporarily, as a result.

in very liquid form.[3] A surplus of assets over liabilities creates a funding requirement. If there is a surplus of liabilities, the bank will need to find efficient uses for those funds. In either case, the bank has a liquidity gap. This liquidity can be projected over time, so that one knows what the situation is each morning, based on net expiring assets and liabilities. The projection will change daily of course, due to new business undertaken each day.

We could eliminate liquidity gap risk by matching assets and liabilities across each time bucket. Actually, at individual loan level this is a popular strategy: if we can invest in an asset paying 5.50% for three months and fund this with a three-month loan costing 5.00%, we have locked in a 50-basis point gain that is interest-rate risk free. However, while such an approach can be undertaken at individual asset level, it would not be possible at an aggregate level, or at least not possible without imposing severe restrictions on the business. Hence, liquidity risk is a key consideration in ALM. A bank with a surplus of long-term assets over short-term liabilities will have an ongoing requirement to fund the assets continuously, and there is the ever-present risk that funds may not be available as and when they are required. The concept of a future funding requirement is itself a driver of interest-rate risk, because the bank will not know what the future interest rates at which it will deal will be.[4] So a key part of ALM involves managing and hedging this forward liquidity risk.

## Definition and illustration

To reiterate then, the liquidity gap is the difference in maturity between assets and liabilities at each point along the term structure. Because for many banks ALM concerns itself with a medium-term management of risk, this will not be beyond a five-year horizon, and in many cases will be considerably less than this. Note from Figure 5.2 how the longest-dated time bucket in the ALM profile extends out to only "12-month plus", so that all liabilities longer than one year were grouped in one time bucket. This recognises that most liabilities are funded in the money markets, although a proportion of funding will be much longer term, up to 30 years or so.

For each point along the term structure at which a gap exists, there is (liquidity) gap risk exposure. This is the risk that funds cannot be raised as

---

[3] Such assets would be very short-term, risk-free assets such as T-bills.
[4] It can of course lock in future funding rates with forward-starting loans, which is one way to manage liquidity risk.

required, or that the rate payable on these funds is prohibitive.[5] To manage this risk, a bank must perforce:

- disperse the funding profile (the liability profile) over more than just a short period of time. For example, it would be excessively risky to concentrate funding in just the overnight to one-week time bucket, so a bank will spread the profile across a number of time buckets. Figure 5.3 shows the liability profile for a European multi-currency asset-backed CP programme, with liabilities extending from one month to one year;
- manage expectations so that large-size funding requirements are diarised well in advance, as well as not planned for times of low liquidity such as the Christmas and New Year period;
- hold a significant proportion of assets in the form of very liquid instruments such as very short term cash loans, T-bills and high-quality short-term bank CDs.

Observing the last guideline allows a bank to maintain a reserve of liquidity in the event of a funding crisis, because such assets can be turned into cash at very short notice.

The size of the liquidity gap at any one time is never more than a snap-shot in time, because it is constantly changing as new commitments are entered into on both the asset and liability side. For this reason some writers speak of a "static" gap and a "dynamic" gap, but in practice one recognises

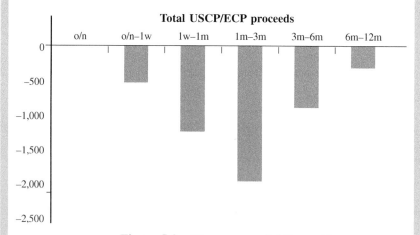

**Figure 5.3**  CP programme liability profile

---

[5] Of course the opposite applies: the gap risk refers to an excess of liabilities over assets.

that there is only ever a dynamic gap, because the position changes daily. Hence we will refer only to one liquidity gap.

A further definition is the "marginal" gap, which is the difference between the change in assets and change in liabilities during a specified time period. This is also known as the "incremental" gap. If the change in assets is greater than the change in liabilities, this is a positive marginal gap, while if the opposite applies this is a negative marginal gap.[6]

We illustrate these values in Table 5.1. This is a simplified asset–liability profile from a regional European bank, showing gap and marginal gap at each time period. Note that the liabilities have been structured to produce an "ALM Smile", which is recognised to follow prudent business practice. Generally, no more than 20% of the total funding should be in the overnight to one-week time bucket, and similarly for the 9–12 month bucket. The marginal gap is measured as the difference between the change in assets and the change in liabilities from one period to the next.

Figure 5.4 shows the graphical profile of the numbers in Table 5.1; and Figure 5.2 shown earlier illustrates the "ALM Smile".

| | One week | One month | 3–month | 6–month | 9–12 month | > 12 months | Total |
|---|---|---|---|---|---|---|---|
| **Assets** | 10 | 90 | 460 | 710 | 520 | 100 | 1890 |
| **Liabilities** | 100 | 380 | 690 | 410 | 220 | 90 | 1890 |
| **Gap** | –90 | –290 | –230 | 300 | 300 | 10 | |
| **Marginal gap** | | 200 | –60 | –530 | 0 | 290 | |

**Table 5.1**   Simplified ALM profile for regional European bank

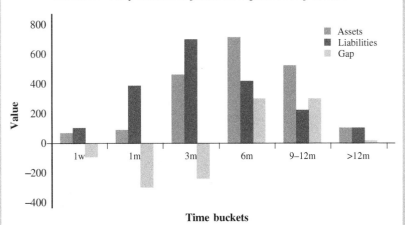

**Figure 5.4**   ALM time profile

---

[6] Note that this terminology is not a universal convention.

## Liquidity risk

Liquidity risk exposure arises from normal banking operations. That is, it exists irrespective of the type of funding gap, be it excess assets over liabilities for any particular time bucket or an excess of liabilities over assets. In other words, there is a funding risk in any case, either funds must be obtained or surplus assets laid off. The liquidity risk in itself generates interest-rate risk, due to the uncertainty of future interest rates. This can be managed through hedging, and we discuss interest-rate hedging in chapters 13, 14 and 15.

If assets are floating-rate, there is less concern over interest-rate risk because of the nature of the interest-rate reset. This also applies to floating-rate liabilities, but only insofar that these match floating-rate assets. Floating-rate liabilities issued to fund fixed-rate assets create forward risk exposure to rising interest rates. Note that even if both assets and liabilities are floating-rate, they can still generate interest-rate risk. For example, if assets pay six-month Libor and liabilities pay three-month Libor, there is an interest-rate spread risk between the two terms. Such an arrangement has eliminated liquidity risk, but not interest-rate spread risk.

Liquidity risk can be managed by matching assets and liabilities, or by setting a series of rolling term loans to fund a long-dated asset. Generally, however, banks will have a particular view of future market conditions, and manage the ALM book in line with this view. This would leave in place a certain level of liquidity risk.

## Matched book

The simplest way to manage liquidity and interest-rate risk is the matched book approach, also known as cash matching. This is actually very rare to observe in practice, even among conservative institutions such as the smaller UK building societies. In matched book, assets and liabilities, and their time profiles, are matched as closely as possible. This includes allowing for the amortisation of assets.[7] As well as matching maturities and time profiles, the interest-rate basis for both assets and liabilities will be matched. That is, fixed loans to fund fixed-rate assets, and the same for floating-rate assets and liabilities. Floating-rate instruments will further need to match the period of each interest-rate reset, to eliminate spread risk.

Under a matched book, also known as *cash flow matching*, in theory there is no liquidity gap. Locking in terms and interest rate bases will also lock in profit. For instance, a six-month fixed-rate loan is funded with a six-month fixed-rate deposit. This would eliminate both liquidity and interest-rate risk. In a customer-focused business it will not be possible to precisely match assets and liabilities, but from a macro level it should be possible to match the profiles fairly closely, by netting total exposure on both sides and matching this. Of course, it may not be desirable to run a matched book, as this would mean the ALM book was not taking any view at all on the path of future interest rates. Hence a part of the banking book is usually left unmatched, and it is this part that will benefit (or lose out) if rates go the way they are expected to (or not!).

## Managing the gap with undated assets and liabilities

We have described a scenario of liquidity management where the maturity date of both assets and liabilities is known with certainty. A large part of retail and commercial banking operations revolves around assets that do not have an explicit maturity date however. These include current account overdrafts and credit card balances. They also include drawn and undrawn lines of credit. The volume of these is a function of general economic conditions, and can be difficult to predict. Banks will need to be familiar with their clients' behaviour and their requirements over time to be able to assess when and for how long these assets will be utilised.

Undated assets are balanced on the other side by non-dated liabilities, such as non-interest-bearing liabilities (NIBLs), which include cheque accounts and instant-access deposit accounts. The latter frequently attract very low rates of interest, and are usually included in the NIBL total. Undated liabilities are treated in different ways by banks; the most common treatment places these funds in the shortest time bucket, the overnight to one-week bucket. However, this means the firm's gap and liquidity profile can be highly volatile and unpredictable, which places greater strain on ALM management. For this reason some bank's take the opposite approach and place these funds in the longest-dated bucket, the greater-than-12-month bucket. A third approach is to split the total undated liabilities into a "core" balance and an "unstable" balance, and place the first in the long-dated bucket and the second in the shortest dated bucket. The amount recognised as the core balance will need to be analysed over time, to make sure that it is accurate.

## Managing liquidity

Managing liquidity gaps and the liquidity process is a continuous, dynamic one because the ALM profile of a bank changes on a daily basis. Liquidity management is the term used to describe this continuous process of raising and laying off funds, depending on whether one is long or short cash that day.

The basic premise is a simple one: the bank must be "squared off" by the end of each day, which means that the net cash position is zero. Thus, liquidity management is both very short-term, as well as projected over the long term, because every position put on today creates a funding requirement in the future on its maturity date. The ALM desk must be aware of their future funding or excess cash positions and act accordingly, whether this means raising funds now or hedging forward interest-rate risk.

## The basic case: the funding gap

A funding requirement is dealt on the day it occurs. The decision on how it will be treated will factor the term that is put on, as well as allowing for any new assets put on that day. As funding is arranged, the gap at that day will be zero. The next day there will be a new funding requirement or surplus, depending on the net position of the book.

This is illustrated in Figure 5.5 on page 222. Starting from a flat position on the first day $(t_0)$ we observe a gap (the dotted line) on $t_1$, which is closed by putting on funding to match the asset maturity. The amount of funding to raise, and the term to run it to, will take into account the future gap as well as that day's banking activities. So at $t_2$ we observe a funding excess, which is then laid off. We see at $t_3$ that the assets invested in run beyond the maturity of the liabilities at $t_2$, so we have a funding requirement again at $t_3$. The decision on the term and amount will be based on the market view of the ALM desk. A matched book approach may well be taken where the desk does not have a strong view, or if its view is at odds with market consensus.

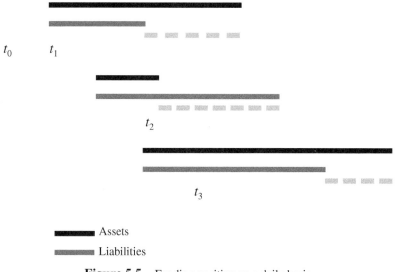

$t_0$        $t_1$

$t_2$

$t_3$

■■■■■ Assets

■■■■■ Liabilities

**Figure 5.5**    Funding position on a daily basis

There are also external factors to take into account. For instance, the availability of funds in the market may be limited, due to both macro-level issues and to the bank's own ability to raise funds. The former might be during times of market correction or recession (a "credit crunch"), while the latter includes the bank's credit lines with market counterparties. Also some funds will have been raised in the capital markets and this cash will cover part of the funding requirement. In addition, the ALM desk must consider the cost of the funds it is borrowing; if, for example, it thought that interest rates in the short term, and for short-term periods, were going to fall, it might cover the gap with only short-term funds so it can then refinance at the expected lower rates. The opposite might be done if the desk thought rates would rise in the near future.

Running a liquidity gap over time, beyond customer requirements, would reflect a particular view of the ALM desk. So maintaining a consistently underfunded position suggests that interest rates are expected to decline, at which longer-term funds can be taken at cost. Maintaining an over-funded gap would imply that the bank thinks rates will be rising, and so longer-term funds are locked in now at lower interest rates. Even if the net position is dictated by customer requirements (for example, customers placing more on deposit than they take out in loans), the bank can still manage the resultant gap in the wholesale market.

Excess liabilities generally is a rare scenario in a bank and it is not, under most circumstances, a desirable position to be in. This is because the bank will have target return on capital ratios to achieve, and this requires that funds be put to work, so to speak, by acquiring assets. In the case of equity capital it is imperative that these funds are properly employed.[8] The exact structure of the asset book will depend on the bank's view on interest rates and the yield curve generally. The shape of the yield curve and expectations on this will also influence the structure and tenor of the asset book. The common practice is to spread assets across the term structure, with varying maturities. There will also be investments made with a forward start date, to lock in rates in the forward curve now. Equally, some investments will be made for very short periods so that if interest rates rise, when the funds are reinvested they will benefit from the higher rates.

## The basic case: illustration

The basic case is illustrated in Table 5.2, in two scenarios. In the first scenario, the longest-dated gap is $-130$, so the bank puts on funding for $+130$ to match this tenor of three periods. The gap at period $t_2$ is $-410$, so this is

---

[8] The firm's capital will be invested in risk-free assets such as government T-bills or, in some cases, bank CDs. It will not be lent out in normal banking operations because the ALM desk will not want to put capital in a credit-risk investment.

matched with a 2-period tenor funding position of +280. This leaves a gap of $-180$ at period $t_1$, which is then funded with a 1-period loan. The net position is zero at each period ("squared off"), and the book has been funded with three bullet fixed-term loans. The position is not a matched book as such, although there is now no liquidity risk exposure.

In the second case, the gap is increasing from period 1 to period 2. The first period is funded with a three-period and a two-period borrowing of +50 and +200 respectively. The gap at $t_2$ needs to be funded with a position that is not needed *now*. The bank can cover this with a forward-start loan of +390 at $t_1$ or can wait and act at $t_2$. If it does the latter it may still wish to hedge the interest-rate exposure.[9]

(i)

| Time | $t_1$ | $t_2$ | $t_3$ |
|---|---|---|---|
| Assets | 970 | 840 | 1,250 |
| Liabilities | 380 | 430 | 1,120 |
| Gap | 590 | −410 | −130 |
| Borrow 1: tenor 3 periods | 130 | 130 | 130 |
| Borrow 2: tenor 2 periods | 280 | 280 | |
| Borrow 3: tenor 1 periods | 180 | | |
| Total funding | +590 | +410 | +130 |
| Squared off | 0 | 0 | 0 |

(ii)

| Time | $t_1$ | $t_2$ | $t_3$ |
|---|---|---|---|
| Assets | 970 | 840 | 1,250 |
| Liabilities | 720 | 200 | 1,200 |
| Gap | −250 | −640 | −50 |
| Borrow 1: tenor 3 periods | 50 | 50 | 50 |
| Borrow 2: tenor 2 periods | 200 | 200 | |
| Borrow 3: tenor 1 periods | 0 | 390 | |
| Total funding | +250 | +640 | +50 |
| Squared off | 0 | 0 | 0 |

**Table 5.2** Funding the liquidity gap: two examples

[9] We look at the mechanics of this, using different derivative instruments, in chapters 13, 14 and 15.

CASE STUDY 5.1    Hypothetical derivatives trading house
ALM policy and profile

We conclude this introduction to the basic concept of ALM with a look at the ALM policy and profile of a hypothetical securities and derivatives trading house, which we will call XYZ Securities Limited. The business is a financial institution based in London, with a number of business lines in FX, equity, and credit derivatives trading and market-making. We outline the various firm-wide policies on ALM, cash management, liquidity and investment that have been formalised at XYZ Securities.

## XYZ Securities Limited

### Funding and ALM

This note outlines the approach to managing the asset–liability profile that is generated by the funding requirements of XYZ Securities Limited ("XYZ"). The principal source of funding is the parent bank. Funds are also taken from a variety of external sources (prime brokerage, bank lines, TRS and repo lines, a repo conduit and an ABCP programme). The overall management of the ALM profile is centralised within XYZ Treasury desk.

The key objective of the Treasury desk is to undertake prudent management of XYZ's funding requirement, with regard to liquidity management, interest-rate management (gap profile) and funding diversification. This process includes management information and reporting. The primary deliverable of the Treasury desk is the ALM report. This is presented in Table 5.3 on page 233.

### ALM report

The ALM profile of all combined XYZ business lines is shown in Table 5.3. The report comprises the following segments:

- the ALM report;
- asset liquidity profile;
- liabilities.

We consider each part next.

### *ALM report*

This report summarises the total funding requirement of each of XYZ's business lines. The business lines are: FX, interest-rate and credit derivatives market-making; equity derivatives proprietary trading, asset management and equity brokerage. The funding is pro-filed against the asset profile to produce the firm-wide ALM profile. Liability represents the funding taken by each business line. They are set out in accordance with the maturity term structure of each constituent loan of the total funding requirement. The maturity buck-ets used are:

- overnight
- overnight – one week
- one week – one month
- one month – three months
- three months – six months
- six months – 12 months
- over 12 months.

The asset pool is distributed along the same maturity buckets in accordance with certain assumptions. These assumptions are con-cerned with the expected turnover of assets in each business, and the time estimated to liquidate the business under enforced conditions.[11] Underneath the ALM profile is the gap profile (see Figure 5.6 on page 233). Gap is defined as the difference between assets and liabilities per maturity bucket; it shows how the liability profile differs from the asset profile. It is also a snapshot that reflects where the forward funding requirement lies at the time of the snapshot.

### Asset liquidity profile
This report is a detailed breakdown of the funding requirement of each business line. Assets and liabilities are split according to desk within each business line, set out by maturity profile.

### Liabilities
This is the detailed liability profile breakdown of all the business lines. Funding is split into term structure of liabilities. A separate table is given for each business line. There is also a detailed breakdown of use of funds from each source of funds.

### Aims and objectives

Historically, the funding of XYZ business was concentrated over-whelmingly on a very short-term basis. This reflected primarily the

---

[11] The percentage breakdown that reflects senior management assumptions of the maturity profile of assets is an input into the ALM report.

short-term trading nature of XYZ's assets, which meant that the asset profile was effectively changing on a high frequency. Over time, XYZ's business evolved into dealing in more longer-term asset classes and as a consequence XYZ moved to funding in the longer-term to more adequately match its asset profile. The Treasury objective is based on the following reasoning:

- to match asset profile with liability profile and to minimise forward gap;
- to term out the funding away from the very short-dated tenors used hitherto;
- to construct an ALM profile that recognises the differing requirements of individual business lines. For example, the market-making businesses are expected to have a more flexible liquidity profile than the asset management business. Hence, the liability profile of the former will be concentrated along the short end of the funding term structure when compared to the latter;
- to even out the liability profile such that no one maturity bucket contains more than 20% of the total funding requirement. This will be treated as a funding limit.

A 20% gap limit will apply to the overall XYZ funding requirement.

### Application of cost of funds

The effect of terming out funding is to produce a cost of funds that is not explicitly observable without calculation. That is, the cost of funds must be determined as a pooled or weighted-average cost of funds (WAC). XYZ uses a simplified version of this calculation that is essentially the interest charged on each loan as a proportion of the total borrowing, or, put another way, the daily interest payable on all loans divided by the total notional amount. This is standard market practice and is used, for example, at a number of European investment banks. Treasury applies the WAC interest rate to each business line.

### XYZ Securities Limited

### Funding and ALM: enhanced procedures

As XYZ increases in size and complexity, it becomes necessary to implement a more sophiscated ALM approach. This is described below.

## ALM report

The ALM report summarises the total funding requirement of each of XYZ's business lines. The funding is profiled against the asset profile to produce the firm-wide ALM profile. Liability represents the funding taken by each business line. They are set out in accordance with the maturity term structure of each constituent loan of the total funding requirement. The asset pool is distributed along the same maturity buckets in accordance with certain assumptions. These assumptions are concerned with the expected turnover of assets in each business, and the time estimated to liquidate the business under enforced conditions. Underneath the ALM profile is shown the gap profile. Gap is defined as the difference between assets and liabilities per maturity bucket; it shows how the liability profile differs from the asset profile. It is also a snapshot that reflects where the forward funding requirement lies at the time of the snapshot.

## Aims and objectives

The aims and objectives remain the same as described on pages 227–8.

## Modifications and updates

The new ALM policy includes the following improvements:

- the ALM profile of XYZ has been structured in line with market good practice, with more accurate matching of liabilities to assets; it now resembles a banking ALM profile more accurately;
- the overnight funding profile of XYZ, which represented significant liquidity risk, has now been transformed such that overnight funding now represents 13% of overall funding, compared with over 40% at the start of the new policy;
- the 20% gap limit has been formalised and put in place, and now is a formal limit that is observed by Treasury;
- there is regular weekly reporting of ALM and funding for XYZ (see Table 5.3 and Figure 5.6);
- greater diversity in funding sources has been achieved, with bank lines in place for XYZ access to unsecured, un-guaranteed funding, secured funding using repo and total return swaps, a repo conduit and an asset-backed CP programme.

The Treasury desk will continue to observe and implement market best practice with regard to ALM and funding policy.

## Funding cost allocation

The major change in policy is now a move from a WAC-funding cost allocation to each of the business lines to a Treasury "pool" funding method.[12] In this approach, all funding, both overnight and term loans, is placed in a central Treasury pool. These funds are lent out, on an overnight basis, to the various business lines in accordance with their funding requirement. This removes interest-rate risk hedging considerations from the business lines and places them with Treasury. All business lines receive the same funding rate, the overnight Libor rate, so no business line has a funding cost advantage over another.

Treasury moves from being a cost-centre to a profit-centre, with any savings it makes in structuring the funding, below that of Libor-flat at which it lends funds, being retained within it.

## Interest-rate hedge

Under the new funding regime, all interest-rate risk exposure generated when putting on term loans is hedged within the Treasury book. The policy is as follows:

- Treasury has an interest-rate exposure limit of USD30,000 total interest-rate risk, measured as present value of a basis point (PVBP, or "DV01"), for all time buckets greater than 30 days.
- This exposure is generated by the use of term loans. Exposure is offset by lending funds in matching terms, running the liquidity book of CP, CDs, sovereign bonds and FRNs.
- Remaining DV01 is hedged using Eurodollar, Bund and short-sterling futures contracts.

The interest-rate exposure is monitored daily and subject to dynamic hedging as term loans are replaced.

## Cash management

Cash management at XYZ is undertaken by the Treasury desk. Its aim is to undertake prudent management of XYZ's funding requirement, with regard to liquidity management, interest-rate management (gap profile and gap risk) and funding diversification. It is also responsible for producing management information and ALM reporting. The Treasury desk carries out its responsibilities working in conjunction

---

[12] This approach is described fully in Chapter 28.

with the middle office and back office. The back office reports each day's funding requirement, and the funding itself is carried out by Treasury in accordance with its view. The middle office reports the funding allocated to each line of business as part of regular p&l reporting.

The objective of ALM policy is to apply market-standard guidelines to the XYZ business and to follow prudent market practice. It is also to make the whole funding process more transparent with regard to management reporting and to centralise funding into one desk within the group.

### ALM and funding report

The firm-wide ALM report is shown in Table 5.3 and Figure 5.6. From Table 5.6 we observe the following:

- the "gap" is defined as the absolute value of the assets and liabilities added together, which, because liabilities are reported as negative numbers, is essentially assets minus liabilities;
- the funding within each time bucket is reported as a percent of total funding. This is a key control measure, as prudent ALM policy suggests that the liability profile should be humped in shape ("the ALM Smile"), so that each bucket should not hold more than approximately 15–20% of the total funding;
- the next control value is the "gap as percent of total gap". This is noted to prevent an excessive forward gap developing in one time bucket;
- the key control measure is the gap as percent of total funding, which at XYZ is set at a 20% limit. We see that on this date there was no breach of this limit in any of the time buckets;
- the report also lists cumulative assets and liabilities, as well as the "net gap", which is the sum of the two cumulative values for each time bucket.

We observe that the ALM profile at XYZ follows roughly the ALM Smile shape that is recommended as the ideal profile over the term structure, and accepted good business practice.

The firm-wide funding report is shown in Figure 5.7. This is reported in graphical form to observe adherence to funding limits and indicate breaches. Unlike the ALM report, which is produced by Treasury (a front-office function), the funding report is produced by the bank's Middle Office, which is a control function. Figure 5.8 shows the breakdown by business line.

| | o/n | o/n–1 | 1w–1 m | 1 m–3 m | 3 m–6 m | 6 m–12 m | 12 m+ | Total |
|---|---|---|---|---|---|---|---|---|
| Assets | 481 | 4,104 | 5,325 | 6,954 | 4,478 | 3,845 | 4,128 | 29,315 |
| Liabilities | –3,947 | –844 | –5,107 | –7,579 | –5,053 | –3,799 | –2,986 | (29,315) |
| Gap | 3,466 | 3,260 | 218 | 625 | 575 | 46 | 1,142 | 9,332 |
| Percent of total funding | 13% | 3% | 17% | 26% | 17% | 13% | 10% | 100% |
| Gap as % of total gap | 37% | 35% | 2% | 7% | 6% | 0% | 12% | 100% |
| Gap as % of total funding | 12% | 11% | 1% | 2% | 2% | 0% | 4% | |
| Gap limit | 20% | 20% | 20% | 20% | 20% | 20% | 20% | |
| Limit breach | – | – | – | – | – | – | – | |
| Cumulative assets | 481 | 4,585 | 9,910 | 16,864 | 21,342 | 25,187 | 29,315 | |
| Cumulative liabilities | –3,947 | –4,791 | –9,898 | –1,747 | –22,530 | –26,329 | –29,315 | |
| Net gap | –3,466 | –206 | 12 | –613 | –1,188 | –1,142 | 0 | |

**Table 5.3**  XYZ Securities Limited ALM report and profile

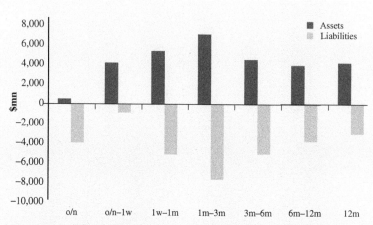

**Figure 5.6**    Cornerstone of ALM philosophy

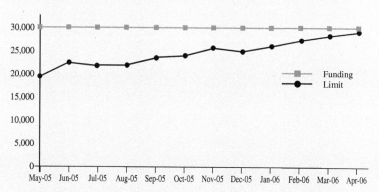

**Figure 5.7**    XYZ Securities Limited funding usage and limit report

## ALM reporting

XYZ Treasury follows the ALM policy previously described to and approved by senior management. One strand of the ALM discipline is the regular reporting of the firm's ALM profile, by means of the ALM report. This is produced by Treasury using data recorded by itself as well as data from Middle Office (MO).

## ALM procedures

The ALM report for XYZ Securities Limited is sent to senior management. The liabilities side of the report is determined by the actual liability profile of all XYZ loans, from overnight to one-year maturity and

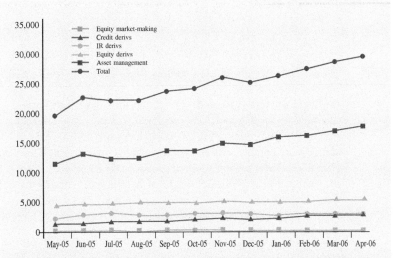

**Figure 5.8**    XYZ Securities Limited funding usage by business line

beyond. The asset side of the report is determined by senior management breakdown of the liquidation profile of all XYZ assets, and input
as the "asset-liquidation input". The basis for this breakdown is senior
management opinion on the length of time it would take to liquidate
the trading book of each business in an enforced "fire sale" situation.[13]

The process of assigning liquidation maturity buckets is based
on the subjective view of senior management. For each business line,
senior management ask the question, "What reasonable time period
would it take to liquidate positions if it were decided to close down
the business?" The answer to this question is a function of the secondary market trading liquidity of the assets in question.[14] Hence,
for frequently traded assets such as Eurobonds, we assume that one
week would be sufficient time to trade out of all assets. For business
lines with illiquid assets, such as some part of the asset management
book, a longer time period (specifically in this case, in excess of one
year) is noted. Management allocate this estimated time period in the
same time buckets as we have established for the liabilities.

We assume that assets equal liabilities.

---

[13] The liquidity duration of the asset pool is unrelated to the actual duration of the
assets themselves.

[14] In practice, other factors (such as whether the market was aware that this was an
enforced sale or not) would also influence this timing but cannot be factored into any
estimation.

The procedure for compiling the report is as follows:

- Treasury compiles its own funding report, independent of MO, from its own record of overnight and term funding for XYZ. The procedure for creating this document is documented internally;
- the Treasury report is used to populate the "Liabilities" segment on the ALM report. This segment lists the current funding profile (liabilities) of XYZ by business line;
- senior management will instruct any change to the asset liquidation breakdown, otherwise these values are retained;
- the "asset liquidity profile" segment is linked directly to the asset liquidation segment (for the asset side) and liabilities input segment (for the liability side).

The ALM graph is automatically updated when the input tabs are populated.

### The Treasury liquidity book

Following conventional banking business practice, XYZ Treasury maintains a liquidity book of T-bills, CDs, sovereign bonds and bank FRNs. The firm's capital as well as a proportion of long-term cash is held in the liquidity book.

In the next case study we set out the firm's policy for maintaining the FRN book.

---

**CASE STUDY 5.2    XYZ SECURITIES LIQUIDITY BOOK: FRN PORTFOLIO**

Banks maintain a pool of low-risk FRNs issued by other banks and building societies as part of their reserve and liquidity requirements. This well-established practice is favoured because of low capital requirements against these assets and because it enables institutions that are funded at sub-Libor to hold Libor-plus floating-rate assets with funding locked in.

The XYZ Treasury desk is able to secure sub-Libor funding via its commercial paper vehicle. Within the parent group funding limit of USD30 billion, Treasury maintains a low-risk portfolio of bank and building society assets to employ spare capacity by holding a low-risk, locked-in funding portfolio of bank and building society FRNs.

## Objectives of the business activity

To maintain a portfolio of short- to medium-dated bank and building society FRNs, all rated A or better, and held to maturity. These will be FRNs paying a spread over three-month Libor, and denominated in USD, EUR or GBP.

Bonds are funded in their own currency by means of three-month CP issued from the CP conduit, funded at sub-Libor. There is no gap funding risk.

## Motivation behind the business

A portfolio of bank and building society FRNs enables XYZ Securities Ltd to:

- earn a low-risk but material return over locked-in funding;
- utilise spare capacity in funding availability.

Bonds will be purchased at par or below par so there is no capital loss if held to maturity.

Building society paper carries particular value relative to their credit rating. There has never been a default in the history of the building society movement (traditionally building societies merge or are taken over if in any financial difficulty) and this implies that their financial risk warrants stronger than the A-rating they receive. In effect, we would carry bank risk (AA-rated) for A-rated return.

## Booking procedure

The FRN book is held in a separate trading book within the Treasury book, in order to ring-fence the match-funded positions. The booking procedure is shown in Figure 5.9.

## Expected return

Assume that the portfolio stands at USD350 million. A sample of the securities held in the book is shown in Table 5.4, all funded using 3-month CP issuance. This eliminates gap funding risk as the bonds all pay quarterly coupon.

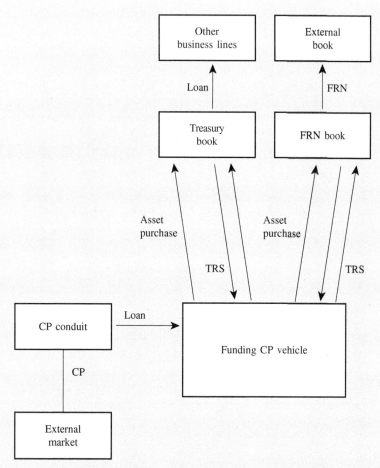

**Figure 5.9**   FRN book: schematic of booking cash flows

For a $350 million portfolio earning an average spread of 12 basis points, the net p&l (assuming L-2 basis points funding cost) would be approximately an average net gain of $490,000 per annum.

## Capital and taxation issues

There are no taxation issues in the name of XYZ Securities, which is a UK-incorporated legal entity. The capital implications are that the securities are all 20% risk-weighted under Basel I.

| Currency | Bond | Maturity | Offer price | Spread3-m Libor | Rating |
|---|---|---|---|---|---|
| USD | Kaupthing Bank | Feb-07 | 100.15 | 12.9 | A2 |
| USD | Bradford & Bingley | Dec-07 | 99.935 | 16.7 | A1 |
| USD | NIB Capital Bank | Mar-08 | 99.94 | 9.0 | AA3 / AA– |
| EUR | HBOS | Jun-09 | 99.835 | 9.9 | AA2 / AA |
| EUR | ANZ | Sep-09 | 100.03 | 11.4 | AA3 / AA– |
| EUR | Alliance & Leicester | Sep-09 | 99.81 | 14.0 | A1 / A+ |
| EUR | ABN Amro | Sep-11 | 99.75 | 13.4 | Aa3 / AA– |
| GBP | Anglo Irish Bank | Dec-06 | 99.96 | 10.3 | A2 |
| GBP | Bradford & Bingley | Dec-06 | 99.925 | 13.4 | A1 |
| GBP | MacQuarie Bank | Feb-07 | 99.95 | 12.6 | A2 |
| GBP | Anglo Irish Bank | Mar-07 | 100.02 | 14.0 | A2 |
| GBP | Fin Danish | Oct-08 | 99.92 | 14.7 | A1 |
| GBP | Bradford & Bingley | Feb-09 | 99.725 | 19.5 | A1 |

**Table 5.4** Assumed XYZ Securities Ltd FRN book (yields represent market rates as at September 2004)

## Foundations of ALM

The general term *asset and liability management* entered common usage from the mid-1970s onwards. In the changing interest-rate environment, it became imperative for banks to manage both assets and liabilities simultaneously, in order to minimise interest rate and liquidity risk and maximise interest income. ALM is a key component of any financial institution's overall operating strategy. ALM is defined in terms of four key concepts, which are described below.

The first is *liquidity*, which in an ALM context does not refer to the ease with which an asset can be bought or sold in the secondary market, but the ease with which assets can be converted into cash.[4] A banking book is required by the regulatory authorities to hold a specified minimum share of its assets in the form of very liquid instruments. Liquidity is very important to any institution that accepts deposits because of the need to meet customer demand for instant-access funds. In terms of a banking book the most liquid assets are

---

[4] The marketability definition of liquidity is also important in ALM. Less liquid financial instruments must offer a yield premium compared to liquid instruments.

overnight funds, while the least liquid are medium-term bonds. Short-term assets such as T-bills and CDs are also considered to be very liquid.

The second key concept is the money market *term structure* of interest rates. The shape of the yield curve at any one time, and expectations as to its shape in the short- and medium-term, impact to a significant extent on the ALM strategy employed by a bank. Market risk in the form of *interest-rate sensitivity* is significant, in the form of present-value sensitivity of specific instruments to changes in the level of interest rates, as well as the sensitivity of floating-rate assets and liabilities to changes in rates. Another key factor is the *maturity profile* of the book. The maturities of assets and liabilities can be matched or unmatched; although the latter is more common the former is not uncommon, depending on the specific strategies that are being employed. Matched assets and liabilities lock in return in the form of the spread between the funding rate and the return on assets. The maturity profile, the absence of a locked-in spread and the yield curve combine to determine the total interest-rate risk of the banking book.

The fourth key concept is *default risk*: the risk exposure that borrowers will default on interest or principal payments that are due to the banking institution.

These issues are placed in context in the simple hypothetical situation described in Example 6.1 "ALM considerations".

---

EXAMPLE 6.1   ALM considerations

Assume that a bank may access the markets for three-month and six-month funds, whether for funding or investment purposes. The rates for these terms are shown in Table 6.1. Assume no bid–offer spreads. The ALM manager also expects the three-month Libor rate in three-months to be 5.10%. The bank can usually fund its book at Libor, while it is able to lend at Libor plus 1%.

| Term | Libor | Bank rate |
| --- | --- | --- |
| 90-day | 5.50% | 6.50% |
| 180-day | 5.75% | 6.75% |
| Expected 90-day rate in 90 days' time | 5.10% | 6.10% |
| 3v6 FRA[1] | 6.60% | |

**Table 6.1**   Hypothetical money market rates
[1]FRA – forward rate *agreement*

The bank could adopt any of the following strategies, or a combination of them:

- Borrow three-month funds at 5.50% and lend this out in the three-month period at 6.50%. This locks in a return of 1% for a three-month period.
- Borrow six-month funds at 5.75% and lend in the six-month at 6.75%; again this earns a locked-in spread of 1%.
- Borrow three-month funds at 5.50% and lend this in the six-month term at 6.75%. This approach would require the bank to re-fund the loan in three months' time, which it expects to be able to do at 5.10%. This approach locks in a return of 1.25% in the first three-month period, and an expected return of 1.65% in the second three-month period. The risk of this tactic is that the three-month rate in three months does not fall as expected by the ALM manager, reducing profits and possibly leading to loss.
- Borrow in the six-month at 5.75% and lend these for a three-month period at 6.50%. After this period, lend the funds in the three-month or six-month period. This strategy does not tally with the ALM manager's view, however, who expects a fall in rates and so should not wish to be long of funds in three months' time.
- Borrow three-month funds at 5.50% and again lend this in the six-month period at 6.75%. To hedge the gap risk, the ALM manager simultaneously buys a 3v6 FRA to lock in the three-month rate in three months' time. The first period spread of 1.25% is guaranteed, but the FRA guarantees only a spread of 15 basis points in the second period. This is the cost of the hedge (and also suggests that the market does not agree with the ALM manager's assessment of where rates will be three months from now!), the price the bank must pay for reducing uncertainty, the lower spread return. Alternatively, the bank could lend in the six-month period, funding initially in the three-month, and buy an interest-rate cap with a ceiling rate of 6.60% and pegged to Libor, the rate at which the bank can actually fund its book.

Although simplistic, these scenarios serve to illustrate what is possible, and indeed there are many other strategies that could be adopted. The approaches described in the last option show how derivative instruments can be used actively to manage the banking book, and the cost that is associated with employing them.

## Liquidity and gap management

We noted in Chapter 5 that the simplest approach to ALM is to match assets with liabilities. For a number of reasons, which include the need to meet client demand and to maximise return on capital, this is not practical and banks must adopt more active ALM strategies. One of the most important of these is the role of the gap, and gap management. This term describes the practice of varying the asset and liability gap in response to expectations about the future course of interest rates and the shape of the yield curve. Simply put, this means increasing the gap when interest rates are expected to rise, and decreasing it when rates are expected to decline. The gap here is the difference between floating-rate assets and liabilities, but gap management must also be pursued when one of these elements is fixed rate.

Such an approach is of course an art and not a science. Gap management assumes that the ALM manager is proved to be correct in his or her prediction of the future direction of rates and the yield curve.[5] Views that turn out to be incorrect can lead to an unexpected widening or narrowing of the gap spread, and losses. The ALM manager must choose the level of trade-off between risk and return.

Gap management also assumes that the profile of the banking book can be altered with relative ease. This is not always the case, and even today may still present problems, although the evolution of a liquid market in off-balance sheet interest-rate derivatives has eased this problem somewhat. Historically it has always been difficult to change the structure of the book, as many loans cannot be liquidated instantly and fixed-rate assets and liabilities cannot be changed to floating-rate ones. Client relationships must also be observed and maintained – this is a key banking issue. For this reason it is much more common for ALM managers to use off-balance sheet products when dynamically managing the book. For example, FRAs can be used to hedge gap exposure, while interest-rate swaps are used to alter an interest basis from fixed to floating, or vice-versa. The last strategy presented in Example 6.1 presented, albeit simplistically, the use that could be made of derivatives. The widespread use of derivatives has enhanced the opportunities available to ALM managers, as well as the flexibility with which the banking book can be managed, but it has also contributed to the increase in competition and the reduction in margins and bid–offer spreads.

## Interest-rate risk and source: Banking book

### The Banking book

Traditionally, ALM has been concerned with the Banking book. The conventional techniques of ALM were developed for application to a bank's banking book; that is, the lending and deposit-taking transactions. The

---

[5] Or, is proved to be correct at least three times out of five!

core banking activity will generate either an excess of funds, when the receipt of deposits outweighs the volume of lending the bank has undertaken, or a shortage of funds, when the reverse occurs. This mis-match is balanced via financial transactions in the wholesale market. The Banking book generates both interest-rate and liquidity risks, which are then monitored and managed by the ALM desk. Interest-rate risk is the risk that the bank suffers losses due to adverse movements in market interest rates. Liquidity risk is the risk that the bank cannot generate sufficient funds when required; the most extreme version of this is when there is a "run" on the bank, and the bank cannot raise the funds required when depositors withdraw their cash.

Note that the asset side of the Banking book, which is the loan portfolio, also generates credit risk.

The ALM desk will be concerned with risk management that focuses on the quantitative management of the liquidity and interest-rate risks inherent in a Banking book. The major areas of ALM include:

- *measurement and monitoring of liquidity and interest-rate risk*. This includes setting up targets for earnings and volume of transactions, and setting up and monitoring interest-rate risk limits;
- *funding and control of any constraints on the balance sheet*. This includes liquidity constraints, debt policy and *capital adequacy* ratio and solvency;
- *hedging of liquidity and interest-rate risk*.

## Interest-rate risk

Put simply, interest-rate risk is defined as the potential impact, adverse or otherwise, on the net asset value of a financial institution's balance sheet and earnings resulting from a change in interest rates. Risk exposure exists whenever there is a maturity date mis-match between assets and liabilities, or between principal and interest cash flows. Interest-rate risk is not necessarily a negative thing; for instance, changes in interest rates that increase the net asset value of a banking institution would be regarded as positive. For this reason, active ALM seeks to position a banking book to gain from changes in rates. The Bank for International Settlements (BIS) splits interest-rate risk into two elements: *investment risk* and *income risk*. The first risk type is the term for potential risk exposure arising from changes in the market value of fixed interest-rate cash instruments and off-balance sheet instruments, and is also known as *price risk*. Investment risk is perhaps best exemplified by the change in value of a plain vanilla bond following a change in interest rates, and from Chapter 4 we know that there is an inverse relationship between changes in rates and the value of such bonds (see Example 4.1). Income risk is the risk of loss of income when there is a non-synchronous change in deposit and funding rates, and it this risk that is known as gap risk.

ALM covering the formulation of interest-rate risk policy is usually the responsibility of what is known as the asset–liability committee or ALCO, which is made up of senior management personnel including the Finance Director and the heads of Treasury and Risk Management. ALCO sets bank policy for balance sheet management and the likely impact on revenue of various scenarios that it considers may occur. The size of ALCO will depend on the complexity of the balance sheet and products traded, and the amount of management information available on individual products and desks.

The process employed by ALCO for ALM will vary according to the particular internal arrangement of the institution. A common procedure involves a monthly presentation to ALCO of the impact of different inter-est-rate scenarios on the balance sheet. This presentation may include:

- an analysis of the difference between the actual net interest income (NII) for the previous month and the amount that was forecast at the previous ALCO meeting. This is usually presented as a gap report, broken by maturity buckets and individual products;
- the result of discussion with business unit heads on the basis of the assumptions used in calculating forecasts and impact of interest-rate changes; scenario analysis usually assumes an unchanging book position between now and one month later, which is essentially unrealistic;
- a number of interest-rate scenarios, based on assumptions of (a) what is expected to happen to the shape and level of the yield curve, and (b) what may happen to the yield curve; for example, extreme scenarios. Essentially, this exercise produces a value for the forecasted NII due to changes in interest rates;
- an update of the latest actual revenue numbers.

Specific new or one-off topics may be introduced at ALCO as circumstances dictate; for example, the presentation of the approval process for the introduction of a new product or business line.

## Sources of interest–rate risk

Assets on the balance sheet are affected by absolute changes in interest rates, as well as increases in the volatility of interest rates. For instance, fixed-rate assets will fall in value in the event of a rise in rates, while funding costs will rise. This decreases the margins available. We noted that the way to remove this risk was to lock in assets with matching liabilities; however, this is not only not always possible, but also sometimes undesirable, as it prevents the ALM manager from taking a view on the yield curve. In a falling interest-rate environment, deposit-taking institutions may experience a decline in available funds, requiring new funding sources that may be accessed at less favourable terms. Liabilities are also impacted by a changing interest-rate environment.

There are five primary sources of interest-rate risk inherent in an ALM book, which are described below.

*Gap risk* is the risk that revenue and earnings decline as a result of changes in interest rates, due to the difference in the maturity profile of assets, liabilities and off-balance sheet instruments. Another term for gap risk is *mismatch risk*. An institution with gap risk is exposed to changes in the level of the yield curve, a so-called *parallel shift*, or a change in the shape of the yield curve or *pivotal shift*. Gap risk is measured in terms of short- or long-term risk, which is a function of the impact of rate changes on earnings for a short or long period. Therefore the maturity profile of the book, and the time to maturity of instruments held on the book, will influence whether the bank is exposed to short-term or long-term gap risk.

*Yield curve risk* is the risk that non-parallel or pivotal shifts in the yield curve cause a reduction in NII. The ALM manager will change the structure of the book to take into account their views on the yield curve. For example, a book with a combination of short-term and long-term asset- or liability-maturity structures[6] is at risk from a yield curve inversion, sometimes known as a *twist* in the curve.

*Basis risk* arises from the fact that assets are often priced off one interest rate, while funding is priced off another interest rate. Taken one step further, hedge instruments are often linked to a different interest rate to that of the product they are hedging. In the US market the best example of basis risk is the difference between the prime rate and Libor. Term loans in the United States are often set at prime, or a relationship to prime, while bank funding is usually based on the Eurodollar market and linked to Libor. However, the prime rate is what is known as an "administered" rate and does not change on a daily basis, unlike Libor. While changes in the two rates are positively correlated, they do not change by the same amount, which means that the spread between them changes regularly. This results in the spread earned on a loan product changing over time. Figure 6.1 illustrates the change in spread during 2005–2006.

Another risk for deposit-taking institutions such as clearing banks is *run-off risk*, associated with the non-interest bearing liabilities (NIBLs) of such banks. The level of interest rates at any one time represents an opportunity cost to depositors who have funds in such facilities. However, in a

---

[6] This describes a *barbell* structure, but this is really a bond market term.

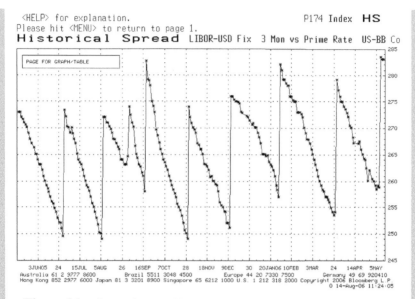

**Figure 6.1**    Change in spread between the 3-month prime rate and 3-month
Libor 2005–06.

rising interest-rate environment, this opportunity cost rises and depositors
will withdraw these funds, available at immediate notice, resulting in an
outflow of funds for the bank. The funds may be taken out of the banking
system completely; for example, for investment in the stock market. This
risk is significant and therefore sufficient funds must be maintained at short
notice, which is an opportunity cost for the bank itself.

Many banking products entitle the customer to terminate contractual
arrangements ahead of the stated maturity term; this is sometimes referred
to as *option risk*. This is another significant risk as products such as CDs,
cheque account balances and demand deposits can be withdrawn or liquidated at no notice, which is a risk to the level of NII should the option
inherent in the products be exercised.

## Gap and net interest income

We noted earlier that gap is a measure of the difference in interest-rate sensitivity of assets and liabilities that revalue at a particular date, expressed as
a cash value. Put simply it is:

$$Gap = A_{ir} - L_{ir} \qquad (6.1)$$

where $A_{ir}$ and $L_{ir}$ are the interest-rate sensitive assets and interest-rate-
sensitive liabilities. Where $A_{ir} > L_{ir}$ the banking book is described as being

*positively gapped*, and when $A_{ir} < L_{ir}$ the book is said to be *negatively gapped*. The change in NII is given by:

$$\Delta NII = Gap \times \Delta r \qquad (6.2)$$

where $r$ is the relevant interest rate used for valuation.

The NII of a bank that is positively gapped will increase as interest rates rise, and will decrease as rates decline. This describes a banking book that is asset sensitive; the opposite, when a book is negatively gapped, is known as liability sensitive. The NII of a negatively gapped book will increase when interest rates decline. The value of a book with zero gap is immune to changes in the level of interest rates. The shape of the banking book at any one time is a function of customer demand, the treasury manager's operating strategy, and view of future interest rates.

Gap analysis is used to measure the difference between interest-rate-sensitive assets and liabilities, over specified time periods. Another term for this analysis is *periodic gap*, and the common expression for each time period is maturity *bucket*. For a commercial bank the typical maturity buckets are:

* 0–3 months;
* 3–12 months;
* 1–5 years;
* > 5 years.

Another common approach is to group assets and liabilities by the buckets or grid points of the *Riskmetrics* VaR methodology (see Chapter 17). Any combination of time periods may be used, however. For instance, certain US commercial banks place assets, liabilities and off-balance sheet items in terms of *known maturities, judgemental maturities* and *market-driven maturities*. These are defined as:

* *known maturities*: fixed-rate loans and CDs;
* *judgemental maturities*: passbook savings accounts, demand deposits, credit cards, non-performing loans;
* *market-driven maturities*: option-based instruments such as mortgages, and other interest-rate sensitive assets.

The other key measure is *cumulative gap*, defined as the sum of the individual gaps up to one-year maturity. Banks traditionally use the cumulative gap to estimate the impact of a change in interest rates on NII.

## Assumptions of gap analysis

A number of assumptions are made when using gap analysis, assumptions that may not reflect reality in practice. These include:

- the key assumption that interest rate changes manifest themselves as a parallel shift in the yield curve; in practice, changes do not occur as a parallel shift, giving rise to basis risk between short-term and long-term assets;
- the expectation that contractual repayment schedules are met; if there is a fall in interest rates, prepayments of loans by borrowers who wish to refinance their loans at lower rates will have an impact on NII. Certain assets and liabilities have option features that are exercised as interest rates change, such as letters of credit and variable rate deposits; early repayment will impact a bank's cash flow;
- that repricing of assets and liabilities takes place in the mid-point of the time bucket;
- the expectation that all loan payments will occur on schedule; in practice, certain borrowers will repay the loan earlier.

Recognised weaknesses of the gap approach include:

- no incorporation of future growth, or changes in the asset–liability mix;
- no consideration of the time value of money;
- arbitrary setting of time periods.

Limitations notwithstanding, gap analysis is used extensively. Gup and Brooks (1993, pp. 59) state the following reasons for the continued popularity of gap analysis:

- it was the first approach introduced to handle interest-rate risk, and provides reasonable accuracy;
- the data required to perform the analysis are already compiled for the purposes of regulatory reporting;
- the gaps can be calculated using simple spreadsheet software;
- it is easier (and cheaper) to implement than more sophisticated techniques;
- it is straightforward to demonstrate and explain to senior management and shareholders.

Although there are more sophisticated methods available, gap analysis remains in widespread use.

# The ALM desk

The ALM desk or unit is a specialised business unit that fulfils a range of functions. Its precise remit is a function of the type of the activities of the financial institution that it is a part of. Let us consider the main types of activities that are carried out.

If an ALM unit has a profit target of zero, it will act as a cost centre with a responsibility to minimise operating costs. This would be consistent with a strategy that emphasises commercial banking as the core business of the firm, and where ALM policy is concerned purely with hedging interest-rate and liquidity risk.

The next level is where the ALM unit is responsible for minimising the cost of funding. That would allow the unit to maintain an element of exposure to interest-rate risk, depending on the view that was held as to the future level of interest rates. As we noted above, the core banking activity generates either an excess or shortage of funds. To hedge away all of the excess or shortage, while removing interest-rate exposure, has an opportunity cost associated with it since it eliminates any potential gain that might arise from movements in market rates. Of course, without a complete hedge, there is an exposure to interest-rate risk. The ALM desk is responsible for monitoring and managing this risk, and of course is credited with any cost savings in the cost of funds that arise from the exposure. The saving may be measured as the difference between the funding costs of a full hedging policy and the actual policy that the ALM desk adopts. Under this policy, interest-rate risk limits are set which the ALM desk ensures the bank's operations do not breach.

The final stage of development is to turn the ALM unit into a profit centre, with responsibility for optimising the funding policy within specified limits. The limits may be set as *gap* limits, VaR limits or by another measure, such as level of earnings volatility. Under this scenario the ALM desk is responsible for managing all financial risk.

The final development of the ALM function has resulted in it taking on a more active role. The previous paragraphs described the three stages of development that ALM has undergone, although all three versions are part of the "traditional" approach. Practitioners are now beginning to think of ALM as extending beyond the risk management field, and responsible for adding value to the net worth of the bank, through proactive positioning of the book and hence, the balance sheet. That is, in addition to the traditional function of managing liquidity risk and interest-rate risk, ALM should be concerned with managing the regulatory capital of the bank and with actively positioning the balance sheet to maximise profit. The latest developments mean that the there are now financial institutions that run a much more sophisticated ALM operation than that associated with a traditional banking book.

Let us review now the traditional and developed elements of an ALM function.

## Traditional ALM

Generally, a bank's ALM function has in the past been concerned with managing the risk associated with the banking book. This does not mean that this function is now obsolete, rather that additional functions have now been added to the ALM role. There are a large number of financial institutions that adopt the traditional approach; indeed, the nature of their operations would not lend themselves to anything more. We can summarise the role of the traditional ALM desk as follows:

*Interest-rate risk management*. This is the interest-rate risk arising from the operation of the banking book. It includes net interest income sensitivity analysis, typified by maturity gap and duration gap analysis, and the sensitivity of the book to parallel changes in the yield curve. The ALM desk will monitor the exposure and position the book in accordance with the limits as well as its market view. Smaller banks, or subsidiaries of banks that are based overseas, often run no interest-rate risk; that is, there is no short gap in their book. Otherwise the ALM desk is responsible for hedging the interest-rate risk or positioning the book in accordance with its view.

*Liquidity and funding management*. There are regulatory requirements that dictate the proportion of banking assets that must be held as short-term instruments. The liquidity book in a bank is responsible for running the portfolio of short-term instruments. The exact make-up of the book is however the responsibility of the ALM desk, and will be a function of the desk's view of market interest rates, as well as its opinion on the relative value of one asset over another. For example, it may decide to move some assets into short-dated government bonds, above what it normally holds, at the expense of high-quality CDs, or vice-versa.

*Reporting on hedging of risks*. The ALM fulfils a senior management information function by reporting on a regular basis on the extent of the bank's risk exposure. This may be in the form of a weekly hardcopy report, or via some other medium.

*Setting up risk limits*. The ALM unit will set limits, implement them and enforce them, although it is common for an independent "middle office" risk function to monitor compliance with limits.

*Capital requirement reporting*. This function involves the compilation of reports on capital usage and position limits as a percentage of capital allowed, and the reporting to regulatory authorities.

All financial institutions will carry out the activities described above.

---

| EXAMPLE 6.2 | Gap analysis |
|---|---|

*Maturity gap* analysis measures the cash difference or *gap* between the absolute values of the assets and liabilities that are sensitive to movements in interest rates. Therefore the analysis measures the relative interest-rate sensitivities of the assets and liabilities, and thus determines the risk profile of the bank with respect to changes in rates. The *gap ratio* is given as (6.3):

$$Gap\ ratio = \frac{Interest - rate\ sensitive\ assets}{Interest - rate\ sensitive\ liabilities} \quad (6.3)$$

and measures whether there are more interest-rate sensitive assets than liabilities. A gap ratio higher than one for example, indicates that a rise in interest rates will increase the NPV of the book, thus raising the return on assets at a rate higher than the rise in the cost of funding. This also results in a higher income spread. A gap ratio lower than one indicates a rising funding cost. *Duration gap* analysis measures the impact on the net worth of the bank due to changes in interest rates by focusing on changes in market value of either assets or liabilities. This is because duration measures the percentage change in the market value of a single security for a 1% change in the underlying yield of the security (strictly speaking, this is *modified duration* but the term for the original "duration" is now almost universally used to refer to modified duration). The duration gap is defined as (6.4):

$$Duration\ gap = Duration\ of\ assets - w\left(Duration\ of\ liabilities\right) \quad (6.4)$$

where *w* is the percentage of assets funded by liabilities. Hence, the duration gap measures the effects of the change in the net worth of the bank. A higher duration gap indicates a higher interest rate exposure. As duration only measures the effects of a linear change in the interest rate – that is, a parallel shift yield curve change – banks with portfolios that include a significant amount of instruments with elements of optionality, such as callable bonds, asset-backed securities and convertibles, also use the *convexity* measure of risk exposure to adjust for the inaccuracies that arise in duration over large yield changes.

# Liquidity and interest–rate risk

## The liquidity gap

Liquidity risk arises because a bank's portfolio will consist of assets and liabilities with different sizes and maturities. When assets are greater than resources from operations, a funding gap will exist that needs to be sourced in the wholesale market. When the opposite occurs, the excess resources must be invested in the market. The differences between the assets and liabilities is called the *liquidity gap*. For example, if a bank has long-term commitments that have arisen from its dealings and its resources are exceeded by these commitments, and have a shorter maturity, there is both an immediate and a future deficit. The liquidity risk for the bank is that, at any time, there are not enough resources, or funds available in the market, to balance the assets.

Liquidity management has several objectives; possibly the most important is to ensure that deficits can be funded under all foreseen circumstances, and without incurring prohibitive costs. In addition there are regulatory requirements that force a bank to operate certain limits, and state that short-term assets be in excess of short-run liabilities, in order to provide a safety net of highly liquid assets. Liquidity management is also concerned with funding deficits and investing surpluses, with managing and growing the balance sheet, and with ensuring that the bank operates within regulatory and in-house limits. In this section we review the main issues concerned with liquidity and interest-rate risk.

The liquidity gap is the difference, at all future dates, between assets and liabilities of the banking portfolio. Gaps generate liquidity risk. When liabilities exceed assets, there is an excess of funds. An excess does not of course generate liquidity risk, but it does generate interest-rate risk, because the present value of the book is sensitive to changes in market rates. When assets exceed liabilities, there is a funding deficit and the bank has long-term commitments that are not currently funded by existing operations. The liquidity risk is that the bank requires funds at a future date to match the assets. The bank is able to remove any liquidity risk by locking in maturities, but of course there is a cost involved as it will be dealing at longer maturities.[7]

## Gap risk and limits

Liquidity gaps are measured by taking the difference between outstanding balances of assets and liabilities over time. At any point a positive gap between assets and liabilities is equivalent to a deficit, and this is measured as a cash amount. The *marginal gap* is the difference between the changes of assets and liabilities over a given period. A positive marginal gap means that the variation of value of assets exceeds the variation of value of liabilities. As new assets and liabilities are added over time, as part of the ordinary course of business, the gap profile changes.

The gap profile is tabulated or charted (or both) during and at the end of each day as a primary measure of risk. For illustration, a tabulated gap report is shown in Table 6.2 on page 266 and is an actual example from

---

[7] This assumes a conventional upward-sloping yield curve.

**Time periods**

| | Total | | 0–6 months | | 6–12 months | | 1–3 years | | 3–7 years | | 7+ years | |
|---|---|---|---|---|---|---|---|---|---|---|---|---|
| Assets | 40,533 | 6.17% | 28,636 | 6.08% | 3,801 | 6.12% | 4,563 | 6.75% | 2,879 | 6.58% | 654 | 4.47% |
| Liabilities | 40,533 | 4.31% | 30,733 | 4.04% | 3,234 | 4.61% | 3,005 | 6.29% | 2,048 | 6.54% | 1,513 | 2.21% |
| Net cumulative positions | 0 | 1.86% | (2,097) | | 567 | | 1,558 | | 831 | | (859) | |

| | |
|---|---|
| Margin on total assets: | 2.58% |
| Average margin on total assets: | 2.53% |

**Table 6.2**  Example gap profile: UK bank

**Table 6.3**   Detailed gap profile: UK bank

| Assets | Total (£m) | Up to 1 month | 1–3 months | 3–6 months | 6 months to 1 year |
|---|---|---|---|---|---|
| Cash & interbank loans | 2,156.82 | 1,484.73 | 219.36 | 448.90 | 3.84 |
| CDs purchased | 1,271.49 | 58.77 | 132.99 | 210.26 | 776.50 |
| FRNs purchased | 936.03 | 245.62 | 586.60 | 12.68 | 26.13 |
| Bank bills | 314.35 | 104.09 | 178.36 | 31.90 | 0.00 |
| Other loans | 13.00 | 0.00 | 1.00 | 0.00 | 0.00 |
| Debt securities/gilts | 859.45 | 0.00 | 25.98 | 7.58 | 60.05 |
| Fixed-rate mortgages | 4,180.89 | 97.72 | 177.37 | 143.13 | 964.98 |
| Variable & capped rate mortgages | 14,850.49 | 14,850.49 | 0.00 | 0.00 | 0.00 |
| Commercial loans | 271.77 | 96.62 | 96.22 | 56.52 | 0.86 |
| Unsecured lending and leasing | 3,720.13 | 272.13 | 1,105.20 | 360.03 | 507.69 |
| Other assets | 665.53 | 357.72 | 0.00 | 18.77 | 5.00 |
|  | 29,239.95 | 17,567.91 | 2,523.06 | 1,289.77 | 2,345.05 |
|  |  |  |  |  |  |
| Swaps | 9,993.28 | 3,707.34 | 1,462.32 | 1,735.59 | 1,060.61 |
| FRAs | 425.00 | 0.00 | 50.00 | 0.00 | 220.00 |
| Futures | 875.00 | 0.00 | 300.00 | 0.00 | 175.00 |
| **TOTAL** | 40,533.24 | 21,275.24 | 4,335.38 | 3,025.36 | 3,800.66 |

**LIABILITIES (£m)**

|  | Total (£m) | Up to 1 month | 1–3 months | 3–6 months | 6 months to 1 year |
|---|---|---|---|---|---|
| Bank deposits | 3,993.45 | 2,553.85 | 850.45 | 233.03 | 329.06 |
| CDs issued | 1,431.42 | 375.96 | 506.76 | 154.70 | 309.50 |
| CP & Euro | 508.46 | 271.82 | 128.42 | 108.21 | 0.00 |
| Subordinated debt | 275.00 | 0.00 | 0.00 | 0.00 | 0.00 |
| Eurobonds + other | 2,582.24 | 768.75 | 1,231.29 | 121.94 | 53.86 |
| Customer deposits | 17,267.55 | 15,493.65 | 953.60 | 311.70 | 340.50 |
| Other liabilities (incl capital/reserves) | 3,181.83 | 1,336.83 | 0.00 | 0.00 | 741.72 |
|  | 29,239.96 | 20,800.86 | 3,670.52 | 929.58 | 1,774.64 |
|  |  |  |  |  |  |
| Swaps | 9,993.28 | 1,754.70 | 1,657.59 | 1,399.75 | 1,254.24 |
| FRAs | 425.00 | 0.00 | 150.00 | 70.00 | 55.00 |
| Futures | 87 5.00 | 0.00 | 0.00 | 300.00 | 150.00 |
| **TOTAL** | 40,533.24 | 22,555.56 | 5,478.11 | 2,699.33 | 3,233.89 |
|  |  |  |  |  |  |
| **Net Positions** | 0.00 | −1,351.09 | −1,234.54 | 265.58 | 583.48 |

| 1–2 years | 2–3 years | 3–4 years | 4–5 years | 5–6 years | 6–7 years | 7–8 years | 8–9 years | 9–10 years | 10+ years |
|---|---|---|---|---|---|---|---|---|---|
| 0.00 | 0.00 | 0.00 | 0.00 | 0.00 | 0.00 | 0.00 | 0.00 | 0.00 | 0.00 |
| | | | | | | | | | |
| 92.96 | 0.00 | 0.00 | 0.00 | 0.00 | 0.00 | 0.00 | 0.00 | 0.00 | 0.00 |
| 45.48 | 0.00 | 0.00 | 19.52 | 0.00 | 0.00 | 0.00 | 0.00 | 0.00 | 0.00 |
| 0.00 | 0.00 | 0.00 | 0.00 | 0.00 | 0.00 | 0.00 | 0.00 | 0.00 | 0.00 |
| 7.00 | 0.00 | 1.00 | 0.00 | 0.00 | 2.00 | 2.00 | 0.00 | 0.00 | 0.00 |
| 439.06 | 199.48 | 26.81 | 100.50 | 0.00 | 0.00 | 0.00 | 0.00 | 0.00 | 0.00 |
| 1,452.91 | 181.86 | 661.36 | 450.42 | 22.78 | 4.30 | 3.65 | 3.10 | 2.63 | 14.67 |
| 0.00 | 0.00 | 0.00 | 0.00 | 0.00 | 0.00 | 0.00 | 0.00 | 0.00 | 0.00 |
| | | | | | | | | | |
| 2.16 | 1.12 | 3.64 | 8.85 | 1.06 | 0.16 | 0.17 | 0.16 | 4.23 | 0.00 |
| 694.86 | 400.84 | 195.19 | 79.98 | 25.45 | 14.06 | 10.03 | 10.44 | 10.82 | 33.42 |
| | | | | | | | | | |
| 0.00 | 0.00 | 0.00 | 0.00 | 0.00 | 0.00 | 0.00 | 0.00 | 0.00 | 284.03 |
| 2,734.43 | 783.31 | 888.00 | 659.26 | 49.28 | 20.53 | 15.85 | 13.71 | 17.68 | 332.12 |
| | | | | | | | | | |
| 344.00 | 146.50 | 537.60 | 649.00 | 70.00 | 5.32 | 200.00 | 75.00 | 0.00 | 0.00 |
| 5.00 | 150.00 | 0.00 | 0.00 | 0.00 | 0.00 | 0.00 | 0.00 | 0.00 | 0.00 |
| 400.00 | 0.00 | 0.00 | 0.00 | 0.00 | 0.00 | 0.00 | 0.00 | 0.00 | 0.00 |
| 3,483.43 | 1,079.81 | 1,425.60 | 1,308.26 | 119.28 | 25.84 | 215.85 | 88.71 | 17.68 | 332.12 |
| | | | | | | | | | |
| 21.07 | 1.00 | 0.00 | 5.00 | 0.00 | 0.00 | 0.00 | 0.00 | 0.00 | 0.00 |
| 60.00 | 20.00 | 3.50 | 1.00 | 0.00 | 0.00 | 0.00 | 0.00 | 0.00 | 0.00 |
| 0.00 | 0.00 | 0.00 | 0.00 | 0.00 | 0.00 | 0.00 | 0.00 | 0.00 | 0.00 |
| 0.00 | 0.00 | 0.00 | 0.00 | 0.00 | 0.00 | 200.00 | 75.00 | 0.00 | 0.00 |
| 9.77 | 13.16 | 150.43 | 150.53 | 0.00 | 7.51 | 0.00 | 0.00 | 0.00 | 75.00 |
| 129.10 | 6.60 | 24.90 | 0.00 | 7.50 | 0.00 | 0.00 | 0.00 | 0.00 | 0.00 |
| 0.00 | 0.00 | 0.00 | 0.00 | 0.00 | 0.00 | 0.00 | 0.00 | 0.00 | 1,103.28 |
| | | | | | | | | | |
| 219.93 | 40.76 | 178.83 | 156.53 | 7.50 | 7.51 | 200.00 | 75.00 | 0.00 | 1,178.28 |
| | | | | | | | | | |
| 1,887.97 | 281.44 | 905.06 | 770.52 | 15.76 | 6.48 | 7.27 | 8.13 | 13.06 | 31.30 |
| 150.00 | 0.00 | 0.00 | 0.00 | 0.00 | 0.00 | 0.00 | 0.00 | 0.00 | 0.00 |
| 425.00 | 0.00 | 0.00 | 0.00 | 0.00 | 0.00 | 0.00 | 0.00 | 0.00 | 0.00 |
| 2,682.90 | 322.20 | 1,083.90 | 927.05 | 23.26 | 13.99 | 207.27 | 83.13 | 13.06 | 1,209.58 |
| | | | | | | | | | |
| 929.10 | 803.46 | 341.70 | 404.88 | 104.28 | 11.85 | 8.58 | 5.57 | 4.62 | −877.45 |

a UK banking institution. It shows the assets and liabilities grouped into maturity *buckets* and the net position for each bucket. It is a snapshot today of the exposure, and hence funding requirement of the bank for future maturity periods.

Table 6.2 is very much a summary report, because the maturity gaps are very wide. For risk management purposes the buckets would be much narrower; for instance, the period between zero and 12 months might be split into 12 different maturity buckets. An example of a more detailed gap report is shown in Table 6.3 on pages 268–9, which is from another UK banking institution. Note that the overall net position is zero, because this is a balance sheet and therefore, not surprisingly, it balances. However, along the maturity buckets or grid points there are net positions which are the gaps that need to be managed.

Limits on a banking book can be set in terms of gap limits. For example, a bank may set a six-month gap limit of £10 million. The net position of assets and maturities expiring in six months' time could then not exceed £10 million. An example of a gap limit report is shown at Figure 6.2 on page 270, with the actual net gap positions shown against the gap limits for each maturity. Again this is an actual limit report from a UK banking institution.

The maturity gap can be charted to provide an illustration of net exposure, and an example is shown in Figure 6.3 on page 270, from yet another UK banking institution. In some firms' reports both the assets and the liabilities are shown for each maturity point, but in our example only the net position is shown. This net position is the gap exposure for that maturity point. A second example, used by the overseas subsidiary of a Middle Eastern commercial bank, which has no funding lines in the interbank market and so does not run short positions, is shown in Figure 6.4 on page 271, while the gap report for a UK high-street bank is shown in Figure 6.5 on page 271. Note the large short gap under the maturity labelled "non-int"; this stands for *non-interest bearing liabilities* and represents the balance of current accounts (cheque or "checking" accounts), which are funds that attract no interest and are in theory very short-dated (because they are demand deposits, so may be called at instant notice).

Gaps represent cumulative funding required at all dates. The cumulative funding is not necessarily identical to the new funding required at each period, because the debt issued in previous periods is not necessarily amortised at subsequent periods. The new funding between, for example, months 3 and 4 is not the accumulated deficit between months 2 and 4 because the debt contracted at month 3 is not necessarily amortised at month 4. Marginal gaps may be identified as the new funding required or

| Time periods | 0–1 | 1–3 | 3–6 | 6–12 | 1–2 | 2–3 | 3–4 | 4–5 | 5–6 | 6–7 | 7–8 | 8–9 | 9–10 | 10+ |
|---|---|---|---|---|---|---|---|---|---|---|---|---|---|---|
| Individual | | 0–6 | | | | 1–3 | | | 3–7 | | | 7–10 | | years |
| Cumulative | | months | | | | years | | | years | | | years | | |
| **Current gaps** | | | | | | | | | | | | | | |
| Individual | 0 | 0 | 0 | 710 | –520 | 771 | 417 | 484 | 104 | 7 | 4 | 2 | 2 | –117 |
| Cumulative | | –1,864 | | | | 251 | | | 1,011 | | | 9 | | |
| **Limits** | | | | | | | | | | | | | | |
| Individual (+/–) | | | | +/–1250 | –2000 | +/–1000 | +1000–200 | +1000–200 | +250–100 | +200–75 | +/–50 | +/–25 | +/–25 | –125 |
| Cumulative | | +500 to –2500 | | | | +750 to –1000 | | | 2,000 | | | +100 | | |
| **Excess** | | 0 | | | | 0 | | | 0 | | | 0 | | |

**Figure 6.2**   Gap limit report

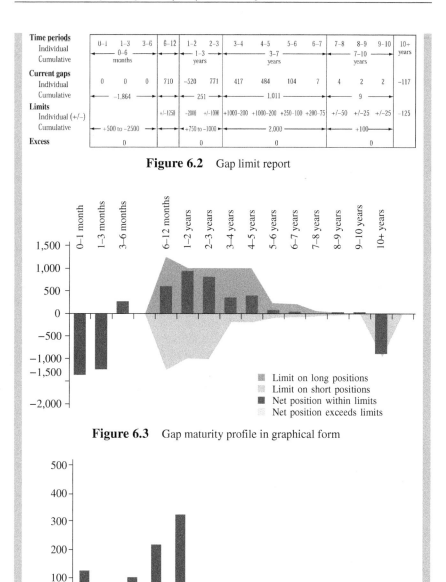

**Figure 6.3**   Gap maturity profile in graphical form

**Figure 6.4**   Gap maturity profile, bank with no short funding allowed

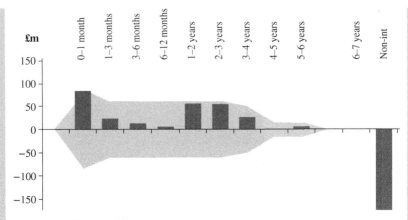

**Figure 6.5** Gap maturity profile, UK high-street bank

the new excess funds of the period that should be invested in the market. Note that all the reports are snapshots at a fixed point in time and the picture is of course a continuously moving one. In practice the liquidity position of a bank cannot be characterised by one gap at any given date, and the entire gap profile must be used to gauge the extent of the book's profile.

The liquidity book may decide to match its assets with its liabilities. This is known as *cash matching* and occurs when the time profiles of both assets and liabilities are identical. By following such a course the bank can lock in the spread between its funding rate and the rate at which it lends cash, and run a guaranteed profit. Under cash matching, the liquidity gaps will be zero. Matching the profile of both legs of the book is done at the overall level; that is, cash matching does not mean that deposits should always match loans. This would be difficult as both result from customer demand, although an individual purchase of, say, a CD can be matched with an identical loan. Nevertheless, the bank can elect to match assets and liabilities once the net position is known, and keep the book matched at all times. However, it is highly unusual for a bank to adopt a cash matching strategy.

## Liquidity management

The continuous process of raising new funds or investing surplus funds is known as liquidity management. If we consider that a gap today is funded, thus balancing assets and liabilities and squaring-off the book, the next day a new deficit or surplus is generated that also has to be funded. The liquidity management decision must cover the amount required to bridge the gap that exists the following day, as well as position the book across future dates in line with the bank's view on interest rates. Usually in order to define the maturity structure of debt a target profile of resources is defined. This may be done in several ways. If the objective of ALM is to replicate the asset profile with resources, the new funding should contribute to bringing the resources profile closer to that of the assets; that is, more of a matched book looking forward. This is the lowest risk option. Another target profile may be imposed on the bank by liquidity constraints. This may arise if, for example the bank has a limit on borrowing lines in the market so that it could not raise a certain amount each week or month. For instance, if the maximum that could be raised in one week by a bank is £10 million, the maximum period liquidity gap is constrained by that limit. The ALM desk will manage the book in line with the target profile that has been adopted, which requires it to try to reach the required profile over a given time horizon.

Figure 6.6 is a liquidity analysis for a UK bank, showing the maturity of funding going forward and where liquidity requirements arise.

Managing the banking book's liquidity is a dynamic process, as loans and deposits are known at any given point, but new business will be taking place continuously and the profile of the book looking forward must be continuously re-balanced to keep it within the target profile. There are several factors that influence this dynamic process, the most important of which are reviewed below.

### Demand deposits

Deposits placed on demand at the bank, such as current accounts (known in the United States as "checking accounts") have no stated maturity and are available on demand at the bank. Technically they are referred to as "non-interest-bearing liabilities" because the bank pays no or very low rates of interest on them, so they are effectively free funds. The balance of these funds can increase or decrease throughout the day without any warning, although in practice the balance is quite stable. There are a number of ways that a bank can choose to deal with these balances. These are:

- to group all outstanding balances into one maturity bucket at a future date that is the preferred time horizon of the bank, or a date beyond this. This would then exclude them from the gap profile. Although this is considered unrealistic because it excludes the current account balances from the gap profile, it is nevertheless a fairly common approach;

- to rely on an assumed rate of amortisation for the balances, say 5% or 10% each year;
- to divide deposits into stable and unstable balances, of which the core deposits are set as a permanent balance. The amount of the core balance is set by the bank based on a study of the total balance volatility pattern over time. The excess over the core balance is then viewed as very short-term debt. This method is reasonably close to reality as it is based on historical observations;
- to make projections based on observable variables that are correlated with the outstanding balances of deposits. For instance, such variables could be based on the level of economic growth plus an error factor based on the short-term fluctuations in the growth pattern.

### Pre-set contingencies

A bank will have committed lines of credit, the utilisation of which depends on customer demand. Contingencies generate outflows of funds that are by definition uncertain, as they are contingent upon some event; for example, the willingness of the borrower to use a committed line of credit. The usual way for a bank to deal with these unforeseen fluctuations is to use statistical data based on past observation to project a future level of activity.

### Prepayment options of existing assets

Where the maturity schedule is stated in the terms of a loan, it may still be subject to uncertainty because of prepayment options. This is similar to the prepayment risk associated with a mortgage-backed bond. An element of prepayment risk renders the actual maturity profile of a loan book to be uncertain; banks often calculate an "effective maturity schedule" based on prepayment statistics instead of the theoretical schedule. There are also a range of prepayment models that may be used, the simplest of which use constant prepayment ratios to assess the average life of the portfolio. The more sophisticated models incorporate more parameters, such as one that bases the prepayment rate on the interest rate differential between the loan rate and the current market rate, or the time elapsed since the loan was taken out.

### Interest cash flows

Assets and liabilities generate interest cash inflows and outflows, as well as the amortisation of principal. The interest payments must be included in the gap profile as well.

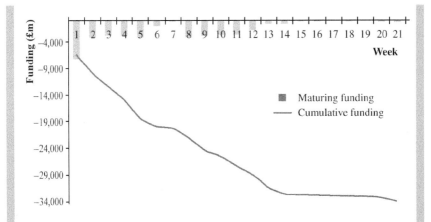

**Figure 6.6**    Liquidity analysis – example of UK bank profile of maturity of funding

## Interest-rate gap

The interest-rate gap is the standard measure of the exposure of the banking book to interest-rate risk. The interest-rate gap for a given period is defined as the difference between fixed-rate assets and fixed-rate liabilities. It can also be calculated as the difference between interest-rate sensitive assets and interest-rate liabilities. Both differences are identical in value when total assets are equal to total liabilities, but will differ when the balance sheet is not balanced. This only occurs intra-day, when, for example, a short position has not been funded yet. The general market practice is to calculate interest-rate gap as the difference between assets and liabilities. The gap is defined in terms of the maturity period that has been specified for it.

The convention for calculating gaps is important for interpretation. The "fixed-rate" gap is the opposite of the "variable-rate" gap when assets and liabilities are equal. They differ when assets and liabilities do not match and there are many reference rates. When there is a deficit, the "fixed-rate gap" is consistent with the assumption that the gap will be funded through liabilities for which the rate is unknown. This funding is then a variable-rate liability and is the bank's risk, unless the rate has been locked in beforehand. The same assumption applies when the banks run a cash surplus position, and the interest rate for any period in the future is unknown. The gap position at a given time bucket is sensitive to the interest rate that applies to that period.

The gap is calculated for each discrete time bucket, so there is a net exposure for, say, 0–1 month, 1–3 months and so on. Loans and deposits do not, except at the time of being undertaken, have precise maturities like that, so they are "mapped" to a time bucket in terms of their relative weighting. For example, a £100 million deposit that matures in 20 days' time will have most of its balance mapped to the three-week time bucket, but a smaller amount will also be allocated to the two-week bucket. Interest-rate risk is measured as the change in present value of the deposit, at each grid point, given a 1 basis point change in the interest rate. So a £10 million one-month CD that was bought at 6.50% will have its present value move upwards if on the next day the one-month rate moves down by a basis point.

The net change in present value for a 1 basis point move is the key measure of interest-rate risk for a banking book and this is what is usually referred to as a "gap report", although strictly speaking it is not. The correct term for such a report is a "PVBP" or "DV01" report, which are acronyms for "present value of a basis point" and "dollar value of a 01 [1 basis point]" respectively. The calculation of interest-rate sensitivity assumes a *parallel shift* in the yield curve; that is, that every maturity point along the term structure moves by the same amount (here one basis point) and in the same direction. An example of a PVBP report is given in Table 6.4, split by different currency books, but with all values converted to sterling.

The basic concept in the gap report is the NPV of the banking book, which is introduced in Appendix 6.1. The PVBP report measures the difference between the market values of assets and liabilities in the banking book. To calculate NPV we require a discount rate, and it represents a *mark-to-market* of the book. The rates used are always the zero-coupon rates derived from the government bond yield curve, although some adjustment should be made to this to allow for individual instruments.

Gaps may be calculated as differences between outstanding balances at one given date, or as differences of variations of those balances over a time period. A gap number calculated from variations is known as a *margin gap*. The cumulative margin gaps over a period of time, plus the initial difference in assets and liabilities at the beginning of the period are identical to the gaps between assets and liabilities at the end of the period.

The interest-rate gap differs from the liquidity gap in a number of ways; note that:

- whereas for liquidity gap all assets and liabilities must be accounted for, only those that have a fixed rate are used for the interest-rate gap;
- the interest-rate gap cannot be calculated unless a period has been defined because of the fixed-rate/variable-rate distinction. The interest-rate gap is dependent on a maturity period and an original date.

| | 1 day | 1 week | 1 month | 2 months | 3 months | 6 months | 12 months | 2 years |
|---|---|---|---|---|---|---|---|---|
| GBP | 8,395 | 6,431 | 9,927 | 8,856 | (20,897) | (115,303) | (11,500) | (237,658) |
| USD | 1,796 | (903) | 10,502 | 12,941 | 16,784 | 17,308 | (13,998) | (18,768) |
| Euro | 1,026 | 1,450 | 5,105 | 2,877 | (24,433) | (24,864) | (17,980) | (9,675) |
| Total | 11,217 | 6,978 | 25,534 | 24,674 | (28,546) | (122,859) | (43,478) | (266,101) |

| | 3 years | 4 years | 5 years | 7 years | 10 years | 15 years | 20 years | 30 years |
|---|---|---|---|---|---|---|---|---|
| GBP | (349,876) | (349,654) | 5,398 | (5,015) | (25,334) | (1,765) | (31,243) | (50,980) |
| USD | (66,543) | (9,876) | (1,966) | 237 | 2,320 | (5,676) | (1,121) | 0 |
| Euro | (11,208) | (3,076) | 1,365 | 1,122 | 3,354 | (545) | (440) | (52) |
| Total | (427,627) | (362,606) | 4,797 | (3,656) | (19,660) | (7,986) | (32,804) | (51,032) |

**Table 6.4**   Banking book PVBP grid report

*GBP total*: (1,160,218); *USD total*: (56,963); *USD total*: (75,974); *Euro total*: (56,963); *Grand total*: (1,293,155) All figures in £.

The primary purpose in compiling the gap report is to determine the sensitivity of the interest margin to changes in interest rates. As we noted earlier the measurement of the gap is always "behind the curve" as it is a historical snapshot; the actual gap is a dynamic value as the banking book continually undertakes day-to-day business.

## Generic ALM policy for different banks

The management of interest-rate risk is a fundamental ingredient of commercial banking. Bank shareholders require comfort that interest-rate risk is measured and managed in a satisfactory manner. A common approach to risk management involves the following:

- the preparation and adoption of a high-level interest-rate risk policy at managing board level; this sets general guidelines on the type and extent of risk exposure that can be taken on by the bank;
- setting limits on the risk exposure levels of the banking book; this can be by product type, desk, geographic area and so on, and will be along the maturity spectrum;
- actively measuring the level of interest-rate risk exposure at regular, specified intervals;
- reporting to senior management on general aspects of risk management, risk exposure levels, limit breaches and so on;
- monitoring of risk management policies and procedures by an independent "middle office" risk function.

The risk management approach adopted by banks will vary according to their specific markets and appetite for risk. Certain institutions will have their activities set out or proscribed for them under regulatory rules. For instance, building societies in the United Kingdom are prohibited from trading in certain instruments under the regulator's guidelines.[8] In this section we present, purely for the purposes of illustration, the ALM policies of three hypothetical banks, called Bank S, Bank M and Bank L. These are respectively, a small banking entity with assets of £500 million, a medium-sized bank with assets of £2.5 billion and a large bank with assets of £10 billion. The following serves to demonstrate the differing approaches that can be taken according to the environment that a financial institution operates in.

---

[8] This is the UK Financial Services Authority, which was established as a "super regulator" for all financial market activities in 2000, through a merger of all the industry-specific regulatory authorities.

# ALM policy for Bank S (assets = £500 million)

The aim of the ALM policy for Bank S is to provide guidelines on risk appetite, revenue targets and rates of return, as well as risk management policy. Areas that may be covered include capital ratios, liquidity, asset mix, rate-setting policy for loans and deposits, and investment guidelines for the banking portfolio. The key objectives should include:

- to maintain capital ratios at the planned minimum, and to ensure safety of the deposit base;
- to generate a satisfactory revenue stream, both for income purposes and to further protect the deposit base.

The responsibility for overseeing the operations of the bank to ensure that these objectives are achieved is lodged with the ALM Committee. This body monitors the volume and mix of the bank's assets and funding (liabilities), and ensures that this asset mix follows internal guidelines with regard to banking liquidity, capital adequacy, asset base growth targets, risk exposure and return on capital. The norm is for the committee to meet on a monthly basis; at a minimum the membership of the committee will include the finance director, head of Treasury and risk manager. For a bank the size of Bank S the ALM committee membership will possibly be extended to the chief executive, the head of the loans business and the chief operating officer.

As a matter of course the committee will wish to discuss and review the following on a regular basis:

- overall macroeconomic conditions;
- financial results and key management ratios, such as share price analysis and rates of return on capital and equity;
- the bank's view on the likely direction of short-term interest rates;
- the current lending strategy, and suggestions for changes to this, as well as the current funding strategy;
- any anticipated changes to the volume and mix of the loan book, and that of the main sources of funding; in addition, the appropriateness or otherwise of alternative sources of funding;
- suggestions for any alteration to the bank's ALM policy;
- the maturity gap profile and anticipated and suggested changes to it.

The committee will also wish to consider the interest rates offered currently on loans and deposits, and whether these are still appropriate.

Interest-rate sensitivity is monitored and confirmed as lying within specified parameters; these parameters are regularly reviewed and adjusted if deemed necessary according to changes in the business cycle and economic conditions. Measured using the following ratio:

$$A_{ir} / L_{ir}$$

typical risk levels would be expected to lie between 90–120% for the maturity period 0–90 days, and between 80–110% for the maturity period over 90 days and less than 365 days.

Put simply, the objective of Bank S would be to remain within specified risk parameters at all times, and to maintain as consistent a level of earnings as possible (and one that is immune to changes in the stage of the business cycle).

## ALM policy for Bank M (assets = £2.5 billion)

Bank M is our hypothetical "medium-sized" banking institution. Its ALM policy would be overseen by an ALCO. Typically, the following members of senior management would be expected to be members of the ALCO:

- deputy chief executive
- finance director
- head of retail banking
- head of corporate banking
- head of Treasury
- head of risk management
- head of internal audit

together with others such as product specialists who are called to attend as and when required. The finance director will often chair the meeting.

The primary responsibilities of the Bank M ALCO are detailed below.

### Objectives

The ALCO is tasked with reviewing the bank's overall funding strategy. Minutes are taken at each meeting, and decisions taken are recorded on the minutes and circulated to attendees and designated key staff. ALCO members are responsible for undertaking regular reviews of the following:

- minutes of the previous meeting;
- the ratio of the interest-rate-sensitive assets to liabilities, gap reports, risk reports and the funding position;

- the bank's view on the expected level of interest rates, and how the book should be positioned with respect to this view; and related to this, the ALCO view on anticipated funding costs in the short- and medium-term;
- stress testing in the form of "what if?" scenarios, to check the effect on the Banking book of specified changes in market conditions; and the change in parameters that may be required if there is a change in market conditions or risk tolerance;
- the current interest rates for loans and deposits, to ensure that these are in accordance with the overall lending and funding strategy;
- the maturity distribution of the liquidity book (expected to be comprised of T-bills, CDs and very short-dated government bonds); the current liquidity position and the expected position in the short and medium term.

As the ALCO meets on a regular monthly basis, it may not be the case that every aspect of their responsibility is discussed at every meeting; the agenda is set by the chair of the meeting in consultation with committee members. The policies adopted by ALCO should be dynamic and flexible, and capable of adaptation to changes in operating conditions. Any changes will be made on agreement of committee members. Generally, any exceptions to agreed policy can only be with the agreement of the CEO and ALCO itself.

### Interest-rate risk policy

The objective will be to keep earnings volatility resulting from an upward or downward move in interest rates to a minimum. To this end, at each ALCO meeting members will review risk and position reports and discuss these in the light of the risk policy. Generally, the six-month and 12-month $A_{ir}/L_{ir}$ cumulative ratio will lie in the range of 90–110%. A significant move outside this range will most likely be subject to corrective action. The committee will also consider the results of various scenario analyses on the book, and if these tests indicate a potential earnings impact of greater than, say, 10%, instructions may be given to alter the shape and maturity profile of the book.

### Liquidity policy

A primary responsibility of the ALCO is to ensure that an adequate level of liquidity is maintained at all times. We define liquidity as:

*. . . the ability to meet anticipated and unanticipated operating cash needs, loan demand, and deposit withdrawals, without incurring a sustained negative impact on profitability.*

**Gup and Brooks (1993), p. 238**

Generally, a Bank M-type operation would expect to have a target level for loans to deposits of around 75–85%, and a loans to core deposits ratio of 85–95%. The loan/deposit ratio is reported to ALCO and reviewed on a monthly basis, and a reported figure significantly outside these ranges (say, by 5% or more) will be reviewed and asked to be adjusted to bring it back into line with ALCO policy.

# ALM policy for Bank L (assets = £10 billion)

The management policy for ALM at a larger entity will build on that described for a medium-sized financial institution. If Bank L is a group company, the policy will cover the consolidated balance sheet as well as individual subsidiary balance sheets; the committee will provide direction on the management of assets and liabilities, and the off-balance sheet instruments used to manage interest-rate and credit risk. A well-functioning management process will be proactive and concentrate on direction in response to anticipated changes in operating conditions, rather than reactive responses to changes that have already taken place. The primary objectives will be to maximise shareholder value, with target returns on capital of 15–22%.

The responsibility for implementing and overseeing the ALM management policy will reside with the ALCO. The ALCO will establish the operating guidelines for ALM, and review these guidelines on a periodic basis. The committee will meet on a more frequent basis than would be the case for Bank M, usually on a fortnightly basis. As well as this, it will set policies governing liquidity and funding objectives, investment activities and interest-rate risk. It will also oversee the activities of the investment banking division. The head of the ALM desk will prepare the interest-rate risk sensitivity report and present it to the ALCO.

### Interest-rate risk management

The ALCO will establish an interest-rate risk policy that sets direction on acceptable levels of interest-rate risk. This risk policy is designed to guide management in the evaluation of the impact of interest-rate risk on the bank's earnings. The extent of risk exposure is a function of the maturity profile of the balance sheet, as well as the frequency of repricing, the level of loan prepayments and funding costs. Managing interest-rate risk is, in effect, the adjustment of risk exposure upwards or downwards, which will be in response to ALCO's views on the future direction of interest rates. As part of the risk management process the committee will monitor the current risk exposure and duration gap, using rate sensitivity analysis and simulation modelling to assess whether the current level of risk is satisfactory.

## Measuring interest-rate risk

Notwithstanding the widespread adoption of VaR as the key market risk measurement tool, funding books such as repo books continue to use the gap report as a key measure of interest-rate risk exposure. This enables ALCO to view the risk sensitivity along the maturity structure. Cumulative gap positions, and the ratio of assets revaluation to liabilities revaluation, are calculated and compared to earnings levels on the current asset/liability position. Generally, the 90-day, six-month and one-year gap positions are the most significant points along the term structure at which interest-rate risk exposure is calculated. The ratio of gap to earnings assets will be set at the ±15% to ±20% level.

As it is a traditional duration-based approach, gap reporting is a static measure that measures risk sensitivity at one specific point in time. It for this reason that banks combine a VaR measure as well.

Reproduced from *Bank Asset and Liability Management* (2007)

# THE BALANCE SHEET RISK TRIUMVIRATE: THE INTERACTION OF THE ALM FUNCTION WITH MARKETS, FINANCE, AND RISK[1]

Arranging the ALM function to deliver the most effective and efficient balance sheet management discipline for the bank requires a genuine detailed understanding of the interaction between Treasury, Markets, Finance, and Risk. By "understanding" we mean a view on the best way to organise the operating model so that the interaction is the most effective, and enables the successful implementation of the strategic ALM process. This requires necessarily a high level review of all the departments involved.

We have referred previously to the balance sheet risk management "triumvirate" of Treasury, Finance, and Risk. Using the traditional definition of the ALM function, as the desk that is the internal "clearer" for the bank, what is the interaction of ALM with Finance, Risk, and front-office money markets desk (which we call here "Markets")?

Before we consider this, let's first summarise ALM functions themselves and their interactions with other departments:

- Interest rate risk, liquidity risk, and exchange rate risk management (*"What do we do?"*);
- Target assets and liabilities structure (*"Where do we go?"*);
- Internal funds transfer pricing (*"How to get there?"*);
- Interest income allocation (*"What will we get?"*).

---

[1] This section was co-authored with Polina Bardaeva.

Most commonly (but not always) these roles are allocated across the triumvirate as at Figure 11.1, which we call "Model A".

Generally, the ALM function is contained within Treasury, although it is not uncommon to observe it as a separate standalone function outside of "external" Treasury and also outside of Risk and Finance. There are sound logical reasons why it should stand outside of Markets, Finance, and Risk, but at the same time placing ALM within a Treasury department that *includes* the profit-centre money markets desk, which is very common in banks, raises potential conflict of interest issues. We illustrate these in "Model B" at Figure 11.2.

Model B highlights the potential conflict of interest that has to be addressed if the ALM function is placed within the profit-centre Treasury function, which is the profit centre versus cost centre one: Treasury Markets tends to make positions under risk, whereas the ALM desk seeks to minimise them. On the other hand, a cost centre may exhibit a certain lack of efficiency and higher expenditure because a lack of profit incentive may drive it to "only" hedge risk exposure (according to ALM recommendations) without considering more efficient instruments and strategies. Paradoxically, both these issues can be addressed by placing ALM within Treasury and Markets but ensuring that the reported P&L of Treasury is concerned with only external business, and not internal clearing business.

We summarise the ALM interaction with the triumvirate in "Model C" at Figure 11.3.

In conclusion, we reiterate that the Treasury operating model, which we covered in Chapter 10, is the critical cornerstone of the bank's operating

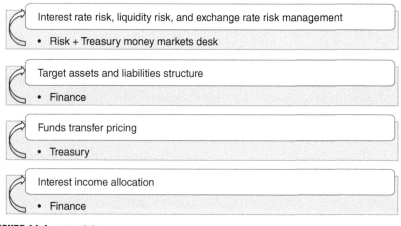

Interest rate risk, liquidity risk, and exchange rate risk management
- Risk + Treasury money markets desk

Target assets and liabilities structure
- Finance

Funds transfer pricing
- Treasury

Interest income allocation
- Finance

**FIGURE 11.1**   Model A

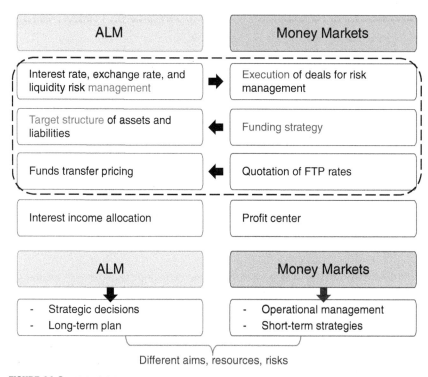

**FIGURE 11.2** Model B

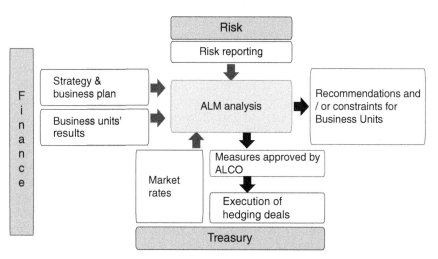

**FIGURE 11.3** Model C

infrastructure and essential to get right if we are to implement a strategic ALM process successfully. It is responsible for:

- Front office P&L generation (Money markets, Repo, Liquid Asset Buffer, Portfolio Management);
- Liquidity and Funding policy, governance, strategy, and management;
- Balance sheet management (capital / RWAs, governance, and policy);
- ALCO-related governance and MI.

In addition, Treasury is also a "Centre of Excellence" working with the bank's business lines and support functions to provide advice and implementation assistance regarding optimum deployment of capital and funding. Hence it is very important to get the operating model right. There is of course no "one size fits all" and the correct model is the one that is the best fit for the bank in question. What works in one firm may not be ideal in another, even another peer bank, so the review of the operating model must be specific to the bank in question.

This conundrum is one of those very rare ones that can be addressed using a management consultant's standard PowerPoint template.

## STRATEGIC ALM

The extracts from the author's earlier book *Bank ALM* (2007) illustrated very much the traditional approach to bank ALM. The description we presented remains nevertheless, more or less, an accurate picture of the ALM department's art as it is practised today by virtually every bank in the world.

Consider for a moment just exactly how ALM is undertaken in almost every bank, irrespective of size, business model, or location. A business line in a bank, following an understood medium-term "strategy" articulated either explicitly or implicitly (but in reality aiming usually simply to meet that year-end's budget target), goes out and originates customer business, be this originating assets or raising liabilities. It will most likely have little interaction with any other business line, and only the formal review interaction with the Risk department. In some banks it may have practically zero interaction with Treasury. In this respect it will be similar to all the other business lines.

Each of these business lines will proceed to undertake business, ostensibly as part of a grand strategy intertwined with other business lines, but in reality to a certain extent in isolation. The actions of all the customer-facing desks in the banks will then give rise to a balance sheet that must be "risk managed". And the ALM part of this risk management process is then undertaken by Treasury, in conjunction with Finance and Risk.

There is little, or no, interaction between business lines and little, or no, influence of the Treasury function or the risk triumvirate in the balance sheet origination process. In other words, ALM is a reactive, after-the-fact process. The balance sheet shape and structure is arrived at, if not by accident, certainly not by active design and certainly not as the result of a process that integrates the assets and liabilities origination process. The people charged with stewarding the balance sheet through the economic cycle and market crashes have very little to do with creating the balance sheet in the first place. But isn't this all good risk management stuff, separation of duties, four lines of defence, etc.? In a word, no. There is no problem with one department originating assets and another one managing the risk on them. That is fine. The issue with the traditional approach to ALM is that the balance sheet that is arrived at often lacks a coherent shape, or logic, and this makes the risk management of it more problematic. It hinders optimisation.

Would one wish to have a balance sheet that was composed overwhelmingly of illiquid long-dated assets funded by wholesale overnight deposits? Or a liabilities strategy that raised wholesale or corporate funding that was treated punitively by Basel III liquidity requirements? What about funding trade finance assets (overwhelmingly very short term) by 10-year MTNs?[2]

In the era of Basel III, it is evident that balance sheet risk management must become more proactive. The shape and structure of the balance sheet must be arrived at as a result of an integrated approach to origination. What does this mean? Quite simply, the discipline of ALM must recognise that asset origination and liability raising has to be a related, intertwined process. For the ALM function to be fit-for-purpose for the 21st century, banks must transition and adapt from a traditional reactive ALM process to a proactive strategic ALM process.

### Addressing the Three-Dimensional (3D) Balance Sheet Optimisation Problem

The market environment is creating a 3D optimisation challenge for banks, or at least for those banks that are serious about competing and serious about being well-respected by customers and peers alike. This challenge requires banks to run optimised balance sheets in order to maximise effectiveness and stakeholder value; however, when we speak of "balance sheet optimisation" we do not mean what it used to mean in the pre-crash era, basically doing whatever was needed to deliver higher Return on Capital (RoC). Today, optimising the balance sheet has to mean structuring the balance sheet to meet the competing needs of Regulators, Customers, and Shareholders. This is the 3D optimisation challenge that we speak of.

---

[2] These illustrations are made to emphasise a point, but they are a few of very many such incongruous examples observed by the author at different banks over the years.

A bank's risk management practice is an integral part of meeting this optimisation challenge. From the Board level downwards, policy must be geared towards achieving this goal, and strategic ALM is a vital part of the optimising process. However, before we consider this let us refresh the regulatory aspects first. We will not cover the myriad requirements of Basel III capital, liquidity, and leverage requirements here, which are discussed in depth in other publications. The essence of implementing the demands of Basel III as stipulated by regulators is that many banks' business models will have to change, to ensure compliance. Figures 11.4 and 11.5 illustrate this in stylised fashion.

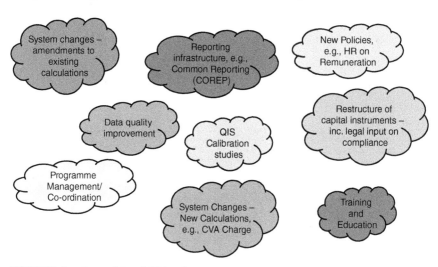

**FIGURE 11.4**   Cost of Basel III implementation
*Source*: © Chris Westcott 2017. Used with permission.

**FIGURE 11.5**   Mitigating the Impacts of Basel III
*Source*: © Chris Westcott 2017. Used with permission.

The inescapable conclusion since the bank crash of 2008 is that banks must manage their balance sheet more efficiently. This gives rise to our 3D optimisation problem. We articulate it thus:

1. **Regulator requirements:** banks must adhere to the capital, liquidity, and leverage ratio requirements of their regulator. With only a handful of exceptions, this means meeting the demands of the Basel III guidelines. The larger the bank, and/or the more complex its business model, the more complicated and onerous this requirement becomes. Related stipulations such as the Fundamental Review of the Trading Book (FRTB) add to the regulatory demands imposed on banks. Every bank must meet its supervisory requirements;

2. **Customer franchise requirements:** this is not necessarily anything new. In a competitive world, any bank would always wish to meet the demands of its customers. In a more constrained environment, this requirement becomes more urgent of course, and this gives rise to the challenge. For instance, a "full service" bank will wish to provide all the products that its customers may demand, and sometimes these products will not be the most optimum from the viewpoint of (1) above. To illustrate one case: the deposits of large corporate customers and non-bank financial customers are considered "non-sticky" under Basel III rules (what the UK PRA calls "Type A" liabilities) and so carry a greater liquidity cost for banks. From that perspective such deposits are not optimum from a regulatory efficiency view, but the bank must accept them if it wishes to satisfy this part of its customer base;

3. **Shareholder requirements:** this aspect is definitely now new. The shareholder has always demanded a satisfactory rate of return, and so all else being equal a bank will always want to maximise its net interest income (NII) and enhance or at least preserve its net interest margin (NIM) through changing economic conditions and interest rate environments. But of course the balance sheet mix that meets this objective will not necessarily be the one that is most efficient for (1) and/or (2) above. One example: from a NII perspective the bank will maximise its funding base in non-interest bearing liabilities (NIBLs) such as current accounts ("checking" accounts) or instant access deposit accounts, whereas the demands of Basel III liquidity will often call for an amount of contractual long-term funding, which is more expensive and thus inimical to NII.

We see therefore that the demands of each stakeholder are, in a number of instances, contradictory to each other. To maximise efficiency a bank will need to work towards a balance sheet shape and structure that is optimised towards each stakeholder, and it is not a linear problem. Hence, the 3D optimisation challenge arises.

This illustrates, we hope self-evidently, the need for a new approach to balance sheet origination and the role of the ALM function. We call this approach strategic ALM.

## Principles of Strategic ALM Practice

Strategic ALM is a single, integrated process that ties in asset origination with liabilities raising. It works to break down "silos" in the organisation, so that asset type is relevant and appropriate to liability type and source, and vice versa. We define it as follows:

> *A business strategy approach at the bank-wide level driven by balance sheet ALM considerations.*

Strategic ALM addresses the three-dimensional optimisation problem of meeting with maximum efficiency the needs of:

- The regulatory requirements;
- The NII requirements;
- The customer franchise requirements;

and is a high-level process overseen by ALCO. It is by nature proactive and not reactive.

Implementing a strategic ALM process will make it more likely that the bank's asset type(s) is relevant and appropriate to its funding type and source, and that its funding type and source is appropriate to its asset type. By definition then, it would also mean that a bank produces an explicit, articulated liabilities strategy that looks to optimise the funding mix and align it to asset origination. Thus, strategic ALM is a high-level, strategic discipline driven from the top down.[3]

Proactive balance sheet management (BSM) is just that, and not the "reactive" balance sheet management philosophy of traditional banking practice. Proactive BSM means the asset-side product line is managed by a

---

[3] My good friend Colin Johnson once stated to me that the way they undertook "strategic ALM" at the Birmingham & Midshires Building Society was, "by having the head of lending sat next to the head of deposit taking!". Joking apart, this is actually a very effective way of ensuring, practically at least if not necessarily in theory, a genuine strategic ALM approach to balance sheet management. Of course once these two particular individuals or teams are situated in different cities or countries, let alone buildings, then this fairly straightforward method will break down and a more formal approach to Strategic ALM implementation becomes necessary.

business head who is closely aligned (in strategic terms) with the liabilities-side product line head. To be effective the process needs to look in granular detail at the product types and how they are funded or deployed; only then can the bank start to think in terms of optimising the balance sheet.

Implementing strategic ALM practice is not a trivial exercise, and can only be undertaken from the top, with Board approved instruction (or at least approval) and control by ALCO. Elsewhere in this book we consider the bank strategy setting cycle, which is also important to the success of the strategic ALM approach. Here we consider another essential prerequisite, which is the Board articulated risk appetite statement.

## IMPLEMENTING STRATEGIC ALM

The approach to implementing an effective strategic ALM practice has several strands. We describe each in turn.

### Recommended Risk Appetite Statement

The Risk Appetite Statement is an articulated, explicit statement of Board appetite for and tolerance of balance sheet risk, incorporating qualitative and quantitative metrics and limits. It becomes the most important document for Board approval. This may appear to be a contentious statement but it is self-evident when one remembers that *the balance sheet is everything*. The over-riding objective of every bank executive is to ensure the long-term sustainability and viability of the bank, and unless the balance sheet shape and structure enable this viability, achieving this objective is at risk.

Figure 11.6 shows a template summary risk appetite statement drafted by the author and recommended for application at any commercial bank. This statement would be presented for Board approval. It may be applied to most banking entities irrespective of their business model, although large multinational banking institutions will need to develop the list of risk metrics much further. It provides a formal guide on the desired Board risk appetite framework, including a description of each of the risk appetite pillars, and the key measures that will be used to confirm on a monthly basis that the bank is within risk appetite.

As we see from Figure 11.6, for each of the measures identified, an overall bank-wide "macro-tolerance" is set, which is then broken down into tolerances for individual business lines (for example, Retail, Corporate). The range of quantitative limits is user-defined. For example, in the section on liquidity limits:

## Strategic Objective

ABC Bank aims to become the Commercial Bank that is respected and trusted by all its stakeholders providing "concierge banking services for ultimate customer service quality", through: committed people; recognising that our long-term sustainability is dependent on having sufficient capital and liquidity to meet liabilities as they fall due through the cycle; the protection of our reputation; and the integrity of our relationship with our customers and wider stakeholders.

## Target Credit Rating

Credit rating in line with ABC's closest peers and UK bank average (A/A-)

## Risk appetite pillars

| Capital Adequacy | Stable Earnings Growth | Liquidity & Funding | Stakeholder Confidence |
|---|---|---|---|
| Maintain sufficient capital, quantity, and quality, substantially over Regulatory minimums, to cover existing and projected risks in extreme but plausible scenarios | Be an agile, sustainable UK Retail and Corporate commercial bank that maintains its capital adequacy in terms of amount and quality, and hence is able to withstand appropriate capital related stress. | Be an agile, sustainable UK Retail and Corporate bank that has stable and efficient access to funding and liquidity, and hence is able to withstand appropriate liquidity related stress, with relevant liquid asset holdings. | Be an agile, sustainable UKK Retail and Corporate commercial bank that is respected and trusted by all its stakeholders and hence maintains stakeholder confidence at all times. |
| 1. CT1 ratio<br>2. Leverage ratio<br>3. Available capital<br>4. Capital buffer minimum over regulatory requirement (ICG) | 1. Earnings volatility<br>2. Return on Capital<br>3. Return on RWA<br>4. Cost to income ratio | 1. Loan to deposit ratio<br>2. HQLA buffer minimum<br>3. Concentration risk<br>4. NSFR minimum<br>5. Wholesale funding limits<br>6. Internal funds pricing regime | 1. Employees<br>2. Regulators<br>3. Investors<br>4. Customers<br>5. Ratings agencies |

**FIGURE 11.6** Recommended Board risk appetite statement template

- A vanilla institution with no cross-border business may content itself with setting limits for the primary liquidity metrics such as loan-deposit ratio and liquidity ratios, as well the regulatory metrics such as LCR and NSFR;
- A bank transacting across currencies will wish to also incorporate FX funding exposure tolerance;
- A bank employing a significant amount of secured funding will wish to add asset encumbrance limits.

The Board risk appetite statement is the single most important policy document in any bank and should be treated accordingly. It requires regular review and approval, at least on an annual basis, or whenever changes have been made to the business model and/or customer franchise. It also should be updated in anticipation or in the event of market stress.

Armed with the Board risk appetite statement, which must be a genuine "working" document and not just a list of platitudes, with specific quantitative limits, the implementation of a strategic ALM process becomes feasible. As well as the Board risk statement, the other ingredient that is required to make strategic ALM a reality is an asset–liability committee (ALCO) with real teeth. One cannot emphasise enough the paramount importance of a bank's ALCO in making this process a reality.

### Elements of Strategic ALM: Paramountcy of ALCO

Consider the executive committees, below Board level, that are responsible for the strategic direction as well as the ongoing viability and sustainability of the bank. Which of them has responsibility for oversight of balance sheet risk? Perhaps it is one or more of the following:

- Executive committee (or "management committee"): this is the primary committee responsible for running the bank, chaired by the CEO;
- Risk management committee: chaired by the CRO, responsible for overall management of all the risk exposures the bank may face, from market and credit risk to technology risk, conduct risk, regulatory risk, employee fraud risk, etc.;
- Credit risk committee: chaired by the head of credit or the credit risk officer, this committee is responsible for managing credit policy including credit risk appetite, limit setting, and credit approvals. As credit risk is the single biggest driver of regulatory capital requirement in banks (in some vanilla institutions representing 75–80% of total requirement) it can be seen that the credit risk committee is also a balance sheet risk committee;

- ALCO: the asset–liability committee, which is described elsewhere in this Anthology. A template Terms of Reference for a commercial bank ALCO was given at Appendix 10.A.

While all of these committees have an element of responsibility for the bank's balance sheet, it is the ALCO that is responsible solely for this and nothing else. It alone has the bandwith to discharge this responsibility effectively and to help ensure that the balance sheet shape and structure are long-term viable. The other committees either also look at other issues unconnected with the balance sheet or only at one part of the balance sheet risk exposure. Thus the executive committee that is most closely concerned with balance sheet risk on a strategic and integrated basis (both sides of the balance sheet and all aspects of risk) is ALCO. Given this, what is the most effective way to ensure above-satisfactory and effective governance from Board perspective? We suggest that it is to ensure the paramountcy of ALCO, as illustrated in the organisation chart given at Figure 11.7.

The key highlight of the structure shown at Figure 11.7 is that ALCO ranks *pari passu* with the ExCo and that it also has an oversight role over the Credit Committee. The former ensures that balance sheet strength and robustness is always given equal priority with shareholder return, and the latter ensures that ALCO really does exercise control over all the *assets and liabilities* on the balance sheet, as suggested by its name. For instance, it would be ALCO, and not ExCo or the Risk Committee, that would design, drive, and monitor the bank's early warning indicator (EWI) metrics, as it would be the committee with the required expertise and understanding of the balance sheet. (An example of an EWI template was given at Appendix 10.B.)

With this structure in place, strategic ALM discipline becomes a reality.

### Elements of Strategic ALM: Integrated Balance Sheet Origination

At its heart, the objective of the strategic ALM process is to remove the "silo mentality" in place at banks in order to ensure a more strategically coherent origination process. This will help the bank to arrive at a balance sheet shape and structure more by design than by well-intentioned accident.

In the first instance, a bank's liquidity and funding policy should not be concerned solely with its liabilities. The type of assets being funded is as important a consideration as the type of liabilities in place to fund those assets. For a bank's funding structure to be assessed on an aggregate balance sheet approach, it must measure the quality and adequacy of the funding structure (liabilities) alongside the asset side of the balance sheet. This gives a more holistic picture of the robustness and resilience of the funding model, in normal conditions and under stress. The robustness of funding is as much

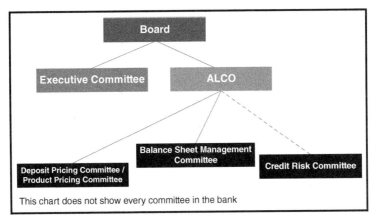

**FIGURE 11.7**    Recommended bank executive committee organisation structure

a function of the liquidity, maturity, and product type of the asset base as it is of the type and composition of the liabilities.

Typical considerations would include:

- Share of liquid assets versus illiquid;
- How much illiquid assets are funded by unstable and/or short-term liabilities;
- Breakdown of liabilities:
  - Retail deposits: stable and less stable;
  - Wholesale funding: secured, senior unsecured;
  - Capital: subordinated / hybrid; equity.

As part of an active liabilities strategy, on the liability side ALCO should consider:

- Debt buy-backs, especially of expensive instruments issued under more stressful conditions at higher coupon;
- Developing a wide investor base;
- A private placement programme;
- Fit-for-purpose allocation of liquidity costs to business lines (FTP);
- Design and use of adequate stress testing policy and scenarios;
- Adequate risk management of intra-day liquidity risk;
- Strong public disclosure to promote market discipline.

On the asset side, strategic action could include:

- Increasing liquid assets as share of the balance sheet (although liquidity and ROE concerns must be balanced);
- De-linking the bank – sovereign risk exposure connection;
  - The HQLA doesn't have to be all sovereign debt.

- Avoiding lower loan origination standards as the cycle moves into bull market phase;
- Addressing asset quality problems:
  - Ring-fence NPLs and impaired loans? (A sort of "non-core" part of the balance sheet that indicates you are addressing the problem and looking at disposal).
- Review the bank's operating model. Retail-wholesale mix? Franchise viability? Comparative advantage?;
- Limit asset encumbrance: this contradicts the pressure for more secured funding.

In essence, as far as possible a bank's balance sheet should aim to maximise those assets and liabilities that hit the "sweet spot" shown in the Venn diagram at Figure 11.8, where the requirements of all three stakeholders are served. What this shows is that different types of balance sheet products meet the requirements of the three key stakeholders differently, and optimising the balance sheet addresses this. Of course, a "full service" commercial bank will still need to offer loan and deposit products that meet customer needs but may be less optimum from a regulator or shareholder requirement perspective. The process of strategic ALM seeks to maximise origination of assets and liabilities that cover off all three stakeholder needs, and minimise the origination of product types that meet the needs of one or two stakeholders (Figure 11.8).

We emphasise especially strongly one of the bullet points above, namely:

*Strong public disclosure to promote market discipline.*

A bank that shouts loudly about the structure and strength of its balance sheet is assisting the industry as a whole, as regulators point to it (informally, it is unlikely that a bank supervisor would make this point formally) as a benchmark and as its peers look to it when comparisons are made by analysts.

Table 11.1 is a summary of a high-level asset–liability policy guide, to be followed as part of a strategic ALM process.

### Elements of Strategic ALM: Peer-Review and Benchmarking

To be more, rather than less, certain that one is following best-practice demands a benchmarking process with the market and with one's peers. Any bank that has a genuine desire to be respected by peers and customers alike will wish to engage in peer review. Managing a bank in blissful ignorance, often with a belief that one knows best, is a recipe, ultimately, for disaster. However one wishes to undertake it – market statistics, attending trade events, presenting at conferences, interacting and networking, and so on – it is a vital part of the proactive balance sheet management and strategic ALM process. It can be a formal process (see Figures 11.9 to 11.12) and/or an informal one but either way it must be done.

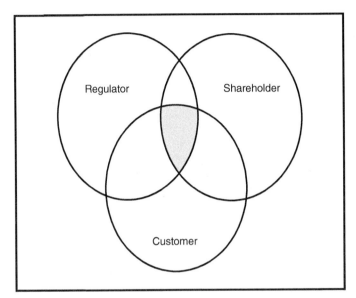

**FIGURE 11.8** Balance sheet mix optimisation

**TABLE 11.1** Summary of asset–liability policy guide

| Assets | Liabilities |
|---|---|
| Strong asset quality, based on resilience of (i) borrowers and (ii) collateral value | Diversity of funding by (i) investors (ii) instruments (iii) geography (iv) currency where appropriate |
| Adequate share of genuinely liquid assets (liquid in times of stress) | Stability of retail and wholesale investor base, based on (i) their investment constraints and preference (ii) their resilience (iii) their behaviour |
| Reduced / limited leverage | Maintaining mismatches by (i) maturity and (ii) currency between assets and liabilities to what is manageable through the cycle. Know the risk |
| Minimum asset encumbrance | High level of capital and deposits |
| "Simple" assets and appropriate disclosure / documentation | Minimise use of complex funding instruments |

| | Loan : deposit ratio | Wholesale funding % of Total Funding | STWF % of Wholesale Funding | STWF Primary Liq Coverage | RWAs % of Funded Assets | Tier 1 % | Basel III Fully Loaded CET % | T1 Leverage % | Overall "Score" |
|---|---|---|---|---|---|---|---|---|---|
| Bank of America Merrill Lynch | 80% | 22% | 28% | 433% | 56% | 12.9% | 9.3% | 7.5% | 20 |
| Citigroup | 68% | 24% | 32% | 374% | 54% | 14.1% | 8.7% | 7.9% | 20 |
| Bank of Montreal | 84% | 21% | 41% | 261% | 43% | 12.6% | 8.7% | 5.5% | 20 |
| HSBC | 74% | 23% | 47% | 242% | 48% | 13.4% | 9.0% | 6.6% | 19 |
| Standard Chartered | 75% | 23% | 64% | 168% | 51% | 13.4% | n.d. | 7.0% | 19 |
| JP Morgan | 60% | 23% | 34% | 166% | 56% | 12.6% | n.d. | 7.2% | 19 |
| Wells Fargo | 78% | 18% | 21% | 352% | 77% | 11.8% | 8.2% | 9.2% | 19 |
| Santander UK | 130% | 33% | 20% | 253% | 29% | 14.6% | 11.1% | 4.3% | 18 |
| UBS | 75% | 32% | 43% | 132% | 23% | 21.3% | 9.8% | 5.0% | 18 |
| Bank of Nova Scotia (Scotiabank) | 87% | 6% | 100% | 319% | 40% | 13.6% | 8.6% | 5.5% | 18 |
| RBS Group | 100% | 29% | 39% | 220% | 53% | 12.4% | 7.7% | 6.7% | 17 |
| Deutsche Bank | 73% | 28% | 53% | 188% | 27% | 15.1% | 8.0% | 4.1% | 17 |
| Credit Suisse | 79% | 39% | 40% | 161% | 25% | 19.4% | 8.3% | 5.0% | 17 |
| Royal Bank of Canada | 76% | 37% | 0% | | 38% | 13.1% | 8.4% | 5.1% | 16 |
| Lloyds Banking Group | 121% | 29% | 30% | 173% | 36% | 13.8% | 8.1% | 5.0% | 16 |
| Barclays | 110% | 38% | 43% | 129% | 38% | 13.3% | 8.2% | 5.1% | 16 |
| Toronto Dominion Bank | 85% | 18% | 71% | 117% | 33% | 12.6% | 8.2% | 4.2% | 14 |
| BNP Paribas | 118% | 38% | 64% | 104% | 37% | 13.6% | 9.9% | 5.1% | 13 |
| Grupo Santander | 120% | 37% | 38% | 97% | 48% | 11.2% | n.d. | 5.6% | 13 |
| Societe Generale | 117% | 46% | 65% | 78% | 32% | 12.5% | n.d. | 4.0% | 13 |
| Average | 91% | 28% | 44% | 209% | 42% | 13.9% | 8.8% | 5.8% | 19 |

Key

| | | | | | | | | |
|---|---|---|---|---|---|---|---|---|
| High risk | >115% | >35% | >45% | <100% | >55% | <12% | <8% | <5% |
| Medium | 85–115% | 25–35% | 30–45% | 100–200% | 45–55% | 12–15% | 8–10% | 5–6% |
| Low risk | <85% | <25% | <30% | >200% | <45% | >15% | >10% | >6% |

**FIGURE 11.9**  Example of peer-review benchmarking: funding and capital
Data Source: BoE 2013; Annual Reports.

| | RBS Group Dec-12 | Barclays Dec-12 | Lloyds Banking Dec-12 | Santander UK Dec-12 | Peer Average | Var to Average |
|---|---|---|---|---|---|---|
| *Funding and Liquidity* | | | | | | |
| Loan: deposit ratio | 100% | 110% | 121% | 130% | 120% | (21%) |
| Customer Funding (Gap) / Surplus £bn | 2 | (40) | (90) | (44) | (58) | 60 |
| Wholesale funding % of Total Funding | 29% | 38% | 29% | 33% | 33% | (4%) |
| ST Wholesale % of Wholesale Funding | 39% | 43% | 30% | 20% | 31% | 8% |
| ST Wholesale Liquidity Coverage (times) | 3.5 | 1.5 | 4.0 | 4.1 | 3.2 | 0.3 |
| LCR (published est.) | 100% | 126% | n.d. | n.d. | 126% | (26%) |
| NSFR (published est.) | 117% | 104% | n.d. | n.d. | 104% | 13% |
| Primary Liquidity % of Funded Assets | 11% | 13% | 10% | 14% | 12% | (2%) |
| Liquidity Portfolio Cash £bn | 70 | 85 | 77 | 28 | 63 | 11% |
| Total Primary Liquidity £bn | 92 | 131 | 88 | 37 | 85 | 7% |
| Total Liquidity Portfolio £bn | 147 | 150 | 205 | 60 | 138 | 6% |
| *Capital and Leverage* | | | | | | |
| CT1% | 10.3% | 10.9% | 12.0% | 12.2% | 11.7% | (1.38%) |
| Tier 1% | 12.4% | 13.3% | 13.8% | 14.6% | 13.9% | (1.49%) |
| Basel III Fully-loaded CET1% | 7.7% | 8.2% | 8.1% | 11.1% | 9.1% | (1.4%) |
| T1 Leverage % | 6.7% | 5.1% | 5.0% | 4.3% | 4.8% | 1.89% |
| *Balance Sheet and RWAs (£bn)* | | | | | | |
| Total Assets | 1,312 | 1,490 | 925 | 293 | 903 | 45% |
| Funded Assets | 870 | 1,021 | 868 | 262 | 717 | 21% |
| RWAs | 460 | 387 | 310 | 77 | 258 | 78% |

**FIGURE 11.10** Example of peer-review benchmarking: funding, capital, and profitability Data Source: BoE 2013; Annual Reports.

| *Profitability (%)* | | | | | | |
|---|---|---|---|---|---|---|
| Net Interest Margin | 1.93% | 1.85% | 1.93% | 1.24% | 1.67% | 0.26% |
| Return on Equity | 9.8% | 7.8% | (3.1%) | 7.3% | 4.0% | 5.8% |
| Cost: Income Ratio | 59% | 64% | (53%) | 53% | 21% | 38% |
| *Business Mix (%)* | | | | | | |
| Geographic - Domestic % | 66% | 41% | 94% | 100% | 78% | (12%) |
| Segmental - R&C, Wealth and AM % | 69% | 60% | 81% | 96% | 79% | (10%) |

**FIGURE 11.10**   (*Continued*)

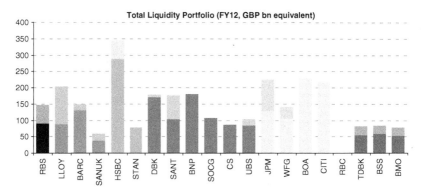

**FIGURE 11.11**   Example of peer-review benchmarking: liquid asset buffer
Data Source: BoE 2013.

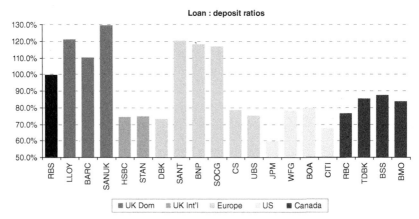

**FIGURE 11.12**   Example of peer-review benchmarking: loan-deposit ratio
Data Source: BoE 2013; Annual Reports.

## Elements of Strategic ALM: Analysing and Understanding Net Interest Margin (NIM)[4]

A more intelligent approach to net interest margin (NIM) management is part of the strategic ALM process, and we address this issue in this section. Before covering this, we provide a primer on the related topic of interest rate benchmarks and net interest income.

**Interest Rate Benchmarks**   A transparent and readily accessible interest rate benchmark is a key ingredient in maintaining market efficiency. Countries that do not benefit from such a benchmark are markedly less liquid as a result. Possibly the most well-known interest rate benchmark is the London Interbank Offered Rate or LIBOR. It is calculated and published daily by ICE, and was described and illustrated in Chapter 1.

**Net Interest Income (NII)**   Net Interest Income or NII is defined as the interest income received from lending activities or debt instruments held (for example, subordinated debt, senior debt, or Certificates of Deposit issued by other financial institutions) minus the interest expense incurred on deposits or issued debt instruments. It is expressed as a currency amount over a period of time, normally 3, 6, or 12 months, in line with reporting frequencies. Thus more formally:

Net interest income is the total interest income earned on a bank's loans, investment securities, and money market deposits, minus the cost of (interest expense related to) the funds used to make loans and investments.

Examples of banking products which would typically contribute to NII include: loans, mortgages, overdrafts, credit cards, asset finance, instant access deposits, savings accounts, and fixed or variable rate bonds. Income earned from activities such as asset management, broking, insurance, corporate finance, investment management, and trusts and estate planning are classified under Fees and Commissions Receivable / Payable. Dividends received on equity positions held are classified as Other Income. Figure 11.13 illustrates the major components of bank P&L. NII is a key element and often makes up the largest constituent part.

**Net Interest Margin (NIM)**   NIM is a key bank profitability metric, given by NII divided by assets (UK and US banks use "average interest earning assets"; Eurozone banks usually use average total assets). Average Interest-Earning Assets is an average of all of a bank's assets that generate

---

[4] This section was co-authored with Christopher Westcott.

|  | £m |
|---|---|
| Interest Income | x |
| Interest Expense | x |
| **Net Interest Income** | x |
| Fees and Commissions Receivable/Payable | x |
| Other Non-Interest Income | x |
| **Total Income** | x |
| Operating Expenses | x |
| Impairment Losses | x |
| **Operating Profit** | x |
| Tax Charge | x |
| **Post Tax P&L Attributable to Shareholders** | x |

**FIGURE 11.13**   Components of Bank P&L

interest income during a specific time period. This excludes certain assets that are not interest-bearing, like cash holdings and fixed assets, but includes non-performing assets.

Hence NIM is expressed thus:

$$NIM = \frac{Net \text{ interest income } (NII)}{\text{Average interest} - \text{earning assests}} \qquad (11.1)$$

The margin is calculated for a specific period, say quarter or year, and expressed as a percentage.

Average interest-earning assets is an average of all of a bank's assets that generate interest income during a specific time period. This excludes certain assets that are not interest-bearing.

NIM is often confused with the net interest-rate spread, although some banks refer to the spread or net interest income as the margin. The difference between the average interest rate on all of a bank's interest-earning assets and the interest rate on all of its sources of funds is usually called the net interest-rate spread. The spread doesn't take into account the size of the interest-earning asset base. NIM, which does take into account the size of the interest-earning asset base, will change when the interest-earning asset base expands or contracts. It is the bank's return on its assets that generate interest income.

NIM is normally expressed as an annual percentage rate. In 2014, the NIMs for major UK banks ranged between 1.8 and 3.6% (source: BoE).

Is there a NIM Gold Standard, a level to which all banks should aspire? The answer is, "No". Comparisons between banks are not really valid as NIMs will differ due to factors such as:

- The amount of equity capital held: a high level will tend to boost the NIM as this form of capital is non-interest bearing, so will tend to reduce a bank's interest expense;
- The amount of credit and or interest rate risk: a bank which engages in risky lending may generate more interest income relative to competitors, but may also carry more non-performing assets, which would act as a drag on the NIM;
- The proportion of non-interest bearing liabilities (for example, current accounts): these may be good for NIM as they do not carry any interest expense, but there are other issues to consider (cost of attracting / maintaining these accounts via branches, handling complaints, etc.);
- The relative sizes of Small and Medium-sized Enterprise and Retail business versus Corporate and Wholesale business: the former would tend to be associated with a higher NIM;
- The amount of residential mortgage lending: often associated with a lower NIM as this type of business is low risk.

Whilst there is not a NIM level that all banks should aim for, it is important for this measure of profitability to be relatively constant over time. Stable sources of income are more highly valued than volatile income streams by the investment community and can be built into valuation models for future years, whilst items like abnormal trading profits cannot be assumed to recur.

According to *Forbes Magazine* in November 2014: "The importance of NIM figures for banks is demonstrated by the fact that the share price of every single US bank jumped last month after the Federal Reserve hinted at a hike in benchmark interest rates in early 2015."

The objective for all banks, therefore, becomes to preserve and maximise whatever NIM they have. Careful management of interest rate risk in the banking book can help to achieve this objective, together with an integrated approach to balance sheet origination. However, the most important challenge facing a bank is to achieve a level of understanding of the sensitivities of its NIM value in relation to products, markets, and customers. We consider this next.

**Managing and Planning of the NIM[5]**  A close understanding of NIM and its sensitivity to various factors is a required part of the strategic ALM process. It was always a metric that banks should monitor and attempt to plan for, but

---

[5] This section was co-authored with Cormac O'Connor.

in the low-interest rate post-2008 era it is imperative that a bank's ALCO be able to get to grips with it. As such, banks' approach to NII and NIM forecasting and stressing requires closer scrutiny given current and anticipated operating challenges.

Some of the main issues concerning NIM analysis include the following:

- Business lines often cannot be compared for similar underlying economic pressures;
- The extent of vulnerability of NII to future shocks or underlying business pressures is not understood;
- At the bank-wide level it if often difficult to obtain a total return view of the banking book on the balance sheet. For instance, the bank may struggle to evaluate the all-in costs of different types of funding (and which is central to developing a Liability Strategy);
- Inability to compare the gross yield on current and new business with the current and marginal costs of liabilities that fund it. This makes accurate evaluation of potential trade-offs between capital, loan-deposit ratio (LDR), and NIM difficult.

Treasury and Finance often have different non-aligned and non-integrated interests in looking at NIM. Typically, Treasury's focus is on management of NII volatility within risk limits, with underdeveloped capability in looking at basic lending and deposit NIM and yields in the divisions. Often Finance NII and NIM focus is on month-to-month and quarter-to-quarter trends. The common case of the lack of a bank-wide information technology platform means that systems in use are not necessarily fit-for-purpose. For example, the IRRBB system may have forward-looking NII stress capabilities but lack significant other functionality capabilities (if it does not capture or hold actual real-time data). Often such systems do not take any form that would allow it to be incorporated into normal Finance forecasting. In essence, the key problem is that, as part of bank governance and overall strategy, NIM is rarely treated as the complex inter-disciplinary inter-departmental challenge that it is. Banks are prone to poor NIM management information (MI) and analytics because Finance and Treasury departments approach NIM from different angles.

**Finance Versus Treasury Focus** A major issue hindering effective NIM management is that Finance and Treasury generally do not view the bank's balance sheet on necessarily comparable terms. Finance reporting usually involves business lines submitting high level product views of the balance sheet, but there may be no standard product view across divisions that have similar business lines (as the lending example in Table 11.2 shows).

**TABLE 11.2**  Lending Products across Divisions

|  | Retail | Corporate | Wholesale |
|---|---|---|---|
| Mortgages | Y | Y | |
| Loans | Y | | |
| Cards | Y | | |
| Overdrafts | Y | Y | |
| Other – centre | | | Y |
| Investments | | | Y |

Within business lines, there may be different product views (although each has a balance sheet asset and liability impact) and hence they may be split sub-optimally.

Treasury may often use a different product view, more targeted at IRRBB (Table 11.3).

This difference in approach creates the main issue: that there is no overall map that unifies all product views in one place, hence no framework for relating the products on which Group Treasury reach certain conclusions on NII sensitivity, in terms that are comprehensible to Finance and the Business Lines. There are other views of the balance sheet that are also relevant to NIM assessment, including those of collateralised assets, securitisations, and the NPL book.

**TABLE 11.3**  Third Party Assets and Liabilities

| Third Party Assets | Third Party Liabilities |
|---|---|
| Overdrafts GBP | Current Account NIBB |
| Overdrafts Currency | Current Account IB |
| Loans Floating | Currency NIBB |
| Loans Fixed | Currency IB |
| Loans LIBOR | SIBA |
| Loans NPL | Reserve Accounts |
| Lease HP / Finance | Fixed Rate Deposits |
| Lease Operating | Client Monies |
| Invoice Finance | Money Market Deposits |
| Group Overdrafts GBP | Other Deposits |
| Group Overdrafts Currency | Notice Accounts ILAAP |
| Inactive Products Base | Notice Accounts Non-ILAAP |
| Inactive Products LIBOR | Group Current Accounts NIBL |
| | Group Current Accounts IBL |
| | Inactive Products Base |
| | Inactive Products LIBOR |

## THE "FINANCE VERSUS TREASURY" FOCUS

Finance department often focuses on headline NIM per business line, and its historical and forecast performance is based on observed trends and known contractual (as opposed to behavioural) balance sheet products run-on and run-off. Finance forecasts carry a high degree of assumption that gains or losses outside of plan *will happen*. However, the finance focus often may not highlight changes in maturity or re-pricing, or rate sensitivity of the balance sheet. Consideration of business-line level NIM is focused on its improvement but without consideration of other possible costs elsewhere in the Group. Those costs can include central funding and liquidity management, and capital costs from excess risk exposure (measured using value-at-risk or VaR).

Within Treasury the focus starts with risk limits and liquidity and capital buffers held at legal entity level. Capital buffers are affected by VaR behaviours and so, once known the VaR limits are set. Treasury looks at mismatch and re-pricing. Re-pricing is measured through VaR (and PV01) which is effectively the present value (PV) of mismatched cash flows. This may be presented pictorially. Since VaR measures mismatch, it can impact real NII. However, VaR is a probability-based measure which says losses or gains might happen, but this is not a forecast that these *will* happen. This analysis is not always factored into Finance-led forecasting (because of modelling approach difference, and lack of visibility of VaR to non-legal entity business lines. In fact, business lines may not necessarily have VaR limits).

Treasury's other concerns are on the NII / NIM performance of centrally managed assets and liabilities.

**Articulating a NIM Framework** Banks often lack a framework for examining the drivers of NII and NIM that is meaningful for business lines, Finance, and Treasury together. For example, the Finance department may not view business line, or Group NIM, or capture the components of its performance on a comprehensive tree of variances or value drivers, whereas doing just that would allow for comparison of similar drivers across all business lines in the Group.

A temporary solution to this would be for a business line to build its own value-driver models for forecasting. These could be split into separate lending and deposits models and also customised for individual businesses. The use of these models for forecasting by the relevant businesses may not be optimal though, from a Group perspective. The recommended solution would be to implement an NII value-driver model that could be used to integrate Finance and Treasury modelling perspectives. Ultimately, the end-goal is for a bank to understand what its NIM sensitivity is – to what extent NIM is expected to change given changes in balance sheet, product type, product mix, customer type, indeed any relevant variable or parameter.

However, building a defined and desired NIM analytics framework is not a trivial task. Post-2008 and in an era of consistently low interest rates and extreme competitive pricing pressure, it is common for a bank to have underway several relatively unconnected initiatives to attempt to resolve specific NIM problems (as they are perceived). This is not optimum. The need instead is for a fresh top-down look at building a joined-up NIM capability that is more fit for purpose to meet onerous business and regulatory requirements, in an environment where performance demands weigh heavily on increasingly scarce balance sheet resources. Those demands include new metrics that are also performance constraints (including NSFR and LCR requirements), increased focus on pricing and the cost of funding, and the continuing need to build capital levels in the face of subdued economies and shareholder interest.

Ideally there would be a central reference source for all NIM-related information whether originated from Treasury or Finance, driven by improved data flows and an improved chart of accounts and product hierarchy. Such an infrastructure is necessary because the NIM space is packed with large quantities of fast changing data, assumptions, metrics, and rules. To try to get a handle on things using different approaches will not produce desired results. A bank requires an ability to dynamically interact and model the components and drivers of NIM, to assist with strategic planning and decision-making.

**The NIM Platform**    A meaningful NIM analytical capability requires that the balance sheet can be aggregated and viewed according to its differing economic risks. We assume for the purposes of this "End State" that products have been suitably mapped; also that a multi-view hierarchy exists to report these. Thus we need a deep product hierarchy in place that in addition to our normal view of products, allows us to switch between different views of the balance sheet. We illustrate this at Figure 11.14. The NIM system should incorporate a facility to view all products, structured along the lines shown at Figure 11.15.

This centralised view of NIM needs certain minimal data feeds, such as:

- A dynamic map of all products;
- Value-driver calculations and results (actual / forecast);
- Funds transfer pricing (FTP) and Treasury Allocations data, and drivers;
- Results of interest-rate risk analysis;
- Economic assumptions and scenario rates.

**1. By CCY**

| Loans | | Deposits | |
|---|---|---|---|
| GBP | | GBP | |
| EUR | | EUR | |
| USD | | USD | |
| Other | | Other | |

**2. By Type**

| Loans | | Deposits | |
|---|---|---|---|
| Investments | | Deposits | |
| Loans-Good Book | | Bonds | |
| Loans-Bad Book | | Other Liabilities | |
| Non-Performing Loans | | | |
| BS Provisions | | | |
| Other Assets | | | |

**3. By Rate**

| Loans | | Deposits | |
|---|---|---|---|
| LIBOR | | LIBOR | |
| Fixed Rate | | Fixed Rate | |
| Base Rate | | Base Rate | |
| Non-interest earning | | T-Bid | |
| | | Non-interest bearing | |

**4. By Liquidity (Cont + Behave)**

| Loans | | Deposits | |
|---|---|---|---|
| Loans <= 3 months | | Deposits as for loans | |
| Loans <= 6 months | | | |
| Loans <= 12 months | | | |
| Loans >12 months | | | |
| Loans >3 years | | | |

**FIGURE 11.14**   NIM System View Selections

| Product | GBP/CCY | Interest Rate Behaviour | | | | | Liquidity Behaviour | | Asset Distribution | |
|---|---|---|---|---|---|---|---|---|---|---|
| | | Control | Fixed / Var | Cust Rate | Internal Rate | Hedging | Tenor | Type A / B | Encumbered | Security? |
| Lending 001 | GBP | | Variable | LIBOR+ | NSFR | STMF VaR | | | | |
| Lending 002 | GBP | | Variable | Base Rate | NSFR | STMF VaR | | | | Y |
| Lending 003 | GBP | | Variable | | SIRE | | | | | N |
| Deposit 001 | GBP/CCY | Managed | Variable | LIBOR+ | NSFR | STMF VaR | <= 1yr | A | | N |
| Deposit 002 | | Managed | Fixed | Base Rate | NSFR | Fixed rate | <= 1 mth | B | | |
| Deposit 003 | | Panel | | T-Bid | | | | | | |

**FIGURE 11.15**   NIM System Product Lines

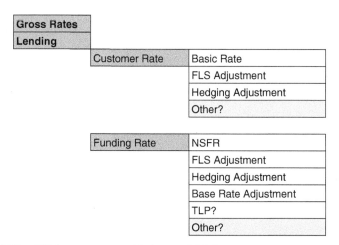

**FIGURE 11.16**   NIM system general ledger and P&L structure

To enable improved backward- and forward-looking NIM analysis, the General Ledger P&L structure would ideally seek to capture the components of internal FTP rates and customer rates. We show a suggested format at Figure 11.16.

Product margins are often affected by the introduction or withdrawal of funding "ingredients"; for example, base rate programme adjustments, hedging overlays, and so on. The Chart of Accounts (CoA) should capture for actuals and forecasts this level of detail per product, to allow Finance or Treasury (or ALCO) to de-construct the reasons for movements in the NIM. It would also be helpful if the CoA had some expansion capability built into it to accommodate introduction of new funding / FTP ingredients / product types / customer types, and so on, as the bank's strategy and supervisory regulation develops. This level of data should also be available to scrutinise within the NIM analytics system.

In order to support dynamic NIM analysis, the NIM system requires the following additional functionality:

- A table to document business line expected linkage of business drivers to economic assumption changes (format shown at Figure 11.17). This would be a reference capable of being called up to show our view on how certain economic "key performance indicator" (KPI) movements affect the bank's business drivers. It would also be a useful document of record within the NIM system;
- Clear user interface, structured to enable a logical walk-through of the data.

| Assumption | vs previous | Deposit | | | Lending | | |
| | | Outflow | Switching | Inflow | New | Re-finance | Pay down |
|---|---|---|---|---|---|---|---|
| LIBOR | up | | | | | | |
| | down | | | | | | |
| Base Rate | up | | | | | | |
| | down | | | | | | |
| M4 | up | | | | | | |
| | down | | | | | | |
| GDP | up | | | | | | |
| | down | | | | | | |
| PNFC Cash | up | | | | | | |
| | down | | | | | | |

**FIGURE 11.17**  Business line linkage to economic KPIs

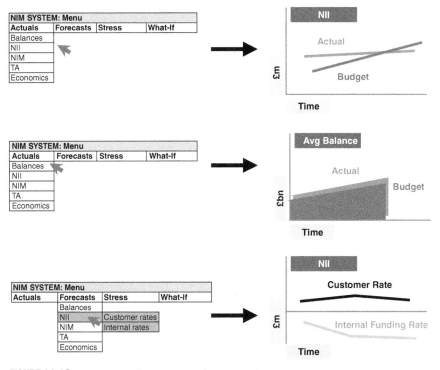

**FIGURE 11.18**  Example illustrations of NIM analysis

A fit-for-purpose NIM-System would allow for NIM to be de-constructed in a phased, orderly manner, with an example illustrated at Figure 11.18. Equally, the balance sheet and P&L should be able to be viewed from different perspectives, as shown at Figure 11.19. Either Finance or Treasury (or Risk) should be able to drill into and preview only those aspects of gross interest flows (or any other trends) that they are interested in. This is shown

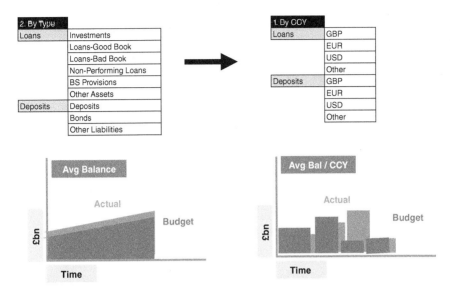

**FIGURE 11.19**   Example illustrations of Balance Sheet and P&L analysis

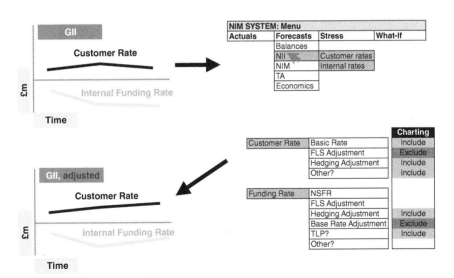

**FIGURE 11.20**   Gross interest income expected after user-specified adjustment to customer and/or funding rates

| NIM SYSTEM: Menu | | | |
|---|---|---|---|
| Actuals | Forecasts | Stress | What-If |

| Chose scenario | Reconciliation |
|---|---|
| | BAU |
| 2012 4+8 Eurozone Meltdown | Scenarios |

| 2012 4+8 Emerging Markets Crisis |
|---|
| Chose stress condition |
| 100 basis points parallel yield curve |
| Non-parallel yield curve |

**FIGURE 11.21**   Example of drill-down NIM stress testing capability

at Figure 11.20, an example of the change in expected gross interest income (GII) after adjustment to the customer and funding rates.

**NIM Stress Testing**   Stress testing should be carried out in an integrated fashion with the NIM system. The results of all stressing activity (together with the underlying economic assumptions guiding this) would be loaded to the NIM system and overlaid on regular NIM analysis. The NIM system should allow for call down of the details of (say) interest-rate stress scenarios or the conditions that Treasury oversees. This is illustrated at Figure 11.21.

**End Result of NIM Analytics Capability**   A purpose-designed NIM system would facilitate the integration of NIM views with other, related, aspects of Treasury and Finance analysis, such as liquidity risk management views, risk appetite, regulatory capital, and so on. By building a joined-up view of the normal financial performance of the bank's products, linked to their economic sensitivities and P&L volatility, and by then linking this with liquidity analysis, the bank can begin to build a total view of factors such as its liability / funding base, customer behaviour, and impact on NIM and the balance sheet. This would provide an enhanced capability to plan for funding that is optimised to support the bank's lending base, and which would give the most economic all-in P&L impact over the economic cycle. An example of the functionality required is shown at Figure 11.22, while a recommended approach is given as a template in the box below.

Thus, we see why a genuine NIM analytics capability is an integral part of implementing a strategic ALM process in balance sheet management. It is also essential in liabilities strategy planning, required to build an optimum liabilities mix. We discuss this further in Chapter 12.

| LIABILITY MANAGEMENT | | | Funding Costs | | | | NII stress response | | Liquidity | | | Basel 3 | |
| | | | Customer Rate | | | | | | | | Outflows | | |
| Product | GBP/CCY | Control | Gross Rate | Rate Range | Margin | Margin range | Volatility | 12m Stress | Supply | Elasticity | Stress | LCR? | NSFR? |
| Deposit 001 | GBP | Managed | 2.0% | 2.0%–2.5% | 1.0% | 1.0% – 1.5% | Low | Low | Poor | Low | | |
| Deposit 002 | GBP | Managed | 2.4% | 2.0%–2.5% | 0.6% | 0.4% – 1.1% | High | High | Good | Medium | | |
| Deposit 003 | GBP | Panel | 2.0% | 2.0%–2.5% | 1.0% | 1.0% – 1.5% | | | Very good | High | | |

**FIGURE 11.22** Integrated NIM analytics and liquidity management functionality

## NIM ANALYTICS CAPABILITY: TEMPLATE OF RECOMMENDATIONS

- **Product Table (Treasury and Finance):** draw up a table of lending and deposit products denoting their systems flags, and economic and regulatory characteristics. This would show their GL codes, their degree of LIBOR or Base Rate sensitivity, their liquidity characteristics (Type A or B where identifiable), and behavioural tenor, whether GBP or multicurrency, etc. The aim is to ensure that there is a uniform approach to segmenting the balance sheet for views such as base rate sensitivity and to provide a foundation for further analysis.
- **Operating Model (Treasury and Finance):** work together on a more formal basis to deepen NIM analysis. More fundamentally, ALCO and the Board should review the Treasury Operating Model to confirm whether it is still optimum.
- **New NIM views:** embed more NIM analysis into the bank's ALCO MI deck. This analysis should aim to add new perspectives such as gross customer rate analysis, linkage of spot and average trends, and overall NIM *(to get a view on the elasticity of the bank's NII and NIM to sudden balance sheet inflows and outflows)*.
- IRRBB system:
  (i.) Develop a Finance and Business-friendly set of displays and metrics (in addition to what is provided to Group Treasury) to highlight NII volatility risk, to feature in ALCO and product committees;
  (ii.) Improve the extent to which IRRM stress test outputs can be combined with Finance forecast views;
  (iii.) Implement a programme to improve the education of Finance and the Business lines on market risk.

## INVESTOR RELATIONS (IR) AND THE CREDIT RATING PROCESS[6]

At first sight it may not appear obvious why the credit ratings process, let alone investor relations, should be part of the strategic ALM discipline. Traditionally, these fields have been seen as separate, and managed out of different areas in the bank. However, it is not uncommon in smaller banks (and some large banks) for the credit ratings relationship to be maintained within the Treasury function. This becomes more obvious if the bank's Board risk appetite statement (see Figure 11.3) has an explicit credit rating target. Because a bank's credit rating is influenced so heavily by the robustness and viability of its balance sheet, and since balance sheet management planning is what strategic ALM is all about, one can see why credit rating strategy should be "owned" by Treasury, or at least by ALCO.

---

[6] This section was co-authored with Ed Bace.

In this section, we highlight the importance of communicating properly with shareholders and other investors and intermediaries, regulators, rating agencies, and other stakeholders. We also look briefly at the credit ratings process, describing the key aspects of the Standard & Poor's (S&P) rating agency process by way of example. Credit ratings reflect an implied default probability of the company being assigned the rating; elsewhere in this book we reference a first-principles approach to extracting default probabilities from market prices (yields).

## What is Investor Relations?

The "investor relations" (IR) discipline is a strategic management responsibility required for publicly-traded companies; it integrates finance, communication, marketing, and securities law compliance issues, from a holistic perspective. It enables effective two-way communication between a company, its shareholders, and the financial community. In this way it contributes to achieving fair valuation for the company, thereby helping to create shareholder value. Finally, it is a form of (technical) marketing and risk management, to help a bank optimise its position in financial markets.

The IR function should be designed to provide company information to investors to help them make informed buy and sell decisions. It promotes access to capital, and encourages a climate of trust for a deep and liquid shareholder base (institutional investors prefer highly liquid companies in order to facilitate large trades). Thus it contributes to a fair valuation for the company.

The IR function can be handled by an individual within a company (such as the Director of Investor Relations), or a department within a company (for example, Corporate Communications or Investor Relations).

In smaller banks, the Treasury department often fulfils this function. The IR function organisationally is sometimes placed under the CFO (Chief Financial Officer) to encourage efficient information transfer and financial disclosure, or within the communications division. Otherwise it may reports into Treasury. In any case, it is desirable to have open communication between IR and the CEO (Chief Executive Officer), for the preservation and enhancement of the bank's reputation.

IR activities primarily target individual investors, institutional investors / money managers / hedge funds, and securities analysts (buy side, sell side, paid-for research). Secondary audiences for IR activities include employees and other internal constituents, as well as customers, communities, media, legal advisors, consultants and regulators.

Primary responsibilities for the IRO (Investor Relations Officer) include developing an overall strategy, setting goals and objectives, developing key messages to support the strategy, overseeing the IR programme development and execution, providing feedback from the investor community to the management team, providing regulatory guidance, and monitoring markets, proxy solicitations, dividends, and share repurchases.

The following are typical duties of an IRO:

- Working with wholesale funding and capital teams; designing and implementing an overall investor strategy;
- Working with colleagues on optimising investor targeting, along with the CFO and others; speaking on behalf of the company;
- Being an acknowledged expert on key industry, ratings, and regulatory developments;
- Designing and implementing an internal IR plan;
- Cultivating relationships with key investors / investment banks / sell side analysts / rating agencies and the wider investment and financial community;
- Providing a feedback mechanism to shape IR and funding strategies;
- Maintaining a database of key investors;
- Supporting presentations and leading the preparation thereof; and
- Preparing for investment bank due diligence to support public issuance.

There needs to be close coordination with the PR (Public Relations) and other communications units. The combined teams are strategic corporate assets, working together, in order to avoid sending conflicting messages.

### What Builds an Effective IR Strategy?

The value drivers need to be identified, in targeting income versus value investors. There is a necessity for market research and analysis, to understand investor perceptions, and to formulate the story. IR has to identify those investors most likely to respond to a tailored and well-crafted message, which means that revisions to strategy must be considered at least annually.

Market research has to be conducted on an ongoing basis. This includes market intelligence (brokers, daily trading metrics, comparisons of relative performance), audience analysis (of the company's shareholders, potential investors, their expectations), and exploration of how well the strategies are recognised. Has the investment community absorbed the information? What are the investment community attitudes towards the bank? How do investors evaluate management and communications? The IRO must be aware of actions that trigger share purchase or sale, while undertaking benchmarking, i.e., tracking changes in investor knowledge, perceptions, and attitudes (on at least an annual basis).

In order to formulate the investment proposition, IR needs to study the medium- and long-term business plan to identify themes (value, growth, income). For this reason, it is logical for IR to at least attend ALCO and have an understanding of the bank's strategic ALM premise. There is a need for understanding of various valuation techniques, including Price / book ratio, P/E ratio, earnings growth, and others appropriate to banks.

Relationships are built with shareholders and debtholders (whose composition is regularly analysed), both institutional and retail, enhanced by an annual perception analysis. Potential investors / analysts are courted through bi-yearly road shows, onsite visits, and follow-up meetings. The media are cultivated through lunch briefings, executive meetings, project and onsite tours. The success of an IR program may be measured by comparing key ratios with the peer group, for example, P/E ratio, the number of analysts following the company and their ratings, the number of requests for information, the stock trading activity, the shareholder mix, and the share price.

Ultimately, the IR process is a long-term one (as is the strategic ALM one!). Effectiveness of the strategy with the buy side can be gauged by: increased positions of current investors, a broadened shareholder base, and changing shareholder mix. With the sell side, effectiveness is shown by more analysts following the company.

The IR effort is equally applicable to bondholders. Keeping investors (and potential investors) happy can help with reducing funding cost, preserving the ability to issue debt. In this respect, updates are mandatory about business plan implementation, revenue streams and related projections, and changes in the bank's asset base. Timely and continuous information gives comfort to bondholders and encourages them to buy more bonds.

Inevitably, IR will find itself in situations of "crisis management". It is essential that "pre-crisis" preparations and early warning systems are installed, which are related to perception and feedback audits. This demands organisation of a crisis team, including the IRO, PRO (Public Relations Officer), CFO, and the company lawyer.

### The Credit Rating Process

This section examines the role and methodology of the credit rating agencies in assessing banks, including liquidity, solvency, and regulatory factors.

Why should a bank, or any entity, whether issuing public bonds or not, have or maintain a credit rating? There are several good reasons:

- It helps to focus strategy development. Management needs a strong business plan to present to the rating agencies, as well as to investors.
- It is meant to provide an independent "verification" of the financial strength of the bank or issuing entity.
- It provides access to wholesale markets for issuance of additional Tier 1 or Tier 2 capital, covered bonds, or senior unsecured bonds.

Many banks have at least one credit rating, from one of the three major global credit rating agencies (S&P, Moody's, and Fitch). Ratings are typically noted by a letter scale, with AAA denoting the highest level of credit quality (minimal risk of default), followed by AA, A, BBB (all of the foregoing considered "investment grade", due to historically low observed default rates), then BB, B, CCC (showing significantly higher default rates), down to D for Default.

The following are the key factors that determine what a bank's credit rating will be:

- Future strategy and objectives;
- Capital levels;
- Asset quality;
- Funding and liquidity profile and robustness;
- Risk appetite / profile;
- Financial and operating performance;
- Product and customer diversification;
- Strength and experience of management;
- Business profile and franchise strength;
- Economic conditions;
- Competitive landscape.

To give an example of S&P's bank rating methodology, for instance, the starting point is a macro view of the environment where the bank operates. This results in an economic risk score and an industry risk score, translating into an "anchor" rating. The next step will be to look at bank specific factors, such as business position, capital and earnings, risk position, funding, and liquidity. The combination of all these results in what S&P terms the "Stand Alone Credit Profile" (SACP), which could be above or below (or equal to) the initial anchor rating. This SACP can then be adjusted upward if there are any meaningful external support factors, such as government ownership, or other pledges from a creditworthy party to stand behind the bank in event of difficulties. Generally, this uplift ranges from one to two rating gradations, or "notches", to arrive at the final rating, termed the Issuer Credit Rating (ICR). Usually this is the rating applied to issues of senior unsecured debt. Ratings on lower-ranking securities would be notched downwards from the ICR to reflect their subordinate position.

Consider, for example, a bank with an anchor rating of BBB+. The bank specific factors reveal particular strength in business position (resulting in a notch uplift), and weakness in capital (resulting in a notch downwards), which largely offset each other. This makes the SACP unchanged at BBB+. However, there is strong expression or even demonstration of government support, which lifts the ICR up one notch to an A–.

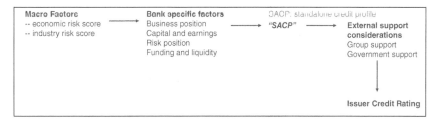

**FIGURE 11.23**   S&P bank ratings approach

This process is illustrated at Figure 11.23. A summary of the approach is shown in the diagram at Figure 11.24.

In arriving at its assessment, a rating agency will consider a number of financial metrics in relation to rated peers; these include:

- Core Tier 1 capital;
- Total Tier 1 capital;
- Total capital;
- RWAs and their quality;
- The LDR (loan to deposit ratio);
- NIM (net interest margin);
- RoE (Return on Equity).

Typical characteristics of A-range banks include factors both qualitative and quantitative:

- Qualitative:
  - Includes the largest banks with diversified business lines;
  - Can include smaller "national champions" with a solid multi-regional franchise;
  - Likely to benefit from 1 or 2 notches of government support uplift.

- Quantitative:
  - Strong financial metrics (capitalisation, liquidity, underlying profitability);
  - Strong deposit base for stable funding;
  - High quality asset base.

BBB-range banks are relatively weaker than their A-rated counterparts, qualitatively and quantitatively:

- Qualitative:
  - They may be more geographically concentrated;
  - Having less product diversification;

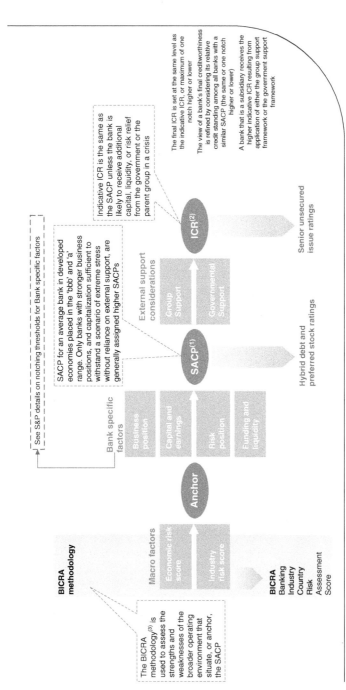

**BICRA methodology**

The BICRA methodology[3] is used to assess the strengths and weaknesses of the broader operating environment that situate, or anchor, the SACP

**Macro factors**

Economic risk score

Industry risk score

BICRA Banking Industry Country Risk Assessment Score

**Bank specific factors**

See S&P details on notching thresholds for Bank specific factors

SACP for an average bank in developed economies placed in the 'bbb' and 'a' range. Only banks with stronger business positions, and capitalization sufficient to withstand a scenario of extreme stress without reliance on external support, are generally assigned higher SACPs

Business position

Capital and earnings

Risk position

Funding and liquidity

Anchor

SACP[1]

**External support considerations**

Group Support

Governmental Support

Indicative ICR is the same as the SACP unless the bank is likely to receive additional capital, liquidity, or risk relief from the government or the parent group in a crisis

ICR[2]

The final ICR is set at the same level as the indicative ICR, or maximum of one notch higher or lower

The view of a bank's final creditworthiness is refined by considering its relative credit standing among all banks with a similar SACP (the same or one notch higher or lower)

A bank that is a subsidiary receives the higher indicative ICR resulting from application of either the group support framework or the government support framework

Hybrid debt and preferred stock ratings

Senior unsecured issue ratings

Source: S&P, Banks: Rating Methodology and Assumptions, 09.11.2011

(1) SACP: Stand Alone Credit Profile
(2) ICR: Issuer Credit Rating
(3) "Banking Industry Country Risk Assessment Methodology And Assumptions", published Nov. 9, 2011

STANDARD &POOR'S

**FIGURE 11.24** Standard & Poor's (S&P) banks rating methodology summary

- Enjoying smaller market share;
- Experiencing challenges to underlying earnings (for example, difficulties with internal capital generation);
- Facing potential execution risks due to acquisitions / new product areas;
- Operational and/or risk management issues (*of course!*).

- Quantitative:
  - More challenged operating performance;
  - Overall weaker financial metrics than A-rated expectations;
  - Limited diversification of funding sources (for example, wholesale funding reliance or lack of access, paradoxically);
  - Concentrations in higher risk portfolios (for example, commercial real estate, buy-to-let).

Sometimes the rating agencies will conduct a rating advisory exercise, which gives banks the ability to "test" various capital and funding scenarios before a formal application, thus enabling management action to try to secure the required rating. It can be useful in that it provides relative certainty of the ratings outcome (all else being equal!) of one or more of the financing scenarios, before selection of a structure to rate. The strategy for engaging with the agencies is important to extracting value from the RAS (Ratings Assessment Service – Moody's) and/or RES (Ratings Evaluation Service – S&P) process.

## CONCLUSIONS

Bank assets and liabilities are inextricably linked. Banks cannot manage risk and return without considering both sides of the balance sheet. All areas of the bank must come together to understand interest rate and liquidity risks in setting and pursuing high-level strategy.

Traditionally "ALM" meant managing liquidity risk and interest-rate risk. But this isn't full "ALM" if what one wishes to manage is all the assets and all the liabilities from one integrated, coherent aggregate viewpoint. The balance sheet is everything – the most important risk exposure in the bank. Managing ALM risk on the balance sheet therefore is managing everything that generates balance sheet risk. Proactive ALM or what we have called "Strategic ALM" is best-practice in the Basel III environment, where one can't expect to originate assets and raise liabilities in isolation from each other and still "optimise" the balance sheet.

We have addressed a number of factors with respect to implementing strategic ALM, of course this is from the high-level viewpoint. The correct approach to ALM discipline demands a keen appreciation and understanding of other related factors, including:

- Product type and behaviour;
- Behavioural tenor characteristics of assets and liabilities (something required to some depth now anyway with implementation of Basel III);
- Relevant reference interest rate benchmarks;
- The Libor-OIS spread, the Libor term premium and determinants of the swap spread (see Chapter 2);

as well as the aspects we have discussed here such as peer benchmarking and understanding, and analysing NIM. ALM really is an all-encompassing discipline and one that should be understood by all senior bankers.

One could say that the best way to implement "strategic ALM" – which at heart means a proactive management of the balance sheet, such that one arrives at a structural balance sheet position by design rather than well-intended accident – is, as Colin Johnson (formerly Birmingham and Midshires Building Society) suggested to the author once, to have the Head of Lending sitting next to the Head of Deposits. Failing that, and as banks get larger, in the Basel III era in order to meet the 3D optimisation challenge one must seek to achieve maximum balance sheet efficiency, and that calls for the risk "triumvirate" of Treasurer, CFO, and CRO to have a bigger influence in origination and customer pricing policy. This is now the recommended approach to "risk management" in banks. Without this approach, it will be difficult to optimise the asset–liability mix that addresses the three-pipe problem of regulatory compliance, NIM enhancement, and customer franchise satisfaction.

## SELECTED BIBLIOGRAPHY AND REFERENCES

Bessis, J., (2015). *Risk Management in Banking*, 4th edition, John Wiley & Sons Ltd.
Skoglund, J., (2015). *Financial Risk Management: Applications in Market, Credit, Asset and Liability Management and Firmwide Risk*, John Wiley & Sons Ltd.

*"Neil Armstrong seemed more the observer than the participant, but when you looked at his eyes you knew that he was the commander and had all the pieces assembled in his mind. I don't think he ever raised his voice. He just saved his energy for when it was needed."*
—Gene Kranz, *Failure Is Not an Option: Mission Control from Mercury to Apollo 13 and Beyond,* New York, NY: Berkley Books, 2000

# CHAPTER 12

# Liquidity and Funding: Policy, Management, and Risk Management

This is a long chapter. But justifiably so. Liquidity management in the banking sector is quite possibly the most important discipline in the entire financial markets industry, and by extension the global economy. When a bank fails there is a significant negative knock-on effect on society as a whole, and when large banks fail, the impact can be severe indeed, as the events of 2007–2008 demonstrated. The very act of undertaking ordinary bank business creates liquidity and funding risk, and so this risk must be managed competently, and in perpetuity. That's why liquidity management is such a vital issue in finance.

Thankfully, pure liquidity stress events are rare. Historically, more banks have gone bust as a result of credit-related losses wiping out their capital than have failed because they could not "roll over" their funding requirement when due; in recent history that is because governments (usually in the form of the central bank) generally step in to rescue banks experiencing liquidity problems. That said, the demise of the UK bank Northern Rock in 2007 is a rare recent example of a bank falling over purely because of liquidity problems, and the one silver lining in this terrible cloud was that it re-emphasised the need for banks and their Boards to focus their energies on a topic that many of them had begun to take for granted: the need to structure balance sheets and risk management policies to ensure that maintenance of continuous liquidity *never* is a reason for a bank to fail.

In this chapter, relevant and still pertinent extracts from previous works are provided to furnish a solid background on the main tenets of liquidity risk management. In addition, previously unpublished material is presented as a form of template and guideline for liquidity risk policy at a bank. These guides and templates are recommended, and applicable, to any banking institution, irrespective of size or business model. In fact, this chapter has been designed in effect to be used as a standalone handbook for bank liquidity risk managers and ALCO members; one could call the book *Bank Liquidity and Funding: Principles and Risk Management.*

In Part 1 of the chapter we provide the essential principles of liquidity risk management. Part 2 covers strategic implications of managing a bank's balance sheet in line with best practice principles. Part 3 is a demonstration, by way of discussing one example from the UK regulator (the Prudential Regulation Authority or PRA), of how the consultation paper process from regulators should itself feed into the risk management process. When banks consider the content of a regulatory authority's consultative paper, they should of course also be reviewing not just their risk management process and any gaps in delivery but also their overall philosophy towards managing risk. In other words, banks need to move away from the standard bureaucratic and process-driven "tick box" approach to meeting regulator requirements and instead seek to understand fully what their risks are and how best to manage them. The example paper we look at in Part 3 describes requirements that we expect to remain a benchmark for some years to come, so is a good case for us now and for the future.

Finally, in Part 4 of the chapter we provide (via the book's website) some real-world examples of policy documents related to liquidity and funding that practitioners can use as benchmark templates at their own employing institutions.

Note that in Part V of the book itself, which is the case studies section, we also provide examples of different funding structures for the period 1989–2008 which readers can use to observe the differing approaches to liability structure planning undertaken at different banks.

## PART 1: LIQUIDITY RISK AND LIQUIDITY RISK MANAGEMENT

In this chapter, we introduce the concept of liquidity risk in banking and provide an overview of the liquidity risk framework that should be in place at all banking institutions. The art of managing liquidity is the art of banking, precisely because banking involves maturity transformation: the act of taking in short-dated deposits and using these to fund long-dated assets. A definition of banking therefore must include the ability to manage liquidity continuously, throughout the economic cycle, and in perpetuity – or at least as long as the bank's managers and shareholders wish it to remain a going concern.

## Defining Liquidity

The first step in undertaking effective and fit-for-purpose liquidity risk management is to understand precisely what it is. We define liquidity risk as follows:

*In banking, liquidity is the ability to meet all cash obligations as and when they become due.*

In other words, at all times a bank must be able to service its obligations as they arise, on both sides of the balance sheet. Maintenance of liquidity at all times is the paramount order of banking. In fact to undertake banking is to assume a continuous ability to roll-over funding, otherwise banks would never originate long-dated illiquid assets such as residential mortgages or project finance loans. As it is never safe to assume anything in life, banks need to set in place an infrastructure and a management ability to ensure that liquidity is always available, to cover for times when market conditions deteriorate. In every jurisdiction, a country's central bank operates as a "lender of last resort", in that it comes to the aid of a bank which finds itself with difficulties in liquidating assets. However, a bank which has to resort to the central bank has failed and this is a failure of its management. Hence the objective must be to remain standalone self-sufficient for funding at all times.

Being continuously liquid means, therefore, an ability to be able to fund assets throughout their life, and to be able to meet demand for withdrawals of liabilities as and when they arise. With respect to the former, these can be very long-dated assets, as well as committed but as yet undrawn assets such as credit cards or contingency funding lines. With the latter, a large proportion of customer liabilities are demand deposits, be they current accounts (otherwise known as "checking accounts" or money transmission accounts (MTAs) or operational deposits) or instant-access savings accounts, so the bank needs to be able to meet requests for withdrawal of such funds from customers. So the challenge of bank liquidity management is a simple one to understand: have available funding for very long periods (a project finance loan may have a 50-year maturity) and be able to meet requests for withdrawal of that funding at immediate notice.

It is important to make the distinction between, and understand, what is meant by bank liquidity, which is funding liquidity (of the type we defined above) and other meanings of liquidity. A common other use of the term is with respect to *trading liquidity*, which is something quite different although the two are related. Trading liquidity refers to the ease with which an asset may be bought or sold in the market, in size and with no material impact on the asset price arising as a result. It is often defined as the ease with which an asset can be turned into cash, but that's not quite the same. A liquid asset can be traded easily at a narrow bid-offer spread (the wholesaler's buying and selling prices) and in size. An illiquid asset cannot. One also comes across the expression *redemption liquidity*, which is similar to trading liquidity but is only relevant as an asset approaches maturity.

The relationship between the two types of liquidity comes about because one can facilitate the other. Holding a portion of the bank's balance sheet in the form of liquid assets will assist the process of maintaining continuous liquidity. We consider this further in the section on the liquid asset buffer.

### Sources of Liquidity

Bank funding instruments and sources of liquidity vary considerably depending on the operating model of the bank in question, but in essence they fall into two types: customer funds and wholesale funds. We would not need to make any further distinction if the different types within each category all exhibited similar *behavioural* characteristics with respect to their tenor. However, they do not, which is why a proper understanding of customer and wholesale funding types is necessary.

This is not to say that all retail funding is good and all wholesale funding is bad. The issue of behavioural quality of liabilities is only pertinent with respect to contractually short-dated funds. Liabilities that are contractually

---

## LIQUIDITY VALUE OF LIABILITIES

Banks fund their balance sheet using a variety of liability types. The liquidity value of each type is different, and in some cases the behavioural aspect of a certain type of liability renders it a more stable and long-term form of funding than would be implied by its contractual maturity. For this reason, regulators review liquidity management principles on both a contractual and behavioural basis. When supplying liquidity metrics to the regulator, banks will include historical analyses of certain types of liabilities, such as retail current accounts, that will seek to demonstrate how stable a customer liability type is. (The Basel III guidelines refer to "stable" and "non-stable" funds, whereas the UK PRA speaks of "sticky" and "non-sticky" funds, also known as Type A and Type B funds respectively.)

Retail current accounts are the best example of this: they are contractually payable on demand, so therefore of immediate maturity, but observation of their behaviour reveals that typically customers maintain large stable balances in such accounts over a long time period. Therefore it is logical to treat a proportion of the amount of such liabilities as "term funding" (the exact amount and tenor is a function of what the historical statistical behaviour of the accounts demonstrates). The exact tenor to apply is, of course, specific to each bank and the Treasury and Risk functions need to understand their different liabilities behaviour and observe over time before they can draw conclusions.

But on this basis, it is apparent that some forms of liabilities have greater term liquidity value for a bank than others. At one end of the scale are retail current accounts; at the other are short-term unsecured wholesale liabilities, sourced in the inter-bank market, which have much more volatile characteristics in stressed market conditions and, therefore, are less valuable for liquidity management purposes. This assumption is based on historical observation, when such funds were seen to flow out much more aggressively than other funding types during stress events, and also because of a perception that wholesale market or "professional" depositors are deemed to be savvier when it comes to anticipating stress events.

Illustrated below is an accepted hierarchy of value of different types of liability. It suggests that a bank should seek to maximise funding based on higher liquidity value liabilities, and minimise its reliance on wholesale inter-bank funding. This is a best-practice principle of liquidity risk management. Of course, it is not only "liquidity value" that should drive medium-term liabilities strategy, there is also a trade off with NII/NIM considerations and customer franchise considerations. But that said, a good starting point for understanding liquidity value of customer deposits would look like the following, with the most stable funding type at the top:

- Retail current accounts;
- Retail deposit accounts;
- Corporate cash-flow accounts/call accounts;
- Retail savings accounts;
- Retail fixed-term deposits;
- Private bank deposits;
- Corporate savings accounts;
- Corporate fixed-term deposits;
- Corporate fixed-term deposits;
- Wholesale market fixed-term deposits;
- Money market term funding (CD/CP);
- Money market deposits/inter-bank deposits.

*(Continued)*

Whilst it is good liquidity risk management practice to be aware of the "sticky" nature (or otherwise) of different types of liabilities, ultimately this remains a generalisation and it is important to be aware of the behavioural characteristics of customer deposits under "business as usual" (BAU) *and* stressed conditions. There may be nuances of behaviour specific to individual banks; for example, internet and mobile-based bank accounts amongst certain customer types (based on age groups, for instance, with respect to retail customers) may behave differently to branch-based or postal accounts.

That said, pure liquidity stress events are rare in any country. It is often the case that senior managers in banks have never experienced one, so it is difficult to draw firm conclusions on expected behaviour of deposits under stress simply from historical observation. So the watchword for optimum liability strategy and liquidity risk management must be to adopt a conservative approach in funding policy.

long-dated are "good" irrespective of where they are sourced from. A capital markets issue of 3-year bonds by a bank is solid, stable funding. Equally as unambiguous, a deposit from customer types such as non-bank financial institutions is seen as behaviourally non-stable, because they are sensitive to market conditions and liable to be withdrawn at no notice if either economic conditions or the specific bank in question are seen as weak.

A "last resort" source of funding liquidity is the central bank, but this should not under any circumstances be seen as a BAU source. Other than daily open market operations, a bank that has to have recourse to central bank funding is in reality compromised as a standalone viability entity. The primary objective of any bank, large or small, is to be self-sufficient for capital and liquidity at all times and throughout the economic cycle. Anything less is a failure of the bank's management.

That said, in the post-crash environment after 2009, banks have indeed been accessing central banks for BAU funding – the best example of this is the 3-year and 4-year term repo facilities implemented by the European Central Bank (ECB). However, this instrument was introduced precisely because in the Eurozone after the crash many banks suffered from unstable funding structures. In theory, this facility will be withdrawn once the Eurozone returns to "normal" conditions. (This may be some years away. . .)

## Liquidity Risk Management

Liquidity risk limits are set in a variety of different ways, and are often a function of the type of metrics used to report liquidity risk exposure in a bank. There are a large number of potential metrics and the important thing for Treasury is that the suite of metrics used – and it is a suite, as liquidity risk cannot be measured adequately with just one or two metrics – is fit for purpose. Measuring liquidity exposure and gleaning a realistic idea of future funding requirements and pressure points requires an array of metrics. The specific types of metrics used are a function of the business model of the bank in question.

The point of calculating and reporting liquidity risk metrics is to enable senior management to have the most accurate and up-to-date estimation of the liquidity exposure of the bank at any time. This assists with planning, but more importantly it enables management to structure the bank's balance sheet and funding mix in the way that best meets its risk tolerance. It also provides management with the ability to respond more knowledgeably to market stresses. Finally, the Basel III regime obliges banks to report specified liquidity metrics on a regular basis, so they have no option but to implement systems that enable the liquidity numbers to be calculated.

The first step in liquidity risk management limit setting is the Board liquidity risk appetite statement. This is a formal articulation of the bank's tolerance for liquidity risk, and it comprises both qualitative and quantitative elements. The actual liquidity limits that a bank has to operate under are contained here – this ensures that they are taken seriously, because they have been sanctioned at Board level. Example 12.1 shows a template for a Board liquidity risk appetite statement, as set up at the hypothetical "ABC Bank".

---

### EXAMPLE 12.1    BOARD LIQUIDITY RISK APPETITE STATEMENT

Risk appetite is an expression of the maximum level of risk that ABC Bank (ABC) is prepared to accept in order to deliver its business strategy. This target of maximum level of risk exposure should be measurable and forms part of the Bank's risk appetite statement. This is referred to as risk tolerance within this statement.

This statement focuses on the Liquidity Risk Appetite which is covered by the Liquidity and Funding Policy. The purpose of the Liquidity Policy is to support the realisation of the strategic plan

---

*(Continued)*

through establishing a control framework consistent with the Bank's liquidity risk tolerance (see Liquidity Metrics and Limits below).

The Liquidity Policy sets out the obligations of ABC Bank to ensure:

- Financial obligations can be met as they fall due;
- Effective and prudent management of liquidity, which is fundamental to the financial strength and soundness of the Bank;
- Funding sources are managed to keep reliance on short-term, volatile funding sources to a minimum and encourage long-term, stable funding as a structural indicator of the Bank's balance sheet strength;
- Market and depositor confidence is maintained in the ability of the Bank to meet its obligations, both in normal market conditions and in the event of extraordinary circumstances or market illiquidity;
- Compliance with evolving regulatory liquidity requirements throughout the jurisdictions within which the Bank operates.

The Liquidity Policy sets out:

- The liquidity risk tolerance of the Bank in accordance with ABC's strategic metrics and targets;
- The governance framework for identifying, monitoring, and controlling Liquidity Risk;
- The activities to plan, manage, and report liquidity through Funding Plans, stress tests (refer to the ILAA document), and contingency plans (refer to the CFP document);
- The foundation for the Bank to fully meet all relevant regulatory requirements on liquidity.

Treasury has proposed the Liquidity Risk Appetite to ALCO and the Board for their approval. The Board owns the Liquidity Risk Appetite. Once approved, Treasury will monitor and report the metrics against the limits. Treasury will notify any breach of the limits to ALCO. Treasury and ALCO will agree an appropriate action plan to remedy the breach.

Refer to the Liquidity Policy Document for more details.

Quantitative limits will be set for the specific liquidity metrics that the bank monitors. This is considered next.

**This extract from** *The Principles of Banking* **(2012)**

## Principles of Bank Liquidity Management

**Principles of Bank Liquidity Management**

The banking system in both the US and Western Europe was on the brink of collapse in September and October 2008, in the wake of the Lehman bankruptcy. Government intervention using taxpayer funds, which in many countries extended to a blanket guarantee of banks' complete liabilities, prevented this collapse from taking place. In the aftermath of the crisis, national regulators and the BIS circulated consultative papers and recommendations that addressed new requirements on bank capital, liquidity and risk management. The UK FSA was perhaps most demanding; its *Policy Statement 09/16*, which was issued in October 2009, outlined measures on capital treatment, liquidity requirements and stress testing that implied a fundamental change in the bank business model going forward.[1] Many of the elements of this change in regulatory requirements were not new, however, but rather a turning of the clock back to earlier times, when conservative principles in liquidity management were actually quite common practice. The crisis of 2007 and 2008 was as much a crisis of bank liquidity as it was of capital erosion, and the events of that period restated the importance of efficient liquidity management in banking.

In this and the next three chapters we discuss the "water of life" of banking: liquidity management. The recommended practices described in this chapter should not be followed because they are required by the national regulator or by the BIS, but because they are essential for any bank that wishes to continue in business on a sustained basis over the business cycle. In other words, sensible banking demands this practice; that regulators have to enforce it by fiat demonstrates the extent to which poor bank management exists in countries around the world. The central tenet of the principles of banking is that of liquidity risk management; therefore, by definition it should be part of the strategy of every bank to be able to survive a liquidity crisis. Liquidity management is the most important risk management function in banking, at the individual bank level and at the aggregate industry level. Failure to survive a liquidity crisis is a failure of management.

---

[1] The UK government announced shortly after it was elected in May 2010 that the banking supervision role was to be handed back to the BoE, and that the role of the FSA would be subsumed within the bank.

This chapter introduces and defines the concept of liquidity risk. It then covers the principles of sound liquidity management, before looking in detail at the elements of a bank liquidity policy statement, including (i) the liquid asset buffer, (ii) central bank funding facilities and (iii) the contingency funding plan.

This is a long chapter, but worth persevering with as it is perhaps the most important chapter in the book.

# BANK LIQUIDITY

A search of "bank liquidity" on Google undertaken when writing this chapter returned "about 8,160,000 results" in 0.24 seconds. The first line of the first website on the list offered the following:

*Liquidity for a bank means the ability to meet its financial obligations as they come due. Bank lending finances investments in relatively illiquid assets, but it funds its loans with mostly short-term liabilities. Thus one of the main challenges to a bank is ensuring its own liquidity under all reasonable conditions.*[2]

This definition is accurate and sufficient for our purposes, although we preferred Wikipedia's definition, which stated,

*In banking, liquidity is the ability to meet obligations when they become due.*

In other words, maintenance of liquidity *at all times* is the paramount order of the day in banking. As we saw in Chapter 1, the business of banking itself creates maturity mismatches between assets and liabilities, and hence liquidity risk. In fact, to undertake banking is to assume a continuous ability to roll over funding, otherwise banks would never originate long-dated illiquid assets such as residential mortgages or project finance loans. As it is never safe to assume anything, banks need to set in place an infrastructure and management capability to ensure that liquidity is always available, to cover for all times when market conditions deteriorate. Because banks are so important to the economy's health, central banks operate as "lenders of last resort" to come to the aid of a bank that finds itself in liquidity difficulties. However, a bank that has to resort to the central bank for funding has failed, and this is a failure of its management.

---

[2] The website was www.wfhummel.cnchost.com and the link was http://wfhummel.cnchost .com/bankliquidity.html, found during a Google search undertaken one night in September 2010.

In this section we provide some historical background to the nature of liquidity risk management, and a more in-depth definition of what it involves.

## Elements of Liquidity Risk Management

The importance of liquidity risk management is such that it must be addressed at the highest level of a bank's management, which is the Board of Directors. The Board will delegate this responsibility to a management operating committee, usually the ALCO, but it is the Board that owns liquidity policy. If it does not own it, then it is not following business best-practice. Given this, it is important that the Board understands every aspect of liquidity risk management. We suggest that this covers the following strands, all of which are covered in Part III of this book:

- definition of liquidity risk;
- the role of liquidity risk management;
- board responsibilities;
- liquidity strategy, policy and processes;
- regulatory requirements and reporting obligations;
- funding strategy and policy;
- liquidity risk tolerance;
- institution-specific and market-wide stress scenarios, and stress testing;
- forecasting funding cash flows over different time horizons;
- the liquidity buffer;
- intra-group and cross-border group lending;
- liquidity contingency funding plan and stress testing;
- the link between liquidity and capital adequacy;
- the benefits of robust business intelligence.

In other words, liquidity management is devised and dictated from the highest level, and influences every aspect of the bank's business strategy and operating model. The UK FSA identified the following failures in bank liquidity management during the lead-up to the 2007–2009 financial crisis:

- an inconsistent approach to qualitative and quantitative reporting, across different firms, to senior management and to the regulator;
- an excessive reliance on short-term wholesale funding and the securitisation market, to the detriment of more stable funding sources such as retail deposits;
- funding long-dated illiquid assets with short-term wholesale liabilities;

- for the branches and subsidiaries of overseas banks, an excessive reliance on parental support for funds;
- the lack of a sufficiently diverse funding base; excessive reliance on only one or two sources of liabilities, with no alternatives available in a stress situation;
- the running down, or complete abolition, of a pool of genuinely liquid assets that would have remained liquid, and providing a pool of funding, during the inter-bank liquidity crisis.

To these we would add the following:

- organisational models and processes inadequate to cope with crisis events;
- poor and ineffective tools for controlling liquidity risk, not fully implemented into banks' internal processes.

The primary lesson to be learned from the financial crisis was that banks needed to return to their roots and manage liquidity risk on a more conservative basis, along the lines that they would have done in the past. An assumption by management that inter-bank liquidity will always be available is the first step towards generating funding difficulties for itself during a period of market or economic downturn.

Liquidity crises are endemic in banking and finance. That is why it is essential to maintain liquidity principles throughout the economic cycle, a discipline that may break down during a bull market or a period of cheap and plentiful cash availability. An excellent paper by John Boyd and Mark Gertler, published in 1994, highlights the lessons learned from the US banking crisis of 1980–1982. The authors' findings and recommendations remain current, and this paper should be required reading for all bank senior management today.[3]

Among the conclusions from Boyd and Gertler were that the larger, more systemically important banks were ultimately responsible for the performance of the overall industry, and contributed disproportionately to aggregate loan losses. This they ascribed to two factors: (i) deregulation and financial innovation leading to increased overall competition in the banking industry; and (ii) the regulatory environment, which had the indirect effect of subsidising risk taking by larger banks. The second factor arises from the existence of "too-big-to-fail" banks, a term that the authors employ. Both factors were in place during 2002–2007. It is worth quoting directly from

---

[3] Boyd, J.H. and Gertler, M., "The Role of Large Banks in the Recent U.S. Banking Crisis", *Federal Reserve Bank of Minneapolis Quarterly Review*, Winter 1994, Volume 18, No. 1.

the paper, because all of the observations could be made about the later crisis; we comment on the authors' remarks with reference to the events of 2007–2008:

> . . . *rationale behind too-big-to-fail was that . . . the failure of a large bank could be contagious. It could greatly disturb the rest of the financial system and cause severe consequences for the entire US economy. But this well-intentioned policy had an unfortunate side effect: it unduly subsidized risk-taking by large banks.* (Boyd and Gertler 1994; p. 2)

The actions of US Federal Reserve chairman Alan Greenspan in assisting the market in the 10 years leading to 2007, and which became known as the "Greenspan Put", contributed to a subconscious belief that the larger banks could not be allowed to fail, and so indirectly led to ever-larger risk taking during a period of cheap liquidity.

> *Most striking are the rise in the share [of bank assets] allocated to loans and the fall in shares allocated to [liquid] securities and to cash and reserves. The drop in the latter reflects mainly a sequence of reductions in reserve requirements . . . The increased access to short-term money [markets] permitted banks to reduce precautionary holdings of securities.* (Boyd and Gertler 1994; p. 3).

Precisely this same pattern of behaviour was repeated in the period leading up to the 2007–2009 crisis.

> *Judged by a variety of criteria, the composition of bank liabilities appears to have become riskier . . . the increased use of managed liabilities relative to deposits . . . In contrast to deposits, which are relatively immobile in the short run, managed liabilities are highly interest elastic. The increased use of managed liabilities – and of money market instruments in particular – has had a number of important effects. One obvious effect is downward pressure on banks' net interest margins . . . Another effect is a rise in the interest rate sensitivity of bank liabilities . . . With the efficiency gains of the money market came the cost of increased exposure to liquidity risk.* (Boyd and Gertler 1994; p. 3).

Again, this remains an accurate description of what happened at the last crisis. As well as higher liquidity risk, lower NII often leads to banks looking at higher risk business to maintain return on capital ratios:

> *The relative use of core deposits (checkable and savings and time deposits) shrinks with size, while the relative use of money market instruments increases.*

*About 85 percent of small bank liabilities are core deposits. Conversely, money market instruments constitute roughly 42 percent of large bank liabilities and 54 percent of money center bank liabilities. Further, the money centre banks obtain more than half of their purchased funds from abroad.*

*An implication of the differences in liability structure is that larger banks have smaller net interest margins . . . In addition to holding riskier asset portfolios and employing greater use of money market instruments, larger banks have lower capital/assets ratios.* (Boyd and Gertler 1994; p. 5).

During 2002–2007 the increased use of non-core funds was not restricted to the large banks, but it is notable that the use of such liabilities rose during the bull market. Failed banks such as Northern Rock embarked on an aggressive expansion strategy that relied heavily on the use of non-core deposits.

*The too-big-to-fail policy contributed by subsidizing risk-taking and thereby increasing the vulnerability of the banking system to these disturbances . . . With large banks as with the savings and loans, the key issue is whether the portfolio structure these financial firms adopted was distorted by regulatory bias . . . It is hard to believe that the portfolio structure of very large banks (for example, heavy investment in LDC [less-developed countries] and commercial real-estate lending, in conjunction with thin capital/ assets ratios) could be explained simply by scale economies.* (Boyd and Gertler 1994; p. 8).

If we substitute US sub-prime mortgages for LDC loans above, those same words published in 1994 would apply to any analysis of 2007–2008. For example, for the UK failed bank HBOS, poor quality commercial real-estate lending was the principal factor in its demise, and which required the nationalisation of Lloyds TSB Bank (which had taken over HBOS a few months previously).

Boyd and Gertler welcomed the 1988 Basel Accord, which instituted minimum regulatory capital rules for banks worldwide, just as policymakers in 2010 welcomed the Basel III rules. They suggested that the Basel rules confronted what they saw as the main risk factor: the implicit subsidy to risk taking by large banks. They state:

*. . . an important way the subsidy has played out has been that large banks have held less capital than they might have otherwise.* (Boyd and Gertler 1994; p. 9).

They conclude:

*. . . the main stress on the system has not been the raw number of failures; rather it has been the poor performance of large banks.* (Boyd and Gertler 1994; p. 9).

These last two quotes would not be out of place in an analysis of the 2008 banking crisis. The liquidity crisis was, in many respects, history repeating itself. It is clear that liquidity management and risk taking remain areas of bank risk management that must be addressed throughout the business cycle. So far, they have not been. We have cited this paper in detail here for two reasons. First, to highlight that liquidity crises are not new, that similar crises have occurred in the past, often because of the same causal factors, and will occur again; and second, to note that banks that do not learn the lessons of history will be at high risk of repeating the same mistakes as the failed banks of previous crises.

## Principles of Banking: Liquidity Adequacy

The lesson learned from all bank liquidity crises, of which the most recent one in 2007–2008 was the most noteworthy, is that the majority of banks do not adhere to sound principles of liquidity management during a bull market, when funds are readily available. Many firms cease maintaining an adequate liquidity buffer, and thus encounter difficulties when faced with a firm-specific and/or market-wide liquidity shock. The subsidiaries of foreign-based banks often have trouble obtaining funds from parent groups. In line with the thinking of the UK FSA, we believe that a bank's liquidity policy should be based on: (i) an adequate reserve of liquidity at all times; and (ii) in principle, the ability to be self-sufficient in funding. These can be taken to be part of the principles of banking. The key point to emphasise is that it is the responsibility of the bank itself, and thereby its Board and senior management, to undertake effective liquidity risk management, and not that of the regulator. A bank's management should incorporate sound liquidity principles into its own objectives and performance measurement, rather than wait to obtain direction from the regulator. Liquidity management is to the benefit of the bank's shareholders and stakeholders.

In principle, every bank should aim to achieve self-sufficiency in funding. For some banks, particularly the overseas branches and subsidiaries of banks headquartered elsewhere, this may not be possible; for others, the particular business model being employed may not permit it. However, funding self-sufficiency should always be the overriding goal of a bank, because that is the only way that a bank can be certain of surviving a liquidity crisis. Where self-sufficiency is not possible, the liquidity policy in place must incorporate a funding strategy that emphasises diversity on funding sources and an adequate liquidity contingency plan.

The UK FSA's *Policy Statement 09/16* states that:

> *UK banks are expected to be able to stand alone, and therefore should normally monitor and manage their own liquidity separately from the liquidity of other institutions in the group.* (page 21)

Applying this principle will help to maintain confidence in the banking system. Adopting a robust liquidity management policy will reduce the probability of a bank's failure in the event of market disruption or a specific firm bankruptcy. The rest of this chapter looks at the principles of sound liquidity management.

# THE BANK LIQUIDITY POLICY STATEMENT

The approach to liquidity risk management at a bank will vary depending on how conservative its liquidity policy is. A bank will be more or less risk averse than other banks, including those in its immediate peer group, in its tolerance to market and credit risk as well as liquidity risk. As such it will apply the basic principles of liquidity discussed in the previous section with more or less enthusiasm, depending on its particular business model and liquidity risk appetite. Irrespective of an individual bank's specific approach to liquidity risk, it is important that this is documented formally in a liquidity policy. This is a policy statement of the bank's *"high-level principles and concepts that provide the framework for liquidity risk measurement, management and control within the bank"*.

The liquidity policy statement is designed to be a regularly updated, go-to-working document, as well as part of the bank's governance structure. We provide two templates for a standard policy statement on the Wiley website (see Chapter 19 for details), the first for a small- to medium-sized commercial bank and the second for a larger banking group that operates across multiple jurisdictions. Either would serve as a first-cut and reasonably robust framework for liquidity and funding governance, and so may be adopted by any bank for its own purposes, and modified accordingly as required. In other words, the liquidity policy templates in this book are designed to be standard frameworks that are adaptable for use at most banks. The value-added element of any policy, of course, is the section that details specific tolerances to risk and specific responses to particular market situations. This part of the policy statement is unique to each bank. We provide an example of this part of the policy statement later in this chapter.

## Liquidity Policy Statement

We quote directly from page 1 of our own template framework statement (the one designed for a medium-sized commercial bank). This defines liquidity as:

> . . . *the ability to ensure that the bank will always be able to maintain or generate sufficient cash resources to meet its payment obligations in full as they fall due, on acceptable terms, under all market conditions.*

This definition should be adopted at all banks. Formally, the objectives of the liquidity policy are to:

- set out the bank's policy for measuring, monitoring and managing liquidity risk;
- set out how the bank governs its tolerance or appetite for liquidity risk;
- set out arrangements for the approval and review of liquidity policies and procedures;
- document the bank's policy for pricing liquidity risk; this includes setting a logical and appropriate internal funding policy (known variously as internal funds pricing, transfer pricing or term liquidity premium);
- document the bank's policy for managing intra-day liquidity risk;
- document the bank's policy for managing the liquidity risk related to collateral cash flows;
- if applicable, document the relationship of the bank to the group of which it is a part and the impact of this relationship on liquidity risk management;
- set out the bank's policy regarding the diversity required in sources of funds and the policy regarding the bank's access to various markets where such funds are applied;

- document the stress testing to be applied to the liquidity position of the bank;
- document the bank's contingency funding plan and policies regarding the timing, responsibility and extent of its use.

The author's stylised depiction of this is shown at Figure 12.2.

The policy statement should be owned at board level, but disseminated and understood at dealing level. It is important that the statement provides an accurate and accessible picture of the bank's view of liquidity risk, as well as its appetite for liquidity risk. Risk appetite is described in both quantitative and qualitative terms. The former is prescribed by means of liquidity metrics and hardwired limits. As we note in our policy template:

> *In defining the bank's appetite for liquidity risk, the bank considers regulatory requirements, internal constraints, external factors and its key stakeholders' liquidity management objectives.*
>
> *The key stakeholders have been identified as:*

- *shareholders*
- *regulators*
- *management.*

Stakeholders may also include customers, employees, the central bank and other persons or entities.

The organisation chart governing the risk management process, which is extracted from the liquidity policy, is shown at Figure 12.3.

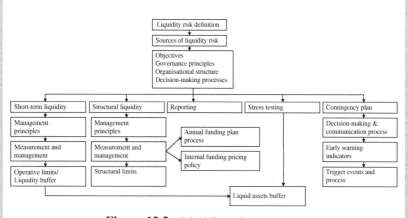

**Figure 12.2** Liquidity policy structure.

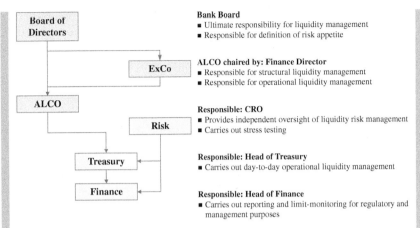

**Figure 12.3**   Liquidity policy statement: risk management governance structure.

Readers are encouraged to review the framework policy statement included as part of this book's supplementary material, available on the Wiley website, which is supplied as a template in MS Word format. We also include a summary of the statement in PowerPoint format.

### Bank Board
• Ultimate responsibility for liquidity management
• Responsible for definition of risk appetite

### ALCO chaired by: Finance Director
• Responsible for structural liquidity management
• Responsible for operational liquidity management

### Responsible: CRO
• Provides independent oversight of liquidity risk management
• Carries out stress testing

### Responsible: Head of Treasury
• Carries out day-to-day operational liquidity management

### Responsible: Head of Finance
• Carries out reporting and limit-monitoring for regulatory and management purposes

## Liquidity Policy Standards

Policy statements are often augmented by policy standards, which may be used to keep the statement up-to-date; for example, with new or modified liquidity metric limits.[6] The rationale behind the liquidity policy statement is to describe in explicit terms how the bank's liquidity and funding policy should be applied. In other words, it is a lower level working document, whose primary objective is to set the framework to ensure that the bank's funding arrangements enable all the bank's assets to be funded through to asset maturity. The policy standard may be composed as follows:

## Objective

- To ensure that liquidity stress for the bank is maintained within a manageable range to ensure continuous liquidity;
- To ensure that funding arrangements are maintained to enable assets to be funded through to maturity;
- To ensure that the bank operates to all required liquidity limits of the national regulator;[7]
- To identify explicitly, via the bank's internal funds pricing policy (or "Funds Transfer Pricing" policy), the cost of liquidity for the bank, and to ensure that this cost is understood by the business lines and feeds correctly into the bank's asset origination process;
- To ensure that liquidity risk reporting is carried out to an acceptable standard.

## Risk appetite

- The bank's approach to liquidity risk in qualitative terms is set out in the liquidity policy statement;
- The bank's approach to liquidity risk in quantitative terms is set out in the section on target liquidity metrics;
- All assets originated at the bank must be able to be transformed into liquid cash within [ ] days, or if not otherwise be (i) able to be funded from a contingency source; (ii) securitised into an existing programme at short notice; or (iii) eligible as collateral at the central bank;[8]

---

[6] The metrics may be changed exogenously; for example, by regulatory authority fiat. Liquidity metrics are considered in Chapter 13.

[7] Note that this objective is implicitly accorded a lower priority, when viewed by its position in the list, than the first objective of ensuring continuous liquidity. This is not to deny its importance – maintenance of all regulatory requirements is vital to ensure that the bank keeps its operating licence – but because simply meeting regulator limits is in itself not sufficient, the bank should apply its own sense and judgement to ensure that it can always source liquidity.

[8] The target number of days is for individual bank appetite. A common figure is 90 days.

- Business-as-usual funding sources are limited to retail customer deposits, corporate customer deposits, long-dated capital market funds, and . . .

## Target liquidity metrics

- Loan-to-deposit ratio of 100%;
- Liquidity gap for
  - 1-week: [ ] million
  - 1-month: [ ] million
  - 3-month: [ ] million;
- Long-dated funding (defined as over 1-year funds) minimum of 25%;
- Undrawn commitments limit of [ ] million.

## Liquidity buffer

- The bank must hold a buffer of truly liquid assets that are "unencumbered" and funded with long-dated liabilities;
- The cost of the buffer will be passed to the business lines. The exact share of each cost is a function of the amount of funding required and the extent of the balance sheet liquidity stress that the business line creates.

The liquidity buffer or "liquid asset buffer" is discussed later in this chapter.

## Liquidity Policy Statement: Banking Group

The definition of liquidity and the basic ingredients of liquidity risk management are identical for all well-run banks. Additional items in a liquidity policy statement adopted at a banking group will cover the requirements necessary for operation in a multi-jurisdictional environment. We provide a template for a group liquidity policy statement on the Wiley website; the filename is "LiquidityPolicyStatement_BankGroup_Template.docx".

The governance structure for a group entity presents problems in control and monitoring. There is more than one way to organise it, but business best-practice favours a centralised Group Treasury, tasked with formulating policy and implementing it throughout the group. Group Treasury also undertakes the money market dealing and term funding issuance at the home country location. Overseas subsidiaries and branches will have local Treasury functions to undertake the local currency dealing and liquidity management. For larger banking groups, it is useful to designate the main business centres as "Liquidity Hubs", which oversee and coordinate policy for their regional area. For example, for a UK bank the London office would be the liquidity hub for GBP and EUR, whereas its New York and Tokyo offices would be the hubs for USD and JPY. For a MENA-based bank, its overseas offices may well be the liquidity hubs for the major currencies USD, EUR and GBP.

The ALCO governance structure follows the regional arrangement of the group's Treasury desks, as we see in Figure 12.4.

The policy statement will describe the liquidity and funding policy for the group, which would be followed at all its operating locations. Regional variations are addressed at local ALCO level. The roles and responsibility of the Group ALCO ("GALCO") will include:

- liquidity risk policy
- group limits
- group liquidity buffer
- group funding plan
- pricing of liquidity risk
- policy on internal funds pricing ("Funds Transfer Pricing")
- collateral management
- stress testing
- group contingency funding plan
- group liquidity risk reporting.

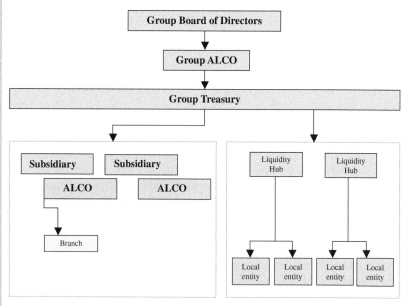

**Figure 12.4** Bank Group ALCO governance structure.

The subsidiary legal entity ALCOs will have responsibility for the same areas with respect to their local legal entity and balance sheet, in line with Group policy. "Liquidity hub" ALCOs will coordinate policy and governance for their defined liquidity region. The policy statement will describe the escalation procedure for liquidity problems from local money market desks upwards to the GALCO level.

Table 12.1 sets out the responsibilities of the GALCO, subsidiary (local entity) ALCOs and liquidity hub ALCOs.

| Roles and responsibilities | |
| --- | --- |
| **Group Asset & Liability Management Committee (GALCO)** | Approving liquidity management framework and liquidity policy for the Group |
| | Overseeing the implementation of balance sheet and liquidity management across the Group |
| | Monitoring and managing liquidity risk against limits set by the regulator and CRO |
| | Setting and reviewing liquidity management targets for each Subsidiary and Liquidity Hub in accordance with Group limits |
| **Subsidiary ALCOs** | Ensure compliance with Group Treasury standards and local regulatory requirements |
| | Oversee local Asset and Liability Management risks, and monitor the liquidity and funding positions in line with Group risk appetite |
| | Act as subject matter experts on local regulations and market developments |
| | Highlight any cross-border constraints and local liquidity needs |
| **Liquidity Hub ALCOs** | Undertake a coordination role between regional legal entity ALCOs |
| | Ensure that Group Treasury policy standards are understood, implemented, and embedded globally and locally |
| | Provide regional summaries to GALCO |

**Table 12.1** Group organisation ALCO roles.

## POLICY ON INTRA-GROUP LENDING

Intra-group lending (IGL) is a significant driver of liquidity risk exposure in a banking group and it is important to address it, at group level, in the liquidity policy statement. IGL policy must adhere to the regulatory requirements of all the jurisdictions that the bank operates in, and in addition to this a bank must ensure that it puts in place adequate risk management processes to monitor IGL activity. Lending that cuts across legal entities within a group usually impacts a bank's IGL limit, although sometimes transactions across jurisdictions or country borders may also impact the IGL limit.

The regulatory environment will differ according to the jurisdiction one operates in. Among the UK FSA's four statutory objectives is consumer protection, which involves securing the appropriate degree of protection for consumers. This influences its approach to monitoring and controlling IGL exposure for UK banks. The FSA is focused on protecting UK depositors' funds and limiting the maximum risk that a bank can enter into. This drives various regulatory requirements, with the main one in relation to IGLs being to limit concentration risk.

Reproduced from *The Principles of Banking* (2012)

This extract from *The Principles of Banking* (2012)

### Liquidity Risk Metrics

### Liquidity Risk Metrics

One of the principles of bank liquidity management we introduced in the last chapter stated that liquidity risk cannot be represented by a single metric, but rather by an array of metrics. This reflects the fact that the business of liquidity risk, like the wider field of asset–liability management, is as much art as science. It is essential that banks use a range of liquidity measures for risk estimation and forecasting, and deploy the widest variety of tools available in order to produce full and accurate MI.

In some instances banks will not have a choice with regard to the liquidity metrics they report. In the wake of the 2008 crisis, national regulators and the BCBS proposed a consistent set of monitoring metrics for all firms. This was so as to assist supervisors across jurisdictions in looking at the liquidity risk in global banks, and to create a common language for MI, reducing the risk of misinterpretation of information by bank boards and regulators. (This also has the added advantage of reducing systems costs in reporting liquidity risk being run by such entities.) Thus banks can only add to the range of metrics they use, because a benchmark minimum is required under Basel III.

The point of calculating and reporting liquidity risk metrics is to enable senior management to have the most accurate, and up-to-date, estimation of the liquidity exposure of the bank at any time. This assists with planning, but more importantly it enables management to structure the bank's balance sheet and funding mix in the way that best meets its risk tolerance. It also provides management with the ability to respond more knowledgeably to market stresses. Finally, regulators oblige banks to report specified liquidity metrics on a regular basis, so the banks have no option but to implement systems that enable the liquidity numbers to be calculated.

In this chapter we detail the range of liquidity metrics that should be employed by all banks, looking beyond simply what is required under regulators' rules, and at a full set of metrics that will provide the best possible liquidity reporting for bank senior management.

## SIX KEY LIQUIDITY METRICS

Liquidity reports help in providing early warning of any likely funding stress points. On their own, the reports enable the Treasury desk to estimate when or if in the future they may encounter some difficulty in rolling over their funding. When combined with the results of liquidity stress tests (see Chapter 14), they provide a reasonable idea of whether the current funding structure of the bank is acceptable. All metrics should be transparent, and ideally disclosed as public information (although often a bank will report them to the regulator, who can release peer group statistics).

We begin with six key baseline liquidity metrics, which all banks irrespective of their size or line of business should calculate and monitor as a matter of course. These are the:

- loan-to-deposit ratio;
- 1-week and 1-month liquidity ratios;
- cumulative liquidity model;

- liquidity risk factor;
- concentration and funding source report;

and one that is relevant to Group entities:

- the inter-entity lending report.

These reports measure different elements of liquidity risk. For consolidated or group entities, reports must be at country level, legal entity level and group level. Taken together, the reports provide detail on:

- the exposure of the bank to funding rollover or "gap" risk;
- the daily funding requirement, and a forecast or estimate of what this is likely to be at a forward date;
- the extent of "self-sufficiency" of a branch or subsidiary.

We examine them each individually.

## Loan-to-Deposit Ratio (LTD)

This is the standard and commonly used metric, typically reported monthly. It is most pertinent to commercial banking entities. It measures the relationship between lending and customer deposits, and is a measure of the self-sustainability of the bank (or the branch or subsidiary). A level above 100% is an early warning sign of excessive asset growth, and of a potentially risky reliance on wholesale funds (which, if they are short-dated, are riskier still). Of course, a level below 70% implies excessive liquidity and implies a potentially inadequate return on funds. Generally, a limit of between 95% and 105% represents business best-practice, but this will vary widely depending on the particular business model and risk-tolerance of the individual bank. All else being equal, a value in excess of 100% is not recommended as a viable, sustainable business model.

The LTD is a good measure of the contribution of customer funding to the bank's overall funding, and as such it is worth monitoring against a specified limit. A number significantly above 100% is an indicator of funding stress for the bank in the event of market instability. However, it is not predictive and does not account for the tenor, concentration and volatility of funds. As such it is insufficient as a liquidity risk measure on its own and must be used in conjunction with other measures.

A related measure is the LTD gap, also known as the Customer Funding Gap, which is the extent to which the bank's total customer lending exceeds total customer deposits. It is used to monitor and control the bank's reliance on wholesale funding markets. A negative number indicates a funding gap; that is, customer deposits are insufficient to fund customer loans and other sources of funding are required. A maximum aggregate actual gap limit should be set to define the level of appetite for the funding gap. A bank can set a quantitative limit for this gap; this is shown at Figure 13.1. The definitions and assumptions are shown at Table 13.1.

## 1-week and 1-month Liquidity Ratios

These are the standard liquidity ratios that are commonly measured against a regulatory limit requirement. An example of a report for a group-type entity comprised of four subsidiaries is shown at Table 13.2.

Liquidity ratios are an essential measure of "gap" risk. They show net cash flows, including the cash effect of liquidating "liquid" securities, as a percentage of liabilities, for a specific maturity "bucket". These are an effective measure of structural liquidity, and help to provide an early warning of likely stress points. A worsening liquidity ratio that is moving closer to an internal or regulatory limit is crucial MI that should drive a change in funding strategy, if not rapid structural changes to the composition of the balance sheet.

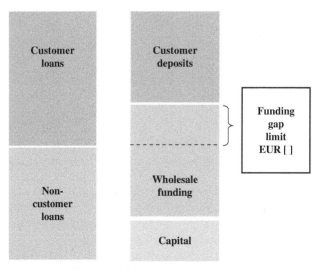

**Figure 13.1**   LTD funding gap limit.

| Metric components | Definition | Measurement |
|---|---|---|
| Customer lending | All loans and advances to retail and corporate customers (excludes reverse repurchase arrangements) | Customer funding gap = |
| Customer deposits | All customer deposits including branch retail deposits and corporate deposits; excludes repurchase agreements | Total customer lending minus Total customer deposits |

**Table 13.1**    LTD gap assumptions and definitions.

| Country | 1-week Gap USD mm | 1-week Liquidity | | | 1-month Liquidity | | |
|---|---|---|---|---|---|---|---|
| | | This week | Limit | Excess | This week | Limit | Excess |
| F | −1586 | −22.83% | −30.00% | | −39.11% | −50% | |
| D | 188 | 15.26% | 0.00% | | 1.62% | −5% | |
| H | 786 | 22.57% | 0.00% | | 19.12% | −5% | |
| G | 550 | 53.27% | 25.00% | | 69.83% | 25.00% | |
| Regional total | −62 | −0.48% | | | −10.64% | | |

**Table 13.2**    Sample liquidity ratio report extract, banking group.

A more detailed liquidity ratio report is shown at Table 13.3. This shows the breakdown of cash inflows and outflows per time bucket, and also the liquidity ratio. The ratio itself is calculated by dividing the selected time bucket liability by the cumulative liability. So in this example the 8-day ratio of 17.3% is given by the fraction [781,065/4,511,294].

The "liquidity gap" is assets minus liabilities in the relevant tenor bucket. The Total Available Funds is the liquidity gap plus marketable securities and CDs, and minus committed facilities that are as yet undrawn. As we note above, the liquidity ratio is the total available funds divided by the total liabilities. Note that it is the liquidity gap element that drives the 30-day ratio much lower than the 8-day ratio.

The full model of the spreadsheet shown at Table 13.3 is provided on the Wiley website (see Chapter 19 for details).

## Cumulative Liquidity Model

This is an extension of the liquidity ratio report and is a forward-looking model of inflows, outflows and available liquidity, accumulated for a 12-month period. It recognises, and helps to predict, liquidity stress points on a cash basis. A report such as this, like the liquidity ratios, will be prepared daily at legal entity level and group level.

Figure 13.2 is an example of a cumulative outflow output graph rising from the cumulative liquidity model. This gives a snapshot view of forward funding stress points.

## Liquidity Risk Factor

The liquidity risk factor (LRF) measure is a static snapshot that shows the aggregate size of the liquidity gap: it compares the average tenor of assets to the average tenor of liabilities. It is also known as the "maturity transformation" value. The ratio may be calculated using years or days as the unit of time, as desired. Table 13.4 is an example of the risk factor for a bank where the unit of measurement is given in days. In this example, (262/19) is 13.79, rounded to 14 in the report.

The higher the LRF, the larger the liquidity gap and hence the greater the liquidity risk that is being run by the bank. On its own, a one-off LRF number is of little value; it is important to observe the trend over time and the change to long-run averages, so as to get early warning of the build-up of a potentially unsustainable funding structure. The limit value, which is subjective and set by ALCO, will differ according to the risk profile and funding structure of the individual bank. Clearly, a bank that wishes to run a more conservative funding profile, or that is concerned about potential future liquidity stresses, will set a lower limit.

The author recommends that the national regulator releases peer-group average and outlier values for the LRF, for banks to compare their statistics to.

**XYZ Bank Liquidity Report 28-Nov-10 (EUR)**

|  | Sight | 2–8 Days | 9 Days–1 Month | 1–3 Months |
|---|---|---|---|---|
| Corporate Current/Call | 24,289 | 0 | 0 | 0 |
| Corporate Time Loan | 28,433 | 14,203 | 151,471 | 106,637 |
| Government Current/Call | 342 | 0 | 0 | 0 |
| Government Time Loan | 250 | 3 | 805 | 63 |
| Inter-bank Current/Call | 41,752 | 0 | 0 | 0 |

**Table 13.3**   Liquidity report and liquidity ratio calculation.

*(continued)*

**XYZ Bank Liquidity Report 28-Nov-10 (EUR)**

| | Sight | 2–8 Days | 9 Days–1 Month | 1–3 Months |
|---|---|---|---|---|
| Inter-bank Time Loan | 339,276 | 201,745 | 6,251 | 31,906 |
| Repos | 0 | 0 | 0 | 47,500 |
| Inter-Group Current/Call | 4,445 | 0 | 0 | 0 |
| Inter-Group Time Loan | 210,177 | 348,414 | 277,964 | 76,268 |
| Marketable Secs & CDs – <1Mth to Maturity | 5,009 | 0 | 55,358 | 0 |
| Retail Current/Call | 8,215 | 0 | 0 | 0 |
| Retail Time Loan | 238 | 41 | 221 | 2,643 |
| Additional Corporate Time Lending | 0 | 8 | 1,313 | 43 |
| Receivables | 0 | 0 | 0 | 0 |
| **Total Assets** | **662,426** | **564,414** | **493,383** | **265,060** |
| Corporate Current/Call | 51,033 | 0 | 0 | 12,758 |
| Corporate Time Deposit | 32,303 | 122,955 | 114,627 | 299,551 |
| Government Current/Call | 1,946 | 0 | 0 | 0 |
| Government Time Deposit | 2,056 | 8,112 | 24,391 | 23,503 |
| Inter-bank Current/Call | 82,087 | 0 | 0 | 0 |
| Inter-bank Time Deposit | 83,898 | 83,684 | 349,461 | 86,979 |
| Repos | 0 | 0 | 0 | 50,000 |
| Inter-Group Current/Call | 47,095 | 0 | 0 | 0 |
| Inter-Group Time Deposit | 302,879 | 418,383 | 629,809 | 225,314 |
| Retail Current/Call | 65,273 | 0 | 0 | 16,318 |
| Retail Time Deposit | 203 | 54,128 | 167,090 | 683,288 |
| Additional Govt/Local Authority Time Deposits | 8,656 | 9,319 | 50,508 | 82,531 |
| Share Capital | 0 | 0 | 0 | 0 |
| Payables | 0 | 0 | 0 | 0 |
| **Total Liabilities** | **677,429** | **696,581** | **1,335,886** | **1,480,242** |
| Ratio Calculation | | | | |
| Marketable Securities | | | | |
| Repos Adj | | | | |
| CDs | | | | |
| Unutilised Commitments | | | | |

**Table 13.3**    (*Continued*)

**XYZ Bank Liquidity Report 28-Nov-10 (EUR)**

| | Sight | 2–8 Days | 9 Days–1 Month | 1–3 Months |
|---|---|---|---|---|
| Liquidity Gap | | | | |
| Total Available Funds | | | | |
| Total Liabilities | | | | |
| **Liquidity Ratio** | | | | |
| Internal Limit | | | | |
| FSA Limit | | | | |
| Stress testing | | | 10% Fall in Marketable Securities | |
| Stress testing | | | 10% Fall in Stickiness | |
| Stress testing | | | Combined Effect of above | |

**XYZ Bank Liquidity Report 28-Nov-10 (EUR)**

| 3–6 Months | 6 Mths to 1 Yr | 1–3 Years | 3–5 Years | +5 Years | Total |
|---|---|---|---|---|---|
| 0 | 0 | 0 | 0 | 0 | **24,289** |
| 98,959 | 47,608 | 357,872 | 573,993 | 642,563 | **2,021,738** |
| 0 | 0 | 0 | 0 | 0 | **342** |
| 3,383 | 2,942 | 12,656 | 7,016 | 76,853 | **103,971** |
| 0 | 0 | 0 | 0 | 0 | **41,752** |
| 18,704 | 28,428 | 11,971 | 0 | 0 | **638,281** |
| 0 | 0 | 0 | 0 | 0 | **47,500** |
| 0 | 0 | 0 | 0 | 0 | **4,445** |
| 13,981 | 30,047 | 156 | 101 | 0 | **957,108** |
| 0 | 0 | 0 | 0 | 0 | **60,367** |
| 0 | 0 | 0 | 0 | 0 | **8,215** |
| 2,427 | 310 | 6,294 | 38,755 | 10,204 | **61,133** |
| 624 | 0 | 21,608 | 7,857 | 75,724 | **107,177** |
| 0 | 0 | 0 | 0 | 0 | **0** |
| **138,078** | **109,335** | **410,557** | **627,722** | **805,344** | **4,076,318** |
| 0 | 0 | 0 | 0 | 0 | **63,791** |
| 28,387 | 928 | 0 | 0 | 0 | **598,751** |
| 0 | 0 | 0 | 0 | 0 | **1,946** |

**Table 13.3**  (*Continued*)

**XYZ Bank Liquidity Report 28-Nov-10 (EUR)**

| 3–6 Months | 6 Mths to 1 Yr | 1–3 Years | 3–5 Years | +5 Years | Total |
|---|---|---|---|---|---|
| 22,687 | 1,200 | 0 | 0 | 0 | **81,949** |
| 0 | 0 | 0 | 0 | 0 | **82,087** |
| 23,967 | 1,205 | 0 | 0 | 0 | **629,194** |
| 0 | 0 | 0 | 0 | 0 | **50,000** |
| 0 | 0 | 0 | 0 | 0 | **47,095** |
| 88,464 | 78,769 | 375 | 0 | 0 | **1,743,993** |
| 0 | 0 | 0 | 0 | 0 | **81,591** |
| 27,925 | 13,273 | 9,224 | 0 | 0 | **955,131** |
| 15,252 | 8,500 | 1,000 | 0 | 0 | **175,766** |
| 0 | 0 | 0 | 0 | 0 | **0** |
| 0 | 0 | 0 | 0 | 0 | **0** |
| **206,682** | **103,875** | **10,599** | **0** | **0** | **4,511,294** |

| Sight | Sight – 8 Days | Sight – 1 M |
|---|---|---|
| 0 | 630,536 | 630,536 |
| 0 | 0 | 0 |
| 0 | 353,219 | 353,219 |
| (55,520) | (55,520) | (55,520) |
| (15,003) | (147,170) | (989,673) |
| (70,523) | 781,065 | (61,438) |
| 4,511,294 | 4,511,294 | 4,511,294 |
| **−1.56%** | **17.31%** | **−1.36%** |
| 45 | 45 | 45 |
| | 3.00% | −3.00% |
| | 0.00% | −5.00% |
| | 15.13% | −3.54% |
| | 17.32% | −2.79% |
| | 15.14% | −4.97% |

*Notes*: THE Sight-8 Day AND THE Sight-30 Day RATIOS ARE SUBJECT TO FSA LIMIT. THE RATIO MUST NOT FALL BELOW THESE LIMITS. THESE REPRESENT 1-WEEK AND 1-MONTH LIQUIDITY LIMITS. MARKETABLE SECURITIES AND CDS ARE PLACED IN A 8-DAY BUCKET WHEN MAKING THE TOTAL AVAILABLE FUNDS CALCULATION.

**Table 13.3**   (*Continued*)

## Concentration Report and Funding Source Report

This report shows the extent of reliance on single sources of funds. An excess concentration to any one lender, sector, or country is an early warning sign

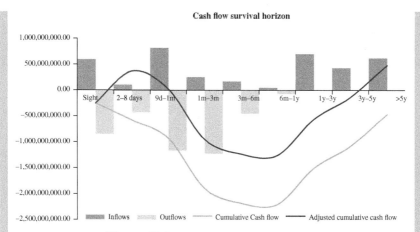

**Figure 13.2**   Cumulative liquidity model.

of potential stress points in the event of a crash. Banks should not become over-reliant on any one source of funds; outside the retail deposit sector they should be wary of excessive reliance on one class of depositor.

An example of a concentration report is shown at Table 13.5. In Table 13.5A, "Customer 1" clearly should be the focus of a potential stress point, and a bank would need to put in a contingency in the event that this source of funds dried up. In Table 13.5B a bank is reporting its largest five depositors by name, again with the purpose of identifying potential future funding risk should one of these customers withdraw some or all of its deposits. In this example, the bank has set a limit of 10% of its aggregate funding base being sourced from one customer (this number is unusually high. Most banks would set a single-customer deposit limit lower than this, at between 2% and 5%); its biggest customer, the "Commercial Bank of Surrey" is well over this limit at 14%. The bank therefore needs to take action to reduce this level or otherwise increase its deposit base at the aggregate level so that this ratio comes down.

A related report is the sector funding source report, an example of which is shown at Table 13.6. This is a summary of the share of funding

| Report date | Average liabilities tenor (days) | Average assets tenor (days) | Maturity transformation effect | Limit | Breach |
|---|---|---|---|---|---|
| 9/30/2010 | 19 | 262 | 14 | 24 | N |

**Table 13.4**   Liquidity risk factor.

| Customer | Deposit amount | Percentage of bank funding | Percentage of group external funding |
|----------|----------------|----------------------------|--------------------------------------|
| Customer 1 | 836,395 | 17.1% | 2.6% |
| Customer 2 | 595,784 | 7.9% | 1.8% |
| Customer 3 | 425,709 | 5.8% | 1.3% |
| Customer 4 | 241,012 | 0.6% | 0.7% |
| Customer 6 | 214,500 | 1.2% | 0.7% |
| Customer 21 | 190,711 | 4.5% | 0.6% |
| Customer 17 | 123,654 | 2.9% | 0.4% |
| Customer 18 | 97,877 | 2.3% | 0.3% |
| Customer 14 | 89,344 | 2.1% | 0.3% |
| Customer 15 | 88,842 | 2.1% | 0.3% |
| Customer 31 | 83,272 | 2.0% | 0.3% |
| Customer 19 | 74,815 | 0.5% | 0.2% |
| Customer 10 | 64,639 | 1.5% | 0.2% |
| Customer 29 | 59,575 | 1.4% | 0.2% |
| Customer 16 | 58,613 | 1.4% | 0.2% |
| Total | 6,562,116 | 53.3% | 20.1% |

**Table 13.5A**    Large depositors as percentage of total funding report.

| Bank top 5 deposit counterparties | Balance (€000,000s) | % Funding | Limit | Breach |
|-----------------------------------|---------------------|-----------|-------|--------|
| Commercial Bank of Surrey | 575 | 14.0% | 10% | Y |
| Central Bank of Mordor | 227 | 5.5% | 10% | N |
| Syldavian Sovereign Wealth Fund | 220 | 5.4% | 10% | N |
| Bordurian Defence Office | 130 | 3.2% | 10% | N |
| Arab Khemed Bank | 105 | 2.6% | 10% | N |
| Total | | **30.7%** | | |

**Table 13.5B**    Largest depositors report.

| Source | Balance (€000,000s) | % Funding | Limit | Within limit (Y/N) |
|---|---|---|---|---|
| Customer – Corporate | 508 | 15.9% | >15% | N |
| Customer – Local Authority | 139 | 4.4% | >10% | Y |
| Customer – Private | 1,198 | 37.4% | >30% | N |
| Institutional – Financial Institutions | 792 | 24.7% | <25% or 1bn | Y |
| Inter-bank | 303 | 9.5% | <25% or 1bn | Y |
| Inter-Group (Net balance) | 249 | 7.8% | <25% or 1bn | Y |
| Other | 15 | 0.5% | <25% or 1bn | Y |
| **Total Liabilities** | **3,204** | **100%** | | |

**Table 13.6**  Sector funding source report.

obtained from all the various different sectors, and is used to flag potential concentration risk by sector.

## Inter-entity Lending Report

This report is relevant for Group and consolidated banking entities. Intragroup lending is common in banking entities, and in some jurisdictions subject to cross-border and cross-legal entity regulatory limits. Hence, this report is a valuable tool used to determine both how reliant a specific

| **Group Treasury** | | | |
|---|---|---|---|
| As at (date) | Total borrowing | Total lending | Net inter-group lending |
| London | 1,713,280 | 883,133 | −830,157 |
| Paris | 3,345,986 | 978,195 | −2,367,617 |
| Frankfurt | 17,026 | 195,096 | 178,089 |
| Dublin | 453,490 | 83,420 | −370,070 |
| Hong Kong | 0 | 162,000 | 162,000 |
| New York | 690,949 | 1,516,251 | 825,302 |

**Table 13.7**  Sample inter-group lending report.

banking subsidiary is on Group funds, and also to what extent it is approaching regulatory limits. An example of a report for a group entity is shown at Table 13.7.

The six reports above represent the primary baseline liquidity metrics. They are the benchmark essential metrics in the measurement of liquidity risk, and the minimum management information that banks and group Treasuries will wish to prepare, both as business best-practice and as part of adherence to regulatory standards.

# TACTICAL LEVEL LIQUIDITY METRICS

We now describe additional liquidity metrics that we recommend banks to adopt.[5]

## Contractual Maturity Mismatch

This is given by assets at their latest possible maturity against liabilities at their earliest possible maturity. It is a measure of the theoretical maximum funding risk, in gap terms, that the bank is running. The objective is to identify the gaps between the contractual inflows and outflows of liquidity for specified time bands. The metric measures contractual cash flow from all on- and off-balance sheet items. Other factors are:

- asset flows should be reported according to their latest possible maturity;
- liability cash flows should be reported according to their earliest possible date of outflow;
- contractual cash flows related to any open-maturity, callable, puttable or extendable issuance should be analysed, based on the earliest possible repayment date;
- instruments that have no specific maturity should be reported separately, with details on the instruments, with no assumptions applied.

This is a straightforward metric to calculate. However, for accurate MI analysis, the contract maturity date of an asset is often longer than its actual maturity date in practice, while the contract maturity of liabilities is for retail products often shorter than its actual maturity in practice. For example, Figure 13.4A shows the maturity profile for retail mortgages. For this reason the liquidity ratio and other metrics use adjusted tenors to consider the amortisation and "stickiness" of assets and liabilities.

---

[5] Thanks to Millie Teasdale at Tonbridge Grammar School for preparing the charts used in this section.

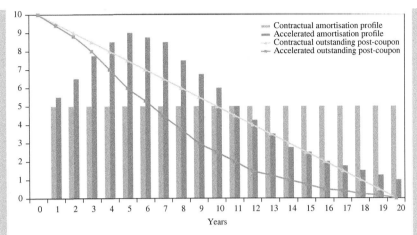

**Figure 13.4A**    Contractual and accelerated amortisation profile, retail mortgages.

Vento and La Ganga (2009) formalise two metrics that are essentially contractual maturity mismatch numbers. The first is the long-term funding ratio (LTFR), which is based on the cash flow profile arising from all on- and off- balance sheet items. It reports the share of assets with a maturity of *n* years or more that is funded through liabilities of the same maturity, given by:

$$LTFR = \frac{\Sigma_i \ out \ flows_i \left( > n \ years \right)}{\Sigma_i \ in \ flows_i \left( > n \ years \right)}$$

It is essentially the long-term contractual funding position and therefore a measure of the bank's structural funding position.

Their second metric is the cash capital position (CCP). This is calculated on the premise that to ensure a long term stable funding outlook, ideally total marketable assets (TLA) should be funded only by total volatile liabilities (TVL), and that otherwise illiquid assets should be funded only by stable liabilities. This mirrors one of the principles of liquidity we noted in Chapter 12.

The CCP approach is illustrated at Figure 13.4B. It is the difference between TLA and the sum of TVL and commitments to lend (CTL), that is,

$$CCP = TLA - TVL - CLT$$

and measures a bank's ability to fund its assets on a collateralised basis. If the result is negative, it shows that illiquid assets are greater than long-term funding and therefore a potentially unstable liquidity arrangement.

The drawback of CCP and LTFR of course is that the exact maturity of both assets and liabilities, when comparing contractual to behavioural

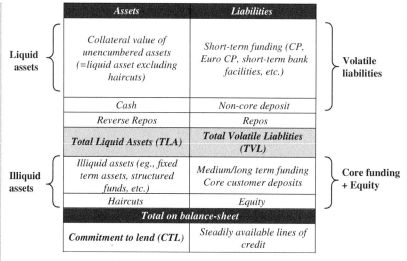

**Figure 13.4B**    The cash capital position
(*Source*: Vento and La Ganga (2009)).

values, may be difficult to estimate. Also, it is a judgement call as to how exactly to define "liquid", unless one takes the conservative view that only risk-free sovereign assets are genuinely liquid in a stressed situation.

## Available Unencumbered Assets

The aggregate marketable assets are acceptable as collateral in secondary markets, and/or eligible for central banks' standing facilities, by currency. The objective of this metric is to provide supervisors with quantitative and qualitative data of the banks' available unencumbered assets, which may potentially be used as collateral to raise additional secured funding in secondary markets, and as such may potentially be additional sources of liquidity. The parameters required for this metric include:

- the amount, type and location of available unencumbered assets that could serve as collateral for secured borrowing in secondary markets;
- the amount, type, and location of available unencumbered assets that are eligible for secured financing with relevant central banks;
- each of the above categorised by currency;
- estimated haircuts that the secondary market and/or relevant central bank would require for each asset;
- expected monetised value of the collateral (rather than the notional amount); where the assets are actually held and what business lines in the bank have access to those assets.

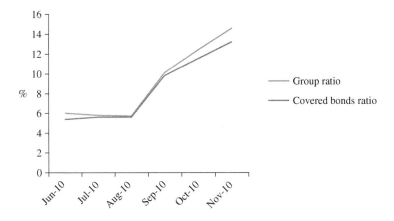

Group ratio:
All encumbered assets / Total funded balance sheet

Covered bonds ratio:
Covered bonds issed / Total assets

**Figure 13.5**     Encumbered asset ratio trend.

Again, this is a straightforward metric that provides excellent transparency for the Board and regulators. The trend of the ratio of encumbered to unencumbered assets is reported as part of the MI metrics in the ALCO pack, with an example shown at Figure 13.5.

## Funding Concentration by Time Bands

This includes the following types of metric:

- Significant counterparties/Bank balance sheet total;
- Significant product or instrument/Bank balance sheet total;
- List of asset and liability balances by significant currency.

These are similar to the concentration and funding source metrics described in our key liquidity metrics section earlier. The second of these is a worthwhile metric to report, because it can highlight potentially risky reliance on one particular type of funding product.

## Market Lock-out Horizon

This metric measures the number of consecutive weekdays the bank can continue to be cash flow positive if there is no access to unsecured funding and no funding rollover is possible. A bank may apply a variety of stress

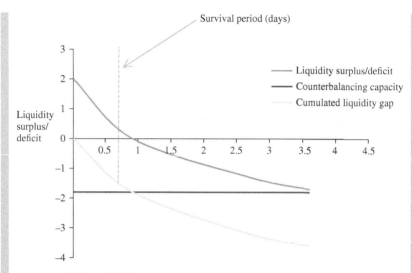

**Figure 13.6** Market lock-out period or "survival period".

scenarios against its cash flows to ensure that it is able to maintain funding in stress scenarios for a minimum period of time. One such stress scenario is a market lockout scenario where the bank has (i) no access to unsecured wholesale markets, and (ii) finds that maturing unsecured wholesale funding cannot be rolled over. In this situation, the bank will need to rely on a portfolio of unencumbered liquid assets to withstand the market lockout. The bank should then define a limit, as a minimum number of days that it can stay funding positive.

Another expression for this metric is the "survival period". It is defined in the same way as the lockout horizon: the time during which the bank is able to meet its liquidity needs without accessing the unsecured funding market. In other words, this indicator represents the "break-even point" between the gap created by the cumulative cash positions and the "counterbalancing capacity" available via the bank's stock of eligible collateral. This is illustrated at Figure 13.6.

Setting a minimum number of days for this period creates another liquidity limit for the bank.

## Cash Outflow Liquidity Reserves: Survival Period

This reports the same metric as the preceding one, but we describe it separately because it is presented in a different format. Table 13.10 shows the values for the current month and the previous month, and note that in this case the bank has set a limit for the absolute dollar size of the outflow, as well as one for the survival period (which is set by the regulator in any case). The report is sent to the regulator every two weeks. In this example, we observe that the bank was within its own absolute limits throughout, but was outside the regulator 2-week limit in the previous month. The report acted as a catalyst for the mitigating action taken.

The trend over time is shown at Figure 13.7.

| | 1/11/2010 | Compliant | 1/10/2010 | Compliant |
|---|---|---|---|---|
| Survival horizon | 23 days versus target of 14 days | Y | 9 days versus target of 14 days | N |
| 2-week outflow metric | −$56 billion versus −$100 billion limit | Y | −$91 billion versus −$100 billion limit | Y |
| 3-month outflow metric | +$41 billion surplus versus target surplus number | Y | +$16 bln versus target surplus number | Y |

*Metric reported twice-monthly to regulator*

**Table 13.10**   Cash flow survival horizon and outflow limit metric.

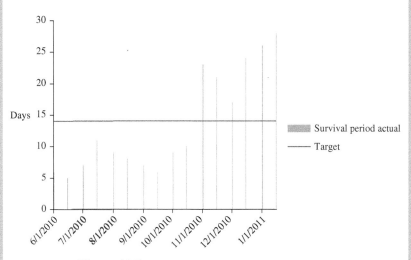

**Figure 13.7**   Trend of cash outflow survival period.

## Undrawn Commitments Report

Undrawn commitments are funds which the bank has committed to make available to customers, but which have not yet been called upon. These include:

- credit card facilities;
- undrawn formal standby lending facilities and credit lines;
- liquidity facilities to customer CP programmes;
- unused overdraft facilities;
- revolving underwriting facilities;
- documentary letters of credit;
- forward asset purchases and forward deposits.

This report measures the aggregate actual level of total undrawn commitments. It is used to control the maximum amount of contractual liquidity outflow possible at a particular point in time if all the bank's customers drew upon the committed facilities that were available to them. To manage this risk a bank should set limits on the maximum cash amount of potential funded draw-downs. The higher this limit number, the larger will be the liquidity exposure for the bank.

The two common risk metrics used to monitor undrawn exposure changes are:

- undrawn commitment/aggregate lending ratio;
- undrawn commitment movements. This number may have an "early warning" limit of (say) 10% or 20% set against it, so that ALCO can monitor increases in the size of commitments.

In an LCR or LAB-related stress test, all undrawn commitments will be assumed to be drawn down and hence viewed as cash outflows. Therefore it is important to monitor this metric closely, as it is a significant driver of the liquidity buffer size.

## Surplus Funding Capacity

This is a measure of the amount of funding capacity that exists after taking into account the headroom required to survive a stress event (whether a firm-specific event and/or market-wide), the extent that existing liabilities and assets will be rolled over, and the amount of new business that will be put on, over a given period of time.

## Aggregate Limit Metrics

Liquidity management procedure will include the setting of actual limits for specific funding types. The level of each limit will be a function of the bank's appetite for funding risk and the structure of its funding base. Limits may be set as per the following:

| | |
|---|---|
| Wholesale funding < 1 year (unsecured wholesale funding) | Max.[ ] bln |
| Liquidity reserves (cash and central bank eligible securities) | Min.[ ] bln |
| Amount of short-term wholesale funding (Total amount of unsecured short-term wholesale funding less than one year) | Max.[ ] bln |

The composition of short-term and long-term wholesale funding is observed over time, to observe the trend and also to use in forecasting, planning and contingency planning. Figures 13.8A and 13.8B are examples of these reports. A bank will also set absolute and relative share limits against each source of funding, which these reports are used to monitor against. Table 13.11 is an example of a further breakdown of the short-term wholesale funding numbers.

For banks that engage in significant cross-border or foreign currency operations, it is important when analysing liquidity metrics not to assume that currencies will remain transferrable in a stress situation, even for currencies which in normal times are highly convertible. The experience of the 1997 Asian currency crisis serves to remind us that individual country jurisdictions may impose restrictions on the convertibility of their currency, or on the outflow of foreign currency deposits. This cross-border risk needs to be monitored against limits.

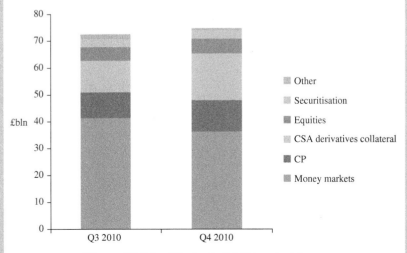

**Figure 13.8A**   Wholesale liabilities: short term.

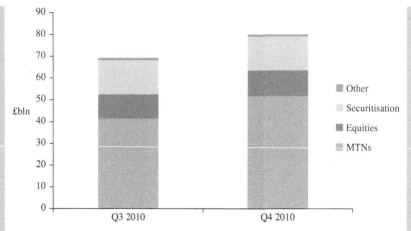

**Figure 13.8B**   Wholesale liabilities: long term.

|  | *Actual* | | | | *Forecast* |
|---|---|---|---|---|---|
|  | **Q1 2010** | **Q2 2010** | **Q3 2010** | **Q4 2010** | **Q1 2011** |
| Bank deposits | 31.8 | 21.7 | 20.6 | 23.1 | 24.5 |
| Debt securities | 48.7 | 51.6 | 51.9 | 51.8 | 50.4 |

**Table 13.11**   Short-term wholesale funding report.

**EXAMPLE 13.2**   SPECIFYING THE LIQUIDITY RISK APPETITE

Table 13.12 is an extract from the liquidity policy statement of a medium-sized UK commercial banking institution. It articulates the liquidity risk appetite that the bank follows. This is an important part of liquidity and ALM risk management: a coherent statement of the bank's risk tolerances, defined as part of an overall ALM strategy framework. From the example illustrated, we observe that apart from the maturity transformation limit, this bank is currently within its board-approved risk tolerances. It also has an objective of reducing the ALM gap to increase its liquidity ratios, but these are to meet internal targets; it is within its regulatory limits for this metric.

| Assumptions | | Actual position |
|---|---|---|
| 1. Funding liabilities | *Total liabilities – Capital (Shareholders equity + Subordinated debt + Reserves) – Other liabilities* | £3,950 mm |
| 2. Customer deposits | *Private customer deposits + Corporate customer deposits + Financial institutions deposits* | £1,905 mm |
| 3. Private customer deposits | Deposits from private customers that behave in line with FSA description of *retail deposits* | £1,235 mm |
| 4. Funding source | Counterparties with similar characteristics, especially a shared trigger that would see this funding evaporate | |
| 5. Liquid currencies | USD, EUR, GBP, JPY, CAD, SEK, NOK, DKK, CHF, AUD, NZD | |

| Limits | Actual position | Target position |
|---|---|---|
| **Liquidity ratio ("maturity mismatch")** | | |
| *Regulatory* | | |
| --- Sight – 8 days > 0.00% | 13.95% | N/A |
| --- Sight – 1 month > –5.00% | 1.66% | N/A |
| *Internal* | | |
| --- Sight – 8 days > 3.00% | 13.95% | 15.00% |
| --- Sight – 1 month > 0.00% | 1.66% | 2.00% |
| **Maturity transformation** | | |
| Average asset tenor < 24 times average liability tenor | Average funding tenor = 39 days | Funding increases to 50 days |
| | Average lending = 1,192 days | Transformation = 24 times |

**Table 13.12** Liquidity risk appetite.

*(continued)*

| Assumptions | | Actual position |
|---|---|---|
| | Maturity transformation = 30 times | |
| **Funding source concentration** | | |
| No individual counterparty > 10% of funding | Largest counterparty = 95% | OK. 10% = £395 mm |
| No source > 25% or £1,000 mm (except private retail) | Largest source = Local authority deposits (£670 m) = 17% | OK. Max = £1,000 mm |
| Customer deposits > 40% of funding | £1,905 m/£3950 = 48% | |
| **FX mismatch** | | |
| No mismatch > 50% of currency volume | | |
| No mismatch > £50 mm per currency | | |
| **Cash buffer** | | |
| Cash buffer minimum 2% of liabilities at all times | £100 mm | OK. 2% = £80 mm |

**Table 13.12**   (*Continued*)

Reproduced from *The Principles of Banking* (2012)

## Example Illustration: A Process to Set Liquidity Risk Limits

We discuss now how liquidity limits and their rationale may be set out in the risk appetite statement. The reporting frequency for all of them should be set to user requirement, typically in a range of daily to monthly depending on the bank business model. (To be clear, the following set of metrics and the associated limits, which are pertinent to the specific bank in question, would be part of the bank's liquidity risk appetite statement.)

1. Loan to Deposit Ratio (LDR):
   - The LDR represents the extent to which customer deposits cover customer lending, so that customer loans are nearly fully funded by customer deposits. The metric also measures the extent of reliance upon wholesale funding;
   - Limit: maximum of 95%, target less than 95%, target 85–90%;
   - Rationale: Target long-term, stable funding.
2. Short-term Wholesale Funding Reliance:
   - It represents wholesale funding which is less than one year;
   - Limits: Short-term Wholesale Funding (less than 3-month tenor) set at maximum of 30% of wholesale funding. In addition, Wholesale Funding (less than 1-year tenor) set at maximum of 30% of wholesale funding;
   - Rationale: Funding sources should be managed to keep reliance on short-term, volatile funding sources to a minimum and encourage long-term, stable funding.
3. Liquidity Reserves:
   - Liquidity reserves capture the amount of liquid assets held in the liquid asset buffer (LAB), now referred to as the high quality liquid asset (HQLA) portfolio, and are available for use in times of funding stress;
   - Limit: LAB minimum 105% of the 90-day stress outflows identified as part of the internal liquidity stress testing regime or at 110% of the LCR metric;
   - Rationale: Hold enough liquid assets to offset 30-day stress outflows as defined in Basel III;
   - Regulatory requirements to hold liquid assets must be observed at all times.
4. Off-balance Sheet Commitments:
   - It refers to the maximum amount of off-balance sheet commitments (undrawn formal standby facilities, credit lines and other commitments to lend). Off-balance sheet Commitments (maximum amount of off-balance sheet commitments; undrawn formal standby facilities, credit lines, etc.) are set at 25% of assets;
   - Limits: to be coordinated with Risk. The percentage limit of assets matters, but the target also max outflows under off-balance sheet activities in the ILAA analysis.
5. Market Lockout:
   - It measures the horizon over which the Bank can survive in a market stress environment without access to the wholesale funding markets;
   - Limit: 120 days minimum (internal limit);
   - Limit: 31 days minimum (regulatory limit) or 91 days under "Pillar 2 liquidity".

6. Funding Concentration:
   ▪ It measures the concentration of deposits, CP, and CD against a single client. Limiting this metric reduces the risk of a single counterparty, or correlated highest volume counterparties;
   ▪ Limit: maximum of 2% liabilities from single counterparty/customer (internal limit);
   ▪ Internal Target less than 1% from single customer;
   ▪ Rationale: A Bank with a sufficiently flexible funding strategy should be able to reduce its liquidity risk by diversifying its liquidity resources.
7. Regulatory Metrics:
   a. Net Stable Funding Ratio:
      This ratio measures the amount of long-term stable funding relative to funded assets and off-balance sheet liquidity exposures. The ratio forms part of the Basel III requirements and is intended to promote longer-term structural funding of the Bank's balance sheet.
   b. Liquidity Coverage Ratio:
      This ratio measures the amount of unencumbered, high-quality liquid assets that can be converted into cash to meet liquidity needs for a 30 calendar day time horizon under a significantly severe liquidity stress scenario. The ratio forms part of the Basel III proposals and is intended to promote short-term resilience of the bank's liquidity risk profile.
   c. Other local regulatory metrics:
      The local regulator may require banks to implement other specific liquidity metrics. For example in the UK the PRA asks that banks adhere to the following reporting:
      ▪ 2-week Wholesale Refinancing;
      ▪ 3-month Liquidity Buffer Surplus;
      ▪ PRA Gap 2 Calendar Days, PRA Gap 2 Weekdays; when applicable.
8. Encumbrance Ratio:
   ▪ This ratio measures the amount of encumbered assets (not available for use in times of a stress) against total assets. The purpose of monitoring is to understand the extent to which the Balance Sheet is encumbered and to understand opportunities for further pledging of assets and to comply with regulatory requirements for covered bond and securitisation programmes;
   ▪ Limit: maximum 15% of balance sheet Bank of England DWF-eligible assets – internal target;
   ▪ The target is less than 15% – this guidance is from the PRA during a conference call;
   ▪ Rationale: Keep assets (marketable and non-marketable) available and ready (pre-positioned) to be used to raise funds in times of stress.

9. Type A : Type B Ratio:
   - This ratio compares the amount of Type A customer deposits ("non-stable" is the Basel III term) to the amount of Type B customer deposits ("stable"). The purpose of monitoring is to ensure that lending is funded through stable customer deposits;
   - Limit: Type A : Type B Liabilities ratio limit 35% – internal.
   - Target Type B no less than 70%, Target 75 % to 80%;
   - Rationale: Target long-term, stable funding.

## Liquidity Cash Inflows and Outflows

All liquidity management applications require a bank to have an understanding of, and to present, both contractual and behavioural tenor profiles and asset–liability gap profiles. The calculation of LCR uses behavioural profiles, while the LAB is also based on behavioural tenors. Finally, the FTP process is applied to behavioural or expected tenors for assets and liabilities.

**Measuring Contractual Maturity Gaps**   A common enquiry from the regulator during the annual liquidity adequacy review is "How does the balance sheet maturity ladder (contractual and behaviouralised) feed into the FTP process?" The two profiles of course are different.

Figure 12.1 shows a contractual ALM gap profile. This is straightforward to calculate. The bank selects the time buckets it wishes to report the balance sheet gap in and places cash flows in the appropriate bucket as at the time of the calculation. The choice of bucket range is user-defined; a common set-up is as follows:

> Overnight (i.e. o/n) to 3-month
> 6-month
> 12-month
> 2-year
> 3-year
> 4-year
> 5-year
> 6-year
> 7-year
> 8-year
> 9-year
> 10-year
> 15-year
> 20-year
> Greater than 20-year.

The behavioural profile will be different. A comparison of the same bank at the same date as shown at Figure 12.1, but where the ALM gap reflects behavioural tenors, is shown at Figure 12.2.

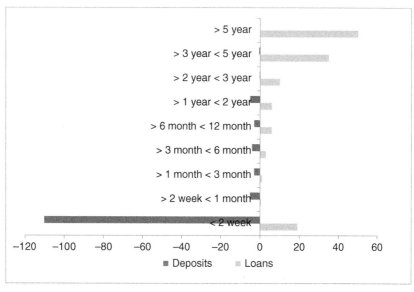

**FIGURE 12.1** Contractual ALM gap

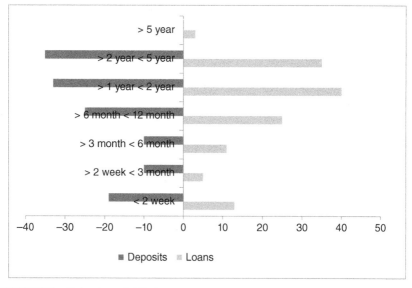

**FIGURE 12.2** Behavioural ALM gap

**Modelling Behaviour of Demand Deposits** Modelling the behavioural tenor of contractually short-dated deposits is generally preferred to be an exercise in observation and statistics. The first principles are as follows:

- Observe month-end spot and average balances over time to build a picture of behavioural tenor, by product type (for example, operational accounts – retail customer and operational accounts – corporate customer). Note that the precise definition of an "operational" account or "money transmission account" (MTA) is not universally agreed. Ultimately the local regulator will opine to the banks it supervises. Essentially, however, a bank can apply its own conservative definition and thereby ensure that it will always be more stringent than the bank's regulator. For most practical purposes a current or "checking" account is an MTA;
- Observe the behaviour at expected outflow points like quarter- and month-ends;
- Observe behaviour at times of stress.

To better understand their liability as well as customer types, banks should also analyse them along other contextual lines, including the following:

1. Are these deposits protected under a government-backed insurance compensation scheme?
2. Are the funds under the actual control of the named depositor?
3. Is there a relationship with the customer that the regulatory authority would recognise (for example, the customer has been with the bank for at least three years, and/or has at least three different products with the bank)?
4. Are deposits sourced via internet access or in-branch?
5. Is the customer retail individual, high net worth individual, small corporate or large corporate (this implies the level of financial sophistication)?
6. Has the deposit come from the customer direct or via another source such as a broker or insurance?

A picture of stable balances over a time period enables the bank to set the appropriate tenor, perhaps with a level of "haircut" (for example, 90% of MTA balances treated as 5-year tenor). This approach satisfies the regulator.

Table 12.1 shows the MTA balances for a UK commercial bank. We only show the extract over two years, in fact this bank had data going back over 20 years and the balances were stable throughout this period (ignoring the steady rise in overall balance over time). Citing stable aggregate balances over say, five years or seven years, is a strong case to treat the funds as possessing this behavioural tenor characteristic.

Table 12.2 is the same bank, this time showing instant access savings deposits.

**TABLE 12.1**  MTA balances observation

## CURRENT ACCOUNTS (MTA)

| | Dec-12 | Jan-13 | Feb-13 | Mar-13 |
|---|---|---|---|---|
| Type | MT | MT | MT | MT |
| SAV | FALSE | FALSE | FALSE | FALSE |
| SAV | FALSE | FALSE | FALSE | FALSE |
| SAV | FALSE | FALSE | FALSE | FALSE |
| SAV | FALSE | FALSE | FALSE | FALSE |
| SAV | FALSE | FALSE | FALSE | FALSE |
| SAV | FALSE | FALSE | FALSE | FALSE |
| SAV | FALSE | FALSE | FALSE | FALSE |
| SAV | FALSE | FALSE | FALSE | FALSE |
| MT | 1,243,753.15 | 2,070,912.09 | 3,583,390.61 | 4,861,114.14 |
| MT | 104,673.30 | 107,598.16 | 193,873.93 | 214,532.62 |
| SAV | FALSE | FALSE | FALSE | FALSE |
| SAV | FALSE | FALSE | FALSE | FALSE |
| SAV | FALSE | FALSE | FALSE | FALSE |
| SAV | - | - | - | - |
| MT | 29,896,369.18 | 28,527,504.79 | 30,527,041.27 | 33,173,736.00 |
| MT | 309,323.48 | 269,960.11 | 315,196.49 | 351,621.12 |
| MT | 105,349,850.19 | 98,667,475.75 | 112,343,134.57 | 125,385,022.88 |
| MT | 16,440,940.24 | 13,899,024.02 | 15,303,602.06 | 15,528,261.05 |
| MT | 3,502,768.24 | 2,969,867.79 | 3,535,211.73 | 4,413,423.93 |
| MT | 59,407,724.76 | 45,909,171.89 | 50,950,954.52 | 55,454,036.76 |
| MT | 3,457,229.71 | 3,113,385.79 | 3,544,889.92 | 3,671,256.53 |
| MT | 48,018,109.73 | 31,701,908.33 | 37,068,297.76 | 43,290,520.44 |
| SAV | FALSE | FALSE | FALSE | FALSE |
| SAV | FALSE | FALSE | FALSE | FALSE |
| SAV | FALSE | FALSE | FALSE | FALSE |

2,020,782,762.68  1,553,868,212.81  1,674,721,972.57  1,812,967,989.07

< *observe over 3, 5 or 10 years.*

What approach should be adopted to set behavioural tenor for Retail Bank liabilities with 1-day contractual tenor such as call accounts and similar demand deposits? The process is essentially a drill-down of the above.

**TABLE 12.2**   Savings deposits balances observation

DEPOSIT/INST ACC SAVINGS

|  | Dec-12 | Jan-13 | Feb-13 | Mar-13 |
|---|---|---|---|---|
| Type | SAV | SAV | SAV | SAV |
| SAV | FALSE | FALSE | FALSE | FALSE |
| SAV | FALSE | FALSE | FALSE | FALSE |
| SAV | FALSE | FALSE | FALSE | FALSE |
| SAV | 1,398,662,962.36 | 1,353,055,834.27 | 1,330,398,863.54 | 1,327,718,097.10 |
| MT | - | - | - | - |
| MT | - | - | - | - |
| MT | - | - | - | - |
| MT | - | - | - | - |
| MT | - | - | - | - |
| MT | - | - | - | - |
| MT | - | - | - | - |
| MT | - | - | - | - |
| SAV | FALSE | FALSE | FALSE | FALSE |
| SAV | FALSE | FALSE | FALSE | FALSE |
| SAV | FALSE | FALSE | FALSE | FALSE |
|  | 5,985,042,938.04 | 5,904,987,542.95 | 5,903,821,549.72 | 5,935,460,144.08 |

1. Group accounts by cohort:
   - By opening date;
   - By product;
   - By customer type.
2. Graph the aggregate balances over time by cohort.

Then, the behavioural tenor is set according to actual observation. This is quite a granular exercise, down to groups of individual account level.

Table 12.3 is a stylised illustration of an extract from such a data mining exercise, while Figure 12.3 is how one might expect the graphical representation to look. We should also note that there are multiple uses for this analysis, for instance:

- FTP;
- Calculating the LCR;
- Determining a LAB that may be above the LCR =100% test;
- Determining a strategic setting for customer pricing.

**TABLE 12.3**  Behavioural tenor via balance observation, by account cohort

Cohort

| | Jan-08 | Feb-08 | Mar-08 | ... | Jan-12 | Feb-12 |
|---|---|---|---|---|---|---|
| Account balances | x | x | x | | x | x |
| | x | x | x | | x | x |
| | x | x | x | | x | x |
| | x | x | x | | x | x |
| | x | x | x | | x | x |
| | x | x | x | | x | x |
| | x | x | x | | x | x |
| | x | x | x | | x | x |
| | x | x | x | | x | x |
| | x | x | x | | x | x |
| | x | x | x | | x | x |
| | x | x | x | | x | x |
| | x | x | x | | x | x |
| | x | x | x | | x | x |
| | x | x | x | | x | x |
| | x | x | x | | x | x |
| | x | x | x | | x | x |
| | x | x | x | | x | |
| | x | x | x | | | |
| | x | x | | | | |
| | x | | | | | |
| | x | | | | | |

**Modelling Prepayment Behaviour**  Asset behavioural profiles, where these fall short of contractual maturity, are obtained by a combination of historical observation and pre-payment assumption. So, for example, historical experience elicits that the average life of a UK variable rate residential mortgage is 6.7 years, so this tenor is set as expected life in many banks for FTP purposes (assuming the customer interest rate is floating-rate).

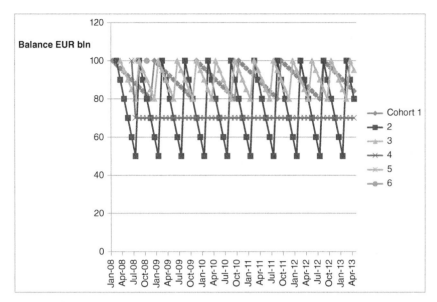

**FIGURE 12.3**   Graphical observation to set tenor

For undrawn facilities or revolving credit facilities, for FTP purposes the best-practice approach is to treat the asset as exhibiting full contractual tenor. This is the correct conservative approach.

Until recently, commitment lines and back-up facilities usually attracted a flat standing charge, say 10bps or 20bps. If the line was drawn, this fee was paid on top of the actual borrowing charge. In other words, the facility tenor was ignored. But post-crash these types of assets are treated as running to full contractual maturity, even if they are undrawn at the time. However, the bank will still wish to perform behavioural analysis of the different types of product offerings.

Figures 12.4 to 12.6 illustrate the utilisation behaviour of committed facilities in general, compared to a vanilla term loan, showing (i) back-up facility; (ii) revolving credit facility; and (iii) term loan respectively.

**Modelling Behaviour of Contingency Funding Obligations**   Contingent, off-balance sheet, and collateral obligations also generate a term funding requirement for a bank. The principle challenge is to understand the tenor characteristics of these cash flows.

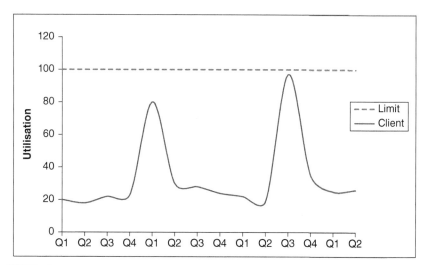

**FIGURE 12.4**   Committed back-up facility usage behaviour

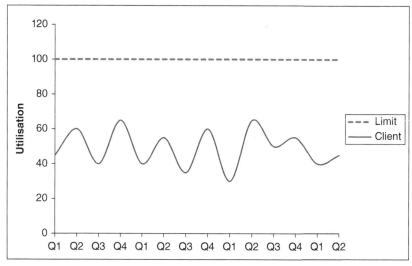

**FIGURE 12.5**   Committed revolving credit facility usage behaviour

For derivatives, the impact of two-way collateralisation requirements under the Credit Support Annexe (CSA) requires one to understand the term funding implications. Inter-bank derivatives trading takes place under the CSA arrangement in the standard International Swaps and Derivatives Association (ISDA) contract. This means that the mark-to-market value of each derivative contract is passed over as collateral, usually in the form of cash.

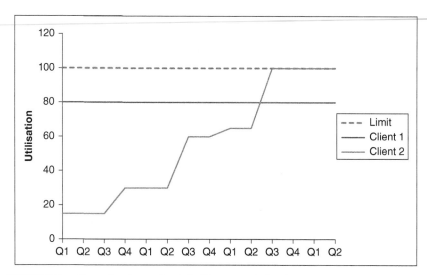

**FIGURE 12.6**  Committed term loan facility usage behaviour

In general, the collateral requirements under a two-way CSA agreement should result in a netted zero cash flow position, because what a bank needs to pass over as collateral on a derivative that is offside, it will receive from the counterparty to the hedge on this derivative. However, a number of counterparties, such as corporates, sovereign authorities, sovereign debt management offices, and central banks, do not sign CSA agreements. This one-way CSA arrangement will create a funding requirement for a bank, as it will have to transfer cash if it is mark-to-market negative, while it will not receive any cash if it is mark-to-market positive.

Therefore, to incorporate the correct discipline with regard to the liquidity effects generated by uncollateralised derivatives business, the bank needs to apply the correct tenor liquidity premium charge. This will apply to the net mark-to-market value of all uncollateralised derivatives on the balance sheet. To do this, the *net* cash flow profile is necessary.

Figure 12.7 is an example of such a profile, time bucketed in the same way as a cash asset or liability.

### Scenario Analysis and Stress Testing

This topic will be covered in greater depth later in this chapter. However, it is introduced here.

Sound business practice dictates that a bank be aware of the behaviour of its assets and liabilities under "business as usual" conditions and under conditions of stress. For the latter to be effective, a bank must review the balance sheet for possible impacts upon it during conditions of stress. This would be

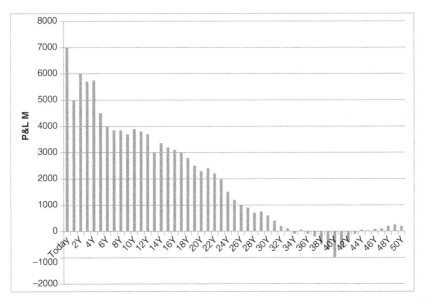

**FIGURE 12.7**   Derivatives portfolio net cash-flow tenor profile

logical management action in its own right; today a bank has no choice in the matter because it is required under international regulatory requirements to undertake such analysis and report the results to the national regulator. In the UK, the regulator required each bank to submit an "Individual Liquidity Adequacy Assessment" (ILAA) which is an internal exercise using the bank's own scenario planning and stressed deposit outflow assumptions. The regulator would then review this and issue its Individual Liquidity Guidance (ILG) which would dictate the size of the bank's LAB. This process is now superseded by the CRDIV/CRR regime in the European Union.

**Importance of Scenario Testing for Understanding Liquidity Risk**   Stress tests are prescribed by the regulator and fall into idiosyncratic (name-specific), market-wide, and combined idiosyncratic and market-wide stresses. Banks are also required to come up with their own scenario analyses and stress event types. It is important for Treasury to formulate some expectation of what the results will look like. For example, all else being equal, an idiosyncratic scenario presents a greater risk to a bank than a combined idiosyncratic and market scenario. In an idiosyncratic scenario, the bank is the focus of market/media attention and will stand out as a bank with particular problems. Customers will withdraw funds to safer havens. There is also the expected impact on wholesale funding. But in a combined scenario, there are market-wide issues to consider as well, so customers would be more cautious about moving funds – the next bank may not be any safer. As an example, in May 2012 Italian banks were downgraded by Moody's, but suffered very little cash outflow as a result, because their relative positions were unchanged.

Therefore, there should be lower cash outflow in such a combined stress scenario. A bank may even benefit as customers spread deposits around. All else being equal, idiosyncratic outflow assumptions should be higher than the combined outflow assumptions, for deposits and undrawn commitments.

The output is essentially assumptions-based. Each product type is assigned a percentage outflow value, which may differ according to scenario. The first step is to classify deposits into "Stable" or "non-Stable" types for Basel III purposes based on the customer type and then classification based on product. Classification of deposits is enhanced by analysing the product types and identifying groups of products whose behaviour is considered to be similar. Banks generally divide deposits into MTA, Interest Bearing (IB), Instant Access accounts, and Term deposits.

MTAs include all current account balances or vostro accounts. These products are used by customers to manage day-to-day cash operations. Generally there is a "customer minimum" balance: what is required to meet daily cash needs, as surplus funds are moved to interest-bearing accounts. These balances are considered "sticky" as the customer cannot move funds without damaging daily operations. Term deposits are those with a fixed term. They may have unbreakable clauses or a 95-day notice clause to withdraw, which would put them outside the LCR denominator scope.

Stressed outflow assumptions are not cast in stone, and continual observation is necessary. Treasury must spread its knowledge of assumptions across the business and ensure this is part of the bank's liabilities strategy, and to do this it will develop granular assumptions by product type and customer type. Basel gives overview guidelines (for example, short-term wholesale deposits are stressed at 100% outflow, whereas, Retail MTA deposits can range in outflow from 2% to 10%) but the final treatment is signed off by the national regulator.

If there is a desire to reduce the LAB number requirement, the bank can target stressed outflow results using some of the following, recognising that some deposits have greater "value" for LCR purposes than others. We discuss in a later section.

The LCR seeks to ensure that banks have sufficient funds to be able to meet "stressed" withdrawals over a 30-day period without recourse to wholesale market funding. The Basel III limit requires that the above result must be greater than 100%. The metric can be managed by (a) increasing the buffer held; and/or (b) by reducing outflows or by doing both. With respect to (b), it becomes important for banks to understand the LCR value of all their deposit types. For example, Retail and SME deposits may make up a majority of the deposit portfolio but generate only a minority of the stressed deposit outflows, while Fixed-term/Notice (greater than 30 days) deposits do not attract any outflows under LCR. Table 12.4 and Table 12.5 show an extract from a UK bank LCR analysis which illustrates this; the top bar chart is the breakdown of liabilities, and the bottom chart is the impact of applying the LCR outflow assumptions to each deposit type. This understanding is very important and needs to be applied to deposits strategy.

The bank may have to deal with differing stressed outflow results between its LCR treatment and its local regulator treatment. Tables 12.5 and 12.6 show the LCR analysis and the UK PRA analysis for the same bank. Clearly the bank needs to be compliant with both requirements.

### Stress Testing in Liquidity Risk Management

A bank's liquidity stress testing regime is a significant element of its overall risk management framework. Under the Basel III regime, a bank is required to undertake such testing in order to demonstrate compliance with the requirements of the national regulatory authority. However, liquidity stress testing should not be seen as a regulatory compliance exercise, but rather the means by which the bank can better understand the liquidity risks faced by the organisation, and the steps that need to be taken in order to minimise and manage these risks. The tests prescribed by the regulator should therefore be seen only as a minimum; in order to acquire as full an understanding of balance sheet cash flow behaviour under stressed circumstances as possible, a bank should devise specific scenarios and "what if" analyses pertinent to its business and operating model. These stress tests should be based on an internal view of the risks faced by the banks and not only those risks prescribed by the regulator.

**TABLE 12.4**  Deposit outflow results, UK commercial bank

|  | Outflow % | Liquidity Value |
|---|---|---|
| Retail | 5%–10% | 90%–95% |
| SME | 5%–10% | 90%–95% |
| MTAs | 25% | 75% |
| Corporate – Non-MTAs | 40% | 60% |
| Banks/FI – Non-MTAs | 10% | 90% |
| Local Authorities | 40% | 60% |
| Fixed Term > 30 days | 0% | 100% |

**TABLE 12.5** LCR report summary

| Depositor Type | Stability | 30-day outflow |
|---|---|---|
| Retail | Stable | 5% |
| Retail | Less Stable | 10% |
| SME | Stable | 5% |
| SME | Less Stable | 10% |
| Non-Financial Corporates | <£85k | 5% |
| Non-Financial Corporates | MTA | 25% |
| Non-Financial Corporates | Non-MTA | 40% |
| Sovs, CBs, PSEs, and MDBs | MTA | 25% |
| Sovs, CBs, PSEs, and MDBs | Non-MTA | 40% |
| Banks & Financial Institutions | MTA | 25% |
| Banks & Financial Institutions | Non-MTA | 100% |
| Fixed Term Depos > 30 Days | | 0% |

**TABLE 12.6** UK PRA ILAA report summary

ILAA Outflows

| Retail/Corporate | Deposit Type | Type A/B | 90-day outflow |
|---|---|---|---|
| Retail | Balance < £85k | B | 4% |
| | Excess balance > £85k | A | 15% |
| Corporate (decision tree applied) | MTA | B | 12% |
| | Bank | A | 50% |
| | Financial Institution | A | 50% |
| | Public Sector | A | 50% |
| | SME | B | 15% |
| | Relationship Account | B | 15% |
| | Other Corporate deposits | A | 50% |

This section will cover aspects of liquidity risk stress testing, including stress testing frameworks and governance.

**Liquidity Stress Testing Policy Approach** Much stress testing involves the undertaking of "scenario analysis". In essence, this involves measuring the impact on the balance sheet of a sudden change in market parameters. For example, the sensitivity of a banking book to a change in interest rates may be given as the change in net interest margin for (say) a 200-basis-point upward parallel shift in interest rates. This type of test helps bank management to position its book in anticipation of rate changes; for instance, a book may be more "liability sensitive" than "asset sensitive", such that a rise in interest rates results in a significant loss of income. Management may then decide to alter the make-up of the book, or perhaps shift to more floating-rate assets, if they expect market rates to rise.

For the Treasury desk, the aim of liquidity stress testing is to determine the impact of a liquidity stress on the bank's funding gap and its ability to survive a specified liquidity stress. Liquidity stress testing can be performed using internally formulated stress tests (that are based on the bank's own liquidity risk appetite) or based on regulatory rules, such as those published by the Basel Committee on Banking Supervision, or a mixture of both. Banks will firstly want to ensure that they hold sufficient liquid resources to meet its internal liquidity risk appetite. However, if regulatory stress tests lead to greater liquidity requirements, then banks will have to increase their liquid resources further in order to ensure regulatory compliance.

Liquidity stress tests are usually conducted to determine the impact of certain events on the bank. Three broad categories are often used to formulate the nature of the event, as outlined in Table 12.7.

A brief description of three regulatory frameworks covered in this chapter is provided in Table 12.8. Further details are provided in the remaining sections.

**TABLE 12.7** Three broad categories used to formulate the nature of certain events in a bank

| Event | Description |
| --- | --- |
| Name-specific | An event occurs that is specific to an individual bank, leading to a liquidity stress. Examples of such events are a large trading loss, operating loss, a loss of senior management capacity, or an event which is damaging to the bank's reputation. |
| Market-wide | A systemic stress event occurs, such as a recession, systemic shock, breakdown in payment system, or a severe dislocation in prices or rates, leading to a liquidity stress being experienced by most banks in the market. |
| Combined | A combination of a market-wide and name-specific stress. |

**TABLE 12.8** Three sample regulatory frameworks

| Regulator | Name of framework | Description |
|---|---|---|
| South African Reserve Bank | BA 300 regulatory return | The regulatory return that South African banks are required to complete on a monthly basis. The return covers the contractual, business as usual, and bank-specific stress mismatch position of the bank, based on assumptions used for internal ALCO processes and approved by the Board. |
| Basel Committee on Banking Supervision | Basel III liquidity risk framework | A global framework for liquidity risk management, phased in from 1 January 2015. The framework consists mainly of two liquidity risk metrics, the Liquidity Coverage Ratio and the Net Stable Funding Ratio. In addition, the framework also outlines public disclosure requirements. |
| Prudential Regulatory Authority | Individual Liquidity Adequacy Assessment (ILAA) | A liquidity risk management framework developed by the Financial Services Authority, the predecessor to the Prudential Regulatory Authority. The framework requires banks to conduct their own internal liquidity stress testing and to report the results to the regulator in the form of a comprehensive report referred to as the "ILAA". The regulator has the ability to increase the liquidity requirements of the bank in areas where the stress testing conducted is felt to be inadequate. This process is usually referred to as Individual Liquidity Guidance (ILG). The ILAA framework introduces the concept of a "survival horizon", being the length of time for which a bank is expected to survive a defined liquidity stress. The liquidity risk appetite of the bank is often defined in terms of its minimum required survival horizon. This assumption is usually approved by the Board, or an appropriate Board risk committee. Three broad categories of stress tests are usually performed, being Name-Specific, Market-Wide, and Combined (as defined in Table 12.7 above). |

Most stress testing frameworks aim to segment the balance sheet (and in particular the liability side of the balance sheet, where the most liquidity risk resides) into components that are likely to exhibit different levels of liquidity risk. For instance, deposits received from retail customers might be deemed less likely to flow out during a liquidity stress than those provided by a large institutional investor.

For it to be a value-adding function, stress testing must feed through to the general risk management process. That is, the results of stress testing need to be considered continuously by senior management, and changes made to strategy and, if possible, the balance sheet if the results suggest an unacceptable vulnerability to changes in certain market parameters. Changes to the shape and size of a balance sheet take time, which is why frequent reviews of stress test results are necessary. Once a decision has been taken to, for instance, withdraw from a business sector or reduce exposure to it, the stress testing needs to continue to see if the sensitivity of the balance sheet has been reduced. If not, further action may need to be taken.

Best-practice is for banks to know on a daily basis what their liquidity risk position is under a specified set of liquidity stress tests. Regulators typically request that banks report their liquidity position on a monthly basis but usually also want comfort that banks meet the regulatory requirements throughout the month and that "window dressing" was not applied at the end of the month to appear liquid.

**Governance Aspects Relating to Liquidity Stress Testing**  A bank should formalise its liquidity stress testing framework (including regulatory compliance aspects) and scenario analysis in a formal policy document, which is approved by a senior committee of the bank, typically the ALCO. A template suitable for application at a medium-sized commercial bank is supplied on the companion's website to the core reference text. The policy sets out the framework within which stress testing and scenario analysis are conducted. It formalises the function and the responsibilities, as well as the reporting line for escalation of results.

An extract from such a policy document is shown in Chapter 11 of *The Principles of Banking*.

The purpose of such a stress test is to assess the bank's likelihood of surviving for a minimum amount of time as a going concern in the event of a name-specific event (such as a large operational or a credit loss), a market-wide event (such as a severe economic downturn), or a combined event (which combines a name-specific event with a market-wide event). The required survival horizon usually varies between 30 days and 3 months.

The objective of the test is to determine the impact of the downturn on three aspects of the bank's performance:

- The profit and loss position;
- The regulatory capital position;
- The liquidity position.

If the results of the report suggest it, action can be taken to alter the profile and sensitivity of the balance sheet to mitigate the impact of any crash. This may take the form of raising additional capital and/or contingency funding arrangements, or hedging to reduce asset exposure.

**Stress Test Reports**    Stress test output results should help senior management to understand the liquidity position of the bank, enabling them to take mitigating action if deemed necessary.

The primary stress test output is the cash flow survival report. This report shows the period (usually measured in days) for which a bank is expected to survive a defined liquidity stress event, the most severe form of which is a market "lock-out", that is no access to any external funding of any sort. Alternatively, the survival period can be specified and the information can then be summarised in a ratio. The next section looks at the Basel III Liquidity Coverage Ratio.

In Figures 12.8 and 12.9, examples of reports under BAU conditions and one after the mitigating actions have been taken, are illustrated (such as liquidating securities, and accessing contingency funding sources) respectively.

Figure 12.9 shows the stressed cumulative cash flow forecast taking into account the immediate sale or repo of securities from the liquid asset buffer. In this example, the survival period has been extended from 49 days to 93 days after taking into account the impact of the stress.

The assumptions used to produce the stress test results outlined above will have to be clearly articulated, and will have to be approved by a senior committee in the bank, possibly the ALCO or in certain cases even a Board risk committee.

A line-by-line stress test result report should be produced on a monthly basis, or as required by the regulator. It would show the results of individual shocks on the liquidity ratio, and the probability of each result occurring. Assigning probabilities to liquidity stress events is a very challenging task and it is not possible to do this with a high level of accuracy. However, best-practice is for banks to assign an approximate likelihood to the occurrence of the event, often based on past events that have occurred, combined with management judgement.

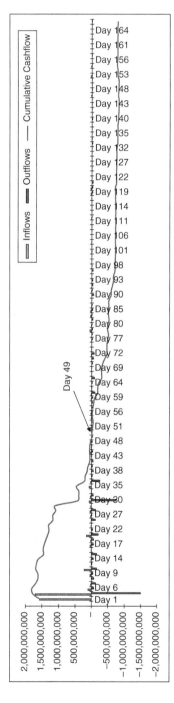

**FIGURE 12.8** Stress test results: cash-flow survival horizon

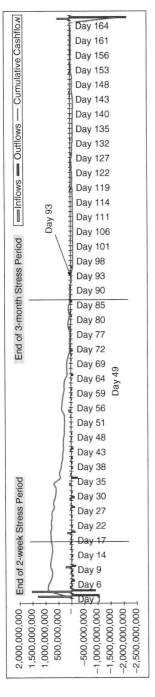

**FIGURE 12.9** Stress test results, after mitigating actions

The report should be comprehensive and cover all sources and uses of liquidity during the stress. Examples are provided below:

- Reduction in liquid assets as a result of the stress, including the impact of increased "haircuts";
- Decrease in liabilities, split by key liability segment (for example, Retail, Small Business, Corporate, Institutional);
- The liquidity impact of forex (FX) mismatches (for example, where the bank has sufficient liquidity in a certain currency, but liability outflows are occurring in a different currency);
- Outflows due to off-balance sheet exposures, such as guarantees, letters of credit, and other facilities provided to clients.

This report would be produced as part of the routine stress testing, undertaken by Treasury or in some instances the CRO's department.

### Implementing Basel III Liquidity Risk Metrics

During the early "liquidity phase" of the financial crisis that began in 2007, many banks – despite adequate capital levels – still experienced difficulties because they had not been managing their liquidity and funding positions in a prudent manner. The crisis drove home the importance of liquidity to the proper functioning of financial markets and the banking sector. Prior to the crisis, asset markets were buoyant and funding was readily available at low cost. The rapid reversal in market conditions illustrated how quickly liquidity can evaporate, and that illiquidity can last for an extended period of time. The banking system came under severe stress, which necessitated central bank action to support both the functioning of money markets and, in some cases, individual institutions.

The difficulties experienced by some banks were due to lapses in the basic principles of liquidity risk management. In response, as the foundation of its liquidity framework, the Committee in 2008 published Principles for Sound Liquidity Risk Management and Supervision.

To complement these principles, the Basel Committee on Banking Supervision (BCBS) introduced two minimum standards for liquidity as summarised in Table 12.9.

The Basel III liquidity framework also contains guidelines regarding liquidity risk monitoring tools and disclosure requirements.

**Liquidity Coverage Ratio (LCR)**    The Basel III short-term liquidity metric is the Liquidity Coverage Ratio (LCR). The calculation of this involves assumptions of the behaviour of liabilities, both customer and wholesale, under both normal and stressed environments. In this section, we consider the issue of stressed behaviours and how a bank should incorporate its LCR results into its liabilities strategy.

**TABLE 12.9** Two minimum standards for liquidity

| Risk metric | Purpose of metric | Timeframe for compliance |
|---|---|---|
| Liquidity Coverage Ratio | To promote short-term resilience of a bank's liquidity risk profile by ensuring it has sufficient high-quality liquid assets to survive a significant stress scenario lasting for one month. | 60% LCR required by 1 January 2015, increasing to 100% by 1 January 2019. |
| Net Stable Funding Ratio | To promote resilience over a longer time horizon (one year) by creating additional incentives for banks to fund their activities with more stable sources of funding on an ongoing basis. | Based on current guidance, compliance is required by 1 January 2018. |

The LCR metric is given by:

$$\frac{\text{Stock of high-quality liquid assets}}{\text{Total net cash outflows over the next 30 calendar days}} > 100\% \quad (12.1)$$

The scenario for this standard entails a combined idiosyncratic and market-wide shock that would result in:

- The run-off of a proportion of retail deposits;
- A partial loss of unsecured wholesale funding capacity;
- A partial loss of secured, short-term financing with certain collateral and counterparties;
- Additional contractual outflows that would arise from a downgrade in the bank's public credit rating by up to and including three notches, including collateral posting requirements;
- Increases in market volatilities which impact the quality of collateral or potential future exposure of derivative positions and thus require larger collateral haircuts or additional collateral, or lead to other liquidity needs;
- Unscheduled draws on committed but unused credit and liquidity facilities that the bank has provided to its clients; and
- The potential need for the bank to buy back debt or honour non-contractual obligations in the interest of mitigating reputational risk.

The LCR also allows for a defined set of inflows that the bank is expected to receive during a liquidity stress. The framework has been developed to allow only for inflows that can be expected to be received during a liquidity stress with a high level of certainty. The inflows that can be allowed for in the calculation are capped at 75% of the cash outflows.

The LCR does not only consider on-balance-sheet items, but also liquidity flows that might occur due to off-balance sheet commitments that the bank has made. For example, if clients have unutilised facilities with the bank that may be drawn at short notice, then the framework allows for cash outflows arising from these facilities during a liquidity stress.

In essence, LCR is a regulatory-defined stress scenario, in that regulators define assumptions on the rate of fund withdrawals, for example, Basel III assigns pre-determined weights which reflect assumed behavioural outflow/inflow rates. However, there is scope for nuancing this for specific product and customer types in liaison with the national regulatory authorities. The concept is illustrated at Figure 12.10.

The LCR calculation is simple, but understanding the requirements and the impacts requires focus on the assumptions being applied per asset and liability type and counterparty type, as well as:

- Type of counterparty to which the facility is provided;
- Type of deposit product provided;
- Understanding what constitutes an "operational deposit".

A bank needs to have in place a database that calculates the LCR requirement by:

- Exposure (in particular the exposures with 30 days or less to maturity);
- Transaction;
- Account;
- Customer type;

and which generates a bottom-up LCR calculation that can be aggregated by customer or business line, and segmented as required by the Basel III LCR requirements into Retail, SME, public sector, and so on. This is essential to understanding how the liabilities mix should be framed.

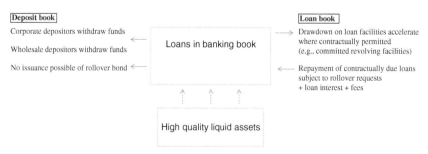

**FIGURE 12.10**   LCR coverage

**High Quality Liquid Assets (HQLA)**   For the purpose of the calculation of the LCR, high quality liquid assets are defined as assets that can be converted with ease and immediacy into cash to meet the liquidity needs of the bank. These assets need to be unencumbered and have the following fundamental characteristics:

- Low risk;
- Be easy to value and with a high level of certainty regarding the valuation;
- Have a low correlation with risky assets;
- Be listed on a developed and recognised exchange.

HQLA are further divided into "Level 1" and "Level 2" HQLA, depending on characteristics such as whether they were issued by a sovereign or not, and what their risk ratings are under the Basel II Standardised Approach for credit risk. Only 40% of the total stock is allowed to be represented by "Level 2" HQLA.

**Sample Stressed Outflow Report**   The initial assessment will involve applying the BIS guidelines on expected outflow in stress. An example of such an output is given at Table 12.10.

Table 12.10 demonstrates some of the more obvious treatments under the Basel regime. For example, deposits from financial institutions (FI) with less than 30 days to maturity, both in respect of banks and non-banks, are assumed to flow completely in the first 30 days of a stressed environment. Deposits from small corporates (and the Basel Committee has published a definition of what constitutes an "SME" corporate, which is reproduced in the second edition of

**TABLE 12.10**   Example LCR denominator calculation

| Deposits Classification | Corporate Bank | Retail Bank | LCR Weight | Buffer |
|---|---|---|---|---|
| Deposits over 30 days | 5.4 | 3.3 | 0% | 0.0 |
| Deposits under 30 days: | | | | |
| SME – covered by deposits insurance scheme | 0.2 | 5.4 | 5% | 0.3 |
| SME – not covered by deposit insurance scheme | 7.1 | 35.9 | 10% | 4.4 |
| Corporates – operational deposits | 9.1 | 1.2 | 25% | 2.6 |
| Financial customer – operational deposits | 3.3 | 1.6 | 25% | 1.3 |
| Corporates – non-operational | 9.5 | 2.4 | 75% | 9.2 |
| Financial customer – non-operational | 11.2 | 2.7 | 100% | 13.9 |
| | 45.8 | 52.5 | | 31.7 |

the core text) are assigned much lower outflow assumptions, in this case 5% or 10%. Retail customer "operational" deposits (such as current accounts or checking accounts) are assigned lower weights still, often 2% to 4%.

Table 12.11 provides a definition of "operational" and "non-operational" deposits. As operational deposits receive a more favourable treatment, the criteria for being operational are more stringent.

A further distinction that is made by the LCR is between "stable" and "less stable" deposits provided by retail and small business customers as summarised in Table 12.12.

**Example Outflow Assumptions**    As an example from the UK prior to the full implementation of Basel III/CRDIV, when the previous "ILAA" regime was in place, Table 12.13 shows the detailed breakdown by product and customer type for a medium-sized European commercial bank at the 2-week

**TABLE 12.11**    Operational and non-operational deposits

| Deposit type | Definition |
| --- | --- |
| Operational deposits | Deposits where the client has a substantive dependency on the bank for activities such as clearing, custody, and cash management. The customer needs to be reliant on the bank to perform these clearing, custody, or cash management services in order to fulfil its normal banking activities over the next 30 days, and the services must be provided under a legally binding agreement. The client must not be able to terminate the services with fewer than 30 days' notice. |
| Non-operational deposits | Deposits that do not meet the criteria for being "operational". |

**TABLE 12.12**    Stable and less stable deposits

| Deposit type | Definition |
| --- | --- |
| Stable deposits (5% run-off factor) | Deposits which are fully covered by a deposit insurance scheme or by a public guarantee where the depositors have other relationships with the bank which makes withdrawal unlikely, and where the deposits are in transactional accounts. |
| Stable deposits (3% run-off factor) | In addition to the above criteria, the deposit insurance scheme is based on a system of prefunding via the periodic collection of levies from banks with insured deposits, and the scheme has adequate means of ensuring ready access to funds where required. |
| Less stable deposits (10% run-off factor) | All those deposits from retail and small business investors that are not covered by a deposit insurance scheme. |

**TABLE 12.13** Deposit outflow assumptions, extract of product and customer breakdown for a UK bank

| Business Line | Customer Type | Product | Idiosyncratic | | Market | | Combined | |
|---|---|---|---|---|---|---|---|---|
| | | | 2-week | 3-month | 2-week | 3-month | 2-week | 3-month |
| Corporate | 45 - UK Credit Institutions | IBs (non-MTA) | 40.0% | 50.0% | 20.0% | 25.0% | 30.0% | 35.0% |
| Corporate | 45 - UK Credit Institutions | MTA | 10.0% | 12.0% | 5.0% | 8.0% | 8.0% | 10.0% |
| Corporate | 49 - Non-financial large enterprises – Type A | MTA | 10.0% | 12.0% | 5.0% | 8.0% | 8.0% | 10.0% |
| Corporate | 49 - Non-financial large enterprises – Type A | Time deposits % of deposits broken | 30.0% | 60.0% | 15.0% | 40.0% | 20.0% | 50.0% |
| Corporate | 53 - SME deposits | 95-day notice | 0.8% | 2.5% | 0.4% | 1.8% | 0.6% | 2.2% |
| Corporate | 53 - SME deposits | IBs (non-MTA) | 12.0% | 15.0% | 8.0% | 10.0% | 10.0% | 12.0% |
| Corporate | 54 - Retail – Type A | 95-day notice | 0.8% | 2.5% | 0.4% | 1.8% | 0.6% | 2.2% |
| Corporate | 54 - Retail – Type A | IBs (non-MTA) | 12.0% | 15.0% | 8.0% | 10.0% | 10.0% | 12.0% |
| Corporate | 54 - Retail – Type A | MTA | 10.0% | 12.0% | 5.0% | 8.0% | 8.0% | 10.0% |
| Corporate | 54 - Retail – Type A | Time deposits % of deposits broken | 10.0% | 35.0% | 5.0% | 25.0% | 8.0% | 30.0% |
| Corporate | 54 - Retail – Type A | Fixed Rate Deposits % of deposits broken | 1.0% | 6.0% | 1.0% | 6.0% | 1.0% | 6.0% |
| Corporate | 55 - Retail – Type B | MTA | 10.0% | 12.0% | 5.0% | 8.0% | 8.0% | 10.0% |
| Corporate | 55 - Retail – Type B | Time deposits % of deposits broken | 10.0% | 35.0% | 5.0% | 25.0% | 8.0% | 30.0% |

*(continued)*

**TABLE 12.13**  (*Continued*)

| Business Line | Customer Type | Product | Current ILAA assumptions | | | | | |
|---|---|---|---|---|---|---|---|---|
| | | | Idiosyncratic | | Market | | Combined | |
| | | | 2-week | 3-month | 2-week | 3-month | 2-week | 3-month |
| Corporate | 55 - Retail – Type B | Fixed Rate Deposits % of deposits broken | 1.0% | 6.0% | 1.0% | 6.0% | 1.0% | 6.0% |
| Corporate | 55 - Retail deposits – Type B | 95-day notice | 0.8% | 2.5% | 0.4% | 1.8% | 0.6% | 2.2% |
| Retail | 52 - Non-financial large enterprises – Type B | Non-financial large enterprises – Type B | 25.0% | 25.0% | 25.0% | 25.0% | 25.0% | 25.0% |
| Retail | 53 - SME deposits | Wholesale Funding Type B | 22.5% | 22.5% | 22.5% | 22.5% | 22.5% | 22.5% |
| Retail | 54 - Retail deposits – Type A | Retail Funding Type A | 15.8% | 15.3% | 11.4% | 10.2% | 12.5% | 11.6% |
| Retail | 55 - Retail deposits – Type B | Retail Funding Type B | 0.2% | 4.2% | 0.3% | 3.0% | 0.3% | 3.3% |
| Retail | 66 - Overdraft and credit card facilities provided | Cards | 0.3% | 2% | 0.3% | 2.0% | 0.3% | 2.0% |
| Retail | 66 - Overdraft and credit card facilities provided | Overdrafts | 0.3% | 2% | 0.3% | 2.0% | 0.3% | 2.0% |
| Retail | 66 - Overdraft and credit card facilities provided | Committed loan facilities | 0.3% | 2% | 0.3% | 2.0% | 0.3% | 2.0% |

and 3-month stressed outflow tenors. (Under Pillar 2 liquidity requirements, banks would still need to assess and report the beyond the 30-day metric required by the LCR, so the analysis is still required!) This is very detailed, and in some cases unnecessary. Note that, however, the range from stable to non-stable across the different product and customer types.

An alternative approach is to apply a blanket but conservative estimate – the author applied 15% once – for customer deposits that are non-FI, and in most cases this will be more than acceptable to the regulator. This avoids the over-engineering that may sometimes arise with tinkering between 2%, 4%, 10%, 15%, and 20%, and all points in between for every different type of product and counterparty. An over-engineered approach leads to excessive bureaucracy and process which it is always best to try to avoid.

## Example LCR Calculation

A European commercial bank of approximately GBP25bn of assets reported this LCR value in 2014, with an estimate (following implementation of a deposits raising strategy) for 2015 (see Table 12.14).

The breakdown of how each type of liability led to the LCR denominator value and what this means for the bank's liquid asset buffer (or High Quality Liquid Assets portfolio, as described for the LCR metric) is shown at Figure 12.11. In this figure, "LAB" refers to the liquid asset buffer, and "MTAs" to money transmission accounts.

The following are apparent conclusions from the analysis above:

- Retail deposits are LCR efficient. The £10.8 of deposits form 43% of the bank's deposits, but due to the lower outflows expected retail outflows are only 15% of the LCR Buffer required.
- SMEs are another type of deposits which are LCR efficient as SME deposits at 2015 are expected to form ˜17% of the overall deposit base, however, the outflow requirements for SME deposits are only 5% of the overall LCR outflows.
- MTAs are relatively neutral to buffer requirements as those deposits form 10% of the bank's overall 2015 deposit base, and are judged to be 11% of the outflow buffer requirements.

**TABLE 12.14**   LCR calculation for a European commercial bank

|                  | Dec13 Proxy[1] | Dec15 Forecast |
|------------------|----------------|----------------|
| HQLA (£'bn)      | 4.0            | 6.0            |
| Outflows (£'bn)  | 5.5            | 6.0            |
| LCR (£'bn)       | 73%            | 100%           |

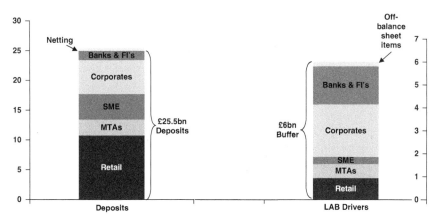

**FIGURE 12.11**    Bank LCR calculation and HQLA result

- The deposits which carry the highest outflows risk are large corporates, banks, and financial institutions. Corporate deposits are estimated to be at 22% for 2015, with the LCR outflows for those deposits forming 38% of the overall buffer.
- Banks and financial institutions are forecast to be only 6% of the overall deposits base, however, they impact 27% of the overall LCR outflows.

A bank should use its LCR analysis to inform its deposit strategy and also as input towards estimating its optimum liabilities mix.

**Factors Which Determine the Liquidity Value of Deposits**    A bank should be aware of the regulatory liquidity value of its deposits base. The liquidity value of a deposit determines the amount of liquid asset buffer (LAB, or HQLA) which must be held to withstand a liquidity stress event. The following factors are relevant in assigning liquidity value to a deposit:

1. Counterparty Type:
   Retail customers are often considered to be "stickier" than large corporate customers. This is based on the thinking that retail customers tend to have smaller amounts deposited with banks, but with banks having more retail depositors than large corporate depositors. As a result, the risk of funds being withdrawn is spread across a larger number of smaller depositors. Furthermore, retail depositors are often less financially astute than corporates, which often have their own Treasury functions responsible for the management of their deposits with banks. Corporate clients are also more likely to have a second bank account at a different bank into which the funds could be transferred during times of a liquidity stress.

Financial institutions and public sector customers are considered to be less sticky than other corporates. This is because these institutions are deemed more financially astute than other corporates, and more likely to have Treasury functions that manage their funds. Their deposits are also likely to be concentrated in a smaller number of larger deposits.

2. Deposit Type:
   Money Transmission Accounts (MTAs) are considered to be "stickier" as there is a lead time to setting up such an account and hence a customer would find it difficult to transfer such an account within the stress timescale.

3. Counterparty Relationship:
   Customers who have an established relationship with the bank are deemed to be "stickier", taking into consideration length of relationship and number of products held.

4. Maturity:
   For corporate deposits with a residual maturity which falls outside the stress period, a breakage rate is assumed, thereby implying that these customers would be reluctant to withdraw their funds before contractual maturity, due to the financial loss they may suffer when doing so. This can result in "Cliff Risk" when the residual maturity comes within the 1-month period that is used for the LCR. Cliff Risk refers to the risk that a large outflow is experienced due to a large term deposit reaching maturity, or due to a number of large deposits reaching maturity in the same month. In these cases, the bank experiences a higher re-financing requirement, potentially leaving it with no choice but to pay a higher rate to obtain funding, or having to borrow from the central bank.

Once these characteristics are understood, a bank is in a better position to frame its liabilities mix and medium-term strategy. There is also a business model issue. A bank that offers, or wishes to offer, a "full service" commercial banking operation must accept that certain of its customers – such as non-bank financial institutions and large corporates – will be placing deposits that have lower value as stable funding, and so will drive a higher HQLA and also impact the net stable funding ratio (NSFR) metric. It must accept this as the cost of providing a full service. The alternative is to offer a reduced service and target only specific customer types.

## LCR and Liabilities Strategy

If a bank has a desire to either improve its LCR metric (primarily, but not necessarily always, because the number is below the required 100% or far above it) then it would, in the first instance, address either or both of the numerator or the denominator. Addressing the numerator is a straightforward exercise requiring no particular additional analysis: simply increase the size of the HQLA. The HQLA itself needs to be funded with long-term liabilities, so increasing the size of the portfolio may also require raising additional customer and/or wholesale term liabilities.

Whereas in more developed economies, raising the size of HQLA is a relatively straightforward exercise, the situation in an emerging market economy such as South Africa is more challenging. There is a limited supply of HQLA in the South African market, with government paper (Treasury bills and government bonds) being the only allowable "Level 1" asset available to banks. As these instruments are only issued in limited quantities by National Treasury, it is generally felt that the South African economy will not have sufficient HQLA to enable South African banks to comply with the requirements of the LCR.

When BCBS drafted the requirements for the LCR, they made available an option for jurisdictions with insufficient liquid assets. Under this option, the local regulator has the ability to make available a "Committed Liquidity Facility" to banks which can be used as a further source of liquidity during a liquidity stress. The facility has to be made available to banks for a fee, and as part of the facility, banks need to pledge appropriate assets as collateral to the central bank. The SARB has made such a committed liquidity facility available in South Africa, under which banks can pledge assets such as their mortgage portfolios as security.

That said, there is nothing which insists an HQLA be comprised of bonds or other financial instruments. One could simply hold it as cash. A shortage of assets does not mean it is difficult to increase the size of the HQLA. One could simply place it as cash at the central bank. That a bank would prefer to have a stand-by liquidity line at the central bank is just a profit-and-loss (P&L) consideration.

Addressing the LCR denominator is not necessarily a trivial task. In fact, what a bank that wishes to raise additional liabilities must do is target an optimal liabilities profile and mix, and implement a strategy which results in a robust and sustainable funding profile that, at the same time, helps deliver a strong LCR value.

If there is desire to reduce the HQLA number requirement, a bank would generally target the Net Cash Outflow results to identify areas where this number could be reduced. Its liabilities strategy will therefore address measures needed to reduce the ILAAP, for example:

- Greater targeting towards longer-term fixed deposits, which fall outside a 30-day maturity bucket for the purpose of the LCR;
- Greater focus on SME/Operational/Stable deposit customers;

- Introduction of unbreakable fixed-term deposits that reduce risk of out-flow in stress;
- Reducing undrawn commitment levels;
- Pricing for liquidity risk to, for example, encourage customers to invest in longer-term products, and deter customers from holding borrowing limits that (a) they don't use, and/or (b) are higher than their borrowing requirements.

This list is not exhaustive and, of course, in some cases may not simply apply. However, it gives a flavour of expected action. Additional potential strategic initiatives in detail may include the following:

- Margin improvement: fixed-term deposits are re-priced where possible, to reduce costs, and/or volumes; accounts with bonus rates could be added: introduce a bonus cap to reduce leakage; and move out of nego-tiated rate accounts to managed rate products;
- Customer optimisation: target a specific sector, for example, universi-ties, trade unions with a package to attract stable deposits from growing customer sectors; and also target online accounts that are set at only 10% outflow in stress;
- Longer-term account initiatives: base-rate strategy and widen margins; type A/B deposits strategy: manage book-to-price customers according to cost and not solely value; standalone customers: minimise number of "rate chaser" customers that have been acquired during periods of aggressive balance sheet growth, that generate no income; introduce 91-day or 95-day notice accounts to generate more ILAAP (and LCR) friendly liabilities; remove 7-day or 14-day or 30-day notice accounts which are not ILAA friendly to focus on 31-day, 60-day, or 95-day accounts; introduce a clause in fixed-rate fixed-term deposits which states that a customer will not get funds for 95 days on breakage.

Again, this is a sample list only.

**Deposits Analysis Template**　A bank, as any institution in a competitive industry, does not operate in isolation. When assessing the LCR value of customer deposits, it is important to include a competitor watch in the reg-ular deposits analysis that is carried out on a weekly or fortnightly basis by the products committees.

The standard deposits analysis template would include an executive summary which features at least the following:

- Year-end and next-year deposits forecast;
- Articulation of the high-level deposits strategy, for example, "2015 strategy is to retain current balances and enhance the value of those

retained balances for NIM" or "Medium-term strategy is to grow the deposit book by £2 billion";

- View on market rates and impact on FTP from Treasury to the business, for example, "falling 3-month Libor rates are an issue for forecast income in 2015";
- Product emphasis: focus on MTAs, instant access savings, or term deposits;
- Regular competitive analysis.

The primary theme is generally to focus on a holistic view of customer needs, focusing on valued relationships and not necessarily rates payable, although the pressure on NIM is always there. There will be a secondary theme to "manage for value", for example, a focus on retaining deposit balances and enhancing value for NIM.

A regular competitor watch is essential. In general, a bank will want to be in the middle range of rates obtainable by customers, although large international institutions are able to pay deposit rates at the lower end and still attract deposits. Table 12.15 is an example of how a UK commercial bank, say XYZ Bank, reports this market intelligence in its weekly deposits reporting template.

**TABLE 12.15**  Competitor deposit interest rates template, UK banking market. XYZ Bank is "our" bank

| Deposit Terms | ABC Bank | XYZ Bank | County Bank | Friendly Bank | Life Bank | Trust Bank |
|---|---|---|---|---|---|---|
| Instant Access | 0.10 | | 1.50 | 0.50 | 0.95 | 0.90 |
| 30-day notice | 1.25 | 0.60 | 1.00 | 1.35 | 1.10 | 1.00 |
| 90-day notice | | 1.55 | 2.00 | 1.75 | 0.95 | 1.35 |
| 95-day notice | 1.95 | | 2.00 | | | 1.35 |
| 3-month | | 1.55 | | 2.00 | | |
| 6-month | 2.00 | 1.75 | 2.25 | | 2.25 | 1.75 |
| 12-month | 2.20 | 2.15 | | 2.50 | 2.65 | 2.00 |
| 2-year | | 2.35 | | | | 2.50 |
| 3-year | | | | 2.60 | | |
| 5-year | | 2.65 | | | | |

## Net Stable Funding Ratio (NSFR)

A significant aspect of Basel III is the long-term liquidity measurement metric known as the net stable funding ratio (NSFR). The NSFR promotes resilience over the longer term; setting a limit whereby it should ensure that sufficient long-term funding is in place to support the bank's balance sheet over the cycle. In other words, maintaining an adequate NSFR should help considerably in ensuring a stable funding structure.

The stated objective of the NSFR is to encourage more medium and term funding, and the metric itself highlights the level of long-term funding compared to short-term liabilities. The metric measures the amount of stable funding as a proportion of the total requirement for such stable funding. The requirements for stable funding are determined with reference to the assets on the balance sheet, with longer-term assets (such as mortgages) requiring more stable funding than shorter-term assets. It is typically used to monitor and control the level of dependency on volatile, short-term wholesale markets, as a key structural balance sheet ratio. A low ratio indicates a concentration of funding in shorter maturities (under 1-year tenor) which can give rise to roll-over and mismatch risks. Setting a minimum percentage level for term funding would reduce dependency on short-term funding, while increasing cost of business, as more liabilities are moved into longer-term funding.

The ratio aims to "promote more medium and long-term funding of the assets and activities of banking organisations".

NSFR is given by:

$$\frac{\text{Available amount of stable funding}}{\text{Required amount of stable funding}} > 100\% \qquad (12.2)$$

Table 12.16 describes the calculation in greater detail.

**Understanding the Calculation**    A bank must understand the ASF and RSF levels and how they impact its balance sheet and business model. To improve a given NSFR an institution has two options:

- The institution can increase the ASF by adjusting the liability side of its balance sheet (for example, liabilities with higher roll-over factors or longer duration); or
- The institution can decrease the RSF by adjusting the asset side of its balance sheet (for example, assets with lower roll-over factors or shorter duration). As outlined earlier in this section, changing the shape of the balance sheet is very challenging and takes a long time. It is therefore not possible to make changes to a bank's NSFR over a short time period, and banks will have to start preparing now in order to ensure compliance by the regulatory deadline of January 2019.

**TABLE 12.16**    NSFR calculation

| Available Stable Funding | Required Stable Funding |
|---|---|
| The sum of:<br>■ 100% of total Tier 1 and Tier 2 capital and preferred stock;<br>■ 100% of liabilities with a contractual maturity greater than 1 year;<br>■ 85% of "stable" retail and small business deposits with maturity less than 1 year;<br>■ 70% of "less stable" retail and small business with maturity less than 1 year;<br>■ 50% of large corporate deposits with maturity less than 1 year. | The sum of:<br>■ 0% cash, securities with a maturity less than 1 year, interbank loans with a maturity less than 1 year, securities held with an offsetting reverse repo;<br>■ 5% unpledged high-quality liquid securities (similar definition to central bank eligible collateral);<br>■ 20% corporate and covered bonds with a proven record of liquidity (i.e., no major increases in repo haircut in the last 10 years);<br>■ 50% other corporate bonds, gold, equities, loans to corporates with a maturity less than 1 year;<br>■ 85% retail loans with a maturity less than 1 year;<br>■ 100% all loans with maturity greater than 1 year, all other assets;<br>■ 10% of all undrawn committed credit lines and overdraft facilities;<br>■ % of percentage of guarantees, uncommitted credit lines, letters of credit, money market mutual fund repo obligations, etc. |

The NSFR is a whole balance sheet assessment and every bank needs to understand the impact of all its business lines on the metric, on both sides of the balance sheet, in order to ensure that its business model is correctly aligned with regulatory requirements. Where sufficient available funding was not available to meet the requirements given by "required funding", it may be necessary to revise the business model and possibly withdraw some particular business activities.

**Addressing NSFR Compliance**    If adjusting the asset side, the measures would include reducing maturities, shifting to assets with lower RSF, and so on. If adjusting the liability side, measures might include increasing maturities and shifting to liabilities with higher ASF values.

In some cases, it may be that a major realignment in business model is called for, which may include compressing the net position of derivatives, cutting credit lines, focusing on advisory business, or reviving a form of "originate and distribute" model.

## Individual Liquidity Adequacy Assessment Process (ILAAP) Framework

The ILAAP framework is based on an internal stress testing process, where banks are required to conduct name-specific, market-wide, and combined stress tests in order to determine their liquidity requirements. At the process conclusion, the regulatory authority will direct any further steps, including raising the size of the HQLA, that the bank may have to take. This is the individual liquidity guidance (ILG).

**The ILAAP Stress Testing Framework**   The UK framework is more "principles based" than the Basel III framework, with banks required to determine their own stress test levels, based on their understanding of their business and their liquidity risk appetite. Banks are required to account for 10 risk areas when formulating their liquidity stresses as summarised in Table 12.17.

**TABLE 12.17**   Risk areas banks account for when formulating liquidity stresses

| Liquidity risk area | Description |
| --- | --- |
| Wholesale funding risk | The risk that wholesale funds mature and are unable to be refinanced in the event of a liquidity stress. |
| Retail and commercial funding risk | The risk that retail and commercial funding is lost in the event of a liquidity stress. |
| Intra-day liquidity risk | The risk arising from a bank's direct participation in a payment or settlement system. |
| Intra-group liquidity risk | The risk arising from relying on other parts of the group for liquidity or having to provide liquidity to other parts of the group. |
| Cross-currency liquidity risk | The risk of outflows in currencies in which the bank has material positions during liquidity stress. |
| Off-balance sheet liquidity risk | The risk that off-balance sheet commitments/activities might affect the bank's cash flows. |
| Franchise viability risk | The risk that under stress the bank does not have resources available to maintain its core business and reputation. |
| Marketable assets risk | The risk that marketable assets behave differently under liquidity stress than under normal conditions, for example, haircuts increase. Marketable assets are those which the bank can sell outright or repo. |
| Non-marketable assets risk | The risk that cash inflows from these assets may in stressed conditions be affected by counterparty behaviour. |
| Funding concentration risk | The risk that concentration exists in the funding portfolio and that some funding providers reduce or terminate their funding provision. |

The results of the stress testing is written down in a detailed document, referred to as the ILAAP, which contains the approach followed, assumptions made, and results obtained. Banks are required to justify the key assumptions made as part of this process. The regulator reviews the ILAAP submissions of individual banks. If there are areas where it is felt that inadequate provision has been made, then banks are required to hold additional liquidity resources.

**Additional Reporting Requirements in the UK**  Over and above the ILAA process, banks are also required to submit a liquidity return to the PRA which summarises their liquidity risk position (contained in forms FSA 047 and FSA 048). Banks need to be able to produce the information at short notice, so that the PRA and the bank itself are able to quickly understand its liquidity position during periods where the liquidity position is starting to experience a stress.

For this purpose, a distinction is made between "Type A" and "Type B" deposits as outlined in Table 12.18.

**TABLE 12.18**   Type A versus Type B deposits

| Deposit type | Definition |
| --- | --- |
| Type A deposits (more risky) | Contains at least the following types of wholesale deposits:<br>■ Is accepted from a credit institution, local authority, insurance undertaking, pension fund, money market fund, asset manager (including a hedge fund manager), government-sponsored agency, sovereign government, or sophisticated non-financial corporation; or<br>■ Is accepted through the Treasury function of a sophisticated nonfinancial corporation which may be assumed to respond swiftly to negative news about a firm's credit-worthiness; or<br>■ Is accepted on wholesale market terms as a part of a firm's money market operations; or<br>■ Is accepted from a depositor with whom a firm does not have a long-established relationship or to whom a firm does not supply a range of services; or<br>■ Is accepted from overseas counterparties other than those in the country or territory of incorporation of a firm's parent undertaking or, in the case of a UK branch, of the firm of which it forms part; or is obtained through unsecured debt instruments (such as certificates of deposit, medium-term notes, and commercial paper); or<br>■ Is obtained from counterparties with a relatively low creditor seniority on the liquidation of the firm. |

*(continued)*

**TABLE 12.18** *(Continued)*

| Deposit type | Definition |
|---|---|
| | Contains at least the following types of retail deposits:<br>▪ Has been accepted through the internet; or<br>▪ Is considered to have a more than average sensitivity to interest rate changes (such as a deposit whose acceptance can reasonably be attributed to the use of price-focused advertising by the firm accepting the deposit); or<br>▪ In relation to any individual depositor exceeds to a significant extent the amount of that individual's deposits with the accepting firm that are covered by a national deposit guarantee scheme; or<br>▪ Is not accepted from a depositor with whom the firm has had a long relationship; or<br>▪ Is accepted from retail depositors who can access their deposits before their residual contractual maturity subject to a loss of interest or payment of another form of early access charge (as a general proposition, the behaviour of liabilities to retail depositors is likely to depend in part on the contractual terms and conditions which give rise to those liabilities); or<br>▪ Is not held in an account which is maintained for transactional purposes. |
| Type B deposits (less risky) | Those deposits that do not have the characteristics outlined above for Type A deposits. |

# PART 2: ILAAP AND STRESS TESTING

In Part 2 we look further at the ILAAP regime and stress testing, and also what this means from a wider policy and strategy angle. Liquidity management is more than simply "risk management" of the funding rollover exposure, it also must be a key input to strategy setting and overall balance sheet management.

## Liquidity Reporting, Stress Testing, and ILAAP; Intra-Day Liquidity Risk and Asset Encumbrance Policy[1]

This section continues our detailed look into the liquidity risk management process. We consider further the regulatory aspect and the process of the "individual liquidity adequacy assessment". We also review intra-day liquidity risk and the importance of understanding the liquidity risk aspects of having encumbered assets on the balance sheet.

---

[1] This section was co-authored with Jamie Paris and Chris Westcott.

**Liquidity Reporting** Liquidity reporting is necessary because:

- It obliges banks to monitor their liquidity risk on a daily or intra-day basis.
- The data required by the regulator would normally be required by firms for their own purposes in undertaking prudent liquidity risk management (regulatory guidance).
- It enables the regulator to identify and challenge outliers.
- Supervisors can apply their own stress testing scenario analysis to data provided by a firm.
- It enables the regulator to form firm specific, sector, and industry-wide views on liquidity risk during good and bad times and provide feedback to firms on their liquidity positioning within their peer group.

In the UK, in 2009–2010, in the wake of the financial crisis, the Financial Services Authority (now Prudential Regulation Authority) introduced a series of new liquidity reports. The most well-known of these reports are the FSA 047 (Daily Flows) and the FSA 048 (Enhanced Mismatch Report), which show respectively, contractual liquidity flows out to three months (for the analysis of survival periods and potential liquidity squeezes) and liquidity mismatch positions across the whole maturity spectrum.

Other key reports include: FSA 050 (Liquidity Buffer Qualifying Securities), FSA 051 (Funding Concentration), FSA 052 (Pricing Data), FSA 053 (Retail, SME and Large Enterprise Type B (Stable) Funding), FSA 054 (Currency Analysis), and FSA 055 (Systems and Controls Questionnaire). These too are all based upon contractual maturities, where relevant.

Reporting frequency ranged between Daily and Quarterly depending upon: the size and complexity of the bank, the nature of the report (for example, money/financial market updates were required more often than those on retail/corporate accounts), and the market conditions (reporting frequency was increased in a stress situation).

The FSA reports were required to be submitted at a consolidated group level, as well as for key banking subsidiaries.

Since October 2015, the FSA suite of reports has largely been replaced by EU Common Reporting or COREP. COREP is a standardised reporting framework issued by the European Banking Authority for the Capital Requirements Directive. It covers credit risk, market risk, operational risk, own funds capital adequacy, and liquidity risk. The reporting framework has been adopted by around 30 countries in Europe (including the UK) and applies to all banks (credit institutions), building societies, and investment firms (and, in some cases, significant branches of credit institutions).

COREP requires data to be reported at a more granular level than hitherto. Separate reports must be prepared for all "significant" currencies, which make up more than 5% of the total balance sheet.

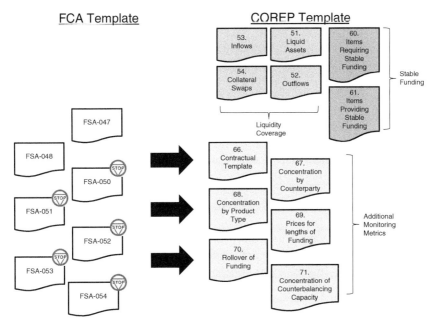

**FIGURE 12.12**    Transition to COREP in the European Union

As illustrated at Figure 12.12, the FSA reports (apart from FSA 047 and 048 which are retained) are being replaced by four returns on the Liquidity Coverage Ratio, two on the Net Stable Funding Ratio, and six reports on Additional Monitoring Metrics. The LCR and Additional Monitoring Metrics reports must be submitted each month, whilst the NSFR templates are required on a quarterly basis.

The Additional Monitoring Metrics cover a range of data, which helps supervisors to identify potential liquidity difficulties for a single institution or across the market as a whole and to take pre-emptive action if necessary:

- **Contractual Maturity Ladder:** provides an insight into the extent to which an organisation relies on maturity transformation and provides advanced warning of potential future liquidity stress;
- **Concentration of Funding by Counterparty:** the top 10 largest counterparties from which funding obtained exceeds 1% of total liabilities – identifies those sources of wholesale and retail funding of such significance that their withdrawal could trigger liquidity problems;
- **Concentration of Funding by Product Type:** the total amount of funding received from each product category when it exceeds a threshold of 1% of total liabilities – identifies those sources of wholesale and retail

funding of such significance that their withdrawal could trigger liquidity problems;

■ **Concentration of Counterbalancing Capacity by Issuer/Counterparty:** the 10 largest holdings of assets or liquidity lines granted – demonstrates potential borrowing capacity in a stress;
■ **Prices for Various Lengths of Funding:** average transaction volume and prices paid by institutions for funding with different maturities – provides advanced warning of a deteriorating liquidity position through a peer group comparison;
■ **Rollover of Funding:** volume of funds maturing and new funding obtained on a daily basis over a monthly time horizon – provides a validation for behavioural assumptions and advanced warning of a deteriorating liquidity position through a peer group comparison.

**Liquidity Stress Testing** The liquidity stress testing process (illustrated at Figure 12.13) involves the modelling of assumptions on how assets and liabilities of a bank (inventory) will behave in various stress scenarios, to produce an output for review and action by senior management.

**Inventory** The inventory is the composition and maturity profile of the balance sheet (including off-balance sheet exposures) on a given date – a basic building block for all modelling activity.

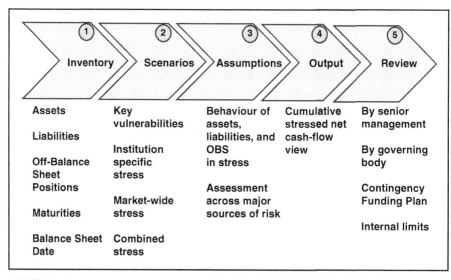

**FIGURE 12.13**　End-to-End Liquidity Stress Testing Process

**Stress Scenarios** The calculation of the LCR is based upon a stress scenario set by the regulatory authorities. In contrast, the scenarios used for liquidity stress testing should be generated by banks and include a range of idiosyncratic, market, and macroeconomic stresses. These should be severe, but plausible and focus upon key vulnerabilities. Examples could include: a sustained period of systems failure, a vulnerability to previously liquid markets becoming illiquid (for example, commercial paper or securitisation), heavy reliance on a particular sector for funding which becomes no longer available (local authorities in a credit downgrade scenario).

**Assumptions** Assumptions about the response of assets and liabilities to a given stress scenario are based on their historic behaviour in both normal and stressed conditions. The level of sophistication adopted will depend upon the amount of historic data available to support the modelling process. For example, if there is little or no history, assumptions might be developed at a product level only. Alternatively, if the product data can be broken down by customer type and cohort (by account opening date), a more advanced modelling approach may be adopted.

In forming behavioural assumptions, banks should consider the likely consequences of the stress scenario for the Major Sources of Risk they face, which include: Retail Funding Risk, Wholesale Secured and Unsecured Funding Risk, Correlation and Concentration of Funding, Additional Contingent Off-Balance Sheet Exposures, Funding Tenors, Intraday Liquidity Risk, Deterioration in the Firm's Credit Rating, Foreign Exchange Convertibility and Access to Foreign Exchange Markets, Ability to Transfer Liquidity across Entities, Sectors and Countries, Future Balance Sheet Growth, Impact on a Firm's Reputation and Franchise, Marketable and Non-Marketable Asset Risk, and Internalisation Risk (which relates to the potential close-out of customer short-positions leading to outflows).

**Output** A key output from the stress testing process is the calculation of a cash flow survival period. This details how many days a bank's sources of liquidity (liquid assets, cash inflows, and drawdown of contingent liquidity facilities) will be able to offset the outflows that are assumed in a stress scenario. Banks will set a minimum acceptable survival period as part of their Liquidity Risk Appetite Statements.

**Review** The output of the stress testing process should be shared with the ALCO and be included in periodic updates to the Board. If the cash flow survival period exceeds the bank's risk appetite, then no further action is necessary, other than continuously reviewing the stress testing process and investing in areas like data collection to improve the quality of outputs over time. Alternatively, if the cash flow survival period is less than the risk appetite, then some form of corrective action is required, such as:

- Reduce exposures to certain products and markets;
- Reduce limits applied to contractual outflows (i.e., the amount of maturity transformation undertaken by the bank);
- Review strategies to address liquidity shortfalls in the Contingency Funding Plan. The Contingency Funding Plan is a statement setting out a bank's strategies for addressing liquidity shortfalls in emergency situations; it will demonstrate how a bank will survive a given stress scenario. Quick, decisive, pre-planned action is important in times of great uncertainty when confidence is low and may make the difference between bank survival and failure.

### Individual Liquidity Adequacy Assessment Process

The ILAAP should incorporate:

- A clearly articulated risk appetite defining the duration and type of stress the firm aims to survive;
- A range of stress scenarios focusing upon key vulnerabilities of the firm;
- The results of stress tests; and
- Those measures set-out in the Contingency Funding Plan that it would implement.

It should also be:

- Recorded in a document approved by the Board;
- Proportionate to the nature scale and complexity of a bank's activities; and
- Updated annually or more frequently if the business model of the firm changes.

The UK PRA provides a suggested format and table of contents for an ILAAP submission in Annexe 1 of its document SS24/15 (Dec 2016 update). A bank is not obliged to use this template, it is only a guide. We show the author's recommended schedule of contents in Table 12.19. Above all, banks must ensure that their ILAAP informs decision-making and risk management and are not seen to be just a compliance exercise. This is known as passing the regulator's "Use Test".

**Liquidity Supervisory Review and Evaluation Process (L-SREP)**   This is the review of the ILAA by the regulator. It is a broad assessment which will also capture items like:

- Whether the institution has an appropriate framework and IT system for identifying liquidity risk;
- Whether the governance framework around the liquidity risk management process is sufficient;

---

**TABLE 12.19**   Specimen ILAA Contents

 1  Executive Summary (incl. ILAAP scope and purpose)
 2  Institution Strategy
 3  Liquidity Risk Ownership
 4  Funding Profile
 5  Forecast Balance Sheet
 6  Liquidity Risk Management Framework (incl. ownership and risk appetite)
 7  Liquidity Risk Appetite
 8  ILAAP Coverage
 9  Stress Scenarios
10  Stress Testing Results (covering all sources of risk)
11  Liquidity Risk Assessment
12  High Quality Liquid Assets policy and portfolio
13  Other sources of funding/mitigants
14  ILAAP Challenge and Internal Approval Process
15  Use of ILAAP in the firm
16  Recovery and Resolution
17  Appendix A. Internal Funds Transfer Pricing Policy
18  Appendix B. Outflow Assumptions
19  Appendix C. Contingency Funding Plan

---

- Whether there is an adequate transfer pricing mechanism for liquidity;
- Whether there are adequate controls over the liquid asset buffer;
- Whether the institution defines and communicates its liquidity risk strategy and tolerance;
- Whether there is a comprehensive internal limit and control framework for liquidity risk management.

**Individual Liquidity Guidance**   Following the L-SREP, the PRA (in the UK) will give Individual Liquidity Guidance to banks. Typically, this will cover whether the quantity and quality of liquid assets held by the bank are sufficient, whether the firm's funding profile is appropriate, and any further qualitative arrangements the firm should undertake to mitigate its liquidity risk. Note, the quantitative guidance extends beyond the liquidity buffer the firm is required to maintain under the LCR and will cover liquidity risks to which the firm is exposed, but which are not captured by the LCR.

A similar process exists in other jurisdictions subject to the Basel regulations.

## Intra-Day Liquidity Risk

Principle 8 of the Basel Committee Principles for Sound Liquidity Risk Management and Supervision states:

"A bank should actively manage its intraday liquidity positions and risks to meet payment and settlement obligations on a timely basis under both normal and stressed conditions and thus contribute to the smooth running of payment and settlement systems."

Intraday Liquidity is defined as funds which can be accessed during the business day to enable firms to make payments in real time. Intraday Liquidity Risk is the risk that a bank fails to manage its intraday liquidity effectively, which could leave it unable to meet a payment obligation at the time expected, thereby affecting its own liquidity position and that of other parties.

Intraday sources of liquidity include:

- Reserve balances and collateral pledged at central banks;
- Unencumbered liquid assets that can be freely transferred to the central bank;
- Secured or unsecured committed or uncommitted credit lines available intraday;
- Balances with other banks that can be used for settlement same day;
- Payments received from other payment system participants and ancillary systems.

Intraday liquidity needs arise from:

- Payments needing to be made to other system participants and ancillary systems;
- Contingent payments (for example, as an emergency liquidity provider) relating to a payment systems failure to settle procedures;
- Contingent intraday liquidity liabilities to customers;
- Payments arising from the provision of correspondent banking services.

The Basel Committee recommend that a bank's usage of and requirement for intraday liquidity is monitored in both normal and stressed conditions via eight metrics:

1. Daily Maximum Liquidity Requirement;
2. Available Intraday Liquidity at the Start of the Business Day;
3. Total Payments;
4. Time Specific and Other Critical Obligations;
5. Value of Payments Made on Behalf of Correspondent Bank Customers;
6. Intraday Credit Lines Extended to Customers;
7. Timing of Intraday Payments;
8. Intraday Throughput.

In the EU, firms have been required to provide quarterly reports on the above measures since October 2015.

Of particular note are the Daily Maximum Liquidity Requirement, Time Specific and Other Critical Obligations, and Intraday Throughput.

**The Daily Maximum Liquidity Requirement** Banks need to calculate their net intraday liquidity position (the difference between the total value of payments received and payments made at any point in the day) during the course of the day. The bank's largest net cumulative position during the day will determine its maximum intraday requirement on that day. If a bank runs a negative net cumulative position at some point during the day, it will need to access intraday liquidity to fund this balance. In the example at Figure 12.14, this is just over 10 currency units.

**Time Specific and Other Critical Obligations** Banks must identify the volume and value of time-specific obligations and any missed payments. This enables supervisors to assess whether these obligations are being effectively managed. Examples include payments required to settle positions in payment and settlement systems and those related to market activities, such as the delivery or return of money market transactions or margin payments. A bank's failure to settle such obligations on time could result in financial penalty, reputational damage, or loss of future business.

**Intraday Throughput** This metric shows the proportion, by value, of a bank's outgoing payments that settle by specific times during the day (for example, by 9.00 a.m., by 10.00 a.m., etc.) and enables supervisors to identify specific times during the day when a bank may be more vulnerable to liquidity or operational stresses and any changes in its payment and settlement behaviour.

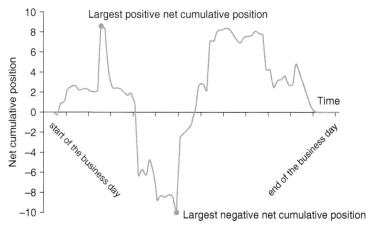

**FIGURE 12.14**  Specimen Daily Maximum Liquidity Requirement

**Intraday Liquidity Stress Testing**    The monitoring tools discussed provide supervisors with information on a bank's intraday liquidity profile in normal conditions. However, the availability and usage of intraday liquidity can change markedly in times of stress. As guidance, the Basel Committee have developed four stress scenarios relating to own financial stress, customer stress, counterparty stress, and market-wide credit or liquidity stress. Banks should use the scenarios to assess how their intraday liquidity profile in normal conditions would change in a stressful situation and discuss with their supervisor how any adverse impact would be addressed either through contingency planning and/or the wider intraday liquidity risk management framework.

**How are the Intraday Liquidity Rules Influencing Banks?**    The intraday liquidity rules have encouraged banks to focus on IT development to generate the required metrics and real time information flows. Senior management understanding of sources and uses of intraday liquidity have improved rapidly and banks are employing their available liquidity resources more efficiently, for example, through payment scheduling to reduce maximum intraday liquidity usage and ensuring that liquid assets are held in the right place to support payment systems as necessary. Also, banks have considered what might happen in a stress situation and put plans in place to mitigate the outcomes.

### Asset Encumbrance[2]

Asset encumbrance, also known as earmarking or pledging assets refers to a situation where assets secure liabilities in the event that an institution fails to meet its financial obligations. It originates from transactions such as repurchase agreements, securitisations, covered bonds, central bank funding, or derivatives hedging. Asset encumbrance is critical to the Asset and Liability Manager because unsecured creditors are unable to benefit from the liquidation of encumbered assets in the case of insolvency and encumbered assets are not available to obtain emergency liquidity in the case of an unforeseen stress event.

   Since the 2007–2008 global financial crisis, the level of encumbrance amongst financial institutions has increased rapidly. According to the European Systemic Risk Board, encumbrance in the EU rose from 11% in 2007 to 32% in 2011. Since the end of 2014, the European Banking Authority has been collecting data from 200 banks across 29 countries – in March 2015 this revealed an encumbrance position that was still high relative to historic norms at 27.1%.

   The challenge for regulators is the very different levels of encumbrance across the countries in the EU. The asset encumbrance ratio ranges from 0%

---

[2] This section was co-authored with Enrique Benito.

in Estonia to 44% in the case of both Denmark and Greece. Higher encumbrance ratios are driven by a variety of factors, such as:

- Large and established covered bond markets (for example, Sweden and Denmark);
- A high share of central bank funding in countries affected by the sovereign debt crisis (for example, Greece);
- A high share of repo financing and collateral requirements for over the counter derivatives (for example, UK and Belgium).

Due to the disparity across EU institutions, there are no formal limits imposed by the EU authorities as a whole (note, in the UK, the PRA has applied capital add-ons for some banks where the asset encumbrance level exceeded 20%). However, a clear framework should be adopted by institutions containing the following components:

- Establishment of an approach to Asset Encumbrance by the governing body, including regular review;
- Monitoring and active management of the Asset Encumbrance position;
- Incorporation of Asset Encumbrance into stress testing scenarios;
- Provision of information to the governing body on contingent encumbrance requirements from stress scenarios;
- Incorporation of strategies to address Asset Encumbrance into contingency funding and Recovery and Resolution plans.

**Stylised Illustration** Figure 12.15 shows the principle issues associated with asset encumbrance. In essence, the main problem lies with the fact that measuring the level of encumbrance in real-time, to a degree of reasonable

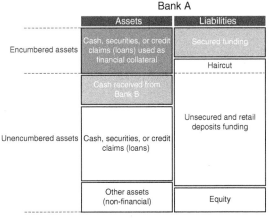

**FIGURE 12.15** Bank balance sheet and asset encumbrance

accuracy, is not a trivial task for all but the smallest and/or simplest banking institutions.

We noted above the range of transactions that result, to differing degrees of administrative complexity, in certain assets being encumbered on the balance sheet. All these transactions differ on their legal and accounting treatment and therefore their impact on asset encumbrance measures will differ.

**Measuring Asset Encumbrance**   Measuring asset encumbrance presents difficulties and there is currently no global consensus as to what measure should be used. For example, a bank may adopt one of the following approaches:

1. Ratio of encumbered assets to total assets
   - Does not consider the amount of structural subordination;
   - Considered by the BoE to assess the financial resilience of the UK banking sector.
2. Ratio of encumbered assets and collateral to total assets and collateral
   - Captures encumbrance arising from off-balance sheet activities;
   - Selected by the EBA and EC to discriminate between banks in order to apply more comprehensive regulatory reporting requirements on asset encumbrance.
3. Ratio of unencumbered assets to unsecured liabilities
   - Provides an indication of the amount of structural subordination;
   - Also considered as effective by the BoE;
   - Considered the best ratio to assess encumbrance by CGFS.

There is also the issue of "looking through" to the ultimate encumbrance of assets given or received as collateral. We illustrate this at Figure 12.16(a) and (b). Most regulators and central clearing counterparties will only accept an asset that has no more than one level of "rehypothecation", which is the extent to which assets received as collateral have been pledged as such to someone else as collateral.

There is also the issue of contingent encumbrance. This refers to additional assets which may need to be encumbered when the firm faces adverse developments triggered by an external event over which the reporting institution has no control. The European Banking Authority has provided two independent scenarios for reporting purposes:

- Decrease of the fair value of the encumbered assets by 30%;
- A 10% depreciation in each significant currency.

The scenarios above account only for changes in collateral value under very particular scenarios. A more comprehensive approach entails an assessment of risk factors as well as stress scenarios (for example, rating downgrade) and associated collateral requirements. A historical approach can be used as backstop.

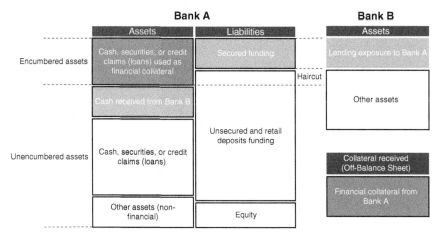

**FIGURE 12.16(a)** Stylised example collateral and encumbrance, Banks A and B

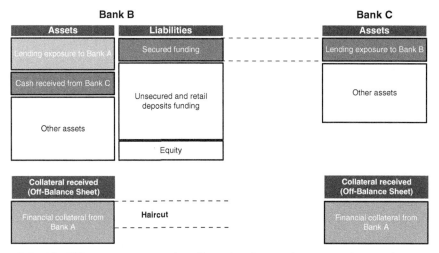

**FIGURE 12.16(b)** Stylised example collateral and encumbrance, Banks B and C

**Implications for Funding and Collateral Management** The overall cost of funding for European banks has increased significantly in recent times in consonance with increases in asset encumbrance. Published estimates from the IMF show that under a framework with depositor preference, higher levels of asset encumbrance could increase spreads of senior unsecured debt of European banks by 30 to 120 basis points. Despite the current environment of historically low interest rates, banks issuance of senior unsecured debt has been in decline, pointing to structural shifts in bank funding structures.

In this environment, visibility of and data on collateral sources and usages is paramount and a key technology/data analytics challenge for banks. Implementation of collateral pooling systems managing repo and asset inventory as well as derivatives collateral, at an aggregate balance sheet level, is very important. In other words, asset encumbrance policy must state that data management is undertaken at the overall level – moving from product silos to holistic management.

It is recommended that banks maintain an asset encumbrance policy, with the following broad pointers:

- Include a policy framework and guidance that addresses the need to take into account:
  - Current level of encumbrance;
  - Type of encumbrance;
  - Contractual obligations.
- Address 3rd-party (regulator, investors, rating agencies) perception;
- Calculate and report the true economic cost of encumbrance;
- Ensure ALCO is aware of the quality of assets on the balance sheet left unencumbered, versus those encumbered;
- Ensure coverage and impact of Repo/Reverse Repo guidelines.

## BANK INTERNAL FUNDS TRANSFER PRICING (FTP OR IFP)

In this section, we cover the concept of bank internal funding; policy, which regulators see now as a key component of a bank's overall liquidity risk management framework. FTP is also known as liquidity transfer pricing (LTP) or funds transfer pricing (FTP). Although FTP is probably the most commonly used acronym, we believe that IFP captures more accurately what the process actually involves. That said, in this book the terms are used interchangeably.

The IFP regime in place at a bank is a key segment of the bank's overall liquidity risk management regime. This is because it influences product pricing, and also acts as an incentivising mechanism for the type of business a bank's customer relationship managers seek. Thus, it is important for the IFP mechanism to be appropriate to a bank's specific business and operating model. There is no "one size fits all" IFP framework, and rightly so: what is appropriate for one bank may well not be correct for another bank, even for another bank in the same peer group. Therefore, all banks need to keep their IFP policy and associated product funding policies, under regular review and revise them as and when necessary. Reflecting the financial markets generally, a bank's IFP policy needs to be dynamic.

That said, FTP is at its best when kept as simple and straightforward as possible. At the end of the day, it is essentially "left-hand, right-hand" stuff, an internal mechanism that the shareholder or customer knows little and cares less about. Complicated FTP regimes ultimately become self-defeating.

## The Concept of Bank Internal Funds Pricing

The process of actually managing the IFP function in a bank sits usually, although not always, within the bank's Treasury department. (Some banks place the function within an asset–liability management (ALM) desk that is outside Treasury.) Irrespective of where the IFP desk sits, it must always be a central one, dealing in two-way funding with all the business lines. Within this context, "two-way" refers to the process whereby asset business lines are charged an appropriate rate for the funding they consume, whereas liability business lines are paid an appropriate rate for the funding they provide to the bank. There must only be one internal funding desk at a bank, for a number of reasons that will be elaborated on later in the chapter. For banking Groups, operating across multiple national jurisdictions and legal entities, it is common to observe local internal funding desks for a specific geographical region or legal entity. However, the IFP policy and key principles under which local desks operate must be a uniform, Group-wide one. This will ensure that all parts of the bank adhere to a minimum benchmark acceptable standard, and also follow Group operational procedure.

**Framework Design and Economic Basis of Transfer Pricing**   Internal bank funds pricing is a key element in liquidity risk management. An inappropriate or artificial internal funds pricing policy may lead to poor business decision-making, and could generate excessive liquidity and funding risk exposure. It is therefore imperative for banks to operate a robust and disciplined internal funding mechanism, one that is integrated into the overall liquidity risk management framework.

FTP – the price at which an individual business line raises funds from its own Treasury desk – is essential to the risk management process. It is the key parameter in business decision-making which drives sales, asset allocation, and customer product pricing. It is also a key hurdle rate behind the product approval process and in an individual business line's performance measurement. Just as capital allocation decisions affecting front-office business units need to account for the cost of that capital (in terms of return on regulatory and economic capital), funding decisions exercised by corporate treasurers carry significant implications for sales and trading teams at the trade level.

The problem arises because banks undertake maturity transformation, funding long-dated assets with shorter-dated liabilities, where the date of an asset or liability is the expected date of the associated cash flows (also referred to as the behavioural term) and not necessarily the contractual term. Moreover, certain assets, such as mortgages and corporate loans, are frequently illiquid in nature. The combination of a funding gap and illiquid asset base makes it imperative that, each time an asset is originated, business lines correctly price in the term liquidity risk they are generating. Conversely, a business line that raises funds can also be valued at the internal term liquidity premium. Certain liabilities might be contractually short-term but longer on a behavioural basis, and therefore need to be rewarded for the true funding benefit that they bring to the bank.

Hence, the internal funding rate is important in driving business decision-making. For example, a uniform cost of funds (something practised by many banks during the lead-up to the 2008 financial crisis) will mean that the different liquidity stresses on the balance sheet, created by different types of asset, are not addressed adequately at the aggregate funding level. Different asset types place different liquidity pressures on the Treasury funding desk, thereby demanding a structurally sound internal funding pricing policy which is appropriate to the type of business line being funded.

In addition to being a key liquidity risk management tool, IFP is also a key mechanism for the identification and management of interest-rate risks which arise from conducting banking business. This is done by ensuring that the FTP rate paid or charged to the business unit is linked to the same rate as is used by the business unit to determine the interest-rate charged or paid to the client. By doing this, the Treasury function can ensure that any interest-rate risks are centralised in the bank's Treasury function, from where it can be more efficiently managed.

For example, in the UK, most retail loans re-price against the central bank base rate or 3-month Libor, and therefore the IFP rate is set as a function of the Base or Libor rate.

The IFP rate is usually set to reflect:

- The base cost of funds, which reflects the general level of interest rates in the relevant market;
- The term liquidity premium (TLP), which reflects the additional "spread" above the base cost which is required by depositors (or investors) to deposit funds, within the bank, for an agreed term;
- The re-pricing characteristics of the product, as explained above.

As a further example, a South African bank might issue a floating-rate note to a local money market fund. This instrument will be priced based on a spread above the 3-month JIBAR rate. The FTP rate for this instrument will therefore be set as 3-month JIBAR (the base rate) plus a TLP. The same bank might issue a fixed deposit to a retail client. The FTP rate for this instrument will be set as a fixed rate, based on the level of the swap curve at the time and representing the base rate, plus a TLP.

### Behavioural Tenor of Deposits, Lending Facilities, and Other Optionality Characteristics

In principle, the price at which cash is internally transferred within a bank should reflect the true economic cost of that cash for the bank (at each maturity band), and its impact on overall bank liquidity. This internal price of cash is often referred to as the bank's "FTP curve" or its "funding curve". This would ensure that each business aligns its commercial propensity to maximise profit with the correct maturity profile of associated funding. Of course, the very act of taking deposits and advancing loans creates liquidity risk exposure on the balance sheet. This must be managed appropriately, and one of the key instruments with which this management takes place is the internal funding rate.

A measure of discipline in business decision-making is enforced via the imposition of minimum return-on-capital (ROC) targets. Independent of the internal cost of funds, a business line would ordinarily seek to ensure that any transaction it entered into achieved its targeted ROC. However, relying solely on this measure is not sufficient discipline. For this to work, each business line should set ROC levels which are commensurate with its (risk-adjusted) risk-reward profile. However, banks do not always set different target ROCs for each business line. The FTP rate has a direct impact on these metrics and it is therefore important that FTP reflects the underlying economics of the transaction as accurately as possible, in order to ensure that these metrics are not distorted.

In contrast, a uniform cost of funds, even allowing for different ROCs, will mean that the different liquidity stresses on the balance sheet, created by different types of asset across different term structures, are not addressed adequately at the aggregate funding level.

As a key driver of the economic decision-making process, the cost at which funds are lent from central Treasury to the bank's businesses needs to be set at a rate that reflects the true liquidity risk position of each business line transaction. If this cost is unrealistic, there is a risk that transactions are entered into, which produce an unrealistic profit. This profit will reflect the artificial funding gain, rather than the true economic value-added of the business. It also creates a risk that the bank's price testing of products out to the market is set at inappropriate levels.

There is empirical evidence of the damage that can be caused by artificially low transfer pricing. In an OECD paper from 2008, Adrian Blundell-Wignall and Paul Atkinson discussed the losses at the Swiss bank,

UBS AG, in its structured credit business. The credit business originated and invested in collateralised debt obligations (CDO). Quoting a UBS shareholder report,

> "...*internal bid prices were always higher than the relevant London inter-bank bid rate (LIBID) and internal offer prices were always lower than the relevant London inter-bank offered rate (LIBOR).*" (p. 97)

In other words, UBS's structured credit business was able to fund itself at prices better than in the market (which is, implicitly, inter-bank risk), despite the fact that it was investing in assets of considerably lower liquidity than inter-bank assets. There was no adjustment for tenor mismatch, to better align term funding to liquidity.

Another example is KBC Bank's London investment banking arm, which entered into the "fund derivatives" business. This was lending to investors in hedge funds via a leveraged structured product. These instruments were illiquid, with maturities of two years or longer. Once dealt, they could not be unwound, thus creating significant liquidity stress for the lender. However, banks funded these business lines from central Treasury at Libor-flat or Libor plus a small spread, rolling the funding in the short-term. The liquidity problems that resulted became apparent during the 2007–2008 financial crisis, when interbank liquidity dried up.

**Concept of Pricing Term Liquidity**  Trading liquidity is a much researched topic in financial economics. The trading liquidity of the secondary market in bonds and equities is usually measured with a proxy metric such as the price bid-offer spread; a narrower spread indicates a more liquid market. There are a number of other proxies which may be used, such as trading volume, market turnover, average daily trading frequency, average quote size, average trade size, and theoretical yield spread, amongst others. No one proxy measure provides a complete picture of trading liquidity, however, so analysts often consider a range of them when attempting to determine how liquid a secondary market is.

Measuring funding liquidity is an even more opaque process. It is further complicated because there are two elements to it, the market liquidity (overall) and the term liquidity premium specific to one bank. It is reasonably straightforward to calculate the cost of term liquidity for the larger multinational banks, because there are transparent and accurate market prices available for their secondary market debt and for the prices at which they issue money market instruments, not to mention a ready reference of liquid CDS prices for comparison. The exercise is slightly more involved for smaller banks, which will have fewer points of external reference. Just as with trading liquidity, a bank should consider a number of proxies when setting its funding liquidity measure.

It is worth remembering what the point of an FTP mechanism is when setting the internal funds curve. Business lines originate assets that create liquidity "stress" for the banks, because the business of banking involves maturity transformation. In this context, "stress" refers to the fact that the assets brought on to the balance sheet need to be funded by obtaining funding from customers, other banks or the central bank. It does not refer to a liquidity stress as outlined elsewhere in this chapter, where there is a specific concern around the liquidity position of the bank, leading to an unexpected withdrawal of funds. The cost of sourcing that liquidity in the market needs to be covered by the business line (via the FTP charge), first so that the business can undertake its project appraisal as efficiently as possible, and second so as not to create artificial profits which do not reflect the cost of the bank's funds. Especially for smaller banks, bearing this in mind is important, because an element of judgement is called for when setting the internal funds curve.

The FTP curve should not be blended with additional business incentives. Such incentives should, if applied, be clearly ring-fenced in order to first articulate the justification of the FTP curve and separately any incentives that the bank may wish to apply. That said, in many banks it is blended with other factors such as incentivising certain business types, the cost of maintaining the liquidity buffer, the cost of raising term funds, and certain other business costs.

We consider first the shape of the FTP curve, and then look at what proxies are available when setting it.

**FTP Curves**  Given the foregoing, it is now possible to understand the logic of an FTP curve (or in this case, grid) as shown in Table 12.20. This is a positively sloping pricing structure (mid-prices are shown but in practice there should be a minimum 1 to 2 bps bid-offer spread).

The rates are the bank's cost of liquidity, relative to its external funding cost. The derivation of these rates is discussed in the next section. This curve is the bank Treasury's FTP curve for its internal customers. Note this is not the same as the bank's external cost of funds (COF) of which there is more than one because a bank will raise liabilities from more than one source.

In a stable and liquid banking market, the asset–liability gap is generally not an issue. If one is always able to roll-over funding, it does not matter if the gap is 12 months, 60 months, or 120 months – if funding is always available, then the gap can usually be funded. However, there is a

**TABLE 12.20**    Hypothetical bank internal funds price curve ("FTP" or "TLP" curve)

| Term | FTP (bps) |
|---|---|
| 0–6 months | 0 |
| 6–12 months | 5 |
| 1–2 years | 15 |
| 3 years | 35 |
| 4 years | 40 |
| 5 years | 50 |
| 6 years | 60 |
| 7 years | 70 |
| 8 years | 80 |
| 9 years | 90 |
| 10 years | 100 |
| >10 years | 135 |

risk that the cost of rolling this funding will increase, due to increases in the general level of interest rates in the market, or due to increases in term liquidity premiums for the bank in question. Strangely enough, if one is not able to roll-over funding, then the term structure of the gap is immaterial as well – any gap is fatal. In other words, in a liquidity crisis situation it does not really matter if the gap is 12 months or 120 months. If the bank cannot obtain funds, then it will have to seek assistance at the central bank acting as a lender of last resort (or go bust). Basel III focuses on the 30-day funding gap.

**Summary of the Logical Basis for Sound FTP**    The foregoing has illustrated why a bank needs to ensure its internal funds pricing mechanism is fit for purpose. In the first instance, banks operate on the basis of maturity transformation, which means tenors and behaviours of assets and liabilities are mismatched and assets are longer than liabilities. Of course, in normal trading conditions, the extent of this ALM gap is less than the contractual tenors might suggest. We saw this in Figures 12.1 and 12.2, which showed the ALM profiles for a UK bank, the first one contractual tenor-based and the second one behavioural tenor-based. They showed the difference clearly. That does not mean that the second, more "real" gap profile, carries any less liquidity or funding risk. As we noted above, during a stress event it does not matter if a funding gap is small or large – if the bank cannot roll-over funding, it ceases to be a going concern.

The IFP regime is designed to manage the price setting process such that it reflects this gap profile.

The second clear rationale of the IFP regime is that it acts to ensure liquidity and funding risk, and, if constructed properly, interest-rate risk is removed from the business lines and centralised in Treasury. We illustrate this mechanism later in the chapter.

The third and overriding clear rationale behind the IFP regime is to ensure that the asset price setting process reflects the true extent of liquidity risk generation that such asset origination creates, which in turn makes the returns attribution reported to each business line more clearly reflective of genuine SVA.

It is emphasised, however, that the IFP mechanism, while an important part of a bank's liquidity management regime, is not any form of liquidity risk mitigation. It does not address the liquidity and funding risks which arise out of a bank's normal course of business, and which must be addressed by measures such as terming out funding and maintaining an adequate liquidity buffer of risk-free liquid assets. IFP is essentially a "left-hand – right-hand" exercise, and not any form of substitute for a robust liquidity risk management regime.

## Calculating the Term Liquidity Premium

It is important, then, that all banks put in place an internal funding structure which correctly charges for the term liquidity risk placed on the balance sheet by each business line. An artificially low funding rate can create as much potentially unmanageable risk exposure as a risk-seeking loan origination culture.

**Calculation**   The principle debate concerns exactly what Treasury is pricing when it sets the FTP. If one accepts that a bank undertakes maturity transformation, then logic dictates that the FTP charge should be a *term liquidity premium*. For example, the internal rate from Treasury to the Corporate Banking division looking to price a 5-year bullet corporate loan would be the 5-year TLP. The FTP would then be:

$$\text{FTP} = \text{Short-term funding rate} + \text{TLP} \qquad (12.3)$$

As explained above, the base rate should reflect the underlying level of interest rates in the market, and should reflect the re-pricing characteristics of the product. Examples of base rates in South Africa are:

- Jibar, for Jibar-linked instruments (the most frequently used rate is 3-month Jibar, as this is the reference rate used in the South African swap market);
- A fixed rate, for fixed-rate instruments;
- The prime rate, for prime-linked assets.

In the UK, the proxy for the short-term funding rate is usually 3-month Libor, but it could equally be 1-month Libor or the central bank base rate. Or it may be some specific funding rate peculiar to the bank. ALCO should approve the appropriate proxy. Note that the 5-year FTP rate does not necessarily equate to the bank's 5-year wholesale cost of funds (COF) rate. That is because the overall loan pricing calculator, which will incorporate the target rate of return, which is in turn a function of the bank's cost of capital, will already incorporate the bank's cost of credit. To add it to the internal FTP input would be to double count this factor.

If we were to ignore the reality of maturity transformation and assume matched funding, then in this example we would have FTP = COF.

But this would not be realistic because banks do not practise matched funding. Furthermore, while it is always important to ensure that the correct cost of liquidity is allowed for in the internal funding model, it needs to be set in line with commercial and practical reality. As a result, the FTP is often set in between these two approaches, guided by the behavioural structure of the balance sheet as well as some allowance for term liquidity premiums.

**Difficulties with Calculating the TLP**   When used in the way defined here, it is not a straightforward exercise to extract the TLP from market and customer rates. Often one needs to have recourse to proxies, and instead of one specific value being available, one may need to be satisfied with a range and/or average. The calculation is perhaps easiest for larger banks which have a range of external pricing points across wholesale and retail markets.

The base case scenario would be for a bank to have access to the wholesale markets at Libor across the entire term structure. Then there is a case here for saying that the FTP can be Libor-flat; however, this is the current state now, with the future state of the markets being unknown. Thus a zero FTP spread can be justified only on a match-funded basis. Given this logic, a bank needs to determine its cost of term liquidity. There may be more than one answer, so an element of judgement is called for.

The starting point is the rate at which the bank can raise funds in the market. For a large bank, its primary issuance level will, in a stable market, lie above the secondary market level. If we ignore this difference for the time being, a logical first step would be to take the cost of its funds in the market as the primary input to its internal funding curve. Two things must be considered: (i) this funding rate includes the credit risk of the bank, which needs to be stripped out; and (ii) not every bank has a public funding curve. It is necessary then to consider proxies to establish the cost of liquidity.

While a number of proxy measures can be considered, the following are theoretical contenders:

- The difference between the funded and the unfunded rate for the bank; that is, the swap rate versus the bond rate paid by the bank. In other words, what it pays floating in an interest-rate swap against what it pays floating in an asset swap on a bond it issues (of the same tenor);
- The difference between:
  - Paying fixed on a term interest-rate swap; and
  - Paying fixed on the same-tenor money market swap or OIS swap.
- The increase in the cost of funds for the bank for each incremental upward change in tenor. For example, a bank's cost of borrowing along the term structure, as a spread over Libor, may look like this:
  - 1-year: 20 bps;
  - 2-year: 30 bps;
  - 3-year: 35 bps;
  - 4-year: 40 bps;
  - 5-year: 50 bps.

While the above example approach assumes a flat credit term structure for the bank (which, from observation of the credit derivative market is known not to be accurate), this approach does still give some idea of the liquidity premium. The difference between the bank's CDS spread and the asset-swap spread (ASW) for the bank is the CDS basis, and in theory represents the cost of cash borrowing and liquidity premium for the bank against its pure credit risk. Since a CDS is, theoretically, the price of credit only, the basis should represent its liquidity premium.

In the above context, an "asset-swap spread" refers to the spread obtained above the relevant floating-rate (such as 3-month LIBOR) when a fixed-rate instrument, such as a bond, is packaged with a pay-fixed swap with the same tenor as the bond in order to create a floating-rate instrument.

The FTP charge can be based on a simple average of the above measures. Alternatively, given an individual bank's structure, it may choose to give higher weight to certain proxies. Since there is no transparent explicit cost of liquidity, a bank will have to exercise some judgement when setting the rate.

A worked example of this calculation is presented in Example 12.2.

## EXAMPLE 12.2     EXTRACTING THE TLP

The true or "fair value" TLP is difficult to observe. Banks' cost of funds (COF), whether raised in the customer or the wholesale markets, incorporate both the bank's perceived credit risk as well as an element of term premium, so the task here is to extract the term liquidity element from the overall cost. As there is no direct observable, TLP proxies have to be used. In this chapter, the types of proxies that one can consider are detailed. Here, these proxies are then used to determine an estimate for a bank's 5-year TLP.

Consider the following market rates for Euros (EUR), observed on Bloomberg for an A+ rated European bank in January 2013:

**5-Year Rates**
| | |
|---|---|
| CDS | 97 bps |
| Asset Swap (actual bond) interpolated | 103 bps |
| Interest-rate swap | 95 bps |
| Risk-free | 52 bps |

The above imply a 5-year TLP of 6bps (against the CDS) and 8bps (against the swap). Note that the combined credit and liquidity cost as implied by spread over risk-free is 51 bps.

Further implied TLP by proxy can be ascertained from the following:

**Pay-Fixed in 5-Year Swap**
| | |
|---|---|
| Vanilla IRS | 95 bps |
| OIS | 56 bps |

This implies a 5-year TLP of 39 bps. Note this is the 5-year TLP and not the overnight – 3-month TLP. For the 1-year TLP we would use the 1-year swap.

**Cost of Funds Term Structure (Wholesale Market Bonds)**
| | |
|---|---|
| 3-month | 50 bps |
| 1-year | 61 bps |
| 2-year | 79 bps |
| 5-year interpolated | 103 bps |

This implies a 5-year TLP of 53 bps.

**New Issue Premium**
| | |
|---|---|
| New issue | 132 bps |
| Secondary market asset-swap | 103 bps |

This implies a 5-year TLP of 29 bps.

From the above, one has five inputs for the 5-year TLP in the range of 6 bps to 53 bps. The average is 27 bps and the median is 29 bps. If one removes the outlier, the highest value and the lowest value, the average is 25.3 bps. One can then conclude that a logical rate to set for the 5-year TLP is of the order of 25–30 bps. This calculation should be updated periodically, say every quarter.

At first sight this may appear insufficient value for a 5-year liquidity premium. But bear in mind that the bank's 5-year asset swap is trading at 103 bps, and it is able to issue new 5-year wholesale market FRNs at 132 bps. If the bank's COF for this tenor is in this range, it is not unexpected that the pure liquidity premium element of this cost should appear to be around one third of this figure, with the balance representing the issuer credit risk of the bank.

In countries with a well-developed market for money-market instruments such as floating-rate notes and negotiable certificates of deposit (for medium and long tenors (for example, tenors of three years and longer)), and a developed market in capital markets funding instruments (referred to as the "senior unsecured" market), the TLP is most realistically set by determining the spread between these instruments and the bank's swap curve.

**FTP Curves**  The actual internal funding curve template, be it the TLP or all-in FTP curve, should be included in the bank's funding policy document and reviewed on a regular basis. While it is common for the FTP rates to be posted as a grid (as shown earlier), this is not recommended because of the implied linear interpolation relationship between odd-date tenors. Instead, the FTP curve should be drawn as a curve such as at Figure 12.17. Here an example for a bank that operates across the retail, corporate and wholesale banking space and has calculated a "weighted average" funding curve (WACF), is illustrated. Many banks choose the grid presentation, however. When a grid is used, assets or liabilities with maturities that are not exact full years, and thus fall in between the tenors on the grid, should be priced on a straight-line interpolation basis between the shorter and longer date prices.

The FTP curve will state explicitly the rate paid or received by the business lines for assets and liabilities across the term structure. If the FTP

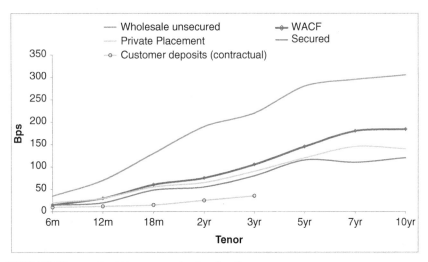

**FIGURE 12.17**    Bank FTP curve and other funding curves

policy assumes matched funding, and applies full marginal cost pricing (FMC), then this disregards the fact that, in reality, the bank is engaging in maturity transformation. While this is logically tenable, it may not be practical for commercial or economic reasons. It is preferable to understand the market consistent pricing framework and make incentive adjustments over and above this to allow for the impact of maturity transformation in the behavioural balance sheet. The final customer pricing would incorporate cost of capital, required margin, and an add-on for customer credit risk.

Of course, the final choice for the FTP policy is a matter of individual bank judgement, and again, should be decided by ALCO. It is also influenced by the bank's current balance sheet shape and structure, and planned shaped and structure. (For example, a bank running a customer loans-deposits ratio of 180% would be advised to have an FTP regime that is different to that in place at a bank running an LDR of 80%.)

Where behavioural analysis indicates that the term to maturity of an item differs from its contractual term to maturity, the expected maturity is used to set the appropriate FTP rate.

For assets and liabilities, good examples are:

- *Residential mortgages*: in many jurisdictions mortgages are issued commonly with a contractual term of 20 years. However, in the UK from observation and behavioural analysis point of view the expected life is approximately 6–7 years, hence a 6-year rate, or lower, would be applied for new asset origination pricing. Fixed-rate mortgages, on the other hand, are priced at the product rate tenor, but take pre-payment behaviour into account.

▪ *Current accounts*: this product has a 1-day (or 0-day) contractual maturity but balances are sticky and, typically, at least half of the aggregate balance is static over 2, 3, or even 5 years. It is logical to assign such tenors for FTP purposes. In a similar vein, if a call account balance is shown to be 50% sticky for one year, the 1-year FTP would be earned on 50% of the funds. No TLP would be payable on the 50% of the funds deemed to not be sticky, because these funds are deemed to be of a short-term (overnight) nature.

For trading book assets, which are generally assumed to be liquid and expected to be sold within 6 months of being bought, the FTP charge would be set according to the expected holding duration and not the legal maturity of the traded asset. Typically, this will be at the 6-month FTP rate, however, this depends on the type of asset and the level of liquidity. In general, a bank will set different tiers of liquidity, with Tier 1 (such as G7 government bonds) being the most liquid and thus attracting a 1-week or 1-month FTP, down to Tier 3 for the least liquid and attracting the 6-month internal funds rate. Note this would apply to the unsecured funding element of trading book assets: often, such assets are funded in repo so except for the haircut element they are "self-funded".

## Template Bank FTP Regime

Though there is no "one size fits all" FTP regime, but best-practice guidelines for the FTP approach in retail, corporate, and wholesale market business lines are presented here.

The guidelines assume a standard internal funding arrangement, whereby internal funding operations are arranged via a "bank account" in Treasury. (Note that this is not necessarily implemented in the form of a physical bank account – it might simply be an accounting process whereby all assets and liabilities are charged and paid appropriate FTP rates on a regular basis, usually monthly.) When a loan is made, this internal "account" is overdrawn and then funded on an overnight basis to the business line. The standard overnight FTP charge is 3-month Libor, but it could be 1-month Libor or 6-month Libor, or the central bank base rate, depending on the opinion of the bank's ALCO. Note this is simply a cash management process, the FTP rate is set on a month-end basis but of course the cash account is drawn down (or up) every day. Assets or liabilities are set at the relevant tenor FTP, although another option is to operate a net rather than gross funding basis, and either charge or pay the net position long or short in each relevant tenor bucket at the relevant FTP.

**Commercial Bank FTP Policy**   The funding provided by retail customers tends to be of a more stable nature than funding provided by other types of customer. A large proportion of retail funding is of a zero-rate or low-rate liabilities nature (termed non-interest bearing liabilities or NIBLs, or non-interest bearing current accounts or NIBCAs). The FTP tenor for retail assets can generally be set safely at less than the contractual tenor – often the expected life (EL) tenor is used to set the FTP rate for retail assets. This is because retail assets tend to have a behavioural life that is shorter than the contractual term, due to the tendency of these loans to be pre-paid. Using the EL tenor preserves the competitive position of the bank, as the TLP is lower for shorter tenors, thereby reducing the overall FTP rate charged on the retail assets. Liabilities are also priced at behavioural tenor. So here the FTP rate is determined as the base rate plus the TLP, and not determined with reference to COF. For residential mortgage assets, we assume that all are capital and repayment products, with no interest-only mortgages. The main principles are shown at Figure 12.18. If a bank has a large exposure to interest-only mortgages, it is advisable to set FTP rates for these separately, using a "bullet" structure to price the loans rather than the usual "amortising" structure.

Note here that the tenors quoted are behavioural or, as is common, can be adjusted downwards for competitive reasons. If operating a net charging regime (i.e., a regime under which the funding provided by a business unit is first used to offset the funding needed to fund the business unit's assets, before the net funding requirement from Treasury is determined), it is possible to set and net nearly matching tenors, for example, 3-year deposits against 3-year assets. A net charging regime runs the risk of leaving some liquidity risk within the business unit, and if such a regime is used it needs to be carefully managed.

From Figure 12.18, for the floating-rate asset, FTP is 3M Libor plus TLP. The TLP tenor will be the behavioural life of the asset, so we have suggested seven years. For the fixed-rate asset, FTP is the fixed-rate equivalent to 3M Libor plus TLP, where the TLP tenor matches the product life (for example, a 2-year fixed rate on a mortgage that moves to floating, or can be re-fixed at a new rate after two years). This transfers interest-rate risk from the business line and centralises it in Treasury.

In practice, it is unlikely that any particular business unit has exactly the same amount of assets and liabilities. The business unit is therefore "surplus funded" (if it has more liabilities than assets) or has a "funding gap". It is important that the FTP framework is designed in such a way that business units receive fair value for their liabilities, and receive a fair charge for their assets, regardless of the business unit's funding position.

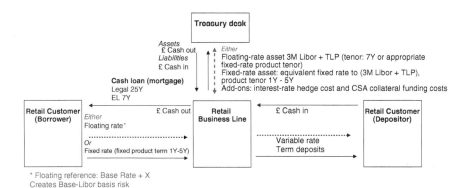

**FIGURE 12.18** Retail banking FTP regime

The reality of FTP policy is that it must reflect the two-way relationship between assets and liabilities. We summarise, with reference to Figure 12.19, the practical considerations that FTP should reflect:

- Critically: whether the bank is surplus customer-funded (so a loan-deposit ratio materially below 100%) or short customer funded;
- Actual rates paid by both sides;
- Competitive position;
- Properly priced products;
- Behavioural match-funding where applicable, for example, match-funded or not:
  - Banks that treat current account balances as 5Y or even longer tenor;
  - Banks that treat such liabilities as shorter tenor;
- The funding position of the business unit.

The longer-dated assumption allows a retail bank to consider itself as "almost match-funded". This is the attraction, from a liquidity risk management point of view, of stable customer deposits ("stable" liabilities as opposed to "non-stable" in the Basel III terminology).

Figure 12.19 also makes clear another important fact: that many banks are price takers and not price makers. They have to pay customer rates in the wholesale markets and cannot set loan pricing with complete freedom, because the positioning of larger banks means that smaller banks must follow this lead. Irrespective of what a bank's own funding costs might dictate the FTP pricing element of its loan pricing overall cost should be, the fact remains that banks needs to take into account their competitive position, and where they stand in product pricing terms relative to their peer group.

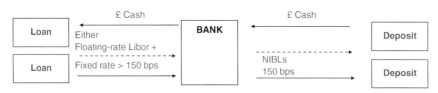

**FIGURE 12.19**   Asset and liabilities interaction

If the FTP regime applied results in product pricing which are uncompetitive, the bank will lose business. Rates can either be changed to improve customer pricing vis-à-vis the peer group, or the bank can exit that business line. In that respect, the FTP regime is an important part of the planning process at a bank.

**Wholesale Bank FTP Regime**   The wholesale banking business model, requires a more prescribed FTP regime. There is little, if any, concept of a "customer deposits" funding business and the asset side is often funded with Repo (secured funding) and wholesale unsecured funding (money markets and capital markets).

This makes the FTP model more straightforward to implement. For example, a summary template could look like this:

- Trading book: funded in repo at repo rate. Any unsecured funding is funded at 6-month or 12-month Libor. However, not all trading book assets are of an equal liquidity level. The funding policy may break down the asset types into the following:
  - Tier 1: G7 currency bonds;
  - Tier 2: Bonds denominated in AUD, CHF, DKK, HKD, NOK, NZD, SEK, SGD;
  - Tier 3: Bonds rated below A–/A3.

Most banks will not have FTP grids for currencies other than for their domestic currency, US Dollars, and Euros. The base currency grid can be converted to a required currency rate by applying the FX basis swap rate to it – not an exact science but the approach should be sufficient for most purposes.

Where trading book assets cannot be funded in Repo, they will be funded at the money market's unsecured rate for the tenor that the trading book operates to (most banks' trading books have a "churn" rule that requires assets purchased on it to be sold after 90 or 180 days. So, the unsecured money market rate would be the matching 90-day or 180-day one). Where Repo funding is used, the haircut amount is also funded at this unsecured money market rate. Setting haircut levels needs to be a joint business line and Treasury process, and reviewed regularly.

- Securitisable assets: origination of assets that are eligible for securitisation often receive a lower funding rate, say a specified reduction in basis points, because in theory they do not expose the bank to a need for more unsecured wholesale funding;
- Derivatives book: contractual and collateral funding cash-flows are modelled into tenor buckets, as expected positive exposure (EPE) and expected negative exposure (ENE), with the net number ("expected exposure" or EE) charged or credited with the appropriate wholesale market COF, rather than on the basis of Base Rate plus TLP.

A bank which operates across all markets will need to carefully consider how to construct its FTP curve and whether there should be one unified curve across the bank or variations by business line. For instance, consideration should be given to whether funding is sourced centrally (for instance, where US Dollars are sourced by a "hub" at the centre), or whether funding is sourced by each business unit individually. In the case of the former, it might be sensible to have a uniform curve for US Dollars across the bank.

**Illustration** The chart at Figure 12.20 shows examples of how the FTP process might be applied in practice. In reality, business lines transact large

---

⫽ Liability: MTA balance agreed as 5-year behavioural tenor

   ⫽ MTA treated as "floating rate" liability

   ⫽ Notional balance £X stated on internal ticket (this may be "haircut" to [ ]% of actual aggregate balance as determined by behavioural profile)

   ⫽ Current 5-yr TLP [ ] bps

      ⫽ (Curve or grid updated weekly/monthly/quarterly as desired)

   ⫽ FTP is 3-mo Libor + TLP spread on £X shown in month-end management accts


⫽ Asset: 2-year standby liquidity facility

   ⫽ Assume it will be drawn down to max term so FTP is STFR + 2-year TLP on *floating* basis

⫽ Asset: 25-year legal maturity residential mortgage, dealt at 3-year fixed rate

   ⫽ Assume 3-year behavioural profile so FTP is 3-mo Libor + 3-year TLP at *fixed* rate equivalent

   ⫽ Assume re-fixed in 3 years and retained on balance sheet, so will reprice then

---

**FIGURE 12.20**   FTP operation illustration examples

volumes of tickets each day, so it would be impractical to write internal funding tickets for each transaction. In practice, Treasury will write a ticket for each business line at month-end for the aggregate volume of business in that month. Large ticket transactions (such as a large corporate syndicated loan) may still have their own FTP ticket transacted at the time of the deal.

The FTP mechanism itself is implemented operationally through various "funding policies" that describe the specific nuances to the regime for each product type. For example, there would be a Banking Book Funding Policy, Trading Book Policy, and (for banks that are market makers in derivatives), a Derivatives Funding Policy.

For example, undrawn commitments such as liquidity lines need to be priced based on the liquidity risk they represent. This differs according to the type of customer; bank and non-bank FI customers are deemed to represent a greater liquidity risk with such products compared to small corporates. The FTP policy for committed facilities is a crucial part of the overall discipline of internal funds pricing. Back-up and other liquidity lines supplied to the bank's customers are likely to be drawn on at precisely the time when the bank will itself most want to be preserving liquidity and lend less: during a funding crisis. It is imperative, therefore, that these facilities be allocated the appropriate charge when they are originated, given the liquidity risk exposure they represent.

Figure 12.21 reprises the expected usage profile for a committed funding line shown earlier at Figure 12.4, but this time with an indication of what implies a stress event.

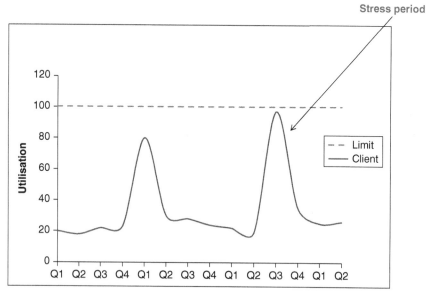

**FIGURE 12.21**   Committed facility usage profile

**TABLE 12.21** Undrawn commitments FTP pricing grid

| | | Facility Tenor | | |
|---|---|---|---|---|
| | Rating | 1-year | 2–4 year | > 5-year |
| Revolving Credit Facility | A1/P1 | 20 | 20 | 30 |
| | A2/P2 | 25 | 25 | 35 |
| Committed Back-Up Line | A1/P1 | 35 | 40 | 50 |
| | A2/P2 | 40 | 50 | 75 |
| Conduit Liquidity Line | A1/P1 | 35 | 40 | n/a |
| | A2/P2 | 40 | 50 | n/a |

From this understanding, we conclude that a committed standing back-up facility represents the highest risk to a bank's liquidity stress position. The FTP for this facility must therefore be set as term FTP. This is the basic position; exceptions can be made depending on the type of client, and to what extent the client is dependent on the facility in the event of market stress. Table 12.21 is an example of a pricing grid for inclusion in an FTP policy. It would be reviewed on a semi-annual basis, to reflect changes in market conditions.

### Implementation: Case Study Example

Until the Lehman default in September 2008, for many bankers, it was a long-held assumption that their firms would be able to fund at Libor-flat along the term structure. As long as inter-bank markets were reasonably stable, which, despite the Western economies recessions of 1980–1982 and 1990–1991, was generally the case, this assumption was not wholly unreasonable. What was unreasonable was the expectation that this would always be the case.

The Lehman experience resulted in a general freezing of inter-bank markets and all but the most robust banks found themselves paying above Libor for wholesale funding. Figure 12.22 shows how the generally stable Libor-OIS spread in USD blew out at this time.

This experience was a lesson learned in many aspects of liquidity risk management, including FTP. Banks found themselves having to revise their FTP regimes, not least because of the regulator's scrutiny.

One example of this occurred at the A-rated London subsidiary of a MENA-domiciled bank in 2009. The London subsidiary revamped its FTP regime and its model was then adopted throughout the Group. In fact, the London office was designated the "liquidity hub" for GBP, EUR, and USD

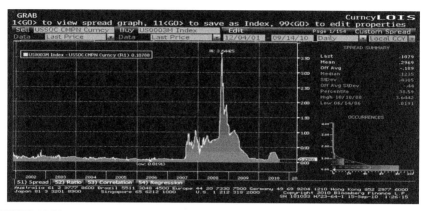

**FIGURE 12.22** USD Libor-OIS spread 2002–2010
*Source*: © Bloomberg LLP. Reproduced with permission.

(as well as CHF) pricing. Details on the business in London and its funding arrangements at the time are given in the case studies in Chapter 19.

## Treasury Allocation and FTP

"Treasury allocation" (TA) is the generic term for the process of passing on central entity obligations – Liquid Asset Buffer (net funding cost, so "carry") and wholesale market term funding costs – to the business lines. Sometimes there is an element of "capital income" to allocate if no aspect of TA is held centrally or in something like an "ALCO book", which may be comprised of capital income on the "equity hedge" and previous years' profit interest income.

In most banks, the LAB operates at a net loss, although in some banks it operates at a profit. The cost of the LAB is in effect a cost of liquidity risk mitigation, and would be the net of the LAB asset income, the funding cost of the assets and any interest-rate hedge costs. This is quantified as a net basis point cost. This cost can be held centrally in the bank, added on to the FTP charge, or "allocated" back to the business lines.

The extent of allocation is a function of how much the business line contributes to the size of the liquidity buffer and the requirement to generate term funding, which is a function of how short-funded the business line is. Usually an extent of the "funding gap", often calculated with respect to the Basel III Liquidity Coverage Ratio stressed cash outflow results, or the cash outflow results obtained by performing internal stress testing exercises in line with the bank's own liquidity risk appetite framework, drives this calculation. Different banks set their TA methodologies differently, and one can observe considerable variation in type. However, the relevance to FTP is that TA is an element of cost allocation that drives ultimate performance reporting – just as correct FTP does – and in some banks the cost of the TA is incorporated as an add-on to the FTP rate.

Given that FTP itself is a front-book principle – one is pricing something today that will be on the balance sheet going forward – it would appear to be illogical to pass on the cost of something that has just been determined and relates to the past onto new front book business. That is why it is recommended that the liquidity buffer and term funding costs be passed on at month-end in management accounts, rather than incorporated into new business pricing.

Keeping the TA costs separate from the FTP process also preserves transparency with a pricing mechanism that is in essence placing a value on term liquidity premium, and nothing else.

## Conclusions

With FTP it is important that the mechanism put in place is the one most appropriate to the business model of the bank in question, and set up to reflect the type of business that is in line with the objectives of the bank's shareholders and Board.

Implementing an internal funds pricing policy that explicitly charges each business line for its cost of liquidity is not always a painless task, due in part to inertia and resistance from the business lines themselves. This is particularly acute when the businesses have historically always paid a Libor-flat or a Libor plus fixed spread charge.

The FTP framework can also form an important risk management tool by ensuring that liquidity risk and interest-rate risk are centralised within the Treasury function. FTP can also be used strategically, but the impact on return and performance metrics needs to be fully understood first.

---

**CASE STUDY: FTP QUESTION FROM MEDIUM-SIZED COMMERCIAL BANK**

The Treasury and Risk departments in a medium-sized commercial bank in the Americas posed this question connected to FTP policy:

> When funding a loan, there is an internal loan between the ALM unit and the business unit. This loan could be considered as a risk-free loan since the business unit should always repay the loan to the ALM unit. Also, capital is allocated to all business units (including the Treasury business units but ALM) and ALM pays a capital rebate to the business units as compensation.

---

*(Continued)*

When a loan defaults, there is a provision charge which impacts the business unit's P&L, reducing its capital. This capital reduction can be seen as a transfer from the business unit to ALM, and since the ALM desk should not pay any more capital rebate for this portion, this amount can be seen as a prepayment of the loan initially given by ALM to the business unit.

Our view is that since in the case of a full default the ALM gets the loan fully prepaid, defaults should be considered when calculating the actual behaviour of the loan initially given by ALM desk and therefore the duration (and the FTP rate) of such loans could be lower in the case of riskier loans (everything else the same). Currently our bank does not include defaulted loans when calculating the actual behaviour its loan portfolio.

The Author's response:

- Provisions ordinarily will hit P&L and capital at the end of the period; if credit performance improves then the impact can be compensated in following periods.
- There is only one reason to allocate capital to the business units and it is for the finance department to calculate a return on capital for each business line.
- No individual business line "owns" the bank's capital, the capital is owned by the ALCO and should be recorded in an ALCO book.
- Provisions are unusable capital, they sit on the balance sheet and aren't available to use, it should be transferred to the ALCO book.
- If the loan defaults, it can't be repaid to the ALM unit unless it recovers.
- The expected life can be used for FTP. Behavioural tenor should be used for FTP. There should not be a specific adjustment for defaults, but they must be included in the estimation of the portfolio's behaviour.
- If having two identical portfolios but one with a riskier profile, then the riskier would have a shorter life. When including credit risk, then the expected life will be higher, but for funding (where no credit risk should be included) the tenor is lower.
- Including defaults in the expected life of the portfolio shouldn't make that much difference.
- Credit risk should not be included in FTP, but can be included in the calculation of the expected life of a product.

The bank's FTP policy, whether it is an update or is being set up for the first time, should always be owned by the Board, delegated to ALCO, and implemented by the Treasury and Finance department.

# OPTIMUM LIABILITIES STRATEGY AND MANAGING THE LIQUID ASSETS BUFFER[3]

In this section, we examine the interdependency between the Liability Strategy and the link that it has on the Liquid Asset Buffer (LAB) requirement. This topic should be read in conjunction with the regulatory reporting chapter in order to ensure that this interdependency is understood in the context of stress testing. We will start by looking at the liabilities strategy, formulated through a coherent and integrated funding plan, and then examine the LAB.

## Liabilities Strategy

As part of an integrated liquidity risk management framework, a bank should articulate an optimum liabilities strategy. This sits at the heart of the strategic ALM balance sheet planning process. The liabilities strategy of an organisation needs to take into consideration the diversification of the liability base to ensure that it is not concentrated in any particular aspect such as tenor, client, industry sector, or product type.

Under the Strategic ALM umbrella, there are a few core components that are directly relevant to the liabilities strategy:

- A single, integrated balance sheet approach that ties in asset origination with liabilities raising;
- Thus, asset type must be relevant and appropriate to funding type and source. . .;
- . . . .and the funding type and source must be appropriate to the asset type.

In order to apply these three key principles, it is important to undertake a comprehensive review of the bank's balance sheet liabilities as a first step towards determining both the optimum liability profile and then the overall liabilities strategy. This exercise is more involved, the larger and more complex businesses, but critical nonetheless.

The strategy setting is not a static or one-off process. The objective is to arrive at a balance sheet liability mix and structure by design, and one which is optimum from a strategic ALM perspective, rather than one that is a result simply of history and business line BAU activity – in other words, a passive inherited liability shape.

**The Changing Liability Structure of Banks** The liability structure of many EU and MENA banks has changed since 2007–2008 and has focused on moving away from wholesale funds, both short-term (supply) and long-term (demand), and moving towards more non-interest bearing liabilities (NIBLs)

---

[3] This section was co-authored with Jamie Paris.

|  | UK banks average | | Your bank's split and interest cost |
|---|---|---|---|
|  | 2007 | 2012 | |
| Deposits by banks | 6.00% | 3.80% | |
| Customer accounts | 31% | 31% | |
| Debt securities | 12.30% | 10.60% | |
| NIBLs | 24.30% | 27.50% | |
| Equity | 4.40% | 5.00% | |
| Other | 21.90% | 22.10% | |
| Total liabilities and equity | 100% | 100% | |
| (Source: SEC 20-F filings) | | | |

**FIGURE 12.23** Funding breakdown UK banks average, 2007 and 2012

and equity (Figure 12.23). This has largely been driven by the introduction of the ILAS regime and subsequent LCR stress testing regulatory metrics. Both of these stress tests penalise the use of wholesale funding and hence banks have diversified and focused on retail and NIBLs balances. For one high street UK bank, NIBLs rose from 28% of liabilities and equity in 2007 to 41% in 2012.

**The Liability Structure: What Is the Optimum Mix?** In compiling the optimum liability mix targets, there are some important considerations that need to be applied in the planning process. These revolve around:

- Regulation;
- Liquidity value (to what extent is a type of customer deposit or type beneficial towards the final LCR or NSFR metric?);
- Funding diversification/concentration;
- Impact to Net Interest Income and Net Interest Margin;
- NII sensitivity;
- Customer franchise value and funding diversity value;
- How to build the customer franchise;
- Set up costs of new products.

Banks fund their balance sheets using a variety of liability types. The liquidity value of each type is different. Ideally, a funding type has high liquidity value as well as high NII value, customer franchise value, etc. This is essentially the "Strategic ALM" optimisation problem, attempting to structure the balance sheet mix, in this case with respect to liabilities, that best serves the competing requirements of the regulator, the customer stakeholder, and the shareholder.

In practice, there is usually a trade-off amongst these factors as some liabilities have greater term liquidity value for a bank than others. At one end of the scale are retail current accounts; at the other are short-term unsecured wholesale liabilities, sourced in the inter-bank market, which have much more volatile characteristics in stressed market conditions and therefore are less valuable for liquidity management purposes.

Consider a bank funded by:

- Customer NIBLs;
- Customer deposits;
- Wholesale funding;
- Secured funding (Repo, RMBS, and Covered Bonds);
- Private placements including structured notes.

This mix would give the (stylised) funding curve shown at Figure 12.24. What is the optimum mix of these funds? To answer this question requires us to investigate and report on the value of each liability type in accordance with the parameters above. This is a non-trivial exercise that Treasury should undertake under direction of ALCO. Some of the considerations include the following:

- Review the liability structure of the bank, and changes over time historically;
- Look at funding costs as interest paid over the entire liability structure (for this exercise exclude equity: its balance is heavily influenced by regulatory requirements and it doesn't drive a customer franchise strategy with respect to deposit mix);
- Review the bank's CDS premium if it has one, but recognise there is a disconnect in the CDS-Asset Swap basis relationship and so CDS price may not be relevant for understanding actual funding costs;
- Review the importance (weight) of NIBLs and its share of total funding;
- Review interest costs versus peer group levels, to determine how the bank is perceived in the customer and market space;
- Compare your deposit costs versus peer levels;
- Review individual business line contribution to trends identified, and assess for optimum share. Which type of funding do you want to maximise, and which to minimise?;
- Obtain a better understanding of the movement in NIBL balances.

Table 12.22 highlights the detailed considerations that need to be applied during the planning process.

We already considered earlier in this chapter the "hierarchy" of value of different types of liabilities. From a liquidity value perspective, a bank should seek to maximise funding from customer relationship balances and minimise its reliance on wholesale inter-bank funding.

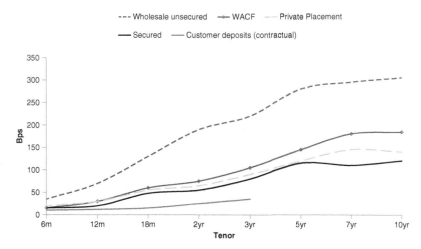

**FIGURE 12.24**   Hypothetical bank funding curve for an institution raising multiple different liability types

**TABLE 12.22**   Considerations during the liabilities strategy setting stage

| Factor | Consideration |
| --- | --- |
| Regulation | Deposit Guarantee Scheme? Is a regulated sales force required to distribute the product? |
| Liquidity | What is the liquidity value of the deposit? |
| Concentration | Does the deposit type improve the diversity of the funding base? |
| NII/NIM | Contribution to NII per FTP system, not gross cost? |
| NII Sensitivity | Does the deposit act as a natural hedge for assets? Some banks do not use derivatives to manage NII sensitivity |
| Customer Franchise | Does the product reinforce the franchise value of the organisation? E.g., Santander 123 account |
| Other Costs | Explicit costs associated with the product? |

The mix of these should be arrived at through design as much as possible and a bank's Funds Transfer Pricing process may be used to help drive liabilities raising of the "right" type and through incentivising businesses by rewarding them with a higher commission or sales credit for the higher value liquidity type.

**Peer Group Analysis**   In the UK, the Bank of England (BoE) publishes monthly data showing effective interest rate paid on (sterling) deposit balances of UK household and UK non-FI corporate sectors, split by deposit type. It is a measure of back-book deposit costs (in the UK), not front book (that is, marginal cost of new funds).

Through this peer review, one can compare the current bank levels to peer levels, to establish whether your bank is paying above the sector-wide average and to establish a better understanding of what your bank is paying for its deposits and assess if this can be improved.

In addition to data published by central banks, a bank should survey the market itself to determine the current pricing associated with certain liability products. Earlier in this chapter we presented the results of such a comparison, and noted that "XYZ bank" is exactly where it most probably wishes to be, in the middle of the range amongst its peers and not an outlier for rates at either end. The highest deposit rate payers are sometimes perceived by customers to be struggling to raise deposits, and such a customer perception would not be welcome for a bank.

An analysis of front-book deposit prices versus competitors would provide additional colour to the liabilities review. This information should also be presented regularly to either the Products Pricing Committee or Deposits Pricing Committee (sub-committee of ALCO). As noted above, the general rule of thumb is not to be an outlier at either end.

**Product Volume Sensitivity to Interest Rate Movements**   Some liability products are sensitive to movements in interest rates and are referred to as NII sensitive products. A high volume sensitivity may not be a good thing as this could lead to certain challenges notably cannibalisation from other product types and "hot money".

Cannibalisation from other deposit products offered by the bank can lead to a dramatically different impact on NII than originally anticipated, especially, if large volumes of deposits switch to the new/re-priced product from high margin accounts. Placing restrictions on who can apply for certain products can attract the attention of the regulators.

"Hot money" from interest rate seekers (standalone customers): if a new/re-priced account attracts deposits from customers who are only interested in the rate being paid, then you may finish up with expensive funding which has no liquidity value. For this reason, many banks have withdrawn from offering offshore instant access Internet-based accounts.

The same can also be said around products that have been offered at below par rate. Deposit products often have tiered rates and/or customer relationship managers are given the discretion to pay a higher rate

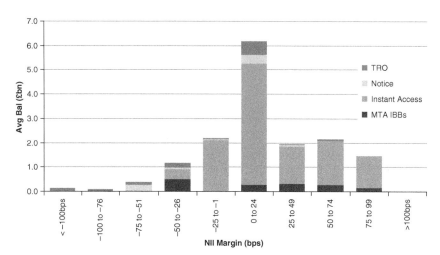

**FIGURE 12.25**   Deposit product analysis

to protect/attract business. Average product margins can mask underlying trends. Figure 12.25 is an example of this type of review in more detail.

As part of the liability strategy, a bank should conduct a granular review to understand which deposits are being written at negative margins and consider the options to reduce the size of this segment of business as it is value destroying.

**Output of the Liability Review**   The result of the liabilities mix review should be a medium-term (for example, 3- to 5-year) strategy that specifies a precise target for:

- The liabilities mix: how much do we wish of each funding type, and why;
- What the drivers are;
- What if any funding types are of less value and should be reduced or withdrawn from;
- Plan for implementation.

This liabilities strategy review would be presented for ALCO approval and subsequent implementation. This plan could include a series of initiatives that would be tracked at ALCO on a regular basis to ensure that the balance sheet is tracking in the right direction and is being measured by some key performance indicators.

Initiatives could include any or all of those listed in Table 12.23.

The ALCO review should have a level of product emphasis aligned to the specific initiatives that the plan has identified such as: focus on Instant Access savings or term deposits. There should be a regular competitive

**TABLE 12.23** Sample of potential range of liabilities strategies

| Target | Initiative |
|--------|------------|
| Customer Optimisation | Target specific sectors, e.g., universities, charities. Package an offering to growing customer segments Rationalise geographies Volume caps on retail customer business (e.g., £1m) Remove from sale any products offering lifetime guarantees |
| Margin Improvement | Increase range of managed rate products by reducing those that price according to a fixed formula (e.g., Base Rate + . . .%) |
| Other Initiatives | Standalone customers: target reduction in "rate chaser" customers acquired during periods of aggressive balance sheet growth |
| | Lengthen notice period on notice accounts, from 7/14 days to 90+ |
| | Remove the facility to break fixed rate deposits early |
| | Stop paying liquidity premia on accounts without liquidity value |

analysis as previously described to ensure that pricing is still relevant in the market and that process against key performance indicators is tracked monthly and any variations clearly understood.

**Summary** A balance sheet funding review is an essential start to the bank's drafting of its optimum funding mix and liabilities strategy. The larger and more complex the bank (IB, Corporate, Retail), the more complex the review. It is important to understand the share of the balance sheet and costs currently and review these in the context of what the balance sheet should look like in one to three years' time.

The overall optimum liabilities strategy will consist of a series of tactical/strategic initiatives that will help bank re-engineer the funding profile to achieve an optimal mix. This is the start of a more logical and coherent approach to balance sheet funding.

## The Liquid Asset Buffer

We consider now the Liquid Asset Buffer (LAB), also known globally as the high quality liquid assets portfolio (HQLA, the term used by the Basel Committee) which can be a sizeable item on the asset side of the balance sheet. The size of the LAB is determined purely by the quality of the liabilities mix on the balance sheet, as it is required to offset the potential outflow of liabilities in a time of stress, for example, the Financial Crisis.

All firms are required to hold buffers of liquid assets and it forms a key part of the PRA requirement for liquidity, and this is now enshrined in global regulation by Basel III (the HQLA). These assets must be uncorrelated to the institution – so it cannot be the bank's own debt issued – nor can they be repo funded (i.e., they must be unencumbered) and should preferably be funded by long-term (>90 days) liabilities.

Liquid assets are those that can be easily converted to cash at any time (including times of stress), with little or no loss of value. They have certain characteristics that need to be fulfilled in order to qualify as liquid assets. These characteristics can be divided into fundamental and market components.

The fundamental characteristics of LAB assets are described as:

- Low Credit and Market Risk:
  Low degree of subordination, low duration, low volatility, low inflation risk and denominated in a convertible currency;
- Ease and Certainty of Valuation:
  - Pricing formula must be easy to calculate with no strong assumptions and inputs must be publicly available;
- Low Correlation with Risky Assets:
  - Should not be subject to wrong way risk;
- Listed on a Developed and Recognised Exchange Market:
  - Increases transparency;

The Market characteristics are described as:

- Active and Sizeable Market:
  - Outright sale and repo markets at all times. Historical evidence of market breadth and market depth;
- Presence of Committed Market-Makers:
  - Quotes are always available for buying and selling the asset Low Market Concentration;
  - Diverse group of buyers and sellers in the assets' market;
- Flight to Quality:
  - Historic evidence of these types of asset being traded in a systemic crisis.

Under the Basel III LCR calculation, the liquidity value of differing types of Liquid Assets is pre-determined within the confines of the stress test. Table 12.24 highlights what these haircuts are and highlights that a minimum of 60% of the portfolio would need to be made up of Level 1 assets (most liquid).

**TABLE 12.24**  Requirements for LAB (or HQLA) eligibility

| HQLA Eligibility Criteria | Cap | Haircut |
|---|---|---|

**Level 1**  Min 60%

- Cash at Central Banks
- Central Bank Reserves
- Government Bonds issued or guaranteed by ECB, member state government or central bank

| | Cap | Haircut |
|---|---|---|
| Government Bonds (AAA to AA-) | | 0% |
| Public Sector Debt guart'd by sovereign (AAA to AA-) | | |
| Government Bonds (<A+) for CCY specific stress | | |
| Multinational Banks | | |
| Covered Bonds (EEA) (AAA to AA-) | 70% | 7% |

**Level 2 A**

| | Cap | Haircut |
|---|---|---|
| Government Bonds (A+ to A-) | | |
| Public Sector Debt guart'd by sovereign (A+ to A-) | | |
| Covered Bonds (Non EEA) (AAA to AA-) | | 15% |
| Corporate Bonds (AAA to AA-) | | |
| Covered Bonds (EEA) (A+ to A-) | 40% | |

**Level 2 B**  Max 15%

| | Cap | Haircut |
|---|---|---|
| Corporate Bonds (A+ to BBB-) | | 50% |
| Major Index Equities | | 50% |
| Covered Bonds (Unrated) | | 30% |
| Restricted Use Central Bank Committed Liquidity Facility | | 35% |
| Asset Backed Securities (AAA to AA-) | 15% | |
| ‣ RMBS | | 25% |
| ‣ Auto-ABS | | 25% |
| ‣ CMBS – SME | | 35% |
| ‣ Consumer Loans ABS | | 35% |

**Hedging the Liquid Asset Buffer**  Part of the LAB will be comprised of longer-term securities and so ALCO must direct the Interest-Rate Risk (and credit risk) hedging approach, particularly for those assets that are fixed rate.

| IR Swap – Pros | IR Swap – Cons |
|---|---|
| •A liquid instrument – GBP swap market is transparent and served by a large number of market makers<br><br>•An accurate hedge can be achieved by matching asset tenor precisely | •Remain exposed to the counterparty risk of the swap bank (mitigated in part by the use of collateral via a CSA)<br>•Uses up precious swap lines which may be better saved for other books<br>•Difficult to use for dynamic hedging (loss of bid-offer spread on unwind) |

| IR Futures – Pros | IR Futures – Cons |
|---|---|
| •No counterparty risk<br>•Liquid instant market with narrow bid-offer spread<br>•Dynamic hedging is straightforward – adjust the hedge by buying or selling additional contracts as necessary<br>•Does not use swap lines | •Requires account at clearing house and daily margining<br>•Requires rollover each time the "front month" is reached, which is on or before the 1st of the delivery month |

**FIGURE 12.26**    Pros and cons of employing the different interest-rate risk hedging instruments

For portfolios denominated in GBP, interest-rate risk hedges may be transacted using IR swaps, short sterling futures (fixed-rate instruments up to three years), or LIFFE Gilt Futures (fixed-rate instruments of over three years). There are equivalent OTC and exchange-traded derivative instruments for other liquid currencies.

The pros and cons of using each instrument type is summarised at Figure 12.26.

A point worth noting is that, in the UK, there is a requirement that LAB be demonstrated to be truly liquid through an element of "churn" (sold and repurchased), so the assets will be designated as Available for Sale (AFS) and not Held to Maturity (HTM) from an accounting perspective.

## Liquid Asset Buffer Policy

Given the importance of the LAB, it is important to ensure that investment criteria are established in line with the Board Risk Appetite of the firm. An integral part of the Board-approved liquidity risk management policy is that all banks must maintain a portfolio of high-quality genuinely liquid assets to act as a funding reserve against liabilities outflow in times of stress.

The amount of liquid assets should cover the outflows projected from the Bank's Liquidity Stress Tests, provide collateral for payment systems, and satisfy minimum regulatory requirements.

The Liquid Asset Buffer Policy sets out the parameters in respect of the ownership, size, maturity, and composition of the liquidity portfolio.

This policy document is approved by ALCO and reviewed on an annual basis.

The policy will set out some key principles around the governance of the portfolio. These principles are typically as follows:

- The LAB Policy will be proposed by the Treasurer and approved by ALCO.
- ALCO will review the parameters within the policy on a semi-annual or ad-hoc basis as required.
- Internal Audit and Risk will oversee implementation of the policy.
- To ensure segregation of duties, the quantum of the portfolio and breaches will be reported through Finance to the Treasurer (or delegated authority).
- The Liquidity Portfolio Policy applies to all high-quality liquid assets held by Treasury for the provision of liquidity to prudential, operational (for example, to support payment systems), and regulatory requirements.
- The sell down test must be representative of the constitution of the LAV and must be randomly tested in size at least once a quarter via sale or repurchase agreement.
- The relevant Discount Window Facilities operated by the Central banks should be tested in size and regularity. This exercise should be pre-notified to the Central Bank and only done if there is no market stigma associated with the testing.

**Summary**   The LAB is an integral part of the balance sheet and is predominantly derived from the quality of the liability base through the lens of stress tests. It needs to be representative of the risk appetite of the Board and commensurate with the underlying breakdown of the balance sheet. The LAB needs to be easily and quickly liquefiable and this needs to be tested regularly via sale or repo of a test sample of the portfolio.

**This extract from *PRMIA, "Intelligent Risk",* November, 2013.**

### Bank Liquidity Principles and Liabilities Strategy

### Bank Liquidity Principles and Liabilities Strategy

In this section we review the key liquidity risk principles and describe how they fit into a banks' customer deposit strategy, including its pricing strategy. Although no bank operates in a vacuum and deposit pricing must always reflect the overall market and competitor position, we state why liquidity preservation principles cannot be relegated to second position behind the profit objective. We also consider the regulatory requirements for liquidity as required under Basel III, and how these must influence overall liability strategy and structure.

## Liquidity Risk Principles and Liability Strategy

In the conventional bank business model, the desire to maximise return and P&L is as much a driver of liabilities strategy as it is of asset origination strategy. A commercial bank will generally look to pay the lowest possible rate on its deposits, particularly funds such as current accounts and instant access deposit accounts which often pay zero or very low interest (hence characterised as non-interest bearing liabilities or NIBLs. The availability of NIBLs is a significant element of the shareholder value proposition in a bank).

Post-crash and the requirements of LCR mean that principles of liquidity risk must also carry equal weight in developing liability strategy. In the UK the PRA assigns customer deposits as either "Type A" or "Type B", as part of the Individual Liquidity Adequacy Assessment (ILAA) process at each UK-regulated bank. Type A deposits are deemed less "sticky" than Type B deposits in times of market stress, and therefore carry a higher outflow assumption.

For example, the PRA view is that 100% of the contractually maturing deposits from Type A customers would be expected to leave during the first 2 weeks of a stress event. This reduces to 2% for certain Type B deposits and therefore a Type A/B mix weighted to Type B customers is beneficial for LAB requirement purposes.

A summary of Type A and B funding is given in Figure 2.

Deposits that are contractually longer than 90-day maturity – for example a fixed term unbreakable 1-year deposit or a 95-day Notice Account – are deemed not to outflow in a crisis.

---

TYPE A
- Deposits from Financial Institutions and Government agencies/public sector
- Deposits from customers with short relationships with the Bank
- Money market funds
- Funds not held in an account maintained for transactional purposes
- In relation to any individual depositor funds that exceed by a significant amount the level included in a national deposit guarantee scheme (in EU, above EUR 100,000)

TYPE B
- Deposits from Retail customers
- Deposits from SME customers
- Deposits from customers with a long relationship with the Bank or holding more than 3 products with the Bank
- Deposits held on Money Transmission Accounts, eg current accounts

---

**Figure 2** Definition of Type A and B customer deposits

All else being equal, therefore, Type B deposits are more attractive for LAB optimisation purposes, as are all notice or unbreakable fixed-term deposits. These, of course, are more expensive for banks than NIBLs or certain Type A deposits, so from a P&L perspective would be less likely to be emphasised in a bank's liability strategy. But the dictates of sound liquidity risk principles, and the need for an external perception of a robust and stable funding structure at a bank, should mean that a bank will aggressively target a higher share of its funding as Type B funding and/or contractually > 90-day funding.

## A RISK AND P&L TRADE OFF?

It is frequently suggested that the need to preserve liquidity strength implies a trade-off with P&L generation in the type of funding raised. While this is true to a certain extent (for example, a 95-day Notice Account or a 2-year Fixed Rate Deposit will cost the bank more than a vanilla current account or corporate customer deposit account), it is not an accurate assessment when considering the cost of wholesale market funding. Capital markets issuance will be more expensive than customer deposits. This can be material; during Q2 2013 an A-rated bank in Europe might expect to pay 140–160 bps over Libor for 3-year bond issuance and up to 220 bps for 5-year issuance. This is contractually explicit term funding, so of value towards the LCR and long-term Net Stable Funding Ratio (NSFR) metrics of Basel III, but it is not uncommon for many Type B deposits such as retail current accounts and savings accounts to be treated behaviourally as 3-year or even 5-year funding. Such funds would not have cost a bank more than 100 bps during the same period, so a liability strategy that emphasises a customer funding surplus can meet both liquidity risk and P&L requirements.

In practice this will translate into a customer loan-deposit ratio (LDR) of between 80% and 90%. Any higher than this and the mechanics of the LCR calculation will mean that the bank will be running an aggregate funding gap, which can only be plugged with wholesale funds. Maintaining sufficient customer deposits will ensure:

- Reduction in the wholesale markets funding requirement, thereby lowering the bank's cost-of-funds (COF) and weighted-average COF (WACF);
- A beneficial impact on liquidity metrics (PRA, Basel III and ILAA);
- Positive impact on the bank's credit rating;
- A rise, or at least preservation, of the bank's net interest margin (NIM).

Given the importance of sound liquidity risk management principles to ensure minimum target credit rating and Basel III LCR compliance, a bank's articulated "Deposits Strategy" drivers must reflect parallel needs of Liquidity Risk objectives as well as P&L and income improvement, with explicit liquidity limit metrics including LDR, cash flow survival horizon minimum, and so on.

## DRAFTING LIABILITIES STRATEGY

Ownership of a bank's funding strategy will lie with the business lines, but the document itself will require approval at ALCO and hence will need extensive Treasury input. In effect, liabilities strategy is a co-authored effort, with parallel tracks related to liquidity risk and NIM enhancement.

The Treasury elements would be expected to include discussion on the following:

- Decisions to re-price customer deposit rates downwards ("de-tuning") should be accompanied by analysis on expected impact on retention levels and volume impact to ensure compliance with liquidity limits, as well as an analysis of what peer-group competitors are offering at present;
- Liquidity and funding policy requirements, approved by ALCO, are articulated at bank level but the individual business lines (Retail and Corporate) would be expected to adhere to them as standalone businesses, to ensure risk exposure is maintained within manageable proportions. For example, business lines would be expected to be self-funded, or otherwise present clear and realistic plans on how funding gaps are being met, with confirmation that these are within the business model;
- Strategy targeting lower deposit pricing would be expected to also include a clear outline and approach on how the bank will replace expected deposit attrition, or otherwise cover off liquidity risk policy requirements with respect to how funding limits, funding concentration and funding diversity will be addressed;
- Asset origination strategy that targets continued growth in balance sheet assets, to meet P&L targets, must also address how any resultant funding gap will be dealt with. For example, detail on the P&L impact of saving on deposit costs versus cost of raising new funds in the wholesale market;

- For ILAA and LCR compliance purposes, the liabilities strategy is expected to target the desired Deposits Type A/B split explicitly and how this will be achieved. An A/B split of around 30:70 is considered optimum for most bank business models, but of course depends on franchise requirements – banks servicing a Type A customer base will expect to have a larger share of such deposits;
- A bank-wide Products Pricing Committee should be set up to meet regularly outside of ALCO, with representation including Treasury and Finance. This committee would review deposits pricing.

In general, a deposit strategy is constructed to meet the dual objectives of a stable funding structure, meeting all regulatory requirements, and a P&L-driven desire to preserve and enhance NII/NIM. This requires the following content:

- Agree the broad shape of actions to drive deposit raising; items such as retail versus corporate customer mix and principles of fund raising approach. This then feeds into specific plans in detail for pricing approval;
- Determining the size of customer funding gap where deposit raising action is required, and phasing of deposit raising, to meet regulatory and P&L objectives as well as the loan-deposit ratio (LDR) target and other liquidity metrics targets.

The content of the strategy is reviewed and updated on a regular basis and would include:

- Performance year-to-date and summary of pricing decisions taken;
- Future deposit target and waterfall of risks and upsides, with deposit raising/reducing challenge agreed;
- Principles of deposit generation; that is, how the bank will evaluate priority activities; for example cost of funds, ease of fund raising, customer clarity, relationship deepening (no reliance on financial institutions deposits, higher share of sticky deposits, Type A:B ratio target desired, and so on);
- Retail and Corporate potential deposit raising opportunities, evaluated by principles above, with Treasury recommended approach and phasing.

We drill down into deposits strategy itself in the next section.

# DEPOSIT STRATEGY TEMPLATES

The content of a bank's deposits strategy will reflect its overall liabilities objective. This cannot be understood without a deep understanding of the institution's current balance sheet structure, and value-for-money of each type of liability. This "value" extends not just to P&L and NIM impact but also the value from a regulatory perspective (bearing in mind that the most valuable deposits from an LCR viewpoint can also be the most beneficial to NIM: for example, retail current account balances).

Deposits strategy should reflect the objectives for the overall balance sheet structure of the bank. In general a bank will draft a detailed template addressing:

- maintaining current customer funding types and levels;
- increasing levels, or concentrating on different types of customer and product; or
- where there is excess surplus liabilities, reducing current levels.

We introduce templates for retail and corporate banking businesses.

# RETAIL DEPOSITS STRATEGY: AGENDA POINTS

A Retail bank template may be set out as shown in Figure 3. This is a summary of the content and includes essential management information (MI). In this case we observe a declining market share in a growing deposit market, an issue that would be addressed in the regular updates on strategy progress.

Any strategy plan must be dynamic and respond as necessary to changes in market and performance below plan. This demands timely and accurate MI. A template of contents for the monthly MI would look similar to Figure 4.

Figure 5 is an example of the type of analysis that would accompany the MI - it reflects strategic imperatives in a bank that has a deposits reduction target due to a surplus of liabilities.

### 2014 Retail Bank Customer Liabilities Strategy

1. Retain and grow deposit balances by £2bln over next 12 months
2. Maintain the main bank relationship
3. Focus, retain and grow the strategy on "sticky" deposits (PRA-designated "Type B" balances)
4. Acquire additional balances through improved understanding of customer requirements
5. Stimulate demand through incremental pricing changes, and not by "chasing money"
6. Maintain an holistic view of the aggregate balance sheet: monitor liabilities surplus and funding of illiquid assets

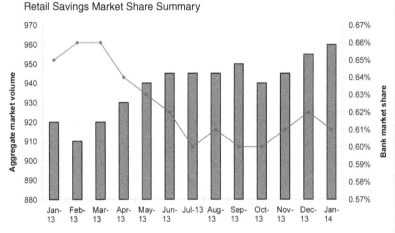

Retail Savings Market Share Summary

**Figure 3**    Sample retail bank customer liabilities strategy

* Performance by product—Bank versus market
* Instant access—Bank versus market
* Fixed term fixed rate bonds—Bank versus market
* Tax-free savings—Bank versus market
* Strategy and Funding: Type A/B mix
* Bank customer pricing versus market
* Retail Savings versus Fixed Term maturity profile
* Market share and context—Bank versus market
* Retail savings growth by product
* Product margins

**Figure 4**    Contents of the strategy progress template

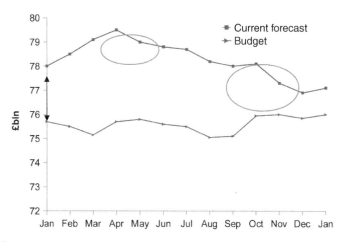

- Stronger end to preceding year due to back-book performance is projected to continue this year

- The back-book repricing downwards from April resulted in outflows as planned, generating NII improvement

- Removal of e-savings retention offer in September expected to generate further outflow

**Figure 5**   Retail bank performance outlook

# CONCLUSIONS

Good banking practice dictates that sound liquidity principles take equal precedence with returns and P&L targets when setting liquidity and funding strategy. This dictum should carry through into a bank's customer deposit strategy. We have seen how the conservative liquidity regime that is Basel III now enforces by regulatory fiat what was previously only followed at banks that adopted a sound liquidity regime. This necessarily creates a regulator requirement versus P&L trade-off, but it is possible to meet both objectives in a way that preserves shareholder value.

A prevailing theme in any bank's liability strategy is this P&L and liquidity risk management trade-off. A bank that is in the position of having a strong, stable customer funding base has less need of wholesale market contractual long-term liabilities to meet regulatory requirements. This is worth bearing in mind for strategy because raising "sticky" customer deposits is cheaper than raising wholesale funds. So for certain banks the trade-off may not be so onerous a problem. Ultimately, liabilities strategy must be appropriate to the overall strategy and business model of the bank in question.

Reproduced from *PRMIA, "Intelligent Risk"*, November, 2013.

## COLLATERAL FUNDING MANAGEMENT, FVA, AND CENTRAL CLEARING FOR OTC DERIVATIVES[4]

A commonly used misnomer is the expression "off-balance sheet" to refer to derivative instruments. From the viewpoint of the ALM manager, there is nothing off the balance sheet of these products: they have a cash flow impact on the balance sheet that is material and must be managed as closely and effectively as any cash flows arising out of on-balance sheet products.

In this section, we look at the practical impact on the ALM discipline arising out of the use of derivatives for hedging or trading purposes; first, the funding value adjustment (FVA), and then the use of central clearing counterparties (CCP) to clear over-the-counter (OTC) derivatives.

### Derivative Risks and CVA

Entering into a derivative transaction creates a number of balance sheet risks for both counterparties. A key one is counterparty risk, *viz.*,

- Derivatives are typically entered free of payment at zero initial cost;
- The value can go up (buyer has performance risk on seller) or down (seller has performance risk on buyer) through the whole life of the contract.

Counterparty risk remains live for a long period of time. For this reason, most derivatives business is undertaken under a Credit Support Annexe (CSA) which dictates that collateral must be passed from the counterparty offside on the trade to the party onside. CSA agreements are mostly standardised with the following terms:

- Cash collateral and no substitution option;
- Zero threshold;
- Zero minimum transfer amount;
- Daily continuous margining.

Certain counterparties (such as some sovereign authorities and central banks) do not enter into CSAs and their trades remain uncollateralised to the market-maker.

Banks apply a credit valuation adjustment (CVA) to the price of the derivative contract, which is an adjustment to the risk-neutral derivative price. It allows for the chance that a loss might result if the counterparty defaults, that is, the bank has a receivable on a derivative that the counterparty cannot pay.

---

[4] Acknowledgements and special thanks to Stephen Laughton for his FVA presentations at BTRM Cohort 4 and Cohort 5, which has been used as a source for much of the data and exhibits in this section.

## Exposures and CVA

A vanilla interest-rate swap (IRS) exhibits the following characteristics:

- No exchange of principal at inception;
- Parties exchange fixed for floating (i.e., a variable rate such as LIBOR) through the life;
- No re-exchange or principal at termination.

A Cross Currency Swap (XCY) has the following characteristics:

- Full exchange of principal at inception, one currency vs another;
- Exchange of floating payments, one currency for the other through the life;
- Full re-exchange or principal at termination.

The counterparty risks on the IRS are as follows:

- Traded "at market" at inception, hence no net counterparty risk on day 1;
- Unless yield curves are (exactly) flat, IRS has implied payments through the life: as time passes payments are made;
- Net payable/receivable remain on structure.
- Interest rates fluctuate throughout the life:
  - Expected payments on floating leg vary;
  - Discounting of implied cash-flows vary.
- The counterparty risks on the XCY are:
  - Traded "at market" at inception, hence no net counterparty risk on day 1;
  - Unless yield curves are (exactly) flat, XCY has implied payments throughout its life;
  - As time passes payments are made;
  - Net payable/receivable remain on structure.
- Interest rates fluctuate throughout the life:
  - Expected payments on floating leg vary;
  - Discounting of implied cash flows vary.
- FX rates fluctuate throughout the life:
  - Value of the re-exchange of principal varies.

The fact that market rates vary from day 1 onwards throughout the life of the contract presents the problem with estimating counterparty risk exposure. "At market" derivatives start with a zero net present value; however, over time and the movement of markets, the structure will develop a present value (PV); but we don't know how much, because we don't know how market prices will evolve. Therefore, the amount of our counterparty exposure is uncertain. The questions to answer are (1) How do we know how much to price for counterparty risk at inception? and (2) How can we hedge this counterparty risk?

We don't know exactly how (i.e., in which direction) market prices will evolve but we do know (can hypothesise) their dynamics and distribution. For example, under the Black-Scholes model assumption we assume a log-normal interest rate and foreign exchange rate movements profile. Hence the most common approach is to simulate the variation in PV. For instance, how will interest rates develop? Figure 12.27 shows a set of interest rate simulations, where we assume a yield-curve flat at 4%, and a set of possible profiles on how the remaining maturity swap rate may develop over the next five years. Solid lines are one standard-deviation move.

The future distribution of possible market rates and FX rates expands at a decreasing rate (the $\sqrt{T}$ law), converging to a log-normal distribution. But what about the remaining Mark-to-Market (MtM) value on the swap, and hence the counterparty risk? Over time, fewer cash flows remain on the IRS as duration shortens, and on the XCY the exposure is dominated by the principal occurring in one bullet payment at maturity. So again we run the simulation; expected exposure on an IRS peaks at between 18 and 30 months, then falls back towards zero at maturity. Figure 12.28 shows an example of remaining maturity IRS MtM simulations.

However, with an XCY the expected exposure grows throughout the life, peaking at maturity (due to the bullet exchange of principal on maturity). We show this at Figure 12.29.

To reiterate, XCY swaps involve principal exchange, whereas interest rate swaps involve only coupon exchanges, therefore, expected exposures are much larger on the XCY than on the IRS, as we compare at Figure 12.30.

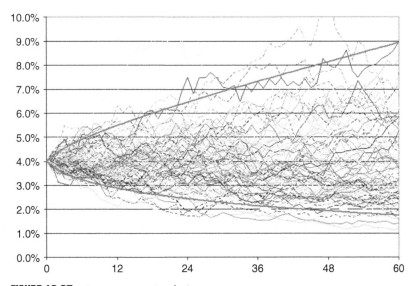

**FIGURE 12.27** Interest rate simulations

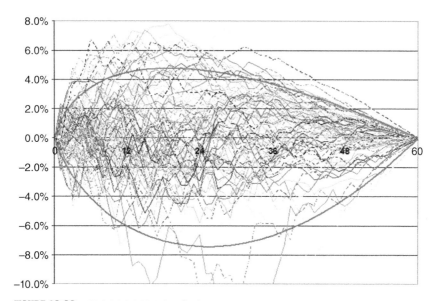

**FIGURE 12.28** IRS MtM PV simulations

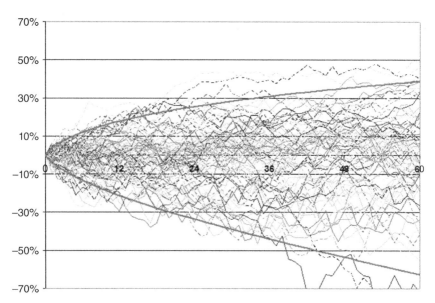

**FIGURE 12.29** Cross Currency Swap Mark-to-Market PV simulations

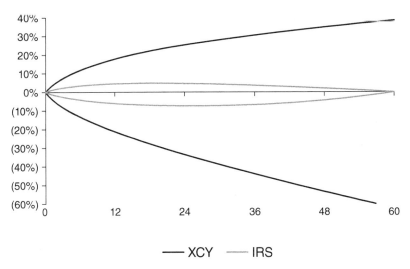

**FIGURE 12.30**   Comparing IRS and XCY expected exposures

So how do we use these PV MtM distributions to calculate counterparty risk, and hence the counterparty credit valuation adjustment (CVA)? The most common approach involves:

1. Price the cost of insuring expected exposure on day 1;
2. Only increase the hedge if realised exposure exceeds expected exposure.

Using this approach, CVA is therefore the cost of insuring the area under the curve shown at Figure 12.31, given by

$$CVA = LGD_C \sum_{i=1}^{T} EPE(t_i) Q_C(t_{i-1}, t_i) D(t_i) \qquad (12.4)$$

where   $LGD_C$ is the counterparty loss given default;
         $Q_C(t_{i-1}, t_i)$ is the counterparty default probability.

LGD and Q can be estimated from market credit curves (CDS) or estimated from fundamental credit analysis. So we see that CVA is the cost of hedging expected counterparty credit exposure.

We should be aware that there are some obvious problems with the standard CVA approach:

- Where one party has a positive mark, the other has a negative mark:
  - Both should be charging each other CVA;
  - No agreed, open market price therefore no trade;

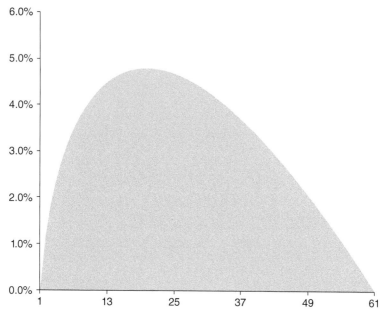

**FIGURE 12.31**    Expected swap exposure through life

- In reality there is usually a significant disparity between (bank) dealer credit and customer credit, which partly explains the need for collateralisation between inter-dealer/trading counterparties;
- Dealers are typically unable to monetise a negative market (their own payable).
- Exposure is not capped at the expected exposure:
  - This is only an arbitrarily chosen percentile exposure (normally one standard deviation);
  - Exposures (and hence potential losses) can be much higher.
- Credit curves may be unobservable and/or untradeable.

As one can appreciate there is more than way to approach this issue!

While CVA relates to the credit exposures from derivatives, FCA relates to funding costs. An uncollateralised derivative hedged with a collateralised one can give rise to a funding requirement: if markets move such that the collateralised trade has a negative MtM, then collateral must be posted. There would be no offsetting flows on the uncollateralised derivative, thus giving rise to a net funding requirement. At the same time, the CVA will increase due to the net counterparty exposure. So we see that CVA and FCA operate in the same direction. We consider FVA next.

## Derivatives Funding Policy

As part of sound liquidity management policy, all banks should have articulated funding policies in place for each of their business lines. These set out the liquidity and funding treatment of each product type within the businesses, including FTP rates, required tenor of funding, and so on. The treatment of the derivatives book can sometimes be particularly problematic. But if we stop using the misnomer "off-balance sheet", and treat the funding requirement that arises out of derivatives business in exactly the same way we should be treating the cash business, then the issue regains clarity.

In practice, this means banks that run derivatives portfolios. Generally, the derivatives dealers plus large users of derivatives, must treat the cash flow requirements arising out of this business with the same discipline and liquidity risk principles as they do any other business line. The divergence in bank cost-of-funds (COF) from Libor since 2008 confirms the importance of valuing and risk managing derivatives using such an approach, in a way that recognises the bank's term funding rates.

**First Principles**  Inter-bank derivatives trading takes place under the CSA arrangement in the standard ISDA agreement. This means that the mark-to-market value of each derivative contract is passed over as collateral, usually in the form of cash but sometimes as risk-free sovereign securities. In general, the collateral requirements under a two-way CSA agreement should result in a netted zero cash flow position, because what a bank needs to pass over as collateral on a derivative that is offside, it will receive from the counterparty to the hedge on this derivative. However, a number of counterparties, such as corporates, sovereign authorities, sovereign debt management offices, and central banks, do not sign CSA agreements. This one-way CSA arrangement will create a funding requirement for a bank, as it will have to transfer cash if it is MtM negative, while it will not receive any cash if it is MtM positive.

To incorporate the correct discipline with regard to the liquidity effects generated by uncollateralised derivatives business, the funding policy needs to incorporate an appropriate liquidity premium charge. This will apply to the net MtM value of all uncollateralised derivatives on the balance sheet. By charging the right rate, the business lines are incentivised to work towards reducing uncollateralised business wherever possible.

A bank will fund its balance sheet at its specific COF, which splits into four categories:

- Secured short-term funding costs: the rate at which the bank borrows against collateral. This is generally the OIS curve, and thus the lowest funding rate available (OIS lies below Libor). It is not relevant in an uncollateralised derivative context, because such instruments cannot be used as collateral (even if they are positive MtM);

- Secured long-term funding costs: the rate at which the bank can borrow by issuing term secured liabilities such as covered bonds and mortgage-backed securities;
- Short-term unsecured funding costs: the bank's COF for short-dated (0–12-month) tenors. At its lowest this will be around Libor, although many banks' ST unsecured borrowing rate is at a spread above Libor. That said, for certain banks the ST unsecured funding will be at zero, for example, retail deposits such as current ("checking") account balances;
- Long-term unsecured funding costs: the bank's COF for long-dated (2–10-year) tenors, also referred to as the term liquidity premium (TLP).

A general position of OIS, Libor and TLP curves is shown at Figure 12.32.

The above of course is in the "wholesale" or investment bank space. In reality, derivatives dealers are often part of "universal" banking groups that also include retail and corporate business lines. A large part of the balance sheet will be funded therefore by low-cost liabilities of contractual short-dated but behaviourally long-dated maturity. These also need to be factored into the pricing curve in a way that is appropriate. One approach might be to derive the derivatives COF off a "weighted average cost of funds" (WACF) curve that is an average of all balance sheet liabilities. Either way, care needs to be taken that business lines in the wholesale bank, which includes the derivatives desk, are charged an appropriate price and not necessarily the retail or corporate COF rate, particularly since customer deposits have short contractual tenors but long behavioural tenors, and so do not inflict a term liquidity premium (TLP) on the bank.

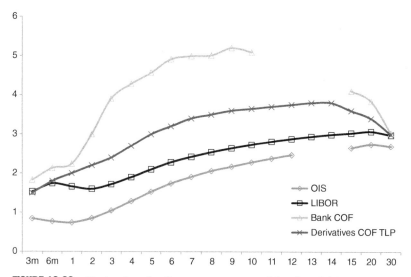

**FIGURE 12.32**    Derivatives funding curve as secured funding COF

**Derivative Liabilities and Assets**  Derivative liabilities correspond to what is termed an overall expected negative exposure (ENE), the most basic example of which is a deposit. A derivative asset corresponds to an overall expected positive exposure or EPE, and at its simplest would be a loan.

An appreciation of the terms of a derivatives funding policy requires an understanding of credit valuation adjustment (CVA), debt value adjustment (DVA), and funding value adjustment (FVA). Following existing literature (for example, see Picault (2005) and Gregory (2009)), under a set of simplifying assumptions we have:

$$
\begin{aligned}
CVA &= EPE \times PD \times LGD \qquad\qquad (12.5)\\
&= EPE \times \text{Counterparty Credit Spread}
\end{aligned}
$$

where EPE is expected positive earnings, and PD and LGD are standard credit analyst expressions for default probability and loss-given-default. More formally we write:

$$
CVA = (1-R)\int_{t=0}^{T} q(t)v(t)\,dt
$$

where  $R$  is the recovery rate;
   $q$  is the probability density function of counterparty default; and
   $v$  is the value of the derivative payoff.

In discrete time we write:

$$
CVA = (1-R)\sum_{i=1}^{n} q_i v_i
$$

where $q_i$ is the probability of default between times $t_{i-1}$ and $t_i$.

$$
DVA = ENE \times RBS\,\text{Credit Spread}
$$

and

$$
\text{Funding Cost} = (EPE + ENE) \times \text{Derivative Funding Spread.}
$$

In other words, the discounting to be applied for valuation is at the appropriate tenor bank funding cost.

The funding cost to apply to the derivatives portfolio cash flows may sometimes be selected depending on what assumption we make about the ease of unwinding the portfolio:

- Assume no easy unwind: if we cannot unwind the portfolio without punitive costs, we must assume we will have to fund the transaction for the full term. The funding cost of this commitment is given by the bank's LT COF. If we fund (value) at ST COF, we run the risk that sudden spikes in the ST COF will create funding losses, or that a liquidity squeeze in general will impact our ability to roll-over funding for the position. To avoid this risk, we would fund with LT borrowing, and discount unsecured derivatives off the LT COF (TLP) curve;

- Assume easy unwind: if we can unwind the position with no extraneous cost, we can apply the ST COF, say the 1-year TLP. The assumption of easy unwind means that we are not committed to rolling over funding; in the event of liquidity stress we would simply unwind the portfolio and eliminate the funding commitment. This is a strong assumption to make, particularly at a time of stress, and would be a high-risk policy.

Therefore in theory, we recommend that the derivative asset be discounted at TLP and the funding for collateral postings be substantially term funded. That said, in some cases the funding generated from a derivative book (assuming no counterparty default) is contractually for a long maturity, and so the case may be made that this should be charged for/receive the secured funding rate as opposed to the unsecured COF rate. That being the case, the Derivatives funding curve then sits below the bank's COF curve, and closer to the secured funding curve. This is shown at Figure 12.32.

In general, when applying derivatives funding policy we assume no netting arrangements are in place, but in practice these are quite common and will have an impact on the bank's collateral funding position in the event of default.

**Derivative Portfolio Maturity**    The tenor period to apply when applying the correct funding cost to derivative book cash flows can be the contractual maturity of the derivative in question, but not necessarily so. An alternative approach is to split the portfolio into tenor buckets commensurate with the tenors at which we wish to fund the cash flows, with each bucket funded at the appropriate tenor COF.

Placing the derivative portfolio cash flows into appropriate term tenor buckets is a logical position on which to base how we choose to fund these cash flows. In practice, the derivative valuation model itself can be used to produce this tenor bucket breakdown, in the form of a "funding risk per basis point" (FR01) delta ladder. Using this model output removes the need for a subjective analysis of the maturity profile of the portfolio. In other words, the maturity profile of the portfolio is given by the model output. The appropriate tenor TLP is charged on the amount in each bucket. This is shown at Figure 12.33.

In practice, of course, the profile is unlikely to look like the one at Figure 12.33 (although it might do). Rather, it is more likely to be all one way – either net long or short across most if not all tenor buckets.

In summary, cash flows arising out of the derivatives business, both contractual and collateral, must be funded at the appropriate TLP COF for their tenor. This means term funding a large part of the portfolio cash flows.

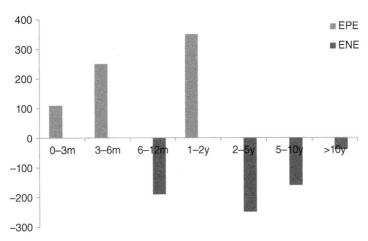

**FIGURE 12.33** Uncollateralised derivatives net position FTP pricing

**Funding Valuation Adjustment** Funding value adjustment is as important in derivative pricing as CVA, if not more so, and a vital part of an effective derivatives funding policy. When incorporating CVA, FVA, and where desired the cost of associated regulatory capital (CRC) into a transaction, we take a portfolio view with each individual counterparty. FVA represents the value adjustment made for the funding and liquidity cost of undertaking a derivative transaction.

To illustrate, consider a portfolio of just one plain vanilla interest-rate swap (IRS) transaction. Assume it is fully collateralised with no threshold and daily cash collateral postings. This means that on a daily basis collateral is posted or received (MtM value). The bank exhibiting negative MtM borrows funds to post collateral at its unsecured COF, while collateral posted earns interest at the OIS rate (Fed Funds, SONIA, or EONIA). This is an asymmetric arrangement that impacts the pre-crash norm of Libor-based discounting of the IRS, which was acceptable when the bank was funding at Libor or at the interbank swap curve. But post-crash the higher bank COF means that funding adds to the cost of transacting the swap. The magnitude of this cost is a function of [OIS% – COF%] for the bank.

If we consider now a book of derivative transactions, the funding cost for the counterparty banks ("Banks A and B") is a function of the size of the net MtM for the entire portfolio. Therefore, exactly as with CVA, to calculate the impact of the asymmetric funding cost we need to consider the complete portfolio value with each counterparty, as well as the terms of the specific CSA. This means in practice that when pricing the single swap, unless Banks A and B have the same funding costs – unlikely unless one is being very approximate – we see that the banks will not agree on a price for the instrument, irrespective of their counterparty risk and CVA.

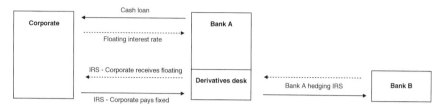

**FIGURE 12.34**   Customer IRS and hedging IRS

That means a bank can choose to use FVA for a profitability-type analysis only, not impacting swap MTM, or it can choose to cover this cost in which case it will impact swap valuation. The decision may depend on the counterparty and the product/trade type, or it can be a universal one. But not passing it on or adjusting the price for FVA means the derivatives business line is not covering its costs correctly.

The position is not markedly different with uncollateralised derivatives, generally ones where one counterparty is a "customer", for example, a corporate that is using the swap to hedge interest-rate risk. The bank providing the swap will hedge this exposure with another bank, and this second swap will be traded under a CSA. This is shown at Figure 12.34.

The first swap has no collateral posting flows, but the second one does. This is in itself an asymmetric CSA position; moreover the second swap cost will include an FVA element. The bank may wish to pass on this FVA hedge cost into the customer pricing, which means making the FVA adjustment to the swap price.

In both of the above illustrations, at any time the transaction (or hedge transaction) or portfolio MTM is negative, the bank will be borrowing cash to post as collateral. This borrowing is at the bank's cost of funds (COF), which we denote Libor + $s$ where $s$ is the funding spread. (Ignore specific tenor at this point.) If we look at FVA intuitively, it is an *actual* cost borne by the derivatives desk (and therefore, the bank) as part of maintaining the derivatives portfolio – no different in cost terms than funding the cash asset side of the balance sheet. So at the very least, a bank needs to incorporate FVA into its derivatives business returns and profitability analysis. Ideally, the governance of FVA will be incorporated alongside all collateral management functions, including CVA, and overseen by the bank's Treasury/ALM function.

Notwithstanding the strategic objective of a balanced portfolio policy, the net impact of uncollateralised derivatives transactions or any asymmetric derivatives and hedging arrangement is to generate an ongoing unsecured funding requirement. We should expect this funding requirement to be in place as long as a bank is a going concern, in other words as ordinary business. Therefore it should be funded in LT tenors, with only a minority proportion funded in ST tenors.

The cost of funding a derivatives portfolio, whether as a market maker or simply for hedging purposes, is an important part of the overall profitability of a bank and needs to be treated exactly as would the funding cost of a cash asset. FVA is one approach to measure funding cost. It can be passed on in customer pricing or the bank can choose to wear it, but the business line still needs to be charged for it (exactly as with cash asset funding).

The magnitude of FVA is a direct function of a bank's COF which fluctuates, and so it is important for FVA to reflect current reality. By definition, banks with the highest COF (highest *s* and lowest perceived credit quality) will suffer a competitive disadvantage in this space.

## Centralised Clearing and ALM[5]

One of the policy decisions taken in the wake of the 2008 bank crash was the demand from regulators that hitherto "over-the-counter" (OTC) derivative transactions be settled, or "cleared", through a centralised clearing counterparty (CCP), in the same way that exchange-traded derivatives are settled at the clearing house. This would remove bilateral counterparty risk because every transaction participant would, in effect, be dealing with the clearing house. In theory, this removes counterparty credit risk, because the clearing house would be sufficiently collateralised so as to never go bankrupt.[6]

The role of CCP is being carried out by existing clearing houses such as London Clearing House in the European Union. Whilst there are technical issues to consider when dealing in, say USD IRS (because of the basis that exists between IRS cleared in US and EU), from an ALM perspective the issues that should be addressed may include:

- What price FVA to consider? The bank's TLP vs capital arbitrage;
- Who "owns" the collateral in the bank?;
- Impact on the Basel III NSFR liquidity requirement: all market participants will have to post a significant amount of "initial margin" with the CCP (or their agent bank). Thus IM will act as a permanent drain of funding, with negative impact on the NSFR metric value;
- Optimising collateral (placing the cheapest available, in the cheapest currency, to the bank as collateral at the CCP);
- Impact on securities financing;
- The role of the XVA desk;
- Incentivising the right behaviour at business lines.

---

[5] This section was co-authored with Kevin Liddy.

[6] Or, as one might say, in their rush to remove the liability of the taxpayer to "Too Big to Fail" banks, the regulators have created an institution that is, if not necessarily the largest TBTF institution in existence, certainly one of the most systemically important. . .

The collateral management impact of dealing via CCPs is considerable, and the orthodox treatment would be to place collateral management as a direct responsibility of the Treasury department.

The box below summarises the key issues for consideration surrounding CCPs.

---

## CENTRALISED CLEARING COUNTERPARTY KEY POINTS

### A Bigger Role for CCPs

- CCPs have been growing in importance for many years.
- A particularly important boost to growth came after the financial crisis, with the G20 requirement that standardised OTC derivatives should be centrally cleared.
- CCPs are, in effect, being tasked with helping to mitigate the effects of the next financial crisis.

### Financial Stability: Advantages of CCPs Over Bilateral Clearing

**De Facto Advantages**
- More risk absorbed by the defaulter itself (i.e., higher "initial margin" or "defaulters-pay collateral");
- More rigorous risk management processes (e.g., re collection of margin, transparency).

**Intrinsic Advantages**
- Multilateral netting;
- Mutualisation of risk – risk born by the non-defaulting clearing members (e.g., through the default fund).

### Are CCPs Safe Enough?
- This question has been increasingly asked over the past year;
- Whatever the *potential* advantages, if *in practice* CCP risk management is not good enough those advantages won't be realised;
- Concern about banks' large and growing exposures to CCPs . . .;
- . . . and what is seen as the resulting "concentration" of risk and "single points of failure".

### Largely an Empirical Issue
CCPs are subject to international standards, the CPMI-IOSCO *Principles for financial market infrastructures* (PFMI), issued in 2012.

- Are the standards being observed?
  - Lags in adopting and enforcing the standards;
  - Differences in interpreting the standards.
- Are the standards enough? Are they effective?

### A Key Difference Between CCPS and Banks

- CCPs are not like banks. In particular, capital plays a different role.
- CCPs exist to provide protection against member default.
  - They *don't* do this primarily by absorbing the loss themselves through their capital.
  - Rather, it's more accurate to see a CCP as being there to help the market *manage* risk effectively.
  - Specifically, they try to ensure that, if the losses are so great that they exceed the collateral put up by the defaulter itself, they are *mutualised* by the surviving members in a safe and effective way.
- In this sense, CCPs are risk "distributors" more than "concentrators".

### Should Capital Play a Bigger Role?

- In principle, you can imagine a world where CCP capital *does* play the primary role in absorbing losses from participant default.
- We'd need to think carefully about whether this was:
  - "Fair";
  - Realistic.
- But even if CCPs don't become like banks in their use of capital, capital *is* nevertheless important:
  - "Skin in the game" (incentive for good CCP risk management);
  - Other risks (e.g., business risk), where a CCP *is* more like a bank;
  - Even for absorbing losses from participant default, could play a *bigger* role than today.

### Optimal Allocation of Losses

May need to focus more broadly on two issues simultaneously:
- Quantity (and quality) of the pre-funded financial resources the CCP should have *in total* to deal with clearing member default? How extreme an event should be assumed?

- Who provides those resources:
  - The defaulting clearing member(s)?
  - The surviving clearing members (i.e., mutualisation)?
  - The owners (i.e., capital)?
  - Others (e.g., insurance)?

It seems clear that clearing members themselves will continue to play the primary role in absorbing the risk that they create. The issue is how best that can be done.

---

## EXAMPLE 12.3    XVAs AND DERIVATIVES VALUATION[7]

The "xVAs" are a series of adjustments required to be made to the valuation of derivatives contracts to account for variations in counterparty credit risk, funding cost, capital impact, and collateral requirement amongst different participants. Generally the "screen" price of (say) an interest-rate swap reflects the price of a contract that is cleared through a CCP, under the collateral rules of the CCP (which generally requires cash in the currency of the contract, thus minimising an optionality with respect to type of collateral posted).

The valuation of a vanilla OTC derivative is now therefore an extremely complex process due to the ever increasing number of potential valuation adjustments, as shown with this expression:

$$Value = Reference\ value - CVA + DVA \pm FVA \pm CollVA - KVA - MVA$$

| Risk–free value | Counterparty risk | Funding | Collateral | Capital | Initial Margin |

XVA can be envisaged as the total lifetime cost (or benefit) of a derivative, including all the economically relevant terms. When a transaction is in-the-money then the uncollateralised component gives rise to counterparty risk and funding cost. When the transaction is out-of-the money there is counterparty risk from the party's own default and a funding benefit to the extent they are uncollateralised.

---

[7] This section was co-authored with Kevin Liddy.

Other points to note:

- Best market practice (and a regulatory push) requires the use of observable market CDS and/or index prices to compute CVA for both pre-deal pricing and accounting purposes. The resulting market implied PDs lead to increased levels of CVA reserve and accounting volatility.
- There has been a significant amount of debate on the validity of DVA and its overlap with FVA
- It is now readily accepted that FVA has two flavours, FCA and FBA although determining the funding level for calculating FVA is debated and varies across institutions.
- CollVA reflects collateral optionality to the extent it exists in collateral agreements
- Recent debate has focused on whether KVA is a capital valuation adjustment or a target hurdle/threshold.
- MVA is a member of the FVA family explicitly defined as the cost of funding the Initial Margin at CCP's or segregated margin for non-cleared derivatives as a result of the new bilateral margin rules.

Figure 12.35 is a summary of these different factors.

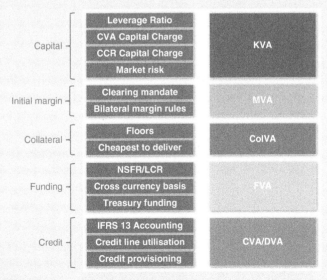

**FIGURE 12.35**   Factors related to xVAs and derivatives valuation
*Source*: © Solum Capital / Jon Gregory 2017. Used with permission.

## NEGATIVE INTEREST RATES AND THE IMPACT ON ALM POLICY[8]

Finance is not a complex subject. Ultimately every financial product, irrespective of its outward complexity, is a series of cash flows. And the basis of all financial market valuation and practice is the concept of net present value (NPV) and fair market discounting. When we discount a series of cash flows, we do this in an environment of positive interest rates. This reflects the time value of money. If money has no time value, or worse still a negative time value, then NPV becomes a pointless irrelevance. Orthodox corporate finance gets turned on its head as the conventional rules of the market break down. That said, many banks have had to adjust to working in a low or negative interest rate environment since the 2008 crash. This has had an impact on the approach to ALM in these banks.

### A New Normal

In response to the financial crisis, central banks worldwide cut official interest rates to historically very low levels, approaching 0.00%, for example, at the US Federal Reserve and the Bank of England. Japan of course had rates moving into negative territory for some time before the crash. Non-conventional monetary policy measures, such as large-scale bond purchases, depressed medium to long-term risk-free interest rates, and compressed risk premiums (so the yield curve has flattened). In the Eurozone, the European Central Bank cut base rates to –0.20% and then –0.40%, and the sovereign bond yields curve was only very small positive even at the 10-year tenor. A similar picture was observed in Switzerland. This meant that institutional deposits were paying interest on EUR and CHF deposits placed at banks.

Figures 12.36 and 12.37 show the level of rates in developed economies since the 2008 crash. Figure 12.38 reproduced with the kind permission of Wolfgang Marty, shows the discount function for positive and negative interest rates.

### ALM Policy Considerations

Initially, banks tend to benefit from parallel downward shifts in the yield curve as the duration of deposits is typically shorter than the duration assets. This curve flattening is often supported by a zero floor on interest rates on deposits, as it is generally not possible or appropriate to charge negative interest rates to commercial clients. Consequently, NIM is compressed and the income from maturity transformation is reduced. Of course as we have noted in the EU and Switzerland, the bank refinancing rate has fallen into negative territory and corporate depositors are paying a negative rate, hence interest rate margins have expanded.

However, in such environments the loss of lending margin means that often banks will enter into increased risk-taking in their desire to preserve

---

[8] This section was co-authored with Chris Westcott.

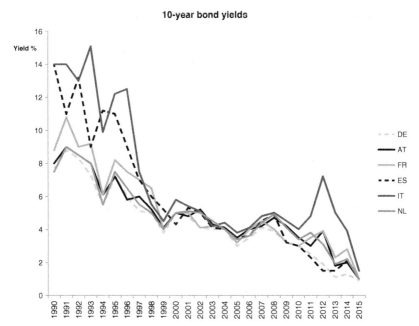

**FIGURE 12.36** 10-year bond yields
*Data Source*: Thomson Reuters.

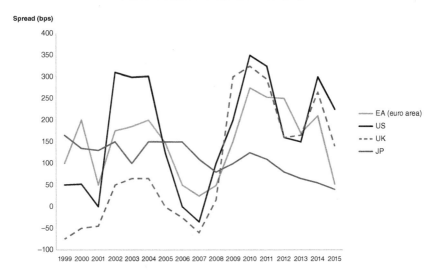

**FIGURE 12.37** Flattening yield curves
*Data Source*: Thomson Reuters.

## Discount factors

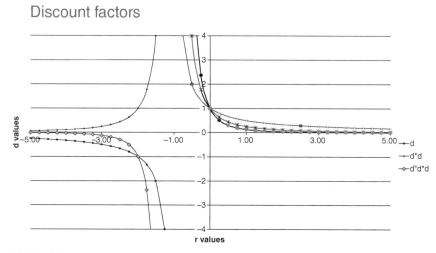

**FIGURE 12.38**   Discount function for positive and negative interest rates
*Source*: © Wolfgang Marty, 2017.

or enhance NII and NIM. Another consequence is a delayed balance sheet repair (for example, the ever-greening of loans). Ultimately though the gradual erosion of earnings from non- and low-interest bearing liabilities re-enforces NIM compression and also can create negative margin retail liabilities, as customer deposit prices can be above a bank's funding curve. On the other hand, the reduced interest rate volatility, as central banks keep rates stable for a long period, results in lower risk of loss from fixed rate drawdowns and lower prepayment risk.

Other impacts include the following:

- The difficulties in increasing NII leads to a focus on fee income and cost control (intensified by the development of the P2P market in corporate and SME lending);
- There is a new spotlight on second order IR risk, as basis risks are more in evidence; for example, the spread between Base Rate, LIBOR, and the bank's mortgage standard variable rate (SVR);
- Negative rates potentially affect the stability of bank deposits; for example, depositors may respond to very low rates or negative rates by holding their savings in the form of bank notes. (Of course this option is not open to corporate customers who simply must place their cash on deposit, but of course there is a lower incentive to hoard cash.);
- Potential reduction in natural duration hedging capacity, with changes in the balance sheet structure – on the liability side, customers tend to

move from fixed-term deposits into non maturing sight deposits. On the asset side, customers can increasingly prefer longer tenors for fixed-rate loans. As a result, there may be a tendency for the net asset duration gap to widen, implying less natural offsetting positions in the balance sheet and more reliance upon external markets to hedge interest rate positions;

- Potential technical and operational problems: banks need to ensure that their business infrastructure (for example, derivative models, VaR models, and IT systems) can handle negative rates and yield reasonable results.

In terms of cash management, there is little incentive for a bank to run a large surplus cash position especially in EUR or CHF. In a more risk-seeking environment, this could lead to banks deploying spare surplus funding in ever more risky areas, but in the circumstances prevailing after the global crash such behaviour has been less in evidence. The alternative approach is to "de-tune" the deposit base and try to lose deposits, starting with those that are less Basel III-friendly. This is not always possible of course, as corporate depositors are often obliged to place their cash in a bank.

The other key ALM policy consideration, other than to minimise surplus cash position, is to try to maximise duration gap in order to enhance NIM.

## PART 3: SUMMARY AND ANALYSIS OF PRA CP21/16 AND CP13/17: "PILLAR 2: LIQUIDITY"[9]

Taking their cue from the Bank for International Settlements (BIS), typically regulators and supervision authorities will publish a draft or "consultation paper" that outlines new proposals or requirements, before any new or changed rules become law. Banks are able to respond to the draft with their comments before the final regulation is published. This consultation process should not be viewed merely as an opportunity to send back opinion on the proposals; rather, a bank should also review its internal philosophy and culture with respect to regulation and risk management, and use the review period to inform its own approach and understanding.

In the first instance, the bank should undertake a "gap analysis" on what is required and what it is doing now compared to what will be required

---

[9] This section was co-authored with Graeme Wolvaardt.

under the new proposals. But the bank should also ascertain what exactly the new proposals are seeking to achieve, and try to determine if this is the optimum way to go about things. In other words, is there a more efficient and effective way to achieve the same result? Is the overall concept in question logical? Responses to consultation papers should always seek to include strategic as well as tactical considerations.

The purpose of this section is to present a summary of the PRA Consultation Paper CP21/16, which was issued in October 2016, together with context and consideration of some of the potential policy and procedure impacts on banks. Although the paper is specific to UK banks, the approach herein is relevant to any bank in the world. We also believe that the requirements in the paper will become a general benchmark for liquidity risk management looking beyond the Basel III LCR requirement. In essence though, this section confirms that the PRA is continuing the previous 90-day liquidity regime pre-Basel III into its new Pillar 2 liquidity requirement in the era of Basel III.

### Summary of CP21/16

The consultation paper is the first of two regarding "Pillar 2 Liquidity" that the PRA put to the industry. The purpose of "Pillar 2 Liquidity" rules will be to ensure that firms retain sufficient available liquidity to cover risks that, in the opinion of the PRA, are not covered (or not fully covered) by the Liquidity Coverage Ratio (LCR), which represents the "Pillar 1 Liquidity" requirement. The PRA divides these uncovered risks into two categories:

- Risks not covered by the LCR that were *not* previously covered by the BIPRU 12 (ILAS) rules; and
- Risks not covered by the LCR that were previously covered by the BIPRU 12 (ILAS) rules.

The purpose of the CP (according to the PRA) is to elicit feedback on areas where the regulator's "thinking is advanced enough to make specific proposals"; that is, the CP contains draft policies regarding these areas and to invite the industry to contribute its views on key areas where the regulator's views are as yet somewhat less fixed.

The areas for which the PRA has developed draft guidance are:

- Franchise viability: debt buyback and early termination of non-margined derivatives;
- Intraday liquidity.

## Pillar 2 Liquidity Risks

The risks that the PRA identifies as not being covered by the Basel III LCR standard can be summarised as follows:

### Risks not covered by the LCR that were previously covered by the BIPRU 12 rules

1. Funding risks, including "cliff" risk: the risk that outflows beyond the 30-day LCR horizon systematically exceed inflows, leading to liquidity shortfalls outside of the LCR window. "Cliff" risk refers to a subset of this risk where the risk is that outflows (usually deposit maturities) cluster or concentrate around single dates (for example, month-ends, quarter-ends) beyond the 30-day LCR window (usually due to firms "terming out" liabilities) leading to liquidity shortages that cannot be met with available liquidity resources.
2. Cash flow mismatch risk: the risk generated by using a "point-in-time" approach in the LCR against the maximum net cumulative outflow, i.e., a firm may meet the LCR requirement at 30 days but fall below that requirement at some point within that 30-day period.
3. Liquid asset management risk: the risk generated by widening the definition of "liquid assets" to include assets that perhaps cannot be monetised as quickly as those defined as liquid under BIPRU 12. Essentially, this is the risk that the firm will not or cannot actively manage the liquid assets it holds to ensure that at any given moment they can be turned promptly into cash.
4. Funding concentration risks: the risk of over-reliance on a single source or restricted sources of funding (where source can be very broadly defined as counterparty/customer name, industry, region, customer type, product, or maturity, etc.) leading to liquidity shortages if this funding is withdrawn or interrupted.

### Risks not covered by the LCR that were not previously covered by the BIPRU 12 rules

1. Franchise viability risks:
   - Debt buyback: non-contractual request by debt holder to buy back issued debt resulting in cash outflow;
   - Non-margined derivatives: non-contractual request by non-margined derivative counterparty (who is "in-the-money") to terminate derivative contract resulting in cash outflow;
   - Prime brokerage: short-term financing provided by clients is withdrawn leading to liquidity stress (for example, proceeds of short sales

are withdrawn but the firm continues to fund long positions for franchise reasons);

- Matched books: matched books may not behave contractually under stress (for example, the firm may decide to extend financing to franchise clients, for example, via a reverse repo, for longer than their contractual terms while losing repo funding); and

- Settlement failure risk: increased likelihood that settlements will fail during increased activity of a liquidity stress leading to failed incoming payments generating increased liquidity needs.

2. Intraday liquidity risk: a firm fails to manage its intraday liquidity effectively, which leaves it unable to meet a payment/settlement obligation on time, thereby impairing its own liquidity position and that of other parties;

3. Underwriting risk: risk that lack of take-up of an underwritten new issue(s) leads to additional assets being added to a firm's balance sheet, thus impairing its liquidity position and funding position;

4. Inadequate systems and controls: having a direct impact on liquidity risk;

5. Risks relating to derivative outflows: where not included under the LCR standard;

6. Risks relating to securities financing margin requirements: risk of cash outflows resulting from increased margin requirements caused by deteriorating collateral credit quality;

7. Risks relating to intragroup flows: risk that liquidity may not move freely from non-EU entities within a group to EU entities within the same group.

## Evaluation of Cash Flow Mismatch Risk

This section of the CP explains how a firm may meet its LCR requirement at the end of the 30-day period but have fallen significantly below that standard at some point within that period. Figures 12.39 and 12.40 are two graphs that summarise the issue – in this illustration both banks have the same LCR (103%) and HQLA size, but the graph at Figure 12.40 shows a net cumulative liquidity shortfall throughout most of the LCR period.

This is where a simple compliance with LCR is not sufficient to provide confidence on a robust liquidity position. The CP states that the PRA will be adding requirements to evaluate and monitor this risk, note:

- The PRA is considering two approaches:
  - Quantity-based approach; that is, largest net cumulative outflow over given time horizon and stress scenario (either including or excluding

Liquidity surplus while meeting LCR

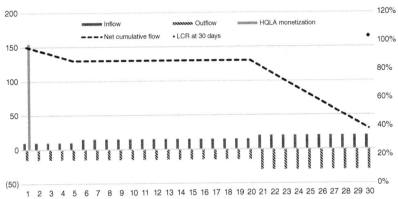

**FIGURE 12.39**   Cash flow illustration and compliant LCR value – no cumulative liquidity shortfall bank

Liquidity shortfall while meeting LCR

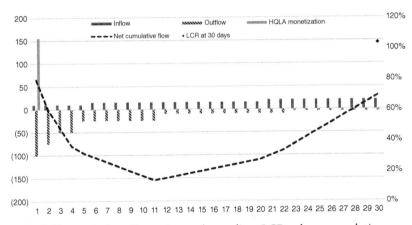

**FIGURE 12.40**   Cash flow illustration and compliant LCR value – cumulative liquidity shortfall bank

HQLA) – very similar to the approach taken in the FSA047 liquidity report; or

■ A time-based approach, that is, demonstrating the number of days until a firm's net cash flow becomes negative, given a stress scenario and taking into account HQLA;

- The PRA considers measurement of cash flow mismatch important because:

  - A firm may meet the LCR requirement yet "fail the stress scenario"; that is, show a liquidity shortfall within the LCR horizon; and
  - The regulator is concerned about the level of short-dated wholesale funding in use by firms: sudden withdrawal of these may lead to a large number of firms attempting to monetise HQLA at the same time, potentially impairing the value of HQLAs across the industry.

- The PRA will monitor cash flow mismatch risk and will require reporting to allow it to perform this monitoring;

- The PRA intends to develop policy to allow it to:

  - Impose specific liquidity requirements (calculations/metrics) including limiting maturity mismatches between assets and liabilities;
  - Require specific reporting to monitor cash flow mismatch risk: it would appear this means daily granularity (although the CP references the contractual maturity ladder template in the EBA Implementing Technical Standards for additional liquidity monitoring metrics);
  - Specify the time horizon which this specific reporting must cover – at least over the 30-day LCR time horizon; there is an implication that this is a minimum and the period may be longer;
  - Specify the assumptions for inflows, outflows, and HQLA to use in mismatch calculations/metrics.

**Franchise Viability: Debt Buyback and Early Termination of Non-Margined Derivatives**   Franchise viability risk arises from the fact that a firm may feel compelled to take actions not required by contract in order to protect its reputation (its franchise) which give rise to unexpected cash outflows.

This section contains principles for rules and guidance as to the approach the PRA will use to assess:

- *Debt buyback risk*: (non-contractual request by debt holder to buy back issued debt resulting in cash outflow) indicating that the supervisor may consider:

  - The quantity of debt with maturity beyond the 30-day LCR horizon, taking into account the Minimum Requirement for Own Funds and Eligible Liabilities (MREL) under stressed conditions; and
  - Activity in the secondary debt market – market-makers may experience greater frequency of buyback requests.

- *Early termination of non-margined derivatives risk*: (non-contractual request by non-margined derivative counterparty (who is "in-the-money") to terminate derivative contract resulting in cash out-flow) indicating that the supervisor may, in relation to the firm's percentage of outstanding exposure:

- Choose either the peak or the average exposure;
- Identify a historical period which allows the supervisor to assess unusual events regarding frequency of early termination requests;
- Take into account other factors as a guide to quantifying the add-on:

  - Exposure to non-margined derivatives as a proportion of total balance sheet; and
  - Exposure to derivatives with more volatile mark-to-market valuations (greater volatility causing greater liquidity outflows given a frequency for early termination and a given exposure).

**Intraday Liquidity**    This section contains principles for rules and guidance as to the approach the PRA will use to assess intraday liquidity risk. This is the risk that the timing of payments against receipts within a working day results in a firm exhausting its available capacity to make payment before it has made all the payments it is obligated to make on the day. From an earlier PRA paper, SS24/15: "the risk that a firm is unable to meet its daily settlement obligations, for example, as a result of timing mismatches arising from direct and indirect membership of relevant payments or securities settlements systems".

The PRA considers all firms connected to payment or securities settlement systems to be subject to intraday liquidity risk, i.e., the overwhelming majority of all firms regulated by the PRA.

The CP distinguishes between two types of participant in payment or securities settlement systems:

- Direct participants: directly connected to the system and responsible to the settlement agent (or all other participants) for settlement of its own transactions, those of its customers, and those of indirect participants on whose behalf it is acting; and
- Indirect participants: who have engaged direct participants to act on their behalf (for example, a firm making payments via its nostro account would be an indirect participant with the entity providing the account acting as a direct participant).

The CP emphasises that one of the prime reasons for including intraday risk in the assessment of the firm's required liquid assets is to mitigate the risk of "double duty; that is, the risk that the HQLAs identified as being used to mitigate a firm's liquidity position are also used to support payments and securities settlement activities intraday. The PRA has identified the following manifestations of double duty:

- Impaired balance sheet resilience: if the HQLAs are supporting intraday liquidity they cannot be effective against a run on liabilities;
- Increased intraday liquidity risk: if a firm suffers a prolonged balance sheet liquidity stress the HQLAs are exhausted, leaving insufficient funds to operate effectively in payment and securities settlement systems.

This section contains principles for rules and guidance as to the approach the PRA will use to assess intraday liquidity risk:

- The firm's mean maximum net debits (net payment position);
- The firm's stress testing framework;
- Relevant characteristics of the firm;
- The markets within which the firm operates.

The CP states that the PRA considers the *mean average of maximum net debits combined with stress uplift* to be the most appropriate measurement for assessing intraday liquidity risk.

The mean average of maximum net debits is defined as follows:

- Maximum net debit for a given day means the maximum amount by which cumulative payments outward exceeded cumulative receipts inward for a given settlement system (see Table 12.25);

**TABLE 12.25**   Illustration maximum net debit for given day

**Day 1**

| Time | Payments | Receipts | Cumulative payments | Cumulative receipts | Cumulative net (debit)/ credit |
|------|----------|----------|---------------------|---------------------|-------------------------------|
| 7:00 | (10) | 10 | (10) | 10 | 0 |
| 8:00 | (35) | 10 | (45) | 20 | (25) |
| 9:00 | (15) | 10 | (60) | 30 | (30) |
| 10:00 | (10) | 12 | (70) | 42 | (28) |
| 11:00 | (10) | 40 | (80) | 82 | 2 |
| 12:00 | (5) | 10 | (85) | 92 | 7 |
| 13:00 | (5) | 10 | (90) | 102 | 12 |
| 14:00 | (10) | 10 | (100) | 112 | 12 |
| 15:00 | (10) | 10 | (110) | 122 | 12 |
| 16:00 | (10) | 10 | (120) | 132 | 12 |
| | | | | Maximum net debit | (30) |

- Mean average means the average for the above metric across all the days in the assessment period (for example, one month) – see Table 12.26.

The CP makes a number of points regarding the PRA's view of maximum net debit as the appropriate measurement:

- Mean average maximum net debit is assessed for a firm on a system by system basis and the PRA does not consider any cross-system efficiencies to be quantifiable on a systematic basis. However, the PRA will give such efficiencies due consideration during the Liquidity Supervisory Review and Evaluation Process (L-SREP) should a firm be able to demonstrate these efficiencies appropriately.
- A firm should not assume that a reduction in mean average maximum net debit will necessarily lead to a reduction in the PRA's assessment of intraday liquidity risk.

**TABLE 12.26**　Illustration mean average maximum net debit

| Working Day | Maximum net debit |
|---|---|
| 1 | (30) |
| 2 | (12) |
| 3 | 0 |
| 4 | (5) |
| 5 | 0 |
| 6 | 0 |
| 7 | (12) |
| 8 | (15) |
| 9 | (7) |
| 10 | (19) |
| 11 | (21) |
| 12 | 0 |
| 13 | (1) |
| 14 | (2) |
| 15 | (5) |
| 16 | (6) |
| 17 | (11) |
| 18 | (3) |
| 19 | (25) |
| 20 | (29) |
| 21 | (31) |
| Mean average net debit | (11) |

- The PRA expects all direct participants to be able to calculate mean average maximum net debit and encourages any indirect participants that are currently unable to calculate this value to engage with their correspondent banks in order to obtain sufficiently granular and timely settlement data to enable such participants to begin calculating this metric.

The CP then discusses alternative measurement methodologies for assessing intraday liquidity risk where a firm is unable to calculate the PRA's preferred metric (mean average maximum net debit):

- Liquidity recycling: the ratio between value of payments sent and liquidity usage, for example, if for a system a firm has liquidity usage of €1mn and gross outflows of €10mn, the firm's liquidity recycling ratio would be 10 (€10mn/€1mn);
- Secured, disclosed intraday credit facilities in *securities settlement* systems: intraday risk equivalent to the sum of the haircut value of settled trades plus a stress uplift, provided the following conditions are met:

  - The settlement venue provides a secured and disclosed intraday credit facility to the direct participant; and
  - The direct participant in the system secures that facility by holding a pool of assets of value equivalent to the haircut value of the underlying security being settled.

A discussion of how stresses may impact intraday liquidity risk concludes the section and the CP lists ways in which an intraday stress may manifest (based on BCBS Monitoring tools for intraday liquidity management – see BCBS 248):

- A credit or liquidity shock affects the firm itself, causing counterparties to delay or suspend payments to the firm (potentially causing correspondent banks to withdraw intraday credit lines and requiring the firm to prefund or collateralise its intraday credit lines);
- An operational, credit, or liquidity shock affects a major counterparty of the firm's ability to make payments to the firm as expected (delayed, suspended, or failed);
- A credit or liquidity shock affects the firm's customers (either a major customer, or a group of customers), causing delays or suspensions of payments due to the customer(s);
- A change in market conditions causes a given pool of assets to generate less intraday liquidity.

The first three scenarios impact the payment/receipt profile of the firm, thus affecting the maximum net debit, while the last scenario impacts the firm's ability to fund its intraday liquidity position. All of the scenarios can affect both direct and indirect participants in payment and settlement systems.

## Impact of Pillar 2 and Implications for Banks

If a firm has carried out its obligations to assess its own risks and carry out its own stress testing, some or all of the Pillar 2 risks should already be identified in the firm's ILAAP. However, the assessment/quantification of these risks by the bank may not accord with the specific policy guidance given for franchise viability risk (debt buyback and non-margined derivatives) and intraday liquidity risk. In general, banks should expect that a final policy document will not deviate much from the CP draft policy. Consequently, firms should set about ensuring that their ILAAP documents can demonstrate compliance with the draft policy (see comments at start of Part 3).

Regarding the risks that the PRA has identified, a significant number of these are more relevant to market-making firms and firms with a "flow"-focused business model:

- Franchise viability liquidity risk: debt buyback – the CP states clearly that "Firms that are market makers in their secondary debt market may experience a greater frequency of buyback requests";
- Franchise viability liquidity risk: non-margined derivatives – firms with high levels of non-margined derivatives (that is, derivatives with non-FI counterparties) are likely to have a "flow" business model. In addition, derivatives with high volatility (for example, non-linear or leveraged products) which will attract greater add-ons are likely to be offered only by larger firms making markets or conducting "flow" business;
- Prime brokerage risk: again only larger firms making markets or conducting "flow" business are likely to undertake significant underwriting business;
- Matched book risk: specific risk attaching to firms which try to match customers' buy and sell orders, i.e., "flow" business.

Although it may be difficult to identify appropriate courses of action for firms which may be impacted by any draft CP proposals, including the one we discussed here, nevertheless this is what each bank must do. It is part of the approach to applying Strategic ALM, to determine what impact new or changed rules have on the viability of the current business model and customer franchise. For instance, a bank in which the activities captured by the above proposals do not constitute a core or major part of the business may wish to consider actions to minimise the proportion of their business affected by these potential policy changes, or indeed withdraw from such areas completely. Firms that are focused in these areas should present detailed comments and also, if appropriate, alternative policy proposals that may meet the objectives more efficiently.

The CP mentions curtailing reliance on short-dated wholesale funding as a desired outcome:

*"The PRA is concerned about firms running high levels of short-dated wholesale funding risk: even with adequate amounts of liquid assets, the sudden withdrawal of short-term funding could result in firms trying to liquidate large amounts of securities, impacting the value of other firms' liquid asset holdings."*

In response, affected banks may need to take steps to amend their liquidity profile and/or identify additional sources of funding as the PRA moves to make short-dated wholesale funding less useful in demonstrating adequate levels of liquidity. This is particularly relevant as the NSFR rules also penalise such short-dated wholesale funding.

It appears that the PRA is contemplating an acceptable method for reinstituting some of the requirements previously embodied in BIPRU 12.5: essentially daily cumulative cash flow metrics under stressed assumptions for at least 30 days and probably for a longer period. Firms should look to the FSA047 and FSA048 reports (which are still required by the PRA) to form a basis for assessing the impacts of any new requirements.

The detailed description accompanying draft policy for intraday liquidity risk implies that the PRA is very unlikely to deviate from the draft in the final policy. Consequently, firms should make arrangements as soon as possible to follow the PRA's suggestion that they *"engage with their correspondent bank(s), with the aim of improving the granularity and timeliness of payment settlement data to enable them to"* calculate the "mean average maximum net debit" (plus stress uplift). In the absence of such data, firms should at the very least make attempts to begin calculating an appropriate proxy or alternate metric as specified in the CP, i.e., the liquidity recycling ratio, or (for securities settlement systems) the sum of the haircut value of settled trades (plus a stress uplift).

## Implementation of Pillar 2 Requirement

In keeping with what we consider best-practice response to any consultation process, this section is not derived from the CP itself but is the result of internal discussions and sessions within industry forums.

The implementation of Pillar 2 liquidity requirements appears to be achieved by converting the Pillar 2 add-on (defined as a fixed amount) to an equivalent LCR percentage (by dividing by net outflows) and adding this to the Pillar 1 requirement – we provide a worked example at Table 12.27.

In the example, the bank has been allocated two additional Pillar 2 add-ons as part of its Individual Liquidity Guidance (ILG): €25mn for intraday liquidity risk and €15mn for funding concentration liquidity risk. These add-ons are divided by the absolute value of the net outflow amount (€210mn) to obtain LCR-equivalent percentages of 12% and 7% which are added to

**TABLE 12.27**  Worked example of "Pillar 2" implementation of liquidity risk and LCR calculation

| LCR calculation | Amount | |
|---|---|---|
| **High quality liquid assets** | | |
| **HQLA** | 450 | **(A)** |
| Outflows | | |
| Retail deposits | (185) | |
| Corporate, sovereign, central banks deposits | (175) | |
| Financial institution deposits | (200) | |
| **Total outflows** | (560) | |
| Inflows | | |
| Retail loans | 50 | |
| Corporate, sovereign, central banks loans | 200 | |
| Financial institution loans | 100 | |
| **Total inflows** | 350 | |
| Adjusted inflows (lesser of actual inflows and 75% of outflows) | 350 | **(B)** |
| Net outflows (A + B) | (210) | **(C)** |

| Pillar 1 requirement | | Percentage | |
|---|---|---|---|
| Minimum level (2016 = 80%, 2017 = 90%, 2018 = 100%) | | 80% | **(P)** |

(*continued*)

**TABLE 12.27**     (*Continued*)

| LCR calculation | Amount | | |
|---|---|---|---|
| Pillar 2 requirement | Amount | Percentage | |
| Intraday risk (X) | 25 | 12% | = X/–C |
| Funding concentration risk (Y) | 15 | 7% | = Y/–C |
| Total Pillar 2 requirement | | 19% | (Q) |
| Overall assessment | | Percentage | |
| Overall requirement (P + Q) | | 99% | |
| Overall LCR ratio (A/–C) | | 214% | |
| Therefore the firm meets the combined Pillar 1 and Pillar 2 requirement. | | | |

the Pillar 1 minimum requirement (80% from 01 January 2016, 90% from 01 January 2017, and 100% from 01 January 2018) to get an overall combined Pillar 1 and Pillar 2 requirement of 99% (80% + 12% + 7%).

The firm's actual LCR ratio is the proportion of HQLA to the absolute value of net outflows (€560mn/€210mn); that is, 214%. This exceeds the combined Pillar 1 and Pillar 2 requirement, therefore this bank meets its ILG requirement.

## Conclusion

We have provided this detailed review and response of one particular regulatory authority's consultation paper as an example of what the process should look like, and what every bank should be doing during these consultation processes. In this specific case, the CP provided clarity as to the specific methods the PRA will use to assess the Pillar 2 risks of franchise viability liquidity risk (debt buy-back and non-margined derivatives) as well as intraday liquidity risk.

The CP also indicates the path of future PRA policy development and provides a summary of the Pillar 2 risks that it plans to make the subject of policy requirements. The observation to take away from this review is a uniform one for all draft paper reviews: to provide input to the question, To what extent do new and/or changed rules and requirements impact the bank's overall business model and strategy? And do any new requirements generate a need for a bank to modify aspects of its current business model, particularly (in this specific case) those having significant short-term wholesale deposits, and those engaged in market-making and/or "flow"-based activities?

This approach to the consultation process is one we recommend for all banks irrespective of their regulatory jurisdiction.

## PART 4: SAMPLE POLICY STATEMENTS

In this last part of the chapter, we refer the reader to sample policy statements in the liquidity risk management space, which are held on the associated website for this book. (Please see Chapter 20 for details on accessing the website.)

These sample statements may be used as templates at any bank. There are two in the relevant section of the website:

- ALCO annual review of the bank's Liquidity Policy Statement. This is a comprehensive review that should be undertaken at least annually at ALCO, and refers to a hypothetical UK bank called ABC Bank which is part of a larger global banking group called ChoudBank Group;
- An example of a small bank Liquidity Reserve policy. This appears to be relatively unsophisticated and perhaps not sufficiently detailed, but we should always remember that finance is not a complex topic. A small commercial bank with a significant portion of its regulatory capital driven purely by credit RWAs is not necessarily expected to have a sophisticated liquid asset buffer. For most banks in the world we would recommend no more than Cash and T-bills as HQLA components, but such a policy needs to be argued vehemently at ALCO to counter the views of those who believe that the HQLA should also feed into overall bank profitability. We suggest that the format template shown here is reasonable given its objectives.

Other related policy documents that may be used as template guidelines by any bank are provided on the book's website. Full details of these templates may be found in Chapter 20.

## SELECTED BIBLIOGRAPHY AND REFERENCES

Basel Committee on Banking Supervision, *Principles for sound stress testing practices and supervision*, May 2009.

Choudhry, M., "The Bank Treasury Function: Bank Internal Funds Pricing Mechanism", *Lafferty Retail Banking Insights*, October 2013, pp. 24–26.

*Basel III: The Liquidity Coverage Ratio and liquidity risk monitoring tools*, BIS, January 2013, http://www.bis.org/publ/bcbs238.htm.

*Basel III: the Net Stable Funding Ratio – consultative document*, BIS, January 2014, http://www.bis.org/publ/bcbs271.htm.

*EU Banks' Funding Structures and Policies*, ECB, May 2009, http://www.ecb.europa.eu/pub/pdf/other/eubanksfundingstructurespolicies0905en.pdf.

Frequently Asked Questions on Basel III's January 2013 Liquidity Coverage Ratio, BIS April 2014, http://www.bis.org/publ/bcbs284.htm.

Guidance for Supervisors on Market-Based Indicators of Liquidity, BIS, January 2014, http://www.bis.org/publ/bcbs273.htm.

*Guidelines on liquidity cost benefit allocation*, EBA, October 2010, http://www.eba.europa.eu/-/guidelines-on-liquidity-cost-benefit-allocati-1.

*Liquidity stress testing: a survey of theory, empirics and current industry and supervisory practices*, BIS, October 2013, http://www.bis.org/publ/bcbs_wp24.htm.

*Liquidity transfer pricing: a guide to better practice*, BIS, December 2011, http://www.bis.org/fsi/fsipapers10.htm.

Prudential Regulatory Authority, Policy Statement 09/16 Strengthening liquidity standards.

South African Reserve Bank, Regulations as published in Government Gazette No. 35950, December 2012, Chapter 26: Liquidity Risk (Form BA300).

*"It was clear to me that many Naval Academy graduates and senior officers did whatever it took to please their bosses. Such sycophants taught me one of the most important lessons I learned from my Vietnam experience: there will always be people who pursue power by ingratiating themselves with those in power without pausing to assess the goals of those leaders. I came to understand this as a POW, but I have witnessed it in all institutions since: corporations, bureaucracies, schools, churches, you name it."*

—Robert Wideman, *Unexpected Prisoner: Memoir of a Vietnam POW*, 2 May 2016

# Market Risk and Non-Traded Market Risk (Interest-Rate Risk in the Banking Book)

In a discipline that is more art than science, the subset of finance that is "hedging" is often an even more imprecise and approximate art. The Head of Treasury at the UK subsidiary of a European bank was fond of telling the author that "hedging was for gardeners". That is a perhaps understandable attitude if one is running a "Banking Book", where assets and liabilities do not re-mark every day. In a Trading Book environment, hedging is arguably a more precise technique. One of the best examples the author ever observed personally was at NatWest Bank's Global Financial Markets division in 1998; the FX Exotic Options desk, run at the time by a gentleman named Luke Ding, had structured the book so that the P&L was positive whichever direction the underlying FX rate moved. That was impressive, but then again an options trading book does lend itself better to hedging than vanilla assets and liabilities on the balance sheet of a commercial bank. It's the nature of the beast.

Most banks do not run material amounts of traded market risk. The main risk exposure they *do* run, borrower credit risk, is difficult if not impossible to hedge in any practical sense. The high-profile but in reality infrequently applicable credit default swap (CDS) is not available for most of the credits that banks lend to (a survey in *The Economist* at the time of the 2008 crash suggested that the CDS was used by less than 3% of the developed world's banks). The market risk that most banks run is the non-traded kind, also called interest-rate risk in the banking book (IRRBB).

Hence in this chapter we concentrate on IRRBB, particularly as it now drives a Pillar 2 regulatory capital requirement under Basel III. For reference we also discuss, in the book extracts, market risks approach for interest-rate risk and credit risk of bond portfolios. The new material for this book discusses key aspects of IRRBB management, and also considers the Strategic ALM approach to interest-rate risk origination and hedging.

**This extract from *Bank Asset and Liability Management* (2007)**

The primary hedge measure: bond modified duration and PV01

# THE PRIMARY HEDGE MEASURE: BOND MODIFIED DURATION AND PV01[2]

The main risk sensitivity measure used in calculating hedges is modified duration, or minor variations of this. We observed this earlier in the chapter when we described how to hedge a bond position using futures. The market uses variations of modified duration including the following:

- PV01: the present value of 1 basis point, also referred to as PVBP or DV01 ("dollar value of an 01"). This is the change in the bond's value for a 1 basis point change in market yields.
- Dollar duration: this is the change in bond value for a 1 basis point change in the bond's yield.

In fact both measures are essentially the same thing, and, strictly speaking, only the first one is totally correct if one is following modified duration principles. In any case, once we know an instrument's risk sensitivity, we can construct the hedge, because the futures contract DV01 is fixed and known. Here we use Excel spreadsheets to calculate PV01 for a plain vanilla bond.

Table 15.4 on pages 732–3 shows an hypothetical four-year 5% annual coupon bond, valued given an assumed zero-coupon curve. Table 15.5 on pages 734–5 is the same spreadsheet but with the Excel formulas shown in the cells. The PV01 value shows the change in the value of the bond for a 1 basis point parallel shift in the curve; the second calculation shows dollar durations which is the change in the bond price for a 1 basis point change in the bond's yield. The difference between the two calculations is minor.

Table 15.6 on pages 736 shows a three-year bond, with additional calculations of convexity and the change in bond value for a 1 point change in the yield curve. Table 15.7 on pages 737 shows the spreadsheet formulas.

---

[2] Very big, big thanks to Professor Carol Alexander at the ICMA Centre, University of Reading, who let me use her spreadsheets in this section! It is a privilege to work with her.

| A1 | B | C | D | E |
|----|----|----|----|----|
| 2 | | | | |
| 3 | Time | Cash flow | PV | Time*PV |
| 4 | 1 | 4 | 3.8095 | 3.8095 |
| 5 | 2 | 4 | 3.6281 | 7.2562 |
| 6 | 3 | 104 | 89.8391 | 269.5173 |
| 7 | Price | | 97.2768 | |
| 8 | Macaulay duration | | | 2.8844 |
| 9 | Modified duration | | | 2.7470 |
| 10 | Dollar duration | | | 0.0267 |
| 11 | Yield | 5.00% | | |
| 12 | | | | |

13 Example 4-year bond: assuming zero-coupon curve given, calculation of bond price, yield and interest-rate risk sensitivities

| | Years to maturity | Interest rate | Cash flow | PV | PV × Maturity |
|----|----|----|----|----|----|
| 14 | | | | | |
| 15 | 1 | 4.5% | 5 | 4.78 | 4.78 |
| 16 | 2 | 4.75% | 5 | 4.56 | 9.11 |
| 17 | 3 | 4.85% | 5 | 4.34 | 13.01 |
| 18 | 4 | 5% | 105 | 86.38 | 345.54 |
| 19 | | Macaulay duration | 3.72 | 100.0630 | 372.45 |

**Table 15.4**  Calculation of interest-rate risk sensitivities for a 4-year bond, given a zero-coupon curve

| A1 | B | C | D | E | F | G | H | I |
|----|---|---|---|---|---|---|---|---|
| 20 | | | | | | | | |
| 21 | | | | | | | | |
| 22 | | | | | | | | |
| 23 | | Years to maturity | Cash flow | Interest rate | PV | Yield –1bp | PV | PV01 |
| 24 | | 1 | 5 | 4.5% | 4.7847 | 4.49% | 4.7851 | 0.00046 |
| 25 | | 2 | 5 | 4.75% | 4.5568 | 4.74% | 4.5577 | 0.00087 |
| 26 | | 3 | 5 | 4.85% | 4.3378 | 4.84% | 4.3390 | 0.00124 |
| 27 | | 4 | 105 | 5.0% | 86.3838 | 4.99% | 86.4167 | 0.03292 |
| 28 | | | | | 100.0630 | | 100.0985 | 0.03549 |
| 29 | | | | | | | | |
| 30 | | Years to maturity | Cash flow | Yield | PV | Yield –1bp | PV | Dollar duration |
| 31 | | 1 | 5 | 4.97% | 4.7633 | 4.96% | 4.7638 | 0.00045 |
| 32 | | 2 | 5 | 4.97% | 4.5379 | 4.96% | 4.5388 | 0.00086 |
| 33 | | 3 | 5 | 4.97% | 4.3231 | 4.96% | 4.3243 | 0.00124 |
| 34 | | 4 | 105 | 4.97% | 86.4885 | 4.96% | 86.5214 | 0.03297 |
| 35 | | | | | 100.1128 | | 100.1483 | 0.03552 |
| 36 | | | | | | | | |
| 37 | | Solver objective: | 0.002479757 | | | | | |
| 38 | | | | | | | | |

**Table 15.4**   (*Continued*)

| A1 | B | C | D | E |
|---|---|---|---|---|
| 2 | | | | |
| 3 | Time | Cash flow | PV | Time*PV |
| 4 | 1 | 4 | =C4/(1+$C$11) | =B4*D4 |
| 5 | 2 | 4 | =C5/(1+$C$11)^2 | =B5*D5 |
| 6 | 3 | 104 | =C6/(1+$C$11)^3 | =B6*D6 |
| 7 | Price | | =SUM(D4:D6) | |
| 8 | Macaulay duration | | | =SUM(E4:E6)/D7 |
| 9 | Modified duration | | | =E8/(1+C11) |
| 10 | Dollar duration | | | =D7*E9*0.0001 |
| 11 | Yield | 5.00% | | |
| 12 | | | | |

Example 4-year bond: assuming zero-coupon curve given, calculation of bond price, yield and interest-rate risk sensitivities

| Years to maturity | Interest rate | Cash flow | PV | PV × Maturity |
|---|---|---|---|---|
| 1 | 4.5% | 5 | =E16/(1+D16) | =F16*C16 |
| 2 | 4.75% | 5 | =E17/(1+D17)^C17 | 9.11 |

**Table 15.5** Table showing Excel formulas

| A1 | B | C | D | E | F | G | H | I |
|---|---|---|---|---|---|---|---|---|
| 17 | | 3 | 4.85% | 5 | =E18/((1+D18)^C18) | 13.01 | | |
| 18 | | 4 | 5% | 105 | =E19/((1+D19)^C19) | 345.54 | | |
| 19 | | | Macaulay duration | =G20/F20 | =SUM(F16:19) | =SUM(G16:G19) | | |
| 20 | | | | | | | | |
| 21 | | | | | | | | |
| 22 | | | | | | | | |
| 23 | | Years to maturity | Cash flow | Interest rate | PV | Yield −1bp | PV | **PV01** |
| 24 | | 1 | 5 | =D16 | =D25/(1+E25) | =E25−0.0001 | =D25/((1+G25)^C25) | =H25−F25 |
| 25 | | 2 | 5 | =D17 | =D26/((1+E26)^C26) | =E26−0.0001 | =D26/((1+G26)^C26) | =H26−F26 |
| 26 | | 3 | 5 | =D18 | =D27/((1+E27)^C27) | =E27−0.0001 | =D27/((1+G27)^C27) | =H27−F27 |
| 27 | | 4 | 105 | =D19 | =D28/((1+E28)^C28) | =E28−0.0001 | =D28/((1+G28)^C28) | =H28−F28 |
| 28 | | | | | **=SUM(F25:F28)** | | =SUM(H25:H28) | =SUM(125:128) |

**Table 15.5**  *(Continued )*

| A1 | B | C | D | E | F | G | H | I |
|---|---|---|---|---|---|---|---|---|
| 29 | | | | | | | | |
| 30 | | Years to maturity | Cash flow | Yield | PV | Yield −1bp | PV | Dollar duration |
| 31 | | 1 | 5 | 4.97% | =D32/(1+E32) | =E32−0.0001 | =D32/(1+G32) | =H32−F32 |
| 32 | | 2 | 5 | 4.97% | =D33/(1+E33)^C33 | =E33−0.0001 | =D33/((1+G33)^C33 | =H32−F32 |
| 33 | | 3 | 5 | 4.97% | =D34/(1+E34)^C34 | =E34−0.0001 | =D34/(1+G34)^C34 | =H32−F32 |
| 34 | | 4 | 105 | 4.97% | =D35/(1+E35)^C35 | =E35−0.0001 | =D35/((1+G35)^C35 | =H32−F32 |
| 35 | | | | | **=SUM(F32:F35)** | | =SUM(H325:H35) | =SUM(132:135) |
| 36 | | | | | | | | |
| 37 | | | Solver objective: | =(F36−F29)^2 | | | | |
| 38 | | | | | | | | |

**Table 15.5**  (*Continued*)

| A1 | B | C | D | E | F | G | H | I | J |
|---|---|---|---|---|---|---|---|---|---|
| 2 | Market interest rates | | Coupon = | 5% | Face value = | 100 | | | |
| 3 | 4% | | | | | | | | |
| 4 | **4.25%** | | | | | | | | |
| 5 | **4.50%** | | | | | | | | |
| 6 | **4.25%** | | | | | | | | |

| Maturity | Interest rate | Cash flow | PV | | MaCaulay duration | **2.86** |
|---|---|---|---|---|---|---|
| 1 | 4.00% | 5 | 4.81 | | Modified duration | **2.74** |
| 2 | 4.25% | 5 | 4.60 | | Convexity | **10.31** |
| 3 | 4.50% | 105 | 92.01 | | Duration–convexity approximation | |
| Bond 1 | | **Price** | **101.419** | | Yield change | 1% |

| Maturity | Yield | Cash flow | PV | PV*maturity |
|---|---|---|---|---|
| 1 | 4.48% | 5 | 4.79 | 4.79 |
| 2 | 4.48% | 5 | 4.58 | 9.16 |
| 3 | 4.48% | 105 | 92.05 | 276.16 |
| Bond 1 | **4.48%** | 0.00 | 101.42 | |

| Percentage price change | −2.686% |
|---|---|
| Actual percentage price change | −2.687% |

**Table 15.6**   Bond convexity calculation

| Maturity | Yield | Cash flow | PV |
|---|---|---|---|
| 1 | 5.48% | 5 | 4.74 |
| 2 | 5.48% | 5 | 4.49 |
| 3 | 5.48% | 105 | 89.46 |
| Bond 1 | 5.48% | 7.43 | **98.69** |

**Table 15.6** *(Continued)*

| A1 | B | C | D | E | F | G | H |
|---|---|---|---|---|---|---|---|
| 2 | **Market interest rates** | | Coupon = | **5%** | Face value = | **100** | |
| 3 | 4% | | | | | | |
| 4 | **4.25%** | | Maturity | Interest Rate | Cash flow | PV | |
| 5 | **4.50%** | | 1 | =B3 | =$E$2*$G$2 | =F5/(1+E5) | |
| 6 | **4.25%** | | 2 | =B4 | =$E$2*$G$2 | =F6/(1+E6)^D6 | |
| 7 | | | 3 | =B5 | =$E$2*$G$2+G2 | =F7/(1+E7)^D7 | |
| 8 | | | Bond 1 | | **Price** | **=SUM(G5:G7)** | |
| 9 | | | | | | | |
| 10 | | | Maturity | **Yield** | Cash flow | PV | PV*Maturity |
| 11 | | | 1 | =E14 | =F5 | =F11/(1+E11) | =G11*D11 |
| 12 | | | 2 | =E14 | =F6 | =F12/(1+E12)^D12 | =G12*D12 |
| 13 | | | 3 | =E14 | =F7 | =F13/(1+E13)^D13 | =G13*D13 |
| 14 | | | Bond 1 | **4.48%** | =(G8-G14)^2 | =SUM(G11:G13) | |
| 15 | | | | | | | |

**Table 15.7**   Convexity calculation spreadsheet formula

| | Maturity | Yield | Cash flow | PV |
|---|---|---|---|---|
| | 1 | =E20 | =F5 | =F17/(1+E17) |
| | 2 | =E20 | =F6 | =F18/((1+E18)^D18) |
| | 3 | =E20 | =F7 | =F19/((1+E19)^D19) |
| Bond 1 | =E14+1% | =(G14-G20)^2 | **=SUM(G17:G19)** |

| | |
|---|---|
| Macaulay dauration | **=SUM(H11:H13)/G8** |
| Modified duration | **=J5/(1+E14)** |
| Convexity | **=(2\*F5/(1+E14)^3+6\*F6/((1+E14)^4+12\*F7/ (1+E14)^5)/G8** |
| Duration–convexity approximation | |
| Yield change | **1%** |
| Percentage price change | **=-J6\*J9+0.5\*J7\*J9^2** |
| Actual percentage price change | **=(G20-G8)/G8** |

**Table 15.7**　(*Continued*)

# HEDGING THE BOND ELEMENT
# IN A CREDIT BASIS TRADE

Credit traders and investors now undertake basis-type trades using cash bonds, or asset swaps, and credit derivative contracts such as credit default swaps. While this is not the preserve of the ALM or Treasury desk, well not usually anyway, we do not need to consider these types of trades here (although credit derivatives themselves, which are important credit risk management tools, are covered in detail in Chapter 16). However, we briefly describe a basis-type trade here so that we can then illustrate the interest-rate risk hedge put on for the cash bond element of the trade, which may be undertaken by the Treasury desk in some banks.

In a "positive basis" trade, the CDS trades above the cash spread, which can be measured using the asset-swap spread (ASW) or the z-spread.[3] The potential arbitrage trade is to sell the basis; that is, sell the cash bond and sell protection on the same reference name. We would do this if we expected the basis to converge or narrow.

To illustrate this we describe an example of a basis trade in France Telecom credit. The cash side of the trade is an EUR-denominated bond issued by it, the 3.625% 2015, rated A3/A– and which is trading on 8 December 2005 as follows:[4]

| | |
|---|---|
| Bond: | France Telecom 3.625% 2015 |
| ISIN: | FR0010245555 |
| Maturity: | 14 October 2015 |
| Price: | 97.52–97.62 clean |
| ASW: | 42.9 bps |
| z-spread: | 45.2 bps |
| CDS price: | 77–87 bps (10-year CDS) |
| Repo rate: | 2.06 – 2.02 (Libor minus 35 bps). |

The asset-swap spreads can be seen in Figure 15.2 (they are slightly different to the levels quoted above because the screens were printed the next day and the market had moved). This is Bloomberg screen ASW for the bond. The basis for this bond is positive, as shown in Figure 15.3, which is Bloomberg screen CRVD.

---

[3] See Chapter 11 for a description of the different ways to measure the basis and an example of a z-spread calculation.
[4] Prices are taken from Bloomberg L.P. (bond and repo) and market-makers (CDS).

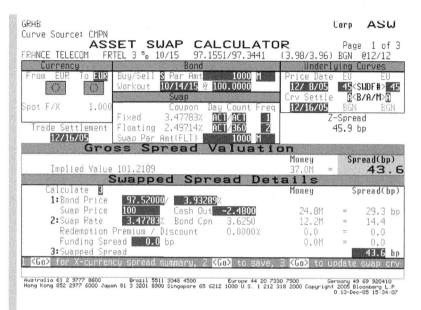

**Figure 15.2**   Asset-swap spread on screen ASW, France Telecom
3.625% 2015 bond, 9 December 2005
© 2005 Bloomberg L.P. Reproduced with permission. All rights reserved.

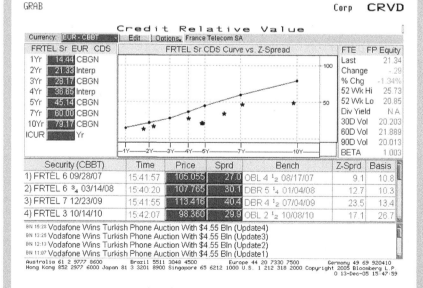

**Figure 15.3**   Cash–CDS basis for France Telecom, 9 December 2005
© 2005 Bloomberg L.P. Reproduced with permission. All rights reserved.

**Figure 15.4**    One-year historical CDS–ASW spread, France Telecom, December 2005

Above we see that the basis is (77 – 45.2) or +31.8 basis points. If we have the view that the bond will underperfom, or the basis will otherwise narrow and go towards zero and/or negative, we will sell the basis. We consider historical data on the basis during our analysis, as shown in Figure 15.4 on page 740 which is from screen BQ and shows the one-year historical ASW spread against the five-year CDS spread.[5]

The trade is put on in the following terms:

- sell EUR6 million nominal of the bond at 97.52 clean price, 98.1158 dirty price;
- sell protection EUR5.85 million CDS at 77 basis points.

As we are shorting the bond we fund it in reverse repo, which is done at 2.02 basis points, or Libor minus 35 basis points.

The credit risk on the bond position is hedged using the CDS. The interest-rate risk ("DV01") is hedged using Bund futures contracts. The

---

[5] Our view on where the basis is going may be based on any combination of factors; these can include speculation about future direction based on historical trade patterns, specific company intelligence such as expectations of a takeover or other buy-out, views on credit quality, and so on. We do not discuss the rationale behind the trades in this article, merely the trade mechanics!

| A1 | B | C |
|----|---|---|
| 2 | **Hedging bonds with futures** | |
| 3 | | |
| 4 | | |
| 5 | $Number\ of\ contracts\ =\ \dfrac{M_{bond}}{M_{fut}} \times \dfrac{BPV_{bond}}{BPV_{fut}}$ | |
| 6 | | |
| 7 | | |
| 8 | | |
| 9 | | |
| 10 | **Inputs** | |
| 11 | | |
| 12 | **Nominal value of the bond ($M_{bond}$)** | 10,000,000.00 |
| 13 | | |
| 14 | **Nominal value of futures contract ($M_{fut}$)** | 100,000.00 |
| 15 | | |
| 16 | **BPV of the futures CTD bond** | 7.484 |
| 17 | | |
| 18 | **Conversion factor of CTD** | 0.852 |
| 19 | | |
| 20 | **BPV of the Bond ($BPV_{bond}$)** | 7.558 |
| 21 | | |
| 22 | **BPV of the future ($BPV_{fut}$)** | 8.780 |
| 23 | | |
| 24 | | |
| 25 | **Number of contracts to hedge** | **86.083** |
| 26 | | |
| 27 | | |
| 28 | | |

**Table 15.8**    Futures hedge calculation spreadsheet
© *Stuart Turner. Reproduced with permission.*

hedge calculation is a straightforward one and uses the ratio of the respective DV01 of the bond and futures contract; see earlier in this chapter for the hedge calculation mechanics.[6] From this we determine that we need to buy 52 lots of the Bund future to hedge the bond position.

We show the DV01 hedge calculation in Table 15.8, which is the Excel spreadsheet used to determine the futures hedge. Note that the example

---

[6] The hedge calculation is based on a ratio of BPV ("DV01") of the bond to be hedged and the futures contract. See Table 15.8 and Table 15.9 for the calculation spreadsheet.

shown is for an hypothetical hedge, not our example – we show it here for instructional purposes. Table 15.9 on page 742 shows the Excel formulas used in the spreadsheet.

The analysis is undertaken with reference to Libor, not absolute levels such as the YTM. The cash flows are:

| | |
|---|---|
| Sell bond: | pay 42.9 bps |
| Sell protection: | receive 62 bps. |

| A1 | B | C |
|---|---|---|
| 2 | **Hedging bonds with futures** | |
| 3 | | |
| 4 | | |
| 5 | $Number\ of\ contracts\ = \dfrac{M_{bond}}{M_{fut}} \times \dfrac{BPV_{bond}}{BPV_{fut}}$ | |
| 6 | | |
| 7 | | |
| 8 | | |
| 9 | | |
| 10 | **Inputs** | |
| 11 | | |
| 12 | **Nominal value of the bond (M$_{bond}$)** | 10,000,000.00 |
| 13 | | |
| 14 | **Nominal value of futures contract (M$_{fut}$)** | 100,000.00 |
| 15 | | |
| 16 | **BPV of the futures CTD bond** | 7.484 |
| 17 | | |
| 18 | **Conversion factor of CTD** | 0.852 |
| 19 | | |
| 20 | **BPV of the bond (BPV$_{bond}$)** | 7.558 |
| 21 | | |
| 22 | **BPV of the future (BPV$_{fut}$)** | =C16/C18 |
| 23 | | |
| 24 | | |
| 25 | **Number of contracts to hedge** | =((C12/C14)*(C20/C22)) |
| 26 | | |
| 27 | | |
| 28 | | |

**Table 15.9**   Table 15.8 with Microsoft Excel formulas shown
© *Stuart Turner. Reproduced with permission*

In addition, the reverse repo position is 35 basis points below Libor; as it represents interest income we consider this spread a funding loss so we incorporate this into the funding calculation; that is, we also pay 35 basis points. We ignore the futures position for funding purposes. This is a net carry of:

$$62 - (42.9 + 35)$$

or −15.9 basis points. In other words, the net carry for this position is negative. Funding cost must form part of the trade analysis. Funding has a greater impact on the trade net p&l the longer it is kept on. If the trade is maintained over one month, the funding impact will not be significant if we generated, say, a 5 basis points gain in the basis, because that is 5 basis points over a 10-year horizon (the maturity of the bond and CDS), the present value of which will exceed the 15.9 basis points loss on one month's funding. If the position is maintained over a year, the impact of the funding cost will be greater.

## Position after one month

On 10 January 2006 we recorded the following prices for the France Telecom bond and reference name:

| Bond: | France Telecom 3.625% 2015 |
|---|---|
| Price: | 98.35–98.45 |
| ASW: | 42.0 bps |
| z-spread: | 43.8 bps |
| CDS price: | 76–80 bps. |

Spreads are shown in Figure 15.5.

To unwind this position we would take the other side of the CDS quote, so the basis is now at (80 − 43.8) or 36.2 basis points. In other words, it has not gone the way we expected but has widened. As we sold the basis, the position has lost money if we unwind it now. The decision to unwind would be based on the original trade strategy: if the trader's time horizon was six months or longer, then the decision may be made to continue holding the position. If the trader's time horizon was shorter, it is probably sensible to cut one's losses now. Note that this trade is running at negative net carry so it incurs a carry loss if maintained irrespective of where the basis is going.

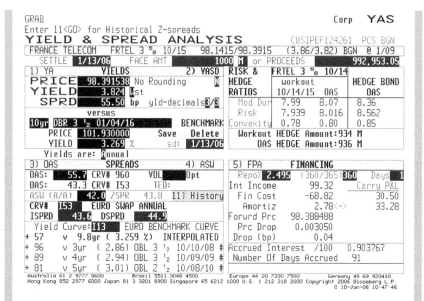

**Figure 15.5** France Telecom bond YAS page for asset-swap and z-spreads, 10 January 2006

# CONCLUSIONS

Exchange-traded bond futures contracts are very important as interest-rate risk hedging tools, and as such are widely used by bank ALM desks. Because ALM desks frequently maintain a portfolio of short-dated (on average, about three-year) government bonds for capital and liquidity purposes, they sometimes use bond futures to hedge the portfolio interest-rate risk. In this chapter we have described the contracts in the USD and GBP markets, the Treasury bond and long gilt future. We also illustrated the calculation of the hedge, which uses the relative basis point values of the cash instrument and the futures contract.

The modified duration method is still commonly used in risk hedging. We showed the calculation of "PV01" as well as "Dollar Duration" for an hypothetical bond. A Treasury desk would use this approach to calculate the hedge for a portfolio of government bonds.[7] In some banks, the Treasury or

---

[7] It is by no means always the case that a liquidity portfolio of government bonds would be hedged against interest-rate risk exposure. In many case the bonds held in such a portfolio are purchased on a "buy-to-hold" basis and held to maturity, so hedging may be considered unnecessary. However an ALM desk sometimes will hedge against anticipated yield curve shifts on a short-term basis.

repo desk would be responsible for arranging the hedge for a proprietary trade, and we illustrated this in our discussion of a credit derivative basis trade.

---

**EXAMPLE 16.5**  **CDS HEDGE**

XYZ plc credit spreads are currently trading at 120 basis points relative to government-issued securities for five-year maturities and 195 basis points for 10-year maturities. A portfolio manager hedges a $10 million holding of 10-year paper by purchasing the following CDS, written on the five-year bond. This hedge protects for the first five years of the holding, and in the event of XYZ's credit spread widening, it will increase in value and may be sold before expiry at profit. The 10-year bond holding also earns 75 basis points over the shorter-term paper for the portfolio manager.

| | |
|---|---|
| Term: | Five years |
| Reference credit: | XYZ plc five-year bond |
| Credit event payout date: | The business day following occurrence of specified credit event |
| Default payment: | Nominal value of bond × [100 − price of bond after credit event] |
| Swap premium: | 3.35% |

Assume now that midway into the life of the swap there is a technical default on the XYZ plc five-year bond, such that its price now stands at $28. Under the terms of the swap the protection buyer delivers the bond to the seller, who pays out $7.2 million to the buyer.

The CDS enables one party to transfer its credit risk exposure to another party. Banks may use default swaps to trade sovereign and corporate credit spreads without trading the actual assets themselves; for example, someone who has gone long a default swap (the protection buyer) will gain if the reference asset obligor suffers a rating downgrade or defaults, and can sell the default swap at a profit if he or she can find a buyer counterparty.[4] This is because the cost of

---

[4]Be careful with terminology here. To "go long" of an instrument generally is to purchase it. In the cash market, going long of the bond means one is buying the bond and so receiving coupon; the buyer has therefore taken on credit risk exposure to the issuer. In a CDS, to go long is to buy the swap, but the buyer is purchasing protection and therefore paying premium; the buyer has no credit exposure on the name and has in effect "gone short" on the reference name (the equivalent of shorting a bond in the cash market and paying coupon). So buying a CDS is frequently referred to in the market as "shorting" the reference entity.

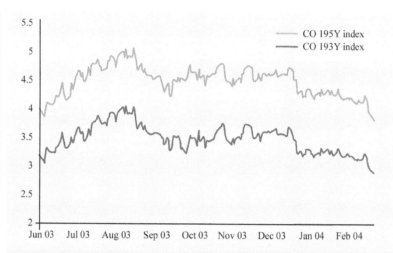

**Figure 16.11**     Investment-grade credit default swap levels, 2003–2004
*Source*: Bloomberg.

protection on the reference asset will have increased as a result of the credit event. The original buyer of the default swap need never have owned a bond issued by the reference asset obligor. CDS are used extensively for flow trading (that is, the daily customer buys and sells business) of single reference name credit risks or, in *portfolio swap* form, for trading a basket of reference credits. CDSs and CLNs are also used in structured products, in various combinations, and their flexibility has been behind the growth and wide application of the synthetic collateralised debt obligation and other credit hybrid products.

Figure 16.11 shows US dollar CDS price levels (in basis points) during 2003 and 2004 for BBB-rated reference entities, for three- and five-year CDS contracts. The graph shows the level of fluctuation in CDS prices, it also shows clearly the term structure of credit rates, as the five-year CDS price lies above the three-year rate at all times.

Figure 16.12 shows the Bloomberg screen WCDS, which contains CDS prices for a wide range of reference names, grouped according to industry category. Our example, from 1 December 2005, shows a selection of industrial corporate names.

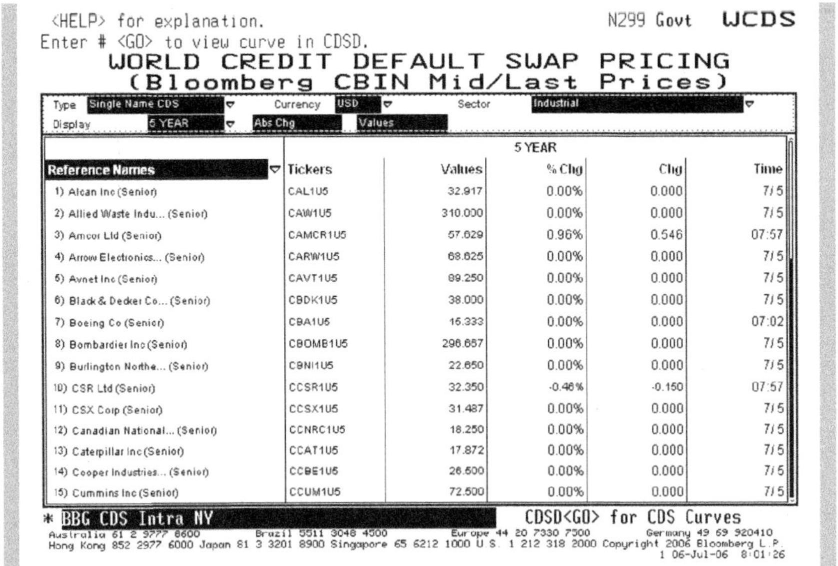

**Figure 16.12** Bloomberg screen WCDS showing extract of world CDS prices, as at 6 July 2006

© 2006 Bloomberg L.P. All rights reserved. Reprinted with permission.

---

**EXAMPLE 16.6(i)** **CALCULATING THE NOTIONAL AMOUNT OF THE CREDIT RISK HEDGE[29]**

It is intuitively easy to view a credit hedge as a straight par-for-par trade of notionals. That is, we would buy (or sell) USD10 million nominal of a bond against buying (or selling) USD10 million of notional in the CDS. This is still quite common due to its simplicity. However, unless the cash bond in question is priced at par, this approach is not correct and the analysis will not be accurate. The biggest errors will arise when the bond is trading significantly away from par.

To avoid the risk of being over- or under-hedged we must assess how much CDS protection to put on against a set amount of the bond. There is no one way to approach this; the key is the assumption made

---

[29] With special thanks to Niall Considine and Suraj Gohil for their assistance with the technical details in this section.

about the recovery rate in the event of default. In practice traders will adopt one of the following methods:

- par/par: this is a common approach. In such a trade, identical par amounts of the bond and the CDS are traded. The advantage of this method is that the position is straightforward to maintain. The disadvantage is that the trader is not accurately credit-risk hedged if the bond is priced away from par. The CDS pays out par (minus the deliverable asset or cash value on default) on default, but if the bond is priced above par greater cash value is at risk. Therefore this approach is recommended for bonds priced near to par or for trades with a long-term horizon. It is not recommended for use with bonds at higher risk of default (for instance, sub-investment-grade bonds) as default events will expose this approach to be under-hedged;
- delta-neutral: this is a similar approach used to duration-weighted bond spread trades such as butterfly/barbell trades (see Choudhry 2004). It is appropriate when the maturity of the bond does not match precisely the maturity of the CDS;
- DV01: this approach sets the CDS notional relative to the actual price of the bond. For example, if the bond is trading at 120 then we would buy 120% notional of the CDS. This is a logical approach and recommended if the bond is trading away from par.

An assumption of the recovery rate will influence the choice of hedging approach and the notional amount of CDS protection to buy.

A key risk factor is the recovery rate assumed for the bond. The rate of recovery cannot be hedged and the actual recovery after event of default will impact the final profit/loss position. The impact is greatest for bonds that are priced significantly away from par. To illustrate this, consider a bond priced at $110.00. To hedge a long position of $10 million of this bond, assume we buy protection in $11 million nominal of the CDS. We do not use a par/par approach because otherwise we would be under-hedged. Now consider, in the event of default, the following recovery rates:

- 0% recovery: we receive $11 million on the CDS, and lose $11 million ($1.10 × 10,000,000) on the bond, so net we are flat;
- 50% recovery: we receive $5.5 million on the CDS, and lose $6 million on the bond (the bond loss is $5 million nominal and

so we receive back $5 million, having paid out $11 million), so net we are down $500,000.

So in other words, under a 50% recovery rate scenario we are under-hedged still and would need more notional of CDS to cover the loss on the bond. If the recovery rate is 30%, we will lose on the position, while at 50% or more we will lose progressively more. Note that the reverse analysis applies when the bond is priced below par. Overall then we conclude that the assumption of the recovery rate must influence the notional size of the CDS position.

Generally, the market assumes the following recovery rates:

- investment-grade 40%;
- insurance companies and corporates 30%;
- sub-investment grade 20%.

Some banks assume a 50% recovery rate in their pricing models. While a more robust approach might be to use historical data of actual defaults and ultimate recovery rates, at the current time some markets, notably those in Europe and Asia, suffer from a paucity of data and so for the time being market participants use assumed recovery rates.

To construct the correct hedge, we use the following formula for a bond priced over par:

$$\text{Hedge} = N + \left[ \left( \frac{P-100}{1-R} \right) \times N \right] \qquad 16.22$$

where

$N$     is the bond notional
$P$     is the bond price
$R$     is the (assumed) recovery rate.

In the earlier example of a bond priced at 110.00, a CDS notional of USD11,428,571 would provide an adequate hedge if the recovery rate was at 30%.

For a bond priced over par, we subtract the adjustment from the bond notional.

---

**ExAMPLE16.6 (ii)**   COMPARING CASH AND SYNTHETIC
BOND PRICE

The existence of a liquid market in credit derivatives allows banks and
fund managers to calculate a theoretical cash market bond price from
the CDS curve. By comparing the actual market price to the theoretical price, investors can determine relative value and any mispricing
in one market vis-à-vis the other. The cash market price is observed
in the market. The CDS curve implies the theoretical bond price: we
can use the CDS curve and an assumed recovery rate to calculate the
default probability of the reference name for any point along the CDS
term structure. With a term structure of default probabilities, we can
imply the likelihood of default or that all the bond's coupons and
redemption payments will be made. If no default occurs, the bondholder receives the expected cash flows; if default occurs, the investor's payout is determined by the recovery rate. The theoretical bond
price is the net present value of all probability-weighted payments, in
the event of default or no default.

In other words, using prices observed in the CDS market we
can calculate the theoretical value of a bond's cash flows, given the
value of the same name as implied in the CDS market. We can then
consider whether the bond is cheap or dear relative to the synthetic
credit market.

Bloomberg screen HG can be used to make the calculation.[30]
It is used with a single bond position, and we illustrate this here.
Figure 16.31 shows the page selected for use with a bond issued by
British Airways plc, the 10⅞% June 2008. The analysis was conducted on 11 December 2006. This page uses the CDS spreads for
British Airways plc plus an assumed recovery rate of 30% to determine future default probability. The model price (shown in the bottom
left-hand corner, beneath the market price) is the net present value of
the bond's probability-weighted cash flows. We see that the model
price of 107.151 differs from the observed market offer price of
107.02, a matter of 13 pence or so.

The "Default Adj Spread" field shows the number of basis points
by which the CDS curve would need to be moved in order to equate
the theoretical price to the market price. In this case we see that this
adjustment is around 8.5 basis points.

---

[30] This screen has more than one application, and can also be used for a number of
interest-rate risk ("DV01") and credit risk hedge calculations.

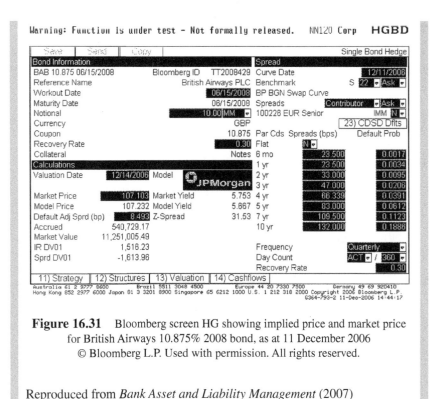

**Figure 16.31** Bloomberg screen HG showing implied price and market price for British Airways 10.875% 2008 bond, as at 11 December 2006
© Bloomberg L.P. Used with permission. All rights reserved.

Reproduced from *Bank Asset and Liability Management* (2007)

# UNDERSTANDING AND MANAGING MARKET AND INTEREST-RATE RISKS

In this chapter, we introduce the concept of interest and market risk in a banking operation. These risks differ from credit risk, and instead relate to how changes in interest rates and prices for market instruments affect the profitability and value of a bank. A bank can be extremely effective at managing its credit portfolio, but still perform poorly if it fails to manage its interest-rate and market risk. That said, credit risk remains by far the main type of risk exposure for the majority of the world's retail banks. Most banks run very little genuine market risk, the exception of course are the large global investment banks which routinely manage trading books.

## Interest-Rate Risk and Interest-Rate Risk Management

Banks provide loans to customers, funding these loans with deposits, inter-bank borrowing, debt issuance, and capital. In the process, interest-rate risk arises on the balance sheet in a number of forms. While loans can be sold or securitised, the vast majority are retained and are not characterised as trading book assets managed with a market risk approach, as they are banking book assets.

**Forms of Interest-Rate Risk**     The forms of interest-rate risk are as follows:

- Gap Risk: assets (generally loans) do not match liabilities (funding) in terms of tenure, duration, and currency. Where assets and liabilities are mismatched, adverse interest rate movements can lead to profitability being reduced or eliminated, and, in extreme situations, losses can arise;
- Optionality: the bank may have match-funded a loan, but the client has an option to pre-pay that may be exercised. If rates fall, the matching assets need to be replaced at a lower rate than the original loan, which would reduce profitability or could result in a loss. For example, mortgages can often be pre-paid, with the decision to do so being based not solely on interest rate movements;
- Basis Risk: assets and liabilities can be linked to floating rates off different benchmarks. For example, loans could be based on T-bills, while borrowing is based on LIBOR. These rates would not necessarily move by the same magnitude or in the same direction. If an asset and liability are priced off the same floating rate but both do not reset on the same date, risk exposure is created;
- Yield Curve Risk: rates may not change generally, but rather in only one part of the yield curve. In a short / lend long funding scenario, profitability is reduced if short-term rates increase.

A key performance and "current state" measure in commercial and retail banking is Net Interest Income (NII), which is defined as interest income from loans less interest costs on funding, together with net interest margin (NIM). The higher these measures, the better performing a bank can feel itself to be. However, NIM values are not comparable across banks because of the different way that banks in different jurisdictions compute the measure. In essence, IRRBB is concerned with minimising the negative risk to NII arising from a change in market interest rates (including customer rates).

**Risk Measurement and Sensitivity**     With the types of risk identified, the next step is to establish measurements to help manage the risk.

The traditional method used is called a gap analysis, where assets and liabilities are each grouped together by maturity "buckets" (e.g., one day, one week, one month, two months). Banks estimate and use probable maturities for assets and liabilities with optionality (effective maturity as opposed to contractual maturity). Floating-rate obligations are measured according to their next repricing date as opposed to their final maturity date.

The mismatch of assets and liabilities is calculated for each bucket. With gaps identified, modified duration formulas allow for the time value of money and are applied to calculate price sensitivity to changes in interest rates.

The process described above is simplistic, with numerous limitations:

- Gap analysis is only a "snapshot" of the balance sheet, and does not incorporate likely future developments in the bank's business.
- Interest rate changes do not always occur across the yield curve.
- Asset performance (for example, loan loss, rescheduling) is uncertain.
- Client exercise of optionality may or may not be linked to interest rate movements.

The gap periods used are by their nature arbitrary. However, large banks must attempt to calculate every measure with precision given the size of the balance sheet and potentially large swings in profit and loss. For example, a floating-rate asset and a floating-rate liability could be in the same bucket, but reprice on different days at considerable risk.

ALM policies may be built around certain key simulations. For example, management could determine that a 100 basis point change in interest rates or a 25 basis point shift in the yield curve should not result in a change in NII of more than 10%.

## PRODUCT TENOR

Note that when we speak of the tenor of assets and liabilities, contractual or behavioural, we must remember the application that the tenor value is being used for. It is important to distinguish between reports that help in the management of interest-rate risk and those that help with liquidity or funding risk, or are used for FTP purposes. Interest-rate risk is concerned with when assets and liabilities reprice, whereas liquidity / funding risk is primarily focused upon when they mature. An interest rate gap report is used to measure interest-rate risk. It is perhaps not best to use the term "funding gap report" in the context of a discussion on interest-rate risk, because that implies the report will depict the maturity, not the repricing of assets and liabilities. Furthermore, the term "ALM report" is a generic term and could apply to any report containing ALM related information, whether for liquidity reporting or IRRBB reporting.

## Market Risk and Market Risk Management

Market risk is defined as the risk of loss from movements in prices in the financial markets. Market risk can arise from any position, whether on- or off-balance sheet, in cash or securities or derivatives, or from customer lending, or market making or trading. Interest-rate risk is therefore a form of market risk. Banks also have market risk from foreign exchange, commodities, and equities, depending on the scale of their global operations and trading businesses.

**Value at Risk (VaR)**   Banks often utilise Value at Risk (VaR) models to analyse correlations and yield curve sensitivity. These models rely on historical simulations, the most sophisticated of which is the Monte Carlo method, which uses powerful computers to randomly generate a large number (often in excess of 10,000) of interest rate and market scenarios. These are aggregated to estimate probable and possible swings in P&L. One of the more desirable features of using Monte Carlo simulation is that it allows one to generate a distribution of possible outcomes, as opposed to a point estimate. This can then be extended to estimating a confidence interval for the results.

VaR focus is on P&L probabilities out to two standard deviations (95% confidence level). For example, if one-day 5% VaR is $25 million, there is an estimated 5% chance of a single trading day a loss of more than $25 million. In rough terms, a loss of $25 million or more is expected in one out of twenty trading days (about once a month). A "VaR break" is when losses exceed the VaR threshold.

**Market and Systemic Risk, and Funding**   Money market funding includes deposits, inter-bank, commercial paper, certificates of deposit, Repo, and medium-term notes (see Chapter 1). Accessibility to funding markets can be curtailed not only because of investor concerns about a given bank, but also because of "systemic" concerns with an instrument or the broader financial system. As globalisation increased, many banks adopted the same risk management methodologies and built balance sheets of similar assets. When the crisis hit, it was not possible for all to find liquidity to unwind positions and mitigate risk.

It is sound policy to establish a funding programme in as many instruments across as many regions as practical, maintaining a minimum borrowing presence even if rates are not always attractive. Investors can then be accessed quickly so borrowings can increase sharply, should rates rise or liquidity contract in other markets.

Banks can seek to reduce the cost of borrowing in one currency by issuing in another and swapping. This depends on swap rate arbitrage opportunities and the swap capabilities of the bank, and credit lines with counterparties.

Money market liquidity diminished significantly in the crisis. Short-term investors are the most conservative, and can withdraw funding at any hint of trouble. As the most a short-term investor can gain is a slightly better yield than that offered by a deposit with a leading bank or government T-bill (and no capital gain), there is simply no point in tolerating risk. It does not matter to investors that short-term debt instruments will mature over a few months or less. Money market funds must convince their cash investors that their portfolio has no possibility of loss, and are very sensitive to negative headlines.

Repo, while secured, is not immune to the same liquidity problems as commercial paper and CDs. Investors know that underlying securities can lose liquidity, fall in value, or even default. The credit worthiness of the cash borrower remains tantamount despite collateral, if only for "reputational risk" and the desire to avoid being associated with a troubled institution.

**Hedging: Tools, Strategy, and Risks**  Banks must mitigate risk when exposures become too large. Limits are set for each bucket. The most straightforward way to address large exposures would be to sell assets, but most are illiquid or would find only unattractive bids.

**Forward Rate Agreements**  Forward Rate Agreements (FRAs) and futures are popular instruments for hedging ALM books. Both involve agreeing to buy or sell a deposit in the future, with the amount, term, and rate fixed. At maturity, there is no actual settlement of a cash deposit, but funds are exchanged to reflect the change in value from interest rate movements. FRAs are over-the-counter (OTC) trades between two parties who can agree whatever terms suit (amounts, term, and forward start date).

**Futures**  Futures are exchange traded and have fixed terms. For example, Eurodollar futures contracts are $1 million for 90-day periods settling in March, June, September, and December. Banks can sell consecutive futures contracts, or "strips", to create longer hedges. Futures positions are margined (the exchange takes an "initial" margin to cover potential losses and then "variation" margin as needed) to mitigate credit risk. The fixed nature of futures contracts and strictly enforced margining allows for liquid trading. Both FRAs and futures are priced off the forward yield curve.

**Overnight Index Swaps**  Overnight Index Swaps (OIS) are another popular form of interest rate hedging. One party agrees to pay a fixed rate for a fixed period on a nominal amount, while the other will pay the average floating overnight rates based on a benchmark index. As with FRAs and futures, the nominal amounts are not exchanged and settlement involves paying the difference between the two rates. OIS allows a treasury team to separate interest rate and liquidity positions. Funds can be borrowed for a term period and if the view is that rates will decline, the fixed rate paid can be swapped for floating overnight rates.

**Options**    Options are an alternative hedging tool and are valuable because of entirely different characteristics. Futures, FRAs, and OIS are firm commitments to take on exposure. (American) options represent the right to buy or sell at a given price within a specific time frame. Buying an option is similar to buying an insurance policy in that a premium is paid which represents maximum exposure, and that premium depends on the likelihood there will be a pay-out. Prices increase with market volatility. The buyer of financial options can insure against small or large rate movements. Options can be purchased against contingent exposures, or as general protection. A buyer of protection against interest rates rising above a certain level can offset the cost of the premium by selling an option that pays out if rates fall below a certain level, creating a "collar".

Cash instruments can be used to hedge exposures. For example, sovereign debt securities (such as T-bills) can be sold short to protect against rising rates. It is imperative that the repo desk is able to borrow the security to complete delivery. In a hedging trade, securities are sold against cash and simultaneously borrowed from a repo desk or client against cash. When the short position is covered eventually by buying the security in the market, the seller will pay cash including accrued interest. The security will be returned to the lender against cash plus the repo rate. Until the security is borrowed, the seller does not receive the sale price and is short the coupon without receiving the repo rate.

A bank could see strong demand for its issuance at small spreads over its benchmark, but have the view that general interest rates would fall. One strategy would be to issue right away to take advantage of the tight credit spread, but also execute an "anticipatory" hedge, buying treasuries financed through repo.

The "basis" is a great challenge in hedging. This means that there is no certainty that rates on the bank's exposure will move in tandem with the instrument used to hedge. As explained earlier, credit considerations meant that in the crisis LIBOR rates lost much of their correlation with cash settled derivatives that have no element of credit risk. Shorting sovereign debt as a hedge can backfire if there is a "flight to quality" and it outperforms. Securities can become difficult to borrow to maintain short positions, triggering a "short squeeze" rally. On the other hand, buying certain securities as a hedge can go wrong if they underperform because their perceived liquidity makes them attractive for others to short.

It is vital that risk management reports identify hedging, so that basis risk can be analysed. A report aggregating various types of long and short positions could show little or no risk, while the basis risk was substantial.

**Trading and Funding Policy**   Treasury teams manage liquidity in varying degrees by holding security portfolios that can be sold as funds are required. Most of the securities are highly liquid, even in periods of stress. Bank Floating Rate Notes (FRNs) incur less interest-rate risk and price volatility than notes with a fixed coupon. Traders will want to maximise profits and trade actively – and have varying incentives to do so – but liquidity management is the primary objective.

Banks have invested their own capital through the treasury function. Beyond the liquid securities buffer, securities with an attractive risk–return profile can be purchased using capital surpluses. This may occur when loan demand is weak, or the bank is defensive in its view of credit risk. Sometimes bonds are attractive relative to loans, as corporations with access to the markets are often of higher quality. While many loans can be sold or syndicated, bonds usually are more liquid.

Trading book exposures must be managed actively and held for "trading intent", or short-term gain. Positions may be proprietary or arise from market-making to serve clients. Capital should be allocated to cover losses from a very short period (10–20 days). Standardised methods banks must use set parameters, but advanced banks with approved internal models banks can use their own EAD and VaR.

During the financial crisis, losses from market risk in most trading books were higher than VaR indicated and regulators required. A new incremental risk capital charge (to include default and migration risk) and a stressed VaR requirement have been added. The stressed VaR requirement is designed to reduce pro-cyclicality, i.e. downturns are exacerbated because banks are forced to sell as asset prices fall, necessitating cutbacks in lending or new capital.

## MANAGING INTEREST-RATE RISK IN THE BANKING BOOK (IRRBB)[1]

Conventional bank loan and deposit products that do not reprice while they are on the balance sheet are held on the "banking book", also referred to as an "accruals" book. An absence of marking-to-market does not mean that the book is without market risk, however, or at least P&L risk, because of

---

[1] This section was co-authored with Chris Westcott.

the funding structure that banks use. Assets are long-dated and liabilities are in the main short-dated, so if the cost of funding rises there is a potential negative impact on net interest income. Also the origination of fixed-rate assets and liabilities gives rise to what one might term "accounting risk", because if market rates rise or fall then there is a potential "opportunity cost foregone" impact and this will also be viewed negatively.[2] This explains the focus on IRRBB by the Basel Committee and national regulators.

### Interest-Rate Risk in the Banking Book

Interest-rate risk in the banking book refers to the current or prospective risk to a bank's earnings and ultimately capital arising from movements in interest rates.

When interest rates change, the present value and timing of future cash flows change. This in turn affects the underlying value of a bank's assets, liabilities, and off-balance sheet instruments, and hence its economic value. Changes in interest rates also influence a bank's earnings by altering interest income and expense from assets and liabilities which reprice within a 12-month time horizon, affecting its NII. This risk is inherent to the banking business and its successful management can have an important impact on the NIM and shareholder value. Excessive interest-rate risk could, just possibly (if the move was large enough and/or the balance sheet was structured badly enough), pose a material threat to a bank's current capital base and/or future earnings if not properly managed.

There are a number of different types of interest-rate risk faced by banks in their banking books, which we introduced earlier. The first step required is to calculate the risk exposure as a quantitative value.

### The Interest Rate Gap Report

A static interest rate gap report is used as a basis to assess gap risk, whether it is in relation to the effect of interest rate movements on income (NII Sensitivity) or economic value.

---

[2] One could argue that this opportunity cost foregone issue lacks logic, however. Fixing interest rates, whether for loans or assets or both, removes uncertainty so unarguably is a "good" thing. Does it matter if, having lent 5-year money at 3%, in 6 months' time the 4.5-year interest rate rises to 3.5%? The bank would not be re-marking the loan as it isn't a trading book asset, so in real-world terms are we concerned about the rise in rates? As long as the loan is repaid on maturity then all is good. Of course the cost of funding the loan, if it is not fixed, will rise in this case so the net P&L on the loan will reduce. So there is certainly a NII exposure here, but it would be an extremely poorly structured bank that collapsed because of NII exposure. Is reduced NII a "loss" of income? Yes by orthodox logic of the banking industry and the accounting world, but part of what banking is about. The accounting world is concerned about this opportunity cost issue, but that doesn't necessarily give the argument logic.

The report has separate columns for assets and liabilities and is divided into a number of distinct time buckets, ranging from 0–1 month to a period normally in excess of 10 years. All cash items in the balance sheet (not accounting adjustments) are included in the report according to when they reprice or, in the case of fixed rate items, when they mature.

The difference between the assets and liabilities repricing in a given period is known as the interest rate gap. The cumulative gap captures the net position on all the assets and liabilities which reprice between 0 months and a given time bucket.

A specimen Interest Rate Gap report is illustrated in Table 13.1.

Within a given time bucket, a bank may have a positive, negative, or neutral gap. The gap is positive when more assets reprice or mature than liabilities. In this case, the bank is said to be asset sensitive for the time band. An asset sensitive bank is generally expected to benefit from rising interest rates because its assets are expected to reprice more quickly than its liabilities. A similar situation applies to the cumulative gap; if this is positive out to a given time bucket, a bank will gain for that period from any rise in interest rates.

**TABLE 13.1**  Specimen Interest Rate Gap Report

| Repricing Bucket | Assets | Liabilities | Interest Rate Gap | Cumulative Gap |
|---|---|---|---|---|
| Currency (£m) | | | | |
| 0 – 1 month | 500 | 4,600 | –4,100 | –4,100 |
| 1 – 2 months | 443 | 324 | 119 | –3,981 |
| 2 – 3 months | 156 | 1,781 | –1,625 | –5,606 |
| 3 – 4 months | 342 | 430 | -88 | –5,694 |
| 4 – 5 months | 213 | 24 | 189 | –5,505 |
| 5 – 6 months | 224 | 69 | 155 | –5,350 |
| 6 – 9 months | 356 | 17 | 339 | –5,011 |
| 9 – 12 months | 324 | 46 | 278 | –4,733 |
| 12 – 15 months | 614 | 32 | 582 | –4,151 |
| 15 – 18 months | 459 | 123 | 336 | –3,815 |
| 18 – 24 months | 875 | 275 | 600 | –3,215 |
| 2 years – 3 years | 1,365 | 135 | 1,230 | –1,985 |
| 3 years – 4 years | 845 | 86 | 759 | –1,226 |
| 4 years – 5 years | 725 | 58 | 667 | –559 |
| 5 years – 6 years | 413 | 0 | 413 | –146 |
| 6 years – 7 years | 45 | 0 | 45 | –101 |
| 7 years – 10 years | 89 | 0 | 89 | –12 |
| 10 years + | 12 | 0 | 12 | 0 |
| Total | 8,000 | 8,000 | | |

The converse is true for a negative gap, which occurs when more liabilities than assets mature in a given time bucket. A bank in this situation will be liability sensitive for the time band and expected to gain from falling rates (but lose from rising rates) as in this instance, its liabilities would re-price downwards more quickly than its assets. A bank with an interest rate gap report like that illustrated at Figure 13.1 would be liability sensitive.

If the gap is zero in all time buckets, the NII of the bank would not be subject to any gap risk.

**What Should Be Included in a Static Interest Rate Gap Report?**     A static interest rate gap report is focused on the assets and liabilities making up the balance sheet at a particular point in time. It takes no account of future levels of business or how the interest rate gap is likely to develop over time in response to different levels of interest rates.

All principal balances must be included in the gap report (though see later discussion on the treatment of non-interest bearing balances in the calculation of NII sensitivity). When it comes to interest flows though, there is a trade-off between technical accuracy and practicality. Technically speaking, banks should include interest payments on tranches of principal that have not yet been repaid or repriced and the spread component of floating-rate instruments, but capturing and reporting this data is no easy task and the

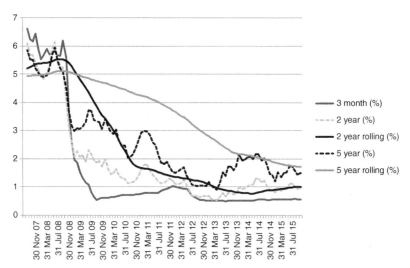

**FIGURE 13.1**     The Volatility of UK Interest Rates over time
*Data Source*: Bank of England Bank Liability Curve Estimates (cash and interest rate swap rates) 2007–2015.

majority of gap risk, in most interest rate environments, tends to arise from principal rather than interest flows.

Whilst the static interest rate gap report has the benefit of being relatively simple and easy to calculate, it is not readily able to capture basis and option risks, though the Basel Committee have sought to address the problem in their framework for the Management of Interest-Rate Risk in the Banking Book.

For the purposes of simplification, the product treatments discussed below will focus on the representation of principal balances in the Static Interest Rate Gap Report.

**The Treatment of Variable-Rate Products**   Variable-rate products are normally linked to a benchmark rate that either does (for example, 1-month or 3-month LIBOR) or can (for example, Bank Base Rates or Standard Variable Rates) reprice in the short term. As a result, principal balances on variable-rate products will generally be shown in the repricing buckets of 2–3 months or below.

**The Treatment of Fixed Maturity Products**   The principal amounts of fixed-rate loans and deposits, with market-related early repayment / redemption charges, should be reflected in the interest rate gap report according to their contractual repayment profile. These would normally be associated with wholesale, corporate, or commercial clients.

For bullet repayment loans, the entire principal balance should be shown in the gap report in a time bucket corresponding to the maturity of each loan. In the case of amortising loans, though, the regular repayments of principal are allocated to the time period in which they are scheduled to occur.

When it comes to fixed rate retail bank products, these tend to be homogenous and are characterised by early repayment charges that do not reflect the potential underlying funding cost to banks. Given the nature of the products and the desire to avoid losses from early repayment / redemption, banks often build models to estimate the behavioural run-off profile of the loans and deposits (how they expect it to happen in practice, which may be different to the run-off profile agreed with the customer in the contract) and this is what should be captured in the interest rate gap report.

**The Treatment of Non-Interest Bearing Balances**   Typical examples of items in this category include Non-Interest Bearing deposits and Cash (notes and coin) balances. Neither of them carry an interest rate, so cannot reprice as such. However, the items need to be included in the gap report if it is being used to calculate the Economic Value sensitivity of the balance sheet.

Banks should aim for a stable NIM over time. With these balance sheet items, this will be best achieved by treating them as long term as possible in the gap report.

We have already noted that a commercial bank seeking to run an interest rate neutral position will aim to minimise the size of both the gaps in each repricing bucket as well as the overall cumulative gap. So, with this in mind, representing Non-Interest Bearing balances as notionally repricing in the long term will require the bank to obtain matching assets and liabilities at the same long-term tenor on the other side of the balance sheet (see the later section on the management of Gap Risk).

Using Non-Interest Bearing Current Accounts as an example, a time series analysis will reveal that a proportion of the aggregate balance is volatile and between 5% and 20% of accounts are closed each year due to demographic factors, switching to competitors, etc. So, even if a bank continues to offer this product *ad infinitum*, it would be unwise to treat the balances as having a notional repricing maturity beyond 5 years (as they could disappear from the balance sheet altogether in that time frame).

Figure 13.1 illustrates that 5-year interest rates are more stable over time than either 3-month or 2-year interest rates. In addition, if choosing to invest or borrow over 5 years, with a potential requirement to extend the arrangement after 5 years, it is better to do so on a rolling basis (by spreading the borrowing or investment over 5 years and renewing a proportion each year) to avoid any potential "cliff effects" (for example, the 5-year swap rate in May 2008 was 5%, but only 1% by May 2013).

Putting all of these factors together, banks will often decide to represent a proportion (say 20%) of non-interest bearing deposits as notionally repricing in the short term and spread the remainder between 1 month and 3 or 5 years in the interest rate gap report. This will ensure that a relatively stable return, which is insensitive to interest rate movements, is generated on the core element of the balances.

**The Treatment of Managed Rate Products**   Examples of products in this category include credit cards, interest-bearing current accounts, and obsolete accounts that are no longer on sale. In these instances, a bank may not reprice these products in line with an established market benchmark rate.

This is where production of the Static Interest Rate Gap report becomes part art and part science. To establish the treatment of managed rate products in the Gap report, the ALM Manager must estimate which market benchmark rate their interest rate correlates most closely to. Also, he or she must consider how long the balances are likely to remain on the balance sheet. Based on these two factors, a notional repricing treatment is allocated. Akin to non-interest bearing accounts, to avoid "cliff risk" with the corresponding asset or liability, it is preferable to spread the balances over all the time buckets within the repricing maturity than allocate the full sum to the time bucket corresponding to the agreed repricing maturity.

## NII Sensitivity

There are a range of different mechanisms used by banks to calculate the sensitivity of their NII to movements in interest rates.

In its simplest form, the repricing profile of assets and liabilities, established in the production of the Interest Rate Gap report is subjected to a parallel shock of 1% or 2%, either upwards or downwards, in the level of interest rates across the yield curve, which is assumed to be sustained for 12 months.

If, by way of example, interest rates are currently 5% at all tenors, that will result in a given level of forecast NII for a bank over the next 12 months. In this analysis, we are not concerned with the forecast itself, but want to estimate how it would change if interest rates at all tenors were to move to 6% or 7% or alternatively, were to fall to 3% or 4%.

In the basic calculation, we would multiply the gap in each period out to 12 months by the rate shock and the number of months between the repricing bucket and 1 year, divided by 12, for example, instruments repricing between 4 and 5 months' time could only affect NII for between 7 and 8 months over the next year, so we would calculate: gap × rate shock × 7.5/12. Note, it is assumed that the repricing of the assets and liabilities occurs at the mid-point of each repricing bucket.

In Table 13.2, an NII sensitivity analysis has been performed on the specimen Interest Rate Gap report from Table 13.1. This reveals that the NII for the bank in question would fall by £48.1m in the event of a parallel 1% upward shift in the yield curve sustained for 12 months.

For the purposes of this analysis, non-interest bearing balances should be removed from the Interest Rate Gap report before the calculation is performed, as they do not reprice in response to interest rate movements.

This basic calculation contains a number of simplifying assumptions, and therefore, in this form only provides a rough guide to an organisation's NII sensitivity. In reality:

- Bank balance sheets are seldom constant over time, which is the implication here;

**TABLE 13.2**   Specimen NII sensitivity calculation

| Repricing Bucket Currency (£m) | Interest Rate Gap | IR Gap x Rate Shock x Remaining Months/12 | | (£m) |
|---|---|---|---|---|
| 0 – 1 month | –4,100 | –4,100 × 1% × 11.5/12 | = | –39.29 |
| 1 – 2 months | 119 | 119 × 1% × 10.5/12 | = | 1.04 |
| 2 – 3 months | –1,625 | –1,625 × 1% × 9.5/12 | = | –12.86 |
| 3 – 4 months | –88 | –88 × 1% × 8.5/12 | = | –0.62 |
| 4 – 5 months | 189 | 189 × 1% × 7.5/12 | = | 1.18 |
| 5 – 6 months | 155 | 155 × 1% × 6.5/12 | = | 0.84 |
| 6 – 9 months | 339 | 339 × 1% × 4.5/12 | = | 1.27 |
| 9 – 12 months | 278 | 278 × 1% × 1.5/12 | = | 0.35 |
| 12 – 15 months | 582 | | | |
| 15 – 18 months | 336 | | | |
| 18 – 24 months | 600 | | | |
| 2 years – 3 years | 1,230 | | | |
| 3 years – 4 years | 759 | | | |
| 4 years – 5 years | 667 | | | |
| 5 years – 6 years | 413 | | | |
| 6 years – 7 years | 45 | | | |
| 7 years – 10 years | 89 | | | |
| 10 years + | 12 | | | |
| | | | | –48.10 |

- Parallel shifts in the yield curve are rare – more often than not, the movement at the short-end of the yield curve will exceed that at the long-end;
- Not all assets and liabilities will reprice by the exact amount of the shock in rates.

Limits on NII sensitivity, which will be discussed and approved by a bank's Asset and Liability Committee, are normally expressed as a currency amount or percentage of NII relative to a given rate shock. For example, Bank X might wish to restrict NII sensitivity to +0 or –£10m (or 5% of NII) to a parallel shock of + or – 1% in the level of interest rates at all tenors.

As a first step to developing the analysis, banks will look to factor in how much and when products are likely to be repriced in response to a given rate shock:

- Depending upon the competitive environment and P&L and market share aspirations, management may choose to reprice managed rate products by either more than, less than, or by the same amount as the underlying market interest rate movement;

- Leads or lags that management may choose to impose on when managed rate products are repriced.

## Economic Value of Equity (EVE) Sensitivity

The starting point for an EVE sensitivity calculation is also the static interest rate gap report. In this case, the gaps in each time bucket are turned into a net present value (NPV) by discounting using discount factors based upon the current level of interest rates. As a second step, the NPVs for each time bucket are summed to produce a high level estimate of the bank's economic value.

The exercise is repeated for a given interest rate shock, for example, a 1% parallel upward movement in the yield curve. Note, application of the rate shock will give rise to a new set of discount factors and a revised estimate of economic value. It is the difference between the two sums that gives rise to the EVE sensitivity. In this example, we would say [calculation 2 minus calculation 1] is the EVE sensitivity of the balance sheet to a 1% parallel upward shock in interest rates.

Table 13.3 illustrates the EVE calculation output.

Typically, banks will evaluate their EVE sensitivities to a variety of different shock scenarios (see section on Interest Rate Shock Scenarios). Based on risk appetite, a bank's ALCO will set limits on the change in EVE it is prepared to accept to a sudden movement in interest rates.

It is arguable how much real value this EVE calculation actually represents. Discounting all balance sheet cash flows to their maximum tenor (which for some banks could be beyond 30 or even 50 years) produces a very approximate figure. To then calculate a straight-line sensitivity of this number to a large interest rate movement produces an even more approximate number. We are then supposed to inform management actions based on this almost "finger-in-the-air" estimation! Nevertheless, it is the requirement.

**Interest Rate Shock Scenarios** The interest rate shocks employed should reflect a stressful rate environment that is both plausible and severe.

The relatively simple NII sensitivity calculations rely only on parallel shifts in the yield curve, for example, + or − 2% at all tenors.

EVE sensitivity calculations do not face these constraints. To capture a full range of scenarios, banks often choose to assess the consequences of a steepening or flattening in the yield curve or material shocks to short-term rates, in addition to the parallel shifts. ALCO committees will focus upon

**TABLE 13.3**   Illustrative Maturity Schedule Time Buckets for EVE Calculation

|  | A | B | A-B | C | (A-B)*C |
|---|---|---|---|---|---|
|  | Assets | Liabilities | Net Position | Discount Factor Weighting |  |
| 1   Overnight |  |  |  |  |  |
| 2   Overnight – 1 month |  |  |  |  |  |
| 3   1 month – 3 months |  |  |  |  |  |
| 4   3 months – 6 months |  |  |  |  |  |
| 5   6 months – 9 months |  |  |  |  |  |
| 6   9 months – 1 year |  |  |  |  |  |
| 7   1 year – 18 months |  |  |  |  |  |
| 8   18 months – 2 years |  |  |  |  |  |
| 9   2 years – 3 years |  |  |  |  |  |
| 10   3 years – 4 years |  |  |  |  |  |
| 11   4 years – 5 years |  |  |  |  |  |
| 12   5 years – 6 years |  |  |  |  |  |
| 13   6 years – 7 years |  |  |  |  |  |
| 14   7 years – 8 years |  |  |  |  |  |
| 15   8 years – 9 years |  |  |  |  |  |
| 16   9 years – 10 years |  |  |  |  |  |
| 17   10 years – 15 years |  |  |  |  |  |
| 18   15 years – 20 years |  |  |  |  |  |
| 19   20 years + |  |  |  |  |  |

Sum = EVE

those scenarios which lead to the biggest negative effect on EVE, as this may influence capital requirements under Pillar 2 of the Basel framework.

**Simulation Analysis**   Simulation models, adopted by some banks, can be used to assess either NII or economic value sensitivities. Rather than relying upon a constant or static balance sheet, these models allow management to introduce assumptions on how prepayment / early redemption, levels of new business and margins will be affected by interest rate movements. Also, they allow multiple interest rate shocks or rate paths to be modelled using Monte-Carlo analysis.

The key steps in the analysis are:

- Develop a bottom-up forecast of NII for the next 1–5 years;
- Capture assumptions for all conceivable interest rate environments on:
  - How all products would be repriced;
  - New business volumes;
  - Forecast prepayments / early redemptions;
  - The level of loan defaults.

- Run a simulation to evaluate the impact of multiple different interest rate paths on NII and economic value;
- Review the distribution of NII and economic value outputs;
- Focus on outlying values, particularly on the downside. If these are of concern to management, consider what mitigants can be put in place to reduce the exposure.

### The Management of Gap Risk

There are a number of tools at the disposal of banks to reduce NII or EVE sensitivities if they are operating close to or in excess of approved limits. These may be categorised as either "cash hedges" or "derivative hedges".

**Cash Hedges**  Banks may write assets or liabilities at specific repricing maturities to reduce the size of gap exposures. For example, a 2-year fixed rate deposit bond product might be offered to customers to offset the interest-rate risk arising on 2-year fixed-rate mortgages. Alternatively, fixed rate amortising business loans might provide a useful match for a book of non-interest bearing current accounts that is spread over 5 years in the interest rate gap report.

**Derivative Hedges**  The main derivative instruments used to manage gap risk are Forward Rate Agreements, futures, and interest rate swaps. Interest rate derivatives are more flexible than cash hedges and will be the instrument of choice of most medium / larger banks. Smaller banks, on the other hand, may prefer to maintain all operations in cash instruments, either for simplicity and/or to avoid the additional accounting (for example, potential P&L volatility if hedge accounting arrangements are not put in place) and operational challenges (for example, collateral posting for negative mark to market positions) posed by derivatives.

By way of an illustration, if a bank had a 5-year fixed-rate loan of £100m funded by a 3-month deposit, it would have a cumulative interest rate gap exposure between 3 months and 5 years, as shown in Table 13.4.

**TABLE 13.4**   Specimen interest-rate gap report for a 5-year fixed-rate bullet loan funded by a 3-month deposit

| Repricing Bucket Currency (£m) | Assets | Liabilities | Interest Rate Gap | Cumulative Gap |
|---|---|---|---|---|
| 0 – 1 month | 0 | 0 | 0 | 0 |
| 1 – 2 months | 0 | 0 | 0 | 0 |
| 2 – 3 months | 0 | 100 | –100 | –100 |
| 3 – 4 months | 0 | 0 | 0 | –100 |
| 4 – 5 months | 0 | 0 | 0 | –100 |
| 5 – 6 months | 0 | 0 | 0 | –100 |
| 6 – 9 months | 0 | 0 | 0 | –100 |
| 9 – 12 months | 0 | 0 | 0 | –100 |
| 12 –15 months | 0 | 0 | 0 | –100 |
| 15 – 18 months | 0 | 0 | 0 | –100 |
| 18 – 24 months | 0 | 0 | 0 | –100 |
| 2 years – 3 years | 0 | 0 | 0 | –100 |
| 3 years – 4 years | 0 | 0 | 0 | –100 |
| 4 years – 5 years | 100 | 0 | 100 | 0 |
| 5 years – 6 years | 0 | 0 | 0 | 0 |
| 6 years – 7 years | 0 | 0 | 0 | 0 |
| 7 years – 10 years | 0 | 0 | 0 | 0 |
| 10 years + | 0 | 0 | 0 | 0 |

This position could be hedged by writing a 5-year pay fixed, receive 3m LIBOR interest rate swap, with a notional principle of £100m.

From the perspective of the interest rate gap report, writing the swap creates an asset of 100 in the 3-month repricing bucket and a liability of 100 in the 5-year repricing bucket, which would eliminate the bank's gap risk and NII would equate to the margin above the 5-year rate on the customer loan plus the margin below the 3-month rate on the customer deposit, as illustrated at Figure 13.2 and Table 13.5.

**Hedge Accounting**   Derivatives used to hedge IRR are "trading book" instruments which must be marked-to-market. That creates no special problems if they are being used to hedge a trading book, but when used to hedge non-traded risk in a banking book, they generate P&L volatility which is not mirrored on the other side (the product being hedged), which is not repriced daily. Hedge accounting is the process by which this volatility

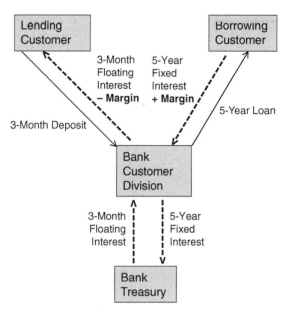

**FIGURE 13.2**   Interest-rate swap hedge

can be addressed, although the procedure to apply it is not necessarily straightforward.

There are two basic approaches in hedge accounting:

- Fair value hedge: changes in both the asset and the hedge instrument (derivative) are recorded through the P&L. So a hedged asset creates zero volatility in reported P&L;
- Cash flow hedge: for example, a fixed-rate loan. Split results of hedge into an effective and ineffective hedge. The "ineffective" part reflects that the hedge instrument does not match the P&L moves of the hedged asset 1-for-1. This ineffective part is reported in P&L, and effective part through to equity. Movements in the P&L are recognised when the asset cash flow affects it.

Hedge accounting only applies to a micro hedge; that is, hedges used for specific transactions. Because IRR of the Banking book is often on a macro basis, that is, booked for an aggregate portfolio as a whole (such as the cumulative gap for one tenor bucket), the macro hedge is marked-to-market with consequent volatility impact on the P&L. It is possible to obtain an external auditor's sign-off of a hedge accounting process at a macro level, but this is an involved process!

Further details on hedge accounting were given in Chapter 2.

**TABLE 13.5**    Specimen interest-rate gap report for a 5-year fixed-rate bullet loan funded by a 3-month deposit hedged by an interest rate swap

| Repricing Bucket Currency (£m) | Assets | Liabilities | Interest Rate Gap | Cumulative Gap |
|---|---|---|---|---|
| 0 – 1 month | 0 | 0 | 0 | 0 |
| 1 – 2 months | 0 | 0 | 0 | 0 |
| 2 – 3 months | 100 | 100 | 0 | 0 |
| 3 – 4 months | 0 | 0 | 0 | 0 |
| 4 – 5 months | 0 | 0 | 0 | 0 |
| 5 – 6 months | 0 | 0 | 0 | 0 |
| 6 – 9 months | 0 | 0 | 0 | 0 |
| 9 – 12 months | 0 | 0 | 0 | 0 |
| 12 – 15 months | 0 | 0 | 0 | 0 |
| 15 – 18 months | 0 | 0 | 0 | 0 |
| 18 – 24 months | 0 | 0 | 0 | 0 |
| 2 years – 3 years | 0 | 0 | 0 | 0 |
| 3 years – 4 years | 0 | 0 | 0 | 0 |
| 4 years – 5 years | 100 | 100 | 0 | 0 |
| 5 years – 6 years | 0 | 0 | 0 | 0 |
| 6 years – 7 years | 0 | 0 | 0 | 0 |
| 7 years – 10 years | 0 | 0 | 0 | 0 |
| 10 years + | 0 | 0 | 0 | 0 |

## The Management of Basis and Option Risks

**Basis Risk**    As a reminder, basis risk is present when assets and liabilities price off different benchmark rates at the same tenor or the same benchmark rate at different tenors. The risk arises, as these rates might not all move by the same amount at the same time. For a commercial bank, examples might include an asset written off the Bank of England Bank Rate funded by a liability linked to short-term LIBOR rates or, alternatively, an asset priced in relation to 3m LIBOR funded by a liability priced in relation to 1m LIBOR.

In normal market conditions basis risk is often overlooked, the index you receive is assumed to be correlated to the index you pay and the risk is regarded as small. As Figure 13.3 shows however, it can often be material.

Basis risk cannot be measured by the static interest rate gap report. However, the Basel Committee has developed a methodology based upon historic differentials between the various reference rates.

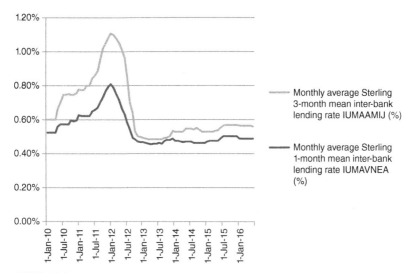

**FIGURE 13.3** A Comparison between Sterling 1-month and 3-month Inter-bank Lending Rates
*Source*: Bank of England Statistics.

**The Management of Basis Risk** Banks faced with basis risk can manage their exposure using a variety of different techniques, such as:

- Develop products pricing off the same underlying interest rate on both sides of the balance sheet to provide a natural hedge;
- Hedge the exposure with basis swaps, which is not a market with any great liquidity or depth, even in G7 currencies;
- Adjust product pricing.

**Option Risks** Commercial banks face a range of option risks that are embedded in the products they offer to customers. We will concentrate on three types:

- **Prepayment or Early Redemption Risk:** applies on fixed-rate loans and deposits, where customers have the right (or an option) to repay loans or redeem deposits ahead of the scheduled maturity date, on payment of an early repayment or redemption charge.
  Banks may be exposed to loss of income if assets must be replaced at a lower rate or deposits at a higher rate and any early repayment or redemption charges collected are insufficient to offset the reduction in interest income or increase in interest expense over the residual life of the replaced assets or liabilities. For example, assume a bank has made a 5-year loan for £10,000 at 7%, which is repaid 2 years before

its contractual maturity date by a customer on payment of an early repayment charge equating to 1% of the principal amount outstanding. For simplicity, ignoring the impact of discounting on future cash flows, the bank will suffer a loss of NII unless it is able to re-lend the repaid amount to a similar customer (from a credit risk perspective) for the remaining 2 years of the original contract at an interest rate of at least 6.50%.

Loans to and deposits from corporate and wholesale counterparties will normally be subject to full market related early repayment charges, so this risk tends to be more prevalent with retail and small business counterparties, where governments or regulators may have placed restrictions on the charges that banks are able to levy.

- **Pipeline Risk:** also applies on fixed-rate loans and deposits and occurs when customers have an option (but not a contractual obligation) to draw down on a fixed-rate loan or enter into a fixed-rate deposit at a given interest rate. In the case of certain fixed-rate loans, such as mortgages, the borrower may be required to pay a booking or commitment fee to secure the option.

Similar to prepayment risk, pipeline risk is most in evidence with retail products. Banks may be exposed to loss of income if interest rates move, either upwards or downwards, between the time when the fixed-rate offer is made to customers and the time when loan drawdown takes place or the deposit is received. Consider a 2-year fixed-rate deposit bond offered to customers at 3%. If interest rates rise during the offer period, customers may be able to obtain better rates from depositors, with the result that bond sales are below expectations and the bank is required to close out a surplus hedging position (normally achieved with forward-starting interest rate swaps) at a loss. Alternatively, if interest rates fall during the offer period, the bond starts to look particularly attractive in the market place, relative to those offered by competitors, with the result that the bank may be flooded with applicants and forced to undertake more hedging activity at a reduced or negative margin.

- **Cap and Floor Risk:** the former relates to loans which are offered to customers with a maximum rate and the latter to deposits (and possibly loans) which cannot be repriced downwards in response to a reduction in the general level of interest rates, for example, when interest rates are low.

In both cases, banks are exposed to a reduction in NII and NIM. With cap risk, as interest rates rise, interest sensitive liabilities reprice upwards, but the interest rate on corresponding assets that have reached their rate ceiling (for example, capped rate loans) remains at existing levels. Alternatively, with floor risk, the margin is squeezed as interest rate sensitive assets reprice in response to a downward movement in the general level of interest rates, but deposits that would normally be interest rate sensitive may not be capable of repricing if the interest rate being paid is close to 0%.

## The Management of Prepayment Risk

Prepayment or early redemption occurs either due to social factors (such as death, divorce, etc.) or when the customer has a financial incentive (for example, he or she can borrow more cheaply elsewhere taking into account any early repayment charges payable).

In respect of the financial incentive, there is no naturally offsetting item on the other side of the balance sheet; if rates fall, fixed rate borrowers may be encouraged to prepay, but fixed rate depositors are much more likely to be happy with their existing arrangements in this situation. Equally, if interest rates rise, fixed-rate depositors may consider moving to other products available in the market, but fixed-rate borrowers will face a negative financial incentive to do the same.

In theory, at least, banks could purchase derivative products called swaptions giving them the right to enter into an interest rate swap during the life of a cohort of loans / deposits at a pre-determined rate, to replace lost cash flows from customer prepayment / early redemption. However, swaptions tend to be relatively expensive, with the upfront premium payable likely to make a serious dent in the product margin. In addition, the swaptions market is not deep or liquid enough to support large-scale portfolio hedging by banks.

Another, more realistic alternative for banks to adopt is a dynamic hedging approach. In this case, a model is built, based upon historic experience of fixed-rate loan prepayment or early redemption of fixed-rate deposits, to predict the run-off profile of a particular cohort in a variety of interest rate scenarios. At inception of the fixed-rate loans or deposits, a funding / hedging profile is aligned to their expected run-off based on the anticipated level of interest rates over the life of the cohort. Each month, the expected run-off profile is re-evaluated according to the latest expectation for interest rates and the level of balances outstanding and the funding/hedging position adjusted accordingly.

Banks will tend to impose levels of tolerance, so that the funding / hedge is only amended for material movements in the expected run-off profile of the loans / deposits. In following this approach, they hope that the cost of periodically re-aligning the funding hedge is less than any early repayment or redemption fees collected.

The dynamic hedging process is illustrated at Figure 13.4 to Figure 13.6.

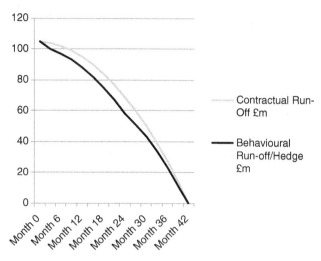

**FIGURE 13.4**   Period 1 – Amortising Pay Fixed Swap hedge aligned to anticipated behavioural run-off profile of a loan cohort

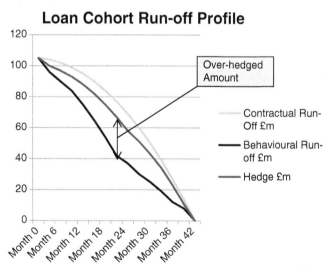

**FIGURE 13.5**   Period 2 – General level of interest rates falls so loans anticipated to repay quicker than original assumption

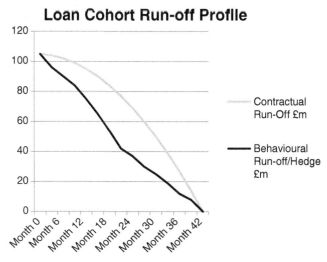

**FIGURE 13.6**  Period 2 – Balloon receive fixed swap is written to re-align swap hedge to behavioural loan run-off profile

## The Management of Pipeline Risk

Conceptually, the management of pipeline risk is similar to that of pre-payment risk.

In both cases, there is no natural hedge between loans and deposits and although the drawdown risk faced by banks could be hedged by the use of swaptions, this is expensive and will tend to offset most if not all of any prospective interest margin.

So, as with the management of prepayment risk, banks tend to adopt a dynamic hedging approach. Based upon historical experience and management's assessment of competitive conditions, a forward starting hedge (such as an interest rate swap) will be booked when the loan or deposit is first offered to customers, based upon the anticipated level of draw-downs or product take-up. As the offer period progresses, regular re-assessments of likely draw-downs will be made and the hedge adjusted accordingly. Again, similar to the position with prepayment risk, any hedge re-alignment is likely to carry a cost and management will be hoping that this is less than or equal to any booking or commitment fees collected.

For fixed-rate mortgages, the final amount of any draw-downs may not be known until up to 9 months after the terms of the offer are first developed by the Product Marketing department. This is illustrated at Figure 13.7.

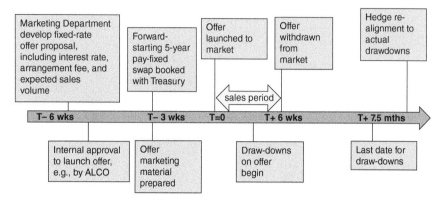

**FIGURE 13.7**  Typical Timeline for a 5-year Fixed Rate Mortgage Offer

## The Management of Cap and Floor Risk

Historically, it was common for banks in the UK to offer loan products with published minimum rates which would act as a natural hedge to floor risk on deposits. However, this type of product is no longer prevalent in the market place, as it was not favoured by the regulatory authorities. As a result, banks must look to interest rate caps and interest rate floors offered in the financial markets, if they wish to hedge their exposures to caps and floors that are embedded in the products they offer.

Interest rate caps and floors are generally based on money market interest rates (such as LIBOR) and pay-out if interest rates move above (for caps) or below (for floors) pre-agreed levels or strike prices. The pay-out is determined by the notional principal of the contract and the amount by which the strike price is breached. Banks pay an upfront premium to secure protection for a specific period of time.

The amount of protection sought by a bank will depend on factors such as:

- The internally held view on future interest rate movements (the likelihood that embedded product caps and floors will be triggered);
- The bank's risk appetite (the amount it can afford to lose if embedded product caps and floors are triggered);
- The depth of the financial markets in the provision of interest rate caps and floors;
- The accounting treatment of the arrangement – a lesser factor, which should nevertheless be understood by management.

## BCBS386: THE BASEL COMMITTEE AND HIGH LEVEL PRINCIPLES FOR INTEREST-RATE RISK IN THE BANKING BOOK

Interest-rate risk in the banking book (IRRBB) is part of Pillar 2 in the Basel capital framework. This risk area is subject to guidance published by the Basel Committee in the form of a set of principles, which were first issued in 2004 and updated in 2016.

Principles 1 to 9 are intended to be of general application for the management of interest-rate risk arising through banks' non-trading activities. They cover expectations for a bank's interest-rate risk management process, including the development of a business strategy, the structure of assets and liabilities and the system of internal controls. Principles 10 to 12 focus on the supervisory approach to banks IRRBB management framework and internal capital adequacy.

Each of the principles is summarised below:

**Principle 1. IRRBB is an important risk for all banks that must be specifically identified, measured, monitored, and controlled. In addition, banks should monitor and assess Credit Spread Risk in the Banking Book (CSRBB).**
It is essential that an adequate control system is in place to identify the interest-rate risk inherent in both new and existing products / services and to approve hedging / risk-taking strategies. CSRBB refers to any kind of asset–liability spread risk of credit-risky instruments that is not explained by IRRBB and the expected credit / jump to default risk, i.e., the risk of loss associated with the deterioration of an entity that remains a going concern.

**Principle 2. The governing body of each bank is responsible for oversight of the IRRBB management framework, and the bank's risk appetite for IRRBB.** Monitoring and management of IRRBB may be delegated by the governing body to senior management, expert individuals or an asset and liability committee. Banks must have an adequate IRRBB management framework, involving regular independent reviews and evaluations of the effectiveness of the system.
In most banks, it will be the Board of Directors that has ultimate responsibility and must ensure that senior management have the requisite skills to manage IRRBB. The Board should receive updates on a semi-annual basis as a minimum. Also, monitoring and control processes should be regularly reviewed by an independent party (for example, an internal or external auditor).

**Principle 3. The banks' risk appetite for IRRBB should be articulated in terms of the risk to both economic value and earnings. Banks must implement**

policy limits that target maintaining IRRBB exposures consistent with their risk appetite.

A risk appetite statement is a written articulation of the levels and types of IRRBB exposures that a bank will accept or avoid. The policy framework should delineate delegated powers, lines of responsibility and accountability over IRRBB management decisions and clearly define limits, authorised instruments, hedging strategies, risk-taking opportunities, and the procedure for exceptions. Limits should be appropriate to the nature, size, and complexity of the organisation. Policies should be reviewed at least annually and be approved by the Board.

**Principle 4. Measurement of IRRBB should be based on outcomes of both economic value and earnings-based measures, arising from a wide and appropriate range of interest rate shock and stress scenarios.**

The EV measure should focus on instruments already on the balance sheet (static approach). The earnings measure, in addition to the static view, may incorporate future business flows (dynamic view). Interest rate shock scenarios assessed should include: internally selected rate shock scenarios to comply with the ICAAP process, the six supervisory prescribed interest rate shock scenarios and any additional rate shock scenarios required by the supervisor. The bank should estimate how interest rates that are administered or managed will reprice in each of the scenarios.

**Principle 5. In measuring IRRBB, key behavioural and modelling assumptions should be fully understood, conceptually sound and documented. Such assumptions should be rigorously tested and aligned with the bank's business strategies.**

Key behavioural assumptions are required for items such as: expected prepayments of loans / early redemption of deposits, non-maturity deposits, and pass-through assumptions for market interest rate changes. The most significant assumptions should be documented, together with supporting evidence and regularly reviewed.

**Principle 6. Measurement systems and models used for IRRBB should be based on accurate data, and subject to appropriate documentation, testing and controls to give assurance on the accuracy of calculations. Models used to measure IRRBB should be comprehensive and covered by governance processes for model risk management, including a validation function that is independent of the development process.**

As every risk measurement system has its limitations, the Basel Committee recommends that banks should rely on a variety of measures; both earnings and EV based with both static and dynamic views. An effective validation framework should include: evaluation of conceptual soundness, ongoing monitoring, including process verification and benchmarking, and outcomes analysis, including back-testing.

**Principle 7. Measurement outcomes of IRRBB and hedging strategies should be reported to the governing body or its delegates on a regular basis, at relevant levels of aggregation (by consolidation level and currency).**
Reports prepared for the Board and various levels of management should include: summaries of the bank's aggregate exposures, reports demonstrating compliance with policies and limits, key assumptions, results of stress tests, and summaries of findings of internal and external auditors.

**Principle 8. Information on the level of IRRBB exposure and practices for measuring and controlling IRRBB must be disclosed to the public on a regular basis.**
Banks should notify their supervisors ahead of any significant changes planned for: internal limits, internal modelling systems or methodologies, and behavioural assumptions on options. Public disclosure should cover EV and earnings measures using the Bank's internal model as well as the Standardised framework (if appropriate), together with key assumptions across both processes.

**Principle 9. Capital adequacy for IRRBB must be specifically considered as part of the Internal Capital Adequacy Assessment Process approved by the governing body, in line with the bank's risk appetite on IRRBB.**
Banks should not only rely on supervisory measures of capital required for IRRBB, but should also develop their own methodologies for internal capital allocation. In determining the appropriate level of capital, banks should consider both the amount and quality of capital needed.

**Principle 10. Supervisors should, on a regular basis, collect sufficient information from banks to be able to monitor trends in banks IRRBB exposures, assess the soundness of banks IRRBB management, and identify outlier banks that should be subject to review and/or should be expected to hold additional regulatory capital.**
The information collected by supervisors should be consistent across the banks they supervise and may include: the modelling of non-maturity deposits, the impact of the assumptions used on products with embedded options, the treatment of own equity in a bank's internal calculations of IRRBB, repricing gaps, the exposure to automatic interest rate options, the change in EVE in each interest rate shock scenario under the Standardised

framework and EVE, and earnings-based sensitivities under both prescribed and bank internal stress scenarios.

**Principle 11.** Supervisors should regularly assess banks' IRRBB and the effectiveness of the approaches that banks use to identify, measure, monitor and control IRRBB. Supervisory authorities should employ specialist resources to assist with such assessments. Supervisors should cooperate and share information with relevant supervisors in other jurisdictions regarding the supervision of banks' IRRBB exposures.

When assessing a bank's IRRBB, supervisors are guided to consider, as a minimum:

- The complexity and level of risk posed by a bank's assets, liabilities, and off-balance sheet activities;
- The adequacy of governance oversight;
- Knowledge and ability to identify and manage IRRBB;
- The adequacy of both internal validation of IRRBB measures and internal monitoring;
- The effectiveness of risk limits and of the bank's IRRBB stress testing programme;
- The adequacy and effectiveness of internal review, audit, and IRRBB management practices as evidenced by past and projected financial performance;
- The effectiveness of hedging strategies; and
- The appropriateness of the level of IRRBB in relation to a bank's capital, earnings, and risk management systems.

**Principle 12.** Supervisors must publish their criteria for identifying outlier banks. Banks identified as outliers must be considered as potentially having undue IRRBB. When a review of a bank's IRRBB exposure reveals inadequate management or excessive risk relative to capital, earnings or general risk profile, supervisors must require mitigation actions and/or additional capital.

When a national supervisor concludes that a bank has undue interest-rate risk in the banking book relative to its capital or earnings (for example, change in EVE under any of the six prescribed scenarios exceeds 15% of Tier 1 capital), it should require the bank to undertake one or more of the following actions within a specified timeframe: reduce interest rate exposure, improve its risk management framework, raise additional capital, and/ or set constraints on the internal risk parameters used until improvements have been made.

One technical observation that may be made on the principles is as fol lows: note a particular requirement under the IRRBB finalised standards, *viz.*,

> *"ΔNII should be computed assuming a constant balance sheet, where maturing or repricing cash flows are replaced by new cash flows with identical features with regard to the amount, repricing period and spread components".*
>
> *"In order to be able to calculate changes in expected earnings under different interest rate shocks and stress scenarios, an institution will need to be able to project future earnings under both the expected economic scenario that informs its corporate plan, and the interest rate shock and stress scenarios so that the differences can be measured. Such projections involve a range of further assumptions about client / market behaviour, and the bank's own management response to the evolving economic climate. In practical terms, this may result in modelling of earnings under three different states; constant balance sheet: total balance sheet size and shape maintained by assuming like-for-like replacement of assets and liabilities as they run off";*

Should a bank interpret the requirements literally, i.e., replacement of assets and liabilities done at the individual transaction level, rather than at aggregate level? This is not practically viable so an aggregate approach will be the norm.

## ILLUSTRATION: STRATEGIC ALM POLICY AND APPROACH TO IRRBB

Undertaking banking business is, or should be, the act of providing financial products to customers that the customers want and benefit from. This will include arranging loans and deposits at fixed-rate or floating-rate bases, as required. Thus the very act of produces "IRRBB", because there will be a mix of interest rate bases on the balance sheet. IRR can arise as a result of carrying out the following:

- Writing fixed-rate assets funded by floating-rate liabilities;
- Writing floating-rate assets funded by floating-rate liabilities referencing another index, or by fixed-rate deposits;
- To lengthen the funding profile of the bank, raising term funding across the curve at fixed-term deposit rates that reprice only on maturity;

- Offering short-term demand funding products that reprice to different short-term base rates;
- Offering non-repricing transactional deposits (such as current or "checking" accounts) that are non-rate-sensitive;
- Running a mismatch in net non-rate-sensitive balances, including shareholders' funds that do not reprice for interest rate changes.

This normal business produces our IRRBB report, another example of which is shown in Table 13.6. Its approximate nature is self-evident. Assets and liabilities are placed in repricing tenor buckets, but the treatment is not exact. For example:

- How shall we handle fixed-coupon assets? Generally as a series of zero-coupon bullet cash flows split into relevant coupon date buckets;
- Equity liabilities present another issue: it is considered (as it should be) very long-dated for ALM funding purposes, but for repricing gap purposes this may not be correct. It is sometimes placed in the non-IR sensitive bucket (which is correct from an accounting and NII perspective) but the bank's cost of equity (always a problematic concept anyway) is related to interest rates, generally a function of the sovereign long-bond rate) so one cannot necessarily say it is not IR sensitive. Perhaps we should place equity liabilities in the 10-year bucket, if we place it anywhere at all. Then again, equity is a zero-coupon instrument (any dividend is the issuer's discretion) - what is the IRR of a zero-coupon non-maturing liability? The simplest approach is to invest equity in T-bills and, despite being long-dated, treat as negligible IRR.

The upshot of all this is that IRRBB is not an optional risk taking position but rather a by-product of repricing mismatches between lending and deposit taking positions that arise out of the normal course of business. Hedging, on the other hand, is not conventional "banking". The need for it arises because of the risks generated by BAU banking. Put artlessly, banking is "normal" whereas "hedging" is not.

Given the approximate nature of the hedger's art, certainly when it comes to the Banking Book, it stands to reason that the less hedging we need to do, especially when it involves derivative instruments, the better. A strategic ALM approach to balance sheet origination will assist this process. Wherever possible it is advantageous to use cash products to hedge IRR exposure rather than have recourse to derivatives. This is not only because of the P&L volatility issue, but also because there may be a desire

**TABLE 13.6** Bank IRR repricing gap example

| | Rollover date or nearest interest-rate adjustment date (£mm) | | | | | |
|---|---|---|---|---|---|---|
| | O/n – 3mo | 3mo – 6mo | 6mo – 1yr | 1yr – 5yr | >5yr | Non-IR sensitive |
| Assets | 270,959 | 16,813 | 21,375 | 115,831 | 35,893 | 139,475 |
| Liabilities | 331,496 | 25,271 | 26,344 | 67,256 | 20,754 | 128,775 |
| Repricing gap | –60,537 | –8,908 | –4,969 | 48,575 | 15,139 | 10,700 |
| Cumulative gap | –60,537 | –69,445 | –74,414 | –25,839 | –10,700 | 0 |

to preserve precious swap lines with dealer banks, or to reduce collateral funding requirements. Using derivatives comes at a cost.

In the first instance, one can mitigate IRR in specific business lines with piece-meal approaches; actual examples the author has undertaken in the past have included the following:

- At Hambros Bank: using Gilts to hedge the interest-rate swap market-making book (which was net pay fixed but hedging often undertaken on an individual swap basis);
- At KBC Bank: using US Treasuries to hedge the investment bank's fixed-rate long-dated term liability issuance;
- At Europe Arab Bank: using issuing fixed-rate medium-term notes (MTNs) to hedge the market risk on the HQLA portfolio.

As the above examples suggest, in most banks natural hedges exist on-balance sheet using cash products, and banks should use such hedges to reduce reliance on derivatives. Further examples might include using a portion of the liquid asset portfolio (LAB) as repricing and basis risk hedges for senior unsecured and subordinated debt issuance respectively. Table 13.7 shows how current account credit balances "hedge" current accounts in overdraft as well as credit card balances, all of which are on the same interest-rate basis.

A more scientific approach would be to set strategy around business lines at the aggregate level that is integrated. Some assets and liabilities naturally hedge each other, such as:

- Variable rate mortgages and floating-rate liabilities of similar behavioural tenor;
- Fixed rate mortgages and Fixed Rate Deposits;
- 1-, 2- or 3-year fixed-rate personal finance loans with 1-, 2- or 3-year fixed rate deposits;
- Credit card loans with variable-rate deposits.

The origination of loans on the asset side should be matched, as far as possible and practical, with the origination of deposits with identical interest-rate bases and similar behavioural tenor. This will mitigate the IRRBB that is generated, with resulting reduced derivative usage and minimising the Pillar 2a regulatory capital requirement.

To undertake customer business on this basis is an example of strategic ALM implementation *par excellence*, and needs to be led, and managed, from ALCO downwards as it requires coordination of marketing and customer strategies across business lines. This is why it needs to be driven by ALCO.

**TABLE 13.7** Natural cash hedging arising out of normal customer business (fixed-rate against fixed-rate and current account in credit against overdrafts)

*Liabilities*

| "Convention" hedging | Retail MTA | | Corporate MTA | |
| --- | --- | --- | --- | --- |
| Current accounts in credit | 2012 | 675.3 | 2012 | 2140.3 |
| | 2013 | 675.3 | 2013 | 2140.3 |
| | 2014 | 675.3 | 2014 | 2140.3 |
| | 2015 | 675.3 | 2015 | 2140.3 |
| Fixed Rate | | | | |
| Savings and Deposit Accounts | 2012 | 611.2 | 2012 | 905.2 |
| | 2013 | 611.2 | 2013 | 905.2 |
| | 2014 | 611.2 | 2014 | 905.2 |
| | 2015 | 611.2 | 2015 | 905.2 |

*Assets*

| Fixed rate | Retail Loans | | Corporate Loans | |
| --- | --- | --- | --- | --- |
| Loans | 2012 | 570.5 | 2012 | 1875.6 |
| | 2013 | 570.5 | 2013 | 1875.6 |
| | 2014 | 570.5 | 2014 | 1875.6 |
| | 2015 | 570.5 | 2015 | 1875.6 |
| "Convention" hedging | | | | |
| Credit Cards / Current Accounts overdrawn | 2012 | 237.5 | 2012 | 60.6 |
| | 2013 | 237.5 | 2013 | 60.6 |
| | 2014 | 237.5 | 2014 | 60.6 |
| | 2015 | 237.5 | 2015 | 60.6 |

## INTEREST-RATE RISK POLICY AND ALCO

As introduced in Chapter 10, the ALCO is a senior management committee that sets and implements ALM policy. In this section, we present a template IRR risk policy.

A Board-approved interest-rate risk policy template for drafting under ALCO auspices may exhibit the following:

- Details on the size and stability of net interest margins, and interest-sensitive fee income;
- An evaluation if the component and aggregate levels of interest-rate risk, including repricing, basis, yield curve and option risk, relative to earnings and capital;
- An analysis on the size, complexity, and components of each type of interest-rate risk position;
- Management, monitoring, and controlling interest-rate risk over both the short and long term;
- An assessment of the character of risk, such as the volume and price sensitivity of various products;
- A determination of the complexity of risk positions such as optionality of mortgage products and changing value of servicing portfolios;
- Ensuring a process independent of the ALCO function that measures and analyses risk in all the significant activities, including interest rate movements under a variety of scenarios;
- An examination of the vulnerability of earnings and capital positions under interest rate changes, such as parallel rate shifts, as well as changes in the shape and slope of the yield curve. The rate scenarios should be compared within the context of the current rate environment;
- An assessment of the relative volume and future prospects of continued support from low cost or stable funding sources, especially deposits that are non-maturing;
- A determination as to whether satisfactory risk position changes are occurring to reflect changing market conditions;
- Ensuring that appropriate levels of procedures, controls, and self-monitoring techniques are implemented and properly administered.

The size of the bank, the nature, and complexity of its activities, earning, and the adequacy of its capital and earnings must be considered when developing the interest-rate risk policy.

## SELECTED BIBLIOGRAPHY AND REFERENCES

*Fundamental review of the trading book: A revised market risk framework*, BIS, October 2013, www.bis.org/publ/bcbs265.pdf.

*Interpretive issues with respect to the revisions to the market risk framework*, BIS, July 2011, www.bis.org/publ/bcbs193a.pdf.

*Principles for the Management and Supervision of Interest Rate Risk*, BIS, July 2004, http://www.bis.org/publ/bcbs108.htm.

*Regulatory Consistency Assessment Programme (RCAP) – Second report on risk-weighted assets for market risk in the trading book*, BIS, December 2013, www.bis.org/publ/bcbs267.htm.

*"I was thinking about how [UK prime minister] David Cameron had been saying in the media that he was a fan of* The Smiths. . .*I picked up my phone and typed, "David Cameron, stop saying you like The Smiths, no you don't. I forbid you to like them." . . . There was the inevitable reaction from some scathing types, like. . . "I bet Johnny Marr wouldn't give back the £10 David Cameron spent on buying* The Queen Is Dead." *I was amazed. Anyone who didn't see any humour in the situation had to be a bit stupid, and anyone who seriously thought that David Cameron had actually bought* The Queen Is Dead *had to be very stupid indeed."*
—Johnny Marr, Set the Boy Free: The Autobiography,
Century, 2016

*"The whole thing with David Cameron saying 'Eton Rifles' was one of his favourite songs. . . I just think, 'Which bit didn't you get?'"*
—Paul Weller, MOJO magazine, 23 April 2015

# CHAPTER 14

# The Future of Bank Treasury and Balance Sheet Risk Management

P art III could be described as the "heart" of this book, with its focus on the balance sheet, the art of asset–liability management (ALM), and liquidity risk in particular. The reader will have noted some of the previous book extracts date from some time ago – the manuscript for *Bank Asset and Liability Management* (BALM) was completed in 2006, for example – but they are still relevant, more so than ever as the events of 2008 demonstrated. Having a mantra of "take care of the balance sheet" and maintaining a conservative approach to both asset origination and funding profile are not new things, in fact one would be accurate if describing them as being as old as banking itself. But it is apparent that the importance of these two things needs to be reiterated every 10 years or so, otherwise as history shows some of the next generation of senior bankers is apt to forget them.

In this chapter, we look at the operating model once again and attempt to recommend best-practice for the future. The aim here is to formulate, and formalise, an organisation structure for governance of the balance sheet that remains fit-for-purpose for many years to come. In other words, a reader should be able to turn to this chapter in 40 or 50 years' time and find the contents still of relevance and value. A bold objective on the author's part perhaps – only time will tell if it's realised!

We set the scene with an extract from *The Principles of Banking*; we then consider the future of the bank Treasury function, the issue of "lines of defence" for Treasury, and finally how best to integrate the triumvirate of Treasury, Risk, and Finance into a wider "enterprise" risk management framework.

**This extract from *The Principles of Banking* (2012)**

## Macro-Level Risk Management and Strategy

# MACRO-LEVEL RISK MANAGEMENT AND STRATEGY

The high-level strategy and risk appetite of a bank is set by its Board of Directors.[14] Such a process is a very real, serious one, or at least it should be, because board direction must set the overall approach of the bank. In other words, this direction must be a practical working document because the bank's entire appreciation of its risk-reward profile will come from it. An unclear or ambiguous board direction can come back to haunt the bank's shareholders, and embarrass its directors, if the bank ends up taking large losses on a particular trade or line of business.

We summarise now the correct process by which this overall risk appetite for a bank should be set.

## Setting the Formal Risk–Reward Profile

The Board sets the high-level guidelines for the bank's risk appetite and its expected return. Risk appetite is in the form of upper limits on risk exposures. We do not mean that the Board sets trading limits; we mean that the Board defines broad measures such as capital ratio ranges and leverage ratios. If it does not, then it will be held accountable if the bank is seen to have taken on too much risk exposure or allowed its capital base to fall to unacceptable levels. So in this context, when we refer to "limits" we mean the broad upper limit – in other words, the risk tolerance and risk appetite.

---

[14] Just to be clear, the Board of Directors of a bank will comprise the executive directors, who are full-time senior officers of the bank and will typically include the chief executive officer (CEO) and the finance director, plus (say) one to five other senior officers (such as the head of investment banking or the head of commercial banking), and the non-executive directors (NEDs), who are not employees of the bank but retained as members of the Board (they are paid a fee for this). Often, significant shareholders of the bank may also have representation on the Board. Generally, the NEDs should be individuals with considerable banking and finance experience and/or expertise, but it is not uncommon to find some whose experience and expertise lie in other, very different fields. The chairman of the Board is often, in effect, a NED because he/she will not have a formal line function at the bank. NEDs usually chair the various board sub-committees of the bank, so one would hope that they do indeed possess extensive banking experience, as well as a proven track record of excellence within banking, and an ability to take decisions. A strong track record in other fields such as retail (supermarkets, shops and so on) is no indicator of effective judgement and decision-making ability when applied in a bank. We discuss bank corporate governance in Chapter 18.

The same applies to expected return. The Board should set the target, or benchmark, levels of return on an annual basis. Of course, traditionally higher risk means higher reward, so the return expected should reflect the risk tolerance of the bank.

We described the various bank risk exposures earlier. For a commercial bank the key risk exposure is credit risk. At this level, the Board is not setting credit risk limits for individual borrowers. Rather, it should set aggregate or upper limits for countries and sectors. Below this, risk limit setting is delegated to operating business lines. Credit risk setting and monitoring is a discipline that is as old as banking itself, and its basic principles remain unchanged; essentially, credit risk management starts and ends with avoiding concentration – concentration with a single customer, industry, sector or country. The capital base of the bank also acts as a constraint on lending. Other risk limits, for market risk and FX risk for instance, are set at a lower operating level.

The point of setting a high-level risk tolerance guideline is to ensure that the bank's risk exposure does not exceed the appetite of the Board and shareholders. For this reason, limits on capital structure may be set; for instance, these could include:

- leverage limits: a limit on how much a multiple of the bank's capital base it can lever up to;
- funding gap limits: how much of a tenor mismatch between assets and liabilities a bank can run;
- wholesale funding limits: how much of the bank's balance sheet can be funded by wholesale, as opposed to retail deposit, funds.

By definition, staying within the overall risk culture, and adhering to the formal limits that are part of it, acts as a brake on business volume. That is the point. The whole concept of "risk management" is to prevent a bank over-reaching itself in a bull market or expanding economy, and to maintain its business within manageable levels. Hence procedures to constrain unlimited growth are vital.

Banking is a relationship business. The customer relationship must always remain the most important principle in banking. Viewed purely from a business angle, the logical approach might be to continuously enhance the relationship through more and more transactions. This implies a continuous increase in risk exposure as more and more business was put on the balance sheet. This would be an unsustainable strategy, because it would come unstuck at the first sign of an economic downturn. The risk management framework acts as a limit to continuous new business, thus constraining risk exposure to a manageable level. The same principle applies to market risks and capital structure risks.

Of course, it is possible to hedge risk exposures. Interest-rate risk can be neutralised, at least in theory, using derivatives. Credit risk can be removed using credit derivatives, insurance or some form of securitisation. In this way a bank can increase its business volume, but still remain within both the high-level risk culture and the specific risk limits. This is true only if the bank's senior management remains aware of the bank's true risk. In other words, to what extent in reality, and under all market conditions, is the risk really hedged? Risk hedging does not remove the need for the bank to "know your risk".

## Target Return Rates

It is essential that a bank's Board sets the target return rates for business lines to meet. The level of return is itself part of the risk culture of a bank. A high target, relative to, for instance, long-run average return rates or the bank's peer group average, sends a message from management that the bank is willing to take greater risks in order to meet the higher return.

The key objective in return setting is sustainability. A bank must set targets that it believes can be sustained over the business cycle. If they are too high, then they risk being unwound at the next downturn; conversely, if they are too low then shareholders may find it unacceptable. Of course, a key part of the Board's role is to educate shareholders about the concept of a sustainable return.

There are a number of return measures that can be set. They will usually include RoE or its close relation RoC, and RoA. It is quite common to set different RoE targets for different business lines, reflecting the different risk exposures across each business line. An important ingredient in the target-setting discipline is the cost at which a business line obtains its funds. This is known as the internal funding rate (IFR), internal funds pricing or funds transfer pricing (FTP or just TP). We prefer the first term because the cost at which a Treasury desk lends funds to the other business lines of the bank is not really a "transfer" and it isn't really a "price" either; however, FTP is the most commonly used expression. FTP is important because it itself is a discipline, and also because it feeds into the return calculation. It is therefore a vital part of risk management policy. It is discussed in Chapter 15.

Another ingredient in return target setting is the risk-adjusted return. This allows for the different risk exposure of a particular business line, and is allied to how much capital it consumes. The amount of capital consumed by a business should be commensurate with the risk exposure it represents and also the return it generates. The Sharpe ratio is commonly used to compare returns levels for different businesses in order to make a fair risk-adjusted comparison.[15]

A sustainable return target, together with a robust FTP mechanism and a logical capital allocation methodology, are essential ingredients in the high-level risk management mechanism in a bank.

---

[15] There are countless references in the financial literature, as well as on the Internet, to this calculation.

## Dynamic Risk Management

The process of risk management in a bank is a dynamic and not static one. In other words, it is not enough to simply set up the infrastructure and then leave it at that. The Board and senior management need to remain aware of changes in market conditions, and act accordingly. What seemed like a worthwhile transaction a few months ago may not be now, in light of other events, and bank management must be able to react to these. Of course, prevention is better than cure. Ideally, the risk impact of all ongoing business should be captured and assessed as part of the decision-making process; that is, before the decision is made rather than after. Once a transaction is entered into, changing circumstances may dictate that the exposure is no longer worth maintaining, in which case the risk management response should be to re-hedge it or otherwise dispose of the transaction.

The risk management process is therefore dynamic with regard to the existing portfolio of business and all new business. Each new business transaction decision, both at the individual as well as portfolio level, should seek to answer clearly the following questions:

- Does it adhere to existing risk-reward guidelines and bank risk culture?
- What is the impact of the transaction(s) on risk exposure?
- Does it meet specified return-on-capital requirements?

Notice how we placed the revenue question last. This is deliberate. It is not sufficient to consider only the revenue raised and the net profit generated. To do so would result in excessive risk generation, often beyond the acceptable tolerance of the shareholders. Therefore it is imperative that the risk review process stays within an acceptable framework.

Exactly the same process applies to off-balance sheet transactions. Derivative and other OTC transactions, whether undertaken for hedging or speculative purposes, or as part of a customer product offering, must still fall under the high-level risk review process.

## Bank Risk Management Structure and Organisation

A 20th century development in banks worldwide has been the introduction of a bank-wide risk management function. This was a response to the increasing sophistication and internationalisation of banking operations.[16] Risk management is now a centralised operation, whereas previously credit risk would have

---

[16] Globalisation was an indirect causal factor of the 2007–2009 financial crisis. What began as a downturn in one particular sector of the US housing market ended up as global recession, and banking failure, partly arising as a result of the extensive cross-border and integrated nature of banking operations.

been managed separately to market risk, liquidity risk, operational risk and so on. These are still individual departments within a bank, but are overseen by a head of risk or chief risk officer (CRO). The CRO will typically report to the chief operating officer (COO) or a non-executive member of the Board.

By definition a firm-wide risk management function will mean a separation between the business lines and the risk supervising lines of a bank. This is an essential organisational requirement. The ALM function of the bank, usually delegated to the Treasury division, is part of this centralised risk management framework. The ALM desk is usually a separate desk within Treasury (in small banks it can be just two persons) and is responsible for the entire bank's interest-rate risk and liquidity management. For banks that have overseas branches, the head office ALM desk is ultimately responsible for the entire bank's ALM risk. Global banking groups, with overseas subsidiaries, will still place overall firm ALM risk management supervision with its Global Treasury, even if the foreign subsidiaries are required to be independent stand-alone entities with their own funding.

Placing interest-rate risk and liquidity management within one centralised function is essential for efficient ALM. Individual bank business lines cannot be allowed to run interest-rate or liquidity risk, otherwise there would be a severe danger of the bank's senior management being unable to effectively control it. Each business line, be it project finance, or corporate banking or private banking, generates interest-rate risk, and this is managed at an aggregate portfolio level by the ALM desk. Transferring this risk from the individual businesses to Treasury also means that the business lines do not have to worry about interest-rate and liquidity risk: this is managed for them. The banking portfolio also generates credit risk, which is monitored by the credit risk unit. The hedging of credit risk, either by securitisation or the use of credit derivatives, insurance or guarantees, may be left to the business line (or, in the case of securitisation, to Treasury) or a dedicated unit.

### Centralised Risk Management

Figure 1.15 is a stylised view of the centralised risk management function in a bank. We observe that the business lines originate the various risk exposures, and these are overseen, monitored and managed by the risk function. The senior management – which we can take to be the Board – will set the overall risk culture and this must be dynamic and up-to-date with events.

The centralised risk function will break down into individual departments monitoring specific risks. This is illustrated at Figure 1.16. Note that the Valuation Control function is sometimes situated within the Finance department. It is also sometimes known as "product control", although this term does not describe what it actually does, which is the independent checking of market prices. All three of the principal department heads will meet regularly on the ALCO. The role, objectives and responsibility of ALCOs are described in detail in Chapter 9.

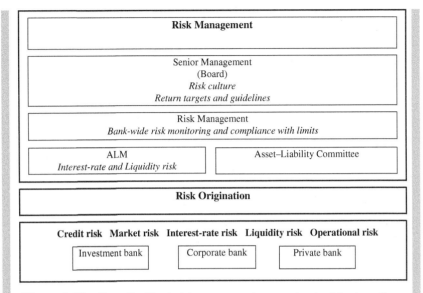

**Figure 1.15**  Centralised bank risk management, overseeing bank business lines.

## Asset–Liability Management and the ALM Committee

The art of banking is the art of asset and liability management or ALM. Or rather we should say that the art of banking is maturity transformation. This is the term for the mechanism by which banks "lend long" and "borrow short". This is an unavoidable fact of life for banks, and the need for ALM arises precisely because assets (loans) are always, on average, longer dated than liabilities (borrowings). It is not really practical to run a bank, except one with a very narrow and specific remit, any other way. Customer assets such as corporate loans and mortgages will always have a longer legal final maturity than liabilities such as customer deposits.

The ALM department, which is organised in different ways in different banks, is the unit responsible for managing the bank's liquidity, its interest rate and foreign exchange risk, and also its internal funds pricing. The stewardship of ALM is in the hands of the ALM Committee or ALCO. The ALCO sets policy for a number of different areas in the bank, and is the most important committee in the bank, including the bank's Board. It is possible to have an incompetent Board and still survive a market crisis; however, it is not possible for a bank to have an incompetent ALCO and survive the same crisis.

The ALCO terms of reference are larger than mere implementation of ALM decisions, important and onerous though that task is. They include overall balance sheet management, as well as the responsibility of ensuring that policies adopted by the individual business lines fall within the boundaries required by the global ALM policy. This latter is an important, "political" task.

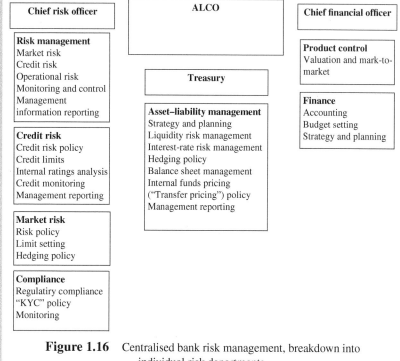

**Figure 1.16**    Centralised bank risk management, breakdown into individual risk departments.

ALM itself addresses the following:

- defining the extent of the actual structure of the balance sheet, both assets and liabilities: one sees how this must perforce drill down into more detailed issues such as allowed tenor of assets and liabilities, as well as sources of liabilities;
- hedging policy for all risk exposures, including interest-rate, FX and liquidity risk;
- defining actual risk measures: how risks will be measured, how they will be reported, and what the limits are; monitor (or delegate monitoring) the risk exposures themselves.

We state at the outset that liquidity risk and market risk (including interest-rate risk) are inter-related and inter-dependent issues. They cannot be managed, monitored or controlled separately or independently of each other. This reflects a number of factors, the main one being that an expectation of funding difficulty in the future must be addressed today, with consequent impact on the funding cost and interest rate exposure.

Notwithstanding that larger and more sophisticated banks will have different levels of complexity compared to smaller or more narrowly focused banks, the scope of the ALM function will be identical at all banks. The one key functional difference across banks is whether the ALM, and Treasury, function, operates as a cost centre or a profit centre. We discuss this further in Chapter 9. However, setting up the ALM desk as a profit centre does not obviate the need for it to adhere to all the required levels of ALM control.

The ALCO then is the controlling arm for bank ALM. It is not an administrative function, however, as it also sets policy and guidelines. Note that banks comprised of more than one legal entity, for example across multiple legal jurisdictions, will have a Group ALCO that sets policy for the banking group as a whole. In some banks ALCO is known as the ALMAC (Asset–Liability Management Action Committee) or ALPCO (Asset–Liability Policy Committee).

Reproduced from *The Principles of Banking* (2012)

## THE NEW TREASURY

We've already discussed in Chapter 10 how, given the more onerous regulatory scrutiny of every aspect of a bank's operations from capital, liquidity, and leverage, to conduct, and technology, banks need to make their Treasury departments more all-encompassing, more outward looking, and market aware. The new Treasury is "Strategic Treasury" or, as the author has termed it in the past, Strategic ALM. In what ways is this new, more proactive approach to ALM different, and is it possible to codify it into an explicit, formal discipline?

Let us take a look again at the business model impact of Basel III, as summarised at Figure 14.1.

The key part of Figure 14.1 is the last segment, "manage balance sheets more efficiently". This is essential if a bank is to maintain viability and robustness. Two main ingredients are required to make this part work: first, a technology suite that allows, as far as possible, every department in the bank to use the same system and work off the same dataset,[1] and secondly a Strategic ALM approach to balance sheet risk management.

---

[1] For anything other than brand new start-up banks (and even for them it's still something of a challenge), this would be a major undertaking. To have just the Finance, Treasury, and Risk departments, without even considering the Front Office, Operations, Compliance, and HR departments, all using the same system would make balance sheet management more efficient. To take just one example: the author is familiar with a bank in which, depending on which department runs the report, one will obtain IRR reports for the same day stating different values. Just getting the general ledger and the ALM system on the same piece of kit would be a major, major improvement for large banks.

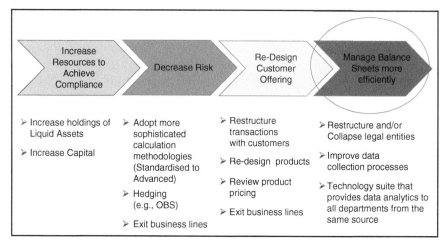

**FIGURE 14.1**    Managing the impact of Basel III

Conventional approaches to organising the Treasury operating model were discussed in Chapter 10. Let's reprise the figure from then, shown here as Table 14.1. What can we add to this table to make it more long-term permanent and fit-for-purpose? In essence, we suggest the following:

- Business line liaison and interaction (a "Business Treasury" function);
- ALCO standardisation;
- Group Treasury standardisation;
- Chairing the new approvals process;
- Overseeing the Strategic ALM process;
- Chairing the Product Pricing Committee;
- Being the "centre of excellence" for markets.

With this added functionality it becomes more feasible to implement a strategic ALM process and help to make balance sheet management more efficient.

For banking groups that have multiple legal entities and/or overseas locations, the Group standardisation function is very important. Figure 14.2 shows our recommended best-practice approach to setting up the organisation structure for such groups. Generally Group Treasury will define Treasury policy for the entire bank and implement this across the group. It will also manage and be responsible overall for the relationship with the national and all external regulators, and the rating agencies. Overseas entities will manage the local regulatory relationship on a day-to-day basis but in line always with Group stated policy. As a standard template, Group ALCO (GALCO) on an overview basis and Group Treasury on a delegated

**TABLE 14.1** Scope of Treasury activities, reprised

| | Capital and balance sheet | Liquidity | Net Interest Income / NIM |
|---|---|---|---|
| **STRATEGIC MANAGEMENT** | **Capital management** <br> Risk limits (RWA) <br> Cost of capital <br> Budget forecasting <br> Setting capital policy <br> Setting return metrics <br> Defining capital structure and ratios <br> Capital allocation | **Liquidity risk management** <br> Liquidity limits <br> Liquidity stress tests <br> Liquidity policy <br> Contingency funding plan <br> LAB policy <br> Liquidity cost calculation <br> Funding strategy <br> Internal funds pricing policy (FTP) | **Banking book interest rate risk** <br> Interest rate risk management <br> Interest rate risk modelling <br> Forecasting NII / NIM |
| **MARKET FACING FUNCTIONS** | **Term Liabilities Issuance** <br> Senior unsecured debt <br> Subordinated debt <br> Equity instruments <br> Securitisation <br> Secured <br> ■ ABS / MBS <br> ■ Covered bonds <br><br> **Investor Relations** <br> Rating Agencies <br> Investors | **Money Markets Desk** <br> Cash management <br> Money markets <br> – Depos <br> – CD / CP <br> Repo <br> Collateral management <br> Counterparty risk management | **Swaps and Derivatives desks** <br> Banking book <br> Trading book <br> Market risk hedging |
| **GOVERNANCE** | **Finance and Risk Management** <br> Financial control and reporting <br> Regulatory reporting <br> Risk and product control | | |

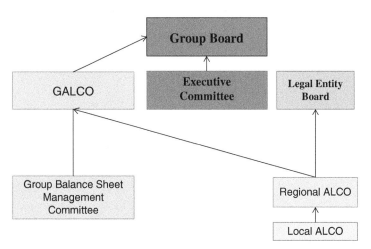

**FIGURE 14.2**     Group Treasury structure

basis are responsible for all Treasury-related issues in the bank. These would include but not be limited to the following:

- Managing the capital base of the bank;
- Monitoring and managing the Group's balance sheet risk, interest rate risk for the Banking book, FX exposure risk;
- Compiling for Board approval the Group's liquidity risk appetite and funding policy (capital raising, including equity, hybrid capital instruments, and senior and subordinated debt);
- Managing the Group's funding structure, in line with approved guidelines, with respect to regulatory requirements and internal funding policy;
- Putting in place the procedures to allow a strategic ALM process to function, and managing the Business Treasury function.

Business Treasury is the interface between the business lines and the internal Treasury function. It also acts as the centre of excellence for all matters capital, liquidity, and regulation for the businesses.

We provide a template GALCO brief or Terms of Reference in the companion website, in the folder for Chapter 14 (see Appendix 14.A).

## THE TREASURY "SECOND LINE OF DEFENCE"

In this section we present the rationale behind our recommendation for a "second line of defence" (2LD) arrangement for governance of capital, liquidity, and funding in a bank. We suggest that all banks other than the very smallest should implement a variation of what we describe; allied with the authority of ALCO it should help ensure that the bank's balance sheet is always robust and long-term viable.

## The Rationale for a Treasury Second Line of Defence

The traditional and still current objective of the Treasury function is to be the guardian and steward of the bank's balance sheet, with a primary mission of protecting the bank's financial resources of capital and liquidity and to be able to withstand a bank run or similar stress event. The majority of the world's banks also assign a revenue and P&L target to the Treasury function, but this can only ever be a secondary mission behind the primary, balance sheet management function.

In the era of Basel III and beyond, the regulatory requirements on capital and liquidity serve to constrain those resources to a material degree, if we define constraint in terms of cost as well as availability. This suggests that the Treasury function, which is the first line of defence, should add a second line of defence to ensure that the management and optimisation of these constrained resources is always in line with Board appetite and guidance. In other words, institute a risk department with specific oversight over capital, liquidity, and funding. We can call this 2LD the "Treasury Risk" function. Consider the summarised operating models observed in most banks:

- Type A: this is the most common operating model observed:
  - First line: Treasury owns planning, execution, and risk controls, and reports to the CEO;
  - Second line: there is no dedicated Treasury Risk function. The CRO will include the Treasury space as part of its overall mission;

- Type B: this is a limited scope 2LD set-up:
  - First line: Treasury owns planning, execution, and risk controls, and reports to either the CEO or the CFO;
  - Second line: a dedicated Treasury Risk function with responsibility for reviewing and assessing the 1LD risk controls. The 2LD may report to the Treasurer or the CRO (that is, the Treasury Risk team may still be part of Treasury);

- Type C: an independent 2LD set-up:
  - First line: Treasury owns planning and execution, and supports risk controls;
  - Second line: Treasury Risk ultimately owns key risk controls and reports to the CRO.

In the Basel III era it is logical and adds value for there to be a Treasury Risk function. In essence, the real operating model question for debate is where this department should sit, whether in the Treasury space, Risk, or elsewhere.

### Concept and Mandate of Treasury Risk

Treasury Risk may be defined under the following parameters:

- Mandate: explicit and clear mandate;
- Segregation of duty: the reporting line should be sufficiently independent from front office Treasury. This does not necessarily mean Treasury Risk cannot report to the Treasurer, especially if the Treasury function has no direct P&L responsibility. In other words it does not mean that the Treasurer cannot manage both the external market facing function and the Treasury Risk function. After all, the bank's CEO will manage both P&L and control functions! However, if explicit segregation is desired then the Treasury 2LD should report to either the CRO or the CFO. The author's preferred alternative arrangement is for Treasury Risk to have "dual" reporting lines to the Treasurer and CRO;
- Legal entity and jurisdiction focus: a clear organisation and reporting responsibility defined by legal entity and overseas subsidiary;
- Credibility: necessary and sufficient experience, knowledge base, and resource capability.

The mandate is the starting point. What exactly is Treasury Risk here to do? The objective of the Treasury 2LD is to provide an effective challenge, through a review and oversight process, to Treasury and the business lines regarding capital and liquidity management processes. In formal terms, we suggest the 2LD function should focus on five key areas:

- Governance and internal guidelines including effectiveness of ALCO;
- Monitoring and oversight;
- Methods, models, and assumptions;
- Stress testing;
- Organisation structure and operating model.

Figure 14.3 shows how this might work with respect to Treasury, Treasury Risk, and a third function Regulatory Reporting.

Banking groups that have overseas operations, typically as subsidiary legal entities, need to ensure that the correct dedicated regional coverage is in place. This may involve Treasury Risk working from head office or regional offices as necessary.

| | Data collection, preparation, and control | Model assumptions and validation | Aggregation and Reporting | Stress Testing | Planning and Forecasting | Execution |
|---|---|---|---|---|---|---|
| **Current observed model** | Regulatory Reporting | Treasury | Regulatory Reporting | Treasury | Treasury | Treasury |
| **Target operating model** | Regulatory Reporting | Treasury Risk | Regulatory Reporting | Treasury Risk | Treasury | Treasury |

Legend: Treasurer / CRO or Treasurer / CFO

**FIGURE 14.3**  Sample separation of duties

## Structure and roles

The suggested target operating model for Treasury Risk is summarised at Figure 14.4. This illustrates a dedicated 2LD model and risk methodology function that owns model calibration and validation, and stress testing parameters.

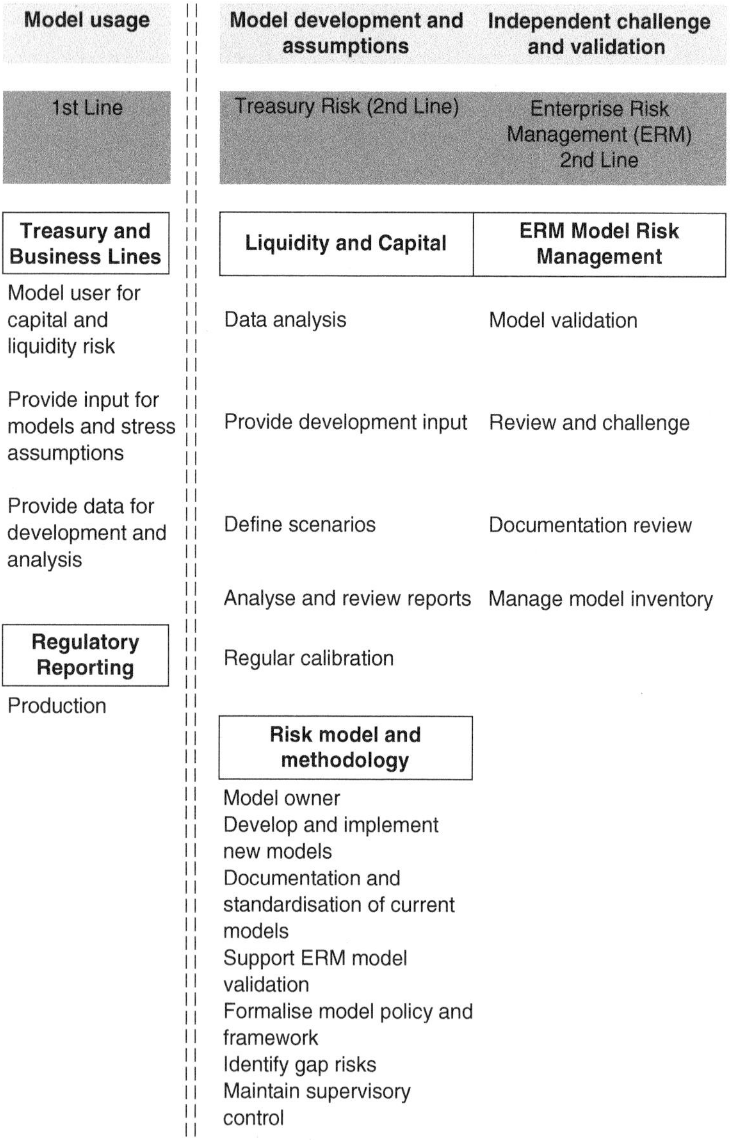

| Model usage | Model development and assumptions | Independent challenge and validation |
|---|---|---|
| 1st Line | Treasury Risk (2nd Line) | Enterprise Risk Management (ERM) 2nd Line |

| **Treasury and Business Lines** | **Liquidity and Capital** | **ERM Model Risk Management** |
|---|---|---|
| Model user for capital and liquidity risk | Data analysis | Model validation |
| Provide input for models and stress assumptions | Provide development input | Review and challenge |
| Provide data for development and analysis | Define scenarios | Documentation review |
| | Analyse and review reports | Manage model inventory |

| **Regulatory Reporting** | Regular calibration |
|---|---|
| Production | |

| **Risk model and methodology** |
|---|
| Model owner |
| Develop and implement new models |
| Documentation and standardisation of current models |
| Support ERM model validation |
| Formalise model policy and framework |
| Identify gap risks |
| Maintain supervisory control |

**FIGURE 14.4**    Treasury Risk target operating model

To provide genuine added value rather than simply evolve into yet another middle office monitoring function, Treasury Risk *should* also provide a strategic project function. This would include:

- Driving regulatory projects relevant to capital, liquidity, and funding, and project managing for delivery;
- Leading the impact analysis process:
  - Regulatory impact analysis;
  - Methodology and models impact analysis;
  - Business change impact analysis;
- Review the governance structure on a regular basis to ensure it remains fit-for-purpose.

The effectiveness of the second line of defence is also a function of the committee structure in place at the bank. We described (in Chapter 10) our recommended ALCO model and how the authority of ALCO needs to be formalised to ensure its pre-eminence as a management *and* risk committee. The best way to achieve this is to have ALCO operate under direct Board delegated authority or as a sub-committee of the Board. To facilitate a value-added Treasury Risk function we recommend the committee structure shown at Figure 14.2. This is at the level immediately below ALCO (or Group ALCO) and should be straightforward to appreciate for those already familiar with our recommended ALCO operating model. Note that not every bank needs to have all these committees; the full model will be necessary for larger banking groups only. However, the key pointer here is our guideline to set up a new Treasury Risk Management committee, with a focus on capital, liquidity, and funding, and chaired by the Treasurer. By having such a committee structure the bank will ensure that these critical balance sheet resource constraints are on a par with the management and importance of the traditional risk areas such as credit risk or (in larger banks) market risk.

## TREASURY AND THE RISK TRIUMVIRATE: THE NEED FOR AN AGGREGATE APPROACH ENABLING INTEGRATED MANAGEMENT OF THE BALANCE SHEET

By now readers will be familiar with our description of the bank risk management "triumvirate" of Treasury, Risk, and Finance, the three departments that are concerned principally with management of the balance sheet. In this section, we describe what we consider to be an essential part of the future strategic Treasury function: that of integrating the risk management process across the triumvirate. Some banks and consulting firms describe a concept known as enterprise risk management (ERM) but for the author what ERM has meant in practice is yet another department that is in the middle office; in other words, merely an added ingredient in the recipe for bureaucracy. The concept of ERM

**FIGURE 14.5**  Areas benefitting from integrated risk management

may be sound in theory, but the key to an effective risk culture is not so much ERM as simply integrating work processes of the risk triumvirate and implementing an aggregate approach to balance sheet origination and management.

In the Basel III era, there is no shortage of workstreams that cut across departments. A possibly somewhat amusing illustration is given at Figure 14.5, with the drivers being Basel, the European Banking Authority (for banks in the European Union), the national regulatory authority, and the bank itself.

All of these areas are part of the bank that are reviewed as part of the bank-wide stress testing process. This is the primary means by which the Board determines the bank's resilience to adverse scenarios. Stress testing results provide the regulatory authorities with relevant insights about individual and systemic risks; they also enable banks to assess the viability of their strategies and business models under different scenarios. Stress testing techniques are now the norm in banks worldwide, and are used across the entire banking infrastructure, so this makes obvious the need for integration between Treasury, Risk, and Finance, overseen on behalf of the Board by ALCO. By definition, what banks call ERM stress testing is designed to be a macro-level aggregate analytical process across the bank. For this to be effective requires strong coordination between Risk, Finance, and Treasury units, in sharing data and setting common metrics and views. Ideally, all three departments will work from the same technology suite and also the same data sets; however, this is by no means common, especially at larger banks.

As illustration, consider Figure 14.6 and a sample of workstreams that cut across disciplines and are part of the stress testing process. Figure 14.7 further illustrates the ways that the balance sheet risk triumvirate will need to coordinate data analytics and planning.

In all this the role of ALCO is paramount. It must set the parameters for oversight of the risk management and stress testing process and approve the methodology. Banks generally adopt either a "top down" or a "bottom up" approach to the stress testing process, but in fact the best-practice

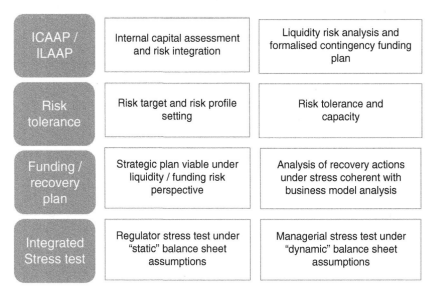

**FIGURE 14.6**   Samples of workstreams as part of regulatory requirements

**FIGURE 14.7**   Sample of areas requiring cross-departmental coordination and cooperation

approach would be to conduct *both* a top-down and bottom-up process. This is because (i) bottom-up metrics are needed in order to quantify the sensitivity of P&L, capital, and liquidity variables to individual risk factors (interest and FX rates, default probabilities, recovery rates, and so on); and (ii) a top-down logic is needed in order to quantify the dependency of risk factors (interest and FX rates, PD, RR, etc.) to macroeconomic variables. Figure 14.8 shows the defining points of each (again, banks outside the European Union can ignore "EBA").

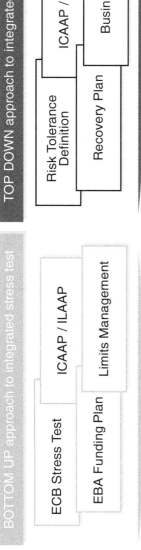

**TOP DOWN approach to integrated stress test**

Risk Tolerance Definition

ICAAP / ILAAP

Recovery Plan

Business Plan

- Based on aggregated data feeding
- Both deterministic and stochastic analysis
- High level of integration with planning processes
- Calculated by "light" analytical solution (typically Excel) in order to run an high number of interactions

- PROs: Easy and not time consuming
- CONS: High level of approximation, limited view and no drill-down capabilities

**BOTTOM UP approach to integrated stress test**

ECB Stress Test

ICAAP / ILAAP

EBA Funding Plan

Limits Management

- Based on single deal data feeding
- Deterministic scenario analysis (internal or regulatory)
- Standardized analysis, usually based on regulatory approaches, in particular for Credit Risk
- Calculated by "vertical" analytical solutions for each risk factor (ALM platform, RWA parallel run engines)

- PROs: full consistency with Risk solutions
- CONs: "silo approach" very time consuming

**FIGURE 14.8** Stress testing approaches

The foregoing makes obvious the necessity to have in place an effective fit-for-purpose collaboration model between the CRO, CFO, and Treasurer. A bank should be aware of the most appropriate operating model for ownership and final responsibility for the different liquidity, stress test, and capital planning processes, and submit this to the regulator for approval.

## APPENDIX 14.A: Sample Group ALCO Template

For a template Terms of Reference for a bank's Group ALCO, please see the book's companion website, where the template is provided as a Word document in the folder for Chapter 14.

### SELECTED BIBLIOGRAPHY AND REFERENCES

Bardaeva, P., *Concepts of Asset and Liability Management in Commercial Banks*, Saarbruecken: Lambert Academic Publishing, 2011

*"I had the good fortune to have grown up under several outstanding leaders who had given me a lot of hands-on experience with people and technically complex missions. I didn't have innate talent, so I surrounded myself with smart people and relied on them to work with me as a team to get the job done. My credo: always hire people who are smarter and better than you are, and learn with them."*

—Gene Kranz, *Failure Is Not an Option: Mission Control from Mercury to Apollo 13 and Beyond,* New York, NY: Berkley Books, 2000

# CHAPTER 15

# Regulatory Reporting and Principles of Policy Documentation

This chapter, which is also the last in Part III, may at first glance give the impression of being something of an "odds and ends" piece or even worse, no more than a filler, but in reality from a perpetual viability standpoint it's as important as any of the chapters preceding it. Regulatory reporting is a vital fact of life for a bank and one would expect it to continue to be so for the foreseeable future, thus justifying the presence of this chapter in the "future" part of the book's sub-title. As for policy documentation, that subject may elicit a yawn from many readers but since just about every relationship with all stakeholders including the regulator, the central bank daily monetary operation, rating agencies, customers, employees, and investors revolves around and is governed by formal policy statements, then it is apparent that there is a need to implement and adhere to best-practice principles governing how policies should be drafted and documented.

We summarise the main tenets of regulatory reporting and for illustration provide a description of the process that UK banks would follow. This is followed by a discussion on the main principles of organising a bank's policy documentation process.

The final section is a listing of the various template policy documents that are contained on the book's companion website. These are all relevant to the topics and disciplines discussed in the last section of this chapter and are applicable at most banks, irrespective of size or business model specificities. To access the templates, please see the instructions in Chapter 20.

## REGULATORY REPORTING FOR CAPITAL AND LIQUIDITY[1]

In this section, we consider the regulatory reporting requirements for capital and liquidity for banks based in the European Union as part of the CRDIV requirements (implementation of Basel III provisions). This material is provided as illustration of the basic principles; banks outside the EU will of course have variations on what is discussed here.

### Capital Regulatory Reporting

Regulatory reporting of capital and liquidity is necessary because:

- It obliges banks to monitor their capital adequacy and liquidity risk on a daily or intra-day basis;
- The data required by the regulator would normally be required by firms for their own purposes in undertaking prudent risk management;
- It enables the regulator to identify and challenge outliers;
- Supervisors can apply their own stress testing scenario analysis to data provided by a firm;
- It enables the regulator to form firm specific, sector, and industry-wide views on capital adequacy and liquidity risk during good and bad times, and provide feedback to firms on their positioning within their peer group.

**EU Common Reporting** In 2006, the Committee of European Bank Supervisors (CEBS) established common reporting framework guidelines with the aim of achieving four key objectives:

- Increase the comparability of financial information reported to different supervisors within the European Union (EU);
- Increase the cost-effectiveness of supervision across the EU;
- Reduce the reporting burden on cross-border credit institutions;
- Remove potential obstacles to financial market integration.

In this context, the European Banking Authority (EBA) mandated COREP ("Common Reporting") and FINREP ("Financial Reporting") as the new European reporting frameworks to achieve harmonised supervisory reporting standards for regulated institutions in over 30 countries across the EU. In the UK, COREP and FINREP were adopted in 2014.

COREP implementation has required institutions to increase the volume and granularity of regulatory data they report from approximately 2,000 data elements to more than 10,000 for larger banks.

COREP and FINREP reports must be delivered to the EBA in the XBRL (Extendable Business Reporting Language) format, using the European

---

[1] This section was co-written with Chris Westcott and Jamie Paris.

Banking Authority's reporting requirement, format, and layout (Data Point Model). The Data Point Model (DPM) is a structured representation of the data, identifying all the business concepts and their relationships, as well as validation rules and the associated taxonomy (the vehicle that enables data to be shared in line with the DPM structure). In the UK, this is collected via the Financial Conduct Authority's (FCA) GABRIEL system.

EU supervisory reporting is required in the following areas (on either a quarterly, semi-annual, or annual basis):

- Own funds requirements and the Leverage Ratio;
- Losses stemming from lending collateralised by immovable property;
- Large exposures and other largest exposures;
- Liquidity Coverage and Net Stable Funding requirements; and
- Asset encumbrance.

Capital Adequacy is covered by the Own Funds requirements. In total, there are 29 reporting templates, split into capital adequacy, transitional provisions, group solvency, credit risk, market risk, and operational risk categories.

Abridged versions of templates 1 (Own Funds), 2 (Own Funds Requirements), and 3 (Capital Ratios and Capital Levels) are illustrated at Figures 15.1, 15.2, and 15.3.

The EBA reporting on the Leverage Ratio consists of four templates:

- A table reconciling the figures of the Leverage Ratio denominator with those reported under the relevant accounting standards;
- A table providing a breakdown of the leverage ratio denominator by exposure category;
- A table providing a further breakdown of the leverage ratio denominator by group of counterparty; and
- A table with qualitative information on leverage risk.

In the UK, prior to the implementation of COREP, banks were required to submit a variety of FSA (the UK regulator at that time) returns on various aspects of capital adequacy. Since 2014, as illustrated in Table 15.1, a number of these reports have been discontinued, whilst others have been retained, either in full or with an amended application by the Financial Conduct Authority.

**Challenges Posed by COREP**    COREP (and FINREP) poses a range of potential issues for banks to manage.

**Organisational**    Reporting processes, frequency, and related technology must be aligned across traditionally silo'd areas such as Risk and Finance. In addition, there are data mapping and data modelling challenges, since

| C 01.00 - OWN FUNDS (CA1) | | | |
|---|---|---|---|
| Rows | ID | Item | Amount |
| 010 | 1 | OWN FUNDS | |
| 015 | 1.1 | TIER 1 CAPITAL | |
| 020 | 1.1.1 | COMMON EQUITY TIER 1 CAPITAL | |
| 030 | 1.1.1.1 | Capital instruments eligible as CET1 Capital | |
| 130 | 1.1.1.2 | Retained earnings | |
| 180 | 1.1.1.3 | Accumulated other comprehensive income | |
| 200 | 1.1.1.4 | Other reserves | |
| 210 | 1.1.1.5 | Funds for general banking risk | |
| 220 | 1.1.1.6 | Transitional adjustments due to grandfathered CET1 Capital instruments | |
| 230 | 1.1.1.7 | Minority interest given recognition in CET1 capital | |
| 240 | 1.1.1.8 | Transitional adjustments due to additional minority interests | |
| 250 | 1.1.1.9 | Adjustments to CET1 due to prudential filters | |
| 300 | 1.1.1.10 | (-) Goodwill | |
| 340 | 1.1.1.11 | (-) Other intangible assets | |
| 370 | 1.1.1.12 | (-) Deferred tax assets that rely on future profitability and do not arise from temporary differences net of associated tax liabilities | |
| 380 | 1.1.1.13 | (-) IRB shortfall of credit risk adjustments to expected losses | |
| 390 | 1.1.1.14 | (-) Defined benefit pension fund assets | |
| 430 | 1.1.1.15 | (-) Reciprocal cross holdings in CET1 Capital | |
| 440 | 1.1.1.16 | (-) Excess of deduction from AT1 items over AT1 Capital | |
| 450 | 1.1.1.17 | (-) Qualifying holdings outside the financial sector which can alternatively be subject to a 1.250% risk weight | |
| 460 | 1.1.1.18 | (-) Securitisation positions which can alternatively be subject to a 1.250% risk weight | |

**FIGURE 15.1** COREP Own Funds Reporting Template (CA1)

| Rows | ID | Item | Amount |
|------|-----|------|--------|
| 470 | 1.1.1.19 | (-) Free deliveries which can alternatively be subject to a 1.250% risk weight | |
| 471 | 1.1.1.20 | (-) Positions in a basket for which an institution cannot determine the risk weight under the IRB approach, and can alternatively be subject to a 1.250% risk weight | |
| 472 | 1.1.1.21 | (-) Equity exposures under an internal models approach which can alternatively be subject to a 1.250% risk weight | |
| 480 | 1.1.1.22 | (-) CET1 instruments of financial sector entities where the institution does not have a significant investment | |
| 490 | 1.1.1.23 | (-) Deductible deferred tax assets that rely on future profitability and arise from temporary differences | |
| 500 | 1.1.1.24 | (-) CET1 instruments of financial sector entities where the institution has a significant investment | |
| 510 | 1.1.1.25 | (-) Amount exceeding the 17.65% threshold | |
| 520 | 1.1.1.26 | Other transitional adjustments to CET1 Capital | |
| 524 | 1.1.1.27 | (-) Additional deductions of CET1 Capital due to Article 3 CRR | |
| 529 | 1.1.1.28 | CET1 capital elements or deductions - other | |
| 530 | 1.1.2 | ADDITIONAL TIER 1 CAPITAL | |
| 540 | 1.1.2.1 | Capital instruments eligible as AT1 Capital | |
| 660 | 1.1.2.2 | Transitional adjustments due to grandfathered AT1 Capital instruments | |
| 670 | 1.1.2.3 | Instruments issued by subsidiaries that are given recognition in AT1 Capital | |
| 680 | 1.1.2.4 | Transitional adjustments due to additional recognition in AT1 Capital of instruments issued by subsidiaries | |
| 690 | 1.1.2.5 | (-) Reciprocal cross holdings in AT1 Capital | |
| 700 | 1.1.2.6 | (-) AT1 instruments of financial sector entities where the institution does not have a significant investment | |

**FIGURE 15.1** (*Continued*)

| Rows | ID | Item | Amount |
|------|------|------|--------|
| 710 | 1.1.2.7 | (-) AT1 instruments of financial sector entities where the institution has a significant investment | |
| 720 | 1.1.2.8 | (-) Excess of deduction from T2 items over T2 Capital | |
| 730 | 1.1.2.9 | Other transitional adjustments to AT1 Capital | |
| 740 | 1.1.2.10 | Excess of deduction from AT1 items over AT1 Capital (deducted in CET1) | |
| 744 | 1.1.2.11 | (-) Additional deductions of AT1 Capital due to Article 3 CRR | |
| 748 | 1.1.2.12 | AT1 capital elements or deductions - other | |
| 750 | 1.2 | TIER 2 CAPITAL | |
| 760 | 1.2.1 | Capital instruments and subordinated loans eligible as T2 Capital | |
| 880 | 1.2.2 | Transitional adjustments due to grandfathered T2 Capital instruments and subordinated loans | |
| 890 | 1.2.3 | Instruments issued by subsidiaries that are given recognition in T2 Capital | |
| 900 | 1.2.4 | Transitional adjustments due to additional recognition in T2 Capital of instruments issued by subsidiaries | |
| 910 | 1.2.5 | IRB Excess of provisions over expected losses eligible | |
| 920 | 1.2.6 | SA General credit risk adjustments | |
| 930 | 1.2.7 | (-) Reciprocal cross holdings in T2 Capital | |
| 940 | 1.2.8 | (-) T2 instruments of financial sector entities where the institution does not have a significant investment | |
| 950 | 1.2.9 | (-) T2 instruments of financial sector entities where the institution has a significant investment | |
| 960 | 1.2.10 | Other transitional adjustments to T2 Capital | |
| 970 | 1.2.11 | Excess of deduction from T2 items over T2 Capital (deducted in AT1) | |
| 974 | 1.2.12 | (-) Additional deductions of T2 Capital due to Article 3 CRR | |
| 978 | 1.2.13 | T2 capital elements or deductions - other | |

**FIGURE 15.1**  (*Continued*)

| C 02.00 - OWN FUNDS REQUIREMENTS (CA2) | | | |
| --- | --- | --- | --- |
| Rows | Item | Label | Amount |
| 010 | 1 | TOTAL RISK EXPOSURE AMOUNT | |
| 040 | 1.1 | RISK WEIGHTED EXPOSURE AMOUNTS FOR CREDIT, COUNTERPARTY CREDIT, AND DILUTION RISKS AND FREE DELIVERIES | |
| 050 | 1.1.1 | Standardised approach (SA) | |
| 240 | 1.1.2 | Internal ratings based Approach (IRB) | |
| 460 | 1.1.3 | Risk exposure amount for contributions to the default fund of a CCP | |
| 490 | 1.2 | TOTAL RISK EXPOSURE AMOUNT FOR SETTLEMENT/DELIVERY | |
| 500 | 1.2.1 | Settlement/delivery risk in the non-Trading book | |
| 510 | 1.2.2 | Settlement/delivery risk in the Trading book | |
| 520 | 1.3 | TOTAL RISK EXPOSURE AMOUNT FOR POSITION, FOREIGN EXCHANGE AND COMMODITIES RISKS | |
| 530 | 1.3.1 | Risk exposure amount for position, foreign exchange and commodities risks under standardised approaches (SA) | |
| 580 | 1.3.2 | Risk exposure amount for Position, foreign exchange, and commodities risks under internal models (IM) | |
| 590 | 1.4 | TOTAL RISK EXPOSURE AMOUNT FOR OPERATIONAL RISK (OpR ) | |
| 600 | 1.4.1 | OpR Basic indicator approach (BIA) | |
| 610 | 1.4.2 | OpR Standardised (STA) / Alternative Standardised (ASA) approaches | |
| 620 | 1.4.3 | OpR Advanced measurement approaches (AMA) | |
| 630 | 1.5 | ADDITIONAL RISK EXPOSURE AMOUNT DUE TO FIXED OVERHEADS | |
| 640 | 1.6 | TOTAL RISK EXPOSURE AMOUNT FOR CREDIT VALUATION ADJUSTMENT | |
| 650 | 1.6.1 | Advanced method | |

**FIGURE 15.2** Own Funds Requirements (CA2)

| Rows | Item | Label | Amount |
|------|------|-------|--------|
| 660 | 1.6.2 | Standardised method | |
| 670 | 1.6.3 | Based on OEM | |
| 680 | 1.7 | TOTAL RISK EXPOSURE AMOUNT RELATED TO LARGE EXPOSURES IN THE TRADING BOOK | |
| 690 | 1.8 | OTHER RISK EXPOSURE AMOUNTS | |
| 700 | 1.8.1 | *Of which: Additional risk exposure amount due to application of Basel I floor* | |
| 710 | 1.8.2 | Of which: Additional stricter prudential requirements based on Art 458 | |
| 750 | 1.8.3 | Of which: Additional stricter prudential requirements based on Art 459 | |
| 760 | 1.8.4 | *Of which: Additional risk exposure amount due to Article 3 CRR* | |

**FIGURE 15.2** (*Continued*)

## C 03.00 - CAPITAL RATIOS AND CAPITAL LEVELS (CA3)

| Rows | ID | Item | Amount |
|------|----|------|--------|
| 010 | 1 | CET1 Capital ratio | |
| 020 | 2 | Surplus(+)/Deficit(-) of CET1 capital | |
| 030 | 3 | T1 Capital ratio | |
| 040 | 4 | Surplus(+)/Deficit(-) of T1 capital | |
| 050 | 5 | Total capital ratio | |
| 060 | 6 | Surplus(+)/Deficit(-) of total capital | |
| Memorandum Items: Capital ratios due to Pillar II adjustments | | | |
| 070 | 7 | CET1 capital ratio including Pillar II adjustments | |
| 080 | 8 | Target CET1 capital ratio due to Pillar II adjustments | |
| 090 | 9 | T1 capital ratio including Pillar II adjustments | |
| 100 | 10 | Target T1 capital ratio due to Pillar II adjustments | |
| 110 | 11 | Total capital ratio including Pillar II adjustments | |
| 120 | 12 | Target Total capital ratio due to Pillar II adjustments | |

**FIGURE 15.3** Capital Ratios and Capital Levels (CA3)

**TABLE 15.1**   Changes to Gabriel Reporting under COREP and FINREP

| Data items replaced for CRD IV Firms | Data items that remain for CRD IV Firms but application differs under CRD IV rules | Data items retained for CRD III Firms | Data items unaffected by COREP / FINREP |
|---|---|---|---|
| COREP Own Funds | FSA005 - Market Risk: Only 2 data elements for Capital Add-ons will be completed | FSA001 Balance sheet on a consolidated and solo basis | CRD: |
| FSA003 - Capital Adequacy | | | FSA001 Balance Sheet |
| FSA004 - Credit Risk | FSA006 - Market Risk (supp.): Retained to support RNIV Framework | FSA002 Income Statement on a consolidated and solo basis | FSA002 Income Statement |
| FSA005 - Market Risk | | | FSA014 - Forecast data |
| FSA007 - Operational Risk | FSA045 - IRB Portfolio Data: Guidance will change | FSA003 - Capital Adequacy | FSA015 - Sectoral analysis |
| FSA028 - Non EEA Sub groups | FSA018 - UKIGs Large exposures: Guidance will change as this will be applied to entities with Core UK Group and Non-Core LE Group Waiver (Applies to PRA Firms Only At Present) | FSA004 - Credit Risk | FSA016 - Solo consolidation |
| FSA045 - IRB Portfolio Data | | FSA005 - Market Risk | FSA017 - Interest rate gap |
| FSA046 - Securitisation | | FSA007 - Operational Risk | FSA019 - Pillar 2 Questions |
| FSA058 - Securitisation | | FSA028 - Non EEA Sub groups | LIQUIDITY |
| COREP LE | | FSA058 - Securitisation | FSA011, 047 – 055 |
| FSA008 - Large Exposures | | | Non CRD: |
| FINREP IFRS | | | FSA029 – 042 |
| FSA001 Balance Sheet | | | Payment Services: |
| FSA002 Income Statement | | | FSA056 / 057 |
| | | | MLAR |
| | | | RMAR |
| | | | Complaints |

reported information will be underpinned by the same set of regulations and assumptions, for the same reporting dates. This can be extremely challenging, given that most organisations are embedded with multiple layers of source systems and complex data transformations. There are also organisational challenges related to regulatory interpretation, as the lack of subject matter experts and different interpretations of the same data definition could only add to the level of complexity.

**Operational** Data needs to be correct and consistent across each of the reporting submissions, requiring a robust financial and risk control framework. Maintenance of the template rules and hierarchies is also vital. "Hard-coding" of business rules to hit reporting deadline is likely to be a costly approach. A robust operational process to understand both the Prudential Regulation Authority (PRA) and EBA requirements and implement any changes to the DPM is important. The operational impact of the new reporting requirements and maintenance of the DPM and templates can be minimised by utilising a granular business data model to assemble reporting information, aggregated and mapped to the EBA reporting model. That way, if the view of the data required for reporting changes, essentially all that is required is a tweak to the aggregation and mapping process.

**Process** In the areas of data mapping and data modelling, for example, data may not be stored in a single data warehouse, in which case it may prove problematic to source the information required for the reporting templates. As a result, many institutions have created or enhanced reporting systems to collate, normalise, and output the required data.

For many firms, the final XBRL format of the reports also proved to be a large technical challenge. As the XBRL reports are subject to a large set of validation rules embedded in the XBRL taxonomy, the reports need to be created with a high degree of accuracy, with appropriate pre-submission formatting and validation checks. Many organisations have purchased third-party software to facilitate the formatting of the reports to XBRL.

**Additional UK PRA Capital Reporting Requirements** The collection and availability of data obtained under the European regime, for example, COREP and FINREP, form the baseline against which any additional data requirements are assessed in the context of the PRA's review of reporting requirements in the UK.

In addition to regulatory reporting, the PRA requires a wide variety of data to be collected from firms including management information, financial accounts, and other ad-hoc data, which are used to support supervisory reviews and risk assessment. The PRA also collects data to support the work of the Financial Policy Committee (FPC) in identifying and understanding common sectoral risks that have the potential to affect the stability of the UK financial system as a whole and to monitor the impact of the Committee's decisions and recommendations.

Additional data collected by the PRA includes, but is not confined to:

- **Pillar 2 Data Items:** Since 1 January 2016, UK firms have been required to report Pillar 2 data items, alongside the submission of their Internal Capital Adequacy Assessment Process (ICAAP) assessment. This information, together with data already collected in other regulatory reports supports the PRA's review of a firm's ICAAP and enables it to calculate capital benchmarks for Pillar 2 risks.
- **Capital+ Return:** In 2017 the PRA introduced the Capital+ return into the existing regulatory framework for PRA-regulated banks, building societies, and designated investment firms. On the Capital+ return, data is collected on actual figures and firms' own forecasts, with the data definitions aligned with various COREP templates. The level of detail and the frequency at which data will be collected will be proportionate to the importance of a firm to the PRA in meeting its objectives. For example, the largest UK deposit-takers would report actual and forecast data on a monthly or quarterly basis (PRA101), whereas the smallest firms would report forecasts only on an annual basis (PRA103).
- **Branch Return:** On 30 April 2015, the PRA published a policy statement setting out a rule requiring incoming firms and third country firms to submit a Branch Return on a 6-monthly basis. The Branch Return provides the PRA with information about the UK activities of these firms.

### Liquidity Regulatory Reporting

We examine the evolution of liquidity regulatory reporting through the eyes of the European regulators, notably the Prudential Regulatory Authority (PRA) and the Basel Committee on Banking Supervision (BCBS).

During the early "liquidity phase" of the financial crisis that began in 2007, many banks – despite adequate capital levels – still experienced difficulties because they did not manage their liquidity in a prudent manner. The crisis drove home the importance of the industry having a standard set of liquidity metrics to correctly assess the state of the participants in the financial markets and the banking sector.

The PRA introduced a series of new liquidity reporting standards called the ILAS stress test effective from 1 December 2009[2] established under the

---

[2] http://www.fca.org.uk/static/pubs/policy/ps09_16.pdf.

Policy Statement entitled "Strengthening liquidity standards". This regime focused on a 3M stress test, which needed to be adequately covered by a prescribed set of liquid assets. The stress test has a prescribed set of outflow assumptions and was standardised in its approach. It enabled the PRA to consistently assess the liquidity positions of each banking institution in the market simultaneously. The banks reported to the regulators on a Monday the Friday's close of business position and subsequent qualitative discussions followed. This was founded under the overarching principle outlined in BIPRU 12.2.1R:

> *" A firm must at all times maintain liquidity resources which are adequate, both as to amount and quality, to ensure that there is no significant risk that its liabilities cannot be met as they fall due".*

The PRA followed a principle-based approach for the overall framework while using a more prescriptive approach for reporting and quantitative measures.

The key elements of this regime included the following:

- Over-arching principles of self-sufficiency and adequacy of liquidity resources;
- Enhanced systems and control requirements, which implement the Basel Committee's updated Principles for Sound Liquidity Risk Management and Supervision;
- New quantitative requirements, coupled with a narrow definition of liquid assets;
- A new modifications regime for branches and subsidiaries; and
- Granular and frequent reporting requirements.

This set of monitoring metrics was designed to assist supervisors in the analysis of bank specific and system wide liquidity risk trends. Whilst this practice had already existed in the UK since the introduction of the Independent Liquidity Assessment Supervision (ILAS) regime under BIPRU 12, there was no single worldwide standardised set of metrics to evaluate the quantum of liquidity risk in the banking sector.

The relevance of the framework established by the PRA was that it founded the basis of the Liquidity Coverage Ratio and Net Stable Funding Ration[3] established by the Basel Committee in January 2013, which built on the standards set out in the 2008 Principles for Sound Liquidity Risk Management and Supervision[4].

---

[3] http://www.bis.org/publ/bcbs238.pdf.

[4] http://www.bis.org/publ/bcbs144.pdf.

See Chapter 12 for detail on the Liquidity Coverage Ratio (LCR), Net Stable Funding Ratio (NSFR), and a discussion on potential business model impacts of the requirement to adhere to these funding metrics. From a reporting perspective, the LCR should be produced on an ongoing basis to help monitor and control liquidity risk. The LCR should be reported to supervisors at least monthly and in most instances weekly, with the operational capacity to increase the frequency to weekly or even daily in stressed situations at the discretion of the supervisor. Banks are expected to meet the NSFR requirement on an ongoing basis and the NSFR should be reported at least quarterly. Over time, it is expected that the NSFR reporting frequency aligns to that prescribed for the LCR.

## Reporting Requirements to Regulatory Authorities

In order to ensure a high level of consistency and harmonisation, the European Banking Supervisors (EBA) devised a set of guidelines and reporting requirements covering all aspects of Basel III. These are titled "Guidelines on Common Reporting" (COREP) which form part of the overall CRD IV EU legislative package. This section will focus on the elements of COREP that apply to the reporting of key liquidity metrics pertaining to LCR and in the future will cover NSFR, which is currently covered by separate legislation under Capital Requirements Regulation (CRR).

The European Banking Authority (EBA) is specifying all liquidity reporting data requirements for via COREP and this will continue to be collected via the Financial Conduct Authority's (FCA) GABRIEL system. The GABRIEL system was introduced under the BIPRU 12 regime in 2009. It is the PRA's centralised online system for collecting and storing regulatory data on firms.

In the UK, the sole reporting format for this data will be via XBRL (eXtensible Business Reporting Language), which is a global standard for exchanging business information. This will cover all data currently included within the EBA Implementing Technical Standards (ITS).

Under the EBA ITS standards, the following reporting frequencies have been agreed:

- Monthly reporting: on the last day of each month;
- Quarterly reporting: 31 March, 30 June, 30 September, and 31 December;
- Semi-annual reporting: 30 June and 31 December;
- Annual reporting: 31 December.

In times of stress, it is expected that these metrics can be run on a daily basis and some regulators are asking to see these numbers on a weekly basis. Whilst this is not hard wired into the regulations, it is a request being made and one that banks can easily adhere to given that they will be managing these ratios on a daily basis to ensure adherence.

In addition to the reporting frequencies, the ITS also specified the template format that need to be populated. This is to ensure that all firms are reporting the key liquidity metrics in a standardised controlled format. These templates can be found on the EBA website[5].

These templates (for LCR) are broken down into the following main components:

- Template C72.00 of Annex XXIV Liquidity coverage: liquid assets broken down into the qualifying components Level 1 assets or as Level 2 assets in accordance with Chapter 1 and 2 of Title II of the delegated act and which comply with the general requirements set out in Article 7 as well as the operational requirements defined in Article 8 of the LCR delegated act;
- Template C73.00 of Annex XXIV Liquidity coverage: liquidity outflows measured over the next 30 days, for the purpose of reporting the liquidity coverage requirement as specified in the delegated act. This template contains both outflows from unsecured transactions / deposits and from liabilities resulting from secured lending and capital-market driven transactions;
- Template C74.00 of Annex XXIV Liquidity coverage: liquidity inflows measured over the next 30 days, for the purpose of reporting the liquidity coverage requirement as specified in the delegated act. This template contains both inflows from unsecured transactions / deposits and from secured lending and capital-market driven transactions;
- Template C75.00 of Annex XXIV Liquidity coverage: collateral swaps maturing within 30 days in which non-cash assets are swapped for other non-cash assets;
- Template C76.00 of Annex XXIV Liquidity coverage: calculation of the LCR for the purpose of reporting the liquidity coverage requirement as specified in the delegated act.

The reporting requirements outlined for NSFR are covered under the Capital Requirements Regulation (CRR) and follow the templates outlined in the Quantitative Impact Study (QIS). These templates can be found on the Bank for International Settlements (BIS) website[6] under the tab entitled NSFR. The reporting frequency of these templates is designed to be in line with the publication of financial statements, which typically is on a quarterly, semi-annual, and annual basis. Further information can be obtained on the BIS website contained within the "Net Stable Funding Ratio disclosure

---

[5] https://www.eba.europa.eu/.../Annex+XXIV+-+LCR+templates_for+publication.xlsx.
[6] https://www.bis.org/bcbs/qis/biiiimplmoniwb_aug16.xlsx.

standards"[7]. Note that at time of writing the final form of NSFR calculation and assumptions is still to be published. LCR was the first metric to go live while NSFR should go live in 2019. There is still a lot of work to agree the templates and reporting frequencies around NSFR, but the dates that have been outlined in this chapter are good proxy for what the market expects to occur.

## Intra-day Risk Monitoring and Reporting

In April 2013, the Basel Committee on Banking Supervision (BCBS) published the requirements "Monitoring tools for intra-day liquidity management". The document referenced as BCBS248 set out the key metrics that need to be monitored and reported to the regulator. The management of intra-day liquidity risk is probably one of the more challenging liquidity risks to manage by the simple nature that it requires up to the minute data on transaction information that is occurring real time in the bank.

Intra-day liquidity and risk were described in Chapter 12.

**Background** Under the Principles of Sound Liquidity Risk Management and Supervision, Principle 8 identified six operational elements that should be included in a bank's strategy for managing intra-day liquidity risk. These state that a bank should:

1. Have the capacity to measure expected daily gross liquidity inflows and outflows, anticipate the intra-day timing of these flows where possible, and forecast the range of potential net funding shortfalls that might arise at different points during the day;
2. Have the capacity to monitor intra-day liquidity positions against expected activities and available resources (balances, remaining intra-day credit capacity, available collateral);
3. Arrange to acquire sufficient intra-day funding to meet its intra-day objectives;
4. Have the ability to manage and mobilise collateral as necessary to obtain intra-day funds;
5. Have a robust capability to manage the timing of its liquidity outflows in line with its intra-day objectives; and
6. Be prepared to deal with unexpected disruptions to its intra-day liquidity flows.

The set of monitoring tools established within BCBS248 are listed in Table 15.2.

---

[7] http://www.bis.org/bcbs/publ/d324.pdf.

**TABLE 15.2** Intra-day monitoring tools

**The set of monitoring tools**

Tools applicable to all reporting banks
- A(i)   Daily maximum intra-day liquidity usage
- A(ii)  Available intraday liquidity at the start of the business day
- A(iii) Total payments
- A(iv)  Time-specific obligations

Tools applicable to reporting banks that provide correspondent banking services
- B(i)   Value of payments made on behalf of correspondent banking customers
- B(ii)  Intraday credit lines extended to customers

Tool applicable to reporting banks which are direct participants
- C(i)   Intraday throughput

These monitoring tools are explained in more detail in Chapter 12.

**Reporting Templates for Intra-day Risk**   The PRA's intra-day liquidity data template is closely aligned with the Basel Committee on Banking Supervision "Monitoring Tools for Intra-day Liquidity Management" to follow in the common format of reporting across Basel III. In similar format to other types of liquidity reports, these are submitted in XML format on a quarterly basis with a 15-day delay time period allowed given the volumes of data required to submit.

The reporting templates are broken into three main categories:

1. Table A – Direct participants;
2. Table B – Banks that use correspondent banks;
3. Table C – Banks that provide correspondent banking services.

These tables are reproduced at Figure 15.4.

This is designed to ensure that all the associated intra-day risk from both sides of market participants – payers and receivers – are fully captured. Currently all of these reports are being disclosed to the regulators but on a quarterly basis. It is expected over time that this frequency of reporting is increased. Nevertheless, in order to ensure that they can demonstrate that they can manage intra-day risk, banks need to evaluate this on a daily basis and set controls and procedures around the management of this liquidity risk.

| Direct participants | | | | Table A |
|---|---|---|---|---|
| Reporting month | | | | |
| Name of the large value payment system | | | | |

| A(i) Daily maximum intraday liquidity usage | Max | 2d max | 3d max | Avg |
|---|---|---|---|---|
| 1. Largest positive net cumulative position | | | | |
| 2. Largest negative net cumulative position | | | | |

| A(ii) Available intraday liquidity at the start of the business day | Min | 2d min | 3d min | Avg |
|---|---|---|---|---|
| Total | | | | |
| Of which: | | | | |
| 1. Central bank reserves | | | | |
| 2. Collateral pledged at the central bank | | | | |
| 3. Collateral pledged at ancillary systems | | | | |
| 4. Unencumbered liquid assets on a bank's balance sheet | | | | |
| 5. Total credit lines available[26] | | | | |
| 5a. Of which secured | | | | |
| 5b. Of which committed | | | | |
| 6. Balances with other banks | | | | |
| 7. Other | | | | |

| A(iii) Total payments | Max | 2d max | 3d max | Avg |
|---|---|---|---|---|
| 1. Gross payments sent | | | | |
| 2. Gross payments received | | | | |

| A(iv) Time-specific obligations | Max | 2d max | 3d max | Avg |
|---|---|---|---|---|
| 1. Total value of time-specific obligations | | | | |

| C(i) Intraday throughput (%) | Avg | -- | -- | --- |
|---|---|---|---|---|
| 1. Throughout at 8:00 | | --- | --- | --- |
| 2. Throughout at 9:00 | | --- | --- | --- |
| 3. Throughout at 10:00 | | --- | --- | --- |
| 4. Throughout at 11:00 | | --- | --- | --- |
| 5. Throughout at 12:00 | | --- | --- | --- |
| 6. Throughout at 13:00 | | --- | --- | --- |
| 7. Throughout at 14:00 | | --- | --- | --- |
| 8. Throughout at 15:00 | | --- | --- | --- |
| 9. Throughout at 16:00 | | --- | --- | --- |
| 10. Throughout at 17:00 | | --- | --- | --- |
| 11. Throughout at 18:00 | | --- | --- | --- |

**FIGURE 15.4** Reporting Templates for Table A, B and C

**Banks that use correspondent banks**　　Table B

| | |
|---|---|
| Reporting month | |
| Name of the correspondent bank | |

| A(i) Daily maximum liquidity usage | Max | 2d max | 3d max | Avg |
|---|---|---|---|---|
| 1. Largest positive net cumulative position | | | | |
| 2. Largest negative net cumulative position | | | | |

| A(ii) Available intraday liquidity at the start of the business day | Min | 2d min | 3d min | Avg |
|---|---|---|---|---|
| Total | | | | |
| Of which: | | | | |
| 1. Balance with the correspondent bank | | | | |
| 2. Total credit lines from the correspondent bank[27] | | | | |
| 2a. Of which secured | | | | |
| 2b. Of which committed | | | | |
| 3. Collateral pledged at the correspondent bank | | | | |
| 4. Collateral pledged at the central bank | | | | |
| 5. Unencumbered liquid assets on a bank's balance sheet | | | | |
| 6. Central bank reserves | | | | |
| 7. Balances with other banks | | | | |
| 8. Other | | | | |

| A(iii) Total payments | Max | 2d max | 3d max | Avg |
|---|---|---|---|---|
| 1. Gross payments sent | | | | |
| 2. Gross payments received | | | | |

| A(iv) Time-specific obligations | Max | 2d max | 3d max | Avg |
|---|---|---|---|---|
| 1. Total value of time-specific obligations | | | | |

**Banks that provide correspondent banking services**　　Table C

| | |
|---|---|
| Reporting month | |

| B(i) Value of payments made on behalf of correspondent banking customers | Max | 2d max | 3d max | Avg |
|---|---|---|---|---|
| 1. Total gross value of payments made on behalf of correspondent banking customers | | | | |

| B(ii) Intraday credit lines extended to customers | Max | 2d max | 3d max | --- |
|---|---|---|---|---|
| 1. Total value of credit lines extended to customers[28] | | | | --- |
| 1a. Of which secured | | | | ---- |
| 1b. Of which committed | | | | --- |
| 1c. Of which used at peak usage | | | | --- |

**FIGURE 15.4**　(*Continued*)

## PRINCIPLES OF POLICY DOCUMENTATION

These days, policy documents are a staple of the banker's art. Regulators lay great importance on the existence of detailed and "robust" policies for essentially every aspect of a bank's operations, from its recruitment policy to its staff sickness policy. The two examples just noted may not be that relevant to the discipline of ALM, however, included within the ambit of policy documentation are such important ones as the liquidity risk appetite statement and the interest-rate risk policy. From the Board risk appetite policy downwards, it is indeed vital that the main principles of a bank's balance sheet management approach are documented formally, and that these principles are approved at the highest level and reviewed at least annually.

Therefore we can see why practitioners in the ALM and balance sheet risk management space must be well versed in what constitutes an effective policy document, and the best way to ensure that it is drafted, reviewed, approved, and implemented correctly. Ultimately, having an efficient and strong policy formulation and documentation process is connected with the long-run well-being of the bank.

Note that while policy statements are available for public inspection, in essence they are *internal* governance documents. As such they are more flexible and accessible than formal external-facing documents such as an ILAAP or Pillar 3 disclosure document. A question the author has been asked is, "Why does the bank need to have a Liquidity Policy Statement when all that would be contained within such a policy is already contained within the ILAAP?" But the bank should have such a statement for the same reason it might have an HR policy or a customer complaints policy, to dictate governance and process discipline. And the fundamental benefit is that as an internal policy, any changes to (in this case) the funding operating model or indeed any aspect of the liquidity risk regime, whether enforced or by design, can be updated quickly in the policy statement compared to the considerably longer time it would take to edit and approve an ILAAP document. So the fact that much of what a bank does may be described in a regulatory submission does not obviate the need to maintain sound internal policy documentation.

In this section, we present an overview recommendation of best-practice principles of the policy documentation process, and provide a template for a document format. We also provide a policy approval process template.

## Baseline Approach

It is very important that every aspect of balance sheet risk management is articulated in a formal policy document, approved at ALCO. This is to ensure that every stakeholder is aware of the requirements, operating procedures, and minimum / maximum tolerances of the bank relating to any and all factors that impact the balance sheet.

Policies should be reviewed by ALCO on a regular basis; depending on the type of policy in question we suggest once every 6 to 12 months. Drafting and ownership responsibilities of each policy must be known by all relevant bank staff and appropriate stakeholders.

The key principles underpinning policy documentation are as follows:

- Ownership and drafting responsibilities clear;
- Transparent, accessible language;
- Principle objectives of the policy clear;
- Who is affected by the policy;
- Regular review timetable;
- Relevant procedures and guidelines that form part of the policy;
- Balance sheet limits.

The Treasury (or possibly, Risk) must ensure that all critical aspects of the balance sheet management function are covered with the appropriate and relevant policy. For example, at every bank these would be expected to include:

- ALM policy standard;
- Liquidity management policy (and subsets of this policy thereof);
- Capital management policy;
- Dividend policy;
- Liquid asset buffer (LAB) policy;
- IRRBB policy;
- FX assets–liabilities policy;
- ALCO ToR formulation;
- ALCO papers submission template;
- Asset encumbrance policy;
- Funds transfer pricing policy;
- Securities issuance policy;
- Market risk hedging policy;
- Standard templates.

At this stage it is important to define, if only loosely, what a "policy" is and show how it differs from other forms of rulebooks or instruction manuals. The box below differentiates a policy from, in turn, a guideline, a

## DEFINING A POLICY

*Guideline*
- A piece of advice on how to act in a given situation;
- Recommended but non-mandatory control;
- For example, Employment Discrimination Guidelines, Screening Guideline.

*Procedure*
- A series of detailed steps to accomplish an objective;
- Step-by-step instructions for implementation;
- Standard Operating Procedures (SOPs);
- Derived from "process"; it is an established way of doing something.
- For example, a Medical Procedure.

*Standard*
- Acceptable level of quality or attainment;
- Quantifiable low-level mandatory controls;
- For example, Standard of Living, Standard Size.

*Policy*
- Recommended high-level statement protecting information across the firm;
- Business rules for fair and consistent staff treatment and to ensure compliance;
- For example, Dress Code Policy, Sick Leave Policy, Email, Internet Policy.

procedure, and a "standard" (although some commentators refer to "policy standards" which does confuse things).

### Template Policy Format and Submission Process

We show the author's own recommended template for a policy format at Figure 15.5. This example is a funding concentration policy, however the layout and format is the author's recommended standard template. This may be applied to any policy within the Treasury, Risk, or Finance space, and indeed most parts of the bank.

---

**Template Funding Concentration Policy**

---

**1. Policy Background information**

| Aspect | Details |
|---|---|
| Risk Framework | This policy is one of a number of policies forming part of the Treasury Risk Framework |
| Link to Risk Taxonomy | Level 1: Funding & Liquidity<br>Level 2: Funding Concentration<br>Level 3: N/A |
| Scope | All customer funding raised by ABC falls within the scope of this policy. |
| Application | This policy applies to everyone in ABC Treasury, including permanent and temporary members of staff, contractors, and employees of outsourced suppliers. |
| Policy Owner | Treasurer, ABC Bank |

---

**2. Definition**

Funding concentration risk is the risk that sources of funding may be affected by correlation of source or type.

---

**3. Purpose**

Funding concentration measures the concentration of deposits, CP and CD against a single client and/or group of clients. Limiting this metric reduces the risk of a single counterparty, or correlated highest volume counterparties, influencing the bank's funding strategy or pricing, and prevents over-reliance on a single funding source customer or sector.

---

**4. Regulatory and Legislative Drivers**

UK (pre- CRDIV) BIPRU section 12.3.32:
*Funding Diversification (nature of depositor or counterparty)*

---

**5. Risk Appetite**

Liquidity risk management in ABC Bank is the responsibility of ABC Treasury and its process is described in the Liquidity & Funding policy, which is approved by ABC Asset & Liability Committee (ALCOO).

The management of liquidity risk is controlled via a combination of risk appetite statements, limit monitoring and adherence to regulatory fiat, and through a suite of tools designed to limit or suppress the build up of risk beyond our stated appetite. Overall management is described within four principal disciplines:

---

**FIGURE 15.5**   Funding concentration policy, recommended template example

---

**Template Funding Concentration Policy**

---

- Liquidity Controls & Monitoring Framework
- Managing of Liquidity under stress
- Funding policy statements
- Internal funds pricing

Funding Concentration falls within the Liquidity Controls & Monitoring Framework.

Funding Concentration Risk Appetite is laid out in the following measures:

| Metric | Frequency | Limit |
|---|---|---|
| Single name client exposure across all tenors | Weekly | [%TBC] of total liabilities |
| Single name client exposure sub 3 months | Weekly | [%TBC] of total liabilities sub 3 months |
| Top 10 clients exposure across all tenors | Weekly | [%TBC] of total liabilities |
| Single name client exposure across all tenors | Weekly | [%TBC] of total customer liabilities |
| Single name client exposure sub 3 months | Weekly | [%TBC] of total customer liabilities sub 3 months |
| Top 10 clients exposure across all tenors | Weekly | [%TBC] of total customer liabilities |
| Sector concentration limit | Weekly | [%TBC] of total liabilities |
| Sector concentration limit | Weekly | [%TBC] of total customer liabilities |

---

**6. Policy Principles**

The Funding Concentration Policy sets limits around reliance on a single depositor or group of depositors in order to reduce the risk of a single counterparty, or correlated highest volume counterparties, influencing the bank's funding strategy or pricing. This forms part of the bank's liquidity risk and control framework, ensuring that the bank has access to funding that is adequately diversified. The policy requires that both Treasury and the ALCo are informed of the diversification of the bank's funding sources. The policy requires that corrective action is taken in the case of a breach of policy.

---

**7. Policy Implementation**

Funding concentration limits form part of the Liquidity & Funding Risk Appetite, approved by the ABC Bank Board. Performance against limits (as defined in section 5 - Risk Appetite) will be monitored on a weekly basis by ABC Treasury and reported to the ALCo on a monthly basis.
In the case of a policy breach, corrective action must be taken (as defined in section 9 – Non-Compliance With This Policy).

---

The Information Classification of this document is **Confidential**    2

**FIGURE 15.5**   (*Continued*)

---

**Template Funding Concentration Policy**

---

**8. Responsibilities and Accountabilities**

First Line of Defence
Treasury is responsible for setting governance policy and ensuring effective implementation of the Funding Concentration policy within ABC.

Second Line of Defence
Risk is responsible for monitoring compliance within limits and for reporting breaches, and for ensuring compliance by the business and Treasury with the policy overall.

Third Line of Defence
Internal Audit is responsible for:
- Undertaking risk based independent audits on relevant processes and controls, in line with their Audit Plan.

---

**9. Non-compliance with this Policy**

ABC has no appetite for any non-compliance with this Policy. Any breach must result in either:

- Actions to bring the risk back within Appetite; or
- Amendments to this Policy.

All exceptions to be submitted in writing to the Treasurer, ABC who will submit to the ABC ALCo for agreement as appropriate

All cases of non-compliance will be taken seriously and dealt with by the policy owner. Part of that process will involve consideration of the effectiveness of existing controls.

Non-compliance with this policy  must be managed in accordance with the Operational Risk Issues Management Policy

---

**10. Policy Governance Approval Process**

Reference should be made to the Enterprise Risk Policy Framework which sets out the Policy Governance Approval process.

Treasury policies are recommended  by the ABC ALCo within its delegated authority as a sub-committee of the ABC Board and as laid down within its Terms of Reference (ToR) - Version 7(18 July 2013)

---

The Information Classification of this document is **Confidential**     3

**FIGURE 15.5**   *(Continued)*

| Template Funding Concentration Policy |
|---|

**11. Further information**

ABC Treasury – 020 7672 3806

**12. Policy Approval**

| Policy ref / version | Version 1 |
|---|---|
| Prepared by: | ABC Treasury<br>Professor Moorad Choudhry |
| Date: | 21$^{st}$ May 2014 |
| Approved by: | Professor Moorad Choudhry |
| Date | |

The Information Classification of this document is **Confidential**    4

**FIGURE 15.5**   (*Continued*)

The process of submitting a paper for approval – whether by ALCO, or any other committee up to Board level – should also be contained in a policy document. The process should also supply a standard template for all paper submissions which all business lines must use. We illustrate a recommended process for approval submission in the box below. In this example, the process described is for those business lines wishing to issue private placement or public capital market instruments such as medium-term notes or structured notes. The approval authority in question is the Security Issuance Committee.

## SECURITIES ISSUANCE COMMITTEE: PAPER SUBMISSION POLICY STANDARD

The Committee provides two stages of approval of Debt Issuance Initiatives:

1. **Stage 1 Approval:** to be obtained by the business line or Treasury for proposed Debt Issuance Initiatives before incurring expenses such as legal fees or initiating any external discussions with third parties or regulators;

(*Continued*)

2. **Stage 2 Approval:** to be obtained by the business line or Treasury for proposed Debt Issuance Initiatives after receiving confirmation of all requisite internal and regulatory approvals and completed (if appropriate) New Product Approval Process form before proceeding to ALCO approval.

### Stage 1

Papers submitted in respect of a Stage 1 Approval should provide a paragraph of high-level information setting out the key features of the proposed Debt Issuance Initiative.

Items to be included in the paragraph are:

- Proposed issuing and (where relevant) guaranteeing entity and place in ABC Bank Group structure;
- Estimated size of programme;
- Type of product;
- Target investor category and jurisdiction(s);
- Underlying asset class (if any);
- Collateral (if any);
- Why it is required and why we cannot use any existing programmes;
- Any other key information on the proposal.

### Stage 2

Papers submitted in respect of a Stage 2 Approval should be detailed and in the format set out below.

Pro Forma Stage 2 Paper

| | |
|---|---|
| To: | ABC Bank Securities Issuance Committee |
| Date: | [ ] |
| Subject: | [Type of product] |
| From: | [Division] |
| | [Contact name] |

[N.B. ALL FIELDS BELOW MUST BE COMPLETED. NO FIELD SHOULD BE DELETED. IF ANY ITEMS ARE NOT APPLICABLE, THEY SHOULD BE MARKED AS "NOT APPLICABLE" AND A BRIEF EXPLANATION PROVIDED]

*Background*
[INSERT]

*Product Type*
[INSERT TYPE OF PRODUCT (E.G. MTNs, CERTIFICATES, WARRANTS, ETC.]

*Issuer*
[INSERT NAME AND BRANCH (IF APPLICABLE) AND PLACE IN ABC BANK GROUP STRUCTURE]

*Guarantor (if any)*
[INSERT NAME AND BRANCH (IF APPLICABLE) AND PLACE IN ABC BANK GROUP STRUCTURE]

*Transaction Structure*
[INSERT SUMMARY OF TRANSACTION FEATURES. INCLUDE STRUCTURE DIAGRAM AS AN APPENDIX IF APPROPRIATE]

*Objectives*
We seek to achieve the following objectives:
[INCLUDE OBJECTIVES OF TRANSACTION. INCLUDE EXPLANATION OF WHY EXISTING PROGRAMMES CANNOT BE USED]

*Target Size*
[INSERT ESTIMATED SIZE OF PROGRAMME]

*Currency*
[INSERT CURRENCY OR CURRENCIES]

*Rate of Interest (Spread to be Achieved)*
[INSERT RATE OF INTEREST AND PROPOSED PAYMENT FREQUENCY]

*(Continued)*

*Proposed Maturity*

[INSERT PROPOSED MATURITY]

*Put / Call Options*

[INSERT DETAILS OF ANY PUTS OR CALLS AND WHEN EXERCISABLE]

*Status*

[INSERT STATUS (E.G. SENIOR)]

*Underlying Asset Class (If Any)*

[INSERT ANY UNDERLYING ASSET CLASSES]

*Collateral (If Any)*

[INSERT DETAILS OF COLLATERAL INCLUDING CLASS, JURISDICTION(S), HAIRCUTS]

*Settlement*

[INSERT APPLICABLE CLEARING SYSTEMS]

*Governing Law*

[INSERT GOVERNING LAW(S)]

*Ratings*

[INSERT DETAILS OF REQUIRED RATING AGENCIES]

*Listing*

[INSERT DETAILS OF STOCK EXCHANGE AND MARKET]

*Disclosure*

[SUMMARY OF DISCLOSURE REQUIREMENTS AND PROPOSED SOURCE (E.G., PLC REGISTRATION STATEMENT OR SEC FILINGS)]

[IF BESPOKE DISCLOSURE REQUIRED THIS MUST BE FLAGGED. DETAILS OF ANY DISCUSSIONS OF GROUP SECRETARIAT TO BE INCLUDED]

*Translations*
[INSERT DETAILS OF ANY DOCUMENTS THAT WILL NEED TO BE TRANSLATED AND WHETHER ON A ONE-OFF OR ONGOING BASIS]

*Marketing Strategy*
[INSERT TARGET INVESTOR AUDIENCE AND JURISDICTION(S)]

*Issuance responsibility*
[INSERT WHO WILL ARRANGE THE TRANSACTION AND WHO WILL MANAGE THE TRANSACTION POST-CLOSING]

*Where Will the Funds Be Allocated?*
[INSERT. ABC TREASURY OR ELSEWHERE?]

*Impact on Intra-Group Lending*
[INSERT IGL IMPACT]

*External Legal Advisers*
[INSERT IN RESPECT OF EACH RELEVANT JURISDICTION]

*Legal Contact and Input*
[INSERT NAMES AND INPUT]

*Internal Approvals Received*
[INSERT DETAILS OF ANY INTERNAL APPROVALS RECEIVED TO DATE]

*Indicative Timeline*
[INSERT PLANNED TIMELINE TOGETHER WITH ANY CRITICAL DEADLINE DATES]

*Risks*
[INSERT ANY MATERIAL OR EXCEPTIONAL RISKS.

*(Continued)*

> PLEASE COVER (WITHOUT LIMITATION): LEGAL RISKS, OPERATIONAL RISKS, REPUTATIONAL RISKS, MARKET RISKS, LIQUIDITY RISKS, AND INTEREST RATE RISKS]
>
> *Other*
>
> [INSERT ANY OTHER MATERIAL FEATURES OR CONSIDERATIONS (IF ANY)]

## TEMPLATE POLICY DOCUMENTATION

We list here items contained on the book's accompanying website that are relevant to the chapters in Part III. To access the website, please see login details in Chapter 20. The files described below are held in the website folder "Part III Policy Documentation".

### Chapter 10

- Template for an ALCO Terms of Reference;
- Example of an ALCO operating agenda (which would form part or an appendix of the ALCO ToR);
- Template for the design and format of the ALCO Monthly Pack (slide deck).

### Chapter 12

- Exercise on preferred suite of liquidity risk management metrics summary for ALCO pack;
- Example of the recommended Group Treasury weekly qualitative report summary, provided by Regional / Divisional Treasurers;
- Example strategy implemented at a commercial bank using the FTP mechanism to incentivise the raising of Retail deposits;
- Template for a commercial bank liquidity risk appetite statement. Note that the expression "TBC" alongside a particular risk metrics denotes that this is a limit that is user-defined and user-specified;
- Case study of the suite of liquidity metrics used and reported at a MENA commercial bank. Note that limits are set with the internal Treasury limit as the most conservative, above or below (as necessary) the Board and Regulator limits, to ensure that critical limits are not breached without sufficient advance warning;

- Template ILAA submission document which is based on case study of actual final approved submission for a medium-sized UK commercial bank;
- Template Liquidity reserve book policy.

## Chapter 13

- Template for a commercial bank IRRBB risk management policy.

## Chapter 14

- Template for a commercial bank Group ALCO ToR. (This file is held in the folder "Chapter 14".)

## Chapter 15

- Template for a policy standard document;
- Presentation on principles of policy documentation;
- Template and example of a Funding Concentration Policy document;
- Real-world example of the Terms of Reference of a Treasury-related committee, the Securities Issuance Committee (a committee of the Global Banking and Markets division of RBS) in 2011 of which the author was Chair;
- Template for a bank's Contingency Funding Plan (CFP) document.

Note that a template Trading Book Policy and FX risk hedging policy are held in the folder marked "Chapter 5".

## SELECTED BIBLIOGRAPHY AND REFERENCES

*Regulatory and financial reporting essential for effective banking supervision and financial stability*, https://www.bankingsupervision.europa.eu/press/speeches/date/2014/html/se140603.en.html.

*Regulatory data*, http://www.bankofengland.co.uk/PRA/Pages/regulatorydata/default.aspx.

*Regulatory Reporting: What Banks Can Do to Keep Pace with the Changes*, Tata Consulting, http://www.tcs.com/resources/white_papers/Pages/Regulatory-Reporting-What-Banks-can-do.aspx.

*"Disappointments and setbacks have to be faced in life. There must be no recriminations. I had learnt this lesson when I was dropped from the Marlborough XI on the morning of our match against Rugby at Lord's. There is always something else ahead."*

—Lt. Gen. Sir Hugh Stockwell, quoted in B. Turner, *Suez 1956,* London: Hodder and Stoughton, 2006

# PART IV

# The Future of Banking: Strategy, Governance and Culture

Perhaps rather than Strategic ALM as such, it is Part IV that is "the big one" in terms of idea and permanence? Governance and culture in a bank are ultimately the last word, the two things that can make the difference between survival and failure in a market crash, or between good customer service and outrageous customer mis-selling. But unsurprisingly these are the two things least amenable to being codified into a formal process, or described in a textbook. And the further a process is from one that can be described in scientific terms, the more important it is for those engaged in such a process to exercise sound judgement acquired over time through continuous practice. And even this ingredient is a necessary but not sufficient one to ensure good banking. We've described the content of Part IV as the "future" of banking but it's less a prophecy and more of a wish-list: it's what we'd like banking to be, because it's what banking *should* be. Only time will tell if the industry does travel in the direction we recommend it should.

Michael Lafferty, chairman of the Lafferty Group and one of the founders of the Retail Banking Academy, on receiving a copy of the author's book *The Principles of Banking*, remarked that it was a good text but he had to get to around page 750 before he saw any mention of the customer! Of course all non-public sector commercial institutions are reliant on customers and therefore must pay close attention to them, and banks are no exception. Good customer service is not a discipline unique to banks and doesn't require a skill specific to bankers, whereas managing the balance sheet so that it is long-term sustainable does. But one can't deny the need to repair the image of banks and bankers in the eyes of customers, and we consider some aspects of this in Chapter 18.

In Part IV we discuss strategy setting principles, and the importance of actually knowing where one wants to go, such that one can articulate it explicitly. This includes an idea of the shape and structure of the balance sheet as well as the image, size, customer targeting, and so on. We go on to discuss culture and governance. The latter actually drives the former but in an indirect fashion; in essence, it doesn't matter as much what the governance infrastructure is, what committees there are and who sits on them, if the culture is not appropriate. And the imperative is to have a universal stakeholder focus at the centre of the bank's culture.

Finally, we present an outline of a "model bank" in terms of its customer outlook and attitude to customer service. This is not an exhaustive description, but rather a suggestion of what a good bank should be aiming to provide. Banks are an important part of society as a whole, and it's much more important for them to have a broad stakeholder approach than some other commercial enterprises.

As one might expect with a section of the book entitled "The Future of Banking", there is much more new material here than there are extracts from the author's previous works.

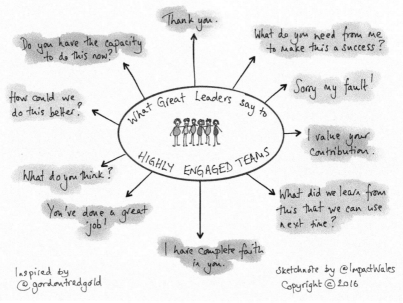

*Source:* Impact School Improvement (@ImpactWales) 2010. Used with permission.

# CHAPTER 16

# Strategy Setting: Principles for Sustained Bank Viability

Not every bank possesses the luxury of having a "strategy" department. Many banks don't even have a single person tasked with carrying out the role of strategist, let alone an entire department. But here's a paradox: the very large banks, which often do possess significant strategy human resources, rarely generate their actual medium-term directional goals from work produced by these teams. It wasn't someone in the RBS Strategy team who thought it was a good idea to acquire (the rubbish parts of) ABN Amro, or someone in HBOS Strategy who suggested they fill their boots with commercial real-estate assets. Likewise the excesses observed at Lehman Brothers in the run-up to its demise, or the Latin American bad debt lending of a generation earlier, both had "CEO" written all over them. Banks generally leave, by accident or design, their strategy setting to the CEO and a small coterie of his (it's usually a he, historically for failed banks anyway) in-house colleagues. Medium-term direction and specific projects are sent upwards for Board approval, but this review process is not necessarily a major hurdle, particularly with the composition of Boards and the character of non-executive directors being what they have been hitherto.[1]

Banks' so-called strategy teams are frequently employed undertaking due-diligence *after* a decision has been taken, or providing background information to support a pet idea proposed by a member of the executive management committee (ExCo). In other words, strategy teams are more often than not data crunchers and PowerPoint slide producers rather than actual authors of the bank's strategic direction. Often these teams have a background in management consulting firms, or move on to work at such companies, which is unsurprising given that often banks bring in such

---

[1] In Chapter 17 we look in more detail at the roles and responsibilities of the Board and what the ideal non-executive director (NED) should look like.

consultants to help them produce a piece of strategy work – even when they have internal resources dedicated to this task.[2]

This is a pity, because a "Head of Strategy" is in theory a genuine value-added function in a bank; indeed readers will note that in Chapter 10 we recommended that this person be included as a member of ALCO. Small- and medium-sized banks generally do not create such roles, the thinking being that it is the responsibility of the ExCo to draft strategy and present it to the Board for approval. There is nothing wrong or illogical in this, it is perfectly sensible. But there is much to be said for having an individual or team that is tasked wholly with developing strategic thinking, with respect to products, customers, geographies, and so on, unencumbered with the day-to-day paraphernalia associated with managing a conventional line function.

Strategy setting takes its direction from the type of firm the bank is, its culture, and antecedents, whether or not there is a dedicated team or individual responsible for generating it. And this is the absolute vital point with strategy: the bosses and owners have to set the tone. For any corporate entity, one assumes the Board of Directors is the ultimate controller, the entity that is in charge. Boards being Boards, they will often respond to input from their executive committee rather than set the direction themselves, but the overarching parameters within which strategy is set *must* be set by the Board. Only under this (albeit simple, let's face it) condition can strategy setting be successful over the long term.

Because the long term is what it is all about. This is unsurprising, given that the definition of strategy is:

*"a plan of action designed to achieve a long-term or overall aim".*[3]

For any strategy to be successful then, it's evident that the long-term or overall aim must not only be known, but articulated explicitly. This is not as straightforward as it seems. Of course in some banks even the first part isn't really known with certainty, so one can see how it would be hard for such banks' Boards to articulate anything intelligible. Family-owned banks are particularly prone to this handicap.

---

[2] This part does exhibit a certain irony. People who more often than not have never worked at a commercial bank are asked to develop the strategy for a commercial bank. . .

[3] It being 2016 as I write this, the source of this definition wasn't the Oxford English Dictionary but rather Google.

But as the clichéd saying goes, this isn't rocket science. If one stops to think about it, developing a long-term aim does not sound particularly difficult; one just has to know what one wants. It does, however, take boldness: the character and ability to take decisions. This is not always so easy for some senior executives. Often banks describe themselves as being "conservative", as if this was some sort of badge of honour; certainly there is nothing wrong with this trait, indeed it has much to commend it. But occasionally a fall-back to "conservatism" becomes a euphemism for not making a decision, and there are times when the act of not deciding what to do (in itself a decision) can result in dangerous inaction.

In this chapter, we consider best-practice principles of strategy setting in a bank. We will assume that the Board has set the overall long-term aim, down to specific quantitative targets and risk appetites, because unless and until it has done this, drafting strategy is actually a sophisticated form of time wasting. So we make this assumption and then we can proceed.

The previous book extracts are pertinent today and also we believe will remain so in the future. After the extracts, we present our recommended approach on principles for setting strategy and the correct inputs to this process.

**This extract from *The Principles of Banking* (2012)**

**Strategy Inputs**

## STRATEGY INPUTS

Notwithstanding that all banks are ultimately similar beasts, the strategy formulated for an individual bank will be unique to it and reflects its particular market, business model, customer base and operating environment. Unlike some of the other subjects dealt with in this book, it would be difficult (and of questionable value) to come up with a "template" strategy document. Instead, in this section we will illustrate business best-practice with a description of the relevant inputs to a coherent strategy. These would then be modified for each specific case.

It is important that a bank articulates its strategic vision, and publicly announces its quantitative and qualitative targets. This may sound obvious, but one would be surprised how many financial institutions do not actually do this beyond bland platitudes, and simply bumble along from one year to the next.

## Vision Statement

The concept of a vision statement is beloved of management consultants and therefore care must be taken to avoid writing one that is simply verbiage and platitudes, and thereby a worthless, pointless document. To be of value, it should capture succinctly and accurately what the bank aspires to be. In a top-down strategy origination process, it would drive the quantitative and qualitative elements of the bank strategy; hence, if the statement is well formulated it becomes a worthwhile input to the strategy. It can set the risk-reward culture at the bank. If the bank wishes to deviate from this culture, it would then look to revise the statement (and its strategy). In other words, a vision statement serves as a statement of intent, so that all the bank's stakeholders know what its business model and objectives are.

For example, a framework vision statement might encompass one or more of the following:

- to be a stable commercial bank serving the requirements of customers in the EMEA region;
- to achieve a consistent RoE of 12%–14% and RoA of 4%–5% throughout the business cycle;
- to maintain an AA–/Aa2 credit rating;
- to generate revenue from customer business, within core business lines;
- to focus on customer requirements, emphasising a robust risk management culture;
- to limit cost base, including employee remuneration, to [ ]% of revenue base.

Note how the above almost explicitly restricts proprietary trading business. A bank whose primary focus lay outside some or all of the above would craft a different vision statement. Equally, if the bank that drafted the above statement wished to move into new businesses or products that were not covered by its current vision, it would modify it, thereby giving intent of its new focus.

With the vision set, the bank should drill down from it and articulate its strategic plan. This is still a general statement; it is the next layer down that will describe detailed target metrics. For example, the hypothetical bank that drafted our vision statement above might describe its strategic plan in the following terms:

## BANK STRATEGIC PLAN

- Business focus
  - home market, euro-zone and Gulf Co-operation Council (GCC) region;

- customer base for corporate and institutional banking: corporate and financial institutions;
- customer base for retail banking: high net worth individuals (HNWIs) in home market and GCC region;
- limit balance sheet to EUR [ ] billion;
- limit wholesale funding share to 20%.
- Management focus
  - limit cost base to [ ]% of revenue base;
  - explicit metric for balance sheet usage;
  - return target set at 12%–14% on a sustained basis;
  - robust risk management organisation, policy and reporting line;
  - incentivise long-term customer-focused business.

The above would be built on and developed into greater detail. The next input to the strategy is the next level down, the target metrics.

## Strategy Setting : Performance Parameters

The second tier of strategy development is the formulation of a bank-wide business plan and target return metrics. This should set key performance indicators (KPIs) in actual quantitative terms. The base KPIs are:

- capital: return on capital; RAROC; assets-to-capital ratio;
- liquidity: loan-to-deposit ratio; liquidity ratio; wholesale funding ratio;
- cost base: front-office/back-office ratio; cost–income ratio;
- risk appetite: provisions/lending; NPLs/lending; VaR;
- growth: asset growth; liability growth.

We emphasise that the targets are not necessarily minimum levels, and in some cases they can be maximum levels. A sustained performance of 12% RoC over a 10–15-year period is infinitely preferable, from an aggregate market viewpoint (or from society's viewpoint), to several years of 22% RoE followed by losses for a year or two. Equally, a market share target of 10% does not mean that a level of 20% is desirable: an emphasis on market share as a KPI was one of the forces that drove Northern Rock and Bradford & Bingley to their demise. In any case, market share is not a value-added KPI for banks. It should have no place in bank strategy.

The next level down is quantitative target setting. We imagine a mediumsized commercial bank with three business lines: Treasury, corporate banking and domestic retail banking. Table 16.1 shows the elements of quantitative returns targets that would be set into the strategy, at the

| Bank level | | |
|---|---|---|
| Core Tier 1 capital | | |
| Return on equity | | |
| Return on assets | | |
| Wholesale funding share | | |
| Leverage ratio | | |
| Cost–income ratio | | |
| **Treasury** | **Corporate banking** | **Retail banking** |
| Return on capital | Return on capital | Return on capital |
| Return on equity | Return on equity | Return on equity |
| Liquidity ratio, 1-week and 1-month | Loan-to-deposit ratio | Weighted average cost of deposits |
| Front office/Back office cost ratio | Front office/Back office cost ratio | Front office/Back office cost ratio |
| Cost–income ratio | Cost–income ratio | Cost–income ratio |
| VaR limit | Provisions/Lending ratio | Loan growth |
| Securities growth year-on-year (y-o-y) | Loan growth | Deposit growth |
| Sharpe ratio | Deposit growth Unfunded asset growth | |

**Table 16.1**   Bank strategy setting: quantitative targets.

bank-wide level and at the individual business unit level. These are not set in stone; they should be set as part of 1-year and 3-year plans, but reviewed on an annual basis. Note how some of them are control targets (such as the Treasury department's liquidity ratio) and cost targets. Not all the elements of the strategy are revenue or returns orientated. The control and cost elements are an important part of the strategy.

The extent of the bank's achievement against the 3-year strategic target should be reported on a regular quarterly basis, as shown at Table 16.2. Given the dynamic situation of the markets and the need to respond to events, there is less worth in setting a longer term (say 5-year) strategic target in anything but the broadest terms; that is, at the level of the vision statement. However, some banks still do this. One would be right to question the actual practical value of such targets on a day-to-basis, although they do serve a purpose in communicating to stakeholders a coherent view of the Board's strategic vision and direction.

| | Quarter-end actual | 3-year target |
|---|---|---|
| Core Tier 1 capital | 7% | 10% |
| Return on equity | 9.80% | 11% |
| Wholesale funding share | 33% | 20% |
| Leverage ratio | 23:1 | 15:1 |
| Cost–income ratio | 66% | 50% |

**Table 16.2**  Performance against strategy: example quarterly report. Reproduced from *The Principles of Banking* (2012)

**This extract from *The Principles of Banking* (2012)**

## An Integrated Capital and Liquidity Management Strategy

### AN INTEGRATED CAPITAL AND LIQUIDITY MANAGEMENT STRATEGY

In the Basel III environment, banks will wish to ensure that their high level strategy setting integrates both capital management and liquidity management. We describe a template of objectives for banks to consider when formulating strategy.

## Capital Management Issues: Strategy Level

As a strategic imperative a bank should review its complete business model and identify which businesses have the most attractive funding and cost base under Basel III, and remain viable, and which do not. The result of this exercise is then an action plan that describes which businesses in the bank's portfolio it should be growing, maintaining, and exiting.

Other considerations include:

- ensure that an appropriate and sustainable incentive scheme is in place to drive correct senior management behaviour and optimise use of capital;
- ensure that specified, consistent, quantified capital objectives are explicitly stated and applied throughout every business line in the bank or group;
- ensure the bank is set up with the infrastructure to enable senior management to measure and report on the capital position and requirements on a sufficiently timely basis;
- review whether existing business models, if they are being retained, should continue in the form they are currently organised or should

be re-modelled on a more efficient basis (for example, branch versus subsidiary) in a way that makes better use of capital;
- prepare to be able to meet more accelerated implementation times-cales if required.

The above should not be a worthless management consultant-style strategy document, but rather a working document that sets out exactly how the bank's businesses should be set up in a way that uses capital the most effectively.

## Capital Management Issues: Tactical Level

Capital management at the tactical level is first and foremost about ensuring that senior management is intimately familiar with the capital requirements and return on assets of every business line. This requires efficient and timely MI.

The main considerations are:

- ensure that business lines are charged the correct level for the capital costs of their activity;
- ensure that Basel III capital implications are taken into account for new business proposals;
- review all long-dated business on the balance sheet from a capital efficiency and RoA viewpoint, and consider whether this is still SVA business. If not, can it be divested efficiently?
- maintain focus on Basel II as well as Basel III implications of all business lines, because Basel III amplifies any increases in RWAs arising from Basel II;
- review performance of existing regulatory capital calculation methodologies where these are internal models (for example, IRB under Basel II);
- ensure procedures are in place that enable Treasury and the business lines to consider the pricing implications arising from changes in the capital requirements for specified product lines.

The above process is a regular review, and not a one-off exercise.

## Liquidity Management Strategy

Liquidity management at the detailed technical level was considered in Part III of this book. For senior management it should be closely integrated into capital management strategy. Liquidity management strategy should be contained in an up-to-date policy document that includes the CFP and liquidity risk tolerances, as well as the strategy and tactical plan for diversi-fying sources of funds.

The principal considerations for liquidity management strategy are:

- bank senior management must be aware of the current liquidity position at all times, as well as what the forward stress points are. This knowledge must be to sufficient detail;
- the incentive structure for management should ensure optimal use of liquidity. This demands an appropriate and effective internal funds pricing policy (FTP policy);
- ensure that regulatory requirement for liquidity are always taken into consideration when assessing profitability and RoA on existing business and on new business proposals;
- ensure robust and wide-ranging stress testing and scenario planning, and review results regularly. Test results must be acted on through mitigating action and an enhanced CFP;
- review regularly the bank's liquidity strategy and ensure that infra-structure and MI adequately meet all requirements.

The liquidity strategy document should drill down to detailed metric requirements. For example, it could be stated along the following lines:

- the bank will maintain sufficient liquidity buffer to address 115% of 90-day regulatory stressed cash outflows;
- specified liquidity metrics will be:
  - loan-to-deposit ratio of 95%;
  - an LAB size of $10 billion;
  - maximum short-term wholesale funding usage of $1 billion;
- liquidity risk appetite should be made explicit.

Bank senior management should strive to ensure that their liquidity management strategy is always business best-practice. Regular peer-group review and comparison will assist with this. Industry practice should be reported at ExCo and ALCO level.

---

**EXAMPLE 17.2**   A CAPITAL ADEQUACY AND LIQUIDITY TRADE-OFF

Figure 17.5 is reproduced with permission from the UK FSA and shows an hypothetical arrangement with two different banks, posing the question "Which is riskier?". The bank on the top is running a

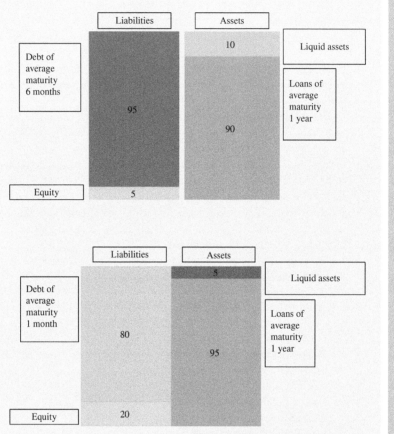

**Figure 17.5**   Capital and liquidity trade-off.
© FSA 2010. Reproduced with permission

more conservative liquidity policy, with longer dated liabilities as well as a larger liquidity buffer. The bank on the bottom is running a higher risk liquidity policy, but has a larger capital buffer. Its higher capitalisation would, all else being equal, make it higher rated than the other bank and thereby able to access cheaper funding.

There is not necessarily one right answer to the question. If the first bank has a high risk appetite and has acquired higher risk assets on the balance sheet, then it is in the riskier position because its capital base is low and may be reduced to below regulatory minimum should it start to experience losses. That said, in the event of a liquidity crisis it is in the better position. A liquidity event will finish a bank as a going concern if it cannot roll over liabilities, so ultimately we must conclude that the riskier bank is the second, well-capitalised bank. This sounds paradoxical but we can understand it.

The author's preferred solution is "neither of the above", and is instead shown at Figure 17.6.

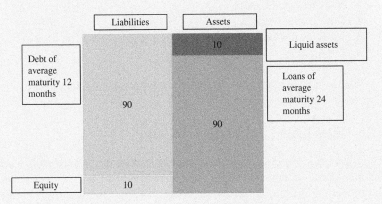

**Figure 17.6**   Recommended capital and liquidity position.

Reproduced from *The Principles of Banking* (2012)

This extract from *The Future of Finance* (2010)

## A Sustainable Bank Business Model: Capital, Liquidity, and Leverage

## A Sustainable Bank Business Model: Capital, Liquidity, and Leverage

The global financial crisis has had the effect of making all participants in the banking industry—from regulators, central banks, and governments to bank boards, directors, and trade associations—take a fundamental look at the principles of banking. Issues such as capital and liquidity management and systemic risk became the subject of renewed focus. In practical terms, legislators realized that they needed to address the issue of the too-big-to-fail bank, and this issue remains unresolved.

From the point of view of bank practitioners, the most important task is to address the issues of capital, liquidity, and risk management and work them into a coherent strategy that is designed to produce sustainable returns over the business cycle. In this chapter we discuss these topics and consider how bank strategy can be formulated to handle the changed requirements of the post-crisis age. The contents are laid out as follows:

- Bank business models
- Corporate governance
- Liqudity risk management
- Liquidity asset buffer

We list recommendations for the new banking approach in the conclusion at the end of this chapter.

## THE NEW BANK BUSINESS MODEL

The basic bank business model has remained unchanged since banks were first introduced in modern society. Of course, as it is as much art as science, the model parameters themselves can be set to suit the specific strategy of the individual bank, depending on whether the strategy operates at a higher or lower risk/reward profile. But the basic model is identical across all banks. In essence, banking involves taking risks, and then the effective management of that risk. This risk can be categorized as follows:

- Managing the bank's capital.
- Managing the liquidity mismatch. A fundamental ingredient of banking is *maturity transformation*, the recognition that loans (assets) generally have a longer tenor than deposits (liabilities).

If we wished to summarize the basic ingredients of the historical bank model, we might describe it in the following terms:

- Leverage: A small capital base is levered up into an asset pool that can be 10, 20, 30 times greater, or even higher.
- The gap: essentially funding short to lend long. The gap is a function of the conventional positively sloping yield curve, and dictated by the recognition of the asset-liability mismatch previously noted.
- Liquidity: an assumption that a bank will always be able to roll over funding as it falls due.
- Risk management: an understanding of credit or default risk.

These fundamentals remain unchanged. The critical issue for bank management, however, is that some of the assumptions behind the application of these fundamentals *have* changed, as demonstrated by the crash of 2007–2009. The changed landscape in the wake of the crisis has resulted in some hitherto seemingly safe or profitable business lines being viewed as risky. Although favorable conditions for banking may well return in due course, for the foreseeable future the challenge for banks will be to set their strategy only after first arriving at a true and full understanding of economic conditions as they exist today. The first subject for discussion is to consider what a realistic, sustainable return on capital target level should be, and that it is commensurate with the level of risk aversion desired by the board. The board should also consider the bank's capital availability, and what sustained amount of business this would realistically support. These two issues need to be addressed before the remainder of the bank's strategy can be considered.

## Bank Strategy

The most important function that a bank board can undertake is to set the bank's strategy. This is not as obvious as it sounds. It may be surprising to a layperson to see how often banks, both large and small, both sophisticated and plain vanilla, have no real articulated strategy, but this is a fact. What is vital is that banks have in place a coherent, articulated strategy that sets the tone for the entire business, from the top down.

In the first instance the board must take into account the current regulatory environment. This includes the requirements of the forthcoming Basel III rules. A bank cannot formulate strategy without a clear understanding of the environment in which it operates. Once this is achieved, before proceeding with a formal strategy the bank needs to determine in what markets it wishes to operate, with what products, and for what class of customer. All its individual business lines should be set up to operate within the main strategy, having identified the markets and customers.

In other words, a bank cannot afford to operate by simply meandering along, noting its peer group market share and return on equity (ROE), and making up strategy as it goes along. This approach, which again is evidently what many banks do indeed follow, however inadvertently, results in a senior management and board that are not fully aware of what the bank's liabilities and risk exposures are.

The first task is to understand one's operating environment, and then to incorporate a specific target market and product suite as the basis of its strategy. Concurrent with this, the bank must set its ROE target, which drives much of the bank's culture and ethos. It is important to get this part of the process right and at the start. Prior to the recent crash, it was common for banks to seek to increase revenue by adding to their risk exposure. Assets were added to the balance sheet or higher risk assets were taken on. In the bull market environment of 2001–2007, and allied to low funding costs as a result of low base interest rates, this resulted in ever higher ROE figures, to the point where it was common for even Tier 2 banks to target levels of 22 to 25 percent ROE in their business appraisal. This process was, of course, not tenable in the long run.

The second task, following immediately from the first, is to set a realistic ROE target and one that is sustainable over the entire business cycle. This cannot be done without educating board directors as well as shareholders, who must appreciate the new, lower ROE targets. Managing expectations will contribute to a more dispassionate review of strategy. As importantly, risk-adjusted ROE should also be set at a realistic level and not be allowed to increase. Hence, the board and shareholders must accept that lower ROE levels will become the standard. This should also be allied to lower leverage levels and higher capital ratios.

Concurrently with this process, a bank must also ask itself where its strength lies, and formulate its strategy around that. In other words, it is important to focus on core competencies. Again, the experience of the crash has served to demonstrate that many banks found themselves exposed to risk exposures that they did not understand. This may have been simply the holding of assets (such as structured finance securities) whose credit exposures, valuation, and secondary market liquidity they did not understand, or embarking on investment strategies such as negative basis trading without being aware of all the measurement parameters of such strategies.[1] To properly implement a coherent, articulate strategy, a bank needs to be aware of exactly what it does and does not have an expertise for undertaking, and not operate in products or markets in which it has no genuine knowledge base.

Allied to an understanding of core competence is a review of core and noncore assets. Bank strategy is not a static process or document, but rather a dynamic process. Regular reviews of the balance sheet need to be undertaken to identify any noncore assets, which can then be assessed to determine whether they remain compatible with the strategy. If they are not, then a realistic disposal process would need to be drawn up. In the long run, this is connected with an understanding of where the bank's real strengths lie. Long-term core assets may well differ from core assets, but this needs to be articulated explicitly. The decision of whether an asset is core or noncore, or core or long-term core, is a function of the bank's overall strategy of what its expertise is and what markets and customers it wishes to serve. These decisions will be embedded in the strategy and the bank's business model. This drives the choice of products and business lines that the bank feels it can add value in.

## Leverage Ratios

Elsewhere we discuss bank capital structure. There is no doubt that the new model for banking assumes higher capital ratios and buffers for all banks during the next 10 years. The higher level of capital will be substantial in some cases, because under the proposed Basel III rules, trading businesses will be required to hold up to three times as much capital as vanilla banking businesses. It is also evident that many bank jurisdictions will, in addition, implement leverage ratio limits.

A *leverage ratio* is the total value of a bank's assets relative to its equity capital. The financial crash highlighted the extent of risk taking by certain banks when measured using leverage ratios. As a measure of the ratio of assets to owner's equity, they are an explicit indication of risk exposure. Lehman Brothers' leverage ratio increased from approximately 24:1 in 2003 to over 31:1 by 2007. Such aggressive asset growth generated tremendous profits during the boom years, but exposed the bank to such an extent that even a 3 or 4 percent decline in the value of its assets would completely eliminate its equity. This duly happened.

The Basel Committee for Banking Supervision (BCBS), as well as some national regulatory authorities, will introduce a limit on leverage ratios as an added safety measure alongside capital requirements. In the aftermath of the crash it is accepted that bank leverage ratios have to adjust downward, and the prevailing sentiment today dictates that boards should be wary of a business model that ramps up the ratio to an excessive level. Figure 9.1 shows levels during 2007–2009; prudent management suggests average levels will be much lower than these figures during the next 10 to

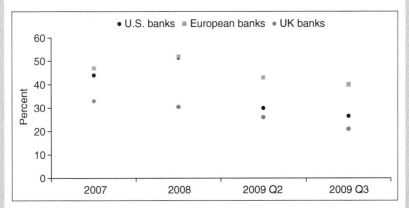

**Figure 9.1**  Bank Median Leverage Ratios, 2007–2009
*Source*: Bank of England (2009)

15 years. Not only is this business best practice, but lower average leverage ratio levels will also contribute to greater systemic stability.

Bank management will have to adjust to a concept of an explicit ratio limit, the rationale for which is clear. The experience of the recent and previous crises has shown that during a period of upside growth, banks' risk models tend to underestimate their exposure. This has two consequences: (1) The bank takes on ever greater risk, as it targets greater revenue and profit during a bull market, and (2) the amount of capital set aside is below what is adequate at the time the crash occurs.

Figure 9.2, which shows a sample of bulge-bracket banks, suggests that banks focused on trading assets as they expanded their balance sheets. In such an environment, capital ratio requirements are an insufficient safeguard against instability, and it becomes necessary to monitor leverage ratios. Hence, in the post-crash environment banks need to adjust their business strategy to allow for this constraint.

As we noted earlier in the case of Lehman Brothers, excessively high leverage results in a higher sensitivity of the balance sheet to trading and/or default losses. Limiting the amount of leverage acts as an additional risk control measure, backing up the safety net provided by a regulatory capital buffer. In advance of the introduction of a standardized ratio, as part of a future Basel III, banks can address this issue themselves as part of their prudential capital and risk management.

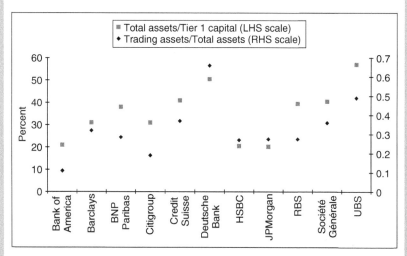

**Figure 9.2**   Selected Bank Ratios of Total Assets to Tier 1 Capital and Trading Assets to Total Assets
*Source*: Bank of England (2009).

Note that a number of jurisdictions already employ a leverage ratio limit, although there is no uniform definition (see Table 9.1). It is likely that the new Basel III rules will incorporate a limit, with a common definition of capital and an agreed measure of all assets, both on- and off-balance-sheet.

## Core Competence: Know Your Risk

Regulatory authorities noticed a considerable decline in cross-border lending flows in the aftermath of the Lehman bankruptcy (for instance, see the Bank of England's *Financial Stability Report* dated June 2009). This is significant. During the bull market of 2001–2007, international lending volumes had expanded steadily (see Figure 9.4), as banks grew their balance sheets and sought higher yield opportunities elsewhere.

It is evident that during and after the bank crisis, when interbank market liquidity had dried up, banks pulled back from overseas markets, irrespective of whether these were deemed peripheral, and concentrated on core markets. This reflects informational advantages in core markets compared to overseas and noncore markets. The UK corporate lending sector makes a case in point: Between 2002 and 2009, lending volume from UK banks fell by approximately 16 percent (the figure between 2006 and 2009 was a decline of 14 percent). However, the equivalent figures for foreign subsidiaries was a fall of 10.5 percent and 20 percent while for foreign branches the decline was even more dramatic, at 17 percent and 46 percent. Foreign banks would, on average, have less depth and breadth of corporate

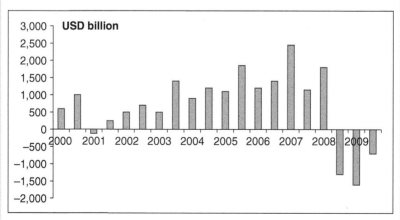

**Figure 9.4** Cross-Border Bank Lending Volumes, 2000–2009
*Source*: Bank of England (2009).

relationships, while branches would be expected to have even less developed relationships in the domestic market.

The lessons for the bank business model are clear: During an expansionary phase, it is important to remain focused on areas of core competence and sectors in which the bank possesses actual knowledge and strength. Concentrating on areas in which the bank carries a competitive advantage makes it less likely that loan origination standards will decline, resulting in lower losses during an economic downturn. There is also a technical reason for ensuring that overseas lending standards are maintained strictly, and limits set carefully, because it is often undertaken in foreign currency. A bank's ability to fund such lending is more dependent on external markets and wholesale counterparties relative to domestic lending, thus making the bank more vulnerable to a market downturn. For example, the cross-currency swap market in U.S. dollars came under pressure, resulting in higher swap prices, following the Lehman default, and many banks struggled to obtain dollar funding.

Reproduced from *The Future of Finance* (2010)

## BANK STRATEGY INPUTS AND SETTING

This section provides an overview of the development of a strategy for a bank, as well as the identification of the likely key elements of a strategic plan for a bank. Of course strategy is a vast topic, so those wishing to have a deeper understanding should become familiar with some of the writings in this domain.

The development of an effective strategy is as much an art as a science. Fundamental analytic work is a key element of the process, however, the crafting of an effective strategy requires much more. Equally important is a deep understanding of the organisation itself – its key strengths ("core competencies" which we will return to later) and its key weaknesses in the environment within which the entity operates – the markets, the competitors, and the regulatory framework – and the emerging trends and forces likely to shape the future environment. The art lies in the integration of all this information and the distillation of the relevant actions that the organisation needs to implement to improve its competitive positioning – the essence of strategy.

Many different methodologies are employed to assist with this process. Robust analytics assist with the understanding of internal financial dynamics (for example, the profitability of business units or products) and some elements of market and consumer dynamics. Insightful analysis of competitor performance can also be of value in the process. However, strategy is all about changing course for some preferred future positioning of the organisation (strategy is seldom, if ever, about what needs to be done to maintain the current "status quo"), and this is where intuition is often as powerful a player as logic. The preferred future positioning needs to be identified and articulated, and a bridge needs to be built from where the organisation currently stands to that future positioning. An overview of this process is discussed later.

For most corporate entities, the lack of an effective strategy raises the risk of leading to a "slow death" – the gradual loss of a commercial franchise in its chosen marketplace, as it succumbs to the efforts of its competitors – unless it is in the unusual position of being a monopoly, without any threat of substitution. This effect leads to attrition – loss of clients, loss of profitability, loss of talented staff, consolidation, and eventual bankruptcy or takeover.

A similar process may happen with a bank as well, but there is one key aspect of a bank that normally hastens this process: banking is built on trust and confidence and when that erodes, the effects can be and usually are a "rapid death". When a bank loses the trust of its clients and the market, deposits are withdrawn, new funding dries up, and bad debts may increase. Sometimes it is the increase in bad debts (credit losses) to unforeseen levels that erodes confidence in a bank, and if the bank has insufficient capital to weather the storm, it will have a rapid demise. Similarly, a bank with an unsustainable asset–liability mismatch may suddenly experience a liquidity crisis, the triggering of which may also lead to a credit crisis, which will be followed by a rapid demise. The actual failure of a bank is seldom a slow process, but rather a rapid one and is usually led by a liquidity or credit crisis, but often by both. That said, banks can also suffer a slow death, leading to irrelevance and insignificance without actually going bust. Such firms may find themselves takeover targets or being asked by the regulator to merge if they are deemed unsustainable.

For this reason, it is essential that the strategic plan of a bank includes at its centre robust capital and liquidity management plans which can deal with all challenges through the various expected (and unexpected) phases of the business cycle – it has to be financially robust through the business cycle and not just when the "weather is fair". The strength of the bank's balance sheet throughout the business cycle lies at the heart of any effective strategic plan for a bank.

In this chapter, we distinguish between the annual business plan or budget and the strategic plan. A strategic plan typically describes a process of development or change in the entity, including high-level financial outcomes over an extended period of time (three to five years). The business plan or budget captures the planned set of activities and expected financial outcomes for the next year, by month / quarter, and possibly for the following year. The annual business plan or budget is the year-by-year roll out of the longer-term strategic plan and must therefore be structured to deliver the strategic plan one year at a time, for the duration of the strategic plan period. This chapter focuses on the development and shape of an effective strategic plan and not the annual business plan.

## The Strategic Planning Process

Strategy is about defining a path from where an organisation is at present to where it would prefer to be in the future and preparing a plan to get there. This involves the enquiry and development of responses to a number of basic questions:

- Where are we today? What is the imperative to change? (Often described as the "Current Reality");
- What should we aim to become? Why? (The "Preferred Future" or "Vision");
- What do we need to do to take us from our "Current Reality" to our "Preferred Future"? ("Strategic Initiatives"); note the answer to this may not be something substantial, it may well be just some minor tweaks that are required;
- What enablers are required to ensure that we can execute the planned "Strategic Initiatives"?

This is the start of a multi-year commitment to some form of organisational change, possibly of significant magnitude, and the importance thereof is reflected in the fact that the Board of the enterprise must agree on the strategic plan.

It is often said that 80% of strategic plans fail to deliver their expected results. Much of this is due to execution failure, where the combination of lack of resources, change fatigue, and executive impatience undermine the implementation of the strategic plan. Frequently, this is a direct result of a lack of executive commitment to the plan in the face of various difficulties that are encountered. Consequently, the commitment of both the Board and executive management to the desired outcome and the associated strategic plan is critical to a successful execution of the plan.

**Step 1**    The first stage in the process is an honest and open interrogation of the "current reality" of the enterprise: How are we performing? What is being done well? What are the weaknesses? Where do our strengths lie?

What are our customers saying? What are our competitors doing to improve their position? How well are we responding to changes in our environment / market / industry? This is not a simple exercise, as it requires insight and honesty and is based on an in-depth analysis which together leads to a thoughtful assessment. It is easy to be overly complacent or overly critical, but neither is helpful.

There are three key outputs from this stage of the process:

- First, a good understanding of the imperative for change – do we have to do something other than "business as usual", and if so what should that be? This is crucial to ensuring internal alignment with the strategic objectives. Also, it is often the point at which Boards, often at small banks and/or family-owned banks, fall down and fail to proceed forward in a genuine fashion;
- Secondly, a clear view of aspects of the business around which future developments can take place ("core competencies"), or where changes need to be made, or where new skills may be needed;
- Thirdly, how the entity's current market positioning affects its ability to realise their goals.

**Step 2**    Based on this assessment, the next step is to consider what the entity should become, for example, over the following five years. This is often crafted in the form of a "vision statement", which describes the organisation in five years' time. It articulates what the organisation strives to be and the manner in which it intends to operate, and the statement should further be crafted in a form that captures the imagination of both internal and external stakeholders. It is always short on detail (the "how"); this is explained later. There is also no template; such statements can be brief or a "one pager", depending on the organisation and audience, but what it has to do is articulate a preferred high-level future state for the entity.[4]

Sometimes, as this is organisation dependent, a vision statement will precede or be in existence prior to the assessment of the current reality, and it may be that failure to achieve the previously crafted vision is what drives the re-evaluation. It is also possible that the vision statement exists in the form of a "grand ambition" – "to be the best / biggest. . ." – to the extent that such a statement is far removed from the organisation's current reality.

It remains important, however, that any "vison statement" is built on a thorough understanding of the organisation and the environment

---

[4] At this point many banks, indeed many corporates generally, fall victim to bureaucratic processes and produce no more than meaningless platitudes. Vision statements rarely articulate a genuine "vision".

within which it operates. In the absence of this, any "vison statement" runs the real risk of being no more than wishful thinking, detached from reality, and doomed to failure.

Few strategic plans survive in the absence of a compelling "vision statement", simply because without a vision statement in one form or other, the strategic plan lacks a motive – why are we trying to do all this?

**Step 3**   The third stage involves identifying those developments that the entity needs to undertake to enable it to approximate the organisation described in the vision or "preferred future". These often take the form of high level "strategic initiatives" which, in turn, are supported by many detailed projects spread throughout the organisation. It may not be important to scope or identify all the supporting projects at the outset, but it is imperative that the eventual outcome is kept clearly in mind throughout. These strategic initiatives, in turn, define the strategic priorities throughout the organisation and should also shape the allocation of resources. Annual business plans / budgets should also make it clear how they intend to advance the agreed strategic initiatives.

The definition of the strategic initiatives is seldom a trivial matter; appropriate scoping must always be based on a deep understanding of the resource base available to support an initiative. For example, if a strategic initiative within a bank calls for geographical expansion, problems are foreseen if the bank has minimal scalable and transportable business processes or significant depth of management, or, especially, if the bank has little risk management experience in the targeted region.

**Step 4**   Finally, consideration should be applied to which resources and support needs are to be provided to enable the strategic initiatives. Day-to-day business activities will continue for most of the organisation, and to simply add strategic initiative work to the workload of people responsible for normal operations often results in failure. How to resource for the strategic initiatives and type of support needed by those involved, is also a key consideration. Often, this aspect of a plan needs to address matters such as corporate culture and the relationship the entity has with its employees because such "soft" matters will often define the manner in which employees respond to the challenges in the strategic plan.

Of fundamental importance to the strategic plan is the commitment of senior management, up to and including the Chief Executive (and the Board). Operational management may not welcome changes that affect their daily lives and there may be resistance to requirements for change or additional effort. Management at all levels has a keen ability to find ways to test the commitment of senior management to a plan, and any cvidence of hesitation or ambivalence on the part of executive management will initiate the process of erosion for the foundations of a strategic plan. It is thus vital that the commitment of the executive management be seen continuously by everyone throughout the entity for the strategic plan to have any chance of success.

The overall process may be represented diagrammatically at Figure 16.1.

There are many tools, approaches, and techniques that can be of help with the development of an integrated strategy as described above, but irrespective of the methods used the output of such a process must cover all five aspects of Figure 16.1 if it is to be successful.

## Considerations in the Development of Strategy

The previous section considered the *process* involved in the development of a strategic plan. In this section we consider the *key influencers and drivers* of a strategic plan, particularly in the context of a bank. These are the factors that will have to be analysed and understood in order to develop the plan as described previously.

**Stakeholder Expectations** What is expected of the entity by its various stakeholders, including shareholders, regulators, and clients? Shareholder expectations assist in defining financial targets. Client expectations – considering both current and future clients – may assist in defining product and service delivery expectations. The expectations (and requirements) of regulators, particularly in the banking industry, may have a significant impact on what is possible, and the resources, both financial (often in the form of capital), and people are required to support a particular plan.

Within a banking environment (and generally), these expectations provide an important input into the development of a bank's "risk appetite", which will in turn provide an important overlay to the development

**FIGURE 16.1** Leadership Commitment

of the bank's strategic plan. The overall "risk appetite" will also be guided by a number of factors.

**The Macro (Economic) and Micro (Market and Market Segment) Environment**   Views on development with regard to future macroeconomic and market developments will play a significant role in the shaping of the plan. However, one has to bear in mind that predictions can be dangerous and therefore any chosen business strategy should be robust under various scenarios. For a bank, this is particularly important, where capital and liquidity management under various scenarios is a key aspect of any plan. (Note that the regulator will be a keen reviewer of the bank's articulated medium-term strategy.)

**The Competitive Landscape**   No entity, including a bank, operates in a vacuum. Peers, both direct and indirect, are continuously seeking some form of competitive advantage and any strategic plan will have to take into account the changing competitive landscape. This will include a deep understanding of the customer franchise and their changes in response to both the entity's actions and those of its competitors. This analysis will suggest product and market segment developments, or perhaps some form of geographical expansion or change; it may also suggest marketing initiatives designed to reposition the entity within its chosen market and market segments.

The entity is in control of its response to its environment and the changing competitive landscape: for a bank, all actions should be designed to reinforce an image of trustworthiness and stability, whatever other attributes they may seek to highlight. In addition, dramatic changes to how or where the bank operates are likely to be negatively viewed.

**Resource Capacity**   This simply asks the question: Does the entity have the resources to undertake the plan? We will separately (see below) consider the balance sheet implications because this is such an important matter for banks in particular – here we limit the question to people, skills, and processes. This is linked to the question of core competencies, but also addresses the issue of "capacity". This will inform the assessment for the resources required to support the plan, covering aspects as varied as financial / budgets, people and training, management support and communication, and equipment. Failure to address this will fuel employee discontent and build resistance to the implementation of the plan.

**Organisational Structure**   It has been said that "structure follows strategy", and for good reason. A key element in the development of the overall plan is the organisational structure required to properly support the plan. Structure should be shaped by a number of factors that emerge from the strategic plan, and would typically address how:

- To best engage with its chosen markets;
- To best deliver the products / services to the chosen markets;
- To best leverage and/or build the identified "core competencies"; and
- To operate within acceptable cost and pricing constraints.

Within an entity such as a bank, the resultant structures are seldom simple, and care needs to be taken to ensure that clear accountability is maintained.

This also suggests the need for clarity of purpose: the future of business units that do not naturally fit into the defined strategy should be considered with care as such entities are often management diversions and potential sources of unwanted problems.

**Capital and Funding**  For most organisations, the question of capital and funding is limited to the access to sufficient funding and capital to enable the execution of the strategy. There may also be questions of risk management should there be reliance on third parties for the funding. For banks, however, capital and funding are central to any strategic plan. The bank should be able to demonstrate its robustness, within the context of its chosen strategy, throughout a full business cycle as well as under extreme stress scenarios. Such a consideration is a regulatory requirement in any case, and needs to cover both the sufficiency of capital and access to liquidity under both "fair weather" and adverse business conditions.

For this reason, capital and liquidity management (in effect, the structure of the bank's balance sheet) lie at the heart of the bank's strategic plan and will guide the bank's capacity for embarking on the strategic plan. For many banks, in the Basel III era the issue will be building their capital base to meet the new requirements and restructuring their depositor and funding base to improve their liquidity profile; for the lucky few it may be more an issue of maintenance of appropriate capital levels and funding profiles. Whatever the position of a bank, these issues remain central to the development of their strategic plan and any plan will continuously be tested against its potential impact on capital levels and liquidity profiles. Similarly, the strategic plan will have to take an account of the bank's ability to attract appropriate duration funding, and where necessary, to raise capital over the entire planning period. Hence, the capital management plan and liquidity management plan will both be core elements of any bank's strategic plan.

**Risk Appetite**  Risk appetite is a key Board-driven factor that shapes bank strategy. Risk appetite is defined by a number of factors, including:

- Board and shareholder appetite for variations in financial performance and expected levels of profitability (for example, return on equity or return on capital – see below);
- Absolute and relative levels of loss absorption of capital and regulatory requirements;
- Funding structures and liquidity profiles;
- Reputational and market positioning of the bank;
- Operational robustness and managerial capacity.

A recommended template Board risk appetite statement was presented in Chapter 10. Its content drives the strategic plan. For example, rapid growth of the balance sheet is unlikely to be a choice for a bank with a low tolerance for credit risk surprises, while geographical expansion might not be a top priority for a bank with a low tolerance for operational risk – however, this may well be a strategic option for a bank with significant capital buffers, robust operational processes, and a deep pool of managerial talent. For this reason, the strategic plan will have to be assessed against the framework of the risk appetite approved by the Board. An element of this includes the capital and liquidity management plans as discussed previously.

## Universal Objectives

It is unsurprising that there are a number of strategic objectives that will be found universally within banking, particularly following the implementation of the Basel III regulatory regime. These may be summarised as:

- To **ensure adequate capital buffers,** in terms of both quantity and quality, to meet the requirements of Basel III; for many banks, this called for an increase in capital, a process that is not complete at the time of writing this chapter. It also requires effective ongoing management of capital buffers;
- To **improve capital efficiency** via, for example, existing loan book restructuring and "optimising" collateral management;
- To investigate **"capital-light" growth opportunities** within existing knowledge and resource base;
- To **lower cost structures** via a combination of improving business processes to reduce operational costs, simplifying operating models, headcount reduction or out-sourcing; and/or
- To **review the portfolio of business units** within the bank; this may lead to the disposal of unprofitable or non-core business lines for reasons

such as strategic fit or failure to achieve target risk adjusted return on capital;

- To implement more **robust and stable funding structures**, particularly with respect to higher-cost longer-term funds.

The first and last of these are demanded explicitly in the Basel III regime, in the form of higher capital buffers of varying types and adherence to structural liquidity metrics. Of course the first three are essentially platitudes – all businesses would seek to maximise capital efficiency and minimise the cost–income ratio at all times, simply as good operating practice.

However, to be considered a genuine long-term contender in banking requires more than this in fact: no less than a specific defined customer-orientated differentiation of one's business model. The competitive environment for banks remains challenging. This is particularly the case for banks domiciled in countries that experienced a sovereign bail-out, where there is additional pressure associated with continuing poor public image and reputation. Under such circumstances, it is unsurprising that differentiating oneself from the competition presents difficulties for bank Boards and senior management, particularly in view of the commoditised nature of the basic bank product.

The requirements of Basel III standards and those of national regulators will play a major role in influencing bank strategy. Of course, the Board must have its own view on sustainable banking, and consider the regulatory standards to be a minimum requirement. The specific areas of capital and liquidity, as well as sound asset origination policy, must be set by the Board in line with its own beliefs and understanding. To summarise, the basic strategy is identical for all banks in that it must ensure that the entity meets regulatory requirements. At the individual bank level, strategy should reflect core competence and risk appetite strengths.

## FROM VISION TO A STRATEGIC PLAN

The most important function that a bank's Board and senior executives can undertake is to set the firm's strategy. The process that should be followed, at least in broad outline, is as described earlier in this chapter. In the following we will discuss certain specific aspects of a bank strategic plan.

The first subject for discussion is to consider what a realistic, sustainable return on capital target level should be, and that it is commensurate with the level of risk aversion desired by the Board as defined in the risk appetite statement. Setting these targets at appropriate levels and in a manner that does not encourage behaviour that is inconsistent with the risk appetite or general ethos of the bank is very important. It is also important that the target be clearly understood as a "through-the-cycle" target – on average, through both good and bad years!

Investment markets relate more easily to Return on Equity (RoE) and Return on Assets (RoA) targets, but they suffer because they are not "risk adjusted", as a result, the use of RoE and RoA is no longer best-practice. There are a number of ways to approach the question of an appropriate risk adjusted return metric that reflects the changing risk profile of the bank's underlying business:

- "Return on Capital" could be defined as return on the total regulatory capital required for the bank, combining both Pillar I and Pillar II requirements. By definition, this is a "risk adjusted" metric. However, a bank may, and often does, choose to keep a higher level of capital, including its own defined capital buffers. If such additional capital margins are included in the "C", as they are at the discretion of the bank, the robustness of the definition of "C" should be carefully considered;
- Alternatively, one could use "risk adjusted" return or capital metrics. This calls for the use of "economic profit" rather than accounting profit, or "economic capital" rather than regulatory capital. These approaches would provide "risk adjusted return on capital" (RARoC) and return on risk adjusted capital (RoRAC or RoEC) measures respectively. Both would need careful definition and to satisfy the challenge of both robustness and transparency;
- Return on Risk-Weighted Assets (RoRWA) is also a commonly used risk adjusted metric.

Ultimately both RoC (and the other variations) and RoRWA link to "equity", as the bank needs sufficient "equity" to back the capital implicit in both numbers. In addition, the quite natural question from investors is: "What return is the bank generating on the funds we, as investors, have left in the bank?" Even if the bank uses RoE targets in discussion with the investment community, it would be wise to adopt a risk-adjusted measure for strategic plan purposes, and deal with the link between "equity" held and "capital" requirements as a separate investor discussion.

The choice of the target return metric is not necessarily a simple one and is evidently an important part of the strategy formulation process; the target chosen (form and level) will influence much of the bank's culture and ethos. The two key issues, the return target – both unadjusted and adjusted for risk – and the availability of capital to support business within the bank's risk appetite need to be addressed before the remainder of the bank's strategy can be considered.

The regulatory environment has become a major factor in all banks' strategic deliberations; often, an actual or even anticipated, regulatory environment will be shaping a bank's strategy. The Board must take into account the current regulatory environment, as well as trends and developments likely to shape future activities. This includes of course the requirements of Basel III, as well as any specific requirements of the national regulator. It will also consider carefully its competitive environment and the developments within the markets it serves (and does not!). To assist with the decision as to its chosen product / market focus areas, the bank will need to consider where its genuine expertise resides and the extent of its capacity – its "core competencies".

To properly implement a coherent, articulate strategy, a bank needs to be aware of exactly what it does and does not have an expertise for undertaking, and not operate in products or markets in which it has no genuine knowledge base. The experience of the crash showed that many banks found themselves with balance sheet risk exposures that they did not realise they had, and did not understand. This may have been simply the holding of assets (such as structured finance securities) whose credit exposures, valuation, and secondary market liquidity they did not understand, or otherwise embarking on investment strategies such as cash-synthetic negative basis trading without being aware of all the risk measurement parameters of such strategies.

The lessons for the bank business model and strategy-setting are clear: during an expansionary phase, it is important to remain focused on areas of core competence and those sectors in which the bank possesses genuine knowledge and understanding. Concentrating on areas in which the bank carries competitive advantage makes it less likely that loan origination standards will decline, resulting in lower losses during an economic downturn. There is also a technical reason for ensuring that overseas lending standards are strictly maintained, and limits set carefully, because it is often undertaken in foreign currency. Where no customer funding base exists in the overseas location, a bank's ability to fund such lending is more dependent on external markets and wholesale counterparties relative to domestic lending, thus making the bank more vulnerable to a market downturn.

Based on this capacity assessment (including capital availability), the bank needs to make strategic choices such as what markets it should operate in, what products it sells, and what class of customer it wishes to serve. This defines the specific target markets and product suites chosen by the bank as the basis of its strategy, after taking into account what resources are currently in place, and if these are insufficient, what additional resources are needed before embarking on the strategy.

Individual business lines should be set up to operate in alignment with the overall strategy. *In other words, all the business lines exist as ingredients of the same one strategy.* If a business line is not a fit with the current or future strategy, it should be exited. Equally, if a bank wishes to enter into new business where the fit with the agreed strategy is not clear, either the strategy or the acquisition should be challenged; put simply, it is difficult, if not impossible to "ride two horses at once". This sounds obvious, but there are many cases of banks entering piecemeal into different businesses, or maintaining unsuitable lines that have been inherited through previous growth or acquisition, all usually leading to some future difficulty.

As previously noted, to compete effectively in most banking markets, a clearly defined customer-orientated differentiation of one's business model that is experienced by customers in the target markets is required. There are many elements to this, but all will be underpinned by the "core competencies" of the bank if they are to be robust and sustainable.

One element of this may be the pricing strategy applied by the bank. Banks charge for their products and services in many different ways; in some countries, banking is portrayed as being "free", which, of course, it is not. Elsewhere bank charges are more explicit and have become a competitive element. Pricing also relates to the setting of interest rate margins and fees, and the extent to which these prices reflect the risk of a particular product and client – applied at client level, this is an element of the so-called "use test" applied by regulators since the introduction of Basel II – while appropriate pricing to match the cost of longer duration funding that may be required for specific products helps balance the supply of and demand for longer dated funds and hence the bank's overall matching. Most of the deliberations around pricing naturally take place at business unit and/or product owner level, but from time to time, pricing may be a component of the overall strategic plan. Ultimately, there needs to be a clear link of pricing into the returns objectives of the plan.

Finally, a comment on the "cost to income" ratio: The cost to income ratio is a widely used measure of the efficiency of a bank, and there is a natural and ongoing drive to improve efficiency. There are always new demands being placed on how a bank interacts with its customers, and there seems to be a constant upgrading of the technology at play. Regulation, too, plays a part in the need for additional technology, whether because of growing regulation relating to customer information or additional information required by the regulator for oversight purposes. However, the construct of this measure within a bank needs to be carefully understood before setting targets, as different parts of a bank's operation may have distinctly different cost structures. This also suggests some caution before simply comparing one bank's cost to income ratio with another, as the relative sizes and structures of the different business units may differ.

## Bank Strategy Setting Cycle

Figure 16.2 is a stylised representation of the typical bank strategy (and typically, budget setting) cycle as practised by banks for many years prior to 2008. However, the crash showed the obvious flaw in this paradigm, in that it is too heavily skewed towards a profit and unconstrained Return on Equity (RoE) incentive without regard to or adjustment for risks being undertaken by the bank. This in turn leads to "market share" targets set by senior executives. A market share target, while logical and understandable for a clothes retailer or a supermarket, is quite possibly the most inappropriate target to set at a banking institution.

The problem with this approach to strategy formulation is that it pays insufficient attention to the risks being undertaken by the bank, and the impact on the balance sheet itself, including capital and liquidity risk management – with results that were apparent in 2008 and 2009 in the USA and Europe, as well as a number of banks in the MENA and GCC regions. The direction of strategy setting – with the unconstrained RoE target driving the process in a clockwise direction – also results in business lines extending into areas of the market that they may not necessarily possess any genuine expertise in. The obvious flaw in the process lies in the dangerous assumption it makes about capital and funding liquidity: *that they will always be*

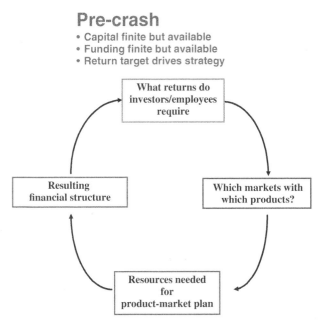

**FIGURE 16.2**   Strategy-setting cycle, pre-crash

*available.* Such an approach means that balance sheet risk management is secondary to profit and growth ambitions.

The recommended approach to strategy formulation emphasises the primacy of balance sheet risk management in the process when it comes to bank strategy setting. This reflects more prudent management practices, and is illustrated at Figure 16.3. It shows clearly the change in strategy-setting culture that has been demanded as a result of the crash. The cycle is now resource-constraint driven, and anti-clockwise in direction on the diagram, compared to the clockwise process that was heavily influenced by return target, often unadjusted for risk, in the pre-crash era.

Figure 16.3 states that a bank's resource base, and its ability to grow it over the economic cycle, including the availability of funding from capital markets, should drive the strategy forward, rather than the other way round. In practice, the process is more iterative than may be suggested, and the stages may be considered simultaneously during the strategy setting cycle. The key point is that this approach recognises the importance of the balance sheet and its shape and structure over the economic cycle (and indeed, in perpetuity – unless the bank has an objective to wind itself up at some point in the future), and the critical resource constraints that may arise with respect to capital and liquidity from time to time.

## Post-crash

- Capital and liquidity more expensive and constrained
- Funding now driven by regulatory requirements
- Resource base constraints drives strategy
- Balance sheet optimisation need drives strategy: decide on optimum financial structure first

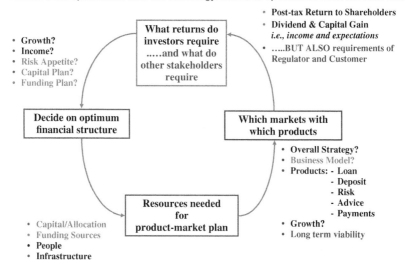

**FIGURE 16.3** Strategy-setting cycle, post-crash

## Strategy Setting: Sustainable Banking Through the Cycle

Inherent to the strategic framework for a bank is the belief that strategy should be *sustainable*. That is, it should focus on preserving returns and capital strength through the business cycle. This belief needs to be a genuine part of the Board's thinking. In other words, the bank needs to stick to its core strengths and not be overly influenced by KPIs which emphasise growth, such as balance sheet growth or market share, over resilience during a bull market phase in the economic cycle.

Allied to this is governments' and regulators' conversion to the idea of "macro-prudential" strategy: Although the practical impact of this sort of thinking is not new, it had just been forgotten in recent years.

As a result, bank strategy needs to consider two key aspects of sustainable banking:

- **Macro-prudential:** Banks should strengthen their balance sheets and liquidity ratios during the expansionary period of the economic cycle, while profits are growing and conditions are benign. This can be done by:
  - Limiting the asset-side growth of their balance sheet;
  - Retaining a greater proportion of profits as reserves during the bull market phase;
  - Setting a leverage ratio limit (the Basel III leverage ratio limit of 3% can be set as an upper bound with a more conservative internal limit).
- **Micro-prudential:** At all times, banks should maintain an appropriate level, and quality of capital and liquid asset buffers; they should also seek to increase the average tenor of liabilities in order to improve the mismatch position. Both elements work towards preserving a bank as a going concern irrespective of the state of the economy. Higher capital ratios and absolute levels per se should act as a more effective buffer to cushion the impact of an economic downturn, when business volumes decrease and loan losses increase; at the same time a more conservative liquidity regime, with limits on use of wholesale funding and larger gaps means that a bank will be less able to grow rapidly during a boom period in the cycle.

The importance of the macro-prudential aspect of a bank's strategy arises from the phenomenon of "herd mentality", found in all industries and not just banking. Senior executives, inexplicably, often find it difficult to resist a prevailing trend even if that runs counter to one's better instincts. This is illustrated at Figure 16.4. This shows the increase in the funding gap, measured as customer loans less customer deposits, on an aggregate basis for four large UK banks during the period 1997–2009. The worsening customer loan-deposit ratio (LDR) during this time, which was mirrored across the individual banks, is a perfect example of how banks can end up adopting the same approach when the latest fad is mistaken for business best-practice. Bank management needs to be mindful of this danger during a bull market.

In assessing what factors should form part of strategy formulation, it is also worth noting those factors that should be viewed with extreme caution when they make an appearance as part of a bank's strategy. The bank crisis of 2007–2008, as well as previous banking failures such as the US bank crash of 1980–1982 and the "zombie" banks experience in Japan in the 1990s, all resulted from banks adopting a management approach that allowed them to become over-extended through:

- Ever greater risk-taking and leverage levels;
- Over-reliance on wholesale funding;
- Increasing exposure to higher-risk product classes, such as 100% LTV mortgages, adjustable-rate mortgages, buy-to-let mortgages, or derivatives trading;
- Poor management decisions involving overly ambitious acquisitions or expansion of new business lines;
- Emphasis on market share and high RoE as KPI targets, thereby driving excessive risk-taking.

Evidence of any of the above in a bank's strategic plan should serve as a warning light with regard to the sustainability of the plan through the cycle.

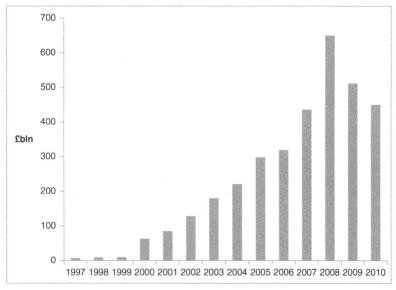

**FIGURE 16.4**   UK banks customer funding gap, 1997–2009
*Data Source*: ECB.

## Capital Management as Part of the Strategic Plan

As noted above, capital management is an integral part of a bank's strategic plan. The capital strategy follows on from the overall strategy, and describes how and what capital is allocated to each business line. It should be a coherent, articulated, and formal plan of action which builds on a regular review of the business, allocation of capital to those businesses, and the desired return on capital, adjusted and unadjusted for risk.

As a key part of strategy, the capital management framework at a bank should address the requirements of all the various stakeholders. It should be communicated in a transparent fashion to all internal and external stakeholders, articulating:

- How the risk appetite is aligned to their needs and expectations;
- How and why capital allocation and capital constraints are integrated with funding capabilities and assigned to each business line;
- The extent of tolerance for earnings volatility;
- The framework in which each of the business lines operate, with respect to risk exposure and the type of business undertaken;
- Strategy and implications on business plans.

Stress testing is an important part of the process; the results of this testing feed into an assessment of the robustness of the plan through different business conditions, as well as testing the plan against the bank's risk appetite. An integrated approach to stress test design and processing is vital, as described in Chapter 14.

However, capital management is as much about the quality of the capital as it is about the quantity; while regulators have raised the amount of capital required by a bank significantly, post-2008, they have also required significant changes to the quality of the capital, with a much stronger focus on the accessibility of the capital in times of crisis. Accordingly, capital management strategy also has to address the structure of the capital base over the planning period, ensuring the maintenance of the quality of the capital.

## Typical Elements of a Bank's Strategic Plan

This section considers what might be expected in a typical bank's strategic plan. Some would consider this an ambitious goal because one finds in practice so many different presentations and areas of focus. What follows therefore can best be described as an attempt to highlight those features that should be present in some form or other, if the plan is to succeed.

## Objectives

As discussed above, the strategic objectives of the bank should be framed by a vision statement that is embraced by the Board and executive management.

These strategic objectives will range in nature and in character, but there are a few that should be found in all plans, due to the nature of banking. We would expect to find strategic objectives covering the following four aspects of a bank's operations at least, and under each we set out some of the issues that may be specifically addressed. Note the points are not exhaustive:

Financial:
- Capital strength: What capital the bank will have as it executes its strategy, both quantity and quality; target ratios; sources of capital; steps to be taken to ensure the maintenance of confidence in the bank by customers, markets, and regulators;
- Profitability: What profitability / return targets the bank has and the key drivers of the planned change in return; business actions to be taken to impact the drivers;
- Balance sheet structure: Planned changes in the nature and structure of the bank's balance sheet with a specific focus on liquidity management; funding strategies; limits to balance sheet growth;
- Cost structures: Planned cost targets (for example, cost to income); specific cost reduction targets or planned extraordinary expenditure;
- Sources of income: Plans for improving the "quality" of the bank's income – annuity vs once off; net interest income vs fee income;
- Risks to the planned financial outcomes and actions to mitigate the risks.

Customers and the competitive environment:
- Which markets the bank intends to serve and segments within those markets, and why;
- The positioning of the bank within those markets and segments and how it will achieve this;
- The differentiation of the bank's market propositions;
- Business objectives and targets for the targeted segments and markets;
- Dealing with challenges from competitors (both current and potential);
- Improving the bank's relationship with customers;
- Positioning the bank as a "good corporate citizen".

Business capacity and capabilities:
- What core competencies are to be leveraged and how;
- Structure of the organisation; acquisition and divestment plans;
- How the bank intends dealing with changes in the regulatory environment and other environmental impacts such as market changes, technology, and even climate change;

- Information technology infrastructure development (critical within a bank);
- Revisions to major product / business lines;
- Expense reduction activities.

Skills and people:
- Development and retention of the talent pool within the bank;
- Development of new core competencies;
- Major training and development programmes;
- Support activities for major strategic initiatives.

The above categorisation of potential issues within a typical strategic plan is based on the "Balanced Scorecard" approach developed by Kaplan and Norton in their book *The Strategy Focussed Organisation* (Harvard Business School Press, 2001).

**Financial Targets and metrics ("KPIs")**   Table 16.1 illustrates a set of key metrics and targets that should be covered in a bank's strategic plan, as well as the annual budgets. Within the strategic plan, explicitly longer-term targets for certain of the key metrics should be set. The table also shows how the metrics might apply to a bank with three lines of business: Treasury, Corporate Banking, and Retail Banking.

**Strategy as a Dynamic Process**   Notwithstanding that "strategy" is geared towards the medium- and long term, the process by which it is formulated and approved needs to be flexible in order to respond quickly and efficiently to changing events. This includes changes in the competitive arena, changes enforced by regulatory fiat, market events that result in higher balance sheet resource costs, and so on.

Part of the strategy will therefore have to include the so-called "Plan B" or action to be taken in the event of any of these types of occurrences. A good example would be the contingency funding plan (CFP) that is part of the liquidity risk management regime (nowadays, by regulatory requirement). Although the CFP is not part of a bank's strategy, the part of the strategy document that deals with liquidity and funding strategy would refer to it.

Larger banks and banking groups are also now required, by regulators, to develop and maintain "recovery and resolution" plans. The recovery plan describes, in some detail, how the bank would respond to an event that had a major negative impact on its capital position, while remaining solvent. This may include responses like major cost reduction exercises, the sale of non-core assets / businesses, and would also have to deal with the market repercussions of such an event (for example, liquidity and credit issues). The resolution plan, which belongs as much to the regulator as it does to the

**TABLE 16.1**   Strategic metrics and Kpis

| Metric / KPI | Bank Overall | Treasury | Corporate Banking | Retail Banking |
|---|---|---|---|---|
| Tier 1 Capital ratio | | | | |
| Core Tier 1 ratio | | | | |
| Return on Capital (RoC) | | | | |
| Return on Risk Weighted Assets | | | | |
| Loan to Deposit ratio | | | | |
| Loan growth | | | | |
| Deposit growth | | | | |
| Risk Weighted Assets | | | | |
| Wholesale Funding ratio | | | | |
| Leverage ratio (Assets / Capital) | | | | |
| Liquidity ratio | | | | |
| Net Stable Funding ratio | | | | |
| Unfunded Asset growth | | | | |
| Cost / Income ratio | | | | |
| FO / BO cost ratio | | | | |
| Non-interest income per cent revenue | | | | |
| Credit Loss ratio | | | | |
| VAR limits | | | | |
| Securities growth (yoy) | | | | |

individual bank, would consider the necessary steps to be taken in the event that recovery is no longer an option – i.e., solvency is an issue.

In addition to balance sheet management and related risk management activities, the customer franchise and the (hopefully "unique") customer proposition that the bank is offering, will be an important part of the overall strategy. To ensure that this remains relevant, the bank must be aware of its marketplace and what is happening within it, both at the macro and the individual customer-facing level. For this to happen, the senior executives cannot be too far removed from the "coalface". For large banks, this becomes a practical difficulty, but it is incumbent on the bank's leadership that they remain in touch with the marketplace through whatever means best suits their circumstances. This is an important aspect of keeping the strategy and risk appetite in tune with changes in the operating environment.

Internal communication and management involvement are key elements of ensuring the continued relevance of the strategic plan; all key players must be involved in both the development of the plan as well as its monitoring and review. Within a banking environment, this often means that the process is owned and driven by the Finance Director (CFO), given the centrality of the financial, capital, and liquidity issues, but this does not minimise the importance of the contributions required of other functional and business unit leaders.

An analogy may be drawn between the strategic planning process and the actuarial control cycle: they both begin with an analysis phase, a solution is proposed and implemented, and the results are monitored and examined with a view to adjusting the proposed solution. It is a process well known to actuaries – as is the understanding that the ongoing review of outcomes is an essential part of the process.

A final observation is that while some flexibility is called for, it should be remembered that tactical process setting exists to handle short-term adjustments. A strategy that was regularly modified would not be much of a strategy. Consider the following text, taken from the website of a MENA-based commercial bank:

> The Directors set the strategic direction of the Bank (with due consideration given to risk tolerance, shareholder expectations, business development opportunities and other macro-economic factors) which senior management then uses to design the Bank's annual strategic plan and prepare the annual budget for Board approval. Thereafter, quarterly updates are provided by senior management to the Board of Directors to monitor progress and permit any necessary modifications or adjustments in strategic direction.

This description appears text book and has much to commend it – it sets essentially the right tone and is largely indisputable. One could place it on one's strategy setting template. However, the reference to quarterly updates should not be taken to suggest a quarterly adjustment to the strategic plan; strategy is forward looking and long term. Therefore, stakeholders should consider the long term. Quarterly aberrations in performance would not necessarily be a reason to change strategic direction.

## Evaluation of the Strategic Plan

It is useful to consider the issues to raise as part of the review of a proposed strategic plan.

The questions asked should include:

- How helpful is the vision statement that frames the strategic plan? Are the two congruent and aligned?
- Would the execution of the strategy advance the realisation of the vision? How quickly?
- How realistic is the evaluation of the "current reality" of the bank? Is there a clear understanding of the strengths and weaknesses of the bank? Does the bank understand its "core competencies"?
- Are the proposed strategic initiatives grounded in reality? Can they be achieved? Is there adequate resourcing and support? Does the bank have the skills and competencies to deliver?
- Are the strategic targets and objectives clear?
- Is there clear accountability for delivery?
- Does management have the capacity to focus on the initiatives amidst "business as usual"? Where will pressure be felt in the delivery of the plan?
- Can progress be monitored effectively and how will "success" be measured?
- Is leadership committed to the plan? How well are the plan and its implications understood by management and other staff?
- Will the bank have sufficient capital to fund the initiatives, as well as the balance sheet to support the planned book of business? Where will this capital come from? Will the bank's capital targets be realised?
- Will any of the new initiatives – for example, new business units and/or lines of business – impact on the risk profile of the bank?
- What can be done to make the balance sheet more robust over the planning period – restructuring of liabilities; restructuring of debt; improving the liquidity profile?
- What is the risk profile of the planned new balance sheet and does this fit within the agreed risk appetite of the bank?
- Do the pricing policies in place adequately reflect the underlying risk of the key product areas, both financial and operational? Do the transfer pricing policies properly reflect the cost of funds and the duration of the liabilities?

There are clearly many more questions that may be asked, depending on the particular circumstances, but the above list provides an indication of what might be covered.

This extract from *PRMIA,"Intelligent Risk"*, August 2014.

**Future Bank Strategy: Fewer Choices, Tougher Calls**

# Future bank strategy: fewer choices, tougher calls

The most important function that a bank's Board and senior executive can undertake is to set the firm's strategy. It is vital that banks put in place a coherent, articulated strategy that sets the tone for the entire business, from the top down.

In the first instance the Board must take into account the current regulatory environment and the bank's own capital, liquidity and human capital constraints. This includes of course the requirements of Basel III, as well as any specific requirements of the national regulator. A bank cannot formulate strategy without a clear and genuine understanding of the environment in which it operates. Once this is achieved, before proceeding with a formal strategy the bank needs to determine what markets it should operate in based on the resources it possesses, what products it sells and what class of customer it wishes to serve. Individual business lines should be set up to operate within the main strategy. In other words, all the business lines exist as ingredients of the strategy. If a business line is not a fit with the strategy, it should be divested; equally, if a bank wishes to enter into new business, the strategy should be reviewed and realigned if it does not naturally suggest the new business. This sounds obvious, but there are many cases of banks entering piecemeal into different businesses, or maintaining unsuitable lines that have been inherited through previous growth or acquisition.

The first task then is to understand one's operating environment. It is then to incorporate a specific target market and product suite as the basis of its strategy, after taking into account what resources are currently in place and, if these are insufficient, what additional resources are needed before embarking on the strategy. Concurrent with this, the bank must set its Return on Capital (RoC) and Return on Risk-Weighted Assets (RoRWA) targets, the level of which will influence much of the bank's culture and ethos. A realistic RoC target is one that is sustainable over the entire business cycle.

Concurrently with the above process, a bank must ask itself where its strength lies and formulate its strategy around that. In other words, it is important to focus on core competencies. The experience of the crash showed that many banks found themselves with balance sheet risk exposures that they did not realise they had. This may have been simply the

holding of assets (such as structured finance securities) whose credit exposures, valuation and secondary market liquidity they did not understand, or
otherwise embarking on investment strategies such as cash-synthetic negative basis trading without being aware of all the risk measurement parameters of such strategies. To properly implement a coherent, articulate strategy,
a bank needs to be aware of exactly what it does and does not have an expertise for undertaking, and not operate in products or markets in which it has
no genuine knowledge base.

Figures 1A and 1B are a summary of the change in strategy-setting
culture that was demanded as a result of the crash. The cycle is now
resource-constraint driven, and anti-clockwise on our diagram, compared
to the clockwise process that was heavily influenced by return target in the
pre-crash era.

| Pre-crash | Post-crash |
|---|---|
| • Capital finite but available | • Capital more expensive and limited |
| • Funding finite but available | • Funding now driven by regulatory requirements |
| • Return target drives strategy | • Resource base constraints drives strategy |

In this article we consider the various strategy alternatives for commercial banks and their feasibility: as we will see, the choice is limited for all
but the largest or the most nimble firms. Furthermore, none of them is any
easier to implement than the other.

## specific strategy choices

The competitive environment for banks remains extremely tough. The issue
is even more challenging for banks domiciled in countries that experienced
a sovereign bail-out, where there is additional pressure associated with continuing poor public image and brand association. Under such circumstances
it is unsurprising that differentiating oneself from the competition presents
difficulties for bank Boards and senior management, particularly when one
considers the commoditised nature of the basic bank product.

All banks are aware of universal strategic imperatives in the wake of the
crash and the Basel III regulatory regime. These are summarised as follows:

- To improve capital efficiency via existing loan book restructuring
  and "optimising" collateral management
- To investigate "capital-light" growth opportunities within existing
  knowledge and resource base;

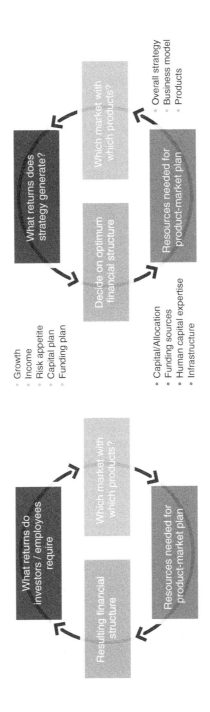

- Overall strategy
- Business model
- Products

Which market with which products?

What returns does strategy generate?

Resources needed for product-market plan

Decide on optimum financial structure

- Growth
- Income
- Risk appetite
- Capital plan
- Funding plan

- Capital/Allocation
- Funding sources
- Human capital expertise
- Infrastructure

Which market with which products?

What returns do investors / employees require

Resources needed for product-market plan

Resulting financial structure

- To lower costs via a combination of simplifying operating models, headcount reduction, out-sourcing or disposing of unprofitable or non-core business lines;
- To implement more robust and stable funding structures, particularly with respect to higher-cost longer-term funds.

Of course the first three are essentially platitudes – all businesses would seek to maximise capital efficiency and minimise the cost-income ratio at all times, simply as good operating practice. To be considered a genuine long-term contender in banking requires more than this in fact: no less than a specific defined customer-orientated differentiation of one's business model.

## strategy and outperformance

The overwhelming majority of retail and corporate customer banking requirements can be met with simple deposit and loan products. The plain vanilla nature of bank products makes brand differentiation not a straightforward process, and requires that banks place a great emphasis on customer service. This fact, together with traditional high barriers to entry, limits the strategy choices available to both established and new challenger banks. We summarise below six distinct strategic paths that a bank might consider.

- **Global integrated multinational:** our first strategy choice is, in fact, hardly any choice at all. The barriers to entry to a bank electing this option are so considerable as to make this strategy unfeasible for virtually all banks that are not already in this space. Outside of a handful of names such as HSBC, Citibank and Bank of America it is difficult to think of any institution that would consider this strategy today, realistically, particularly in the wake of the more stringent capital and liquidity requirements of Basel III. Unless a bank derives a significant share of its revenue from outside home markets, say at least 35% - 40%, it is not credible for banks to adopt this approach.
- **Basic banking:** this approach concentrates on delivering simple product with maximum efficiency. The key metrics to follow are customer satisfaction (or, customer complaints volume) and cost-income ratio. Adopting this strategy is only feasible if the bank exhibits, or plans to exhibit, a below-average cost base compared to its peers. Almost by definition, such banks would run low balance sheet risk exposure compared to other banks, but the key to competitive advantage is in keeping costs low – and by responding to mass customer desire for simple, easy-to-understand products. By running a

low cost operation, a bank following this strategy can supply low-cost products. At the same time, the bank would need to adopt a conservative credit origination policy, to maintain relatively low risk exposure on the balance sheet and also to ensure that it understood fully the credit and market risks it was running.

- **Specialist customer base:** a bank adopting this strategy will target a specific customer franchise, in essence those customers that are willing to pay a premium in return for a more "modern" banking experience. This would include products with a dynamic image and a leading edge digital and mobile platform. Note that such a customer base does not exist in every jurisdiction; it is also more of a retail rather than corporate customer base. While we emphasise the importance of strong customer service at all banks irrespective of their strategy, this particular approach requires a markedly superior reputation for truly excellent customer care, if it is to succeed as a strategy – the difference has to be such that customers are happy to pay the cost premium involved. As important is the cultural ethos in place at the bank, treating every customer as a special relationship in which all their financial needs are met from one source.

- **Market growth strategy:** fast-growing economies are able to support banks that adopt a market-growth strategy. Almost by definition it suits more those banks that are early entrants and thus able to help shape the country's financial system. Later entrants can still apply this approach but will need to demonstrate creativity and innovation as they also seek to influence the market's development. Domestic banks may have an advantage in that they "know your customer" better than foreign banks; multinational banks need to ensure they are familiar with the customer base if they are to adopt this strategy for their local branch or subsidiary. This strategy is more realistic in those countries that have a comparatively faster growing economy than more mature economies, such as certain regions of Asia-Pacific and the Arabian Gulf.

- **Private banking:** an alternative approach to mainstream banking is to concentrate on high net worth customers and target this franchise. As such this strategy is a sub-set of the specific customer base approach described earlier; however, it is more specialist – it demands a capital- and funding-light balance sheet model, and one in which returns are generated more from wealth management and asset management activities than mainstream banking. In fact, for this to be a realistic and distinct strategy the bank would have to derive over 60% of its revenues from such activities, and most likely outsource more traditional banking operations such as ATMs and cheque clearing to other banks. It would concentrate on efficient capital/asset and revenue/asset ratios, and be funded exclusively by customer deposits. Larger banks may choose to set up a separately branded arm specifically so as to incorporate this strategy for part of their revenue base.

- **Hybrid strategy:** this strategy combines two or more of the above strategies but presents a greater challenge in implementation and delivery because of the need to excel in all selected fields. This applies equally to the need to control costs. That said, it may be the logical choice for comparatively larger institutions that currently offer a full service product across all customer types but are struggling to deliver shareholder value in some or all of their customer proposition. For example, a bank may elect both the "back-to-basics" strategy but at the same time develop and enhance a niche or boutique business arm – perhaps with its own brand – that delivers a private banking or asset management service.

This list is not claimed to be the complete universe of possible strategic direction for all banks. Equally, there is always scope for an approach that is more tailored, or perhaps simply a hybrid one as we suggest above, for specific individual banks. But it does present almost the complete range of distinct strategy types that are available. This should not come as a surprise: as we note at the start, financial services are a commoditised product. There are only so many ways one can seek to deliver them well, consistently, and at the same time also differentiate one's brand and customer offering.

## concierge banking

Irrespective of the strategy selected and the customer franchise targeted, some requirements are universal. All banks will need to invest capital and resource into enhancing their digital capability. Internet and mobile technology are paramount because of customer demand for them and must be delivered with efficiency. This is the one area where the barrier to entry for new banks is less of an issue; established banks, particularly large banks and/or banks that have grown through acquisition, suffer from legacy systems and data management platforms that do not necessarily lend themselves to modification or enhancement. Challenger banks at least have the luxury of being able to develop new systems that are fit-for-purpose, albeit at cost. All the strategies, with the exception perhaps of the global multinational approach, require high quality data analysis ability and interface skills that integrate the physical (branch) and digital channels, to the benefit of all customers. The benchmark for banks is companies such as Amazon or Google, which have a customer-orientated data management and analytics capability that is highly efficient.

The other universal is customer service. Simply selecting and attempting to implement a strategy is no guarantee of success or outper-formance. In essence, a bank needs to make every one of its customers feel as if he or she is the only customer it has. This is perhaps less of an issue in the Basic Banking model, where customers' expectations will be slightly lower, but all of the strategies demand exceptional customer service. For certain strategy options such as specific customer franchise this will require heavy investment in staff technical and service skills, but every bank will need to pay close attention to this requirement. The emphasis on customer care, and the staff training requirements that this will drive, is paramount.

In effect, banking culture needs to move to that of a service one. Cul-ture is set from the top and it is essential that senior management drive change through personal example. The author's own term is "Concierge Banking", the qualitative philosophy that states that each and every inter-action with every customer, however large or small, must be treated as if the future of the company depends on it. This is a skillset that must be taught by example, from the top downwards. The way that senior executives deal with their subordinates, and they in turn with theirs, is crucial to inculcating this cultural skillset. The way a team operates in a bank will help drive this cultural change. "Total banking" demands that every member of a team can cover for everyone else (to an extent, but certainly amongst peers), are open and honest in their interaction with each other without fear of impact on career progression, and enthusiastic about assisting each other in their daily tasks. This creates a genuine team environment.

Each customer must be made to feel as if it is the bank's only customer. Adopting a concierge banking approach is the key to success.

## delivering on the strategy

Strategy selection is, of course, only the start. In any case, the options are limited. Notwithstanding that, we have outlined six distinct strategies; the reality for most banks is that only 2 or 3 of them present a feasible course of action. For example, the market growth approach is dependant on the state of the economy, and non-domestic banks with no existing presence in-country would struggle with it. The capital- and funding-light private bank or asset management strategy would involve a fundamental change of operating model for banks that are not already involved, to a significant degree, in this business. And the multinational integrated bank strategy presents simply too high a barrier to entry for banks that are not, already, large universal banks.

This leaves essentially two paths: the "basic bank" strategy that emphasises tight control of costs, or the more "up market" approach that targets a more sophisticated customer franchise and product base. The latter also requires genuine brand, service and product differentiation if it is to succeed. Both approaches require exceptional, or at least above peer-group average, levels of customer service. For larger banks, adopting either strategy will require substantial cost-cutting and possibly divestment of "non-core" businesses.

The hybrid strategy is in our list precisely because many larger banks will not be nimble enough to adopt one focused approach but will nevertheless be too small to adopt the universal strategy. Instead they will take the perceived "easy option" of a combined strategy. This can still be a winning course of action; however, it requires a knowledgeable and intellectually strong senior executive. It is not uncommon for larger banks to wish to offer a "one stop shop" for all customers ranging from retail to SMEs and larger corporates. The big danger is that the bank provides an average service for all customers. To make this strategy work, middle management must be cut to a minimum and the line of control from senior executive to operating businesses must be clear and transparent. Otherwise the bank will drift and become a jack-of-all-trades and master of none. In a crowded field, this could prove fatal.

## conclusions

Selecting a defined, and definite, strategy is the first step to becoming a more focused financial institution. As we noted earlier, for the majority of banks the choice is limited to at most 2 or 3 distinct approaches. And irrespective of the strategy path embarked upon, the need to deliver first-class customer service is paramount. Another universal is the need to have efficient technology platforms, to simplify products, and to narrow the product range. Every bank would testify to the popularity of this action in the past with both retail and corporate customers. This also benefits the bank's risk management function: a simpler product range generates less exotic and more "vanilla" risk exposure on the balance sheet, which is easier to understand and mitigate.

The shift to a high-class customer service culture is the key to success. This requires investment in staff training, both technical and qualitative, especially for customer-facing teams. But customer service is more than simply having senior executives spouting platitudes, it is a change in internal environment to one that is genuine and open. A working culture free of politics and bureaucracy creates naturally an ethos of caring customer service. This, beyond mere selection of a distinct strategy, is the biggest challenge faced by banks.

Reproduced from *PRMIA, "Intelligent Risk"*, August 2014.

## EXAMPLE: "SWOT" ANALYSIS FOR MEDIUM-SIZED UK COMMERCIAL BANK

From the foregoing we may conclude that the strategy setting process is quite involved and requires significant data analysis of the firm in breadth and depth. This is not untrue. If there is a difficult part, however, it's at the beginning: making a start in crafting one's strategic direction is the hardest stage of the cycle. Knowing where wants to be in five or seven years' time, and what shape and structure, takes some thought as well as the boldness to make decisions. The best aid to making the start is knowing precisely where the bank is now, and where the market in which it operates is as well. In other words, the strategy team must have in-depth knowledge of the bank they're in as well as their peer banks, and the wider market.

A good start to the process is the "strengths-weaknesses-opportunities-threats" (SWOT) analysis. This should be conducted at the ExCo and ALCO level, as well as one level below. The results of the SWOT review can form the initial input to crafting the strategy but of course this does not obviate the need for the Board and for ExCo to have an idea of where the bank should aim to be in the medium and long term.

In this section, we present the results of a SWOT analysis for a medium-size UK commercial banking institution ("XYZ Bank Ltd") with the following characteristics:

| | |
|---|---|
| Balance sheet: | GBP 35bln |
| Business lines: | Retail banking, Corporate banking, Treasury |
| Products Assets: | Residential and commercial mortgages, corporate loans, personal finance loans, credit cards |
| Liabilities: | Current accounts, deposit accounts, notice accounts, term accounts |
| Funding: | Customer deposits and short-term wholesale funding (CP / CD); no access to long-dated wholesale funding as yet |
| Franchise: | UK retail and corporate customers only; GBP balance sheet |

The report shows the form of the analysis and the thinking involved when conducting the SWOT review. As one sees from a read of the SWOT, the work undertaken has identified areas for development and direction, but not to any great depth. When the ExCo of this bank moves onto drafting the 5–7-year plan it will need to build out much more granularity and focus as it seeks to identify and articulate how opportunities will be exploited and threats addressed.

Readers will also note that this SWOT reports on market share as a performance metric. This is not an appropriate metric for banks as we have noted (two failed UK banks in 2007 and 2008, Northern Rock and HBOS, were obsessed with growing market share in residential and commercial mortgages respectively, while UBS in Switzerland, which required state aid to survive in 2008 was obsessed with growing its share of the infamous structured credit market), but nevertheless it is a hard one for ExCo members to let go of. On the other hand, the initiative to obtain a credit rating and submit itself to that process, which the SWOT report recognises, will help ExCo to crystallise its thoughts on strategy, is encouraging to see. In essence though, this SWOT looks unrealistically optimistic. For a bank to identify only one weakness arising out of an internal review suggests it may not have been looking very hard for them.

Note that SWOT analysis is also discussed in our primer on marketing, presented at Appendix 18.A.

### XYZ Bank Limited: SWOT Analysis

XYZ Bank is a financial services company based in the UK. The company's stable capital ratios and robust business performance are its strengths. XYZ has only limited access to wholesale markets so faces certain limitation to raise funds for expansion. The company faces challenges due to fluctuating interest rates, Basel III requirements on capital and long-term structural funding (NSFR), and the stringent rules and regulations set by the Board. Inorganic growth initiatives coupled with the improving economy would provide expanded scope and growth opportunities.

#### Strengths

- Stable Capital Ratios;
- Robust Business Performance;
- Strong Financial Performance.

**Stable Capital Ratios**    XYZ reported stable capital position, meeting all the regulatory requirements. Stable ratios indicate efficient management of capital and could provide good base for growth and expansion in future.

During the fiscal year ended December 2015, XYZ's core tier 1 ratio was 13.9% in 2014 and 13.7% in 2013; and the company's tier 1 ratio was at 14% in 2015 and 13.8% in 2014. The core tier 1 ratio increased in 2015 and 2013 on account of capital buyback. XYZ improved the overall quality of its capital while providing liquidity to holders of capital securities. XYZ reported £12,595.4m in risk weighted assets in 2015, and £11,905.7m in 2014. The company's tier 1 capital was £1,805.9m in 2015, compared to £1,694.4m in 2014. The company also reported its solvency ratio as 14.3% in 2015.

**Robust Business Performance**  XYZ reported robust business performance during the year 2015. The company reported a stable market share of gross lending at 3.8% in 2015 compared to 3.2% in 2014. The market share of net lending in 2015 was 17.4% compared to 8.1% in 2012. Mortgage balances increased by 7% to £29.5 billion in 2015 from £27.6 billion in 2014. The average indexed loan to value in 2015 was 54% and 55% in 2014. Asset quality was strong with the percentage of retail mortgages with arrears of three months or more falling to 1.57% in 2015 compared to 1.69% in 2014. The company has a total asset base of £34.5 billion in 2015 compared to £33.5 billion in 2014. Savings balances and general reserves accounted for 96.7% of mortgage lending in 2015 and 104.7% in 2014. Nearly 89% of savings balances earn more than the official bank rate and reported a 2.2% share of household savings market. First time buyers comprised 36% of all house purchase mortgages and gross lending above 85% loan to value rose to £675m, indicating an increase of 38% over £490m in 2014. XYZ provided support to small and medium-sized companies in our communities with gross lending rising 48% to £88.5m in 2015; compared to £60m in 2014. Significantly improved complaints processes and experienced only 6% of complaints from customers being upheld by the Financial Services Ombudsman as compared to an industry average of 64%.

**Strong Financial Performance**  The company reported a strong financial performance during the fiscal year 2015. Stable financial performance indicates strong performance of the company. It reported net interest income of £531.6m in 2015, compared to £346m in 2014. The interest income in 2015 was £1,405.6m compared to £1,380.7m in 2014. Total income in 2015 increased to £543.4m as compared to £460.4m in 2014. The net interest margin in 2015 was stable at 1.56% compared to 1.05% in 2014. The profit before tax reported in 2015 was £199.3m, an increase of 26% over £158.1m. It reported a healthy leverage ratio of 4.6% in 2015 compared to 4.8% in 2014.

### Weakness

* Limitation of Wholesale Funding.

**Limitation of Wholesale Funding** XYZ being an un-rated organisation Does not have easy access to capital markets. It may require a huge amount of capital in case of expansion through acquisitions. The company has to forgo the benefit of raising money from the public, which is relatively less costly when compared to debt. This absence costs the company and would have to forgo on available investment opportunity, as debt issuance is a slower process. Moreover, it would be difficult for the company to raise debt for risky ventures, as debt is usually not issued for risky ventures. These restrictions do not give the company a competitive advantage when compared with public companies.

### Opportunities

* Strategic Initiatives;
* Positive Economic Growth Outlook;
* Obtain Credit Rating.

The company has a substantial focus on expanding its business operations and it has undertaken several initiatives to augment its growth. In the past the company has grown significantly through acquisition of mortgage and savings books and three mergers. The company unveiled a new multi-platform site, which is fully adaptable to tablet devices, desktop computers, and mobile phones. This will improve accessibility and the customers can view the full range of products and services through the internet. XYZ's substantial focus on expanding its business operations through strategic initiatives would strengthen its competitive position in the market.

**Positive Economic Growth Outlook** The positive economic growth outlook of the UK is expected to drive demand for the company's solutions. The UK's gross domestic product is among the strongest in western economies. The growth in the UK economy is expected to remain positive for the foreseeable future. XYZ expects GDP growth of around 2.5%. The Bank of England forecasts growth of 2.4% in 2016. Unemployment in the UK fell quickly than policy makers and independent forecasters' expectations in 2015. ILO unemployment fell to 7.2% in December from 7.8% at the end of 2014. XYZ forecasts a slower rate of improvement in the next three years, a modest improvement over the current consensus expectation. The latest XYZ forecast assumes the bank rate will increase by 25 basis points in Q3 2016 and rise very modestly thereafter. Bank rate is expected to reach c.2% by the end of 2019. House price inflation increased rapidly over the course of 2015 to an average of around 8%. This was driven by government programmes reducing the cost of mortgages, easing of credit availability, and the improvement in the general economic environment. Gross mortgage lending in the UK totalled £176 billion in 2015, an increase of over 20% over the previous year. The company forecast the market to return to a size of £200 billion by 2019. Net lending in the UK remained weak at £11.2 billion in 2015, an increase of 11% over 2014. XYZ expects this to return to a level of around £40 billion in 2019.

**Obtain Credit Rating** The lack of an investment-grade credit rating from S&P / Moody's / Fitch prevents the bank from accessing wholesale markets, which is an obstacle to both asset growth and mitigating the risk of compliance with NSFR. The bank's internal analysis suggests a public rating of BB+ or possibly BBB– could be achieved. For the rating to be of value, it cannot be below BBB– (IG level) but undertaking an informal "ratings advisory service" (RAS) with Moody's or S&P before a formal credit rating application would enable ExCo to understand what management actions needed to be taken to ensure an IG-level rating.

### Threats

- Fluctuations in Interest Rates;
- Basel III Capital Requirements;
- Stringent Rules and Regulations.

**Fluctuations in Interest Rates** The low level of interest rates has depressed NIM and made the objective of raising NIM difficult. This is a threat but also an opportunity to consider forms of lending with higher spreads that remain within the Board credit risk appetite.

**Basel III Capital Requirements** Basel III requirements are intended to protect the global banking industry from financial meltdowns. The new norms require banks to hold more and better quality capital, carry more liquid assets, and limit leverage. These will not only restrict banks to hold more capital on hand, which will limit the amount of money they can lend out, but also reduce the risk of insolvency given many loan defaults. According to the new rules, Basel III increases the minimum Tier 1 capital ratio to 6%. The ratio was set at 6% from 1 January 2015. Predominance of common equity would reach 82.3% of Tier 1 capital, inclusive of capital conservation buffer. The minimum total capital ratio remains at 8%. Such regulations would engage companies to incur high costs, putting extra pressure on banks, which are already in the process of improving their own governance processes.

## CONCLUSIONS

Developing a strategy for a bank is a complex task as banks are complex institutions operating within a complex industry. Banks are also potentially fragile, notwithstanding their often formidable looking balance sheets. The imperative for effective strategic planning that is found in any business is therefore of greater importance within banking, and particular attention has to be placed on the sustainability of the bank through an entire business cycle as part of the strategic planning process. The banking regulators take a specific interest in both the process as well as the outcome, which adds a further dimension to the process within the banking industry.

For that reason, while banks need to deal with all the usual strategic issues in the planning process, the balance sheet and its robustness takes central stage – everything takes a cue from the evolving balance sheet, and the health of the bank which is measured by capital and liquidity metrics, remains of the utmost importance. As noted, banking rests on trust and confidence, and unfortunately banking is a business where perceptions can drive reality with undesirable consequences. The strategic plan has to take all this into account, and at the same time meet the expectations of the various stakeholder groups, including most importantly the shareholders. Stakeholders generally care for a constant and sustainable performance from the bank. That is why we have emphasised "the balance sheet is everything" tone for the strategy setting process. This will prove ultimately beneficial for shareholder and wider society interests.

Banking is also a difficult industry in which to carve out a distinctive "niche", due to the nature of the products and services offered. This is not to say it is an impossible quest as there are numerous examples of banks which have achieved this. However, this invariably takes time, suggesting that if the goal of the strategy is to build a distinctive positioning for itself as a bank, it is going to entail perseverance. This makes the commitment of executive management and the Board and shareholders even more important.

The strategy setting process requires input at both the conceptual and detail level; it is a process requiring clear logical analysis and thinking, as well as creative and lateral thinking. The end result has to contain both the "call to arms" – the vision statement – as well as the much more detailed "battle plan", and be supported by regular reports from the front and progress reviews.

## SELECTED BIBLIOGRAPHY AND REFERENCES

Altunbas, Yener; Manganelli, Simone; and Marques-Ibanez, David, *Bank Risk During the Financial Crisis: Do Business Models Matter?* ECB, November 2011. http://www.ecb.europa.eu/pub/pdf/scpwps/ecbwp1394.pdf.

*Bank business models, managerial discretion and risk efficiency*, BIS, May 2010. http://www.bis.org/bcbs/events/sfrworkshopprogramme/baele.pdf.

Blundell-Wignall, Adrian; Atkinson, Paul; and Roulet, Caroline, *Bank business models and the Basel system: Complexity and interconnectedness*, OECD Journal: Financial Market Trends 2014, 2014 http://www.oecd.org/finance/Bank-Business-Models-Basel-2013.pdf.

Choudhry, Moorad, *The Principles of Banking*, Singapore: John Wiley & Sons Ltd, 2012, Chapters 16, 17.

Dombret, Andreas, *Business models and the banking sector seen in terms of financial stability*, Bundesbank, September 2012. http://www.bis.org/review/r120925d.pdf.

Gambacorta, Leonardo and Van Rixtel, Adrian, *Structural bank regulation initiatives: approaches and implications*, BIS, June 2013. http://www.bis.org/publ/work412.pdf.

Post-crisis evolution of the banking sector, BIS 82 Annual report, June 2012. http://www.bis.org/publ/arpdf/ar2012e6.pdf.

Tumpel-Gugerell, Gertrude, *Business models in banking – is there a best practice?* ECB, September 2009. http://www.bis.org/review/r090923e.pdf.

*U.S. bank-level data*, De Nederlandsche Bank, August 2013. http://www.dnb.nl/en/binaries/Working per cent20Paper per cent20387_tcm47-295326.pdf.

Van Ewijk, Saskia and Arnold, Ivo, *How bank business models drive interest margins: Evidence from U.S. Bank-Level Data*, Working Paper No. 387, August 2013.

*"Someone once said, 'Great men talk about ideas, good people talk about things, and everybody else talks about people'. . .Consequently, I seldom enjoy talking about people, either within our own group or outside."*
—Neil Armstrong, quoted in C. Nelson, *Rocket Men: The Epic Story of the First Men on the Moon,* John Murray Publishers, 2009

# CHAPTER 17

# Present and Future Principles of Governance and Culture

Corporate governance is a discipline in its own right. For example, the academic journal *Corporate Governance – An International Review* celebrated its 25th year in 2017. While that may not necessarily make the subject a "science", it does indicate that it's a reasonably distinct specialism that deserves to be taken seriously. Culture, on the other hand, is a slightly more elusive topic to define. However, both of these arts are very important aspects of finance in general and bank management in particular. Anyone who disagrees with this, especially with respect to wider financial markets and not just banking, should read *What They Do With Your Money* by Stephen Davis, Jon Lukomnik, and David Pitt-Watson (Yale University Press, 2016). A more damning indictment of the financial system in place in most Western countries would be hard to find: the authors identify culture and governance as being at the heart of much of what is negative in the industry.

The governance framework and culture was self-evidently flawed in every crashed Western bank of 2007–2008. That nothing overmuch was said, let alone done, about either beforehand was simply because it's difficult to speak up when things are going well and one set of stakeholders, the executives and employees, are being paid above-average salaries. Once the bank goes bust, then the flaws expose themselves. The most glaring feature of the bank failures of 2007–2008 or the ones of an earlier generation in the early 1980s is that they expose the supreme incompetence at the heart of all of them.

Banking is not a difficult art in which to make money. Just the act of being a bank extracts a certain monopoly rent; being on the high street with a banking license and an unspectacular credit rating means customers will always deposit their daily cash requirement with you for a few basis points, money that the bank can lend at several hundred basis points higher even if the borrower supplies quality collateral. That's why even banks with poor service, poorer product range, a laughable image, and limited intellectual capital can still make a profit every year. For a bank to run out of capital is the equivalent of an aeroplane crashing because it turns out the person at the flight controls wasn't actually a pilot. For a bank to fail because of liquidity management inadequacy is even more unforgivable: analogous to someone tasked with being in charge of the water supply on a lifeboat in the middle of the Pacific who realises he's forgotten to pack the water bottles.

This chapter is worthy of inclusion in Part IV, the "future of banking" section of the book, rather than Part III because its subject matter is so important. Banks need to get the governance and culture bits right in order to regain, and retain, a status as trusted pillars of the community that exist to do good for society. The book extracts in this chapter address cultural aspects to an extent, including the topic of remuneration, as well as governance imperatives. The new material concentrates more on governance and provides recommendations and principles for best-practice in banks. We believe that the material is applicable to all banks, irrespective of their business model, product suite, or customer franchise. (There are of course detail differences in approach to this discipline depending on jurisdiction, so we speak here only in general terms. Note that one of the biggest differences in governance framework is between what is seen at "Anglo-Saxon" banks, with their unitary Board structure, and banks on the European continent and elsewhere which tend to have the dual Board structure. What is important is to realise precisely where and with whom specific responsibilities lie.)

**This extract from *The Principles of Banking* (2012)**

## Effective Bank Corporate Governance: Conclusions from the Market Crash

### EFFECTIVE BANK CORPORATE GOVERNANCE: CONCLUSIONS FROM THE MARKET CRASH

Banks are the critical infrastructure component in an economy. They provide financing for individuals and corporations, and facilitate the transmission of funds across payment systems. The effective functioning of any economy depends on banks ensuring the supply of credit and liquidity throughout the business cycle and in all market conditions. The importance of banks to human well-being and societal development is recognised by the fact that in virtually every country banking is a regulated industry and protected by taxpayer-funded safety nets. The efficient mobilisation and allocation of funds is dependent on efficient corporate governance at banks. When they are able to undertake this, the cost of capital is lowered for all market participants. This in turn increases capital formation and raises productivity growth. Therefore the management of banks has implications for corporate as well as national prosperity. This in turn highlights the importance, and central function, of bank governance. It is self-evident then, that bank corporate governance must be robust, effective, adaptable to changing circumstances and fit for purpose.

In the banking industry corporate governance refers to the manner in which the business and strategy of the institution are governed by the firm's board and senior management. An accurate and succinct description of it is given in BIS (1999), which describes the mechanics of bank corporate governance as (i) setting the bank's objectives, including target rate of return for shareholders; (ii) setting the control framework that oversees the daily operations of the bank; (iii) protecting customer deposits; (iv) setting strategy that accounts for the interests of all stakeholders, including shareholders, employees, customers and suppliers; and (v) maintaining the bank as a going concern irrespective of economic conditions and throughout the business cycle.

A banking crisis highlights the failure of bank corporate governance with dramatic effect. The financial crash and economic recession of 2007–2009 resulted in the demise of a number of banks, of varying size and systemic importance, in the US and Europe. The evidence from the crash is that corporate governance at many banks failed completely, at least with respect to points (iv) and (v) above, and in many cases with respect to all five governance objectives. This was despite the fact that the banking sector is heavily regulated and subject to internationally agreed rules on capital buffers and accounting transparency.

## The Conventional Bank Corporate Governance Framework

We noted in the literature review that there is no universal bank corporate governance model. Differences in organisation and infrastructure differ by regulatory jurisdiction and also within them, depending on the type of institution being considered. The Basel Committee, as noted in BCBS (1998) and BIS (1999), suggest the following, *inter alia*, as elements of strategy and technique that are essential to an effective corporate governance arrangement:

- a coherent and explicit statement of strategy for the business, with stated required return and performance measures;
- clear and transparent outline of responsibilities for the executive management;

- explicit lines of authority and communication, from the Board downwards and from business lines upward;
- strong framework of internal control, and accountability, and review procedures and processes for this control (including internal and external audit arrangements and a Board audit-risk committee);
- an effective risk management framework that also describes the monitoring and reporting of all risk exposures;
- transparent information flows both internally and externally.

These principles would always be required, in any economic environment. In the wake of the crash, it is reasonable to conclude that the above principles were not observed at many banks. However, that does not suggest that these principles need to be changed, but rather observed and enforced more adequately and, in a number of key respects, added to.

Irrespective of the regulatory jurisdiction of a bank, at the top level there are five areas of governance over which strong oversight must be established. These are (i) genuine controlling supervision by the Board of Directors; (ii) supervision by individuals who do not work within the business lines; (iii) direct executive supervision of each business line; (iv) independent audit and risk management sub-boards; and (v) senior personnel who are sufficiently expert in their jobs. In other words, a "rubber stamp" Board is not acceptable.

The Board should establish a coherent, articulated strategy for the bank. This is stated in BIS (1999), but was not always observed. However, strategy objectives must be reviewed on a frequent basis, so that they can be altered as necessary to respond to changes in economic circumstances. Such macroprudential oversight is perhaps the most difficult aspect of a Board's responsibilities. Further, board directors must be qualified to perform their role and must be able to access all necessary information, on a timely basis, to enable them to perform their duties. The events during the crash suggest that this was not always the case.

## Board Structure and Role

The most effective composition of a bank board remains an issue for debate. Heidrick and Struggles (2009) define three different forms of board structure that are common in Western Europe and North America, which we summarise at Figure 18.1.

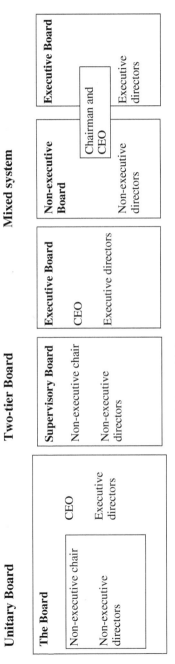

**Figure 18.1**  Examples of board structure.

The fully unitary system is common in UK banks, as well as in Spain, while the two-tier format is required by law in Germany, and also observed in Switzerland and Holland. The mixed system is observed in Belgium. All these countries, with the exception of Germany, suffered a banking crisis of one type or another in 2008, while a number of German *landesbanks* had to be rescued by the federal government. On anecdotal evidence therefore we conclude that the form of the Board itself does not have a bearing on the ability of a bank to survive a capital or liquidity crisis. A checklist of accepted business best-practice operating mechanisms, as contained in Heidrick and Struggles (2009), confirms further that simple observation of form for board supervision did not prevent banks from failing to meet the challenges of the crisis. For instance, UK banks are reported as exhibiting the highest rating on corporate governance in the study, yet suffered possibly the most serious banking crisis. A country ranked in the study with a low governance rating, such as Denmark, experienced fewer bank liquidity and capital problems in the crash.

Other metrics reported in the study are also uncorrelated with the experience of banks during the crisis; for instance, the average number of board members at European banks is 11.8; however, countries above this figure (Belgium, with 12.7 on average) and below it (the UK, with an average of 8.5) both suffered banking crises. Yet, the issue of the most effective size of a Board remains contentious. Advocates of large boards believe that these allow scope for representation of diverse interests, as well as a wider range of expertise. The experience of banks in the crisis, however, suggests that large boards are unwieldy, as well as unable to react quickly enough to fast-moving events.

Reproduced from *The Principles of Banking* (2012)

This extract from *The Principles of Banking* (2012)

Policy Recommendations

## POLICY RECOMMENDATIONS

From our observation of a number of failed banks, we conclude that current bank corporate governance culture and legislation is insufficient to deal with the risk of failure when markets crash. We recommend a number of measures designed to strengthen the infrastructure of corporate governance, and to increase the effectiveness of boards when dealing with dynamic and volatile market environments. If necessary, these measures should be imposed by regulatory fiat:

*Correct board representation.* At none of the failed firms was a representative of the major debt holders placed on the Board. Market observations suggest that risk behaviour is related to the type of representative on the Board, and insofar as they represent any stakeholder, NEDs usually represent the shareholders. Increased scrutiny of company earnings has forced listed companies to report their results on a quarterly basis; the short-term focus on corporate results makes boards focus overmuch on share price and peer comparison. A board membership representing solely the management and shareholders, and concentrating on such performance parameters, will be predisposed to lower risk discipline in a rising market. Furthermore, Levine (2004) suggests that shareholders "have incentives to raise the bank's risk profile. Debt holders, however, do not enjoy any upside potential from risk-taking, but do suffer on the downside if the bank cannot service its debts." Rarely, however, if ever, are bondholders represented on the Board. If they were, the accent on policies and strategies would be more risk averse. Therefore we recommend that bank boards be required to appoint at least one member who is a representative of the major debt holders in the company.

*Expert knowledge of board members.* In our observation of the events at KBC Bank, we noted that board members were not familiar with securitisation techniques and structured credit products, and with specific structures in use within their own group. For board membership, financial services expertise is a prerequisite. Non-executive directors must have financial services expertise, and executive directors – including CEOs – must have direct relevant experience. We noted that Bradford & Bingley and HBOS, two failed UK banks, appointed CEOs from the retail sector. We recommend therefore that the regulator approve only suitably qualified persons for board membership. The expertise of board members must be reviewed annually by bank regulators.

*Management understanding of core strategy.* A frequent refrain in risk management principles is to know one's risk. This maxim is also relevant for senior management from a governance point of view. We observed that a Board that has no clear understanding of the bank's direction, beyond a simple one of growth in absolute size and market share, can be easily influenced into higher risk business. This was the case at Northern Rock and DBS. We recommend that boards articulate a clear, coherent definition of strategy and *raison d'être* that explicitly outlines the areas of business competence the bank should engage in.

**Board size.** We observed that direction and risk management can easily stray into higher risk and inappropriate business sectors without effective checks and balances on management. Bank boards would be more effective with fewer but more committed members. Large-size boards diminish a sense of personal responsibility, with each board member taking refuge in the collective position. This makes it harder to restrain management and the cult of personality. As long as there are sufficient checks and balances to ensure that business lines cannot force their own agenda, we recommend that a Board of 6–10 persons rather than the norm of 12–20 would make for more effective supervision and control.

**Frequency of board meetings.** The frequency of board meetings was not able to meet the challenge of a dynamic market environment, of the kind observed in 2008. However, it may be administratively difficult for a full board to meet more frequently than once every 4–6 weeks. We recommend that a smaller sub-group of the Board, an "alpha-team" of key executive directors (the CEO, CFO, one business line head, Treasury head and one or two non-executive directors) meet more often – say one or two days every month rather than 6–12 days every year. This would provide more solid direction and awareness of bank business, especially during times of crisis or negative sentiment when markets are fast-moving.

**Expertise of board sub-committees.** It is common practice for boards to appoint an independent risk committee of non-executive directors; for example, the Board Audit & Risk committee. However, while such committees have an important function, they are ineffective unless the membership is composed of market experts able to understand the nature of the bank's risk exposures. Otherwise, the role is more effectively undertaken by an internal board sub-committee. We recommend therefore that such board sub-committees consist only of those with proven bank experience and expertise gained over the business cycle.

**Transparency.** We observed that frequently senior management did not issue transparent notices of strategy, intent and risk exposure to shareholders. In the case of DBS, the description of events in the annual report was kept opaque. We recommend that regulators enforce a requirement, reviewed annually, that management communicate to shareholders in a precise and clear fashion the extent of the bank's risk and losses.

At many banks the performance of senior management and boards during the crisis of 2008 was unsatisfactory. It is apparent that current corporate governance infrastructure is not sufficiently robust to handle market corrections. We have outlined a range of recommendations that should, if implemented by banks and enforced by regulators, assist management to better handle events during the next crash.

## MANAGEMENT STRUCTURE

There is no one right way for a bank to organise its governance structure; rather, there is an optimum way that best suits the particular bank's business model. The basic structure might follow the principles first outlined by Coase (1937), his treatise that founded the discipline of industrial economics. However, banks often arrive at what they believe to be their optimum governance structure after a period of trial and error and learning from experience. The purpose of this section is to describe what we consider to be business best-practice. It should be viewed as a benchmark template that is suitable for implementation at any medium- or large-size commercial bank, with detail modifications applied relevant to its specific environment.

Figure 18.4 illustrates the typical bank management structure. We add the Board "Alpha Team" as well to it, to manage decision-making during stress events. The independence of the chief operating officer (COO), and hence CRO function is paramount here, to ensure the avoidance of the Lehmans-type situation that was recounted in Sorkin (2009). However, in some cases a "dotted line" reporting connection to the CEO, for communications and policy setting, is logical.

This structure drills down to a committee arrangement that is kept as simplified and transparent as possible. It is important to avoid overlap and to minimise drag on decision-making, as experience of the crash demonstrates that these factors prevent effective control during a stress period. We illustrate the recommended committee structure at Figure 18.5.

The matrix diagram at Table 18.1 describes the terms of reference and objectives of each of the committees shown in Figure 18.5.

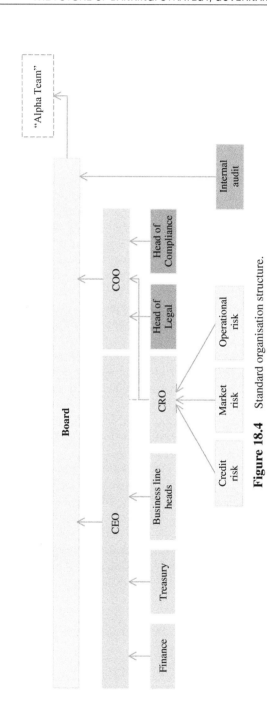

**Figure 18.4** Standard organisation structure.

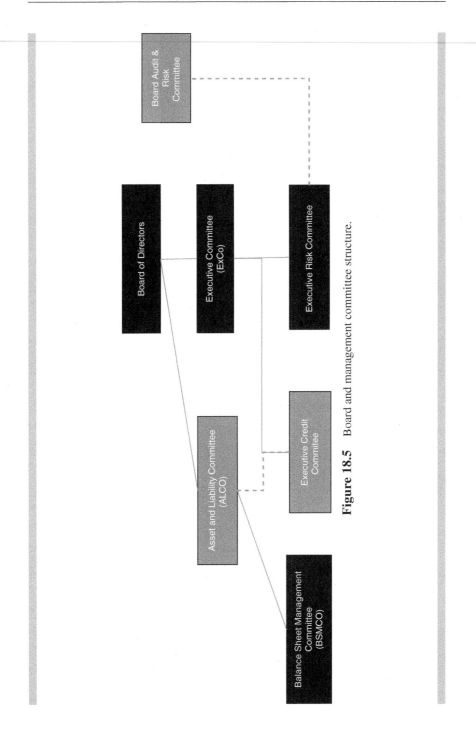

**Figure 18.5** Board and management committee structure.

| Board of Directors | ▪ Sets the bank's medium- and long-term strategy and objectives, and monitors performance |
| --- | --- |
| | ▪ Defines and describes the bank's high-level business model |
| | ▪ Sets the bank's target ROE/ROC/ROA and approves the desired risk-return profile |
| | ▪ Monitors the risk exposure and stress scenarios, ensures they are within a specified risk profile |
| | ▪ Identifies medium- and long-term opportunities and threats to the bank's business operations |
| | ▪ Assumes overall responsibility for managing liquidity risk for the bank, and specifying liquidity risk tolerance |
| "Alpha" Committee | ▪ Smaller committee of principal executives and non-executive directors, meets during crisis or stress periods |
| | ▪ Executive authority from the Board to manage the bank as and when required |
| | ▪ Organised to meet on a frequent basis |
| Executive Committee (ExCo) | ▪ Implements the Board-approved strategy across the business lines |
| | ▪ Responsible for management of the balance sheet |
| | ▪ Manages risk exposure and ensures risk stays within specified tolerance |
| | ▪ Sets risk limits at business line level |
| | ▪ Manages the regulatory relationships |
| | ▪ Manages the liquidity risk position under the delegated authority of the Board |
| | ▪ Responsible for stewardship of the bank's capital |
| | ▪ Approves capital allocation to business line transactions |
| Board Audit & Risk Committee | ▪ Delegated board authority to oversee and control all aspects of bank finance and accounting policies, internal control and regulatory reporting functions |
| | ▪ Executive and implementation assistance to the Board on any business matters referred to it by the Board |
| | ▪ Undertakes the role of audit committee for the bank |
| | ▪ Oversees every aspect of the bank's business on an investigative basis and reports to the Board with recommendations for improvement |
| | ▪ Responsible for reporting on all risk and control issues across the bank, at a both strategic and tactical level, including financial, capital, liquidity and operational risk |

**Table 18.1** Bank governance: committee overview.

| Executive Credit Committee | ■ Reviews decision-making on all capital allocation issues, as well as the approval of requests for credit limits <br> ■ Delegated authority from the Board <br> ■ Delegates authority to the ALCO and relevant Credit Committees as required <br> ■ Approves credit and loss provisions |
| --- | --- |
| Executive Risk Committee | ■ Delegated authority from the Board with responsibility for overseeing risk and control issues at the strategic and tactical level <br> ■ Review risk tolerances for regulatory, funding and liquidity risk exposures |
| Management Committee | ■ Delegated authority from ExCo to implement and manage the bank's business lines' strategy <br> ■ Monitors and reports on capital and revenue targets <br> ■ Reports on bank's performance against business lines' strategy and budget <br> ■ Recommends strategy and implementation therefore to ExCo for board approval <br> ■ Not necessary for smaller banks and/or non-group structures |
| Asset and Liability Committee (ALCO) | ■ Discussed in Part II of the book <br> ■ Meets on a more frequent basis than the Board, and on a weekly basis if the Alpha Committee is meeting |
| Balance Sheet Management Committee | ■ Technical advisory committee that feeds in to ALCO <br> ■ Reviews all strategic, external market, peer group and regulatory developments of relevance and/or those expected to impact the bank <br> ■ Reviews the current and forecast state of the bank's balance sheet and the impact of external developments <br> ■ Monitors trends and forecasts on capital state, capital requirements, customer deposits, customer funding gap, net interest margin and net interest-rate risk <br> ■ Monitors external macroeconomic indicators and uses this to recommend policy to ALCO and ExCo <br> ■ Meets on a more frequent basis than the Board and other committees, and on a weekly basis if the Alpha Committee is meeting |

**Table 18.1**    *(Continued)*

Reproduced from *The Principles of Banking* (2012)

**This extract from *The Future of Finance* (2010)**

## Corporate Governance and Remuneration in the Banking Industry

### Corporate Governance and Remuneration in the Banking Industry

Corporate governance in the banking industry was severely criticized in the aftermath of the financial crisis of 2007–2009. Much of the debate centered on banks' remuneration, although the failures in corporate governance were not limited to the bonus culture, which in reality had little connection with the causes of the crisis. More relevant causal factors that should be looked at included the type of representatives on the board, the expertise of these board members, and the partnerships of investment banks.

In this chapter we review the failings of bank corporate governance during the buildup to the crisis, and present recommendations for improvements to the model.

# BONUSES AND A MORAL DILEMMA

The bonus culture is the first topic that is raised when talking about bank corporate governance. The bonuses that have been paid out to investment bankers are objectionable in the eyes of many legislators and the mainstream media, and came under populist attack after banks had to be rescued with taxpayer money. This became an emotional debate which has the potential to lead to flawed decision making that could jeopardize the future prospects of the banking industry. Therefore this is also the most controversial and sensitive chapter in this book.

We should be careful about automatically condemning bonuses. As Jack Welch, the former CEO of General Electric, once noted, it is important to reward the outperformers. These are people who make the difference in corporate performance. In a free-market capitalist system we need such people as these, on the one hand, but on the other hand society also needs a safety net for those who fall out of the system. However, for the continued success of the system we must be careful not to level out the high performers, who continuously lift standards and boundaries. Instead of discouraging such people, society actually needs to encourage them, as without them there would be less for governments and citizens to share.

That said, it is unarguable that there were and still are unjustifiable excesses and distortions in the remuneration system employed at banks.

Of course, the problems discussed elsewhere in this book, including failures in regulation, bank liquidity management, credit standards, and excess leverage, are more to blame for causing the crisis than the bonus culture. The argument that high bonuses were the incentive to adopt extreme leverage and poor liquidity standards is a sophism. The impression that bankers would sit together in a meeting room discussing the potential bonus they could take home if they set up a structured investment vehicle (SIV) or a collateralized debt obligation squared (CDO-squared) is simply wrong. That is not how the system works. It would be more correct to argue that high remuneration arose from the mistakes that were made in the other areas, but which are not being made a scapegoat. In fact, to concentrate on bonuses is to abrogate the responsibility for the real errors that were made in banks, central banks, and government.

Notwithstanding this state of affairs, it is true that in certain cases there was greed involved and that this greed skewed decision making. But this is not limited to the banking industry. Consider, for example, the events at WorldCom, the excesses of CEO Dennis Kozlowski from Tyco, and of course the Enron saga, which led to the demise of that company's audit firm Arthur Andersen.

## A DISTORTED REMUNERATION MODEL

Greed is undoubtedly, since prehistory, a trait of humankind. But of course this does not mean that we should simply accept it and close our eyes to certain practices.

Let us consider first the type of malpractices that occurred in the banking industry. A major issue connected with excessive risk taking at banks is the tendency to calculate the net present value (NPV) of the future profits made on deals, and add this to the annual profit-and-loss (P&L) budget of a sales or trading desk. The following hypothetical example is typical of what occurs regularly at many investment banks.

A salesperson closes a transaction with a client that is a 20-year inflation hedge, for an amount of €250 million. The future cash flows over that period would create a profit of €4.5 million, which would be a substantial contribution to the salesperson's annual budget. However, the €4.5 million will be realized over the lifetime of the deal (that is, 20 years) and represents a net present value. There is always the possibility that during the next 20 years the client could go bankrupt and be incapable of fulfilling its liabilities. Potentially this could mean that the bank would be stuck with a negative mark-to-market on the transaction that could not be recovered from the client. If we assume this happens three years into the deal, then unwinding the transaction would create a loss of €1.3 million for the bank.

The problem, however, is that the salesperson would in all probability have already been remunerated on this deal three years earlier. And furthermore, as is not unusual in the industry, it is also possible that the salesperson has left the bank and is no longer an employee. A transaction that the salesperson originated and received additional compensation for (in addition to his annual salary) has now created a loss for the bank that paid him.

These practices have been abandoned at certain banks, which have replaced them with a system whereby part of the profit realized on long-dated transactions is placed in a reserve account and allocated to the budget of the trader or salesperson on a year-by-year basis as long as the trade remains profitable.

Nevertheless, there are still many banks that do not apply this system and stimulate instead something akin to hit-and-run behavior. The preceding example refers to a long-dated inflation swap, but similar parallels can be made with the selling or trading of collateralized debt obligations (CDOs) and other structured credit deals that have maturities of 7 to 10 years or even longer. In the case of the CDO-type product, the authors are familiar with examples where the profit or fees paid out to sales desks were dependent on the quality of the tranche of the note that was sold. At a Belgian bank, salespeople received a 5 percent commission of the notional of the tranche added to their P&L budget whenever they sold to an investor client the BB+ tranche of a CDO, which is the poorest quality (just above the equity tranche) of the structure. Investors in a BB+ note, one would hope, are always sophisticated market participants who understand fully the risk/ reward behavior of such products. But this is not always the case. And such a remuneration arrangement can stimulate potentially reckless behavior. For instance, what if the desk, spurred on by such a remuneration arrangement, starts selling CDO tranches to clients of its commercial paper desk? A CDO tranche is not in the first instance a suitable investment for money-market investors.

Is this greed? To a certain extent it is. But it is the natural outcome of a system in which senior management does not look at the quality of P&L realized by its traders or salespersons, but rather its immediate impact. What system should be adopted? Is there a benefit for the bank and all stakeholders if instead of closing, for instance, 5,000 tickets with low margins in order to realize its budget, a trading desk closes 10 to 15 deals that generate a similar profit? This type of mentality created the possibility that some fixed-income sales desks would focus only on high-commission deals and would neglect the daily plain-vanilla flow business.

Nevertheless, we must still downplay the hysteria about big bonuses. Only a very small minority of bank employees receive excessive remuneration packages. (Then again, everything is relative.) For example, during the period 2002–2007 approximately 4,000 people in the city of London received a bonus greater than £1 million. Out of a total of approximately 325,000 people in London employed in financial services, this is only 1 percent of the total population. In this respect the state of affairs in the financial industry is replicated in other industries.

This does not mean that there are not certain anomalies. An interesting observation was made by Clementi, Richardson, and Walter (in Acharya and Richardson 2009), to wit that something is not quite right when board members' remuneration is higher than the return from the underlying stock or the return earned by shareholders, who ultimately take the risk. Or the way they phrased it: "Would you rather manage a Wall Street firm or own the shares in one?"

Their analysis produced some surprising results. First of all, they compared the total remuneration package of CEOs among several industries (mining, manufacturing, transport, wholesale, retail, and the financial industry, including the insurance sector). A first observation is that the average wealth of a CEO in the financial industry outperforms that of other industries. This comes as no surprise as this was already a general belief. Second—and this could explain at first glance why the performances are higher compared to other sectors—CEOs in the financial industry receive a higher amount of company shares.

Given this feature, one would think their wealth would be much more related to the performance of the underlying share. However, if one looks at the relationship between the wealth of CEOs and shareholders one observes surprising results. The authors measured the extent to which CEOs' wealth would change if the shareholders' wealth would rise by 1 percent—in other words, the elasticity of CEOs' wealth versus shareholders' wealth. Apparently CEOs' wealth is less affected in this case compared to shareholders' wealth performance. And this answers the earlier question: In a downturn market, CEOs' wealth is less affected than that of shareholders. This we understand goes against the fair principles of capitalism. CEOs are guiding the firm, with the backing from the shareholders, and are taking risks to produce profit. But if their strategy does not work out, they should be penalized to the same extent as the shareholders.

## UNSUITABLE PERSONAL BEHAVIOUR

As in certain other industries, as well as in the world of politics, the investment banking industry attracts personalities with a more than healthy interest in acquiring wealth and control. These individuals are often more driven, and more motivated, than those around them and consequently it is not unusual to see these types promoted to senior positions.

Senior management in banking is from time to time dominated by eccentric personalities who manage strategic desks or indeed the entire firm. This is evident from Sorkin (2009) and McDonald and Robinson (2009).

Reading about the Lehman collapse, one repeatedly comes across the remark that former Lehman CEO Dick Fuld and his president, Joe Gregory, did not give the impression that they understood the risks involved in the new investment banking environment from the 1990s onward. In the two references just noted, the words *remote* and *denial* are often used when describing the personalities of the top two Lehman executives. What is implied—which, if true, would be worrying if it is repeated in other banks' management—is that these shortcomings were often due to megalomania, excessive ego, and envy.

An example of this is given in McDonald and Robinson (2009), describing the way Dick Fuld dealt with the rise of the private equity firm Blackstone, which was run by two ex-Lehman managing directors, Peter Peterson and Stephen Schwarzman, who it appears were not on speaking terms with the Lehman CEO. Instead of focusing on the core business and listening to the advice of his senior investment banking team (Larry McCarthy, Mike Gelband, and Alex Kirk), who had been warning since 2005 about the growing risks that Lehman was facing, Fuld was driven by frustration and envy to start investing in hedge funds, energy companies, credit cards, commodities, and leveraged mortgages, apparently not only to match the success of the private equity firm, but also because of a desire to top the league tables published on Wall Street. This obsession arose to such irrational levels that at certain times when strategic acquisitions were being discussed at the executive committee, the head of risk management was asked to leave the room. Clearly, if we accept this anecdote as fact, this is not only worrying but also extremely dangerous for any firm.

It is certainly possible to run a big organization without getting into detail on the technicalities of the operation. Genuinely effective business leaders are wise to surround themselves with experts and talented people who can guide them into making the right decisions and have the personality to motivate their troops. However, from the moment that ego is prioritized over all else, then an organization is in great danger. This danger is exacerbated if the person at the top is surrounded by sycophantic acolytes whose only purpose would appear to be simply to keep the monarchy in place.

It is difficult, from a corporate governance point of view, to make recommendations or formulate regulations on how to deal with these types of phenomena. At the end of the day it is not up to the government or regulator to remove such people, or better still not to promote them in the first place, but rather up to the shareholders to vote them out of the organization.

# CONCLUSION

In order to tackle these excesses and incentives of unnecessary risk taking, we recommend that remuneration policy should have some long-term prospects built into it.

One such policy that is noteworthy is in place at two European banks with which the authors are familiar. The UK FSA is considering imposing a similar system at the banks it regulates. The bonus is split up into three parts. For ease of discussion let's say this split is in equal thirds. The first part of the bonus is a straightforward cash payment, paid out immediately. The second part of the remuneration package is in the form of shares of stock options that have to be held for a minimum period of time before they can be sold or exercised. That period should be around three years. The final part of the bonus, also in cash, is placed in a claw-back account, which is also monitored for three years. During that period the bank has the right to reclaim part of this cash back if a trade or deal originated by the individual concerned starts losing money for the bank.

A bonus arrangement with postponement of cash payouts would certainly diminish a hit-and-run mentality among traders and sales. However, one should not forget that this system would not prevent a crash or crisis of the kind we experienced in 2007–2009. If this bonus schedule had been common practice during the beginning of the twenty-first century it would not have prevented some traders and salespersons from receiving considerable amounts of money, even when it would have been spread out over, say, 2003 to 2007. The subprime mortgage crash was created by the buildup of a number issues acting over a decade.

Another initiative that should be investigated is the return of partnerships of the kind that operated on Wall Street and in London among the U.S. investment banks and UK merchant banks. It would be difficult to prove empirically, but if partnerships had still existed today, it is possible that senior management would have thought twice before pursuing certain risky strategies. Accounting firms still operate under this model, and a partner at an audit firm company will be careful before signing off on a balance sheet of an audited client, as the partner can be held legally responsible if the information on the balance sheet does not reflect reality. So the question that should be asked is whether it would make sense to return to this model in investment banking. We believe that risk-taking behavior of senior bankers would be more contained if they were personally liable should a transaction go wrong, as was the case in the past. However, such a model may be unworkable in today's global market and large multinational integrated banks.

Risk behavior is also closely related to the type of representatives on the board. This is not a discussion that is limited to the banking industry, but can be generalized for the corporate world. Board members represent the shareholders. Increased transparency forces listed companies to report their results on a quarterly basis. There is nothing wrong with this. Nevertheless, the very short-term focus on corporate results makes board members focus on the share price. The issue here is that on the boards of banks and companies there are rarely, if ever, members that represent the bondholders (in case the company has outstanding debt).

Having only people on the board who are mostly concerned about a rising share price will certainly influence risk behavior and culture, which always resonates downward from the feelings and beliefs of the highest level. If major investors in the outstanding debt of a company were to have a presence on the board, the accent on policies and strategies would be more risk contained.

There is also the issue of the expertise of board members. Certainly in banks the sophistication of financial products reached a high level over time. There are well-known anecdotes of board members of European bailed-out banks who were not up to speed with, for example, securitization techniques and structured credit in general. The authors are personally familiar with senior management at European banks who displayed this lack of knowledge of modern banking.

Therefore we recommend that regulators monitor the financial knowledge of all board members and force them to take relevant courses on a regular basis, in order that they stay updated about developments in the industry.

Reproduced from *The Future of Finance* (2010)

## CORPORATE GOVERNANCE WITHIN BANKING

Banks are the critical infrastructure component in every economy. They provide financing for individuals and corporations, and facilitate the transmission of funds across payment systems. The effective functioning of any economy depends on banks ensuring the supply of credit and liquidity throughout the business cycle and in all market conditions. The importance of banks to human well-being and societal development is recognised by the fact that banking is a regulated industry and protected by taxpayer-funded safety nets in virtually all countries worldwide.

The efficient mobilisation and allocation of funds is predicated on an inherent trust in the system by all participants; when trust fails, so too does the system, which is clearly illustrated by events following the 2008 banking crisis. While effective regulation is an important component of building this trust, *the* most critical element is the corporate governance regime in place at banks. If the corporate governance regime in place at banks is seen to be efficient and effective, the cost of capital is lowered for all market participants. This in turn increases capital formation and raises productivity growth. Therefore the management of banks has implications for corporate as well as national prosperity. It is self-evident that bank corporate governance must be robust, effective, and adaptable to changing circumstances, and fit for purpose.

In general, corporate governance may be described as the manner in which an entity is governed. This refers to the sets of relationships that exist between the Board of the entity, its management, employees, shareholders, and other external stakeholders. These relationships include the manner in which the various players interact and the steps taken to ensure that the entity delivers, in terms of the expectations that the various players have of each other. The UK Corporate Governance Code includes the following recommended key features:

- An effective Board to provide leadership;
- Accountability, which also covers transparent processes for the management of risk;
- Effective remuneration policies, to ensure the alignment of interests between management and all other stakeholders;
- Effective and open relationships with shareholders.

Corporate governance, of course, is not only an issue for banks. Corporate governance codes have been developed in a number of countries (for example, the King code in South Africa, *Code of Governance Principles for South Africa 2009*), setting out good practice with regards to the governance of corporate entities. In both South Africa and the UK, all listed entities are required to either comply with the relevant code or explain any deviation. Each code has its own areas of focus, and may have styles which differ. However, all emphasise the need for transparency, accountability, and long-term sustainability as necessary ingredients for the long-term growth and success of the entity.

In the banking industry, it is noted that corporate governance is of particular importance. This refers to the manner in which the business and strategy of the institution are governed by the firm's Board and senior management. An accurate and succinct description is provided in BIS (1999 & 2006), which describes the mechanics of bank corporate governance as:

1. Setting the bank's objectives, including a target rate of return for shareholders;
2. Setting the control framework that oversees the daily operations of the bank;

3. Protecting customer deposits;
4. Setting strategy that accounts for the interests of all stakeholders, including shareholders, employees, customers, and suppliers; and
5. A bank must be maintained as a going concern, irrespective of economic conditions and throughout the business cycle.

In this chapter, we describe the principles of good corporate governance within banking, what drives the shape of governance structures, and how they are typically implemented. This is included together with the view to managing risk throughout the economic cycle and under volatile market conditions.

### Principles of Sound Corporate Governance Within Banking

There is no universal bank corporate governance model. Differences in organisation and infrastructure exist by regulatory jurisdiction and also within them, depending on the type of institution being considered. However, a number of publications suggest sets of principles or key elements of a robust corporate governance framework which have common elements. The World Bank publication, *Analysing Banking Risk* sets out the following elements for a sound corporate governance framework within a bank:

- A well-articulated corporate strategy against which the success of the firm and individual contributions can be assessed;
- Setting and enforcing clear assignment of responsibilities, decision making authority, and accountabilities appropriate for the bank's selected risk profile;
- A strong financial risk management function (independent of business lines), adequate internal control systems (including internal and external audit functions), and functional process design with the necessary checks and balances;
- Adequate corporate values, codes of conduct and other standards of appropriate behaviour, and effective systems to monitor compliance;
- Financial and managerial incentives to act in an appropriate manner;
- Transparent and appropriate information flows both internally and externally.

Underpinning any effective structure will display an engaged and competent Board that has both the skills and experience to effectively engage with management in a constructive fashion. The focus on the role of the Board is emphasised in the following eight principles suggested by the Basel Committee on Banking Supervision (BIS 2006), which relate to corporate governance for banking organisations:

Principle 1: Board members should be qualified for their positions, have a clear understanding of their role in corporate governance, and be able to exercise sound judgement about the affairs of the bank.

Principle 2: The Board should approve and oversee the bank's strategic objectives and corporate values that are communicated throughout the organisation.
Principle 3: The Board should set and reinforce clear lines of responsibility and accountability throughout the organisation.
Principle 4: The Board should ensure that there is appropriate supervision by senior management consistent with Board policy.
Principle 5: The Board and senior management should effectively utilise the work conducted by the internal audit function, the external auditors, and other internal control functions.
Principle 6: The Board should ensure that compensation policies and practices are consistent with the bank's corporate culture, long-term objectives, and strategy and control environment.
Principle 7: The bank should be governed in a transparent manner.
Principle 8: The Board and senior management should understand the bank's operational structure, including where the bank operates in jurisdictions or through structures that impede transparency (that is, "know your structure").

Taking the above into account, key features of an effectively governed bank will include the following:

- Genuine controlling supervision by the Board of Directors; the Board will be engaged with (and not distant from) the organisation, and the Board's role within the bank will be discernible to both management and other employees (Board involvement and engagement);
- Clear articulation of the vision and strategy for the bank, in a manner that is understood and embraced by all layers of management and staff (Clear direction);
- Direct executive supervision of each business line (Executive accountability);
- Supervision of business line activities by individuals who do not work within the business lines (Effective management challenge and over-seeing);
- Independent audit and risk management functions (Effective and independent control functions);
- Senior personnel who are sufficiently expert in their jobs (Executive competence).

Following the 2009 banking crisis, a number of key questions relating to governance became topical. These included the following:

- Were bank Boards sufficiently engaged with their organisations?
- Were bank Boards sufficiently competent to properly challenge management?
- Did bank Boards have a sufficient understanding of the operations and methodologies used within their bank to assess risks?

- How transparent was the reporting of control issues within the bank?
- How effective was the Board's control of executive incentives?

In reviewing the role of corporate governance in banks (and other financial institutions) following the well-publicised banking failures in the UK around 2008, the Walker Committee (*A review of corporate governance in UK banks and other financial industry entities*, HM Treasury 2009) developed five key themes around which the report (and its more detailed 39 recommendations) was structured:

- The "unitary Board" structure adopted in the UK and the "Combined Code" (as the UK Corporate Governance Code was then called) remains "fit for purpose" – i.e., there is no reason to seek to change either the essential structure of UK Boards or the standards / principles by which good corporate governance may be assessed;
- The principal deficiencies observed in bank (and other financial institution) Boards related to patterns of behaviour, rather than organisation. In other words, problems arose because of how (effectively) Boards functioned rather than the structure of Boards;
- Given that the overriding strategic objective of a bank is the successful management of financial risk, Board level engagement in risk supervision should be materially increased;
- There is a need for better engagement between shareholders (in particular fund managers acting on behalf of the beneficial owners) and the Boards of investee companies (the banks) – to ensure that the shareholders do not operate in a disengaged fashion and do hold the Board and management accountable;
- Enhanced Board supervision of remuneration policies, in particular, variable pay, as well as improved disclosure.

As a result, there is now a significantly greater focus on the role of the Board within the governance structure, and regulators have significantly enhanced their interaction with the Board, while, at the same time, taking a careful look at the role played by shareholders in ensuring the effectiveness of the Board.

### Key Role Players in a Typical Bank Governance Structure

While a typical governance structure is shaped partly by a number of external "drivers", the following are the key role players within a banking governance structure in most jurisdictions.

**The Regulator(s)**     While the majority of countries enshrine the role of supervisory and conduct authorities within the central bank, the UK incorporates a "Twin Peaks" regulatory structure, where one regulator – the Prudential Regulatory Authority, part of the Bank of England – is responsible for prudential supervision, while another – the Financial Conduct Authority – is responsible for market conduct regulation.

The nature and form of the regulatory interface between the banking entity (at both a management and Board level) is key in setting the "tone" for governance activities. Effective regulatory interaction can and should heighten both management's and the Board's appetite for appropriate governance activities and structures, while assisting them both by broadening their perspective on the activities of the bank. Unfortunately, the interaction is not always that constructive, and in this case, it can be seen as an implementation failure of this important step in the overall governance process.

**Shareholders** This body plays a key role in three important respects:

- Ensuring that the elected Board is both competent and engaged. (See "Board stupid", *Euromoney*, February 2008);
- Holding the Board and management accountable for outcomes;
- Demanding appropriate levels of transparent reporting of activities.

Because of these roles, recent reviews of governance processes within banks (such as the Walker Committee report) have included a focus on the role of shareholders in the overall governance process. It is important that shareholders take their responsibility for the election of a competent Board seriously, as well as willingness to challenge the Board and management when relevant opportunities are presented (such as at annual general meetings).

However, it can prove difficult for shareholders to exercise genuine control and influence in practice (note the rise in so-called "activist shareholders"). This is because they are diverse and diffuse in nature and in practice they often prefer to leave governance to the paid agents. This does not mean that they should not seek to act towards achieving the three targets above.

**The Board** The Board plays the pivotal role in the overall governance structure. This is where the internal tone / culture is established, the internal governance structure is set and final oversight of activities takes place. However, the role of the Board is not to manage the business – that is the role of management. The Board plays a supervising role and provides a challenge to management as they act on the agreed strategic plan. But to do this it must have a good idea of where it wants the bank to be and to go.

The most effective structure of a bank Board remains an issue for debate; this issue was discussed in one of the earlier book extracts in this chapter. That said, the form of the Board itself does not have a significant bearing on the ability of a bank to survive a capital or liquidity crisis. Indeed, the report of the Walker Committee concluded that UK bank failures had more to do with the effectiveness of the Board than their structure.

An important feature of the unitary Board structure is the emphasis on the separation of duties between the Chairman of the Board and the CEO. This requirement, particularly for banks, is for an independent non-executive to fill the role as Chair, allowing for the governance process to function effectively. This separation is not necessarily the case in other countries, such as the US.

In practice, the size of the Board is a function of the activities that the Board is expected to undertake, and when linked to the absolute imperative which is now better recognised, bank Boards should comprise persons with sufficient experience and knowledge to fully understand the operations of the bank, resulting in a Board size which may be bigger than some might suggest. Indeed the size of bank Boards is growing rather than shrinking, due mainly to the increased demands on Board member involvement. For example, the Board of Barclays PLC in the UK has grown from 13 members (10 non-executive) in 2009 to 15 members (13 non-executive) in 2013, with the number of Board committees growing from four in 2009 to six in 2013.

In many countries, bank Boards tend to be larger than they are in the UK, for example, in South Africa as Table 17.1 shows.

**TABLE 17.1**    Examples of Board sizes and committees

| | # Directors | # Non-executive Directors | # Board Committees | Notes |
|---|---|---|---|---|
| First Rand Group | 20 | 17 | 6 | *Excludes mandatory Board credit committees which are located at subsidiary bank level* |
| Standard Bank Group | 17 | 14 | 7 | |
| Barclays Africa Group | 12 | 10 | 8 | *2 additional Board members to be appointed* |
| Nedbank | 13 | 10 | 9 | |

*Data Source*: 2013 Annual Integrated Reports.

It is clear that the demands on a bank Board arc growing and that the time commitment required is substantial. However, the commitment is more than just time – it also requires the ability to respond quickly to market developments. Of the bank failures of 2008–2009 discussed in Choudhry (2012), none of the banks had conducted Board and sub-committee meetings more than once a month, with an average frequency of one meeting every eight weeks. The pace of events in 2008 suggests that such a frequency is insufficient to meet risk management demands, as the extract from PoB shows.

Table 17.2 illustrates how a bank Board needs to be flexible in responding to market conditions as well as how extensive the demands of Board members are, in terms of committee meetings.

Barclays is one of the largest UK listed banking groups, while Barclays Africa / Absa (Absa Group was reconstituted as Barclays Africa in 2013) is one of the largest South African banking groups. The Barclays Africa / Absa Board met a similar number of times each year over the period represented in the table, but they faced few of the external (and internal) issues that confronted the Board of Barclays over the same period. It is also evident how much time is dedicated to committee work.

Given the above it would be dangerous to be prescriptive about the structure and size of a bank Board. However, it is clear that:

- The Board should be large enough to ensure that all the necessary activities of the Board, including committee work, can be effectively addressed, while small enough to react appropriately to emerging issues;

**TABLE 17.2**   Example of Board meeting frequencies over time

| | Barclays Group PLC | | Barclays Africa / Absa | |
| --- | --- | --- | --- | --- |
| Year | # Board meetings | # Board committee meetings | # Board meetings | # Board committee meetings |
| 2007 | 21 | 26 | 9 | 46 |
| 2008 | 30 | 21 | 8 | 41 |
| 2009 | 27 | 34 | 8 | 32 |
| 2010 | 11 | 33 | 6 | 30 |
| 2011 | 16 | 33 | 8 | 30 |
| 2012 | 23 | 43 | 7 | 38 |
| 2013 | 13 | 29 | 8 | 36 |

*Data Source*: Bank Annual reports: 2007–2013.

■ Membership of a bank Board is not something to be lightly undertaken – there are significant demands and responsibilities, and appropriate experience and expertise are vitally important.

Finally, the composition and objectives of the Board should be set to prevent a specific interest group from gaining overall control. Composition of the Board is critical, and independent non-executive directors play an important role in this regard. While banks remain a commercial enterprise (in the main) with responsibilities to shareholders, directors of a bank have a fiduciary responsibility to the bank's depositors as well. Thus Board composition and objectives must be set with this in mind. Transparency in operation and reporting is a key requirement.

**Management Style**   The structures put in place to develop, drive, and monitor the business activities of the bank will be largely influenced by the senior leadership team in general and the CEO in particular. The role of the Board will be to ensure that appropriate attention is paid to the aspects of accountability, transparency, challenge, and control in the structures proposed by senior management, and that appropriate and timely reporting is generated by the established management structures.

Within the overall governance structure, the Board will place significance on the effective functioning of the management / executive committees established to oversee the various activities within the bank. It is also important that the senior leadership accept and understand the governance role of the Board and that the relationship, as evidenced by the nature of reporting, is open and transparent.

Corporate governance is as much an art as it is a science; its impact is a function of the values embraced within an entity and the manner in which people, whether Board members, senior leadership, middle management, or other members of staff, interact with each other. Structures and processes cannot dictate the openness with which management is challenged or the effectiveness of that challenge. Neither can it dictate the willingness of middle management to ensure the open flow of information, both good and bad, through to senior management and the Board. A strong and dominant CEO who brooks no challenge is a strong contra-indicator of good corporate governance, whatever the financial results produced by the firm. Effective governance is thus a function of the firm's culture (how people actually behave) rather than the scale or scope of written (and agreed) policies that may be laid down by leadership. We address at the end of the chapter in the section on leadership.

**Board Skills and Knowledge**   As noted above, and becomes clear as one considers the degree of involvement expected of a non-executive director on the

Board of a bank, it is critical to effective governance that the Board, collectively, has the skills, experience, and understanding of the operations of a bank to provide the appropriate level and form of challenge to executive management. The range of skills and experience required will be a function of the scale and complexity of each individual bank, but the collective skill set and experience base of directors should enable the non-executive Board, *inter alia*, to:

- Understand the financial structure of the bank, the drivers of its financial performance, and the associated risks; in this regard a detailed understanding of the bank's balance sheet, the bank's risk profile, and overall risk appetite is critical;
- Understand the operational structures deployed within the bank and the associated operational risks, with a particular focus on information technology matters;
- Appreciate the marketing and business development strategy of the bank and be able to challenge management on its effectiveness;
- Have a good understanding of the legal and regulatory framework within which the bank functions, and have an appreciation of potential legal and regulatory risks to which the bank may become exposed;
- Guide the development of remuneration policy (rather than being led by management);
- Play a constructive role in the formulation of the bank's strategy, contributing to management thinking and providing an effective challenge;
- Understand the market dynamics of the market segments within which the bank chooses to do business.

Of all the above, financial literacy, encompassing both skill and experience, is perhaps the most important. The Board has to be able to comprehend the implications of financial outcomes and at both Board and relevant committee meetings, to challenge management on emerging trends. At the committee level, both the Audit and Risk committees play vital roles in this step within the governance framework.

The required insight into financial trends and outcomes is perhaps best illustrated by the Risk Appetite Statement and the monitoring of financial outcomes relative to this. Regulators in many jurisdictions, when undertaking the annual review of a bank's ILAAP and ICAAP process, request to review the bank's overall risk appetite statement. This statement should be owned by the Board, and is an explicit statement of the tolerance of the bank for various risk exposures, in both qualitative and quantitative terms.

By "owning" the statement, the Board makes clear that the risk toler-ances contained within are, or should be, as sacrosanct as a market-maker's trading limits; in other words, a breach would be viewed as a disciplinary offence. The statement should also set the tone and culture of risk culture in the bank, and this qualitative feel is as important as the quantitative limits, because it influences customer service attitudes.

Figure 11.6 (in Chapter 11) shows an example of a best-practice Board risk appetite statement, in this case as drafted for a medium-sized UK com-mercial bank. The statement itself should be drafted by ALCO, for upward review and sign-off by the Board. In the example at Figure 11.6, we see the various parameters by which risk exposure is measured (for example, loan–deposit ratio and minimum size of liquid asset buffer). The "live" statement would list the actual limits for each parameter, depending on the specific bank's risk tolerance under business-as-usual conditions. So it might state an LDR maximum of 85% and an LAB minimum of 110% of 30-day stressed environment cash outflows, for example.

Note that the objective here is to illustrate the format, not the specific risk tolerances which will differ with each bank. The example of a Board risk appetite statement given at Figure 11.6 is a recommended template applicable at most banks.

## Board and Management Governance Structures

**Board Committees**  As noted above, both Board and management govern-ance structures will vary by jurisdiction, size, and complexity of the bank in question. There is thus no agreed template, but, the following summarises what can be observed around the world. Not every bank necessarily exhib-its every committee described below and the smaller banks will have fewer sub-committees, but some or all of the following committees are likely to be found within the Board governance structure and normally comprise mostly independent non-executive directors:

- **Audit committee:** This is required by regulation, as well as the governance codes. This may include Compliance within its mandate. All members of this committee are required to be independent non-executive directors.
  **Risk committee:** Chaired by the CRO or a NED, this includes "capital management", and generally includes all forms of risk – financial and otherwise.
  (Note that in many banks these two are combined into an "Audit and Risk Committee" (ARC) or Audit, Risk and Compliance Committee (ARCC). A template ARCC Terms of Reference is available on the book's companion website; see Chapter 20 for further details.)

- **Nominations and Remuneration committee:** This committee is responsible for remuneration policy for the bank, with a special focus on the important issue of executive remuneration; the mandate sometimes is extended to other human resource matters, but this overlaps if there is a specific HR-related committee.
- **Governance committee:** This committee is responsible for reviewing all governance processes within the bank, as well as ensuring the effective functioning of the Board; this leads into recruitment and selection of new Board members and reviews of Board and individual director performance. This may or may not include the appointment (and removal) of key executive positions.
- **Social and Ethics committee:** In some countries this committee is required (and is not necessarily banking specific), and has a wide remit. The essential purpose is to ensure, that, in a focused manner, company Boards effectively review the various actions that make the entity a "good corporate citizen". Matters range from HR policies and practices, the manner in which the entity interacts with its clients, environmental and sustainability issues and, importantly in the South African context, "transformation" of the workforce.
- **Executive committee:** An exception to the rule of non-executive director participation, the Executive Committee (ExCo) is the vehicle, common to most banks, through which the delegation of operational responsibility and accountability takes place. As suggested, this is an executive committee, led by the CEO, and comprising the other executive directors as well as other senior executives, depending on the structure of the bank. Typically, there is no NED involvement in ExCo.

Good practice would require that the mandates for each element of the Board (and management) structures are guided by a written mandate that is reviewed and agreed by a suitable oversight body. For the Board itself, this often takes the form of a "Board Charter". Such documents ensure that the responsibilities and accountabilities are clear. Figure 17.1 represents a typical Board governance structure.

**Management Committees** The structure of management governance committees is just as important as the Board committees, as these provide the interface with the "coalface" of the banking operations and determine, to a large extent, the quality of the information that flows to the Board committees. Ignoring the complexity introduced when a bank has multiple business lines, perhaps spread over multiple jurisdictions, the core management governance committees and control functions might be as follows.

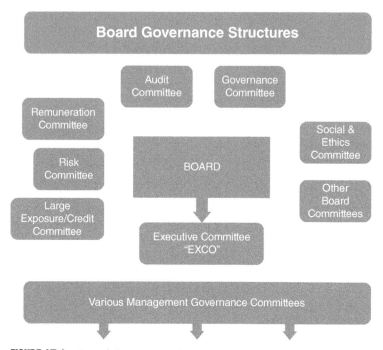

**FIGURE 17.1**   Board Governance Structures

**Control Functions**   Control functions, critical to the integrity of the governance / oversight processes within a bank, typically have direct access to Board committees, and the heads of these functions are appointed by the relevant Board committee, on the recommendation of the executive. Their independence from the business executive teams is an important aspect of the overall governance structure of the bank.

- **Internal audit:** Typically reports directly to the Board audit committee, with its key function being to provide an independent assessment of the effectiveness of internal control systems and procedures;
- **Risk management:** Typically reports directly to the Board risk committee, and provides oversight on all risk and control issues. It also provides input to the Risk committee and Board on the setting of risk strategy, and is the primary interface with the regulators on risk matters;
- **Compliance:** Generally reports to either the Audit or Risk Board committees and is responsible for oversight of all the bank's compliance related activities, both at client / customer and at entity / bank level.

Governance (Related) Committees   There are a number of key committees typically found in a bank structure that are critical to both the operations of the bank and overall governance process. All management committees would report into ExCo, but some would also have an indirect link into relevant Board committees or ALCO as well. The committees described below may appear to overlap with the control functions described above. They do – but they describe the mechanism whereby management and business takes accountability for the controls necessary to run the bank, while the control functions, described above, are separate from business units and are accountable, for their oversight function, to the Board rather than the executive.

These management committees would include:

- **Lending (credit approval) committees:** Credit approvals will be delegated to different levels within the bank and may follow different processes for different business units. However, it is usual to find a main credit approval committee for each key business unit (for example, Retail / Commercial / Corporate) that links, finally to the Board credit committee, if this exists. What is important here is that the final credit approvals, especially on significant transactions, are independent of business unit management to ensure the integrity of the process. Note that ALCO or ExCo would normally approve limits above which a transaction size is deemed significant and so requiring higher approval.
- **Risk committees:** Management risk committees are established to ensure proper risk management reviews across all risk types, and, in some instances, they also perform vital management functions. These committees typically address a specific risk type, and the following are the management risk committees typically found in a bank:
- **Credit risk committee:** Responsible for the overall management, monitoring and reporting of credit risk across the bank.
- **Market risk committee:** Where a bank assumes market risk on its balance sheet to any significant degree – depending on the scale and scope of the bank and its activities – this committee would be responsible for the management, monitoring and reporting of market risk across the bank.
- **Operational risk committee:** Responsible for the overall management, monitoring and reporting of operational risk across the bank. As this includes reviewing of process failures, this may be where the management reviews of internal audit reports takes place.
- **Compliance committees:** These committees would review the bank's compliance with legislative and regulatory requirements. The compliance requirements on banks arise not only from the traditional

(prudential) regulators, but also from legislation that addresses issues such as anti-money laundering (where the sanctions for non-compliance may be significant) and consumer protection (where non-compliance can have a significant impact on the bank's position and reputation in the market).

In addition to the above, there are likely to be a number of other management committees, such as the CRO-chaired Risk committee, the Credit Committee, and so on, in place, which will be part of the overall governance fabric of the bank, but where the main focus will be on operational matters. Again, these structures will be a function of the size and complexity of the bank. What is important, from a governance perspective, is the effectiveness of these committees with regard to decision-making and the transparency of the decision-making process, and it is important to ensure that the executives do not spend their entire working days in committee meetings.

In summary, given the crucial role of corporate governance within banks, the corporate governance frameworks and structures put in place are an important element of the proper functioning of the bank. Effective governance is critical, whatever the size of the bank, but the shape and form of the governance structures may differ. What is important, however, is that they have an impact on the manner in which the bank operates and that they add to the stability of both the bank and the banking system within which the bank operates.

Perhaps the real lesson learned from 2008 is the simplest of all: banks are the custodians of other people's funds and should act in a manner that is consistent with this simple fact. To put these funds at significant risk is simply immoral, and effective governance structures, policies, and procedures play a key role in making sure that we limit the risk associated with funds entrusted to banks.

## NON-EXECUTIVE DIRECTOR IMPERATIVES

Increasing levels of boardroom regulation and risk have placed greater demands on the non-executive director (NED) community and specifically on the personal characteristics and technical skills and knowledge of NEDs.[1] "The days of turning up for a quick hour and a good lunch are long gone," attributed to Sir Bryan Nicholson,

---

[1] The principles we describe here are equally applicable to both NEDs and independent NEDs (INEDs).

former chairman of the Financial Reporting Council, in an interview with PwC is quite true. As the role and responsibilities of the NED are now under regulator scrutiny, the decision to embark on a fresh directorship must be made with a thorough understanding of the challenges and changes facing an NED.

The pressures of today's business environment, in conjunction with recent high-profile bank governance failures, are driving corporate demand for more diverse and specialised NEDs as businesses appreciate the benefits of having the right people on their Boards. Before accepting an appointment a prospective NED should undertake their own thorough examination of the company to satisfy themselves that it is an organisation in which they can have faith and in which they will be well suited to working.

Every current or prospective NED must ask themselves:

- Do I have something to contribute to this Board?
- Am I capable of passing judgement on the company's management / strategic plan / risks / alternatives / competition?
- Do I have sufficient time and am I sufficiently committed?
- Am I aware of the risks?

A person who adds value as a Board NED is someone who brings innovation, experience, and technical knowledge and expertise in banking and balance sheet management to the Board whilst monitoring executive decisions. The challenge is to remain independent of the business and its day-to-day operations, while maintaining a level of knowledge that will allow the NED to ask tough, objective questions.

A NED must exhibit the following characteristics:

- Constructively challenging and contributing to the development of strategy;
- Monitoring the performance of management;
- Satisfying themselves that financial information is accurate and that financial controls and systems of risk management are robust;
- Ensuring there is satisfactory succession planning and determining appropriate levels of remuneration for executive directors.

Ultimately it is the Board that runs the bank and is responsible directly if the bank fails or becomes unviable. NEDs are there to hold executives to account, so they must be up to their role.

## THE ROLE OF LEADERSHIP AND TEAMBUILDING EXCELLENCE IN GOOD BANKING

A quote attributed to Richard Branson runs along the following lines: "We don't worry about delivering good customer service – if you treat your staff right, they will treat customers right." There is undoubtedly much truth in this. A satisfied workforce, unfettered by purely monetary incentives, is more likely to deliver good customer service and minimise "conduct risk" exposure for the bank. The working environment has much to do with producing a satisfied workforce. However, this is a book on banking and finance, not leadership and teambuilding, so we will confine ourselves to just a few words, based on the author's experience when he was IPO Treasurer at Royal Bank of Scotland during 2013–2014. (The project to divest part of the bank was known as "Project Bluebird", hence the Treasury team was referred to as Bluebird Treasury.)

As he developed the Bluebird Treasury team, the author realised that he was following, loosely and inadvertently, the equivalent of the "Total Football" concept practised by Rinus Michels, the manager of the 1974 Holland football team and as articulated brilliantly in his book *Teambuilding: The Road to Success*. The key tenets of this philosophy were:

- In practice, a flat management structure because everyone's opinion, from the most junior to the most senior, is respected and invited;
- There is a genuine teamworking spirit because everyone shares the same goal and is therefore willing to assist anyone else in the team; and
- As a result, analogous to the Dutch football team of 1974, up to a point any team player can perform any team function. (There are limits to this: just as "total football" leaves the goalkeeper out of the concept, so one would not necessarily expect the graduate trainee to be able to perform the role of the CEO, or indeed vice versa.)

Following a "Total Banking" leadership style is more likely than not to foster genuine team spirit and attract people who wish to work for the team, rather than just for the pay cheque. Other general pointers:

- Minimise process and bureaucracy. Don't say 300 words when 10 will do. Minimise the process involved in actually delivering work.
- Being courteous, polite, and respectful extends to all facets of your life. It should not stop in a work environment. Beware the boss who speaks meekly to his wife on the telephone and shouts aggressively at his subordinates in a team meeting.
- It is important to treat others how you would want to be treated.
- Be yourself and be true to yourself, especially in instances where people are political or are not overly transparent and open. Of course, if you have an aptitude and taste for office politics, and not being open with colleagues, then you will ignore this advice.

- People skills and soft skills are essential. They are what make a really good team and in turn this is what will make a really good Bank.
- As a leader you should trust your team to get on with what they have been tasked to do. Delegate meaningfully. Don't micromanage. And treat everyone the same, no cliques, and no inner circles, which are divisive and ruin team cohesion.

Figure 17.2 is a summary slide from the Bluebird Treasury team concept presentation. There are also two presentations on leadership on the book's website, in the folder for Chapter 17. See Chapter 20 for further details.

# "Total Banking" concept

Bluebird Treasury Doctrine

Treat people the way you wish to be treated

Everyone is involved in all tasks

No single-person dependencies

Staff can and do step in for each other as required

Open, collaborative, and challenging environment

Effective upward and downward communication

Effective upward and downward delegation

Team answers each other's telephones

Open access: no cliques, no inner circles

"Open door" policy is genuine and not platitude

**FIGURE 17.2**  Total banking leadership concept, Bluebird Treasury team 2013-14

## CONCLUSIONS

When it comes to bank governance and oversight, there is no "one-size-fits-all" and consequently no one "right" way to set the governance framework. What is important is to have in place a structure that ensures, above all else, that the institution remains a going concern throughout the economic cycle and beyond, and that the bank functions for the benefit of all its stakeholders. The individuals that are directly responsible for this are the members of the Board (or Boards for those banks that operate a dual or two-tier structure). Focus on the role of the Board has increased dramatically since 2008.

There are a number of different Board structures that one observes in place at banks around the world. The unitary Board structure is common in "Anglo-Saxon" economies, whereas the dual Board structure is frequently observed in the EU and also in state-owned enterprises in Asia-Pacific economies. Board composition and frequency of meetings also differ markedly across jurisdictions. No one factor of structure, composition, or frequency of meetings define good governance, but there are common features when good practice is found. At the heart of good governance is an engaged and competent Board, and a management team that understands and embraces the importance of challenge and transparency. Much of this is captured in the eight principles set out in BIS (2006) and outlined in this chapter.

Governance failures may trigger a variety of events within a bank, but these usually lead to one conclusion – the bank either fails or gets into significant difficulties. The losses are invariably significant, so the importance of good governance cannot be overstated.

## SELECTED BIBLIOGRAPHY AND REFERENCES

Basel Committee on Banking Supervision: Enhancing corporate governance for banking organisations, 2009, http://www.bis.org/publ/bcbs122.pdf.

Choudhry, M., "Effective bank corporate governance: observations from the market crash and recommendations for policy", *Journal of Applied Finance and Banking*, Vol. 1, No. 1, June 2011.

Euromoney: Board Stupid: Clive Horwood, February 2008, http://www.euromoney.com/Article/1859509/Board-stupid.html?ArticleID=1859509.

Institute of Directors in Southern Africa: King Code of Governance for South Africa 2009, http://c.ymcdn.com/sites/www.iodsa.co.za/resource/collection/94445006-4F18-4335-B7FB-7F5A8B23FB3F/King_Code_of_Governance_for_SA_2009_Updated_June_2012.pdf.

OECD: The Corporate Governance Lessons from the Financial Crisis, 2009, http://www.oecd.org/finance/financial-markets/42229620.pdf.

The Walker Report: A review of corporate governance in UK banks and other financial industry entities, 2009, http://webarchive.nationalarchives.gov.uk/+/http:/www.hm-treasury.gov.uk/d/walker_review_261109.pdf.

The UK Corporate Governance Code, https://www.frc.org.uk/Our-Work/Publications/Corporate-Governance/UK-Corporate-Governance-Code-2014.pdf.

World Bank: *Analysing and Managing Banking Risk: Corporate Governance*, Chapter 3, https://openknowledge.worldbank.org/handle/10986/14949.

World Bank: *Analysing Banking Risk: A Framework for assessing corporate governance*, Chapter 3.

*"A Commanding Officer who flew the most dangerous trips himself contributed immensely to morale. Perhaps the chief reason that he inspired such loyalty and respect was that he took the trouble to know and recognise every single man at RAF Linton. It was no mean feat, learning five hundred or more faces which changed every week. He would not ask them to do anything that he had not done himself."*
—Max Hastings, describing Leonard Cheshire VC (1917–1992), *Bomber Command*, Michael Joseph Limited, 1979

# CHAPTER 18

# Present and Future Principles of Banking: Business Model and Customer Service

I t is surely unarguable to state that before one can achieve a satisfactory result in any endeavour one must first ask what "satisfactory" looks like. A practitioner of any art, and banking is as much art as science, must first define greatness before attempting to create it. Most of us know what banking is and what a bank does; that isn't the hard part. But what does *good* banking look like? Is a bank that is in a satisfactory state the one that has generated the required rate of return for its shareholders? Or the highest rate of return? Or is it the one that pays its employees the highest salaries? Perhaps it is the one that has the most satisfied customers, or conversely the one with the fewest complaints per 1,000 customers? Or the one with the best relationship with the regulator?

Actually it's none of these. As the author is fond of saying, the first principle of good banking is to have principles. Banks are a cornerstone of modern society, and indeed not-so-modern society. Without a banking service in a community, very little commercial activity would get done and the state of the human condition would be much more underdeveloped than it is now. Practically every aspect of modern life has been assisted at some point of its development by bank funding, or government funding that is reliant on the banks. So whilst all of the criteria set out in the first paragraph are undoubtedly important, none of them is the most important one.

The author wrote this in the Preface of his book *The Mechanics of Securitization*:

**This extract from** *The Mechanics of Securitization* **(2013)**

## Preface to *The Mechanics of Securitization*

In 2009 *The Times* newspaper of London carried an interview with Paul Volcker. The former chairman of the Federal Reserve "berated bankers for their failure to acknowledge a problem with personal rewards and questioned their claims for financial innovation." According to *The Times*, Mr. Volcker rebuked "senior figures in the financial world for failing to grasp the magnitude of the financial crisis and belittled their suggested reforms." As bankers demanded that new regulation should not stifle innovation, Mr. Volcker was quoted as saying, "The biggest innovation in the industry over the past 20 years has been the cash machine."

It's a pity that this impression is now fairly commonplace in business, media, and political circles. One only has to look at the mobile telephone industry, and to be aware that it was financed mainly by recourse to financial engineering techniques that included securitization, to understand that innovation in finance has often been a force for much good in the world. It is worthy of preservation, and if one was to observe a rickshaw puller on the streets of Dhaka, Bangladesh (average salary $1 per day) using a cell phone, one would indeed be convinced of this. The technology needed to make the cell phone available to a mass population worldwide required hundreds of billions of dollars in investment, and a fair proportion of these funds were raised via the securitization markets.

This book is not a general textbook on banking or finance, much less a polemic on the virtues of free markets and capitalism. It is a very focused guide aimed at practitioners in structured finance who are involved with originating, structuring, or arranging securitization transactions. Essentially it has been written to act as a checklist of necessary tasks for commercial banks that are interested in closing a securitization of assets either off their own balance sheet or on behalf of a third-party bank. These assets might be corporate loans, mortgages, credit card loans, or other more esoteric "future flow" cash receivables, but the essential principles that must be followed when securitizing any asset class are virtually identical, and differ only in detail. These essential principles are covered here. Much securitization activity in the immediate post-2008 era was of the "in-house" variety, with an objective of creating tradeable securities that could then be used as collateral when obtaining funding from their central bank.

Reproduced from *The Mechanics of Securitization* (2013)

A rickshaw puller using a mobile phone: a genuine improvement in quality of life for those previously without access to a landline telephone. Just one of many thousands of symbols one could use to illustrate the good that finance in general and banks in particular can achieve. One might say that it was the mobile phone companies that created the product, and of course one would be right; but the financing for the project, from design and development to implementation such that a modern-day technological marvel could be accessible to one of the poorest sections of society, came from banks. We can point to any number of similar instances of societal well-being enabled by banks: more people owning their own home, or starting their own business, or being able to save for their retirement or to help put their children through university. Or indeed setting up their own university. The list is a long one.

The purpose of the foregoing is not so that everyone who works in a bank can pat themselves on the back – not at all. Rather, the purpose is to make the point that the key stakeholder of all banks is society itself. Not the shareholder, the customer, or the regulator but the wider community. Of course the three aforementioned are important stakeholders, but a good bank is one that generates good for society. That's pretty much it.

Certainly the customer is very important, although in that respect banks are by no means unique, in fact the contrary. Every corporate institution, excepting certain (but not all) public-sector entities, must ensure it delivers customer satisfaction otherwise it may find its future well-being rather bleak, if not shortened considerably. Banks have to go one further, however, and work to ensure community satisfaction. They form such an essential part of modern society that any other objective would ultimately be short-sighted. So good banking would be that which had as its objective working towards achieving society's well-being and improvement, as far as it is able to influence actions with such an aim.

In this chapter, we present recommendations on the issues banks should be considering in their daily activity and as part of their longer-term goal. This does, as one might expect, focus on the customer. The relationship with the regulator we consider a given – it is (or should be) merely the starting point for all banks that they have an open, constructive, and transparent working partnership with the regulator. Managing the balance sheet shape and structure is also a given – every bank should be working on ensuring the balance sheet is long-term viable, and we addressed this topic in depth in Part III. The issue of marketing, being as it is very important in customer franchise targeting and retention, we consider also a given and a beginner's primer on this topic is provided in the Appendix to this chapter.

Instead we look at the customer and the ideal banking business model that should be in place to ensure the customer is always at the receiving end of good service. We illustrate our recommendations using a hypothetical pitch book of a "model bank" that has just set itself up for business. We hope that this model bank approach gives a clear picture of the customer ethos that all banks should be aiming towards, where the customer is once again identified and treated as an individual and not a number. Other than the very short extract just given at the start and equally brief one at the end, there is no previously published material in this chapter.

## WEBSITE READING

We show below the links for two informal articles on the suggested future course of the banking business model, with respect to customer service.

The Future of Banking: more traditional than one would think
https://www.linkedin.com/pulse/future-banking-more-traditional-than-one-would-think-moorad-choudhry

Banking is going 100% mobile only. . .or is it?
https://www.linkedin.com/pulse/banking-going-100-mobile-onlyor-moorad-choudhry?trk=mp-reader-card

## CUSTOMER SERVICE MODEL: THE MODEL BANK

This is not the place to discuss the failings of banks in the Western world (and by "failings" we are not referring only to failed banks in the crash. The fines paid out by UK banks for derivatives mis-selling or rigging Libor or a number of other tawdry practices are also a form of failing). In the period since 2008 there has been a considerable literature reviewing the state of financial markets and banks, generally by authors much more august and higher up in the "pecking order" than yours truly. Industry issues of trust, remuneration, the usefulness of innovation, product mis-selling, and myriad other problems abound in the business media. There is no need to discuss these issues further here, which are covered elsewhere in abundance.

Instead we will present what we consider are the key principles that *should* be integral to a good bank's customer business model. The recommendations are open to argument of course, and a business philosophy that is not genuinely customer-centric might easily suggest a counter to our proposals. That is perfectly fine, and is what makes a market. Rather, the purpose of this section is to state what we consider to be *principles* of banking; as such they should be, if not timeless at least of validity for a good few years into the future. There is always an alternative approach that one can take. What we recommend here is simply what we consider to be the best approach for truly good banking.

Note that this section is very much a "high level" description and suggestion of best-practice in customer service in a bank. For a more detailed look on marketing bank products and good customer service provision, please see Chapter 2 of the author's book *An Introduction to Banking*, 2nd edition (John Wiley & Sons Ltd).

## Understanding Good Customer Service

Every bank in the world claims to offer "excellent customer service" or insist they "put the customer first". Certainly no bank would admit to poor customer service. It is possibly one of the most frequently encountered platitudes in business. But it is important to avoid platitudes when formalising one's attitude and objectives with regard to customer service. The key is to take such platitudes and turn them into something genuine, by enshrining a customer-centric ethos into the firm's culture. This is something that is much harder to do, particularly in banking, where in all but the very smallest firms there is considerable "silo mentality" at work and most staff never deal with customers.

So, it is certainly important to provide *genuine* good customer service; the concept is one of those that may not be straightforward to define, but one knows it when one sees (or receives) it, and it's also apparent when one receives bad customer service. Consider this section to be a primer on the essential elements of acceptable customer service in banking.

In general any and all customers should expect the following from their bank:

1. The provision of products and services that meet their needs;
2. The provision of the service that customers want, when they want it and without operational errors;
3. The provision of satisfactory and consistent "after care", which is consistent and ongoing backup and response to customer queries.

It is often on (3) that many banks fall down, particularly larger banks with a large number of customers and mass-market business model.

Banking products are essentially commoditised in nature. This being the case, the primary means to differentiate oneself from peer banks is through a reputation for good service and helpful, welcoming staff. While the product base of a bank is determined at the high or strategy level, even the most junior staff in a branch or call centre are in a position to influence the level of service. It is these employees who deal with customers on a daily basis, and so the way they greet customers, how efficiently and error-free they process transactions and requests, and their face-to-face and telephone / email manner will influence heavily the public perception of the bank as a good place to take their financial services requirements. These are all ingredients of good customer service. Paradoxically, it is often these employees, at the "coal-face" of customer contact, who are the least educated and lowest paid staff in the bank. This is something bank executives should think about.

Service provision is an important part of banking and being a banker, amongst others for the following reasons:

- Good customer service leads to customer satisfaction, which results in retained customers;
- Generally it is quicker to deal with a satisfied customer than an unhappy one or one making a complaint, so business volumes should increase as they are processed more efficiently;
- Satisfied customers are a good source of referral business.

Factors that help drive a good customer service experience include:

- Pleasant, helpful and efficient staff;
- Staff who are interested in customers' needs but also possess the detailed product and process knowledge to be able to answer questions and supply solutions accessibly;
- Receiving the products or service that meet the customer's needs and do not experience operational or process errors during their lifetime;
- Modern, attractive, user-friendly branches that may also include free Wi-Fi, a mini business lounge, and so on.

The factors that may contribute to a negative customer service experience include:

- Rude, unhelpful, bored staff;
- Unkempt branches;
- A bureaucratic, patronising and/or process-driven approach to speaking and responding to the customer, whether in person, on phone, or on email;
- Waiting in a long queue (be it in a branch, on call centre phone, or on the internet);
- Call centre staff who don't know anything about you;
- Staff trying to sell products that weren't asked for, in order to meet sales targets;
- Mistakes in processing requests.

The above are just a small sample of the positive or negative factors that determine whether a customer has a good or bad experience. Readers would most likely be able to add items to both lists from their personal experience. It is easy to see from this list how important the approach and motivation of customer-facing in ensuring good service.

All of the issues we list can be addressed by increasing staff, resources, training, and bandwidth. So while addressing customer service costs money, it is unarguably money well spent in the long run. Ultimately it is all about treating the customer with courtesy or, as the author prefers, treating people the way you would like to be treated by people.

---

**EXAMPLE 18.1   IMPORTANCE OF CUSTOMER-FACING STAFF**

The transaction experience between a customer and a bank is often the one that takes the shortest time, certainly compared to the time-span of bank loan products, but it is often the most important part of the customer service experience. The interaction between customer and branch or call-centre staff is one that must be taken seriously by banks. Poor customer service at the "front end" can often result in loss of business and poor reputation developing as the customer spreads the word; at the same time if this experience is a good one then reputation is enhanced.

It stands to reason then that customer-facing staff should be highly motivated, well trained, and reasonably well paid. This will help deliver a good customer service experience.

The private banking arm of a UK bank has a policy that its call centre staff must all be university graduates. This makes them slightly more mature and educated than school leavers; at the same time all management entry-level staff are required to spend one year working in the call centre and in branch before they are eligible for promotion onto more senior roles. This makes the staff motivated to deliver good service, as they cannot progress if they receive poor customer feedback.

---

**Follow Up and After Care**   The automobile industry has a saying that the sales-person may be behind an initial sale, but it is the service department that ensures repeat business. This is applicable to banking as well. The initial loan approval, credit card issue, deposit facility, and so on is less likely to be followed by a long-term relationship if there is no follow up service, or if there are errors in processing, issuing of statements, and so on.

In the first instance the front office staff should follow up with a general call or email; for example if a personal finance loan was taken out to purchase a car, the salesperson might enquire if this had been successful, what type of car was it, and was the customer happy with it. Making this sort of follow up means that:

- The banker is demonstrating good customer service and a personal touch;
- If there has been a problem, the banker has demonstrated a proactive interest in the customer and moreover is in a position to fix it now;
- There is higher chance of repeat business with this customer, because of the positive impression made and the customer perceives the banker has an interest in the customer personally.

Regular, but not intrusive, follow-up calls and efficiency in account settlement and operational processes are the key to good customer service.

**Customer Complaints**   A complaint is any form of grievance that the customer has. In general, if a customer makes a complaint it reflects the fact that one or more aspects of the service or the bank itself has not met with the customer's expectations.

Customers make complaints for all manner of perceived problems or errors, or even slights. It may be a lack of satisfaction with the product, the level of service, the person the customer dealt with, or the bank itself. The bank should have a straightforward and easy-to-follow process for dealing with complaints, but the important thing to remember is that a complaint is an opportunity to put things right, and so end in a positive outcome. For this reason, complaints should be viewed in a favourable light. Most unhappy customers don't complain, they simply take their business elsewhere (and this is easy to do with a commoditised product like banking services). So turning an unhappy customer into a happy one is actually another way to work towards retaining business.

**Customer Satisfaction**   Any commercial enterprise should always concern itself with ensuring that its customers are "satisfied". Good customer service is essential to long-term viability of a business, and working towards ensuring customer loyalty and retention is as important as winning new customers. Across different industries including banking, a number of businesses spend a lot of time and effort undertaking slick and glossy marketing to attract new customers, but then have a poor after-care service such that the customer is left feeling like a number and not a name. This is a trap into which a bank must not fall.

Ascertaining customer satisfaction levels is not straightforward to determine. Satisfaction surveys are a common approach, and certainly worthwhile undertaking, but are sometimes viewed with annoyance by customers, and completion levels can be variable. It is important to act on the results of satisfaction surveys, otherwise over time the completion rate for them will fall to a negligible level. Responding directly to a customer who has made comments or recommendations in a survey is also important (provided the customer has ticked the box indicating they are happy to be contacted. But if they have ticked this box, then the bank should contact them.).

Survey design is important as well: one should follow these general guidelines:

- Ensure the survey is quick and easy to complete;
- Ensure it asks the right questions;
- Ensure that the request for feedback is designed to generate responses that are capable of being acted upon.

Finally, a satisfaction survey conducted in the communications medium of the customer's choice is also an opportunity to highlight any new services or initiatives.

The two main indicators of customer satisfaction are retention levels and number of complaints. It is true that in the financial services industry, customer apathy is high and often people do not switch provider not necessarily because they are satisfied with the bank but because moving is perceived as too much aggravation. That said, customers staying with the bank should still be viewed as something to pursue proactively.

Complaint levels should be monitored regularly and compared to the industry and peer group statistics. A rising number of complaints is a worrying trend, however banking is a mass volume business and as business grows the absolute number of complaints may increase whilst its share of the business is steady (or declining). On the other hand, many dissatisfied customers may not complain at all, they may simply leave. So both this and the satisfaction statistics are important metrics for a bank to monitor, investigate and follow up.

## Genuine Challenger Banking

In response to the events of 2008, the competition authorities and the regulators made various attempts to reduce the barriers to entry in banking, which have always been high and made higher by the capital and liquidity requirements of Basel III. Whether this made any difference or not is a question worthy of study; that said, large numbers of new entrants have come onto the market in many countries. However, with only one or two exceptions, such as Metro Bank or Handelsbanken in the UK, which combined traditional branch networks with a more-or-less full service product offering (although with certain types of corporate customers ruled out), most of the new players have been niche market competitors. Excluding non-bank firms such as peer-to-peer lenders, new licensed banks have tended to fall into the "digital" bank category, with a limited product suite. Taking the UK again as an example, although the approach observed here has also been noted elsewhere in Europe, North America and South-east Asia, new banks generally fall into the following categories:

- SME-only branchless banks: in the UK these include Aldermore and Oak North Bank. The former has subsequently expanded into retail customer business and the latter targeted retail depositors, but the focus of their business was the small corporate;
- Retail-only branchless banks: these are banks such as Tandem, Atom, and Starling banks, which are "digital" only with customer interface via a smartphone mobile app. The product offering is narrow, based around the current account and overdraft.

Not all new or "challenger" banks could be said to fit into these narrow categories, but the point we are making is that in essence such niche banks target a limited section of the customer marketplace.[1] This makes it unlikely that they will truly "challenge" the established large players, most of whom have well-regarded digital and mobile offerings as well. Of course, they can certainly offer ideas and approaches that the industry as a whole may benefit from. Ultimately, some customers will be happy doing all their banking from a smartphone, while some other customers will desire some human interaction for some of their banking. The banking relationship is a lifetime one; all of us require financial services of some kind or another throughout our lives.

In that spirit we would suggest that the modern approach to good banking would encompass *all* of the following:

- **Genuine customer service:** by that we mean the customer is the focus of the business and the bank has a real relationship with it, irrespective of how important or profitable the individual customer may be. To have a real relationship is to know the customer personally, as a name and not a number, to understand his/her/its banking requirements but in the context of the customer's overall lifestyle, and to provide these requirements in a timely, efficient, and error-free manner. This goes beyond the type of computer algorithm understanding of a customer's needs that an online retailer possesses, for example;

- **Name not number:** one cannot emphasise enough how for a bank as opposed to, say, a high-street clothes retailer (although that is in no way intended to denigrate the latter), every customer needs to be treated as an individual, and not merely one of many in a mass-market environment. Only through this approach will a bank be able to provide genuine customer service. Banking needs of individual customers develop and grow over time; for example, the financial services requirements of a single 21-year-old salaried worker are different, or at least less onerous, than those of a 55-year-old married self-employed person with children at school. Treating customers as all purchasers of the same tin of baked beans will not enable true understanding to develop and will hinder the provision of good customer service;

- **Omni channel:** some customers, individuals and SMEs alike, are perfectly happy dealing with their bank through digital interfaces only, and have no desire or need to talk to a member of staff either in person or on the phone (or video link). Some may never step into a bank branch in an entire decade. Still others prefer to deal with a human being for at least some service requirements, such as a mortgage, personal finance loan, or FX exposure hedging requirement. Unless a bank is specifically setting up as a niche provider for a certain group of customers only, it will need to ensure it provides the customer interface infrastructure that

---

[1] The CFO of one of the new banks told the author once, "We're targeting the 18–35 year age group only". This may or may not be wise strategy, but it does mean a large section of the potential market will never be your customers.

all its customers are likely to desire to use *through the entire period of the customer relationship.* This means enabling digital mobile, phone, internet, video, and branch banking, but is also a key reason why the bank branch is unlikely to disappear. To that end:

- Just as many well-known retail brands do not locate a sales outlet in every high street in the country, banks also do not need to. A smaller number of branches is expected over the next 10–20 years, and this is logical: a good yardstick would be to position branches in "major" population centres only. In the UK there are only 21 towns and cities with a population greater than 250,000; thus, a UK bank seeking to serve the whole country, and which is offering mobile and internet banking, would need only a handful of branches and stilll be able to deliver omni-channel services to the whole country;
- The "model bank" we describe in the next section adopts the following strategy: place a branch in every town with a population of 250,000 or over. For the United Kingdom, this would mean just 21 branches for the entire country. This is a far cry from the many hundreds (or even thousands) of branches some banks possess, and so is an opportunity for a significant cost saving. And the branch would remain an important part of the customer interface and relationship maintenance process;
- **Instant response:** in the digital technology era, there is little justifiable reason for any form of delay in the service process, be this approving a loan, responding to an information request, or correcting an error. Any good bank must place instant response service provision at the top of its priorities, measured in hours rather than days;
- **No more "computer says no" banking:** the adoption of "black box" banking relying on models and assumed parameter input has been the significant factor behind the erosion of the relationship with the customer. Computer models are an integral part of the finance industry and will remain so, but an element of judgement call made by a human being is the essential ingredient of genuine good customer service provision. In the UK, banks such as TSB and Handelsbanken are noteworthy for granting local branch managers an element of autonomy in the loan origination decision. This must surely be the way forward for any bank that takes genuine customer service seriously.

Delivering the above requires the right working culture in the bank. To help inculcate the correct culture, there is one imperative: *employee remuneration should not be linked to customer volume, sales levels, or P&L, but rather customer satisfaction levels.* Anyone who disagrees with this should acquaint themselves again with the stories of each of the bank failures in the UK, Europe, or the US in 2007–2008.

The foregoing presents the basic tenets of a "good" bank, but in essence only. There is much more required to flesh out these bones, but the above are the key points. Of course, there is much variety in banking and some will prefer an alternative approach, niche or otherwise. Both mainstream banks and new or challenger banks have some things to learn from each other, in reality. But for banking to re-emerge as a long-term sustainable force for good, the mainstream banks are the key players in this great game.

An article in *American Banker* entitled "How Far Can 'Challenger' Banks Ride Fintech Charters?"[2] suggested that so-called challenger banks need to do more than simply provide a sleek app if they wish to mount a genuine challenge to the established banks. Its premise was that while such fintech banks may thrive in Europe, the US market is too fragmented in comparison and as such established banks will need to be challenged by a full-service digital service provider rather than a niche provider. But the fintech start-ups in Europe may find a similar obstacle in Europe as well. For instance, it is a moot point how many of the 23 new banks, mainly mobile-only entities, that have been licensed in the UK since 2013 will still be around in 2023 or beyond. Any bank needs to present solid USPs and a reason for a customer to move over to it, and it is in this sphere that so many challenger banks may struggle to build critical mass. If a bank cannot present a convincing reason why a customer should change its supplier, it isn't "challenging" anybody.

## CHOUDWEST BANK: THE MODEL BANK AND "CONCIERGE BANKING"[3]

This hypothetical bank presents a business model that is customer-centric and technology savvy. It's credo is in effect to bring "private banking" to everyone, but by private banking we don't mean asset management and tax planning for wealthy individuals; our definition is of a bank that provides a personal service to each of its customers, retail and corporate, irrespective of their size or income generation potential. Doing this by definition sacrifices an element of profit for the bank. Traditionally, it would also necessitate a large physical branch presence and considerable front-office staff numbers, but in the era of fintech this necessity is negated somewhat. In other words, it is by no means inevitable or pre-ordained that, unless one is a high net-worth individual or a large corporate, one has to go without personal service or human contact for one's banking needs. The bank uses the expression "concierge banking" to encapsulate its service offering. It defines this as follows:

> *With Concierge Banking we will make each and every customer feel like they are the most important and valuable customer we have.*

---

[2] https://www.americanbanker.com/news/how-far-can-challenger-banks-ride-fintech-charters, 21 December 2016.
[3] This section was co-authored with Adam Ginty.

The following exhibits set the scene, illustrate the problems with customer service, and how a bank (whether a new start-up or established institution) might look to address the issue. They are self-explanatory. They are designed to be applicable in any jurisdiction, but of course in some countries the problems suggested – and their respective solutions – may not exist, in which case that is already a more satisfactory state of affairs to begin with. Tables 18.1 and 18.2 list some current customer issues with their bank in many countries around the world; Figures 18.1 to 18.4 describe the model bank's response to them.

Below is an example of a model bank introducing their service offerings and ethos, as well as their "vision statement".

**TABLE 18.1**  Sample of customer issues with their banking services

| SMEs | Retail Customers |
|---|---|
| ▪ Limited access to unsecured borrowing, and decline in lending<br>▪ Their bank doesn't understand their business<br>▪ Often feel that charges are excessive, complex, and unfair<br>▪ Overdrafts facilities are being withdrawn at short notice<br>▪ Lending criteria felt to be too onerous<br>▪ Slow response / turnaround times<br>▪ No relationship, they are just one of many customers | ▪ Mass market general customer service not individual focused<br>▪ Attractive interest rates or bonuses "disappear" after a short time without notification<br>▪ Poor customer response: late, inappropriate, inflexible, or conflicting responses<br>▪ Unusual or onerous contract terms; hidden fees and charges<br>▪ No genuine service, unable to speak or meet with a human being who is familiar with personal situation |

**TABLE 18.2**  Crowded competitive landscape – no single bank meets all customer types' requirements

| Existing banks | "Challenger" banks |
|---|---|
| Introductory, free business banking with phone-based account management and a range of savings products | Digital service model, generally serving only a portion of SME and Retail savers' banking needs |
| 1. Business current account and retail savings accounts<br>2. Full suite of lending, credit, and savings products<br>3. SME banking focus<br>4. 18-Month free business current account<br>5. Full product suite<br>6. SME and Retail savers branch and phone | 1. Specialist lender<br>2. Savings, Asset and Invoice Finance, Property Lending<br>3. Telephone, internet, and some limited relationship banking<br>4. Business Lending, Property Finance, and Savings<br>5. Internet and intermediary based<br>6. Regional focus |

The challenge - to build a scalable banking solution that addresses the fundamental inadequacies in the market offering for SME and Retail Customer

Our proposition seeks to address what we believe are three simple customer requirements, that we aim to provide a different banking path for SME and Retail Customers and, in turn, provide genuine good customer service

1. How can I be treated like an individual and not just a number?

2. Why should I settle for "computer says no" banking, or busy call centres where my query is simply passed down the conveyor belt?

3. Why should I need to have two (or more) years trading history when I've got a great business idea?

**FIGURE 18.1**    Creating a value proposition that delivers concierge banking

Implementation of Superior IT infrastructure, free from legacy issues

A single holistic view of the customer

Concierge Service on first contact for *all* customers, irrespective of size or business potential

**FIGURE 18.2**    Addressing customer issues: 1. Why can't I be treated as more than just a number?

Staff empowered to make lending and savings decisions

Product and Relationship Teams that are integrated

Named Relationship Managers supporting SMEs

**FIGURE 18.3**    Addressing customer issues: 2. Why should I settle for "computer says no" banking, or busy call centres where my query is simply passed down the conveyor belt?

We strive to understand your business and will deliver the lending solution that suits *you*

Our Relationship Managers understand what it means to be an SME and will treat every business on its own merit – there are no prescribed sectors

**FIGURE 18.4**   Addressing customer issues: 3. Why should I need two years trading history to get a loan, when I've got a great business idea?

## EXAMPLE 18.2   CHOUDWEST MODEL BANK SERVICE OFFERINGS, ETHOS, AND VISION

### Changing the Face of Banking

**Mission statement:** To be our customers' No. 1 provider of banking services

> **Our Aims:**
> - To deliver exceptional customer service to:
>   - Small and medium-sized businesses (SMEs);
>   - Individuals looking for a better personal service;
> - Each customer to be treated as an important individual: "private banking" for everyone;
> - Business to be conducted via mobile phone, lap top, telephone, or in person at a branch;
> - State of the art technology to facilitate a high standard of personal service and genuine relationship building.

### Delivering a New Kind of Banking

- **Concierge Banking** will deliver a personal banking service for all customers;
- It will be a unique offering for SMEs and people who want to interact with their bank at a time and place convenient for them, in the style and manner that they desire and that they deserve;
- We intend to know every customer personally;
- The value in our business will be derived from our use of technology allied with a unique service ethos.

*(Continued)*

## Planned Product Suite

Personal Banking
- Current Account;
- Deposit Account;
- Term Deposit;
- Notice Account;
- Cash-ISA Account;
- Personal Loan Secured;
- Personal Loan Unsecured;
- Credit Card.

Business Banking
- Current Account;
- Deposit Account;
- USD and EUR Deposit Account;
- Start-up Loan Unsecured;
- Term Loan Secured;
- Term Loan Unsecured;
- Stand-by Liquidity Line;
- Commercial Mortgage;
- Bridging Finance;
- Invoice Discounting;
- Credit Card;
- Foreign Exchange Services.

## Genuine USPs

- Use current technology and social-media style algorithms to enable the bank to have in-depth knowledge of every single customer to a greater degree than possible up to now;
- Provide a comprehensive and secure bank-wide technology platform for the effective operation of all the bank's systems: a feature unique amongst banks where every department from front to back and middle office uses the same system – creating efficient balance sheet management AND great customer service;
- Provide genuine tailor-made loan and deposit products and transaction profiles;
- Utilise blockchain technology in the core banking platform to provide a high level of security and compliance robustness;
- Replace "call centres" with Relationship Manager Centres where the person customers speak to will know them as well as their personal RM;

- Combine leading-edge technology with a personal service ethos to ensure:
  - Customers will not feel as if they are dealing with someone new each time they make contact;
  - No business is ruled out: we will treat every application on its own merit;
  - Genuine instant service and response.

### Vision Statement

"Do good work."*

*The entirety of a speech given by Virgil "Gus" Grissom to the employees of General Dynamics, builders of the Atlas rocket, in 1961. Gus Grissom was the second American to fly in space, and the first to fly in space twice.

To put the foregoing vision into practice will require the right mix of strategic nous, committed senior and middle management, appropriate culture, and sufficient capital. To achieve the stated objectives will require more comprehensive and granular project plan and a coherent marketing strategy. An example of the "high level" approach that must be built on further is shown at Figures 18.5 to 18.7, which address the topic of customer acquisition for the model bank.

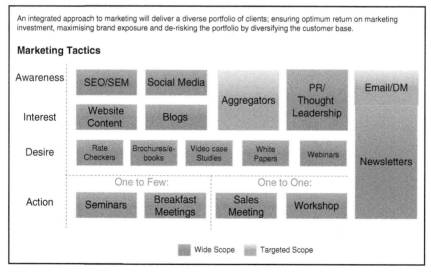

An integrated approach to marketing will deliver a diverse portfolio of clients; ensuring optimum return on marketing investment, maximising brand exposure and de-risking the portfolio by diversifying the customer base.

**Marketing Tactics**

| Awareness | SEO/SEM | Social Media | | | PR/ Thought Leadership | Email/DM |
|-----------|---------|--------------|--|--|------------------------|----------|
| | | | Aggregators | | | |
| Interest | Website Content | Blogs | | | | |
| Desire | Rate Checkers | Brochures/e-books | Video case Studies | White Papers | Webinars | Newsletters |
| | One to Few: | | | One to One: | | |
| Action | Seminars | Breakfast Meetings | | Sales Meeting | Workshop | |

■ Wide Scope ■ Targeted Scope

**FIGURE 18.5**   High level acquisition strategy

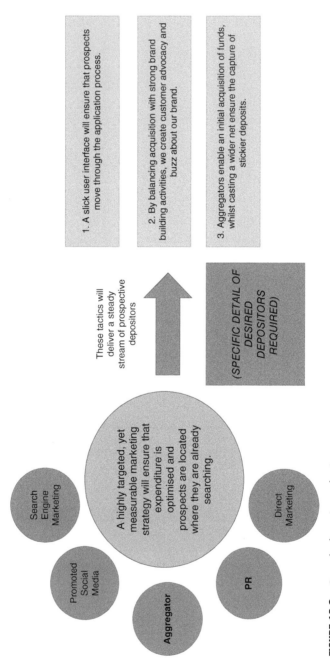

**FIGURE 18.6** Sample deposits gathering strategy

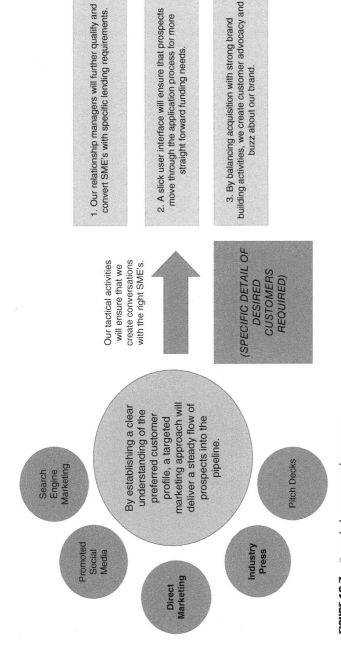

**FIGURE 18.7** Sample loan growth strategy

Obviously we have presented only the bare bones of our model bank. There would be considerable more detail required, and this would form the basis of the banking licence application (if it was a start-up) or the regulatory review submission for an existing bank. A summary of what is presented and reviewed as part of a banking license application in the UK is given at Example 18.3.

We hope that the series of exhibits given at Figures 18.1 to 18.5 provides a flavour of what banks should be doing to ensure they regain the trust and high esteem of society as a whole. It's merely a case of putting the customer first in a genuine way and not in a platitudinous way. Simple, really.

**This extract from** *The Principles of Banking* **(2012)**

## Afterword to *The Principles of Banking*

The profession of banking is an honourable one. To be given a responsibility at any level of a banking institution is to be entrusted with a valuable part of society's well-being. Bankers should never let this thought stray far from their minds.

Sound judgement requires knowledge and experience, of the right kind, if it is to be exercised during both good and bad economic times. This is not always a core belief of those in senior management. In his book *Bounce: The Myth of Talent and the Power of Practice*, (London: Fourth Estate 2010), Matthew Syed notes that:

> *For years, knowledge was considered relatively unimportant in decision-making . . . This was the presumption of top business schools . . . They believed they could churn out excellent managers who could be parachuted into virtually any organisation and transform it through superior reasoning . . . Experience was irrelevant, it was said, so long as you possessed a brilliant mind and the ability to wield the power of logic to solve problems . . .*
>
> *This is nonsense . . . successful decision-making in any situation characterised by complexity – whether in sport, business or wherever – is propelled not by innate ability but by the kind of knowledge that can only be built up through deep experience.*

An understanding of the core principles of banking, acquired over time, is an essential prerequisite of successful banking.

The risk management principles we have discussed in this book are identical whichever way one looks at them: be it from a shareholder-value perspective, hedging or fair-value perspective, regulatory requirement perspective or societal well-being perspective. It is important for bank management to incorporate them into their strategy, even if they think that other banks are ignoring them.

The underlying message remains: the first principle of good banking is to have principles. Or, as the motto of the London Stock Exchange puts it: *my word is my bond.*

Reproduced from *The Principles of Banking* (2012)

## EXAMPLE 18.3   BANKING LICENSE APPLICATION AGENDA

We list here the typical agenda of a banking license application submission to the UK regulatory authorities.

### XYZ Bank – Part I Session

Identity
- USP;
- Purpose, vision and values;
- Brand strategy and positioning;
- SWOT.

Governance
- Ownership structure;
- Management structure and experience;
- Board and board committees (skills);
- SIFs (significant influence functions) / Profiles / Experience;
- Evolution of governance and oversight;
- Internal audit.

Business overview – Day 1 / Customer
- Customer segments;
- Products;
- Pricing strategy;
- Channels;
- Market share;

*(Continued)*

- Risk (high-level, further detail in Part II);
- Conduct agenda (high-level, detail in Part II);
- Capital and liquidity (high-level, detail in Part II);
- Resolution and recovery (high-level).

### Financials

- Financial viability and sustainability (including key assumptions);
- Profitability (including key drivers, margin assumptions);
- Impairment assumptions;
- Cost base;
- Customer franchise targets;
- Key sensitivities / downside risks.

### Risk

- Risk management (including strategy to identify and manage risks to the business);
- Risk appetite;
- Risk structure;
- Risks to the plan;
- Risk MI and reporting;
- Risk policies.

### Future strategy

- Vision / evolution;
- Growth;
- Strategic planning process.

### Challenge Session

- Why should we have confidence in the bank and its management?

## XYZ Bank – Part II Session

Technology platform
Capital

- ICAAP process, assumptions, results;
- Capital structure of XYZ Bank; conclusions from the ICAAP, covering:
  - Structure of capital;
  - Source of capital and sources of additional capital;
  - Control environment (including governance of capital / ICAAP; risk appetite);

- Pillar 1 capital calculations;
- Pillar 2 assessment and quantification of risks;
- Stress testing and scenario analysis;
- Key areas of market risk, credit risk, operational risk, with metrics.

### Liquidity / Funding

- Overview of how Treasury operations are managed in XYZ Bank;
- Approach to hedging (overview);
- Liquidity risk management (including risk appetite and metrics to measure and manage);
- Stress testing, and assumptions;
- ILAAP process, assumptions, results;
- Liquidity buffer;
- Control environment (including governance of liquidity / ILAAP);
- Summary of contingency funding plan (CFP);
- Key liquidity and funding policies;
- Stress testing and scenario analysis.

### Operating Model

- Overview of operating model;
- Overview of IT systems;
- Key supplier relationships;
- Governance;
- Future capacity and plans.

### Conduct

- Conduct agenda in the bank;
- Customer journey;
- Conduct risk assessment by product;
- Issues to be addressed / remediated.

## APPENDIX 18.A: Basic Principles of Bank Marketing

A primer on marketing is provided on the book's companion website, as a Word file in the folder for Chapter 18.

*"One problem was that the older guys in the band seemed to want to just sit in the pub and talk about doing things, whereas I wanted to get out and actually do them."*

—Friend of the author, 7 July 1984

# PART V

# Case Studies: Analysis, Coherent Advice and Problem Solving

The last part of this book is really only one chapter (the second chapter in Part V, Chapter 20, is a guide to the book's associated website). In Chapter 19 we attempt to demonstrate what is perhaps the one thing that the banking industry has in common with the medical profession: namely, that before one can occupy a position as a senior executive or Board member in a bank, one should have demonstrated wide ranging experience as well as exposure to diverse forms of the same problem. In other words, such roles are the equivalent of the hospital consultant. (Another cultural working practice that both industries should adopt is that of learning from one's mistakes – as Matthew Syed makes clear with respect to the medical professional in his book *Black Box Thinking*.) We provide a range of case studies, from very different types of banks, outlining the problem and the approach taken to provide and implement a solution. We hope this demonstrates a best-practice approach to analysis, problem solving, and providing advice. Ultimately, there are always many forms of the same issue to observe, and the more often one comes across them the better it is to aid understanding.

*"But even if we practice diligently, we will still endure real-world failure from time to time. And it is often in these circumstances, when failure is most threatening to our ego that we need to learn most of all. Practice is not a substitute for learning from real-world failure; it is complementary to it. They are, in many ways, two sides of the same coin."*
—Matthew Syed, *Black Box Thinking: The Surprising Truth About Where Success Comes From,*
John Murray Publishers, 2016

# CHAPTER 19

# Case Studies: Analysis, Coherent Advice and Problem Solving

In this chapter, we aim to bring together all the elements of principle and best-practice approach which we have presented in this book and join them together in a coherent, user-friendly format that should serve as a starting template for the "future of bank risk management". A bank is a dynamic thing, always having to serve the needs of a diverse set of stakeholders, often with opposing requirements. Managing the balance sheet to ensure the bank is long-term viable means "risk management" in a bank is really more about understanding the surrounding environment and adapting with it and the times; in the same vein, it should be less of a "tick box" process and more a pragmatic one. Similarly to a hospital consultant, extensive experience in real-world problem solving across different business models is often the best qualification for managing risk in a bank.

To help us in our endeavour we use a number of real-world case studies to illustrate how the principles we have introduced in earlier chapters can be applied to solve issues as they arise. Banks, like all corporate entities, are collections of people with diverse backgrounds and experience. The process undertaken to effect change and/or improvement, principally in the balance sheet risk management space, must take into account the culture and operating process in the specific firm. That said, the aim of the case studies described here is to show that a firm adherence to logical, unemotional best-practice principles is almost invariably the most effective way to approach problem-solving. This calls for a certain level of technical expertise and experience in finance, emphasising at all times that the balance sheet and the importance of a sound balance sheet structure remain the most reliable way to ensure a sustainable, through-the-cycle banking operation.

Previous chapters have shown that the art of banking over the long term is essentially that of managing capital and liquidity in such a way that external market crashes or internal stress events do not "sink" the bank. This is the long-term objective. In the short term and medium term, the challenge is to ensure that day-to-day processes and procedures remain fit-for-purpose in every arena, whether this is an arcane and technical one such as interest-rate risk management or a higher-level topic such as the Board governance framework. By approaching bank management in this way, the bank is better placed to survive continuously, throughout the economic cycle, and in perpetuity – or at least as long as the bank's managers and shareholders wish it to remain a going concern.

## Using this Chapter

This chapter has a different structure than all preceding chapters. There is no material from the author's previous books. Instead it is comprised of real-world case studies representing diverse and wide-ranging problems in banks, selected to illustrate problem solving of specific operational or other issues that have been identified, discussed, analysed, and ultimately fixed through application of the chosen solution. The case studies all illustrate specific technical issues of the kinds discussed in this book. Read this chapter in parallel with a thorough reading of the previous chapters. A sample "question bank" at the end of the chapter is included to suggest ways of directing the reader's understanding.

## COHERENT ADVICE AND PROBLEM SOLVING: CASE STUDIES

### Case Study 1: The Pitfalls of a Risky Liquidity Risk Management Regime

**Northern Rock plc, UK Commercial Banking Institution**    The UK bank Northern Rock was originally a mutual savings-and-loan organisation owned by its members, with no shareholders. The organisation had operated for over a century when it converted into a bank in 1997. Alongside the change in legal entity type was a change in business philosophy, one that emphasised aggressive asset growth and increase in market share. Its main product was residential mortgages, which it marketed nationwide. However, its retail deposit base was still confined to its original home area in the north-east of England, so the new loans were funded via recourse to the wholesale market. Figure 19.1 shows the growth in wholesale and capital markets funding as a share of its total balance sheet liabilities during the 10 years

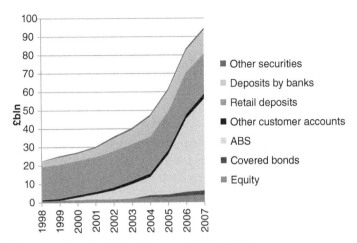

**FIGURE 19.1**   Northern Rock funding types 1998–2007
*Data Source*: Annual reports.

**FIGURE 19.2**   Northern Rock CDS price history Apr–Sep 2007
*Source*: © Bloomberg LLP. Reproduced with permission.

from its transformation to its ultimate demise and government bailout. Figure 19.2 shows the change in its credit default swap price during its last few months.

The case of Northern Rock highlights the pitfalls of a business model based on:

- Rapid asset growth in pursuit of market share (residential real estate), with asset pool far outstripping its retail deposit base;
- Use of securitisation to support asset growth, rather than as funding diversification tool;
- Increasing reliance on an unsustainable funding source.

In fact, "market share" is an inappropriate performance indicator for banks to adopt. While it may have its value in other industries such as supermarket retail, in a banking business model it is vital for the bank to have adequate and robust liabilities support for the assets being originated. In other words, it is vital for the bank to consider both sides of the balance sheet at all times. This is the primary objective of the asset–liability management (ALM) function in a bank.

Following the US sub-prime crash in July 2007, the ability of the bank to continue to issue its mortgage-backed bonds became the subject of rumours circulating in the interbank market. Band banks began reducing the term and size of their interbank lines. One day in September 2007, the bank was not able to roll its overnight funding and turned to the Bank of England (BoE), the lender of last resort. The BoE was obliged to report the borrowing. This news led to media headlines the next day, resulting in a high-street bank run, the first in the UK for over 100 years. The government could not countenance a default and so nationalised it.

The lessons of Northern Rock for all banks are to:

- Term out funding;
- Monitor liquidity ratios, and the customer funding base;
- Arrange diversified funding, and also have alternative sources of funds available;
- Grow slower during a bull market, and set aside reserve liquidity for a "rainy day".

Northern Rock was a rare example of a bank coming unstuck for liquidity reasons only; its loan book was not appreciably damaged. Pure liquidity crises are rare in banking, indeed most banks that went bust in 2007–2008 had suffered large-scale credit losses. As such, this case can expect to be a teaching case study for students in banking and finance for many years to come.

## Case Study 2: Fixing the Internal Yield Curve Construction Process

**UK Multinational Integrated Bank**   In 2010, during a review of the internal liquidity adequacy assessment (ILAA) of a high-street UK bank, the UK regulatory authority made the following observations:

- A reference to the risks created by the bank's public funding curve falling out of line with market prices;
- A material difference between the Group and wholesale banking internal rates and the need for a consistent curve to be applied across the businesses.

This issue was raised by Treasury with the business lines, and it was discovered that the wholesale bank divisional ALM desk did not construct the internal funding curve by any recognised best-practice interpolation method. This had created the risk that the internal prices would not reflect the genuine market (external) prices, and therefore became a sufficient risk management issue to be cited specifically by the regulatory authority.

In response to the ILAA review, the Group Treasury (GT) function seconded a member of its team to the wholesale division ALM desk who would review the curve interpolation procedure existing at the wholesale bank and thereafter make recommendations for improvement. GT found that no recognised interpolation method was in place, and that the ALM desk was not considered sufficiently influential to dictate procedure to the business lines.

GT addressed this issue by formulating a process that was logical and consistent, and based on theoretical principles that were robust in academic terms but also tractable and straightforward to apply by practitioners. Proposals were discussed at a meeting chaired by GT which included representatives from all the business lines and the ALM desk. By holding a discussion on this so publicly, with all business lines in the room, it was difficult for any individual business to object on anything other than what seemed like partisan grounds. In other words, if a proposed solution is demonstrably (a) impartial; (b) based on logic that is proven in the academic literature; and (c) shown not to favour any one product or business line, and then discussed at a public forum, it is difficult for any reasonable objection to be raised.

Following the meeting, GT drafted and presented a paper to the wholesale bank ALCO, where it was subsequently approved. The ALCO submission memo was reproduced earlier in the book in Chapter 3; a quote from it follows:

*A significant risk management decision at every bank is selecting the internal yield curve construction methodology. The internal curve is an important tool in the pricing and risk management process, driving resource allocation, business line transaction pricing, hedge construction and RAROC analysis. It is given therefore that curve construction methodology should follow business best-practice. In this paper, we describe the formal procedure on curve formulation in place at (Investment bank ALM desk), as well as the secondary procedure to liaise with Group Treasury (GT) aimed at maintaining a realistic and market-accurate public issuance curve.*

Via the ALCO process, GT was able to provide a solution that was neutral as well as academically and technically robust but practical. This undoubtedly helped approval and implementation.

In the field of balance sheet risk management, or indeed any aspect of risk management including customer and conduct risk, a bank should have in place internal procedures that ensure that potential pitfalls are picked up by its staff, rather than highlighted by the regulatory authority. This was not the case at this UK bank. Both the central (Group) and divisional Treasury functions were not aware that the method employed for constructing the internal yield curve, a vital input parameter to customer product pricing, was not a best-practice one (in that no firm methodology of any kind was in place). Subsequent to the regulator review, and ALCO approval process, the bank implemented a regular curve procedure methodology.

### Case Study 3: Implementing a Fit-For-Purpose Internal Funds Transfer Pricing (FTP) Process

**UK Subsidiary of MENA Bank Group, Commercial Banking Entity**   The UK-registered and regulated bank EAB is a wholly-owned subsidiary of a MENA-domiciled banking group. In 2009, it had a balance sheet of just over GBP 10bln.

In 2009, EAB comprised three business lines, namely Treasury, Corporate Bank, and Private Bank. These conducted the following activities:

- Treasury: responsible for managing the money market desk and the bank's liquidity portfolio, as well as a Treasury Sales desk that worked with the Corporate Bank to provide risk management solutions to corporate clients;
- Corporate Bank: provided a vanilla commercial bank service to EU-based corporate clients that had a particular interest in the Middle East. The product range included corporate loans, trade finance such as Letters of Credit, bridging loans, and stand-by liquidity lines. Its client base was essentially medium-sized corporates based in the UK;
- Private Bank: provided a private banking service to high-net-worth individuals (HNWI) domiciled in Western Europe, including expatriate citizens of the Gulf state, who had a connection of any kind with the Middle East.

Treasury therefore acted as a front-line business with a P&L target, but crucially also acted as the balance sheet management department of the bank. This meant that it was responsible for capital and liquidity risk management, as well as acting as the internal "clearing house" of the bank providing funding for the Corporate and Private Bank business lines.

Like many banks at the time of the global financial crash of 2008–2009, the bank operated a FTP methodology that was not a true internal funding pricing mechanism, in that all internal funds were transacted between Treasury and the other business lines at Libor-flat. This was simply a tradition that was common at banks around the world, reflecting an assumption – usually unchallenged by the Treasury and Risk departments – that the bank could fund across the term structure at zero spread over Libor. While this assumption was reasonably accurate for large banks during 1992–2007, it was not universally the case and by 2008 was unrealistic.

This was recognised by the Treasury department at the beginning of 2009, which observed that the existing FTP framework was not fit-for-purpose, because at this time EAB was funding at significantly in excess of Libor. As well as facilitating excess liquidity risk creation on the balance sheet, it created artificially high business line returns and did not incentivise customer product pricing that was a true reflection of the cost of raising term liquidity by EAB.

The business lines themselves reflected an understandable but flawed process that concentrated on one side of the balance sheet only. By 2008, Corporate banking operated at a loan-deposit ratio (LDR) approaching 180%, while Private Banking was overweight in customer deposits reflecting the interests of its customers: it operated at approximately 60% LDR. The deposit rates as at January 2009 are shown in Table 19.1.

During Q1 and Q2 2009, Treasury carried out the following steps, in the order shown, that culminated in the FTP methodology being changed and a new best-practice model being implemented:

- Drafted a paper explaining the concept of term liquidity risk, how it arises, and the negative consequences of ignoring and/or mispricing it;
- Presented "teach-ins" on the role of Treasury in the bank, and the concept of asset–liability management and liquidity risk management;

**TABLE 19.1**  EAB deposit rates as at January 2009

| Jan-09 | Basis points |
| --- | --- |
| Base rate | 100 |
| 3M Libor | 118 |
| Current account | 40 |
| Call account | 25 |
| 30-day notice account | 60 |
| 1-year | 75 |
| 2-year | 85 |

- Drafted a paper, to be presented at the bank's ALCO, on the recommended new FTP methodology, in conjunction with the Finance and Risk departments;
- Met bilaterally with the heads of Corporate Banking and Private Banking to discuss the ALCO paper. At these meetings, a strong (and at times emotional) objection was raised by the business lines, used to funding at Libor-flat for as long as anyone could remember, along the lines that Treasury was simply adding a TLP to boost its own P&L from a captive audience that could not fund elsewhere. This objection was addressed in the following way: Treasury confirmed with the IT department that all internal deal tickets, conducted with the business lines, would be identified by a system flag. Finance was asked to ensure that all flagged tickets would not count towards the Treasury P&L. Faced with this fact, the business agreed to the new FTP regime;
- Presented the FTP paper to ALCO, where it was approved.

The paper presented to ALCO, which was co-sponsored by Treasury and Finance, stated the following:

- FTP will be changed (a) by introducing a "term liquidity premium" into the FTP; and (b) by increasing the liquidity premium as a function of the tenor;
- A liquidity-premium-enhanced FTP will transfer more earnings to the liability generating activities and force corporate banking to more accurately price (and re-price) loan assets. It will also incentivise corporate banking to attract more customer deposits;
- More crucially, it will reduce the chances of an artificial funding profit helping to drive the investment decision.

The new FTP regime was implemented at EAB from 1 January 2010. This proved to be timely, as the UK regulator started reviewing bank FTP mechanisms in place at banks from 2010 onwards.

At first a very simple regime was implemented at the London subsidiary for GBP, EUR, and USD, as shown in Table 19.2.

The Private bank rates benefitted and raised net positive liabilities. Note that the rates are shown in Table 19.3.

The fixed-term deposits were "loss making" to the private bank but reflected the need to raise liquidity friendly customer term deposits for the bank as a whole. The impact on corporate banking included:

- Stopped writing back-stop liquidity facilities;
- Term loans now less competitive to market.

**TABLE 19.2** Regime implemented at the London subsidiary

| Old Bid | Old Offer | New Bid | New Offer | Liquidity premium |
|---|---|---|---|---|
| O/N to 2 weeks: | LIBOR - 12.5 bps | LIBOR | LIBOR | LIBOR + 12.5 bps + 12.5 bps |
| 2 weeks to 1 month: | LIBOR - 12.5 bps | LIBOR | LIBOR + 5 bps | LIBOR + 17.5 bps + 17.5 bps |
| > 1 and up to 3 months: | LIBOR - 12.5 bps | LIBOR | LIBOR + 10 bps | LIBOR + 22.5 bps + 22.5 bps |
| > 3 and up to 12 months: | LIBOR - 12.5 bps | LIBOR | LIBOR + 20 bps | LIBOR + 32.5 bps + 32.5 bps |

**TABLE 19.3**   EAB deposit rates as at June 2009

| Jan-09 | Basis points |
|---|---|
| Base rate | 50 |
| 3M Libor | 66 |
| Current account | 60 |
| Call account | 40 |
| 30-day notice account | 75 |
| 1-year | 100 |
| 2-year | 150 |

The crucial operational issue was the need to demonstrate explicitly that Treasury – a front office P&L department – did not generate and report P&L based on FTP regime. Because all internal tickets were flagged as such by the IT booking system and enabled Finance month-end management accounts to be adjusted for Treasury (to strip out impact of internal tickets), this was not an issue. The P&L of FTP tickets was held in the central "ALCO Book".

Ultimately the process at EAB transformed into a best-in-class FTP regime with a curve updated monthly by Treasury, and term liquidity premium rates calculated using market observed external parameters. The full curve format, in reality a "grid", is shown in Table 19.4.

**TABLE 19.4**   Final EAB FTP monthly curve format

| Term | GBP | EUR | USD |
|---|---|---|---|
| <3 mo | 0 | 0 | 0 |
| 6mo | 30 | 25 | 30 |
| 12mo | 85 | 80 | 95 |
| 18mo | 160 | 145 | 180 |
| 2yr | 230 | 205 | 235 |
| 3yr | 250 | 255 | 255 |
| 4yr | 255 | 265 | 260 |
| 5yr | 270 | 280 | 285 |
| 6yr | 275 | 290 | 300 |
| 7yr | 280 | 295 | 305 |
| 8yr | 285 | 300 | 310 |
| 9yr | 295 | 305 | 315 |
| 10yr+ | 305 | 310 | 320 |

The lessons learned for all banks are to:

- Be aware of one's actual TLP, what term funding is available and how it impacts the balance sheet if borrowed at the rate offered;
- Approach ALCO because it is the appropriate forum for such debate, Treasury having previously obtained "buy-in" from all affected parties;
- Ensure adequate support from the business lines ahead of the ALCO presentation. Highlight how the FTP regime does not support Treasury P&L, if arranged to be treated appropriately, so there is no conflict of interest here;
- Demonstrate FTP via a genuine co-written effort from Finance and Treasury. Education is a big priority whenever a bank wants to introduce a new idea.

The above approach was subsequently adapted by the author of the FTP paper and presented at other UK conferences and banks, where its studied objective rationale was generally, although not always, well received.

## Case Study 4: Securities Trading House Funding Mix and Reporting Implementation

**UK Securities and Derivatives Trading House Pre-2008, No Treasury Function**   This firm (referred to here as "XYZ") was a former hedge fund that was acquired by a commercial banking entity in 2000. However, it retained its own internal procedures and culture, because the parent bank did not make any changes to its internal structure and it retained virtually full autonomy. This meant that as the firm grew, the culture and business direction remained one that emphasised balance sheet growth and maximising return on capital. Three years after becoming part of a bank group, the entity comprised a number of business lines (convertibles market-making, equity derivatives, hedge fund derivatives, structured finance origination, and small-cap equities), but no dedicated Treasury or cash management function. Funding was arranged with the parent bank by a single individual in the middle office, who rolled over all funding in the overnight – despite the fact that the balance sheet was at this time over GBP 3 billion. This person was a junior member of staff who reported to a level below that of the head of operations. There was no reporting of the liquidity stress on the firm's (and therefore ultimately the Group's) balance sheet.

The parent bank became aware of this fact in the middle of 2003 but only recommended that the subsidiary should recruit a Treasurer. It did not make any other recommendations or suggest any preferred operating model for the management of balance sheet risk.

The new "Treasury" function comprised initially the one individual recruited in 2003. This person recognised that the management of liquidity risk was severely inadequate. The first requirement was to highlight this to senior management in the form of a report, compiled as quickly as possible and containing only essential, unarguable information. The risk that was emphasised stated that **"the present operating infrastructure runs a high risk of being censured by the regulatory authority"**.
The report highlights were as follows:

*The key objective of the Treasury desk in any bank or non-bank financial is to undertake prudent management of the funding requirement, with regard to liquidity management, interest-rate management and funding diversification. This process includes management information and reporting. The primary deliverable of the Treasury desk is the ALM report. This is presented at Figure 19.3.*

*Historically, the funding of the firm's business was concentrated overwhelmingly on a very short-term basis. The motivation for this was primarily the short-term trading nature of its assets, which meant that the asset profile was effectively changing on a high frequency. Over the last two years, the business has evolved into dealing more in longer term illiquid asset classes and as a consequence the firm must begin a process of rolling out funding into longer term to more adequately fund its asset profile. The Treasury aim going forward is based on the following reasoning:*

- *As much as possible, to fund the asset profile with a more suitable liability profile and to minimise forward gap;*
- *To term out the funding away from the very short-dated tenors used hitherto;*
- *To construct an ALM profile that recognises the differing requirements of individual business lines. For example, the market-making businesses are expected to have a more flexible liquidity profile than the asset management business. Hence the liability profile of the former will be concentrated along the short end of the funding term structure when compared to the latter;*
- *To even out the liability profile such that no one maturity bucket contains more than 20% of the total funding requirement. This will be treated as a funding limit.*

*The 20% limit will apply to the overall XYZ funding requirement.*
*The objective of ALM policy will be to apply market-standard guidelines to the business and to follow prudent market practice. It is also to make the whole funding process more transparent with regard to management reporting and to centralise funding onto one desk within the group.*

Recommendations made included:

▪ To formalise a Treasury middle office function;
▪ To change the Treasury reporting line to the CEO.

The report also highlighted the need to implement management reporting as shown at Figures 19.3 and 19.4, including the need for management to see individual business line funding usage.

| | o/n | o/n – 1w | 1w – 1m | 1m – 3m | 3m – 6m | 6m – 12m | 12m+ | TOTAL |
|---|---|---|---|---|---|---|---|---|
| Assets | 481 | 4,104 | 5,325 | 6,954 | 4,478 | 3,845 | 4,128 | 29,315 |
| Liabilities | –3,947 | –844 | –5,107 | –7,579 | –5,053 | –3,799 | –2,986 | (29,315) |
| Gap | 3466 | 3260 | 218 | 625 | 575 | 46 | 1142 | **9332** |
| | | | | | | | | |
| Percent of total funding | 13% | 3% | 17% | 26% | 17% | 13% | 10% | 100% |
| Gap as % of total Gap | 37% | 35% | 2% | 7% | 6% | 0% | 12% | 100% |
| | | | | | | | | |
| **Gap as % of total Funding** | **12%** | **11%** | **1%** | **2%** | **2%** | **0%** | **4%** | |
| Gap Limit | 20% | 20% | 20% | 20% | 20% | 20% | 20% | |
| Limit breach | – | – | – | – | – | – | – | |
| | | | | | | | | |
| **Cumulative Assets** | 481 | 4585 | 9910 | 16864 | 21342 | 25187 | 29315 | |
| **Cumulative Liabilities** | –3947 | –4791 | –9898 | –17477 | –22530 | –26329 | –29315 | |
| **Net Gap** | –3466 | –206 | 12 | –613 | –1188 | –1142 | 0 | |

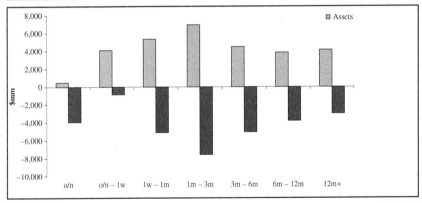

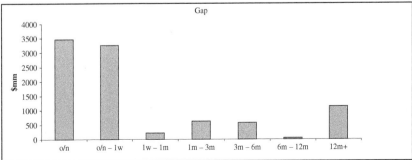

**FIGURE 19.3**   Proposed ALM report in table and graph formats

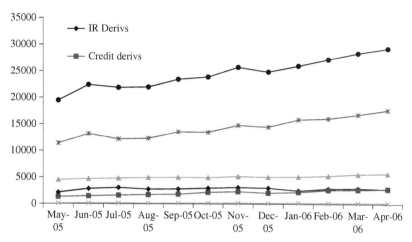

**FIGURE 19.4**    Business line funding usage

On review of the report the senior executive approved all of the recommendations. This process took 12 months to implement but at its conclusion the institution had in place a first-class infrastructure for the risk management, monitoring, reporting, and mitigation of balance sheet risk.

The key lessons learned from this study are:

- Do not allow management strategy to be overwhelmed by the revenue side of the balance sheet. Before embarking on a growth strategy, ensure first that the risk management infrastructure is in place first. (Note that this requirement is explicit now in the UK PRA banking licence application process.);
- The funding function must report to a person of sufficient seniority in the bank, to ensure that any concerns the person has can be aired at the right level;
- The quickest way to ensure management attention and management action on any issue is to highlight what the regulatory authorities would say if they were to be aware of any relevant facts.

### Case Study 5: Improving ALCO Governance Framework

**European Global Integrated Universal Banking Institution**   The bank in question was comprised of three operating divisions, wholesale, corporate, and retail. Each of these was a large banking institution in its own right, with further operating breakdowns within each. For example, as well as the Group CEO each division had its own CEO, and within the division there was a further breakdown into business units, again each with their own "CEO". This case study looks at the operating framework for the asset–liability committee (ALCO) process in place at the corporate banking division (CBD). Note that the bank as a whole also operated a Group ALCO (GALCO).

CDB in this European bank was a large institution, with a balance sheet of over GBP 180 billion. It was split into two parts, Corporate and Institutional Banking (CIB), and Business and Commercial banking (B&C). Both CIB and B&C were run by their respective "CEOs". The framework in place for balance sheet risk management at CBD at the time is shown at Figure 19.5.

Each ALCO had its own ALCO MI pack. The other framework arrangements are shown in Table 19.5.

Note that "CBD" is not a separate legal entity; it is the same legal entity as the wider Group. However, there was a triplication in management staffs, with each operating business line having its own CEO, CFO, Finance department, Risk department, and so on.

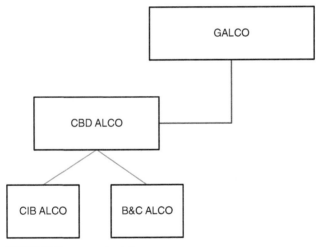

**FIGURE 19.5** CBD ALCO governance structure

**TABLE 19.5** Other arrangements

|  | Meeting Frequency | Chair | MI Pack |
|---|---|---|---|
| **CBD ALCO** | Monthly | CBD CFO (deferred to CDB CEO in practice) | Yes |
| **CIB ALCO** | Monthly | CIB CEO | Yes |
| **B&C ALCO** | Quarterly | B&C CFO | Yes |

It does not take a McKinsey or BCG-trained consultant (not that that is necessarily a measure of bank governance acumen) to see that such an operating infrastructure for risk management is not only grossly inefficient and wasteful in terms of resources, it is also risky. With so many operating committees and separate staffs, there is a material danger of specific exposures "falling through the cracks" and not being picked up. As a governance model, the ALCO structure at this bank's CBD was distinctly *not* fit-for-purpose. There was another issue in that the CBD CEO rarely attended the CBD ALCO, which had two unfortunate side effects: the ALCO was viewed as being not very important (since the CEO didn't attend it) and it made risk management staff view the CIB ALCO as being the "right" one for the important discussions.

CBD Treasury department recognised these issues, and frequently raised them to the CBD CFO. Despite the fact that this individual reported to the CBD CEO, for political and personality reasons he also deferred to the CIB CEO. It was a known fact that the CIB CEO preferred the *status quo* and wished to retain his department's ALCO (and his *de facto* chairmanship of it). Hence the Treasury department was not able to effect any rationalisation to the governance structure, for political reasons.

The approach taken by the Treasury department was to wait until the Internal Audit department conducted its scheduled annual review of Treasury. Generally, internal audit reviews of operating functions rarely throw up anything material for management to consider unless there are serious flaws or issues to uncover, because the audit team have limited time, work to a rigid template, and suffer from a lack of detailed operating knowledge of the department they are auditing. On this occasion, the Treasurer took the opportunity to volunteer information to the auditors, specifically with respect to his concerns on the governance structure, the lack of management challenge in the CIB ALCO, and the non-attendance of key members of the committees. This is detail that it is unlikely the audit team would have uncovered if it had not been volunteered. (For example, the ALCO minutes, which the audit team did review, did not list a register of attendance.) Internal Audit also noted in its report, as suggested by CBD Treasury, that the regulatory authority reviewed Treasury-related Audit reports and may have raised concerns.

Treasury recommendations were agreed to in full by the Internal Audit team, but the draft report sent to CBD senior management implied that these were Audit recommendations. This report carried a force that the Treasury department on its own did not have, and since any final report would be escalated to the Group CFO and Group CRO, the recommendations were difficult for CBD and CIB management to push back.

The result was:

- The two lower-tier ALCOs were abolished, and all relevant members attended the single unified CBD ALCO;
- Attendance was logged with an understanding that it would be monitored by Audit;
- Only one ALCO MI deck was required to be produced each month, which improved efficiency and reduced workload;
- The ALCO pack itself was redesigned by Treasury into one that was more user-friendly, accessible, and succinct. This would have been a pointless exercise when three ALCO decks were being produced, because the CBD ALCO deck was not viewed as being the most important one.

The lessons learned from this experience are:

- To continuously review risk governance and operating model, to ensure it is still optimum;
- To effect improvements to risk practice, it is sometimes necessary to enlist "allies" in the effort, because what is optimum may not suit the internal politics of the organisation. If one can raise a concern that may attract the attention of Audit and/or the regulator, there is a greater likelihood that the concern will be addressed in the proper manner.

### Case Study 6: Improving Interest-Rate Risk in the Banking Book (IRRBB) Hedging Efficiency

**European Commercial Banking Group**  Traditionally, ALM has always been associated with the banking book and conventional ("modified duration") techniques were applied when calculating interest-rate and funding risk exposure in the bank's banking book. With respect to interest-rate risk in the banking book (IRRBB), there are five primary sources of risk (note these were detailed in Chapter 13):

- Gap risk;
- Yield curve risk;
- Basis risk;
- Run-off risk;
- Option risk.

Thus IRRBB is not an optional risk taking position but rather a by-product of re-pricing mismatches between lending and deposit taking positions, which are themselves usually customer-driven. So, banks are exposed to (IRRBB) primarily due to regular customer business.

This case study references an EU commercial bank that operated a common, conventional approach to IRRBB hedging, but one which was recognised by the Treasury department as not being optimum.

The bank in question undertook customer business that generated all of the IRR risks summarised in Chapter 13. It reported its IRRBB risk in two ways, using both the traditional modified duration (DV01) approach and the later value-at-risk (VaR) methodology. Its IRRBB was reported as shown in Table 19.6 and Figure 19.6.

The bank operated the orthodox approach to IRRBB hedging, which one might label "ponderous". Namely, it hedged asset-side IRRBB as it was originated and liabilities-side IRRBB as these appeared, separately. No attempt was made to consider the balance sheet as an integrated whole. Moreover, derivatives were used at all times, no cash hedging was considered.

**TABLE 19.6** UK commercial bank IRRBB reporting

| | Rollover date or nearest interest-rate adjustment date (£mm) | | | | | |
|---|---|---|---|---|---|---|
| | O/n – 3mo | 3mo – 6mo | 6mo – 1yr | 1yr – 5yr | > 5yr | Non-IR sensitive |
| Assets | 270,959 | 16,813 | 21,375 | 115,831 | 35,893 | 139,475 |
| Liabilities | 331,496 | 25,271 | 26,344 | 67,256 | 20,754 | 128,775 |
| Repricing gap | –60,537 | –8,908 | –4,969 | 48,575 | 15,139 | 10,700 |
| Cumulative gap | –60,537 | –69,445 | –74,414 | –25,839 | –10,700 | 0 |

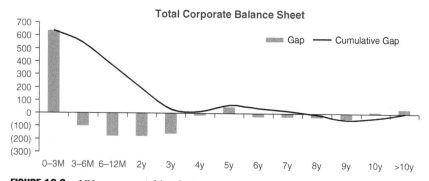

**FIGURE 19.6** UK commercial bank IRRBB reporting

The extract below from the bank's IRR policy summarises the bank's hedging methodology:

*Hedging can be defined as a risk management strategy used in limiting or offsetting probability of loss from fluctuations in interest rates.*

*From an "Interest Rate Risk" perspective, Interest Rate Swaps are the main hedging tool that the bank uses to "hedge" its balance sheet. All fixed rate assets are hedged via "Pay Fixed" and "Receive floating" Interest Rate Swaps; all fixed rate liabilities are hedged via "Receive Fixed" and "Pay Floating" Interest Rate Swaps.*

*Example of Business Line Fixed Rate Asset hedged using internal vanilla interest rate swap (also shows internal funding ticket): see Figure 19.7.*

The approach described above, while common, is not efficient and optimum. It lacks a "strategic ALM" perspective that looks at both sides of the balance sheet, and also makes no effort at minimising the use of derivatives. The use of derivative instruments carries a cost, not least with respect to the cost of collateral which is not always recognised or transparent.

The bank would have continued along these lines for the foreseeable future. The issue was not raised by any of the CFO, CRO, or Treasury departments, nor by the business lines themselves. What happened that ultimately resulted in an improved hedging method was that the CFO and Treasurer attended an industry ALM conference where the author presented on the topic of "Strategic ALM". After listening to this presentation, both individuals invited the author to present the same lecture to their bank's ALCO.

The speaker's lecture included the following points:

*The banks' existing arrangements result in Group or the "Centre" hedging both assets and liabilities individually. It also describes an internal IRS together with the funding ticket for the asset. An alternative procedure is to hedge the net exposure of both assets and liabilities, after allowing for similar, behaviour tenor matching. This benefits from natural hedges already in place and reduces reliance on derivatives. Examples include:*

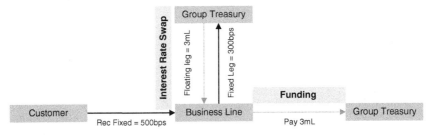

**FIGURE 19.7**   Bank IRRBB hedge structure

- *Fixed rate loans versus fixed rate depos;*
- *Variable rate loans versus floating rate depos.*

*Structural balance sheet hedging should be applied on a net basis: the net A-L position.*
*Some assets and liabilities naturally hedge each other:*

- *Variable rate mortgages and NIBLs of similar behavioural tenor;*
- *Fixed rate mortgages and Fixed rate deposits.*

*Hence we hedge with external market the net un-hedged exposure. There are a number of potential net hedges between fixed-rate assets and liabilities and floating-rate assets and liabilities at the bank, where tenors are approximately similar.*

The recommended approach going forward is, where possible, it may be advantageous to use cash products to hedge IRR exposure rather than have recourse to derivatives. For example, there may be a desire to preserve swap lines or reduce collateral funding requirements. Past examples the author has undertaken at various banks were discussed in Chapter 13.

After hearing this lecture, the bank implemented a change in IRRBB hedging approach. This resulted in a material improvement in operational efficiency as well as lower hedge costs and reduced MTM P&L volatility from hedge instruments (due to lower use of derivatives).

The lessons learned from this case study include:

- To remain in the forefront of market best-practice requires continual knowledge gathered from a variety of sources;
- Seek to continually understand the unintended consequences of any operating method in place at the bank;
- Be open-minded about ideas and strategies that may require you to modify what you think is already optimum.

## Case Study 7: Deposit Strategy

Before considering the specific case study here, please refer to the author's BTRM "Thought Leadership" piece entitled "Basel III LCR is a business model changer: how will it impact your bank?" which is on this book's associated website, in the folder for Chapter 19. It is file number 12 in that folder. This paper highlights considerations for a bank's liability strategy that arise as a result of the need to adhere to the Basel III liquidity regime, and specifically the liquidity coverage ratio (LCR).

**European commercial banking group**   This is a "full service" commercial bank with a sizeable number of large corporate and non-bank financial entity (NBFI) depositors. These deposits are labelled "Type A" by the regulator, classed "non-sticky" and thereby contributing to a higher liquid asset buffer (LAB) requirement than "Type B" sticky deposits. It also had a significant surplus liabilities base, with overall customer loan–deposit ratio well below 100%. Figure 19.8 shows the split of deposit types at the bank. A breakdown of the Type A balances is given at Figure 19.9.

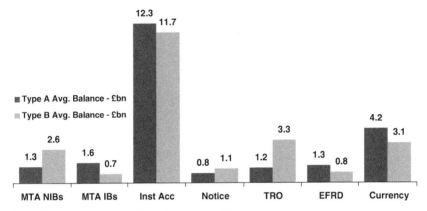

**FIGURE 19.8**   Deposit and product type split

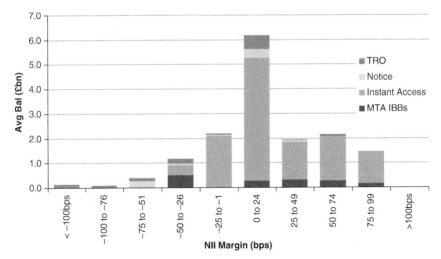

**FIGURE 19.9**   GBP Type A Balances

A review of the deposit base, conducted following the publication of Basel III liquidity requirements, revealed the following:

- Type A Customers place significant deposit balances but contribute a smaller share to income;
- 51% of Bank A's balances are Type A and so attract a higher LAB requirement cost;
- There is a 38% / 62% Type A / B split by e2e value contribution;
- 52% concentration of GBP Instant Access balances which are behaviourally stable but Type A if the customer is a large corporate or NBFI.

This bank operated a centralised Group Treasury allocations function, and each business line received an internal FTP rate from GT for its liabilities. Before the review of deposits strategy, the business line was not aware of the magnitude of its "negative NII" balance size: this where the customer deposit rate is higher than the FTP bid rate received by the business line from GT. The Treasury review highlighted the need to identify those balances that produce a negative NII.

The review revealed:

- Of the bank's Type balances, ~10% of them generated negative NII;
- Approximately 12% of balances which are on instant access attracted the highest LCR outflow buffer costs and therefore generated the lowest end-to-end value;
- Behaviourally, these premium priced balances are highly rate sensitive and carry a high risk of attrition if client rates were to be reduced.

Treasury raised an ALCO agenda item which was a call to address deposit strategy in terms of optimum funding efficiency, and to identify customer balances which attracted the highest portfolio risk as defined by sector concentration (Financial Institutions), and rate sensitivity (client rate higher than FTP bid).

The recommendations arising out of the ALCO discussion and subsequent Treasury follow up included:

- Introduce new products to support migration of some of these balances on to "LCR-friendly" products, delivering reduction in buffer costs;
- Migrating balances to Transactional accounts, which are Type B;
- Migrating Standard Money Market balances to a 35-day Notice Money Market account to take outside the LCR spectrum;
- Draft a wider and higher-level liabilities strategy that also addresses reducing the LCR outflow, for example:
  - Greater targeting towards longer-term fixed deposits;
  - Greater focus on SME / Type B customers;
  - Introduction of unbreakable fixed-term deposits which reduce risk of outflow in stress;

- Pricing for liquidity risk; for example, to encourage customers to invest in longer term products.

The lessons learned from this case study include:

- To maintain a regular review of deposit structure for its impact not only on NII and P&L but also for the regulatory requirement implications;
- To avoid falling into a "business-as-usual" mentality whereby business is undertaken day-to-day without any thought for the medium-term impact or wider strategic picture (without the Treasury initiative and ALCO submission, this state of affairs, and the sub-optimal balance sheet deposit "strategy", could have continued indefinitely);
- Adopting a "Deposits Analysis Template" approach to ensure regular review and update of deposit characteristics including costs, to be "owned" by ALCO and delegated to Treasury or Finance. This is shown in the templates and at Table 19.7 below.

### Deposit Review Template I

- Undertake high level summary of the Bank Deposits book in relation to LCR Stress Testing, in order to illustrate Deposits counterparty splits which drive Type A / B classification and the consequential outflows;
- Highlight specific costs associated with holding certain deposits types, particularly "standalone" deposits which generate no additional value to the bank from additional product lines;
- Present the available options that can be employed to improve overall margin efficiency:
  - LCR Balance Sheet: Type A deposits represent X% or £Xbn of the book, constituted mainly through [Local Authorities, FIs and some non-SME] specific customer types;
  - LCR Outflow summary: Total idiosyncratic scenario outflow of £Xbn.
- Deposit Concentrations: Bank deposit market share is consistent across all sectors, holding c.X% overall deposits share (MTA and Savings), which increases to Y% on a Savings only basis. Indicates that there are no areas of over concentration.
- Appetite to explore pricing differentiated customer pricing for Type A and B counterparties.

### Deposit Review Template II

- Conduct strategic review with objective of finding ways to improve margin efficiency of the Bank Deposit book. For example:
  - £3.2bn of deposits can be classified as "Standalone" (little to no MTA activity, of which £1.4bn are Type A).
  - These deposits have significant cost due to:
    - No value generation beyond the deposit relationship;
    - c.50% are Type A deposits.
- Deposits are typically rate sensitive customer sectors and therefore on low margin pricing;
- Once the business line / bank reaches required self-funding position, these deposits represent an opportunity to improve overall margins through a move to alternative products and deepening relationships.

**TABLE 19.7**     Template to determine cost of holding standalone deposits inclusive of Liquidity Buffer costs

| Standalone Segment | Total Deposits | Average Customer Rate | Average Net Margin including Buffer Cost | Cost of Deposits | Available Management Options |
|---|---|---|---|---|---|
| Fixed Rate Deposits (A&B) Managed Negotiated TYPE A | | | | | ▪ Reprice customer rate<br>▪ Exit Deposits<br>▪ Cross sell MTA/ other product<br>▪ Implement tighter eligibility criteria |

## CASE STUDY: REVIEW OF BANK FUNDING STRUCTURES 1999–2009

Basel III liquidity requirements prescribe somewhat the freedom of action of banks to set their liabilities structure any way they'd like. The liquidity coverage ratio (LCR) and net stable funding ratio (NSFR) minimum requirements mean that today one should observe fewer variations in overall bank funding mixes, in any jurisdiction. Of course that does not mean that banks will all sport identical funding structures, far from it. There is still variety to observe amongst the share of mix of the following funding types:

▪ Tier II capital (for example, long-dated debt);
▪ Senior unsecured debt (for example, Medium-Term Notes);
▪ Other wholesale funding (including short-term interbank instruments);
▪ Customer deposits;
▪ Secured funding long-term (for example, covered bonds);
▪ Secured funding short-term (for example, repo);
▪ Private placements.

Many banks use all these funding types, while a still greater number of banks make no use of any of these types other than customer deposits. So there is still a fair amount of variety to observe. However, this variety was more pronounced prior to the 2008 crash. We show a number of different types of funding structure for a diverse sample of banks during the period 1999–2009, on spreadsheets found on the book's companion website.

We present data for the following banks:

- AIB*;
- Chelsea Building Society ^;
- CIMB;
- Gulf Bank;
- ICICI Bank;
- Northern Rock*;
- Santander;
- Standard Chartered;
- Wells Fargo.

Note: banks marked * went bust in 2007–2008. ^ was later acquired by Nationwide Building Society.

The following spreadsheets are held on the website in the folder for Chapter 19:

1. A dataset of interest rates history for 1980–2009;
2. A dataset of risk-free interest rates 1999–2009;
3. AIB liabilities mix 1999–2008. This bank's funding mix shows what was a common theme in banking during this period, a steady increase in the share of short-term funding as a percentage of the overall funding mix;
4. Chelsea Building Society liabilities mix 2002–2008;
5. CIMB bank (India domicile) liabilities 2002–2008;
6. Gulf Bank (Kuwait domicile) liabilities 2002–2008;
7. Northern Rock liabilities 2001–2008. This bank's experience has been well documented elsewhere; we note the significant increase in share of short-term funding up to 78% of total liabilities in the year of its demise;
8. Santander 1999–2008. This bank's reputation for preferring to run a conservative and robust funding structure is evident in its liabilities mix, throughout the period when other banks were moving in another direction funding-wise;
9. Standard Chartered 1999–2008. Another example of a more conservative approach to funding mix, similar to Santander with a significant share of liabilities comprised of customer deposits;
10. Wells Fargo 1999–2008;
11. A comparison of the split between short-term funding and medium-term funding as a share of the banks' overall non-equity liability structure, as at September 2009. Note the significant increase in share of medium-term funding for all the banks by 2009, an obvious impact of the crash; equally instructive is that this metric was 0.00% for some banks in 1999. (We define "medium-term" as over 12-month tenor.)

The changeover from short-term funding to medium-term funding share is evident from some of the bank's liabilities mixes and from spreadsheet number 11.

## CASE STUDY: HIGH-LEVEL STRATEGIC BANK REVIEW

In Chapter 16 we discussed key concepts in bank strategy. There is a considerable literature out there, certainly very familiar to MBA students at least, that deals with corporate strategy. Often there are significant constraints in place that make any meaningful change in strategy or adoption of a modified strategy difficult. To illustrate this, we present a report written by the author after a strategy review of a small regional EU bank in 2014, and presented to the bank's Board. This bank had a conventional retail and small corporate business model, and its risk-weighted assets were overwhelmingly residential mortgages followed by local authority lending. However, it suffered from extreme constraints in both capital and liquidity, which restricted any material change in direction, or asset growth, unless there was new equity injection from the owner. This is a common issue with small regional banks, which face intense competition from larger full-service banks both national and international.

The background detail on the bank's business lines and balance sheet are introduced in the report itself.

The lessons learned from this exercise included:

- It is important for the Board of a bank to have a clear idea of what exactly they want the bank to be, its shape, structure, size, franchise objectives, and risk appetite, in the medium-term, and work towards achieving that goal;
- Beware of "quick fixes" which are generally never quick and rarely a fix; *ad hoc* transactions are no substitute for a coherent, articulated strategy and business model;
- It is rare for a small bank with little or no presence in wholesale markets to implement a successful new Trading Book strategy and generate acceptable sustained return on capital for the risk incurred: the bank will always suffer from a lack of market intelligence because of insufficient interaction with market counterparties and lack of customer deal flow.

To see the report, please go to the companion website and download the Word file "13_Regional Bank Strategy Review", which is held in the folder for Chapter 19.

## CONCLUSION

This is the last chapter in the book, if one excepts Chapter 20 (which is simply a guide to the files contained on the book's associated website). The book's objective was to provide, as the sub-title states, *Past, Present and Future Principles of Banking and Finance*. Only the reader can confirm whether this has been achieved.

Past principles are perhaps the most straightforward, because these ones are ostensibly timeless and will be forming parts of graduate corporate finance courses for many years to come; one thinks of the time value of money and net present value, for example. But in the 21$^{st}$ century even some of these concepts need to be re-examined: the Eurozone has been living with negative interest rates along the term structure for some years now. In 2016 a senior executive at the Bank of England called for the abolition of physical cash, so as to make it easier for monetary policymakers to implement negative rates whenever they deem fit. So even past principles that have held good for over a thousand years are open to challenge, it seems, in this modern era. Present principles are possibly more problematic, because there is rarely complete agreement amongst practitioners, let alone academics, on many aspects of the mechanics of banking and finance. As for future principles, well ultimately that is only so much speculation.

The common thread uniting the past, present, and future is sound judgement and conservative principles that champion sustainability. But because there is considerable variety in the finance industry, be it with types of products, types of customers, types of banks, and even types of regulators, it is generally sensible to add flexibility to our common thread. What is sensible and works for one set of products or one bank may not be so for another. In that regard, finance is slightly analogous with medicine; one isn't appointed to a position as a hospital consultant until one has had considerable experience and observed many different cases, as well as variations on one type of ailment. Excellence in banking demands the experience level of a hospital consultant. To that end we thought it appropriate to present this set of case studies as the concluding chapter in this book, because banking is as much art as science, there are often variations on a theme when considering just one aspect of balance sheet management or business model strategy. (A good example is internal funds transfer pricing, which is handled in many different ways by banks.)

That is why we opted to conclude with a series of case studies, selected for no particular reason other than that they show variety and intricacy in the art of banking. There is no "one-size-fits-all" in finance and the best solutions to problems arising in bank management are those that are best suited to the organisation in question. A template approach to any issue arising – and we have many templates provided on this book's website, as the next chapter will show – is only good as the starting point. The final decision on anything has to be the one that is best for the bank and all its stakeholders. But like much of finance theory, this makes a strong assumption: that the Board of the bank has a firm idea of what it wants the bank to be and where it should be going, and has communicated that explicitly to the senior executives. It's difficult to generate the best solution if one doesn't know what the problem is.

Our case studies exhibited at least one common feature: the need to work through a problem, and agree a solution amongst all interested parties. This is why the bank's ALCO is often the best forum to debate issues and agree courses of action, although there are numerous other committees in a bank as well. It's just that ALCO contains the right mix of risk and reward around the table. Often one person or department needs to take the initiative and look deeper into a process or management report, and raise it to management, because problems are not always apparent. Without such a person or team, a bank can sleepwalk into trouble without knowing it.

The human element is also present in abundance. Like all corporate entities, banks are groupings of people, and character, personality, and culture play a big part in both success and failure. Some of our case studies highlighted the processes that need to be followed to account for this, when resistance to change or disagreement on the way forward is not because of any lack of logic or technical merit in a solution, but because of conflicting vested interests and what is loosely termed "office politics". This feature of managing a bank must be taken into account and worked around, but there is no textbook on this skill that the author is aware of. Ultimately, as in life itself, all that one could recommend is to be true to oneself and maintain an objective, logical, impartial, and unemotional approach throughout. In the end, one is free to set one's own standards.

# APPENDIX 19.A: Sample Review Questions

Case Study 1: The pitfalls of a risky liquidity risk management regime

1. Discuss the measures that the management of Northern Rock could have implemented over time in managing capital and liquidity to avoid the collapse.
2. Outline the practical challenges that the management could encounter in implementing measures that would ensure ongoing sustainability of the bank.

3. Outline the pros and cons of the Government and the Central Bank intervening in the manner in which they did to prevent Northern Rock from collapsing.
4. Discuss the practical implications in the management of a banking institution, referring to the following lessons learnt from the collapse of Northern Rock:

   a. Term out funding;
   b. Monitor liquidity ratios, and the customer funding base;
   c. Arrange diversified funding, and also have alternative sources of funds available;
   d. Grow slower during a bull market, and set aside reserve liquidity for a "rainy day".

## Case Study 2: Fixing the internal yield curve construction process

1. Discuss the following issues raised by the regulatory authorities and outline their practical implications in the management of a banking operation:

   a. A reference to the risks created by the bank's public funding curve falling out of line with market prices;
   b. A material difference between the group and wholesale banking internal rates and the need for a consistent curve to be applied across the businesses.
2. Discuss the various methods of constructing an internal yield curve, including their advantages and disadvantages, and outline a process that you believe to be best practice. State reasons for your recommendation.

## Case Study 3: Implementing a fit-for-purpose internal funds transfer pricing (FTP) process

1. Describe and discuss what could be considered a best practice internal funds transfer pricing (FTP) model / process.
2. Discuss the practical implications of the following lessons learnt in implementing the best in class FTP regime at EAB.

   a. Being aware of one's actual term liquidity premium (TLP), what term funding is available, and how it impacts the balance sheet if borrowed at the rate offered;
   b. Approaching ALCO because it is the appropriate forum for such debate, with Treasury having already obtained "buy-in" from all affected parties;
   c. Ensuring adequate support from the business lines ahead of the ALCO presentation;

   **d.** Highlighting how the FTP regime does not support Treasury P&L, if arranged to be treated appropriately, so there is no conflict of interest;

   **e.** Demonstrating FTP via a genuine co-written effort from Finance and Treasury;

   **f.** Taking education as a big priority whenever a bank wants to introduce a new idea.

**Case Study 4: Securities trading house funding mix and reporting implementation**

1. Describe how you would go about setting up a Treasury and Cash management function within a medium-sized banking institution experiencing high business growth.

2. Outline the key functions of a Treasury and Cash management division in a banking institution and set out the key strategic objectives of such a division.

**Case Study 5: Improving ALCO governance framework**

1. Describe a typical operating framework for an asset–liability committee process that may be considered to be optimum at a large banking institution.

2. It has been suggested that the following is important:

   **a.** To continuously review risk governance and operating models, to ensure they are still optimal;

   **b.** To effect improvements to risk practice, it is sometimes necessary to enlist "allies" in the effort, because what is optimum may not suit the internal politics of the organisation.

   Discuss these statements and outline their practical implications in the management of a banking institution.

**Case Study 6: Improving interest-rate risk in the banking book (IRRBB) hedging efficiency**

1. Describe and discuss the following primary sources of risks with respect to interest rate risks in a banking book:

   **a.** Gap risk;

   **b.** Yield curve risk;

   **c.** Basis risk;

   **d.** Run-off risk;

   **e.** Option risk.

2. Discuss the key reasons why banks are exposed to IRRBB.

3. Discuss the various mechanisms that banks may apply in managing IRRBB and outline the practical challenges that they are likely to encounter in implementing these hedging mechanisms.

4. Distinguish between derivative based methods and non-derivative based methods of managing IRRBB and comment on the appropriateness of such methods given the circumstances of a particular bank.

### Case study 7: Banks deposit strategy

1. Is there any extent of "negative NII" balances being managed by the bank?
2. Are there large "Type A" or non-sticky deposit balances, the customers for which do not contribute any other revenue to the bank? (Note this raises a strategic and mission-statement issue as well as a customer relationship issue.)
3. Is the deposit strategy aligned with wider balance sheet management concerns, and optimised for maximum balance sheet efficiency?

## SELECTED BIBLIOGRAPHY AND REFERENCES

Accenture, http://www.accenture.com/us-en/Pages/insight-liquidity-transfer-pricing-challenges.aspx.

Barbican Consulting, http://www.barbicanconsulting.co.uk/ftp.

The British Bankers Association, http://www.bba.org.uk/advanced-liquidity-risk-management.

Castagna, A., and Fede, F., (2013), *Measuring and Managing Liquidity Risk*, Hoboken, NJ: John Wiley & Sons.

Choudhry, M. (2003), *Analysing and Interpreting the Yield Curve*, Singapore: John Wiley & Sons Pte Ltd.

European Banking Authority, http://www.eba.europa.eu/regulation-and-policy/liquidity-risk.

James, J., and Webber, N., (2000), *Interest Rate Modelling*, Chichester: John Wiley & Co Ltd.

Nelson, C., and Siegel, A. F. (1987), "Parsimonious Modeling of Yield Curves", *Journal of Business*, 60, pp. 473-489.

Pushkina, N., *A Simple Funds Transfer Pricing Model for a Commercial Bank*, Faculty of Law and Commerce, University of the Witwatersrand, February 2013.

Svensson, Lars E. O. (1994), "Estimating and Interpreting Forward Rates: Sweden 1992-4," *National Bureau of Economic Research*, Working Paper #4871.

Swarup, B., (2012). *Asset Liability Management for Financial Institutions: Balancing Financial Stability with Strategic Objectives (Key Concepts)*, London: Bloomsbury Information Ltd.

Tilman, L., (2003). *Asset, Liability Management for Financial Institutions: Maximising Shareholder Value Through Risk-conscious Investing*, London: Euromoney Books.

US Federal Reserve, http://www.federalreserve.gov/bankinforeg/topics/liquidity_risk.htm

*"When I consider how capable we all are of perverting the truth, and when I remind myself that I was a voluntary participant in the Vietnam debacle, I can only ask: what does it take to be a man? I submit that a real man is not a sycophant, but is someone who pursues the truth in service to his values. It's easy to support the status quo when self-interest is at stake. It takes character to stand up for the truth when it's not in your self-interest – such as opposing war in the face of threats to destroy your reputation."*

——Robert Wideman, *Unexpected Prisoner: Memoir of a Vietnam POW*, 2 May 2016.

# CHAPTER 20

# Guide to the Website

This chapter is a guide to the files contained on the book's companion website. They are held in relevant chapter folders, so that the reader can tie any specific website file back to the associated chapter in the book and become familiar right away with the necessary background information.

To access the website please visit: www.wiley.com/go/mcanthology

Password: MCA1e

As well as policy templates and examples of regulatory submission documents, we include where appropriate teaching aids in the form of PowerPoint slides used by the author for courses and seminars, as well as Excel models that can be applied at most commercial banks. These are placed in the relevant book chapter folder.

## CHAPTER FILES

Most of the material on the website is organised into folders mapping across to the relevant chapter in the book. Other material is grouped into folders relating to generic topics, such as Policy Documentation templates. All of the files are detailed below.

### Chapter 1: A Primer on Banking, Finance and Financial Instruments

1. PowerPoint slide: The Principles of Banking interview
2. PDF file: The Principles of Banking, White Paper, June 2012
3. PowerPoint deck: Introduction to Bank Treasury[1]
4. PowerPoint deck: The Principles of Banking: Aarhus School of Business, MSc course module slides[2]

---

[1] This slide deck was co-written with Chris Westcott.
[2] This slide deck was written by Christian Schmaltz.

### Chapter 2: Derivative Instruments and Hedging

1. PowerPoint deck: CVA and FVA made simple; PRMIA Webinar, November 2012
2. PowerPoint deck: The government futures bond basis
3. PowerPoint deck: The credit default swap basis
4. Word document: Asset swaps and relative value

### Chapter 3: The Yield Curve

1. PowerPoint deck: Fitting the internal yield curve[3]
2. PowerPoint deck: Setting the internal funding curve
3. Excel spreadsheet: Yield curve construction model, using cubic spline methodology[4]
4. Excel spreadsheet: Yield curve model using cubic spline, for versions of Excel earlier then Excel 2013[5]
5. Excel spreadsheet: Yield curve model using Svensson 94 methodology
6. Instruction guide for files (3), (4), and (5), the yield curve models in this folder
7. PowerPoint deck: Analysing and interpreting the yield curve

### Chapter 4: Eurobonds, Securitisation and Structured Finance

1. PowerPoint deck: Introduction to Securitisation
2. PowerPoint deck: Practical issues with originating an own-asset securitisation transaction[6]
3. PowerPoint deck: Credit Rating Considerations
4. PowerPoint deck: Investor Relations Process[7]

### Chapter 5: Banks and Risk Management

1. Trading book policy template, suitable for applying in commercial banks
2. FX risk hedging policy template, applicable to commercial banks
3. PowerPoint deck: Introduction to Value-at-Risk
4. Word document: Template Pillar 3 Disclosure
5. Word document: Template Recovery and Resolution Plan

---

[3] This slide deck was written by Polina Bardaeva.
[4] This model was co-written with Zhuoshi Liu.
[5] This model was co-written with Zhuoshi Liu.
[6] This slide deck was written by Chris Westcott.
[7] This slide deck was co-written with Ed Bace.

## Chapter 8: Regulatory Capital and the Capital Adequacy Assessment Process

1. PowerPoint deck: Sample bank ("ABC Bank") internal capital assessment
2. PowerPoint deck: Sample bank capital stress testing results
3. Excel spreadsheet: Example of balance sheet RWA calculation summary
4. PowerPoint deck: ICAAP best-practice principles

## Chapter 10: The Bank Treasury Operating Model and ALCO Governance Process Best-Practice

1. PowerPoint deck: ALCO governance and culture
2. PowerPoint deck: ALCO processes implementation paper
3. PowerPoint deck: Treasury operating model and Treasury allocations process
4. Word document: Example of Treasury policy statement
5. Word document: ALCO Terms of Reference template

## Chapter 11: Bank Asset–Liability Management (ALM) and "Strategic ALM"

1. Excel spreadsheet: Net interest margin (NIM) analysis model, to study impact on NIM of changes to various internal and external factors.[8] This spreadsheet may be applied to a vanilla commercial banking institution.
2. Excel spreadsheet: ALM simulation model[9]
3. PowerPoint deck: Credit ratings considerations
4. PowerPoint deck: Conference presentation on "Strategic ALM", dated May 2016
5. PowerPoint deck: ALM, Hedging and Net Interest Margin[10]
6. PDF file: Article from *The European Financial Review*, "Strategic ALM and integrated balance sheet management, Aug–Sep 2017.

## Chapter 12: Liquidity and Funding: Policy, Management, and Risk Management

1. PowerPoint deck: Liquidity policy statement template presentation
2. PowerPoint deck: Encumbrance policy
3. PowerPoint deck: Liquidity metrics MI suite

---

[8] This spreadsheet was co-written with Chris Westcott.
[9] This spreadsheet was co-written with Peter Eisenhardt.
[10] This slide deck was co-written with Chris Westcott.

4. PowerPoint deck: Intra-day liquidity risk
5. PowerPoint deck: Principles of funds transfer pricing (FTP)
6. PowerPoint deck: Retail and corporate bank FTP regime
7. PowerPoint deck: FTP and input to loan pricing
8. PowerPoint deck: FTP and business line funding policies
9. PowerPoint deck: FTP policy template
10. Word document: Bank liquidity policy statement template
11. Word document: ILAAP submission template
12. Word document: FTP policy template
13. Word document: FTP issues for discussion and review

### Chapter 13: Market Risk and Non-Traded Market Risk (Interest-Rate Risk in the Banking Book)

1. PowerPoint deck: The Management of Interest Rate Risk in the Banking Book[11]
2. PowerPoint deck: IRRBB Market Realities[12]
3. PowerPoint deck: Fundamental Review of the Trading Book (FRTB); Market Risk from Basel 2.5 to Basel III[13]

### Chapter 14: The Future of Bank Treasury and Balance Sheet Risk Management

1. Word document: Template Group ALCO Terms of Reference

### Chapter 17: Present and Future Principles of Governance and Culture

1. Word document: Template Audit, Risk and Compliance Committee Terms of Reference
2. PowerPoint deck: "Leadership and Teambuilding for senior executives: Seven Steps to Excellence"
3. PowerPoint deck: Presentation by the author to the RBS Multicultural Network, "Inspire Me" series of lectures, 31 July 2014

### Chapter 18: Present and Future Principles of Banking: Business Model and Customer Service

1. Word document: Primer on marketing

---

[11] This slide deck was co-written with Chris Westcott.
[12] This slide deck was written by Chris Westcott.
[13] This slide deck was published originally as part of the BTRM Lecture programme (Cohort 5). It was written by Rita Gnutti.

## Chapter 19: Case Studies: Analysis, Coherent Advice and Problem Solving

1. Excel spreadsheet: Data set for interest rates history 1980–2009
2. Excel spreadsheet: Data set for risk-free interest rates, 1999–2009
3. Excel spreadsheet: AIB liabilities
4. Excel spreadsheet: Chelsea Building Society liabilities
5. Excel spreadsheet: CIMB liabilities
6. Excel spreadsheet: Gulf Bank liabilities
7. Excel spreadsheet: Northern Rock liabilities
8. Excel spreadsheet: Santander liabilities
9. Excel spreadsheet: Standard Chartered liabilities
10. Excel spreadsheet: Wells Fargo liabilities
11. Excel spreadsheet: Comparison of selected bank funding structures, September 2009
12. Basel III and Liabilities Strategy, BTRM Thought Leadership article, December 2016
13. Word document: Regional bank strategy review

### Part III Policy Templates Documentation

The templates for various bank policies are not in the separate chapter folders but instead are grouped together in the folder "Part III Policy Documentation". This should be helpful for individuals or teams working specifically on policy issues, be they in Treasury, Risk, Audit, Compliance, or Finance.

The full list of these files is given in Part III of the book, at the end of Chapter 15.

### Past Templates: ALM Course, March 2007

The files in this folder are a portion of what was presented by the author at an "ALM Master Class" held at the Malaysian Bankers Association in Kuala Lumpur in March 2007. They cover a range of topics within the ALM space, ranging from slide decks on credit derivatives and securitisation to policy templates for a bank's Trading Book and Group Funds Transfer Pricing policies.

1. PowerPoint deck: ALM and ALCO policy
2. Word document: Checklist for market risk limits
3. PowerPoint deck: Hedging and the yield curve
4. PowerPoint deck: Credit derivatives
5. Word document: Group funds transfer pricing policy template
6. Word document: Group trading book policy template

7. PowerPoint deck: Securitisation
8. PowerPoint deck: Securitisation credit rating process
9. Excel spreadsheet: Liquidity ratios report
10. Excel spreadsheet: Instructional sheet for Excel file (9) above
11. PowerPoint deck: Liquidity metrics
12. PowerPoint deck: Liquidity metrics, ALCO guidance
13. Word document: Weekly qualitative Treasury liquidity report template

## Question and Answers Bank for Debt Capital Markets and Money Markets

This document provides questions and model answers on debt capital markets. The questions previously appeared in the author's book, *The Bond and Money Markets* (Butterworth Heinemann, 2001).

## Masters Level Examination Papers and Model Answers

This folder holds the examination papers for the 2016 and 2017 MSc modules in Bank ALM Risk Management at the University of Kent (part of the University's MSc Finance programme), together with the model answers.

1. Word file: 2016 Examination paper
2. Word file: 2016 Examination paper model answers
3. Word file: 2017 Examination paper
4. Word file: 2017 Examination paper model answers

# Afterword

The business of what we call "finance" is as much art as science. Actually, there are grounds for saying that it isn't really a science at all, in which case finance would be just art. In a scientific discipline, theories are (or should be) tested rigorously under controlled conditions and results observed so that the theory can be either proven or disproven. Precision and accuracy are cornerstones of the process, and if a result cannot be replicated exactly by another practitioner under a similar set of circumstances elsewhere then it remains an unproven theory. For instance, mathematical models used in physics produce the same results every time. There isn't any variation depending on who applied it or what country it was applied in or what time of day it was.

Consider, for example, the European Space Agency's *Rosetta* mission. It was launched on 2 March 2004, and on 6 August 2014 it reached its intended destination, the comet 67P/Churyumov–Gerasimenko, which was at that point approximately 317 million miles from Earth. The spacecraft went into orbit around the comet. But that wasn't all – part of the spacecraft, the *Philae* lander, detached itself and performed a soft landing on the comet, which of course wasn't exactly a stationary target – the comet was travelling at around 84,000 miles per hour. *Philae* transmitted pictures back to Earth before its battery ran out.

Now *that* is "rocket science". Engineers and mathematicians had to programme all this into the spacecraft 10 years previously. Precision and accuracy were everything. A 0.01% error in the calculation means you miss the comet by millions of miles and don't get to land on it. Scientists knew to the second when they had to instruct the spacecraft to manoeuvre to go into orbit.

"Rocket scientists" in banks don't work to this accuracy. The actual losses experienced by a bank using a Value-at-Risk exposure calculation will never be what the VaR model predicted they would be. The loan loss provisions set aside by a bank will never equate to the actual loan losses suffered by it. A key parameter input in the credit default swap pricing model (the recovery rate) is merely an estimation. The deposit outflow calculated by Basel III's vaunted liquidity coverage ratio process is based on assumptions. The amount of initial margin (IM) required to be placed by a bank at the derivatives clearing house is calculated via a Monte Carlo simulation within a Monte Carlo simulation, not the sort of process that would enable us to place landers on a comet. The loss-given-default input of a bank's regulatory capital calculation is as accurate as a shotgun blast into the sky at night. The risk-weighting assigned to a credit risky asset (RWA) is based on what could charitably be described as quantitative estimations that rely on strong assumptions about how the risky asset will perform over its life. In a 3-year balance sheet projection (a staple part of an ICAAP submission) there is as much chance of the balance sheet actually looking like what has been predicted for it in three years' time as there is of Elvis Presley playing live at your local pub that same evening. And so on.

Attending the Group ALCO of a foreign banking institution on one occasion, I was astounded to hear the GCC branch Treasurer reporting that the income his department was making from the bank's Eurobond portfolio was the weighted aggregate yield to maturity (YTM) of the bonds in his book. Not one other person present challenged this, not the Group CEO or the Group CRO. When I pointed out that the actual return received from holding a bond purchased in the secondary market at a non-par price was never equal to its YTM, the Treasurer disbelieved me, although any First Year finance undergraduate would have been able to prove this to him. The conversation was taken "off line" and the meeting moved on to the next agenda item.

Why is the practice of finance like this? Because in essence, it has to be in order to move forward. Participants in finance need *something* to base their analysis around, and in the absence of precision an estimate will have to do. Hence we have the prevalence of YTM or RWA and all the other acronyms one encounters in the industry. This is not necessarily a problem as long as *all* practitioners *know* that the calculations are estimates based on assumptions. If one knows that the 1-month VaR number could be out by +/– 20% even in stable conditions, then one can plan for if the number is indeed out by –20%. Regulatory authorities the world over insist on banks using VaR methodology when reporting their risk exposures, but in practice this approach is rarely any more accurate in reality than older more traditional estimation methods. So all the added "quantitative analysis" work undertaken in banks is often a waste of time and resources because it so often does not guarantee any greater precision.

With this in mind, it is self-evident that the most important principle in banking and finance is simply this: always remember it is as much art as science, and although we need something to base our planning around, that something is an estimate at best, so we must be prepared to act and have a plan for when the actual result turns out to be different – which will be frequently. The most important attributes required of a banker are sound judgement based on actual practical experience in the field in question, be it retail, corporate, or wholesale banking, and to be adaptable in response to changing circumstances. Banking is a force for positive societal development in every country, which makes it incumbent on everyone in the industry to apply objective judgement and acceptable risk appetite as they perform their duties. The principal duty of course, is to serve the customer and act in its best interests.

And above all, do good work.

# Index

Page references followed by *f* indicate an illustrated figure; page references followed by *e* indicate an exhibit; and page references followed by *t* indicate a table